The Almanac of American Education

2004

The Almanac of American Education

2004

Edited by Deirdre A. Gaquin and Katherine A. DeBrandt

BERNAN PRESS

Lanham, MD

ISBN: 0-89059-896-7

Cover photo: www.punchstock.com

Composed and printed by Automated Graphic Systems, Inc., White Plains, MD, on acid-free paper that meets the American National Standards Institute Z39-48 standard.

2004 2003   4 3 2 1

BERNAN PRESS
4611-F Assembly Drive
Lanham, MD 20706
800-274-4447
email: info@bernan.com
www.bernan.com

Contents

Tables

PART A—NATIONAL SCHOOL ENROLLMENT AND EDUCATIONAL ATTAINMENT STATISTICS

ENROLLMENT RATES AND BACKGROUND OR FAMILY CHARACTERISTICS

SECONDARY AND POSTSECONDARY EDUCATION

HISTORICAL ENROLLMENT CHARACTERISTICS

EDUCATIONAL ATTAINMENT AND BACKGROUND OR FAMILY CHARACTERISTICS

EDUCATIONAL ATTAINMENT, EMPLOYMENT, AND INCOME

Figures

PART C—COUNTY EDUCATION STATISTICS

Preface

This premier edition of *The Almanac of American Education* serves as a guide to understanding and comparing the quality of education at the national, state, and county levels. Compiled from sources such as the U.S. Census Bureau and the National Center for Education Statistics (NCES), The Almanac contains historical and current data, insightful analysis, and useful graphics that paint a compelling picture of the state of education in America.

The Almanac is organized into three sections—Part A: National School Enrollment and Educational Attainment Statistics; Part B: State Education Statistics; and Part C: County Education Statistics. The data presented in Part A are no longer available in print form from the Census Bureau. The data in Part C have been specially tabulated for this book from computer files of the NCES and from the 2000 Census. *The Almanac* also contains a valuable guide to the wide array of educational resources that are available on the Internet.

The Almanac's contents and coverage allows you to answer—and ask—important questions about education, including:

- What are the nationwide trends in earnings by educational attainment level?
- Is the gap in earnings between high school graduates and college graduates growing or shrinking?
- Which states have the highest dropout rates, and which have the highest completion rates?
- Is there any correlation between a state's average test scores and its rate of college attainment?
- Which states have the most county-to-country variance in student/teacher ratios?
- Is there any correlation between student poverty and county-level, per-student expenditures?

The data in this volume meet the publication standards of the federal statistical agencies and the few non-governmental organizations from which they were obtained. Every effort has been made to select data that are accurate, meaningful, and useful. All statistical data are subject to error arising from sampling variability, reporting errors, incomplete coverage, imputation, and other causes. The responsibility of the editors and publisher of this volume is limited to reasonable care in the reproduction and presentation of data obtained from established sources.

Deirdre A. Gaquin and Katherine A. DeBrandt have edited this edition of *The Almanac*. Ms. Gaquin has been a data use consultant to private organizations, government agencies, and universities for over 20 years. Prior to that, she was Director of Data Access Services at Data Use & Access Laboratories, a pioneer in private sector distribution of federal statistical data. A former President of the Association of Public Data Users, Ms. Gaquin has served on numerous boards, panels, and task forces concerned with federal statistical data and has worked on four decennial censuses. She holds a Master of Urban Planning (MUP) degree from Hunter College. Ms. Gaquin is also an editor of Bernan Press' *The Who, What, and Where of America: Understanding the Census Results*; *County and City Extra: Annual Metro, City, and County Data Book*; and *Places, Towns and Townships*.

Ms. DeBrandt is a senior data analyst with Bernan Press. She received her B.A. in political science from Colgate University. She is also a co-editor of *The Who, What, and Where of America: Understanding the Census Results*; *State Profiles, The Population and Economy of Each U.S. State*; and *Social Change in America, The Historical Handbook*, all published by Bernan Press.

Special thanks go to Kara Gottschlich of Bernan Press for managing the production aspects of this volume, including preparation of the graphics. Additionally, thanks to Christopher Jorgenson for assisting Kara with the layout. Thanks also to Jacalyn Houston, who copy edited this edition, with support from Tamera Wells-Lee. Finally, thanks are due to the federal agency personnel who prepared the original data and generously responded to our requests for assistance.

PART A—NATIONAL SCHOOL ENROLLMENT AND EDUCATIONAL ATTAINMENT STATISTICS

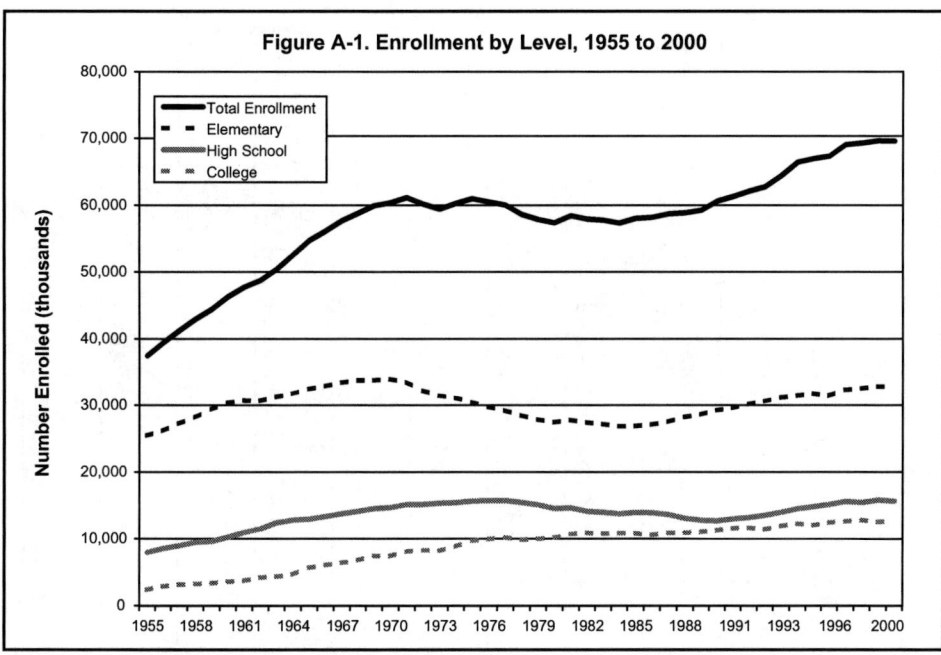

Figure A-1. Enrollment by Level, 1955 to 2000

Source: U.S. Census Bureau, *Current Population Survey*, 2000.

- In 2000, 69.6 million people between the ages of 3 and 34 years were enrolled in school. While this is a slight decrease from 1999, it represents the second highest enrollment yet measured. During the 1990s, the number of Americans between the ages of 3 and 34 years remained steady at about 124 million, while the percentage of this population enrolled in school has steadily increased from about 50 percent to over 55 percent.

- While the number of high school students slightly decreased to 15.6 million in 2000, there was an increase in private school enrollment. The proportion of high school students in private schools rose to 8.5 percent in 2000, a percentage not matched since the mid-1980s. More than 43 percent of high school graduates between the ages of 18 and 24 years went on to college.

- The number of students 14 years and over enrolled in college has continued to grow, reaching 15.3 million in 2000. Over 35 percent of the population 18 to 24 years were enrolled in college. The percentage of 18-to 24-year-old Blacks exceeded 30 percent for the first time in 2000. Over 20 percent of Hispanics were also enrolled in college. Minorities represent 30 percent of students 14 years and over enrolled in college.

- Since 1979, the number of female college students has exceeded male students, and in 2000 the proportion of women marked a new high of 56.4 percent. The greatest disparity is among Black college students, where over 62 percent are women. Women also represented nearly 60 percent of all graduate students.

1

Table A-1. Enrollment Status of the Population 3 Years and Over by Age and Sex, October 2000

(Numbers in thousands, percent.)

| Age and sex | Population | Enrolled in school | | | | | | | | | |
| | | Total | | Nursery or kindergarten | | Elementary | | High school | | College | |
	Number	Number	Percent	Number	Percent	Number	Percent	Number	Percent	Number	Percent
Both Sexes											
3 years and over	263 053	72 214	27.5	8 233	3.1	32 898	12.5	15 770	6.0	15 314	5.8
3 and 4 years	7 869	4 097	52.1	4 097	52.1	*	*	*	*	*	*
5 and 6 years	8 002	7 648	95.6	4 114	51.4	3 535	44.2	*	*	*	*
7 to 9 years	12 320	12 083	98.1	22	0.2	12 061	97.9	*	*	*	*
10 to 13 years	16 492	16 213	98.3	*	*	15 968	96.8	245	1.5	*	*
14 and 15 years	7 993	7 885	98.7	*	*	1 263	15.8	6 615	82.8	7	0.1
16 and 17 years	7 910	7 341	92.8	*	*	33	0.4	7 167	90.6	141	1.8
18 and 19 years	8 045	4 926	61.2	*	*	5	0.1	1 322	16.4	3 599	44.7
20 and 21 years	7 508	3 314	44.1	*	*	2	0.0	143	1.9	3 169	42.2
22 to 24 years	11 105	2 731	24.6	*	*	*	*	48	0.4	2 683	24.2
25 to 29 years	17 782	2 030	11.4	*	*	*	*	68	0.4	1 962	11.0
30 to 34 years	19 429	1 292	6.7	*	*	7	0.0	40	0.2	1 244	6.4
35 to 44 years	44 684	1 632	3.7	*	*	12	0.0	57	0.1	1 563	3.5
45 to 54 years	37 312	810	2.2	*	*	8	0.0	34	0.1	768	2.1
55 years and over	56 604	211	0.4	*	*	4	0.0	31	0.1	176	0.3
Male											
3 years and over	128 044	35 838	28.0	4 194	3.3	16 884	13.2	8 077	6.3	6 682	5.2
3 and 4 years	4 007	2 035	50.8	2 035	50.8	*	*	*	*	*	*
5 and 6 years	4 105	3 903	95.1	2 152	52.4	1 751	42.7	*	*	*	*
7 to 9 years	6 304	6 177	98.0	7	0.1	6 170	97.9	*	*	*	*
10 to 13 years	8 449	8 308	98.3	*	*	8 205	97.1	103	1.2	*	*
14 and 15 years	4 103	4 050	98.7	*	*	719	17.5	3 325	81.0	6	0.1
16 and 17 years	4 064	3 767	92.7	*	*	18	0.4	3 693	90.9	56	1.4
18 and 19 years	4 037	2 353	58.3	*	*	2	0.1	780	19.3	1 570	38.9
20 and 21 years	3 777	1 548	41.0	*	*	*	*	76	2.0	1 472	39.0
22 to 24 years	5 525	1 320	23.9	*	*	*	*	20	0.4	1 300	23.5
25 to 29 years	8 566	860	10.0	*	*	*	*	16	0.2	844	9.8
30 to 34 years	9 547	536	5.6	*	*	2	0.0	17	0.2	517	5.4
35 to 44 years	22 021	651	3.0	*	*	8	0.0	24	0.1	620	2.8
45 to 54 years	18 238	250	1.4	*	*	5	0.0	12	0.1	233	1.3
55 years and over	25 300	80	0.3	*	*	4	0.0	11	0.0	65	0.3
Female											
3 years and over	135 010	36 376	26.9	4 038	3.0	16 014	11.9	7 693	5.7	8 631	6.4
3 and 4 years	3 863	2 062	53.4	2 062	53.4	*	*	*	*	*	*
5 and 6 years	3 897	3 745	96.1	1 961	50.3	1 784	45.8	*	*	*	*
7 to 9 years	6 016	5 906	98.2	15	0.3	5 891	97.9	*	*	*	*
10 to 13 years	8 042	7 905	98.3	*	*	7 763	96.5	142	1.8	*	*
14 and 15 years	3 889	3 836	98.6	*	*	544	14.0	3 290	84.6	2	0.0
16 and 17 years	3 847	3 575	92.9	*	*	15	0.4	3 474	90.3	86	2.2
18 and 19 years	4 008	2 573	64.2	*	*	3	0.1	542	13.5	2 029	50.6
20 and 21 years	3 731	1 766	47.3	*	*	2	0.1	67	1.8	1 697	45.5
22 to 24 years	5 580	1 411	25.3	*	*	*	*	28	0.5	1 383	24.8
25 to 29 years	9 215	1 170	12.7	*	*	*	*	52	0.6	1 118	12.1
30 to 34 years	9 882	757	7.7	*	*	5	0.1	24	0.2	728	7.4
35 to 44 years	22 663	980	4.3	*	*	4	0.0	33	0.1	943	4.2
45 to 54 years	19 073	560	2.9	*	*	3	0.0	22	0.1	535	2.8
55 years and over	31 304	131	0.4	*	*	*	*	20	0.1	111	0.4

* = Represents zero or rounds to zero.

Table A-2. Preprimary School Enrollment of the Population 3 to 6 Years, by Mother's Labor Force Status and Education, and Family Income, October 2000

(Numbers in thousands.)

Mother's labor force status and education, and family income	Population	Not enrolled	Nursery school	Kindergarten	Elementary school
3 TO 6 YEARS	15 871	4 126	4 401	3 809	3 535
3 and 4 Years					
Labor force status of mother	7 869	3 773	3 762	335	*
Children not living with mother	532	295	218	18	*
Mother employed part-time	1 264	517	686	61	*
Mother employed full-time	3 122	1 426	1 546	150	*
Mother unemployed	208	94	109	6	*
Mother not in the labor force	2 743	1 441	1 202	100	*
Education of mother	7 869	3 773	3 762	335	*
Children not living with mother	532	295	218	18	*
Elementary: 0 to 8 years	398	266	121	10	*
High school: 9 to 11 years	803	497	257	48	*
High school graduate	2 083	1 096	912	75	*
Less than a bachelor's degree	2 221	1 037	1 084	100	*
Bachelor's degree or more	1 833	581	1 169	83	*
Family income	7 869	3 773	3 762	335	*
Less than $10,000	682	367	275	40	*
$10,000 to $14,999	485	276	188	20	*
$15,000 to $19,999	432	212	204	16	*
$20,000 to $24,999	504	286	198	20	*
$25,000 to $29,999	502	305	169	28	*
$30,000 to $34,999	495	272	209	14	*
$35,000 to $39,999	440	221	187	32	*
$40,000 to $49,999	623	367	243	14	*
$50,000 to $74,999	1 370	568	739	64	*
$75,000 and over	1 467	430	978	58	*
Not reported	870	468	372	30	*
5 Years					
Labor force status of mother	3 989	239	565	2 931	254
Children not living with mother	397	42	56	255	44
Mother employed part-time	638	38	103	461	37
Mother employed full-time	1 647	85	254	1 200	108
Mother unemployed	96	*	10	81	5
Mother not in the labor force	1 211	75	142	934	60
Education of mother	3 989	239	565	2 931	254
Children not living with mother	397	42	56	255	44
Elementary: 0 to 8 years	155	20	14	113	7
High school: 9 to 11 years	345	19	40	259	27
High school graduate	1 023	56	128	779	60
Less than a bachelor's degree	1 095	51	162	815	67
Bachelor's degree or more	974	52	164	709	49
Family income	3 989	239	565	2 931	254
Less than $10,000	327	33	41	233	20
$10,000 to $14,999	236	15	31	181	8
$15,000 to $19,999	181	17	34	109	21
$20,000 to $24,999	233	19	34	167	13
$25,000 to $29,999	279	34	37	196	12
$30,000 to $34,999	272	17	28	211	17
$35,000 to $39,999	243	3	46	176	18
$40,000 to $49,999	299	19	40	231	9
$50,000 to $74,999	683	31	100	501	52
$75,000 and over	742	15	113	587	27
Not reported	494	37	61	340	56
6 Years					
Labor force status of mother	4 013	114	75	543	3 281
Children not living with mother	288	12	3	37	235
Mother employed part-time	701	10	6	108	577
Mother employed full-time	1 758	49	54	212	1 443
Mother unemployed	99	*	2	14	84
Mother not in the labor force	1 167	43	9	173	942
Education of mother	4 013	114	75	543	3 281
Children not living with mother	288	12	3	37	235
Elementary: 0 to 8 years	203	5	8	19	171
High school: 9 to 11 years	296	7	9	36	243
High school graduate	1 165	34	19	169	944
Less than a bachelor's degree	1 203	29	21	175	979
Bachelor's degree or more	858	26	15	107	710
Family income	4 013	114	75	543	3 281
Less than $10,000	307	4	7	45	250
$10,000 to $14,999	262	8	4	46	204
$15,000 to $19,999	248	*	3	33	211
$20,000 to $24,999	263	6	12	27	219
$25,000 to $29,999	246	6	7	22	212
$30,000 to $34,999	247	1	4	33	209
$35,000 to $39,999	244	13	5	38	189
$40,000 to $49,999	336	12	9	45	270
$50,000 to $74,999	619	10	10	91	508
$75,000 and over	763	21	1	112	627
Not reported	479	33	13	51	381

* = Represents zero or rounds to zero.

Table A-3. Level of Enrollment Below College for Population 3 to 24 Years, by Control of School, Metropolitan Status, Sex, Race, and Hispanic Origin, October 2000

(Numbers in thousands.)

Metropolitan status, sex, race, and Hispanic origin	Total			Nursery school			Kindergarten			Elementary			High school		
	Total	Public	Private	Total	Public	Private	Total	Public	Private	Total	Public	Private	Total	Public	Private
ALL RACES															
Both Sexes															
3 to 24 years	56 639	48 977	7 661	4 401	2 217	2 184	3 832	3 173	659	32 867	29 347	3 520	15 539	14 240	1 299
Central city	16 222	14 032	2 190	1 243	781	462	1 186	958	228	9 513	8 420	1 093	4 281	3 874	407
Outside central city	29 862	25 437	4 425	2 531	1 057	1 474	1 979	1 617	362	17 158	15 281	1 877	8 194	7 482	712
Nonmetropolitan	10 554	9 508	1 046	627	379	248	667	598	69	6 196	5 646	550	3 064	2 885	179
Male															
3 to 24 years	29 057	25 078	3 980	2 212	1 123	1 089	1 983	1 633	349	16 866	14 996	1 870	7 997	7 326	671
Central city	8 312	7 184	1 128	604	387	216	588	471	117	4 891	4 298	593	2 230	2 028	202
Outside central city	15 410	13 085	2 325	1 270	523	747	1 067	872	196	8 836	7 833	1 003	4 236	3 857	379
Nonmetropolitan	5 336	4 809	527	338	212	126	327	291	37	3 139	2 865	274	1 531	1 441	91
Female															
3 to 24 years	27 582	23 900	3 682	2 189	1 094	1 095	1 849	1 540	309	16 001	14 352	1 650	7 542	6 915	627
Central city	7 911	6 848	1 063	639	393	246	598	487	111	4 622	4 122	500	2 051	1 846	206
Outside central city	14 453	12 352	2 100	1 261	534	727	911	745	166	8 322	7 449	874	3 958	3 624	334
Nonmetropolitan	5 218	4 700	519	289	167	122	340	307	32	3 057	2 781	276	1 533	1 444	88
WHITE															
Both Sexes															
3 to 24 years	44 163	37 634	6 530	3 392	1 539	1 853	2 998	2 453	545	25 547	22 523	3 024	12 227	11 120	1 107
Central city	10 180	8 471	1 709	786	441	345	767	600	167	5 986	5 104	882	2 641	2 326	315
Outside central city	25 070	21 223	3 847	2 093	818	1 275	1 676	1 366	310	14 336	12 695	1 641	6 965	6 344	621
Nonmetropolitan	8 912	7 939	974	513	279	234	555	487	68	5 224	4 723	501	2 621	2 449	171
Male															
3 to 24 years	22 695	19 335	3 360	1 724	792	932	1 551	1 256	295	13 087	11 517	1 571	6 333	5 771	563
Central city	5 236	4 372	863	394	232	163	372	279	92	3 102	2 639	463	1 368	1 223	145
Outside central city	12 903	10 903	2 000	1 048	402	646	893	727	166	7 348	6 488	860	3 614	3 287	327
Nonmetropolitan	4 557	4 060	497	282	159	123	287	250	37	2 638	2 390	248	1 351	1 261	90
Female															
3 to 24 years	21 468	18 298	3 169	1 668	746	922	1 447	1 197	250	12 459	11 006	1 453	5 893	5 349	544
Central city	4 945	4 099	846	392	209	182	396	321	75	2 885	2 466	419	1 273	1 103	170
Outside central city	12 168	10 320	1 847	1 045	416	629	783	639	144	6 988	6 207	781	3 351	3 058	294
Nonmetropolitan	4 355	3 879	476	231	120	111	268	237	31	2 587	2 333	253	1 269	1 188	81
NON-HISPANIC WHITE															
Both Sexes															
3 to 24 years	35 928	29 882	6 046	2 854	1 149	1 705	2 346	1 846	500	20 567	17 740	2 827	10 161	9 147	1 013
Central city	6 253	4 784	1 469	526	224	302	450	316	135	3 614	2 842	772	1 663	1 402	261
Outside central city	21 483	17 865	3 618	1 835	662	1 173	1 417	1 115	302	12 180	10 620	1 560	6 051	5 468	583
Nonmetropolitan	8 192	7 233	959	493	263	230	479	415	64	4 773	4 278	495	2 447	2 277	170
Male															
3 to 24 years	18 494	15 365	3 129	1 465	584	882	1 216	946	270	10 540	9 071	1 469	5 272	4 763	509
Central city	3 250	2 497	753	257	114	143	234	156	78	1 884	1 464	420	875	762	113
Outside central city	11 086	9 197	1 889	941	323	619	750	591	159	6 255	5 450	805	3 140	2 833	306
Nonmetropolitan	4 158	3 671	487	267	147	120	232	199	33	2 402	2 158	244	1 258	1 168	90
Female															
3 to 24 years	17 434	14 517	2 917	1 389	565	824	1 130	900	231	10 027	8 668	1 358	4 888	4 384	504
Central city	3 003	2 287	716	268	109	159	217	159	57	1 730	1 378	352	788	640	148
Outside central city	10 397	8 669	1 729	894	339	555	666	524	143	5 925	5 170	755	2 912	2 635	276
Nonmetropolitan	4 034	3 562	472	226	116	110	247	216	31	2 371	2 120	251	1 189	1 109	80
BLACK															
Both Sexes															
3 to 24 years	9 275	8 510	765	726	531	195	629	547	82	5 474	5 127	347	2 446	2 305	141
Central city	4 897	4 533	364	368	286	81	341	296	45	2 903	2 727	176	1 286	1 225	61
Outside central city	3 258	2 881	377	273	167	105	216	179	37	1 909	1 751	158	861	785	76
Nonmetropolitan	1 120	1 095	25	86	78	8	73	72	0	662	649	13	299	296	3
Male															
3 to 24 years	4 691	4 267	424	344	255	89	320	283	37	2 815	2 603	213	1 212	1 126	86
Central city	2 482	2 275	207	173	137	37	175	157	19	1 473	1 363	110	661	619	42
Outside central city	1 684	1 482	202	132	81	51	119	101	18	1 000	910	90	434	391	43
Nonmetropolitan	525	510	15	39	38	1	26	26	*	343	330	13	117	117	1
Female															
3 to 24 years	4 584	4 243	341	382	276	106	309	264	46	2 659	2 524	135	1 234	1 179	55
Central city	2 415	2 258	157	195	150	45	166	139	26	1 430	1 363	67	625	606	19
Outside central city	1 574	1 399	175	141	86	54	97	78	19	909	841	68	427	394	33
Nonmetropolitan	595	585	10	47	40	7	47	47	0	319	319	*	182	179	3

* = Represents zero or rounds to zero.

Table A-3. Level of Enrollment Below College for Population 3 to 24 Years, by Control of School, Metropolitan Status, Sex, Race, and Hispanic Origin, October 2000—*Continued*

(Numbers in thousands.)

Metropolitan status, sex, race, and Hispanic origin	Total			Nursery school			Kindergarten			Elementary			High school		
	Total	Public	Private	Total	Public	Private	Total	Public	Private	Total	Public	Private	Total	Public	Private
ASIAN/PACIFIC ISLANDER															
Both Sexes															
3 to 24 years	2 382	2 086	296	222	91	132	152	124	28	1 345	1 252	93	663	619	43
Central city	970	868	102	68	34	34	69	56	13	521	491	30	312	287	25
Outside central city	1 273	1 103	170	146	55	92	73	58	15	739	691	48	314	300	15
Nonmetropolitan	138	115	24	8	2	6	10	10	*	85	71	14	36	32	3
Male															
3 to 24 years	1 256	1 100	156	111	47	64	83	66	17	698	644	54	365	344	20
Central city	507	456	51	27	12	15	36	31	6	269	251	18	174	162	12
Outside central city	693	595	98	82	34	48	42	30	12	397	367	29	173	164	9
Nonmetropolitan	57	49	8	2	1	1	5	5	*	32	25	7	18	18	*
Female															
3 to 24 years	1 125	985	140	112	44	68	69	58	11	647	608	39	298	275	23
Central city	463	411	52	41	22	19	33	25	8	251	239	12	138	125	13
Outside central city	580	508	72	65	21	44	32	28	3	342	323	19	142	136	6
Nonmetropolitan	82	66	16	6	1	5	5	5	*	53	45	8	18	14	3
HISPANIC[1]															
Both Sexes															
3 to 24 years	8 647	8 137	510	574	419	154	687	639	48	5 213	5 000	213	2 174	2 080	95
Central city	4 160	3 909	252	280	234	46	334	302	33	2 501	2 382	119	1 045	991	54
Outside central city	3 736	3 494	241	271	166	105	273	261	12	2 245	2 160	85	947	908	39
Nonmetropolitan	751	734	17	23	20	4	79	76	4	466	458	8	182	181	2
Male															
3 to 24 years	4 397	4 154	243	274	222	52	357	328	29	2 642	2 534	108	1 124	1 071	54
Central city	2 096	1 980	116	147	125	22	147	132	15	1 271	1 223	47	532	500	33
Outside central city	1 878	1 762	116	109	81	27	152	142	11	1 126	1 069	57	491	470	21
Nonmetropolitan	423	412	11	19	16	3	58	55	4	245	241	4	101	101	*
Female															
3 to 24 years	4 250	3 983	267	300	198	102	330	310	19	2 570	2 466	104	1 050	1 009	41
Central city	2 064	1 929	135	133	109	24	188	170	18	1 231	1 159	72	513	491	21
Outside central city	1 858	1 733	125	162	85	78	121	120	1	1 119	1 090	29	456	438	18
Nonmetropolitan	328	322	6	5	4	1	21	21	*	221	217	4	82	80	2

[1]May be of any race.
* = Represents zero or rounds to zero.

Table A-4. Enrollment of the Population 15 Years and Over, by Attendance Status, Type and Control of School, Age, and Sex, October 2000

(Numbers in thousands.)

Age and sex	Total enrolled	Enrolled Below college	Undergraduate 2-year college Full-time	Undergraduate 2-year college Part-time	Undergraduate 4-year college Full-time	Undergraduate 4-year college Part-time	Graduate Full-time	Graduate Part-time
TOTAL ENROLLED	28 252	12 939	2 193	1 688	6 698	1 822	1 268	1 645
Both Sexes								
Public								
15 years and over	23 888	11 880	2 010	1 581	4 971	1 482	839	1 125
15 to 17 years	10 335	10 214	50	9	57	*	5	*
18 and 19 years	4 149	1 265	885	207	1 672	97	19	6
20 and 21 years	2 604	132	466	197	1 566	195	43	5
22 to 24 years	2 168	48	245	231	914	321	285	124
25 to 29 years	1 567	55	135	233	380	286	228	250
30 to 34 years	993	36	54	170	183	213	130	207
35 to 39 years	714	33	84	200	66	143	49	140
40 to 44 years	565	31	43	142	68	113	38	130
45 to 49 years	388	19	32	105	41	58	22	110
50 to 54 years	239	14	8	55	14	34	15	99
55 to 59 years	86	6	7	20	0	15	3	34
60 to 64 years	25	11	1	3	*	1	*	8
65 years and over	55	16	*	9	10	6	2	11
Private								
15 years and over	4 364	1 059	184	107	1 726	340	429	519
15 to 17 years	971	944	4	0	24	*	*	*
18 and 19 years	777	62	55	22	621	7	8	*
20 and 21 years	711	13	42	6	585	37	24	5
22 to 24 years	563	*	34	16	287	65	129	32
25 to 29 years	463	13	27	21	96	68	132	107
30 to 34 years	299	12	13	20	42	47	54	111
35 to 39 years	199	3	5	2	32	51	26	79
40 to 44 years	153	2	4	9	26	25	16	71
45 to 49 years	112	2	*	3	11	22	19	53
50 to 54 years	71	6	*	5	2	6	12	39
55 to 59 years	28	*	*	*	*	7	8	13
60 to 64 years	6	*	*	2	*	*	*	4
65 years and over	12	2	*	*	*	4	1	5
Male								
Public								
15 years and over	11 343	6 151	869	642	2 298	637	366	381
15 to 17 years	5 295	5 237	31	5	18	*	3	*
18 and 19 years	2 029	745	427	111	678	47	16	5
20 and 21 years	1 194	68	169	76	743	110	24	5
22 to 24 years	1 043	20	111	112	508	148	105	37
25 to 29 years	663	12	47	100	194	148	96	67
30 to 34 years	390	12	15	63	74	82	67	77
35 to 39 years	279	15	32	79	28	49	23	53
40 to 44 years	188	14	12	37	21	22	18	64
45 to 49 years	119	7	12	33	22	14	4	26
50 to 54 years	78	6	8	14	5	16	8	21
55 to 59 years	23	*	4	5	*	1	2	11
60 to 64 years	22	10	*	3	*	*	*	8
65 years and over	21	5	*	3	7	*	*	6
Private								
15 years and over	2 061	571	100	43	792	139	180	236
15 to 17 years	511	507	*	*	4	*	*	*
18 and 19 years	324	37	22	15	242	6	2	*
20 and 21 years	354	8	29	*	287	14	17	*
22 to 24 years	278	*	20	9	159	28	46	16
25 to 29 years	197	5	16	1	49	17	55	53
30 to 34 years	145	7	5	6	18	26	33	50
35 to 39 years	118	*	5	2	19	26	20	45
40 to 44 years	66	2	4	5	12	10	2	32
45 to 49 years	29	2	*	*	1	9	4	13
50 to 54 years	24	2	*	3	1	*	*	19
55 to 59 years	9	*	*	*	*	3	*	6
60 to 64 years	3	*	*	2	*	*	*	1
65 years and over	3	*	*	*	*	*	1	2

* = Represents zero or rounds to zero.

Table A-4. Enrollment of the Population 15 Years and Over, by Attendance Status, Type and Control of School, Age, and Sex, October 2000—*Continued*

(Numbers in thousands.)

Age and sex	Total enrolled	Enrolled Below college	Undergraduate 2-year college Full-time	Part-time	4-year college Full-time	Part-time	Graduate Full-time	Part-time
Female								
Public								
15 years and over	12 545	5 729	1 141	938	2 674	845	473	745
15 to 17 years	5 040	4 976	19	4	39	*	2	*
18 and 19 years	2 121	519	458	96	994	50	3	1
20 and 21 years	1 409	64	297	121	823	86	19	*
22 to 24 years	1 126	28	133	118	406	173	180	88
25 to 29 years	904	43	88	132	186	139	132	183
30 to 34 years	603	24	39	107	109	131	63	130
35 to 39 years	436	18	52	121	38	94	26	87
40 to 44 years	377	16	31	105	47	91	21	66
45 to 49 years	270	12	20	72	19	44	18	84
50 to 54 years	161	8	*	41	10	18	6	78
55 to 59 years	63	6	3	15	0	14	1	23
60 to 64 years	4	1	1	*	*	1	*	*
65 years and over	34	11	*	6	3	6	2	5
Private								
15 years and over	2 304	488	84	64	935	201	249	284
15 to 17 years	460	437	4	0	20	*	*	*
18 and 19 years	453	25	34	7	379	1	7	*
20 and 21 years	357	5	13	6	298	23	7	5
22 to 24 years	285	*	14	7	128	37	84	16
25 to 29 years	266	8	11	19	46	51	76	54
30 to 34 years	154	5	8	14	23	22	21	61
35 to 39 years	81	3	*	*	13	25	5	35
40 to 44 years	87	*	0	5	14	15	14	39
45 to 49 years	83	*	*	3	11	14	15	40
50 to 54 years	47	4	*	2	2	6	12	21
55 to 59 years	19	*	*	*	*	4	8	7
60 to 64 years	3	*	*	*	*	*	*	3
65 years and over	9	2	*	*	*	4	*	3

* = Represents zero or rounds to zero.

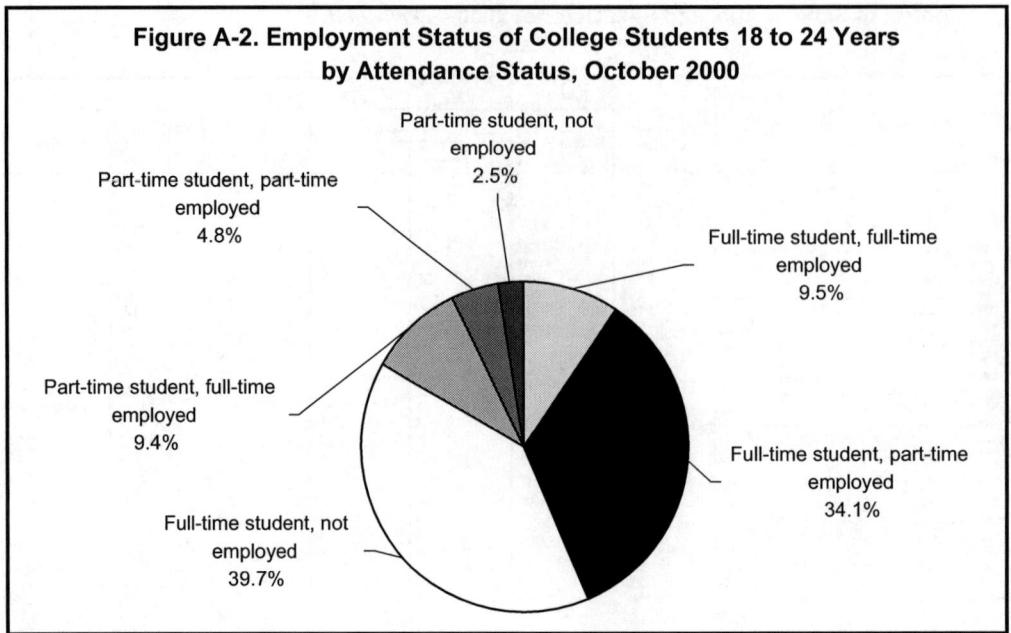

Figure A-2. Employment Status of College Students 18 to 24 Years by Attendance Status, October 2000

Part-time student, not employed 2.5%

Part-time student, part-time employed 4.8%

Full-time student, full-time employed 9.5%

Part-time student, full-time employed 9.4%

Full-time student, part-time employed 34.1%

Full-time student, not employed 39.7%

Source: U.S. Census Bureau, *Current Population Survey*, 2000.

- Over half of all part-time and full-time college students between the ages of 18 and 24 years are employed, and nearly 10 percent of full-time students are employed full-time. More than 4 out of 5 college students this age are enrolled full-time. Fewer than 40 percent of college students over 25 years of age are enrolled full-time.

- More than 100,000 high school students under 18 years are employed full-time while attending school full-time. More than 11 percent of high school students are employed part-time.

- More than 49 percent of female high school and college students of all ages are employed, and 45.6 percent of male students are employed. Male high school students outnumber females by nearly half a million. Although there are nearly 2 million more females enrolled in colleges than males.

Table A-5. Employment Status of High School and College Students 15 Years and Over, by Level of School, Attendance Status, Age, Sex, Race, and Hispanic Origin, October 2000

(Numbers in thousands.)

Age, sex, race, and Hispanic origin	Total	Full-time students				Part-time students			
		Total	Employed full-time	Employed part-time	Not employed	Total	Employed full-time	Employed part-time	Not employed
ALL RACES									
Both Sexes									
15 years and over	28 054	22 900	1 945	6 956	13 999	5 155	3 635	809	711
Enrolled in High School									
15 years	3 831	3 831	18	412	3 401	*	*	*	*
16 and 17 years	7 167	7 167	107	2 276	4 784	*	*	*	*
18 and 19 years	1 322	1 322	113	387	821	*	*	*	*
20 years and over	422	422	112	44	265	*	*	*	*
Enrolled in College									
15 to 17 years	149	139	6	46	87	10	1	9	0
18 and 19 years	3 599	3 261	269	1 258	1 734	339	142	125	71
20 and 21 years	3 169	2 725	291	1 215	1 218	445	232	159	54
22 to 24 years	2 683	1 894	338	753	802	789	510	166	113
25 to 29 years	1 962	998	321	285	392	964	743	115	106
30 to 34 years	1 244	476	156	127	192	769	613	63	93
35 years and over	2 507	667	213	153	302	1 839	1 394	172	273
Male									
15 years and over	13 288	11 211	973	3 238	6 999	2 078	1 585	260	232
Enrolled in High School									
15 years	1 957	1 957	13	219	1 725	*	*	*	*
16 and 17 years	3 693	3 693	43	1 135	2 515	*	*	*	*
18 and 19 years	780	780	83	207	490	*	*	*	*
20 years and over	176	176	59	16	101	*	*	*	*
Enrolled in College									
15 to 17 years	61	56	3	28	25	5	*	5	*
18 and 19 years	1 570	1 387	112	523	752	184	85	61	37
20 and 21 years	1 472	1 268	133	507	628	204	106	70	28
22 to 24 years	1 300	949	168	370	411	351	257	55	39
25 to 29 years	844	458	168	129	161	386	315	40	31
30 to 34 years	517	213	78	53	81	304	277	2	25
35 years and over	918	274	113	52	109	644	544	28	72
Female									
15 years and over	14 766	11 689	971	3 718	7 000	3 077	2 050	549	478
Enrolled in High School									
15 years	1 874	1 874	5	193	1 676	*	*	*	*
16 and 17 years	3 474	3 474	64	1 141	2 268	*	*	*	*
18 and 19 years	542	542	30	181	331	*	*	*	*
20 years and over	245	245	53	28	164	*	*	*	*
Enrolled in College									
15 to 17 years	88	83	3	18	62	4	1	3	0
18 and 19 years	2 029	1 874	157	736	981	155	57	64	34
20 and 21 years	1 697	1 457	159	707	590	241	125	89	26
22 to 24 years	1 383	945	170	382	392	438	253	112	74
25 to 29 years	1 118	540	153	156	231	578	428	75	75
30 to 34 years	728	263	78	74	111	465	336	61	68
35 years and over	1 589	393	100	101	192	1 196	850	144	201
WHITE									
Both Sexes									
15 years and over	22 014	17 959	1 563	5 909	10 487	4 055	2 872	676	507
Enrolled in High School									
15 years	2 997	2 997	13	376	2 608	*	*	*	*
16 and 17 years	5 712	5 712	96	1 984	3 632	*	*	*	*
18 and 19 years	1 004	1 004	103	332	570	*	*	*	*
20 years and over	301	301	87	39	175	*	*	*	*
Enrolled in College									
15 to 17 years	117	110	6	36	68	6	1	5	*
18 and 19 years	2 914	2 634	245	1 058	1 331	280	128	109	43
20 and 21 years	2 590	2 227	247	1 058	922	363	196	127	40
22 to 24 years	2 062	1 431	260	608	563	630	412	143	75
25 to 29 years	1 433	706	237	205	264	727	571	92	65
30 to 34 years	906	340	118	95	127	566	442	57	68
35 years and over	1 978	496	151	118	227	1 482	1 123	143	216
Male									
15 years and over	10 535	8 897	797	2 786	5 314	1 638	1 270	207	161
Enrolled in High School									
15 years	1 517	1 517	9	197	1 311	*	*	*	*
16 and 17 years	2 966	2 966	39	988	1 939	*	*	*	*
18 and 19 years	610	610	72	191	346	*	*	*	*
20 years and over	131	131	50	14	67	*	*	*	*
Enrolled in College									
15 to 17 years	47	42	3	20	19	5	*	5	*
18 and 19 years	1 289	1 137	105	445	587	152	75	54	23
20 and 21 years	1 225	1 066	110	452	505	158	94	45	19
22 to 24 years	1 008	710	126	299	285	297	214	52	31
25 to 29 years	662	379	144	104	130	284	240	27	17
30 to 34 years	367	147	64	31	52	220	210	1	10
35 years and over	713	192	75	45	72	520	436	23	61

* = Represents zero or rounds to zero.

Table A-5. Employment Status of High School and College Students 15 Years and Over, by Level of School, Attendance Status, Age, Sex, Race, and Hispanic Origin, October 2000—*Continued*

(Numbers in thousands.)

Age, sex, race, and Hispanic origin	Total	Full-time students				Part-time students			
		Total	Employed full-time	Employed part-time	Not employed	Total	Employed full-time	Employed part-time	Not employed
WHITE									
Female									
15 years and over	11 480	9 062	766	3 124	5 173	2 417	1 603	469	345
Enrolled in High School									
15 years	1 480	1 480	4	180	1 296	*	*	*	*
16 and 17 years	2 747	2 747	57	997	1 693	*	*	*	*
18 and 19 years	394	394	30	140	224	*	*	*	*
20 years and over	170	170	37	26	108	*	*	*	*
Enrolled in College									
15 to 17 years	70	69	3	16	50	1	1	*	*
18 and 19 years	1 625	1 497	140	613	744	128	53	55	20
20 and 21 years	1 365	1 161	137	606	417	204	102	82	21
22 to 24 years	1 054	721	134	309	278	333	198	91	44
25 to 29 years	770	327	93	101	134	443	330	65	48
30 to 34 years	539	193	55	64	74	346	232	57	57
35 years and over	1 266	304	76	73	155	962	687	120	154
NON-HISPANIC WHITE									
Both Sexes									
15 years and over	18 894	15 363	1 308	5 369	8 685	3 531	2 518	571	442
Enrolled in High School									
15 years	2 515	2 515	13	358	2 143	*	*	*	*
16 and 17 years	4 830	4 830	88	1 862	2 880	*	*	*	*
18 and 19 years	757	757	67	287	403	*	*	*	*
20 years and over	156	156	52	16	88	*	*	*	*
Enrolled in College									
15 to 17 years	92	86	6	26	54	6	1	5	*
18 and 19 years	2 580	2 350	210	925	1 216	230	111	84	35
20 and 21 years	2 333	2 019	216	962	841	314	177	101	37
22 to 24 years	1 796	1 286	231	546	508	510	328	117	65
25 to 29 years	1 275	636	196	196	243	638	512	74	52
30 to 34 years	770	278	94	78	106	492	384	50	57
35 years and over	1 790	449	134	113	202	1 341	1 005	139	197
Male									
15 years and over	9 043	7 623	656	2 527	4 441	1 420	1 111	158	151
Enrolled in High School									
15 years	1 249	1 249	9	182	1 058	*	*	*	*
16 and 17 years	2 534	2 534	36	941	1 557	*	*	*	*
18 and 19 years	471	471	41	164	265	*	*	*	*
20 years and over	74	74	37	2	35	*	*	*	*
Enrolled in College									
15 to 17 years	35	30	3	10	17	5	*	5	*
18 and 19 years	1 138	1 009	92	383	533	129	64	43	22
20 and 21 years	1 109	979	94	412	473	130	83	27	19
22 to 24 years	890	645	112	267	265	245	173	41	31
25 to 29 years	603	354	125	102	126	249	217	20	12
30 to 34 years	296	107	43	20	44	188	184	*	5
35 years and over	646	172	63	41	67	474	390	22	61
Female									
15 years and over	9 850	7 739	652	2 843	4 244	2 111	1 407	412	291
Enrolled in High School									
15 years	1 266	1 266	4	176	1 086	*	*	*	*
16 and 17 years	2 296	2 296	52	920	1 323	*	*	*	*
18 and 19 years	286	286	26	122	138	*	*	*	*
20 years and over	82	82	15	13	53	*	*	*	*
Enrolled in College									
15 to 17 years	57	56	3	16	37	1	1	*	*
18 and 19 years	1 443	1 341	118	542	682	101	47	41	13
20 and 21 years	1 224	1 040	122	550	368	184	93	74	17
22 to 24 years	906	641	120	279	243	265	155	76	34
25 to 29 years	672	282	71	94	117	389	295	55	40
30 to 34 years	474	171	51	58	62	303	200	50	52
35 years and over	1 145	278	71	72	135	867	615	117	135
BLACK									
Both Sexes									
15 years and over	4 221	3 407	286	667	2 455	814	577	89	148
Enrolled in High School									
15 years	610	610	*	24	586	*	*	*	*
16 and 17 years	1 081	1 081	9	218	854	*	*	*	*
18 and 19 years	261	261	9	42	211	*	*	*	*
20 years and over	104	104	23	5	77	*	*	*	*
Enrolled in College									
15 to 17 years	19	16	*	6	10	3	*	3	*
18 and 19 years	454	404	21	128	255	50	14	14	22
20 and 21 years	375	314	37	83	194	61	29	19	12
22 to 24 years	387	277	60	82	135	110	73	15	22
25 to 29 years	325	170	58	50	62	155	119	10	26
30 to 34 years	242	77	33	13	32	165	135	6	24
35 years and over	361	92	37	16	39	270	207	21	41

* = Represents zero or rounds to zero.

Table A-5. Employment Status of High School and College Students 15 Years and Over, by Level of School, Attendance Status, Age, Sex, Race, and Hispanic Origin, October 2000—*Continued*

(Numbers in thousands.)

Age, sex, race, and Hispanic origin	Total	Full-time students				Part-time students			
		Total	Employed full-time	Employed part-time	Not employed	Total	Employed full-time	Employed part-time	Not employed
BLACK									
Male									
15 years and over	1 854	1 547	135	262	1 151	306	222	31	53
Enrolled in High School									
15 years	312	312	*	13	299	*	*	*	*
16 and 17 years	536	536	3	103	430	*	*	*	*
18 and 19 years	147	147	9	14	125	*	*	*	*
20 years and over	43	43	9	2	32	*	*	*	*
Enrolled in College									
15 to 17 years	10	10	*	6	4	*	*	*	*
18 and 19 years	163	134	5	46	83	29	10	7	13
20 and 21 years	137	110	19	23	67	28	8	12	7
22 to 24 years	169	141	32	38	70	28	28	*	*
25 to 29 years	110	42	19	14	9	68	51	4	13
30 to 34 years	92	28	13	2	13	64	48	2	14
35 years and over	133	44	27	*	17	89	76	6	7
Female									
15 years and over	2 367	1 859	151	405	1 304	507	354	58	95
Enrolled in High School									
15 years	298	298	*	12	287	*	*	*	*
16 and 17 years	544	544	6	114	424	*	*	*	*
18 and 19 years	114	114	*	28	86	*	*	*	*
20 years and over	61	61	14	3	45	*	*	*	*
Enrolled in College									
15 to 17 years	9	6	*	*	6	3	*	3	*
18 and 19 years	291	270	17	82	171	21	4	7	10
20 and 21 years	238	205	18	60	127	33	21	7	5
22 to 24 years	218	136	27	44	65	82	44	15	22
25 to 29 years	215	128	39	37	53	87	67	6	13
30 to 34 years	150	49	20	10	19	101	87	4	10
35 years and over	228	47	10	16	21	181	131	15	35
ASIAN/PACIFIC ISLANDER									
Both Sexes									
15 years and over	1 562	1 305	82	343	880	257	171	42	43
Enrolled in High School									
15 years	177	177	4	11	162	*	*	*	*
16 and 17 years	277	277	1	56	220	*	*	*	*
18 and 19 years	45	45	*	12	33	*	*	*	*
20 years and over	14	14	3	*	12	*	*	*	*
Enrolled in College									
15 to 17 years	12	12	*	3	9	*	*	*	*
18 and 19 years	212	203	2	65	136	8	*	2	6
20 and 21 years	200	180	7	74	98	20	6	12	2
22 to 24 years	227	181	18	59	103	46	25	7	13
25 to 29 years	188	112	25	29	57	76	50	12	13
30 to 34 years	81	51	5	20	27	30	30	*	*
35 years and over	130	53	16	14	23	76	60	8	9
Male									
15 years and over	782	659	34	167	459	123	85	22	15
Enrolled in High School									
15 years	103	103	4	10	89	*	*	*	*
16 and 17 years	145	145	1	26	118	*	*	*	*
18 and 19 years	15	15	*	1	14	*	*	*	*
20 years and over	2	2	*	*	2	*	*	*	*
Enrolled in College									
15 to 17 years	4	4	*	2	2	*	*	*	*
18 and 19 years	108	105	2	27	76	2	*	1	2
20 and 21 years	109	92	4	33	55	17	4	11	2
22 to 24 years	120	97	10	32	55	23	15	3	6
25 to 29 years	66	33	4	11	18	33	23	8	2
30 to 34 years	51	38	2	20	16	13	13	*	*
35 years and over	60	26	6	6	13	34	31	*	3
Female									
15 years and over	780	646	49	176	421	134	86	20	28
Enrolled in High School									
15 years	74	74	*	1	73	*	*	*	*
16 and 17 years	132	132	*	29	103	*	*	*	*
18 and 19 years	31	31	3	11	19	*	*	*	*
20 years and over	12	12	3	*	9	*	*	*	*
Enrolled in College									
15 to 17 years	8	8	*	1	7	*	*	*	*
18 and 19 years	104	98	*	38	60	6	*	2	4
20 and 21 years	91	88	4	41	43	3	2	1	*
22 to 24 years	107	84	8	27	48	23	11	5	8
25 to 29 years	122	79	22	19	39	43	28	4	11
30 to 34 years	30	13	3	2	11	17	17	*	*
35 years and over	69	27	10	8	10	42	29	8	5

* = Represents zero or rounds to zero.

Table A-5. Employment Status of High School and College Students 15 Years and Over, by Level of School, Attendance Status, Age, Sex, Race, and Hispanic Origin, October 2000—*Continued*

(Numbers in thousands.)

Age, sex, race, and Hispanic origin	Total	Full-time students				Part-time students			
		Total	Employed full-time	Employed part-time	Not employed	Total	Employed full-time	Employed part-time	Not employed
HISPANIC[1]									
Both Sexes									
15 years and over	3 269	2 716	269	556	1 892	553	376	105	72
Enrolled in High School									
15 years	503	503	*	18	485	*	*	*	*
16 and 17 years	930	930	8	130	791	*	*	*	*
18 and 19 years	263	263	39	45	179	*	*	*	*
20 years and over	148	148	35	24	90	*	*	*	*
Enrolled in College									
15 to 17 years	24	24	*	10	14	*	*	*	*
18 and 19 years	349	297	35	138	125	51	18	25	8
20 and 21 years	268	219	34	100	85	49	19	26	3
22 to 24 years	282	153	36	61	55	130	90	26	14
25 to 29 years	167	71	41	9	21	96	64	17	15
30 to 34 years	142	62	24	17	21	80	61	6	12
35 years and over	194	47	17	5	25	147	124	4	19
Male									
15 years and over	1 571	1 346	150	264	932	225	166	48	11
Enrolled in High School									
15 years	281	281	*	14	267	*	*	*	*
16 and 17 years	462	462	3	52	407	*	*	*	*
18 and 19 years	152	152	34	27	91	*	*	*	*
20 years and over	58	58	13	11	33	*	*	*	*
Enrolled in College									
15 to 17 years	12	12	*	10	2	*	*	*	*
18 and 19 years	160	136	12	62	61	25	13	11	0
20 and 21 years	118	89	16	39	34	29	11	18	*
22 to 24 years	123	70	19	32	20	52	41	11	*
25 to 29 years	61	26	20	2	5	35	23	7	5
30 to 34 years	75	40	21	11	8	35	29	*	6
35 years and over	70	21	12	4	5	49	49	0	*
Female									
15 years and over	1 698	1 370	119	291	960	328	210	56	61
Enrolled in High School									
15 years	221	221	*	4	218	*	*	*	*
16 and 17 years	468	468	5	79	384	*	*	*	*
18 and 19 years	111	111	4	18	88	*	*	*	*
20 years and over	91	91	21	12	57	*	*	*	*
Enrolled in College									
15 to 17 years	13	13	*	*	13	*	*	*	*
18 and 19 years	188	162	22	76	64	27	5	14	8
20 and 21 years	150	130	18	60	52	20	9	8	3
22 to 24 years	160	82	17	30	35	78	49	15	14
25 to 29 years	106	45	21	7	16	61	41	10	10
30 to 34 years	67	22	4	6	13	45	32	6	6
35 years and over	124	26	5	1	20	98	75	4	19

[1] May be of any race.
* = Represents zero or rounds to zero.

Table A-6. Enrollment Status of Primary Family Members 18 to 24 Years, by Family Income, Level of Enrollment, Type of School, Attendance Status, Sex, Race, and Hispanic Origin, October 2000

(Numbers in thousands.)

Enrollment status, sex, race, and Hispanic origin	Total	Family income										
		Less than $10,000	$10,000 to $14,000	$15,000 to $19,999	$20,000 to $24,999	$25,000 to $29,999	$30,000 to $34,999	$35,000 to $39,999	$40,000 to $49,999	$50,000 to $74,999	$75,000 and over	Not reported
ALL RACES												
Male												
18 to 24 years	8 065	374	400	268	335	466	396	374	619	1 528	2 105	1 201
Not enrolled												
Not high school graduate	1 008	98	135	83	70	91	86	52	86	75	67	165
High school graduate, no college	2 220	93	109	85	106	153	113	139	197	454	444	325
Less than a bachelor's degree	745	4	29	7	13	34	46	23	32	190	222	146
Bachelor's degree or more	196	3	*	*	*	10	3	7	23	44	95	11
Enrolled below college	807	88	61	28	58	45	37	42	70	110	130	137
Enrolled in college full-time												
2-year college	669	34	19	15	23	44	31	24	50	147	201	81
4-year college	1 955	51	33	32	51	58	70	80	115	380	804	281
Enrolled in college part-time												
2-year college	244	2	6	13	2	24	*	4	16	85	64	28
4-year college	221	*	8	4	10	7	10	2	31	44	80	25
Female												
18 to 24 years	6 665	364	279	256	327	294	325	315	569	1 157	1 848	931
Not enrolled												
Not high school graduate	493	87	72	20	52	28	26	23	39	28	45	72
High school graduate, no college	1 376	109	84	95	83	91	88	70	135	211	223	186
Less than a bachelor's degree	574	30	36	20	16	8	24	39	36	86	191	88
Bachelor's degree or more	252	2	2	4	6	2	0	7	24	50	119	36
Enrolled below college	533	76	26	30	35	31	44	18	27	71	78	97
Enrolled in college full-time												
2-year college	749	25	22	31	30	38	43	43	52	160	211	95
4-year college	2 273	31	15	46	78	83	86	102	192	476	837	327
Enrolled in college part-time												
2-year college	223	*	14	4	15	8	9	8	39	39	71	14
4-year college	192	5	8	4	13	6	4	5	25	35	73	15
WHITE												
Male												
18 to 24 years	6 441	163	256	179	269	337	304	297	520	1 309	1 895	912
Not enrolled												
Not high school graduate	750	46	84	65	55	74	72	41	69	66	61	118
High school graduate, no college	1 751	57	72	45	88	105	91	108	167	364	397	257
Less than a bachelor's degree	594	*	23	6	10	18	26	14	31	164	197	105
Bachelor's degree or more	177	3	*	*	*	2	3	7	19	43	90	10
Enrolled below college	634	37	40	19	54	41	29	34	60	105	129	86
Enrolled in college full-time												
2-year college	528	4	5	14	14	35	24	19	45	126	172	71
4-year college	1 631	13	24	18	45	42	50	68	97	325	718	232
Enrolled in college part-time												
2-year college	198	2	6	13	*	14	*	4	15	72	56	15
4-year college	179	*	3	*	2	7	10	2	18	44	74	19
Female												
18 to 24 years	5 120	184	176	153	251	208	209	220	441	921	1 613	744
Not enrolled												
Not high school graduate	355	43	46	9	42	24	16	21	32	22	38	61
High school graduate, no college	1 021	57	57	55	54	61	58	42	101	168	211	155
Less than a bachelor's degree	432	23	17	14	16	4	19	34	23	59	159	64
Bachelor's degree or more	190	2	2	*	5	*	0	4	24	42	86	23
Enrolled below college	376	28	24	24	28	20	26	11	24	54	68	69
Enrolled in college full-time												
2-year college	575	15	2	14	23	33	24	27	43	144	177	74
4-year college	1 831	13	13	30	55	56	58	73	152	367	739	273
Enrolled in college part-time												
2-year college	181	*	9	2	15	5	9	8	25	35	64	9
4-year college	160	3	6	4	13	4	*	0	17	29	70	15

* = Represents zero or rounds to zero.

Table A-6. Enrollment Status of Primary Family Members 18 to 24 Years, by Family Income, Level of Enrollment, Type of School, Attendance Status, Sex, Race, and Hispanic Origin, October 2000
—Continued

(Numbers in thousands.)

Enrollment status, sex, race, and Hispanic origin	Total	Family income										Not reported
		Less than $10,000	$10,000 to $14,000	$15,000 to $19,999	$20,000 to $24,999	$25,000 to $29,999	$30,000 to $34,999	$35,000 to $39,999	$40,000 to $49,999	$50,000 to $74,999	$75,000 and over	
NON-HISPANIC WHITE												
Male												
18 to 24 years	5 188	90	141	88	153	184	210	223	407	1 133	1 790	768
Not enrolled												
Not high school graduate	368	10	23	31	24	20	33	20	56	38	48	65
High school graduate, no college	1 439	43	54	21	63	71	63	84	138	314	372	216
Less than a bachelor's degree	528	*	20	4	5	11	26	6	23	144	197	91
Bachelor's degree or more	160	3	*	*	*	2	3	7	19	35	82	10
Enrolled below college	463	19	9	15	26	26	21	29	44	92	118	66
Enrolled in college full-time												
2-year college	399	*	5	6	9	13	5	11	24	105	154	66
4-year college	1 526	13	21	12	24	26	49	62	83	306	702	226
Enrolled in college part-time												
2-year college	154	2	6	*	*	12	*	4	10	57	50	13
4-year college	150	*	3	*	1	3	10	*	10	41	67	16
Female												
18 to 24 years	4 202	108	94	66	138	143	145	192	354	812	1 534	617
Not enrolled												
Not high school graduate	210	18	23	3	18	10	13	19	28	10	29	40
High school graduate, no college	777	43	37	22	30	41	30	35	87	151	193	108
Less than a bachelor's degree	368	17	11	7	8	4	11	29	17	55	152	57
Bachelor's degree or more	177	2	2	*	3	*	0	4	20	42	86	17
Enrolled below college	264	11	6	11	18	11	18	11	9	45	66	59
Enrolled in college full-time												
2-year college	493	8	2	6	19	20	18	23	41	127	162	67
4-year college	1 642	6	7	15	30	51	49	62	121	337	715	248
Enrolled in college part-time												
2-year college	145	*	3	*	10	5	5	8	17	26	61	9
4-year college	124	3	2	2	2	1	*	0	13	18	70	12
BLACK												
Male												
18 to 24 years	1 212	170	122	70	53	102	63	60	62	171	106	234
Not enrolled												
Not high school graduate	228	46	47	18	13	17	14	4	14	8	3	44
High school graduate, no college	384	26	34	36	16	44	16	31	19	75	26	62
Less than a bachelor's degree	100	4	3	1	3	12	11	5	*	14	16	30
Bachelor's degree or more	6	*	*	*	*	5	*	*	*	*	1	*
Enrolled below college	157	49	18	9	4	4	4	8	10	5	*	47
Enrolled in college full-time												
2-year college	87	23	12	*	4	6	4	1	*	19	10	8
4-year college	193	22	7	2	5	10	13	12	11	41	40	29
Enrolled in college part-time												
2-year college	24	*	*	*	*	3	*	*	*	10	3	8
4-year college	33	*	1	4	8	*	*	*	8	*	6	6
Female												
18 to 24 years	1 198	146	97	96	59	75	99	67	95	201	133	131
Not enrolled												
Not high school graduate	124	39	22	11	10	4	11	3	7	6	0	11
High school graduate, no college	296	44	27	38	24	28	28	22	21	38	7	20
Less than a bachelor's degree	115	3	16	6	*	2	6	6	10	21	28	18
Bachelor's degree or more	34	*	*	*	0	*	*	3	*	7	18	7
Enrolled below college	121	41	2	7	7	6	18	3	3	9	*	26
Enrolled in college full-time												
2-year college	140	6	20	17	7	5	16	10	8	13	20	17
4-year college	308	12	2	15	10	26	17	19	35	98	49	26
Enrolled in college part-time												
2-year college	38	*	5	2	*	2	*	*	11	4	8	5
4-year college	22	2	3	*	*	2	4	2	*	6	3	*

* = Represents zero or rounds to zero.

Table A-6. Enrollment Status of Primary Family Members 18 to 24 Years, by Family Income, Level of Enrollment, Type of School, Attendance Status, Sex, Race, and Hispanic Origin, October 2000 —Continued

(Numbers in thousands.)

Enrollment status, sex, race, and Hispanic origin	Total	Family income										
		Less than $10,000	$10,000 to $14,000	$15,000 to $19,999	$20,000 to $24,999	$25,000 to $29,999	$30,000 to $34,999	$35,000 to $39,999	$40,000 to $49,999	$50,000 to $74,999	$75,000 and over	Not reported
ASIAN/PACIFIC ISLANDER												
Male												
18 to 24 years	333	26	17	15	9	26	23	12	33	31	95	46
Not enrolled												
Not high school graduate	21	4	4	*	2	*	*	3	3	*	2	3
High school graduate, no college	49	3	1	1	*	5	1	1	8	7	19	5
Less than a bachelor's degree	38	*	4	*	*	4	9	3	1	6	5	7
Bachelor's degree or more	13	*	*	*	*	3	*	*	4	1	4	1
Enrolled below college	10	3	*	*	*	*	3	*	*	*	1	4
Enrolled in college full-time												
2-year college	52	6	2	2	3	3	4	4	6	2	19	3
4-year college	121	11	2	12	1	5	7	1	7	13	41	20
Enrolled in college part-time												
2-year college	19	*	*	*	2	6	*	*	1	3	5	3
4-year college	9	*	4	*	*	*	*	*	4	*	*	*
Female												
18 to 24 years	316	22	3	7	15	11	14	26	31	31	101	54
Not enrolled												
Not high school graduate	8	*	1	*	*	*	*	*	*	*	6	*
High school graduate, no college	43	2	*	2	3	2	*	4	10	5	5	10
Less than a bachelor's degree	28	4	2	*	*	2	*	*	4	6	4	5
Bachelor's degree or more	28	*	*	4	*	2	*	*	*	1	15	6
Enrolled below college	33	5	*	*	*	5	*	4	*	8	9	2
Enrolled in college full-time												
2-year college	34	4	*	*	*	*	4	6	*	2	14	3
4-year college	129	6	*	*	12	*	11	10	5	9	49	27
Enrolled in college part-time												
2-year college	3	*	*	*	*	*	*	*	3	*	*	*
4-year college	10	*	*	*	*	*	*	2	8	*	*	*
HISPANIC[1]												
Male												
18 to 24 years	1 301	79	121	96	119	153	102	84	113	178	107	148
Not enrolled												
Not high school graduate	392	38	61	34	34	54	42	20	13	28	13	53
High school graduate, no college	323	14	20	28	25	33	28	27	29	50	27	41
Less than a bachelor's degree	70	*	5	3	5	6	1	9	7	21	*	14
Bachelor's degree or more	16	*	5	*	*	*	*	*	*	8	9	*
Enrolled below college	184	22	33	5	28	15	8	12	16	14	11	21
Enrolled in college full-time												
2-year college	132	4	*	7	5	21	22	9	20	20	18	5
4-year college	109	*	2	6	21	16	0	6	14	19	16	10
Enrolled in college part-time												
2-year college	44	*	*	13	*	2	*	*	5	15	6	2
4-year college	30	*	*	1	1	4	0	2	9	3	7	2
Female												
18 to 24 years	963	89	85	91	116	65	67	31	91	120	81	127
Not enrolled												
Not high school graduate	153	25	26	9	27	14	3	1	4	12	9	21
High school graduate, no college	259	21	20	33	24	20	30	8	14	23	19	47
Less than a bachelor's degree	67	6	6	8	8	*	7	5	9	5	7	7
Bachelor's degree or more	13	*	*	*	3	*	*	*	4	*	*	6
Enrolled below college	115	20	18	13	10	9	8	*	15	9	2	10
Enrolled in college full-time												
2-year college	82	7	*	8	3	13	6	4	2	17	15	8
4-year college	199	7	6	15	25	5	9	14	31	34	27	25
Enrolled in college part-time												
2-year college	38	*	5	4	5	*	4	*	8	9	2	*
4-year college	37	2	3	2	10	4	*	*	3	11	*	3

[1]May be of any race.
* = Represents zero or rounds to zero.

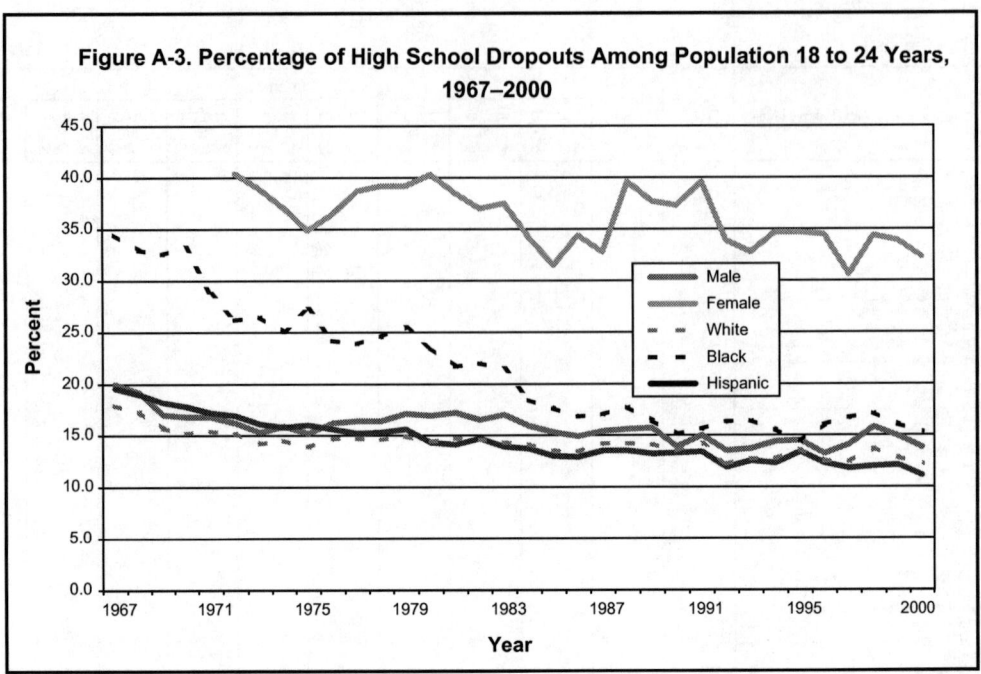

Figure A-3. Percentage of High School Dropouts Among Population 18 to 24 Years, 1967–2000

Source: U.S. Census Bureau, *Current Population Survey*, 2000.

- In 1967, nearly one in five between the ages of 18 and 24 years were high school dropouts. By 2000, the proportion of high school dropouts reached a new low of 12.4 percent.

- The high school dropout rate for grades 10 to 12 dipped slightly to 4.5 percent, with a significant drop to 3.9 percent for females, offsetting an increase among males. Both Blacks and Asian and Pacific Islanders had lower than average female dropout rates, and above average male rates. Since 1967, the dropout rates have dropped among all races, however, the change among Blacks has been more dramatic, going from 34.5 percent in 1967 to 15.3 percent in 2000.

Table A-7. Population 14 to 24 Years by High School Graduate Status, College Enrollment, Attainment, Sex, Race, and Hispanic Origin, October 1967 to 2000

(Numbers in thousands.)

Year, sex, race, and Hispanic origin	Total	Population 18 to 24 years							High school graduates 14 to 24 years		
		High school graduates		Percent			High school dropouts		All graduates	Percent	
		Total students	Enrolled in college	High school graduates	Enrolled in college	High school graduates enrolled in college	Number	Percent		Enrolled in college	Enrolled or completed some college
ALL RACES											
Both Sexes											
2000	26 658	21 822	9 452	81.9	35.5	43.3	3 315	12.4	22 080	43.5	66.7
1999	26 041	21 127	9 259	81.1	35.6	43.8	3 413	13.1	21 390	44.0	67.2
1998	25 507	20 567	9 322	80.6	36.6	45.3	3 544	13.9	20 775	45.5	68.0
1997	24 973	20 338	9 204	81.4	36.9	45.2	3 236	13.0	20 577	45.6	67.3
1996	24 671	20 131	8 767	81.6	35.5	43.5	3 147	12.8	20 465	44.0	67.2
1995	24 900	20 125	8 539	80.8	34.3	42.4	3 471	13.9	20 359	42.7	67.1
1994	25 254	20 581	8 729	81.5	34.6	42.4	3 365	13.3	20 779	42.7	66.9
1993r	25 522	20 844	8 630	81.7	33.8	41.4	3 349	13.1	21 060	41.6	65.3
1993	24 100	19 772	8 193	82.0	34.0	41.4	3 070	12.7	19 979	41.6	65.4
1992	24 278	19 921	8 343	82.1	34.4	41.9	3 083	12.7	20 194	42.3	65.6
1991	24 572	19 883	8 172	80.9	33.3	41.1	3 486	14.2	20 065	41.4	60.7
1990	24 852	20 311	7 964	82.3	32.0	39.1	3 379	13.6	20 571	39.6	58.9
1989	25 261	20 461	7 804	81.0	30.9	38.1	3 644	14.4	20 749	38.5	57.9
1988	25 733	20 900	7 791	81.2	30.3	37.3	3 749	14.6	21 204	37.6	57.4
1987	25 950	21 118	7 693	81.4	29.6	36.4	3 751	14.5	21 477	36.9	56.2
1986	26 512	21 768	7 477	82.1	28.2	34.3	3 687	13.9	22 086	34.8	55.0
1985	27 122	22 349	7 537	82.4	27.8	33.7	3 687	13.9	22 722	34.3	54.3
1984	28 031	22 870	7 591	81.6	27.1	33.2	4 142	14.8	23 252	33.7	53.0
1983	28 580	22 988	7 477	80.4	26.2	32.5	4 410	15.4	23 359	33.1	52.8
1982	28 846	23 291	7 678	80.7	26.6	33.0	4 500	15.6	23 708	33.5	52.7
1981	28 965	23 343	7 575	80.6	26.2	32.5	4 520	15.6	23 705	32.9	51.7
1980	28 957	23 413	7 400	80.9	25.6	31.6	4 515	15.6	23 856	32.1	51.1
1979	27 974	22 421	6 991	80.1	25.0	31.2	4 560	16.3	22 911	31.9	51.6
1978	27 647	22 309	6 995	80.7	25.3	31.4	4 388	15.9	22 759	31.9	51.4
1977	27 331	22 008	7 142	80.5	26.1	32.5	4 313	15.8	22 499	33.0	52.0
1976	26 919	21 677	7 181	80.5	26.7	33.1	4 276	15.9	22 158	33.7	53.4
1975	26 387	21 326	6 935	80.8	26.3	32.5	4 110	15.6	21 824	33.1	52.5
1974	25 670	20 725	6 316	80.7	24.6	30.5	4 070	15.9	21 267	31.2	51.3
1973	25 237	20 377	6 055	80.7	24.0	29.7	3 973	15.7	20 895	30.4	50.7
1972	24 579	19 618	6 257	79.8	25.5	31.9	4 068	16.6	20 107	32.6	52.9
1971	23 668	18 691	6 210	79.0	26.2	33.2	4 025	17.0	19 130	33.9	53.1
1970	22 552	17 768	5 805	78.8	25.7	32.7	3 908	17.3	18 218	33.5	52.3
1969	21 362	16 703	5 840	78.2	27.3	35.0	3 769	17.6	17 152	35.7	52.5
1968	20 562	15 683	5 356	76.3	26.0	34.2	3 929	19.1	16 165	35.2	51.5
1967	20 009	15 114	5 100	75.5	25.5	33.7	3 967	19.8	15 642	34.9	50.5
Male											
2000	13 338	10 622	4 343	79.6	32.6	40.9	1 837	13.8	10 736	41.0	63.1
1999	12 905	10 201	4 396	79.1	34.0	43.1	1 818	14.9	10 331	43.3	64.5
1998	12 764	9 915	4 403	77.7	34.5	44.4	2 018	15.8	10 006	44.5	64.9
1997	12 513	9 933	4 374	79.4	35.0	44.0	1 765	14.1	10 025	44.2	64.9
1996	12 285	9 815	4 187	80.0	34.1	42.6	1 628	13.2	9 960	43.0	65.6
1995	12 351	9 789	4 089	79.3	33.1	41.8	1 791	14.5	9 884	42.1	64.2
1994	12 557	9 970	4 152	79.4	33.1	41.6	1 804	14.4	10 051	41.9	64.9
1993r	12 712	10 142	4 237	79.8	33.3	41.8	1 745	13.7	10 229	42.0	63.9
1993	11 898	9 541	3 994	80.2	33.6	41.9	1 575	13.2	9 625	42.0	64.1
1992	11 965	9 576	3 912	80.0	32.7	40.9	1 617	13.5	9 706	41.3	64.1
1991	12 036	9 493	3 954	78.9	32.9	41.7	1 810	15.0	9 564	41.9	59.2
1990	12 134	9 778	3 922	80.6	32.3	40.1	1 689	13.9	9 894	40.5	58.0
1989	12 325	9 700	3 717	78.7	30.2	38.3	1 941	15.7	9 810	38.6	57.2
1988	12 491	9 832	3 770	78.7	30.2	38.3	1 950	15.6	9 947	38.5	56.5
1987	12 626	10 030	3 867	79.4	30.6	38.6	1 948	15.4	10 207	39.0	56.0
1986	12 921	10 338	3 702	80.0	28.7	35.8	1 924	14.9	10 465	36.2	54.4
1985	13 199	10 614	3 749	80.4	28.4	35.3	2 015	15.3	10 784	36.0	54.6
1984	13 744	10 914	3 929	79.4	28.6	36.0	2 184	15.9	11 052	36.4	53.6
1983	14 003	10 906	3 820	77.9	27.3	35.0	2 379	17.0	10 959	35.5	52.7
1982	14 083	11 120	3 837	79.0	27.2	34.5	2 329	16.5	11 295	35.0	53.0
1981	14 127	11 052	3 833	78.2	27.1	34.7	2 424	17.2	11 203	35.1	52.1
1980	14 107	11 125	3 717	78.9	26.3	33.4	2 390	16.9	11 309	33.7	51.4
1979	13 571	10 657	3 508	78.5	25.8	32.9	2 320	17.1	10 838	33.6	52.4
1978	13 385	10 614	3 621	79.3	27.1	34.1	2 200	16.4	10 789	34.5	52.6
1977	13 218	10 440	3 712	79.0	28.1	35.6	2 170	16.4	10 626	36.0	54.2
1976	13 012	10 312	3 673	79.2	28.2	35.6	2 109	16.2	10 492	36.0	55.7
1975	12 724	10 214	3 693	80.3	29.0	36.2	1 928	15.2	10 415	36.7	56.1
1974	12 315	9 835	3 411	79.9	27.7	34.7	1 958	15.9	10 073	35.3	55.6
1973	12 111	9 716	3 360	80.2	27.7	34.6	1 853	15.3	9 908	35.1	55.4
1972	11 712	9 647	3 601	79.0	30.7	38.2	1 898	16.2	9 461	38.8	59.0
1971	11 092	8 669	3 599	78.2	32.4	41.5	1 865	16.8	8 855	42.1	60.1
1970	10 385	8 087	3 331	77.9	32.1	41.2	1 746	16.8	8 279	41.8	59.2
1969	9 649	7 445	3 392	77.2	35.2	45.6	1 640	17.0	7 609	46.2	61.2
1968	9 251	6 864	3 152	74.2	34.1	45.9	1 777	19.2	8 038	46.7	61.1
1967	8 999	6 678	2 982	74.2	33.1	44.7	1 804	20.0	6 829	45.1	58.8

r = Revised, controlled to the 1990 census-based population estimates; previous 1993 data controlled to 1980-based population estimates.

Table A-7. Population 14 to 24 Years by High School Graduate Status, College Enrollment, Attainment, Sex, Race, and Hispanic Origin, October 1967 to 2000—*Continued*

(Numbers in thousands.)

Year, sex, race, and Hispanic origin	Total	Population 18 to 24 years							High school graduates 14 to 24 years		
		High school graduates		Percent			High school dropouts		All graduates	Percent	
		Total students	Enrolled in college	High school graduates	Enrolled in college	High school graduates enrolled in college	Number	Percent		Enrolled in college	Enrolled or completed some college
ALL RACES											
Female											
2000	13 319	11 200	5 109	84.1	38.4	45.6	1 478	11.1	11 344	45.8	70.1
1999	13 136	10 926	4 863	83.2	37.0	44.5	1 594	12.1	11 058	44.6	69.8
1998	12 743	10 651	4 919	83.6	38.6	46.2	1 526	12.0	10 768	46.4	70.7
1997	12 460	10 403	4 829	83.5	38.8	46.4	1 471	11.8	10 549	46.8	69.6
1996	12 386	10 317	4 582	83.3	37.0	44.4	1 519	12.3	10 507	44.9	68.6
1995	12 548	10 338	4 452	82.4	35.5	43.1	1 679	13.4	10 477	43.4	69.8
1994	12 696	10 611	4 576	83.6	36.0	43.1	1 561	12.3	10 729	43.4	68.7
1993r	12 810	10 702	4 393	83.5	34.3	41.0	1 604	12.5	10 831	41.3	66.6
1993	12 202	10 232	4 199	83.9	34.4	41.0	1 494	12.2	10 355	41.2	66.7
1992	12 313	10 344	4 429	84.0	36.0	42.8	1 466	11.9	10 486	43.3	66.9
1991	12 536	10 391	4 218	82.9	33.6	40.6	1 676	13.4	10 502	41.0	62.1
1990	12 718	10 533	4 042	82.8	31.8	38.4	1 690	13.3	10 676	38.7	59.8
1989	12 936	10 758	4 085	83.2	31.6	38.0	1 702	13.2	10 936	38.4	58.6
1988	13 242	11 068	4 021	83.6	30.4	36.3	1 799	13.5	11 257	36.8	58.2
1987	13 324	11 086	3 826	83.2	28.7	34.5	1 803	13.5	11 268	35.0	56.4
1986	13 591	11 430	3 775	84.1	27.8	33.0	1 751	12.9	11 623	33.5	55.5
1985	13 923	11 736	3 788	84.3	27.2	32.3	1 804	13.0	11 937	32.8	54.0
1984	14 287	11 956	3 662	83.7	25.6	30.6	1 958	13.7	12 199	31.3	52.4
1983	14 577	12 082	3 657	82.9	25.1	30.3	2 031	13.9	12 294	31.0	52.8
1982	14 763	12 171	3 841	82.4	26.0	31.6	2 171	14.7	12 411	32.1	52.4
1981	14 838	12 290	3 741	82.8	25.2	30.4	2 097	14.1	12 503	31.0	51.3
1980	14 851	12 287	3 682	82.7	24.8	30.0	2 124	14.3	12 547	30.6	50.8
1979	14 403	11 763	3 482	81.7	24.2	29.6	2 240	15.6	12 074	30.4	50.8
1978	14 262	11 694	3 373	82.0	23.7	28.8	2 188	15.3	11 969	29.6	50.3
1977	14 113	11 569	3 431	82.0	24.3	29.7	2 143	15.2	11 875	30.3	50.0
1976	13 907	11 365	3 508	81.7	25.2	30.9	2 168	15.6	11 666	31.6	51.4
1975	13 663	11 113	3 243	81.3	23.7	29.2	2 181	16.0	11 407	29.9	49.2
1974	13 355	10 889	2 905	81.5	21.8	26.7	2 112	15.8	11 194	27.4	47.5
1973	13 126	10 663	2 696	81.2	20.5	25.3	2 119	16.1	10 986	26.1	46.5
1972	12 867	10 371	2 724	80.6	21.2	26.3	2 170	16.9	10 644	27.0	47.4
1971	12 576	10 020	2 610	79.7	20.8	26.0	2 159	17.2	10 272	26.9	47.1
1970	12 167	9 680	2 474	79.6	20.3	25.6	2 163	17.8	9 908	26.3	46.6
1969	11 713	9 259	2 448	79.0	20.9	26.4	2 128	18.2	9 499	27.1	45.7
1968	11 311	8 820	2 205	78.0	19.5	25.0	2 150	19.0	9 072	25.9	44.4
1967	11 011	8 436	2 117	76.6	19.2	25.1	2 162	19.6	8 694	26.0	44.7
WHITE											
Both Sexes											
2000	21 257	17 512	7 566	82.4	35.6	43.2	2 598	12.2	17 714	43.4	66.9
1999	20 866	17 052	7 447	81.7	35.7	43.7	2 680	12.8	17 220	43.8	67.5
1998	20 465	16 701	7 541	81.6	36.9	45.2	2 810	13.7	16 855	45.3	68.3
1997	20 020	16 557	7 495	82.7	37.4	45.3	2 476	12.4	16 733	45.6	67.7
1996	19 676	16 199	7 123	82.3	36.2	44.0	2 458	12.5	16 436	44.3	68.4
1995	19 866	16 269	7 011	81.9	35.3	43.1	2 711	13.6	16 439	43.4	68.3
1994	20 171	16 670	7 118	82.6	35.3	42.7	2 553	12.7	16 814	42.9	67.6
1993r	20 493	16 989	7 074	82.9	34.5	41.6	2 595	12.7	17 161	41.8	66.5
1993	19 430	16 196	6 763	83.4	34.8	41.8	2 369	12.2	16 361	41.9	66.7
1992	19 671	16 379	6 916	83.3	35.2	42.2	2 398	12.2	16 586	42.7	67.0
1991	19 980	16 324	6 813	81.7	34.1	41.7	2 845	14.2	16 467	42.0	62.3
1990	20 393	16 823	6 635	82.5	32.5	39.4	2 751	13.5	17 022	39.8	60.1
1989	20 825	17 089	6 631	82.1	31.8	38.8	2 926	14.1	17 329	39.1	58.9
1988	21 261	17 491	6 659	82.3	31.3	38.1	3 012	14.2	17 720	38.4	58.5
1987	21 493	17 689	6 483	82.3	30.2	36.6	3 042	14.2	17 982	37.1	56.8
1986	22 020	18 291	6 307	83.1	28.6	34.5	2 961	13.4	18 554	34.9	55.5
1985	22 632	18 916	6 500	83.6	28.7	34.4	3 050	13.5	19 229	35.0	55.3
1984	23 347	19 373	6 256	83.0	28.0	33.7	3 281	14.1	19 686	34.2	53.8
1983	23 899	19 643	6 463	82.2	27.0	32.9	3 428	14.3	19 948	33.5	53.4
1982	24 206	19 944	6 694	82.4	27.2	33.1	3 523	14.6	20 292	33.6	53.1
1981	24 486	20 123	6 549	82.2	26.7	32.5	3 590	14.7	20 439	33.0	52.1
1980	24 482	20 214	6 423	82.6	26.2	31.8	3 525	14.4	20 583	32.3	51.4
1979	23 895	19 616	6 120	82.1	25.6	31.2	3 571	14.9	20 033	31.8	51.7
1978	23 650	19 526	6 077	82.6	25.7	31.1	3 464	14.6	19 911	31.7	51.3
1977	23 430	19 291	6 209	82.3	26.5	32.2	3 445	14.7	19 712	32.6	52.1
1976	23 119	19 045	6 276	82.4	27.1	33.0	3 407	14.7	19 462	33.5	53.5
1975	22 703	18 883	6 116	83.2	26.9	32.4	3 149	13.9	19 298	32.0	52.7
1974	22 141	18 318	5 589	82.7	25.2	30.5	3 212	14.5	18 794	31.2	51.7
1973	21 766	18 023	5 438	82.8	25.0	30.2	3 085	14.2	18 470	30.8	51.6
1972	21 315	17 410	5 624	81.7	26.4	32.3	3 241	15.2	17 838	33.0	53.9
1971	20 533	16 593	5 594	81.3	27.2	33.5	3 156	15.4	17 087	34.2	54.1
1970	19 608	15 960	5 305	81.4	27.1	33.2	2 974	15.2	16 334	33.9	53.4
1969	18 606	15 031	5 347	80.8	28.7	35.6	2 915	15.7	15 383	36.2	53.5
1968	17 951	14 127	4 929	78.7	27.5	34.9	3 107	17.3	14 506	35.7	52.5
1967	17 500	13 657	4 708	78.0	26.9	34.5	3 141	17.9	14 022	35.2	51.4

r = Revised, controlled to the 1990 census-based population estimates; previous 1993 data controlled to 1980-based population estimates.

Table A-7. Population 14 to 24 Years by High School Graduate Status, College Enrollment, Attainment, Sex, Race, and Hispanic Origin, October 1967 to 2000—*Continued*

(Numbers in thousands.)

Year, sex, race, and Hispanic origin	Total	Population 18 to 24 years							High school graduates 14 to 24 years		
		High school graduates		Percent			High school dropouts		All graduates	Percent	
		Total students	Enrolled in college	High school graduates	Enrolled in college	High school graduates enrolled in college	Number	Percent		Enrolled in college	Enrolled or completed some college
WHITE											
Male											
2000	10 739	8 603	3 522	80.1	32.8	40.9	1 450	13.5	8 690	41.1	63.5
1999	10 532	8 382	3 585	79.6	34.0	42.7	1 462	13.9	8 457	42.8	64.8
1998	10 400	8 194	3 634	78.8	34.9	44.3	1 628	15.7	8 256	44.4	65.5
1997	10 173	8 204	3 633	80.6	35.7	44.3	1 406	13.8	8 274	44.5	65.3
1996	9 897	8 000	3 419	80.8	34.5	42.7	1 275	12.9	8 104	43.0	66.0
1995	9 980	8 001	3 398	80.2	34.0	42.5	1 430	14.3	8 067	42.7	65.3
1994	10 123	8 168	3 406	80.7	33.6	41.7	1 377	13.6	8 227	41.9	65.4
1993r	10 294	8 338	3 498	81.0	34.0	42.0	1 388	13.5	8 411	42.1	65.1
1993	9 641	7 857	3 313	81.5	34.4	42.2	1 379	12.9	7 926	42.3	65.4
1992	9 744	7 911	3 291	81.2	33.8	41.6	1 300	13.3	8 016	42.1	65.8
1991	9 896	7 843	3 270	79.3	33.0	41.7	1 520	15.4	7 899	41.9	59.9
1990	10 053	8 157	3 292	81.1	32.7	40.3	1 430	14.2	8 246	40.7	58.8
1989	10 240	8 177	3 223	79.9	31.5	39.4	1 572	15.4	8 271	39.7	58.5
1988	10 380	8 268	3 260	79.7	31.4	39.4	1 594	15.4	8 365	39.6	57.8
1987	10 549	8 498	3 289	80.6	31.2	38.7	1 593	15.1	8 647	39.2	56.4
1986	10 814	8 780	3 168	81.2	29.3	36.1	1 575	14.6	8 886	36.4	55.1
1985	11 108	9 077	3 254	81.7	29.3	35.8	1 637	14.7	9 229	36.6	55.5
1984	11 521	9 348	3 406	81.1	29.6	36.4	1 744	15.1	9 459	36.8	54.2
1983	11 787	9 411	3 335	79.8	28.3	35.4	1 865	15.8	9 534	35.9	53.5
1982	11 874	9 611	3 308	80.9	27.9	34.4	1 810	15.2	9 761	34.9	53.2
1981	12 040	9 619	3 340	79.9	27.7	34.7	1 960	16.3	9 754	35.1	52.8
1980	12 011	9 686	3 275	80.6	27.3	33.8	1 883	15.7	9 838	34.1	51.8
1979	11 721	9 457	3 104	80.7	26.5	32.8	1 830	15.6	9 615	33.4	52.7
1978	11 572	9 438	3 195	81.6	27.6	33.9	1 722	14.9	9 582	34.3	52.5
1977	11 445	9 263	3 286	80.9	28.7	35.5	1 779	15.5	9 422	35.8	54.5
1976	11 279	9 186	3 250	81.4	28.8	35.4	1 691	15.0	9 340	35.7	55.9
1975	11 050	9 139	3 326	82.7	30.1	36.4	1 490	13.5	9 310	36.9	56.6
1974	10 722	8 768	3 035	81.8	28.3	34.6	1 579	14.7	8 980	35.2	55.9
1973	10 511	8 637	3 032	82.2	28.8	35.1	1 453	13.8	8 817	35.6	56.5
1972	10 212	8 278	3 195	81.1	31.3	38.6	1 506	14.7	8 462	39.2	60.1
1971	9 653	7 807	3 284	80.9	34.0	42.1	1 429	14.8	7 978	42.6	61.4
1970	9 053	7 324	3 096	80.9	34.2	42.3	1 297	14.3	7 496	42.9	60.9
1969	8 420	6 740	3 146	80.0	37.4	46.7	1 248	14.8	6 882	47.3	62.8
1968	8 084	6 221	2 949	77.0	36.5	47.4	1 401	17.3	6 372	48.1	62.7
1967	7 864	6 073	2 761	77.2	35.1	45.5	1 391	17.7	6 210	45.9	60.0
Female											
2000	10 517	8 909	4 044	84.7	38.5	45.4	1 148	10.9	9 024	45.6	70.2
1999	10 334	8 671	3 862	83.9	37.4	44.5	1 218	11.8	8 763	44.7	70.1
1998	10 065	8 507	3 907	84.5	38.8	45.9	1 181	11.7	8 599	46.2	71.0
1997	9 847	8 352	3 863	84.8	39.2	46.3	1 072	10.9	8 458	46.6	70.1
1996	9 778	8 200	3 705	83.9	37.9	45.2	1 182	12.1	8 333	45.6	70.7
1995	9 886	8 271	3 615	83.7	36.6	43.7	1 281	13.0	8 376	44.0	71.3
1994	10 048	8 503	3 714	84.6	37.0	43.7	1 175	11.7	8 588	43.9	69.7
1993r	10 199	8 651	3 576	84.8	35.1	41.3	1 207	11.8	8 750	41.5	67.9
1993	9 790	8 339	3 450	85.2	35.2	41.4	1 125	11.5	8 435	41.6	68.0
1992	9 928	8 468	3 625	85.3	36.5	42.8	1 098	11.1	8 569	43.2	68.1
1991	10 119	8 481	3 544	83.8	35.0	41.8	1 324	13.1	8 568	42.1	64.5
1990	10 340	8 666	3 344	83.8	32.3	38.6	1 322	12.8	8 775	38.9	61.4
1989	10 586	8 913	3 409	84.2	32.2	38.2	1 354	12.8	9 059	38.6	59.2
1988	10 881	9 223	3 399	84.8	31.2	36.9	1 418	13.0	9 355	37.3	59.1
1987	10 944	9 189	3 192	84.0	29.2	34.7	1 449	13.2	9 334	36.2	57.2
1986	11 205	9 509	3 139	84.9	28.0	33.0	1 388	12.4	9 667	33.6	55.8
1985	11 524	9 840	3 247	85.4	28.2	33.0	1 413	12.3	10 001	33.6	55.2
1984	11 826	10 026	3 120	84.8	26.4	31.1	1 535	13.0	10 089	31.8	53.4
1983	12 112	10 233	3 129	84.5	25.8	30.6	1 563	12.9	10 233	31.3	53.4
1982	12 332	10 333	3 285	83.8	26.6	31.8	1 713	13.0	10 530	32.3	52.9
1981	12 446	10 504	3 208	84.4	25.8	30.5	1 629	13.1	10 687	31.1	51.6
1980	12 471	10 528	3 147	84.4	25.2	29.9	1 642	13.2	10 749	30.6	50.9
1979	12 174	10 157	3 015	83.4	24.8	29.7	1 741	14.3	10 417	30.3	50.8
1978	12 078	10 088	2 882	83.5	23.9	28.6	1 742	14.4	10 327	29.3	50.3
1977	11 985	10 029	2 923	83.7	24.4	29.1	1 666	13.9	10 292	29.7	50.0
1976	11 840	9 860	3 026	83.3	25.6	30.7	1 717	14.5	10 118	31.4	51.3
1975	11 653	9 743	2 790	83.6	23.9	28.6	1 658	14.2	9 986	29.4	49.1
1974	11 419	9 551	2 555	83.6	22.4	26.8	1 633	14.3	9 811	27.5	47.8
1973	11 255	9 387	2 406	83.4	21.4	25.6	1 632	14.5	9 653	26.4	47.1
1972	11 103	9 132	2 428	82.2	21.9	26.6	1 735	15.6	9 377	27.4	48.3
1971	10 880	8 887	2 310	81.7	21.2	26.0	1 720	15.0	9 107	26.0	47.7
1970	10 555	8 634	2 209	81.8	20.9	25.6	1 675	15.9	8 837	26.3	47.2
1969	10 186	8 291	2 200	81.4	21.6	26.5	1 668	16.4	8 501	27.2	46.3
1968	9 866	7 906	1 980	80.1	20.1	25.0	1 706	17.3	8 135	26.0	45.1
1967	9 637	7 586	1 949	78.7	20.2	25.7	1 750	18.2	7 815	26.6	45.7

r = Revised, controlled to the 1990 census-based population estimates; previous 1993 data controlled to 1980-based population estimates.

Table A-7. Population 14 to 24 Years by High School Graduate Status, College Enrollment, Attainment, Sex, Race, and Hispanic Origin, October 1967 to 2000—*Continued*

(Numbers in thousands.)

Year, sex, race, and Hispanic origin	Total	Population 18 to 24 years							High school graduates 14 to 24 years		
		High school graduates		Percent			High school dropouts			Percent	
		Total students	Enrolled in college	High school graduates	Enrolled in college	High school graduates enrolled in college	Number	Percent	All graduates	Enrolled in college	Enrolled or completed some college
BLACK											
Both Sexes											
2000	4 013	3 090	1 216	77.0	30.3	39.4	615	15.3	3 129	39.5	61.0
1999	3 827	2 911	1 145	76.1	29.9	39.4	613	16.0	2 985	39.9	60.4
1998	3 745	2 747	1 116	73.4	29.8	40.6	642	17.1	2 790	40.8	61.8
1997	3 650	2 725	1 085	74.7	29.7	39.8	611	16.7	2 762	40.2	60.0
1996	3 637	2 738	983	75.3	27.0	35.9	581	16.0	2 805	36.6	54.6
1995	3 625	2 788	988	76.9	27.3	35.4	522	14.4	2 828	35.8	58.0
1994	3 661	2 818	1 001	77.0	27.3	35.5	568	15.5	2 859	36.3	59.2
1993r	3 666	2 747	897	74.9	24.5	32.7	600	16.4	2 771	32.8	54.0
1993	3 516	2 629	861	74.8	24.5	32.8	578	16.4	2 653	32.9	53.9
1992	3 521	2 625	886	74.6	25.2	33.8	575	16.3	2 668	34.3	53.3
1991	3 504	2 630	828	75.1	23.6	31.5	545	15.6	2 658	31.8	46.0
1990	3 520	2 710	894	77.0	25.4	33.0	530	15.1	2 759	33.7	48.0
1989	3 559	2 708	835	76.1	23.5	30.8	583	16.4	2 750	31.5	49.2
1988	3 568	2 680	752	75.1	21.1	28.1	631	17.7	2 741	28.6	46.3
1987	3 603	2 739	823	76.0	22.8	30.0	611	17.0	2 790	30.6	48.1
1986	3 653	2 795	812	76.5	22.2	29.1	617	16.8	2 837	29.3	47.8
1985	3 716	2 810	734	75.6	19.8	26.1	655	17.6	2 848	26.5	43.8
1984	3 862	2 885	786	74.7	20.4	27.2	712	18.4	2 950	28.0	45.2
1983	3 865	2 740	741	70.9	19.2	27.0	832	21.5	2 790	27.7	45.0
1982	3 872	2 744	767	70.9	19.8	28.0	851	22.0	2 793	28.2	45.5
1981	3 778	2 678	750	70.9	19.9	28.0	821	21.7	2 718	28.7	44.8
1980	3 721	2 592	715	69.7	19.2	27.6	876	23.5	2 656	28.1	45.9
1979	3 510	2 356	696	67.1	19.8	29.5	895	25.5	2 415	30.6	48.4
1978	3 452	2 340	694	67.8	20.1	29.7	850	24.6	2 396	30.6	47.8
1977	3 387	2 286	721	67.5	21.3	31.5	808	23.9	2 342	32.4	46.9
1976	3 315	2 239	749	67.5	22.6	33.5	803	24.2	2 291	34.2	50.4
1975	3 213	2 081	665	64.8	20.7	32.0	877	27.3	2 149	32.6	48.1
1974	3 105	2 083	555	67.1	17.9	26.6	780	25.1	2 145	27.5	44.8
1973	3 114	2 079	498	66.8	16.0	24.0	826	26.5	2 139	25.0	41.6
1972	2 986	1 992	540	66.7	18.1	27.1	782	26.2	2 044	28.0	42.0
1971	2 866	1 789	522	62.4	18.2	29.2	825	28.8	1 833	30.0	42.3
1970	2 692	1 602	416	59.5	15.5	26.0	897	33.3	1 635	26.7	39.4
1969	2 542	1 497	407	58.9	16.0	27.2	828	32.6	1 547	27.5	40.1
1968	2 421	1 399	352	57.8	14.5	25.2	799	33.0	1 432	26.0	38.1
1967	2 283	1 276	297	55.9	13.0	23.3	788	34.5	1 316	23.7	35.0
Male											
2000	1 885	1 389	470	73.7	24.9	33.8	329	17.4	1 409	34.1	53.5
1999	1 747	1 292	501	73.9	28.7	38.8	285	16.3	1 336	40.2	57.7
1998	1 724	1 163	445	67.5	25.8	38.2	354	20.5	1 186	38.5	57.5
1997	1 701	1 214	425	71.4	25.0	35.0	297	17.5	1 232	35.1	56.3
1996	1 682	1 199	422	71.3	25.1	35.2	292	17.4	1 225	35.8	53.7
1995	1 660	1 247	430	75.1	25.9	34.4	235	14.2	1 262	35.1	56.2
1994	1 733	1 277	440	73.7	25.4	34.5	303	17.5	1 293	35.3	57.9
1993r	1 703	1 240	387	72.8	22.7	31.2	266	15.6	1 247	31.4	50.1
1993	1 659	1 207	379	72.8	22.8	31.4	258	15.6	1 214	31.5	50.0
1992	1 676	1 211	356	72.3	21.2	29.4	259	15.5	1 226	29.7	49.4
1991	1 635	1 174	378	71.8	23.1	32.2	252	15.4	1 188	32.4	47.0
1990	1 634	1 240	426	75.9	26.1	34.4	223	13.6	1 260	35.1	48.8
1989	1 654	1 195	324	72.2	19.6	27.1	307	18.6	1 207	27.5	45.8
1988	1 653	1 189	297	71.9	18.0	25.0	312	18.9	1 205	25.1	42.5
1987	1 666	1 188	377	71.3	22.6	31.7	312	18.7	1 209	32.3	48.0
1986	1 687	1 220	349	72.3	20.7	28.6	300	17.8	1 239	29.1	44.4
1985	1 720	1 244	345	72.3	20.1	27.7	323	18.8	1 258	28.2	43.6
1984	1 811	1 272	367	70.2	20.3	28.9	362	20.2	1 295	29.6	45.2
1983	1 807	1 202	331	66.5	18.3	27.5	435	24.1	1 228	27.9	43.6
1982	1 786	1 171	331	65.6	18.5	28.3	458	25.6	1 188	28.6	44.5
1981	1 730	1 154	325	66.7	18.8	28.2	419	24.2	1 165	28.5	42.3
1980	1 690	1 115	293	66.0	17.3	26.3	440	26.0	1 141	26.9	44.1
1979	1 577	973	304	61.7	19.3	31.2	457	29.0	988	32.0	46.7
1978	1 554	956	305	61.5	19.6	31.9	451	29.0	981	32.4	49.3
1977	1 528	970	309	63.5	20.2	31.9	369	24.1	991	33.0	47.6
1976	1 503	936	331	62.3	22.0	35.4	393	26.1	952	35.9	50.3
1975	1 451	897	294	61.8	20.3	32.8	404	27.8	923	33.4	50.5
1974	1 396	919	280	65.8	20.1	30.5	346	24.8	941	31.1	47.3
1973	1 434	952	266	66.4	18.5	27.9	371	25.9	962	28.4	44.2
1972	1 373	870	287	63.4	20.9	33.0	373	27.2	897	34.0	47.4
1971	1 318	769	262	58.3	19.9	34.1	416	31.6	783	34.9	45.8
1970	1 220	668	192	54.8	15.7	28.7	436	35.7	684	29.5	41.4
1969	1 141	631	202	55.3	17.7	32.0	383	33.6	653	32.5	44.6
1968	1 087	582	170	53.5	15.6	29.2	370	34.0	600	30.3	43.2
1967	1 032	525	167	50.9	16.2	31.8	397	38.5	539	32.3	41.6

r = Revised, controlled to the 1990 census-based population estimates; previous 1993 data controlled to 1980-based population estimates.

Table A-7. Population 14 to 24 Years by High School Graduate Status, College Enrollment, Attainment, Sex, Race, and Hispanic Origin, October 1967 to 2000—*Continued*

(Numbers in thousands.)

Year, sex, race, and Hispanic origin	Total	Population 18 to 24 years								High school graduates 14 to 24 years		
		High school graduates		Percent			High school dropouts		All graduates	Percent	
		Total students	Enrolled in college	High school graduates	Enrolled in college	High school graduates enrolled in college	Number	Percent		Enrolled in college	Enrolled or completed some college
BLACK											
Female											
2000	2 128	1 700	747	79.9	35.1	43.9	287	13.5	1 720	43.9	67.1
1999	2 080	1 619	644	77.9	31.0	39.8	327	15.7	1 650	39.6	62.6
1998	2 021	1 584	671	78.4	33.2	42.4	288	14.3	1 604	42.4	65.0
1997	1 949	1 511	659	77.5	33.8	43.6	314	16.1	1 529	43.1	63.0
1996	1 956	1 539	561	78.7	28.7	36.4	288	14.7	1 580	37.3	55.3
1995	1 965	1 541	558	78.4	28.4	36.2	287	14.6	1 566	36.3	59.5
1994	1 928	1 542	561	80.0	29.1	36.4	265	13.7	1 567	37.1	60.3
1993r	1 965	1 508	511	76.7	26.0	33.9	337	17.2	1 526	34.1	57.2
1993	1 857	1 425	484	76.7	26.1	34.0	319	17.2	1 441	34.1	57.1
1992	1 845	1 417	531	76.8	28.8	37.5	315	17.1	1 446	38.2	56.6
1991	1 869	1 455	450	77.8	24.1	30.9	296	15.8	1 468	31.4	45.2
1990	1 886	1 468	467	77.8	24.8	31.8	306	16.2	1 498	32.4	47.3
1989	1 905	1 511	511	79.3	26.8	33.8	277	14.5	1 541	34.7	51.8
1988	1 915	1 492	455	77.9	23.8	30.5	318	16.6	1 538	31.3	49.2
1987	1 937	1 550	445	80.0	23.0	28.7	298	15.4	1 579	29.4	48.9
1986	1 966	1 574	462	80.1	23.5	29.4	306	15.6	1 598	29.3	50.4
1985	1 996	1 565	389	78.4	19.5	24.9	332	16.6	1 592	25.1	44.0
1984	2 052	1 613	419	78.6	20.4	26.0	349	17.0	1 655	26.8	45.1
1983	2 058	1 539	411	74.8	20.0	26.7	398	19.3	1 561	27.5	46.3
1982	2 086	1 572	436	75.4	20.9	27.7	393	18.8	1 604	27.9	46.3
1981	2 049	1 526	424	74.5	20.7	27.8	402	19.6	1 554	28.8	46.6
1980	2 031	1 475	422	72.6	20.8	28.6	436	21.5	1 511	29.1	47.4
1979	1 934	1 383	392	71.5	20.3	28.3	439	22.7	1 426	29.7	49.8
1978	1 897	1 384	390	73.0	20.6	28.2	398	21.0	1 415	29.3	46.7
1977	1 859	1 317	413	70.8	22.2	31.4	439	23.6	1 354	31.9	46.2
1976	1 813	1 302	417	71.8	23.0	32.0	410	22.6	1 338	32.9	50.3
1975	1 761	1 182	372	67.1	21.1	31.5	473	26.9	1 224	32.0	46.4
1974	1 709	1 167	277	68.3	16.2	23.7	434	25.4	1 207	24.8	42.9
1973	1 681	1 125	231	66.9	13.7	20.5	456	27.1	1 177	22.2	39.4
1972	1 613	1 123	253	69.6	15.7	22.5	408	25.3	1 150	23.2	37.9
1971	1 547	1 019	259	65.9	16.7	25.4	409	26.4	1 049	26.4	39.8
1970	1 471	935	225	63.6	15.3	24.1	461	31.3	955	24.7	39.3
1969	1 402	867	206	61.8	14.7	23.8	444	31.7	896	24.0	38.6
1968	1 334	819	183	61.4	13.7	22.3	430	32.2	834	22.9	35.9
1967	1 249	751	130	60.1	10.4	17.3	391	31.3	778	17.9	33.2
ASIAN/PACIFIC ISLANDER											
Both Sexes											
2000	1 143	1 038	639	90.8	55.9	61.6	52	4.6	1 053	61.8	83.9
1999	1 130	1 019	626	90.2	55.4	61.4	58	5.1	1 035	62.0	85.5
Male											
2000	571	521	337	91.1	58.9	64.7	34	6.0	527	64.7	85.6
1999	505	443	284	87.8	56.2	64.0	39	7.7	454	64.9	82.5
Female											
2000	572	517	302	90.4	52.9	58.5	18	3.1	526	58.9	82.3
1999	626	576	342	92.1	54.7	59.4	19	3.1	582	59.7	87.8

r = Revised, controlled to the 1990 census-based population estimates; previous 1993 data controlled to 1980-based population estimates.

Table A-7. Population 14 to 24 Years by High School Graduate Status, College Enrollment, Attainment, Sex, Race, and Hispanic Origin, October 1967 to 2000—*Continued*

(Numbers in thousands.)

Year, sex, race, and Hispanic origin	Total	Population 18 to 24 years								High school graduates 14 to 24 years		
		High school graduates		Percent			High school dropouts			Percent	
		Total students	Enrolled in college	High school graduates	Enrolled in college	High school graduates enrolled in college	Number	Percent	All graduates	Enrolled in college	Enrolled or completed some college
HISPANIC[1]												
Both Sexes												
2000	4 134	2 462	899	59.6	21.7	36.5	1 335	32.3	2 509	36.8	53.1
1999	3 953	2 325	739	58.8	18.7	31.8	1 340	33.9	2 359	31.7	49.6
1998	4 014	2 403	820	59.8	20.4	34.1	1 383	34.4	2 419	34.3	53.2
1997	3 606	2 236	806	62.0	22.4	36.0	1 103	30.6	2 302	37.1	54.3
1996	3 510	2 019	706	57.5	20.1	35.0	1 210	34.5	2 046	34.5	52.5
1995	3 603	2 112	745	58.6	20.7	35.3	1 250	34.7	2 142	35.7	55.8
1994	3 523	1 995	662	56.6	18.8	33.2	1 224	34.7	2 009	33.4	54.3
1993r	3 363	2 049	728	60.9	21.6	35.5	1 103	32.8	2 081	35.8	55.6
1993	2 772	1 682	602	60.7	21.7	35.8	907	32.7	1 712	36.0	55.8
1992	2 754	1 579	586	57.3	21.3	37.1	936	33.9	1 603	37.6	55.0
1991	2 874	1 498	516	52.1	18.0	34.4	1 139	39.6	1 519	34.6	47.6
1990	2 749	1 498	435	54.5	15.8	29.0	1 025	37.3	1 523	29.4	44.7
1989	2 818	1 576	453	55.9	16.1	28.7	1 062	37.7	1 600	29.4	43.6
1988	2 642	1 458	450	55.2	17.0	30.9	1 046	39.6	1 481	31.3	47.0
1987	2 592	1 597	455	61.6	17.6	28.5	849	32.8	1 612	28.7	44.0
1986	2 514	1 507	458	59.9	18.2	30.4	864	34.4	1 535	30.9	45.6
1985	2 221	1 396	375	62.9	16.9	26.9	700	31.5	1 419	27.6	46.7
1984	2 018	1 212	362	60.1	17.9	29.9	691	34.2	1 223	30.0	46.0
1983	2 025	1 110	349	54.8	17.2	31.4	759	37.5	1 134	32.3	48.4
1982	2 001	1 153	337	57.6	16.8	29.2	740	37.0	1 173	30.0	47.3
1981	2 052	1 144	342	55.8	16.7	29.9	790	38.5	1 166	30.5	45.8
1980	2 033	1 099	327	54.1	16.1	29.8	820	40.3	1 117	30.1	47.3
1979	1 754	968	292	55.2	16.6	30.2	687	39.2	1 001	31.2	45.7
1978	1 672	935	254	55.9	15.2	27.2	656	39.2	965	28.0	43.2
1977	1 609	880	277	54.7	17.2	31.5	622	38.7	900	32.4	43.8
1976	1 551	862	309	55.6	19.9	35.8	566	36.5	891	36.3	48.9
1975	1 446	832	295	57.5	20.4	35.5	505	34.9	849	36.5	50.8
1974	1 506	842	272	55.9	18.1	32.3	558	37.1	858	33.1	47.8
1973	1 285	709	206	55.2	16.0	29.1	500	38.9	732	30.3	43.0
1972	1 338	694	179	51.9	13.4	25.8	541	40.4	709	27.2	36.7
Male												
2000	2 171	1 172	401	54.0	18.5	34.2	800	36.8	1 197	34.5	50.8
1999	2 045	1 122	322	54.9	15.8	28.7	746	36.4	1 131	28.7	45.7
1998	2 109	1 146	346	54.3	16.4	30.2	838	39.7	1 153	30.0	47.2
1997	1 937	1 140	371	58.9	19.2	32.5	643	33.2	1 168	33.0	49.2
1996	1 815	994	300	54.8	16.5	30.2	657	36.2	1 005	30.6	48.8
1995	1 907	1 106	356	58.0	18.7	32.2	653	34.2	1 022	36.2	52.3
1994	1 896	1 021	312	53.8	16.5	30.6	685	36.1	1 026	30.7	52.7
1993r	1 710	1 005	338	58.8	19.8	33.6	591	34.6	1 023	33.7	51.2
1993	1 354	786	266	58.1	19.6	33.8	470	34.7	803	33.9	51.1
1992	1 384	720	247	52.0	17.8	34.3	531	38.4	736	34.8	52.2
1991	1 503	719	211	47.8	14.0	29.3	668	44.4	728	29.7	42.2
1990	1 403	753	214	53.7	15.3	28.4	559	39.8	770	29.4	46.5
1989	1 439	756	211	52.5	14.7	27.9	580	40.3	767	28.2	42.7
1988	1 375	724	228	52.7	16.6	31.5	553	40.2	736	32.2	48.3
1987	1 337	795	247	59.5	18.5	31.1	461	34.5	803	31.1	45.1
1986	1 339	769	233	57.4	17.4	30.3	499	37.3	776	30.5	44.4
1985	1 132	659	168	58.2	14.8	25.5	405	35.8	675	26.4	44.9
1984	956	549	154	57.4	16.1	28.1	338	35.4	554	28.2	45.7
1983	968	476	152	49.2	15.7	31.9	396	40.9	489	33.1	47.4
1982	944	519	141	55.0	14.9	27.2	347	36.8	525	28.0	44.8
1981	988	498	164	50.4	16.6	32.9	428	43.3	506	33.6	48.6
1980	1 012	518	160	51.2	15.8	30.9	431	42.6	521	31.1	49.5
1979	837	454	153	54.2	18.3	33.7	328	39.2	469	34.3	49.5
1978	781	420	126	53.8	16.1	30.0	313	40.1	438	30.4	46.3
1977	754	396	139	52.5	18.4	35.1	295	39.1	404	35.9	46.5
1976	701	378	150	53.9	21.4	39.7	253	36.1	403	39.8	51.8
1975	678	383	145	56.5	21.4	37.9	221	32.6	390	37.9	55.4
1974	720	390	141	54.2	19.6	36.2	279	38.8	401	36.7	51.4
1973	625	348	105	55.7	16.8	30.2	228	36.5	361	32.1	45.4
1972	609	301	92	49.4	15.1	30.6	253	41.5	309	32.0	44.3

[1]May be of any race.
r = Revised, controlled to the 1990 census-based population estimates; previous 1993 data controlled to 1980-based population estimates.

Table A-7. Population 14 to 24 Years by High School Graduate Status, College Enrollment, Attainment, Sex, Race, and Hispanic Origin, October 1967 to 2000—*Continued*

(Numbers in thousands.)

Year, sex, race, and Hispanic origin	Total	Population 18 to 24 years							High school graduates 14 to 24 years		
		High school graduates		Percent			High school dropouts		All graduates	Percent	
		Total students	Enrolled in college	High school graduates	Enrolled in college	High school graduates enrolled in college	Number	Percent		Enrolled in college	Enrolled or completed some college
HISPANIC[1]											
Female											
2000	1 963	1 290	498	65.7	25.4	38.6	535	27.3	1 312	38.9	55.2
1999	1 908	1 203	417	63.0	21.8	34.7	593	31.1	1 228	34.4	53.3
1998	1 906	1 257	474	66.0	24.9	37.7	545	28.6	1 266	38.2	58.7
1997	1 669	1 097	436	65.7	26.1	39.7	460	27.6	1 135	41.4	59.6
1996	1 694	1 026	406	60.6	24.0	39.6	554	32.7	1 043	40.4	56.0
1995	1 696	1 011	389	59.6	22.9	38.4	598	35.4	1 022	38.6	59.6
1994	1 628	973	350	59.8	21.5	36.0	539	33.1	983	36.2	55.9
1993r	1 652	1 045	390	63.3	23.6	37.3	510	30.9	1 059	37.8	60.1
1993	1 418	895	336	63.1	23.7	37.5	439	31.0	907	38.0	60.4
1992	1 369	860	339	62.8	24.8	39.4	405	29.6	867	39.9	57.4
1991	1 372	780	305	56.9	22.2	39.1	473	34.5	791	39.2	52.5
1990	1 346	745	221	55.3	16.4	29.7	465	34.5	753	29.5	43.0
1989	1 377	823	244	59.8	17.7	29.6	482	35.0	836	30.5	44.5
1988	1 267	736	224	58.1	17.7	30.4	492	38.8	747	30.5	45.8
1987	1 256	801	208	63.8	16.6	26.0	387	30.8	808	26.4	43.2
1986	1 175	739	226	62.9	19.2	30.6	365	31.1	759	31.4	46.8
1985	1 091	734	205	67.3	18.8	27.9	295	27.0	743	28.4	48.0
1984	1 061	661	207	62.3	19.5	31.3	353	33.2	667	31.5	46.6
1983	1 057	634	198	60.0	18.7	31.2	363	34.3	644	31.8	49.7
1982	1 056	634	196	60.0	18.6	30.9	393	37.2	648	31.8	49.2
1981	1 064	646	178	60.7	16.7	27.6	362	34.0	662	28.2	43.4
1980	1 021	579	165	56.7	16.2	28.5	389	38.1	595	29.1	45.4
1979	917	516	140	56.3	15.3	27.1	358	39.0	534	28.1	42.3
1978	891	516	128	57.9	14.4	24.8	343	38.5	528	25.8	40.0
1977	855	483	139	56.5	16.3	28.8	326	38.1	495	29.7	41.6
1976	850	483	160	56.8	18.8	33.1	313	36.8	489	33.5	46.5
1975	769	449	150	58.4	19.5	33.4	283	36.8	460	34.8	46.7
1974	786	451	129	57.4	16.4	28.6	280	35.6	459	29.2	43.4
1973	658	362	102	55.0	15.5	28.2	272	41.3	372	28.8	41.1
1972	728	394	88	54.1	12.1	22.3	288	39.6	402	23.6	31.1
NON-HISPANIC WHITE											
Both Sexes											
2000	17 327	15 187	6 709	87.7	38.7	44.2	1 316	7.6	15 344	44.3	69.0
1999	17 080	14 812	6 735	86.7	39.4	45.5	1 404	8.2	14 952	45.6	70.2
1998	16 459	14 259	6 704	86.6	40.7	47.0	1 470	8.9	14 396	47.1	70.7
1997	16 446	14 318	6 700	87.1	40.7	46.8	1 405	8.5	14 429	47.0	70.1
1996	16 261	14 214	6 420	87.4	39.5	45.2	1 303	8.0	14 420	45.5	70.7
1995	16 747	14 440	6 365	86.2	38.0	44.1	1 616	9.7	14 589	44.3	70.4
1994	16 892	14 746	6 466	87.3	38.3	43.9	1 464	8.7	14 875	44.1	69.3
1993	16 895	14 665	6 221	86.8	36.8	42.4	1 524	9.0	14 801	42.6	68.1
Male											
2000	8 670	7 493	3 136	86.4	36.2	41.9	677	7.8	7 556	42.0	65.4
1999	8 580	7 301	3 284	85.1	38.3	45.0	753	8.8	7 369	45.0	67.7
1998	8 296	7 027	3 271	84.7	39.4	46.6	813	9.8	7 082	46.6	68.2
1997	8 277	7 071	3 269	85.4	39.5	46.2	794	9.6	7 113	46.4	68.1
1996	8 119	7 004	3 104	86.3	38.2	44.3	651	8.0	7 097	44.6	68.6
1995	8 347	7 053	3 087	84.5	37.0	43.8	869	10.4	7 110	43.9	67.3
1994	8 353	7 186	3 101	86.0	37.1	43.2	755	9.0	7 242	43.4	67.0
1993	8 403	7 138	3 071	84.9	36.6	43.0	811	9.7	7 192	43.2	67.1
Female											
2000	8 657	7 693	3 573	88.9	41.3	46.4	638	7.4	7 789	46.6	72.5
1999	8 500	7 510	3 451	88.4	40.6	46.0	651	7.7	7 583	46.2	72.5
1998	8 164	7 232	3 433	88.6	42.1	47.5	656	8.0	7 315	47.7	73.2
1997	8 169	7 247	3 431	88.7	42.0	47.3	611	7.5	7 316	47.5	72.1
1996	8 143	7 210	3 316	88.5	40.7	46.0	652	8.0	7 323	46.4	72.8
1995	8 400	7 388	3 278	88.0	39.0	44.3	747	8.9	7 480	44.7	73.2
1994	8 539	7 560	3 365	88.5	39.4	44.5	709	8.3	7 633	44.8	71.5
1993	8 492	7 527	3 150	88.6	37.1	41.9	714	8.4	7 610	42.0	69.1

[1]May be of any race.
r = Revised, controlled to the 1990 census-based population estimates; previous 1993 data controlled to 1980-based population estimates.

Table A-7. Population 14 to 24 Years by High School Graduate Status, College Enrollment, Attainment, Sex, Race, and Hispanic Origin, October 1967 to 2000—*Continued*

(Numbers in thousands.)

Year, sex, race, and Hispanic origin	Total	Population 18 to 24 years							High school graduates 14 to 24 years		
		High school graduates		Percent			High school dropouts			Percent	
		Total students	Enrolled in college	High school graduates	Enrolled in college	High school graduates enrolled in college	Number	Percent	All graduates	Enrolled in college	Enrolled or completed some college
NON-HISPANIC BLACK											
Both Sexes											
2000	3 875	3 002	1 182	77.5	30.5	39.4	581	15.0	3 038	39.6	61.0
1999	3 686	2 841	1 120	77.1	30.4	39.4	561	15.2	2 907	40.0	60.8
1998	3 637	2 678	1 080	76.6	29.7	40.3	606	16.7	2 719	40.5	61.8
1997	3 559	2 677	1 060	75.2	29.8	39.6	576	16.2	2 710	39.9	60.4
1996	3 514	2 665	959	75.9	27.3	36.0	540	15.4	2 728	36.7	55.0
1995	3 534	2 724	971	77.1	27.5	35.7	503	14.2	2 764	36.0	58.5
1994	3 545	2 755	978	77.0	27.6	35.5	527	14.9	2 796	36.3	60.0
1993	3 460	2 597	847	75.0	24.5	32.6	565	16.3	2 620	32.8	54.5
Male											
2000	1 813	1 348	456	74.3	25.1	33.8	311	17.6	1 368	34.1	53.4
1999	1 672	1 260	484	75.4	28.9	38.4	255	15.2	1 301	39.7	57.5
1998	1 672	1 139	436	68.1	26.1	38.3	329	19.7	1 159	38.7	57.7
1997	1 646	1 189	418	72.2	25.4	35.2	274	16.6	1 206	35.2	56.7
1996	1 623	1 171	419	72.2	25.8	35.8	272	16.8	1 197	36.4	54.4
1995	1 617	1 220	421	75.5	26.0	34.5	224	13.9	1 235	35.1	56.3
1994	1 661	1 243	427	74.8	25.7	34.4	268	16.2	1 259	35.2	58.6
1993	1 637	1 194	374	73.0	22.9	31.4	255	15.6	1 201	31.5	50.7
Female											
2000	2 061	1 653	726	80.2	35.0	43.9	270	13.1	1 670	44.1	67.3
1999	2 014	1 581	636	78.5	31.6	40.2	306	15.2	1 606	40.2	63.4
1998	1 965	1 539	643	78.3	32.7	41.8	277	14.1	1 559	41.8	64.8
1997	1 913	1 487	642	77.8	33.6	43.1	303	15.8	1 504	43.6	63.4
1996	1 891	1 494	540	79.0	28.6	36.1	268	14.2	1 530	36.9	55.5
1995	1 918	1 504	550	78.4	28.7	36.6	280	14.6	1 529	36.7	60.3
1994	1 884	1 512	550	80.3	29.2	36.4	258	13.7	1 537	37.2	61.3
1993	1 823	1 402	473	76.9	25.9	33.7	309	17.0	1 419	33.9	57.7

Note: The change in the educational attainment question and the college completion categories from "4 or more years of college" to "at least some college" in 1992 caused an increase in the proportion of 14-to 24-year-old high school graduates enrolled in college or completed some college, of approximately 5 percentage points. High school graduates are people who have completed 4 years of high school or more, for 1967 to 1991. Beginning in 1992, they were people whose highest degree was a high school diploma (including equivalency) or higher.

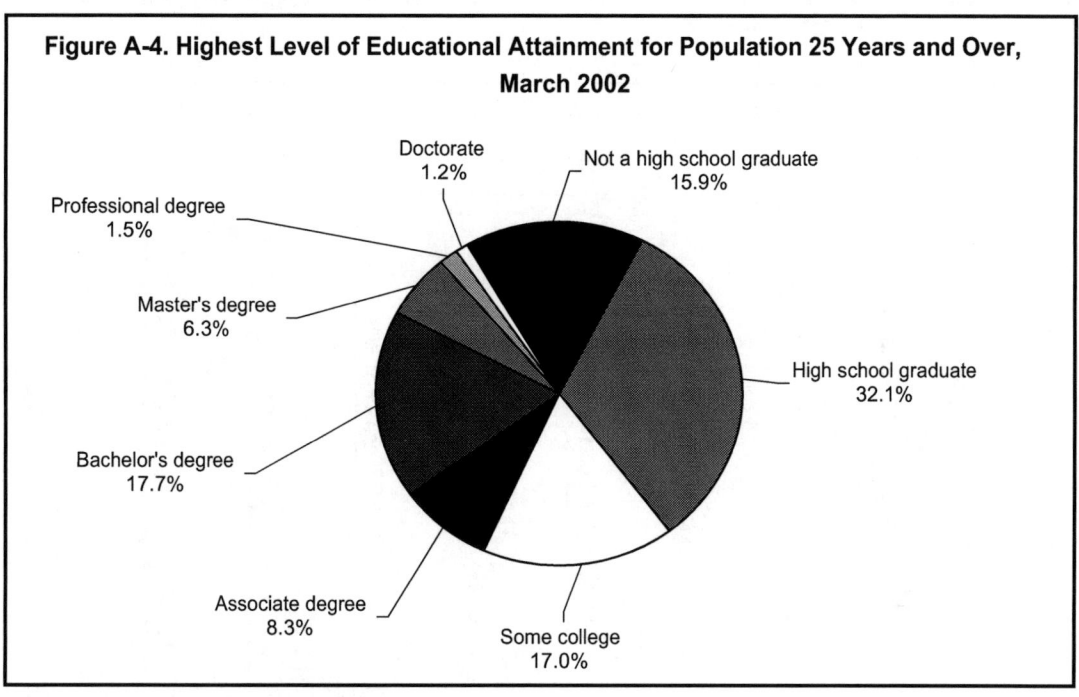

Figure A-4. Highest Level of Educational Attainment for Population 25 Years and Over, March 2002

Source: U.S. Census Bureau, *Current Population Survey*, 2002.

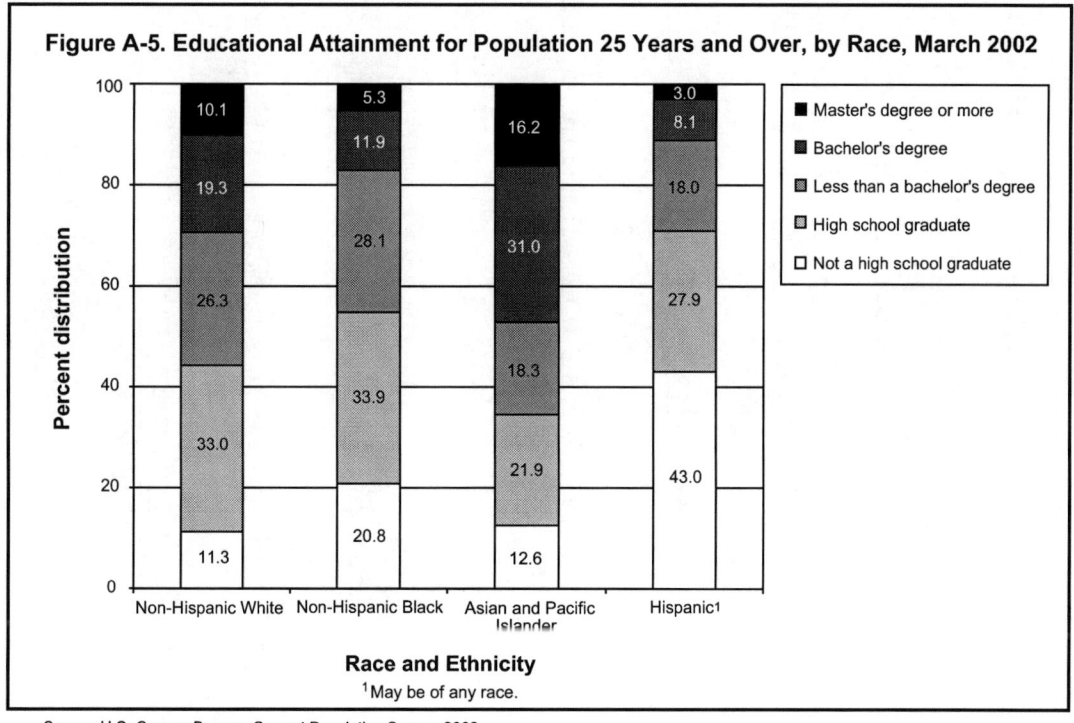

Figure A-5. Educational Attainment for Population 25 Years and Over, by Race, March 2002

Source: U.S. Census Bureau, *Current Population Survey*, 2002.

Table A-8. Educational Attainment of the Population 15 Years and Over, by Age, Sex, Race, and Hispanic Origin, March 2002

(Numbers in thousands.)

Age, sex, race, and Hispanic origin	Total	None	Elementary			High school			
			1st–4th grade	5th–6th grade	7th–8th grade	9th grade	10th grade	11th grade	High school graduate
ALL RACES									
Both Sexes									
15 years and over	221 591	945	2 132	4 153	8 469	8 136	9 879	13 632	66 831
15 to 17 years	12 137	12	9	52	2 247	3 772	3 714	2 117	150
18 and 19 years	7 909	13	16	46	96	217	482	2 608	2 276
20 to 24 years	19 404	51	76	266	247	396	645	1 318	5 949
25 to 29 years	18 310	59	136	393	262	345	405	886	5 200
30 to 34 years	20 360	66	172	411	327	365	433	810	5 789
35 to 39 years	21 648	69	156	384	322	366	481	809	6 854
40 to 44 years	22 636	76	148	322	330	381	468	827	7 455
45 to 49 years	20 988	71	160	327	319	270	422	699	6 764
50 to 54 years	18 557	95	166	297	336	237	329	584	5 667
55 to 59 years	14 667	72	155	272	446	270	384	563	4 733
60 to 64 years	11 208	41	163	246	454	277	385	527	4 070
65 to 69 years	9 597	79	185	274	561	272	466	564	3 524
70 to 74 years	8 526	81	201	229	709	322	436	430	3 043
75 years and over	15 647	160	392	633	1 815	645	828	890	5 359
15 to 17 years	12 137	12	9	52	2 247	3 772	3 714	2 117	150
18 years and over	209 454	933	2 123	4 100	6 222	4 364	6 165	11 515	66 682
15 to 24 years	39 449	76	100	364	2 589	4 385	4 842	6 042	8 375
25 years and over	182 142	870	2 032	3 789	5 880	3 751	5 037	7 589	58 456
15 to 64 years	187 822	626	1 355	3 017	5 383	6 898	8 150	11 748	54 906
65 years and over	33 769	319	778	1 136	3 086	1 238	1 729	1 884	11 926
Male									
15 years and over	106 910	458	1 102	2 132	4 265	4 089	4 881	6 833	31 308
15 to 17 years	6 209	9	4	32	1 252	1 917	1 903	994	74
18 and 19 years	4 026	8	7	29	58	114	276	1 445	1 117
20 to 24 years	9 679	21	55	169	114	221	322	716	3 169
25 to 29 years	9 150	42	79	233	135	185	218	507	2 767
30 to 34 years	10 084	45	114	257	184	199	253	421	2 984
35 to 39 years	10 698	44	91	188	177	206	264	417	3 466
40 to 44 years	11 124	32	81	143	177	214	258	449	3 767
45 to 49 years	10 256	38	80	169	164	134	227	363	3 323
50 to 54 years	9 075	61	86	143	172	112	142	278	2 576
55 to 59 years	7 091	27	66	137	234	145	165	274	2 067
60 to 64 years	5 282	12	82	135	224	119	167	235	1 694
65 to 69 years	4 451	34	83	134	277	131	206	250	1 436
70 to 74 years	3 794	27	106	124	394	141	185	154	1 150
75 years and over	5 991	58	169	239	703	252	295	329	1 717
15 to 17 years	6 209	9	4	32	1 252	1 917	1 903	994	74
18 years and over	100 701	449	1 099	2 100	3 013	2 172	2 977	5 839	31 234
15 to 24 years	19 914	37	66	230	1 424	2 252	2 502	3 156	4 361
25 years and over	86 996	421	1 037	1 902	2 841	1 837	2 379	3 678	26 947
15 to 64 years	92 674	340	744	1 635	2 891	3 565	4 194	6 100	27 005
65 years and over	14 235	118	358	497	1 374	524	687	733	4 303
Female									
15 years and over	114 681	488	1 030	2 021	4 204	4 047	4 998	6 799	35 523
15 to 17 years	5 928	4	5	20	995	1 855	1 811	1 123	75
18 and 19 years	3 883	5	9	17	38	103	206	1 163	1 159
20 to 24 years	9 724	30	20	96	132	175	323	601	2 780
25 to 29 years	9 159	17	57	160	127	160	187	380	2 433
30 to 34 years	10 277	21	58	154	143	166	181	389	2 805
35 to 39 years	10 950	25	65	196	144	161	218	392	3 388
40 to 44 years	11 512	44	67	179	153	167	210	379	3 688
45 to 49 years	10 732	33	80	158	155	136	195	336	3 441
50 to 54 years	9 482	35	80	154	164	126	187	306	3 091
55 to 59 years	7 575	45	89	135	212	125	220	288	2 666
60 to 64 years	5 926	28	81	111	229	159	219	292	2 375
65 to 69 years	5 146	45	102	140	284	141	259	314	2 088
70 to 74 years	4 732	55	95	105	316	181	251	276	1 893
75 years and over	9 656	102	223	394	1 113	393	532	561	3 641
15 to 17 years	5 928	4	5	20	995	1 855	1 811	1 123	75
18 years and over	108 753	484	1 025	2 000	3 209	2 192	3 187	5 676	35 448
15 to 24 years	19 535	38	35	134	1 165	2 133	2 340	2 887	4 014
25 years and over	95 146	449	995	1 887	3 039	1 914	2 658	3 912	31 509
15 to 64 years	95 147	286	610	1 381	2 492	3 333	3 956	5 648	27 900
65 years and over	19 534	201	420	639	1 712	714	1 042	1 151	7 623

Table A-8. Educational Attainment of the Population 15 Years and Over, by Age, Sex, Race, and Hispanic Origin, March 2002—*Continued*

(Numbers in thousands.)

Age, sex, race, and Hispanic origin	College						
	Some college, no degree	Associate degree, occupational	Associate degree, academic	Bachelor's degree	Master's degree	Professional degree	Doctorate degree
ALL RACES							
Both Sexes							
15 years and over	40 333	8 659	7 530	34 372	11 576	2 753	2 190
15 to 17 years	51	1	4	4	2	1	*
18 and 19 years	2 097	34	17	6	2	*	*
20 to 24 years	7 194	554	528	2 081	85	15	*
25 to 29 years	3 746	814	691	4 288	799	207	78
30 to 34 years	3 653	1 024	849	4 694	1 295	274	199
35 to 39 years	3 840	1 156	972	4 348	1 298	351	240
40 to 44 years	3 918	1 229	1 090	4 341	1 436	354	260
45 to 49 years	3 820	1 067	938	3 910	1 553	377	290
50 to 54 years	3 281	895	941	3 348	1 759	331	290
55 to 59 years	2 473	620	558	2 353	1 259	265	243
60 to 64 years	1 753	371	295	1 506	738	189	193
65 to 69 years	1 349	281	221	1 118	431	120	154
70 to 74 years	1 151	192	182	964	387	99	101
75 years and over	2 007	423	243	1 412	531	169	141
15 to 17 years	51	1	4	4	2	1	*
18 years and over	40 282	8 658	7 526	34 368	11 574	2 752	2 190
15 to 24 years	9 343	590	548	2 090	89	16	*
25 years and over	30 991	8 070	6 981	32 282	11 487	2 737	2 190
15 to 64 years	35 828	7 764	6 884	30 878	10 227	2 365	1 794
65 years and over	4 506	895	645	3 494	1 349	388	396
Male							
15 years and over	19 093	3 885	3 123	16 805	5 620	1 803	1 514
15 to 17 years	15	1	2	4	*	1	*
18 and 19 years	944	14	8	5	2	*	*
20 to 24 years	3 473	292	225	871	23	7	*
25 to 29 years	1 843	398	286	2 012	313	93	39
30 to 34 years	1 747	467	390	2 208	570	135	110
35 to 39 years	1 843	546	372	2 095	644	208	138
40 to 44 years	1 820	533	447	2 073	717	228	185
45 to 49 years	1 843	482	364	1 903	698	270	199
50 to 54 years	1 661	413	415	1 711	846	245	215
55 to 59 years	1 141	245	259	1 298	678	186	169
60 to 64 years	792	156	153	811	432	135	136
65 to 69 years	634	135	81	609	234	85	122
70 to 74 years	520	60	59	527	187	76	85
75 years and over	816	142	63	679	277	135	115
15 to 17 years	15	1	2	4	*	1	*
18 years and over	19 078	3 883	3 121	16 801	5 620	1 801	1 514
15 to 24 years	4 432	308	234	880	25	8	*
25 years and over	14 661	3 577	2 889	15 925	5 595	1 795	1 514
15 to 64 years	17 122	3 547	2 920	14 989	4 921	1 507	1 192
65 years and over	1 971	337	203	1 816	698	295	322
Female							
15 years and over	21 240	4 775	4 406	17 567	5 956	950	676
15 to 17 years	36	*	2	*	2	*	*
18 and 19 years	1 154	20	9	1	*	*	*
20 to 24 years	3 721	262	303	1 210	62	8	*
25 to 29 years	1 903	416	405	2 276	486	114	39
30 to 34 years	1 905	557	459	2 486	725	139	89
35 to 39 years	1 997	610	600	2 253	655	144	102
40 to 44 years	2 098	696	644	2 268	720	127	75
45 to 49 years	1 977	584	575	2 007	856	106	92
50 to 54 years	1 621	482	526	1 638	913	86	75
55 to 59 years	1 332	375	299	1 055	582	79	75
60 to 64 years	961	215	143	695	306	54	57
65 to 69 years	714	146	140	509	197	35	32
70 to 74 years	630	131	123	436	200	24	17
75 years and over	1 190	281	180	733	254	34	25
15 to 17 years	36	*	2	*	2	*	*
18 years and over	21 205	4 775	4 404	17 567	5 954	950	676
15 to 24 years	4 910	282	314	1 211	64	8	*
25 years and over	16 330	4 493	4 092	16 357	5 893	942	676
15 to 64 years	18 705	4 217	3 964	15 889	5 305	857	603
65 years and over	2 506	558	443	1 678	651	93	74

* = Represents zero or rounds to zero.

Table A-8. Educational Attainment of the Population 15 Years and Over, by Age, Sex, Race, and Hispanic Origin, March 2002—*Continued*

(Numbers in thousands.)

Age, sex, race, and Hispanic origin	Total	None	Elementary			High school			
			1st–4th grade	5th–6th grade	7th–8th grade	9th grade	10th grade	11th grade	High school graduate
NON-HISPANIC WHITE									
Both Sexes									
15 years and over	158 258	230	466	909	5 326	4 732	6 271	7 980	49 210
15 to 17 years	7 815	8	*	23	1 446	2 471	2 430	1 307	96
18 and 19 years	4 988	3	2	2	42	98	233	1 635	1 468
20 to 24 years	12 038	10	5	8	78	144	320	569	3 648
25 to 29 years	11 252	10	5	25	92	91	184	383	3 062
30 to 34 years	13 068	15	8	24	105	91	214	338	3 615
35 to 39 years	14 760	25	10	27	103	107	247	426	4 786
40 to 44 years	16 269	23	17	32	118	171	286	468	5 489
45 to 49 years	15 545	16	15	44	124	124	266	387	5 095
50 to 54 years	14 188	32	46	50	186	96	210	327	4 340
55 to 59 years	11 486	22	28	68	268	156	240	344	3 821
60 to 64 years	8 876	1	45	66	280	186	260	368	3 354
65 to 69 years	7 493	9	53	107	402	204	341	388	2 917
70 to 74 years	7 057	18	71	104	563	257	350	307	2 648
75 years and over	13 423	38	160	329	1 519	537	692	735	4 872
15 to 17 years	7 815	8	*	23	1 446	2 471	2 430	1 307	96
18 years and over	150 443	222	465	886	3 880	2 261	3 842	6 674	49 114
15 to 24 years	24 841	21	7	33	1 566	2 713	2 982	3 510	5 212
25 years and over	133 417	210	459	875	3 760	2 019	3 289	4 470	43 998
15 to 64 years	130 285	165	182	369	2 843	3 734	4 889	6 551	38 773
65 years and over	27 973	65	284	540	2 483	998	1 383	1 429	10 437
Male									
15 years and over	76 602	127	235	473	2 714	2 383	3 067	4 009	22 992
15 to 17 years	3 973	6	*	12	799	1 249	1 237	607	46
18 and 19 years	2 553	2	*	2	28	55	134	893	761
20 to 24 years	5 993	4	4	8	35	73	161	304	1 988
25 to 29 years	5 591	4	*	12	41	51	110	222	1 688
30 to 34 years	6 551	11	1	14	68	55	133	188	1 960
35 to 39 years	7 337	16	6	10	52	69	134	240	2 439
40 to 44 years	8 080	6	8	19	68	103	157	271	2 816
45 to 49 years	7 742	7	11	23	67	75	160	213	2 558
50 to 54 years	7 024	25	32	29	111	44	89	174	1 936
55 to 59 years	5 631	12	14	39	158	84	98	179	1 660
60 to 64 years	4 261	1	24	42	147	87	115	170	1 390
65 to 69 years	3 515	5	29	52	220	99	148	174	1 189
70 to 74 years	3 174	13	44	65	319	122	147	110	992
75 years and over	5 177	17	62	147	602	217	244	265	1 569
15 to 17 years	3 973	6	*	12	799	1 249	1 237	607	46
18 years and over	72 629	122	235	461	1 915	1 134	1 830	3 402	22 946
15 to 24 years	12 519	11	5	22	862	1 377	1 532	1 804	2 795
25 years and over	64 083	116	230	452	1 852	1 007	1 535	2 205	20 197
15 to 64 years	64 736	93	100	208	1 574	1 945	2 527	3 461	19 242
65 years and over	11 866	34	135	265	1 140	439	540	549	3 751
Female									
15 years and over	81 656	103	231	435	2 612	2 349	3 205	3 971	26 218
15 to 17 years	3 842	2	*	11	648	1 222	1 193	700	50
18 and 19 years	2 435	1	2	*	14	44	98	742	706
20 to 24 years	6 045	6	*	1	43	71	159	264	1 660
25 to 29 years	5 661	6	5	14	51	40	74	160	1 374
30 to 34 years	6 517	4	6	10	36	36	81	150	1 654
35 to 39 years	7 423	9	5	17	51	38	113	186	2 348
40 to 44 years	8 189	18	9	13	50	68	129	198	2 673
45 to 49 years	7 802	9	4	21	57	49	106	175	2 537
50 to 54 years	7 164	7	13	21	76	52	121	153	2 404
55 to 59 years	5 855	10	15	29	109	72	142	165	2 161
60 to 64 years	4 615	*	21	24	133	98	146	198	1 964
65 to 69 years	3 978	4	24	55	182	105	192	214	1 728
70 to 74 years	3 883	6	27	39	244	135	203	197	1 655
75 years and over	8 246	21	98	181	917	319	448	470	3 303
15 to 17 years	3 842	2	*	11	648	1 222	1 193	700	50
18 years and over	77 814	100	231	425	1 964	1 127	2 012	3 271	26 167
15 to 24 years	12 322	9	2	12	704	1 336	1 450	1 706	2 416
25 years and over	69 334	93	228	424	1 907	1 012	1 755	2 265	23 801
15 to 64 years	65 549	72	82	160	1 269	1 789	2 362	3 091	19 531
65 years and over	16 107	30	149	275	1 343	559	843	881	6 686

* = Represents zero or rounds to zero.

Table A-8. Educational Attainment of the Population 15 Years and Over, by Age, Sex, Race, and Hispanic Origin, March 2002—*Continued*

(Numbers in thousands.)

Age, sex, race, and Hispanic origin	College						
	Some college, no degree	Associate degree, occupational	Associate degree, academic	Bachelor's degree	Master's degree	Professional degree	Doctorate degree
NON-HISPANIC WHITE							
Both Sexes							
15 years and over	29 703	6 783	5 748	27 367	9 514	2 250	1 767
15 to 17 years	26	1	2	3	*	1	*
18 and 19 years	1 463	21	17	2	2	*	*
20 to 24 years	4 836	390	367	1 585	67	12	*
25 to 29 years	2 325	579	458	3 217	603	150	69
30 to 34 years	2 437	777	634	3 520	965	181	145
35 to 39 years	2 644	872	717	3 384	978	280	154
40 to 44 years	2 851	971	813	3 413	1 137	284	195
45 to 49 years	2 916	858	747	3 137	1 275	321	220
50 to 54 years	2 614	701	770	2 763	1 511	282	261
55 to 59 years	2 057	524	440	1 959	1 131	224	205
60 to 64 years	1 511	320	234	1 277	642	161	172
65 to 69 years	1 118	220	183	958	364	101	129
70 to 74 years	1 036	168	163	844	347	96	85
75 years and over	1 869	380	206	1 304	492	158	132
15 to 17 years	26	1	2	3	*	1	*
18 years and over	29 677	6 782	5 747	27 364	9 514	2 249	1 767
15 to 24 years	6 325	413	385	1 590	69	14	*
25 years and over	23 378	6 370	5 363	25 777	9 445	2 237	1 767
15 to 64 years	25 680	6 015	5 196	24 261	8 311	1 895	1 421
65 years and over	4 023	769	552	3 107	1 203	355	346
Male							
15 years and over	14 110	3 084	2 401	13 589	4 645	1 531	1 240
15 to 17 years	9	1	2	3	*	1	*
18 and 19 years	659	9	8	1	2	*	*
20 to 24 years	2 374	206	164	648	17	7	*
25 to 29 years	1 158	297	190	1 488	226	71	36
30 to 34 years	1 183	359	295	1 688	418	91	85
35 to 39 years	1 269	429	272	1 670	479	170	84
40 to 44 years	1 339	428	311	1 665	561	193	137
45 to 49 years	1 429	395	297	1 548	576	230	155
50 to 54 years	1 340	326	350	1 437	728	212	192
55 to 59 years	938	209	216	1 104	617	161	142
60 to 64 years	672	142	129	707	392	119	124
65 to 69 years	515	108	64	535	202	74	102
70 to 74 years	470	54	53	471	168	74	72
75 years and over	757	121	53	625	258	130	111
15 to 17 years	9	1	2	3	*	1	*
18 years and over	14 101	3 082	2 399	13 585	4 645	1 530	1 240
15 to 24 years	3 042	217	174	652	19	8	*
25 years and over	11 068	2 867	2 228	12 936	4 626	1 524	1 240
15 to 64 years	12 369	2 801	2 232	11 957	4 017	1 254	956
65 years and over	1 741	283	169	1 631	628	277	284
Female							
15 years and over	15 593	3 699	3 347	13 779	4 869	719	526
15 to 17 years	17	*	*	*	*	*	*
18 and 19 years	804	13	9	1	*	*	*
20 to 24 years	2 462	184	202	937	50	6	*
25 to 29 years	1 168	282	268	1 730	377	79	33
30 to 34 years	1 254	418	340	1 832	546	90	59
35 to 39 years	1 375	443	445	1 714	499	110	70
40 to 44 years	1 512	543	502	1 748	577	91	58
45 to 49 years	1 487	463	450	1 590	699	91	65
50 to 54 years	1 274	375	420	1 327	783	70	69
55 to 59 years	1 119	315	223	855	514	63	63
60 to 64 years	839	178	105	570	249	42	48
65 to 69 years	604	113	119	423	162	28	27
70 to 74 years	566	114	110	373	179	22	13
75 years and over	1 112	259	154	680	235	28	22
15 to 17 years	17	*	*	*	*	*	*
18 years and over	15 576	3 699	3 347	13 779	4 869	719	526
15 to 24 years	3 283	197	211	938	50	6	*
25 years and over	12 309	3 503	3 136	12 841	4 819	713	526
15 to 64 years	13 311	3 214	2 964	12 304	4 294	641	465
65 years and over	2 282	486	383	1 475	575	78	61

* = Represents zero or rounds to zero.

Table A-8. Educational Attainment of the Population 15 Years and Over, by Age, Sex, Race, and Hispanic Origin, March 2002—*Continued*

(Numbers in thousands.)

Age, sex, race, and Hispanic origin	Total	None	Elementary			High school			
			1st–4th grade	5th–6th grade	7th–8th grade	9th grade	10th grade	11th grade	High school graduate
NON-HISPANIC BLACK									
Both Sexes									
15 years and over	25 233	99	231	346	994	1 065	1 556	2 605	7 976
15 to 17 years	1 784	2	4	5	337	546	539	333	11
18 and 19 years	1 147	4	*	1	7	33	109	397	371
20 to 24 years	2 661	3	*	1	16	38	138	299	927
25 to 29 years	2 303	8	6	4	12	20	56	179	787
30 to 34 years	2 475	8	7	8	14	27	55	181	883
35 to 39 years	2 628	7	6	6	23	33	67	178	984
40 to 44 years	2 674	6	6	13	50	34	78	188	916
45 to 49 years	2 357	10	13	20	47	37	79	169	810
50 to 54 years	1 981	5	11	20	35	53	64	160	715
55 to 59 years	1 397	4	22	26	61	54	86	123	459
60 to 64 years	1 026	6	15	34	68	48	65	91	364
65 to 69 years	1 025	9	28	55	85	39	80	111	290
70 to 74 years	698	11	24	39	70	40	58	83	208
75 years and over	1 078	18	88	114	168	62	84	113	250
15 to 17 years	1 784	2	4	5	337	546	539	333	11
18 years and over	23 449	97	227	342	657	519	1 018	2 272	7 965
15 to 24 years	5 591	8	4	7	361	617	785	1 028	1 310
25 years and over	19 642	91	227	340	633	447	772	1 576	6 667
15 to 64 years	22 432	62	91	138	672	924	1 334	2 298	7 228
65 years and over	2 801	37	140	209	322	141	222	307	748
Male									
15 years and over	11 264	44	122	174	456	494	736	1 194	3 599
15 to 17 years	895	2	1	3	189	279	261	152	7
18 and 19 years	556	1	*	*	4	12	58	212	163
20 to 24 years	1 221	*	*	*	7	20	70	144	434
25 to 29 years	1 021	8	5	2	4	4	20	102	347
30 to 34 years	1 105	5	5	4	5	12	28	82	404
35 to 39 years	1 168	3	4	3	15	16	30	72	474
40 to 44 years	1 204	1	1	9	20	14	40	91	434
45 to 49 years	1 065	5	7	14	24	16	37	76	360
50 to 54 years	900	5	6	12	17	27	27	69	341
55 to 59 years	621	*	8	14	26	29	39	60	206
60 to 64 years	414	2	12	19	29	16	26	33	148
65 to 69 years	447	4	16	32	31	18	39	38	122
70 to 74 years	284	4	11	26	33	11	27	24	91
75 years and over	364	5	47	36	53	20	34	38	68
15 to 17 years	895	2	1	3	189	279	261	152	7
18 years and over	10 369	42	121	171	267	216	475	1 042	3 592
15 to 24 years	2 671	3	1	3	199	310	389	508	604
25 years and over	8 593	41	121	171	257	184	347	685	2 995
15 to 64 years	10 168	31	48	80	339	446	636	1 094	3 318
65 years and over	1 095	13	74	94	117	49	100	99	281
Female									
15 years and over	13 969	55	109	172	537	570	821	1 411	4 377
15 to 17 years	889	*	3	2	148	267	278	181	4
18 and 19 years	591	2	*	1	3	22	50	184	208
20 to 24 years	1 440	3	*	1	10	19	67	155	494
25 to 29 years	1 282	*	2	2	9	16	36	77	440
30 to 34 years	1 370	3	1	3	9	15	26	99	479
35 to 39 years	1 460	4	3	3	8	17	37	107	510
40 to 44 years	1 469	5	5	5	30	20	38	97	482
45 to 49 years	1 293	5	6	6	23	20	43	92	450
50 to 54 years	1 081	*	5	9	19	26	37	91	374
55 to 59 years	776	4	15	12	35	24	47	63	253
60 to 64 years	612	4	4	14	39	31	39	58	216
65 to 69 years	577	5	12	23	53	21	41	73	169
70 to 74 years	414	7	13	13	37	29	31	59	116
75 years and over	714	13	42	78	114	43	50	76	182
15 to 17 years	889	*	3	2	148	267	278	181	4
18 years and over	13 080	55	105	170	389	303	543	1 230	4 373
15 to 24 years	2 920	5	3	4	161	307	396	520	706
25 years and over	11 049	50	105	168	376	263	425	891	3 671
15 to 64 years	12 264	31	43	58	333	478	699	1 204	3 910
65 years and over	1 706	25	66	115	205	93	122	207	467

* = Represents zero or rounds to zero.

Table A-8. Educational Attainment of the Population 15 Years and Over, by Age, Sex, Race, and Hispanic Origin, March 2002—*Continued*

(Numbers in thousands.)

Age, sex, race, and Hispanic origin	College						
	Some college, no degree	Associate degree, occupational	Associate degree, academic	Bachelor's degree	Master's degree	Professional degree	Doctorate degree
NON-HISPANIC BLACK							
Both Sexes							
15 years and over	5 118	879	829	2 488	799	142	105
15 to 17 years	5	*	*	*	2	*	*
18 and 19 years	215	6	*	3	*	*	*
20 to 24 years	972	63	46	150	8	*	*
25 to 29 years	632	101	81	360	43	13	*
30 to 34 years	579	116	90	398	74	20	16
35 to 39 years	581	121	128	352	109	18	15
40 to 44 years	607	126	153	336	126	21	13
45 to 49 years	517	110	95	287	128	20	16
50 to 54 years	365	94	88	239	116	12	3
55 to 59 years	241	54	58	139	47	8	16
60 to 64 years	136	24	36	75	47	9	8
65 to 69 years	144	31	24	69	41	10	9
70 to 74 years	59	13	11	43	30	3	7
75 years and over	66	21	20	38	26	8	2
15 to 17 years	5	*	*	*	2	*	*
18 years and over	5 113	879	829	2 488	797	142	105
15 to 24 years	1 193	68	46	153	10	*	*
25 years and over	3 925	811	783	2 335	788	142	105
15 to 64 years	4 849	815	774	2 338	701	121	88
65 years and over	269	65	55	150	98	21	18
Male							
15 years and over	2 338	331	303	1 048	294	66	63
15 to 17 years	1	*	*	*	*	*	*
18 and 19 years	100	1	*	3	*	*	*
20 to 24 years	452	28	15	49	2	*	*
25 to 29 years	295	29	21	171	9	4	*
30 to 34 years	259	49	37	179	21	6	8
35 to 39 years	271	40	50	135	37	10	9
40 to 44 years	266	47	77	134	55	8	8
45 to 49 years	244	44	32	131	50	14	8
50 to 54 years	163	42	30	101	53	8	1
55 to 59 years	117	18	13	58	15	6	11
60 to 64 years	57	6	13	32	15	2	4
65 to 69 years	64	14	11	31	16	5	7
70 to 74 years	24	1	1	13	10	1	5
75 years and over	23	10	3	11	12	3	2
15 to 17 years	1	*	*	*	*	*	*
18 years and over	2 337	331	303	1 048	294	66	63
15 to 24 years	554	30	15	53	2	*	*
25 years and over	1 784	301	288	996	293	66	63
15 to 64 years	2 227	306	288	993	256	57	49
65 years and over	111	25	15	55	38	9	14
Female							
15 years and over	2 780	548	526	1 440	504	76	42
15 to 17 years	4	*	*	*	2	*	*
18 and 19 years	115	4	*	*	*	*	*
20 to 24 years	520	34	31	100	6	*	*
25 to 29 years	337	71	59	189	35	9	*
30 to 34 years	319	67	53	220	53	15	8
35 to 39 years	309	81	78	217	72	9	6
40 to 44 years	341	79	76	202	71	13	5
45 to 49 years	272	66	63	155	78	6	8
50 to 54 years	202	52	59	138	63	4	2
55 to 59 years	123	36	44	80	31	2	5
60 to 64 years	79	17	23	43	33	7	4
65 to 69 years	80	16	13	39	25	5	2
70 to 74 years	35	11	10	30	20	1	2
75 years and over	43	11	17	27	14	5	*
15 to 17 years	4	*	*	*	2	*	*
18 years and over	2 776	548	526	1 440	502	76	42
15 to 24 years	639	39	31	100	8	*	*
25 years and over	2 141	510	495	1 340	496	76	42
15 to 64 years	2 622	509	487	1 345	445	64	38
65 years and over	158	39	39	95	59	12	4

* = Represents zero or rounds to zero.

Table A-8. Educational Attainment of the Population 15 Years and Over, by Age, Sex, Race, and Hispanic Origin, March 2002—*Continued*

(Numbers in thousands.)

Age, sex, race, and Hispanic origin	Total	None	Elementary			High school			
			1st–4th grade	5th–6th grade	7th–8th grade	9th grade	10th grade	11th grade	High school graduate
ASIAN/PACIFIC ISLANDER									
Both Sexes									
15 years and over	9 842	121	84	197	273	269	317	480	1 962
15 to 17 years	591	*	*	*	73	171	174	160	3
18 and 19 years	376	*	*	*	*	5	15	100	79
20 to 24 years	1 009	10	*	1	9	2	8	25	154
25 to 29 years	1 066	*	3	1	3	6	12	27	176
30 to 34 years	1 168	3	2	6	2	11	18	28	229
35 to 39 years	1 081	6	8	7	14	14	17	29	187
40 to 44 years	990	9	2	24	14	7	11	19	225
45 to 49 years	957	11	11	25	31	14	7	10	238
50 to 54 years	766	12	11	36	28	7	9	11	162
55 to 59 years	558	19	7	12	22	4	15	16	139
60 to 64 years	380	8	8	12	25	6	6	14	104
65 to 69 years	315	8	9	18	10	7	10	25	97
70 to 74 years	235	17	10	11	17	3	3	11	66
75 years and over	348	18	13	45	25	11	13	4	102
15 to 17 years	591	*	*	*	73	171	174	160	3
18 years and over	9 251	121	84	197	200	98	143	319	1 959
15 to 24 years	1 976	10	*	1	82	178	197	285	236
25 years and over	7 866	111	84	196	191	91	120	195	1 726
15 to 64 years	8 943	78	51	123	221	248	291	440	1 697
65 years and over	899	43	33	74	52	21	26	40	265
Male									
15 years and over	4 761	27	25	58	122	136	185	268	888
15 to 17 years	315	*	*	*	36	96	99	80	1
18 and 19 years	203	*	*	*	*	3	14	70	35
20 to 24 years	502	1	*	1	3	*	4	22	83
25 to 29 years	539	*	*	*	3	5	7	19	86
30 to 34 years	558	3	1	2	2	6	12	15	101
35 to 39 years	539	2	1	4	4	6	7	14	95
40 to 44 years	470	3	1	2	4	3	8	9	102
45 to 49 years	445	4	4	5	18	4	6	2	108
50 to 54 years	370	6	4	12	7	3	8	2	78
55 to 59 years	259	1	3	7	9	2	6	7	64
60 to 64 years	168	1	*	3	12	*	3	8	42
65 to 69 years	149	3	2	5	4	3	4	15	40
70 to 74 years	103	*	5	2	14	2	*	3	22
75 years and over	139	3	3	15	7	4	6	3	29
15 to 17 years	315	*	*	*	36	96	99	80	1
18 years and over	4 446	27	25	58	86	40	86	188	887
15 to 24 years	1 020	1	*	1	39	99	117	171	119
25 years and over	3 741	26	25	57	82	37	68	97	769
15 to 64 years	4 369	22	14	35	98	127	175	247	796
65 years and over	392	6	11	23	24	9	10	21	92
Female									
15 years and over	5 081	94	59	139	151	133	132	212	1 074
15 to 17 years	277	*	*	*	37	75	75	81	1
18 and 19 years	173	*	*	*	*	2	1	29	45
20 to 24 years	507	8	*	*	6	1	3	4	71
25 to 29 years	527	*	3	1	*	1	4	9	91
30 to 34 years	610	*	1	4	*	5	6	13	128
35 to 39 years	543	5	6	4	11	9	9	15	92
40 to 44 years	520	7	1	21	9	4	4	10	122
45 to 49 years	512	7	6	20	13	11	2	7	130
50 to 54 years	397	6	7	24	20	5	1	10	84
55 to 59 years	299	18	4	6	14	2	8	9	75
60 to 64 years	211	6	8	9	14	6	2	6	62
65 to 69 years	166	5	7	12	6	4	5	10	57
70 to 74 years	132	17	5	9	3	1	3	8	44
75 years and over	209	15	10	30	18	6	7	1	73
15 to 17 years	277	*	*	*	37	75	75	81	1
18 years and over	4 805	94	59	139	114	57	57	131	1 073
15 to 24 years	956	8	*	*	43	78	80	114	117
25 years and over	4 125	85	59	139	108	54	52	98	957
15 to 64 years	4 574	57	37	89	124	120	116	193	900
65 years and over	507	37	22	51	28	12	16	19	174

* = Represents zero or rounds to zero.

Table A-8. Educational Attainment of the Population 15 Years and Over, by Age, Sex, Race, and Hispanic Origin, March 2002—*Continued*

(Numbers in thousands.)

Age, sex, race, and Hispanic origin	College						
	Some college, no degree	Associate degree, occupational	Associate degree, academic	Bachelor's degree	Master's degree	Professional degree	Doctorate degree
ASIAN/PACIFIC ISLANDER							
Both Sexes							
15 years and over	1 575	302	317	2 664	831	214	235
15 to 17 years	9	*	*	1	*	*	*
18 and 19 years	177	*	*	*	*	*	*
20 to 24 years	497	32	39	225	6	1	*
25 to 29 years	190	25	39	432	111	34	8
30 to 34 years	110	38	36	425	184	47	31
35 to 39 years	152	40	48	310	156	36	56
40 to 44 years	105	34	50	320	109	22	39
45 to 49 years	114	40	27	286	92	15	36
50 to 54 years	75	37	36	236	71	19	18
55 to 59 years	48	17	15	166	43	20	14
60 to 64 years	20	8	8	108	31	11	10
65 to 69 years	29	11	8	53	14	6	11
70 to 74 years	24	7	3	47	7	1	8
75 years and over	25	14	9	54	6	3	6
15 to 17 years	9	*	*	1	*	*	*
18 years and over	1 567	302	317	2 663	831	214	235
15 to 24 years	682	32	39	226	6	1	*
25 years and over	893	270	278	2 437	825	213	235
15 to 64 years	1 498	271	298	2 509	804	205	211
65 years and over	78	31	19	155	28	10	25
Male							
15 years and over	762	135	139	1 258	473	127	158
15 to 17 years	2	*	*	1	*	*	*
18 and 19 years	81	*	*	*	*	*	*
20 to 24 years	241	20	14	108	3	*	*
25 to 29 years	94	12	22	219	59	12	2
30 to 34 years	44	16	21	200	97	28	12
35 to 39 years	78	15	17	141	99	18	37
40 to 44 years	41	15	24	140	73	14	31
45 to 49 years	60	18	8	125	45	13	24
50 to 54 years	43	18	15	112	35	13	14
55 to 59 years	21	3	5	80	28	11	13
60 to 64 years	15	1	4	47	15	9	8
65 to 69 years	17	6	4	25	9	5	7
70 to 74 years	12	3	3	24	6	*	6
75 years and over	13	8	3	37	4	3	3
15 to 17 years	2	*	*	1	*	*	*
18 years and over	760	135	139	1 257	473	127	158
15 to 24 years	324	20	14	109	3	*	*
25 years and over	438	114	125	1 148	470	127	158
15 to 64 years	720	118	130	1 172	455	119	142
65 years and over	41	16	9	86	19	8	16
Female							
15 years and over	813	168	178	1 406	358	87	78
15 to 17 years	7	*	*	*	*	*	*
18 and 19 years	95	*	*	*	*	*	*
20 to 24 years	256	12	25	117	3	1	*
25 to 29 years	96	13	17	213	53	21	6
30 to 34 years	66	22	15	226	87	19	19
35 to 39 years	74	25	31	169	57	19	18
40 to 44 years	64	19	27	180	36	8	7
45 to 49 years	55	22	18	161	47	2	12
50 to 54 years	32	18	21	124	36	6	3
55 to 59 years	28	15	10	87	15	9	1
60 to 64 years	5	7	5	61	16	2	2
65 to 69 years	12	5	4	28	5	*	3
70 to 74 years	12	4	*	23	2	*	2
75 years and over	12	6	6	18	2	1	4
15 to 17 years	7	*	*	*	*	*	*
18 years and over	806	168	178	1 406	358	87	78
15 to 24 years	358	12	25	117	3	1	*
25 years and over	455	156	153	1 289	355	86	78
15 to 64 years	777	153	168	1 337	349	85	69
65 years and over	36	15	10	69	9	2	9

* = Represents zero or rounds to zero.

Table A-8. Educational Attainment of the Population 15 Years and Over, by Age, Sex, Race, and Hispanic Origin, March 2002—*Continued*

(Numbers in thousands.)

Age, sex, race, and Hispanic origin	Total	None	Elementary			High school			
			1st–4th grade	5th–6th grade	7th–8th grade	9th grade	10th grade	11th grade	High school graduate
HISPANIC[1]									
Both Sexes									
15 years and over	26 351	488	1 342	2 690	1 781	1 943	1 595	2 408	7 013
15 to 17 years	1 801	3	4	24	351	538	531	302	37
18 and 19 years	1 321	7	14	43	45	73	113	446	336
20 to 24 years	3 559	28	71	256	145	208	173	411	1 147
25 to 29 years	3 537	41	124	363	154	222	147	281	1 112
30 to 34 years	3 457	42	157	372	205	231	136	255	995
35 to 39 years	2 953	31	133	344	178	207	135	165	798
40 to 44 years	2 486	36	123	258	144	155	89	141	739
45 to 49 years	1 938	35	121	238	114	87	65	119	548
50 to 54 years	1 461	47	98	190	79	72	41	77	393
55 to 59 years	1 103	27	97	167	87	50	37	64	276
60 to 64 years	839	25	94	134	71	34	50	51	213
65 to 69 years	680	51	93	90	58	17	27	38	189
70 to 74 years	495	34	94	73	57	19	22	24	109
75 years and over	722	83	121	138	93	32	29	35	122
15 to 17 years	1 801	3	4	24	351	538	531	302	37
18 years and over	24 550	485	1 338	2 666	1 430	1 405	1 065	2 106	6 977
15 to 24 years	6 681	37	89	323	540	818	817	1 159	1 520
25 years and over	19 670	451	1 254	2 367	1 241	1 124	778	1 249	5 493
15 to 64 years	24 454	319	1 034	2 389	1 573	1 875	1 518	2 312	6 594
65 years and over	1 896	168	308	301	208	68	77	96	420
Male									
15 years and over	13 451	258	716	1 424	932	1 000	837	1 287	3 519
15 to 17 years	950	1	2	16	208	265	289	147	17
18 and 19 years	675	5	7	27	25	39	62	254	150
20 to 24 years	1 911	15	51	162	71	125	83	241	625
25 to 29 years	1 933	30	74	220	88	120	79	159	616
30 to 34 years	1 792	28	107	237	107	122	74	129	488
35 to 39 years	1 559	24	82	172	106	111	87	85	412
40 to 44 years	1 279	23	71	115	82	86	52	75	375
45 to 49 years	928	23	57	126	53	37	21	63	263
50 to 54 years	697	25	44	90	33	33	18	29	186
55 to 59 years	516	13	42	78	39	25	17	23	123
60 to 64 years	401	8	46	70	33	12	22	21	98
65 to 69 years	303	22	36	43	20	9	13	21	76
70 to 74 years	219	10	44	30	27	6	9	16	39
75 years and over	287	30	53	37	39	10	9	23	49
15 to 17 years	950	1	2	16	208	265	289	147	17
18 years and over	12 501	257	714	1 407	724	734	548	1 140	3 502
15 to 24 years	3 536	21	60	205	305	430	435	641	792
25 years and over	9 915	237	657	1 219	628	570	402	645	2 727
15 to 64 years	12 642	196	583	1 313	846	976	806	1 226	3 355
65 years and over	809	63	133	111	86	24	32	60	164
Female									
15 years and over	12 900	229	626	1 266	849	943	758	1 121	3 494
15 to 17 years	851	1	2	7	142	273	241	155	20
18 and 19 years	646	2	7	15	20	33	51	192	186
20 to 24 years	1 648	13	20	95	74	82	90	170	522
25 to 29 years	1 604	11	50	144	66	102	68	122	495
30 to 34 years	1 664	14	50	135	97	109	62	126	507
35 to 39 years	1 394	7	51	173	72	96	48	80	385
40 to 44 years	1 206	13	52	142	63	69	37	66	363
45 to 49 years	1 010	11	64	112	61	49	44	56	284
50 to 54 years	764	22	54	100	46	39	23	48	207
55 to 59 years	587	14	55	88	48	24	20	41	153
60 to 64 years	438	16	48	65	38	22	28	29	116
65 to 69 years	376	29	57	46	38	8	14	17	113
70 to 74 years	277	24	49	44	30	13	13	7	71
75 years and over	435	52	68	101	55	22	19	12	73
15 to 17 years	851	1	2	7	142	273	241	155	20
18 years and over	12 049	228	624	1 259	706	670	517	966	3 474
15 to 24 years	3 145	16	29	118	236	389	382	518	728
25 years and over	9 755	214	597	1 149	613	554	376	604	2 766
15 to 64 years	11 812	124	451	1 076	726	899	712	1 085	3 238
65 years and over	1 088	106	175	190	122	44	46	36	256

[1]May be of any race.

Table A-8. Educational Attainment of the Population 15 Years and Over, by Age, Sex, Race, and Hispanic Origin, March 2002—*Continued*

(Numbers in thousands.)

Age, sex, race, and Hispanic origin	College						
	Some college, no degree	Associate degree, occupational	Associate degree, academic	Bachelor's degree	Master's degree	Professional degree	Doctorate degree
HISPANIC[1]							
Both Sexes							
15 years and over	3 594	617	574	1 710	384	143	68
15 to 17 years	10	*	2	*	*	*	*
18 and 19 years	238	7	*	*	*	*	*
20 to 24 years	855	67	75	118	4	1	*
25 to 29 years	565	103	110	267	36	11	1
30 to 34 years	474	86	76	326	71	27	4
35 to 39 years	421	107	76	277	52	17	14
40 to 44 years	307	85	70	242	59	28	12
45 to 49 years	237	47	62	184	51	17	14
50 to 54 years	197	54	39	98	48	18	8
55 to 59 years	117	21	36	80	28	11	5
60 to 64 years	70	16	13	41	17	8	2
65 to 69 years	41	17	6	36	10	2	5
70 to 74 years	27	4	2	27	2	*	2
75 years and over	36	5	7	14	6	1	*
15 to 17 years	10	*	2	*	*	*	*
18 years and over	3 584	617	572	1 710	384	143	68
15 to 24 years	1 104	73	77	118	4	1	*
25 years and over	2 491	544	497	1 592	380	141	68
15 to 64 years	3 491	591	559	1 634	365	139	61
65 years and over	104	26	15	76	19	3	7
Male							
15 years and over	1 758	309	258	844	185	76	47
15 to 17 years	3	*	*	*	*	*	*
18 and 19 years	102	4	*	*	*	*	*
20 to 24 years	402	38	33	64	2	*	*
25 to 29 years	280	57	50	135	17	7	1
30 to 34 years	247	41	33	134	33	10	3
35 to 39 years	212	56	33	136	26	11	7
40 to 44 years	157	38	36	120	28	13	7
45 to 49 years	100	20	25	94	24	11	11
50 to 54 years	97	24	16	54	26	12	8
55 to 59 years	57	14	18	47	8	7	3
60 to 64 years	43	6	6	23	10	4	*
65 to 69 years	24	7	2	17	6	1	5
70 to 74 years	14	2	2	16	2	*	2
75 years and over	19	2	4	5	4	1	*
15 to 17 years	3	*	*	*	*	*	*
18 years and over	1 755	309	258	844	185	76	47
15 to 24 years	506	42	33	64	2	*	*
25 years and over	1 252	267	224	781	184	76	47
15 to 64 years	1 701	297	250	806	173	75	40
65 years and over	58	12	8	39	12	2	7
Female							
15 years and over	1 836	308	316	866	199	66	21
15 to 17 years	7	*	2	*	*	*	*
18 and 19 years	136	3	*	*	*	*	*
20 to 24 years	454	28	41	55	2	1	*
25 to 29 years	285	46	60	132	19	5	*
30 to 34 years	227	45	43	193	38	18	1
35 to 39 years	208	51	43	142	27	7	7
40 to 44 years	149	46	34	122	31	15	5
45 to 49 years	137	27	37	91	27	5	3
50 to 54 years	100	30	23	44	22	6	1
55 to 59 years	60	7	18	33	20	4	3
60 to 64 years	27	10	8	18	7	3	2
65 to 69 years	16	9	4	19	4	2	*
70 to 74 years	13	2	*	11	*	*	*
75 years and over	17	3	3	8	2	*	*
15 to 17 years	7	*	2	*	*	*	*
18 years and over	1 829	308	314	866	199	66	21
15 to 24 years	597	31	44	55	2	1	*
25 years and over	1 239	277	273	811	197	65	21
15 to 64 years	1 790	294	310	828	192	65	21
65 years and over	46	14	7	38	7	2	*

[1]May be of any race.
* = Represents zero or rounds to zero.

Table A-8. Educational Attainment of the Population 15 Years and Over, by Age, Sex, Race, and Hispanic Origin, March 2002—*Continued*

(Numbers in thousands.)

Age, sex, race, and Hispanic origin	Total	None	Elementary			High school			
			1st–4th grade	5th–6th grade	7th–8th grade	9th grade	10th grade	11th grade	High school graduate
WHITE									
Both Sexes									
15 years and over	183 086	691	1 769	3 478	6 998	6 565	7 773	10 258	55 781
15 to 17 years	9 500	10	5	46	1 773	2 970	2 930	1 590	131
18 and 19 years	6 257	9	16	42	86	169	339	2 064	1 791
20 to 24 years	15 387	38	74	246	216	343	472	959	4 728
25 to 29 years	14 574	51	122	381	233	301	329	638	4 114
30 to 34 years	16 322	53	158	380	302	311	349	583	4 524
35 to 39 years	17 537	50	141	347	270	300	374	578	5 539
40 to 44 years	18 618	57	138	281	257	315	370	604	6 178
45 to 49 years	17 342	48	129	266	230	207	328	501	5 600
50 to 54 years	15 563	74	142	236	261	168	246	400	4 703
55 to 59 years	12 530	49	122	229	352	204	274	405	4 076
60 to 64 years	9 666	23	138	194	345	213	308	414	3 557
65 to 69 years	8 137	57	142	194	455	221	365	422	3 094
70 to 74 years	7 531	52	162	176	616	275	371	331	2 754
75 years and over	14 122	121	281	462	1 603	569	719	770	4 992
15 to 17 years	9 500	10	5	46	1 773	2 970	2 930	1 590	131
18 years and over	173 586	681	1 764	3 432	5 226	3 596	4 843	8 668	55 649
15 to 24 years	31 144	58	94	334	2 074	3 482	3 741	4 613	6 650
25 years and over	151 942	634	1 675	3 144	4 924	3 084	4 032	5 645	49 131
15 to 64 years	153 296	461	1 184	2 647	4 325	5 501	6 318	8 736	44 941
65 years and over	29 790	230	585	831	2 674	1 064	1 455	1 522	10 840
Male									
15 years and over	89 291	371	930	1 825	3 598	3 334	3 856	5 227	26 290
15 to 17 years	4 867	7	3	28	996	1 499	1 510	744	62
18 and 19 years	3 194	7	7	26	53	93	191	1 131	905
20 to 24 years	7 786	19	54	153	102	194	238	534	2 580
25 to 29 years	7 418	34	72	228	123	165	189	366	2 272
30 to 34 years	8 248	37	106	241	173	168	206	313	2 409
35 to 39 years	8 810	34	86	166	156	174	216	320	2 831
40 to 44 years	9 295	27	79	131	147	185	207	343	3 163
45 to 49 years	8 606	28	63	137	114	112	178	274	2 805
50 to 54 years	7 679	50	75	119	140	76	105	203	2 102
55 to 59 years	6 114	26	53	113	196	109	112	202	1 774
60 to 64 years	4 637	8	69	110	178	97	135	189	1 480
65 to 69 years	3 805	24	64	96	240	108	160	195	1 261
70 to 74 years	3 379	23	86	94	343	127	156	126	1 029
75 years and over	5 453	48	115	184	637	227	252	287	1 618
15 to 17 years	4 867	7	3	28	996	1 499	1 510	744	62
18 years and over	84 424	365	927	1 798	2 602	1 835	2 346	4 483	26 228
15 to 24 years	15 847	33	64	207	1 151	1 785	1 939	2 409	3 547
25 years and over	73 444	339	866	1 618	2 447	1 548	1 917	2 817	22 743
15 to 64 years	76 654	277	666	1 452	2 378	2 872	3 287	4 618	22 382
65 years and over	12 637	95	264	373	1 220	462	568	608	3 908
Female									
15 years and over	93 795	320	839	1 653	3 401	3 231	3 917	5 031	29 491
15 to 17 years	4 633	4	2	18	777	1 471	1 420	846	69
18 and 19 years	3 063	3	9	16	32	76	147	933	886
20 to 24 years	7 601	19	19	93	113	150	235	425	2 148
25 to 29 years	7 156	17	50	152	110	136	140	272	1 842
30 to 34 years	8 074	15	52	139	129	143	142	270	2 115
35 to 39 years	8 727	16	54	181	114	126	157	258	2 708
40 to 44 years	9 323	30	60	150	110	130	163	261	3 015
45 to 49 years	8 736	20	66	129	116	95	150	228	2 795
50 to 54 years	7 884	24	67	117	121	91	141	198	2 602
55 to 59 years	6 417	24	69	116	156	95	162	203	2 302
60 to 64 years	5 029	14	69	83	167	117	172	225	2 077
65 to 69 years	4 332	33	78	98	215	113	206	227	1 833
70 to 74 years	4 152	29	76	82	273	147	215	204	1 726
75 years and over	8 669	73	166	278	966	341	467	482	3 373
15 to 17 years	4 633	4	2	18	777	1 471	1 420	846	69
18 years and over	89 162	316	837	1 634	2 623	1 761	2 498	4 185	29 422
15 to 24 years	15 297	25	30	127	923	1 696	1 802	2 204	3 103
25 years and over	78 498	295	809	1 526	2 478	1 535	2 115	2 828	26 388
15 to 64 years	76 642	185	518	1 195	1 947	2 630	3 030	4 118	22 559
65 years and over	17 153	135	321	458	1 454	602	887	914	6 932

Table A-8. Educational Attainment of the Population 15 Years and Over, by Age, Sex, Race, and Hispanic Origin, March 2002—*Continued*

(Numbers in thousands.)

Age, sex, race, and Hispanic origin	College						
	Some college, no degree	Associate degree, occupational	Associate degree, academic	Bachelor's degree	Master's degree	Professional degree	Doctorate degree
WHITE							
Both Sexes							
15 years and over	33 062	7 366	6 281	28 960	9 889	2 385	1 828
15 to 17 years	36	1	4	3	*	1	*
18 and 19 years	1 695	26	17	2	2	*	*
20 to 24 years	5 641	452	435	1 699	70	13	*
25 to 29 years	2 843	672	558	3 463	638	161	70
30 to 34 years	2 882	861	709	3 821	1 034	206	148
35 to 39 years	3 039	972	790	3 644	1 030	295	168
40 to 44 years	3 141	1 052	877	3 639	1 194	311	206
45 to 49 years	3 128	901	803	3 304	1 326	338	233
50 to 54 years	2 794	753	802	2 859	1 558	300	267
55 to 59 years	2 167	545	474	2 032	1 156	235	211
60 to 64 years	1 575	335	247	1 317	659	167	175
65 to 69 years	1 159	236	189	994	374	104	131
70 to 74 years	1 061	172	163	867	349	96	87
75 years and over	1 901	386	213	1 317	499	158	132
15 to 17 years	36	1	4	3	*	1	*
18 years and over	33 027	7 365	6 277	28 957	9 889	2 384	1 828
15 to 24 years	7 372	479	456	1 704	73	15	*
25 years and over	25 690	6 887	5 825	27 256	9 816	2 371	1 828
15 to 64 years	28 941	6 572	5 717	25 782	8 667	2 028	1 477
65 years and over	4 121	794	565	3 178	1 222	358	350
Male							
15 years and over	15 758	3 375	2 640	14 372	4 828	1 605	1 282
15 to 17 years	11	1	2	3	*	1	*
18 and 19 years	760	10	8	1	2	*	*
20 to 24 years	2 743	241	194	708	18	7	*
25 to 29 years	1 419	350	236	1 607	243	77	37
30 to 34 years	1 418	398	327	1 810	451	100	89
35 to 39 years	1 470	483	305	1 793	504	180	92
40 to 44 years	1 490	463	345	1 780	587	205	145
45 to 49 years	1 521	414	316	1 638	600	242	165
50 to 54 years	1 431	350	365	1 489	755	224	197
55 to 59 years	991	223	233	1 145	625	168	145
60 to 64 years	711	147	135	729	402	123	124
65 to 69 years	539	115	65	552	208	75	104
70 to 74 years	482	56	53	485	170	74	74
75 years and over	773	123	57	630	262	130	111
15 to 17 years	11	1	2	3	*	1	*
18 years and over	15 747	3 374	2 638	14 368	4 828	1 604	1 282
15 to 24 years	3 514	253	203	713	21	8	*
25 years and over	12 244	3 122	2 436	13 659	4 808	1 598	1 282
15 to 64 years	13 964	3 081	2 465	12 704	4 188	1 327	993
65 years and over	1 794	294	175	1 667	640	278	289
Female							
15 years and over	17 304	3 991	3 642	14 589	5 061	780	546
15 to 17 years	24	*	2	*	*	*	*
18 and 19 years	935	16	9	1	*	*	*
20 to 24 years	2 898	211	241	990	52	7	*
25 to 29 years	1 425	322	322	1 856	395	84	33
30 to 34 years	1 464	463	382	2 010	583	106	60
35 to 39 years	1 569	489	485	1 851	526	115	77
40 to 44 years	1 651	589	532	1 859	606	106	61
45 to 49 years	1 607	487	487	1 666	726	96	68
50 to 54 years	1 363	404	437	1 370	803	76	69
55 to 59 years	1 176	322	241	887	531	67	66
60 to 64 years	864	188	112	588	257	44	51
65 to 69 years	620	121	124	442	166	29	27
70 to 74 years	579	116	110	382	179	22	13
75 years and over	1 129	262	156	687	237	28	22
15 to 17 years	24	*	2	*	*	*	*
18 years and over	17 280	3 991	3 639	14 589	5 061	780	546
15 to 24 years	3 858	227	252	991	52	7	*
25 years and over	13 446	3 764	3 389	13 597	5 009	773	546
15 to 64 years	14 976	3 492	3 252	13 078	4 479	701	484
65 years and over	2 327	499	390	1 511	582	79	61

* = Represents zero or rounds to zero.

Table A-8. Educational Attainment of the Population 15 Years and Over, by Age, Sex, Race, and Hispanic Origin, March 2002—*Continued*

(Numbers in thousands.)

Age, sex, race, and Hispanic origin	Total	None	Elementary			High school			
			1st–4th grade	5th–6th grade	7th–8th grade	9th grade	10th grade	11th grade	High school graduate
BLACK									
Both Sexes									
15 years and over	26 171	112	256	420	1 064	1 144	1 606	2 681	8 255
15 to 17 years	1 856	2	4	6	352	574	553	345	13
18 and 19 years	1 181	4	*	4	9	34	113	408	377
20 to 24 years	2 776	3	2	14	19	45	150	311	957
25 to 29 years	2 439	8	10	10	17	29	58	194	831
30 to 34 years	2 602	10	11	19	22	35	55	185	934
35 to 39 years	2 731	9	7	17	34	43	69	187	1 011
40 to 44 years	2 764	8	7	15	55	41	82	191	953
45 to 49 years	2 445	12	20	28	52	38	79	171	840
50 to 54 years	2 029	5	11	25	40	53	67	164	735
55 to 59 years	1 433	4	23	28	62	56	88	126	473
60 to 64 years	1 063	7	15	39	73	54	68	92	373
65 to 69 years	1 046	11	31	55	88	39	81	111	299
70 to 74 years	717	12	26	41	72	41	60	83	210
75 years and over	1 091	18	88	119	170	62	85	113	251
15 to 17 years	1 856	2	4	6	352	574	553	345	13
18 years and over	24 315	110	251	414	712	570	1 053	2 336	8 243
15 to 24 years	5 812	8	6	24	380	653	816	1 064	1 346
25 years and over	20 359	104	249	395	685	491	790	1 617	6 909
15 to 64 years	23 318	71	111	204	734	1 002	1 380	2 374	7 495
65 years and over	2 853	41	145	215	330	142	226	307	760
Male									
15 years and over	11 721	52	135	215	486	535	756	1 234	3 732
15 to 17 years	928	2	1	4	198	292	266	157	8
18 and 19 years	580	1	*	3	4	13	62	224	166
20 to 24 years	1 282	*	1	11	8	24	74	146	450
25 to 29 years	1 085	8	7	3	5	9	20	111	368
30 to 34 years	1 159	5	7	9	8	20	28	85	424
35 to 39 years	1 216	5	4	10	18	19	30	76	487
40 to 44 years	1 249	3	1	10	23	18	42	94	453
45 to 49 years	1 107	6	11	22	27	16	37	78	372
50 to 54 years	919	5	6	12	21	27	27	69	352
55 to 59 years	640	*	8	16	26	30	40	60	211
60 to 64 years	434	3	12	20	30	19	27	34	156
65 to 69 years	457	6	18	32	31	18	40	38	124
70 to 74 years	296	4	13	27	34	11	27	24	94
75 years and over	369	5	47	37	55	20	36	38	68
15 to 17 years	928	2	1	4	198	292	266	157	8
18 years and over	10 793	50	134	212	288	243	491	1 077	3 725
15 to 24 years	2 790	3	2	18	209	329	402	527	624
25 years and over	8 931	49	133	198	276	206	355	707	3 109
15 to 64 years	10 599	37	58	119	366	487	653	1 134	3 447
65 years and over	1 122	15	78	96	120	49	103	99	286
Female									
15 years and over	14 450	60	120	204	579	609	850	1 447	4 523
15 to 17 years	928	*	3	2	155	282	288	188	5
18 and 19 years	601	2	*	1	5	22	50	184	211
20 to 24 years	1 494	3	1	3	11	21	76	165	507
25 to 29 years	1 354	*	3	7	13	20	38	83	463
30 to 34 years	1 442	6	4	10	14	15	26	100	510
35 to 39 years	1 515	4	4	7	17	24	39	111	524
40 to 44 years	1 515	6	6	5	32	24	39	97	500
45 to 49 years	1 338	5	8	6	25	22	43	93	468
50 to 54 years	1 111	*	5	13	19	26	40	95	382
55 to 59 years	793	4	15	13	36	25	47	66	262
60 to 64 years	628	4	4	18	42	35	40	58	217
65 to 69 years	588	5	13	23	57	21	41	73	175
70 to 74 years	421	8	13	14	38	30	33	59	116
75 years and over	721	13	42	82	115	43	50	76	183
15 to 17 years	928	*	3	2	155	282	288	188	5
18 years and over	13 522	60	117	202	424	327	562	1 259	4 518
15 to 24 years	3 022	5	4	7	170	324	415	537	722
25 years and over	11 428	55	116	198	409	285	435	910	3 801
15 to 64 years	12 719	34	53	85	368	515	727	1 240	4 048
65 years and over	1 731	26	67	119	211	94	123	207	475

* = Represents zero or rounds to zero.

Table A-8. Educational Attainment of the Population 15 Years and Over, by Age, Sex, Race, and Hispanic Origin, March 2002—*Continued*

(Numbers in thousands.)

Age, sex, race, and Hispanic origin	College						
	Some college, no degree	Associate degree, occupational	Associate degree, academic	Bachelor's degree	Master's degree	Professional degree	Doctorate degree
BLACK							
Both Sexes							
15 years and over	5 257	893	860	2 564	805	146	109
15 to 17 years	5	*	*	*	2	*	*
18 and 19 years	221	8	*	3	*	*	*
20 to 24 years	1 005	64	48	150	8	*	*
25 to 29 years	661	106	88	370	44	13	*
30 to 34 years	594	116	92	419	74	20	16
35 to 39 years	592	123	130	365	109	20	15
40 to 44 years	619	128	157	343	129	22	14
45 to 49 years	533	111	100	298	128	20	16
50 to 54 years	370	94	93	242	117	12	3
55 to 59 years	244	54	59	144	48	8	16
60 to 64 years	141	24	36	75	47	10	8
65 to 69 years	144	31	24	69	41	10	11
70 to 74 years	61	13	13	47	30	3	7
75 years and over	67	21	20	39	26	8	2
15 to 17 years	5	*	*	*	2	*	*
18 years and over	5 252	893	860	2 564	803	146	109
15 to 24 years	1 231	72	48	153	10	*	*
25 years and over	4 025	821	812	2 411	795	146	109
15 to 64 years	4 984	828	804	2 409	707	126	89
65 years and over	273	65	56	155	98	21	20
Male							
15 years and over	2 402	339	319	1 086	296	67	65
15 to 17 years	1	*	*	*	*	*	*
18 and 19 years	101	3	*	3	*	*	*
20 to 24 years	472	28	16	49	2	*	*
25 to 29 years	307	33	25	176	9	4	*
30 to 34 years	264	49	38	187	21	6	8
35 to 39 years	276	41	50	146	37	10	9
40 to 44 years	270	48	78	136	56	9	8
45 to 49 years	251	44	37	133	50	14	8
50 to 54 years	163	42	31	103	53	8	1
55 to 59 years	121	18	15	64	15	6	11
60 to 64 years	61	6	13	32	15	2	4
65 to 69 years	64	14	11	31	16	5	9
70 to 74 years	26	1	3	16	10	1	5
75 years and over	24	10	3	11	12	3	2
15 to 17 years	1	*	*	*	*	*	*
18 years and over	2 400	339	319	1 086	296	67	65
15 to 24 years	575	32	16	53	2	*	*
25 years and over	1 827	307	304	1 034	294	67	65
15 to 64 years	2 288	314	302	1 029	258	59	49
65 years and over	114	25	17	57	38	9	16
Female							
15 years and over	2 855	554	541	1 477	509	79	44
15 to 17 years	4	*	*	*	2	*	*
18 and 19 years	121	4	*	*	*	*	*
20 to 24 years	532	36	33	100	6	*	*
25 to 29 years	354	73	63	194	36	9	*
30 to 34 years	330	67	54	232	53	15	8
35 to 39 years	316	83	80	218	72	10	6
40 to 44 years	349	79	79	207	73	13	6
45 to 49 years	281	67	63	165	78	6	8
50 to 54 years	207	52	62	139	65	4	2
55 to 59 years	123	36	44	80	33	2	5
60 to 64 years	80	17	23	43	33	8	4
65 to 69 years	80	16	13	39	25	5	2
70 to 74 years	35	11	10	31	20	1	2
75 years and over	43	11	17	28	14	5	*
15 to 17 years	4	*	*	*	2	*	*
18 years and over	2 851	554	541	1 477	507	79	44
15 to 24 years	657	40	33	100	8	*	*
25 years and over	2 198	514	508	1 377	501	79	44
15 to 64 years	2 696	514	502	1 380	450	67	40
65 years and over	158	39	38	97	60	12	4

* = Represents zero or rounds to zero.

Table A-9. Percentage of High School and College Graduates of the Population 15 Years and Over by Age, Sex, Race, and Hispanic Origin, March 2002

(Numbers in thousands, except where noted.)

Age, sex, race, and Hispanic origin	Total	Percent					
		Total	Not high school graduate	High school graduate or more	Total	Less than bachelor's degree	Bachelor's degree or more
ALL RACES							
Both Sexes							
15 years and over	221 591	100.0	21.4	78.6	100.0	77.0	23.0
15 to 17 years	12 137	100.0	98.2	1.8	100.0	99.9	0.1
18 and 19 years	7 909	100.0	44.0	56.0	100.0	99.9	0.1
20 to 24 years	19 404	100.0	15.5	84.5	100.0	88.8	11.2
25 to 29 years	18 310	100.0	13.6	86.4	100.0	70.7	29.3
30 to 34 years	20 360	100.0	12.7	87.3	100.0	68.3	31.7
35 to 39 years	21 648	100.0	12.0	88.0	100.0	71.2	28.8
40 to 44 years	22 636	100.0	11.3	88.7	100.0	71.8	28.2
45 to 49 years	20 988	100.0	10.8	89.2	100.0	70.8	29.2
50 to 54 years	18 557	100.0	11.0	89.0	100.0	69.1	30.9
55 to 59 years	14 667	100.0	14.7	85.3	100.0	71.9	28.1
60 to 64 years	11 208	100.0	18.7	81.3	100.0	76.6	23.4
65 to 69 years	9 597	100.0	25.0	75.0	100.0	81.0	19.0
70 to 74 years	8 526	100.0	28.2	71.8	100.0	81.8	18.2
75 years and over	15 647	100.0	34.3	65.7	100.0	85.6	14.4
15 to 17 years	12 137	100.0	98.2	1.8	100.0	99.9	0.1
18 years and over	209 454	100.0	16.9	83.1	100.0	75.7	24.3
15 to 24 years	39 449	100.0	46.6	53.4	100.0	94.4	5.6
25 years and over	182 142	100.0	15.9	84.1	100.0	73.3	26.7
15 to 64 years	187 822	100.0	19.8	80.2	100.0	75.9	24.1
65 years and over	33 769	100.0	30.1	69.9	100.0	83.3	16.7
Male							
15 years and over	106 910	100.0	22.2	77.8	100.0	75.9	24.1
15 to 17 years	6 209	100.0	98.4	1.6	100.0	99.9	0.1
18 and 19 years	4 026	100.0	48.1	51.9	100.0	99.8	0.2
20 to 24 years	9 679	100.0	16.7	83.3	100.0	90.7	9.3
25 to 29 years	9 150	100.0	15.3	84.7	100.0	73.1	26.9
30 to 34 years	10 084	100.0	14.6	85.4	100.0	70.0	30.0
35 to 39 years	10 698	100.0	13.0	87.0	100.0	71.2	28.8
40 to 44 years	11 124	100.0	12.2	87.8	100.0	71.2	28.8
45 to 49 years	10 256	100.0	11.5	88.5	100.0	70.1	29.9
50 to 54 years	9 075	100.0	10.9	89.1	100.0	66.8	33.2
55 to 59 years	7 091	100.0	14.8	85.2	100.0	67.1	32.9
60 to 64 years	5 282	100.0	18.4	81.6	100.0	71.4	28.6
65 to 69 years	4 451	100.0	25.1	74.9	100.0	76.4	23.6
70 to 74 years	3 794	100.0	29.8	70.2	100.0	76.9	23.1
75 years and over	5 991	100.0	34.1	65.9	100.0	79.8	20.2
15 to 17 years	6 209	100.0	98.4	1.6	100.0	99.9	0.1
18 years and over	100 701	100.0	17.5	82.5	100.0	74.4	25.6
15 to 24 years	19 914	100.0	48.5	51.5	100.0	95.4	4.6
25 years and over	86 996	100.0	16.2	83.8	100.0	71.5	28.5
15 to 64 years	92 674	100.0	21.0	79.0	100.0	75.6	24.4
65 years and over	14 235	100.0	30.1	69.9	100.0	78.0	22.0
Female							
15 years and over	114 681	100.0	20.6	79.4	100.0	78.1	21.9
15 to 17 years	5 928	100.0	98.1	1.9	100.0	100.0	*
18 and 19 years	3 883	100.0	39.7	60.3	100.0	100.0	*
20 to 24 years	9 724	100.0	14.2	85.8	100.0	86.8	13.2
25 to 29 years	9 159	100.0	11.9	88.1	100.0	68.2	31.8
30 to 34 years	10 277	100.0	10.8	89.2	100.0	66.5	33.5
35 to 39 years	10 950	100.0	11.0	89.0	100.0	71.2	28.8
40 to 44 years	11 512	100.0	10.4	89.6	100.0	72.3	27.7
45 to 49 years	10 732	100.0	10.2	89.8	100.0	71.5	28.5
50 to 54 years	9 482	100.0	11.1	88.9	100.0	71.4	28.6
55 to 59 years	7 575	100.0	14.7	85.3	100.0	76.4	23.6
60 to 64 years	5 926	100.0	18.9	81.1	100.0	81.2	18.8
65 to 69 years	5 146	100.0	25.0	75.0	100.0	85.0	15.0
70 to 74 years	4 732	100.0	27.0	73.0	100.0	85.7	14.3
75 years and over	9 656	100.0	34.4	65.6	100.0	89.2	10.8
15 to 17 years	5 928	100.0	98.1	1.9	100.0	100.0	*
18 years and over	108 753	100.0	16.3	83.7	100.0	76.9	23.1
15 to 24 years	19 535	100.0	44.7	55.3	100.0	93.4	6.6
25 years and over	95 146	100.0	15.6	84.4	100.0	74.9	25.1
15 to 64 years	95 147	100.0	18.6	81.4	100.0	76.2	23.8
65 years and over	19 534	100.0	30.1	69.9	100.0	87.2	12.8

* = Represents zero or rounds to zero.

Table A-9. Percentage of High School and College Graduates of the Population 15 Years and Over by Age, Sex, Race, and Hispanic Origin, March 2002—*Continued*

(Numbers in thousands, except where noted.)

Age, sex, race, and Hispanic origin	Total	Percent					
		Total	Not high school graduate	High school graduate or more	Total	Less than bachelor's degree	Bachelor's degree or more
NON-HISPANIC WHITE							
Both Sexes							
15 years and over	158 258	100.0	16.4	83.6	100.0	74.2	25.8
15 to 17 years	7 815	100.0	98.3	1.7	100.0	99.9	0.1
18 and 19 years	4 988	100.0	40.4	59.6	100.0	99.9	0.1
20 to 24 years	12 038	100.0	9.4	90.6	100.0	86.2	13.8
25 to 29 years	11 252	100.0	7.0	93.0	100.0	64.1	35.9
30 to 34 years	13 068	100.0	6.1	93.9	100.0	63.2	36.8
35 to 39 years	14 760	100.0	6.4	93.6	100.0	67.5	32.5
40 to 44 years	16 269	100.0	6.9	93.1	100.0	69.1	30.9
45 to 49 years	15 545	100.0	6.3	93.7	100.0	68.1	31.9
50 to 54 years	14 188	100.0	6.7	93.3	100.0	66.0	34.0
55 to 59 years	11 486	100.0	9.8	90.2	100.0	69.4	30.6
60 to 64 years	8 876	100.0	13.6	86.4	100.0	74.6	25.4
65 to 69 years	7 493	100.0	20.0	80.0	100.0	79.3	20.7
70 to 74 years	7 057	100.0	23.7	76.3	100.0	80.6	19.4
75 years and over	13 423	100.0	29.9	70.1	100.0	84.5	15.5
15 to 17 years	7 815	100.0	98.3	1.7	100.0	99.9	0.1
18 years and over	150 443	100.0	12.1	87.9	100.0	72.8	27.2
15 to 24 years	24 841	100.0	43.6	56.4	100.0	93.3	6.7
25 years and over	133 417	100.0	11.3	88.7	100.0	70.6	29.4
15 to 64 years	130 285	100.0	14.4	85.6	100.0	72.5	27.5
65 years and over	27 973	100.0	25.7	74.3	100.0	82.1	17.9
Male							
15 years and over	76 602	100.0	17.0	83.0	100.0	72.6	27.4
15 to 17 years	3 973	100.0	98.4	1.6	100.0	99.9	0.1
18 and 19 years	2 553	100.0	43.6	56.4	100.0	99.9	0.1
20 to 24 years	5 993	100.0	9.8	90.2	100.0	88.8	11.2
25 to 29 years	5 591	100.0	7.9	92.1	100.0	67.4	32.6
30 to 34 years	6 551	100.0	7.2	92.8	100.0	65.2	34.8
35 to 39 years	7 337	100.0	7.2	92.8	100.0	67.2	32.8
40 to 44 years	8 080	100.0	7.8	92.2	100.0	68.4	31.6
45 to 49 years	7 742	100.0	7.2	92.8	100.0	67.6	32.4
50 to 54 years	7 024	100.0	7.2	92.8	100.0	63.4	36.6
55 to 59 years	5 631	100.0	10.4	89.6	100.0	64.1	35.9
60 to 64 years	4 261	100.0	13.8	86.2	100.0	68.5	31.5
65 to 69 years	3 515	100.0	20.7	79.3	100.0	74.0	26.0
70 to 74 years	3 174	100.0	25.8	74.2	100.0	75.3	24.7
75 years and over	5 177	100.0	30.0	70.0	100.0	78.3	21.7
15 to 17 years	3 973	100.0	98.4	1.6	100.0	99.9	0.1
18 years and over	72 629	100.0	12.5	87.5	100.0	71.1	28.9
15 to 24 years	12 519	100.0	44.8	55.2	100.0	94.6	5.4
25 years and over	64 083	100.0	11.5	88.5	100.0	68.3	31.7
15 to 64 years	64 736	100.0	15.3	84.7	100.0	71.9	28.1
65 years and over	11 866	100.0	26.1	73.9	100.0	76.2	23.8
Female							
15 years and over	81 656	100.0	15.8	84.2	100.0	75.6	24.4
15 to 17 years	3 842	100.0	98.3	1.7	100.0	100.0	*
18 and 19 years	2 435	100.0	37.0	63.0	100.0	100.0	*
20 to 24 years	6 045	100.0	9.0	91.0	100.0	83.6	16.4
25 to 29 years	5 661	100.0	6.2	93.8	100.0	60.8	39.2
30 to 34 years	6 517	100.0	5.0	95.0	100.0	61.2	38.8
35 to 39 years	7 423	100.0	5.7	94.3	100.0	67.8	32.2
40 to 44 years	8 189	100.0	5.9	94.1	100.0	69.8	30.2
45 to 49 years	7 802	100.0	5.4	94.6	100.0	68.7	31.3
50 to 54 years	7 164	100.0	6.2	93.8	100.0	68.6	31.4
55 to 59 years	5 855	100.0	9.3	90.7	100.0	74.5	25.5
60 to 64 years	4 615	100.0	13.4	86.6	100.0	80.3	19.7
65 to 69 years	3 978	100.0	19.5	80.5	100.0	83.9	16.1
70 to 74 years	3 883	100.0	21.9	78.1	100.0	84.9	15.1
75 years and over	8 246	100.0	29.8	70.2	100.0	88.3	11.7
15 to 17 years	3 842	100.0	98.3	1.7	100.0	100.0	*
18 years and over	77 814	100.0	11.7	88.3	100.0	74.4	25.6
15 to 24 years	12 322	100.0	42.4	57.6	100.0	91.9	8.1
25 years and over	69 334	100.0	11.1	88.9	100.0	72.7	27.3
15 to 64 years	65 549	100.0	13.5	86.5	100.0	73.0	27.0
65 years and over	16 107	100.0	25.3	74.7	100.0	86.4	13.6

* = Represents zero or rounds to zero.

Table A-9. Percentage of High School and College Graduates of the Population 15 Years and Over by Age, Sex, Race, and Hispanic Origin, March 2002—*Continued*

(Numbers in thousands, except where noted.)

Age, sex, race, and Hispanic origin	Total	Percent					
		Total	Not high school graduate	High school graduate or more	Total	Less than bachelor's degree	Bachelor's degree or more
NON-HISPANIC BLACK							
Both Sexes							
15 years and over	25 233	100.0	27.3	72.7	100.0	86.0	14.0
15 to 17 years	1 784	100.0	99.0	1.0	100.0	99.9	0.1
18 and 19 years	1 147	100.0	48.0	52.0	100.0	99.7	0.3
20 to 24 years	2 661	100.0	18.6	81.4	100.0	94.1	5.9
25 to 29 years	2 303	100.0	12.4	87.6	100.0	82.0	18.0
30 to 34 years	2 475	100.0	12.1	87.9	100.0	79.5	20.5
35 to 39 years	2 628	100.0	12.2	87.8	100.0	81.2	18.8
40 to 44 years	2 674	100.0	14.1	85.9	100.0	81.5	18.5
45 to 49 years	2 357	100.0	15.9	84.1	100.0	80.9	19.1
50 to 54 years	1 981	100.0	17.6	82.4	100.0	81.3	18.7
55 to 59 years	1 397	100.0	26.9	73.1	100.0	85.0	15.0
60 to 64 years	1 026	100.0	31.9	68.1	100.0	86.4	13.6
65 to 69 years	1 025	100.0	39.6	60.4	100.0	87.4	12.6
70 to 74 years	698	100.0	46.5	53.5	100.0	88.2	11.8
75 years and over	1 078	100.0	60.1	39.9	100.0	93.1	6.9
15 to 17 years	1 784	100.0	99.0	1.0	100.0	99.9	0.1
18 years and over	23 449	100.0	21.9	78.1	100.0	84.9	15.1
15 to 24 years	5 591	100.0	50.3	49.7	100.0	97.1	2.9
25 years and over	19 642	100.0	20.8	79.2	100.0	82.8	17.2
15 to 64 years	22 432	100.0	24.6	75.4	100.0	85.5	14.5
65 years and over	2 801	100.0	49.2	50.8	100.0	89.8	10.2
Male							
15 years and over	11 264	100.0	28.6	71.4	100.0	86.9	13.1
15 to 17 years	895	100.0	99.1	0.9	100.0	100.0	*
18 and 19 years	556	100.0	51.7	48.3	100.0	99.4	0.6
20 to 24 years	1 221	100.0	19.7	80.3	100.0	95.8	4.2
25 to 29 years	1 021	100.0	14.2	85.8	100.0	82.1	17.9
30 to 34 years	1 105	100.0	12.9	87.1	100.0	80.7	19.3
35 to 39 years	1 168	100.0	12.2	87.8	100.0	83.7	16.3
40 to 44 years	1 204	100.0	14.7	85.3	100.0	83.0	17.0
45 to 49 years	1 065	100.0	16.9	83.1	100.0	80.9	19.1
50 to 54 years	900	100.0	17.9	82.1	100.0	81.9	18.1
55 to 59 years	621	100.0	28.3	71.7	100.0	85.5	14.5
60 to 64 years	414	100.0	33.2	66.8	100.0	87.4	12.6
65 to 69 years	447	100.0	39.8	60.2	100.0	86.9	13.1
70 to 74 years	284	100.0	47.7	52.3	100.0	89.5	10.5
75 years and over	364	100.0	64.0	36.0	100.0	92.4	7.6
15 to 17 years	895	100.0	99.1	0.9	100.0	100.0	*
18 years and over	10 369	100.0	22.5	77.5	100.0	85.8	14.2
15 to 24 years	2 671	100.0	52.9	47.1	100.0	98.0	2.0
25 years and over	8 593	100.0	21.0	79.0	100.0	83.5	16.5
15 to 64 years	10 168	100.0	26.3	73.7	100.0	86.7	13.3
65 years and over	1 095	100.0	49.9	50.1	100.0	89.4	10.6
Female							
15 years and over	13 969	100.0	26.3	73.7	100.0	85.2	14.8
15 to 17 years	889	100.0	98.9	1.1	100.0	99.8	0.2
18 and 19 years	591	100.0	44.6	55.4	100.0	100.0	*
20 to 24 years	1 440	100.0	17.6	82.4	100.0	92.6	7.4
25 to 29 years	1 282	100.0	11.1	88.9	100.0	81.9	18.1
30 to 34 years	1 370	100.0	11.4	88.6	100.0	78.5	21.5
35 to 39 years	1 460	100.0	12.2	87.8	100.0	79.2	20.8
40 to 44 years	1 469	100.0	13.6	86.4	100.0	80.2	19.8
45 to 49 years	1 293	100.0	15.1	84.9	100.0	80.9	19.1
50 to 54 years	1 081	100.0	17.3	82.7	100.0	80.8	19.2
55 to 59 years	776	100.0	25.7	74.3	100.0	84.6	15.4
60 to 64 years	612	100.0	31.0	69.0	100.0	85.8	14.2
65 to 69 years	577	100.0	39.5	60.5	100.0	87.7	12.3
70 to 74 years	414	100.0	45.6	54.4	100.0	87.3	12.7
75 years and over	714	100.0	58.1	41.9	100.0	93.5	6.5
15 to 17 years	889	100.0	98.9	1.1	100.0	99.8	0.2
18 years and over	13 080	100.0	21.4	78.6	100.0	84.3	15.7
15 to 24 years	2 920	100.0	47.8	52.2	100.0	96.3	3.7
25 years and over	11 049	100.0	20.6	79.4	100.0	82.3	17.7
15 to 64 years	12 264	100.0	23.2	76.8	100.0	84.6	15.4
65 years and over	1 706	100.0	48.8	51.2	100.0	90.0	10.0

* = Represents zero or rounds to zero.

Table A-9. Percentage of High School and College Graduates of the Population 15 Years and Over by Age, Sex, Race, and Hispanic Origin, March 2002—*Continued*

(Numbers in thousands, except where noted.)

Age, sex, race, and Hispanic origin	Total	Percent					
		Total	Not high school graduate	High school graduate or more	Total	Less than bachelor's degree	Bachelor's degree or more
ASIAN/PACIFIC ISLANDER							
Both Sexes							
15 years and over	9 842	100.0	17.7	82.3	100.0	59.9	40.1
15 to 17 years	591	100.0	97.9	2.1	100.0	99.8	0.2
18 and 19 years	376	100.0	31.8	68.2	100.0	100.0	*
20 to 24 years	1 009	100.0	5.4	94.6	100.0	77.0	23.0
25 to 29 years	1 066	100.0	4.9	95.1	100.0	45.2	54.8
30 to 34 years	1 168	100.0	6.0	94.0	100.0	41.3	58.7
35 to 39 years	1 081	100.0	8.8	91.2	100.0	48.4	51.6
40 to 44 years	990	100.0	8.7	91.3	100.0	50.5	49.5
45 to 49 years	957	100.0	11.4	88.6	100.0	55.2	44.8
50 to 54 years	766	100.0	14.8	85.2	100.0	55.2	44.8
55 to 59 years	558	100.0	17.0	83.0	100.0	56.3	43.7
60 to 64 years	380	100.0	20.7	79.3	100.0	57.8	42.2
65 to 69 years	315	100.0	27.4	72.6	100.0	73.3	26.7
70 to 74 years	235	100.0	31.1	68.9	100.0	73.4	26.6
75 years and over	348	100.0	37.0	63.0	100.0	79.9	20.1
15 to 17 years	591	100.0	97.9	2.1	100.0	99.8	0.2
18 years and over	9 251	100.0	12.6	87.4	100.0	57.4	42.6
15 to 24 years	1 976	100.0	38.1	61.9	100.0	88.2	11.8
25 years and over	7 866	100.0	12.6	87.4	100.0	52.8	47.2
15 to 64 years	8 943	100.0	16.2	83.8	100.0	58.3	41.7
65 years and over	899	100.0	32.1	67.9	100.0	75.9	24.1
Male							
15 years and over	4 761	100.0	17.2	82.8	100.0	57.7	42.3
15 to 17 years	315	100.0	98.6	1.4	100.0	99.7	0.3
18 and 19 years	203	100.0	42.8	57.2	100.0	100.0	*
20 to 24 years	502	100.0	6.4	93.6	100.0	77.9	22.1
25 to 29 years	539	100.0	6.3	93.7	100.0	45.9	54.1
30 to 34 years	558	100.0	7.1	92.9	100.0	39.7	60.3
35 to 39 years	539	100.0	7.0	93.0	100.0	45.2	54.8
40 to 44 years	470	100.0	6.2	93.8	100.0	45.0	55.0
45 to 49 years	445	100.0	9.8	90.2	100.0	53.4	46.6
50 to 54 years	370	100.0	11.0	89.0	100.0	52.8	47.2
55 to 59 years	259	100.0	13.4	86.6	100.0	49.0	51.0
60 to 64 years	168	100.0	16.2	83.8	100.0	53.1	46.9
65 to 69 years	149	100.0	23.9	76.1	100.0	68.6	31.4
70 to 74 years	103	100.0	26.3	73.7	100.0	65.0	35.0
75 years and over	139	100.0	29.7	70.3	100.0	67.2	32.8
15 to 17 years	315	100.0	98.6	1.4	100.0	99.7	0.3
18 years and over	4 446	100.0	11.5	88.5	100.0	54.7	45.3
15 to 24 years	1 020	100.0	42.1	57.9	100.0	89.0	11.0
25 years and over	3 741	100.0	10.5	89.5	100.0	49.1	50.9
15 to 64 years	4 369	100.0	16.4	83.6	100.0	56.8	43.2
65 years and over	392	100.0	26.6	73.4	100.0	67.2	32.8
Female							
15 years and over	5 081	100.0	18.1	81.9	100.0	62.0	38.0
15 to 17 years	277	100.0	97.1	2.9	100.0	100.0	*
18 and 19 years	173	100.0	18.9	81.1	100.0	100.0	*
20 to 24 years	507	100.0	4.4	95.6	100.0	76.1	23.9
25 to 29 years	527	100.0	3.4	96.6	100.0	44.4	55.6
30 to 34 years	610	100.0	4.9	95.1	100.0	42.7	57.3
35 to 39 years	543	100.0	10.7	89.3	100.0	51.5	48.5
40 to 44 years	520	100.0	10.9	89.1	100.0	55.5	44.5
45 to 49 years	512	100.0	12.8	87.2	100.0	56.9	43.1
50 to 54 years	397	100.0	18.3	81.7	100.0	57.4	42.6
55 to 59 years	299	100.0	20.2	79.8	100.0	62.7	37.3
60 to 64 years	211	100.0	24.3	75.7	100.0	61.5	38.5
65 to 69 years	166	100.0	30.4	69.6	100.0	77.5	22.5
70 to 74 years	132	100.0	34.9	65.1	100.0	79.9	20.1
75 years and over	209	100.0	41.9	58.1	100.0	88.4	11.6
15 to 17 years	277	100.0	97.1	2.9	100.0	100.0	*
18 years and over	4 805	100.0	13.6	86.4	100.0	59.9	40.1
15 to 24 years	956	100.0	33.8	66.2	100.0	87.3	12.7
25 years and over	4 125	100.0	14.5	85.5	100.0	56.2	43.8
15 to 64 years	4 574	100.0	16.1	83.9	100.0	59.9	40.2
65 years and over	507	100.0	36.3	63.7	100.0	82.6	17.4

* = Represents zero or rounds to zero.

Table A-9. Percentage of High School and College Graduates of the Population 15 Years and Over by Age, Sex, Race, and Hispanic Origin, March 2002—*Continued*

(Numbers in thousands, except where noted.)

Age, sex, race, and Hispanic origin	Total	Percent					
		Total	Not high school graduate	High school graduate or more	Total	Less than bachelor's degree	Bachelor's degree or more
HISPANIC[1]							
Both Sexes							
15 years and over	26 351	100.0	46.5	53.5	100.0	91.3	8.7
15 to 17 years	1 801	100.0	97.3	2.7	100.0	100.0	*
18 and 19 years	1 321	100.0	56.0	44.0	100.0	100.0	*
20 to 24 years	3 559	100.0	36.3	63.7	100.0	96.5	3.5
25 to 29 years	3 537	100.0	37.6	62.4	100.0	91.1	8.9
30 to 34 years	3 457	100.0	40.4	59.6	100.0	87.6	12.4
35 to 39 years	2 953	100.0	40.4	59.6	100.0	87.8	12.2
40 to 44 years	2 486	100.0	38.0	62.0	100.0	86.3	13.7
45 to 49 years	1 938	100.0	40.2	59.8	100.0	86.3	13.7
50 to 54 years	1 461	100.0	41.4	58.6	100.0	88.2	11.8
55 to 59 years	1 103	100.0	48.0	52.0	100.0	88.8	11.2
60 to 64 years	839	100.0	54.6	45.4	100.0	91.9	8.1
65 to 69 years	680	100.0	55.0	45.0	100.0	92.2	7.8
70 to 74 years	495	100.0	65.1	34.9	100.0	93.7	6.3
75 years and over	722	100.0	73.5	26.5	100.0	97.1	2.9
15 to 17 years	1 801	100.0	97.3	2.7	100.0	100.0	*
18 years and over	24 550	100.0	42.8	57.2	100.0	90.6	9.4
15 to 24 years	6 681	100.0	56.6	43.4	100.0	98.2	1.8
25 years and over	19 670	100.0	43.0	57.0	100.0	88.9	11.1
15 to 64 years	24 454	100.0	45.1	54.9	100.0	91.0	9.0
65 years and over	1 896	100.0	64.7	35.3	100.0	94.4	5.6
Male							
15 years and over	13 451	100.0	48.0	52.0	100.0	91.4	8.6
15 to 17 years	950	100.0	97.9	2.1	100.0	100.0	*
18 and 19 years	675	100.0	62.2	37.8	100.0	100.0	*
20 to 24 years	1 911	100.0	39.1	60.9	100.0	96.6	3.4
25 to 29 years	1 933	100.0	39.8	60.2	100.0	91.7	8.3
30 to 34 years	1 792	100.0	44.9	55.1	100.0	90.0	10.0
35 to 39 years	1 559	100.0	42.8	57.2	100.0	88.5	11.5
40 to 44 years	1 279	100.0	39.4	60.6	100.0	86.8	13.2
45 to 49 years	928	100.0	41.0	59.0	100.0	85.0	15.0
50 to 54 years	697	100.0	39.2	60.8	100.0	85.7	14.3
55 to 59 years	516	100.0	46.4	53.6	100.0	87.4	12.6
60 to 64 years	401	100.0	52.7	47.3	100.0	90.7	9.3
65 to 69 years	303	100.0	54.3	45.7	100.0	90.6	9.4
70 to 74 years	219	100.0	64.8	35.2	100.0	90.6	9.4
75 years and over	287	100.0	70.3	29.7	100.0	96.4	3.6
15 to 17 years	950	100.0	97.9	2.1	100.0	100.0	*
18 years and over	12 501	100.0	44.2	55.8	100.0	90.8	9.2
15 to 24 years	3 536	100.0	59.3	40.7	100.0	98.2	1.8
25 years and over	9 915	100.0	43.9	56.1	100.0	89.0	11.0
15 to 64 years	12 642	100.0	47.0	53.0	100.0	91.4	8.6
65 years and over	809	100.0	62.8	37.2	100.0	92.7	7.3
Female							
15 years and over	12 900	100.0	44.9	55.1	100.0	91.1	8.9
15 to 17 years	851	100.0	96.6	3.4	100.0	100.0	*
18 and 19 years	646	100.0	49.5	50.5	100.0	100.0	*
20 to 24 years	1 648	100.0	33.0	67.0	100.0	96.5	3.5
25 to 29 years	1 604	100.0	35.0	65.0	100.0	90.3	9.7
30 to 34 years	1 664	100.0	35.6	64.4	100.0	85.0	15.0
35 to 39 years	1 394	100.0	37.7	62.3	100.0	87.0	13.0
40 to 44 years	1 206	100.0	36.6	63.4	100.0	85.7	14.3
45 to 49 years	1 010	100.0	39.3	60.7	100.0	87.4	12.6
50 to 54 years	764	100.0	43.4	56.6	100.0	90.4	9.6
55 to 59 years	587	100.0	49.4	50.6	100.0	90.0	10.0
60 to 64 years	438	100.0	56.3	43.7	100.0	93.0	7.0
65 to 69 years	376	100.0	55.6	44.4	100.0	93.5	6.5
70 to 74 years	277	100.0	65.3	34.7	100.0	96.1	3.9
75 years and over	435	100.0	75.7	24.3	100.0	97.5	2.5
15 to 17 years	851	100.0	96.6	3.4	100.0	100.0	*
18 years and over	12 049	100.0	41.3	58.7	100.0	90.4	9.6
15 to 24 years	3 145	100.0	53.6	46.4	100.0	98.2	1.8
25 years and over	9 755	100.0	42.1	57.9	100.0	88.8	11.2
15 to 64 years	11 812	100.0	43.0	57.0	100.0	90.6	9.4
65 years and over	1 088	100.0	66.1	33.9	100.0	95.8	4.2

[1]May be of any race.
* = Represents zero or rounds to zero.

Table A-9. Percentage of High School and College Graduates of the Population 15 Years and Over by Age, Sex, Race, and Hispanic Origin, March 2002—*Continued*

(Numbers in thousands, except where noted.)

Age, sex, race, and Hispanic origin	Total	Percent					
		Total	Not high school graduate	High school graduate or more	Total	Less than bachelor's degree	Bachelor's degree or more
WHITE							
Both Sexes							
15 years and over	183 086	100.0	20.5	79.5	100.0	76.5	23.5
15 to 17 years	9 500	100.0	98.1	1.9	100.0	100.0	*
18 and 19 years	6 257	100.0	43.5	56.5	100.0	99.9	0.1
20 to 24 years	15 387	100.0	15.3	84.7	100.0	88.4	11.6
25 to 29 years	14 574	100.0	14.1	85.9	100.0	70.3	29.7
30 to 34 years	16 322	100.0	13.1	86.9	100.0	68.1	31.9
35 to 39 years	17 537	100.0	11.7	88.3	100.0	70.7	29.3
40 to 44 years	18 618	100.0	10.9	89.1	100.0	71.3	28.7
45 to 49 years	17 342	100.0	9.9	90.1	100.0	70.0	30.0
50 to 54 years	15 563	100.0	9.8	90.2	100.0	68.0	32.0
55 to 59 years	12 530	100.0	13.0	87.0	100.0	71.0	29.0
60 to 64 years	9 666	100.0	16.9	83.1	100.0	76.0	24.0
65 to 69 years	8 137	100.0	22.8	77.2	100.0	80.3	19.7
70 to 74 years	7 531	100.0	26.3	73.7	100.0	81.4	18.6
75 years and over	14 122	100.0	32.0	68.0	100.0	85.1	14.9
15 to 17 years	9 500	100.0	98.1	1.9	100.0	100.0	*
18 years and over	173 586	100.0	16.3	83.7	100.0	75.2	24.8
15 to 24 years	31 144	100.0	46.2	53.8	100.0	94.2	5.8
25 years and over	151 942	100.0	15.2	84.8	100.0	72.8	27.2
15 to 64 years	153 296	100.0	19.0	81.0	100.0	75.2	24.8
65 years and over	29 790	100.0	28.1	71.9	100.0	82.9	17.1
Male							
15 years and over	89 291	100.0	21.4	78.6	100.0	75.3	24.7
15 to 17 years	4 867	100.0	98.3	1.7	100.0	99.9	0.1
18 and 19 years	3 194	100.0	47.2	52.8	100.0	99.9	0.1
20 to 24 years	7 786	100.0	16.6	83.4	100.0	90.6	9.4
25 to 29 years	7 418	100.0	15.9	84.1	100.0	73.5	26.5
30 to 34 years	8 248	100.0	15.1	84.9	100.0	70.3	29.7
35 to 39 years	8 810	100.0	13.1	86.9	100.0	70.8	29.2
40 to 44 years	9 295	100.0	12.0	88.0	100.0	70.8	29.2
45 to 49 years	8 606	100.0	10.5	89.5	100.0	69.3	30.7
50 to 54 years	7 679	100.0	10.0	90.0	100.0	65.3	34.7
55 to 59 years	6 114	100.0	13.2	86.8	100.0	65.9	34.1
60 to 64 years	4 637	100.0	17.0	83.0	100.0	70.3	29.7
65 to 69 years	3 805	100.0	23.3	76.7	100.0	75.3	24.7
70 to 74 years	3 379	100.0	28.3	71.7	100.0	76.2	23.8
75 years and over	5 453	100.0	32.1	67.9	100.0	79.2	20.8
15 to 17 years	4 867	100.0	98.3	1.7	100.0	99.9	0.1
18 years and over	84 424	100.0	17.0	83.0	100.0	73.8	26.2
15 to 24 years	15 847	100.0	47.9	52.1	100.0	95.3	4.7
25 years and over	73 444	100.0	15.7	84.3	100.0	70.9	29.1
15 to 64 years	76 654	100.0	20.3	79.7	100.0	74.9	25.1
65 years and over	12 637	100.0	28.4	71.6	100.0	77.3	22.7
Female							
15 years and over	93 795	100.0	19.6	80.4	100.0	77.6	22.4
15 to 17 years	4 633	100.0	97.9	2.1	100.0	100.0	*
18 and 19 years	3 063	100.0	39.7	60.3	100.0	100.0	*
20 to 24 years	7 601	100.0	13.9	86.1	100.0	86.2	13.8
25 to 29 years	7 156	100.0	12.3	87.7	100.0	66.9	33.1
30 to 34 years	8 074	100.0	11.0	89.0	100.0	65.8	34.2
35 to 39 years	8 727	100.0	10.4	89.6	100.0	70.6	29.4
40 to 44 years	9 323	100.0	9.7	90.3	100.0	71.8	28.2
45 to 49 years	8 736	100.0	9.2	90.8	100.0	70.7	29.3
50 to 54 years	7 884	100.0	9.6	90.4	100.0	70.6	29.4
55 to 59 years	6 417	100.0	12.8	87.2	100.0	75.8	24.2
60 to 64 years	5 029	100.0	16.9	83.1	100.0	81.3	18.7
65 to 69 years	4 332	100.0	22.4	77.6	100.0	84.7	15.3
70 to 74 years	4 152	100.0	24.7	75.3	100.0	85.6	14.4
75 years and over	8 669	100.0	32.0	68.0	100.0	88.8	11.2
15 to 17 years	4 633	100.0	97.9	2.1	100.0	100.0	*
18 years and over	89 162	100.0	15.5	84.5	100.0	76.5	23.5
15 to 24 years	15 297	100.0	44.5	55.5	100.0	93.1	6.9
25 years and over	78 498	100.0	14.8	85.2	100.0	74.6	25.4
15 to 64 years	76 642	100.0	17.8	82.2	100.0	75.5	24.5
65 years and over	17 153	100.0	27.8	72.2	100.0	87.0	13.0

* = Represents zero or rounds to zero.

Table A-9. Percentage of High School and College Graduates of the Population 15 Years and Over by Age, Sex, Race, and Hispanic Origin, March 2002—*Continued*

(Numbers in thousands, except where noted.)

Age, sex, race, and Hispanic origin	Total	Percent						
		Total	Not high school graduate	High school graduate or more	Total	Less than bachelor's degree	Bachelor's degree or more
BLACK							
Both Sexes							
15 years and over	26 171	100.0	27.8	72.2	100.0	86.2	13.8
15 to 17 years	1 856	100.0	98.9	1.1	100.0	99.9	0.1
18 and 19 years	1 181	100.0	48.4	51.6	100.0	99.7	0.3
20 to 24 years	2 776	100.0	19.6	80.4	100.0	94.3	5.7
25 to 29 years	2 439	100.0	13.4	86.6	100.0	82.5	17.5
30 to 34 years	2 602	100.0	12.9	87.1	100.0	79.6	20.4
35 to 39 years	2 731	100.0	13.4	86.6	100.0	81.4	18.6
40 to 44 years	2 764	100.0	14.4	85.6	100.0	81.6	18.4
45 to 49 years	2 445	100.0	16.3	83.7	100.0	81.1	18.9
50 to 54 years	2 029	100.0	17.9	82.1	100.0	81.6	18.4
55 to 59 years	1 433	100.0	27.0	73.0	100.0	84.9	15.1
60 to 64 years	1 063	100.0	32.7	67.3	100.0	86.7	13.3
65 to 69 years	1 046	100.0	39.8	60.2	100.0	87.4	12.6
70 to 74 years	717	100.0	46.6	53.4	100.0	88.0	12.0
75 years and over	1 091	100.0	60.2	39.8	100.0	93.1	6.9
15 to 17 years	1 856	100.0	98.9	1.1	100.0	99.9	0.1
18 years and over	24 315	100.0	22.4	77.6	100.0	85.1	14.9
15 to 24 years	5 812	100.0	50.8	49.2	100.0	97.2	2.8
25 years and over	20 359	100.0	21.3	78.7	100.0	83.0	17.0
15 to 64 years	23 318	100.0	25.2	74.8	100.0	85.7	14.3
65 years and over	2 853	100.0	49.3	50.7	100.0	89.7	10.3
Male							
15 years and over	11 721	100.0	29.1	70.9	100.0	87.1	12.9
15 to 17 years	928	100.0	99.0	1.0	100.0	100.0	*
18 and 19 years	580	100.0	52.8	47.2	100.0	99.4	0.6
20 to 24 years	1 282	100.0	20.6	79.4	100.0	96.0	4.0
25 to 29 years	1 085	100.0	15.0	85.0	100.0	82.6	17.4
30 to 34 years	1 159	100.0	14.0	86.0	100.0	80.8	19.2
35 to 39 years	1 216	100.0	13.2	86.8	100.0	83.4	16.6
40 to 44 years	1 249	100.0	15.2	84.8	100.0	83.3	16.7
45 to 49 years	1 107	100.0	17.9	82.1	100.0	81.5	18.5
50 to 54 years	919	100.0	18.1	81.9	100.0	82.1	17.9
55 to 59 years	640	100.0	28.1	71.9	100.0	85.0	15.0
60 to 64 years	434	100.0	33.6	66.4	100.0	88.0	12.0
65 to 69 years	457	100.0	40.0	60.0	100.0	86.7	13.3
70 to 74 years	296	100.0	47.2	52.8	100.0	89.1	10.9
75 years and over	369	100.0	64.1	35.9	100.0	92.5	7.5
15 to 17 years	928	100.0	99.0	1.0	100.0	100.0	*
18 years and over	10 793	100.0	23.1	76.9	100.0	86.0	14.0
15 to 24 years	2 790	100.0	53.4	46.6	100.0	98.0	2.0
25 years and over	8 931	100.0	21.5	78.5	100.0	83.6	16.4
15 to 64 years	10 599	100.0	26.9	73.1	100.0	86.8	13.2
65 years and over	1 122	100.0	49.8	50.2	100.0	89.2	10.8
Female							
15 years and over	14 450	100.0	26.8	73.2	100.0	85.4	14.6
15 to 17 years	928	100.0	98.9	1.1	100.0	99.8	0.2
18 and 19 years	601	100.0	44.1	55.9	100.0	100.0	*
20 to 24 years	1 494	100.0	18.7	81.3	100.0	92.9	7.1
25 to 29 years	1 354	100.0	12.0	88.0	100.0	82.3	17.7
30 to 34 years	1 442	100.0	12.1	87.9	100.0	78.7	21.3
35 to 39 years	1 515	100.0	13.6	86.4	100.0	79.7	20.3
40 to 44 years	1 515	100.0	13.8	86.2	100.0	80.3	19.7
45 to 49 years	1 338	100.0	15.1	84.9	100.0	80.8	19.2
50 to 54 years	1 111	100.0	17.8	82.2	100.0	81.1	18.9
55 to 59 years	793	100.0	26.1	73.9	100.0	84.8	15.2
60 to 64 years	628	100.0	32.1	67.9	100.0	85.9	14.1
65 to 69 years	588	100.0	39.6	60.4	100.0	87.9	12.1
70 to 74 years	421	100.0	46.2	53.8	100.0	87.2	12.8
75 years and over	721	100.0	58.2	41.8	100.0	93.5	6.5
15 to 17 years	928	100.0	98.9	1.1	100.0	99.8	0.2
18 years and over	13 522	100.0	21.8	78.2	100.0	84.4	15.6
15 to 24 years	3 022	100.0	48.4	51.6	100.0	96.4	3.6
25 years and over	11 428	100.0	21.1	78.9	100.0	82.5	17.5
15 to 64 years	12 719	100.0	23.8	76.2	100.0	84.8	15.2
65 years and over	1 731	100.0	48.9	51.1	100.0	90.1	9.9

* = Represents zero or rounds to zero.

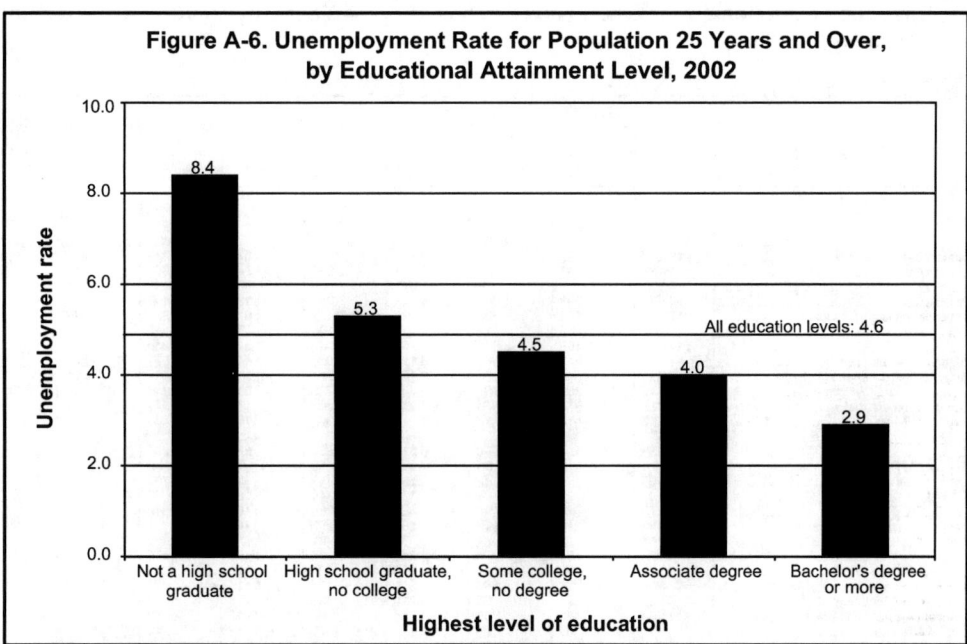

Figure A-6. Unemployment Rate for Population 25 Years and Over, by Educational Attainment Level, 2002

Source: U.S. Department of Labor, Bureau of Labor Statistics, Office of Employment and Unemployment Statistics, *Current Population Survey,* 2002.

- People with higher levels of educational attainment are less likely to be unemployed. In 2002, the unemployment rate for all educational levels was 4.6. The unemployment rate for people holding a bachelor's degree or more, 2.9, differed dramatically from people without a high school diploma, 8.4. The unemployment rate for people ages 20 to 24 years is higher than older workers at all educational attainment levels.

Table A-10. Educational Attainment of Employed Civilians 18 to 64 Years, by Occupation, Age, and Sex, March 2002

(Numbers in thousands.)

Occupation, age, and sex	Total	Elementary		High school		College					
		None–8th grade	9th–11th grade	High school graduate	Some college, no degree	Associate degree	Bachelor's degree	Master's degree	Professional degree	Doctorate degree
Both Sexes											
18 to 64 years	128 654	4 375	9 405	39 353	25 840	11 799	25 421	8 762	2 085	1 615
Executive, administrative, and managerial	19 970	112	450	3 856	3 718	1 873	6 928	2 592	223	219
Professional specialty	21 132	36	153	1 201	1 897	1 884	8 341	4 693	1 633	1 294
Technicians and related support	4 359	6	38	872	1 105	987	1 081	206	34	30
Sales	14 579	208	1 043	4 411	3 648	1 131	3 495	546	61	37
Administrative support, including clerical	17 643	106	694	6 655	5 471	2 017	2 339	313	38	11
Private household	602	108	112	188	105	32	50	3	3	*
Other service	17 078	1 108	2 341	6 766	3 940	1 378	1 343	148	47	6
Precision production, craft, and repair	14 044	842	1 662	6 194	2 850	1 443	891	133	24	5
Machine operators, assemblers, and inspectors	6 335	575	929	3 166	971	374	281	31	3	5
Transportation and material moving	5 345	252	730	2 780	959	342	249	23	7	3
Handlers, equipment cleaners, helpers, and laborers	4 869	548	875	2 248	803	181	170	37	8	*
Farming, forestry, and fishing	2 698	476	377	1 016	372	157	253	37	5	6
18 to 24 years	16 853	482	2 590	5 514	5 635	863	1 694	68	8	*
Executive, administrative, and managerial	1 020	5	55	319	305	76	252	7	*	*
Professional specialty	1 407	6	42	163	347	94	698	53	4	*
Technicians and related support	542	*	8	122	244	83	83	*	3	*
Sales	2 770	25	498	859	1 059	109	219	*	*	*
Administrative support, including clerical	2 781	16	212	881	1 305	162	195	7	2	*
Private household	114	2	24	30	41	8	8	*	*	*
Other service	3 838	131	774	1 249	1 384	160	140	*	*	*
Precision production, craft, and repair	1 523	83	304	694	324	87	31	*	*	*
Machine operators, assemblers, and inspectors	731	38	186	309	137	36	24	*	*	*
Transportation and material moving	502	21	85	234	135	15	14	*	*	*
Handlers, equipment cleaners, helpers, and laborers	1 209	86	309	504	280	15	16	*	*	*
Farming, forestry, and fishing	417	68	95	150	73	17	14	*	*	*
25 to 34 years	30 095	1 127	2 062	8 201	5 843	2 787	7 579	1 829	415	252
Executive, administrative, and managerial	4 221	19	95	614	752	370	1 878	455	15	22
Professional specialty	5 482	9	28	244	429	397	2 717	1 084	360	214
Technicians and related support	1 237	1	11	181	275	300	407	53	2	7
Sales	3 155	48	161	866	732	252	973	108	7	6
Administrative support, including clerical	3 884	31	155	1 259	1 251	456	670	53	9	*
Private household	103	20	16	27	12	7	18	*	2	*
Other service	4 073	272	480	1 526	935	364	450	35	11	*
Precision production, craft, and repair	3 456	284	450	1 394	685	386	228	24	3	3
Machine operators, assemblers, and inspectors	1 452	110	212	702	244	104	72	6	1	*
Transportation and material moving	1 200	45	159	640	222	63	68	3	1	*
Handlers, equipment cleaners, helpers, and laborers	1 283	157	204	562	236	65	53	4	3	*
Farming, forestry, and fishing	550	130	93	186	69	23	44	4	1	*
35 to 44 years	35 309	1 124	2 174	11 211	6 191	3 749	7 357	2 381	654	468
Executive, administrative, and managerial	6 197	39	137	1 229	1 080	655	2 169	764	75	48
Professional specialty	5 866	8	49	309	522	602	2 268	1 225	506	376
Technicians and related support	1 256	3	10	267	261	347	293	52	7	15
Sales	3 780	54	179	1 182	786	333	1 047	164	21	13
Administrative support, including clerical	4 549	21	138	1 766	1 226	645	675	71	5	5
Private household	154	29	29	62	16	7	10	1	*	*
Other service	4 087	250	447	1 793	761	420	352	45	16	5
Precision production, craft, and repair	4 144	202	432	1 899	827	467	268	34	13	2
Machine operators, assemblers, and inspectors	1 839	171	251	970	260	99	78	6	2	1
Transportation and material moving	1 566	62	222	871	225	83	89	5	6	2
Handlers, equipment cleaners, helpers, and laborers	1 161	150	188	581	147	43	44	5	3	*
Farming, forestry, and fishing	712	135	94	283	79	49	64	9	*	*
45 to 64 years	46 396	1 642	2 579	14 426	8 171	4 400	8 791	4 484	1 008	895
Executive, administrative, and managerial	8 532	49	164	1 693	1 580	772	2 630	1 365	132	149
Professional specialty	8 377	12	35	485	599	791	2 658	2 332	763	703
Technicians and related support	1 324	2	10	301	326	257	296	101	22	8
Sales	4 873	80	205	1 503	1 070	437	1 255	274	33	17
Administrative support, including clerical	6 430	38	189	2 750	1 689	755	799	182	21	6
Private household	231	57	43	68	35	11	13	1	2	*
Other service	5 080	455	641	2 198	861	433	402	68	20	1
Precision production, craft, and repair	4 921	273	476	2 207	1 015	503	364	75	8	*
Machine operators, assemblers, and inspectors	2 313	255	280	1 185	329	134	106	20	*	4
Transportation and material moving	2 077	124	264	1 036	377	182	79	14	1	1
Handlers, equipment cleaners, helpers, and laborers	1 217	154	175	602	139	57	58	28	2	*
Farming, forestry, and fishing	1 020	143	96	397	152	68	131	24	4	6
25 to 64 years	111 801	3 894	6 815	33 839	20 205	10 936	23 727	8 694	2 077	1 615
Executive, administrative, and managerial	18 950	107	395	3 536	3 412	1 797	6 677	2 585	223	219
Professional specialty	19 725	30	111	1 038	1 550	1 790	7 643	4 641	1 629	1 294
Technicians and related support	3 817	6	30	750	862	904	997	206	31	30
Sales	11 809	182	545	3 552	2 588	1 022	3 276	546	61	37
Administrative support, including clerical	14 863	90	482	5 774	4 166	1 855	2 144	305	36	11
Private household	488	106	88	158	64	24	42	3	3	*
Other service	13 240	976	1 568	5 517	2 557	1 218	1 203	148	47	6
Precision production, craft, and repair	12 520	759	1 359	5 500	2 526	1 356	859	133	24	5
Machine operators, assemblers, and inspectors	5 604	537	743	2 857	833	337	257	31	3	5
Transportation and material moving	4 842	232	645	2 546	824	327	235	23	7	3
Handlers, equipment cleaners, helpers, and laborers	3 660	462	567	1 744	523	166	154	37	8	*
Farming, forestry, and fishing	2 281	407	283	866	300	140	239	37	5	6

* = Represents zero or rounds to zero.

Table A-10. Educational Attainment of Employed Civilians 18 to 64 Years, by Occupation, Age, and Sex, March 2002—*Continued*

(Numbers in thousands.)

Occupation, age, and sex	Total	Elementary	High school		College					
		None–8th grade	9th–11th grade	High school graduate	Some college, no degree	Associate degree	Bachelor's degree	Master's degree	Professional degree	Doctorate degree
Male										
18 to 64 years	67 997	2 920	5 625	20 937	12 983	5 532	13 144	4 356	1 380	1 119
Executive, administrative, and managerial	10 743	71	270	1 857	1 839	865	3 982	1 564	146	149
Professional specialty	9 459	13	60	449	936	613	3 491	1 917	1 090	891
Technicians and related support	1 914	5	11	332	468	361	556	138	22	21
Sales	7 440	96	362	1 858	1 803	614	2 255	372	51	28
Administrative support, including clerical	3 694	41	223	1 185	1 146	339	647	89	14	10
Private household	30	7	5	6	7	2	3	*	*	*
Other service	7 055	547	940	2 480	1 706	590	690	81	18	2
Precision production, craft, and repair	12 830	751	1 552	5 677	2 607	1 331	774	113	21	5
Machine operators, assemblers, and inspectors	4 075	296	548	2 064	671	277	196	18	3	4
Transportation and material moving	4 780	247	666	2 491	838	287	222	21	5	3
Handlers, equipment cleaners, helpers, and laborers	3 871	459	686	1 739	676	147	131	26	8	*
Farming, forestry, and fishing	2 105	387	301	799	287	107	198	17	4	6
18 to 24 years	8 637	354	1 524	3 013	2 605	417	702	17	5	*
Executive, administrative, and managerial	508	1	36	152	164	50	106	*	*	*
Professional specialty	592	3	17	52	176	41	283	17	3	*
Technicians and related support	251	*	1	65	108	32	46	*	*	*
Sales	1 099	9	162	335	424	56	113	*	*	*
Administrative support, including clerical	751	5	85	219	371	30	39	*	2	*
Private household	7	*	2	*	5	*	*	*	*	*
Other service	1 734	92	404	557	578	55	48	*	*	*
Precision production, craft, and repair	1 403	78	287	660	278	82	17	*	*	*
Machine operators, assemblers, and inspectors	475	17	123	202	86	26	21	*	*	*
Transportation and material moving	460	21	81	219	116	15	9	*	*	*
Handlers, equipment cleaners, helpers, and laborers	1 035	72	252	434	251	15	11	*	*	*
Farming, forestry, and fishing	324	57	75	120	50	14	7	*	*	*
25 to 34 years	16 254	849	1 329	4 728	3 028	1 373	3 784	815	204	144
Executive, administrative, and managerial	2 092	14	53	303	364	165	925	250	5	13
Professional specialty	2 433	3	11	103	232	148	1 206	431	179	120
Technicians and related support	577	1	3	69	132	110	220	36	2	5
Sales	1 598	25	61	373	369	141	572	51	3	3
Administrative support, including clerical	911	7	52	284	261	84	211	6	6	*
Private household	5	2	*	1	*	*	2	*	*	*
Other service	1 815	172	209	585	411	168	254	12	3	*
Precision production, craft, and repair	3 204	267	416	1 309	631	354	206	17	2	3
Machine operators, assemblers, and inspectors	1 040	63	143	522	183	75	48	6	1	*
Transportation and material moving	1 072	45	147	572	189	52	63	3	1	*
Handlers, equipment cleaners, helpers, and laborers	1 049	144	154	450	198	55	43	3	3	*
Farming, forestry, and fishing	457	107	80	156	59	20	33	2	*	*
35 to 44 years	18 766	706	1 309	6 077	3 142	1 716	3 851	1 233	420	311
Executive, administrative, and managerial	3 308	27	76	624	527	265	1 254	458	43	34
Professional specialty	2 641	4	19	124	267	197	915	536	331	248
Technicians and related support	540	2	2	105	102	129	153	39	1	8
Sales	2 054	18	73	545	407	170	700	113	17	12
Administrative support, including clerical	892	7	37	289	214	115	204	21	1	4
Private household	5	2	*	2	*	1	*	*	*	*
Other service	1 540	98	126	613	311	188	177	19	8	1
Precision production, craft, and repair	3 763	179	404	1 706	762	438	231	30	11	2
Machine operators, assemblers, and inspectors	1 178	84	153	629	171	77	58	4	2	*
Transportation and material moving	1 387	61	196	767	202	70	80	5	3	2
Handlers, equipment cleaners, helpers, and laborers	893	118	147	445	115	32	28	5	3	*
Farming, forestry, and fishing	565	108	74	229	63	34	52	4	*	*
45 to 64 years	24 340	1 011	1 462	7 119	4 208	2 027	4 807	2 291	751	664
Executive, administrative, and managerial	4 834	29	105	777	783	386	1 698	856	97	102
Professional specialty	3 793	3	13	171	261	226	1 087	934	577	522
Technicians and related support	546	2	6	93	127	90	138	63	19	8
Sales	2 689	44	67	606	603	249	869	208	31	13
Administrative support, including clerical	1 141	23	49	393	300	110	192	62	6	6
Private household	14	4	3	2	2	2	1	*	*	*
Other service	1 966	186	201	726	405	178	211	51	6	1
Precision production, craft, and repair	4 461	228	445	2 002	937	457	319	66	8	*
Machine operators, assemblers, and inspectors	1 382	131	128	711	231	98	70	9	*	4
Transportation and material moving	1 860	120	241	933	331	150	70	13	1	1
Handlers, equipment cleaners, helpers, and laborers	894	125	133	410	112	45	48	19	2	*
Farming, forestry, and fishing	760	116	71	294	115	38	105	11	4	6
25 to 64 years	59 360	2 566	4 100	17 924	10 378	5 115	12 442	4 340	1 375	1 119
Executive, administrative, and managerial	10 234	70	234	1 705	1 675	816	3 876	1 564	146	149
Professional specialty	8 867	10	43	398	760	572	3 208	1 900	1 087	891
Technicians and related support	1 663	5	11	267	360	329	510	138	22	21
Sales	6 341	87	201	1 524	1 379	559	2 142	372	51	28
Administrative support, including clerical	2 943	36	139	966	775	309	607	89	12	10
Private household	24	7	3	6	2	2	3	*	*	*
Other service	5 321	456	536	1 923	1 128	535	642	81	18	2
Precision production, craft, and repair	11 427	673	1 265	5 017	2 329	1 248	757	113	21	5
Machine operators, assemblers, and inspectors	3 600	278	424	1 862	585	251	175	18	3	4
Transportation and material moving	4 320	226	585	2 272	722	272	213	21	5	3
Handlers, equipment cleaners, helpers, and laborers	2 837	397	434	1 305	425	132	119	26	8	*
Farming, forestry, and fishing	1 782	330	226	679	237	92	190	17	4	6

* = Represents zero or rounds to zero.

Table A-10. Educational Attainment of Employed Civilians 18 to 64 Years, by Occupation, Age, and Sex, March 2002—*Continued*

(Numbers in thousands.)

Occupation, age, and sex	Total	Elementary		High school		College					
		None–8th grade	9th–11th grade	High school graduate	Some college, no degree	Associate degree	Bachelor's degree	Master's degree	Professional degree	Doctorate degree
Female										
18 to 64 years	60 657	1 455	3 780	18 416	12 857	6 266	12 277	4 405	705	496
Executive, administrative, and managerial	9 228	40	180	1 999	1 879	1 008	2 946	1 028	77	70
Professional specialty	11 672	23	93	752	962	1 271	4 850	2 777	543	403
Technicians and related support	2 445	1	26	540	637	626	524	68	12	10
Sales	7 139	112	681	2 553	1 844	517	1 240	174	11	9
Administrative support, including clerical	13 949	65	470	5 470	4 325	1 678	1 693	223	23	1
Private household	571	101	107	183	98	30	48	3	3	*
Other service	10 023	560	1 401	4 286	2 235	788	653	67	30	3
Precision production, craft, and repair	1 214	91	110	517	243	112	117	20	3	*
Machine operators, assemblers, and inspectors	2 260	279	381	1 102	300	97	85	13	1	1
Transportation and material moving	565	6	65	288	121	55	26	1	2	*
Handlers, equipment cleaners, helpers, and laborers	998	89	189	509	127	34	40	11	*	*
Farming, forestry, and fishing	593	89	76	217	86	50	55	19	1	*
18 to 24 years	8 216	128	1 065	2 501	3 030	446	992	51	4	*
Executive, administrative, and managerial	512	4	19	168	141	26	146	7	*	*
Professional specialty	815	3	24	112	172	53	415	36	1	*
Technicians and related support	291	*	7	57	136	51	37	*	3	*
Sales	1 672	16	337	524	635	54	105	*	*	*
Administrative support, including clerical	2 029	11	127	662	934	132	156	7	*	*
Private household	107	2	22	30	36	8	8	*	*	*
Other service	2 104	40	370	692	806	105	92	*	*	*
Precision production, craft, and repair	120	5	16	34	46	5	14	*	*	*
Machine operators, assemblers, and inspectors	256	21	63	107	51	10	4	*	*	*
Transportation and material moving	42	*	4	14	19	*	4	*	*	*
Handlers, equipment cleaners, helpers, and laborers	174	14	57	70	29	*	5	*	*	*
Farming, forestry, and fishing	93	12	19	30	23	3	6	*	*	*
25 to 34 years	13 842	278	733	3 473	2 816	1 414	3 795	1 013	211	108
Executive, administrative, and managerial	2 129	5	42	311	389	205	953	205	10	9
Professional specialty	3 048	6	17	141	197	249	1 511	653	181	94
Technicians and related support	660	*	8	112	143	190	188	18	*	2
Sales	1 557	22	100	494	363	112	401	57	5	3
Administrative support, including clerical	2 973	24	102	974	990	372	459	47	4	*
Private household	98	18	16	26	12	7	16	*	2	*
Other service	2 258	100	271	941	524	196	195	23	8	*
Precision production, craft, and repair	253	17	34	85	54	32	22	7	1	*
Machine operators, assemblers, and inspectors	412	47	69	181	62	28	25	*	*	*
Transportation and material moving	127	*	11	67	33	11	5	*	*	*
Handlers, equipment cleaners, helpers, and laborers	234	14	50	112	38	10	10	1	*	*
Farming, forestry, and fishing	93	24	13	30	11	3	10	2	1	*
35 to 44 years	16 543	418	865	5 135	3 048	2 032	3 505	1 148	234	157
Executive, administrative, and managerial	2 888	12	61	605	553	391	915	307	32	14
Professional specialty	3 225	5	30	185	255	405	1 353	690	176	128
Technicians and related support	715	1	7	163	160	217	141	13	6	7
Sales	1 726	37	107	637	379	163	347	51	4	1
Administrative support, including clerical	3 657	14	100	1 477	1 012	530	471	49	4	1
Private household	149	27	29	60	16	6	10	1	*	*
Other service	2 547	152	321	1 181	450	232	175	26	8	3
Precision production, craft, and repair	381	23	28	193	65	29	37	4	2	*
Machine operators, assemblers, and inspectors	661	87	98	341	89	21	21	2	1	1
Transportation and material moving	178	2	26	104	23	12	9	*	2	*
Handlers, equipment cleaners, helpers, and laborers	268	32	40	136	32	11	16	*	*	*
Farming, forestry, and fishing	147	27	19	54	16	15	12	5	*	*
45 to 64 years	22 056	632	1 116	7 307	3 963	2 374	3 984	2 193	256	232
Executive, administrative, and managerial	3 699	19	59	915	796	386	932	509	35	46
Professional specialty	4 584	9	22	314	338	565	1 571	1 398	186	181
Technicians and related support	779	*	5	209	199	168	159	37	3	*
Sales	2 184	36	137	897	467	188	386	66	1	4
Administrative support, including clerical	5 290	16	140	2 357	1 389	645	607	120	16	*
Private household	217	53	40	66	33	9	13	1	2	*
Other service	3 114	269	440	1 472	455	255	191	18	14	*
Precision production, craft, and repair	460	45	31	205	78	46	45	9	*	*
Machine operators, assemblers, and inspectors	931	124	152	474	98	37	36	11	*	*
Transportation and material moving	217	4	23	103	45	32	8	1	*	*
Handlers, equipment cleaners, helpers, and laborers	322	29	42	192	28	13	10	10	*	*
Farming, forestry, and fishing	260	27	25	103	36	30	26	13	*	*
25 to 64 years	52 441	1 328	2 715	15 915	9 827	5 820	11 284	4 354	701	496
Executive, administrative, and managerial	8 716	36	162	1 831	1 738	981	2 800	1 021	77	70
Professional specialty	10 858	20	69	640	790	1 218	4 435	2 741	542	403
Technicians and related support	2 154	1	19	483	501	575	487	68	9	10
Sales	5 467	95	344	2 028	1 209	463	1 134	174	11	9
Administrative support, including clerical	11 920	54	343	4 808	3 391	1 547	1 537	216	23	1
Private household	464	99	85	152	62	22	39	3	3	*
Other service	7 919	521	1 031	3 594	1 429	683	561	67	30	3
Precision production, craft, and repair	1 093	86	94	483	197	108	103	20	3	*
Machine operators, assemblers, and inspectors	2 004	258	319	995	248	87	82	13	1	1
Transportation and material moving	522	6	60	274	102	55	22	1	2	*
Handlers, equipment cleaners, helpers, and laborers	824	75	132	439	98	34	35	11	*	*
Farming, forestry, and fishing	500	77	57	187	63	48	49	19	1	*

* = Represents zero or rounds to zero.

Table A-11. Educational Attainment of Employed Civilians 18 to 64 Years, by Industry, Age, and Sex, March 2002

(Numbers in thousands.)

Industry, age, and sex	Total	Elementary	High school		College					
		None–8th grade	9th–11th grade	High school graduate	Some college, no degree	Associate degree	Bachelor's degree	Master's degree	Professional degree	Doctorate degree
Both Sexes										
18 to 64 years	128 654	4 375	9 405	39 353	25 840	11 799	25 421	8 762	2 085	1 615
Agricultural, forestry, fisheries	2 750	416	359	1 018	412	175	279	42	20	29
Mining	501	13	50	189	76	47	98	21	1	5
Construction	8 909	751	1 215	3 723	1 628	672	779	119	16	6
Manufacturing	17 838	875	1 523	6 764	3 153	1 490	3 039	808	78	108
Transportation, communication, other public utilities ...	9 373	161	536	3 503	2 269	939	1 569	329	45	22
Wholesale trade	4 754	143	347	1 555	951	402	1 141	183	25	7
Retail trade	20 700	816	2 536	7 851	5 101	1 381	2 561	355	54	45
Finance, insurance, and real estate	8 576	80	200	2 144	1 992	806	2 632	599	92	32
Personal services	4 249	341	507	1 551	820	417	528	59	21	6
Business and repair services	9 034	331	709	2 666	1 789	887	2 009	569	41	34
Entertainment/recreation services	2 306	54	172	600	558	195	580	125	12	12
Professional and related services	33 799	376	1 139	6 485	5 642	3 628	8 723	5 035	1 546	1 227
Public administration	5 864	16	113	1 304	1 450	760	1 484	519	136	83
18 to 24 years	16 853	482	2 590	5 514	5 635	863	1 694	68	8	*
Agricultural, forestry, fisheries	412	56	93	147	88	12	16	*	*	*
Mining	38	*	6	17	6	9	*	*	*	*
Construction	1 073	95	225	469	196	45	43	*	*	*
Manufacturing	1 338	67	242	556	271	73	120	11	*	*
Transportation, communication, other public utilities ...	765	7	69	323	244	51	66	5	*	*
Wholesale trade	407	17	72	145	112	7	54	*	*	*
Retail trade	5 819	149	1 214	1 921	2 074	215	247	*	*	*
Finance, insurance, and real estate	876	1	31	282	353	48	157	2	2	*
Personal services	698	24	127	253	195	44	54	*	*	*
Business and repair services	1 211	31	196	467	320	84	109	4	*	*
Entertainment/recreation services	524	9	79	149	201	39	47	*	*	*
Professional and related services	3 403	26	225	717	1 456	217	712	45	7	*
Public administration	291	*	13	70	118	19	69	2	*	*
25 to 34 years	30 095	1 127	2 062	8 201	5 843	2 787	7 579	1 829	415	252
Agricultural, forestry, fisheries	532	108	86	175	68	37	46	4	3	5
Mining	104	1	11	43	26	8	9	6	*	*
Construction	2 414	289	350	914	433	183	219	25	1	*
Manufacturing	4 047	188	331	1 363	682	355	916	188	10	15
Transportation, communication, other public utilities ...	2 019	36	102	683	521	227	397	46	5	3
Wholesale trade	1 193	36	93	353	254	106	310	36	5	1
Retail trade	4 873	233	491	1 794	1 114	356	785	71	12	17
Finance, insurance, and real estate	2 140	5	52	422	473	194	826	147	16	6
Personal services	1 050	78	124	340	199	123	170	12	5	1
Business and repair services	2 503	84	184	576	515	210	774	148	5	7
Entertainment/recreation services	619	10	19	132	151	49	205	44	4	4
Professional and related services	7 400	57	206	1 168	1 117	766	2 553	1 023	328	183
Public administration	1 201	5	13	240	291	173	370	80	21	9
35 to 44 years	35 309	1 124	2 174	11 211	6 191	3 749	7 357	2 381	654	468
Agricultural, forestry, fisheries	762	126	99	294	97	56	67	12	7	4
Mining	162	5	20	53	22	14	40	4	*	4
Construction	2 632	184	328	1 140	476	211	241	38	10	4
Manufacturing	5 432	220	418	2 118	922	495	912	281	30	36
Transportation, communication, other public utilities ...	2 876	50	166	1 048	634	284	555	115	14	10
Wholesale trade	1 432	30	89	486	249	128	367	71	9	4
Retail trade	4 676	204	398	1 940	916	370	706	117	14	11
Finance, insurance, and real estate	2 437	28	49	555	484	292	820	176	27	5
Personal services	1 072	96	128	398	189	105	139	11	2	3
Business and repair services	2 589	71	154	779	444	306	628	177	15	15
Entertainment/recreation services	532	21	29	153	84	65	147	25	6	2
Professional and related services	9 012	88	265	1 862	1 274	1 161	2 317	1 224	476	344
Public administration	1 695	*	31	386	399	260	418	130	43	27
45 to 64 years	46 396	1 642	2 579	14 426	8 171	4 400	8 791	4 484	1 008	895
Agricultural, forestry, fisheries	1 044	127	81	403	158	70	149	26	9	20
Mining	197	7	13	76	22	16	49	12	1	2
Construction	2 790	183	312	1 200	523	233	276	55	5	2
Manufacturing	7 021	400	532	2 729	1 278	567	1 092	329	39	56
Transportation, communication, other public utilities ...	3 714	69	199	1 450	869	376	552	163	26	10
Wholesale trade	1 722	60	93	571	335	161	411	77	12	3
Retail trade	5 332	230	433	2 197	996	440	824	168	28	16
Finance, insurance, and real estate	3 124	46	68	886	682	271	829	273	46	21
Personal services	1 429	143	129	559	237	145	165	35	14	2
Business and repair services	2 732	145	175	843	510	288	497	240	21	12
Entertainment/recreation services	631	14	45	166	122	41	181	55	1	6
Professional and related services	13 984	206	444	2 738	1 795	1 484	3 139	2 743	735	700
Public administration	2 677	11	55	608	642	308	627	307	72	46
25 to 64 years	111 801	3 894	6 815	33 839	20 205	10 936	23 727	8 694	2 077	1 615
Agricultural, forestry, fisheries	2 338	360	266	872	324	163	262	42	20	29
Mining	463	13	44	172	70	38	98	21	1	5
Construction	7 835	656	990	3 253	1 431	628	736	119	16	6
Manufacturing	16 500	809	1 281	6 209	2 882	1 417	2 919	798	78	108
Transportation, communication, other public utilities ...	8 609	154	467	3 181	2 024	888	1 503	324	45	22
Wholesale trade	4 348	126	275	1 410	839	395	1 087	183	25	7
Retail trade	14 881	668	1 322	5 930	3 026	1 166	2 315	355	54	45
Finance, insurance, and real estate	7 701	79	169	1 862	1 639	758	2 475	597	90	32
Personal services	3 552	317	381	1 297	625	373	474	59	21	6
Business and repair services	7 004	000	519	2 109	1 460	804	1 899	565	41	34
Entertainment/recreation services	1 782	45	93	451	357	156	533	125	12	12
Professional and related services	30 396	350	914	5 769	4 186	3 411	8 010	4 990	1 540	1 227
Public administration	5 573	16	100	1 233	1 332	741	1 415	517	136	83

* = Represents zero or rounds to zero.

Table A-11. Educational Attainment of Employed Civilians 18 to 64 Years, by Industry, Age, and Sex, March 2002—*Continued*

(Numbers in thousands.)

Industry, age, and sex	Total	Elementary None–8th grade	High school 9th–11th grade	High school graduate	College Some college, no degree	Associate degree	Bachelor's degree	Master's degree	Professional degree	Doctorate degree
Male										
18 to 64 years	67 997	2 920	5 625	20 937	12 983	5 532	13 144	4 356	1 380	1 119
Agricultural, forestry, fisheries	2 017	348	294	730	280	106	204	19	15	20
Mining	433	13	46	177	55	41	77	19	1	4
Construction	8 085	741	1 173	3 419	1 408	560	659	103	16	5
Manufacturing	12 384	560	1 074	4 596	2 184	1 079	2 164	582	62	82
Transportation, communication, other public utilities	6 604	142	450	2 526	1 532	647	1 025	240	25	18
Wholesale trade	3 284	103	256	1 069	638	261	809	122	20	7
Retail trade	10 386	516	1 246	3 682	2 522	703	1 414	235	36	32
Finance, insurance, and real estate	3 550	52	88	516	639	276	1 495	400	65	20
Personal services	1 251	85	142	377	285	104	218	25	10	5
Business and repair services	5 669	214	455	1 636	1 084	552	1 261	411	33	23
Entertainment/recreation services	1 312	36	102	328	298	120	336	71	9	12
Professional and related services	9 886	104	244	1 281	1 321	658	2 621	1 834	993	830
Public administration	3 136	7	54	598	737	424	859	297	96	64
18 to 24 years	8 637	354	1 524	3 013	2 605	417	702	17	5	*
Agricultural, forestry, fisheries	294	44	79	113	47	6	5	*	*	*
Mining	36	*	4	17	6	9	*	*	*	*
Construction	1 008	94	220	447	178	39	30	*	*	*
Manufacturing	914	48	182	392	169	49	70	6	*	*
Transportation, communication, other public utilities	503	5	52	222	156	40	27	*	*	*
Wholesale trade	286	17	45	109	81	6	28	*	*	*
Retail trade	2 888	97	640	978	967	108	98	*	*	*
Finance, insurance, and real estate	298	1	13	78	121	14	69	*	2	*
Personal services	203	4	47	63	69	2	18	*	*	*
Business and repair services	804	25	142	307	201	60	69	1	*	*
Entertainment/recreation services	281	9	45	82	90	27	28	*	*	*
Professional and related services	1 000	11	51	169	476	44	236	10	3	*
Public administration	123	*	6	36	44	14	23	*	*	*
25 to 34 years	16 254	849	1 329	4 728	3 028	1 373	3 784	815	204	144
Agricultural, forestry, fisheries	411	91	77	130	52	24	31	2	1	2
Mining	88	1	8	43	18	7	5	6	*	*
Construction	2 229	284	331	873	372	157	190	21	1	*
Manufacturing	2 863	143	261	1 000	472	265	583	126	7	6
Transportation, communication, other public utilities	1 382	33	86	490	338	153	254	26	3	1
Wholesale trade	811	22	70	266	165	65	205	12	5	*
Retail trade	2 561	172	232	929	598	176	404	40	5	6
Finance, insurance, and real estate	851	2	20	103	142	53	442	78	7	3
Personal services	332	28	50	85	64	34	65	3	3	1
Business and repair services	1 547	50	115	363	290	145	464	114	2	4
Entertainment/recreation services	389	6	10	76	96	35	132	26	4	4
Professional and related services	2 109	15	61	252	246	146	802	324	154	109
Public administration	682	3	8	119	174	113	206	38	14	7
35 to 44 years	18 766	706	1 309	6 077	3 142	1 716	3 851	1 233	420	311
Agricultural, forestry, fisheries	583	106	80	225	73	35	51	6	5	2
Mining	136	5	20	52	16	13	27	1	*	2
Construction	2 382	182	324	1 042	415	174	199	34	10	3
Manufacturing	3 714	119	284	1 438	626	345	655	201	20	27
Transportation, communication, other public utilities	2 011	46	133	764	415	195	364	79	7	7
Wholesale trade	986	17	68	334	169	69	264	54	7	4
Retail trade	2 336	114	187	906	442	189	408	74	7	10
Finance, insurance, and real estate	1 059	21	27	137	154	101	475	117	21	5
Personal services	316	24	17	103	70	26	67	6	1	2
Business and repair services	1 618	42	91	464	275	183	412	129	12	10
Entertainment/recreation services	281	12	14	77	53	29	74	16	4	2
Professional and related services	2 432	17	47	339	229	210	619	454	299	218
Public administration	911	*	17	197	206	147	237	62	26	19
45 to 64 years	24 340	1 011	1 462	7 119	4 208	2 027	4 807	2 291	751	664
Agricultural, forestry, fisheries	729	107	59	262	108	41	117	11	9	16
Mining	173	7	13	66	16	12	45	12	1	2
Construction	2 466	181	299	1 057	443	190	240	48	5	2
Manufacturing	4 892	251	348	1 767	917	420	857	249	35	48
Transportation, communication, other public utilities	2 709	57	178	1 050	624	259	380	136	15	10
Wholesale trade	1 201	47	73	360	222	121	312	56	8	3
Retail trade	2 602	134	188	869	515	230	504	122	25	16
Finance, insurance, and real estate	1 342	29	29	197	221	108	509	204	35	11
Personal services	400	29	28	127	82	42	68	16	6	2
Business and repair services	1 700	96	108	502	319	165	317	166	19	8
Entertainment/recreation services	360	8	32	94	59	30	102	29	*	6
Professional and related services	4 345	62	85	522	369	258	963	1 045	537	503
Public administration	1 420	4	23	247	313	151	393	197	56	37
25 to 64 years	59 360	2 566	4 100	17 924	10 378	5 115	12 442	4 340	1 375	1 119
Agricultural, forestry, fisheries	1 723	304	216	617	232	100	200	19	15	20
Mining	397	13	41	161	50	32	77	19	1	4
Construction	7 077	647	954	2 972	1 230	521	629	103	16	5
Manufacturing	11 470	513	893	4 205	2 015	1 030	2 094	576	62	82
Transportation, communication, other public utilities	6 101	136	397	2 304	1 377	607	998	240	25	18
Wholesale trade	2 998	86	211	960	556	255	781	122	20	7
Retail trade	7 498	419	607	2 704	1 555	595	1 316	235	36	32
Finance, insurance, and real estate	3 252	51	76	437	518	262	1 426	400	63	20
Personal services	1 048	81	95	314	216	102	200	25	10	5
Business and repair services	4 865	189	314	1 329	883	493	1 193	409	33	23
Entertainment/recreation services	1 031	26	56	247	207	94	308	71	9	12
Professional and related services	8 886	93	193	1 112	845	614	2 384	1 824	990	830
Public administration	3 013	7	48	562	693	410	836	297	96	64

* = Represents zero or rounds to zero.

Table A-11. Educational Attainment of Employed Civilians 18 to 64 Years, by Industry, Age, and Sex, March 2002—*Continued*

(Numbers in thousands.)

Industry, age, and sex	Total	Elementary None–8th grade	High school 9th–11th grade	High school graduate	College Some college, no degree	Associate degree	Bachelor's degree	Master's degree	Professional degree	Doctorate degree
Female										
18 to 64 years	60 657	1 455	3 780	18 416	12 857	6 266	12 277	4 405	705	496
Agricultural, forestry, fisheries	733	68	64	288	132	69	74	24	5	9
Mining	68	*	4	12	20	6	21	2	*	2
Construction	824	10	42	303	220	112	119	16	*	1
Manufacturing	5 454	315	449	2 168	969	411	875	226	16	26
Transportation, communication, other public utilities	2 769	20	86	977	737	292	544	88	20	5
Wholesale trade	1 471	41	91	486	313	141	332	61	5	1
Retail trade	10 313	300	1 290	4 169	2 579	678	1 147	120	17	13
Finance, insurance, and real estate	5 026	28	111	1 628	1 353	530	1 137	199	27	12
Personal services	2 999	256	365	1 173	535	312	310	34	11	1
Business and repair services	3 366	117	253	1 030	705	335	747	158	8	12
Entertainment/recreation services	994	19	70	271	260	75	243	53	3	*
Professional and related services	23 914	272	895	5 204	4 321	2 970	6 102	3 201	553	397
Public administration	2 728	9	59	705	712	336	625	222	40	19
18 to 24 years	8 216	128	1 065	2 501	3 030	446	992	51	4	*
Agricultural, forestry, fisheries	118	12	14	34	41	6	12	*	*	*
Mining	1	*	1	*	*	*	*	*	*	*
Construction	66	2	6	22	18	6	12	*	*	*
Manufacturing	424	19	60	164	102	24	50	5	*	*
Transportation, communication, other public utilities	262	1	17	100	89	11	39	5	*	*
Wholesale trade	121	*	27	36	31	1	26	*	*	*
Retail trade	2 931	52	574	943	1 107	107	148	*	*	*
Finance, insurance, and real estate	577	*	18	203	231	34	88	2	*	*
Personal services	495	20	80	190	127	42	36	*	*	*
Business and repair services	407	6	54	160	120	24	41	3	*	*
Entertainment/recreation services	243	*	33	67	111	13	19	*	*	*
Professional and related services	2 403	15	173	548	980	173	476	35	4	*
Public administration	168	*	8	35	74	5	46	2	*	*
25 to 34 years	13 842	278	733	3 473	2 816	1 414	3 795	1 013	211	108
Agricultural, forestry, fisheries	121	17	9	45	16	13	14	2	3	3
Mining	17	*	3	1	8	1	4	*	*	*
Construction	184	5	19	40	61	26	28	5	*	*
Manufacturing	1 184	45	70	363	209	89	333	61	3	9
Transportation, communication, other public utilities	638	3	16	193	184	74	143	20	2	2
Wholesale trade	383	13	23	87	89	41	105	23	*	1
Retail trade	2 312	62	259	865	515	180	381	31	7	11
Finance, insurance, and real estate	1 289	3	32	319	331	141	384	69	9	2
Personal services	718	50	73	255	135	88	105	10	2	*
Business and repair services	956	33	69	213	225	65	310	33	4	2
Entertainment/recreation services	230	4	9	56	55	15	73	18	*	*
Professional and related services	5 291	42	145	916	870	620	1 751	699	174	74
Public administration	519	1	6	120	117	60	163	42	7	2
35 to 44 years	16 543	418	865	5 135	3 048	2 032	3 505	1 148	234	157
Agricultural, forestry, fisheries	179	20	19	69	25	21	16	6	2	2
Mining	26	*	*	1	6	2	13	2	*	2
Construction	250	2	4	98	61	37	42	5	*	1
Manufacturing	1 717	101	134	680	297	150	257	80	10	9
Transportation, communication, other public utilities	865	4	33	284	219	89	191	36	7	2
Wholesale trade	445	13	21	152	80	59	103	17	1	*
Retail trade	2 341	90	211	1 034	474	181	298	43	8	1
Finance, insurance, and real estate	1 378	8	22	417	330	191	345	59	6	*
Personal services	756	72	111	295	119	79	72	6	1	1
Business and repair services	970	29	63	316	169	123	216	47	3	5
Entertainment/recreation services	251	9	15	76	31	36	73	9	2	*
Professional and related services	6 580	72	218	1 524	1 045	951	1 699	769	178	125
Public administration	784	*	14	189	193	113	182	69	17	8
45 to 64 years	22 056	632	1 116	7 307	3 963	2 374	3 984	2 193	256	232
Agricultural, forestry, fisheries	314	20	23	141	50	29	32	16	*	3
Mining	24	*	*	10	6	3	4	*	*	*
Construction	324	2	13	143	80	43	36	7	*	*
Manufacturing	2 129	149	184	962	361	147	235	80	3	8
Transportation, communication, other public utilities	1 005	12	20	400	245	117	171	28	11	*
Wholesale trade	521	14	20	211	113	40	99	20	4	*
Retail trade	2 729	97	245	1 327	482	210	319	46	3	*
Finance, insurance, and real estate	1 782	18	40	688	461	164	321	69	12	10
Personal services	1 029	114	101	433	155	103	97	19	8	*
Business and repair services	1 032	48	67	341	192	123	180	75	2	4
Entertainment/recreation services	270	6	13	72	63	11	78	26	1	*
Professional and related services	9 639	144	358	2 216	1 426	1 226	2 176	1 698	198	197
Public administration	1 256	8	32	361	329	158	234	110	16	9
25 to 64 years	52 441	1 328	2 715	15 915	9 827	5 820	11 284	4 354	701	496
Agricultural, forestry, fisheries	615	56	50	254	92	63	63	24	5	9
Mining	67	*	3	12	20	6	21	2	*	2
Construction	758	9	36	281	201	107	107	16	*	1
Manufacturing	5 030	296	388	2 004	867	386	825	221	16	26
Transportation, communication, other public utilities	2 507	18	70	877	648	281	505	84	20	5
Wholesale trade	1 350	40	64	450	282	140	307	61	5	1
Retail trade	7 382	248	716	3 227	1 471	571	999	120	17	13
Finance, insurance, and real estate	4 449	28	93	1 425	1 122	496	1 049	197	27	12
Personal services	2 504	236	285	983	409	270	274	34	11	1
Business and repair services	2 959	110	199	870	586	311	707	155	9	12
Entertainment/recreation services	752	19	37	205	149	62	224	53	3	*
Professional and related services	21 510	257	721	4 656	3 341	2 797	5 626	3 166	549	397
Public administration	2 560	9	52	671	639	331	579	220	40	19

* = Represents zero or rounds to zero.

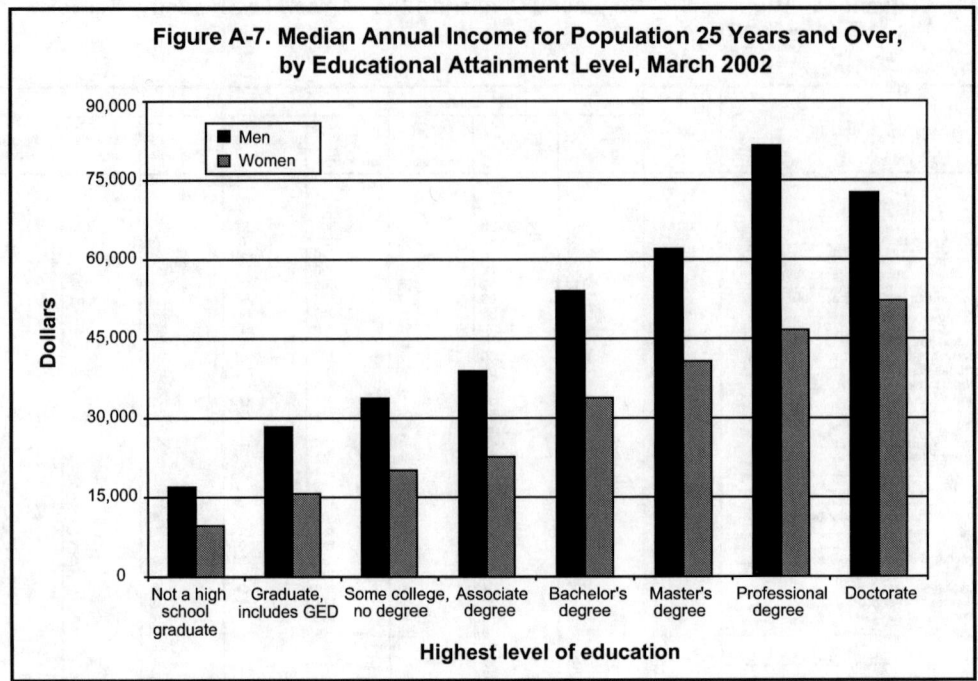

Figure A-7. Median Annual Income for Population 25 Years and Over, by Educational Attainment Level, March 2002

Source: U.S. Census Bureau, *Current Population Survey*, 2002.

- The overall median income from salaries and self-employment for all persons 25 years and over in 2002 was $25,309. For those who did not finish high school, the median was $12,632. For high school graduates, median income rose to more than $21,000, while those with a bachelor's degree had median income of $38,854. The highest median was $71,806 among persons with professional degrees (such as law or medicine).

Table A-12. Income in 2001 by Educational Attainment for Population 18 Years and Over, by Age, Race, and Hispanic Origin, March 2002

(Numbers in thousand, except where noted.)

Income, standard error, age, race, and Hispanic origin	Total	High school		College						
		Not high school graduate	Graduate, includes GED	Some college, no degree	Associate degree	Bachelor's degree or more	Bachelor's degree	Master's degree	Professional degree	Doctorate degree
All Workers, 18 Years and Over										
All races, number with income	195 510	30 373	62 034	37 993	15 566	49 541	33 361	11 349	2 689	2 141
Median income (dollars)	22 575	11 864	19 900	21 658	28 563	41 648	37 203	49 324	71 606	63 952
Standard error (dollars)	85	71	106	127	298	144	174	541	2 098	1 798
Mean income (dollars)	32 875	16 234	24 885	28 264	33 644	56 376	48 892	63 205	96 779	86 036
Standard error (dollars)	126	184	147	212	315	380	402	885	2 298	2 323
White, number with income	163 461	24 503	52 257	31 356	13 161	42 182	28 300	9 745	2 337	1 799
Median income (dollars)	23 298	12 226	20 294	21 978	29 074	42 127	37 600	49 804	74 528	65 372
Standard error (dollars)	94	77	92		328		268	495	1 814	1 898
Mean income (dollars)	33 862	16 653	25 620	29 054	34 092	57 572	49 809	64 315	99 923	88 123
Standard error (dollars)	141	203	170	242	313	419	435	997	2 558	2 525
Black, number with income	21 794	4 473	7 337	4 813	1 671	3 498	2 469	786	140	101
Median income (dollars)	19 083	9 772	17 384	20 961	26 742	37 696	35 510	42 505	54 722	49 421
Standard error (dollars)	213	166	251	362	522	662	512	1 505	5 585	3 870
Mean income (dollars)	24 624	14 083	20 411	24 767	30 196	44 082	39 590	51 255	71 505	59 761
Standard error (dollars)	246	579	232	401	1 059	880	865	2 395	6 030	5 699
Hispanic[1], number with income	20 986	8 391	6 105	3 247	1 083	2 157	1 589	365	136	66
Median income (dollars)	17 011	13 252	17 483	20 733	25 717	34 265	31 235	42 899	48 661	(B)
Standard error (dollars)	124	201	268	376	815	1 126	569	2 281	7 138	(B)
Mean income (dollars)	23 099	16 655	21 681	25 295	30 903	44 949	38 987	53 907	82 953	(B)
Standard error (dollars)	287	393	416	639	1 093	1 549	1 449	4 964	10 223	(B)
Non-Hispanic White, number with income	143 708	16 540	46 546	28 322	12 142	40 156	26 819	9 389	2 208	1 739
Median income (dollars)	24 782	11 807	20 614	22 147	29 400	42 467	38 174	50 065	75 444	65 688
Standard error (dollars)	100	97	101	153	347	223	314	427	1 364	1 777
Mean income (dollars)	35 333	16 608	26 112	29 447	34 313	58 196	50 403	64 706	100 895	88 995
Standard error (dollars)	156	238	184	259	327	433	453	1 019	2 643	2 597
Non-Hispanic Black, number with income	21 061	4 221	7 093	4 694	1 635	3 415	2 401	780	136	97
Median income (dollars)	19 234	9 703	17 347	21 021	26 855	37 790	35 540	42 577	55 501	49 672
Standard error (dollars)	220	170	252	368	528	683	518	1 524	5 802	3 967
Mean income (dollars)	24 737	14 124	20 401	24 825	30 280	44 081	39 535	51 320	70 894	60 552
Standard error (dollars)	251	612	236	408	1 079	873	841	2 413	5 912	5 837
Asian/Pacific Islander, number with income	8 149	871	1 685	1 406	570	3 616	2 422	766	205	222
Median income (dollars)	24 591	12 474	18 028	16 842	27 231	40 682	34 820	56 298	49 201	64 709
Standard error (dollars)	515	534	711	787	1 208	538	1 107	3 810	11 850	5 133
Mean income (dollars)	37 163	16 791	22 428	23 427	35 126	54 601	48 357	61 823	78 471	75 702
Standard error (dollars)	835	879	676	1 377	3 853	1 586	2 104	2 465	6 498	4 673
Year-Round, Full-Time Workers, 18 Years and Over										
All races, number with income	100 231	9 794	31 275	18 810	9 384	30 966	20 618	7 080	1 835	1 432
Median income (dollars)	35 364	21 153	28 576	33 602	36 828	52 190	47 784	60 148	86 878	77 315
Standard error (dollars)	78	116	171	275	203	148	381	485	2 511	1 647
Mean income (dollars)	47 154	26 471	34 390	40 765	43 110	71 694	62 775	79 287	119 810	100 891
Standard error (dollars)	217	488	261	338	448	551	589	1 316	2 970	2 987
White, number with income	83 351	8 033	26 036	15 345	7 902	26 032	17 272	5 987	1 596	1 176
Median income (dollars)	36 095	21 311	29 761	34 922	37 406	53 470	49 575	60 348	87 929	80 199
Standard error (dollars)	86	126	190	259	294	424	441	434	2 534	2 065
Mean income (dollars)	48 594	26 500	35 633	42 067	43 688	73 711	64 379	81 324	123 802	104 019
Standard error (dollars)	244	516	307	386	424	614	642	1 509	3 320	3 239
Black, number with income	11 329	1 243	3 910	2 666	1 084	2 424	1 721	535	96	70
Median income (dollars)	29 868	20 427	25 277	30 339	31 860	42 575	40 644	49 404	71 049	(B)
Standard error (dollars)	266	336	234	434	434	790	464	1 334	6 053	(B)
Mean income (dollars)	35 105	26 794	27 553	33 993	37 271	51 800	46 421	59 448	89 855	(B)
Standard error (dollars)	413	1 976	322	585	1 499	1 154	1 119	3 237	7 306	(B)
Hispanic[1], number with income	11 976	4 255	3 689	1 854	737	1 439	1 055	246	97	40
Median income (dollars)	23 946	19 186	23 219	29 871	31 704	42 231	38 918	51 796	70 454	(B)
Standard error (dollars)	252	249	364	576	714	953	1 489	3 065	10 513	(B)
Mean income (dollars)	31 119	22 924	28 025	34 695	36 952	55 672	48 635	66 112	96 273	(B)
Standard error (dollars)	439	670	623	992	1 026	2 031	1 903	7 025	10 289	(B)
Non-Hispanic White, number with income	72 051	3 978	22 595	13 608	7 193	24 675	16 283	5 749	1 501	1 141
Median income (dollars)	37 999	24 781	30 596	35 623	38 127	54 454	50 258	60 480	90 332	80 497
Standard error (dollars)	175	378	111	182	472	424	198	414	2 632	2 160
Mean income (dollars)	51 327	30 037	36 800	42 983	44 334	74 704	65 352	81 941	125 606	104 678
Standard error (dollars)	273	796	340	416	455	638	671	1 545	3 469	3 324
Non-Hispanic Black, number with income	10 919	1 130	3 759	2 597	1 064	2 366	1 675	528	93	68
Median income (dollars)	30 105	20 765	25 292	30 408	31 895	42 666	40 607	49 456	71 187	(B)
Standard error (dollars)	202	358	242	341	430	817	480	1 322	7 271	(B)
Mean income (dollars)	35 309	27 603	27 600	34 103	37 309	51 659	46 180	59 644	88 528	(B)
Standard error (dollars)	421	2 169	330	597	1 524	1 141	1 077	3 272	7 130	(B)
Asian/Pacific Islander, number with income	4 613	358	944	634	318	2 357	1 519	522	136	178
Median income (dollars)	37 379	19 615	25 526	31 526	36 164	52 477	46 382	67 057	82 576	73 368
Standard error (dollars)	605	847	472	612	1 005	1 360	955	2 171	11 923	6 120
Mean income (dollars)	52 527	25 294	29 543	38 985	48 712	70 039	63 918	77 133	94 048	00 000
Standard error (dollars)	1 358	1 762	1 027	2 801	6 684	2 242	3 163	3 086	7 496	5 298

[1]May be of any race.
(B) = Base less than 75,000.

Table A-12. Income in 2001 by Educational Attainment for Population 18 Years and Over, by Age, Race, and Hispanic Origin, March 2002—*Continued*

(Numbers in thousand, except where noted.)

| Income, standard error, age, race, and Hispanic origin | Total | High school | | College | | | | | | |
		Not high school graduate	Graduate, includes GED	Some college, no degree	Associate degree	Bachelor's degree or more	Bachelor's degree	Master's degree	Professional degree	Doctorate degree
All Workers, 25 Years and Over										
All races, number with income	172 464	25 802	54 899	29 760	14 528	47 473	31 382	11 271	2 677	2 141
Median income (dollars)	25 309	12 632	21 056	26 273	29 916	42 606	38 854	49 626	71 806	63 952
Standard error (dollars)	70	106	89	149	267	238	290	500	2 033	1 798
Mean income (dollars)	35 324	17 283	26 175	32 471	34 697	57 689	50 325	63 460	97 029	86 036
Standard error (dollars)	139	196	161	252	334	391	417	890	2 306	2 323
White, number with income	144 817	20 792	46 484	24 763	12 303	40 473	26 667	9 679	2 326	1 799
Median income (dollars)	25 816	13 126	21 413	26 598	30 263	43 527	39 437	50 049	74 774	65 372
Standard error (dollars)	78	118	100	172	211	297	320	420	1 753	1 898
Mean income (dollars)	36 329	17 856	26 897	33 243	35 115	58 909	51 283	64 570	100 186	88 123
Standard error (dollars)	156	236	185	285	330	431	452	1 003	2 568	2 525
Black, number with income	18 774	3 792	6 282	3 793	1 565	3 341	2 320	778	140	101
Median income (dollars)	21 098	10 563	18 935	25 148	27 633	38 916	36 323	43 084	54 722	49 421
Standard error (dollars)	177	222	357	423	755	781	534	1 629	5 585	3 870
Mean income (dollars)	26 292	14 256	21 598	28 046	31 181	44 499	39 828	51 557	71 505	59 761
Standard error (dollars)	240	272	253	478	1 121	830	720	2 417	6 030	5 699
Hispanic[1], number with income	17 234	7 012	4 894	2 315	958	2 054	1 489	363	134	66
Median income (dollars)	18 752	14 015	19 642	25 256	26 949	35 464	31 994	43 206	49 590	(B)
Standard error (dollars)	212	227	389	551	1 038	732	646	2 336	7 403	(B)
Mean income (dollars)	25 016	17 562	23 135	29 729	32 365	46 199	40 256	54 148	83 365	(B)
Standard error (dollars)	335	464	437	848	1 213	1 618	1 534	4 987	10 300	(B)
Non-Hispanic White, number with income	128 588	14 121	41 913	22 608	11 398	38 546	25 282	9 325	2 198	1 739
Median income (dollars)	26 922	12 726	21 652	26 749	30 427	44 124	40 005	50 213	75 514	65 688
Standard error (dollars)	84	141	108	184	223	304	261	350	1 288	1 777
Mean income (dollars)	37 748	17 954	27 316	33 554	35 292	59 530	51 881	64 962	101 143	88 995
Standard error (dollars)	170	273	200	302	344	446	470	1 025	2 653	2 597
Non-Hispanic Black, number with income	18 165	3 596	6 066	3 709	1 534	3 258	2 252	772	136	97
Median income (dollars)	21 226	10 484	18 925	25 205	27 841	39 029	36 377	43 157	55 501	49 672
Standard error (dollars)	181	226	369	408	807	782	540	1 637	5 802	3 967
Mean income (dollars)	26 398	14 232	21 611	28 094	31 284	44 509	39 776	51 625	70 894	60 552
Standard error (dollars)	243	281	259	486	1 140	818	674	2 435	5 912	5 837
Asian/Pacific Islander, number with income	7 047	779	1 502	839	506	3 419	2 230	762	203	222
Median income (dollars)	27 722	13 360	19 738	26 279	28 346	41 681	36 817	56 617	49 455	64 709
Standard error (dollars)	651	553	740	831	1 315	559	1 116	3 839	12 150	5 133
Mean income (dollars)	40 891	17 943	23 600	31 971	37 198	56 453	50 586	62 011	78 820	75 702
Standard error (dollars)	952	966	742	2 213	4 317	1 667	2 272	2 473	6 522	4 673
Year-Round, Full-Time Workers, 25 Years and Over										
All races, number with income	92 241	8 506	28 004	16 777	8 904	30 048	19 736	7 050	1 829	1 432
Median income (dollars)	36 733	21 799	30 289	35 771	37 471	53 054	49 289	60 240	86 887	77 315
Standard error (dollars)	79	125	99	157	298	399	408	430	2 509	1 647
Mean income (dollars)	49 104	27 239	35 849	42 840	43 946	72 674	63 816	79 466	119 970	100 891
Standard error (dollars)	230	496	282	364	468	561	601	1 321	2 978	2 987
White, number with income	76 703	6 927	23 315	13 718	7 489	25 251	16 519	5 963	1 591	1 176
Median income (dollars)	37 492	21 987	30 984	36 513	38 667	54 926	50 531	60 431	87 787	80 199
Standard error (dollars)	126	137	107	176	454	351	195	402	2 528	2 065
Mean income (dollars)	50 701	27 751	37 212	44 207	44 552	74 804	65 577	81 489	123 923	104 019
Standard error (dollars)	260	593	332	413	443	626	656	1 514	3 328	3 239
Black, number with income	10 356	1 108	3 479	2 379	1 040	2 347	1 651	528	96	70
Median income (dollars)	30 818	20 891	25 983	31 495	32 131	43 369	40 958	49 730	71 049	(B)
Standard error (dollars)	178	358	243	352	518	1 042	456	1 300	6 053	(B)
Mean income (dollars)	35 812	24 592	28 337	35 447	37 831	51 671	45 917	59 823	89 855	(B)
Standard error (dollars)	366	686	340	639	1 557	1 058	867	3 271	7 306	(B)
Hispanic[1], number with income	10 259	3 598	3 059	1 524	679	1 397	1 012	246	97	40
Median income (dollars)	25 537	20 047	25 088	31 202	32 300	43 121	40 162	51 796	70 454	(B)
Standard error (dollars)	196	216	344	386	968	1 314	1 319	3 065	10 513	(B)
Mean income (dollars)	32 824	23 901	29 280	37 110	37 738	56 506	49 488	66 112	96 273	(B)
Standard error (dollars)	493	786	621	1 184	1 099	2 086	1 974	7 025	10 289	(B)
Non-Hispanic White, number with income	67 033	3 495	20 468	12 297	6 836	23 935	15 571	5 725	1 497	1 141
Median income (dollars)	40 178	25 768	31 592	37 075	39 405	55 503	50 974	60 567	90 299	80 497
Standard error (dollars)	94	256	114	185	469	244	199	413	2 625	2 160
Mean income (dollars)	53 268	31 384	38 323	44 985	45 182	75 809	66 572	82 116	125 740	104 678
Standard error (dollars)	288	897	367	440	474	650	686	1 551	3 478	3 324
Non-Hispanic Black, number with income	9 982	1 010	3 342	2 316	1 023	2 289	1 605	522	93	68
Median income (dollars)	30 995	21 243	26 014	31 577	32 172	43 460	40 936	49 783	71 187	(B)
Standard error (dollars)	177	381	250	348	562	1 064	473	1 288	7 271	(B)
Mean income (dollars)	36 020	25 131	28 414	35 601	37 873	51 522	45 652	60 026	88 528	(B)
Standard error (dollars)	371	739	349	653	1 580	1 037	787	3 307	7 130	(B)
Asian/Pacific Islander, number with income	4 328	335	866	531	297	2 297	1 461	522	135	178
Median income (dollars)	39 552	20 123	26 086	35 270	36 771	53 895	46 915	67 057	83 373	73 368
Standard error (dollars)	785	879	513	1 695	1 095	1 660	1 175	2 171	11 788	6 120
Mean income (dollars)	54 421	25 995	30 532	42 173	50 207	70 954	65 070	77 153	95 509	82 323
Standard error (dollars)	1 439	1 871	1 104	3 316	7 140	2 294	3 282	3 086	7 521	5 298

[1]May be of any race.
(B) = Base less than 75,000.

Table A-12. Income in 2001 by Educational Attainment for Population 18 Years and Over, by Age, Race, and Hispanic Origin, March 2002—*Continued*

(Numbers in thousand, except where noted.)

Income, standard error, age, race, and Hispanic origin	Total	High school		College						
		Not high school graduate	Graduate, includes GED	Some college, no degree	Associate degree	Bachelor's degree or more	Bachelor's degree	Master's degree	Professional degree	Doctorate degree
All Workers, 25 to 64 Years										
All races, number with income	139 554	16 050	43 262	25 301	13 011	41 928	27 955	9 931	2 292	1 748
Median income (dollars)	28 733	15 214	23 470	28 245	31 270	45 251	40 696	51 358	77 305	67 404
Standard error (dollars)	115	126	140	227	187	198	173	294	1 634	1 968
Mean income (dollars)	38 416	19 363	27 980	33 920	35 978	59 948	52 134	66 574	104 388	88 978
Standard error (dollars)	162	289	183	272	363	429	452	993	2 593	2 610
White, number with income	115 614	12 713	35 852	20 673	10 963	35 411	23 525	8 463	1 971	1 451
Median income (dollars)	29 907	15 746	24 395	29 109	31 711	46 053	41 219	51 627	80 090	68 757
Standard error (dollars)	119	139	152	255	208	218	196	302	1 652	2 026
Mean income (dollars)	39 749	20 119	28 997	35 017	36 467	61 459	53 330	68 034	108 412	91 124
Standard error (dollars)	185	354	214	318	357	478	496	1 128	2 912	2 829
Black, number with income	16 053	2 456	5 566	3 529	1 446	3 053	2 168	683	120	81
Median income (dollars)	23 411	12 237	20 283	25 949	28 672	40 130	36 885	45 682	61 989	54 053
Standard error (dollars)	314	330	225	360	928	527	527	1 706	5 993	5 430
Mean income (dollars)	28 098	15 822	22 386	28 878	31 927	45 673	40 771	53 344	76 581	66 118
Standard error (dollars)	269	379	274	504	1 193	878	751	2 653	6 541	6 592
Hispanic[1], number with income	15 514	5 917	4 504	2 215	918	1 958	1 420	345	131	60
Median income (dollars)	20 251	15 553	20 572	25 774	27 574	35 958	32 408	43 452	50 668	(B)
Standard error (dollars)	144	181	259	494	1 123	644	1 011	2 418	9 206	(B)
Mean income (dollars)	26 301	18 761	23 927	30 227	32 847	47 037	40 977	54 955	85 169	(B)
Standard error (dollars)	368	543	465	881	1 254	1 688	1 596	5 225	10 502	(B)
Non-Hispanic White, number with income	101 033	7 096	31 655	18 612	10 095	33 573	22 204	8 126	1 846	1 395
Median income (dollars)	31 231	15 926	25 114	29 594	31 974	46 598	41 621	51 847	80 827	69 852
Standard error (dollars)	78	220	125	268	218	225	200	307	965	2 103
Mean income (dollars)	41 675	21 092	29 679	35 520	36 734	62 235	54 059	68 569	109 991	92 240
Standard error (dollars)	204	473	235	339	373	495	517	1 155	3 029	2 921
Non-Hispanic Black, number with income	15 490	2 282	5 363	3 449	1 417	2 977	2 104	677	115	80
Median income (dollars)	23 701	12 157	20 299	26 009	28 880	40 183	36 933	45 730	62 570	54 489
Standard error (dollars)	317	331	225	363	938	502	534	1 680	7 115	5 511
Mean income (dollars)	28 248	15 852	22 410	28 932	32 039	45 670	40 702	53 439	76 051	66 549
Standard error (dollars)	273	399	280	513	1 214	864	700	2 676	6 398	6 645
Asian/Pacific Islander, number with income	6 282	551	1 270	768	458	3 233	2 104	735	194	199
Median income (dollars)	30 630	15 356	21 199	27 127	29 714	42 380	38 401	57 719	52 107	68 148
Standard error (dollars)	362	598	657	1 104	1 369	948	1 334	3 268	12 345	5 720
Mean income (dollars)	42 891	19 444	24 926	31 066	38 928	57 323	51 392	62 714	81 202	76 815
Standard error (dollars)	995	1 240	844	1 269	4 748	1 684	2 281	2 536	6 765	5 034
Year-Round, Full-Time Workers, 25 to 64 Years										
All races, number with income	90 105	8 161	27 307	16 417	8 784	29 434	19 403	6 910	1 763	1 358
Median income (dollars)	36 654	21 633	30 166	35 629	37 433	52 749	49 273	60 163	86 658	76 637
Standard error (dollars)	79	128	99	159	282	355	412	483	2 524	842
Mean income (dollars)	48 754	27 046	35 311	42 343	43 850	72 284	63 535	79 439	119 626	99 387
Standard error (dollars)	228	514	264	339	473	563	597	1 343	3 059	3 039
White, number with income	74 827	6 660	22 691	13 385	7 386	24 703	16 218	5 842	1 531	1 111
Median income (dollars)	37 412	21 830	30 855	36 358	38 608	54 595	50 518	60 312	87 231	77 379
Standard error (dollars)	87	141	107	178	460	423	194	455	2 492	1 851
Mean income (dollars)	50 325	27 553	36 605	43 741	44 429	74 397	65 330	81 426	123 508	102 053
Standard error (dollars)	259	615	310	396	446	630	655	1 539	3 426	3 279
Black, number with income	10 176	1 050	3 427	2 362	1 026	2 310	1 633	520	90	65
Median income (dollars)	30 794	20 700	25 932	31 505	32 117	43 289	40 951	49 687	71 879	(B)
Standard error (dollars)	177	359	242	353	492	1 024	466	1 294	7 442	(B)
Mean income (dollars)	35 798	24 398	28 242	35 442	37 859	51 638	45 938	60 016	90 304	(B)
Standard error (dollars)	371	706	342	642	1 578	1 068	873	3 315	7 454	(B)
Hispanic[1], number with income	10 138	3 536	3 037	1 512	673	1 378	997	244	97	38
Median income (dollars)	25 469	19 930	25 057	31 124	32 358	42 985	40 043	51 696	70 454	(B)
Standard error (dollars)	198	242	347	385	1 000	1 292	1 402	2 973	10 513	(B)
Mean income (dollars)	32 754	23 767	29 198	37 022	37 777	56 512	49 493	65 928	96 273	(B)
Standard error (dollars)	497	798	624	1 192	1 107	2 112	2 003	7 057	10 289	(B)
Non-Hispanic White, number with income	65 273	3 287	19 866	11 976	6 738	23 404	15 284	5 605	1 437	1 077
Median income (dollars)	40 118	25 668	31 460	36 933	39 343	55 315	50 955	60 449	89 498	77 499
Standard error (dollars)	94	258	114	188	476	245	198	414	2 569	1 954
Mean income (dollars)	52 885	31 286	37 667	44 488	45 047	75 389	66 314	82 068	125 374	102 666
Standard error (dollars)	287	950	343	419	478	655	685	1 578	3 588	3 366
Non-Hispanic Black, number with income	9 808	954	3 290	2 299	1 009	2 254	1 588	514	87	63
Median income (dollars)	30 970	21 044	25 961	31 587	32 158	43 378	40 931	49 740	72 016	(B)
Standard error (dollars)	177	382	250	348	537	1 045	479	1 282	7 409	(B)
Mean income (dollars)	36 006	24 926	28 317	35 598	37 902	51 485	45 668	60 224	88 904	(B)
Standard error (dollars)	375	762	351	656	1 601	1 046	792	3 352	7 251	(B)
Asian/Pacific Islander, number with income	4 262	320	850	526	295	2 269	1 447	512	135	173
Median income (dollars)	39 521	20 061	25 955	35 170	36 683	53 838	47 003	67 459	83 692	74 735
Standard error (dollars)	809	861	521	1 720	1 051	1 692	1 257	2 167	11 650	5 147
Mean income (dollars)	53 870	25 877	30 452	39 154	50 296	70 484	64 210	77 380	95 751	82 724
Standard error (dollars)	1 369	1 935	1 121	1 582	7 201	2 223	3 141	3 132	7 534	5 414

[1]May be of any race.
(B) = Base less than 75,000.

Table A-12. Income in 2001 by Educational Attainment for Population 18 Years and Over, by Age, Race, and Hispanic Origin, March 2002—*Continued*

(Numbers in thousand, except where noted.)

Income, standard error, age, race, and Hispanic origin	Total	High school		College						
		Not high school graduate	Graduate, includes GED	Some college, no degree	Associate degree	Bachelor's degree or more	Bachelor's degree	Master's degree	Professional degree	Doctorate degree
All Workers, 25 to 34 Years										
All races, number with income	35 900	4 170	10 066	7 023	3 211	11 428	8 679	2 032	461	255
Median income (dollars)	26 085	15 555	21 420	24 985	28 796	37 102	36 064	41 340	46 639	46 485
Standard error (dollars)	117	223	169	274	531	199	227	509	2 679	3 150
Mean income (dollars)	31 673	19 900	24 260	28 245	31 398	44 683	42 287	49 456	62 563	55 795
Standard error (dollars)	231	857	298	396	499	501	579	1 042	2 839	3 828
White, number with income	28 906	3 477	7 999	5 449	2 675	9 304	7 095	1 643	357	208
Median income (dollars)	26 631	15 844	22 030	25 390	29 801	37 272	36 301	41 503	49 239	47 766
Standard error (dollars)	133	237	196	266	487	210	235	528	2 450	3 459
Mean income (dollars)	32 345	20 505	25 158	29 018	32 291	44 887	42 470	49 789	62 811	57 822
Standard error (dollars)	258	1 012	361	476	572	515	579	1 199	2 852	4 604
Black, number with income	4 560	507	1 566	1 186	377	921	761	118	31	10
Median income (dollars)	22 000	12 888	18 148	23 103	25 857	33 663	32 580	35 520	(B)	(B)
Standard error (dollars)	263	932	630	827	756	1 249	882	2 734	(B)	(B)
Mean income (dollars)	25 353	15 109	19 896	25 921	26 658	39 011	37 969	37 525	(B)	(B)
Standard error (dollars)	404	648	449	793	977	1 280	1 414	2 459	(B)	(B)
Hispanic[1], number with income	6 046	2 173	1 864	969	341	697	551	103	37	5
Median income (dollars)	19 864	15 593	20 058	24 592	24 420	31 459	30 970	32 081	(B)	(B)
Standard error (dollars)	296	297	479	1 061	1 349	630	726	3 002	(B)	(B)
Mean income (dollars)	24 535	19 660	22 242	28 509	29 927	37 681	35 563	39 441	(B)	(B)
Standard error (dollars)	591	1 247	478	1 543	2 504	1 688	1 874	3 242	(B)	(B)
Non-Hispanic White, number with income	23 232	1 408	6 261	4 552	2 354	8 655	6 587	1 542	321	203
Median income (dollars)	29 013	16 451	22 752	25 502	30 318	37 707	36 613	41 692	50 166	47 651
Standard error (dollars)	236	414	301	298	336	407	244	530	2 243	3 532
Mean income (dollars)	34 244	21 767	25 978	29 063	32 524	45 447	43 034	50 430	62 773	58 424
Standard error (dollars)	287	1 739	442	481	556	544	613	1 259	2 954	4 698
Non-Hispanic Black, number with income	4 332	446	1 484	1 145	366	889	731	117	31	9
Median income (dollars)	22 146	12 009	18 145	22 999	26 009	33 684	32 576	35 647	(B)	(B)
Standard error (dollars)	273	772	667	830	771	1 241	866	2 753	(B)	(B)
Mean income (dollars)	25 359	14 801	19 869	25 823	26 760	38 647	37 501	37 647	(B)	(B)
Standard error (dollars)	390	701	463	814	981	1 081	1 142	2 476	(B)	(B)
Asian/Pacific Islander, number with income	1 981	98	339	276	122	1 143	776	261	72	33
Median income (dollars)	30 129	16 895	20 780	24 413	26 212	39 718	37 400	49 077	(B)	(B)
Standard error (dollars)	1 132	1 608	1 104	1 654	2 194	1 180	1 891	3 652	(B)	(B)
Mean income (dollars)	38 372	24 702	23 164	26 011	28 177	48 147	45 499	52 943	(B)	(B)
Standard error (dollars)	1 660	5 356	1 138	1 715	2 262	2 725	3 736	2 892	(B)	(B)
Year-Round, Full-Time Workers, 25 to 34 Years										
All races, number with income	23 670	2 402	6 456	4 535	2 197	8 079	6 184	1 375	336	182
Median income (dollars)	31 856	20 516	26 533	30 655	32 527	42 782	41 354	50 099	55 266	49 296
Standard error (dollars)	104	204	180	218	453	479	267	805	4 571	1 606
Mean income (dollars)	39 170	26 368	30 294	35 201	37 276	52 811	50 313	59 170	70 830	56 308
Standard error (dollars)	310	1 364	419	503	529	634	751	1 293	2 991	2 745
White, number with income	19 243	2 064	5 185	3 521	1 834	6 637	5 096	1 129	271	140
Median income (dollars)	32 209	20 453	27 084	31 171	33 804	43 039	41 445	49 374	55 614	50 464
Standard error (dollars)	114	223	213	246	584	581	314	1 077	4 748	3 288
Mean income (dollars)	39 725	26 680	31 153	36 173	38 317	52 754	50 186	59 137	71 256	58 906
Standard error (dollars)	342	1 565	508	600	600	638	730	1 500	3 258	3 313
Black, number with income	2 925	234	946	785	273	685	571	79	26	8
Median income (dollars)	27 379	20 607	23 876	27 872	27 895	37 186	36 316	40 159	(B)	(B)
Standard error (dollars)	336	531	706	727	1 192	1 080	879	1 499	(B)	(B)
Mean income (dollars)	31 905	22 539	26 006	31 640	29 995	44 323	42 963	43 820	(B)	(B)
Standard error (dollars)	539	942	570	1 034	1 012	1 585	1 748	2 985	(B)	(B)
Hispanic[1], number with income	4 015	1 365	1 272	647	251	478	382	63	29	3
Median income (dollars)	24 035	19 333	23 896	30 121	28 681	37 098	36 465	(B)	(B)	(B)
Standard error (dollars)	401	461	565	814	1 314	1 206	800	(B)	(B)	(B)
Mean income (dollars)	29 822	24 244	26 654	35 140	31 720	45 958	43 781	(B)	(B)	(B)
Standard error (dollars)	764	1 709	537	2 187	1 415	2 193	2 454	(B)	(B)	(B)
Non-Hispanic White, number with income	15 472	765	4 004	2 923	1 593	6 185	4 737	1 068	241	137
Median income (dollars)	35 079	22 294	28 374	31 404	34 732	43 671	41 780	49 673	60 145	50 262
Standard error (dollars)	188	536	421	279	563	609	320	1 038	4 895	5 954
Mean income (dollars)	42 136	30 537	32 479	36 279	39 278	53 328	50 779	59 799	71 466	59 024
Standard error (dollars)	382	3 113	638	566	657	672	773	1 572	3 356	3 387
Non-Hispanic Black, number with income	2 774	198	889	753	267	665	552	78	26	8
Median income (dollars)	27 488	20 846	23 753	27 758	28 000	37 073	36 055	40 254	(B)	(B)
Standard error (dollars)	396	663	700	747	1 288	1 029	949	1 439	(B)	(B)
Mean income (dollars)	31 891	22 943	26 034	31 643	29 878	43 476	41 905	44 111	(B)	(B)
Standard error (dollars)	507	1 047	591	1 070	1 006	1 292	1 352	3 007	(B)	(B)
Asian/Pacific Islander, number with income	1 254	63	230	175	71	713	483	160	39	30
Median income (dollars)	39 230	(B)	25 811	30 710	(B)	50 385	46 591	62 700	(B)	(B)
Standard error (dollars)	1 035	(B)	984	1 513	(B)	1 366	1 411	2 856	(B)	(B)
Mean income (dollars)	49 290	(B)	28 365	34 761	(B)	62 265	61 249	67 298	(B)	(B)
Standard error (dollars)	2 411	(B)	1 368	2 195	(B)	4 011	5 755	3 008	(B)	(B)

[1]May be of any race.
(B) = Base less than 75,000.

Table A-12. Income in 2001 by Educational Attainment for Population 18 Years and Over, by Age, Race, and Hispanic Origin, March 2002—*Continued*

(Numbers in thousand, except where noted.)

Income, standard error, age, race, and Hispanic origin	Total	High school		College						
		Not high school graduate	Graduate, includes GED	Some college, no degree	Associate degree	Bachelor's degree or more	Bachelor's degree	Master's degree	Professional degree	Doctorate degree
All Workers, 35 to 44 Years										
All races, number with income	41 813	4 491	13 348	7 398	4 292	12 281	8 425	2 674	693	488
Median income (dollars)	30 403	16 402	25 370	30 561	32 053	48 369	43 859	53 039	81 169	68 468
Standard error (dollars)	119	209	169	241	354	589	804	1 334	1 551	5 388
Mean income (dollars)	40 359	20 150	29 308	35 434	36 506	64 075	56 745	70 456	109 657	90 861
Standard error (dollars)	318	487	309	466	687	896	935	2 233	5 103	5 706
White, number with income	34 324	3 588	11 015	5 915	3 570	10 234	7 089	2 185	594	365
Median income (dollars)	30 985	16 904	26 066	31 207	32 300	49 708	45 479	52 536	82 331	70 293
Standard error (dollars)	132	230	190	268	506	579	522	1 181	2 059	5 338
Mean income (dollars)	41 621	21 182	30 315	36 755	36 079	65 704	58 325	71 918	114 370	92 577
Standard error (dollars)	360	596	362	551	546	1 010	1 046	2 621	5 780	5 944
Black, number with income	5 078	651	1 782	1 134	520	989	685	232	42	29
Median income (dollars)	25 785	13 610	21 463	27 322	30 691	41 458	39 389	48 632	(B)	(B)
Standard error (dollars)	311	836	423	756	818	602	1 191	1 728	(B)	(B)
Mean income (dollars)	30 054	15 524	23 837	30 153	34 168	48 532	41 638	60 070	(B)	(B)
Standard error (dollars)	549	609	507	892	1 947	2 010	1 223	6 997	(B)	(B)
Hispanic[1], number with income	4 818	1 819	1 362	671	306	657	484	103	44	25
Median income (dollars)	21 274	16 599	21 286	26 680	29 712	37 455	35 442	43 807	(B)	(B)
Standard error (dollars)	254	303	464	932	2 322	2 042	1 694	4 754	(B)	(B)
Mean income (dollars)	28 465	19 824	25 611	32 137	33 781	52 053	44 338	67 109	(B)	(B)
Standard error (dollars)	789	864	1 220	1 593	1 696	4 034	3 489	16 229	(B)	(B)
Non-Hispanic White, number with income	29 780	1 870	9 738	5 277	3 281	9 612	6 633	2 084	552	340
Median income (dollars)	32 267	17 074	26 628	31 613	32 449	50 434	46 220	53 506	83 240	72 375
Standard error (dollars)	142	379	199	292	630	315	560	1 451	2 183	4 768
Mean income (dollars)	43 615	22 186	30 977	37 285	36 264	66 577	59 274	72 130	115 820	94 883
Standard error (dollars)	397	835	377	587	576	1 044	1 091	2 643	5 963	6 306
Non-Hispanic Black, number with income	4 921	596	1 726	1 119	511	967	670	229	39	28
Median income (dollars)	25 990	13 839	21 442	27 424	30 727	41 471	39 271	48 627	(B)	(B)
Standard error (dollars)	321	898	422	822	798	626	1 220	1 719	(B)	(B)
Mean income (dollars)	30 247	15 648	23 883	30 249	34 205	48 495	41 745	60 186	(B)	(B)
Standard error (dollars)	560	632	517	902	1 972	2 032	1 243	7 066	(B)	(B)
Asian/Pacific Islander, number with income	1 891	149	357	246	155	982	585	248	56	91
Median income (dollars)	33 694	16 630	22 268	27 361	37 337	50 364	40 727	65 572	(B)	63 615
Standard error (dollars)	1 477	1 478	967	2 133	1 675	1 975	2 263	3 867	(B)	10 864
Mean income (dollars)	47 457	18 567	26 120	31 446	56 116	62 262	56 808	67 633	(B)	72 408
Standard error (dollars)	1 991	1 319	1 305	1 819	13 535	2 961	4 574	3 028	(B)	5 910
Year-Round, Full-Time Workers, 35 to 44 Years										
All races, number with income	28 783	2 540	9 183	5 133	3 021	8 904	6 021	1 941	550	390
Median income (dollars)	37 320	21 808	30 573	36 401	38 311	57 007	52 180	64 328	88 442	76 754
Standard error (dollars)	147	244	161	293	658	457	309	1 290	3 639	2 451
Mean income (dollars)	49 982	26 849	35 727	43 188	43 996	77 230	68 742	85 195	124 077	102 397
Standard error (dollars)	429	800	409	584	886	1 155	1 212	2 948	5 787	6 847
White, number with income	23 593	2 106	7 621	4 082	2 486	7 296	4 992	1 547	484	287
Median income (dollars)	38 612	22 127	31 148	37 351	39 191	59 615	54 541	65 483	92 088	77 028
Standard error (dollars)	304	254	173	423	758	778	764	1 518	4 245	2 551
Mean income (dollars)	51 606	27 691	36 914	44 944	43 568	80 325	71 617	88 841	129 977	104 755
Standard error (dollars)	487	952	478	692	632	1 321	1 372	3 543	6 581	7 133
Black, number with income	3 515	308	1 180	830	392	804	555	190	34	23
Median income (dollars)	31 469	19 767	26 330	32 068	33 958	43 949	41 178	50 878	(B)	(B)
Standard error (dollars)	314	799	376	623	1 552	1 426	699	1 424	(B)	(B)
Mean income (dollars)	36 744	22 734	29 023	35 481	39 618	53 352	45 261	66 626	(B)	(B)
Standard error (dollars)	722	908	627	1 077	2 408	2 368	1 305	8 379	(B)	(B)
Hispanic[1], number with income	3 304	1 167	952	479	232	472	348	76	31	15
Median income (dollars)	26 419	20 583	25 631	31 510	35 233	45 173	42 097	50 813	(B)	(B)
Standard error (dollars)	333	354	578	725	1 783	1 823	2 131	2 730	(B)	(B)
Mean income (dollars)	34 363	24 352	30 498	38 646	40 054	59 747	51 115	80 888	(B)	(B)
Standard error (dollars)	1 043	1 275	1 669	2 045	1 845	4 175	4 175	21 466	(B)	(B)
Non-Hispanic White, number with income	20 452	984	6 727	3 627	2 263	6 848	4 661	1 473	440	272
Median income (dollars)	40 788	25 341	31 668	38 598	39 738	60 609	55 619	66 327	92 687	77 394
Standard error (dollars)	171	554	183	697	652	452	554	1 561	4 384	2 762
Mean income (dollars)	54 261	31 246	37 835	45 697	43 916	81 663	73 063	89 187	132 142	106 553
Standard error (dollars)	537	1 458	495	736	672	1 370	1 437	3 572	6 907	7 455
Non-Hispanic Black, number with income	3 409	278	1 142	816	387	785	544	187	31	22
Median income (dollars)	31 674	20 488	26 413	32 179	33 931	44 114	41 197	50 873	(B)	(B)
Standard error (dollars)	312	984	385	640	1 544	1 405	748	1 415	(B)	(B)
Mean income (dollars)	36 998	23 452	29 141	35 675	39 592	53 308	45 356	66 854	(B)	(B)
Standard error (dollars)	737	980	639	1 090	2 437	2 396	1 326	8 481	(B)	(B)
Asian/Pacific Islander, number with income	1 400	89	263	180	116	750	428	196	47	77
Median income (dollars)	41 230	19 525	25 906	33 207	39 943	60 233	51 693	70 904	(B)	76 063
Standard error (dollars)	780	1 464	1 287	2 334	1 888	2 101	2 709	3 050	(B)	10 388
Mean income (dollars)	56 178	22 668	30 993	37 360	67 482	71 791	67 251	75 280	(B)	79 525
Standard error (dollars)	2 529	1 876	1 548	1 907	17 837	3 565	5 801	3 216	(B)	6 196

[1]May be of any race.
(B) = Base less than 75,000.

Table A-12. Income in 2001 by Educational Attainment for Population 18 Years and Over, by Age, Race, and Hispanic Origin, March 2002—*Continued*

(Numbers in thousand, except where noted.)

Income, standard error, age, race, and Hispanic origin	Total	High school		College						
		Not high school graduate	Graduate, includes GED	Some college, no degree	Associate degree	Bachelor's degree or more	Bachelor's degree	Master's degree	Professional degree	Doctorate degree
All Workers, 45 to 54 Years										
All races, number with income	37 481	3 666	11 648	6 819	3 723	11 624	7 092	3 260	698	572
Median income (dollars)	31 738	15 207	25 432	31 367	32 783	50 694	44 389	55 268	90 693	76 801
Standard error (dollars)	141	316	209	277	695	294	608	687	4 710	2 351
Mean income (dollars)	42 977	19 572	30 575	36 978	37 893	67 935	57 976	70 716	123 224	108 047
Standard error (dollars)	344	434	444	463	618	895	1 022	1 649	5 005	5 457
White, number with income	31 353	2 760	9 700	5 704	3 163	10 024	6 054	2 844	629	495
Median income (dollars)	32 950	16 068	26 277	31 764	33 920	51 475	45 348	55 779	87 413	76 760
Standard error (dollars)	334	368	235	300	895	308	449	679	3 144	3 284
Mean income (dollars)	44 751	20 549	31 899	38 022	38 572	69 633	59 481	72 019	124 505	110 259
Standard error (dollars)	392	548	523	523	609	989	1 126	1 820	5 453	6 093
Black, number with income	4 122	650	1 443	843	384	800	512	239	30	17
Median income (dollars)	24 988	12 261	21 113	27 838	30 083	45 702	40 916	50 074	(B)	(B)
Standard error (dollars)	622	563	382	1 044	1 862	1 000	1 072	1 961	(B)	(B)
Mean income (dollars)	30 085	15 968	23 399	30 783	35 258	50 390	44 416	56 011	(B)	(B)
Standard error (dollars)	566	659	551	1 151	3 386	1 381	1 460	2 383	(B)	(B)
Hispanic[1], number with income	2 989	1 128	845	404	188	421	271	95	33	21
Median income (dollars)	20 658	15 546	21 099	28 091	29 825	41 398	35 203	55 812	(B)	(B)
Standard error (dollars)	327	448	593	1 534	2 079	1 838	3 014	4 921	(B)	(B)
Mean income (dollars)	27 415	17 736	25 387	31 317	33 392	50 970	42 060	60 667	(B)	(B)
Standard error (dollars)	602	497	909	1 297	2 089	2 799	2 830	4 695	(B)	(B)
Non-Hispanic White, number with income	28 560	1 688	8 920	5 338	2 986	9 626	5 801	2 750	596	477
Median income (dollars)	35 133	16 574	26 726	32 077	34 339	51 698	45 713	55 783	90 334	77 084
Standard error (dollars)	200	584	241	317	839	310	430	684	4 856	3 413
Mean income (dollars)	46 416	22 289	32 436	38 474	38 837	70 360	60 197	72 406	126 806	111 540
Standard error (dollars)	425	838	563	551	633	1 023	1 167	1 876	5 643	6 297
Non-Hispanic Black, number with income	4 006	618	1 399	825	376	786	500	237	30	17
Median income (dollars)	25 227	12 363	21 192	27 992	30 084	45 871	41 074	49 953	(B)	(B)
Standard error (dollars)	570	606	390	1 043	1 850	817	1 076	1 980	(B)	(B)
Mean income (dollars)	30 338	16 046	23 494	30 932	35 453	50 675	44 723	56 015	(B)	(B)
Standard error (dollars)	579	685	563	1 170	3 453	1 397	1 481	2 396	(B)	(B)
Asian/Pacific Islander, number with income	1 593	177	359	184	134	737	495	156	33	51
Median income (dollars)	30 723	15 757	22 077	35 634	28 704	43 217	38 647	52 209	(B)	(B)
Standard error (dollars)	687	943	1 224	2 224	1 549	1 974	2 087	9 869	(B)	(B)
Mean income (dollars)	44 926	18 719	25 878	36 001	30 649	65 357	54 842	71 386	(B)	(B)
Standard error (dollars)	2 059	1 339	1 273	2 044	2 064	4 162	5 038	8 913	(B)	(B)
Year-Round, Full-Time Workers, 45 to 54 Years										
All races, number with income	25 673	1 895	7 858	4 674	2 591	8 653	5 131	2 460	581	479
Median income (dollars)	40 573	22 298	31 375	38 986	40 923	57 367	52 025	60 550	99 875	82 029
Standard error (dollars)	150	318	205	635	358	556	378	554	22 304	2 575
Mean income (dollars)	53 417	27 228	37 728	45 803	46 194	79 678	70 027	79 870	134 458	115 529
Standard error (dollars)	463	744	620	579	766	1 111	1 309	2 037	5 648	5 853
White, number with income	21 625	1 448	6 581	3 954	2 211	7 429	4 354	2 135	523	416
Median income (dollars)	41 593	23 136	32 297	40 118	41 541	59 458	53 668	60 823	97 110	81 760
Standard error (dollars)	164	590	242	483	379	818	796	559	16 000	2 972
Mean income (dollars)	55 359	28 220	39 366	46 929	46 859	81 836	72 338	81 126	135 751	117 049
Standard error (dollars)	523	937	730	651	717	1 230	1 441	2 261	6 183	6 506
Black, number with income	2 668	296	935	542	271	622	382	202	23	14
Median income (dollars)	32 186	20 649	26 730	34 382	35 894	47 654	45 733	50 422	(B)	(B)
Standard error (dollars)	357	607	569	999	1 626	1 002	1 144	1 967	(B)	(B)
Mean income (dollars)	38 073	23 723	28 791	38 798	43 808	55 701	50 281	58 379	(B)	(B)
Standard error (dollars)	759	1 111	674	1 476	4 629	1 512	1 604	2 441	(B)	(B)
Hispanic[1], number with income	1 971	664	567	294	137	308	192	73	26	16
Median income (dollars)	26 168	19 906	25 633	31 829	36 484	51 310	42 313	(B)	(B)	(B)
Standard error (dollars)	621	499	914	1 120	3 910	3 369	2 270	(B)	(B)	(B)
Mean income (dollars)	34 597	22 484	31 718	36 891	39 405	61 599	51 552	(B)	(B)	(B)
Standard error (dollars)	810	698	1 169	1 527	2 278	3 429	3 476	(B)	(B)	(B)
Non-Hispanic White, number with income	19 779	819	6 059	3 683	2 079	7 137	4 174	2 062	497	403
Median income (dollars)	42 516	26 725	32 787	40 567	41 695	59 915	54 197	60 712	99 442	82 188
Standard error (dollars)	272	424	419	360	379	691	798	569	24 443	3 360
Mean income (dollars)	57 257	32 511	39 974	47 672	47 313	82 615	73 196	81 532	137 562	117 891
Standard error (dollars)	565	1 551	786	688	748	1 272	1 494	2 334	6 396	6 694
Non-Hispanic Black, number with income	2 595	278	906	530	266	613	374	201	23	14
Median income (dollars)	32 358	20 854	26 885	34 350	35 847	47 772	45 886	50 289	(B)	(B)
Standard error (dollars)	440	588	581	997	1 631	1 018	861	1 972	(B)	(B)
Mean income (dollars)	38 383	24 087	28 911	38 948	44 000	55 946	50 554	58 398	(B)	(B)
Standard error (dollars)	776	1 161	689	1 501	4 706	1 529	1 625	2 455	(B)	(B)
Asian/Pacific Islander, number with income	1 152	115	252	134	83	566	378	109	31	46
Median income (dollars)	37 321	20 122	26 063	40 303	31 602	52 570	43 291	73 320	(B)	(B)
Standard error (dollars)	1 427	1 646	817	3 281	2 637	2 154	2 043	5 417	(B)	(B)
Mean income (dollars)	55 360	24 185	30 746	43 009	37 112	78 354	64 060	96 014	(B)	(B)
Standard error (dollars)	2 715	1 690	1 536	2 156	2 419	5 184	6 397	11 580	(B)	(B)

[1]May be of any race.
(B) = Base less than 75,000.

Table A-12. Income in 2001 by Educational Attainment for Population 18 Years and Over, by Age, Race, and Hispanic Origin, March 2002—*Continued*

(Numbers in thousand, except where noted.)

Income, standard error, age, race, and Hispanic origin	Total	High school		College						
		Not high school graduate	Graduate, includes GED	Some college, no degree	Associate degree	Bachelor's degree or more	Bachelor's degree	Master's degree	Professional degree	Doctorate degree
All Workers, 55 to 64 Years										
All races, number with income	24 359	3 721	8 199	4 060	1 784	6 593	3 758	1 964	440	431
Median income (dollars)	25 801	12 689	21 059	26 663	31 629	47 326	40 229	52 488	75 547	71 836
Standard error (dollars)	218	313	248	511	673	731	709	1 361	4 668	3 384
Mean income (dollars)	38 002	17 605	26 697	35 844	38 956	64 640	53 512	72 124	110 054	81 186
Standard error (dollars)	410	326	383	1 024	1 326	1 142	1 133	2 661	6 245	3 003
White, number with income	21 029	2 886	7 136	3 603	1 553	5 848	3 286	1 789	390	381
Median income (dollars)	26 657	13 269	21 482	26 811	32 093	48 565	40 694	53 355	80 023	75 124
Standard error (dollars)	241	369	264	548	876	940	651	1 547	5 720	3 290
Mean income (dollars)	39 411	17 836	27 323	36 480	40 264	66 389	54 669	73 718	115 114	83 054
Standard error (dollars)	461	348	420	1 133	1 499	1 254	1 230	2 892	6 858	3 260
Black, number with income	2 291	647	774	364	163	342	208	93	15	24
Median income (dollars)	19 120	10 647	18 551	25 693	29 295	37 887	36 341	42 123	(B)	(B)
Standard error (dollars)	721	658	872	1 797	3 139	2 167	2 038	7 163	(B)	(B)
Mean income (dollars)	25 652	16 534	22 192	30 123	29 128	44 305	39 183	49 858	(B)	(B)
Standard error (dollars)	612	1 000	779	1 480	1 892	2 122	2 213	4 445	(B)	(B)
Hispanic[1], number with income	1 659	795	432	168	82	180	113	42	16	7
Median income (dollars)	16 717	12 110	19 272	25 087	34 418	40 386	34 594	(B)	(B)	(B)
Standard error (dollars)	611	516	1 054	2 337	3 594	2 153	4 152	(B)	(B)	(B)
Mean income (dollars)	24 446	15 327	23 028	29 885	40 213	55 734	50 321	(B)	(B)	(B)
Standard error (dollars)	866	559	1 088	2 231	4 869	5 427	6 736	(B)	(B)	(B)
Non-Hispanic White, number with income	19 459	2 128	6 734	3 443	1 472	5 680	3 180	1 749	376	373
Median income (dollars)	27 679	13 796	21 640	26 879	31 938	49 102	40 917	53 887	80 853	75 249
Standard error (dollars)	310	447	273	569	855	948	685	1 569	5 867	3 162
Mean income (dollars)	40 620	18 734	27 592	36 773	40 249	66 698	54 819	74 292	115 097	83 552
Standard error (dollars)	493	429	440	1 181	1 561	1 281	1 252	2 953	7 058	3 268
Non-Hispanic Black, number with income	2 230	622	753	359	162	333	202	91	14	24
Median income (dollars)	19 110	10 767	18 342	25 933	29 533	37 903	36 309	42 481	(B)	(B)
Standard error (dollars)	725	661	861	1 814	3 069	2 255	1 991	7 598	(B)	(B)
Mean income (dollars)	25 692	16 609	22 029	30 139	29 206	44 404	38 879	50 033	(B)	(B)
Standard error (dollars)	624	1 032	791	1 496	1 904	2 155	2 237	4 508	(B)	(B)
Asian/Pacific Islander, number with income	816	125	214	61	45	369	246	69	31	22
Median income (dollars)	25 280	11 616	17 189	(B)	(B)	42 522	36 355	(B)	(B)	(B)
Standard error (dollars)	2 093	1 705	1 249	(B)	(B)	4 758	4 470	(B)	(B)	(B)
Mean income (dollars)	39 304	17 377	24 131	(B)	(B)	56 556	50 148	(B)	(B)	(B)
Standard error (dollars)	2 194	2 357	3 527	(B)	(B)	3 646	4 338	(B)	(B)	(B)
Year-Round, Full-Time Workers, 55 to 64 Years										
All races, number with income	11 978	1 324	3 808	2 074	973	3 797	2 065	1 132	294	305
Median income (dollars)	39 398	23 754	31 481	38 927	40 795	62 499	56 089	65 746	(B)	86 816
Standard error (dollars)	442	1 103	265	740	553	1 212	710	2 093	44 015	5 318
Mean income (dollars)	54 748	28 395	37 828	48 067	51 994	85 264	71 821	93 249	137 763	95 969
Standard error (dollars)	713	673	677	1 453	2 198	1 764	1 696	4 327	8 216	3 542
White, number with income	10 363	1 041	3 301	1 827	853	3 340	1 774	1 029	268	267
Median income (dollars)	40 433	24 408	32 036	39 241	41 297	65 485	57 148	66 393	(B)	91 742
Standard error (dollars)	265	987	286	818	593	1 475	995	1 912	46 795	5 460
Mean income (dollars)	56 584	28 073	38 953	48 737	53 777	87 908	73 936	95 367	141 073	98 455
Standard error (dollars)	800	662	745	1 609	2 483	1 954	1 852	4 720	8 828	3 885
Black, number with income	1 066	210	365	204	89	197	123	48	7	18
Median income (dollars)	32 482	22 121	28 534	36 950	36 413	51 580	46 345	(B)	(B)	(B)
Standard error (dollars)	832	1 956	1 402	2 129	1 022	3 343	2 873	(B)	(B)	(B)
Mean income (dollars)	37 664	29 868	30 103	40 983	36 114	57 252	49 297	(B)	(B)	(B)
Standard error (dollars)	990	2 614	1 000	2 016	2 084	2 852	2 745	(B)	(B)	(B)
Hispanic[1], number with income	847	339	244	92	53	117	72	31	10	3
Median income (dollars)	26 726	19 454	27 246	36 184	(B)	48 467	(B)	(B)	(B)	(B)
Standard error (dollars)	863	738	1 990	3 423	(B)	8 412	(B)	(B)	(B)	(B)
Mean income (dollars)	36 085	22 349	31 525	42 210	(B)	73 112	(B)	(B)	(B)	(B)
Standard error (dollars)	1 460	857	1 499	2 992	(B)	7 427	(B)	(B)	(B)	(B)
Non-Hispanic White, number with income	9 568	716	3 075	1 741	801	3 233	1 710	1 000	258	263
Median income (dollars)	41 315	28 104	32 318	39 322	41 377	65 937	57 338	66 943	(B)	91 767
Standard error (dollars)	282	1 216	348	800	659	1 416	1 145	1 785	44 110	5 556
Mean income (dollars)	58 287	30 739	39 511	49 019	53 828	88 348	74 158	96 460	140 800	98 080
Standard error (dollars)	856	866	792	1 682	2 614	2 003	1 885	4 848	9 088	3 896
Non-Hispanic Black, number with income	1 028	200	351	198	88	190	117	47	7	18
Median income (dollars)	32 521	22 213	28 015	37 344	36 522	51 710	46 307	(B)	(B)	(B)
Standard error (dollars)	872	1 947	1 311	2 107	1 037	3 143	2 665	(B)	(B)	(B)
Mean income (dollars)	37 820	30 105	29 884	41 327	36 353	57 604	49 259	(B)	(B)	(B)
Standard error (dollars)	1 018	2 731	1 025	2 047	2 097	2 924	2 798	(B)	(B)	(B)
Asian/Pacific Islander, number with income	454	52	104	34	23	239	157	46	17	18
Median income (dollars)	35 636	(B)	26 073	(B)	(B)	54 765	50 291	(B)	(B)	(B)
Standard error (dollars)	2 070	(B)	1 977	(B)	(B)	4 899	4 175	(B)	(B)	(B)
Mean income (dollars)	55 621	(B)	32 978	(B)	(B)	72 277	65 396	(B)	(B)	(B)
Standard error (dollars)	3 474	(B)	6 710	(B)	(B)	4 892	5 950	(B)	(B)	(B)

[1]May be of any race.
(B) = Base less than 75,000.

Table A-12. Income in 2001 by Educational Attainment for Population 18 Years and Over, by Age, Race, and Hispanic Origin, March 2002—*Continued*

(Numbers in thousand, except where noted.)

Income, standard error, age, race, and Hispanic origin	Total	High school		College						
		Not high school graduate	Graduate, includes GED	Some college, no degree	Associate degree	Bachelor's degree or more	Bachelor's degree	Master's degree	Professional degree	Doctorate degree
All Workers, 65 Years and Over										
All races, number with income	32 909	9 752	11 636	4 459	1 517	5 544	3 426	1 340	385	392
Median income (dollars)	14 152	10 509	13 764	17 002	16 639	26 523	23 406	31 146	34 460	49 714
Standard error (dollars)	78	94	118	263	406	461	522	919	1 965	2 616
Mean income (dollars)	22 210	13 860	19 468	24 246	23 705	40 606	35 570	40 387	53 223	72 929
Standard error (dollars)	217	202	329	662	663	794	958	1 157	3 393	4 979
White, number with income	29 203	8 079	10 631	4 090	1 340	5 061	3 142	1 216	354	348
Median income (dollars)	14 601	10 889	13 981	17 403	16 880	26 836	23 851	31 318	34 684	49 891
Standard error (dollars)	82	101	124	277	416	487	520	1 034	1 858	2 531
Mean income (dollars)	22 790	14 295	19 813	24 274	24 053	41 068	35 958	40 472	54 482	75 609
Standard error (dollars)	229	235	357	614	715	804	922	1 206	3 593	5 523
Black, number with income	2 721	1 335	715	263	118	287	152	95	20	19
Median income (dollars)	10 631	8 940	11 467	12 114	14 085	24 927	19 040	30 304	(B)	(B)
Standard error (dollars)	210	205	380	679	1 742	2 085	3 155	2 021	(B)	(B)
Mean income (dollars)	15 642	11 376	15 472	16 908	22 114	32 042	26 402	38 697	(B)	(B)
Standard error (dollars)	382	311	575	1 005	2 465	2 280	2 047	5 005	(B)	(B)
Hispanic[1], number with income	1 720	1 095	389	100	39	96	68	17	3	6
Median income (dollars)	9 132	8 488	9 260	14 431	(B)	19 531	(B)	(B)	(B)	(B)
Standard error (dollars)	170	186	404	1 759	(B)	2 980	(B)	(B)	(B)	(B)
Mean income (dollars)	13 424	11 083	13 976	18 741	(B)	29 160	(B)	(B)	(B)	(B)
Standard error (dollars)	403	364	955	1 769	(B)	3 045	(B)	(B)	(B)	(B)
Non-Hispanic White, number with income	27 554	7 024	10 258	3 995	1 303	4 973	3 078	1 198	352	343
Median income (dollars)	14 961	11 329	14 135	17 477	16 861	26 948	23 960	31 260	34 910	49 770
Standard error (dollars)	89	104	124	284	421	495	523	1 046	1 844	2 516
Mean income (dollars)	23 350	14 784	20 022	24 397	24 122	41 272	36 172	40 501	54 773	75 815
Standard error (dollars)	241	265	368	627	730	816	938	1 219	3 612	5 590
Non-Hispanic Black, number with income	2 675	1 313	703	260	117	281	147	95	20	17
Median income (dollars)	10 638	8 949	11 475	12 169	13 893	25 224	19 601	30 304	(B)	(B)
Standard error (dollars)	212	209	377	736	1 630	2 051	3 364	2 021	(B)	(B)
Mean income (dollars)	15 691	11 415	15 518	16 981	22 163	32 208	26 605	38 697	(B)	(B)
Standard error (dollars)	387	315	583	1 016	2 499	2 325	2 094	5 005	(B)	(B)
Asian/Pacific Islander, number with income	764	227	231	71	47	186	126	26	9	23
Median income (dollars)	12 553	9 028	12 400	(B)	(B)	20 209	14 914	(B)	(B)	(B)
Standard error (dollars)	585	407	843	(B)	(B)	2 638	1 970	(B)	(B)	(B)
Mean income (dollars)	24 452	14 305	16 335	(B)	(B)	41 353	37 137	(B)	(B)	(B)
Standard error (dollars)	3 101	1 341	1 170	(B)	(B)	8 964	12 832	(B)	(B)	(B)
Year-Round, Full-Time Workers, 65 Years and Over										
All races, number with income	2 135	344	697	359	120	613	333	140	65	74
Median income (dollars)	42 027	27 011	37 411	45 936	43 212	63 164	50 867	64 742	(B)	(B)
Standard error (dollars)	882	964	1 148	1 376	3 900	1 992	4 433	4 402	(B)	85 231
Mean income (dollars)	63 892	31 809	56 902	65 526	50 938	91 414	80 165	80 785	(B)	128 254
Standard error (dollars)	2 418	1 147	4 528	6 817	2 926	4 975	7 675	5 985	(B)	14 689
White, number with income	1 875	267	624	333	103	547	301	121	59	65
Median income (dollars)	43 591	27 314	38 232	46 117	43 818	68 566	55 157	70 847	(B)	(B)
Standard error (dollars)	1 330	1 351	1 479	1 110	5 471	4 644	4 705	5 149	(B)	(B)
Mean income (dollars)	65 704	32 706	59 278	62 936	53 315	93 158	78 866	84 535	(B)	(B)
Standard error (dollars)	2 511	1 310	5 035	5 970	3 262	4 894	7 036	6 680	(B)	(B)
Black, number with income	179	58	51	17	14	36	17	7	5	5
Median income (dollars)	35 163	(B)	(B)	(B)	(B)	(B)	(B)	(B)	(B)	(B)
Standard error (dollars)	2 838	(B)	(B)	(B)	(B)	(B)	(B)	(B)	(B)	(B)
Mean income (dollars)	36 642	(B)	(B)	(B)	(B)	(B)	(B)	(B)	(B)	(B)
Standard error (dollars)	2 277	(B)	(B)	(B)	(B)	(B)	(B)	(B)	(B)	(B)
Hispanic[1], number with income	120	62	22	11	5	18	15	1	(B)	2
Median income (dollars)	34 342	(B)	(B)	(B)	(B)	(B)	(B)	(B)	(B)	(B)
Standard error (dollars)	2 889	(B)	(B)	(B)	(B)	(B)	(B)	(B)	(B)	(B)
Mean income (dollars)	38 707	(B)	(B)	(B)	(B)	(B)	(B)	(B)	(B)	(B)
Standard error (dollars)	2 454	(B)	(B)	(B)	(B)	(B)	(B)	(B)	(B)	(B)
Non-Hispanic White, number with income	1 760	208	601	321	97	530	287	120	59	63
Median income (dollars)	44 965	28 361	38 084	46 286	44 998	69 984	55 708	70 410	(B)	(B)
Standard error (dollars)	1 215	1 722	1 418	1 129	6 285	4 835	4 847	5 443	(B)	(B)
Mean income (dollars)	67 467	32 944	59 990	63 477	54 465	94 324	80 316	84 347	(B)	(B)
Standard error (dollars)	2 665	1 492	5 216	6 186	3 391	5 035	7 367	6 745	(B)	(B)
Non-Hispanic Black, number with income	174	56	51	17	14	35	16	7	5	4
Median income (dollars)	35 220	(B)	(B)	(B)	(B)	(B)	(B)	(B)	(B)	(B)
Standard error (dollars)	2 754	(B)	(B)	(B)	(B)	(B)	(B)	(B)	(B)	(B)
Mean income (dollars)	36 789	(B)	(B)	(B)	(B)	(B)	(B)	(B)	(B)	(B)
Standard error (dollars)	2 313	(B)	(B)	(B)	(B)	(B)	(B)	(B)	(B)	(B)
Asian/Pacific Islander, number with income	66	14	15	4	2	28	13	9	(B)	4
Median income (dollars)	(B)	(B)	(B)	(B)	(B)	(B)	(B)	(B)	(B)	(B)
Standard error (dollars)	(B)	(B)	(B)	(B)	(B)	(B)	(B)	(B)	(B)	(B)
Mean income (dollars)	(B)	(B)	(B)	(B)	(B)	(B)	(B)	(B)	(B)	(B)
Standard error (dollars)	(B)	(B)	(B)	(B)	(B)	(B)	(B)	(B)	(B)	(B)

[1]May be of any race.
(B) = Base less than 75,000.

Table A-12. Income in 2001 by Educational Attainment for Population 18 Years and Over, by Age, Race, and Hispanic Origin, March 2002—*Continued*

(Numbers in thousand, except where noted.)

Income, standard error, age, race, and Hispanic origin	Total	High school		College						
		Not high school graduate	Graduate, includes GED	Some college, no degree	Associate degree	Bachelor's degree or more	Bachelor's degree	Master's degree	Professional degree	Doctorate degree
MALE										
All Workers, 18 Years and Over										
All races, number with income	96 139	15 879	29 786	18 250	6 844	25 378	16 558	5 544	1 785	1 488
Median income (dollars)	30 143	15 696	26 217	28 636	36 952	52 405	47 657	61 848	81 580	72 641
Standard error (dollars)	85	123	127	309	280	265	453	535	965	2 321
Mean income (dollars)	41 924	19 759	31 629	35 018	43 334	72 463	63 036	80 483	115 085	96 330
Standard error (dollars)	218	244	242	333	584	653	707	1 576	3 203	3 098
White, number with income	81 426	13 207	25 280	15 190	5 884	21 863	14 232	4 778	1 590	1 262
Median income (dollars)	30 904	16 204	27 022	30 003	37 522	53 901	49 498	62 386	81 673	74 361
Standard error (dollars)	92	130	142	260	449	461	551	701	1 327	2 412
Mean income (dollars)	43 421	20 344	32 806	36 448	43 842	74 366	64 717	82 411	117 457	98 415
Standard error (dollars)	242	282	277	381	529	716	765	1 771	3 509	3 314
Black, number with income	9 653	2 009	3 339	2 202	638	1 463	1 045	289	67	60
Median income (dollars)	22 049	11 979	21 040	24 013	32 230	42 341	40 770	48 537	(B)	(B)
Standard error (dollars)	245	308	307	844	1 128	1 014	2 010	(B)	(B)	(B)
Mean income (dollars)	28 423	16 049	24 130	28 130	38 312	51 339	45 824	61 589	(B)	(B)
Standard error (dollars)	417	445	402	728	2 490	1 780	1 682	5 917	(B)	(B)
Hispanic[1], number with income	11 493	4 979	3 244	1 631	532	1 105	809	173	75	46
Median income (dollars)	20 496	16 471	21 465	25 124	30 976	41 100	36 965	48 570	67 515	(B)
Standard error (dollars)	159	198	286	780	997	1 057	1 610	3 873	11 395	(B)
Mean income (dollars)	27 185	19 769	26 482	30 008	37 479	53 541	45 345	65 241	104 307	(B)
Standard error (dollars)	425	524	720	903	1 908	2 376	1 654	9 939	16 533	(B)
Non-Hispanic White, number with income	70 576	8 466	22 239	13 661	5 387	20 822	13 477	4 606	1 517	1 221
Median income (dollars)	32 477	15 997	27 950	30 384	38 404	54 735	50 226	62 755	81 979	75 220
Standard error (dollars)	141	176	217	204	606	430	268	752	1 846	2 392
Mean income (dollars)	45 888	20 600	33 681	37 134	44 346	75 350	65 753	83 056	117 987	99 238
Standard error (dollars)	271	334	299	412	550	742	801	1 803	3 597	3 410
Non-Hispanic Black, number with income	9 273	1 870	3 217	2 145	615	1 424	1 011	287	65	58
Median income (dollars)	22 238	11 825	20 998	24 178	32 533	42 406	40 781	48 358	(B)	(B)
Standard error (dollars)	254	306	312	862	1 322	1 082	691	2 009	(B)	(B)
Mean income (dollars)	28 663	16 075	24 107	28 266	38 764	51 714	46 172	61 504	(B)	(B)
Standard error (dollars)	431	468	411	744	2 576	1 822	1 728	5 946	(B)	(B)
Asian/Pacific Islander, number with income	4 079	405	790	691	260	1 931	1 195	455	126	155
Median income (dollars)	31 580	14 340	22 578	20 689	31 102	51 292	42 387	65 487	84 544	78 023
Standard error (dollars)	447	1 716	1 276	1 428	1 165	853	1 508	2 573	8 498	3 764
Mean income (dollars)	46 285	20 069	27 326	25 832	44 976	67 043	59 360	72 453	99 275	84 129
Standard error (dollars)	1 367	1 675	1 234	1 306	8 191	2 424	3 469	3 250	9 259	5 805
Year-Round, Full-Time Workers, 18 Years and Over										
All races, number with income	58 621	6 657	18 250	10 549	4 964	18 198	11 886	3 968	1 303	1 041
Median income (dollars)	40 169	22 478	32 217	38 936	41 998	61 589	55 120	70 831	(B)	86 965
Standard error (dollars)	103	214	124	418	270	277	418	687	19 525	3 013
Mean income (dollars)	54 120	27 925	38 852	46 313	49 487	84 803	73 789	93 615	137 488	111 031
Standard error (dollars)	325	451	360	478	730	851	924	2 094	3 920	3 904
White, number with income	49 949	5 663	15 495	8 846	4 311	15 632	10 225	3 390	1 152	864
Median income (dollars)	40 824	22 502	33 343	40 307	42 362	62 604	56 197	71 590	(B)	91 554
Standard error (dollars)	113	249	320	229	409	552	343	808	23 104	3 176
Mean income (dollars)	55 593	28 026	40 145	47 789	49 536	86 981	75 501	96 217	141 222	114 216
Standard error (dollars)	360	508	414	543	624	934	994	2 377	4 336	4 174
Black, number with income	5 485	680	2 009	1 277	450	1 066	763	208	56	37
Median income (dollars)	31 935	22 538	26 932	32 876	38 544	47 343	44 920	54 439	(B)	(B)
Standard error (dollars)	260	739	317	696	1 717	929	1 302	3 536	(B)	(B)
Mean income (dollars)	38 667	26 948	30 553	38 047	45 270	59 387	52 615	71 744	(B)	(B)
Standard error (dollars)	647	989	516	1 066	3 351	2 287	2 135	7 780	(B)	(B)
Hispanic[1], number with income	7 619	3 095	2 275	1 027	406	814	591	129	63	29
Median income (dollars)	25 310	20 346	25 392	32 283	35 157	48 262	44 522	61 704	(B)	(B)
Standard error (dollars)	228	193	397	697	1 364	1 881	1 886	7 032	(B)	(B)
Mean income (dollars)	33 089	23 955	30 943	39 158	40 657	62 359	53 098	77 069	(B)	(B)
Standard error (dollars)	560	687	963	1 237	1 512	2 859	1 992	12 891	(B)	(B)
Non-Hispanic White, number with income	42 728	2 699	13 372	7 879	3 923	14 854	9 662	3 261	1 091	838
Median income (dollars)	43 266	27 179	35 217	40 938	43 213	63 951	56 763	72 054	(B)	92 035
Standard error (dollars)	299	293	184	241	711	745	350	1 082	27 655	2 512
Mean income (dollars)	59 375	32 411	41 625	48 795	50 375	88 245	76 800	96 970	143 056	114 859
Standard error (dollars)	407	762	454	590	668	971	1 044	2 422	4 510	4 285
Non-Hispanic Black, number with income	5 252	608	1 921	1 242	436	1 042	743	207	55	36
Median income (dollars)	32 169	23 802	26 983	33 137	39 224	47 235	44 771	52 840	(B)	(B)
Standard error (dollars)	260	1 039	328	755	1 686	875	1 328	3 427	(B)	(B)
Mean income (dollars)	39 088	27 733	30 604	38 264	45 754	59 540	52 672	71 697	(B)	(B)
Standard error (dollars)	672	1 085	530	1 091	3 450	2 336	2 188	7 835	(B)	(B)
Asian/Pacific Islander, number with income	2 651	206	514	346	165	1 418	840	353	91	133
Median income (dollars)	42 771	19 616	30 002	36 277	40 592	61 585	52 159	71 681	(B)	80 666
Standard error (dollars)	1 251	1 385	1 305	1 019	2 287	798	1 294	2 048	66 711	3 792
Mean income (dollars)	60 334	28 124	33 736	40 212	59 416	79 681	73 364	81 905	116 301	88 528
Standard error (dollars)	1 972	2 941	1 698	2 092	12 653	3 114	4 766	3 760	9 625	6 246

[1]May be of any race.
(B) = Base less than 75,000.

Table A-12. Income in 2001 by Educational Attainment for Population 18 Years and Over, by Age, Race, and Hispanic Origin, March 2002—*Continued*

(Numbers in thousand, except where noted.)

Income, standard error, age, race, and Hispanic origin	Total	High school		College						
		Not high school graduate	Graduate, includes GED	Some college, no degree	Associate degree	Bachelor's degree or more	Bachelor's degree	Master's degree	Professional degree	Doctorate degree
MALE										
All Workers, 25 Years and Over										
All races, number with income	84 388	13 230	25 953	14 340	6 351	24 512	15 722	5 522	1 779	1 488
Median income (dollars)	32 494	16 965	28 342	33 777	38 870	54 068	49 984	61 959	81 601	72 641
Standard error (dollars)	132	133	202	373	573	445	379	534	997	2 321
Mean income (dollars)	45 595	21 480	33 790	40 842	45 067	74 027	64 912	80 672	115 289	96 330
Standard error (dollars)	243	285	269	402	619	671	736	1 582	3 213	3 098
White, number with income	71 766	11 003	22 091	12 038	5 473	21 159	13 554	4 759	1 583	1 262
Median income (dollars)	34 020	17 423	29 543	35 195	39 790	55 393	50 791	62 492	81 697	74 361
Standard error (dollars)	198	153	213	253	491	312	250	719	1 368	2 412
Mean income (dollars)	47 146	22 078	35 043	42 369	45 506	75 959	66 663	82 588	117 696	98 415
Standard error (dollars)	270	330	307	456	556	736	797	1 778	3 521	3 314
Black, number with income	8 274	1 678	2 855	1 737	593	1 408	993	287	67	60
Median income (dollars)	25 243	13 489	22 316	28 395	33 949	43 099	41 197	48 772	(B)	(B)
Standard error (dollars)	273	521	422	890	1 606	1 332	646	2 002	(B)	(B)
Mean income (dollars)	30 673	17 530	25 599	31 968	40 009	51 084	45 082	61 969	(B)	(B)
Standard error (dollars)	445	500	436	874	2 656	1 605	1 197	5 947	(B)	(B)
Hispanic[1], number with income	9 360	4 074	2 560	1 205	470	1 049	754	173	75	46
Median income (dollars)	22 056	17 409	23 853	30 168	32 442	42 311	39 636	48 570	67 515	(B)
Standard error (dollars)	175	254	561	839	1 296	1 422	1 874	3 873	11 395	(B)
Mean income (dollars)	29 646	21 043	28 489	34 955	39 834	55 202	47 055	65 241	104 307	(B)
Standard error (dollars)	494	628	747	1 133	2 108	2 484	1 744	9 939	16 533	(B)
Non-Hispanic White, number with income	62 912	7 108	19 699	10 903	5 029	20 171	12 852	4 587	1 510	1 221
Median income (dollars)	36 146	17 420	30 233	35 696	40 273	55 914	51 208	62 899	82 004	75 220
Standard error (dollars)	122	202	143	244	311	316	254	768	1 887	2 392
Mean income (dollars)	49 581	22 588	35 847	43 096	45 951	76 916	67 681	83 242	118 240	99 238
Standard error (dollars)	299	385	332	490	576	762	834	1 810	3 610	3 410
Non-Hispanic Black, number with income	7 968	1 577	2 748	1 698	573	1 370	959	286	65	58
Median income (dollars)	25 432	13 212	22 277	28 708	34 467	43 297	41 240	48 592	(B)	(B)
Standard error (dollars)	277	531	413	886	1 638	1 388	681	2 000	(B)	(B)
Mean income (dollars)	30 910	17 511	25 611	32 120	40 457	51 466	45 423	61 884	(B)	(B)
Standard error (dollars)	460	522	447	890	2 740	1 642	1 224	5 977	(B)	(B)
Asian/Pacific Islander, number with income	3 505	342	692	415	227	1 827	1 092	453	126	155
Median income (dollars)	36 715	15 620	25 355	31 784	34 577	52 880	45 632	65 671	84 544	78 023
Standard error (dollars)	641	597	1 020	2 094	2 642	1 737	1 659	2 612	8 498	3 764
Mean income (dollars)	51 560	22 403	29 211	35 642	48 829	69 458	62 621	72 621	99 275	84 129
Standard error (dollars)	1 561	1 937	1 373	1 906	9 344	2 542	3 766	3 261	9 259	5 805
Year-Round, Full-Time Workers, 25 Years and Over										
All races, number with income	54 013	5 709	16 314	9 494	4 714	17 780	11 479	3 961	1 298	1 041
Median income (dollars)	41 616	24 364	34 723	41 045	42 776	62 222	55 929	70 898	(B)	86 965
Standard error (dollars)	104	329	298	214	561	279	335	687	19 318	3 013
Mean income (dollars)	56 612	29 350	40 651	48 748	50 531	85 823	74 952	93 701	137 686	111 031
Standard error (dollars)	348	517	392	521	763	866	948	2 097	3 932	3 904
White, number with income	46 040	4 828	13 840	7 996	4 097	15 277	9 881	3 383	1 148	864
Median income (dollars)	42 322	24 510	35 729	41 886	43 565	64 223	57 012	71 675	(B)	91 554
Standard error (dollars)	114	363	176	234	708	730	341	807	22 888	3 176
Mean income (dollars)	58 227	29 540	42 109	50 250	50 530	88 136	76 856	96 322	141 461	114 216
Standard error (dollars)	386	587	451	590	648	953	1 024	2 382	4 351	4 174
Black, number with income	5 000	602	1 789	1 139	431	1 036	733	208	56	37
Median income (dollars)	33 326	23 914	28 174	34 739	39 771	47 405	45 045	54 439	(B)	(B)
Standard error (dollars)	585	1 034	773	752	1 523	940	1 225	3 536	(B)	(B)
Mean income (dollars)	39 730	27 842	31 411	39 764	46 129	58 297	50 802	71 744	(B)	(B)
Standard error (dollars)	651	1 075	541	1 170	3 490	2 014	1 393	7 780	(B)	(B)
Hispanic[1], number with income	6 472	2 568	1 871	861	378	792	569	129	63	29
Median income (dollars)	26 752	21 097	27 158	34 723	35 589	49 695	45 509	61 704	(B)	(B)
Standard error (dollars)	240	207	463	1 159	1 439	1 833	1 616	7 032	(B)	(B)
Mean income (dollars)	35 064	25 230	32 328	41 605	41 378	63 273	54 005	77 069	(B)	(B)
Standard error (dollars)	622	819	952	1 438	1 603	2 929	2 054	12 891	(B)	(B)
Non-Hispanic White, number with income	39 908	2 365	12 101	7 186	3 735	14 519	9 339	3 254	1 086	838
Median income (dollars)	45 756	28 813	36 646	42 431	44 522	65 308	57 656	72 151	(B)	92 035
Standard error (dollars)	165	535	185	403	659	480	655	1 120	27 453	2 512
Mean income (dollars)	61 759	33 884	43 532	51 164	51 378	89 408	78 176	97 081	143 317	114 859
Standard error (dollars)	432	853	496	636	693	990	1 076	2 427	4 526	4 285
Non-Hispanic Black, number with income	4 793	541	1 708	1 110	418	1 013	713	207	55	36
Median income (dollars)	33 766	25 040	28 339	34 936	40 207	47 297	44 956	52 840	(B)	(B)
Standard error (dollars)	581	840	795	753	1 402	886	1 251	3 427	(B)	(B)
Mean income (dollars)	40 164	28 645	31 511	40 012	46 597	58 429	50 810	71 697	(B)	(B)
Standard error (dollars)	675	1 172	557	1 194	3 589	2 058	1 425	7 835	(B)	(B)
Asian/Pacific Islander, number with income	2 484	189	476	283	149	1 385	807	353	91	133
Median income (dollars)	45 782	20 236	30 719	40 134	41 578	62 160	52 796	71 681	(B)	80 866
Standard error (dollars)	857	1 584	752	1 819	1 312	1 141	1 763	2 048	66 711	3 792
Mean income (dollars)	62 760	29 344	34 763	44 235	62 970	80 726	74 895	81 905	116 301	88 528
Standard error (dollars)	2 090	3 181	1 815	2 436	13 931	3 181	4 951	3 760	9 625	6 246

[1]May be of any race.
(B) = Base less than 75,000.

Table A-12. Income in 2001 by Educational Attainment for Population 18 Years and Over, by Age, Race, and Hispanic Origin, March 2002—*Continued*

(Numbers in thousand, except where noted.)

Income, standard error, age, race, and Hispanic origin	Total	High school		College						
		Not high school graduate	Graduate, includes GED	Some college, no degree	Associate degree	Bachelor's degree or more	Bachelor's degree	Master's degree	Professional degree	Doctorate degree
MALE										
All Workers, 25 to 64 Years										
All races, number with income	70 448	9 074	21 748	12 388	5 820	21 416	13 935	4 828	1 486	1 167
Median income (dollars)	36 050	19 308	30 411	35 982	40 310	56 770	51 395	65 531	90 724	77 173
Standard error (dollars)	109	240	127	224	267	304	225	777	2 684	2 236
Mean income (dollars)	48 634	23 223	34 984	42 584	46 129	77 441	67 460	85 190	126 211	102 454
Standard error (dollars)	277	371	276	448	662	742	799	1 777	3 677	3 652
White, number with income	59 306	7 492	18 249	10 253	5 009	18 301	11 896	4 123	1 307	973
Median income (dollars)	37 070	20 003	31 289	37 103	40 781	58 355	52 337	66 333	90 863	79 977
Standard error (dollars)	117	214	137	244	292	681	304	801	3 008	2 536
Mean income (dollars)	50 516	23 898	36 468	44 483	46 592	79 873	69 637	87 683	129 644	105 030
Standard error (dollars)	310	430	317	515	589	824	877	2 015	4 070	3 915
Black, number with income	7 201	1 149	2 585	1 628	551	1 288	935	249	58	44
Median income (dollars)	26 772	15 887	23 195	29 601	34 851	44 743	41 492	50 548	(B)	(B)
Standard error (dollars)	269	635	716	817	1 792	1 438	636	2 009	(B)	(B)
Mean income (dollars)	32 269	19 061	26 066	32 715	40 534	52 397	45 969	64 471	(B)	(B)
Standard error (dollars)	496	667	464	920	2 828	1 710	1 242	6 678	(B)	(B)
Hispanic[1], number with income	8 599	3 603	2 403	1 147	452	991	716	161	73	40
Median income (dollars)	22 883	18 456	24 495	30 674	33 015	43 207	40 315	50 532	(B)	(B)
Standard error (dollars)	340	310	558	527	1 410	1 660	1 713	5 943	(B)	(B)
Mean income (dollars)	30 663	21 906	28 964	35 748	40 300	56 325	47 779	67 189	(B)	(B)
Standard error (dollars)	531	703	784	1 177	2 177	2 612	1 813	10 636	(B)	(B)
Non-Hispanic White, number with income	51 178	4 052	16 007	9 171	4 581	17 366	11 229	3 964	1 235	936
Median income (dollars)	40 196	21 252	31 989	37 971	41 210	59 690	53 204	66 722	91 667	80 632
Standard error (dollars)	120	275	145	461	299	593	580	804	3 029	2 713
Mean income (dollars)	53 634	25 480	37 529	45 468	47 126	81 078	70 876	88 512	130 924	106 180
Standard error (dollars)	347	541	343	559	612	856	922	2 055	4 201	4 045
Non-Hispanic Black, number with income	6 921	1 058	2 483	1 592	532	1 254	904	247	57	44
Median income (dollars)	27 038	15 646	23 116	29 885	35 234	44 847	41 526	50 421	(B)	(B)
Standard error (dollars)	282	785	706	755	1 709	1 390	662	2 046	(B)	(B)
Mean income (dollars)	32 556	19 091	26 089	32 853	40 970	52 767	46 300	64 388	(B)	(B)
Standard error (dollars)	513	709	476	937	2 916	1 749	1 269	6 717	(B)	(B)
Asian/Pacific Islander, number with income	3 181	263	615	379	204	1 718	1 025	434	117	140
Median income (dollars)	39 645	16 414	26 492	32 353	35 914	55 331	47 216	66 958	91 464	78 077
Standard error (dollars)	1 183	662	777	2 137	2 557	2 066	2 162	2 906	7 524	3 618
Mean income (dollars)	53 635	23 360	30 696	36 776	51 171	70 506	63 351	73 710	103 888	84 803
Standard error (dollars)	1 631	2 380	1 499	2 034	10 359	2 531	3 703	3 356	9 656	6 210
Year-Round, Full-Time Workers, 25 to 64 Years										
All races, number with income	52 616	5 471	15 908	9 275	4 647	17 313	11 236	3 858	1 242	975
Median income (dollars)	41 536	24 059	34 396	40 943	42 679	62 094	55 932	70 946	(B)	85 065
Standard error (dollars)	104	342	308	214	534	282	336	681	19 061	2 555
Mean income (dollars)	56 181	29 127	39 909	48 446	50 443	85 367	74 593	93 827	137 753	109 276
Standard error (dollars)	347	536	350	524	771	872	942	2 143	4 070	4 012
White, number with income	44 806	4 636	13 480	7 795	4 038	14 855	9 659	3 294	1 096	805
Median income (dollars)	42 224	24 204	35 544	41 773	43 445	63 797	57 005	71 610	(B)	87 568
Standard error (dollars)	114	377	180	235	703	750	341	801	21 309	3 276
Mean income (dollars)	57 741	29 286	41 266	49 908	50 392	87 682	76 584	96 412	141 352	111 995
Standard error (dollars)	385	606	400	594	654	964	1 025	2 434	4 515	4 274
Black, number with income	4 894	570	1 756	1 128	425	1 013	723	203	52	34
Median income (dollars)	33 310	23 531	28 062	34 763	40 015	47 438	45 082	55 224	(B)	(B)
Standard error (dollars)	592	1 090	741	747	1 446	951	1 194	3 727	(B)	(B)
Mean income (dollars)	39 776	27 703	31 305	39 787	46 389	58 456	50 862	72 221	(B)	(B)
Standard error (dollars)	662	1 110	546	1 178	3 533	2 055	1 407	7 948	(B)	(B)
Hispanic[1], number with income	6 388	2 522	1 857	856	377	775	556	128	63	27
Median income (dollars)	26 659	21 000	27 092	34 520	35 500	49 886	45 611	61 455	(B)	(B)
Standard error (dollars)	242	209	418	1 188	1 438	1 822	1 657	8 039	(B)	(B)
Mean income (dollars)	34 961	25 055	32 216	41 521	41 355	63 418	54 129	76 822	(B)	(B)
Standard error (dollars)	629	831	957	1 445	1 609	2 989	2 098	13 010	(B)	(B)
Non-Hispanic White, number with income	38 754	2 217	11 755	6 991	3 677	14 112	9 128	3 167	1 035	781
Median income (dollars)	45 650	28 592	36 485	42 328	44 413	65 052	57 616	72 097	(B)	89 532
Standard error (dollars)	166	540	189	314	673	578	641	1 086	26 005	3 219
Mean income (dollars)	61 271	33 756	42 613	50 812	51 238	88 934	77 882	97 198	143 293	112 564
Standard error (dollars)	431	900	436	641	700	1 002	1 077	2 482	4 708	4 388
Non-Hispanic Black, number with income	4 690	510	1 676	1 099	412	991	704	202	50	34
Median income (dollars)	33 764	24 831	28 228	34 961	40 332	47 323	44 984	52 479	(B)	(B)
Standard error (dollars)	588	954	777	748	1 311	897	1 237	3 618	(B)	(B)
Mean income (dollars)	40 222	28 536	31 401	40 038	46 872	58 581	50 858	72 176	(B)	(B)
Standard error (dollars)	687	1 214	562	1 203	3 635	2 097	1 438	8 005	(B)	(B)
Asian/Pacific Islander, number with income	2 420	178	468	281	147	1 364	797	344	91	130
Median income (dollars)	45 827	20 435	30 803	40 012	41 411	62 331	52 849	72 069	(B)	81 242
Standard error (dollars)	845	1 578	758	1 866	1 130	1 317	1 766	2 231	66 711	3 820
Mean income (dollars)	62 449	29 565	34 850	44 176	63 267	79 893	73 288	82 124	116 301	88 866
Standard error (dollars)	2 031	3 345	1 842	2 458	14 136	3 032	4 636	3 830	9 625	6 356

[1]May be of any race.
(B) = Base less than 75,000.

Table A-12. Income in 2001 by Educational Attainment for Population 18 Years and Over, by Age, Race, and Hispanic Origin, March 2002—*Continued*

(Numbers in thousand, except where noted.)

Income, standard error, age, race, and Hispanic origin	Total	High school		College						
		Not high school graduate	Graduate, includes GED	Some college, no degree	Associate degree	Bachelor's degree or more	Bachelor's degree	Master's degree	Professional degree	Doctorate degree
MALE										
All Workers, 25 to 34 Years										
All races, number with income	18 532	2 634	5 502	3 499	1 507	5 388	4 159	863	225	140
Median income (dollars)	30 510	18 461	25 927	30 393	35 160	44 802	41 975	52 397	51 345	46 139
Standard error (dollars)	136	357	246	277	630	704	414	1 678	3 960	3 079
Mean income (dollars)	36 887	21 743	28 886	34 169	39 483	53 502	50 541	62 560	70 051	58 964
Standard error (dollars)	334	757	416	580	855	837	957	1 815	4 579	6 316
White, number with income	15 256	2 279	4 547	2 783	1 287	4 357	3 380	681	176	119
Median income (dollars)	30 922	18 599	26 511	31 110	35 740	45 340	42 831	51 796	51 377	46 856
Standard error (dollars)	148	387	286	307	608	554	805	883	4 492	3 531
Mean income (dollars)	37 545	21 927	29 823	35 569	40 468	54 173	51 611	62 541	66 180	61 256
Standard error (dollars)	370	840	486	664	967	914	1 038	2 136	4 099	7 339
Black, number with income	2 026	239	701	544	140	400	355	30	9	5
Median income (dollars)	25 593	17 092	21 565	26 492	29 913	36 154	34 580	(B)	(B)	(B)
Standard error (dollars)	405	1 210	609	975	1 513	2 297	2 057	(B)	(B)	(B)
Mean income (dollars)	28 788	18 214	23 174	29 581	32 035	42 742	40 666	(B)	(B)	(B)
Standard error (dollars)	665	1 054	714	1 529	1 801	1 871	1 849	(B)	(B)	(B)
Hispanic[1], number with income	3 547	1 477	1 061	507	173	327	257	49	16	4
Median income (dollars)	21 583	17 642	22 557	27 521	29 385	34 877	33 003	(B)	(B)	(B)
Standard error (dollars)	259	411	648	1 425	1 646	1 846	1 901	(B)	(B)	(B)
Mean income (dollars)	26 908	21 523	25 972	32 549	36 886	40 207	37 966	(B)	(B)	(B)
Standard error (dollars)	696	1 315	674	1 523	4 590	1 908	1 929	(B)	(B)	(B)
Non-Hispanic White, number with income	11 893	858	3 551	2 306	1 123	4 054	3 147	632	159	114
Median income (dollars)	33 322	20 554	27 516	31 517	36 736	46 010	43 909	52 238	52 023	44 961
Standard error (dollars)	390	433	425	335	627	530	964	1 454	3 345	3 703
Mean income (dollars)	40 513	22 501	30 903	36 122	40 956	55 116	52 506	63 942	66 465	62 190
Standard error (dollars)	429	717	593	739	890	970	1 104	2 263	4 242	7 595
Non-Hispanic Black, number with income	1 916	206	663	527	133	386	341	30	9	5
Median income (dollars)	25 815	16 109	21 495	26 469	30 318	36 398	34 942	(B)	(B)	(B)
Standard error (dollars)	425	2 037	616	971	1 460	2 303	2 109	(B)	(B)	(B)
Mean income (dollars)	29 036	17 982	23 144	29 540	32 129	43 294	41 222	(B)	(B)	(B)
Standard error (dollars)	693	1 179	733	1 567	1 817	1 911	1 890	(B)	(B)	(B)
Asian/Pacific Islander, number with income	1 031	69	164	128	64	604	402	148	39	13
Median income (dollars)	36 006	(B)	26 332	27 225	(B)	47 392	42 155	63 593	(B)	(B)
Standard error (dollars)	765	(B)	1 103	2 590	(B)	2 083	2 247	4 710	(B)	(B)
Mean income (dollars)	45 401	(B)	27 949	27 523	(B)	56 800	51 440	65 626	(B)	(B)
Standard error (dollars)	2 211	(B)	1 818	1 879	(B)	3 502	4 660	3 927	(B)	(B)
Year-Round, Full-Time Workers, 25 to 34 Years										
All races, number with income	14 030	1 793	4 105	2 593	1 227	4 309	3 334	698	177	99
Median income (dollars)	34 520	21 333	29 752	34 205	37 206	49 467	46 738	57 554	65 605	49 350
Standard error (dollars)	380	235	399	743	650	713	476	1 967	7 848	2 283
Mean income (dollars)	41 730	25 348	32 643	39 001	41 916	58 794	55 987	67 777	77 667	56 167
Standard error (dollars)	390	842	516	600	789	962	1 134	2 018	4 394	3 532
White, number with income	11 698	1 578	3 395	2 107	1 057	3 559	2 761	573	143	81
Median income (dollars)	34 927	21 190	30 323	35 015	37 752	49 637	47 126	55 712	61 750	49 852
Standard error (dollars)	309	247	231	562	833	714	627	1 700	9 786	5 581
Mean income (dollars)	42 026	25 010	33 369	39 768	42 569	59 008	56 539	67 091	74 732	58 107
Standard error (dollars)	425	899	607	655	881	1 035	1 207	2 348	4 608	4 150
Black, number with income	1 443	139	507	370	116	309	272	23	9	4
Median income (dollars)	30 101	22 045	26 098	31 307	30 997	41 344	40 820	(B)	(B)	(B)
Standard error (dollars)	541	1 195	518	699	1 179	992	1 615	(B)	(B)	(B)
Mean income (dollars)	34 715	25 342	28 263	36 473	34 553	47 467	45 304	(B)	(B)	(B)
Standard error (dollars)	813	1 318	800	2 002	1 796	2 205	2 188	(B)	(B)	(B)
Hispanic[1], number with income	2 647	1 064	826	369	142	244	189	35	16	3
Median income (dollars)	24 672	20 023	25 505	31 778	30 838	40 614	38 537	(B)	(B)	(B)
Standard error (dollars)	469	382	626	711	1 220	2 445	2 357	(B)	(B)	(B)
Mean income (dollars)	29 930	23 750	28 393	37 996	34 419	47 178	45 190	(B)	(B)	(B)
Standard error (dollars)	691	1 330	692	1 854	1 841	2 169	2 178	(B)	(B)	(B)
Non-Hispanic White, number with income	9 191	557	2 627	1 762	920	3 323	2 580	538	127	78
Median income (dollars)	37 192	25 192	31 153	35 384	39 159	50 215	47 817	56 033	64 202	49 500
Standard error (dollars)	209	747	254	416	930	418	873	1 435	8 235	7 606
Mean income (dollars)	45 300	27 144	34 824	40 010	43 777	59 853	57 346	68 238	76 165	58 282
Standard error (dollars)	502	935	757	696	971	1 097	1 281	2 471	4 801	4 312
Non-Hispanic Black, number with income	1 363	114	476	357	110	304	267	23	9	4
Median income (dollars)	30 286	23 979	26 077	31 191	31 300	41 099	40 548	(B)	(B)	(B)
Standard error (dollars)	461	1 943	551	687	1 114	991	2 126	(B)	(B)	(B)
Mean income (dollars)	35 026	26 452	28 302	36 425	34 518	47 308	45 095	(B)	(B)	(B)
Standard error (dollars)	849	1 482	822	2 061	1 804	2 242	2 227	(B)	(B)	(B)
Asian/Pacific Islander, number with income	743	50	141	87	42	421	284	99	24	12
Median income (dollars)	41 573	(B)	29 163	35 516	(B)	56 868	50 972	69 496	(B)	(B)
Standard error (dollars)	832	(B)	2 145	2 205	(B)	3 607	1 195	2 225	(B)	(B)
Mean income (dollars)	52 590	(B)	30 844	35 372	(B)	66 443	62 158	75 513	(B)	(B)
Standard error (dollars)	2 764	(B)	1 924	1 896	(B)	4 492	6 318	3 944	(B)	(B)

[1]May be of any race.
(B) = Base less than 75,000.

Table A-12. Income in 2001 by Educational Attainment for Population 18 Years and Over, by Age, Race, and Hispanic Origin, March 2002—*Continued*

(Numbers in thousand, except where noted.)

| Income, standard error, age, race, and Hispanic origin | Total | High school | | College | | | | | | |
		Not high school graduate	Graduate, includes GED	Some college, no degree	Associate degree	Bachelor's degree or more	Bachelor's degree	Master's degree	Professional degree	Doctorate degree
MALE										
All Workers, 35 to 44 Years										
All races, number with income	21 165	2 559	6 948	3 590	1 859	6 208	4 117	1 343	432	314
Median income (dollars)	38 339	20 628	31 358	38 459	41 358	64 267	58 241	71 051	95 525	82 465
Standard error (dollars)	378	258	205	753	398	1 019	1 140	1 543	9 150	3 077
Mean income (dollars)	51 886	24 447	36 480	45 296	47 554	85 548	76 473	92 197	134 928	107 987
Standard error (dollars)	560	801	460	825	1 376	1 589	1 699	4 000	7 502	8 407
White, number with income	17 683	2 156	5 804	2 917	1 567	5 237	3 547	1 079	382	228
Median income (dollars)	40 088	21 182	32 134	40 565	41 717	66 052	60 501	73 968	97 306	85 717
Standard error (dollars)	260	267	223	438	493	624	707	2 250	14 906	4 781
Mean income (dollars)	53 760	25 585	38 003	47 713	46 369	88 402	78 925	96 562	139 679	111 219
Standard error (dollars)	623	936	528	960	885	1 772	1 867	4 748	8 328	8 811
Black, number with income	2 285	290	872	520	205	395	268	92	18	16
Median income (dollars)	29 405	16 340	25 377	31 404	40 411	47 606	45 197	51 258	(B)	(B)
Standard error (dollars)	941	1 199	649	837	1 203	1 594	1 513	3 010	(B)	(B)
Mean income (dollars)	34 694	17 548	27 293	34 263	45 343	58 630	49 340	77 078	(B)	(B)
Standard error (dollars)	1 064	992	814	1 668	4 474	4 504	2 421	16 962	(B)	(B)
Hispanic[1], number with income	2 681	1 115	717	359	153	335	248	48	23	14
Median income (dollars)	25 333	20 155	25 758	32 005	36 505	48 311	46 604	(B)	(B)	(B)
Standard error (dollars)	438	445	714	968	2 393	2 135	1 814	(B)	(B)	(B)
Mean income (dollars)	33 693	23 325	31 293	38 847	41 275	64 350	51 232	(B)	(B)	(B)
Standard error (dollars)	1 229	1 352	2 198	2 716	2 370	6 234	2 770	(B)	(B)	(B)
Non-Hispanic White, number with income	15 138	1 091	5 132	2 574	1 421	4 918	3 313	1 032	359	213
Median income (dollars)	41 969	22 172	33 310	41 487	42 044	66 930	61 339	74 860	97 161	86 935
Standard error (dollars)	207	470	641	453	532	662	667	2 047	14 249	4 800
Mean income (dollars)	57 108	27 543	38 945	48 847	46 881	89 900	80 849	96 589	139 668	114 122
Standard error (dollars)	694	1 325	525	1 026	946	1 843	1 984	4 742	8 511	9 307
Non-Hispanic Black, number with income	2 206	264	842	513	202	384	258	91	17	16
Median income (dollars)	29 971	16 617	25 378	31 570	40 490	47 515	45 288	51 105	(B)	(B)
Standard error (dollars)	773	1 297	694	830	1 181	1 668	1 461	1 483	(B)	(B)
Mean income (dollars)	35 003	17 520	27 354	34 406	45 472	59 111	49 788	77 034	(B)	(B)
Standard error (dollars)	1 097	1 011	833	1 690	4 549	4 632	2 480	17 198	(B)	(B)
Asian/Pacific Islander, number with income	966	61	176	117	70	540	271	168	31	67
Median income (dollars)	43 746	(B)	28 204	31 486	(B)	64 740	57 131	71 346	(B)	(B)
Standard error (dollars)	2 085	(B)	2 601	3 543	(B)	2 184	3 005	3 397	(B)	(B)
Mean income (dollars)	60 131	(B)	32 016	36 232	(B)	76 322	73 894	73 228	(B)	(B)
Standard error (dollars)	3 454	(B)	1 961	2 646	(B)	4 514	8 268	3 589	(B)	(B)
Year-Round, Full-Time Workers, 35 to 44 Years										
All races, number with income	16 992	1 659	5 464	2 889	1 612	5 365	3 546	1 164	379	274
Median income (dollars)	42 403	24 863	35 005	42 163	42 894	67 289	61 333	75 674	(B)	89 181
Standard error (dollars)	263	505	402	424	940	765	590	1 171	44 575	4 252
Mean income (dollars)	58 203	30 186	40 706	50 188	50 467	91 334	81 266	99 027	143 085	117 146
Standard error (dollars)	670	1 181	546	945	1 539	1 787	1 921	4 542	7 863	9 398
White, number with income	14 400	1 445	4 647	2 382	1 373	4 552	3 082	941	331	197
Median income (dollars)	44 012	25 444	35 777	44 700	43 568	69 384	62 325	77 000	(B)	91 703
Standard error (dollars)	601	373	300	928	1 163	1 022	1 047	1 480	51 687	4 482
Mean income (dollars)	59 588	31 001	41 902	52 229	48 699	93 849	83 293	103 307	149 104	120 690
Standard error (dollars)	735	1 344	620	1 087	932	1 981	2 093	5 369	8 785	9 844
Black, number with income	1 637	144	600	398	168	325	221	73	18	11
Median income (dollars)	35 381	22 022	30 132	34 844	41 482	50 084	46 213	(B)	(B)	(B)
Standard error (dollars)	692	1 150	1 126	1 312	957	1 228	1 120	(B)	(B)	(B)
Mean income (dollars)	41 588	24 762	32 657	39 427	49 591	64 051	52 596	(B)	(B)	(B)
Standard error (dollars)	1 393	1 326	993	2 007	5 272	5 326	2 571	(B)	(B)	(B)
Hispanic[1], number with income	2 091	816	577	283	140	273	205	41	19	7
Median income (dollars)	28 039	22 060	27 407	35 391	37 091	50 882	48 012	(B)	(B)	(B)
Standard error (dollars)	763	389	1 047	1 553	2 439	1 663	2 319	(B)	(B)	(B)
Mean income (dollars)	37 438	26 758	34 080	43 892	42 507	67 105	53 508	(B)	(B)	(B)
Standard error (dollars)	1 468	1 795	2 672	3 275	2 421	6 752	2 944	(B)	(B)	(B)
Non-Hispanic White, number with income	12 398	653	4 105	2 111	1 239	4 288	2 884	901	313	190
Median income (dollars)	47 046	29 417	36 603	45 788	44 392	70 552	64 270	77 276	(B)	91 758
Standard error (dollars)	309	1 064	294	507	1 098	725	1 463	1 798	53 313	4 415
Mean income (dollars)	63 160	35 880	43 027	53 246	49 338	95 465	85 330	103 158	150 758	121 666
Standard error (dollars)	817	2 090	608	1 154	999	2 061	2 222	5 355	9 194	10 172
Non-Hispanic Black, number with income	1 581	129	577	390	165	317	216	71	17	11
Median income (dollars)	35 635	23 110	30 232	35 143	41 647	50 044	46 290	(B)	(B)	(B)
Standard error (dollars)	620	1 075	1 039	1 318	1 823	1 276	1 106	(B)	(B)	(B)
Mean income (dollars)	42 064	25 773	32 818	39 716	49 871	64 384	52 799	(B)	(B)	(B)
Standard error (dollars)	1 436	1 425	1 016	2 039	5 353	5 457	2 625	(B)	(B)	(B)
Asian/Pacific Islander, number with income	800	43	147	80	50	459	217	148	29	63
Median income (dollars)	51 310	(B)	31 240	39 790	(B)	71 064	64 146	72 206	(B)	(B)
Standard error (dollars)	1 808	(B)	1 168	2 647	(B)	2 418	2 405	2 038	(B)	(B)
Mean income (dollars)	67 482	(B)	34 988	42 488	(B)	83 796	84 397	77 320	(B)	(B)
Standard error (dollars)	4 073	(B)	2 155	2 847	(B)	5 163	10 113	3 672	(B)	(B)

[1]May be of any race.
(B) = Base less than 75,000.

Table A-12. Income in 2001 by Educational Attainment for Population 18 Years and Over, by Age, Race, and Hispanic Origin, March 2002—*Continued*

(Numbers in thousand, except where noted.)

Income, standard error, age, race, and Hispanic origin	Total	High school		College						
		Not high school graduate	Graduate, includes GED	Some college, no degree	Associate degree	Bachelor's degree or more	Bachelor's degree	Master's degree	Professional degree	Doctorate degree
MALE										
All Workers, 45 to 54 Years										
All races, number with income	18 768	1 983	5 680	3 419	1 651	6 032	3 582	1 525	515	409
Median income (dollars)	41 104	19 757	33 394	40 784	43 380	63 358	55 035	69 931	(B)	86 387
Standard error (dollars)	201	542	508	434	1 071	1 205	852	1 413	39 115	4 426
Mean income (dollars)	55 176	23 936	38 404	46 444	48 538	88 009	75 819	89 933	140 068	121 948
Standard error (dollars)	590	733	635	746	1 119	1 524	1 820	2 919	6 347	7 120
White, number with income	15 898	1 547	4 753	2 891	1 425	5 281	3 108	1 346	465	359
Median income (dollars)	42 627	20 525	35 528	42 018	44 920	65 714	56 961	70 846	(B)	87 970
Standard error (dollars)	367	491	315	504	996	755	1 014	1 159	32 371	5 143
Mean income (dollars)	57 832	25 181	40 503	48 168	49 601	90 511	78 363	92 019	140 975	124 500
Standard error (dollars)	662	903	739	831	1 012	1 665	1 975	3 199	6 929	7 884
Black, number with income	1 885	317	667	393	154	352	225	96	22	8
Median income (dollars)	27 824	15 937	22 874	30 996	35 574	48 229	44 338	48 947	(B)	(B)
Standard error (dollars)	1 120	1 593	1 307	1 597	2 722	1 778	2 895	4 517	(B)	(B)
Mean income (dollars)	34 108	18 882	26 684	34 366	44 289	57 136	50 369	59 740	(B)	(B)
Standard error (dollars)	1 040	1 082	975	2 072	7 835	2 432	2 623	4 219	(B)	(B)
Hispanic[1], number with income	1 525	599	423	188	82	232	144	46	23	18
Median income (dollars)	24 845	19 105	26 124	34 682	32 247	55 567	42 617	(B)	(B)	(B)
Standard error (dollars)	771	692	1 242	4 250	4 055	4 290	2 945	(B)	(B)	(B)
Mean income (dollars)	33 901	21 554	31 978	39 237	37 608	63 635	53 526	(B)	(B)	(B)
Standard error (dollars)	993	778	1 480	2 127	3 266	4 344	4 569	(B)	(B)	(B)
Non-Hispanic White, number with income	14 472	982	4 365	2 717	1 350	5 056	2 969	1 299	442	344
Median income (dollars)	44 898	22 261	35 981	42 217	45 296	66 152	57 515	70 960	(B)	90 601
Standard error (dollars)	379	955	332	631	931	764	1 482	1 343	40 896	4 736
Mean income (dollars)	60 133	27 184	41 214	48 715	50 183	91 662	79 498	92 707	143 335	126 146
Standard error (dollars)	717	1 348	793	872	1 050	1 726	2 054	3 304	7 158	8 198
Non-Hispanic Black, number with income	1 827	297	645	386	147	350	222	96	22	8
Median income (dollars)	28 671	15 850	23 166	31 245	35 906	48 256	44 431	48 947	(B)	(B)
Standard error (dollars)	1 316	2 049	1 398	1 400	3 200	1 776	2 941	4 517	(B)	(B)
Mean income (dollars)	34 454	18 994	26 745	34 556	45 277	57 151	50 310	59 740	(B)	(B)
Standard error (dollars)	1 068	1 134	1 000	2 100	8 146	2 450	2 651	4 219	(B)	(B)
Asian/Pacific Islander, number with income	784	76	178	99	56	373	233	75	25	38
Median income (dollars)	40 148	15 541	27 052	46 172	(B)	53 785	43 168	70 189	(B)	(B)
Standard error (dollars)	1 976	1 427	1 972	2 786	(B)	2 967	2 215	8 929	(B)	(B)
Mean income (dollars)	56 584	20 881	31 086	44 938	(B)	82 569	68 272	90 348	(B)	(B)
Standard error (dollars)	3 576	2 404	1 914	2 676	(B)	7 029	9 444	14 024	(B)	(B)
Year-Round, Full-Time Workers, 45 to 54 Years										
All races, number with income	14 616	1 180	4 338	2 643	1 304	5 149	3 020	1 313	457	357
Median income (dollars)	46 657	25 553	37 288	46 175	48 263	69 235	60 423	72 786	(B)	91 702
Standard error (dollars)	247	443	349	462	1 235	1 278	801	1 752	43 161	4 016
Mean income (dollars)	63 135	30 779	43 458	53 090	53 962	94 612	82 904	94 764	147 571	125 142
Standard error (dollars)	711	1 134	791	863	1 290	1 694	2 069	3 202	6 857	7 367
White, number with income	12 577	937	3 693	2 290	1 143	4 511	2 635	1 152	412	311
Median income (dollars)	48 341	25 907	39 459	47 022	49 098	70 975	61 797	74 548	(B)	93 398
Standard error (dollars)	553	448	666	468	1 298	731	656	1 865	46 820	8 051
Mean income (dollars)	65 326	31 748	45 352	54 337	54 306	97 027	85 415	96 766	148 578	128 000
Standard error (dollars)	786	1 388	910	944	1 105	1 845	2 228	3 526	7 517	8 205
Black, number with income	1 286	166	463	251	112	292	176	89	19	6
Median income (dollars)	35 446	23 452	28 529	36 382	43 102	50 358	47 712	50 460	(B)	(B)
Standard error (dollars)	743	1 734	1 247	1 370	3 589	3 306	2 410	5 134	(B)	(B)
Mean income (dollars)	42 434	26 926	31 528	43 345	55 201	62 881	56 464	62 774	(B)	(B)
Standard error (dollars)	1 384	1 603	1 169	2 815	10 442	2 629	2 871	4 264	(B)	(B)
Hispanic[1], number with income	1 152	420	330	146	61	193	117	41	19	15
Median income (dollars)	30 300	21 479	30 858	42 760	(B)	60 648	48 936	(B)	(B)	(B)
Standard error (dollars)	944	522	2 553	3 074	(B)	4 300	5 846	(B)	(B)	(B)
Mean income (dollars)	39 287	25 076	36 077	44 344	(B)	70 832	59 857	(B)	(B)	(B)
Standard error (dollars)	1 219	976	1 741	2 400	(B)	4 874	5 134	(B)	(B)	(B)
Non-Hispanic White, number with income	11 498	545	3 389	2 152	1 085	4 324	2 520	1 111	393	299
Median income (dollars)	50 287	29 004	40 195	47 179	49 920	71 421	62 166	75 083	(B)	94 433
Standard error (dollars)	224	1 204	412	557	1 052	788	986	1 875	47 175	15 642
Mean income (dollars)	67 705	36 356	46 131	54 791	54 890	98 125	86 565	97 440	150 351	129 419
Standard error (dollars)	849	2 260	978	992	1 144	1 912	2 315	3 647	7 759	8 501
Non-Hispanic Black, number with income	1 244	153	444	247	109	289	173	89	19	6
Median income (dollars)	35 754	24 317	28 915	36 511	43 442	50 373	47 728	50 460	(B)	(B)
Standard error (dollars)	676	2 132	1 238	1 387	3 693	3 300	2 393	5 134	(B)	(B)
Mean income (dollars)	42 966	27 556	31 706	43 570	55 997	62 937	56 465	62 774	(B)	(B)
Standard error (dollars)	1 424	1 699	1 206	2 851	10 707	2 650	2 908	4 264	(B)	(B)
Asian/Pacific Islander, number with income	632	52	131	80	37	330	202	65	24	38
Median income (dollars)	44 831	(B)	32 014	48 143	(B)	59 685	44 835	(B)	(B)	(B)
Standard error (dollars)	1 905	(B)	2 846	2 723	(B)	4 765	3 294	(B)	(B)	(B)
Mean income (dollars)	64 829	(B)	35 720	49 069	(B)	89 230	73 598	(B)	(B)	(B)
Standard error (dollars)	4 300	(B)	2 281	2 778	(B)	7 776	10 781	(B)	(B)	(B)

[1]May be of any race.
(B) = Base less than 75,000.

Table A-12. Income in 2001 by Educational Attainment for Population 18 Years and Over, by Age, Race, and Hispanic Origin, March 2002—*Continued*

(Numbers in thousand, except where noted.)

Income, standard error, age, race, and Hispanic origin	Total	High school		College						
		Not high school graduate	Graduate, includes GED	Some college, no degree	Associate degree	Bachelor's degree or more	Bachelor's degree	Master's degree	Professional degree	Doctorate degree
MALE										
All Workers, 55 to 64 Years										
All races, number with income	11 981	1 896	3 616	1 879	801	3 787	2 076	1 095	312	302
Median income (dollars)	35 637	17 777	30 409	35 833	38 564	60 767	53 221	62 910	92 013	78 739
Standard error (dollars)	352	551	340	958	1 300	881	1 235	1 731	6 531	5 330
Mean income (dollars)	50 810	22 882	36 018	46 052	50 353	81 377	69 056	87 837	131 728	90 446
Standard error (dollars)	723	536	740	1 763	2 205	1 780	1 831	4 258	8 143	3 754
White, number with income	10 467	1 508	3 143	1 660	728	3 425	1 859	1 015	283	266
Median income (dollars)	36 903	18 793	31 115	36 575	39 537	61 784	54 474	63 709	96 596	85 451
Standard error (dollars)	363	647	357	957	1 349	964	1 272	1 839	12 785	7 435
Mean income (dollars)	52 828	23 150	37 148	47 338	52 004	83 127	70 102	89 366	136 898	93 082
Standard error (dollars)	803	550	807	1 954	2 397	1 921	1 942	4 554	8 799	4 066
Black, number with income	1 003	300	342	170	50	139	86	29	8	14
Median income (dollars)	23 843	14 149	22 381	32 764	(B)	43 067	41 973	(B)	(B)	(B)
Standard error (dollars)	1 445	1 313	1 661	2 167	(B)	3 675	3 158	(B)	(B)	(B)
Mean income (dollars)	30 320	21 389	27 658	34 181	(B)	50 427	45 853	(B)	(B)	(B)
Standard error (dollars)	1 060	1 879	1 448	2 075	(B)	3 870	4 045	(B)	(B)	(B)
Hispanic[1], number with income	844	410	201	92	43	96	66	16	10	2
Median income (dollars)	21 549	16 374	26 104	26 674	(B)	41 220	(B)	(B)	(B)	(B)
Standard error (dollars)	715	691	2 609	3 580	(B)	2 050	(B)	(B)	(B)	(B)
Mean income (dollars)	30 968	19 939	30 101	34 157	(B)	65 574	(B)	(B)	(B)	(B)
Standard error (dollars)	1 459	907	1 820	3 406	(B)	9 006	(B)	(B)	(B)	(B)
Non-Hispanic White, number with income	9 673	1 119	2 958	1 573	686	3 335	1 799	998	272	263
Median income (dollars)	38 287	20 112	31 321	37 088	38 976	62 198	54 920	64 422	96 990	85 383
Standard error (dollars)	462	708	366	959	1 410	1 068	1 192	1 895	13 769	7 414
Mean income (dollars)	54 609	24 256	37 590	48 030	51 714	83 586	70 417	90 267	137 055	92 835
Standard error (dollars)	857	673	850	2 052	2 502	1 957	1 975	4 621	9 042	4 064
Non-Hispanic Black, number with income	969	289	331	165	49	133	81	29	8	14
Median income (dollars)	23 972	14 300	22 078	33 189	(B)	42 925	41 905	(B)	(B)	(B)
Standard error (dollars)	1 432	1 347	1 535	1 891	(B)	3 598	3 050	(B)	(B)	(B)
Mean income (dollars)	30 366	21 419	27 496	34 608	(B)	50 442	45 558	(B)	(B)	(B)
Standard error (dollars)	1 087	1 939	1 480	2 116	(B)	3 992	4 215	(B)	(B)	(B)
Asian/Pacific Islander, number with income	399	56	96	33	11	200	117	41	20	20
Median income (dollars)	32 833	(B)	19 979	(B)	(B)	56 174	52 378	(B)	(B)	(B)
Standard error (dollars)	4 191	(B)	4 431	(B)	(B)	5 657	5 049	(B)	(B)	(B)
Mean income (dollars)	53 380	(B)	32 248	(B)	(B)	73 647	69 893	(B)	(B)	(B)
Standard error (dollars)	3 992	(B)	7 497	(B)	(B)	5 761	7 796	(B)	(B)	(B)
Year-Round, Full-Time Workers, 55 to 64 Years										
All races, number with income	6 977	836	1 999	1 148	503	2 488	1 334	682	227	244
Median income (dollars)	46 751	29 995	39 157	43 557	46 054	73 162	68 605	73 552	(B)	94 626
Standard error (dollars)	466	925	900	1 330	1 084	1 216	1 844	1 960	58 158	6 458
Mean income (dollars)	65 748	32 799	44 954	54 696	62 027	99 397	84 544	109 788	156 025	98 820
Standard error (dollars)	1 116	948	1 166	2 485	3 265	2 473	2 406	6 533	10 067	4 266
White, number with income	6 130	674	1 744	1 015	464	2 231	1 180	626	208	215
Median income (dollars)	47 992	30 017	40 214	43 974	46 684	74 942	70 314	73 792	(B)	96 863
Standard error (dollars)	731	989	590	1 482	1 270	1 167	1 190	2 009	59 390	13 363
Mean income (dollars)	67 832	32 193	46 290	55 519	63 558	101 943	86 243	112 241	160 493	101 201
Standard error (dollars)	1 234	901	1 269	2 751	3 512	2 687	2 544	7 061	10 726	4 629
Black, number with income	526	119	185	107	28	86	52	18	4	10
Median income (dollars)	36 748	30 221	33 670	41 648	(B)	55 969	(B)	(B)	(B)	(B)
Standard error (dollars)	1 518	2 812	2 061	2 773	(B)	6 208	(B)	(B)	(B)	(B)
Mean income (dollars)	41 519	35 136	34 689	44 195	(B)	61 816	(B)	(B)	(B)	(B)
Standard error (dollars)	1 578	4 165	1 661	2 317	(B)	5 217	(B)	(B)	(B)	(B)
Hispanic[1], number with income	497	221	122	56	33	63	43	10	7	1
Median income (dollars)	30 719	21 436	35 564	(B)	(B)	(B)	(B)	(B)	(B)	(B)
Standard error (dollars)	1 187	761	4 258	(B)	(B)	(B)	(B)	(B)	(B)	(B)
Mean income (dollars)	41 307	25 003	38 791	(B)	(B)	(B)	(B)	(B)	(B)	(B)
Standard error (dollars)	2 234	1 180	2 377	(B)	(B)	(B)	(B)	(B)	(B)	(B)
Non-Hispanic White, number with income	5 666	461	1 632	964	432	2 175	1 143	616	201	213
Median income (dollars)	50 125	32 512	40 330	44 104	46 492	75 256	70 402	74 652	(B)	96 462
Standard error (dollars)	552	912	540	1 486	1 210	1 069	1 171	2 095	60 668	10 722
Mean income (dollars)	69 991	35 663	46 801	55 940	63 397	102 223	86 290	113 330	160 378	100 682
Standard error (dollars)	1 317	1 167	1 345	2 887	3 717	2 736	2 578	7 167	11 036	4 625
Non-Hispanic Black, number with income	501	113	177	103	26	80	47	18	4	10
Median income (dollars)	36 926	29 290	32 995	42 680	(B)	55 852	(B)	(B)	(B)	(B)
Standard error (dollars)	1 584	2 661	2 107	5 068	(B)	6 125	(B)	(B)	(B)	(B)
Mean income (dollars)	41 738	35 099	34 352	45 308	(B)	62 644	(B)	(B)	(B)	(B)
Standard error (dollars)	1 639	4 349	1 718	2 326	(B)	5 483	(B)	(B)	(B)	(B)
Asian/Pacific Islander, number with income	262	29	48	22	8	154	92	31	12	16
Median income (dollars)	47 383	(B)	(B)	(B)	(B)	63 908	60 986	(B)	(B)	(B)
Standard error (dollars)	4 561	(B)	(B)	(B)	(B)	5 573	6 219	(B)	(B)	(B)
Mean income (dollars)	69 270	(B)	(B)	(B)	(B)	84 992	80 729	(B)	(B)	(B)
Standard error (dollars)	5 579	(B)	(B)	(B)	(B)	6 987	9 293	(B)	(B)	(B)

[1]May be of any race.
(B) = Base less than 75,000.

Table A-12. Income in 2001 by Educational Attainment for Population 18 Years and Over, by Age, Race, and Hispanic Origin, March 2002—*Continued*

(Numbers in thousand, except where noted.)

Income, standard error, age, race, and Hispanic origin	Total	High school		College						
		Not high school graduate	Graduate, includes GED	Some college, no degree	Associate degree	Bachelor's degree or more	Bachelor's degree	Master's degree	Professional degree	Doctorate degree
MALE										
All Workers, 65 Years and Over										
All races, number with income	13 940	4 155	4 205	1 952	531	3 095	1 787	693	292	321
Median income (dollars)	19 688	13 714	19 472	22 493	25 009	34 772	31 368	40 094	38 558	50 811
Standard error (dollars)	178	194	319	443	918	725	997	1 985	2 011	3 256
Mean income (dollars)	30 238	17 673	27 614	29 790	33 440	50 404	45 052	49 226	59 888	74 079
Standard error (dollars)	428	405	839	736	1 365	1 267	1 681	1 886	4 146	5 248
White, number with income	12 460	3 511	3 841	1 784	464	2 858	1 657	635	276	288
Median income (dollars)	20 331	14 221	19 917	23 000	25 165	35 138	31 926	40 811	38 184	51 829
Standard error (dollars)	187	212	310	532	936	815	953	2 034	2 262	4 439
Mean income (dollars)	31 107	18 196	28 274	30 223	33 787	50 894	45 322	49 524	61 119	76 113
Standard error (dollars)	456	467	912	772	1 478	1 255	1 572	1 963	4 357	5 738
Black, number with income	1 072	529	269	109	42	120	57	38	8	16
Median income (dollars)	13 775	11 454	14 990	15 917	(B)	27 416	(B)	(B)	(B)	(B)
Standard error (dollars)	428	367	998	1 674	(B)	5 462	(B)	(B)	(B)	(B)
Mean income (dollars)	19 951	14 206	21 122	20 878	(B)	37 059	(B)	(B)	(B)	(B)
Standard error (dollars)	730	610	1 213	1 850	(B)	3 881	(B)	(B)	(B)	(B)
Hispanic[1], number with income	761	471	156	57	18	58	37	12	1	6
Median income (dollars)	12 337	9 836	15 253	(B)	(B)	(B)	(B)	(B)	(B)	(B)
Standard error (dollars)	559	369	1 222	(B)	(B)	(B)	(B)	(B)	(B)	(B)
Mean income (dollars)	18 167	14 442	21 184	(B)	(B)	(B)	(B)	(B)	(B)	(B)
Standard error (dollars)	759	691	2 013	(B)	(B)	(B)	(B)	(B)	(B)	(B)
Non-Hispanic White, number with income	11 733	3 055	3 691	1 732	447	2 805	1 622	623	275	284
Median income (dollars)	20 855	14 792	20 105	23 258	25 254	35 280	32 060	40 913	38 381	51 434
Standard error (dollars)	189	224	298	552	919	853	947	2 019	2 256	3 161
Mean income (dollars)	31 904	18 753	28 555	30 537	33 933	51 154	45 567	49 721	61 279	76 370
Standard error (dollars)	481	527	946	791	1 515	1 276	1 602	1 991	4 369	5 822
Non-Hispanic Black, number with income	1 047	519	265	106	40	115	54	38	8	14
Median income (dollars)	13 769	11 488	14 791	16 283	(B)	28 223	(B)	(B)	(B)	(B)
Standard error (dollars)	428	368	972	1 873	(B)	5 473	(B)	(B)	(B)	(B)
Mean income (dollars)	20 037	14 288	21 131	21 166	(B)	37 396	(B)	(B)	(B)	(B)
Standard error (dollars)	744	619	1 234	1 892	(B)	4 009	(B)	(B)	(B)	(B)
Asian/Pacific Islander, number with income	324	79	76	36	22	108	67	18	8	14
Median income (dollars)	15 824	12 729	13 504	(B)	(B)	27 532	(B)	(B)	(B)	(B)
Standard error (dollars)	976	1 374	2 124	(B)	(B)	3 576	(B)	(B)	(B)	(B)
Mean income (dollars)	31 219	19 223	17 326	(B)	(B)	52 931	(B)	(B)	(B)	(B)
Standard error (dollars)	5 199	2 712	2 428	(B)	(B)	14 854	(B)	(B)	(B)	(B)
Year-Round, Full-Time Workers, 65 Years and Over										
All races, number with income	1 396	238	405	218	66	466	242	102	55	65
Median income (dollars)	47 325	30 118	44 705	48 602	(B)	75 415	55 680	68 131	(B)	(B)
Standard error (dollars)	1 200	1 732	1 697	2 404	(B)	4 963	5 814	7 897	(B)	(B)
Mean income (dollars)	72 823	34 447	69 717	61 550	(B)	102 740	91 563	88 989	(B)	(B)
Standard error (dollars)	3 229	1 525	7 583	4 126	(B)	6 364	10 346	7 820	(B)	(B)
White, number with income	1 233	192	360	200	58	422	222	89	51	59
Median income (dollars)	49 568	30 842	45 996	49 348	(B)	79 305	57 817	78 638	(B)	(B)
Standard error (dollars)	1 475	1 040	1 475	3 074	(B)	4 426	7 088	8 726	(B)	(B)
Mean income (dollars)	75 867	35 662	73 674	63 514	(B)	104 091	88 644	92 994	(B)	(B)
Standard error (dollars)	3 438	1 709	8 500	4 436	(B)	6 166	9 337	8 793	(B)	(B)
Black, number with income	105	32	32	11	5	23	10	4	4	3
Median income (dollars)	34 081	(B)	(B)	(B)	(B)	(B)	(B)	(B)	(B)	(B)
Standard error (dollars)	3 262	(B)	(B)	(B)	(B)	(B)	(B)	(B)	(B)	(B)
Mean income (dollars)	37 637	(B)	(B)	(B)	(B)	(B)	(B)	(B)	(B)	(B)
Standard error (dollars)	2 606	(B)	(B)	(B)	(B)	(B)	(B)	(B)	(B)	(B)
Hispanic[1], number with income	83	45	14	5	1	16	13	1	(B)	2
Median income (dollars)	38 804	(B)	(B)	(B)	(B)	(B)	(B)	(B)	(B)	(B)
Standard error (dollars)	2 751	(B)	(B)	(B)	(B)	(B)	(B)	(B)	(B)	(B)
Mean income (dollars)	42 915	(B)	(B)	(B)	(B)	(B)	(B)	(B)	(B)	(B)
Standard error (dollars)	3 054	(B)	(B)	(B)	(B)	(B)	(B)	(B)	(B)	(B)
Non-Hispanic White, number with income	1 153	147	345	195	57	407	210	87	51	57
Median income (dollars)	51 092	31 024	46 148	49 674	(B)	80 468	61 787	78 283	(B)	(B)
Standard error (dollars)	1 566	834	1 577	3 317	(B)	4 307	6 959	8 771	(B)	(B)
Mean income (dollars)	78 152	35 803	74 776	63 744	(B)	105 815	90 945	92 853	(B)	(B)
Standard error (dollars)	3 659	1 987	8 838	4 552	(B)	6 368	9 850	8 914	(B)	(B)
Non-Hispanic Black, number with income	102	31	32	11	5	21	9	4	4	2
Median income (dollars)	33 869	(B)	(B)	(B)	(B)	(B)	(B)	(B)	(B)	(B)
Standard error (dollars)	3 258	(B)	(B)	(B)	(B)	(B)	(B)	(B)	(B)	(B)
Mean income (dollars)	37 522	(B)	(B)	(B)	(B)	(B)	(B)	(B)	(B)	(B)
Standard error (dollars)	2 666	(B)	(B)	(B)	(B)	(B)	(B)	(B)	(B)	(B)
Asian/Pacific Islander, number with income	44	11	7	2	2	20	9	8	(B)	2
Median income (dollars)	(B)	(B)	(B)	(B)	(B)	(B)	(B)	(B)	(B)	(B)
Standard error (dollars)	(B)	(B)	(B)	(B)	(B)	(B)	(B)	(B)	(B)	(B)
Mean income (dollars)	(B)	(B)	(B)	(B)	(B)	(B)	(B)	(B)	(B)	(B)
Standard error (dollars)	(B)	(B)	(B)	(B)	(B)	(B)	(B)	(B)	(B)	(B)

[1]May be of any race.
(B) = Base less than 75,000.

Table A-12. Income in 2001 by Educational Attainment for Population 18 Years and Over, by Age, Race, and Hispanic Origin, March 2002—*Continued*

(Numbers in thousand, except where noted.)

Income, standard error, age, race, and Hispanic origin	Total	High school		College						
		Not high school graduate	Graduate, includes GED	Some college, no degree	Associate degree	Bachelor's degree or more	Bachelor's degree	Master's degree	Professional degree	Doctorate degree
FEMALE										
All Workers, 18 Years and Over										
All races, number with income	99 371	14 494	32 248	19 742	8 722	24 163	16 802	5 804	903	652
Median income (dollars)	17 122	9 085	15 046	17 168	22 075	32 595	30 267	40 591	46 343	52 181
Standard error (dollars)	71	84	101	153	241	235	168	340	1 903	1 865
Mean income (dollars)	24 120	12 373	18 657	22 020	26 040	39 481	34 953	46 700	60 614	62 567
Standard error (dollars)	123	274	165	257	297	327	348	780	1 998	2 584
White, number with income	82 035	11 296	26 976	16 166	7 276	20 319	14 067	4 967	747	536
Median income (dollars)	17 176	9 212	15 037	16 957	21 931	32 453	30 001	40 645	48 854	53 344
Standard error (dollars)	79	96	111	171	257	226	270	381	1 896	2 103
Mean income (dollars)	24 374	12 337	18 885	22 106	26 207	39 501	34 727	46 911	62 615	63 881
Standard error (dollars)	137	288	193	292	338	353	360	876	2 206	2 979
Black, number with income	12 141	2 464	3 998	2 610	1 032	2 035	1 423	497	73	40
Median income (dollars)	16 679	8 404	15 170	19 252	23 458	34 913	32 765	41 094	(B)	(B)
Standard error (dollars)	207	209	300	431	1 067	571	552	789	(B)	(B)
Mean income (dollars)	21 604	12 480	17 304	21 930	25 176	38 865	35 014	45 243	(B)	(B)
Standard error (dollars)	288	986	246	399	690	779	824	1 490	(B)	(B)
Hispanic[1], number with income	9 492	3 411	2 860	1 615	551	1 052	779	192	60	19
Median income (dollars)	12 949	9 585	13 484	17 388	21 139	30 074	26 293	40 737	(B)	(B)
Standard error (dollars)	232	201	447	597	823	1 028	1 335	2 344	(B)	(B)
Mean income (dollars)	18 152	12 110	16 235	20 535	24 561	35 927	32 387	43 678	(B)	(B)
Standard error (dollars)	361	580	308	882	1 004	1 910	2 369	2 662	(B)	(B)
Non-Hispanic White, number with income	73 131	8 073	24 307	14 661	6 754	19 333	13 341	4 783	691	517
Median income (dollars)	17 843	9 077	15 184	16 916	21 975	32 728	30 128	40 625	50 106	54 126
Standard error (dollars)	105	110	113	179	273	303	226	401	1 773	2 177
Mean income (dollars)	25 147	12 422	19 186	22 284	26 311	39 721	34 896	47 035	63 399	64 836
Standard error (dollars)	147	332	212	309	357	360	360	905	2 306	3 063
Non-Hispanic Black, number with income	11 787	2 350	3 876	2 549	1 019	1 991	1 389	492	70	38
Median income (dollars)	16 786	8 374	15 163	19 314	23 497	34 979	32 827	41 168	(B)	(B)
Standard error (dollars)	210	212	305	437	1 091	570	553	785	(B)	(B)
Mean income (dollars)	21 648	12 572	17 326	21 930	25 159	38 621	34 702	45 367	(B)	(B)
Standard error (dollars)	288	1 033	251	404	692	704	687	1 501	(B)	(B)
Asian/Pacific Islander, number with income	4 069	465	895	714	309	1 684	1 227	311	78	67
Median income (dollars)	19 208	10 662	14 993	15 135	24 224	30 899	27 361	37 762	31 295	(B)
Standard error (dollars)	554	736	669	1 096	1 715	725	1 847	2 998	5 904	(B)
Mean income (dollars)	28 018	13 934	18 104	21 102	26 820	40 333	37 643	46 269	45 217	(B)
Standard error (dollars)	927	723	608	2 391	1 425	1 883	2 358	3 521	5 787	(B)
Year-Round, Full-Time Workers, 18 Years and Over										
All races, number with income	41 609	3 136	13 025	8 260	4 419	12 767	8 731	3 112	532	391
Median income (dollars)	30 430	17 619	24 267	28 832	31 743	43 653	40 288	50 577	61 673	62 122
Standard error (dollars)	88	256	175	269	226	392	233	328	3 984	2 227
Mean income (dollars)	37 341	23 385	28 139	33 679	35 947	53 009	47 783	61 018	76 517	73 927
Standard error (dollars)	244	1 184	364	454	451	510	545	1 266	2 566	2 908
White, number with income	33 401	2 370	10 541	6 499	3 591	10 400	7 046	2 597	443	312
Median income (dollars)	30 858	17 567	24 714	29 296	32 096	44 521	40 623	50 775	68 461	65 102
Standard error (dollars)	98	288	288	310	257	419	261	326	5 467	2 620
Mean income (dollars)	38 127	22 852	29 001	34 280	36 667	53 765	48 239	61 887	78 519	75 773
Standard error (dollars)	275	1 257	443	515	530	560	564	1 467	2 787	3 336
Black, number with income	5 844	562	1 900	1 388	634	1 357	958	326	40	32
Median income (dollars)	27 317	17 397	22 302	27 395	29 777	40 236	36 554	46 437	(B)	(B)
Standard error (dollars)	246	520	330	459	829	726	638	2 228	(B)	(B)
Mean income (dollars)	31 762	26 609	24 380	30 263	31 585	45 842	41 485	51 599	(B)	(B)
Standard error (dollars)	517	4 199	356	518	854	967	1 033	1 666	(B)	(B)
Hispanic[1], number with income	4 356	1 159	1 413	826	331	625	463	116	34	11
Median income (dollars)	21 989	16 361	21 070	25 912	28 843	36 981	34 147	49 099	(B)	(B)
Standard error (dollars)	221	264	350	598	1 236	1 004	1 671	2 962	(B)	(B)
Mean income (dollars)	27 675	20 174	23 327	29 143	32 411	46 963	42 937	53 858	(B)	(B)
Standard error (dollars)	702	1 631	453	1 581	1 272	2 773	3 482	3 186	(B)	(B)
Non-Hispanic White, number with income	29 322	1 278	9 223	5 728	3 270	9 821	6 620	2 487	410	302
Median income (dollars)	31 801	19 769	25 293	29 931	32 391	45 072	40 968	50 826	70 121	65 466
Standard error (dollars)	104	466	154	285	349	346	263	334	6 547	2 880
Mean income (dollars)	39 600	25 024	29 805	34 988	37 088	54 223	48 646	62 233	79 246	76 452
Standard error (dollars)	298	1 875	502	544	569	573	563	1 525	2 889	3 423
Non-Hispanic Black, number with income	5 666	521	1 837	1 354	628	1 324	932	321	38	31
Median income (dollars)	27 421	17 706	22 341	27 361	29 661	40 347	36 608	46 728	(B)	(B)
Standard error (dollars)	277	573	354	453	852	671	663	2 174	(B)	(B)
Mean income (dollars)	31 807	27 451	24 459	30 286	31 439	45 452	41 005	51 886	(B)	(B)
Standard error (dollars)	515	4 525	365	526	856	827	783	1 679	(B)	(B)
Asian/Pacific Islander, number with income	1 962	151	430	288	153	938	678	169	45	44
Median income (dollars)	31 283	19 615	21 664	28 145	31 846	42 303	40 607	50 076	(B)	(B)
Standard error (dollars)	510	1 080	660	1 270	2 419	1 293	1 022	4 840	(B)	(B)
Mean income (dollars)	41 980	21 455	24 533	37 509	37 126	55 468	52 224	67 251	(B)	(B)
Standard error (dollars)	1 718	1 037	901	5 631	1 937	3 001	3 845	5 289	(B)	(B)

[1]May be of any race.
(B) = Base less than 75,000.

Table A-12. Income in 2001 by Educational Attainment for Population 18 Years and Over, by Age, Race, and Hispanic Origin, March 2002—*Continued*

(Numbers in thousand, except where noted.)

Income, standard error, age, race, and Hispanic origin	Total	High school		College						
		Not high school graduate	Graduate, includes GED	Some college, no degree	Associate degree	Bachelor's degree or more	Bachelor's degree	Master's degree	Professional degree	Doctorate degree
FEMALE										
All Workers, 25 Years and Over										
All races, number with income	88 075	12 572	28 945	15 420	8 176	22 960	15 659	5 749	898	652
Median income (dollars)	18 548	9 636	15 664	20 100	22 638	33 841	30 972	40 744	46 635	52 181
Standard error (dollars)	96	87	105	173	341	285	177	343	1 891	1 865
Mean income (dollars)	25 483	12 866	19 348	24 685	26 641	40 247	35 680	46 929	60 875	62 567
Standard error (dollars)	130	261	177	296	313	329	345	786	2 005	2 584
White, number with income	73 050	9 788	24 392	12 724	6 830	19 313	13 113	4 920	743	536
Median income (dollars)	18 527	9 788	15 588	19 740	22 370	33 746	30 711	40 793	49 137	53 344
Standard error (dollars)	104	98	115	206	311	331	200	386	1 853	2 103
Mean income (dollars)	25 702	13 109	19 519	24 608	26 788	40 230	35 386	47 143	62 874	63 881
Standard error (dollars)	145	329	205	328	356	352	347	883	2 214	2 979
Black, number with income	10 500	2 113	3 427	2 055	971	1 932	1 327	490	73	40
Median income (dollars)	18 319	8 818	16 204	22 210	24 625	35 682	33 540	41 285	(B)	(B)
Standard error (dollars)	303	222	317	531	947	549	628	784	(B)	(B)
Mean income (dollars)	22 841	11 655	18 265	24 731	25 790	39 698	35 896	45 460	(B)	(B)
Standard error (dollars)	239	265	272	464	720	807	863	1 505	(B)	(B)
Hispanic[1], number with income	7 873	2 937	2 333	1 109	487	1 004	735	190	59	19
Median income (dollars)	14 198	10 037	14 760	20 959	21 199	30 528	27 237	40 884	(B)	(B)
Standard error (dollars)	262	211	475	511	880	688	1 464	2 105	(B)	(B)
Mean income (dollars)	19 510	12 734	17 261	24 052	25 162	36 790	33 280	44 029	(B)	(B)
Standard error (dollars)	429	669	356	1 240	1 113	1 992	2 504	2 674	(B)	(B)
Non-Hispanic White, number with income	65 676	7 013	22 213	11 704	6 369	18 374	12 430	4 737	688	517
Median income (dollars)	19 195	9 707	15 676	19 586	22 443	34 060	30 862	40 772	50 254	54 126
Standard error (dollars)	110	112	120	219	348	336	209	406	1 732	2 177
Mean income (dollars)	26 414	13 257	19 750	24 666	26 876	40 444	35 545	47 262	63 635	64 836
Standard error (dollars)	155	379	223	339	374	358	343	912	2 311	3 063
Non-Hispanic Black, number with income	10 197	2 018	3 318	2 010	960	1 888	1 292	486	70	38
Median income (dollars)	18 463	8 779	16 207	22 207	24 745	35 768	33 608	41 360	(B)	(B)
Standard error (dollars)	311	225	322	536	936	560	620	780	(B)	(B)
Mean income (dollars)	22 873	11 670	18 298	24 692	25 808	39 460	35 584	45 587	(B)	(B)
Standard error (dollars)	233	274	277	470	722	727	713	1 516	(B)	(B)
Asian/Pacific Islander, number with income	3 541	436	809	423	278	1 592	1 137	309	77	67
Median income (dollars)	21 109	11 142	15 696	21 741	25 171	31 647	30 039	37 956	31 609	(B)
Standard error (dollars)	421	727	786	1 152	1 733	750	1 741	2 972	5 868	(B)
Mean income (dollars)	30 327	14 444	18 803	28 367	27 712	41 526	39 024	46 486	45 653	(B)
Standard error (dollars)	1 054	757	656	3 955	1 526	1 983	2 534	3 531	5 850	(B)
Year-Round, Full-Time Workers, 25 Years and Over										
All races, number with income	38 228	2 796	11 689	7 282	4 190	12 268	8 257	3 088	530	391
Median income (dollars)	31 356	18 096	25 302	30 418	32 152	44 775	40 994	50 668	61 747	62 122
Standard error (dollars)	91	306	132	185	231	366	231	327	3 975	2 227
Mean income (dollars)	38 497	22 930	29 147	35 137	36 537	53 619	48 335	61 211	76 647	73 927
Standard error (dollars)	246	1 072	387	472	472	501	514	1 275	2 568	2 908
White, number with income	30 663	2 099	9 474	5 722	3 392	9 974	6 637	2 580	443	312
Median income (dollars)	31 808	18 135	25 668	30 746	32 633	45 452	41 391	50 837	68 461	65 102
Standard error (dollars)	101	357	148	205	433	287	256	325	5 467	2 620
Mean income (dollars)	39 401	23 639	30 059	35 764	37 332	54 383	48 786	62 043	78 519	75 773
Standard error (dollars)	282	1 415	471	524	556	542	504	1 475	2 787	3 336
Black, number with income	5 356	506	1 690	1 239	609	1 310	917	320	40	32
Median income (dollars)	28 450	17 544	23 245	28 821	30 197	40 707	37 072	47 185	(B)	(B)
Standard error (dollars)	369	623	654	616	702	545	771	2 108	(B)	(B)
Mean income (dollars)	32 155	20 722	25 082	31 478	31 955	46 429	42 008	52 060	(B)	(B)
Standard error (dollars)	355	736	382	559	881	993	1 067	1 683	(B)	(B)
Hispanic[1], number with income	3 787	1 030	1 188	663	300	604	443	116	34	11
Median income (dollars)	22 880	16 612	22 060	27 448	29 735	37 301	35 145	49 099	(B)	(B)
Standard error (dollars)	413	273	423	824	1 482	1 327	1 663	2 962	(B)	(B)
Mean income (dollars)	28 998	20 591	24 478	31 273	33 145	47 645	43 683	53 858	(B)	(B)
Standard error (dollars)	801	1 829	514	1 946	1 381	2 858	3 633	3 186	(B)	(B)
Non-Hispanic White, number with income	27 125	1 129	8 366	5 111	3 101	9 415	6 232	2 470	410	302
Median income (dollars)	32 864	20 247	26 091	31 073	33 131	45 860	41 719	50 891	70 121	65 466
Standard error (dollars)	219	377	155	221	538	296	258	333	6 547	2 880
Mean income (dollars)	40 775	26 151	30 790	36 297	37 720	54 838	49 183	62 399	79 246	76 452
Standard error (dollars)	302	2 115	529	537	595	552	490	1 535	2 889	3 423
Non-Hispanic Black, number with income	5 189	469	1 633	1 205	605	1 276	891	315	38	31
Median income (dollars)	28 639	17 865	23 325	28 837	30 162	40 823	37 156	47 476	(B)	(B)
Standard error (dollars)	379	680	652	644	717	545	841	2 054	(B)	(B)
Mean income (dollars)	32 191	21 071	25 175	31 538	31 837	46 040	41 520	52 360	(B)	(B)
Standard error (dollars)	334	780	392	569	881	847	803	1 697	(B)	(B)
Asian/Pacific Islander, number with income	1 844	146	390	247	147	912	654	169	44	44
Median income (dollars)	32 014	20 066	22 273	29 659	31 839	43 157	40 789	59 875	(B)	(B)
Standard error (dollars)	549	1 128	815	1 488	2 431	1 596	1 001	4 840	(B)	(B)
Mean income (dollars)	43 187	21 656	25 373	39 804	37 260	56 127	52 953	67 251	(B)	(B)
Standard error (dollars)	1 821	1 073	967	6 549	1 990	3 080	3 984	5 289	(B)	(B)

[1]May be of any race.
(B) = Base less than 75,000.

Table A-12. Income in 2001 by Educational Attainment for Population 18 Years and Over, by Age, Race, and Hispanic Origin, March 2002—Continued

(Numbers in thousand, except where noted.)

Income, standard error, age, race, and Hispanic origin	Total	High school		College						
		Not high school graduate	Graduate, includes GED	Some college, no degree	Associate degree	Bachelor's degree or more	Bachelor's degree	Master's degree	Professional degree	Doctorate degree
FEMALE										
All Workers, 25 to 64 Years										
All races, number with income	69 105	6 975	21 514	12 913	7 191	20 511	14 020	5 103	806	581
Median income (dollars)	21 806	10 912	17 858	21 685	24 974	35 747	32 071	42 227	50 336	53 461
Standard error (dollars)	89	151	153	175	337	189	179	365	1 535	2 404
Mean income (dollars)	28 000	14 341	20 899	25 609	27 762	41 683	36 902	48 959	64 171	61 931
Standard error (dollars)	155	450	229	292	343	357	374	868	2 139	2 350
White, number with income	56 308	5 221	17 603	10 419	5 954	17 110	11 629	4 339	664	477
Median income (dollars)	21 972	10 914	17 971	21 485	24 786	35 866	31 941	42 430	52 030	55 572
Standard error (dollars)	101	171	171	197	414	205	204	474	1 520	2 562
Mean income (dollars)	28 408	14 696	21 252	25 702	27 949	41 764	36 648	49 362	66 627	62 732
Standard error (dollars)	178	592	274	347	393	383	377	983	2 373	2 651
Black, number with income	8 851	1 307	2 981	1 901	895	1 765	1 232	434	61	37
Median income (dollars)	21 017	10 397	17 581	23 350	25 578	36 460	34 108	42 153	(B)	(B)
Standard error (dollars)	235	413	377	716	628	551	645	1 106	(B)	(B)
Mean income (dollars)	24 704	12 974	19 195	25 592	26 629	40 765	36 823	46 961	(B)	(B)
Standard error (dollars)	267	381	299	487	757	839	904	1 546	(B)	(B)
Hispanic[1], number with income	6 915	2 313	2 100	1 067	466	966	704	184	57	19
Median income (dollars)	15 852	11 295	16 031	21 273	21 456	30 942	28 268	40 850	(B)	(B)
Standard error (dollars)	224	235	403	501	875	616	1 615	2 133	(B)	(B)
Mean income (dollars)	20 876	13 863	18 162	24 289	25 626	37 505	34 054	44 251	(B)	(B)
Standard error (dollars)	483	843	382	1 285	1 151	2 061	2 604	2 734	(B)	(B)
Non-Hispanic White, number with income	49 855	3 044	15 647	9 441	5 514	16 207	10 974	4 162	611	458
Median income (dollars)	23 075	10 557	18 285	21 520	25 053	36 126	32 163	42 555	53 159	56 183
Standard error (dollars)	155	255	183	216	376	212	214	512	1 710	2 394
Mean income (dollars)	29 399	15 250	21 648	25 857	28 100	42 044	36 851	49 577	67 684	63 764
Standard error (dollars)	191	821	304	358	415	390	373	1 019	2 487	2 726
Non-Hispanic Black, number with income	8 569	1 224	2 879	1 857	884	1 723	1 199	429	58	35
Median income (dollars)	21 173	10 394	17 603	23 369	25 654	36 553	34 150	42 227	(B)	(B)
Standard error (dollars)	237	444	393	721	613	562	637	1 168	(B)	(B)
Mean income (dollars)	24 768	13 053	19 237	25 570	26 659	40 503	36 481	47 123	(B)	(B)
Standard error (dollars)	259	399	306	494	759	745	736	1 558	(B)	(B)
Asian/Pacific Islander, number with income	3 101	288	654	388	254	1 514	1 078	301	76	58
Median income (dollars)	23 052	13 935	17 379	22 740	26 741	32 355	30 872	38 661	31 829	(B)
Standard error (dollars)	656	882	892	1 221	1 653	926	804	2 850	5 831	(B)
Mean income (dollars)	31 869	15 867	19 503	25 497	29 064	42 368	40 021	46 861	46 065	(B)
Standard error (dollars)	1 075	877	751	1 456	1 623	2 068	2 655	3 594	5 957	(B)
Year-Round, Full-Time Workers, 25 to 64 Years										
All races, number with income	37 489	2 690	11 398	7 142	4 136	12 121	8 166	3 051	520	382
Median income (dollars)	31 304	17 738	25 184	30 283	32 120	44 687	40 951	50 602	61 898	62 357
Standard error (dollars)	91	304	133	185	231	385	231	328	4 057	2 295
Mean income (dollars)	38 330	22 815	28 894	34 417	36 442	53 597	48 321	61 248	76 396	74 150
Standard error (dollars)	242	1 113	394	354	476	506	519	1 289	2 579	2 970
White, number with income	30 020	2 024	9 210	5 589	3 347	9 848	6 559	2 548	435	306
Median income (dollars)	31 755	17 723	25 546	30 586	32 592	45 383	41 338	50 763	69 158	65 216
Standard error (dollars)	101	346	150	203	427	289	254	326	6 234	2 625
Mean income (dollars)	39 256	23 582	29 784	35 139	37 236	54 357	48 757	62 052	78 561	75 895
Standard error (dollars)	281	1 467	480	428	560	548	508	1 493	2 816	3 391
Black, number with income	5 282	479	1 671	1 233	600	1 296	909	317	38	31
Median income (dollars)	28 398	17 409	23 150	28 808	30 115	40 646	37 022	47 149	(B)	(B)
Standard error (dollars)	372	596	658	614	748	555	739	2 103	(B)	(B)
Mean income (dollars)	32 112	20 468	25 023	31 469	31 813	46 309	42 023	52 163	(B)	(B)
Standard error (dollars)	355	750	384	560	886	986	1 073	1 681	(B)	(B)
Hispanic[1], number with income	3 749	1 013	1 179	656	296	603	441	116	34	11
Median income (dollars)	22 833	16 568	22 045	27 354	29 898	37 283	35 123	49 099	(B)	(B)
Standard error (dollars)	407	273	422	807	1 452	1 308	1 686	2 962	(B)	(B)
Mean income (dollars)	28 994	20 562	24 447	31 158	33 219	47 634	43 650	53 858	(B)	(B)
Standard error (dollars)	808	1 858	515	1 964	1 399	2 866	3 647	3 186	(B)	(B)
Non-Hispanic White, number with income	26 518	1 069	8 110	4 985	3 060	9 292	6 155	2 437	402	296
Median income (dollars)	32 754	19 995	25 966	30 904	33 062	45 794	41 667	50 814	70 668	65 579
Standard error (dollars)	227	486	158	219	546	298	257	334	6 284	3 115
Mean income (dollars)	40 629	26 162	30 500	35 619	37 608	54 817	49 158	62 412	79 306	76 592
Standard error (dollars)	300	2 234	541	414	600	558	494	1 554	2 922	3 482
Non-Hispanic Black, number with income	5 117	443	1 614	1 199	596	1 262	884	312	37	29
Median income (dollars)	28 582	17 667	23 230	28 823	30 080	40 764	37 104	47 440	(B)	(B)
Standard error (dollars)	382	652	660	642	763	556	810	2 049	(B)	(B)
Mean income (dollars)	32 141	20 773	25 114	31 529	31 692	45 913	41 531	52 468	(B)	(B)
Standard error (dollars)	334	797	394	570	886	834	806	1 695	(B)	(B)
Asian/Pacific Islander, number with income	1 822	142	382	244	147	904	650	167	44	42
Median income (dollars)	31 933	19 784	22 057	29 452	31 869	43 331	40 602	60 145	(D)	(B)
Standard error (dollars)	526	1 181	750	1 521	2 429	1 634	1 045	4 728	(B)	(B)
Mean income (dollars)	42 386	21 278	25 063	33 388	37 302	56 298	53 076	67 631	(B)	(B)
Standard error (dollars)	1 635	1 066	967	1 797	1 993	3 106	4 009	5 327	(B)	(B)

[1]May be of any race.
(B) = Base less than 75,000.

Table A-12. Income in 2001 by Educational Attainment for Population 18 Years and Over, by Age, Race, and Hispanic Origin, March 2002—*Continued*

(Numbers in thousand, except where noted.)

Income, standard error, age, race, and Hispanic origin	Total	High school		College						
		Not high school graduate	Graduate, includes GED	Some college, no degree	Associate degree	Bachelor's degree or more	Bachelor's degree	Master's degree	Professional degree	Doctorate degree
FEMALE										
All Workers, 25 to 34 Years										
All races, number with income	17 367	1 535	4 563	3 523	1 704	6 040	4 520	1 168	236	115
Median income (dollars)	21 472	10 604	16 639	20 171	22 177	32 561	31 580	35 848	42 113	47 098
Standard error (dollars)	162	305	242	286	488	367	246	462	2 400	4 484
Mean income (dollars)	26 110	16 738	18 682	22 361	24 246	36 816	34 693	39 768	55 430	51 952
Standard error (dollars)	310	1 928	407	518	483	560	655	1 118	3 341	3 578
White, number with income	13 650	1 198	3 452	2 665	1 387	4 947	3 714	962	181	88
Median income (dollars)	21 830	10 639	16 818	19 752	22 492	32 692	31 587	36 027	46 340	48 344
Standard error (dollars)	194	335	273	390	686	434	265	498	3 956	4 947
Mean income (dollars)	26 534	18 003	19 012	22 177	24 705	36 708	34 151	40 756	59 539	53 210
Standard error (dollars)	350	2 464	516	652	552	506	530	1 285	3 952	4 324
Black, number with income	2 533	268	864	642	237	520	405	88	22	5
Median income (dollars)	20 377	10 297	15 820	21 425	22 517	32 406	32 023	31 940	(B)	(B)
Standard error (dollars)	339	917	578	542	1 532	938	791	2 391	(B)	(B)
Mean income (dollars)	22 606	12 331	17 237	22 824	23 472	36 143	35 604	33 497	(B)	(B)
Standard error (dollars)	488	730	548	652	1 057	1 734	2 092	2 338	(B)	(B)
Hispanic[1], number with income	2 499	695	803	462	167	370	293	54	21	(B)
Median income (dollars)	15 949	10 901	15 456	20 572	20 016	29 880	28 845	(B)	(B)	(B)
Standard error (dollars)	373	426	623	841	2 240	1 511	1 980	(B)	(B)	(B)
Mean income (dollars)	21 165	15 701	17 312	24 069	22 744	35 446	33 450	(B)	(B)	(B)
Standard error (dollars)	1 030	2 707	602	2 753	1 609	2 688	3 079	(B)	(B)	(B)
Non-Hispanic White, number with income	11 338	550	2 710	2 246	1 231	4 600	3 440	910	161	88
Median income (dollars)	23 372	10 503	17 247	19 590	23 054	33 208	31 782	36 219	47 038	48 496
Standard error (dollars)	291	600	315	428	832	524	278	492	3 998	4 974
Mean income (dollars)	27 668	20 622	19 524	21 816	24 833	36 924	34 370	41 036	59 111	53 529
Standard error (dollars)	368	4 308	637	565	589	524	549	1 337	4 087	4 323
Non-Hispanic Black, number with income	2 415	240	820	618	233	503	389	87	22	4
Median income (dollars)	20 474	9 888	15 807	21 349	22 926	32 352	31 917	32 046	(B)	(B)
Standard error (dollars)	349	918	588	554	1 615	887	737	2 407	(B)	(B)
Mean income (dollars)	22 441	12 075	17 221	22 653	23 686	35 077	34 231	33 675	(B)	(B)
Standard error (dollars)	418	759	567	663	1 068	1 190	1 326	2 360	(B)	(B)
Asian/Pacific Islander, number with income	950	29	174	147	57	539	374	112	33	19
Median income (dollars)	21 595	(B)	16 900	20 757	(B)	31 523	29 163	35 784	(B)	(B)
Standard error (dollars)	792	(B)	1 886	2 108	(B)	3 031	3 209	4 519	(B)	(B)
Mean income (dollars)	30 744	(B)	18 664	24 699	(B)	38 464	39 120	36 189	(B)	(B)
Standard error (dollars)	2 460	(B)	1 269	2 751	(B)	4 184	5 889	3 447	(B)	(B)
Year-Round, Full-Time Workers, 25 to 34 Years										
All races, number with income	9 640	608	2 350	1 942	970	3 769	2 850	677	158	83
Median income (dollars)	29 720	17 046	23 228	26 504	29 026	38 749	37 167	41 996	50 233	49 176
Standard error (dollars)	273	444	318	315	634	512	300	485	2 161	4 729
Mean income (dollars)	35 443	29 377	26 191	30 127	31 409	45 969	43 675	50 296	63 188	56 476
Standard error (dollars)	505	4 778	708	842	600	780	927	1 512	3 889	4 302
White, number with income	7 545	486	1 790	1 413	777	3 078	2 334	556	127	59
Median income (dollars)	30 343	17 029	23 744	26 790	29 974	38 730	37 113	42 083	51 432	(B)
Standard error (dollars)	182	476	359	412	564	580	319	612	2 151	(B)
Mean income (dollars)	36 159	32 101	26 950	30 812	32 536	45 525	42 673	50 941	67 350	(B)
Standard error (dollars)	568	5 963	907	1 114	692	647	667	1 767	4 561	(B)
Black, number with income	1 482	95	439	414	156	376	299	56	16	3
Median income (dollars)	25 960	16 812	21 725	25 836	26 116	35 878	34 843	(B)	(B)	(B)
Standard error (dollars)	370	1 480	446	590	817	681	1 026	(B)	(B)	(B)
Mean income (dollars)	29 169	18 426	23 401	27 330	26 585	41 733	40 833	(B)	(B)	(B)
Standard error (dollars)	700	1 110	785	711	1 039	2 237	2 671	(B)	(B)	(B)
Hispanic[1], number with income	1 367	300	446	277	108	234	192	27	13	(B)
Median income (dollars)	22 810	16 346	21 682	26 765	24 766	35 673	35 037	(B)	(B)	(B)
Standard error (dollars)	604	729	701	1 119	2 750	2 188	2 115	(B)	(B)	(B)
Mean income (dollars)	29 614	25 987	23 434	31 343	28 154	44 682	42 393	(B)	(B)	(B)
Standard error (dollars)	1 802	6 161	807	4 444	2 141	3 869	4 371	(B)	(B)	(B)
Non-Hispanic White, number with income	6 281	208	1 377	1 161	672	2 861	2 157	530	114	59
Median income (dollars)	31 396	18 113	24 437	26 831	30 424	39 088	37 292	42 066	51 425	(B)
Standard error (dollars)	196	762	410	456	510	601	376	587	2 239	(B)
Mean income (dollars)	37 505	39 608	28 006	30 616	33 124	45 750	42 926	51 230	66 231	(B)
Standard error (dollars)	583	11 131	1 153	925	731	666	685	1 843	4 600	(B)
Non-Hispanic Black, number with income	1 410	84	413	395	156	361	285	55	16	3
Median income (dollars)	26 008	16 602	21 744	25 811	26 116	35 785	34 493	(B)	(B)	(B)
Standard error (dollars)	370	1 508	432	576	817	730	1 077	(B)	(B)	(B)
Mean income (dollars)	28 860	18 199	23 417	27 320	26 585	40 247	38 924	(B)	(B)	(B)
Standard error (dollars)	549	1 177	823	734	1 039	1 419	1 554	(B)	(B)	(B)
Asian/Pacific Islander, number with income	510	12	89	87	28	292	198	61	14	18
Median income (dollars)	35 352	(B)	21 391	26 978	(B)	42 270	41 811	(B)	(B)	(B)
Standard error (dollars)	1 785	(B)	1 419	1 336	(B)	1 512	1 275	(B)	(B)	(B)
Mean income (dollars)	44 488	(B)	24 452	34 149	(B)	56 251	59 943	(B)	(B)	(B)
Standard error (dollars)	4 331	(B)	1 679	3 959	(B)	7 324	10 686	(B)	(B)	(B)

[1]May be of any race.
(B) = Base less than 75,000.

Table A-12. Income in 2001 by Educational Attainment for Population 18 Years and Over, by Age, Race, and Hispanic Origin, March 2002—Continued

(Numbers in thousand, except where noted.)

Income, standard error, age, race, and Hispanic origin	Total	High school		College						
		Not high school graduate	Graduate, includes GED	Some college, no degree	Associate degree	Bachelor's degree or more	Bachelor's degree	Master's degree	Professional degree	Doctorate degree
FEMALE										
All Workers, 35 to 44 Years										
All races, number with income	20 647	1 932	6 400	3 808	2 433	6 073	4 307	1 330	260	174
Median income (dollars)	22 471	12 245	19 074	22 892	25 426	35 583	32 362	41 539	52 153	49 246
Standard error (dollars)	197	276	280	449	462	405	430	731	3 947	2 640
Mean income (dollars)	28 543	14 458	21 521	26 137	28 065	42 123	37 891	48 501	67 636	59 956
Standard error (dollars)	261	350	380	398	532	667	707	1 712	3 935	3 911
White, number with income	16 641	1 432	5 211	2 997	2 003	4 996	3 541	1 105	212	137
Median income (dollars)	22 399	12 241	19 246	22 571	24 956	35 443	32 195	40 273	54 053	51 833
Standard error (dollars)	208	326	312	461	676	425	494	1 051	5 551	4 660
Mean income (dollars)	28 722	14 555	21 752	26 089	28 026	41 911	37 692	47 845	68 745	61 559
Standard error (dollars)	300	429	453	461	611	745	766	2 005	4 244	4 665
Black, number with income	2 792	360	909	613	314	593	417	140	23	12
Median income (dollars)	23 030	11 892	18 745	25 348	26 444	37 414	34 106	44 456	(B)	(B)
Standard error (dollars)	626	796	715	757	844	1 542	887	3 120	(B)	(B)
Mean income (dollars)	26 256	13 891	20 521	26 664	26 866	41 799	36 692	48 868	(B)	(B)
Standard error (dollars)	470	741	583	808	1 096	1 392	1 186	2 581	(B)	(B)
Hispanic[1], number with income	2 136	704	644	312	153	322	236	54	20	11
Median income (dollars)	16 641	12 478	16 915	21 807	22 044	31 140	28 091	(B)	(B)	(B)
Standard error (dollars)	366	482	594	791	2 068	1 025	2 398	(B)	(B)	(B)
Mean income (dollars)	21 905	14 278	19 280	24 404	26 268	39 295	37 099	(B)	(B)	(B)
Standard error (dollars)	857	544	701	1 204	2 198	4 933	6 488	(B)	(B)	(B)
Non-Hispanic White, number with income	14 642	778	4 606	2 703	1 860	4 693	3 320	1 051	193	127
Median income (dollars)	23 711	11 770	19 623	22 744	25 153	35 753	32 600	40 056	59 124	53 519
Standard error (dollars)	295	509	335	520	661	452	630	1 098	8 740	4 728
Mean income (dollars)	29 665	14 677	22 098	26 276	28 153	42 132	37 751	48 115	71 399	62 581
Standard error (dollars)	321	652	505	495	638	730	695	2 094	4 526	4 989
Non-Hispanic Black, number with income	2 714	331	883	606	309	583	411	138	21	11
Median income (dollars)	23 317	12 091	18 780	25 399	26 532	37 536	34 137	44 766	(B)	(B)
Standard error (dollars)	653	829	758	733	837	1 544	887	3 152	(B)	(B)
Mean income (dollars)	26 380	14 151	20 575	26 728	26 850	41 505	36 681	49 147	(B)	(B)
Standard error (dollars)	466	785	596	814	1 084	1 327	1 197	2 585	(B)	(B)
Asian/Pacific Islander, number with income	925	88	180	129	84	442	313	79	24	23
Median income (dollars)	24 897	14 498	17 513	22 927	36 275	33 904	30 773	47 544	(B)	(B)
Standard error (dollars)	969	2 351	2 129	1 863	4 141	2 414	2 112	6 014	(B)	(B)
Mean income (dollars)	34 230	17 177	20 381	27 102	35 654	45 100	41 999	55 826	(B)	(B)
Standard error (dollars)	1 742	1 306	1 570	2 415	2 721	3 340	4 406	5 260	(B)	(B)
Year-Round, Full-Time Workers, 35 to 44 Years										
All races, number with income	11 790	880	3 718	2 243	1 408	3 539	2 474	777	170	116
Median income (dollars)	31 323	17 392	25 385	30 533	32 591	46 036	42 217	50 731	73 152	59 069
Standard error (dollars)	164	347	229	346	734	497	571	906	6 031	3 248
Mean income (dollars)	38 134	20 563	28 411	34 171	36 587	55 850	50 796	64 471	81 804	67 631
Standard error (dollars)	376	540	590	473	646	916	916	2 609	4 830	4 384
White, number with income	9 193	660	2 974	1 700	1 113	2 743	1 909	606	136	89
Median income (dollars)	31 715	17 240	25 793	30 716	33 369	47 197	44 627	50 910	78 852	60 683
Standard error (dollars)	184	333	259	382	992	596	1 027	861	3 679	2 050
Mean income (dollars)	39 104	20 449	29 122	34 741	37 241	57 880	52 772	66 395	83 594	69 808
Standard error (dollars)	450	649	720	556	769	1 082	1 038	3 260	5 146	5 295
Black, number with income	1 878	164	579	431	224	478	334	117	15	11
Median income (dollars)	29 115	17 641	23 238	29 849	30 235	40 396	36 087	48 148	(B)	(B)
Standard error (dollars)	667	929	1 099	1 221	1 070	1 024	1 305	3 390	(B)	(B)
Mean income (dollars)	32 523	20 945	25 261	31 838	32 139	46 080	40 394	52 581	(B)	(B)
Standard error (dollars)	572	1 223	709	874	1 140	1 529	1 245	2 704	(B)	(B)
Hispanic[1], number with income	1 212	350	375	195	91	198	143	35	11	8
Median income (dollars)	23 146	16 585	22 080	26 967	31 606	38 373	35 270	(B)	(B)	(B)
Standard error (dollars)	814	407	852	1 157	2 898	2 288	2 188	(B)	(B)	(B)
Mean income (dollars)	29 058	18 753	24 981	31 055	36 315	49 612	47 690	(B)	(B)	(B)
Standard error (dollars)	1 270	618	930	1 372	2 776	6 888	9 225	(B)	(B)	(B)
Non-Hispanic White, number with income	8 053	331	2 622	1 515	1 024	2 559	1 777	572	126	82
Median income (dollars)	32 643	18 471	26 121	31 114	33 620	48 178	45 583	50 986	80 074	61 215
Standard error (dollars)	352	884	265	401	1 111	818	776	1 032	2 878	2 602
Mean income (dollars)	40 561	22 098	29 707	35 180	37 359	58 537	53 159	67 200	86 137	71 825
Standard error (dollars)	481	1 143	809	602	804	1 050	872	3 437	5 419	5 663
Non-Hispanic Black, number with income	1 828	148	564	425	221	468	327	116	14	10
Median income (dollars)	29 434	18 008	23 423	29 907	30 224	40 486	36 139	48 367	(B)	(B)
Standard error (dollars)	657	1 046	1 137	1 201	1 067	990	1 304	3 304	(B)	(B)
Mean income (dollars)	32 617	21 420	25 378	31 963	31 918	45 807	40 450	52 953	(B)	(B)
Standard error (dollars)	559	1 319	723	879	1 121	1 439	1 259	2 701	(B)	(B)
Asian/Pacific Islander, number with income	599	44	116	90	57	291	210	48	18	14
Median income (dollars)	32 051	(B)	22 173	29 522	(B)	42 585	37 553	(B)	(B)	(B)
Standard error (dollars)	1 440	(B)	1 274	2 802	(B)	2 658	3 305	(B)	(B)	(B)
Mean income (dollars)	41 093	(B)	25 930	32 208	(B)	52 917	49 528	(B)	(B)	(B)
Standard error (dollars)	2 092	(B)	2 074	2 367	(B)	3 915	5 071	(B)	(B)	(B)

[1]May be of any race.
(B) = Base less than 75,000.

Table A-12. Income in 2001 by Educational Attainment for Population 18 Years and Over, by Age, Race, and Hispanic Origin, March 2002—*Continued*

(Numbers in thousand, except where noted.)

Income, standard error, age, race, and Hispanic origin	Total	High school		College						
		Not high school graduate	Graduate, includes GED	Some college, no degree	Associate degree	Bachelor's degree or more	Bachelor's degree	Master's degree	Professional degree	Doctorate degree
FEMALE										
All Workers, 45 to 54 Years										
All races, number with income	18 713	1 682	5 967	3 399	2 071	5 591	3 510	1 735	182	163
Median income (dollars)	24 135	11 725	19 764	23 923	26 127	40 774	35 248	48 163	57 449	60 931
Standard error (dollars)	254	261	291	548	509	375	547	900	5 809	2 881
Mean income (dollars)	30 743	14 426	23 122	27 459	29 405	46 279	39 769	53 826	75 718	73 127
Standard error (dollars)	326	333	601	481	583	744	763	1 605	4 929	5 857
White, number with income	15 454	1 212	4 947	2 813	1 738	4 743	2 945	1 497	163	136
Median income (dollars)	24 503	11 661	19 858	23 740	26 040	40 993	35 217	48 491	61 701	60 994
Standard error (dollars)	279	309	308	588	547	406	653	1 000	6 000	3 127
Mean income (dollars)	31 294	14 638	23 633	27 595	29 526	46 387	39 555	54 035	77 563	72 627
Standard error (dollars)	375	402	717	549	639	816	826	1 761	5 298	6 381
Black, number with income	2 237	332	775	450	230	447	287	142	8	9
Median income (dollars)	22 041	11 232	19 742	26 139	25 539	42 293	38 311	50 367	(B)	(B)
Standard error (dollars)	479	580	730	1 489	1 574	1 984	2 152	2 017	(B)	(B)
Mean income (dollars)	26 693	13 185	20 570	27 658	29 215	45 074	39 747	53 473	(B)	(B)
Standard error (dollars)	550	725	562	1 147	1 976	1 490	1 520	2 764	(B)	(B)
Hispanic[1], number with income	1 463	528	422	216	106	189	127	48	10	2
Median income (dollars)	16 370	12 026	16 517	21 816	25 727	32 129	24 406	(B)	(B)	(B)
Standard error (dollars)	461	432	1 092	1 334	3 920	2 815	3 664	(B)	(B)	(B)
Mean income (dollars)	20 654	13 404	18 790	24 433	30 129	35 424	29 102	(B)	(B)	(B)
Standard error (dollars)	593	501	904	1 338	2 650	2 668	2 477	(B)	(B)	(B)
Non-Hispanic White, number with income	14 088	705	4 555	2 621	1 636	4 569	2 832	1 450	153	133
Median income (dollars)	25 656	11 275	20 149	24 015	26 067	41 263	35 438	48 723	64 850	61 214
Standard error (dollars)	239	430	280	619	566	417	540	1 041	6 309	3 063
Mean income (dollars)	32 325	15 472	24 024	27 860	29 476	46 787	39 962	54 211	79 160	73 751
Standard error (dollars)	406	595	775	581	660	840	852	1 810	5 429	6 463
Non-Hispanic Black, number with income	2 178	320	753	439	228	436	277	141	8	9
Median income (dollars)	22 201	11 338	19 925	26 185	25 399	42 466	39 089	50 219	(B)	(B)
Standard error (dollars)	551	692	701	1 447	1 575	2 019	2 099	2 038	(B)	(B)
Mean income (dollars)	26 885	13 304	20 707	27 749	29 100	45 480	40 239	53 457	(B)	(B)
Standard error (dollars)	560	751	571	1 164	1 987	1 509	1 539	2 788	(B)	(B)
Asian/Pacific Islander, number with income	808	101	181	84	77	363	261	81	7	13
Median income (dollars)	24 600	15 892	18 503	24 255	28 386	33 540	32 650	32 356	(B)	(B)
Standard error (dollars)	976	1 208	1 608	2 398	1 600	1 886	1 630	3 259	(B)	(B)
Mean income (dollars)	33 607	17 096	20 750	25 396	28 069	47 689	42 828	53 846	(B)	(B)
Standard error (dollars)	1 989	1 467	1 552	2 525	2 502	4 079	4 250	10 716	(B)	(B)
Year-Round, Full-Time Workers, 45 to 54 Years										
All races, number with income	11 057	714	3 520	2 030	1 287	3 503	2 110	1 147	124	121
Median income (dollars)	32 661	19 037	25 698	31 672	33 819	48 971	44 857	51 780	76 059	67 932
Standard error (dollars)	324	766	268	314	1 065	719	665	444	6 451	4 948
Mean income (dollars)	40 572	21 359	30 668	36 316	38 328	57 732	51 600	62 826	86 128	87 186
Standard error (dollars)	489	534	967	644	744	1 022	1 008	2 249	5 631	7 154
White, number with income	9 048	510	2 888	1 663	1 067	2 918	1 719	982	110	105
Median income (dollars)	33 723	19 923	25 971	31 641	34 348	49 941	45 129	51 774	76 441	64 987
Standard error (dollars)	442	726	300	336	1 044	616	652	444	6 770	4 595
Mean income (dollars)	41 507	21 743	31 712	36 730	38 882	58 348	52 298	62 771	88 014	84 666
Standard error (dollars)	568	636	1 171	754	813	1 132	1 085	2 499	6 089	7 579
Black, number with income	1 381	129	472	290	158	330	206	112	3	7
Median income (dollars)	30 499	16 232	25 319	31 774	31 930	46 382	45 042	50 404	(B)	(B)
Standard error (dollars)	466	1 546	1 074	1 174	1 734	885	2 342	2 083	(B)	(B)
Mean income (dollars)	34 010	19 585	26 104	34 855	35 743	49 356	44 995	54 886	(B)	(B)
Standard error (dollars)	672	1 363	651	1 214	2 539	1 533	1 552	2 713	(B)	(B)
Hispanic[1], number with income	819	243	236	147	76	115	75	32	7	(B)
Median income (dollars)	22 384	16 592	22 363	27 290	32 264	39 479	35 208	(B)	(B)	(B)
Standard error (dollars)	614	542	894	2 259	2 914	2 766	3 204	(B)	(B)	(B)
Mean income (dollars)	28 004	18 011	25 620	29 480	36 905	46 165	38 599	(B)	(B)	(B)
Standard error (dollars)	854	774	1 243	1 587	2 668	3 584	3 136	(B)	(B)	(B)
Non-Hispanic White, number with income	8 281	274	2 669	1 530	993	2 812	1 653	951	103	104
Median income (dollars)	35 211	22 718	26 257	32 001	34 547	50 123	45 361	51 766	76 787	64 868
Standard error (dollars)	262	930	307	358	1 003	522	619	437	3 961	4 552
Mean income (dollars)	42 751	24 876	32 156	37 407	39 038	58 771	52 814	62 946	89 154	84 835
Standard error (dollars)	614	950	1 262	806	852	1 166	1 118	2 570	6 212	7 638
Non-Hispanic Black, number with income	1 351	124	462	283	157	323	200	111	3	7
Median income (dollars)	30 605	16 686	25 434	31 641	31 788	46 496	45 244	50 210	(B)	(B)
Standard error (dollars)	465	1 655	1 000	1 062	1 631	875	2 186	2 079	(B)	(B)
Mean income (dollars)	34 163	19 836	26 226	34 909	35 644	49 680	45 420	54 882	(B)	(B)
Standard error (dollars)	682	1 400	660	1 236	2 564	1 548	1 560	2 743	(B)	(B)
Asian/Pacific Islander, number with income	519	62	120	54	46	235	176	43	6	8
Median income (dollars)	31 458	(B)	22 457	(B)	(B)	46 626	41 236	(B)	(B)	(B)
Standard error (dollars)	833	(B)	1 766	(B)	(B)	3 588	3 610	(B)	(B)	(B)
Mean income (dollars)	43 835	(B)	25 315	(B)	(B)	63 088	53 168	(B)	(B)	(B)
Standard error (dollars)	2 862	(B)	1 857	(B)	(B)	5 806	5 863	(B)	(B)	(B)

[1]May be of any race.
(B) = Base less than 75,000.

Table A-12. Income in 2001 by Educational Attainment for Population 18 Years and Over, by Age, Race, and Hispanic Origin, March 2002—*Continued*

(Numbers in thousand, except where noted.)

Income, standard error, age, race, and Hispanic origin	Total	High school		College						
		Not high school graduate	Graduate, includes GED	Some college, no degree	Associate degree	Bachelor's degree or more	Bachelor's degree	Master's degree	Professional degree	Doctorate degree
FEMALE										
All Workers, 55 to 64 Years										
All races, number with income	12 377	1 824	4 582	2 181	982	2 806	1 681	868	127	128
Median income (dollars)	17 823	8 723	15 485	19 855	25 218	34 164	29 233	44 375	33 758	58 311
Standard error (dollars)	272	265	305	553	861	1 186	1 178	1 080	7 598	2 854
Mean income (dollars)	25 602	12 120	19 343	27 051	29 648	42 050	34 321	52 304	56 730	59 372
Standard error (dollars)	362	302	308	1 108	1 522	1 014	895	2 524	5 142	4 095
White, number with income	10 561	1 377	3 992	1 942	825	2 423	1 426	773	107	114
Median income (dollars)	18 100	8 810	15 492	19 643	24 814	34 717	29 034	44 922	38 268	57 118
Standard error (dollars)	295	329	324	581	877	1 241	1 247	1 046	8 563	3 635
Mean income (dollars)	26 116	12 018	19 588	27 198	29 898	42 731	34 554	53 183	57 781	59 777
Standard error (dollars)	412	331	343	1 228	1 773	1 140	1 000	2 793	5 620	4 439
Black, number with income	1 288	346	431	194	112	202	121	63	7	9
Median income (dollars)	16 024	8 374	15 442	21 481	28 926	36 184	33 266	(B)	(B)	(B)
Standard error (dollars)	794	544	1 193	2 160	3 383	1 458	2 552	(B)	(B)	(B)
Mean income (dollars)	22 015	12 313	17 849	26 577	27 326	40 100	34 429	(B)	(B)	(B)
Standard error (dollars)	686	816	701	2 052	2 256	2 333	2 329	(B)	(B)	(B)
Hispanic[1], number with income	815	384	230	76	39	83	47	25	5	5
Median income (dollars)	11 584	8 199	12 753	20 844	(B)	36 906	(B)	(B)	(B)	(B)
Standard error (dollars)	566	661	1 691	4 142	(B)	4 699	(B)	(B)	(B)	(B)
Mean income (dollars)	17 695	10 409	16 849	24 740	(B)	44 404	(B)	(B)	(B)	(B)
Standard error (dollars)	817	472	1 060	2 544	(B)	4 974	(B)	(B)	(B)	(B)
Non-Hispanic White, number with income	9 786	1 009	3 776	1 869	785	2 344	1 381	750	103	109
Median income (dollars)	18 805	9 047	15 609	19 595	25 040	34 545	28 802	44 829	33 923	57 742
Standard error (dollars)	311	378	323	600	861	1 302	1 363	1 047	8 203	3 122
Mean income (dollars)	26 793	12 611	19 760	27 297	30 230	42 671	34 490	53 027	57 044	61 261
Standard error (dollars)	439	419	358	1 273	1 854	1 167	1 013	2 870	5 813	4 505
Non-Hispanic Black, number with income	1 260	332	421	193	112	200	121	62	6	9
Median income (dollars)	16 144	8 342	15 284	21 315	28 926	36 184	33 266	(B)	(B)	(B)
Standard error (dollars)	801	580	1 152	2 153	3 383	1 444	2 552	(B)	(B)	(B)
Mean income (dollars)	22 099	12 426	17 734	26 309	27 326	40 372	34 429	(B)	(B)	(B)
Standard error (dollars)	697	847	709	2 047	2 256	2 350	2 329	(B)	(B)	(B)
Asian/Pacific Islander, number with income	416	69	117	27	33	168	128	27	10	1
Median income (dollars)	18 418	(B)	16 009	(B)	(B)	28 097	26 658	(B)	(B)	(B)
Standard error (dollars)	1 564	(B)	1 820	(B)	(B)	2 658	4 220	(B)	(B)	(B)
Mean income (dollars)	25 822	(B)	17 480	(B)	(B)	36 208	32 128	(B)	(B)	(B)
Standard error (dollars)	1 601	(B)	1 502	(B)	(B)	3 207	3 270	(B)	(B)	(B)
Year-Round, Full-Time Workers, 55 to 64 Years										
All races, number with income	5 000	487	1 808	926	469	1 309	730	449	67	61
Median income (dollars)	31 679	18 205	26 334	34 193	37 018	49 718	41 933	56 011	(B)	(B)
Standard error (dollars)	250	725	355	830	842	1 077	1 334	1 902	(B)	(B)
Mean income (dollars)	39 399	20 831	29 948	39 843	41 230	58 399	48 592	68 138	(B)	(B)
Standard error (dollars)	626	678	539	966	2 810	1 745	1 500	4 174	(B)	(B)
White, number with income	4 232	366	1 556	811	389	1 108	594	402	60	51
Median income (dollars)	32 076	18 117	26 501	34 466	37 586	50 044	41 994	56 274	(B)	(B)
Standard error (dollars)	276	865	383	789	1 148	988	1 326	1 643	(B)	(B)
Mean income (dollars)	40 292	20 494	30 732	40 247	42 099	59 662	49 509	69 109	(B)	(B)
Standard error (dollars)	719	702	612	1 035	3 360	2 017	1 780	4 616	(B)	(B)
Black, number with income	540	91	180	96	61	111	70	30	2	8
Median income (dollars)	29 914	18 618	25 747	31 729	(B)	50 551	(B)	(B)	(B)	(B)
Standard error (dollars)	887	1 333	1 480	2 397	(B)	2 925	(B)	(B)	(B)	(B)
Mean income (dollars)	33 909	22 992	25 380	37 410	(B)	53 717	(B)	(B)	(B)	(B)
Standard error (dollars)	1 177	2 334	921	3 338	(B)	2 987	(B)	(B)	(B)	(B)
Hispanic[1], number with income	350	118	121	35	19	54	29	21	2	1
Median income (dollars)	23 345	16 776	22 593	(B)	(B)	(B)	(B)	(B)	(B)	(B)
Standard error (dollars)	1 306	606	1 434	(B)	(B)	(B)	(B)	(B)	(B)	(B)
Mean income (dollars)	28 669	17 381	24 230	(B)	(B)	(B)	(B)	(B)	(B)	(B)
Standard error (dollars)	1 431	847	1 444	(B)	(B)	(B)	(B)	(B)	(B)	(B)
Non-Hispanic White, number with income	3 902	255	1 442	777	369	1 058	566	384	57	50
Median income (dollars)	32 689	20 175	26 818	34 414	37 747	50 226	42 267	56 263	(B)	(B)
Standard error (dollars)	468	1 109	398	870	1 240	899	1 397	1 666	(B)	(B)
Mean income (dollars)	41 291	21 838	31 257	40 429	42 625	59 829	49 665	69 382	(B)	(B)
Standard error (dollars)	769	927	649	1 075	3 533	2 095	1 822	4 827	(B)	(B)
Non-Hispanic Black, number with income	526	86	174	95	61	109	70	29	2	8
Median income (dollars)	29 944	19 140	25 651	31 580	(B)	50 724	(B)	(B)	(B)	(B)
Standard error (dollars)	883	1 320	1 622	2 315	(B)	2 900	(B)	(B)	(B)	(B)
Mean income (dollars)	34 091	23 530	25 335	37 019	(B)	53 912	(B)	(B)	(B)	(B)
Standard error (dollars)	1 199	2 444	940	3 361	(B)	3 018	(B)	(B)	(B)	(B)
Asian/Pacific Islander, number with income	191	23	56	12	14	85	64	14	4	1
Median income (dollars)	29 811	(B)	(B)	(B)	(B)	45 098	(B)	(B)	(B)	(B)
Standard error (dollars)	1 219	(B)	(B)	(B)	(B)	6 766	(B)	(B)	(B)	(B)
Mean income (dollars)	36 896	(B)	(B)	(B)	(B)	49 266	(B)	(B)	(B)	(B)
Standard error (dollars)	2 191	(B)	(B)	(B)	(B)	3 902	(B)	(B)	(B)	(B)

[1]May be of any race.
(B) = Base less than 75,000.

Table A-12. Income in 2001 by Educational Attainment for Population 18 Years and Over, by Age, Race, and Hispanic Origin, March 2002—*Continued*

(Numbers in thousand, except where noted.)

Income, standard error, age, race, and Hispanic origin	Total	High school		College						
		Not high school graduate	Graduate, includes GED	Some college, no degree	Associate degree	Bachelor's degree or more	Bachelor's degree	Master's degree	Professional degree	Doctorate degree
FEMALE										
All Workers, 65 Years and Over										
All races, number with income	18 969	5 596	7 430	2 506	985	2 449	1 639	646	92	71
Median income (dollars)	11 312	8 783	11 363	13 309	13 813	19 284	17 372	24 695	17 158	(B)
Standard error (dollars)	78	93	122	273	308	420	470	1 412	2 200	(B)
Mean income (dollars)	16 311	11 029	14 858	19 927	18 456	28 222	25 231	30 900	32 041	(B)
Standard error (dollars)	192	170	173	1 018	633	730	705	1 150	4 396	(B)
White, number with income	16 742	4 567	6 789	2 305	876	2 203	1 484	581	78	59
Median income (dollars)	11 620	9 062	11 470	13 614	14 170	19 334	17 575	23 876	17 180	(B)
Standard error (dollars)	82	105	129	285	318	427	494	1 476	3 657	(B)
Mean income (dollars)	16 600	11 295	15 026	19 668	18 897	28 323	25 501	30 575	31 227	(B)
Standard error (dollars)	193	197	185	897	690	774	746	1 170	4 211	(B)
Black, number with income	1 649	806	446	153	76	167	95	56	11	3
Median income (dollars)	9 050	7 613	9 740	10 556	11 276	22 735	18 040	(B)	(B)	(B)
Standard error (dollars)	180	220	331	693	749	3 511	3 716	(B)	(B)	(B)
Mean income (dollars)	12 841	9 516	12 053	14 081	15 965	28 419	23 878	(B)	(B)	(B)
Standard error (dollars)	393	300	463	1 024	1 823	2 702	2 350	(B)	(B)	(B)
Hispanic[1], number with income	958	623	233	42	21	38	30	5	1	(B)
Median income (dollars)	7 585	7 362	7 245	(B)	(B)	(B)	(B)	(B)	(B)	(B)
Standard error (dollars)	211	222	327	(B)	(B)	(B)	(B)	(B)	(B)	(B)
Mean income (dollars)	9 656	8 546	9 138	(B)	(B)	(B)	(B)	(B)	(B)	(B)
Standard error (dollars)	333	318	606	(B)	(B)	(B)	(B)	(B)	(B)	(B)
Non-Hispanic White, number with income	15 820	3 968	6 566	2 263	855	2 167	1 455	575	77	59
Median income (dollars)	11 928	9 381	11 644	13 618	14 193	19 443	17 692	23 850	17 414	(B)
Standard error (dollars)	83	116	129	282	318	435	504	1 462	3 660	(B)
Mean income (dollars)	17 006	11 727	15 224	19 667	18 985	28 481	25 698	30 511	31 619	(B)
Standard error (dollars)	203	222	189	912	704	784	757	1 177	4 278	(B)
Non-Hispanic Black, number with income	1 627	794	438	153	76	165	93	56	11	3
Median income (dollars)	9 066	7 607	9 802	10 547	11 276	23 206	18 141	(B)	(B)	(B)
Standard error (dollars)	183	222	357	693	749	3 486	4 009	(B)	(B)	(B)
Mean income (dollars)	12 894	9 537	12 124	14 082	15 965	28 564	24 039	(B)	(B)	(B)
Standard error (dollars)	398	304	469	1 025	1 823	2 731	2 396	(B)	(B)	(B)
Asian/Pacific Islander, number with income	440	148	154	34	24	77	58	8	1	8
Median income (dollars)	9 986	7 731	12 024	(B)	(B)	14 465	(B)	(B)	(B)	(B)
Standard error (dollars)	607	492	864	(B)	(B)	1 787	(B)	(B)	(B)	(B)
Mean income (dollars)	19 463	11 679	15 843	(B)	(B)	25 043	(B)	(B)	(B)	(B)
Standard error (dollars)	3 759	1 395	1 268	(B)	(B)	4 472	(B)	(B)	(B)	(B)
Year-Round, Full-Time Workers, 65 Years and Over										
All races, number with income	738	105	291	140	53	146	90	37	9	9
Median income (dollars)	35 098	22 971	32 240	40 830	(B)	52 015	45 538	(B)	(B)	(B)
Standard error (dollars)	805	1 465	1 572	3 575	(B)	3 979	3 394	(B)	(B)	(B)
Mean income (dollars)	46 997	25 849	39 043	71 709	(B)	55 438	49 537	(B)	(B)	(B)
Standard error (dollars)	3 295	1 225	1 868	16 175	(B)	2 939	3 186	(B)	(B)	(B)
White, number with income	642	75	264	132	44	125	78	32	8	5
Median income (dollars)	34 841	22 297	31 739	40 770	(B)	52 876	48 069	(B)	(B)	(B)
Standard error (dollars)	823	1 051	1 618	3 555	(B)	3 771	5 455	(B)	(B)	(B)
Mean income (dollars)	46 185	25 157	39 645	62 064	(B)	56 366	51 235	(B)	(B)	(B)
Standard error (dollars)	3 013	1 148	2 028	13 408	(B)	2 898	3 498	(B)	(B)	(B)
Black, number with income	73	26	18	5	8	13	7	3	1	1
Median income (dollars)	(B)	(B)	(B)	(B)	(B)	(B)	(B)	(B)	(B)	(B)
Standard error (dollars)	(B)	(B)	(B)	(B)	(B)	(B)	(B)	(B)	(B)	(B)
Mean income (dollars)	(B)	(B)	(B)	(B)	(B)	(B)	(B)	(B)	(B)	(B)
Standard error (dollars)	(B)	(B)	(B)	(B)	(B)	(B)	(B)	(B)	(B)	(B)
Hispanic[1], number with income	37	16	8	6	4	1	1	(B)	(B)	(B)
Median income (dollars)	(B)	(B)	(B)	(B)	(B)	(B)	(B)	(B)	(B)	(B)
Standard error (dollars)	(B)	(B)	(B)	(B)	(B)	(B)	(B)	(B)	(B)	(B)
Mean income (dollars)	(B)	(B)	(B)	(B)	(B)	(B)	(B)	(B)	(B)	(B)
Standard error (dollars)	(B)	(B)	(B)	(B)	(B)	(B)	(B)	(B)	(B)	(B)
Non-Hispanic White, number with income	606	60	255	126	40	123	76	32	8	5
Median income (dollars)	35 392	(B)	31 953	40 632	(B)	52 678	47 791	(B)	(B)	(B)
Standard error (dollars)	860	(B)	1 603	4 085	(B)	3 775	5 412	(B)	(B)	(B)
Mean income (dollars)	47 155	(B)	39 992	63 064	(B)	56 447	51 238	(B)	(B)	(B)
Standard error (dollars)	3 179	(B)	2 079	14 094	(B)	2 919	3 536	(B)	(B)	(B)
Non-Hispanic Black, number with income	72	25	18	5	8	13	7	3	1	1
Median income (dollars)	(B)	(B)	(B)	(B)	(B)	(B)	(B)	(B)	(B)	(B)
Standard error (dollars)	(B)	(B)	(B)	(B)	(B)	(B)	(B)	(B)	(B)	(B)
Mean income (dollars)	(B)	(B)	(B)	(B)	(B)	(B)	(B)	(B)	(B)	(B)
Standard error (dollars)	(B)	(B)	(B)	(B)	(B)	(B)	(B)	(B)	(B)	(B)
Asian/Pacific Islander, number with income	21	3	8	2	(B)	7	4	1	(B)	1
Median income (dollars)	(B)	(B)	(B)	(B)	(B)	(B)	(B)	(B)	(B)	(B)
Standard error (dollars)	(B)	(B)	(B)	(B)	(B)	(B)	(B)	(B)	(B)	(B)
Mean income (dollars)	(B)	(B)	(B)	(B)	(B)	(B)	(B)	(B)	(B)	(B)
Standard error (dollars)	(B)	(B)	(B)	(B)	(B)	(B)	(B)	(B)	(B)	(B)

[1]May be of any race.
(B) = Base less than 75,000.

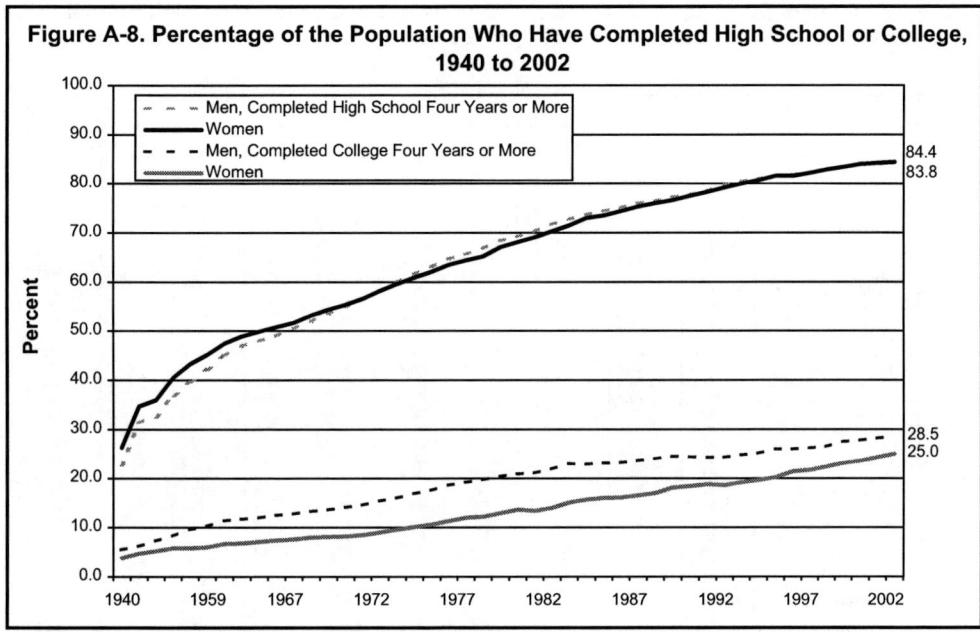

Figure A-8. Percentage of the Population Who Have Completed High School or College, 1940 to 2002

Source: U.S. Census Bureau, *Current Population Survey*, 2000.

- In 1940, only one in four Americans had completed high school. As recently as 1966, less than half of the U.S. population 25 years or older had high school diplomas. By 2002, 84.1 percent of Americans in that age group were high school graduates. In 2002, the high school graduation rate for women (84.4 percent) exceeded that of men (83.8 percent), marking the first statistical difference between the two sexes in over a decade.

- The percentage of college graduates, who constituted less than 5 percent of the 1940 population, rose to almost 10 percent by 1966 and included close to 27 percent of the over-25 population by 2002. In recent years, women, non-Hispanic Whites, and Blacks have seen the most significant increases in college graduates.

Table A-13. Percentage of Population 25 Years and Over Who Have Completed High School or College, by Race, Sex, and Hispanic Origin, Selected Years 1940 to 2002

(Percent.)

Age and year	All races			White			Black			Hispanic origin[1]		
	Total	Male	Female	Total	Male	Female	Total	Male	Female	Total	Male	Female
25 YEARS AND OVER												
Completed 4 Years of High School or More												
2002*	84.1	83.8	84.4	88.7	88.5	88.9	79.2	79.0	79.4	57.0	56.1	57.9
2002	84.1	83.8	84.4	84.8	84.3	85.2	78.7	78.5	78.9	57.0	56.1	57.9
2001*	84.1	84.1	84.2	88.6	88.6	88.6	79.1	79.5	78.8	56.8	55.5	58.0
2001	84.1	84.1	84.2	84.8	84.4	85.1	78.8	79.2	78.5	56.8	55.5	58.0
2000*	84.1	84.2	84.0	88.4	88.5	88.4	78.9	79.1	78.7	57.0	56.6	57.5
2000	84.1	84.2	84.0	84.9	84.8	85.0	78.5	78.7	78.3	57.0	56.6	57.5
1999*	83.4	83.4	83.4	87.7	87.7	87.7	77.4	77.2	77.5	56.1	56.0	56.3
1999	83.4	83.4	83.4	84.3	84.2	84.3	77.0	76.7	77.2	56.1	56.0	56.3
1998*	82.8	82.8	82.9	87.1	87.1	87.1	76.0	75.2	76.7	55.5	55.7	55.3
1998	82.8	82.8	82.9	83.7	83.6	83.8	76.0	75.2	76.7	55.5	55.7	55.3
1997*	82.1	82.0	82.2	86.3	86.3	86.3	74.9	73.5	76.0	54.7	54.9	54.6
1997	82.1	82.0	82.2	83.0	82.9	83.2	74.9	73.5	76.0	54.7	54.9	54.6
1996*	81.7	81.9	81.6	86.0	86.1	85.9	74.3	74.3	74.2	53.1	53.0	53.3
1996	81.7	81.9	81.6	82.8	82.7	82.8	74.3	74.3	74.2	53.1	53.0	53.3
1995*	81.7	81.7	81.6	85.9	86.0	85.8	73.8	73.4	74.1	53.4	52.9	53.8
1995	81.7	81.7	81.6	83.0	83.0	83.0	73.8	73.4	74.1	53.4	52.9	53.8
1994*	80.9	81.0	80.7	84.9	85.1	84.7	72.9	71.7	73.8	53.3	53.4	53.2
1994	80.9	81.0	80.7	82.0	82.1	81.9	72.9	71.7	73.8	53.3	53.4	53.2
1993*	80.2	80.5	80.0	84.1	84.5	83.8	70.4	69.6	71.1	53.1	52.9	53.2
1993	80.2	80.5	80.0	81.5	81.8	81.3	70.4	69.6	71.1	53.1	52.9	53.2
1992	79.4	79.7	79.2	80.9	81.1	80.7	67.7	67.0	68.2	52.6	53.7	51.5
1991	78.4	78.5	78.3	79.9	79.8	79.9	66.7	66.7	66.7	51.3	51.4	51.2
1990	77.6	77.7	77.5	79.1	79.1	79.0	66.2	65.8	66.5	50.8	50.3	51.3
1989	76.9	77.2	76.6	78.4	78.6	78.2	64.6	64.2	65.0	50.9	51.0	50.7
1988	76.2	76.4	76.0	77.7	77.7	77.6	63.5	63.7	63.4	51.0	52.0	50.0
1987	75.6	76.0	75.3	77.0	77.3	76.7	63.4	63.0	63.7	50.9	51.8	50.0
1986	74.7	75.1	74.4	76.2	76.5	75.9	62.3	61.5	63.0	48.5	49.2	47.8
1985	73.9	74.4	73.5	75.5	76.0	75.1	59.8	58.4	60.8	47.9	48.5	47.4
1984	73.3	73.7	73.0	75.0	75.4	74.6	58.5	57.1	59.7	47.1	48.6	45.7
1983	72.1	72.7	71.5	73.8	74.4	73.3	56.8	56.5	57.1	46.2	48.6	44.2
1982	71.0	71.7	70.3	72.8	73.4	72.3	54.9	55.7	54.3	45.9	48.1	44.1
1981	69.7	70.3	69.1	71.6	72.1	71.2	52.9	53.2	52.6	44.5	45.5	43.6
1980	68.6	69.2	68.1	70.5	71.0	70.1	51.2	51.1	51.3	45.3	46.4	44.1
1979	67.7	68.4	67.1	69.7	70.3	69.2	49.4	49.2	49.5	42.0	42.3	41.7
1978	65.9	66.8	65.2	67.9	68.6	67.2	47.6	47.9	47.3	40.8	42.2	39.6
1977	64.9	65.6	64.4	67.0	67.5	66.5	45.5	45.6	45.4	39.6	42.3	37.2
1976	64.1	64.7	63.5	66.1	66.7	65.5	43.8	42.3	45.0	39.3	41.4	37.3
1975	62.5	63.1	62.1	64.5	65.0	64.1	42.5	41.6	43.3	37.9	39.5	36.7
1974	61.2	61.6	60.9	63.3	63.6	63.0	40.8	39.9	41.5	36.5	38.3	34.9
1973	59.8	60.0	59.6	61.9	62.1	61.7	39.2	38.2	40.1	...	...	...
1972	58.2	58.2	58.2	60.4	60.3	60.5	36.6	35.7	37.2	...	...	...
1971	56.4	56.3	56.6	58.6	58.4	58.8	34.7	33.8	35.4	...	...	...
1970	55.2	55.0	55.4	57.4	57.2	57.6	33.7	32.4	34.8	...	...	...
1969	54.0	53.6	54.4	56.3	55.7	56.7	32.3	31.9	32.6	...	...	...
1968	52.6	52.0	53.2	54.9	54.3	55.5	30.1	28.9	31.0	...	...	...
1967	51.1	50.5	51.7	53.4	52.8	53.8	29.5	27.1	31.5	...	...	...
1966	49.9	49.0	50.8	52.2	51.3	53.0	27.8	25.8	29.5	...	...	...
1965	49.0	48.0	49.9	51.3	50.2	52.2	27.2	25.8	28.4	...	...	...
1964	48.0	47.0	48.9	50.3	49.3	51.2	25.7	23.7	27.4	...	...	...
1962	46.3	45.0	47.5	48.7	47.4	49.9	24.8	23.2	26.2	...	...	...
1959	43.7	42.2	45.2	46.1	44.5	47.7	20.7	19.6	21.6	...	...	...
1957	41.6	39.7	43.3	43.2	41.1	45.1	18.4	16.9	19.7	...	...	...
1952	38.8	36.9	40.5	...	...	...	15.0	14.0	15.7	...	...	...
1950	34.3	32.6	36.0	...	...	...	13.7	12.5	14.7	...	...	...
1947	33.1	31.4	34.7	35.0	33.2	36.7	13.6	12.7	14.5	...	...	...
1940	24.5	22.7	26.3	26.1	24.2	28.1	7.7	6.9	8.4	...	...	...

[1]May be of any race.
* = Data for non-Hispanic White (1993–2002) and non-Hispanic Black (1999–2002).
. . . = Not available.

Table A-13. Percentage of Population 25 Years and Over Who Have Completed High School or College, by Race, Sex, and Hispanic Origin, Selected Years 1940 to 2002—*Continued*

(Percent.)

Age and year	All races			White			Black			Hispanic origin[1]		
	Total	Male	Female	Total	Male	Female	Total	Male	Female	Total	Male	Female
25 YEARS AND OVER—*Continued*												
Completed 4 Years of College or More												
2002*	26.7	28.5	25.1	29.4	31.7	27.3	17.2	16.5	17.7	11.1	11.0	11.2
2002	26.7	28.5	25.1	27.2	29.1	25.4	17.0	16.4	17.5	11.1	11.0	11.2
2001*	26.2	28.2	24.3	28.7	31.3	26.3	15.7	15.3	16.0	11.1	10.8	11.4
2001	26.2	28.2	24.3	26.6	28.7	24.6	15.7	15.3	16.1	11.1	10.8	11.4
2000*	25.6	27.8	23.6	28.1	30.8	25.5	16.6	16.4	16.8	10.6	10.7	10.6
2000	25.6	27.8	23.6	26.1	28.5	23.9	16.5	16.3	16.7	10.6	10.7	10.6
1999*	25.2	27.5	23.1	27.7	30.6	25.0	15.5	14.3	16.5	10.9	10.7	11.0
1999	25.2	27.5	23.1	25.9	28.5	23.5	15.4	14.2	16.4	10.9	10.7	11.0
1998*	24.4	26.5	22.4	26.6	29.3	24.1	14.7	13.9	15.4	11.0	11.1	10.9
1998	24.4	26.5	22.4	25.0	27.3	22.8	14.7	13.9	15.4	11.0	11.1	10.9
1997*	23.9	26.2	21.7	26.2	29.0	23.7	13.3	12.5	13.9	10.3	10.6	10.1
1997	23.9	26.2	21.7	24.6	27.0	22.3	13.3	12.5	13.9	10.3	10.6	10.1
1996*	23.6	26.0	21.4	25.9	28.8	23.2	13.6	12.4	14.6	9.3	10.3	8.3
1996	23.6	26.0	21.4	24.3	26.9	21.8	13.6	12.4	14.6	9.3	10.3	8.3
1995*	23.0	26.0	20.2	25.4	28.9	22.1	13.2	13.6	12.9	9.3	10.1	8.4
1995	23.0	26.0	20.2	24.0	27.2	21.0	13.2	13.6	12.9	9.3	10.1	8.4
1994*	22.2	25.1	19.6	24.3	27.8	21.1	12.9	12.8	13.0	9.1	9.6	8.6
1994	22.2	25.1	19.6	22.9	26.1	20.0	12.9	12.8	13.0	9.1	9.6	8.6
1993*	21.9	24.8	19.2	23.8	27.2	20.7	12.2	11.9	12.4	9.0	9.5	8.5
1993	21.9	24.8	19.2	22.6	25.7	19.7	12.2	11.9	12.4	9.0	9.5	8.5
1992	21.4	24.3	18.6	22.1	25.2	19.1	11.9	11.9	12.0	9.3	10.2	8.5
1991	21.4	24.3	18.8	22.2	25.4	19.3	11.5	11.4	11.6	9.7	10.0	9.4
1990	21.3	24.4	18.4	22.0	25.3	19.0	11.3	11.9	10.8	9.2	9.8	8.7
1989	21.1	24.5	18.1	21.8	25.4	18.5	11.8	11.7	11.9	9.9	11.0	8.8
1988	20.3	24.0	17.0	20.9	25.0	17.3	11.2	11.1	11.4	10.1	12.3	8.1
1987	19.9	23.6	16.5	20.5	24.5	16.9	10.7	11.0	10.4	8.6	9.7	7.5
1986	19.4	23.2	16.1	20.1	24.1	16.4	10.9	11.2	10.7	8.4	9.5	7.4
1985	19.4	23.1	16.0	20.0	24.0	16.3	11.1	11.2	11.0	8.5	9.7	7.3
1984	19.1	22.9	15.7	19.8	23.9	16.0	10.4	10.4	10.4	8.2	9.5	7.0
1983	18.8	23.0	15.1	19.5	24.0	15.4	9.5	10.0	9.2	7.9	9.2	6.8
1982	17.7	21.9	14.0	18.5	23.0	14.4	8.8	9.1	8.5	7.8	9.6	6.2
1981	17.1	21.1	13.4	17.8	22.2	13.8	8.2	8.2	8.2	7.7	9.7	5.9
1980	17.0	20.9	13.6	17.8	22.1	14.0	7.9	7.7	8.1	7.9	9.7	6.2
1979	16.4	20.4	12.9	17.2	21.4	13.3	7.9	8.3	7.5	6.7	8.2	5.3
1978	15.7	19.7	12.2	16.4	20.7	12.6	7.2	7.3	7.1	7.0	8.6	5.7
1977	15.4	19.2	12.0	16.1	20.2	12.4	7.2	7.0	7.4	6.2	8.1	4.4
1976	14.7	18.6	11.3	15.4	19.6	11.6	6.6	6.3	6.8	6.1	8.6	4.0
1975	13.9	17.6	10.6	14.5	18.4	11.0	6.4	6.7	6.2	6.3	8.3	4.6
1974	13.3	16.9	10.1	14.0	17.7	10.6	5.5	5.7	5.3	5.5	7.1	4.0
1973	12.6	16.0	9.6	13.1	16.8	9.9	6.0	5.9	6.0	...	...	...
1972	12.0	15.4	9.0	12.6	16.2	9.4	5.1	5.5	4.8	...	...	...
1971	11.4	14.6	8.5	12.0	15.5	8.9	4.5	4.7	4.3	...	...	...
1970	11.0	14.1	8.2	11.6	15.0	8.6	4.5	4.6	4.4	...	...	...
1969	10.7	13.6	8.1	11.2	14.3	8.5	4.6	4.8	4.5	...	...	...
1968	10.5	13.3	8.0	11.0	14.1	8.3	4.3	3.7	4.8	...	...	...
1967	10.1	12.8	7.6	10.6	13.6	7.9	4.0	3.4	4.4	...	...	...
1966	9.8	12.5	7.4	10.4	13.3	7.7	3.8	3.9	3.7	...	...	...
1965	9.4	12.0	7.1	9.9	12.7	7.3	4.7	4.9	4.5	...	...	...
1964	9.1	11.7	6.8	9.6	12.3	7.1	3.9	4.5	3.4	...	...	...
1962	8.9	11.4	6.7	9.5	12.2	7.0	4.0	3.9	4.0	...	...	...
1959	8.1	10.3	6.0	8.6	11.0	6.2	3.3	3.8	2.9	...	...	...
1957	7.6	9.6	5.8	8.0	10.1	6.0	2.9	2.7	3.0	...	...	...
1952	7.0	8.3	5.8	...	...	...	2.4	2.0	2.7	...	...	...
1950	6.2	7.3	5.2	...	...	...	2.3	2.1	2.4	...	...	...
1947	5.4	6.2	4.7	5.7	6.6	4.9	2.5	2.4	2.6	...	...	...
1940	4.6	5.5	3.8	4.9	5.9	4.0	1.3	1.4	1.2	...	...	...

[1]May be of any race.
* = Data for non-Hispanic White (1993–2002) and non-Hispanic Black (1999–2002).
... = Not available.

Table A-13. Percentage of Population 25 Years and Over Who Have Completed High School or College, by Race, Sex, and Hispanic Origin, Selected Years 1940 to 2002—*Continued*

(Percent.)

Age and year	All races			White			Black			Hispanic origin[1]		
	Total	Male	Female	Total	Male	Female	Total	Male	Female	Total	Male	Female
25 TO 29 YEARS												
Completed 4 Years of High School or More												
2002*	86.4	84.7	88.1	93.0	92.1	93.8	87.6	85.8	88.9	62.4	60.2	65.0
2002	86.4	84.7	88.1	85.9	84.1	87.7	86.6	85.0	88.0	62.4	60.2	65.0
2001*	86.8	85.3	88.3	93.4	93.1	93.7	86.8	86.0	87.5	62.4	58.3	67.3
2001	86.8	85.3	88.3	86.4	84.6	88.3	86.3	85.4	87.0	62.4	58.3	67.3
2000*	88.1	86.7	89.4	94.0	92.9	95.2	86.8	87.6	86.2	62.8	59.2	66.4
2000	88.1	86.7	89.4	88.3	86.6	90.0	85.9	86.6	85.3	62.8	59.2	66.4
1999*	87.8	86.1	89.5	93.0	91.9	94.1	88.7	88.2	89.2	61.6	57.4	66.0
1999	87.8	86.1	89.5	87.6	85.8	89.3	88.2	87.7	88.6	61.6	57.4	66.0
1998*	88.1	86.6	89.6	93.6	92.5	94.6	87.6	87.6	87.6	62.8	59.9	66.3
1998	88.1	86.6	89.6	88.1	86.3	90.0	87.6	87.6	87.6	62.8	59.9	66.3
1997*	87.4	85.8	88.9	92.9	91.7	94.0	86.2	85.2	87.1	61.8	59.2	64.9
1997	87.4	85.8	88.9	87.6	85.8	89.4	86.2	85.2	87.1	61.8	59.2	64.9
1996*	87.3	86.5	88.1	92.6	92.0	93.1	85.6	87.2	84.2	61.1	59.7	62.9
1996	87.3	86.5	88.1	87.5	86.3	88.8	85.6	87.2	84.2	61.1	59.7	62.9
1995*	86.8	86.3	87.4	92.5	92.0	93.0	86.5	88.1	85.1	57.1	55.7	58.7
1995	86.8	86.3	87.4	87.4	86.6	88.2	86.5	88.1	85.1	57.1	55.7	58.7
1994*	86.1	84.5	87.6	91.1	90.0	92.3	84.1	82.9	85.0	60.3	58.0	63.0
1994	86.1	84.5	87.6	86.5	84.7	88.3	84.1	82.9	85.0	60.3	58.0	63.0
1993*	86.7	86.0	87.4	91.2	90.6	91.8	82.8	85.0	80.9	60.9	58.3	64.0
1993	86.7	86.0	87.4	87.3	86.1	88.5	82.8	85.0	80.9	60.9	58.3	64.0
1992	86.3	86.1	86.5	87.0	86.5	87.6	80.9	82.5	79.5	60.9	61.1	60.6
1991	85.4	84.9	85.8	85.8	85.1	86.6	81.7	83.5	80.1	56.7	56.4	57.1
1990	85.7	84.4	87.0	86.3	84.6	88.1	81.7	81.5	81.8	58.2	56.6	59.9
1989	85.5	84.4	86.5	86.0	84.8	87.1	82.2	80.6	83.6	61.0	61.0	61.0
1988	85.7	84.4	87.0	86.5	84.8	88.2	80.7	80.6	80.7	62.0	59.4	65.0
1987	86.0	85.5	86.4	86.3	85.6	87.0	83.3	84.8	82.1	59.8	58.6	61.0
1986	86.1	85.9	86.4	86.5	85.6	87.4	83.4	86.5	80.6	59.1	58.2	60.0
1985	86.1	85.9	86.4	86.8	86.4	87.3	80.6	80.8	80.4	60.9	58.6	63.1
1984	85.9	85.6	86.3	86.9	86.8	87.0	78.9	75.9	81.5	58.6	56.8	60.2
1983	86.0	86.0	86.0	86.9	86.9	86.9	79.4	78.9	79.8	58.3	57.8	58.9
1982	86.2	86.3	86.1	86.9	87.0	86.8	80.9	80.5	81.3	60.9	60.7	61.2
1981	86.3	86.5	86.1	87.6	87.6	87.6	77.3	78.4	76.4	59.8	59.1	60.4
1980	85.4	85.4	85.5	86.9	86.8	87.0	76.6	74.8	78.1	58.6	58.3	58.8
1979	85.6	86.3	84.9	87.0	87.7	86.4	74.8	73.9	75.4	57.0	55.5	58.5
1978	85.3	86.0	84.6	86.3	86.8	85.8	77.3	78.5	76.3	56.6	58.5	54.7
1977	85.4	86.6	84.2	86.8	87.6	86.0	74.4	77.5	72.0	58.1	62.1	54.8
1976	84.7	86.0	83.5	85.9	87.3	84.6	73.8	72.5	74.9	58.1	57.6	58.4
1975	83.1	84.5	81.8	84.4	85.7	83.2	71.0	72.2	70.1	51.7	51.1	52.1
1974	81.9	83.1	80.8	83.4	84.1	82.7	68.2	71.1	66.0	52.5	55.1	49.9
1973	80.2	80.6	79.8	82.0	82.4	81.6	64.2	63.1	64.9	. . .	. . .	. . .
1972	79.8	80.5	79.2	81.5	82.3	80.8	64.1	61.8	66.2	. . .	. . .	. . .
1971	77.2	78.1	76.4	79.5	80.8	78.3	57.5	54.1	60.7	. . .	. . .	. . .
1970	75.4	76.6	74.2	77.8	79.2	76.4	56.2	54.5	57.9	. . .	. . .	. . .
1969	74.7	75.6	73.8	77.0	77.5	76.6	55.8	59.8	52.3	. . .	. . .	. . .
1968	73.2	73.7	72.7	75.3	75.5	75.0	55.8	58.1	53.6	. . .	. . .	. . .
1967	72.5	72.1	72.9	74.8	74.3	75.3	53.4	51.7	55.0	. . .	. . .	. . .
1966	71.0	70.9	71.2	73.8	73.2	74.4	47.9	48.9	47.0	. . .	. . .	. . .
1965	70.3	70.5	70.1	72.8	72.7	72.8	50.3	50.3	50.4	. . .	. . .	. . .
1964	69.2	68.8	69.5	72.1	71.8	72.4	45.0	41.6	47.9	. . .	. . .	. . .
1962	65.9	65.8	66.1	69.2	69.2	69.3	41.6	38.9	43.8	. . .	. . .	. . .
1959	63.9	63.9	64.0	67.2	66.9	67.4	39.5	40.6	38.6	. . .	. . .	. . .
1957	60.2	57.9	62.4	63.3	60.7	65.7	31.6	27.4	35.2	. . .	. . .	. . .
1952	57.1	55.3	58.7	. . .	. . .	. . .	28.1	27.9	28.3	. . .	. . .	. . .
1950	52.8	50.6	55.0	. . .	. . .	. . .	23.6	21.3	25.5	. . .	. . .	. . .
1947	51.4	49.4	53.3	54.9	52.9	56.8	22.3	19.6	24.7	. . .	. . .	. . .
1940	38.1	36.0	40.1	41.2	38.9	43.4	12.3	10.6	13.6	. . .	. . .	. . .

[1]May be of any race.
* = Data for non-Hispanic White (1993–2002) and non-Hispanic Black (1999–2002).
. . . = Not available.

Table A-13. Percentage of Population 25 Years and Over Who Have Completed High School or College, by Race, Sex, and Hispanic Origin, Selected Years 1940 to 2002—*Continued*

(Percent.)

Age and year	All races			White			Black			Hispanic origin[1]		
	Total	Male	Female	Total	Male	Female	Total	Male	Female	Total	Male	Female
25 TO 29 YEARS—*Continued*												
Completed 4 Years of College or More												
2002*	29.3	26.9	31.8	35.9	32.6	39.2	18.0	17.9	18.1	8.9	8.3	9.7
2002	29.3	26.9	31.8	29.7	26.5	33.1	17.5	17.4	17.7	8.9	8.3	9.7
2001*	28.4	25.5	31.3	33.7	30.4	36.9	17.2	16.0	18.2	10.5	8.2	13.3
2001	28.4	25.5	31.3	28.5	25.1	32.1	16.8	15.6	17.9	10.5	8.2	13.3
2000*	29.1	27.9	30.1	34.0	32.3	35.8	17.8	18.4	17.4	9.7	8.3	11.0
2000	29.1	27.9	30.1	29.6	27.8	31.3	17.5	18.1	17.0	9.7	8.3	11.0
1999*	28.2	26.8	29.5	33.6	32.0	35.1	15.0	13.1	16.5	8.9	7.5	10.4
1999	28.2	26.8	29.5	29.3	27.6	30.9	15.0	13.1	16.5	8.9	7.5	10.4
1998*	27.3	25.6	29.0	32.3	30.5	34.2	15.8	14.2	17.0	10.4	9.5	11.3
1998	27.3	25.6	29.0	28.4	26.5	30.4	15.8	14.2	17.0	10.4	9.5	11.3
1997*	27.8	26.3	29.3	32.6	31.2	34.1	14.4	12.1	16.4	11.0	9.6	10.1
1997	27.8	26.3	29.3	28.9	27.2	30.7	14.4	12.1	16.4	11.0	9.6	10.1
1996*	27.1	26.1	28.2	31.6	30.9	32.3	14.6	12.4	16.4	10.0	10.2	9.8
1996	27.1	26.1	28.2	28.1	27.2	29.1	14.6	12.4	16.4	10.0	10.2	9.8
1995*	24.7	24.5	24.9	28.8	28.4	29.2	15.3	17.2	13.6	8.9	7.8	10.1
1995	24.7	24.5	24.9	26.0	25.4	26.6	15.3	17.2	13.6	8.9	7.8	10.1
1994*	23.3	22.5	24.0	27.1	26.8	27.4	13.7	11.7	15.4	8.0	6.6	9.8
1994	23.3	22.5	24.0	24.2	23.6	24.8	13.7	11.7	15.4	8.0	6.6	9.8
1993*	23.7	23.4	23.9	27.2	27.2	27.1	13.2	12.6	13.8	8.3	7.1	9.8
1993	23.7	23.4	23.9	24.7	24.4	25.1	13.2	12.6	13.8	8.3	7.1	9.8
1992	23.6	23.2	24.0	25.0	24.2	25.7	11.3	12.0	10.6	9.5	8.8	10.3
1991	23.2	23.0	23.4	24.6	24.1	25.0	11.0	11.5	10.6	9.2	8.1	10.4
1990	23.2	23.7	22.8	24.2	24.2	24.3	13.4	15.1	11.9	8.1	7.3	9.1
1989	23.4	23.9	22.9	24.4	24.8	24.0	12.7	12.0	13.3	10.1	9.6	10.6
1988	22.5	23.2	21.9	23.5	24.0	22.9	12.2	12.6	11.9	11.4	12.1	10.6
1987	22.0	22.3	21.7	23.0	23.3	22.8	11.4	11.6	11.1	8.7	9.2	8.2
1986	22.4	22.9	21.9	23.5	24.1	22.9	11.8	10.1	13.3	9.0	8.9	9.1
1985	22.2	23.1	21.3	23.2	24.2	22.2	11.5	10.3	12.6	11.1	10.9	11.2
1984	21.9	23.2	20.7	23.1	24.3	21.9	11.6	12.9	10.5	10.6	9.6	11.6
1983	22.5	23.9	21.1	23.4	25.0	21.8	12.9	13.1	12.8	10.4	9.6	11.1
1982	21.7	23.3	20.2	22.7	24.5	20.9	12.6	11.8	13.2	9.7	10.7	8.7
1981	21.3	23.1	19.6	22.4	24.3	20.5	11.6	12.1	11.1	7.5	8.6	6.5
1980	22.5	24.0	21.0	23.7	25.5	22.0	11.6	10.5	12.5	7.7	8.4	6.9
1979	23.1	25.6	20.5	24.3	27.1	21.5	12.4	13.3	11.7	7.3	7.9	6.8
1978	23.3	26.0	20.6	24.5	27.6	21.4	11.8	10.7	12.6	9.6	9.6	9.7
1977	24.0	27.0	21.1	25.3	28.5	22.1	12.6	12.8	12.4	6.7	7.2	6.4
1976	23.7	27.5	20.1	24.6	28.7	20.6	13.0	12.0	13.6	7.4	10.3	4.8
1975	21.9	25.1	18.7	22.8	26.3	19.4	10.7	11.4	10.1	8.8	10.0	7.3
1974	20.7	23.9	17.6	22.0	25.3	18.8	7.9	8.8	7.2	5.7	7.2	4.6
1973	19.0	21.6	16.4	19.9	22.8	17.0	8.1	7.1	8.8	...	...	...
1972	19.0	22.0	16.0	19.9	23.1	16.7	8.3	7.1	9.4	...	...	...
1971	16.9	20.1	13.8	17.9	21.3	14.6	6.4	6.4	6.5	...	...	...
1970	16.4	20.0	12.9	17.3	21.3	13.3	7.3	6.7	8.0	...	...	...
1969	16.0	19.4	12.8	17.0	20.6	13.4	6.7	8.1	5.5	...	...	...
1968	14.7	18.0	11.6	15.6	19.1	12.3	5.3	5.3	5.3	...	...	...
1967	14.6	17.2	12.1	15.5	18.3	12.7	5.4	4.2	6.3	...	...	...
1966	14.0	16.8	11.3	14.7	17.9	11.8	5.9	5.4	6.4	...	...	...
1965	12.4	15.6	9.5	13.0	16.4	9.8	6.8	7.3	6.8	...	...	...
1964	12.8	16.6	9.2	13.6	17.5	9.9	5.5	7.5	3.9	...	...	...
1962	13.1	17.2	9.2	14.3	18.7	10.0	4.2	5.7	3.0	...	...	...
1959	11.1	14.8	7.6	11.9	15.9	8.1	4.6	5.6	3.7	...	...	...
1957	10.4	13.5	7.5	11.1	14.5	7.8	4.1	3.3	5.0	...	...	...
1952	10.1	13.8	6.7	...	...	...	4.6	3.2	5.8	...	...	...
1950	7.7	9.6	5.9	...	...	...	2.9	2.4	3.2	...	...	...
1947	5.6	5.8	5.4	5.9	6.2	5.7	2.8	2.6	2.9	...	...	...
1940	5.9	6.9	4.9	6.4	7.5	5.3	1.6	1.5	1.7	...	...	...

Note: The data in 2001 and 2002 are from the expanded CPS sample and were calculated using population controls based on Census 2000. Data are for Black and other races for 1940 to 1962; for 1963 to 1981, data are for Black people only. Beginning 1992, High School Graduate or more. Beginning 1992, Bachelor's degree or more.
[1]May be of any race.
* = Data for non-Hispanic White (1993–2002) and non-Hispanic Black (1999–2002).
. . . = Not available.

Table A-14. Mean Earnings of Workers 18 Years and Over, by Educational Attainment, Race, Sex, and Hispanic Origin, 1975 to 2001

(Mean annual earnings [dollars]. Total number with earnings in thousands. Standard error of the mean.)

Age, sex, race, and Hispanic origin	Total			Not a high school graduate			High school graduate		
	Mean	Number with earnings	Standard error	Mean	Number with earnings	Standard error	Mean	Number with earnings	Standard error
ALL RACES									
Both Sexes									
2001	35 805	147 829	155	18 793	17 293	308	26 795	45 641	186
2000	34 514	147 966	148	17 738	17 425	269	25 692	45 977	142
1999	32 356	144 640	183	16 121	16 737	299	24 572	46 082	186
1998	30 928	142 053	183	16 053	16 742	306	23 594	45 987	203
1997	29 514	140 367	183	16 124	16 962	346	22 895	45 976	206
1996	28 106	138 703	176	15 011	17 075	286	22 154	45 908	209
1995	26 792	136 221	164	14 013	16 990	201	21 431	44 546	225
1994	25 852	135 096	153	13 697	16 479	288	20 248	44 614	170
1993	24 674	133 119	148	12 820	16 575	237	19 422	44 779	162
1992	23 227	130 860	99	12 809	16 612	152	18 737	45 340	110
1991	22 332	130 371	93	12 613	17 553	153	18 261	46 508	104
1990	21 793	130 080	91	12 582	18 698	115	17 820	51 977	95
1989	21 414	129 094	92	12 242	19 137	112	17 594	51 846	100
1988	20 060	127 564	88	11 889	19 635	118	16 750	51 297	98
1987	19 016	124 874	83	11 824	19 748	133	15 939	50 815	91
1986	18 149	122 757	72	11 203	19 665	149	15 120	50 104	77
1985	17 181	120 651	67	10 726	19 692	133	14 457	49 674	74
1984	16 083	118 183	57	10 384	20 206	130	13 893	48 452	68
1983	15 137	115 095	. . .	9 853	20 020	. . .	13 044	47 560	. . .
1982	14 351	113 451	52	9 387	20 789	101	12 560	46 584	64
1981	13 624	113 301	48	9 357	22 296	110	12 109	47 332	59
1980	12 665	111 919	45	8 845	23 028	95	11 314	46 795	54
1979	11 795	110 826	43	8 420	23 783	75	10 624	45 497	50
1978	10 812	106 436	41	7 759	23 787	71	9 834	43 510	49
1977	9 887	103 119	35	7 066	24 854	60	9 013	41 696	41
1976	9 180	100 510	32	6 720	25 035	57	8 393	40 570	39
1975	8 552	97 881	31	6 198	24 916	53	7 843	39 827	38
Male									
2001	43 648	78 342	251	21 508	10 572	347	32 363	24 239	277
2000	42 772	78 319	250	21 007	10 535	372	31 446	24 439	223
1999	40 257	76 233	308	18 855	9 917	277	30 414	24 235	294
1998	38 134	75 213	301	19 155	10 085	426	28 742	24 155	312
1997	36 556	74 596	307	19 575	10 348	493	28 307	24 152	348
1996	34 705	73 955	291	17 826	10 583	440	27 642	23 966	364
1995	33 251	72 634	275	16 748	10 312	296	26 333	23 473	349
1994	32 087	72 246	251	16 633	9 981	457	25 038	23 418	286
1993	30 568	71 183	244	14 946	10 151	233	23 973	23 388	259
1992	28 448	70 409	158	14 934	10 335	212	22 978	23 610	173
1991	27 494	70 145	148	15 056	10 679	187	22 663	24 110	163
1990	27 164	70 218	151	14 991	11 412	155	22 378	26 753	158
1989	27 025	69 798	155	14 727	11 774	150	22 508	26 469	172
1988	25 344	69 006	146	14 551	11 993	163	21 481	26 080	166
1987	24 015	67 951	138	14 544	12 117	188	20 364	25 981	150
1986	23 057	67 189	120	13 703	12 208	217	19 453	25 562	131
1985	21 823	66 439	111	13 124	12 137	185	18 575	25 496	125
1984	20 452	65 005	92	12 775	12 325	170	18 016	24 827	116
1983	19 175	63 816	89	12 052	12 376	160	16 728	24 449	108
1982	18 244	63 489	85	11 513	12 868	144	16 160	24 059	107
1981	17 542	63 547	79	11 668	13 701	146	15 900	24 435	101
1980	16 382	62 825	73	11 042	14 273	129	15 002	24 023	92
1979	15 430	62 464	70	10 628	14 711	102	14 317	23 318	87
1978	14 154	60 586	67	9 894	14 550	93	13 188	22 650	85
1977	12 888	59 441	56	8 939	15 369	81	12 092	21 846	70
1976	11 923	58 419	52	8 522	15 634	79	11 189	21 499	65
1975	11 091	57 297	49	7 843	15 613	71	10 475	21 347	64
Female									
2001	26 962	69 487	162	14 524	6 720	569	20 489	21 402	232
2000	25 228	69 647	131	12 739	6 890	360	19 162	21 538	152
1999	23 551	68 409	165	12 145	6 819	604	18 092	21 847	196
1998	22 818	66 840	180	11 353	6 657	401	17 898	21 832	237
1997	21 528	65 771	163	10 725	6 614	415	16 906	21 824	179
1996	20 570	64 748	165	10 421	6 492	193	16 161	21 942	160
1995	19 414	63 587	144	9 790	6 678	208	15 970	21 073	263
1994	18 684	62 850	143	9 189	6 498	165	14 955	21 195	149
1993	17 900	61 937	141	9 462	6 425	482	14 446	21 391	174
1992	17 145	60 451	96	9 311	6 277	178	14 128	21 730	117
1991	16 320	60 226	91	8 818	6 875	161	13 523	22 398	109
1990	15 493	59 862	86	8 808	7 286	169	12 986	25 224	103
1989	14 809	59 296	84	8 268	7 363	167	12 468	25 377	98
1988	13 833	58 558	84	7 711	7 642	165	11 857	25 217	100
1987	13 049	56 923	80	7 504	7 631	171	11 309	24 834	100
1986	12 214	55 568	67	7 109	7 457	169	10 606	24 542	78
1985	11 493	54 212	63	6 874	7 555	179	10 115	24 178	76
1984	10 742	53 178	56	6 644	7 881	203	9 561	23 625	69
1983	10 111	51 279	. . .	6 292	7 644	. . .	9 147	23 111	. . .
1982	9 403	49 962	50	5 932	7 921	123	8 715	22 525	66
1981	8 619	49 754	44	5 673	8 595	165	8 063	22 897	57
1980	7 909	49 094	42	5 263	8 755	134	7 423	22 772	53
1979	7 099	48 362	38	4 840	9 072	106	6 741	22 179	48
1978	6 396	45 850	35	4 397	9 237	111	6 192	20 860	46
1977	5 804	43 678	30	4 032	9 485	86	5 624	19 850	39
1976	5 373	42 091	28	3 723	9 401	76	5 240	19 071	37
1975	4 968	40 584	26	3 438	9 303	75	4 802	18 480	34

. . . = Not available.

Table A-14. Mean Earnings of Workers 18 Years and Over, by Educational Attainment, Race, Sex, and Hispanic Origin, 1975 to 2001—*Continued*

(Mean annual earnings [dollars]. Total number with earnings in thousands. Standard error of the mean.)

Age, sex, race, and Hispanic origin	Some college/associate degree			Bachelor's degree			Advanced degree		
	Mean	Number with earnings	Standard error	Mean	Number with earnings	Standard error	Mean	Number with earnings	Standard error
ALL RACES									
Both Sexes									
2001	30 782	43 214	203	50 623	27 980	452	72 869	13 700	880
2000	29 939	43 874	194	49 595	27 488	451	71 194	13 200	924
1999	28 403	42 860	262	45 678	26 215	531	67 697	12 749	1 122
1998	27 566	41 412	302	43 782	25 818	533	63 473	12 095	1 018
1997	26 235	40 802	289	40 478	25 035	489	63 229	11 591	1 162
1996	25 181	40 410	279	38 112	24 028	436	61 317	11 281	1 204
1995	23 862	40 142	245	36 980	23 285	463	56 667	11 258	490
1994	22 226	40 135	193	37 224	22 712	491	56 105	11 155	961
1993	21 539	39 429	173	35 121	21 815	425	55 789	10 521	1 140
1992	20 867	37 339	109	32 629	21 091	288	48 652	10 479	571
1991	20 551	35 732	116	31 323	20 475	275	46 039	10 103	571
1990	20 694	28 993	165	31 112	18 128	300	41 458	12 285	488
1989	20 255	28 078	161	30 736	17 767	304	41 019	12 265	506
1988	19 066	27 217	171	28 344	17 308	286	37 724	12 109	458
1987	18 054	26 404	156	26 919	16 497	289	35 968	11 411	447
1986	17 073	26 113	135	26 511	15 788	251	34 787	11 087	393
1985	16 349	25 402	127	24 877	15 373	238	32 909	10 510	367
1984	14 936	24 463	107	23 072	14 653	191	30 192	10 410	281
1983	14 245	23 208	. . .	21 532	13 929	. . .	28 333	10 377	. . .
1982	13 503	22 602	105	20 272	13 425	181	26 915	10 051	272
1981	13 176	21 759	101	19 006	12 579	173	25 281	9 336	266
1980	12 409	21 384	97	18 075	12 175	171	23 308	8 535	254
1979	11 377	21 174	90	16 514	11 751	163	21 874	8 621	251
1978	10 357	20 121	85	15 291	11 001	159	20 173	8 017	248
1977	9 607	18 905	76	14 207	10 357	136	19 077	7 309	222
1976	8 813	17 786	76	13 033	10 132	120	17 911	6 985	218
1975	8 388	16 917	70	12 332	9 764	121	16 725	6 457	206
Male									
2001	37 429	21 390	321	63 354	14 507	772	90 130	7 631	1 411
2000	37 372	21 526	349	62 609	14 375	779	88 077	7 442	1 468
1999	35 326	21 173	471	57 706	13 683	888	84 051	7 225	1 836
1998	34 179	20 545	531	55 057	13 486	901	77 217	6 942	1 543
1997	32 641	20 359	499	50 056	13 008	818	78 032	6 728	1 865
1996	31 426	20 208	488	46 702	12 562	720	74 406	6 636	1 792
1995	29 851	19 918	433	46 111	12 251	802	69 588	6 679	1 570
1994	27 636	19 859	324	46 278	12 324	796	67 032	6 663	1 422
1993	26 614	19 532	301	43 499	11 810	669	68 221	6 302	1 756
1992	25 660	18 768	169	40 039	11 353	456	58 324	6 344	837
1991	25 345	18 076	183	38 484	11 126	432	54 449	6 154	837
1990	26 120	14 844	288	38 901	9 807	505	49 768	7 402	751
1989	25 555	14 384	278	38 692	9 737	510	50 144	7 434	777
1988	23 827	14 019	285	35 906	9 466	479	45 677	7 449	689
1987	22 781	13 433	268	33 677	9 286	472	43 140	7 134	663
1986	21 784	13 502	229	33 376	8 908	406	41 836	7 009	583
1985	20 698	13 385	208	31 433	8 794	386	39 768	6 627	548
1984	18 863	12 818	178	29 203	8 387	301	35 804	6 648	403
1983	18 052	12 261	187	27 239	8 010	295	33 635	6 719	388
1982	17 108	12 103	172	25 758	7 865	285	32 109	6 594	390
1981	16 870	11 784	168	24 353	7 393	273	30 072	6 235	376
1980	15 871	11 663	158	23 340	7 132	272	27 846	5 733	360
1979	14 716	11 781	145	21 482	6 889	260	26 411	5 765	358
1978	13 382	11 352	137	19 861	6 611	250	24 274	5 422	351
1977	12 393	10 848	122	18 187	6 341	210	22 786	5 038	311
1976	11 376	10 282	122	16 714	6 135	186	21 202	4 868	301
1975	10 805	9 851	112	15 758	5 960	188	19 672	4 526	283
Female									
2001	24 268	21 824	241	36 913	13 472	396	51 160	6 068	790
2000	22 779	22 348	161	35 328	13 113	357	49 368	5 757	842
1999	21 644	22 687	215	32 546	12 533	477	46 307	5 523	802
1998	21 056	20 867	273	31 452	12 332	467	44 954	5 153	1 018
1997	19 856	20 442	277	30 119	12 027	460	42 744	4 863	863
1996	18 933	20 202	406	28 701	11 466	421	42 625	4 646	1 333
1995	17 962	20 224	213	26 841	11 034	341	37 813	4 578	702
1994	16 928	20 276	199	26 483	10 388	463	39 905	4 493	1 040
1993	16 555	19 897	155	25 232	10 005	441	37 212	4 218	986
1992	16 023	18 571	138	23 991	9 738	272	33 814	4 135	594
1991	15 643	17 657	141	22 802	9 348	258	32 929	3 948	594
1990	15 002	14 149	154	21 933	8 321	270	28 862	4 883	459
1989	14 688	13 694	155	21 089	8 030	264	26 977	4 831	469
1988	14 009	13 198	179	19 216	7 842	253	25 010	4 660	451
1987	13 158	12 971	155	18 217	7 211	261	24 004	4 277	447
1986	12 029	12 611	133	17 623	6 880	233	22 672	4 078	367
1985	11 504	12 017	134	16 114	6 579	207	21 202	3 883	334
1984	10 614	11 645	110	14 865	6 266	193	20 275	3 762	313
1983	9 981	10 947	. . .	13 808	5 919	. . .	18 593	3 658	. . .
1982	9 348	10 499	108	12 511	5 560	167	17 009	3 457	272
1981	8 811	9 975	98	11 384	5 186	156	15 647	3 101	264
1980	8 256	9 721	99	10 628	5 043	152	14 022	2 802	241
1979	7 190	9 393	89	9 474	4 862	137	12 717	2 856	231
1978	6 441	8 769	79	8 408	4 390	128	11 603	2 595	222
1977	5 856	8 057	69	7 923	4 016	115	10 848	2 271	191
1976	5 301	7 504	70	7 383	3 997	102	10 345	2 117	199
1975	5 019	7 066	62	6 963	3 804	98	9 818	1 931	187

. . . = Not available.

Table A-14. Mean Earnings of Workers 18 Years and Over, by Educational Attainment, Race, Sex, and Hispanic Origin, 1975 to 2001—*Continued*

(Mean annual earnings [dollars]. Total number with earnings in thousands. Standard error of the mean.)

Age, sex, race, and Hispanic origin	Total			Not a high school graduate			High school graduate		
	Mean	Number with earnings	Standard error	Mean	Number with earnings	Standard error	Mean	Number with earnings	Standard error
WHITE									
Both Sexes									
2001	36 844	122 930	174	19 120	14 012	337	27 700	37 969	218
2000	35 527	123 039	169	18 285	14 172	322	26 444	38 133	162
1999	33 326	120 916	210	16 623	13 585	359	25 270	38 428	211
1998	32 057	119 201	211	16 474	13 531	362	24 409	38 397	236
1997	30 515	117 985	210	16 596	13 780	409	23 618	38 409	240
1996	28 844	117 230	192	15 358	13 972	340	22 782	38 463	235
1995	27 556	115 636	181	14 234	13 869	234	22 154	37 802	261
1994	26 696	114 586	173	13 941	13 119	350	20 911	37 562	196
1993	25 440	113 342	165	13 171	13 480	283	19 918	37 826	166
1992	23 932	112 120	106	13 193	13 494	174	19 265	38 692	123
1991	22 998	111 830	103	12 914	14 041	178	18 766	39 764	115
1990	22 401	111 972	101	12 773	15 191	126	18 257	44 635	105
1989	22 035	111 243	102	12 654	15 628	124	18 011	44 726	111
1988	20 616	110 159	97	12 236	16 042	129	17 183	44 399	107
1987	19 599	108 407	93	12 502	16 165	145	16 339	44 235	99
1986	18 698	106 384	79	11 605	16 094	134	15 514	43 593	84
1985	17 709	104 818	75	11 115	16 149	118	14 815	43 347	81
1984	16 546	103 022	62	10 732	16 559	113	14 274	42 547	74
1983	15 556	101 035	. . .	10 239	16 568	. . .	13 357	42 007	. . .
1982	14 767	99 488	57	9 719	17 132	95	12 854	41 157	70
1981	14 027	99 510	53	9 737	18 298	105	12 355	42 080	64
1980	13 040	98 358	49	9 743	18 925	86	11 524	41 600	58
1979	12 155	97 544	47	8 827	19 504	80	10 431	40 458	54
1978	11 135	94 002	44	8 135	19 516	83	10 020	38 915	53
1977	10 191	91 254	37	7 415	20 492	65	9 173	37 521	44
1976	9 469	89 099	35	7 018	20 625	62	8 559	36 523	41
1975	8 815	86 894	33	6 438	20 696	57	8 005	35 799	41
Male									
2001	45 071	66 216	279	22 006	8 833	400	33 545	20 465	319
2000	44 181	66 222	282	21 561	8 859	431	32 528	20 553	253
1999	41 598	64 856	349	19 320	8 286	313	31 279	20 526	326
1998	39 638	64 181	341	19 632	8 430	490	29 782	20 388	359
1997	37 933	63 738	347	20 071	8 670	563	29 298	20 426	402
1996	35 821	63 532	320	18 246	8 899	514	28 591	20 329	405
1995	34 276	62 520	298	17 032	8 660	338	27 467	19 982	403
1994	33 292	62 029	283	16 835	8 133	547	26 125	19 833	330
1993	31 719	61 356	270	15 295	8 430	265	24 781	19 835	264
1992	29 515	60 919	174	15 414	8 487	241	23 844	20 259	192
1991	28 516	60 770	163	15 499	8 720	211	23 475	20 765	179
1990	28 105	60 676	167	15 319	9 476	168	23 135	23 088	174
1989	28 013	60 877	171	15 217	9 805	165	23 291	23 029	191
1988	26 184	60 221	160	14 943	10 008	175	22 216	22 707	181
1987	24 898	59 468	152	15 303	10 132	202	21 012	22 682	162
1986	23 892	58 932	131	14 168	10 239	183	20 128	22 392	143
1985	22 604	58 385	122	13 579	10 163	158	19 203	22 357	136
1984	21 174	57 362	100	13 248	10 280	148	18 681	21 989	125
1983	19 812	56 641	96	12 573	10 387	140	17 281	21 733	117
1982	18 859	56 364	92	11 952	10 816	129	16 662	21 436	116
1981	18 141	56 397	86	12 094	11 523	142	16 352	21 809	109
1980	16 945	55 772	79	11 539	11 937	114	15 382	21 453	99
1979	15 971	55 556	76	11 127	12 291	109	13 916	20 834	94
1978	14 627	54 113	72	10 358	12 141	103	13 534	20 328	91
1977	13 329	53 174	60	9 366	12 903	86	12 377	19 773	74
1976	12 342	52 312	56	8 867	13 117	85	11 497	19 446	69
1975	11 448	51 510	53	8 110	13 191	77	10 726	19 361	69
Female									
2001	27 240	56 714	181	14 197	5 178	596	20 866	17 503	278
2000	25 441	56 816	148	12 823	5 313	458	19 330	17 579	173
1999	23 756	56 061	189	12 405	5 299	770	18 381	17 902	230
1998	23 213	55 020	211	11 255	5 102	498	18 327	18 009	280
1997	21 779	54 247	189	10 700	5 111	527	17 166	17 983	207
1996	20 590	53 697	161	10 290	5 073	210	16 270	18 134	178
1995	19 647	53 117	164	9 582	5 208	239	16 196	17 820	304
1994	18 912	52 557	163	9 220	4 987	192	15 078	17 729	168
1993	18 028	51 986	154	9 624	5 050	606	14 557	17 991	174
1992	17 289	51 200	106	9 428	5 007	207	14 233	18 434	129
1991	16 431	51 060	98	8 677	5 321	174	13 621	18 999	118
1990	15 559	50 905	94	8 725	5 715	186	13 031	21 547	113
1989	14 810	50 366	91	8 338	5 823	182	12 406	21 697	107
1988	13 902	49 938	93	7 747	6 034	184	11 915	21 692	110
1987	13 161	48 939	89	7 798	6 033	190	11 421	21 553	110
1986	12 247	47 452	72	7 123	5 855	181	10 641	21 201	84
1985	11 555	46 433	70	6 931	5 986	172	10 142	20 990	82
1984	10 732	45 660	61	6 614	6 279	175	9 561	20 558	74
1983	10 126	44 394	. . .	6 317	6 181	. . .	9 150	20 274	. . .
1982	9 419	43 124	55	5 896	6 316	135	8 714	19 721	72
1981	8 646	43 113	48	5 727	6 775	148	8 054	20 271	61
1980	7 926	42 586	45	6 675	6 988	127	7 415	20 147	57
1979	7 105	41 988	41	4 909	7 213	110	6 731	19 624	51
1978	6 398	39 889	38	4 476	7 375	138	6 176	18 587	49
1977	5 808	38 080	32	4 097	7 589	95	5 604	17 748	41
1976	5 383	36 787	31	3 788	7 508	86	5 214	17 077	40
1975	4 982	35 384	28	3 500	7 505	80	4 800	16 438	36

. . . = Not available.

Table A-14. Mean Earnings of Workers 18 Years and Over, by Educational Attainment, Race, Sex, and Hispanic Origin, 1975 to 2001—*Continued*

(Mean annual earnings [dollars]. Total number with earnings in thousands. Standard error of the mean.)

Age, sex, race, and Hispanic origin	Some college/associate degree			Bachelor's degree			Advanced degree		
	Mean	Number with earnings	Standard error	Mean	Number with earnings	Standard error	Mean	Number with earnings	Standard error
WHITE									
Both Sexes									
2001	31 482	35 722	224	51 631	23 531	492	74 398	11 694	990
2000	30 638	36 334	224	50 969	23 110	517	71 983	11 288	1 006
1999	29 105	35 634	305	46 894	22 322	609	68 910	10 949	1 236
1998	28 318	34 540	342	44 852	22 266	604	65 379	10 467	1 147
1997	26 906	34 274	337	41 439	21 528	556	65 058	9 994	1 279
1996	25 511	34 087	293	38 936	20 846	489	61 779	9 861	1 230
1995	24 349	33 850	264	37 711	20 203	503	57 054	9 914	1 040
1994	22 648	34 006	218	37 996	19 917	551	56 475	9 981	1 020
1993	21 924	33 728	193	35 846	18 922	469	56 964	9 386	1 241
1992	21 357	32 014	120	33 092	18 555	312	49 347	9 363	611
1991	21 013	30 973	127	31 837	18 033	301	46 498	9 019	611
1990	21 095	25 105	182	31 626	15 993	328	41 908	11 049	522
1989	20 678	24 212	177	31 266	15 723	331	41 610	10 952	546
1988	19 384	23 643	187	28 886	15 221	314	38 129	10 854	489
1987	18 265	23 083	171	27 741	14 624	317	36 175	10 300	477
1986	17 371	22 653	146	27 061	14 055	271	35 265	9 987	422
1985	16 701	22 131	138	25 376	13 670	261	33 401	9 522	391
1984	15 197	21 451	117	23 472	13 056	207	30 515	9 409	298
1983	14 486	20 452	. . .	21 914	12 577	. . .	28 532	9 430	. . .
1982	13 799	19 967	114	20 760	12 103	195	27 040	9 127	286
1981	13 424	19 102	112	19 389	11 450	185	25 564	8 582	280
1980	12 677	18 888	106	18 434	11 067	183	23 466	7 876	267
1979	11 574	18 835	98	16 758	10 807	172	22 085	7 940	266
1978	10 504	18 022	91	15 463	10 171	168	20 531	7 376	265
1977	9 771	16 968	82	14 462	9 534	144	19 337	6 739	235
1976	8 958	16 127	82	13 279	9 325	127	18 153	6 498	230
1975	8 525	15 423	75	12 597	8 955	129	16 920	6 021	217
Male									
2001	38 501	17 957	344	65 046	12 396	838	92 304	6 562	1 577
2000	38 476	18 179	398	64 831	12 271	880	89 812	6 359	1 617
1999	36 518	17 928	544	59 606	11 851	1 004	85 345	6 265	2 016
1998	35 277	17 407	588	56 620	11 874	1 001	79 734	6 083	1 716
1997	33 691	17 423	571	51 678	11 340	920	80 322	5 879	2 023
1996	32 238	17 418	534	48 014	11 065	800	75 481	5 821	1 871
1995	30 529	17 136	451	47 016	10 851	852	70 155	5 891	1 634
1994	28 240	17 091	361	47 575	10 992	880	67 629	5 979	1 504
1993	27 297	16 000	334	44 505	10 452	722	70 000	5 680	1 914
1992	26 387	16 335	187	40 893	10 118	488	59 329	5 720	890
1991	26 090	15 873	198	39 547	9 893	468	55 257	5 519	890
1990	26 841	13 003	317	39 780	8 770	546	50 385	6 731	798
1989	26 260	12 582	303	39 654	8 750	553	51 031	6 710	831
1988	24 462	12 277	310	36 637	8 467	521	46 181	6 762	728
1987	23 310	11 771	295	34 865	8 384	510	43 440	6 499	702
1986	22 303	11 846	248	34 273	8 041	437	42 480	6 413	618
1985	21 240	11 831	224	32 165	7 970	416	40 358	6 064	580
1984	19 344	11 387	193	29 781	7 624	321	36 219	6 081	423
1983	18 388	10 974	202	27 726	7 379	309	33 981	6 168	409
1982	17 571	10 822	186	26 404	7 242	302	32 266	6 047	406
1981	17 303	10 448	184	24 943	6 824	289	30 396	5 794	393
1980	16 313	10 400	171	23 803	6 618	286	27 991	5 363	373
1979	15 043	10 572	157	21 785	6 464	271	26 645	5 395	374
1978	13 589	10 350	146	20 085	6 205	263	24 635	5 088	369
1977	12 657	9 853	131	18 521	5 941	219	23 093	4 704	325
1976	11 616	9 394	130	16 995	5 765	194	21 490	4 589	314
1975	11 028	9 096	119	16 079	5 587	197	19 858	4 275	295
Female									
2001	24 387	17 764	276	36 698	11 135	407	51 499	5 131	895
2000	22 790	18 155	184	35 273	10 838	413	48 982	4 929	849
1999	21 598	17 705	242	32 507	10 471	550	45 741	4 684	832
1998	21 246	17 132	321	31 406	10 393	536	45 462	4 384	1 249
1997	19 892	16 852	325	30 041	10 188	523	43 236	4 114	967
1996	18 482	16 669	185	28 667	9 781	467	42 049	4 041	1 202
1995	18 011	16 714	246	26 916	9 352	383	37 864	4 022	709
1994	16 998	16 915	225	26 198	8 925	525	39 816	4 002	1 113
1993	16 490	16 769	168	25 161	8 470	501	36 988	3 705	967
1992	16 116	15 679	149	23 738	8 437	295	33 675	3 643	635
1991	15 677	15 100	155	22 471	8 140	276	32 687	3 500	635
1990	14 922	12 102	165	21 725	7 223	294	28 694	4 318	486
1989	14 640	11 630	170	20 741	6 973	272	26 709	4 242	510
1988	13 898	11 366	198	19 169	6 754	274	24 824	4 092	488
1987	13 015	11 312	167	18 170	6 240	289	23 753	3 801	482
1986	11 964	10 807	140	17 418	6 014	245	22 320	3 574	397
1985	11 488	10 300	148	15 883	5 700	229	21 202	3 458	357
1984	10 504	10 064	119	14 617	5 432	209	20 092	3 328	332
1983	9 969	9 478	. . .	13 664	5 198	. . .	18 230	3 262	. . .
1982	9 336	9 145	117	12 352	4 861	181	16 779	3 080	287
1981	8 740	8 654	107	11 196	4 626	167	15 523	2 788	279
1980	8 221	8 488	108	10 447	4 449	159	13 809	2 513	253
1979	7 135	8 263	96	9 275	4 343	145	12 420	2 545	243
1978	6 342	7 672	85	8 231	3 966	131	11 404	2 288	235
1977	5 774	7 115	73	7 750	3 593	123	10 655	2 035	203
1976	5 250	6 733	74	7 262	3 560	109	10 131	1 909	207
1975	4 926	6 327	65	6 822	3 368	105	9 728	1 746	199

. . . = Not available.

Table A-14. Mean Earnings of Workers 18 Years and Over, by Educational Attainment, Race, Sex, and Hispanic Origin, 1975 to 2001—Continued

(Mean annual earnings [dollars]. Total number with earnings in thousands. Standard error of the mean.)

Age, sex, race, and Hispanic origin	Total			Not a high school graduate			High school graduate		
	Mean	Number with earnings	Standard error	Mean	Number with earnings	Standard error	Mean	Number with earnings	Standard error
BLACK									
Both Sexes									
2001	27 031	16 683	300	17 248	2 382	1 062	21 743	5 729	260
2000	26 204	16 756	260	15 201	2 434	419	21 789	6 020	325
1999	24 979	16 936	313	13 569	2 393	426	20 991	6 112	432
1998	22 829	16 201	264	13 672	2 402	508	19 236	6 053	307
1997	21 909	15 873	254	13 185	2 437	401	18 980	5 964	322
1996	21 978	15 255	485	13 110	2 383	434	18 722	5 844	554
1995	20 537	14 847	374	12 956	2 389	437	17 072	5 453	315
1994	19 772	14 754	274	12 705	2 290	463	16 446	5 596	276
1993	18 614	14 315	316	11 065	2 352	370	16 122	5 521	584
1992	17 416	13 836	210	11 077	2 451	345	15 260	5 379	249
1991	16 809	13 865	197	11 248	2 860	335	15 060	5 512	264
1990	16 627	13 731	186	11 184	2 853	298	14 794	6 049	213
1989	16 072	13 600	177	10 066	2 883	266	14 613	5 894	206
1988	15 318	13 356	191	10 202	2 970	343	13 835	5 760	236
1987	14 136	13 023	171	9 976	3 015	264	12 862	5 699	224
1986	13 494	12 729	167	9 365	3 028	282	12 276	5 470	190
1985	12 926	12 427	153	9 116	3 009	275	11 791	5 223	192
1984	12 002	11 948	131	8 725	3 127	292	10 882	4 927	170
1983	11 299	11 296	...	7 867	3 035	...	10 557	4 692	...
1982	10 612	11 081	124	7 799	3 188	227	10 287	4 591	161
1981	10 117	11 088	109	7 520	3 514	208	9 994	4 388	159
1980	11 085	5 576	170	8 421	2 054	291	11 563	2 119	260
1979	8 720	10 856	97	6 424	3 776	187	8 723	4 267	135
1978	7 981	10 420	91	5 918	3 841	160	8 152	3 944	133
1977	7 271	10 014	70	5 406	3 946	126	7 553	3 604	116
1976	6 716	9 744	66	5 304	4 008	127	6 805	3 515	95
1975	6 190	9 368	57	4 989	3 922	116	6 281	3 495	83
Male									
2001	30 502	7 727	487	18 543	1 210	656	25 037	2 759	430
2000	30 109	7 700	478	17 992	1 235	717	25 219	2 942	504
1999	28 821	7 806	509	16 391	1 199	686	25 849	2 934	791
1998	26 090	7 488	444	16 013	1 190	744	22 698	2 974	480
1997	25 080	7 370	428	15 423	1 304	647	22 440	2 862	517
1996	25 067	7 125	785	15 461	1 290	648	22 267	2 836	1 034
1995	23 876	7 090	718	14 877	1 280	652	19 514	2 812	443
1994	22 614	7 009	445	15 984	1 191	770	18 527	2 818	413
1993	21 108	6 833	518	13 074	1 305	574	18 668	2 775	903
1992	19 278	6 822	342	12 661	1 457	510	16 978	2 683	382
1991	18 607	6 830	284	15 714	1 624	423	17 352	2 731	382
1990	18 859	6 781	300	13 031	1 563	430	17 046	3 013	332
1989	18 108	6 654	283	11 827	1 614	355	16 658	2 848	328
1988	17 782	6 593	326	12 439	1 671	529	16 345	2 795	404
1987	16 171	6 505	283	11 899	1 711	375	14 800	2 769	374
1986	15 441	6 326	256	11 248	1 691	409	14 214	2 666	294
1985	14 932	6 237	254	10 802	1 716	396	13 721	2 572	308
1984	13 560	5 899	212	10 216	1 780	374	12 382	2 339	280
1983	12 789	5 707	205	9 094	1 768	339	11 956	2 312	265
1982	12 203	5 535	203	9 153	1 798	340	11 952	2 213	268
1981	11 937	5 651	174	9 266	1 925	318	11 905	2 191	261
1980	11 085	5 576	170	8 421	2 054	291	11 563	2 119	260
1979	10 403	5 581	157	7 938	2 138	278	10 662	2 087	225
1978	9 651	5 350	147	7 423	2 156	233	9 869	1 982	219
1977	8 710	5 220	110	6 648	2 230	187	9 332	1 770	184
1976	7 991	5 156	105	6 670	2 289	187	8 056	1 766	155
1975	7 541	4 864	89	6 364	2 247	173	7 847	1 684	138
Female									
2001	24 036	8 956	363	15 912	1 172	2 049	18 683	2 970	289
2000	22 884	9 056	252	12 321	1 198	401	18 510	3 078	403
1999	21 694	9 130	375	10 734	1 194	465	16 506	3 178	345
1998	20 026	8 713	299	11 372	1 212	675	15 892	3 078	357
1997	19 161	8 503	286	10 607	1 132	399	15 789	3 102	371
1996	19 271	8 129	592	10 337	1 094	526	15 379	3 008	433
1995	17 485	7 757	277	10 739	1 108	544	14 473	2 641	433
1994	17 200	7 745	326	9 150	1 099	423	14 333	2 777	356
1993	16 336	7 481	371	8 562	1 048	388	13 550	2 746	730
1992	15 605	7 014	241	8 756	995	376	13 550	2 696	312
1991	15 065	7 034	231	9 151	1 237	524	12 810	2 781	301
1990	14 449	6 950	221	8 946	1 290	402	12 560	3 046	269
1989	14 122	6 946	215	7 827	1 269	403	12 701	3 046	255
1988	12 916	6 763	203	7 325	1 299	391	11 469	2 965	255
1987	12 106	6 518	193	7 452	1 304	360	11 030	2 930	256
1986	11 571	6 403	215	6 984	1 337	375	10 434	2 804	244
1985	10 904	6 190	170	6 879	1 293	366	9 918	2 651	233
1984	10 482	6 049	157	6 754	1 347	464	9 527	2 588	201
1983	9 778	5 589	...	6 154	1 267	...	9 197	2 380	...
1982	9 024	5 546	141	6 047	1 390	279	8 737	2 378	186
1981	8 225	5 437	129	5 404	1 589	252	8 088	2 197	183
1980	7 684	...	121	4 685	...	242	7 508	...	164
1979	6 940	5 275	112	4 448	1 638	232	6 866	2 180	154
1978	6 219	5 070	104	3 993	1 685	212	6 417	1 962	149
1977	5 704	4 794	84	3 793	1 716	158	5 837	1 834	142
1976	5 283	4 588	74	3 486	1 719	162	5 541	1 749	108
1975	4 732	4 504	68	3 145	1 675	140	4 825	1 811	96

. . . = Not available.

Table A-14. Mean Earnings of Workers 18 Years and Over, by Educational Attainment, Race, Sex, and Hispanic Origin, 1975 to 2001—*Continued*

(Mean annual earnings [dollars]. Total number with earnings in thousands. Standard error of the mean.)

Age, sex, race, and Hispanic origin	Some college/associate degree			Bachelor's degree			Advanced degree		
	Mean	Number with earnings	Standard error	Mean	Number with earnings	Standard error	Mean	Number with earnings	Standard error
BLACK									
Both Sexes									
2001	26 907	5 481	448	40 165	2 212	911	55 771	877	2 320
2000	26 324	5 431	351	41 513	2 060	1 198	52 373	809	1 921
1999	25 176	5 417	447	37 422	2 140	986	52 437	873	2 705
1998	23 927	4 559	413	36 373	1 897	1 005	44 760	764	2 020
1997	22 899	4 902	456	32 062	1 846	773	42 791	724	2 139
1996	23 628	4 783	1 084	31 955	1 655	1 080	48 731	590	5 269
1995	21 824	4 727	885	29 666	1 684	876	46 654	595	3 603
1994	19 631	4 610	573	30 938	1 679	907	48 653	579	3 282
1993	18 867	4 279	413	29 953	1 638	1 015	41 221	525	2 456
1992	18 719	4 054	338	27 457	1 429	819	41 439	523	1 885
1991	17 850	3 581	327	25 630	1 383	709	38 002	528	1 885
1990	18 209	3 004	411	26 448	1 217	745	32 962	607	1 461
1989	17 385	3 008	340	25 357	1 121	779	32 740	694	1 422
1988	16 760	2 802	443	23 689	1 204	702	30 802	621	1 346
1987	15 491	2 617	363	20 805	1 097	608	29 163	596	1 411
1986	14 743	2 662	423	21 403	1 004	810	27 503	564	1 130
1985	13 805	2 615	348	20 533	1 046	579	26 246	535	1 254
1984	12 890	2 396	277	19 330	937	551	24 072	561	884
1983	12 426	2 206	. . .	17 207	828	. . .	23 506	535	. . .
1982	11 119	2 067	271	15 152	747	494	22 959	488	1 162
1981	11 456	2 078	255	14 587	708	457	19 463	398	788
1980	12 393	964	417	15 616	283	739	19 960	353	1 026
1979	9 895	1 826	237	13 473	622	534	18 182	366	872
1978	9 026	1 689	230	12 870	557	544	15 076	389	573
1977	8 321	1 578	182	11 088	532	342	14 749	354	494
1976	7 331	1 370	184	10 331	547	314	15 013	305	696
1975	7 212	1 193	170	9 473	517	280	12 333	241	433
Male									
2001	31 084	2 457	887	46 511	943	1 767	67 007	356	5 050
2000	30 966	2 291	686	49 270	880	2 526	60 207	349	3 911
1999	28 442	2 338	712	42 530	971	1 635	59 587	365	4 070
1998	26 586	2 215	707	42 539	792	1 889	51 198	318	4 289
1997	27 215	2 108	847	35 792	818	1 243	49 940	278	4 564
1996	26 365	2 047	1 442	35 558	700	1 664	65 981	253	11 509
1995	26 846	2 047	1 948	36 026	659	1 815	57 186	293	6 801
1994	23 748	1 959	844	34 073	758	1 628	52 829	281	5 010
1993	21 734	1 804	691	35 147	721	1 811	47 372	228	4 974
1992	22 697	1 796	527	30 989	643	1 489	48 968	244	3 719
1991	20 548	1 570	542	26 075	650	966	43 927	255	3 719
1990	21 152	1 372	708	29 471	564	1 291	39 104	269	2 888
1989	20 253	1 352	566	27 493	515	1 201	38 166	326	2 655
1988	19 265	1 311	818	28 506	533	1 220	36 452	283	2 650
1987	18 081	1 250	612	23 345	482	1 091	34 073	294	2 645
1986	17 419	1 226	693	23 412	480	1 161	31 054	263	2 035
1985	16 415	1 230	628	23 818	477	1 072	31 947	243	2 484
1984	14 960	1 106	471	21 986	424	961	27 893	250	1 670
1983	15 113	996	500	20 370	363	1 033	25 466	268	1 470
1982	12 926	953	458	17 658	319	861	26 452	253	2 006
1981	13 740	1 002	432	16 624	327	776	21 082	205	1 197
1980	12 393	964	417	15 616	283	739	23 346	156	1 986
1979	11 971	931	384	16 161	259	1 071	21 092	166	1 673
1978	11 197	770	409	16 009	260	944	18 083	181	1 031
1977	10 023	799	300	12 978	234	641	16 385	188	808
1976	8 688	726	300	12 246	233	597	17 859	143	1 388
1975	8 505	599	267	11 318	213	572	13 720	121	702
Female									
2001	23 511	3 023	360	35 448	1 269	860	48 080	521	1 713
2000	22 937	3 140	324	35 719	1 179	851	46 416	459	1 532
1999	22 699	3 080	560	33 184	1 170	1 149	47 358	509	3 569
1998	20 371	2 870	470	31 952	1 105	1 012	40 214	448	1 496
1997	19 643	2 794	452	29 091	1 027	946	38 392	448	1 902
1996	21 581	2 736	1 555	29 311	954	1 402	35 785	337	1 542
1995	17 985	2 679	429	25 577	1 025	768	36 585	304	1 616
1994	16 589	2 651	472	28 356	921	946	44 618	297	4 220
1993	16 778	2 475	495	25 865	917	1 073	36 485	296	1 862
1992	15 553	2 256	440	24 572	786	821	34 902	281	1 272
1991	15 743	2 010	400	25 235	733	912	32 467	273	1 272
1990	15 734	1 632	466	23 837	653	827	28 074	338	1 265
1989	15 044	1 656	411	23 541	606	1 017	27 933	368	1 290
1988	14 557	1 491	419	19 862	671	804	26 072	338	1 094
1987	13 123	1 367	412	18 815	615	668	24 383	302	1 062
1986	12 459	1 436	516	19 562	524	1 129	24 400	301	1 149
1985	11 488	1 385	347	17 779	569	569	21 502	292	1 003
1984	11 115	1 290	318	17 134	513	618	21 000	311	860
1983	10 215	1 210	. . .	14 738	465	. . .	21 539	267	. . .
1982	9 574	1 114	315	13 284	428	576	19 198	235	1 077
1981	9 329	1 076	285	12 839	381	527	17 743	193	1 011
1980	8 544	. . .	266	12 389	. . .	568	17 278	. . .	951
1979	7 735	895	273	11 555	363	504	15 766	200	785
1978	7 207	919	248	10 122	297	598	12 459	208	585
1977	6 576	779	203	9 604	298	347	12 896	166	524
1976	5 801	644	199	8 910	314	321	12 501	162	465
1975	5 908	594	211	8 180	304	258	10 934	120	505

. . . = Not available.

Table A-14. Mean Earnings of Workers 18 Years and Over, by Educational Attainment, Race, Sex, and Hispanic Origin, 1975 to 2001—*Continued*

(Mean annual earnings [dollars]. Total number with earnings in thousands. Standard error of the mean.)

Age, sex, race, and Hispanic origin	Total			Not a high school graduate			High school graduate		
	Mean	Number with earnings	Standard error	Mean	Number with earnings	Standard error	Mean	Number with earnings	Standard error
NON-HISPANIC WHITE									
Both Sexes									
2001	38 711	106 384	195	19 659	7 812	466	28 426	33 050	241
2000	37 346	106 709	187	19 147	7 957	468	27 122	33 231	180
1999	34 838	106 573	232	16 957	8 219	447	25 847	34 121	231
1998	33 336	105 523	229	16 837	8 488	379	24 801	34 344	249
Male									
2001	47 973	56 528	316	23 096	4 749	549	34 627	17 672	352
2000	47 084	56 675	318	23 296	4 763	706	33 669	17 733	281
1999	44 032	56 575	390	20 256	4 842	471	32 321	18 047	362
1998	41 612	56 246	372	20 781	5 152	584	30 429	18 048	374
Female									
2001	28 210	49 856	197	14 328	3 062	816	21 301	15 378	313
2000	26 315	50 034	158	12 962	3 194	474	19 631	15 498	192
1999	24 436	49 998	199	12 227	3 378	838	18 579	16 074	247
1998	23 891	49 277	226	10 746	3 336	268	18 568	16 295	305
NON-HISPANIC BLACK									
Both Sexes									
2001	27 171	16 079	306	17 465	2 190	1 152	21 750	5 521	266
2000	26 165	16 227	249	15 041	2 304	422	21 734	5 854	332
1999	25 066	16 423	320	13 441	2 241	436	20 979	5 942	440
1998	22 887	15 793	268	13 473	2 252	530	19 225	5 964	308
Male									
2001	30 816	7 392	506	18 728	1 093	709	25 070	2 645	441
2000	29 979	7 427	446	17 835	1 151	725	25 131	2 859	514
1999	28 959	7 542	522	16 288	1 111	707	25 853	2 850	808
1998	26 142	7 289	452	15 768	1 099	786	22 658	2 930	482
Female									
2001	24 068	8 686	363	16 206	1 096	2 188	18 697	2 875	296
2000	22 945	8 800	256	12 252	1 153	412	18 490	2 994	413
1999	21 761	8 881	381	10 640	1 130	475	16 488	3 093	348
1998	20 097	8 504	304	11 283	1 153	696	15 910	3 034	360
HISPANIC[1]									
Both Sexes									
2001	24 786	17 575	327	18 334	6 533	495	22 866	5 265	443
2000	23 855	17 161	348	17 156	6 428	441	22 009	5 145	340
1999	22 096	15 122	397	16 106	5 601	615	20 704	4 539	418
1998	22 117	14 372	508	15 832	5 281	752	20 978	4 219	759
1997	20 766	13 972	421	15 069	5 238	600	19 558	4 082	605
1996	19 439	13 365	458	13 287	5 062	263	18 528	3 783	444
1995	18 262	12 434	428	13 068	4 784	305	18 333	3 594	1 070
1994	18 568	12 035	478	13 733	4 686	944	17 323	3 444	401
1993	17 102	11 644	344	11 852	4 425	263	16 591	3 367	419
1992	16 824	10 171	252	11 836	3 962	273	16 714	2 991	425
1991	16 300	10 006	237	11 335	3 906	230	16 142	3 045	344
1990	15 943	9 729	222	10 368	3 929	210	15 417	3 282	297
1989	15 714	9 570	234	11 500	3 985	222	14 901	3 188	296
1988	15 007	9 226	245	11 045	3 824	240	14 667	2 953	315
1987	14 695	8 817	250	10 961	3 457	272	13 958	2 982	342
1986	13 558	8 393	205	9 896	3 379	237	13 389	2 835	300
1985	13 120	7 840	195	9 956	3 223	257	13 044	2 661	297
1984	12 583	7 349	228	9 671	3 129	293	12 858	2 457	343
1983	11 901	6 222	. . .	9 473	2 674	. . .	12 077	2 030	. . .
1982	11 307	5 914	221	8 498	2 583	283	11 539	1 967	317
1981	10 872	5 930	194	8 645	2 648	255	11 046	1 966	304
1980	10 062	5 723	197	8 119	2 649	284	10 182	1 824	309
1979	9 248	5 545	175	7 683	2 533	272	9 338	1 812	272
1978	8 460	4 898	169	7 138	2 345	305	8 512	1 554	258
1977	7 761	4 752	130	6 547	2 306	205	8 079	1 461	226
1976	7 081	4 303	128	5 984	2 107	199	7 580	1 309	215
1975	6 567	4 078	124	5 462	2 028	198	6 759	1 293	183

[1]May be of any race.
. . . = Not available.

Table A-14. Mean Earnings of Workers 18 Years and Over, by Educational Attainment, Race, Sex, and Hispanic Origin, 1975 to 2001—*Continued*

(Mean annual earnings [dollars]. Total number with earnings in thousands. Standard error of the mean.)

Age, sex, race, and Hispanic origin	Some college/associate degree			Bachelor's degree			Advanced degree		
	Mean	Number with earnings	Standard error	Mean	Number with earnings	Standard error	Mean	Number with earnings	Standard error
NON-HISPANIC WHITE									
Both Sexes									
2001	31 905	32 118	240	52 300	22 204	514	74 932	11 198	1 017
2000	31 217	32 836	243	51 351	21 824	528	72 356	10 859	1 027
1999	29 557	32 454	328	47 401	21 272	630	68 910	10 507	1 237
1998	23 897	31 459	364	45 342	21 175	630	65 461	10 059	1 153
Male									
2001	39 133	16 114	370	66 196	11 692	881	92 954	6 299	1 613
2000	39 379	16 435	431	65 459	11 594	899	90 150	6 149	1 641
1999	37 224	16 343	585	60 384	11 307	1 036	85 918	6 036	2 057
1998	29 555	15 849	625	57 346	11 335	1 042	79 524	5 862	1 709
Female									
2001	24 628	16 004	294	36 844	10 512	404	51 756	4 898	930
2000	23 038	16 401	199	35 362	10 230	414	49 126	4 710	876
1999	21 779	16 112	258	32 667	9 964	573	45 943	4 470	859
1998	18 198	15 610	347	31 516	9 840	554	45 805	4 196	1 294
NON-HISPANIC BLACK									
Both Sexes									
2001	26 957	5 348	458	39 999	2 153	879	55 720	864	2 332
2000	26 450	5 285	358	41 072	1 991	986	51 859	792	1 897
1999	25 190	5 290	454	37 531	2 100	998	52 746	849	2 755
1998	28 753	4 964	419	36 543	1 861	1 019	44 939	753	2 047
Male									
2001	31 234	2 388	909	46 761	914	1 814	67 317	351	5 115
2000	31 120	2 219	705	47 746	853	1 953	59 504	343	3 854
1999	28 404	2 277	721	42 572	954	1 656	61 078	350	4 165
1998	35 841	2 168	714	42 745	779	1 913	51 523	313	4 349
Female									
2001	23 507	2 960	364	35 014	1 239	692	47 769	513	1 649
2000	23 069	3 065	328	36 067	1 138	871	46 009	449	1 507
1999	22 762	3 014	569	33 332	1 146	1 162	46 969	500	3 604
1998	33 330	2 795	480	32 076	1 082	1 026	40 275	440	1 515
HISPANIC[1]									
Both Sexes									
2001	27 523	3 842	600	40 586	1 416	1 570	62 194	517	4 311
2000	25 276	3 737	459	44 661	1 395	2 676	63 908	455	5 138
1999	24 577	3 392	713	36 212	1 117	2 063	55 352	472	5 416
1998	23 091	3 289	925	35 014	1 156	1 650	62 583	425	7 812
1997	22 001	3 075	546	33 465	1 140	1 685	58 571	437	6 897
1996	22 209	3 096	1 185	32 955	1 027	2 746	49 873	398	7 497
1995	19 923	2 856	904	30 602	866	1 678	45 612	334	3 004
1994	21 041	2 723	693	29 165	844	1 337	51 898	337	6 534
1993	19 043	2 728	548	30 359	799	3 355	45 034	325	4 169
1992	19 778	2 242	446	28 260	702	1 272	46 736	274	2 871
1991	19 123	2 080	456	26 623	665	1 249	40 154	311	2 871
1990	19 206	1 534	540	25 703	601	1 208	38 075	382	2 477
1989	18 707	1 513	608	28 157	535	1 519	39 273	349	2 861
1988	18 101	1 511	716	23 745	596	1 134	33 843	340	3 064
1987	16 899	1 400	524	23 105	644	1 139	34 413	335	3 055
1986	16 523	1 411	584	22 707	471	1 248	28 316	295	1 822
1985	15 318	1 226	513	20 878	458	1 104	28 357	273	1 843
1984	14 359	1 116	622	19 924	381	1 226	26 327	265	2 222
1983	13 371	976	. . .	17 972	320	. . .	24 352	222	. . .
1982	13 108	873	546	18 186	303	1 463	28 167	186	2 784
1981	12 971	834	516	16 114	320	1 174	24 082	161	2 557
1980	11 891	808	558	15 676	283	1 267	21 910	157	2 623
1979	10 181	768	458	14 940	240	1 315	18 273	190	1 780
1978	9 575	661	446	13 985	213	1 195	17 333	125	1 903
1977	8 172	656	333	12 572	210	864	16 660	118	1 753
1976	7 252	592	333	11 242	177	887	14 000	118	1 667
1975	7 154	474	351	10 573	173	796	15 756	111	1 994

[1]May be of any race.
. . . = Not available.

Table A-14. Mean Earnings of Workers 18 Years and Over, by Educational Attainment, Race, Sex, and Hispanic Origin, 1975 to 2001—*Continued*

(Mean annual earnings [dollars]. Total number with earnings in thousands. Standard error of the mean.)

Age, sex, race, and Hispanic origin	Total			Not a high school graduate			High school graduate		
	Mean	Number with earnings	Standard error	Mean	Number with earnings	Standard error	Mean	Number with earnings	Standard error
HISPANIC[1]									
Male									
2001	27 964	10 258	456	20 614	4 289	598	26 745	2 985	727
2000	27 253	9 996	516	19 501	4 236	460	25 629	2 940	532
1999	24 970	8 713	527	18 020	3 592	378	23 736	2 597	560
1998	25 534	8 288	775	17 756	3 428	883	24 739	2 413	1 248
1997	23 520	8 261	595	17 447	3 444	712	22 253	2 391	918
1996	21 870	7 975	657	14 986	3 382	347	21 593	2 116	628
1995	20 312	7 337	544	14 774	3 140	347	20 882	2 039	1 467
1994	21 288	7 117	754	16 355	3 111	1 409	19 667	1 937	557
1993	19 460	6 957	526	13 572	2 928	357	18 765	1 954	566
1992	18 842	6 034	365	13 313	2 633	366	19 357	1 665	662
1991	18 516	5 932	316	13 133	2 548	263	18 582	1 705	471
1990	18 320	5 745	332	13 182	2 562	276	18 100	1 812	455
1989	18 087	5 641	352	13 167	2 632	265	17 579	1 711	452
1988	17 357	5 477	361	12 836	2 517	316	17 446	1 621	475
1987	17 048	5 248	372	12 823	2 281	369	16 774	1 616	523
1986	15 624	5 037	305	11 262	2 262	313	15 948	1 546	476
1985	15 293	4 702	285	11 671	2 111	342	15 602	1 491	464
1984	14 957	4 344	344	11 441	2 022	385	15 763	1 319	549
1983	14 265	3 577	324	11 353	1 678	400	14 584	1 074	549
1982	13 484	3 480	339	10 108	1 622	392	13 883	1 083	488
1981	13 052	3 504	292	10 447	1 686	342	13 513	1 037	489
1980	12 310	3 401	303	9 825	1 707	394	13 108	961	526
1979	11 332	3 269	268	9 393	1 615	378	11 714	952	448
1978	10 473	2 915	258	8 836	1 498	427	10 940	815	426
1977	9 655	2 833	198	8 192	1 460	281	10 386	776	372
1976	8 787	2 571	195	7 440	1 321	272	9 640	712	345
1975	8 162	2 456	189	6 745	1 287	268	8 546	691	289
Female									
2001	20 330	7 316	450	13 976	2 243	867	17 786	2 279	336
2000	19 115	7 164	415	12 622	2 191	930	17 180	2 204	314
1999	18 187	6 409	594	12 684	2 010	1 567	16 653	1 943	593
1998	17 461	6 804	557	12 273	1 854	1 377	15 952	1 806	539
1997	16 781	5 711	554	10 503	1 794	1 072	15 747	1 691	637
1996	15 841	5 390	578	9 867	1 680	332	14 635	1 667	577
1995	15 310	5 096	685	9 809	1 644	565	14 989	1 555	1 541
1994	14 631	4 918	404	8 559	1 576	304	14 313	1 508	546
1993	13 602	4 687	329	8 489	1 498	297	13 584	1 413	595
1992	13 880	4 137	304	8 913	1 330	334	13 396	1 326	435
1991	13 069	4 072	273	4 809	1 358	307	13 043	1 339	380
1990	12 516	3 984	254	5 093	1 367	309	12 109	1 470	354
1989	12 307	3 929	266	8 256	1 353	401	11 799	1 477	365
1988	11 573	3 749	290	7 597	1 307	349	11 284	1 332	392
1987	11 234	3 569	286	7 350	1 176	354	10 627	1 366	417
1986	10 457	3 356	231	7 130	1 117	338	10 319	1 289	332
1985	9 865	3 138	236	6 699	1 112	367	9 784	1 170	327
1984	9 150	3 005	252	6 438	1 107	436	9 492	1 138	380
1983	8 704	2 645	. . .	6 305	996	. . .	9 261	956	. . .
1982	8 195	2 434	233	5 781	961	373	8 668	884	374
1981	7 723	2 426	215	5 486	962	364	8 292	929	342
1980	6 770	2 322	199	5 028	942	358	6 923	863	287
1979	6 255	2 276	184	4 675	918	347	6 708	860	286
1978	5 501	1 983	173	4 135	847	377	5 834	739	273
1977	4 964	1 919	137	3 707	846	276	5 466	685	236
1976	4 548	1 732	132	3 537	786	273	5 124	597	229
1975	4 152	1 622	122	3 233	741	277	4 708	602	209

[1]May be of any race.
. . . = Not available.

Table A-14. Mean Earnings of Workers 18 Years and Over, by Educational Attainment, Race, Sex, and Hispanic Origin, 1975 to 2001—*Continued*

(Mean annual earnings [dollars]. Total number with earnings in thousands. Standard error of the mean.)

Age, sex, race, and Hispanic origin	Some college/associate degree			Bachelor's degree			Advanced degree		
	Mean	Number with earnings	Standard error	Mean	Number with earnings	Standard error	Mean	Number with earnings	Standard error
HISPANIC[1]									
Male									
2001	32 595	1 962	882	45 445	748	1 713	75 746	272	7 676
2000	30 155	1 873	797	55 050	722	4 651	81 447	223	9 696
1999	29 387	1 698	1 211	42 733	577	3 697	66 745	250	9 708
1998	26 483	1 652	1 677	40 889	569	2 451	83 754	226	13 919
1997	25 923	1 598	852	37 963	557	2 021	68 097	272	10 265
1996	26 682	1 687	2 101	38 130	531	5 090	49 307	259	6 300
1995	22 171	1 475	978	35 109	466	2 695	50 802	215	4 151
1994	24 517	1 410	855	33 797	450	2 185	60 858	210	10 036
1993	22 417	1 444	859	37 554	438	5 974	52 441	194	6 150
1992	23 033	1 193	596	33 430	380	1 957	53 645	164	4 216
1991	21 974	1 131	693	31 699	356	1 729	45 873	193	4 216
1990	22 376	852	831	31 485	314	1 966	47 479	205	4 339
1989	22 374	810	996	32 767	292	2 536	49 088	196	4 778
1988	21 631	811	1 205	26 935	333	1 807	40 916	194	4 602
1987	19 414	758	773	26 581	383	1 782	39 014	211	4 410
1986	19 675	778	962	27 427	274	1 975	32 538	176	2 705
1985	18 168	678	771	24 723	267	1 723	32 831	155	2 792
1984	17 261	611	1 014	23 835	223	1 878	30 727	168	3 231
1983	16 626	514	864	21 911	170	2 111	28 680	141	2 681
1982	15 560	495	845	22 565	153	2 632	34 474	125	3 995
1981	15 432	489	785	19 201	177	1 928	27 619	114	3 427
1980	14 331	451	890	19 224	167	1 986	24 642	114	3 439
1979	12 489	441	714	18 923	142	2 113	21 299	118	2 619
1978	11 545	393	665	16 898	127	1 861	20 702	82	2 730
1977	9 924	391	501	15 189	120	1 420	19 025	85	2 291
1976	8 843	342	508	13 650	114	1 299	16 184	81	2 339
1975	8 807	279	536	12 881	113	1 142	17 991	86	2 535
Female									
2001	22 229	1 879	783	35 142	668	2 699	47 176	245	2 786
2000	20 372	1 864	413	33 489	672	2 303	47 057	232	3 340
1999	19 754	1 694	694	29 249	540	1 459	42 503	222	2 979
1998	20 460	1 639	689	29 317	587	2 144	38 422	200	3 471
1997	17 759	1 477	611	29 173	584	2 635	43 051	165	6 178
1996	16 856	1 409	581	27 407	495	1 503	50 960	139	17 662
1995	17 521	1 380	1 542	25 338	399	1 722	36 255	118	3 079
1994	17 309	1 313	1 081	23 867	393	1 272	37 269	127	4 428
1993	15 250	1 284	609	21 627	361	1 258	34 001	131	4 391
1992	16 076	1 049	669	22 160	322	1 343	34 551	110	3 141
1991	15 721	948	564	20 791	309	1 377	30 721	117	3 141
1990	15 245	682	629	19 378	287	1 331	27 184	177	1 824
1989	14 482	703	629	22 617	243	1 379	26 700	153	2 265
1988	14 012	700	662	19 707	263	1 171	24 444	146	3 675
1987	13 929	642	688	18 003	261	1 033	26 584	124	3 436
1986	12 648	633	547	16 142	197	1 165	22 071	119	2 096
1985	11 791	548	639	15 503	191	1 098	22 480	118	2 173
1984	10 848	505	619	14 404	158	1 310	18 706	97	2 355
1983	9 750	462	. . .	13 507	150	. . .	16 817	81	. . .
1982	9 896	378	605	13 719	150	1 235	15 244	61	2 247
1981	9 483	345	563	12 292	143	1 101	15 503	47	2 767
1980	8 808	357	576	10 568	116	1 177	14 668	43	2 935
1979	7 069	327	482	9 168	98	1 001	13 313	72	1 905
1978	6 686	268	507	9 684	86	1 098	10 908	43	1 872
1977	5 588	265	367	9 082	90	691	10 569	33	2 119
1976	5 075	250	373	6 884	63	826	9 218	37	1 425
1975	4 790	195	376	6 226	60	805	8 067	25	1 536

Note: The earnings data for 2000 and 2001 are from the expanded CPS sample and were calculated using population controls based on Census 2000. Prior to 1991, Some college/Associate degree equals 1 to 3 years of college completed; Bachelor's degree equals 4 years of college; Advanced degree equals 5 or more years of college completed.
[1]May be of any race.
. . . = Not available.

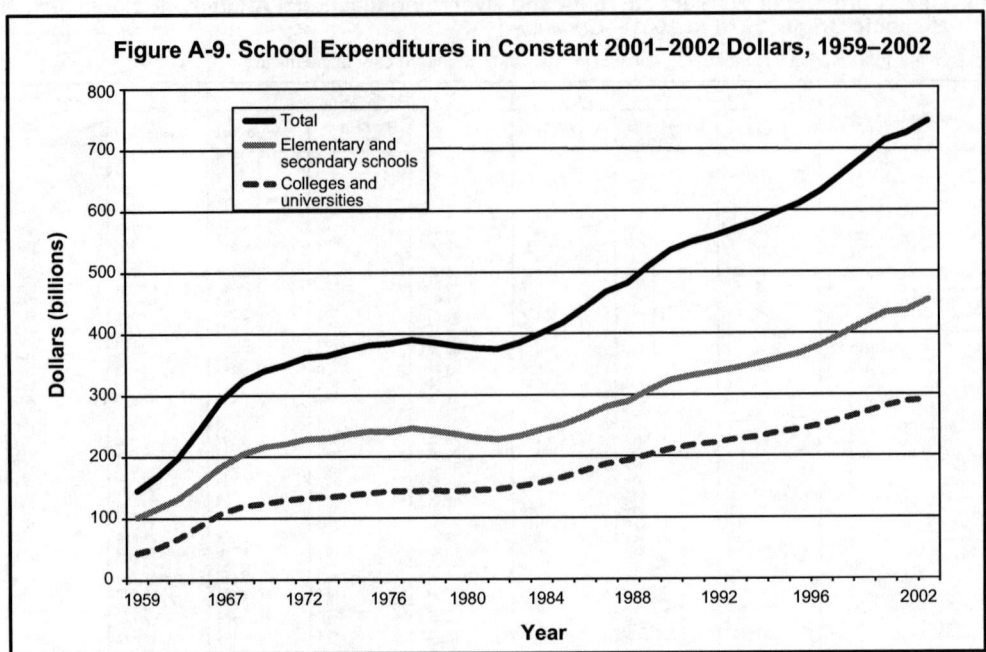

Figure A-9. School Expenditures in Constant 2001–2002 Dollars, 1959–2002

Source: U.S. Department of Education, National Center for Education Statistics. *Digest of Education Statistics, 2002.*

- In 2002, school expenditures increased to $745 billion. More than 60 percent was for elementary and secondary schools, while the remaining amount was spent on higher education. Total expenditures amounted to 7.4 percent of the United States gross domestic product, which is slightly higher than previous years.

NOTES AND DEFINITIONS: NATIONAL SCHOOL ENROLLMENT AND EDUCATIONAL ATTAINMENT

Tables in Part A are derived from the October 2000 *Current Population Survey* and the March 2002 *Current Population Survey*. Comparable tables were disseminated by the U.S. Census Bureau in the P-20 series of *Current Population Reports (CPR)* for most years between 1947 and 1994. Since that time the tables have not been available in printed form, but they are available on the U.S. Bureau of the Census Web site at <www.census.gov>. We have included some tables here covering this entire historical period, including earnings by educational attainment shown in current dollars. In the historical data series, data prior to 1992 are not strictly comparable to those after that date. Before 1992, questions on degrees received were not asked in the *Current Population Survey*, and thus educational attainment was gauged only through years of school completed. For information about the availability of earlier reports or data questions not addressed in this definitions section, contact the Education and Social Stratification Branch, Population Division, U.S. Bureau of the Census at (301) 457-2464.

Age. Age classification is based on the age of the person at his/her last birthday.

Earnings. (See Income)

Educational attainment. Data on educational attainment are derived from a single question that asks, "What is the highest grade of school...has completed, or the highest degree...has received?"

The single educational attainment question now in use was introduced in the CPS beginning January 1992, and is similar to that used in the 1990 Decennial Census of Population and Housing. Consequently, data on educational attainment from the 1992 CPS are not directly comparable to CPS data from earlier years. The new question replaces the previous two-part question used in the CPS that asked respondents to report the highest grade they had attended, and whether or not they had completed that grade.

The questions on educational attainment apply only to progress in "regular" schools. Such schools include graded public, private, and parochial elementary and high schools (both junior and senior high schools), colleges, universities, and professional schools, whether day schools or night schools. Thus, regular schooling is that which may advance a person toward an elementary school certificate or high school diploma, or a college, university, or professional school degree. Schooling in other than regular schools was counted only if the credits obtained are regarded as transferable to a school in the regular school system.

Ethnic origin. People of Hispanic origin were identified by a question that asked for self-identification of the persons' origin or descent. Respondents were asked to select their origin (and the origin of other household members) from a "flash card" listing ethnic origins. People of Hispanic origin, in particular, were those who indicated that their origin was Mexican, Puerto Rican, Cuban, Central or South American, or some other Hispanic origin. It should be noted that people of Hispanic origin may be of any race.

People who were of non-Hispanic White origin, were identified by crossing the responses to two self-identification questions: (1) origin or descent and (2) race. Respondents were asked to select their race (and the race of other household members) from a "flash card" listing racial groups. Beginning with March 1989, the population is divided into five groups on the basis of race: White, Black, American Indian, Eskimo or Aleut, Asian or Pacific Islander, and Other races. The last category includes any other race except the four mentioned. Respondents who selected their race as White and indicated that their origin was not one of the Hispanic origin subgroups Mexican, Puerto Rican, Cuban, Central or South American, were called non-Hispanic White origin.

Family. A family is a group of two people or more (one of whom is the householder) related by birth, marriage, or adoption and residing together; all such people (including related subfamily members) are considered as members of one family. Beginning with the 1980 *Current Population Survey*, unrelated subfamilies (referred to in the past as secondary families) are no longer included in the count of families, nor are the members of unrelated subfamilies included in the count of family members. The number of families is equal to the number of family households; however, the count of family members differs from the count of family household members because family household members include any non-relatives living in the household.

Family household. A family household is a household maintained by a householder who is in a family (as defined above), and includes any unrelated people (unrelated subfamily members and/or secondary individuals) who may be residing there. The number of family households is equal to the number of families. The count of family household members differs from the count of family members, however, in that the family household members include all people living in the household, whereas family members include only the householder and his/her relatives. (See the definition of Family.)

Household. A household consists of all the people who occupy a housing unit. A house, an apartment or other group of rooms, or a single room, is regarded as a housing unit when it is occupied or intended for occupancy as separate living quarters; that is, when the occupants do not live and eat with any other persons in the structure and there is direct access from the outside or through a common hall. A household includes the related family members and all the unrelated people, if any, such as lodgers, foster children, wards, or employees who share the housing unit. A person living alone in a housing unit, or a group of unrelated people sharing a housing unit such as partners or roomers, is also counted as a household. The count of households excludes group quarters. There are two major categories of households, "family" and "nonfamily". (See definitions of Family household and Nonfamily household).

Householder. The householder refers to the person (or one of the people) in whose name the housing unit is owned or rented (maintained) or, if there is no such person, any adult member, excluding roomers, boarders, or paid employees. If the house is owned or rented jointly by a married couple, the householder may be either the husband or the wife. The person designated as the householder is the "reference person" to whom

the relationship of all other household members, if any, is recorded.

The number of householders is equal to the number of households. Also, the number of family householders is equal to the number of families.

Head versus householder. Beginning with the 1980 CPS, the Bureau of the Census discontinued the use of the terms "head of household" and "head of family." Instead, the terms "householder" and "family householder" are used. Recent social changes have resulted in greater sharing of household responsibilities among the adult members and, therefore, have made the term "head" increasingly inappropriate in the analysis of household and family data. Specifically, beginning in 1980, the Census Bureau discontinued its long-time practice of always classifying the husband as the reference person (head) when he and his wife are living together.

Income, Official definition of. For each person in the sample 15 years and over, the CPS asks questions on the amount of money income received in the preceding calendar year from each of the following sources: earnings; unemployment compensation; workers' compensation; Social Security; Supplemental Security Income; Public assistance or welfare payments; veterans' payments; survivor benefits; disability benefits; pension or retirement income; interest, dividends, rents, royalties, and estates and trusts; educational assistance; child support; alimony; financial assistance from outside the household; and other income.
It should be noted that although the income statistics refer to receipts during the preceding calendar year, the demographic characteristics, such as age, labor force status, and family or household composition, are as of the survey date. The income of the family/household does not include amounts received by people who were members during all or part of the income year if these people no longer resided in the family/household at the time of interview. However, the CPS collects income data for people who are current residents but did not reside in the household during the income year.

Data on consumer income collected in the CPS by the Census Bureau cover money income received (exclusive of certain money receipts such as capital gains) before payments for personal income taxes, Social Security, union dues, medicare deductions, etc. Therefore, money income does not reflect the fact that some families receive part of their income in the form of noncash benefits, such as food stamps, health benefits, rent-free housing, and goods produced and consumed on the farm. In addition, money income does not reflect the fact that noncash benefits are also received by some nonfarm residents, which often take the form of the use of business transportation and facilities, full or partial payments by business for retirement programs, medical and educational expenses, etc. Data users should consider these elements when comparing income levels. Moreover, readers should be aware that for many different reasons there is a tendency in household surveys for respondents to underreport their income. Based on an analysis of independently derived income estimates, the Census Bureau determined that respondents report income earned from wages or salaries much better than other sources of income and that the reported wage and salary income is nearly equal to independent estimates of aggregate income.

The Census Bureau collects data for the following income sources.

Earnings. The Census Bureau classifies earnings from longest job (or self-employment) and other employment earnings into three types:

Money wage or salary income is the total income people receive for work performed as an employee during the income year. This category includes wages, salary, armed forces pay, commissions, tips, piece-rate payments, and cash bonuses earned, before deductions are made for items such as taxes, bonds, pensions, and union dues.

Net income from nonfarm self-employment is the net money income (gross receipts minus expenses) from one's own business, professional enterprise, or partnership. Gross receipts include the value of all goods sold and services rendered. Expenses include items such as costs of goods purchased, rent, heat, power, depreciation charges, wages and salaries paid, and business taxes (not personal income taxes). In general, the Census Bureau considers inventory changes in determining net income from nonfarm self-employment; replies based on income tax returns

or other official records do reflect inventory changes. However, when respondents do not report values of inventory changes, interviewers will accept net income figures exclusive of inventory changes. The Census Bureau does not include the value of saleable merchandise consumed by the proprietors of retail stores as part of net income.

Net income from farm self-employment is the net money income (gross receipts minus operating expenses) from the operation of a farm by a person on their own account, as an owner, renter, or sharecropper. Gross receipts include the value of all products sold, payments from government farm programs, money received from the rental of farm equipment to others, rent received from farm property if payment is made based on a percent of crops produced, and incidental receipts from the sale of items such as wood, sand, and gravel.

Operating expenses include items such as cost of feed, fertilizer, seed, and other farming supplies; cash wages paid to farmhands; depreciation charges; cash rent; interest on farm mortgages; farm building repairs; and farm taxes (not state and federal personal income taxes). The Census Bureau does not include the value of fuel, food, or other farm products used for family living as part of net income. In determining farm self-employment income, the Census Bureau considers inventory changes in determining net income only when they are accounted for in replies based on income tax returns or other official records that reflect inventory changes; otherwise, the Census Bureau does not take inventory changes into account.

Unemployment compensation. Unemployment compensation includes payments the respondent received from government unemployment agencies or private companies during periods of unemployment and any strike benefits the respondent received from union funds.

Workers' compensation. Workers' compensation includes payments people receive periodically from public or private insurance companies for injuries received at work.

Social Security. Social Security includes Social Security pensions and survivors' benefits and permanent disability insurance payments made by the Social Security Administration prior to deductions for medical insurance. The Census Bureau does not include Medicare reimbursements for health services as Social Security benefits.

Supplemental Security Income. Supplemental Security Income includes federal, state, and local welfare agency payments to low-income people who are 65 years and over or people of any age who are blind or disabled.

Public assistance or welfare payments. Public assistance or welfare payments include cash public assistance payments low-income people receive, such as aid to families with dependent children (AFDC, ADC), temporary assistance to needy families (TANF), general assistance, and emergency assistance.

Veterans' payments. Veterans' payments include payments disabled members of the armed forces or survivors of deceased veterans receive periodically from the Department of Veterans Affairs for education and on-the-job training, and means-tested assistance to veterans.

Survivor benefits. Survivor benefits include payments people receive from survivors' or widows' pensions, estates, trusts, annuities, or any other types of survivor benefits. Respondents can report payments from 10 different sources: private companies or unions; federal government (Civil Service); military; state or local governments; railroad retirement; workers' compensation; Black lung payments; estates and trusts; annuities or paid-up insurance policies; and other survivor payments.

Disability benefits. Disability benefits include payments people receive as a result of a health problem or disability (other than those from Social Security). Respondents can report payments from 10 sources: workers' compensation; companies or unions; federal government (Civil Service); military; state or local governments; railroad retirement; accident or disability insurance; Black lung payments; state temporary sickness; or other disability payments.

Pension or retirement income. Pension or retirement income includes payments people receive from eight sources: companies or unions; federal government (Civil Service); military; state or local governments; railroad retirement; annuities or paid-up insurance policies; individual retirement accounts (IRAs), Keogh, or 401(k) payments; or other retirement income.

Interest income. Interest income includes payments people receive (or have credited to accounts) from bonds, treasury notes, IRAs, certificates of deposit, interest-bearing savings and checking accounts, and all other investments that pay interest.

Dividends. Dividends include income people receive from stock holdings and mutual fund shares. The CPS does not include capital gains from the sale of stock holdings as income.

Rents, royalties, and estates and trusts. Rents, royalties, and estates and trusts include net income people receive from the rental of a house, store, or other property, receipts from boarders or lodgers, net royalty income, and periodic payments from estate or trust funds.

Educational assistance. Educational assistance includes Pell Grants; other government educational assistance; any scholarships or grants; or financial assistance students receive from employers, friends, or relatives not residing in the student's household.

Child support. Child support includes all periodic payments a parent receives from an absent parent for the support of children, even if these payments are made through a state or local government office.

Alimony. Alimony includes all periodic payments people receive from ex-spouses. Alimony excludes one-time property settlements.

Financial assistance from outside the household. Financial assistance from outside the household includes periodic payments people receive from nonhousehold members. This type of assistance excludes gifts or sporadic assistance.

Other income. Other income includes all other payments people receive regularly that are not included elsewhere on the questionnaire. Some examples are state programs such as foster child payments, military family allotments, and income received from foreign government pensions.

Government transfers. Government transfers include payments people receive from the following sources: (1) unemployment compensation, (2) state workers' compensation, (3) Social Security, (4) Supplemental Security Income (SSI), (5) public assistance, (6) veterans' payments, (7) government survivor benefits, (8) government disability benefits, (9) government pensions, and (10) government educational assistance.

The Census Bureau does not count the following receipts as income: (1) capital gains people received (or losses they incur) from the sale of property, including stocks, bonds, a house, or a car (unless the person was engaged in the business of selling such property, in which case the CPS counts the net proceeds as income from self-employment); (2) withdrawals of bank deposits; (3) money borrowed; (4) tax refunds; (5) gifts; and (6) lump-sum inheritances or insurance payments.

The Census Bureau combines all sources of income into two major types:

Total money earnings. Total money earnings is the algebraic sum of money wages and salary and net income from farm and nonfarm self-employment.

Income other than earnings. Income other than earnings is the algebraic sum of all sources of money income except wages and salaries and income from self-employment.

Labor Force Status

Current job (basic data). For the employed, current job is the job held in the reference week (the week before the survey). Persons with two or more jobs are classified in the job at which the worker spends the most hours during the reference week. The unemployed are classified according to their latest full-time job lasting two or more weeks or by the job (either full time or part time) from which they were on layoff. The occupation/industry classification system for the 1990 Census of Population was used to code CPS data beginning with the January 1992 file.

Labor force. Persons are classified as being in the labor force if they are employed, unemployed, or in the Armed Forces during the survey week. The "civilian labor force" includes all civilians classified as employed or unemployed. The file includes labor force data for civilians age 15 and over. However, the official definition of the civilian labor force is age 16 and over.

Employed. Employed persons comprise (1) all civilians who, during the survey week, did any work at all as paid employees or in their own business or profession, or on their own farm, or who worked 15 hours or more as unpaid workers on a farm or a business operated by a member of the family; and (2) all those who have jobs but who are not working because of illness, bad weather, vacation, or labor-management dispute, or because they are taking time off for personal reasons, whether or not they are seeking other jobs. Each employed person is counted only once. Those persons who held more than one job are counted in the job at which they worked the greatest number of hours during the survey week. If they worked an equal number of hours at more than one job, they are counted at the job they have held the longest.

Unemployed. Unemployed persons are those civilians who, during the survey week, have no employment but are available for work and (1) have engaged in any specific job-seeking activity within the past four weeks such as registering at a public or private employment office, meeting with prospective employers, checking with friends or relatives, placing or answering advertisements, writing letters of application, or being on a union or professional register; (2) are waiting to be called back to a job from which they had been laid off; or (3) are waiting to report to a new wage or salary job within 30 days. The unemployed include job leavers, job losers, new job entrants, and job reentrants.

Not in labor force. All civilians 15 years and over who are not classified as employed or unemployed. These persons are further classified as being engaged in a major activity such as keeping house, going to school, unable to work because of long-term physical or mental illness, and other. The "other" group includes, for the most part, retired persons. Persons who report doing unpaid work in a family farm or business for less than 15 hours are also classified as not in the labor force.

For persons not in the labor force, questions on previous work experience, intentions to seek work again, desire for a job at the time of interview, and reasons for not looking for work are asked only in those households that are in the fourth and eighth months of the sample, that is, the "outgoing" groups—those that had been in the sample for three previous months and would not be in it for the subsequent month.

Finally, it should be noted that the unemployment rate represents the number of unemployed persons as a percentage of the civilian labor force 16 years and over. This measure can also be computed for groups within the labor force classified by sex, age, marital status, race, etc. The job loser, job leaver, reentrant, and new entrant rates are each calculated as a percentage of the civilian labor force 16 years and over; the sum of the rates for the four groups thus equals the total unemployment rate.

Level of school completed. The statistics on level of school indicate the number of persons enrolled at each of five levels: nursery school, kindergarten, elementary school (1st to 8th grades), high school (9th to 12th grades), and college or professional school. The last group includes graduate students in colleges or universities. Persons enrolled in elementary, middle school, intermediate school, or junior high school through the 8th grade are classified as being in elementary school. All persons enrolled in 9th through 12th grade are classified as being in high school.

Metropolitan-nonmetropolitan residence. The general concept of a metropolitan area (MA) is one of a large population nucleus, together with adjacent communities that have a high degree of economic and social integration with that nucleus. Some MAs are defined around two or more nuclei.

The MA classification is a statistical standard, developed for use by federal agencies in the production, analysis, and publication of data on MAs. The MAs are designated and defined by the Federal Office of Management and Budget, following a set of official published standards. These standards were developed by the interagency Federal Executive Committee on Metropolitan Areas, with the aim of producing definitions that are as consistent as possible for all MAs nationwide.

Each MA must contain either a place with a minimum population of 50,000 or a Census Bureau-defined urbanized area and a total MA population of at least 100,000 (75,000 in New England). An MA comprises one or more central counties, and an MA may also include one or more outlying counties that have close economic and social relationships with the central county. An outlying county must have a specified level of commuting to the central counties and also must meet certain standards regarding metropolitan character, such as population density, urban population, and population growth. In New England, MAs are composed of cities and towns rather than whole counties.

The territory, population, and housing units in MAs are referred to as "metropolitan." The metropolitan category is subdivided into "inside central city" and "outside central city." The territory, population, and housing units located outside MAs are referred to as "nonmetropolitan."

To meet the needs of various users, the standards provide for a flexible structure of metropolitan definitions that classify an MA either as a metropolitan statistical area (MSA) or as a consolidated metropolitan statistical area (CMSA) that is divided into primary metropolitan statistical areas (PMSAs). Documentation of the MA standards and how they are applied is available from the Secretary, Federal Executive Committee on Metropolitan Areas, Population Division, U.S. Bureau of the Census, Washington, DC 20233.

Central city. In each MSA and CMSA, the largest place and, in some cases, additional places are designated as "central cities" under the official standards. A few PMSAs do not have central cities. The largest central city and, in some cases, up to two additional central cities are included in the title of the MA; there are also central cities that are not included in an MA title. An MA central city does not include any part of that city that extends outside the MA boundary.

Consolidated and primary metropolitan statistical area. If an area that qualifies as an MA has more than one million people, primary metropolitan statistical areas (PMSAs) may be defined within it. PMSAs consist of a large urbanized county or cluster of counties that demonstrates very strong internal economic and social links, in addition to close ties to other portions of the larger area. When PMSAs are established, the larger area of which they are component parts is designated a consolidated metropolitan statistical area (CMSA).

Metropolitan statistical area. Metropolitan statistical areas are relatively freestanding MAs and are not closely associated with other MAs. These areas are typically surrounded by nonmetropolitan counties.

Modal grade. (see School, Modal grade)

Nonfamily household. A nonfamily household consists of a householder living alone (a one-person household) or where the householder shares the home exclusively with people to whom he/she is not related.

Population coverage. The universe for the CPS includes the civilian noninstitutional population of the United States and members of the Armed Forces in the United States living off post or with their families on post, but excludes all other members of the Armed Forces. The information on the Hispanic population from the CPS was collected in the 50 states and the District of Columbia and, therefore, does not include residents of outlying areas or U.S. territories such as Guam, Puerto Rico, and the Virgin Islands.

Race. The race of individuals was identified by a question that asked for self-identification of the person's race. Respondents were asked to select their race from a "flashcard" listing racial groups. The population is divided into five groups on the basis of race: White; Black; American Indian, Eskimo or Aleut; Asian or Pacific Islander; and Other races beginning with March 1989. The last category includes any other race except the four mentioned. In most of the published tables, "Other races" are included in the total population data line but are not shown individually.

Reference person. The reference person is the person to whom the relationship of other people in the household is recorded. The household reference person is the person listed as the householder (see definition of "Householder"). The subfamily reference person is either the single parent or the husband/wife in a married-couple situation.

Rounding. Percentages are rounded to the nearest 10th of a percent; therefore, the percentages in a distribution do not always add to exactly 100.0 percent.

School, dropout rate, annual high school. The annual high school dropout rate is an estimate of the proportion of students who drop out of school in a single year. This section briefly explains how the annual dropout rate is calculated; for further explanation and details of its derivation; see *Current Population Report*, Series P-20, No. 413, "School Enrollment—Social and Economic Characteristics of Students: October 1983."

Annual dropout rates for a single grade (X) are estimated as the ratio of the number of people who were enrolled in grade (X) in the year preceding the survey and who did not complete grade (X) and are not currently enrolled, to the number enrolled in grade (X) at the start of the year preceding this survey. People reported as enrolled last year but not currently enrolled are presented in table 8 of Current Population Reports on school enrollment, by the highest grade completed and are presumed to have dropped out of the succeeding grade (except those who graduated this year). Thus, individuals counted as 10th grade dropouts are those not enrolled in school whose highest grade completed is the 9th grade. (They include not only those people who were enrolled in the 10th grade in the fall of the year preceding the survey and left school without completing the year, but also those people who finished the 9th grade in the spring preceding the survey and were not enrolled at the survey date.) These estimates form the numerator of estimates of the annual grade-specific dropout rate.

People currently enrolled in high school are presumed to have successfully completed and been enrolled in the preceding grade in the preceding year. Thus, those who have successfully completed the 10th grade are enrolled in the 11th grade. Along with the people who dropped out of that grade, they comprise the denominator of the estimate of the annual grade-specific dropout rate.

$$\frac{\text{Dropout}}{\text{from}} = \frac{\text{Not enrolled and highest grade completed} = n-1}{(\text{Enrolled in } n+1 + \text{Not enrolled and highest grade completed} = n-1)}$$

Since people who complete the 12th grade cannot be presumed to enroll in college, the estimate of the number of people enrolled in the 12th grade one year prior to the survey is constructed as the sum of the number of people reported as having graduated from high school "this year" (both those enrolled in the first year of college and people not currently enrolled whose highest grade completed is the 12th grade) and those people not currently enrolled who were enrolled last year and whose highest grade completed is the 11th grade (dropouts). The annual dropout rate for all grades during one year can be obtained by summing the components of the rates for the individual grades—in other words, those people who were enrolled in the 10th, 11th, or 12th grade last year and who are not currently enrolled and do not have a diploma.

In addition to the annual rate, two other estimates of dropouts are frequently used. The annual dropout rate is different from a "pool" (or status) measure such as the proportion of an age group who are high school dropouts (not enrolled in school, not high school graduates, which does not depend on when the individuals dropped out.) A third measure of dropouts is the cohort measure, most commonly from a longitudinal study, in which one calculates the proportion of a specific group of people enrolled in a specific year, who had not received diplomas (and who were no longer in school) some years later. For example, the proportion of a cohort enrolled in 9th grade in year X, who were not enrolled and had not received a diploma by year X=4.

School enrollment. The school enrollment statistics from the CPS are based on replies to the interviewer's inquiry as to whether the person was enrolled in regular school. Interviewers were instructed to count as enrolled anyone who had been enrolled at any time during the current term or school year in any type of public, parochial, or other private school in the regular school system. Such schools include nursery schools, kindergartens, elementary schools, high schools, colleges, universities, and professional schools. Attendance may be on either a full-time, or part-time basis and during the day or night. Regular schooling is that which may advance a person toward an elementary or high school diploma, a college, university, or professional school degree. Children enrolled in nursery schools and kindergarten are included in the enrollment figures for regular schools and are also shown separately.

Enrollment in schools that are not in the regular school system, such as trade schools, business colleges, and schools for the mentally handicapped, which do not advance students to regular school degrees, is not included.

People enrolled in classes which do not require physical presence in school, such as correspondence courses or other courses of independent study, and in training courses given directly on the job, are also excluded from the count of those enrolled in school, unless such courses are being counted for credit at a regular school.

School enrollment in year preceding current survey. An inquiry on enrollment in regular school or college in October of the preceding year was asked for all people (enrolled and not enrolled). In years before 1988, the question was asked only of people who were not currently attending regular school or were enrolled in college. In the tabulations of people enrolled in secondary school in the previous year, people currently enrolled in high school were assumed to have been enrolled the previous year.

Comparability of enrollment data in previous years. Changes in the edit and tabulation packages used in processing the October CPS school enrollment supplement caused some minor revisions in the estimates. The current edit and tabulation package began with 1987 data. The 1986 data that were published in *Current Population Report*, Series P-20 No. 429, were reprocessed with the rewritten programs in order to clarify comparability. Time series tables usually show only the revised estimates for 1986. The previous edit and tabulation package was used from 1967 to 1986.

Major changes in the data due to the 1987 edit revisions were: (1) Among 14- and 15-year-olds, an edit improvement allowed people with enrollment data not reported, who were previously automatically imputed "not enrolled," to be enrolled; (2) Revisions in tabulation of enrollment in the previous year simplifies calculation of an annual high school dropout rate; (3) Edit improvements caused increases in college enrollment estimates, most notably above age 24; this age group was largely ignored in earlier edits; (4) Type of college is fully allocated (discussed earlier); (5) Tabulations of type of college (2-year, 4-year) are available by race; (6) Dependent family member is defined consistently; (7) New tabulations of employment status, vocational course enrollment, college retention and re-entry, and families with children enrolled in public and private school were available beginning in 1987.

In the series of reports on school enrollment for 1987 to 1992, race and Hispanic origin were erroneously tabulated for a small percentage of children 3 to 14 years. Race and Hispanic origin of an adult in the household were attributed to the child, rather than using the child's reported characteristics. In the vast majority of cases, these characteristics were the same for family members, but for a small percentage of children, they were different. The correction made the following proportional changes in the numbers of children in each group: White (-0.5 percent), Black (+3.1 percent), Hispanic origin (-4.6 percent).

Published data on enrollment from the October CPS for 1981 to 1993 used population controls based on the 1980 Census. Beginning in 1994, estimates were based on 1990 Census population controls, including adjustment for undercount.

Time series tables show two sets of data for 1993; the data labeled "1993r" were processed using population controls based on the 1990 Census, adjusted for undercount. The change in 1994 from a paper and pencil survey to a computer-assisted survey had some affect on the data. Most notable, the enrollment question for children 3 to 5 years was different from the question for older children—it included a reference to nursery school. In 1994 reported nursery school enrollment was significantly higher than in earlier years.

College enrollment. The college enrollment statistics are based on replies to the interviewer's inquiry as to whether the person was attending or enrolled in school and the grade or school or year of college. Interviewers were instructed to count as enrolled anyone who had been enrolled at any time during the current term or school year, except those who have left for the remainder of the term. Thus, regular college enrollment includes those people attending a 4-year or 2-year college, university, or professional school (such as medical or law school) in courses that may advance the student toward a recognized college or university degree (e.g., BA or MA). Attendance may be either full time or part time, during the day or night. The college student need not be working toward a degree, but he/she must be enrolled in a class for which credit would be applied toward a degree. (See "school enrollment.") Students are classified by year of college, based on the academic year (not calendar year) they are attending. Undergraduate years are the 1st through 4th year, or freshman through senior. Graduate or professional school years include the 5th year and higher.

Two-year and four-year colleges: College students were asked to report whether the college in which they were enrolled was a 2-year college (junior or community college) or a 4-year college or university. Students enrolled in the first 4 years (undergraduates) were classified by the type of college they reported. Graduate students are shown as a separate group.

Attendance, full-time and part-time. College students were classified according to whether they were attending school on a full-time or part-time basis. A student was regarded as attending college full time if he/she was taking 12 or more hours of classes during the average school week, and part time if he/she was taking less than 12 hours of classes during the average school week.

Vocational school enrollment. Vocational school enrollment includes enrollment in business, vocational, technical, secretarial, trade, or correspondence courses that are not counted as regular school enrollment and are not for recreation or adult education classes. Courses counted as college enrollment should not also be included as vocational.

School, Level of: The statistics on level of school indicate the number of people enrolled at each of five levels—nursery school, kindergarten, elementary school (1st to 8th grades), high school (9th to 12th grades), and college or professional school. The last group includes graduate students in colleges or universities. People enrolled in elementary, middle school, intermediate school or junior high school through the 8th grade are classified as in elementary school. All people enrolled in 9th through 12th grade are classified as in high school.

School, Modal grade. Enrolled people are classified according to their relative progress in school: that is, whether the grade or year in which they were enrolled was below, at, or above the modal (or typical) grade for people of their age at the time of the survey. The modal grade is the year of school in which the largest proportion of students of a given age is enrolled.

School, Nursery. A nursery school is defined as a group or class that is organized to provide educational experiences for children during the year or years preceding kindergarten. It includes instruction as an important and integral phase of its program of child care. Private homes in which essentially custodial care is provided are not considered nursery schools. Children attending nursery school are classified as attending during either part of the day or the full day. Part-day attendance refers to those who attend either in the morning or in the afternoon, but not both. Full-day attendance refers to those who attend in both the morning and the afternoon. Children enrolled in Head Start programs or similar programs sponsored by local agencies to provide preschool education to young children are counted under nursery school.

School, Public or private. In this report, a public school is defined as any educational institution operated by publicly elected or appointed school officials and supported by public funds. Private schools include educational institutions established and operated by religious bodies, as well as those which are under other private control. In cases where enrollment was in a school or college which was both publicly and privately controlled or supported, enrollment was counted according to whether it was primarily public or private.

Undocumented immigrants or illegal aliens. Because all residents of the United States living in households are represented in the sample of households interviewed by the CPS, undocumented immigrants or illegal aliens are probably included in CPS data. Because the CPS makes no attempt to ascertain the legal status of any person interviewed, these individuals cannot be identified from CPS data.

Work experience. A person with work experience is one who, during the preceding calendar year, did any work for pay or profit or worked without pay on a family-operated farm or business at any time during the year, on a part-time or full-time basis. A full-time worker is one who worked 35 hours or more per week during a majority of the weeks worked during the preceding calendar year. A year-round worker is one who worked for 50 weeks or more during the preceding calendar year. A full-time, year-round worker is a person who worked full time (35 or more hours per week) and 50 or more weeks during the previous calendar year.

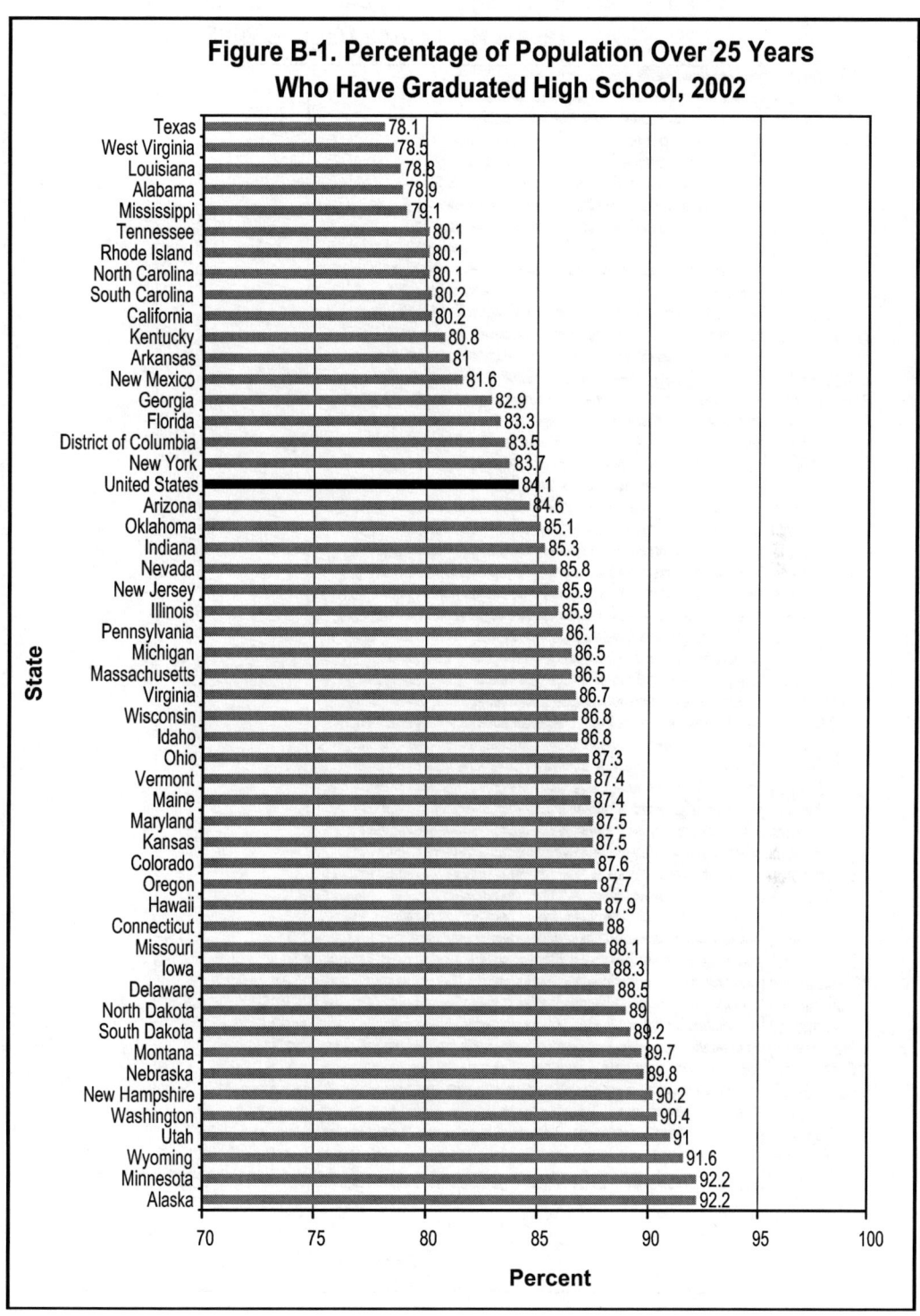

Figure B-1. Percentage of Population Over 25 Years Who Have Graduated High School, 2002

• During the past decade, the proportion of the population 25 years and over with a high school diploma increased from 78 percent to 84 percent. In 2002, Alaska and Minnesota had the highest proportions of high school graduates, with 92.2 percent, and Texas had the lowest with 78.1 percent.

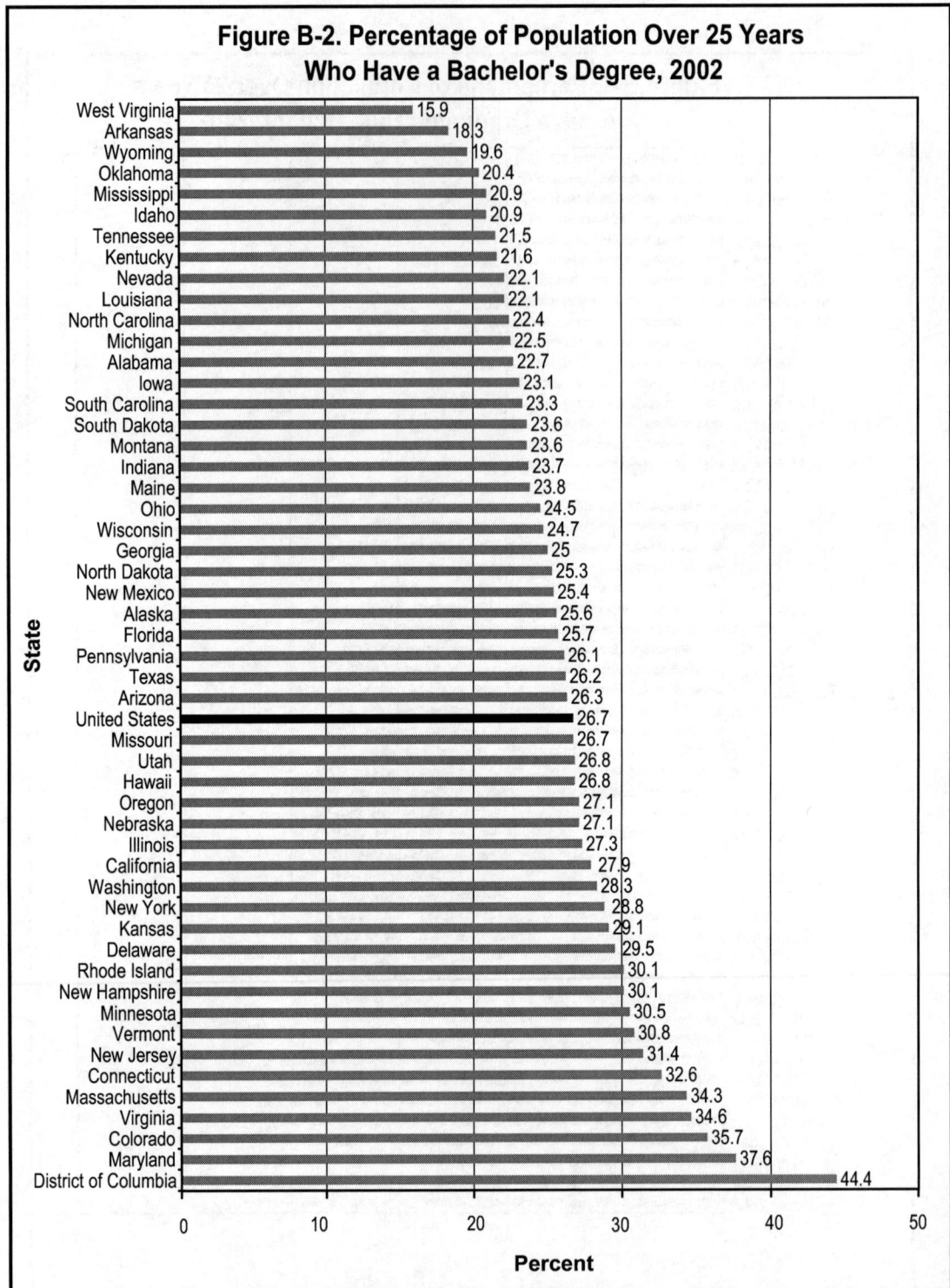

Figure B-2. Percentage of Population Over 25 Years Who Have a Bachelor's Degree, 2002

- The proportion of people 25 years and over with a bachelor's degree increased to 26.7 percent. The proportion of graduates ranged from a high of 44.4 percent in the District of Columbia to 15.9 percent in West Virginia. Indiana had the largest increase, improving from 17.1 percent in 2000 to 23.7 percent in 2002.

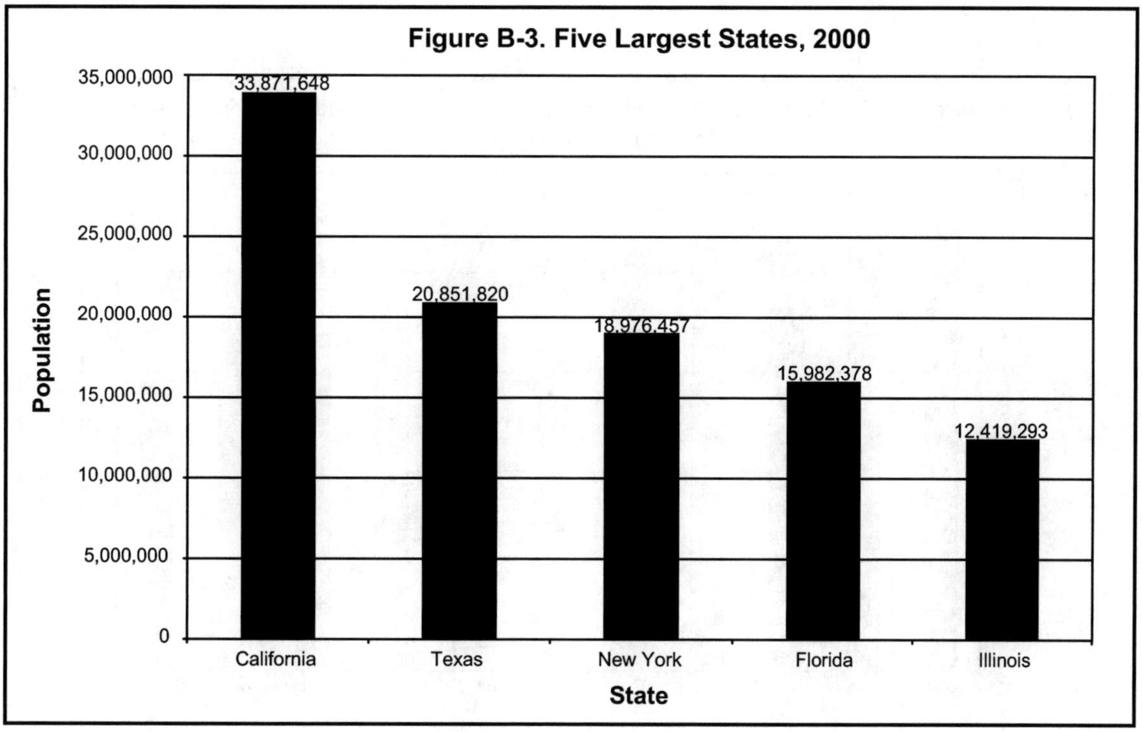
Figure B-3. Five Largest States, 2000
Population
35,000,000
30,000,000
25,000,000
20,000,000
15,000,000
10,000,000
5,000,000
0
33,871,648
20,851,820
18,976,457
15,982,378
12,419,293
California
Texas
New York
Florida
Illinois
State

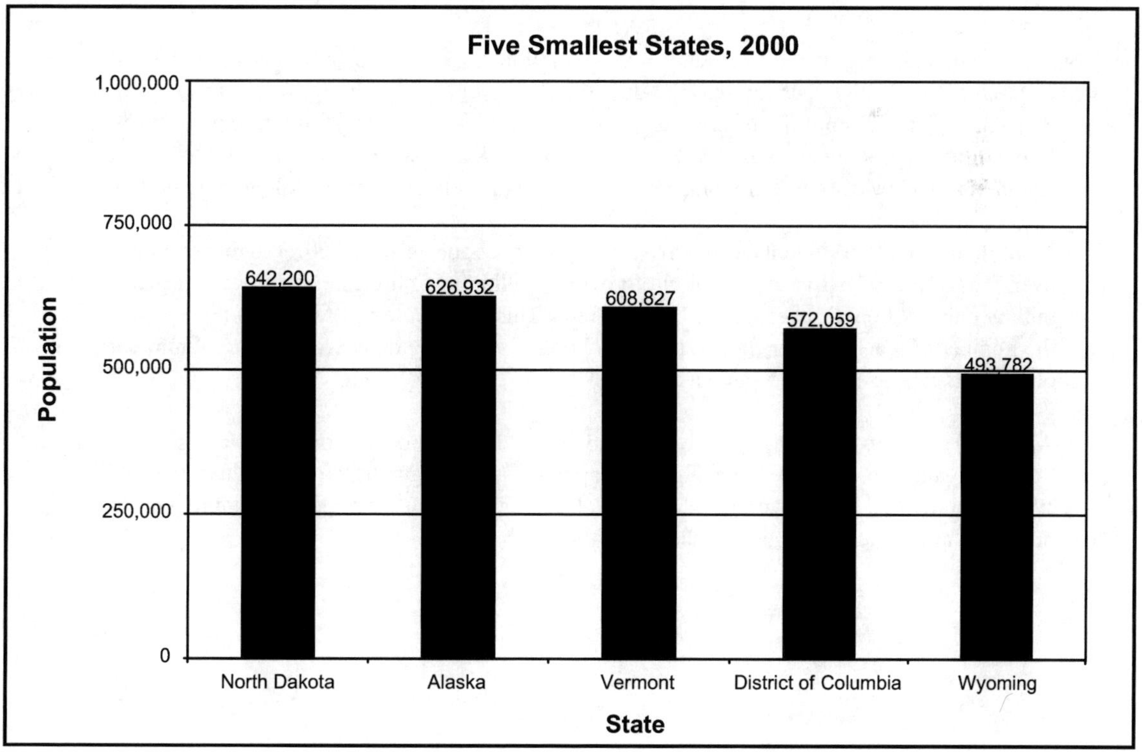
Five Smallest States, 2000
Population
1,000,000
750,000
500,000
250,000
0
642,200
626,932
608,827
572,059
493,782
North Dakota
Alaska
Vermont
District of Columbia
Wyoming
State

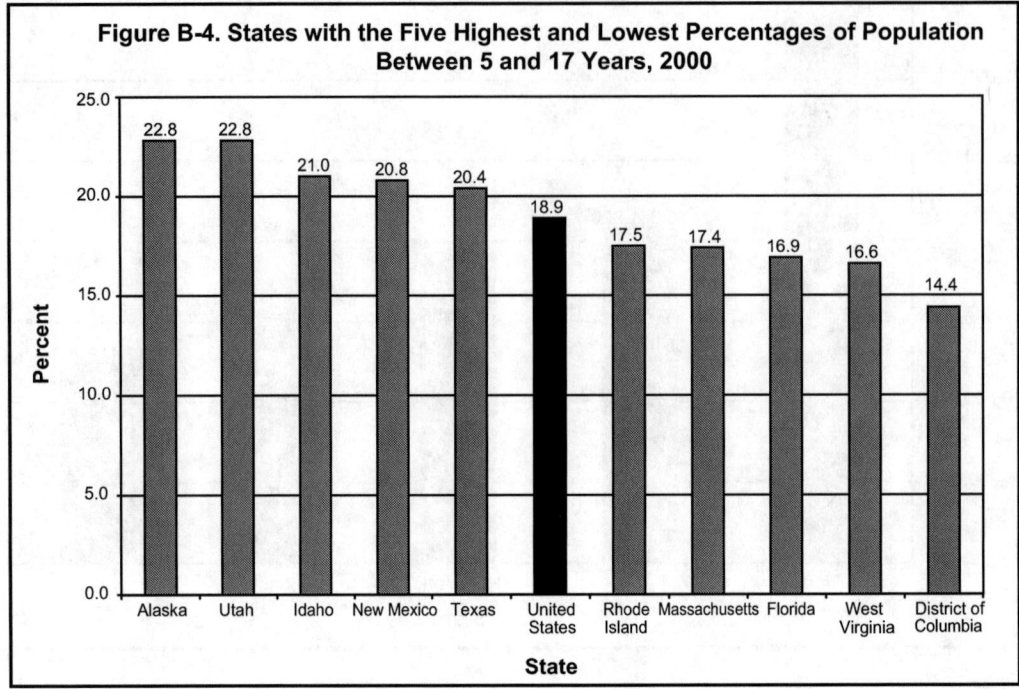

Figure B-4. States with the Five Highest and Lowest Percentages of Population Between 5 and 17 Years, 2000

- States with high proportions of student-age populations tend to have greater costs associated with education. With fewer tax-paying adults, states may not have the resources to direct to education. This often affects student-to-teacher ratios and per student expenditures. Expenditures per student totaled $7,376 in the United States, with $12,046 in the District of Columbia to a low of $4,674 in Utah, a state with a high proportion of school-age population.

- More than 47 million students were enrolled in public schools in 2001–2002, ranging from just over 75,000 in the District of Columbia to over 6 million in California. There were nearly 3 million public school teachers in the United States. This represented a 21.2 percent increase in the number of teachers over the 1991–1992 school year. During this period, the total number of students increased by 11.5 percent.

- About 10 percent of students were enrolled in private elementary or secondary schools. Southern states tended to have higher proportions of private school enrollment, while Western states had below average enrollment. Less than one-fourth of post-secondary enrollment was in private institutes of higher education.

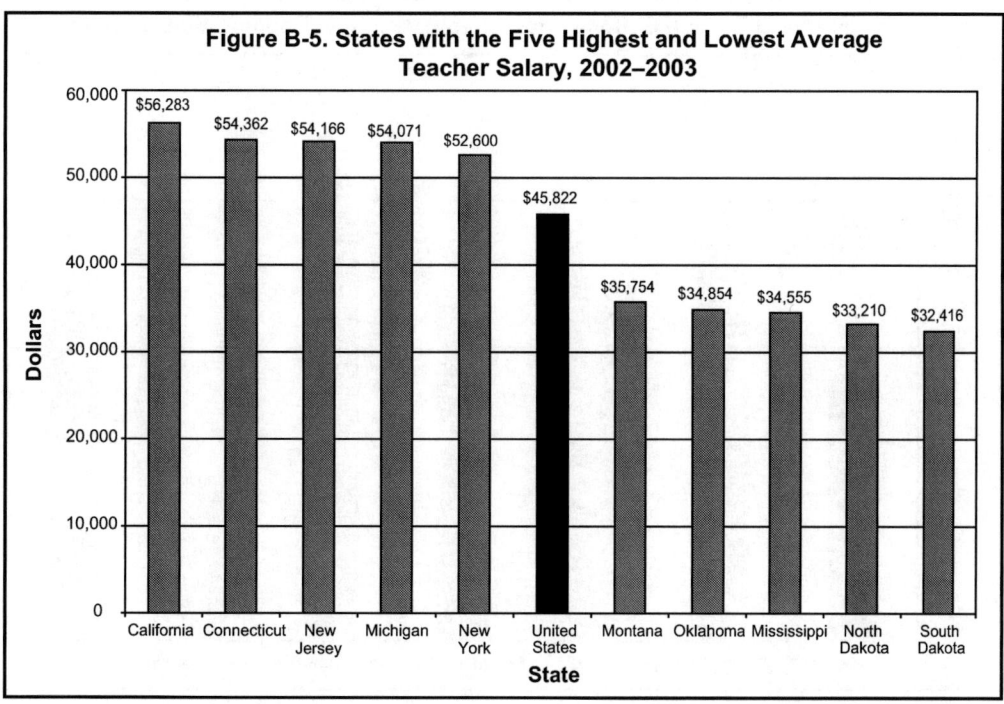

Figure B-5. States with the Five Highest and Lowest Average Teacher Salary, 2002–2003

- The national student/teacher ratio for public schools was 15.9. Vermont had the lowest ratio with 11.8, and Utah had the highest with 21.8. Average teacher salaries ranged from a high of $56,283 in California to a low of $32,416 in South Dakota. The national average in 2002–2003 was $45,822.

- Teachers made up 50.8 percent of staff employed in public schools, the remainder consisted of instructional aides and coordinators, school and district administrators, administrative staff, guidance counselors, school and district support staff, and librarians.

- Public school expenditures reached $348 billion in the 2000–2001 school year. Just over 61 percent went towards instruction, while support services and non-instructional costs accounted for the remaining 39 percent.

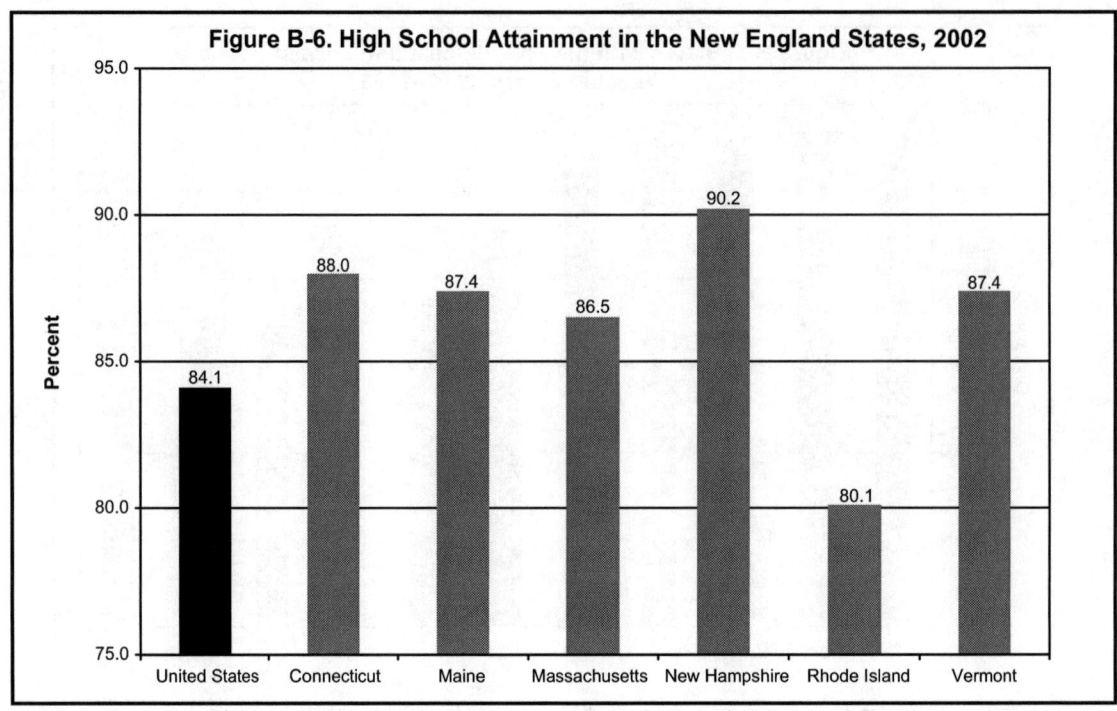

Figure B-6. High School Attainment in the New England States, 2002

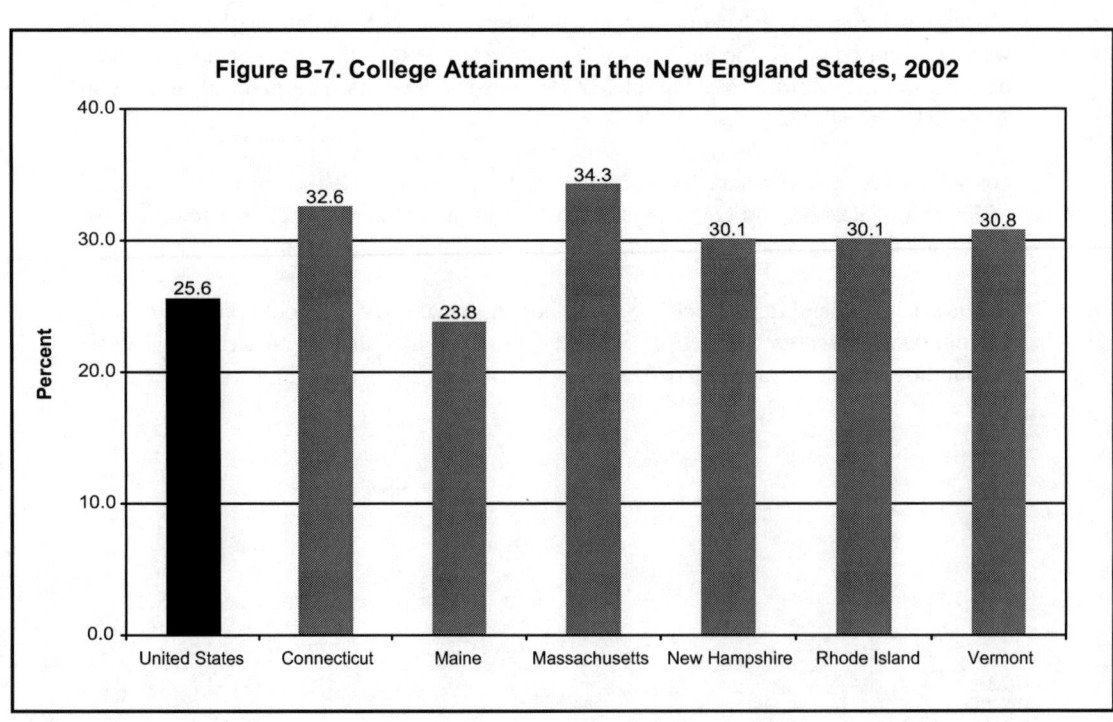

Figure B-7. College Attainment in the New England States, 2002

NEW ENGLAND STATES:

Connecticut, Maine, Massachusetts, New Hampshire, Rhode Island, and Vermont are the New England states. Together, they account for 4.9 percent of the U.S. population, and with 2.2 million students, 4.6 percent of the nation's students. The New England states have 1,136 school districts, ranging from 280 in Maine to 36 in Rhode Island. These states have consistently ranked above average on most educational measures.

With most of the nation's population growth occurring in the West and the South, the six New England states have all had below average growth during the 1990s. Maine is one of 10 states with a decrease in the number of students from 1991 to 2002, when its public school enrollment declined to just over 200,000. Nationally, 18.9 percent of the population is between 5 and 17 years, while in New England only 17.8 percent are school-aged. At 17.4 percent, Massachusetts has the fourth smallest proportion in the United States.

Along with fewer students, these states have below average student-to-teacher ratios. Vermont has the lowest in the nation, with 11.8 students per teacher in 2001–2002. Both Connecticut and Maine are among the lowest 10 in the nation. Rhode Island has the highest in the division, with 14.2 students per teacher, which is still well below the national average of 15.9. With the exception of Maine, all the states in New England have an above average proportion of private school students.

New Hampshire has the smallest proportion of students in the United States who are eligible for free or reduced-price meals. All the New England states have below average proportions of children under 18 years living in poverty. Connecticut and New Hampshire are among 10 states with fewer than 10 percent of children in poverty. Connecticut leads the nation with the highest median income for a family of four. Massachusetts and New Hampshire are also among the five states with incomes of more than $70,000 per family. The national median income is $62,288.

New England's teacher salaries range from a high of $54,362 in Connecticut to $38,121 in Maine. The average in the United States is $45,822. Connecticut ranks second in the nation, just behind California. Connecticut, Rhode Island, Massachusetts, and Vermont all rank among the 10 highest expenditures per student in the nation. New Hampshire spends $7,286 per student, making it the only state in New England with below average

expenditures. All six states direct more than 63 percent of public school expenditures to instruction. Maine ranks first in the nation with 66.9 percent.

Massachusetts and Connecticut have among the highest proportions of students in grades four and eight scoring at or above the proficient level on the National Assessment of Educational Progress project, which tests knowledge and skills in such subjects as math, reading, science, and writing. More than 7 percent of the 1.3 million high school juniors taking the Preliminary Scholastic Assessment Test (PSAT)/National Merit Scholarship Qualifying Test (NMSQT) reside in New England. Connecticut and Massachusetts have among the highest proportion of students scoring above 65, a level that may qualify them for National Merit Scholarships.

High school students in New England tend to choose the SAT over the ACT. In 2002, more than 80 percent of Connecticut's high school graduates took the SAT, the highest proportion in the nation. The other states in New England were well above the national average of 46 percent. As with most states with high proportions of test-takers, the average scores tend to be lower. The New England average scores were close to the national average of 1,020. New Hampshire had the highest scores in the division with 1,038, and Maine, the lowest, with 1,005. All six states had 10 percent or fewer of their students taking the ACT test.

The New England states, with the exception of Rhode Island, all exceed 86 percent with a high school diploma. From 1998 to 2002, New Hampshire had the largest percentage increase in high school attainment levels. In 1998, the state ranked 28th in the nation with 84 percent, and by 2002 had climbed to sixth in the nation with 90.4 percent. Connecticut also showed substantial improvement, and is ranked 14th in the nation with 88 percent of its population having graduated from high school. Just over 80 percent of Rhode Island's residents are high school graduates. It is the only state in New England that is below the U.S. average high school attainment level of 84.1 percent.

The six New England states have college attainment levels among the top in the nation. Massachusetts ranks fifth in the nation, with 34.3 percent of its population holding a bachelor's degree. Despite its lower high school attainment levels, Rhode Island has a high proportion of college graduates, placing it among 10 states and the District of Columbia with proportions exceeding 30 percent. Only Maine has a below average proportion of college graduates and is ranked 33rd in the United States.

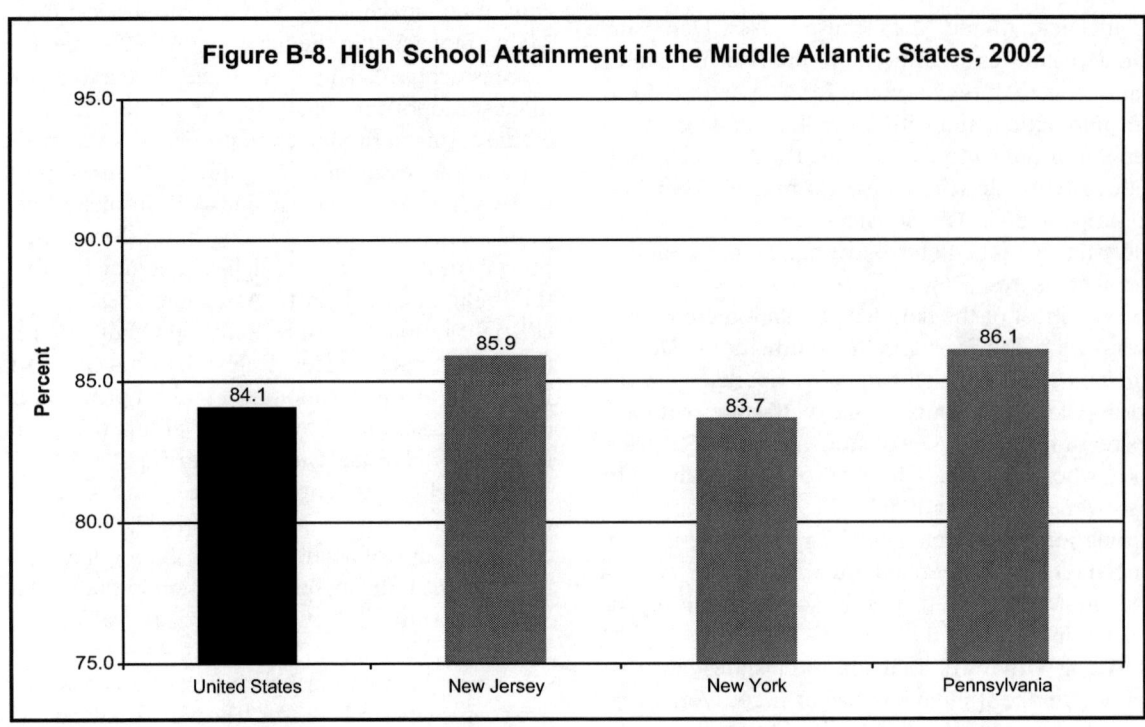

Figure B-8. High School Attainment in the Middle Atlantic States, 2002

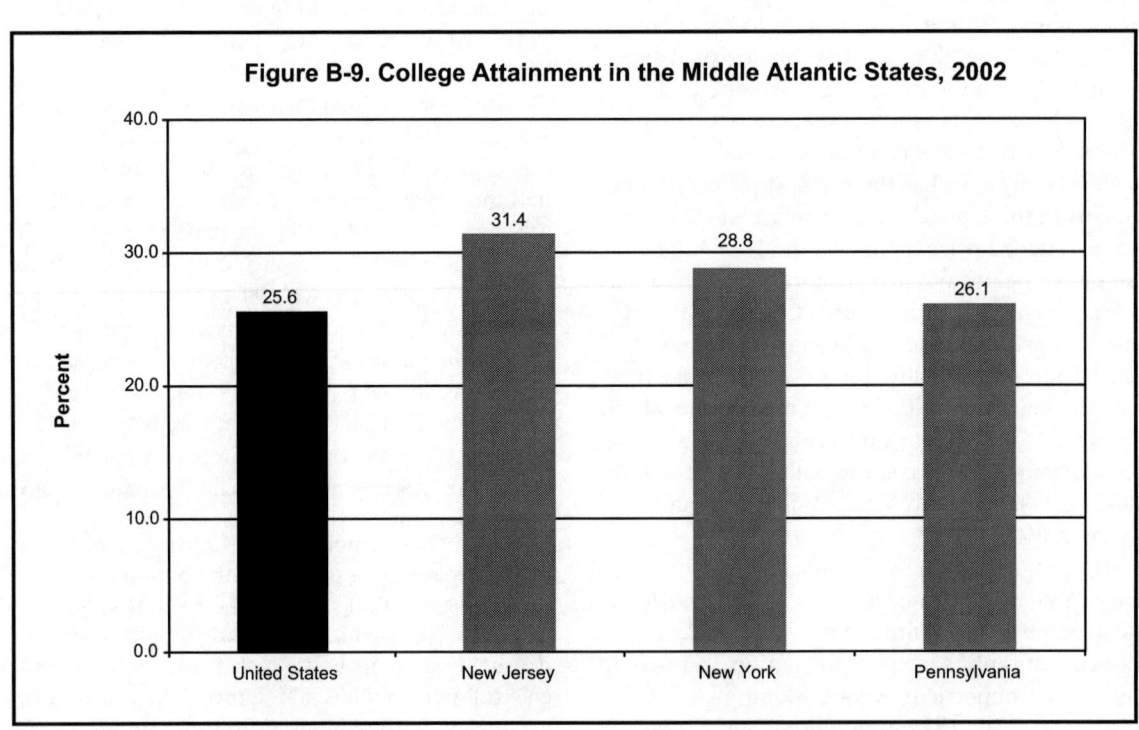

Figure B-9. College Attainment in the Middle Atlantic States, 2002

MIDDLE ATLANTIC STATES:

The Middle Atlantic division of the United States has just three states: New Jersey, New York, and Pennsylvania. However, these states are among the 10 largest in the nation, totaling nearly 40 million people or 14.1 percent of the U.S. population. While the U.S. population grew by 13.2 percent from 1990 to 2000, none of these three states had growth rates above 9 percent. Texas surpassed New York to become the second largest state in the nation.

With 7.1 million people between the ages of 5 and 17 years, the Middle Atlantic states account for 13.5 percent of the nation's student-age population. All three states have below average proportions of school-age children. Together, New Jersey, New York, and Pennsylvania have just over 6 million students enrolled in public elementary and secondary schools. The three Middle Atlantic states have among the 10 highest proportions of students attending private schools, with over 1 million children enrolled in private school during the 1999–2000 school year.

The Middle Atlantic division has 1,782 school districts, with New York having the most of the three (701). Minorities make up nearly half of New York's public school students, while in Pennsylvania they total less than 23 percent. New Jersey has the fourth lowest student-to-teacher ratio in the United States. Both New York, at 13.9, and Pennsylvania, at 15.5, have ratios below the national average. More than 37 percent of teachers in New Jersey and Pennsylvania have 20 years or more of experience, ranking both states among the top 10 in the United States.

New Jersey has the second highest expenditures per student. New Jersey and the District of Columbia are the only jurisdictions where expenditures per student exceed $11,000. New York ranks third with $10,716. The national average during the 2000–2001 school year was $7,376. New York's expenditures for public elementary and secondary schools exceed $30 billion, second only to California.

More than 43 percent of New York students are eligible for free or reduced-price lunch. In both Pennsylvania and New Jersey, fewer than 29 percent qualify. One in five New York children under 18 years of age lived in poverty in 2000. New Jersey is one of 10 states with fewer than 10 percent of students in poverty. The median incomes of a family of four in the Middle Atlantic states exceed the U.S. aver-age. New Jersey has the second highest income in the country with $78,560. The average teacher salary in New Jersey is over $54,000, ranking the state third in the nation. New York and Pennsylvania are also among the top 10, with each surpassing $51,000. The U.S. average teacher salary is $45,822.

Both Pennsylvania and New Jersey had dropout rates at or below 4 percent, ranking them among the bottom 10 of the 36 states that reported dropout rates. New York has no dropout data. However, 8.7 percent of New Yorkers between the ages of 16 and 19 years were not high school graduates and not enrolled in school at the time of the 2000 Census. In New Jersey, this proportion was 7.2 percent, and in Pennsylvania, 7.1 percent. Nationally, 9.8 percent of these teenagers are neither enrolled in school nor high school graduates.

The Middle Atlantic states have average levels of high school attainment, ranging from 83.7 percent in New York to 86.1 percent in Pennsylvania. The U.S. average is 84.1 percent. New Jersey is one of 10 states where the proportion of high school graduates has decreased since 1998.

New Jersey has the second highest proportion of high school graduates taking the SAT in 2002. New York and Pennsylvania are also among the top 10. States along the east coast, especially those in the Northeast, have higher proportions taking the SAT rather than the ACT. The average scores range from 998 in Pennsylvania to 1,011 in New Jersey. The national average is 1,020. Fewer than 10 percent of high school graduates took the ACT in New Jersey and Pennsylvania, and in New York, just 14 percent took the test. New York tied for the fifth highest average ACT score in the United States.

College attainment levels are slightly below average in Pennsylvania, and above average in New Jersey and New York. With 31.4 percent, New Jersey is among the highest in the nation. Pennsylvania's proportion has increased by 4 percentage points to 26.1 percent from 1998 to 2002. Both New York and Pennsylvania have high proportions of enrollment in private institutions of higher education. Both states exceed 44 percent, while nationally fewer than 25 percent of students are enrolled in private colleges. More than 13 percent of the nation's college students are enrolled in schools in the Middle Atlantic states. After California, New York confers the highest number of professional, master's degrees, and doctorates. New York accounts for 9.5 percent of the nation's graduate enrollment, and 6.5 percent of undergraduates.

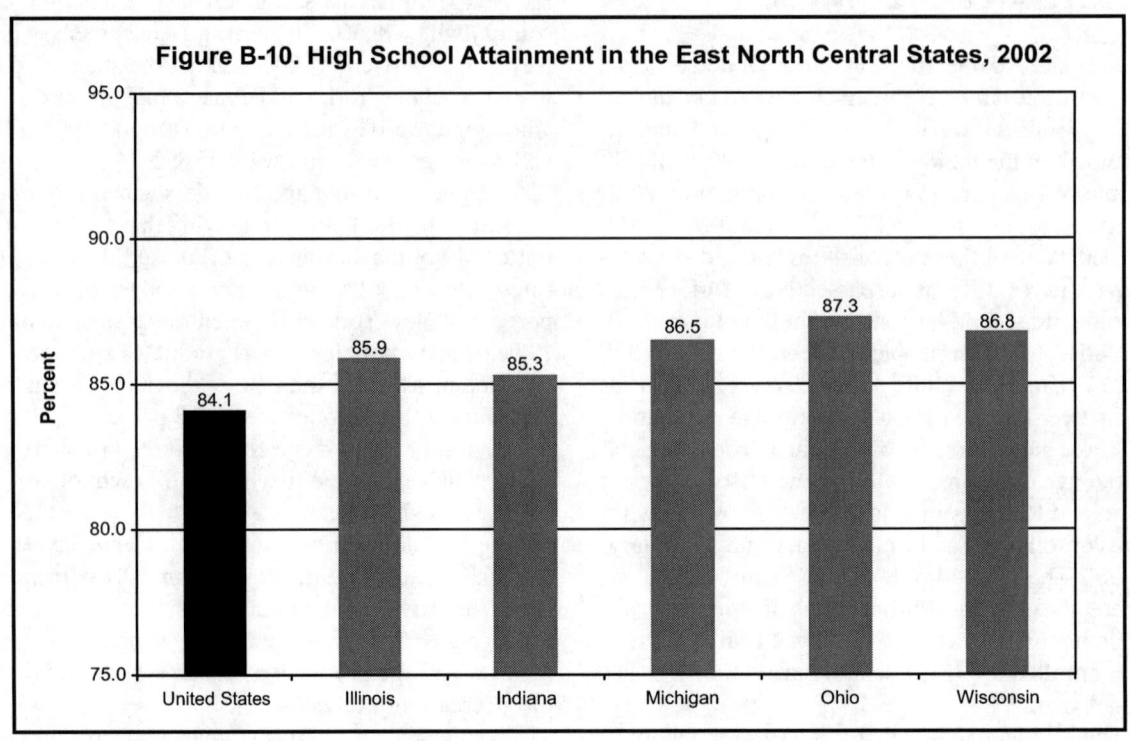

Figure B-10. High School Attainment in the East North Central States, 2002

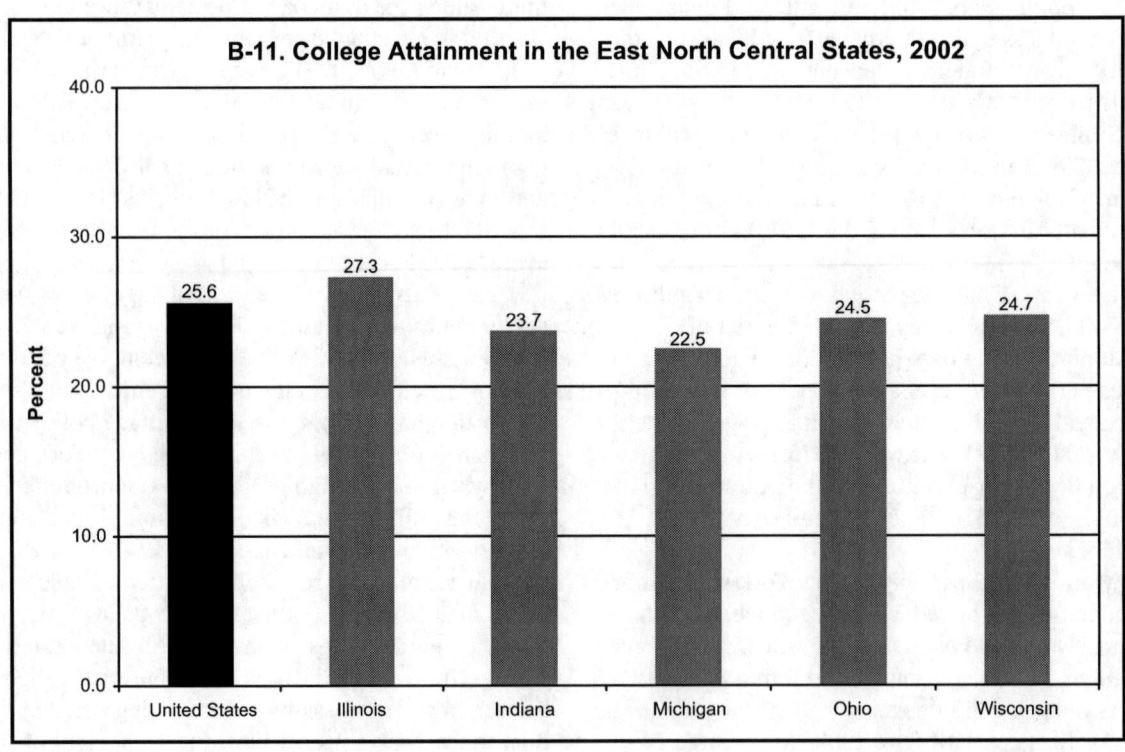

B-11. College Attainment in the East North Central States, 2002

EAST NORTH CENTRAL STATES:

The East North Central division borders the Great Lakes, and is made up of Illinois, Indiana, Michigan, Ohio, and Wisconsin. They account for 45 million people, and 16 percent of the U.S. population. These five states have 8.6 million people between the ages of 5 and 17 years, which amounts to 16.2 percent of the nation's school-age population.

There are more than 7.5 million students enrolled in public schools in the nearly 3,000 school districts in these five states. Wisconsin, Illinois, and Ohio have above average proportions of their students attending private schools. Within all five of the states, nearly 1 million are enrolled in private schools. Illinois has the largest proportion of minority students in the region, with Blacks and Hispanics comprising more than 37 percent of public school students.

Illinois is the only state in the division with above average growth in public school membership from 1991 to 2001. Indiana and Ohio each had below average growth of less than 4.2 percent, well below the U.S. average of 11.5 percent. All five states had below average growth in teachers during the 1990s. The five states had nearly half a million public school teachers during the 2001–2002 school year.

Wisconsin and Ohio have among the lowest percentage of their students in the nation qualifying for free or reduced-price lunch, with less than 27.5 percent eligible. Of the 46 states and District of Columbia reporting data, 36.6 percent of students are eligible. All five East North Central states have a smaller than average proportion of children living in poverty. The states range from a high of 16.2 percent in Ohio to 11.3 percent in Indiana. The U.S. average is 16.3 percent. Both Wisconsin and Michigan have fewer than 4 percent of low-income children without health insurance, which is well below the national average of 7.9 percent.

Michigan has the 8th highest median income of a family of four in the United States, and Illinois is ranked 10th. The other states of the East North Central division all have incomes exceeding $62,000. Average public school teacher salaries in these five states are close to the U.S. average of $45,822. They range from a high of $54,071 in Michigan to $42,871 in Wisconsin.

Michigan has one of the 10 highest student-to-teacher ratios in the nation. The other states in the area are closer to the U.S. average ratio of 15.9, except Wisconsin, which is well below average with 14.4 students per teacher. Michigan and Wisconsin have per student expenditures exceeding $8,200. The other three states of the East North Central division all surpass the U.S. average of $7,376 per student.

All these states by the Great Lakes have high levels of high school attainment, surpassing the national average of 84.1 percent. They range from a high of 87.3 percent in Ohio, to 85.3 percent in Indiana. Wisconsin was one of 10 states with a decrease in the proportion of high school graduates from 1998 to 2000. Overall, Wisconsin ranked 24th in the nation.

Wisconsin has the second lowest reported dropout rate of 2.6 percent. Illinois is one of the 36 states with data with a dropout rate exceeding 6 percent. Ohio has an above average rate of 5 percent, and neither Michigan, nor Wisconsin has data. Just 6.4 percent of Wisconsin teenagers between 16 and 19 years are not in high school, and have not graduated. This places the state among just eight states with proportions of at-risk youth at less than 7 percent. Illinois and Indiana have the highest proportions in the region, both states near the national average of 9.8 percent.

Wisconsin has the third highest average SAT score in the nation, but only 7 percent of graduating students took the test in 2002. Of all the states in this part of the country, only in Indiana do graduates overwhelmingly choose the SAT over the ACT. Indiana also has the lowest average score in the region, with 1,001. In Illinois, 99 percent of graduating seniors took the ACT. Wisconsin, Michigan, and Ohio each had more than 60 percent of its graduates take the test. The scores ranged from a high of 22.2 in Wisconsin to 20.1 in Illinois.

Only Illinois has a proportion of college graduates exceeding the U.S. average. The other states of the East North Central division have proportions lower than 25 percent, ranging from 24.7 percent in Wisconsin to 22.5 percent in Michigan. Indiana has improved by more than 6 percentage points since 1998, going from 48th in the nation to 34th.

There are more than 2.4 million students enrolled in institutions in higher education in the states that border the Great Lakes. One-fourth or more of college students in Illinois and Ohio attend private colleges. Michigan has the lowest proportion of students attending private colleges in the East North Central division with 17.4 percent.

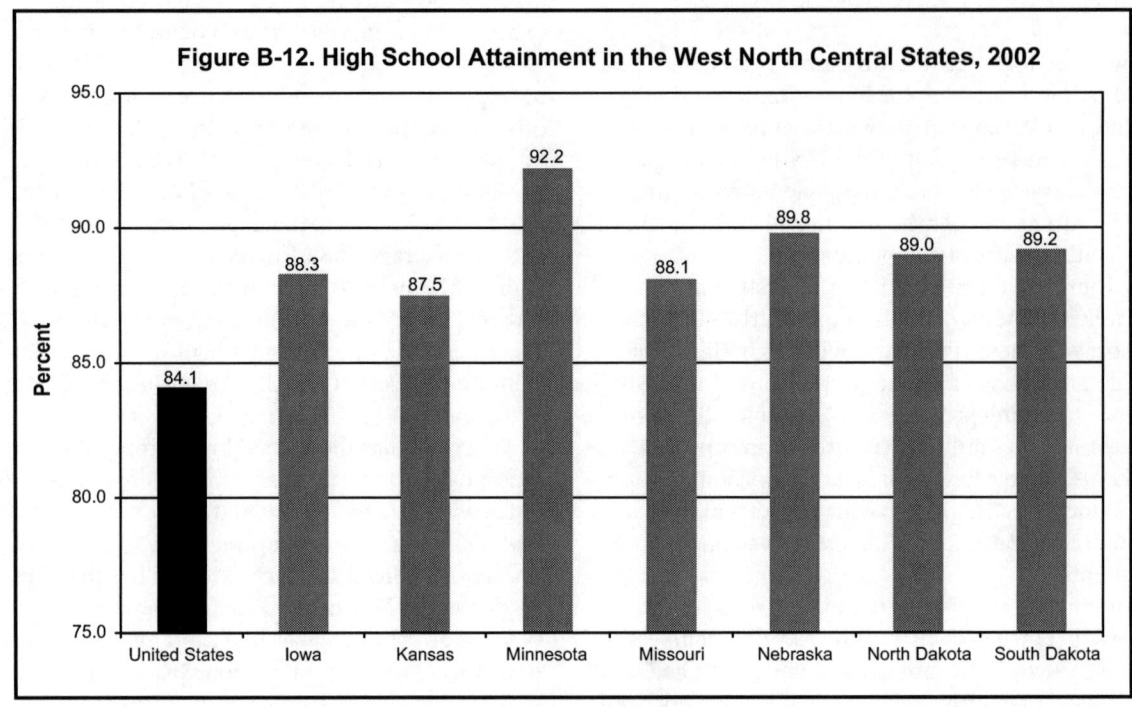

Figure B-12. High School Attainment in the West North Central States, 2002

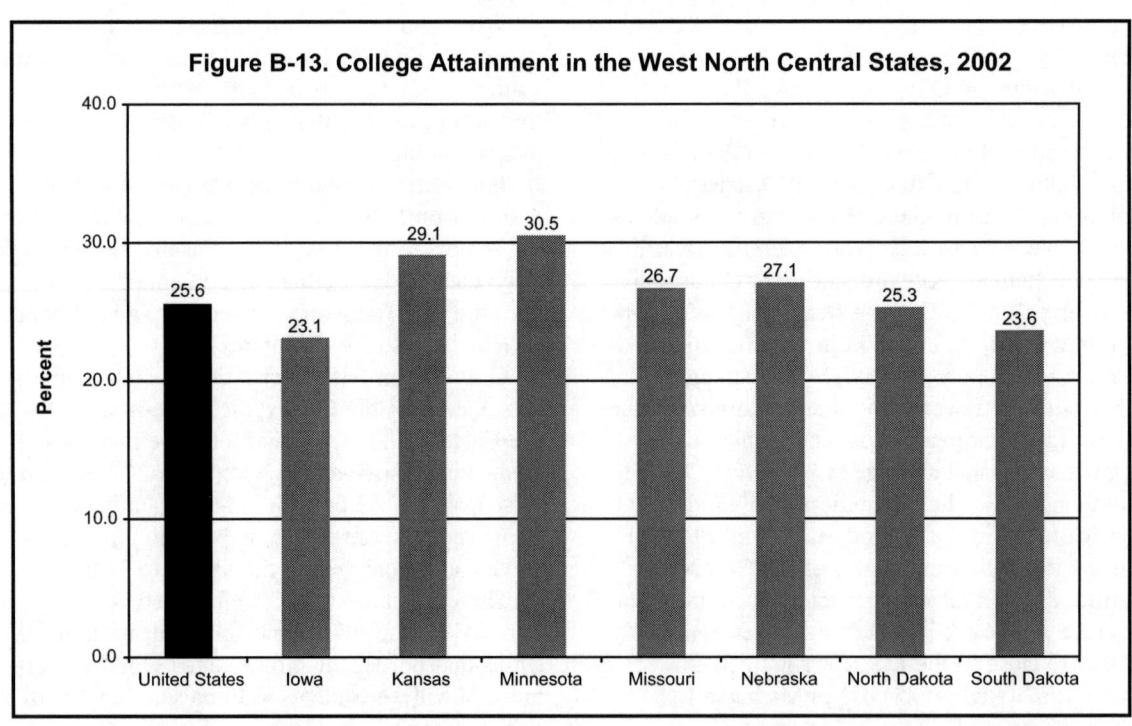

Figure B-13. College Attainment in the West North Central States, 2002

WEST NORTH CENTRAL STATES:

Iowa, Kansas, Minnesota, Missouri, Nebraska, North Dakota, and South Dakota are the seven states of the West North Central division. There are nearly 3.7 million people of student-age living in these states. Expenditures for public schools exceeded $22 billion during the 2000–2001 school year.

The West North Central states total more than 19 million people. With the exception of Missouri and Minnesota, these states rank among the lower half in the nation by population size. Both Dakotas are among the seven states and the District of Columbia with populations less than 1 million. Missouri has the highest total population of the group, and ranks 17th in the nation. All seven states had lower than average population growth from 1990 to 2000. North Dakota grew by 0.5 percent during the decade, ranking only above the District of Columbia for population growth.

Student/teacher ratios are at or below the U.S. average in the West North Central states. North Dakota, Nebraska, and South Dakota rank among the lowest 10 in the nation—each of these states has fewer than 14 students per teacher. The national average is 15.9 students per teacher. Minnesota is the only state in the division with above average per student expenditures. North and South Dakota rank among the lowest 15 in the nation, with less than $6,200 spent per student.

Iowa and Minnesota have small proportions of students eligible for free or reduced-price meals. Of the 45 states and District of Columbia with data, these two states rank among the lowest seven, with less than 27 percent eligible. Iowa, South Dakota, and Minnesota have low proportions of children in poverty. They are among 10 states with a children's poverty rate of less than 10 percent. Nationally, 16.3 percent of children under 18 years live in poverty. In North Dakota, 19.5 percent of children live in poverty.

Minnesota is one of seven states with a median income of a family of four exceeding $70,000 per year. North Dakota has the lowest median income of these seven states with $53,140. The U.S. average is $62,228. Average teacher salaries tend to be lower in the West North Central states. Only Minnesota exceeds $40,000, but the state's average salary remains below the U.S. average of $45,822. North and South Dakota have the two lowest average teacher salaries in the nation. However, the cost of living in these states tends to be lower, and the highest average salaries can be found mostly in states in the northeast.

Minnesota has the second highest high school attainment level in the nation, and is one of six states with attainment levels exceeding 90 percent. The other states in the division range from 89.8 percent in Nebraska to 87.5 percent in Kansas. All of these states are well above the U.S. average of 84.1 percent in 2002. Both Missouri and North Dakota had an increase of 4.7 percentage points or more from 1998 to 2000. Nationally, the high school attainment level increased by 1.3 percentage points during this period.

All the West North Central states except Kansas reported on dropout rates, and these all had rates below 4.5 percent. Of the 36 states and the District of Columbia with dropout data, Iowa, Wisconsin, and North Dakota have the three lowest rates, the only states under 3.0 percent. Missouri (4.4 percent) and Minnesota (4.3 percent) have the highest rates of the division. With the exception of Missouri, these states have 8 percent or lower proportions of children between 16 and 19 years who are neither enrolled in high school, nor have graduated. Missouri is the only one of these states that exceeds the U.S. average of 9.8 percent.

All seven states of the West North Central division are in the top 10 states when ranked by SAT scores, and surpass the national average by more than 100 points. However, in each of these states 10 percent or fewer of high school graduates take the test. High school students in this division tend to take the ACT over the SAT. In each of these states, 65 percent of graduates took the ACT. In Kansas and North Dakota, more than three-fourths of graduates take the ACT, while the U.S. average is 39 percent. In most states with a high proportion of test-takers, the average scores tend to be lower. However, in the West North Central division, the averages in all seven states exceed the national average of 20.8.

College attainment levels in the West North Central division range from 30.5 percent in Minnesota to 23.1 percent in Iowa. Minnesota is one of 10 states and the District of Columbia to surpass 30 percent. The U.S. average is 26.7 percent. Nebraska had the second highest percentage point increase from 1998 to 2000. The state was ranked 36th in the nation in 1998, and 18th in 2002.

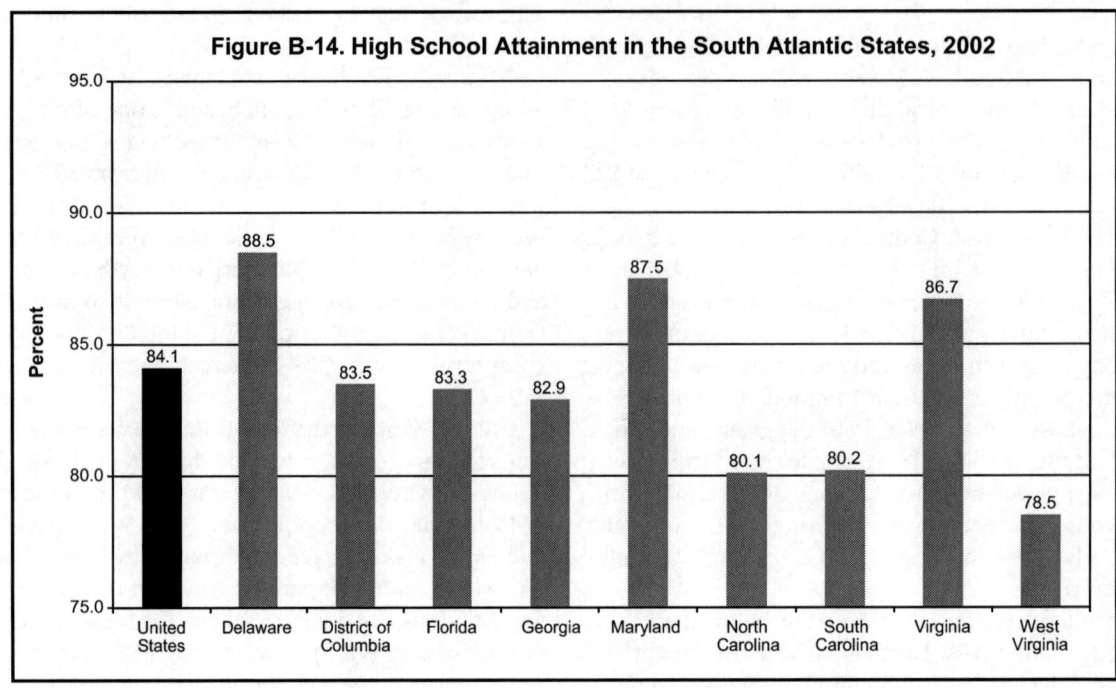

Figure B-14. High School Attainment in the South Atlantic States, 2002

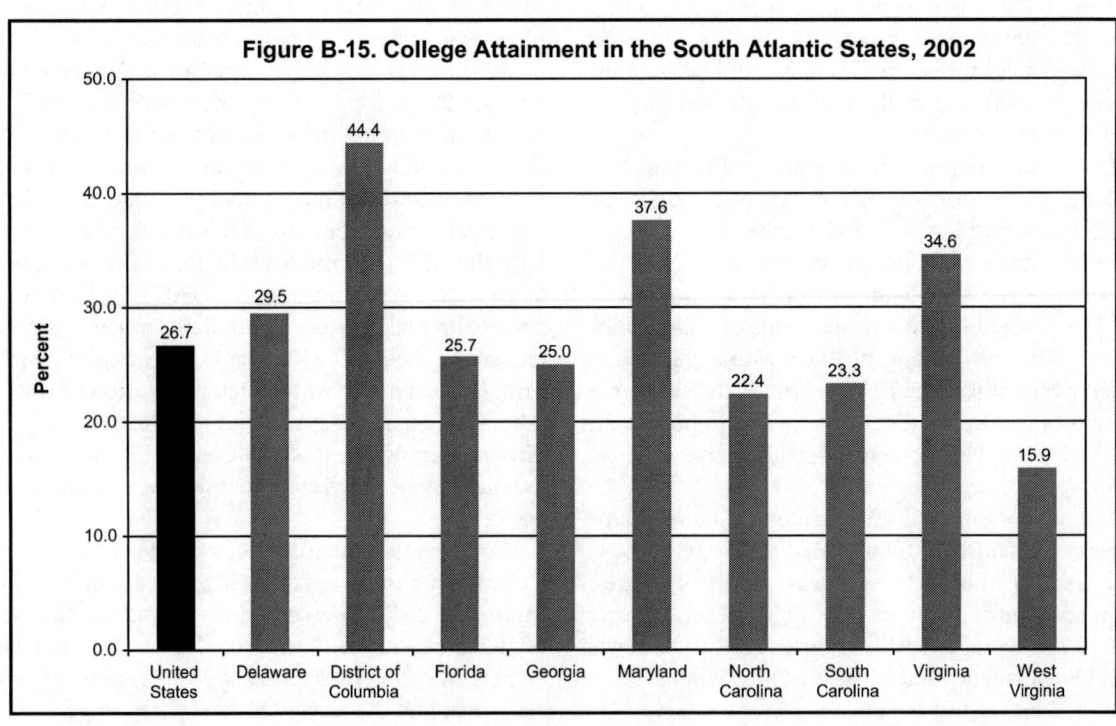

Figure B-15. College Attainment in the South Atlantic States, 2002

SOUTH ATLANTIC STATES:

The South Atlantic division of the United States includes Delaware, the District of Columbia, Florida, Georgia, Maryland, North Carolina, South Carolina, Virginia, and West Virginia. This is the largest division in the nation, with over 67 million people, and over 8 million students enrolled in public elementary and secondary schools.

Most of the South Atlantic states have a lower than average proportion of children between the ages of 5 and 17 years. The District of Columbia has the lowest in the nation, with 14.4 percent. It can be misleading to compare the District of Columbia with the 50 states, rather than with other cities. Unlike any of the states, it has an entirely urban population, so its characteristics are more similar to other large cities. West Virginia and Florida are second and third, respectively, the only two states with proportions of school-age children under 17 percent. Nationally, 18.9 percent of the population is school-aged.

Virginia has the fifth lowest student-to-teacher ratio in the United States. Both West Virginia and the District of Columbia have ratios of less than 14 students per teacher. Of the South Atlantic states, only Florida and Maryland exceed the national average of 15.9 students per teacher. More than 36 percent of teachers in Delaware have less than three years of experience, which is the second highest proportion in the nation. Nearly 49 percent of West Virginia public school teachers have 20 years or more of experience, which is the highest proportion in the United States.

Per student expenditures range from $12,046 in the District of Columbia, which is the highest in the nation, to $6,170 in Florida. Delaware, Maryland, and West Virginia all have per student expenditures exceeding the U.S. average of $7,376. Florida has the highest total expenditures in the division, with $15 billion, one of 10 states exceeding $10 billion per year.

The District of Columbia has the third highest proportion of students who qualified for free or reduced-price meals. Louisiana and Mississippi are the only other states in the division where more than 55 percent of the students qualify. More than 30 percent of children in the District of Columbia live in poverty. South Carolina and West Virginia both have more than 20 percent of children under 18 years living in poverty. With 7.6 percent, Maryland ties with Iowa for the smallest proportion of children in poverty.

Maryland has the fourth highest median income of a family of four. With $69,360, Delaware also ranks among the top 10 states. West Virginia has the third lowest median family income in the nation, at $46,270. Only the District of Columbia, Delaware, and Maryland have average public school teacher salaries exceeding the U.S. average of $45,822. All three states have average salaries above $49,000 per year. The District of Columbia ranks eleventh in the nation, with an average of $50,763. West Virginia has the lowest salary of the South Atlantic states, at $38,508.

Georgia and the District of Columbia tie for the second highest dropout rate in the nation. Of the 37 jurisdictions with data, the other South Atlantic states rank in the lowest third. In both Georgia and Florida, over 12 percent of teenagers between the ages of 16 years and 19 years have not graduated from high school and are not enrolled. These are among the five highest dropout rates in the nation, and well above the U.S. average of 9.8 percent. Both Maryland and Virginia have fewer than 8 percent of teens not enrolled and without diplomas.

With the exception of West Virginia, most high school seniors in the South Atlantic states take the SAT. In the District of Columbia, more than three-fourths of graduates take the SAT. Among the other states in the division, proportions range from Delaware with 69 percent to West Virginia with 18 percent. The District of Columbia, Georgia, South Carolina, Florida, and North Carolina are among seven states with average scores of less than 1,000. The U.S. average is 1,020. As with most states with a small proportion of test-takers, West Virginia has above average scores of 1,040. The proportion of ACT test-takers ranges from 61 percent in West Virginia, the only state in the division that exceeds 50 percent, to 4 percent in Delaware. Not surprisingly, Delaware has the highest score in the South Atlantic division, with 21.3. The District of Columbia, South Carolina, Georgia, and North Carolina have among the lowest 10 ACT scores in the nation.

The District of Columbia has the highest proportion of college graduates in the nation. In 2002, over 44 percent of the city's residents held bachelor's degrees, which is well above the national average of 26.7 percent. Maryland ranks second with 37.6 percent, and Virginia, fourth, with 34.6 percent. West Virginia has the lowest college attainment levels in the nation, with just 15.9 percent of the population holding bachelor's degrees.

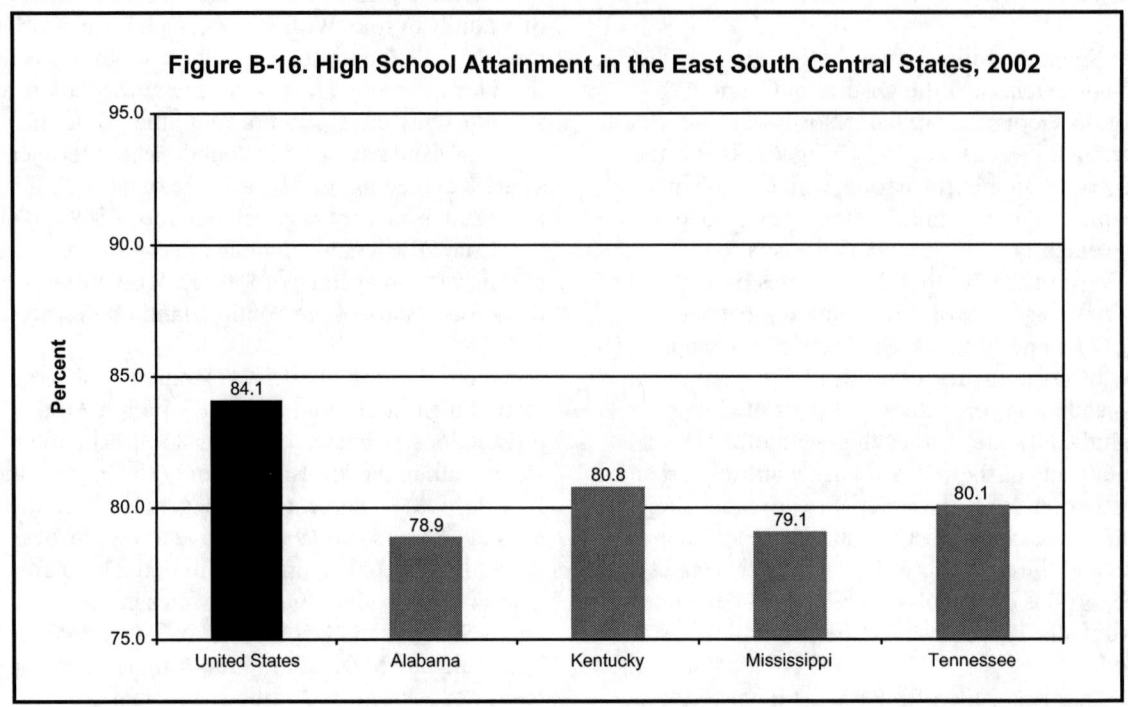

Figure B-16. High School Attainment in the East South Central States, 2002

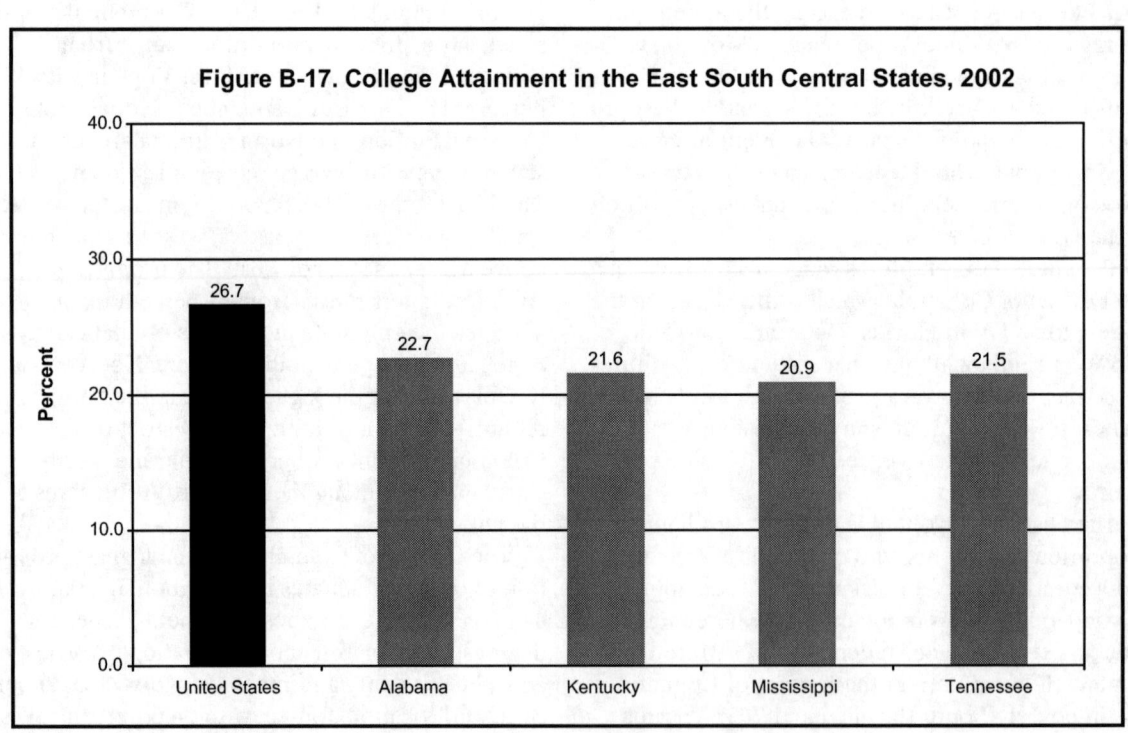

Figure B-17. College Attainment in the East South Central States, 2002

EAST SOUTH CENTRAL STATES:

The East South Central states fall below the U.S. average on most educational measures. This division, comprising Alabama, Kentucky, Mississippi, and Tennessee, accounts for 6 percent of the country's population, or about 17 million people. In 2001–2002, these states totaled 594 school districts and 5,264 schools with 2.8 million public school students.

These four states have over 3 million people between the ages of 5 and 17 years. Mississippi has one of the highest proportions of school-age children in the nation, with more than one in five between the ages of 5 and 17 years. With such a high proportion of young people, it is not surprising that Mississippi's expenditures per student are the second lowest in the nation, just above $5,000. The U.S. average in 2000–2001 was $7,376. Of the four states in the East South Central division, just one exceeded $6,000 per student. Kentucky ranks the highest of the group with $6,079.

Only 46 states and the District of Columbia reported student eligibility for free or reduced-price meals. In most of these states, between 25 percent and 50 percent of the students qualified. Alabama, Kentucky, and Mississippi were among the reporting states and all exceeded 48 percent in 2001–2002. Nearly two-thirds of public school students in Mississippi were eligible for free or reduced-price meals, this is the highest among the reporting states and the District of Columbia. All four of these states top the national average for percentage of children in poverty. In both Alabama and Mississippi, 23.2 percent of the children under 18 were in poverty.

These four states all rank among the lowest 15 in the nation for the proportion of high school graduates in their populations. They range from a high of 80.8 percent in Kentucky to 78.9 percent in Alabama, all below the national average of 84.1 percent. Kentucky is one of five states that have increased by more than 2 percentage points since 2000. In 1998, Kentucky ranked among the five lowest in the United States, and by 2002 it had surpassed the bottom 10 states.

Only 37 states and the District of Columbia reported dropout rates for the 1999–2000 school year. Rates ranged from 2.5 percent to 9.2 percent, with the four East South Central states in the middle with rates of 5 percent or less. Kentucky has the highest dropout rate in the division with 5 percent, and Tennessee the lowest with 4.2 percent. When the 2000 census is used to derive a different estimate of the population of teenage dropouts, Mississippi, Alabama, and Kentucky all have a greater than average population between the ages of 16 and 19 years who are neither enrolled in high school nor high school graduates. For Mississippi and Alabama, these teenagers account for 12 percent or more of those 16 to 19 years of age. Mississippi has the sixth highest proportion of dropouts in the United States.

The states of the East South Central division have average student/teacher ratios, with Kentucky the highest of the group with 16.2 students per teacher. The number of public school students in Kentucky increased by only 1.3 percent from 1991 to 2001, but during the same period the number of teachers jumped 7.5 percent to just over 40,000. Mississippi is one of 10 states where student membership declined during the decade.

Tennessee is among the top 20 states, with nearly 14 percent of its teachers having less than 3 years of experience. With so many young teachers and a cost of living that is lower than some other regions, all four of these states have below average teacher salaries. At $34,555, Mississippi's salaries are the third lowest in the nation, surpassing only North and South Dakota.

In 2002, high school graduates split mostly along regional lines between taking the SAT and the ACT. In the East South Central states, most graduates choose the ACT. Fewer than 15 percent of high school graduates took the SAT in Alabama, Kentucky, Mississippi, and Tennessee. Mississippi tied with North Dakota for the lowest proportion in the nation. However, all of these states had 70 percent or more of 2002 high school graduates taking the ACT, far surpassing the U.S. average of 39 percent. All four states had below average ACT scores, and, as with most states where few graduating seniors took the SAT, each state had average SAT scores over 1,100, surpassing the national average of 1,020 in 2002.

All the states of this division have below average college attainment levels. Kentucky, Tennessee, and Mississippi are among the bottom 10 states in the nation. Only Alabama exceeds 22 percent, which is still well below the U.S. average of 26.7 percent.

Over 5 percent of the nation's college students are enrolled in schools in these four states.

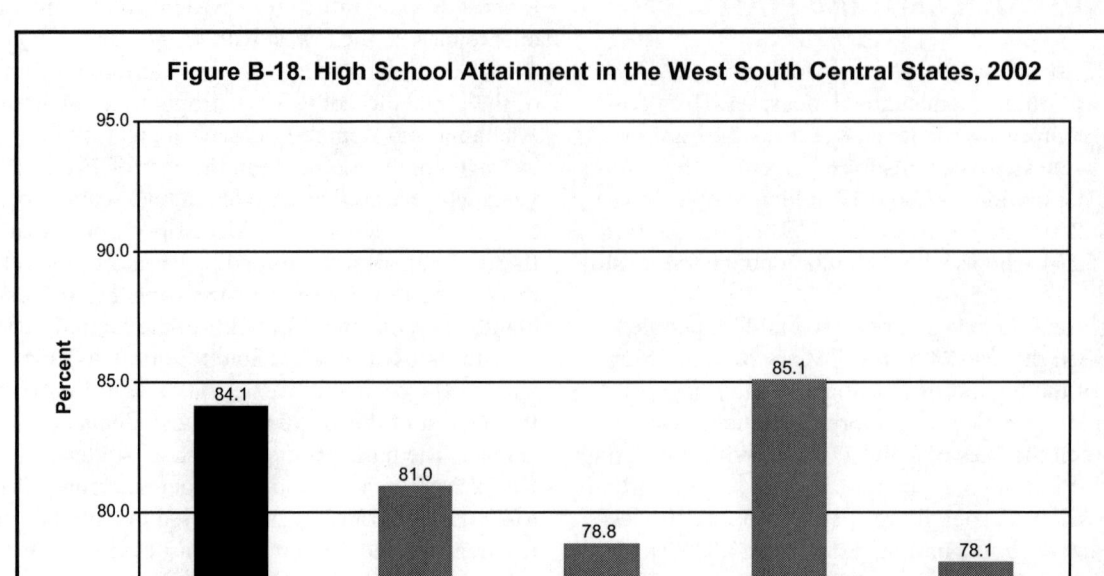

Figure B-18. High School Attainment in the West South Central States, 2002

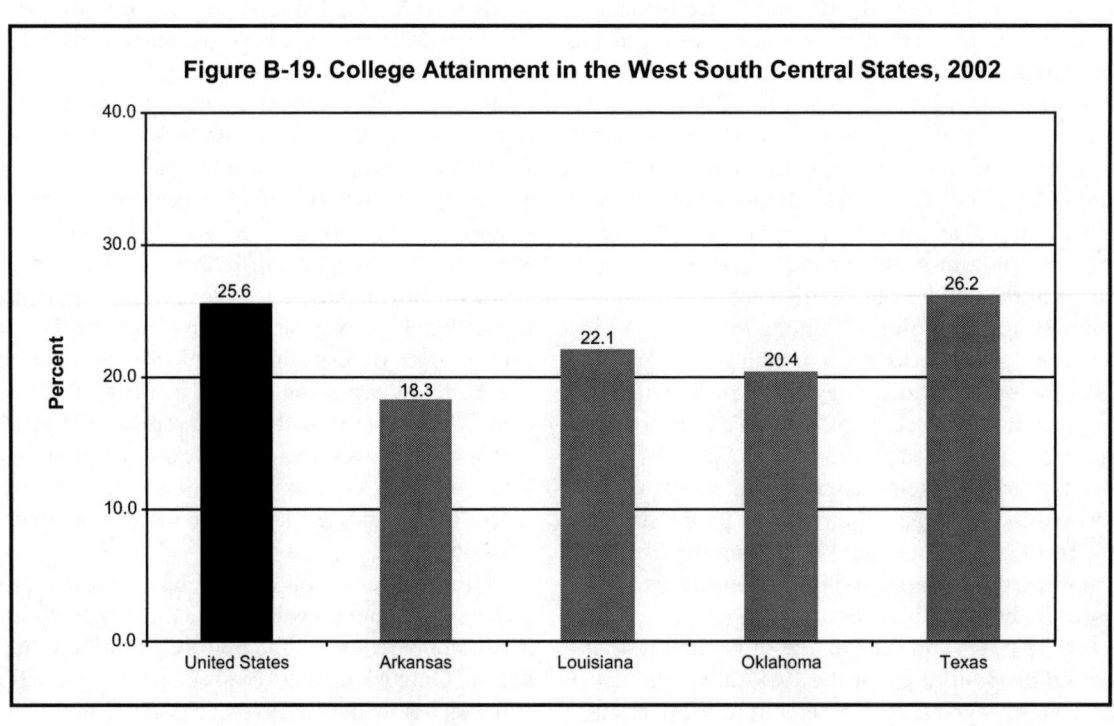

Figure B-19. College Attainment in the West South Central States, 2002

WEST SOUTH CENTRAL STATES:

Arkansas, Louisiana, Oklahoma, and Texas make up the West South Central division of the United States. These four states add up to more than 31 million people, with more than 6 million between 5 and 17 years of age.

With growth of more than 22 percent during the 1990s, Texas surpassed New York to become the second largest state in the nation. More than 20 percent of Texas residents are of school age. Both Texas and Louisiana rank among the top 10 states in the nation for proportion of population between the ages of 5 and 17 years. Arkansas and Oklahoma have proportions close to the national average of 18.9 percent.

More than 12 percent of the nation's public school students attend schools in West South Central states. Texas has more than 4 million students attending public schools. Louisiana is one of nine states and the District of Columbia with a decrease in the number of public school students from 1990 to 2000. The states of the West South Central division have lower than average student-to-teacher ratios. They range from 14.9 in Oklahoma to 13.6 in Arkansas. The number of teachers in Texas grew by more than 30 percent during the 1990s, reaching 282,846 during the 2001–2002 school year.

Texas has the third highest public school expenditures in the United States, with over $26 billion per year. The other three states in the division have expenditures ranging from $4.5 billion to $2.5 billion. Per student expenditures in the West South Central states are lower than average. The average in the United States is $7,376. The amounts in this division range from $6,539 in Texas to $5,568 in Arkansas. Both Arkansas and Oklahoma have among the 10 lowest expenditures per student in the nation.

There are nearly 2,000 school districts in the West South Central States, ranging from 1,040 in Texas to 66 in Louisiana. Texas has the highest number of school districts in the nation. Oklahoma has 543 school districts, but just 15 percent of the number of public school students in Texas. Louisiana has one of the highest proportions of private school students, while Oklahoma, Texas, and Arkansas have among the lowest proportions in the nation. Louisiana has among the highest proportions of minority students. It is one of seven states in the United States where minorities make up the majority of public school students. Nationally, about 60 percent of public school students are non-Hispanic White.

The West South Central states have high proportions of students who qualify for free or reduced price meals. All four states exceed 45 percent and are among the 15 highest in the 46 states with data. In Louisiana, more than 59 percent of students are eligible. All four states have more than 20 percent of their children in poverty, ranging from 28.3 percent in Arkansas, to 21.1 percent in Texas. The U.S. average is 16.3 percent.

The median income of a family of four in this division is less than $54,000. Arkansas has the lowest median income in the nation, with $44,537. The U.S. average is $62,228. The average teacher's salary in Texas is $40,001, which is well below the national average of $45,822. Arkansas, Oklahoma, and Louisiana are among the lowest 10 in the nation, all less than $38,000 a year.

Only Oklahoma surpasses the U.S. average high school attainment level. Texas and Louisiana are among five states with the proportion of high school graduates lower than 80 percent. Louisiana has the highest reported dropout rate in the nation, with 9.2 percent. The other states in the division range from 5.0 percent in Texas to 5.7 percent in Arkansas. In all four states, 9.5 percent or more of teenagers between 16 and 19 years are not enrolled in high school and have not graduated. Texas tied for fourth in the nation, with 12.5 percent.

Most high school graduates in West South Central states opt for the ACT over the SAT. Only Texas has more students taking the SAT. Texas is one of seven states with average scores less than 1,000. Arkansas has one of the smallest proportions of test-takers, with just 5 percent of graduates taking the SAT. More than 70 percent of high school graduates in Arkansas took the ACT. Louisiana (79 percent) and Oklahoma (69 percent) were also well above the national average of 39 percent. All four states had lower than average scores.

Arkansas is one of three states in the United States with a proportion of college graduates lower than 20 percent. The other West South Central states range from 20.4 percent in Oklahoma to 26.2 percent in Texas. The national proportion with a bachelor's degree is 26.7 percent. Oklahoma had a slight decrease in college attainment levels from 1998 to 2002. Texas had an increase of nearly 3 percentage points during this period.

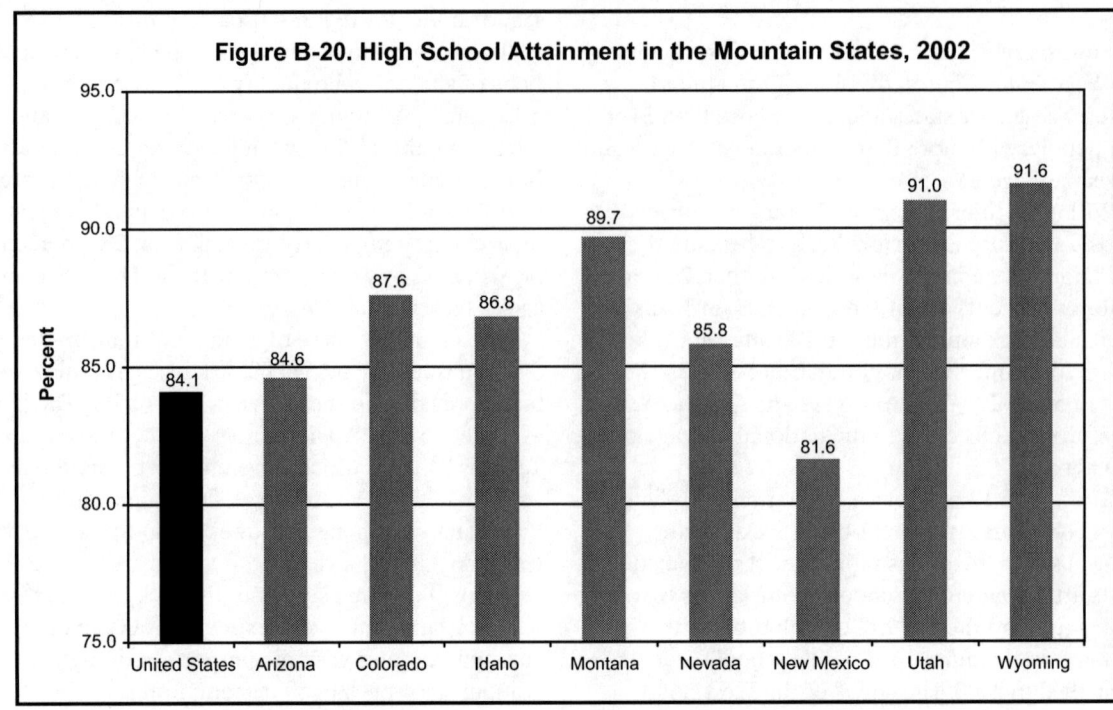

Figure B-20. High School Attainment in the Mountain States, 2002

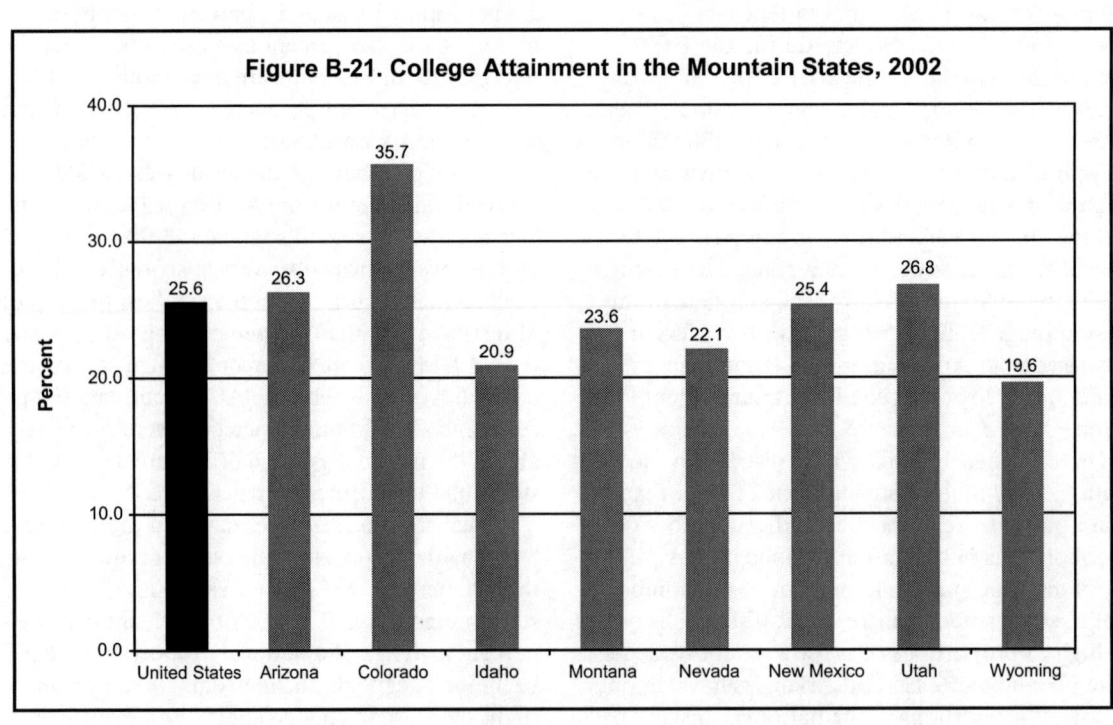

Figure B-21. College Attainment in the Mountain States, 2002

MOUNTAIN STATES:

The Mountain division is composed of Arizona, Colorado, Idaho, Montana, Nevada, New Mexico, Utah, and Wyoming. There are more than 18 million people residing in these eight states, which is about 8.8 percent of the U.S. population.

Utah has the highest student-to-teacher ratio in the United States. Arizona, Nevada, Idaho, and Colorado all rank among the top 10. Many of the states in this division have experienced tremendous population growth in the past decade. All of the Mountain states, except Colorado, have above average proportions of student-age population. Nearly 23 percent of Utah's population is between 5 and 17 years, which is the second highest in the nation. Idaho and New Mexico rank third and fourth in the nation with more than one in five persons of student age.

There are more than 3.3 million students in this division. Wyoming has the highest per student expenditures among the eight Mountain states. It is also the only state of the division that surpasses the U.S. average of $7,376. Utah, Arizona, and Idaho have among the lowest six per student expenditures in the nation. Utah is the only state where less than $5,000 is spent per student.

More than 54 percent of New Mexico students are eligible for free or reduced-price meals, which places the state among the five highest. Colorado has among the lowest of reporting states, with just 27.5 percent eligible. New Mexico and Arizona are among the states with the highest proportion of children under 18 years living in poverty. In New Mexico, one in four children live below the poverty line. In Nevada, less than 10 percent live in poverty. This is among the 10 smallest proportions of children in poverty in the United States.

Colorado is the only Mountain state with an above average median income for a family of four. The other states in this division are all below the national average of $62,228. Montana has the second lowest with $46,142. Nevada has the highest average teacher salary in the division, with $41,795, which is still below the U.S. average of $45,822. The majority of the other Mountain states are in the lowest third of states in the nation. Montana has the fifth lowest average teacher salary in the nation, with $35,754.

Average SAT scores range from 1,027 in Nevada to 1,122 in Utah. All eight states are above the national average of 1,020. However, the majority of graduates in the Mountain states do not take the SAT. In Nevada, 34 percent of high school graduates take the SAT, and in Utah, just 6 percent are test-takers. Most students in this division take the ACT. In Colorado, 99 percent of 2002 high school graduates took the ACT. The other states in the division range from 66 percent in Utah to 26 percent in Arizona. Only New Mexico and Colorado have below average scores. The U.S. average is 20.8.

High school attainment levels tend to be high in the Mountain states. New Mexico is the only state in this division with below average high school attainment levels. Less than 82 percent of New Mexico's population has graduated from high school, placing the state among the lowest 15 proportions in the nation. Wyoming and Utah have among the highest proportions of high school graduates in the nation. They are among just seven states with more than 90 percent of residents holding high school diplomas. Idaho's high school attainment level improved by more than 4 percentage points from 1998 to 2002, improving the state's rank from 33rd to 23rd. While Colorado did have a high proportion of high school graduates, with 87.6 percent in 2002, this was a decline of more than 2 percentage points from 1998. Nevada dropped 3.3 percentage points, changing the state's rank from 8th to 31st in the nation.

Nevada, New Mexico, and Wyoming have among the highest dropout rates among the 36 states and the District of Columbia that reported data. Utah has the lowest rate of the Mountain states reporting (Arizona, Colorado, and Idaho have no data). Among teenagers 16 to 19 years old, Nevada has the highest proportion in the nation who are not in high school, and have not graduated. Arizona ranks second, with 14.8 percent. Both Colorado and New Mexico exceed the U.S. average of 9.8 percent.

Colorado has one of the highest levels of college attainment in the nation. The state is among five states where college graduates account for one-third of their populations 25 years and over. Utah is the only other state in the division that exceeds the national average of 26.7 percent. Wyoming is one of three states in the United States where fewer than 20 percent of residents hold bachelor's degrees. Utah, Montana, and Wyoming were among eight states that had a drop in college attainment level from 1998 to 2002.

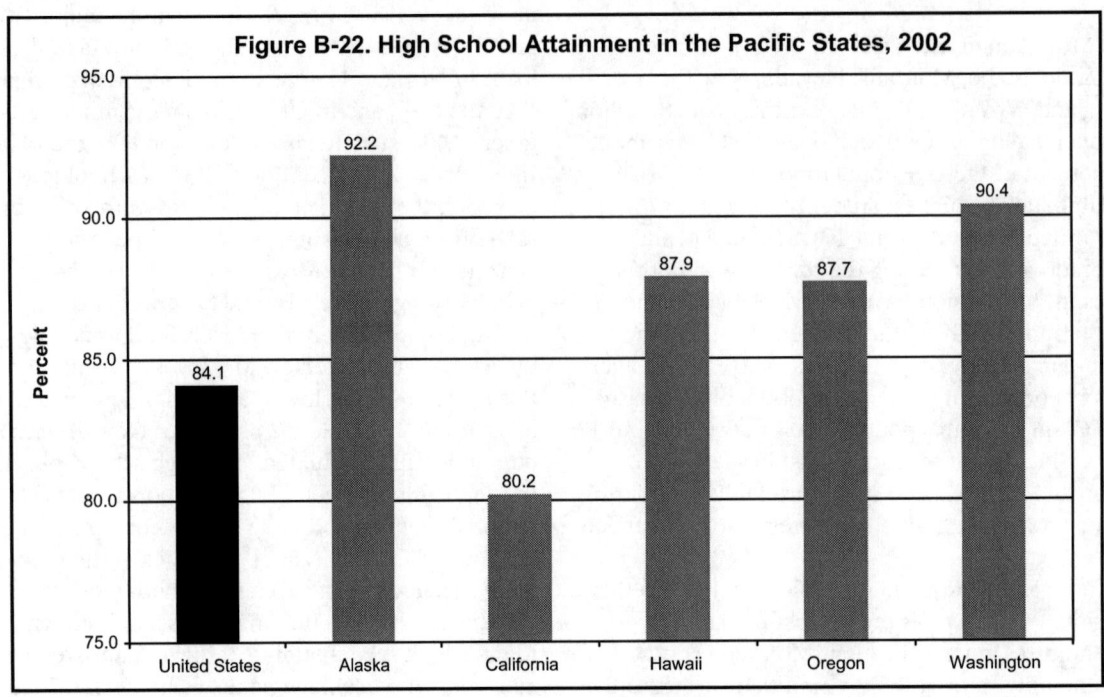

Figure B-22. High School Attainment in the Pacific States, 2002

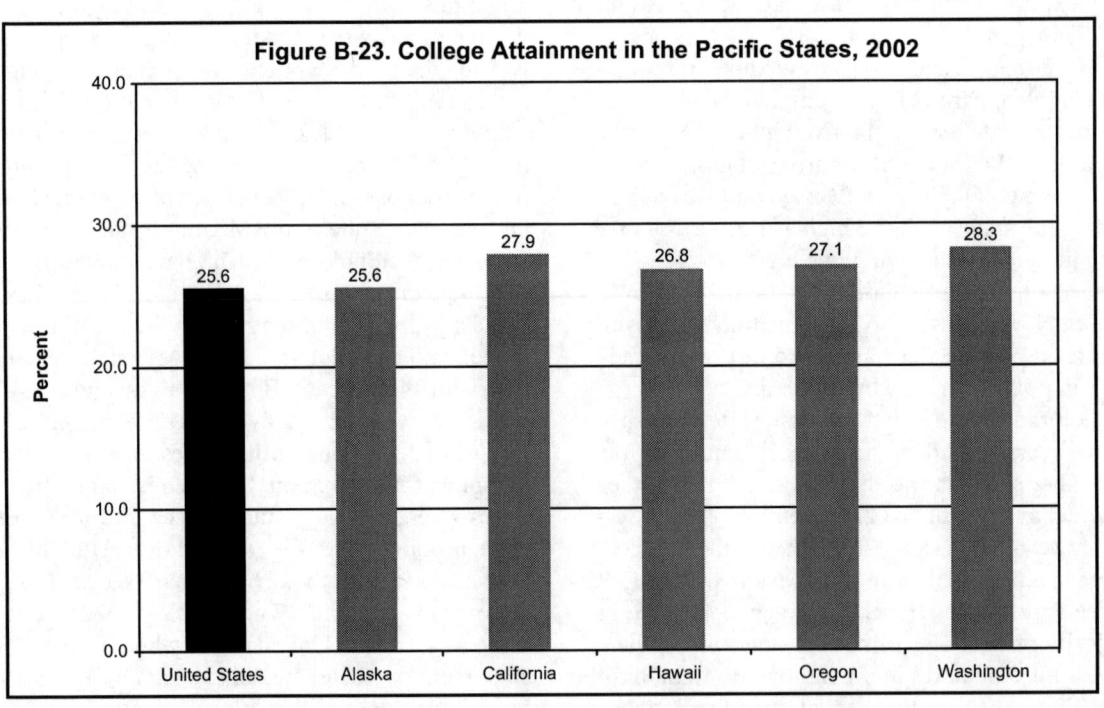

Figure B-23. College Attainment in the Pacific States, 2002

PACIFIC STATES:

The Pacific states are Alaska, California, Hawaii, Oregon, and Washington. The population of the Pacific division, which includes the largest state in the nation, exceeds 45 million. These five states contain 16 percent of the nation's population, and over 8 million students. This is one of the largest divisions in the United States.

The Pacific states account for 16.7 percent of the U.S. population between 5 and 17 years of age. Nearly 23 percent of Alaska's population is school age, giving the state the highest proportion in the United States. Hawaii has the lowest proportion of the group, with 18 percent of the state's population between 5 and 17 years. With the exception of Hawaii, the Pacific states have had above average population growth during the 1990s. Both Washington and Oregon have grown by more than 20 percent during the decade.

The number of school districts ranges from 986 in California to one in Hawaii. States in this division have among the smallest proportion of private school students. Hawaii is the only state with an above average proportion of students attending private schools. There are more than 13,000 schools in these five states, more than two-thirds of which are located in California.

All the Pacific states have above average student-to-teacher ratios. California has the second highest ratio in the nation with 20.5 students per teacher. Washington and Oregon also rate among the top five. Alaska and Hawaii both have student-to-teacher ratios that slightly exceed the national average of 15.9.

California has the highest public school expenditures in the nation. In 2000–2001, more than $42 billion was spent. Hawaii, with considerably fewer students, spent about $1.2 billion. In Alaska, 57.5 percent of expenditures go towards instructional costs; this is among the five lowest proportions in the nation. California is the only state in the division that exceeds the national average of 61.5 percent of expenditures directed for instruction.

Both Oregon and Alaska have above average per student expenditures. With $9,216, Alaska had the seventh highest in the United States. Hawaii has the lowest in the Pacific division, with $6,596 spent per student. California has the highest average teacher salary in the nation. Alaska also ranks among the top 15 states. Both states exceed $49,000 per year, while nationally the average public school teacher salary is $45,822. Hawaii has the lowest average teacher salary in the division, just above $40,000.

Alaska is one of five states with about one-fourth of public school students qualifying for free or reduced-price meals. California and Hawaii both have a high proportion of students who are eligible, each above 40 percent. At 31.4 percent, Washington is below average. The proportion of children living in poverty ranges from 16.4 percent in California to 12.5 percent in Alaska. The U.S. average is 16.3 percent. All the Pacific states have above average median income for a family of four, except for Oregon. Alaska has the highest in the division with $66,874.

About half of the high school graduates in each of the Pacific states take the SAT. Washington has the highest average score in the division, with 1,054, and Hawaii the lowest with 1,008. The U.S. average is 1,020. The proportions that take the ACT range from 31 percent in Alaska to 12 percent in Oregon. Oregon is tied with Maine for the highest average score in the nation. All the states in this division exceed the national average score of 20.8.

Alaska is tied with Minnesota for the highest level of high school attainment in the United States. More than 92 percent of Alaska's population holds a high school diploma. Washington ranks fifth in the nation, with 90.4 percent of the state's residents having graduated from high school. California is the only state in the division with below average high school attainment levels. Nearly one in five people in California have not graduated from high school. Hawaii's high school attainment level improved by more than 3 percentage points from 1998 to 2002, moving the state from 24th in the nation to 15th. Washington is one of nine states and the District of Columbia with a drop in high school attainment level during this period.

Alaska is the only state in the Pacific division with a below average college attainment level. In Alaska, 25.6 percent of residents hold a bachelor's degree, compared with 26.7 percent nationally. Washington is the highest in the division, with 28.3 percent. Oregon is one of eight states with a decline in college attainment levels from 1998.

Among the Pacific division, Hawaii is the only state with an above average proportion of college students attending private institutions. Nationally, 23.5 percent of students are enrolled in private colleges. Alaska has the second lowest proportion in the nation, with just 4.7 percent of students in private colleges. California, with 16.1 percent, has the highest proportion in the division, after Hawaii.

Table B-1. Population, School, and Student Characteristics by State

Fips code	State	Population, 2000		Median income of a family of four in 2000	Children under 18 years in poverty, 2001 (percent)	Poverty and health insurance, 1999–2001 average		
		Total	5 to 17 years (percent)			Total children under 19 years (1,000s)	Low-income children under 19 years (percent)	Low-income children with no health insurance (percent)
		1	2	3	4	5	6	7
00	UNITED STATES	281 421 906	18.9	$62 228	16.3	75 809	38.1	7.9
01	Alabama	4 447 100	18.6	51 451	23.2	1 194	46.0	6.4
02	Alaska	626 932	22.8	66 874	12.5	203	30.6	7.0
04	Arizona	5 130 632	19.2	55 663	22.3	1 526	46.4	12.9
05	Arkansas	2 673 400	18.7	44 537	28.3	725	50.5	8.7
06	California	33 871 648	20.0	63 206	16.4	10 089	43.1	10.4
08	Colorado	4 301 261	18.7	66 624	10.6	1 214	31.0	8.6
09	Connecticut	3 405 565	18.2	82 702	9.3	876	27.3	4.8
10	Delaware	783 600	18.3	69 360	9.3	208	29.8	4.0
11	District of Columbia	572 059	14.4	63 406	30.8	116	50.1	6.5
12	Florida	15 982 378	16.9	55 351	18.8	3 922	42.4	11.3
13	Georgia	8 186 453	19.2	59 489	19.5	2 305	42.3	7.4
15	Hawaii	1 211 537	18.0	65 872	15.9	328	35.2	5.0
16	Idaho	1 293 953	21.0	53 722	15.9	389	43.2	11.1
17	Illinois	12 419 293	19.1	68 117	15.8	3 341	32.9	6.7
18	Indiana	6 080 485	18.9	62 079	11.3	1 561	34.2	6.4
19	Iowa	2 926 324	18.6	57 921	7.6	761	29.2	3.7
20	Kansas	2 688 418	19.5	56 784	14.4	696	34.9	7.1
21	Kentucky	4 041 769	18.0	51 249	17.2	1 020	38.5	6.9
22	Louisiana	4 468 976	20.2	47 363	23.1	1 258	51.5	13.4
23	Maine	1 274 923	18.1	56 186	12.4	301	34.5	3.4
24	Maryland	5 296 486	18.9	77 562	7.6	1 398	22.8	4.6
25	Massachusetts	6 349 097	17.4	78 025	11.9	1 511	33.2	3.6
26	Michigan	9 938 444	19.4	68 740	13.0	2 729	31.9	3.9
27	Minnesota	4 919 479	19.5	70 553	8.4	1 301	23.1	3.0
28	Mississippi	2 844 658	20.1	46 331	23.2	813	48.7	7.7
29	Missouri	5 595 211	18.9	61 173	12.9	1 494	30.9	2.6
30	Montana	902 195	19.4	46 142	16.4	238	44.9	10.2
31	Nebraska	1 711 263	19.5	57 040	13.5	464	31.7	5.0
32	Nevada	1 998 257	18.3	59 614	9.1	603	38.0	11.2
33	New Hampshire	1 235 786	18.9	71 661	8.2	325	23.1	2.5
34	New Jersey	8 414 350	18.1	78 560	9.6	2 044	26.1	5.4
35	New Mexico	1 819 046	20.8	47 314	25.4	541	53.8	14.8
36	New York	18 976 457	18.2	64 520	20.0	4 900	40.0	6.1
37	North Carolina	8 049 313	17.7	57 203	16.4	2 103	41.1	7.5
38	North Dakota	642 200	18.9	53 140	19.5	150	40.2	6.4
39	Ohio	11 353 140	18.8	62 251	16.2	2 933	35.3	5.7
40	Oklahoma	3 450 654	19.0	48 459	21.4	895	45.7	11.7
41	Oregon	3 421 399	18.2	58 315	15.1	904	38.0	7.9
42	Pennsylvania	12 281 054	17.9	65 411	14.0	2 961	33.3	4.3
44	Rhode Island	1 048 319	17.5	68 418	11.0	261	29.4	2.9
45	South Carolina	4 012 012	18.6	56 294	23.0	1 032	40.0	6.9
46	South Dakota	754 844	20.1	55 150	8.2	194	32.3	4.8
47	Tennessee	5 689 283	18.0	54 899	20.4	1 460	40.3	3.6
48	Texas	20 851 820	20.4	53 513	21.1	6 241	46.2	15.9
49	Utah	2 233 169	22.8	57 043	12.5	755	33.4	5.8
50	Vermont	608 827	18.6	59 125	12.2	144	34.6	2.1
51	Virginia	7 078 515	18.0	68 054	8.4	1 845	28.0	6.1
53	Washington	5 894 121	19.0	63 568	13.7	1 557	33.1	6.2
54	West Virginia	1 808 344	16.6	46 270	22.2	403	49.9	7.7
55	Wisconsin	5 363 675	19.1	66 725	12.0	1 448	30.3	3.8
56	Wyoming	493 782	19.8	55 859	10.7	131	38.0	7.5

Table B-1. Population, School, and Student Characteristics by State—*Continued*

Fips code	State	Educational attainment, 2002			Public schools and school districts, 2001–2002					
		Population 25 years and over (1,000s)	High school graduates (percent)	Bachelor's degree or more (percent)	Number of school districts	Total schools	Regular schools	Special education schools	Vocational schools	Alternative schools
								Type of school		
		8	9	10	11	12	13	14	15	16
00	UNITED STATES	182 140	84.1	26.7	14 559	91 380	84 919	1 641	328	4 492
01	Alabama	2 874	78.9	22.7	128	1 381	1 334	18	2	27
02	Alaska	383	92.2	25.6	53	506	473	2	1	30
04	Arizona	3 182	84.6	26.3	323	1 742	1 652	13	9	68
05	Arkansas	1 692	81.0	18.3	312	1 129	1 125	0	0	4
06	California	20 958	80.2	27.9	986	8 914	7 667	122	0	1 125
08	Colorado	2 781	87.6	35.7	178	1 630	1 535	14	2	79
09	Connecticut	2 313	88.0	32.6	166	1 073	992	23	17	41
10	Delaware	518	88.5	29.5	19	197	170	13	5	9
11	District of Columbia	382	83.5	44.4	1	193	178	10	0	5
12	Florida	11 051	83.3	25.7	67	3 314	2 992	122	25	175
13	Georgia	5 135	82.9	25.0	180	1 969	1 940	1	0	28
15	Hawaii	799	87.9	26.8	1	279	275	3	0	1
16	Idaho	811	86.8	20.9	114	654	589	5	0	60
17	Illinois	8 088	85.9	27.3	893	4 292	3 913	253	0	126
18	Indiana	4 058	85.3	23.7	294	1 891	1 832	11	0	48
19	Iowa	1 867	88.3	23.1	371	1 519	1 473	10	0	36
20	Kansas	1 747	87.5	29.1	304	1 423	1 423	0	0	0
21	Kentucky	2 620	80.8	21.6	176	1 387	1 228	9	2	148
22	Louisiana	2 709	78.8	22.1	66	1 509	1 378	28	0	103
23	Maine	916	87.4	23.8	282	681	678	3	0	0
24	Maryland	3 453	87.5	37.6	24	1 340	1 241	50	12	37
25	Massachusetts	4 357	86.5	34.3	350	1 889	1 811	1	43	34
26	Michigan	6 600	86.5	22.5	554	3 782	3 495	90	12	185
27	Minnesota	3 268	92.2	30.5	417	2 119	1 606	195	1	317
28	Mississippi	1 756	79.1	20.9	152	886	886	0	0	0
29	Missouri	3 551	88.1	26.7	524	2 274	2 158	55	0	61
30	Montana	595	89.7	23.6	452	870	863	2	0	5
31	Nebraska	1 063	89.8	27.1	555	1 280	1 229	51	0	0
32	Nevada	1 356	85.8	22.1	17	517	471	12	1	33
33	New Hampshire	873	90.2	30.1	178	472	472	0	0	0
34	New Jersey	5 894	85.9	31.4	603	2 410	2 271	83	38	18
35	New Mexico	1 113	81.6	25.4	89	792	720	15	0	57
36	New York	12 401	83.7	28.8	703	4 298	4 162	26	25	85
37	North Carolina	5 135	80.1	22.4	121	2 223	2 127	20	1	75
38	North Dakota	422	89.0	25.3	222	529	529	0	0	0
39	Ohio	7 509	87.3	24.5	662	3 826	3 700	28	68	30
40	Oklahoma	2 163	85.1	20.4	543	1 814	1 814	0	0	0
41	Oregon	2 216	87.7	27.1	198	1 273	1 193	11	0	69
42	Pennsylvania	8 205	86.1	26.1	501	3 185	3 144	12	16	13
44	Rhode Island	700	80.1	30.1	36	326	313	4	4	5
45	South Carolina	2 588	80.2	23.3	89	1 053	1 047	5	0	1
46	South Dakota	492	89.2	23.6	176	749	720	4	0	25
47	Tennessee	3 708	80.1	21.5	138	1 610	1 574	15	3	18
48	Texas	12 622	78.1	26.2	1 040	7 646	6 715	133	25	773
49	Utah	1 215	91.0	26.8	40	791	719	19	0	53
50	Vermont	421	87.4	30.8	292	359	315	42	0	2
51	Virginia	4 659	86.7	34.6	137	1 839	1 793	10	0	36
53	Washington	3 849	90.4	28.3	296	2 170	1 834	79	10	247
54	West Virginia	1 229	78.5	15.9	55	784	752	7	5	20
55	Wisconsin	3 520	86.8	24.7	433	2 208	2 035	12	1	160
56	Wyoming	323	91.6	19.6	48	383	363	0	0	20

Table B-1. Population, School, and Student Characteristics by State—*Continued*

		Public schools and students, 2001–2002							
		Level of schools				Level of students			
Fips code	State	Number of schools	Primary schools (percent)	Middle schools (percent)	High schools (percent)	Number of students	Primary schools (percent)	Middle schools (percent)	High schools (percent)
		17	18	19	20	21	22	23	24
00	UNITED STATES	91 380	57.5	17.3	19.2	47 687 871	48.8	20.3	27.8
01	Alabama	1 381	51.0	17.0	20.1	737 294	44.0	18.0	25.6
02	Alaska	506	34.4	7.1	13.8	134 358	42.2	13.0	24.5
04	Arizona	1 742	57.2	13.7	20.4	922 180	55.0	16.1	26.5
05	Arkansas	1 129	51.0	16.9	28.7	449 805	45.5	20.7	28.6
06	California	8 914	61.6	14.4	19.1	6 248 610	51.1	18.8	27.4
08	Colorado	1 630	57.8	17.5	20.0	742 145	49.2	20.4	27.6
09	Connecticut	1 073	61.6	18.1	16.6	570 228	49.1	21.9	27.8
10	Delaware	197	52.8	23.4	15.7	115 555	43.2	26.0	28.8
11	District of Columbia	193	60.1	13.0	15.0	75 392	59.2	14.7	18.2
12	Florida	3 314	53.5	14.8	12.3	2 500 478	47.8	21.0	25.6
13	Georgia	1 969	60.5	20.8	16.4	1 470 634	49.2	23.2	25.8
15	Hawaii	279	64.5	13.3	15.4	184 546	52.5	16.4	28.2
16	Idaho	654	52.4	16.8	25.4	246 521	47.6	21.7	27.8
17	Illinois	4 292	61.4	17.0	17.6	2 071 391	54.6	16.2	27.5
18	Indiana	1 891	61.3	17.2	18.1	996 133	49.5	19.6	28.5
19	Iowa	1 519	53.7	19.4	23.9	485 932	45.3	20.4	32.0
20	Kansas	1 423	57.1	17.6	25.1	470 205	49.0	19.7	31.3
21	Kentucky	1 387	55.9	16.7	21.1	654 363	49.0	20.9	28.9
22	Louisiana	1 509	53.1	18.8	16.5	731 328	48.2	20.0	25.7
23	Maine	681	62.7	18.6	16.3	205 586	45.2	23.2	30.0
24	Maryland	1 340	64.8	17.9	15.1	860 640	49.0	21.9	28.0
25	Massachusetts	1 889	63.6	15.8	15.2	973 140	48.1	19.7	26.3
26	Michigan	3 782	57.6	17.2	19.0	1 730 668	47.1	21.3	28.1
27	Minnesota	2 119	49.1	13.4	30.0	851 384	45.4	19.2	32.9
28	Mississippi	886	49.5	20.7	20.3	493 507	45.2	20.9	24.7
29	Missouri	2 274	54.7	16.5	21.7	909 792	48.0	20.2	29.1
30	Montana	870	52.1	27.5	20.2	151 947	46.1	21.2	32.1
31	Nebraska	1 280	65.2	8.0	23.7	285 095	50.3	15.1	34.1
32	Nevada	517	61.9	15.3	20.1	356 814	51.2	22.0	26.4
33	New Hampshire	472	63.3	20.1	16.3	206 847	45.9	24.3	29.6
34	New Jersey	2 410	63.0	17.7	14.9	1 341 656	50.8	20.0	27.7
35	New Mexico	792	55.2	19.9	19.7	320 260	47.2	21.9	28.8
36	New York	4 298	57.8	17.3	18.3	2 872 132	48.3	20.0	27.6
37	North Carolina	2 223	59.3	20.5	15.5	1 315 363	49.0	22.8	26.1
38	North Dakota	529	58.4	6.8	34.2	106 047	48.9	12.8	35.9
39	Ohio	3 826	56.9	19.1	19.7	1 830 985	44.9	20.3	31.5
40	Oklahoma	1 814	54.2	19.0	25.5	622 139	51.9	20.5	25.2
41	Oregon	1 273	59.7	17.4	18.8	551 480	47.3	21.4	29.8
42	Pennsylvania	3 185	60.6	17.8	19.2	1 821 627	45.3	20.9	30.6
44	Rhode Island	326	66.6	17.2	14.4	158 046	47.3	23.6	28.6
45	South Carolina	1 053	57.1	23.8	17.9	691 078	47.9	23.6	27.8
46	South Dakota	749	49.8	23.6	23.5	127 542	46.1	21.9	31.3
47	Tennessee	1 610	60.2	17.6	17.6	925 030	50.6	19.5	27.1
48	Texas	7 646	50.6	20.0	18.1	4 163 447	48.3	22.6	25.7
49	Utah	791	60.0	16.2	19.3	484 677	51.5	21.1	24.7
50	Vermont	359	71.6	6.4	13.1	101 179	51.8	8.8	31.3
51	Virginia	1 839	63.1	18.2	17.0	1 163 091	48.3	21.7	29.2
53	Washington	2 170	54.2	16.2	20.9	1 009 200	47.5	20.4	28.5
54	West Virginia	784	62.8	17.3	16.6	282 885	49.3	21.5	27.0
55	Wisconsin	2 208	56.4	17.5	22.8	879 361	46.1	19.8	32.1
56	Wyoming	383	57.2	20.1	20.1	88 128	46.2	22.8	29.1

Table B-1. Population, School, and Student Characteristics by State—*Continued*

Fips code	State	Characteristics of public school students, 2001–2002						
		Students eligible for free or reduced-price meals (percent)	Students with IEP[1] (percent)	Race and Hispanic origin of students				
				Non-Hispanic White (percent)	Non-Hispanic Black (percent)	Hispanic (percent)	Asian/Pacific Islander (percent)	American Indian/Alaska Native (percent)
		25	26	27	28	29	30	31
00	UNITED STATES	*36.6	13.3	60.3	17.2	17.1	4.2	1.2
01	Alabama	48.7	13.2	60.5	36.5	1.5	0.8	0.7
02	Alaska	25.2	13.3	60.4	4.7	3.6	5.9	25.5
04	Arizona	. . .	10.6	51.3	4.7	35.3	2.1	6.6
05	Arkansas	47.2	12.5	71.1	23.3	4.2	0.9	0.5
06	California	47.3	10.8	35.0	8.4	44.5	11.2	0.9
08	Colorado	27.5	10.0	66.8	5.7	23.3	3.0	1.2
09	Connecticut	. . .	13.0	69.2	13.8	13.7	3.0	0.3
10	Delaware	34.6	13.9	59.6	31.1	6.6	2.4	0.3
11	District of Columbia	55.3	16.7	4.6	84.4	9.4	1.6	0.0
12	Florida	44.6	15.1	52.5	24.9	20.4	1.9	0.3
13	Georgia	44.2	11.6	53.8	38.2	5.5	2.4	0.2
15	Hawaii	41.9	12.4	20.3	2.4	4.5	72.3	0.4
16	Idaho	35.6	11.7	85.4	0.8	11.2	1.3	1.3
17	Illinois	35.2	14.4	59.0	21.2	16.2	3.5	0.2
18	Indiana	31.1	16.1	83.0	11.8	3.9	1.0	0.2
19	Iowa	26.7	14.9	89.6	4.1	4.0	1.7	0.5
20	Kansas	34.1	13.1	77.8	8.9	9.8	2.2	1.3
21	Kentucky	49.1	15.0	87.7	10.3	1.1	0.7	0.2
22	Louisiana	59.1	13.4	48.7	47.8	1.6	1.3	0.7
23	Maine	29.6	15.9	96.2	1.4	0.6	1.1	0.7
24	Maryland	29.7	13.0	52.4	37.2	5.4	4.6	0.4
25	Massachusetts	25.3	15.4	75.7	8.6	10.8	4.5	0.3
26	Michigan	31.2	13.4	73.4	20.0	3.6	2.0	1.0
27	Minnesota	26.4	13.0	82.0	7.0	3.8	5.2	2.0
28	Mississippi	65.3	12.6	47.3	51.0	0.9	0.7	0.2
29	Missouri	35.1	15.4	79.0	17.5	2.0	1.2	0.3
30	Montana	31.5	12.6	85.9	0.6	1.9	1.0	10.6
31	Nebraska	31.2	15.5	81.8	6.9	8.2	1.6	1.6
32	Nevada	29.7	11.3	54.5	10.3	27.4	6.1	1.7
33	New Hampshire	14.8	13.9	95.0	1.2	2.1	1.5	0.2
34	New Jersey	27.8	16.3	59.4	17.9	16.0	6.6	0.2
35	New Mexico	54.7	19.6	34.3	2.4	51.0	1.1	11.3
36	New York	43.2	14.8	54.8	19.9	18.6	6.2	0.4
37	North Carolina	38.4	14.2	60.0	31.3	5.2	1.9	1.5
38	North Dakota	28.0	12.6	88.7	1.1	1.3	0.8	8.1
39	Ohio	27.4	12.4	80.1	16.7	1.9	1.2	0.1
40	Oklahoma	48.7	14.1	63.7	10.8	6.5	1.5	17.5
41	Oregon	36.1	12.7	79.1	3.0	11.5	4.2	2.2
42	Pennsylvania	28.4	12.7	77.7	15.3	4.8	2.1	0.1
44	Rhode Island	33.6	20.0	73.4	8.1	14.8	3.2	0.6
45	South Carolina	48.7	14.6	54.7	41.7	2.4	1.0	0.2
46	South Dakota	30.1	13.1	86.2	1.3	1.4	1.0	10.2
47	Tennessee	. . .	15.9	71.8	24.8	2.1	1.2	0.2
48	Texas	45.4	11.9	40.9	14.4	41.7	2.8	0.3
49	Utah	29.2	11.3	84.7	1.0	9.9	2.8	1.5
50	Vermont	23.8	13.3	95.8	1.2	1.0	1.5	0.5
51	Virginia	29.3	14.1	62.8	27.1	5.5	4.3	0.3
53	Washington	31.4	12.0	73.5	5.4	10.9	7.5	2.6
54	West Virginia	50.4	17.7	94.5	4.4	0.4	0.6	0.1
55	Wisconsin	26.0	14.3	80.1	10.2	5.0	3.4	1.4
56	Wyoming	. . .	13.3	87.3	1.4	7.2	0.9	3.2

[1]IEP = Individual Education Program. See Notes and Definitions at the end of this section.
. . . = Not available.
* = Reporting states.

Table B-1. Population, School, and Student Characteristics by State—*Continued*

Fips code	State	Public school outcomes					Private schools		
		Dropouts, grades 9–12, 1999–2000 (percent)	9th grade membership, 2000–2001	12th grade membership, 2000–2001	Public high school graduates, 2000–2001	High school completion rates, 1998–2000 average	Number of schools, 1999–2000	Enrollment, 1999–2000	High school graduates, 1998–1999
		32	33	34	35	36	37	38	39
00	UNITED STATES	...	4 012 770	2 863 083	2 568 956	85.7	27 223	5 162 684	273 025
01	Alabama	4.5	61 038	42 909	37 082	81.6	374	73 352	4 324
02	Alaska	5.5	11 734	8 340	6 812	93.3	69	6 172	245
04	Arizona	...	72 859	52 162	46 773	73.5	276	44 060	2 399
05	Arkansas	5.7	35 894	28 849	27 100	84.1	192	26 424	1 320
06	California	...	499 505	365 907	315 189	82.5	3 318	619 067	28 097
08	Colorado	...	62 756	44 912	39 241	81.6	339	52 142	2 470
09	Connecticut	3.1	46 621	34 301	30 388	91.7	348	70 058	5 141
10	Delaware	4.1	10 618	7 030	6 614	91.0	96	22 779	1 151
11	District of Columbia	7.2	4 012	2 815	2 808	88.0	89	16 690	1 231
12	Florida	...	248 764	130 613	111 112	84.6	1 545	290 872	12 866
13	Georgia	7.2	128 734	75 814	62 499	83.5	592	116 407	6 819
15	Hawaii	...	16 036	10 632	10 102	91.8	130	32 193	2 533
16	Idaho	...	19 923	17 628	15 941	86.4	94	10 209	459
17	Illinois	6.2	165 529	131 411	110 624	87.1	1 354	299 871	16 652
18	Indiana	...	78 945	62 913	56 172	89.4	677	105 533	4 597
19	Iowa	2.5	39 818	36 469	33 774	90.8	265	49 565	2 693
20	Kansas	...	38 621	33 221	29 360	90.4	237	43 113	2 071
21	Kentucky	5.0	53 583	37 160	36 957	86.2	368	75 084	3 997
22	Louisiana	9.2	57 164	41 611	38 314	82.1	434	138 135	8 716
23	Maine	3.3	16 689	13 410	12 654	94.5	139	18 287	2 050
24	Maryland	4.1	73 300	52 671	49 222	87.4	701	144 131	7 596
25	Massachusetts	4.1	80 394	59 453	54 393	90.9	694	132 154	9 632
26	Michigan	...	145 651	103 839	96 515	89.2	1 012	179 579	9 114
27	Minnesota	4.3	69 032	68 997	56 581	91.9	530	92 795	4 010
28	Mississippi	4.9	38 498	25 816	23 748	82.3	207	51 369	3 649
29	Missouri	4.4	75 156	57 727	54 138	92.6	576	122 387	6 851
30	Montana	4.2	13 004	11 307	10 628	91.1	90	8 711	395
31	Nebraska	4.0	23 855	21 679	19 658	91.3	237	42 141	2 303
32	Nevada	6.2	32 086	19 461	15 127	77.9	80	13 926	639
33	New Hampshire	...	17 646	13 309	12 294	85.1	171	23 383	1 894
34	New Jersey	3.1	98 784	76 271	76 130	90.1	905	198 631	11 072
35	New Mexico	6.0	28 816	18 658	18 199	83.0	182	23 055	1 361
36	New York	...	245 540	153 505	141 884	86.3	1 981	475 942	26 314
37	North Carolina	...	114 236	69 602	63 288	86.1	588	96 262	4 256
38	North Dakota	2.7	8 906	8 661	8 445	94.4	55	7 148	448
39	Ohio	5.0	155 727	117 683	111 281	87.7	974	254 494	13 394
40	Oklahoma	5.4	49 034	38 638	37 458	85.7	179	31 276	1 635
41	Oregon	5.8	45 067	38 379	29 939	82.3	347	45 352	2 376
42	Pennsylvania	4.0	159 919	122 942	114 436	89.0	1 964	339 484	18 002
44	Rhode Island	4.8	13 538	9 507	8 603	87.9	127	24 738	1 404
45	South Carolina	...	64 700	36 057	29 742	85.1	326	55 612	2 915
46	South Dakota	3.5	10 629	9 454	8 881	92.0	83	9 364	442
47	Tennessee	4.2	74 322	51 278	40 642	89.0	533	93 680	6 717
48	Texas	5.0	366 895	226 429	215 316	79.4	1 281	227 645	9 988
49	Utah	4.1	35 029	34 951	31 036	90.0	78	12 614	792
50	Vermont	4.7	8 595	7 422	6 856	90.8	122	12 170	1 273
51	Virginia	3.9	100 599	70 607	66 067	87.3	582	100 171	5 010
53	Washington	...	86 396	69 536	55 081	87.4	494	76 885	3 262
54	West Virginia	4.2	23 328	18 336	18 440	89.6	151	15 895	883
55	Wisconsin	2.6	77 802	65 946	59 341	90.0	991	139 455	5 525
56	Wyoming	5.7	7 443	6 855	6 071	86.5	41	2 221	41

. . . = Not available.

Table B-1. Population, School, and Student Characteristics by State—*Continued*

		Public and private school characteristics								
		Public schools, 2000–2001					Private schools, 1999–2000			Average public school teacher salary, 2002–2003[3]
		Student membership		Teachers[2]		Student/ teacher ratio	Total enrollment	Total teachers[2]	Student/ teacher ratio	
Fips code	State	Total	Percent change from 1990–1991 to 2000–2001	Total	Percent change from 1990–1991 to 2000–2001					
		40	41	42	43	44	45	46	47	48
00	**UNITED STATES**	47 687 871	11.5	2 997 741	21.2	15.9	5 162 684	395 317	13.1	$45 822
01	Alabama	737 294	2.1	46 796	15.6	15.8	73 352	5 934	12.4	38 246
02	Alaska	134 358	13.2	8 026	12.8	16.7	6 172	572	10.8	49 685
04	Arizona	922 180	40.4	46 015	35.4	20.0	44 060	3 319	13.3	40 894
05	Arkansas	449 805	2.6	33 079	28.3	13.6	26 424	2 075	12.7	37 753
06	California	6 248 610	22.4	304 296	35.8	20.5	619 067	43 159	14.3	56 283
08	Colorado	742 145	25.1	44 182	33.5	16.8	52 142	4 353	12.0	41 275
09	Connecticut	570 228	18.5	41 773	21.5	13.7	70 058	6 879	10.2	54 362
10	Delaware	115 555	13.1	7 571	24.2	15.3	22 779	1 784	12.8	50 772
11	District of Columbia	75 392	-14.6	4 951	-22.0	13.8	16 690	1 898	8.8	50 763
12	Florida	2 500 478	29.4	134 684	22.5	18.6	290 872	22 929	12.7	39 465
13	Georgia	1 470 634	24.9	92 732	45.3	15.9	116 407	10 677	10.9	45 533
15	Hawaii	184 546	5.6	11 007	16.5	16.8	32 193	2 475	13.0	44 464
16	Idaho	246 521	9.2	13 854	19.2	17.8	10 209	790	12.9	40 148
17	Illinois	2 071 391	12.1	129 600	17.7	16.0	299 871	19 589	15.3	51 289
18	Indiana	996 133	4.1	59 658	9.4	16.7	105 533	7 362	14.3	45 097
19	Iowa	485 932	-1.1	34 906	11.2	13.9	49 565	3 545	14.0	38 921
20	Kansas	470 205	5.6	33 084	12.8	14.2	43 113	3 166	13.6	38 123
21	Kentucky	654 363	1.3	40 375	7.5	16.2	75 084	5 478	13.7	38 981
22	Louisiana	731 328	-7.9	49 980	8.3	14.6	138 135	9 206	15.0	36 878
23	Maine	205 586	-5.0	16 741	8.6	12.3	18 287	1 760	10.4	38 121
24	Maryland	860 640	16.9	53 774	23.3	16.0	144 131	12 152	11.9	49 677
25	Massachusetts	973 140	15.0	68 942	23.2	14.1	132 154	12 497	10.6	52 043
26	Michigan	1 730 668	8.6	98 849	19.1	17.5	179 579	11 771	15.3	54 071
27	Minnesota	851 384	10.1	53 081	18.2	16.0	92 795	6 467	14.3	42 833
28	Mississippi	493 507	-2.1	31 213	11.0	15.8	51 369	3 884	13.2	34 555
29	Missouri	909 792	7.9	65 240	23.9	13.9	122 387	9 105	13.4	38 826
30	Montana	151 947	-2.5	10 408	5.3	14.6	8 711	740	11.8	35 754
31	Nebraska	285 095	2.0	21 083	10.6	13.5	42 141	2 963	14.2	37 896
32	Nevada	356 814	68.5	19 276	69.0	18.5	13 926	973	14.3	41 795
33	New Hampshire	206 847	16.8	14 677	28.0	14.1	23 383	2 208	10.6	40 519
34	New Jersey	1 341 656	20.9	103 611	28.7	12.9	198 631	15 496	12.8	54 166
35	New Mexico	320 260	3.8	21 823	24.7	14.7	23 055	1 992	11.6	36 687
36	New York	2 872 132	8.6	209 128	21.6	13.7	475 942	37 190	12.8	52 600
37	North Carolina	1 315 363	19.8	85 684	31.2	15.4	96 262	8 962	10.7	43 076
38	North Dakota	106 047	-10.0	8 035	3.9	13.2	7 148	545	13.1	33 210
39	Ohio	1 830 985	2.6	122 115	18.1	15.0	254 494	16 165	15.7	45 452
40	Oklahoma	622 139	5.8	41 632	10.6	14.9	31 276	2 727	11.5	34 854
41	Oregon	551 480	10.6	28 402	6.2	19.4	45 352	3 473	13.1	47 600
42	Pennsylvania	1 821 627	7.6	118 470	17.9	15.4	339 484	24 453	13.9	51 800
44	Rhode Island	158 046	11.2	11 103	14.4	14.2	24 738	1 961	12.6	51 076
45	South Carolina	691 078	10.1	46 616	25.6	14.8	55 612	4 912	11.3	41 279
46	South Dakota	127 542	-3.1	9 370	5.7	13.6	9 364	743	12.6	32 416
47	Tennessee	925 030	11.0	58 357	35.5	15.9	93 680	7 921	11.8	39 677
48	Texas	4 163 447	20.2	282 846	29.0	14.7	227 645	19 777	11.5	40 001
49	Utah	484 677	6.2	22 211	21.3	21.8	12 614	1 091	11.6	38 413
50	Vermont	101 179	4.2	8 554	21.7	11.8	12 170	1 361	8.9	41 603
51	Virginia	1 163 091	14.5	89 314	38.4	13.0	100 171	9 389	10.7	43 152
53	Washington	1 009 200	16.1	52 534	22.4	19.2	76 885	5 697	13.5	44 949
54	West Virginia	282 885	-11.2	20 139	-4.1	14.0	15 895	1 486	10.7	38 508
55	Wisconsin	879 361	7.9	60 918	17.1	14.4	139 455	10 025	13.9	42 871
56	Wyoming	88 128	-14.0	7 026	7.0	12.5	2 221	241	9.2	37 876

[2]Teacher counts are full-time equivalency (FTE) counts.
[3]National Education Association, *Rankings & Estimates Update: Rankings of the States 2002 and Estimates of School Statatistics, 2003*, Table C-11: Average Salaries of Public School Teachers 2001–02, page 19 © NEA; used by permission of the NEA

Table B-1. Population, School, and Student Characteristics by State—Continued

Fips code	State	Staff employed by public elementary and secondary school systems and percentage of total staff, 2001–2002								
		Total staff	Teachers[2]		Instructional aides		Instructional coordinators		Guidance counselors	
			Number	Percent	Number	Percent	Number	Percent	Number	Percent
		49	50	51	52	53	54	55	56	57
00	UNITED STATES	5 902 916	2 997 741	50.8	675 038	11.4	45 934	0.8	100 052	1.7
01	Alabama	88 171	46 796	53.1	6 122	6.9	676	0.8	1 658	1.9
02	Alaska	16 729	8 026	48.0	2 481	14.8	154	0.9	275	1.6
04	Arizona	93 976	46 015	49.0	13 179	14.0	145	0.2	1 215	1.3
05	Arkansas	66 578	33 079	49.7	6 170	9.3	601	0.9	1 459	2.2
06	California	574 559	304 296	53.0	72 554	12.6	6 510	1.1	6 438	1.1
08	Colorado	87 582	44 182	50.4	10 383	11.9	879	1.0	1 277	1.5
09	Connecticut	84 884	41 773	49.2	11 857	14.0	386	0.5	1 279	1.5
10	Delaware	14 172	7 571	53.4	1 332	9.4	166	1.2	240	1.7
11	District of Columbia	11 391	4 951	43.5	1 508	13.2	19	0.2	241	2.1
12	Florida	282 696	134 684	47.6	31 206	11.0	666	0.2	5 547	2.0
13	Georgia	190 054	92 732	48.8	22 625	11.9	1 210	0.6	3 219	1.7
15	Hawaii	19 464	11 007	56.6	1 671	8.6	500	2.6	646	3.3
16	Idaho	24 773	13 854	55.9	2 632	10.6	288	1.2	593	2.4
17	Illinois	255 719	129 600	50.7	32 955	12.9	1 295	0.5	2 983	1.2
18	Indiana	128 938	59 658	46.3	18 337	14.2	1 552	1.2	1 831	1.4
19	Iowa	69 504	34 906	50.2	8 887	12.8	467	0.7	1 230	1.8
20	Kansas	65 155	33 084	50.8	7 153	11.0	136	0.2	1 173	1.8
21	Kentucky	94 826	40 375	42.6	14 302	15.1	742	0.8	1 481	1.6
22	Louisiana	101 552	49 980	49.2	11 094	10.9	1 303	1.3	3 264	3.2
23	Maine	34 072	16 741	49.1	5 705	16.7	198	0.6	643	1.9
24	Maryland	99 282	53 774	54.2	9 361	9.4	863	0.9	2 161	2.2
25	Massachusetts	125 625	68 942	54.9	17 452	13.9	2 633	2.1	2 472	2.0
26	Michigan	214 894	98 849	46.0	25 592	11.9	1 244	0.6	3 136	1.5
27	Minnesota	104 741	53 081	50.7	14 440	13.8	466	0.4	1 056	1.0
28	Mississippi	65 154	31 213	47.9	8 561	13.1	592	0.9	952	1.5
29	Missouri	124 756	65 240	52.3	11 154	8.9	941	0.8	2 673	2.1
30	Montana	19 501	10 408	53.4	2 417	12.4	155	0.8	429	2.2
31	Nebraska	40 541	21 083	52.0	4 479	11.0	350	0.9	777	1.9
32	Nevada	33 967	19 276	56.7	2 652	7.8	185	0.5	693	2.0
33	New Hampshire	29 141	14 677	50.4	5 759	19.8	178	0.6	748	2.6
34	New Jersey	193 337	103 611	53.6	21 474	11.1	1 558	0.8	3 551	1.8
35	New Mexico	44 941	21 823	48.6	5 301	11.8	216	0.5	781	1.7
36	New York	423 199	209 128	49.4	41 660	9.8	2 081	0.5	6 241	1.5
37	North Carolina	166 164	85 684	51.6	27 665	16.6	883	0.5	3 370	2.0
38	North Dakota	14 896	8 035	53.9	1 702	11.4	121	0.8	274	1.8
39	Ohio	230 007	122 115	53.1	14 886	6.5	489	0.2	3 537	1.5
40	Oklahoma	76 405	41 632	54.5	6 594	8.6	199	0.3	1 609	2.1
41	Oregon	57 473	28 402	49.4	8 467	14.7	435	0.8	1 243	2.2
42	Pennsylvania	229 238	118 470	51.7	24 065	10.5	1 460	0.6	4 183	1.8
44	Rhode Island	18 583	11 103	59.7	2 301	12.4	64	0.3	348	1.9
45	South Carolina	71 732	46 616	65.0	10 995	15.3	609	0.8	1 722	2.4
46	South Dakota	18 512	9 370	50.6	2 162	11.7	383	2.1	323	1.7
47	Tennessee	111 926	58 357	52.1	12 661	11.3	1 094	1.0	1 854	1.7
48	Texas	582 555	282 846	48.6	58 283	10.0	1 517	0.3	9 713	1.7
49	Utah	41 111	22 211	54.0	5 496	13.4	622	1.5	666	1.6
50	Vermont	18 050	8 554	47.4	4 007	22.2	278	1.5	399	2.2
51	Virginia	165 249	89 314	54.0	15 725	9.5	1 770	1.1	3 408	2.1
53	Washington	112 021	52 534	46.9	10 044	9.0	4 636	4.1	1 966	1.8
54	West Virginia	37 676	20 139	53.5	3 087	8.2	334	0.9	665	1.8
55	Wisconsin	113 525	60 918	53.7	12 780	11.3	1 581	1.4	2 049	1.8
56	Wyoming	13 919	7 026	50.5	1 663	11.9	104	0.7	361	2.6

[2] Teacher counts are full-time equivalency (FTE) counts.

Table B-1. Population, School, and Student Characteristics by State—*Continued*

Fips code	State	Staff employed by public elementary and secondary school systems and percentage of total staff, 2001–2002									
		Librarians		Support staff		School administrators		School district administrators		School district administrative support staff	
		Number	Percent	Number	Percent	Number	Percent	Number	Percent	Number	Percent
		58	59	60	61	62	63	64	65	66	67
00	UNITED STATES	54 349	0.9	1 392 677	23.6	16 080	6.0	63 351	1.1	41 296	8.0
01	Alabama	1 332	1.5	23 678	26.9	3 307	3.8	1 241	1.4	3 361	3.8
02	Alaska	147	0.9	3 093	18.5	804	4.8	273	1.6	1 476	8.8
04	Arizona	811	0.9	22 941	24.4	2 140	2.3	386	0.4	7 144	7.6
05	Arkansas	1 016	1.5	18 553	27.9	1 734	2.6	673	1.0	3 293	4.9
06	California	1 396	0.2	111 808	19.5	13 225	2.3	2 711	0.5	55 621	9.7
08	Colorado	852	1.0	20 295	23.2	2 289	2.6	932	1.1	6 493	7.4
09	Connecticut	767	0.9	20 439	24.1	2 205	2.6	1 312	1.5	4 866	5.7
10	Delaware	124	0.9	3 365	23.7	359	2.5	262	1.8	753	5.3
11	District of Columbia	119	1.0	3 583	31.5	279	2.4	49	0.4	642	5.6
12	Florida	2 667	0.9	71 093	25.1	6 516	2.3	1 715	0.6	28 602	10.1
13	Georgia	2 114	1.1	51 922	27.3	4 755	2.5	1 764	0.9	9 713	5.1
15	Hawaii	289	1.5	3 642	18.7	517	2.7	139	0.7	1 053	5.4
16	Idaho	188	0.8	5 042	20.4	715	2.9	122	0.5	1 339	5.4
17	Illinois	1 934	0.8	59 350	23.2	6 315	2.5	3 963	1.5	17 324	6.8
18	Indiana	1 065	0.8	34 952	27.1	2 950	2.3	985	0.8	7 608	5.9
19	Iowa	647	0.9	15 419	22.2	2 197	3.2	980	1.4	4 771	6.9
20	Kansas	975	1.5	16 515	25.3	1 754	2.7	1 258	1.9	3 107	4.8
21	Kentucky	1 147	1.2	24 043	25.4	2 461	2.6	1 214	1.3	9 061	9.6
22	Louisiana	1 201	1.2	27 904	27.5	2 585	2.5	398	0.4	3 823	3.8
23	Maine	241	0.7	7 236	21.2	916	2.7	560	1.6	1 832	5.4
24	Maryland	1 112	1.1	23 373	23.5	3 023	3.0	899	0.9	4 716	4.8
25	Massachusetts	823	0.7	20 190	16.1	2 577	2.1	654	0.5	9 882	7.9
26	Michigan	1 612	0.8	66 854	31.1	5 574	2.6	2 084	1.0	9 949	4.6
27	Minnesota	1 015	1.0	21 448	20.5	2 052	2.0	1 909	1.8	9 274	8.9
28	Mississippi	956	1.5	16 387	25.2	1 706	2.6	969	1.5	3 818	5.9
29	Missouri	1 621	1.3	25 865	20.7	2 996	2.4	1 254	1.0	13 012	10.4
30	Montana	359	1.8	3 808	19.5	504	2.6	150	0.8	1 271	6.5
31	Nebraska	565	1.4	9 623	23.7	994	2.5	572	1.4	2 098	5.2
32	Nevada	317	0.9	7 540	22.2	972	2.9	272	0.8	2 060	6.1
33	New Hampshire	286	1.0	5 307	18.2	521	1.8	476	1.6	1 189	4.1
34	New Jersey	1 858	1.0	38 613	20.0	4 790	2.5	1 855	1.0	16 027	8.3
35	New Mexico	283	0.6	10 922	24.3	1 017	2.3	1 250	2.8	3 348	7.4
36	New York	3 180	0.8	117 681	27.8	7 915	1.9	2 954	0.7	32 359	7.6
37	North Carolina	2 289	1.4	39 919	24.0	4 681	2.8	1 601	1.0	72	0.0
38	North Dakota	198	1.3	3 260	21.9	391	2.6	431	2.9	484	3.2
39	Ohio	1 630	0.7	51 310	22.3	5 308	2.3	6 203	2.7	24 529	10.7
40	Oklahoma	1 043	1.4	17 110	22.4	2 043	2.7	723	0.9	5 452	7.1
41	Oregon	582	1.0	11 002	19.1	1 664	2.9	804	1.4	4 874	8.5
42	Pennsylvania	2 217	1.0	57 294	25.0	4 418	1.9	1 578	0.7	15 553	6.8
44	Rhode Island	61	0.3	2 721	14.6	444	2.4	199	1.1	1 342	7.2
45	South Carolina	1 123	1.6	1 562	2.2	3 053	4.3	272	0.4	5 780	8.1
46	South Dakota	167	0.9	4 446	24.0	427	2.3	438	2.4	796	4.3
47	Tennessee	1 506	1.3	23 550	21.0	4 819	4.3	1 117	1.0	6 968	6.2
48	Texas	4 719	0.8	153 550	26.4	28 779	4.9	7 956	1.4	35 192	6.0
49	Utah	311	0.8	7 953	19.3	997	2.4	167	0.4	2 688	6.5
50	Vermont	229	1.3	3 085	17.1	422	2.3	146	0.8	930	5.2
51	Virginia	2 040	1.2	36 003	21.8	4 034	2.4	2 779	1.7	10 176	6.2
53	Washington	1 321	1.2	31 036	27.7	2 709	2.4	1 163	1.0	6 612	5.9
54	West Virginia	393	1.0	9 465	25.1	1 063	2.8	339	0.9	2 191	5.8
55	Wisconsin	1 383	1.2	23 849	21.0	2 567	2.3	949	0.8	7 449	6.6
56	Wyoming	118	0.8	3 078	22.1	323	2.3	251	1.8	995	7.1

Table B-1. Population, School, and Student Characteristics by State—*Continued*

Fips code	State	Highest degree earned and years of experience for teachers in public elementary and secondary schools, 1999–2000						
		Highest degree earned			Years of experience			
		Number of teachers	Bachelor's degree (percent)	Master's degree or higher (percent)	Less than 3 years	3–9 years	10–20 years	20 years or more
		68	69	70	71	72	73	74
00	UNITED STATES	3 002 258	52.0	41.9	12.9	28.8	28.5	29.8
01	Alabama	50 605	41.2	51.2	12.7	28.0	32.3	26.9
02	Alaska	8 340	59.0	36.9	15.6	31.0	34.4	18.9
04	Arizona	48 557	50.8	43.3	16.3	30.2	31.9	21.6
05	Arkansas	30 410	67.4	29.0	10.6	25.4	33.4	30.6
06	California	280 036	61.5	30.3	15.1	33.9	28.3	22.7
08	Colorado	42 352	45.8	50.0	15.6	27.7	27.1	29.6
09	Connecticut	42 178	16.7	65.3	11.5	26.7	26.6	35.2
10	Delaware	7 538	48.7	43.5	11.4	36.3	25.4	26.9
11	District of Columbia	5 712	41.8	46.4	14.6	20.6	23.2	41.6
12	Florida	128 634	61.0	33.6	11.6	30.3	28.8	29.4
13	Georgia	88 161	50.1	37.6	13.0	33.4	27.6	26.0
15	Hawaii	12 112	50.2	23.9	16.0	33.4	24.8	25.8
16	Idaho	14 451	70.3	26.7	13.0	27.3	31.6	28.1
17	Illinois	137 213	46.8	48.9	11.6	27.2	26.5	34.6
18	Indiana	61 184	31.8	63.6	11.1	24.5	23.4	41.1
19	Iowa	38 116	66.0	32.3	10.5	26.2	26.9	36.4
20	Kansas	34 134	60.9	36.8	15.7	25.9	31.3	27.1
21	Kentucky	42 879	27.5	54.0	10.1	31.3	33.5	25.1
22	Louisiana	50 806	63.7	29.3	10.3	30.6	31.0	28.2
23	Maine	17 536	66.3	29.2	10.5	20.3	32.8	36.4
24	Maryland	54 583	45.3	48.5	13.9	30.8	25.3	30.0
25	Massachusetts	78 260	38.6	54.8	11.9	24.9	24.9	38.3
26	Michigan	100 232	42.7	52.2	13.2	30.5	25.3	31.0
27	Minnesota	57 791	54.4	40.8	16.4	28.1	25.0	30.5
28	Mississippi	33 097	58.1	37.0	11.7	24.4	33.5	30.4
29	Missouri	64 094	49.2	46.6	15.1	31.4	26.6	26.9
30	Montana	11 937	70.4	25.7	10.9	25.9	33.4	29.8
31	Nebraska	23 119	59.2	38.8	10.6	25.2	30.5	33.6
32	Nevada	17 273	52.4	43.9	14.9	35.1	25.7	24.3
33	New Hampshire	14 985	51.9	44.4	15.1	22.4	31.5	31.0
34	New Jersey	98 310	58.4	34.7	11.7	25.1	26.0	37.1
35	New Mexico	21 188	56.1	39.1	12.5	38.6	26.5	22.4
36	New York	208 313	21.8	68.4	14.1	25.3	27.6	33.0
37	North Carolina	86 020	67.5	29.5	17.2	28.5	25.2	29.1
38	North Dakota	9 252	77.8	20.0	12.1	25.1	30.4	32.3
39	Ohio	123 370	50.4	45.7	12.0	26.4	29.0	32.6
40	Oklahoma	45 830	63.5	33.3	10.6	30.9	32.1	26.4
41	Oregon	28 584	50.0	46.5	14.0	28.2	32.7	25.1
42	Pennsylvania	126 915	49.5	45.2	9.7	25.2	27.5	37.6
44	Rhode Island	11 616	43.7	51.7	9.4	26.2	30.7	33.8
45	South Carolina	43 754	48.0	43.3	12.0	28.1	31.0	29.0
46	South Dakota	11 708	75.4	23.2	12.9	25.7	35.5	26.0
47	Tennessee	58 296	50.9	41.1	13.9	30.7	27.0	28.4
48	Texas	266 661	69.7	27.1	12.5	32.4	31.2	23.9
49	Utah	23 346	70.4	23.5	15.6	31.5	31.9	21.0
50	Vermont	9 186	49.3	46.1	16.5	24.2	29.1	30.2
51	Virginia	80 987	55.4	40.8	13.3	28.1	28.8	29.8
53	Washington	54 816	46.0	46.8	11.6	28.7	31.6	28.2
54	West Virginia	22 571	37.5	55.6	5.6	14.7	31.0	48.8
55	Wisconsin	67 362	56.5	39.6	12.8	28.7	26.4	32.2
56	Wyoming	7 848	69.8	28.2	10.4	23.5	33.5	32.6

Table B-1. Population, School, and Student Characteristics by State—*Continued*

Fips code	State	National Assessment of Educational Progress: Percentage of public school students at or above the proficient level					Scholastic Assessment Test (SAT) score averages, 2002[4]		
		Math, 2000		Science, 2000		Writing, 2002	Verbal	Math	Percent of graduates taking SAT
		Grade 4	Grade 8	Grade 4	Grade 8	Grade 8			
		75	76	77	78	79	80	81	82
00	UNITED STATES	25	26	28	30	30	504	516	46
01	Alabama	14	16	22	22	20	560	559	9
02	Alaska	...	...	...	...	...	516	519	52
04	Arizona	17	21	22	24	20	520	523	36
05	Arkansas	13	14	24	23	19	560	556	5
06	California	15	18	14	15	23	496	517	52
08	Colorado	...	...	...	...	...	543	548	28
09	Connecticut	32	34	35	35	45	509	509	83
10	Delaware	...	...	...	...	35	502	500	69
11	District of Columbia	6	6	...	...	...	480	473	76
12	Florida	...	...	...	...	32	496	499	57
13	Georgia	18	19	23	23	25	489	491	65
15	Hawaii	14	16	16	15	18	488	520	53
16	Idaho	21	27	30	38	29	539	541	18
17	Illinois	21	27	31	30	...	578	596	11
18	Indiana	31	31	32	35	26	498	503	62
19	Iowa	28	...	37	...	...	591	602	5
20	Kansas	30	34	...	...	32	578	580	9
21	Kentucky	17	21	29	29	25	550	552	12
22	Louisiana	14	12	19	18	18	561	559	8
23	Maine	25	32	38	37	36	503	502	69
24	Maryland	22	29	26	28	35	507	513	67
25	Massachusetts	33	32	43	42	42	512	516	81
26	Michigan	29	28	33	37	24	558	572	11
27	Minnesota	34	40	35	42	...	581	591	10
28	Mississippi	9	8	14	15	13	559	547	4
29	Missouri	23	22	35	36	27	574	580	8
30	Montana	25	37	37	46	29	541	547	23
31	Nebraska	24	31	26	36	32	561	570	8
32	Nevada	16	20	19	23	16	509	518	34
33	New Hampshire	...	...	...	...	...	519	519	73
34	New Jersey	...	...	...	...	...	498	513	82
35	New Mexico	12	13	18	20	18	551	543	14
36	New York	22	26	26	30	30	494	506	79
37	North Carolina	28	30	24	27	34	493	505	67
38	North Dakota	25	31	38	40	24	597	610	4
39	Ohio	26	31	31	41	38	533	540	27
40	Oklahoma	16	19	26	26	27	565	562	8
41	Oregon	23	32	28	33	33	524	528	56
42	Pennsylvania	...	...	...	...	32	498	500	72
44	Rhode Island	23	24	27	29	29	504	503	73
45	South Carolina	18	18	21	20	20	488	493	59
46	South Dakota	...	...	...	...	...	576	586	5
47	Tennessee	18	17	26	25	24	562	555	14
48	Texas	27	24	24	23	31	491	500	55
49	Utah	24	26	32	34	23	563	559	6
50	Vermont	29	32	39	40	41	512	510	69
51	Virginia	25	26	33	31	32	510	506	68
53	Washington	...	...	...	...	34	525	529	54
54	West Virginia	18	18	25	26	21	525	515	18
55	Wisconsin	...	...	...	...	...	583	599	7
56	Wyoming	25	25	33	36	28	531	537	11

[4]"Mean SAT I Verbal and Math Scores by State, with Changes for Selected Years." *College-Bound Seniors, 2002.* Copyright © 2003 by College Board. Reproduced with permission. All rights reserved. <www.collegeboard.com>.

... = Not available.

Table B-1. Population, School, and Student Characteristics by State—*Continued*

Fips code	State	2002 ACT average composite scores[5]		Preliminary SAT (PSAT)/ National Merit Scholarship Qualifying Test (NMSQT) scores, 2002–2003[4]			
		Average score	Percent of graduates taking ACT	Number of high school juniors taking the PSAT/NMSQT	Percent of test-takers achieving scores of 65 or above		
					Verbal	Math	Writing skills
		83	84	85	86	87	88
00	United States	20.8	39	1 364 354	5.9	8.4	7.6
01	Alabama	20.1	71	11 120	6.1	7.7	10.6
02	Alaska	21.3	31	2 410	7.6	7.0	6.4
04	Arizona	21.3	26	15 019	6.4	8.1	8.2
05	Arkansas	20.2	72	6 691	3.9	4.9	9.3
06	California	21.4	13	137 000	6.3	10.1	8.7
08	Colorado	20.1	99	18 273	6.3	8.1	8.6
09	Connecticut	21.6	5	28 324	6.9	9.0	8.9
10	Delaware	21.3	4	4 395	6.7	8.6	7.5
11	District of Columbia	17.5	28	3 972	10.5	10.2	12.5
12	Florida	20.4	39	51 852	6.4	8.8	7.7
13	Georgia	19.8	20	33 687	6.0	8.6	7.8
15	Hawaii	22.0	18	5 734	4.5	11.4	5.8
16	Idaho	21.2	57	4 513	6.0	6.9	7.4
17	Illinois	20.1	99	54 651	6.0	10.2	8.4
18	Indiana	21.5	19	40 339	3.7	5.6	4.7
19	Iowa	22.0	66	10 015	6.0	11.2	8.4
20	Kansas	21.6	76	12 080	6.0	9.2	8.3
21	Kentucky	20.0	72	13 460	5.7	7.5	7.7
22	Louisiana	19.6	79	13 206	5.0	7.2	9.5
23	Maine	22.5	6	8 738	5.2	5.7	5.8
24	Maryland	20.4	11	41 130	6.7	9.1	7.7
25	Massachusetts	21.9	8	45 424	7.8	9.9	9.8
26	Michigan	21.3	68	38 519	5.1	8.2	6.2
27	Minnesota	22.1	65	21 189	7.1	10.9	8.4
28	Mississippi	18.6	84	6 044	4.3	4.7	8.8
29	Missouri	21.5	68	16 194	7.3	10.6	11.0
30	Montana	21.7	52	5 353	4.8	5.6	5.3
31	Nebraska	21.7	72	8 305	3.9	7.7	6.2
32	Nevada	21.3	36	5 134	4.5	7.3	5.8
33	New Hampshire	22.0	7	9 229	6.7	8.6	7.4
34	New Jersey	20.7	5	61 265	6.3	9.9	8.2
35	New Mexico	20.0	63	4 488	6.8	8.0	9.1
36	New York	22.2	14	122 081	5.2	7.4	6.2
37	North Carolina	19.9	13	42 022	4.6	7.1	5.1
38	North Dakota	21.2	78	2 989	3.6	7.6	5.7
39	Ohio	21.4	62	56 168	5.5	8.1	6.9
40	Oklahoma	20.5	69	146 291	6.0	8.3	10.1
41	Oregon	22.5	12	15 527	6.7	8.2	6.6
42	Pennsylvania	21.5	7	74 876	5.5	7.5	7.1
44	Rhode Island	21.9	6	6 155	6.0	7.1	6.8
45	South Carolina	19.2	32	15 511	5.0	7.4	7.1
46	South Dakota	21.4	71	3 773	4.4	6.9	5.3
47	Tennessee	20.0	79	15 503	7.7	8.8	12.4
48	Texas	20.1	32	125 825	4.4	6.6	6.2
49	Utah	21.4	66	4 843	7.2	8.3	10.4
50	Vermont	22.3	10	4 479	6.3	6.9	6.6
51	Virginia	20.6	11	43 704	7.1	7.8	8.0
53	Washington	22.3	16	26 921	7.4	8.6	7.8
54	West Virginia	20.3	61	4 632	4.2	5.8	8.5
55	Wisconsin	22.2	68	22 946	5.6	9.6	7.7
56	Wyoming	21.4	64	2 169	4.1	5.1	5.4

[4]"Mean SAT I Verbal and Math Scores by State, with Changes for Selected Years." *College-Bound Seniors, 2002*. Copyright © 2003 by College Board. Reproduced with permission. All rights reserved. <www.collegeboard.com>.
[5]2000 ACT Composite Averages by State, © 2000 by ACT, Inc. Reprinted with permission.

Table B-1. Population, School, and Student Characteristics by State—*Continued*

Fips code	State	Revenues for public elementary and secondary schools by source, school year 2000–2001					Current expenditures for public elementary and secondary schools, by function, 2000–2001				
		Total revenue ($1,000s)	Percentage from				Total current expenditures ($1,000s)	Percentage for			Per student expenditures
			Local government	Inter-mediate	State government	Federal government		Instruction	Support services	Non-instruction	
		89	90	91	92	93	94	95	96	97	98
00	UNITED STATES	$400 919 024	42.8	0.3	49.7	7.3	$348 170 327	61.5	34.3	4.2	$7 376
01	Alabama	4 812 302	30.5	0.2	59.9	9.4	4 354 794	61.7	31.5	6.8	5 885
02	Alaska	1 370 271	27.1	0.0	57.1	15.8	1 229 036	57.5	39.1	3.4	9 216
04	Arizona	5 797 151	43.1	2.7	43.6	10.6	4 632 539	57.1	36.3	6.6	5 278
05	Arkansas	2 812 169	31.0	0.2	59.6	9.3	2 505 179	61.1	33.3	5.6	5 568
06	California	51 007 510	30.3	0.0	61.5	8.2	42 908 787	62.2	34.0	3.8	6 987
08	Colorado	5 349 899	52.5	0.4	41.5	5.6	4 758 173	57.2	39.2	3.6	6 567
09	Connecticut	6 460 491	56.2	0.0	39.5	4.3	5 693 207	63.9	32.4	3.7	10 127
10	Delaware	1 112 519	26.2	0.0	65.9	7.9	1 027 224	60.8	34.6	4.6	8 958
11	District of Columbia	1 042 711	88.9	0.0	0.0	11.1	830 299	49.7	47.5	2.8	12 046
12	Florida	17 866 868	42.4	0.0	48.7	9.0	15 023 514	58.3	36.8	4.9	6 170
13	Georgia	12 191 113	44.7	0.0	48.9	6.4	10 011 343	63.4	31.4	5.1	6 929
15	Hawaii	1 682 330	1.8	0.0	89.8	8.4	1 215 968	60.2	33.9	5.9	6 596
16	Idaho	1 593 966	30.6	0.0	61.3	8.1	1 403 190	61.3	34.3	4.4	5 725
17	Illinois	18 217 079	58.6	0.0	33.6	7.8	15 658 682	59.7	37.0	3.3	7 643
18	Indiana	9 033 180	40.6	0.7	53.5	5.1	7 548 487	61.6	34.4	4.0	7 630
19	Iowa	3 954 178	44.3	0.2	49.2	6.3	3 430 885	58.6	34.0	7.5	6 930
20	Kansas	3 597 726	30.6	1.8	61.1	6.4	3 258 807	58.6	36.7	4.6	6 925
21	Kentucky	4 509 893	30.1	0.0	59.9	9.9	4 047 392	61.3	33.4	5.3	6 079
22	Louisiana	5 060 133	39.2	0.0	49.4	11.5	4 485 878	60.3	33.2	6.6	6 037
23	Maine	1 934 178	47.5	0.0	44.6	7.9	1 704 422	66.9	29.7	3.4	8 232
24	Maryland	7 846 891	56.6	0.0	37.3	6.1	7 041 586	61.3	33.8	5.0	8 256
25	Massachusetts	10 148 498	51.4	0.0	43.6	5.0	9 272 387	66.3	30.1	3.5	9 509
26	Michigan	16 358 532	28.3	0.0	64.8	6.8	14 243 597	58.4	38.6	3.0	8 278
27	Minnesota	7 873 549	32.1	2.7	60.5	4.7	6 531 198	62.1	33.7	4.1	7 645
28	Mississippi	2 903 534	30.8	0.0	55.4	13.8	2 576 457	60.4	33.1	6.5	5 175
29	Missouri	7 102 501	55.1	0.5	37.5	6.9	6 076 169	60.7	35.0	4.4	6 657
30	Montana	1 140 168	31.9	9.0	47.6	11.5	1 041 760	61.7	34.2	4.1	6 726
31	Nebraska	2 307 804	57.1	0.7	34.9	7.3	2 067 290	62.4	30.2	7.4	7 223
32	Nevada	2 393 494	66.3	0.0	28.6	5.1	1 978 480	62.5	34.3	3.2	5 807
33	New Hampshire	1 714 147	43.9	0.0	51.6	4.5	1 518 792	65.0	31.8	3.2	7 286
34	New Jersey	15 967 075	54.3	0.0	41.8	3.9	14 773 650	59.3	37.7	3.0	11 248
35	New Mexico	2 426 705	15.0	0.0	71.1	13.9	2 022 093	55.6	39.5	4.8	6 313
36	New York	34 266 171	47.6	0.5	46.2	5.7	30 884 292	67.9	29.4	2.7	10 716
37	North Carolina	9 262 181	26.4	0.0	66.3	7.2	8 209 954	63.4	31.0	5.6	6 346
38	North Dakota	767 798	46.4	1.3	39.0	13.4	668 814	59.5	32.2	8.3	6 125
39	Ohio	16 649 361	50.5	0.3	43.2	6.1	13 893 495	58.5	38.0	3.5	7 571
40	Oklahoma	4 034 825	28.9	1.8	59.1	10.2	3 750 542	57.9	35.7	6.4	6 019
41	Oregon	4 564 408	35.0	1.4	56.2	7.4	4 112 069	58.8	37.8	3.4	7 528
42	Pennsylvania	17 053 891	55.6	0.1	37.8	6.5	14 895 316	62.4	33.8	3.8	8 210
44	Rhode Island	1 545 675	51.9	0.0	42.2	5.9	1 465 703	64.5	32.9	2.6	9 315
45	South Carolina	5 459 399	37.9	0.0	53.9	8.2	4 492 161	59.8	34.7	5.5	6 631
46	South Dakota	885 229	50.9	1.6	35.3	12.1	796 133	59.3	35.5	5.2	6 191
47	Tennessee	5 711 950	46.5	0.0	44.3	9.2	5 170 379	64.4	30.6	4.9	5 687
48	Texas	30 469 570	48.9	0.2	42.2	8.7	26 546 557	60.4	34.6	5.0	6 539
49	Utah	2 745 656	34.0	0.0	58.6	7.5	2 250 339	64.7	29.3	6.0	4 674
50	Vermont	1 035 679	23.4	0.0	70.7	5.8	934 031	64.8	32.5	2.7	9 153
51	Virginia	9 313 330	52.1	0.0	42.3	5.6	8 335 805	61.7	34.4	3.9	7 281
53	Washington	8 058 875	29.3	0.0	62.9	7.8	6 782 127	59.4	35.8	4.9	6 750
54	West Virginia	2 375 788	28.6	0.1	61.1	10.2	2 157 568	61.4	32.7	5.8	7 534
55	Wisconsin	8 327 255	41.8	0.0	53.1	5.0	7 249 081	62.0	34.8	3.2	8 243
56	Wyoming	803 414	33.5	7.7	50.2	8.6	704 695	60.5	36.2	3.4	7 835

Table B-1. Population, School, and Student Characteristics by State—*Continued*

Fips code	State	Enrollment in institutions of higher education, fall 1999						Degrees conferred by institutions of higher education, 1999–2000				
		Total	Under-graduate	First profes-sional	Graduate	Public	Private	Associate	Bachelor's	First profes-sional	Master's	Doctorate
		99	100	101	102	103	104	105	106	107	108	109
00	UNITED STATES	14 791 224	12 681 231	303 190	1 806 803	11 309 399	3 481 825	564 933	1 237 875	80 057	457 056	44 808
01	Alabama	223 144	192 026	4 364	26 754	197 173	25 971	8 765	21 293	1 085	8 021	534
02	Alaska	26 948	25 369	. . .	1 579	25 687	1 261	895	1 364	0	517	20
04	Arizona	326 159	285 473	2 328	38 358	276 268	49 891	10 658	20 865	616	10 234	764
05	Arkansas	115 092	105 183	1 675	8 234	103 326	11 766	3 885	9 405	494	2 377	134
06	California	2 017 483	1 778 672	31 729	207 082	1 692 607	324 876	78 360	121 546	8 710	44 257	5 480
08	Colorado	261 744	217 822	3 245	40 677	219 436	42 308	7 720	22 485	866	8 408	796
09	Connecticut	156 907	123 419	3 497	29 991	96 834	60 073	4 298	15 072	951	7 964	667
10	Delaware	46 613	40 507	1 057	5 049	36 895	9 718	1 119	4 665	315	1 450	181
11	District of Columbia	72 118	40 024	8 595	23 499	5 349	66 769	407	6 806	2 602	7 078	603
12	Florida	684 745	602 515	10 576	71 654	540 967	143 778	44 548	51 333	3 144	17 901	2 174
13	Georgia	311 812	263 366	9 821	38 625	237 411	74 401	7 803	29 219	2 437	10 410	1 032
15	Hawaii	62 578	53 991	486	8 101	46 479	16 099	3 266	5 091	131	1 724	171
16	Idaho	64 661	57 316	541	6 804	52 615	12 046	5 040	4 711	174	1 127	105
17	Illinois	733 182	618 649	16 690	97 843	533 522	199 660	26 561	55 036	4 470	26 578	2 498
18	Indiana	304 725	263 888	5 921	34 916	230 810	73 915	11 174	31 970	1 538	8 470	1 215
19	Iowa	186 780	163 729	6 779	16 272	133 753	53 027	9 367	18 750	1 569	3 846	569
20	Kansas	176 737	153 331	2 140	21 266	157 088	19 649	7 288	14 234	685	4 908	418
21	Kentucky	181 626	156 271	5 071	20 284	146 558	35 068	6 492	15 643	1 112	4 795	427
22	Louisiana	221 348	189 412	6 231	25 705	188 573	32 775	5 573	19 844	1 528	5 882	612
23	Maine	57 822	51 122	776	5 924	40 349	17 473	2 208	5 672	215	1 195	49
24	Maryland	268 820	219 172	4 157	45 491	220 809	48 011	7 438	22 089	1 049	10 687	977
25	Massachusetts	419 695	320 370	14 592	84 733	181 514	238 181	10 680	42 308	3 948	24 819	2 283
26	Michigan	558 998	474 676	10 309	74 013	461 825	97 173	18 851	45 754	2 354	20 317	1 496
27	Minnesota	282 756	243 640	6 157	32 959	207 474	75 282	11 030	23 175	1 535	7 797	867
28	Mississippi	133 170	119 395	1 719	12 056	121 369	11 801	6 764	10 988	506	3 263	347
29	Missouri	317 480	263 719	9 911	43 850	199 324	118 156	10 603	30 035	2 573	13 014	791
30	Montana	43 114	40 162	238	2 714	38 336	4 778	1 562	5 171	70	951	65
31	Nebraska	110 806	96 311	3 182	11 313	88 386	22 420	3 893	10 747	794	2 898	363
32	Nevada	89 711	80 834	481	8 396	85 270	4 441	1 988	4 245	53	1 453	115
33	New Hampshire	63 366	53 641	645	9 080	34 927	28 439	3 038	7 776	183	2 438	116
34	New Jersey	330 537	280 649	5 564	44 324	263 752	66 785	12 100	26 939	1 544	9 338	1 001
35	New Mexico	111 896	97 226	1 021	13 649	103 125	8 771	3 783	6 727	226	2 666	271
36	New York	1 020 991	820 973	27 861	172 157	566 306	454 685	50 264	95 558	7 527	47 555	3 783
37	North Carolina	395 907	351 037	7 705	37 165	321 311	74 596	13 505	35 257	1 951	9 636	1 152
38	North Dakota	40 348	37 117	418	2 813	35 940	4 408	2 051	4 877	191	863	58
39	Ohio	548 545	469 558	12 719	66 268	411 541	137 004	19 393	49 849	3 197	16 881	2 124
40	Oklahoma	179 055	155 348	4 066	19 641	155 361	23 694	6 408	15 578	1 001	5 359	437
41	Oregon	175 635	153 373	4 074	18 188	148 177	27 458	6 450	14 428	1 047	4 797	422
42	Pennsylvania	605 283	504 850	17 451	82 982	336 930	268 353	24 350	66 273	4 230	21 988	2 234
44	Rhode Island	74 821	64 370	1 055	9 396	38 650	36 171	3 550	8 402	265	1 864	258
45	South Carolina	183 626	159 408	3 031	21 187	153 496	30 130	6 796	16 033	853	4 533	429
46	South Dakota	42 147	37 384	558	4 205	34 197	7 950	1 833	4 494	195	884	78
47	Tennessee	252 915	219 433	5 617	27 865	193 646	59 269	7 708	22 958	1 518	7 820	724
48	Texas	990 587	867 635	18 566	104 386	862 271	128 316	30 816	75 834	5 288	24 756	2 693
49	Utah	161 591	148 329	1 293	11 969	120 558	41 033	7 867	17 058	382	3 458	350
50	Vermont	36 728	32 237	878	3 613	20 580	16 148	1 594	4 832	233	1 453	65
51	Virginia	377 970	322 241	7 723	48 006	311 536	66 434	11 499	33 599	2 181	11 149	1 122
53	Washington	306 723	278 426	4 420	23 877	263 415	43 308	19 268	24 002	1 075	7 436	647
54	West Virginia	88 657	77 104	1 648	9 905	76 777	11 880	3 049	8 545	376	2 465	134
55	Wisconsin	304 776	270 684	4 180	29 912	249 608	55 168	9 381	27 543	951	6 999	884
56	Wyoming	29 002	26 500	429	2 073	27 944	1 058	1 994	1 797	119	377	73

. . . = Not available.

Table B-1. Population, School, and Student Characteristics by State—*Continued*

Fips code	State	Educational attainment, 2000			Enrollment, 2000						Dropouts, 2000	
		Population 25 years and over	High school graduates (percent)	Bachelor's degree or more (percent)	Total enrollment		K–12 enrollment		College enrollment		Total population 16–19 years	Not high school graduate, not enrolled (percent)
					Number	Percent public	Number	Percent public	Number	Percent public		
		110	111	112	113	114	115	116	117	118	119	120
00	**UNITED STATES**	182 211 639	80.4	24.4	76 632 927	83.6	54 192 083	89.3	17 483 262	74.6	15 930 458	9.8
01	Alabama	2 887 400	75.3	19.0	1 155 504	86.1	837 350	89.4	243 275	85.3	255 315	12.0
02	Alaska	379 556	88.3	24.7	185 760	89.9	142 653	93.2	32 303	85.3	38 321	8.7
04	Arizona	3 256 184	81.0	23.5	1 401 840	89.4	988 818	93.6	331 099	84.5	288 587	14.8
05	Arkansas	1 731 200	75.3	16.7	675 109	89.3	503 693	92.6	128 063	85.2	156 258	9.5
06	California	21 298 900	76.8	26.6	10 129 990	85.9	7 026 326	90.5	2 556 598	80.3	1 925 479	10.1
08	Colorado	2 776 632	86.9	32.7	1 166 004	86.1	804 108	91.2	282 832	80.2	243 396	12.1
09	Connecticut	2 295 617	84.0	31.4	910 869	80.3	639 968	89.5	204 212	61.8	169 277	7.4
10	Delaware	514 658	82.6	25.0	209 979	78.2	143 780	82.7	51 407	74.4	44 154	10.3
11	District of Columbia	384 535	77.8	39.1	157 475	67.3	88 568	84.9	59 498	41.0	32 400	10.1
12	Florida	11 024 645	79.9	22.3	3 933 279	82.8	2 775 141	88.5	886 825	76.2	794 066	11.9
13	Georgia	5 185 965	78.6	24.3	2 211 688	85.6	1 598 291	91.3	436 555	75.2	471 799	13.5
15	Hawaii	802 477	84.6	26.2	320 842	79.5	223 185	84.5	79 748	74.0	64 343	5.8
16	Idaho	787 505	84.7	21.7	368 579	87.8	270 423	93.0	77 392	79.2	87 734	8.2
17	Illinois	7 973 671	81.4	26.1	3 450 604	80.8	2 387 464	86.9	810 038	69.4	704 632	9.9
18	Indiana	3 893 278	82.1	19.4	1 603 554	83.4	1 142 156	88.7	352 687	76.4	360 606	9.8
19	Iowa	1 895 856	86.1	21.2	792 057	84.6	552 637	90.3	187 306	74.0	178 931	5.8
20	Kansas	1 701 207	86.0	25.8	756 960	86.5	529 202	89.6	176 453	85.3	166 014	8.0
21	Kentucky	2 646 397	74.1	17.1	1 007 452	85.3	738 747	88.3	206 367	81.2	228 979	11.5
22	Louisiana	2 775 468	74.8	18.7	1 271 299	81.1	923 702	83.1	258 000	81.7	289 111	11.7
23	Maine	869 893	85.4	22.9	321 041	85.7	236 267	92.2	67 216	71.0	69 770	6.2
24	Maryland	3 495 595	83.8	31.4	1 475 484	79.6	1 024 955	85.1	354 477	72.9	277 834	8.4
25	Massachusetts	4 273 275	84.8	33.2	1 726 111	74.0	1 129 778	88.4	473 403	46.7	330 827	6.6
26	Michigan	6 415 941	83.4	21.8	2 780 378	86.2	1 971 459	89.4	635 836	82.5	566 976	8.7
27	Minnesota	3 164 345	87.9	27.4	1 362 507	84.2	975 733	89.6	296 258	72.9	293 223	5.9
28	Mississippi	1 757 517	72.9	16.9	789 903	87.2	582 848	89.5	152 997	86.7	184 029	12.2
29	Missouri	3 634 906	81.3	21.6	1 479 573	81.5	1 057 556	86.8	319 515	71.8	323 992	10.2
30	Montana	586 621	87.2	24.4	241 754	89.8	176 805	92.7	51 255	88.0	55 369	7.9
31	Nebraska	1 087 241	86.6	23.7	480 705	82.8	338 004	86.5	112 315	79.0	107 180	7.0
32	Nevada	1 310 176	80.7	18.2	492 885	90.9	366 909	94.7	98 631	86.5	98 513	16.0
33	New Hampshire	823 987	87.4	28.7	332 888	79.4	237 188	89.1	74 832	60.2	67 668	7.3
34	New Jersey	5 657 799	82.1	29.8	2 217 832	78.2	1 566 107	86.3	470 302	65.4	408 187	7.2
35	New Mexico	1 134 801	78.9	23.5	533 786	89.2	384 924	91.7	120 265	86.8	113 028	12.1
36	New York	12 542 536	79.1	27.4	5 217 030	76.4	3 584 279	85.9	1 301 375	57.0	1 017 375	8.7
37	North Carolina	5 282 994	78.1	22.5	2 043 225	86.2	1 445 635	92.0	462 275	78.5	428 384	12.5
38	North Dakota	408 585	83.9	22.0	179 667	91.1	123 939	93.3	47 003	89.2	43 073	4.8
39	Ohio	7 411 740	83.0	21.1	3 014 460	82.1	2 157 981	86.6	652 393	75.1	639 825	8.3
40	Oklahoma	2 203 173	80.6	20.3	930 865	89.4	667 503	93.4	203 262	82.3	213 273	9.9
41	Oregon	2 250 998	85.1	25.1	876 492	86.0	621 408	90.6	204 811	81.7	191 546	10.4
42	Pennsylvania	8 266 284	81.9	22.4	3 135 934	76.5	2 228 837	84.6	703 163	59.7	672 849	7.1
44	Rhode Island	694 573	78.0	25.6	290 605	75.6	190 389	87.1	84 009	55.0	61 409	8.2
45	South Carolina	2 596 010	76.3	20.4	1 053 152	85.9	767 586	90.4	216 839	79.4	235 984	11.1
46	South Dakota	474 359	84.6	21.5	208 229	88.6	152 642	92.6	42 894	82.0	49 305	7.9
47	Tennessee	3 744 928	75.9	19.6	1 415 105	85.1	1 037 539	90.1	287 550	75.9	312 760	9.8
48	Texas	12 790 893	75.7	23.2	5 948 260	88.6	4 355 276	93.1	1 202 890	82.6	1 289 185	12.5
49	Utah	1 197 892	87.7	26.1	741 524	87.1	508 724	95.7	186 743	72.3	173 747	8.7
50	Vermont	404 223	86.4	29.4	164 156	81.9	114 318	91.6	40 318	60.4	36 432	5.9
51	Virginia	4 666 574	81.5	29.5	1 868 101	83.8	1 291 600	90.4	450 800	76.3	382 918	7.7
53	Washington	3 827 507	87.1	27.7	1 584 701	86.3	1 127 448	91.1	358 414	81.7	335 082	8.7
54	West Virginia	1 233 581	75.2	14.8	418 553	91.0	304 216	94.7	92 329	84.6	99 445	9.0
55	Wisconsin	3 475 878	85.1	22.4	1 463 038	82.7	1 049 456	85.8	328 537	79.7	319 738	6.4
56	Wyoming	315 663	87.9	21.9	136 139	92.9	98 562	95.6	29 697	91.2	32 130	7.5

NOTES AND DEFINITIONS: STATE EDUCATION STATISTICS

This section provides details about each item's source and relevant definitions. Where available, Internet references are provided. In some cases, the Internet reference will not lead to the precise data included in this volume, but to the general category. Often additional data sources were used, such as the Census Bureau's online FER-RET (Federal Electronic Research and Review Extraction Tool), or CD-ROM databases from the National Center for Education Statistics (NCES.)

POPULATION (ITEMS 1–2)
Source: U.S. Bureau of the Census, Population Estimates Program.

The population data for 2000 are U.S. Bureau of the Census counts for the resident population as of April 1, 2000.

Internet:
<http://www.census.gov/main/www/cen2000.html>

INCOME, POVERTY, AND HEALTH INSURANCE (ITEMS 3–7)
Source: U.S. Bureau of the Census, *Current Population Survey*, March 1999, 2000, 2001

The data on income are derived from the responses of a national sample of persons 15 years and older in about 50,000 households. Total money income is defined by the Bureau of the Census for statistical purposes as the sum of the following: wage or salary income; non-farm self-employment income; Social Security and railroad retirement income; public assistance income; and all other regularly received income such as interest, dividends, veterans payments, pensions, unemployment compensation, and alimony. Receipts not counted as income include various "lump sum" payments such as capital gains or inheritances. The total represents the amount of income received before deductions for personal income taxes, Social Security, bond purchases, union dues, Medicare deductions, etc.

Family income includes the income of all family members 15 years and older. Median family income is usually higher than median household income because many households consist of only one person. The median divides the income distribution into two equal parts, one having incomes above the median, the other with incomes below.

Poverty status is based on the definition prescribed by the U.S. Office of Management and Budget as the standard to be used by federal agencies for statistical purposes. Families are classified as below the poverty level (or "in poverty") if their total family income was less than the poverty threshold specified for the applicable family size, age of householder, and number of related children under 18 years present in the family. The poverty threshold for a 4-person family with two children under 18 years was 17,960 in 2001. Children were defined as low-income if their family's income was less than 200% of the poverty threshold.

Persons lacking health insurance coverage include those who were covered neither by private health plans nor by Medicaid, Medicare, or a military health plan.

Internet:
<http://www.census.gov/hhes/www/income.html>
<http://www.census.gov/hhes/www/poverty01.html>
<http://www.census.gov/hhes/hlthins/liuc01.html>

EDUCATIONAL ATTAINMENT (ITEMS 8–10)
Source: U.S. Bureau of the Census, *Current Population Survey*, March 2002

The data on educational attainment are derived from the responses of a national sample of persons in about 50,000 households. Statistics for educational attainment include only persons 25 years or older. Respondents were asked for the highest grade of school they had attended or the highest degree they had received. Persons who passed a high school equivalency examination were considered high school graduates. Schooling received in foreign schools was to be reported as the equivalent grade or years in the regular American school system.

Internet:
<http://www.census.gov/population/www/socdemo/educ-attn.html>

SCHOOL DISTRICTS (ITEM 11)

Source: U.S. Department of Education, National Center for Education Statistics, Common Core of Data, 2001–2002.

A School District or Local Education Agency (LEA) is an education agency at the local level that exists primarily to operate public schools or to contract for public school services. A public school is controlled and operated by publicly elected or appointed officials and derives its primary support from public funds.

The state numbers are from the CCD state universe and include 14,559 regular school districts with students in membership. Not included are special districts which typically offer research, administrative, or other support services to client agencies.

Internet:
<http://nces.ed.gov/ccd/>

NUMBER OF SCHOOLS AND STUDENTS (ITEMS 12–24)

Source: U.S. Department of Education, National Center for Education Statistics, Common Core of Data, 2000–2001.

The state data are from the CCD state universe as published in NCES' *Overview of Public Elementary and Secondary Schools and Districts: School Year 2001–2002*. There are 91,380 schools represented, including all those that reported membership in 2000–2001.

Regular schools do not focus primarily on special, vocational, or alternative education, although they may offer these programs in addition to the regular curriculum. A special education school focuses primarily on special education, with materials and instructional approaches adapted to meet the students' needs. A vocational education school focuses primarily on vocational, technical or career education and provides education or training in at least one semiskilled or technical occupation. An alternative education school addresses the needs of students that typically cannot be met in the regular school setting, and provides nontraditional education.

Primary schools are those with a low grade of prekindergarten through grade 3 and a high grade of up to 8. Middle schools are those with a low grade of 4 through 7 and a high grade ranging from 4 to 9. High schools have a low grade of 7 to 12 and must extend through grade 12. All other grade configurations, including schools that are completely ungraded, are included only in the totals, but not in the percent distributions.

Internet:
<http://nces.ed.gov/ccd/>

STUDENTS WHO ARE ELIGIBLE FOR FREE OR REDUCED PRICE MEALS (ITEM 25)

Source: U.S. Department of Education, National Center for Education Statistics, Common Core of Data, 2001–2002.

The Free and Reduced-Price Lunch Program is a program under the National School Lunch Act that provides cash subsidies for free or reduced-price meals to students based on family size and income criteria. Because participation in the Free and Reduced-Price Lunch Program depends on income, eligibility is often used to estimate student needs.

The state counts of students eligible for free or reduced price meals are from the NCES *Overview of Public Elementary and Secondary Schools and Districts: School Year 2001–2002*. A state is considered to have missing data if free-lunch-eligibility is reported by less than 70 percent of the schools in the state.

Internet:
<http://nces.ed.gov/ccd/>

STUDENTS WITH INDIVIDUAL EDUCATION PROGRAMS (ITEM 26)

Source: U.S. Department of Education, National Center for Education Statistics, Common Core of Data, 2001–2002.

An Individualized Education Program (IEP) is a written instructional plan for students with disabilities designated as special education students under IDEA (Individuals with Disabilities Education Act). This includes a statement of present levels of educational performance of a child; a statement of annual goals, including short-term instructional objectives; a statement of specific educational services to be provided and the extent to which the child will be able to participate in regular educational programs; a projected date for initiation and anticipated duration of services; appropriate objectives, criteria and evaluation procedures; and schedules for determining, on at least an annual basis, whether instructional objectives are being achieved.

IEP counts for the states are from the NCES *Overview of Public Elementary and Secondary Schools and Districts: School Year 2001–2002.*

Internet:
<http://nces.ed.gov/ccd/>

RACE AND HISPANIC ORIGIN (ITEMS 27–31)
Source: U.S. Department of Education, National Center for Education Statistics, Common Core of Data, 2001–2002.

The race/ethnicity categories used in the CCD are those approved, at the time these data were collected, by the federal Office of Management and Budget. They are mutually exclusive. The state data are aggregated from the CCD school universe file, as published in *Public School Student, Staff, and Graduate Counts by State: School Year: 2001–2002.*

Internet:
<http://nces.ed.gov/ccd/>

DROPOUTS (ITEM 32)
Source: U.S. Department of Education, National Center for Education Statistics, Common Core of Data, 1999–2000.

A dropout is a student who was enrolled in school at some time during the previous school year; was not enrolled at the beginning of the current school year; has not graduated from high school or completed a state or district-approved educational program; and does not meet any of the following exclusionary conditions: has transferred to another public school district, private school, or state- or district-approved educational program; is temporarily absent due to suspension or school-approved illness; or has died.

The state data are from the CCD agency universe as published in the NCES report *Public High School Dropouts and Completers from the Common Core of Data: School Years 1998–1999 and 1999–2000.* Most of the states that reported on dropouts used an October through September cycle but the following states reported on students who dropped out between July and the following June: Alabama, Alaska, Illinois, Maryland, New Jersey, Oklahoma, South Dakota, Tennessee, Vermont, and Virginia. Oregon dropout counts erroneously included students that were completers, these students account for approximately 0.2 percent of Oregon's dropout counts.

Internet:
<http://nces.ed.gov/ccd/>

MEMBERSHIP AND GRADUATES (ITEMS 33–35)
Source: U.S. Department of Education, National Center for Education Statistics, Common Core of Data, 2001–2002.

The data are from the CCD state universe as published in *Public School Student, Staff, and Graduate Counts by State, 2001–2002.* The number of graduates includes individuals who received a regular diploma, individuals who received a diploma from other than the regular school program, and individuals who received a certificate of attendance or other certificate of completion in lieu of a diploma during the previous school year and subsequent summer school. Recipients of high school equivalency certificates are not included.

Internet:
<http://nces.ed.gov/ccd/>

HIGH SCHOOL COMPLETION RATES (ITEM 36)
Source: U.S. Bureau of the Census, Current Population Survey, October 1998, 1999, 2000

The data on high school completion are derived from the responses of a national sample of persons in about 50,000 households. The high school completion rate, as published in the NCES report *Dropout Rates in the United States: 2000*, represents the proportion of the population 18 through 24 years who have completed a high school diploma or an equivalent credential, including a General Educational Development (GED) credential.

The educational attainment and high school completion status data from the October CPS supplement were used to measure high school completion rates. The completion rate is for the young adult population in the years beyond high school—that is, the population 18 through 24 years. These rates are reported at the state level, using a 3- year average to yield more stable estimates for completion rates. State completion rates reflect the experiences of the population 18 through 24 years living in the state at the time of the interview; thus, movements in and out of states to accommodate employment and postsecondary education may be evident in some states. For example, a state with a relatively large unskilled labor employment sector might have a lower high school completion rate than anticipated due to an influx of young workers. Conversely, a state with a disproportionate number of colleges and universities might have a higher high school completion rate than anticipated due to an influx of postsecondary students.

Internet:
<http://nces.ed.gov/ccd/>

PRIVATE SCHOOLS (ITEMS 37–39)
Source: U.S. Department of Education, National Center for Education Statistics, *Private School Universe Survey*, 1999–2000.

Private schools, enrollment and graduate estimates are published by NCES in *Private School Universe Survey, 1999–2000*. The *Private School Universe Survey* (PSS) is designed to collect data from all private schools in the 50 states and the District of Columbia. The survey was conducted in 1999–2000 by the U. S. Bureau of the Census for NCES. The counts presented are estimates derived from an area frame as well as a census of lists. Although the *Private School Survey* has begun to collect limited data on the many private schools for which kindergarten is the highest grade, the data in this volume are for schools (traditional schools) which include at least one grade between 1 and 12.

A private school is controlled by an individual or agency other than a state, a subdivision of a state, or the federal government; is usually supported primarily by other than public funds; and the operation of its program rests with other than publicly elected or appointed officials. Private institutions include both nonprofit and propriety institutions.

Internet:
<http://nces.ed.gov/surveys/pss/>

STUDENT/TEACHER RATIOS (ITEMS 40–47)
Source: U.S. Department of Education, National Center for Education Statistics, Common Core of Data, 2001–2002 for public schools; *Private School Universe Survey*, 1999–2000 for private schools.

The public school numbers are from the CCD state universe, as published in *Public School Student, Staff, and Graduate Counts by State, 2000–2001*. Teacher counts measure the full-time equivalent teachers, including teachers who are employed by agencies and not assigned to specific schools. The student/teacher ratio is calculated by dividing the number of students in all schools by the number of full-time equivalent teachers employed by all schools and agencies.

The private school numbers are from the PSS, as published in *Private School Universe Survey, 1999–2000*. These estimates measure full-time equivalent teachers. The student/teacher ratio is calculated by dividing the number of students enrolled in all schools by the number of full-time equivalent teachers employed by all schools.

Internet:
<http://nces.ed.gov/ccd/>
<http://nces.ed.gov/surveys/pss/>

TEACHER SALARIES (ITEM 48)
Source: National Education Association, Rankings & Estimates database, as shown in *Rankings & Estimates Update, Fall 2002*. Copyright 2002, NEA, Washington, DC. All rights reserved. Reprinted with permission.

The National Education Association publishes average teacher salaries by state in its annual

Estimates of School Statistics. The information is compiled from surveys conducted at the state departments of education. In the fall/winter of each year, NEA Research submits current-year estimates of more than 35 educational statistics to each state's department of education for verification or revision. The figures submitted by NEA Research result from regression analysis, a statistical technique designed to make projections using data from prior years. Only if an education department does not replace these projections with its own estimated data does the NEA use regression- generated figures in its report. In the numbers used in this volume, the following states' estimates were based on the regression analysis: Alabama, Arizona, Michigan, Nevada, New Jersey, and Rhode Island.

The average salary is for public school teachers and is defined as the arithmetic mean of the salaries of the group described. This figure is the average gross salary before deductions for Social Security, retirement, health insurance, etc.

Internet:
<http://www.nea.org/publiced/edstats/salaries.html>

PUBLIC SCHOOL STAFF (ITEMS 49–67)
Source: U.S. Department of Education, National Center for Education Statistics, Common Core of Data, 2001–2002.

The public school staff data are from the CCD state universe, as published in *Public School Student, Staff, and Graduate Counts by State: School Year 2001–2002.* The number of teachers represents full time equivalent teachers employed within the state. Instructional Aides directly assisted teachers in providing instruction. Instructional Coordinators helped teachers through curriculum development and in-service training. Support staff includes food, health, library, maintenance, transportation, security, and other services in public schools. School administrators are principals and assistant principals. School District Administrators include the Local Education Agency superintendents, deputies, assistant superintendents, and other persons with district-wide responsibilities.

Internet:
<http://nces.ed.gov/ccd/>

CHARACTERISTICS OF TEACHERS (ITEMS 68–74)
Source: U.S. Department of Education, National Center for Education Statistics, *Schools and Staffing Survey, 1999–2000.*

The highest degree earned and years of experience are from the 1999–2001 Schools and Staffing Survey, as published in the *Digest of Education Statistics, 2002.*

The Schools and Staffing Survey is a set of linked questionnaires that covers public school districts, public and private schools, principals, and teachers as its core components. The SASS data are collected through a sample survey of schools, the school districts associated with sample schools, school principals, and teachers. The 1999–2000 SASS estimates are based on a sample of approximately 13,500 schools (9,900 public and 3,600 private); 67,000 teachers (56,000 public and 11,000 private); and 5,500 public school districts.

Internet:
<http://nces.ed.gov/surveys/sass/>

NATIONAL ASSESSMENT OF EDUCATIONAL PROGRESS (ITEMS 75–79)
Source: U.S. Department of Education, National Center for Education Statistics, National Assessment of Educational Progress, 2000 and 2002.

The National Assessment of Educational Progress (NAEP) is a congressionally mandated project of the National Center for Education Statistics (NCES) that has, for more than a quarter of a century, continually collected and reported information on what American students know and can do. It is the nation's only ongoing, comparable, and representative assessment of student achievement. Its assessments are based on a national probability sample of public and nonpublic school students enrolled in grades 4, 8, or 12. Results are provided only for group performance. NAEP is forbidden by law to report results at an individual or school level. The assessment questions are written around a framework prepared for each content area—reading, writing, mathematics, science and others—that represents the consensus of groups of curriculum experts, educators, and members of the general public on what should be covered in such a test.

In response to legislation passed by Congress in 1988, the NAEP program includes voluntary state- by- state assessments. To help ensure valid state-by-state results, NCES applies minimum school and student participation rate standards for its reporting activities. Results are not reported for jurisdictions that failed to meet these standards.

This volume includes the proportion of students in specific grades whose NAEP mathematics, science, and writing assessment results were designated to be "proficient" or better for their grades. The achievement level results describe what students participating in the NAEP assessment should know and be able to do. The National Assessment Governing Board (NAGB) adopted three achievement levels: Basic, Proficient, and Advanced. The Basic level denotes partial mastery of fundamental knowledge and skills. The Proficient level defines solid academic performance that demonstrates competency in challenging subject matter, and the Advanced level signifies superior performance. The achievement levels are based on collective judgments, gathered from a broadly representative panel of teachers, education specialists, and members of the general public, about what students should know and be able to do relative to a body of content reflected in the NAEP assessment framework.

Internet:
<http://nces.ed.gov/nationsreportcard/>

SCHOLASTIC ASSESSMENT TEST SCORES (ITEMS 80–82)

Source: *SAT Averages by State for 1990 and 1997–2000*, copyright 2002 by the College Entrance Exam Board. Reprinted with permission. All rights reserved.
<www.collegeboard.com>. Number of high school graduates as projected by the Western Interstate Commission for Higher Education, *Knocking at the College Door: Projections of High School Graduates by State and Race/Ethnicity, 1996–2012*, copyright 1998 by the Western Interstate Commission for Higher Education. All rights reserved.

The Scholastic Assessment Test (SAT) is an examination administered by the Educational Testing Service and used to predict the facility with which an individual will progress in learning college-level academic subjects.

The *Profile of College-Bound Seniors* presents data for 2002 high school graduates who participated in the SAT Program during their high school years. Students are counted once no matter how often they tested, and only their latest scores are summarized.

The College Entrance Examination Board cautions that relationships between test scores and other factors such as educational background, gender, racial/ethnic background, parental education, and household income are complex and interdependent. These factors do not directly affect test performance; rather, they are associated with educational experiences both on tests such as the SAT I and in school work. Moreover, not all students in a high school, school district, or state take the SAT I. Since the population of test takers is self-selected, using aggregate SAT I scores to compare or evaluate teachers, schools, districts, states, or other educational units is not valid, and the College Board strongly discourages such uses.

Interpreting SAT I scores for states requires unique considerations. The most significant factor to consider in interpreting SAT I scores for any group, or subgroup, of test takers is the proportion of students taking the test. For example, it is important to recognize that in some states there are lower participation rates. Typically, test takers in these low participation states have strong academic backgrounds and apply to the nation's most selective colleges and scholarship programs. For these states, it is expected that the SAT I mean scores reported for students will be higher than the national average.

Internet:
<http://www.collegeboard.com/prod_downloads/about/news_info/cbsenior/yr2002/pdf/table3.pdf>

ACT ASSESSMENT AVERAGE COMPOSITE SCORES (ITEMS 83 AND 84)

Source: 2002 ACT Composite Averages by State, copyright 2002 by ACT, Inc. Totals for graduating seniors were obtained from *Projections of High School Graduates by State and Race/Ethnicity 1996–2012*, copyright 1998 by the Western Interstate Commission for Higher Education. All rights reserved.

Founded in 1959 as the American College Testing Program, ACT, Inc. is an independent, not-for-profit organization that provides more than a hundred assessment, research, information, and program management services in the broad areas of educational planning, career planning, and workforce development. The ACT Assessment is designed to assess high school students' general educational development and their ability to complete college-level work. The tests cover four skill areas: English, mathematics, reading, and science reasoning. These data are based on all high school graduates of the class of 2002 who took the ACT Assessment during their sophomore, junior or senior year. For students who took the test more than once, only the most recent scores are used. Those students who tested on campus, used extended time testing or failed to list a valid high school code are not included.

College-bound students who take the ACT Assessment are not representative of college-bound students nationally. First, students who live in the Midwest, the Mountain West, the Plains, and the South are overrepresented among ACT-tested students as compared with college-bound students nationally. Second, ACT-tested students tend to enroll in public college and universities more frequently than do college-bound students nationally.

Caution should be used in comparing state and national norms. State norms may differ from national norms for non-educational reasons such as the representativeness of the ACT-tested population and the demographic makeup of a state.

Internet:
<http://www.act.org/news/data/02/states.html>

PRELIMINARY SAT (PSAT)/NATIONAL MERIT SCHOLARSHIP QUALIFYING TEST (NMSQT) (ITEMS 85–88)
Source: *PSAT scores as published by the College Entrance Examination Board, PSAT/NMSQT® 2002 State Summary Reports*, copyright 2003 by collegeboard.com. Reproduced with permission. All rights reserved.

The PSAT/NMSQT (Preliminary SAT/National Merit Scholarship Qualifying Test) is a program

co-sponsored by the College Board and National Merit Scholarship Corporation. The test serves several functions, including: help assess skills necessary for college-level work, prepare for the SAT, enter the competition for national scholarships (including the National Merit Scholarship Corporation scholarship programs), and receive educational and financial aid information from colleges, universities, and scholarship programs.

Verbal, math, and writing skills scores are each reported on a 20-80 scale. The average scores of juniors are between 47 and 49. Unless students earn scores that are much lower than average, they're probably developing the kinds of critical reading, math problem-solving, and writing skills needed for academic success in college.

The total of the verbal, math, and writing skills scores is the Selection Index used by National Merit Scholarship Corporation to designate groups to be honored in its scholarship programs. The qualifying score varies from state to state, depending on the proportion of test-takers in each state. Scores between 65 and 80 on each skill mark the approximate level of the top students who may qualify. In states with higher percentages of scores in this range, a student must achieve a higher Selection Index to be a designated a semifinalist.

Internet:
<www.collegeboard.com/research/html/2002_psat.html>

REVENUES (ITEMS 89–93)
Source: U.S. Department of Education, National Center for Education Statistics, Common Core of Data, Fiscal Year 2001.

The data are from the National Public Education Financial Survey data file for fiscal year 2001 (school year 2000–2001.) The state data include adjustments made by NCES. Values that were missing and not reported elsewhere in the survey were imputed based on proportions in reporting states. Other adjustments were made when a single value was reported that included two or more categories. NCES distributed portions of the single reported value to the missing items. Revenues from federal sources include direct grants-in-aid from the federal government; federal grants-in-aid through the state or an intermediate agency; and other revenue in lieu of taxes to compensate a school district for nontaxable federal institutions within a district's boundaries.

Revenues from state government sources include those that can be used without restriction; those for categorical purposes; and revenues in lieu of taxation. Included are revenues from payments made by a state for the benefit of the Local Education Agency (LEA) or contributions of equipment or supplies. Such revenues include the payment of a pension fund by the state on behalf of an LEA employee for services rendered to the LEA and contributions of fixed assets (property, plant, and equipment) such as school buses and textbooks.

Revenues from local sources include local property and non-property tax revenues; taxes levied or assessed by an LEA; revenues from a local government to the LEA; tuition received; transportation fees; earnings on investments from LEA holdings; net revenues from food services (gross receipts less gross expenditures); net revenues from student activities (gross receipts less gross expenditures); and other revenues (textbook sales, donations, property rentals).

Intermediate revenues come from sources that are not local or state education agencies, but operate at an intermediate level between local and state education agencies and possess independent fund-raising capability.

Internet:
<http://nces.ed.gov/ccd/>

EXPENDITURES (ITEMS 94–98)
Source: U.S. Department of Education, National Center for Education Statistics, Common Core of Data, Fiscal Year 2001.

The data are from the National Public Education Financial Survey data file for fiscal year 2001 (school year 2000–2001). The state data include adjustments made by NCES. Values that were missing and not reported elsewhere in the survey were imputed based on proportions in reporting states. Other adjustments were made when a single value was reported that included two or more

categories. NCES distributed portions of the single reported value to the missing items.

Current expenditures are defined as expenditures for the categories of instruction, support services, and non-instructional services for salaries, employee benefits, purchased services and supplies; and payments by the state made for or on behalf of school systems. This does not include expenditures for debt service and capital outlay, and property (equipment); or direct costs (Head Start, adult education, community colleges, etc.) and community services expenditures.

Instructional expenses are current expenditures for activities dealing directly with the interaction between students and teachers. These include teacher salaries and benefits, supplies such as textbooks, and purchased instructional services.

Support services expenditures are current expenditures for activities which support instruction. These services include operation and maintenance of buildings, school administration, student support services (nurses, therapists, and guidance counselors), student transportation, instructional staff support (librarians, instructional specialists), school district administration, business services, research, and data processing.

Noninstructional expenditures are mostly for food service with some expenditures for enterprise operations such as bookstores and interscholastic athletics.

Current expenditures per student were derived by dividing total current expenditures by the fall 1999 student membership count from the CCD. Student membership is the count of students enrolled on or about October 1 and is comparable across all states.

Internet:
<http://nces.ed.gov/ccd/>

HIGHER EDUCATION (ITEMS 99–109)
Source: U.S. Department of Education, National Center for Education Statistics, Integrated Postsecondary Education Data System (IPEDS), "Fall Enrollment 2000" for enrollment data, and "Completions" for degrees conferred.

The Integrated Postsecondary Education Data System (IPEDS) surveys approximately 10,000 postsecondary institutions, including universities and colleges, as well as institutions offering technical and vocational education beyond the high school level. This survey, which began in 1986, replaced the Higher Education General Information Survey (HEGIS). IPEDS consists of eight integrated components that obtain information on who provides postsecondary education (institutions), who participates in it and completes it (students), what programs are offered and what programs are completed, and both the human and financial resources involved in the provision of institutionally based postsecondary education. Specifically, these components include: Institutional Characteristics, including instructional activity; Fall Enrollment, including age and residence; Enrollment in Occupationally Specific Programs; Completions; Finance; Staff; Salaries of Full-Time Instructional Faculty; and Academic Libraries.

Institutions of Higher Education include those institutions that have courses leading to an associate degree or higher, or are accepted for credit toward those degrees. A public institution is controlled and operated by publicly elected or appointed officials and derives its primary support from public funds. A private institution is controlled by an individual or agency other than a state, a subdivision of a state, or the federal government; is usually supported primarily by other than public funds; and the operation of its program rests with other than publicly elected or appointed officials. Private institutions include both nonprofit and proprietary institutions.

Undergraduate students are those registered at an institution of higher education who are working in a program leading to a baccalaureate degree or other formal award below the baccalaureate, such as an associate degree.

An associate degree is a degree granted for the successful completion of a sub-baccalaureate program of studies, usually requiring at least 2 years (or equivalent) of full-time college-level study. This includes degrees granted in a cooperative or work-study program.

A bachelor's degree is a degree granted for the successful completion of a baccalaureate program of studies, usually requiring at least 4 years (or equivalent) of full-time college-level study. This includes degrees granted in a cooperative or work-study program.

First-professional enrollment is the number of students enrolled in a professional school or program which requires at least 2 years of academic college work for entrance and a total of at least 6 academic years for a degree, including both prior-required college work and the professional program itself. By NCES definition, first- professional enrollment includes only students in certain programs leading to a degree that signifies both completion of the academic requirements for beginning practice in a given profession and a level of professional skill beyond that normally required for a bachelor's degree. First- professional degrees are awarded in the fields of dentistry (D. D. S. or D. M. D.), medicine (M. D.), optometry (O. D.), osteopathic medicine (D. O.), pharmacy (D. Phar.), podiatric medicine (D. P. M.), veterinary medicine (D. V. M.), chiropractic (D. C. or D. C. M.), law (J. D.), and theological professions (M. Div. or M. H. L.).

Graduate enrollment is the number of students who hold the bachelor's or first- professional degree, or the equivalent, and who are working towards a master's or doctor's degree. First- professional students are counted separately. These enrollment data measure those students who are registered at a particular time during the fall. At some institutions, graduate enrollment also includes students who are in postbaccalaureate classes but not in degree programs.

A master's degree is a degree awarded for successful completion of a program generally requiring 1 or 2 years of full-time college-level study beyond the bachelor's degree. One type of master's degree, including the Master of Arts degree, or M. A., and the Master of Science degree, or M. S., is awarded in the liberal arts and sciences for advanced scholarship in a subject field or discipline and demonstrated ability to perform scholarly research. A second type of master's degree is awarded for the completion of a professionally oriented program, for example, an M. Ed.

in education, an M. B. A. in business administration, an M. F. A. in fine arts, an M. M. in music, an M. S. W. in social work, and an M. P. A. in public administration. A third type of master's degree is awarded in professional fields for study beyond the first-professional degree, for example, the Master of Laws (LL. M.) and Master of Science in various medical specializations.

A doctor's degree is an earned degree carrying the title of doctor. The Doctor of Philosophy degree (Ph. D.) is the highest academic degree and requires mastery within a field of knowledge and demonstrated ability to perform scholarly research. Other doctorates are awarded for fulfilling specialized requirements in professional fields, such as education (Ed. D.), musical arts (D. M. A.), business administration (D. B. A.), and engineering (D. Eng. or D. E. S.). Many doctor's degrees in academic and professional fields require an earned master's degree as a prerequisite. First-professional degrees, such as M. D. and D. D. S., are not included under this heading.

Internet:
<http://nces.ed.gov/ipeds/>

EDUCATIONAL ATTAINMENT (ITEMS 110–112)
Source: U.S. Bureau of the Census, 2000 Census of Population and Housing.

Data on educational attainment were derived from answers to long-form questionnaire Item 9, which was asked of a sample of the population. Data on attainment are tabulated for the population 25 years old and over. People are classified according to the highest degree or level of school completed. The order in which degrees were listed on the questionnaire suggested that doctorate degrees were "higher" than professional school degrees, which were "higher" than master's degrees. The question included instructions for people currently enrolled in school to report the level of the previous grade attended or the highest degree received. Respondents who did not report educational attainment or enrollment level were assigned the attainment of a person of the same age, race, Hispanic or Latino origin, occupation and sex, where possible, who resided in the same or a nearby area. Respondents who filled more than one box were edited to the highest level or degree reported. The question included a response category that allowed respondents to report completing the 12th grade without receiving a high school diploma. It allowed people who received either a high school diploma or the equivalent, for example, passed the Test of General Educational Development (G.E.D.) and did not attend college, to be reported as "high school graduate(s)."

High school graduate or higher. This category includes people whose highest degree was a high school diploma or its equivalent, people who attended college but did not receive a degree, and people who received a college, university, or professional degree. People who reported completing the 12th grade but not receiving a diploma are not high school graduates.

Bachelor's degree or higher. This category includes people whose highest degree was a bachelor's, master's, professional, or doctorate degree. Master's degrees include the traditional M.A. and M.S. degrees and field-specific degrees, such as M.S.W., M.Ed., M.B.A., M.L.S., and M.Eng. Some examples of professional degrees include medicine, dentistry, chiropractic, optometry, osteopathic medicine, pharmacy, podiatry, veterinary medicine, law, and theology. Vocational and technical training, such as barber school training; business, trade, technical, and vocational schools; or other training for a specific trade, are specifically excluded.

SCHOOL ENROLLMENT AND TYPE OF SCHOOL (ITEMS 113–118)
Source: U.S. Bureau of the Census, 2000 Census of Population and Housing.

Data on school enrollment were derived from answers to long-form questionnaire Items 8a and 8b, which were asked of a sample of the population. People were classified as enrolled in school if they reported attending a "regular" public or private school or college at any time between February 1, 2000, and the time of enumeration. The question included instructions to "include only nursery school or preschool, kindergarten, elementary school, and schooling which leads to a high school diploma or a college degree" as regular school or college. Respondents who did not answer the enrollment question were assigned the enrollment status and type of school of a person with the same age, sex, and race/Hispanic or Latino origin whose residence was in the same or a nearby area. All persons 3 years old and over are included.

Public and private school. Public and private school includes people who attended school in the reference period and indicated they were enrolled by marking one of the questionnaire categories for either "public school, public college" or "private school, private college." Schools supported and controlled primarily by a federal, state, or local government are defined as public (including tribal schools). Those supported and controlled primarily by religious organizations or other private groups are private.

DROPOUTS (ITEMS 119 AND 120)
Source: U.S. Bureau of the Census, 2000 Census of Population and Housing.

Not enrolled, not high school graduate. This category includes people of compulsory school attendance age or above who were not enrolled in school and were not high school graduates. These people may be referred to as "high school dropouts." However, there is no criterion regarding when they "dropped out" of school, so they may have never attended high school. This table include only persons 16 to 19 years old.

PART C—COUNTY EDUCATION STATISTICS

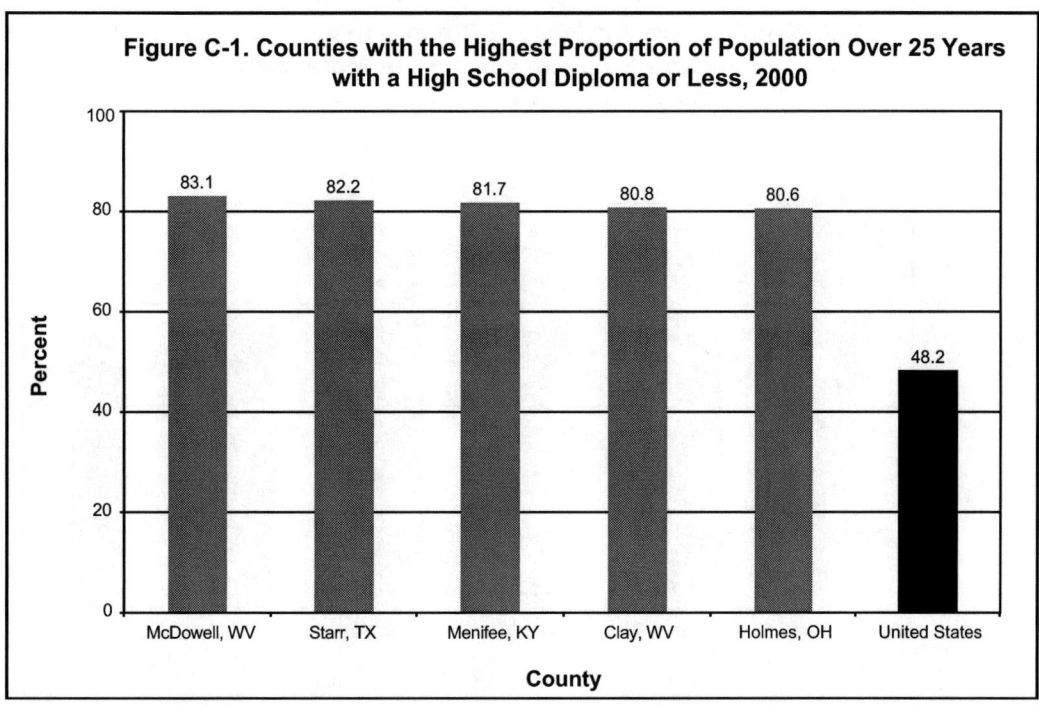

Figure C-1. Counties with the Highest Proportion of Population Over 25 Years with a High School Diploma or Less, 2000

- Expenditures per student range from more than $24,000 in remote North Slope, Alaska to $2,637 in Sierra, California. The median per student expenditure was $5,932 (with half of the counties spending more and half spending less). Los Angeles County had the largest student enrollment as well as the most educational expenditures, with more than $9 billion spent in fiscal 1999. Loving County, Texas had the smallest student enrollment, with just 27 children in kindergarten through 12th grade.

- In the United States, there are approximately 3,100 counties (including county equivalents), more than 15,000 "Local Education Agencies" (school districts), 88,918 public schools, and more than 45 million public school students. Some counties—even large counties such as Miami-Dade County, Florida—have only one school district, while others have many—for example, Maricopa County, Arizona has 166, and Cook County, Illinois has 154 school districts.

- Student/teacher ratios vary greatly from county to county, ranging from a handful of counties exceeding 25 students per teacher, to a low of 5.4 students per teacher in King County, Texas, a county with only 86 students. The median student/teacher ratio is 14.8. More than 800 counties had student/teacher ratios between 14 and 16.

- There are 31 counties, nearly all in the South and 13 specifically in Mississippi, where 90 percent or more of the students are eligible for free or reduced-price lunches. In another 31 counties, fewer than 10 percent of the students are poor enough to qualify for these federal programs. More than 60 percent of all counties with data fall between 20 and 50 percent eligible.

- Colorado has eight of the top 20 counties with the highest proportions of high school graduates, including Douglas, Colorado, where 97 percent of residents over 25 years have a high school diploma. Just 11 counties have high school attainment levels less than 50 percent. Eight of these counties are located in Texas. Twelve counties have college attainment levels exceeding 50 percent. Half of these counties are located in the Washington, DC suburbs. Just two counties have fewer than 5 percent of adults with a bachelor's degree, one in Alaska and the other in Kentucky.

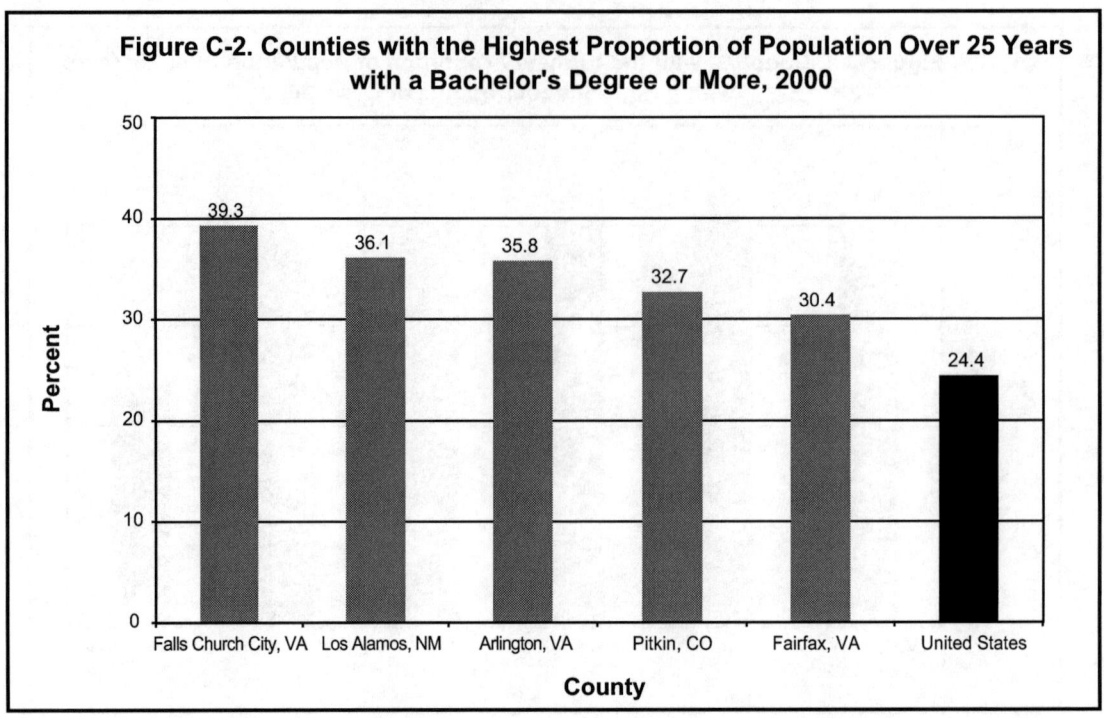

Figure C-2. Counties with the Highest Proportion of Population Over 25 Years with a Bachelor's Degree or More, 2000

Figure C-3. Distribution of Counties by Per Student Expenditures, 1999

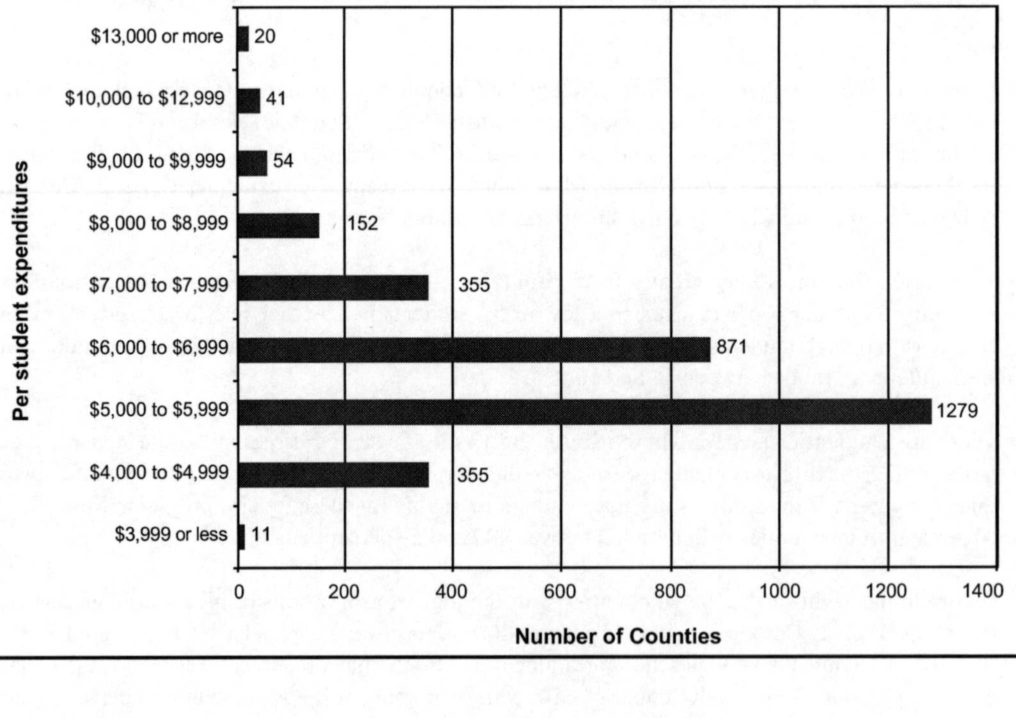

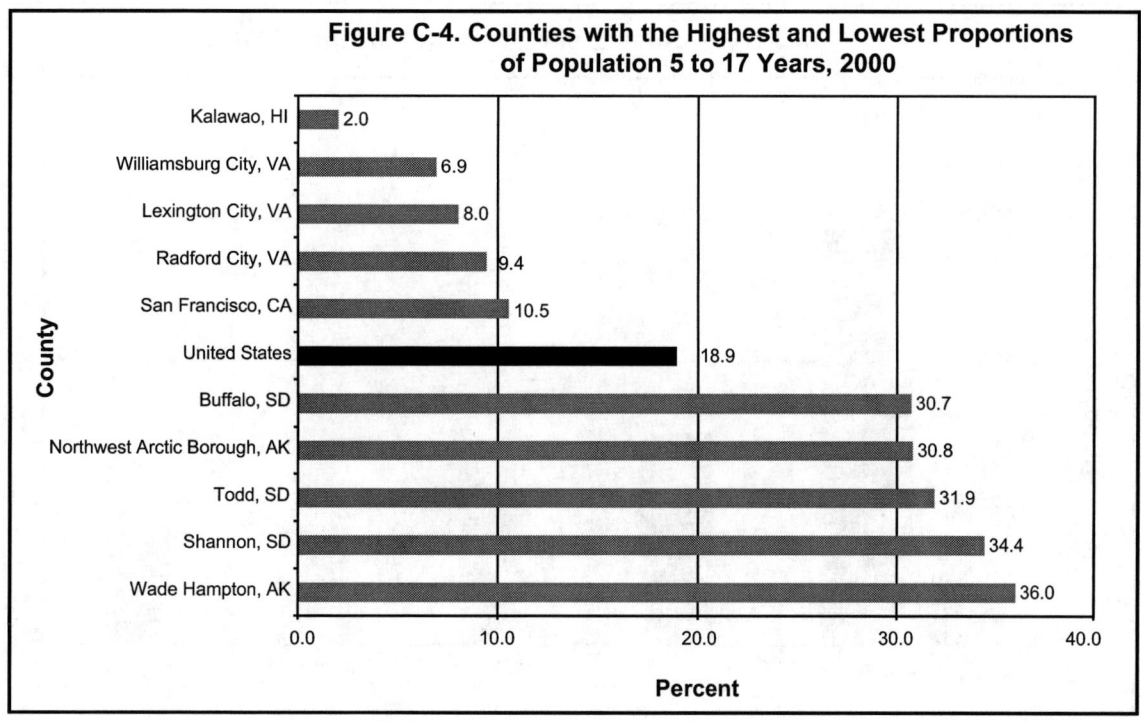

Figure C-4. Counties with the Highest and Lowest Proportions of Population 5 to 17 Years, 2000

Figure C-5. Counties with the Most Students, 2000–2001

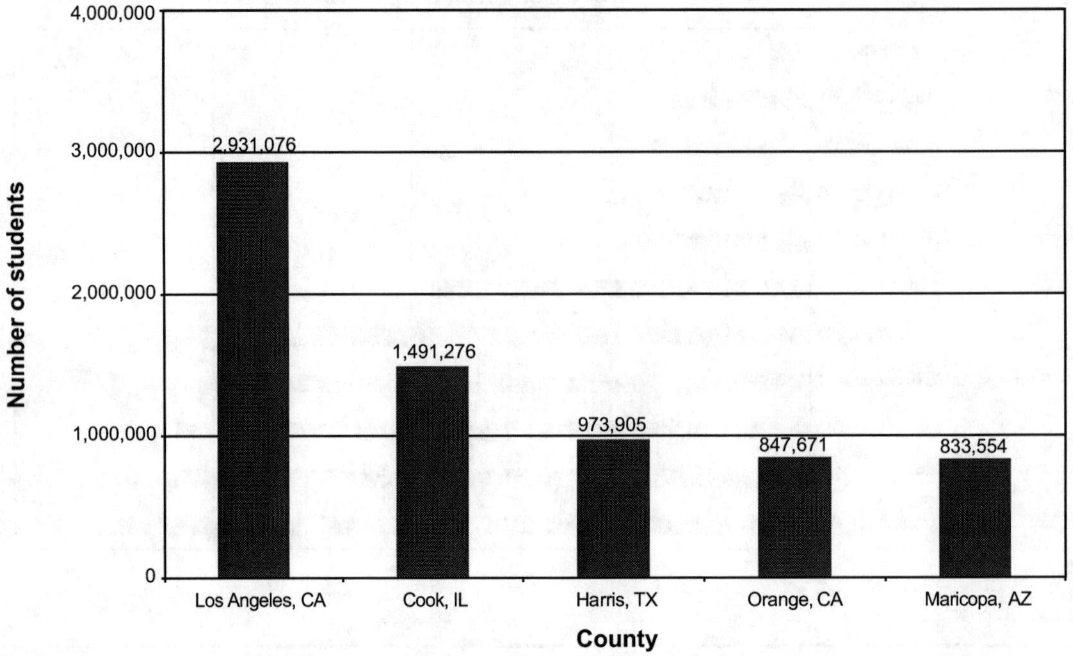

Counties with the Fewest Students, 2000–2001

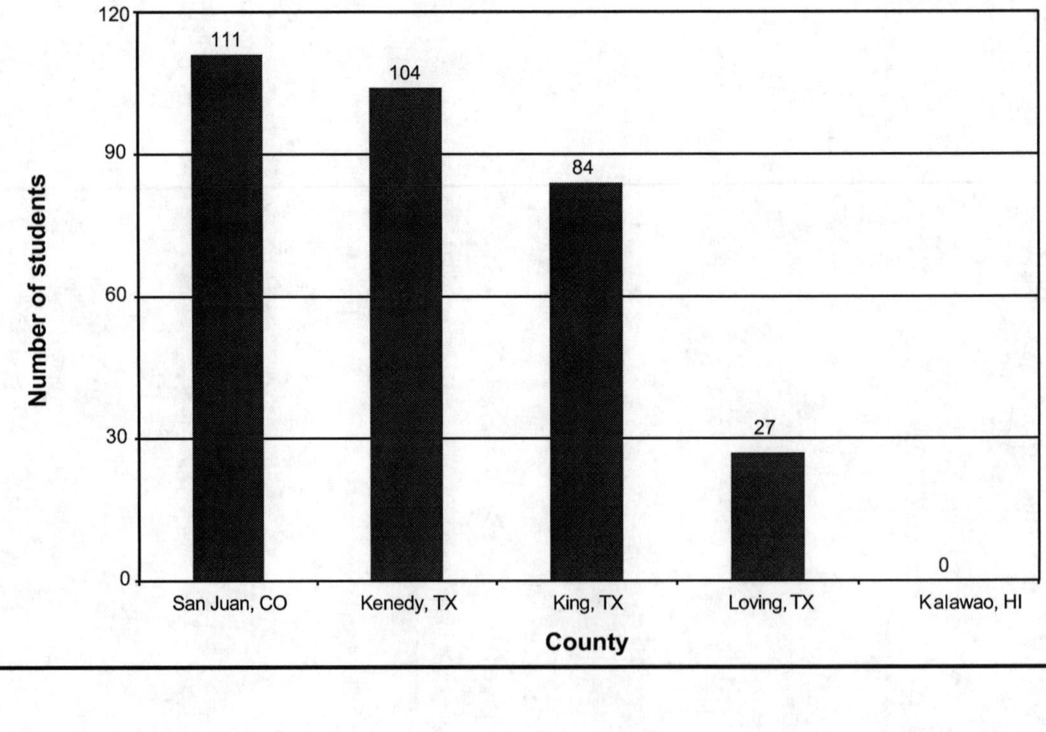

This page
intentionally
left blank

Table C-1. Population, School, and Student Characteristics by County

County	State/County code	County type[1]	Population, 2000		Number of schools and students, 2000–2001			Resident enrollment, 2000			
			Total	Percent 5–17 years	School districts	Schools	Students	Total	Percent public	K–12	Percent public
			1	2	3	4	5	6	7	8	9
UNITED STATES	00000										
ALABAMA	01000										
Autauga, AL	01001	2	43 671	21.7	1	11	8 609	11 887	83.4	9 502	86.9
Baldwin, AL	01003	2	140 415	18.3	1	41	22 656	32 637	83.9	25 805	89.1
Barbour, AL	01005	6	29 038	19.3	2	12	4 671	6 889	88.7	5 760	89.8
Bibb, AL	01007	6	20 826	18.4	1	8	3 556	4 908	87.3	4 142	89.7
Blount, AL	01009	2	51 024	18.5	2	15	8 517	11 833	90.5	9 431	95.3
Bullock, AL	01011	6	11 714	19.8	1	4	1 981	2 884	85.6	2 414	85.9
Butler, AL	01013	7	21 399	20.5	1	7	3 632	5 453	84.6	4 552	84.2
Calhoun, AL	01015	3	112 249	17.4	5	32	18 175	27 855	90.5	19 267	91.6
Chambers, AL	01017	5	36 583	18.0	2	13	5 555	8 386	85.8	6 548	86.7
Cherokee, AL	01019	6	23 988	16.2	1	7	3 919	4 661	93.6	3 836	97.1
Chilton, AL	01021	6	39 593	18.8	1	10	6 785	9 022	91.1	7 509	94.0
Choctaw, AL	01023	9	15 922	19.1	1	6	2 262	3 792	78.2	3 156	77.1
Clarke, AL	01025	7	27 867	20.6	2	12	5 280	6 977	85.5	5 962	88.0
Clay, AL	01027	9	14 254	17.7	1	6	2 426	3 083	92.1	2 567	92.5
Cleburne, AL	01029	6	14 123	18.2	1	7	2 558	3 139	92.4	2 432	95.1
Coffee, AL	01031	4	43 615	18.5	3	16	8 008	11 041	91.8	8 284	95.2
Colbert, AL	01033	3	54 984	17.7	4	23	8 532	12 414	91.7	9 836	92.8
Conecuh, AL	01035	7	14 089	19.7	1	7	2 110	3 355	87.0	2 810	87.7
Coosa, AL	01037	8	12 202	17.5	1	5	1 735	2 688	91.2	2 300	91.4
Covington, AL	01039	7	37 631	17.6	3	14	6 482	8 418	95.8	6 710	98.0
Crenshaw, AL	01041	6	13 665	18.8	1	3	2 387	3 118	90.0	2 599	91.3
Cullman, AL	01043	6	77 483	17.9	2	30	12 217	18 082	92.6	13 754	94.0
Dale, AL	01045	3	49 129	19.1	3	17	7 304	12 680	90.7	9 468	94.0
Dallas, AL	01047	4	46 365	21.2	2	25	9 021	13 032	84.9	10 258	87.3
De Kalb, AL	01049	6	64 452	17.9	2	16	10 443	14 045	94.4	11 435	96.4
Elmore, AL	01051	2	65 874	19.1	2	16	11 909	16 377	85.3	12 967	89.3
Escambia, AL	01053	6	38 440	17.9	2	14	6 185	8 744	91.0	6 955	93.7
Etowah, AL	01055	3	103 459	17.4	3	39	15 818	23 661	88.9	17 868	90.9
Fayette, AL	01057	6	18 495	17.9	1	6	2 780	4 234	94.6	3 301	97.6
Franklin, AL	01059	6	31 223	18.1	2	10	5 533	6 948	94.7	5 687	96.7
Geneva, AL	01061	6	25 764	18.4	2	12	4 141	5 693	93.5	4 715	96.2
Greene, AL	01063	8	9 974	21.5	1	4	1 747	2 616	90.6	2 181	92.4
Hale, AL	01065	6	17 185	21.4	1	7	3 302	4 564	91.3	3 799	91.4
Henry, AL	01067	6	16 310	17.8	1	6	2 794	3 715	90.5	3 026	93.2
Houston, AL	01069	3	88 787	19.1	2	24	14 845	22 033	84.3	17 275	86.2
Jackson, AL	01071	6	53 926	17.9	2	23	8 957	11 505	94.9	9 368	96.4
Jefferson, AL	01073	2	662 047	18.3	10	189	109 528	174 793	84.0	124 485	90.2
Lamar, AL	01075	9	15 904	17.8	1	3	2 684	3 521	95.3	2 890	97.1
Lauderdale, AL	01077	3	87 966	17.1	2	21	13 133	22 201	88.6	15 145	90.6
Lawrence, AL	01079	3	34 803	19.4	1	14	6 118	8 031	91.7	6 667	92.9
Lee, AL	01081	4	115 092	17.0	3	30	17 929	45 855	91.3	19 485	90.2
Limestone, AL	01083	2	65 676	18.3	2	18	10 765	16 015	89.3	12 113	92.6
Lowndes, AL	01085	8	13 473	22.7	1	8	2 620	3 714	88.0	3 192	88.4
Macon, AL	01087	6	24 105	18.7	1	8	3 885	8 743	65.6	4 702	90.0
Madison, AL	01089	2	276 700	18.8	3	75	44 479	78 591	82.6	51 678	87.1
Marengo, AL	01091	7	22 539	21.7	3	11	4 702	5 926	89.3	4 999	90.7
Marion, AL	01093	7	31 214	16.5	2	14	5 096	6 373	92.3	5 123	95.9
Marshall, AL	01095	4	82 231	18.2	4	30	14 875	18 171	93.7	14 556	96.6
Mobile, AL	01097	2	399 843	20.1	1	95	64 894	110 152	78.7	82 148	81.7
Monroe, AL	01099	7	24 324	20.8	1	11	4 438	6 146	86.7	5 059	87.7
Montgomery, AL	01101	2	223 510	18.9	2	62	33 891	65 349	79.2	43 518	81.4
Morgan, AL	01103	3	111 064	18.8	3	37	19 373	26 429	89.2	20 603	92.9
Perry, AL	01105	7	11 861	22.2	1	4	2 302	3 389	87.6	2 585	91.3
Pickens, AL	01107	6	20 949	20.5	1	9	3 708	5 436	89.9	4 382	90.8
Pike, AL	01109	6	29 605	17.9	2	8	4 497	9 104	86.6	5 330	83.5
Randolph, AL	01111	7	22 380	18.5	2	8	3 760	5 262	91.2	4 290	93.2
Russell, AL	01113	2	49 756	19.5	2	18	8 802	12 521	89.7	9 866	92.5
St. Clair, AL	01115	2	64 742	18.8	2	20	10 944	15 126	87.2	12 249	91.4
Shelby, AL	01117	2	143 293	18.8	1	31	20 129	37 311	78.8	26 646	83.3
Sumter, AL	01119	7	14 798	21.9	1	6	2 781	4 704	89.4	3 291	86.6
Talladega, AL	01121	4	80 321	18.6	3	32	13 183	19 125	89.8	15 320	92.7
Tallapoosa, AL	01123	6	41 475	18.0	2	11	6 951	9 775	94.2	7 677	97.0
Tuscaloosa, AL	01125	3	164 875	17.0	2	47	25 211	52 373	89.4	28 564	90.3
Walker, AL	01127	6	70 713	17.1	2	28	10 804	15 536	90.4	12 057	93.0
Washington, AL	01129	8	18 097	21.4	1	7	3 589	4 562	95.3	3 845	96.5
Wilcox, AL	01131	9	13 183	22.6	1	6	2 534	3 626	88.0	3 095	89.3
Winston, AL	01133	6	24 843	17.5	2	11	4 541	5 275	95.1	4 311	97.0
ALASKA	02000										
Aleutians East Borough, AK	02013	9	2 697	12.5	1	6	301	409	98.8	342	100.0
Aleutians West Census Area, AK	02016	9	5 465	12.5	3	7	560	925	88.4	698	96.7
Anchorage, AK	02020	3	260 283	21.5	1	99	49 526	74 625	87.4	55 296	92.0
Bethel, AK	02050	7	16 006	29.8	3	42	4 573	5 584	96.7	4 814	98.1
Bristol Bay, AK	02060	9	1 258	24.2	2	12	1 048	385	95.6	306	95.8
Denali Borough, AK	02068	. . .	1 893	18.6	. . .	. . .	. . .	456	92.3	344	94.2
Dillingham, AK	02070	9	4 922	28.5	1	2	578	1 710	97.3	1 434	98.9
Fairbanks North Star, AK	02090	5	82 840	22.0	2	36	16 509	26 307	89.6	18 063	91.2
Haines, AK	02100	9	2 392	20.3	1	5	402	584	79.6	486	86.0
Juneau, AK	02110	5	30 711	20.9	2	14	6 535	8 777	90.9	6 210	93.1

[1]County type code is from the Economic Research Service of the USDA. See Notes and Definitions at the end of this section.
. . . = Not available.

Table C-1. School and Student Characteristics by County—*Continued*

County	Characteristics of students, 2000–2001			Staff and students, 2000–2001				Revenues, fiscal 1999			
	Percent with IEP[2]	Percent eligible for free lunch	Percent minority	Number of teachers	Student/ teacher ratio	Local school non-teaching staff	Central admin. staff	Total revenue ($1,000s)	Percentage of revenue from		
									Federal govt.	State govt.	Local govt.
	10	11	12	13	14	15	16	17	18	19	20
UNITED STATES											
ALABAMA											
Autauga, AL	12.6	35.6	24.8	516	16.7	370	19	$47 061	6.7	72.0	21.3
Baldwin, AL	16.3	30.6	19.1	1 508	15.0	1 303	73	138 646	6.2	54.6	39.2
Barbour, AL	13.8	67.0	65.7	300	15.6	267	26	30 085	11.4	65.2	23.4
Bibb, AL	17.9	57.0	29.7	220	16.2	196	12	19 808	13.1	71.3	15.6
Blount, AL	12.9	36.1	8.2	491	17.3	437	18	44 058	6.5	69.7	23.8
Bullock, AL	14.0	92.0	99.5	115	17.2	124	12	10 975	18.1	68.4	13.5
Butler, AL	16.4	76.3	62.2	232	15.7	202	18	29 676	11.5	52.0	36.6
Calhoun, AL	14.9	47.4	28.2	1 098	16.6	1 030	73	113 147	7.9	68.0	24.1
Chambers, AL	12.9	62.9	57.0	354	15.7	276	23	33 588	10.8	65.7	23.5
Cherokee, AL	16.2	42.3	8.0	239	16.4	204	18	22 665	8.1	67.8	24.1
Chilton, AL	16.8	40.9	18.1	418	16.2	330	18	34 366	7.6	70.8	21.6
Choctaw, AL	13.4	76.9	73.1	149	15.2	157	13	14 431	14.3	64.9	20.8
Clarke, AL	13.1	60.7	59.4	348	15.2	313	23	35 368	9.9	62.3	27.8
Clay, AL	14.6	54.9	23.9	158	15.4	129	9	14 345	7.9	72.9	19.2
Cleburne, AL	17.1	46.5	5.8	155	16.5	142	10	13 784	8.6	72.5	18.9
Coffee, AL	12.3	40.7	29.1	536	14.9	418	36	48 793	9.0	65.2	25.8
Colbert, AL	12.4	43.6	24.7	563	15.2	454	48	64 406	7.0	51.9	41.1
Conecuh, AL	19.3	81.8	76.6	137	15.4	135	13	12 359	15.8	68.0	16.1
Coosa, AL	17.0	60.6	51.0	94	18.5	103	6	9 747	11.2	71.9	16.9
Covington, AL	14.2	45.9	18.0	418	15.5	312	26	40 515	9.6	65.4	25.0
Crenshaw, AL	11.6	62.3	33.9	150	15.9	113	10	13 155	12.2	69.6	18.3
Cullman, AL	12.9	39.2	3.2	751	16.3	601	34	75 781	12.5	64.6	22.8
Dale, AL	15.2	48.4	33.9	482	15.2	375	27	44 060	10.0	69.8	20.2
Dallas, AL	12.3	80.0	84.4	605	14.9	520	32	53 199	14.7	68.8	16.6
De Kalb, AL	13.6	42.3	19.8	652	16.0	529	33	58 319	8.6	68.2	23.2
Elmore, AL	13.6	38.9	28.7	724	16.4	609	30	63 393	7.2	72.0	20.8
Escambia, AL	12.0	59.1	44.3	413	15.0	403	23	38 771	10.4	65.3	24.3
Etowah, AL	16.2	48.1	23.8	988	16.0	826	60	95 392	8.6	66.6	24.7
Fayette, AL	13.3	40.9	18.6	178	15.6	139	13	16 264	8.2	71.2	20.5
Franklin, AL	11.1	50.5	12.7	363	15.2	252	18	34 405	7.5	64.4	28.1
Geneva, AL	11.6	51.2	19.1	279	14.8	208	13	23 652	8.7	70.1	21.2
Greene, AL	13.3	93.2	99.5	119	14.7	128	18	11 458	19.2	65.9	14.9
Hale, AL	11.1	75.5	75.3	217	15.2	188	11	20 619	12.5	67.8	19.7
Henry, AL	13.3	52.0	48.9	181	15.4	172	7	16 153	9.4	69.8	20.9
Houston, AL	14.7	47.7	38.6	937	15.8	887	63	86 842	10.9	61.4	27.7
Jackson, AL	12.2	47.9	13.7	586	15.3	514	33	58 660	8.1	60.7	31.3
Jefferson, AL	12.7	32.0	53.1	7 012	15.6	5 323	532	752 655	6.9	53.4	39.7
Lamar, AL	10.8	43.1	17.9	156	17.2	138	10	15 540	9.1	71.4	19.5
Lauderdale, AL	10.9	36.5	15.6	870	15.1	662	46	82 044	7.5	60.2	32.4
Lawrence, AL	12.3	47.9	34.7	383	16.0	363	24	37 232	9.8	64.8	25.4
Lee, AL	10.9	40.2	37.6	1 180	15.2	908	73	106 229	6.6	58.8	34.6
Limestone, AL	11.8	34.2	17.9	706	15.2	554	40	68 721	5.3	58.3	36.4
Lowndes, AL	17.4	90.0	99.5	175	15.0	176	18	18 132	24.4	63.4	12.2
Macon, AL	10.4	82.3	96.8	246	15.8	202	18	23 257	15.1	67.5	17.5
Madison, AL	12.6	30.0	34.5	2 858	15.6	2 170	162	277 438	6.1	57.3	36.6
Marengo, AL	11.6	70.9	69.9	306	15.4	248	24	28 862	14.0	65.8	20.2
Marion, AL	13.0	41.4	4.4	335	15.2	237	17	32 226	7.3	69.2	23.5
Marshall, AL	11.3	39.0	7.7	961	15.5	749	73	87 889	7.2	63.7	29.1
Mobile, AL	15.1	63.3	52.8	4 055	16.0	3 355	211	352 925	12.4	65.5	22.1
Monroe, AL	10.7	61.8	59.1	281	15.8	257	18	26 136	10.2	69.9	19.9
Montgomery, AL	12.5	62.5	75.0	2 162	15.7	1 734	173	183 157	11.4	66.6	22.0
Morgan, AL	14.6	35.5	20.8	1 338	14.5	1 142	117	127 649	5.8	54.2	40.0
Perry, AL	16.3	94.0	99.0	144	16.0	119	13	16 147	17.0	69.4	13.6
Pickens, AL	12.8	59.8	64.0	236	15.7	244	22	22 494	15.9	68.1	16.0
Pike, AL	15.5	67.8	56.9	278	16.2	232	24	26 992	14.4	62.3	23.3
Randolph, AL	13.0	51.2	32.3	221	17.0	174	15	20 964	8.7	73.2	18.1
Russell, AL	10.8	62.7	54.2	537	16.4	602	47	56 982	11.9	63.3	24.9
St. Clair, AL	14.2	39.1	11.0	653	16.8	493	34	56 826	7.6	66.9	25.5
Shelby, AL	13.9	20.4	14.4	1 305	15.4	1 215	67	128 238	4.5	52.0	43.5
Sumter, AL	15.9	92.6	99.8	174	16.0	201	18	17 082	17.0	65.4	17.5
Talladega, AL	16.5	59.3	44.3	784	16.8	783	67	78 192	9.8	66.3	23.9
Tallapoosa, AL	15.2	41.2	38.9	446	15.6	330	27	40 883	7.0	64.6	28.4
Tuscaloosa, AL	13.1	48.9	43.7	1 636	15.4	1 407	77	158 998	7.7	60.1	32.2
Walker, AL	15.8	45.6	10.5	699	15.5	651	51	70 901	9.3	61.6	29.1
Washington, AL	9.7	58.3	42.7	227	15.8	205	11	22 096	9.3	64.1	26.6
Wilcox, AL	13.1	96.6	99.6	170	14.9	169	17	18 086	16.9	68.1	15.0
Winston, AL	16.4	47.0	1.5	286	15.9	239	23	28 627	7.9	66.4	25.8
ALASKA											
Aleutians East Borough, AK	15.3	...	88.4	33	9.1	28	5	5 857	32.6	51.9	15.5
Aleutians West Census Area, AK	10.7	...	63.6	45	12.4	48	9	9 983	16.5	53.9	29.6
Anchorage, AK	14.8	...	36.6	2 705	18.3	2 394	200	370 336	9.4	61.2	29.4
Bethel, AK	13.8	71.2	94.9	338	13.5	475	51	76 631	32.5	62.8	4.7
Bristol Bay, AK	12.0	57.2	90.2	86	12.2	94	25	18 676	34.9	49.6	15.5
Denali Borough, AK	...	...	...	...	...	...	...	4 691	5.3	65.8	28.9
Dillingham, AK	16.3	31.0	80.3	41	14.1	44	4	6 486	17.0	60.6	22.4
Fairbanks North Star, AK	13.5	25.9	27.0	913	18.1	689	128	143 310	13.5	61.1	25.3
Haines, AK	12.4	...	26.9	30	13.4	23	3	4 247	5.5	56.2	38.3
Juneau, AK	11.7	8.8	33.4	344	19.0	267	43	49 144	5.7	52.9	41.4

[2]IEP = Individual Education Program. See Notes and Definitions at the end of this section.
... = Not available.

Table C-1. Population, School, and Student Characteristics by County—*Continued*

County	Current expenditures, fiscal 1999			Resident population 16 to 19 years, 2000				Outcomes, 1999–2000	
	Amount ($1,000s)	Amount per student	Percent for instruction	Total population 16 to 19 years	Percent in Armed Forces	Percent high school graduates	Percent not enrolled, not grads, not Armed Forces, not empl.	Number of graduates	Dropouts grades 9–12 (percent)
	21	22	23	24	25	26	27	28	29
UNITED STATES									
ALABAMA									
Autauga, AL	$38 544	$4 540	62.5	2 390	0.0	13.5	7.1	413	4.6
Baldwin, AL	117 883	5 316	62.7	7 374	0.0	10.2	6.1	970	4.7
Barbour, AL	26 169	5 334	61.6	1 664	0.0	10.7	11.4	212	3.4
Bibb, AL	17 669	4 790	63.5	1 144	0.0	15.1	8.0	144	3.5
Blount, AL	37 863	4 654	62.7	2 764	0.2	10.6	9.2	357	6.5
Bullock, AL	10 088	5 187	55.6	654	0.0	8.4	12.5	77	4.2
Butler, AL	19 804	5 144	62.2	1 406	0.0	6.0	9.5	176	10.3
Calhoun, AL	97 438	5 057	59.3	6 252	0.2	8.9	7.2	923	5.7
Chambers, AL	29 452	5 180	61.1	2 082	0.0	11.8	7.1	222	4.5
Cherokee, AL	19 816	5 038	63.2	1 136	0.0	12.5	10.7	216	7.6
Chilton, AL	32 573	4 964	62.5	2 150	0.0	16.6	7.3	275	6.3
Choctaw, AL	13 120	5 397	60.3	951	0.0	6.8	6.6	122	9.4
Clarke, AL	27 692	5 137	60.2	1 624	0.0	10.8	8.9	305	1.6
Clay, AL	12 712	4 979	62.8	655	0.5	9.9	4.9	142	. . .
Cleburne, AL	12 531	4 887	62.2	768	0.0	9.0	8.6	131	5.7
Coffee, AL	43 423	5 188	61.3	2 525	0.2	11.7	8.8	472	5.9
Colbert, AL	50 521	5 894	59.7	2 876	0.0	9.8	6.2	418	4.9
Conecuh, AL	11 707	5 422	59.5	751	0.0	8.0	8.3	83	6.9
Coosa, AL	9 221	5 075	58.7	668	0.0	15.7	6.3	84	7.9
Covington, AL	33 016	4 906	63.2	1 972	0.7	11.8	8.5	366	6.2
Crenshaw, AL	12 307	5 351	64.2	728	0.0	6.3	6.5	138	3.7
Cullman, AL	60 957	4 979	61.4	4 283	0.0	11.9	7.9	684	5.1
Dale, AL	38 754	5 100	61.5	2 775	6.0	16.6	5.7	457	4.6
Dallas, AL	49 402	5 235	60.1	3 125	0.0	6.6	10.1	421	4.1
De Kalb, AL	49 884	4 871	64.4	3 343	0.0	10.7	9.1	509	5.0
Elmore, AL	53 749	4 558	64.9	3 608	0.2	13.1	8.4	556	4.9
Escambia, AL	34 326	5 314	60.0	2 147	0.0	12.0	12.2	330	5.6
Etowah, AL	84 382	5 148	62.9	5 786	0.0	10.1	10.5	839	5.6
Fayette, AL	14 002	4 930	62.0	992	0.0	7.0	11.8	141	7.0
Franklin, AL	30 077	5 322	64.6	1 675	0.0	13.6	7.9	244	2.6
Geneva, AL	20 765	4 837	65.1	1 295	0.5	7.3	6.2	188	5.0
Greene, AL	11 777	5 960	57.9	694	0.0	9.1	16.9	104	6.5
Hale, AL	17 289	5 075	63.0	1 193	0.0	11.1	9.5	153	4.6
Henry, AL	14 829	5 259	62.5	893	0.0	8.4	8.0	139	7.7
Houston, AL	82 640	5 375	60.1	4 832	0.0	8.9	5.5	779	5.2
Jackson, AL	50 094	5 449	60.7	2 794	0.0	14.2	6.4	502	5.1
Jefferson, AL	612 612	5 474	62.9	36 688	0.0	10.2	6.4	6 041	3.6
Lamar, AL	13 454	4 742	61.4	917	0.0	13.8	6.3	193	3.8
Lauderdale, AL	75 552	5 663	62.7	4 930	0.0	7.1	5.7	839	4.7
Lawrence, AL	32 417	5 180	61.6	1 982	0.0	11.5	10.6	281	3.3
Lee, AL	92 601	5 408	61.9	10 016	0.0	5.0	2.9	820	1.9
Limestone, AL	59 970	5 496	65.3	3 229	0.3	12.0	7.9	518	8.3
Lowndes, AL	17 051	6 090	59.9	905	0.1	11.0	11.3	113	5.6
Macon, AL	20 237	4 982	59.8	2 192	0.5	5.7	5.1	189	4.8
Madison, AL	245 487	5 553	62.1	15 636	1.3	8.5	5.7	2 528	2.8
Marengo, AL	25 464	5 232	62.4	1 322	0.1	10.5	7.7	261	2.6
Marion, AL	26 060	4 929	65.0	1 508	0.0	10.4	7.4	299	4.6
Marshall, AL	75 959	5 169	60.8	4 270	0.1	7.8	9.3	697	6.7
Mobile, AL	326 670	5 001	62.5	23 622	0.1	9.1	7.2	3 542	4.3
Monroe, AL	24 401	5 163	63.6	1 505	0.0	8.8	10.6	287	5.2
Montgomery, AL	169 147	4 976	60.1	12 924	0.2	8.7	8.3	1 606	2.5
Morgan, AL	112 659	5 833	59.3	5 898	0.2	10.0	8.4	1 030	5.7
Perry, AL	12 192	5 317	61.5	852	0.0	10.8	9.6	120	3.5
Pickens, AL	20 330	5 289	59.8	1 254	0.0	7.4	7.1	199	3.1
Pike, AL	25 139	5 511	57.7	2 161	0.0	5.5	6.2	216	5.5
Randolph, AL	18 301	4 848	61.2	1 188	0.0	8.7	8.4	195	6.4
Russell, AL	47 882	5 358	57.7	2 663	0.6	9.4	6.8	399	5.8
St. Clair, AL	50 286	4 713	64.1	3 147	0.0	10.8	7.3	470	5.5
Shelby, AL	104 700	5 450	60.0	7 202	0.0	7.7	4.0	1 008	3.8
Sumter, AL	15 638	5 460	61.9	949	0.0	6.1	6.7	165	5.3
Talladega, AL	69 122	5 036	59.2	4 591	0.2	12.5	7.6	708	5.3
Tallapoosa, AL	36 137	5 140	65.0	2 056	0.0	10.9	7.3	365	4.9
Tuscaloosa, AL	139 467	5 412	63.7	12 685	0.0	7.2	4.4	1 339	4.5
Walker, AL	65 440	5 873	61.5	3 756	0.0	9.6	7.9	515	4.2
Washington, AL	18 916	5 101	60.8	1 212	0.0	17.2	6.3	198	1.5
Wilcox, AL	14 727	5 625	57.8	941	0.0	5.4	13.9	139	4.0
Winston, AL	23 115	5 032	62.3	1 145	0.0	11.7	7.7	247	6.2
ALASKA									
Aleutians East Borough, AK	5 595	15 287	60.9	116	0.0	24.1	3.4	13	. . .
Aleutians West Census Area, AK	8 535	14 038	55.0	156	0.0	13.5	1.3	23	1.2
Anchorage, AK	332 985	6 715	61.9	15 210	3.1	16.6	4.7	2 334	3.1
Bethel, AK	68 722	14 985	61.8	1 175	0.0	14.6	8.6	160	15.2
Bristol Bay, AK	15 892	14 317	61.5	75	0.0	18.7	9.3	40	6.0
Denali Borough, AK	4 543	12 515	60.6	104	6.7	18.3	5.8	. . .	. . .
Dillingham, AK	7 057	12 446	61.9	310	0.0	16.1	8.7	22	12.9
Fairbanks North Star, AK	135 186	7 651	64.0	5 230	5.6	16.1	4.7	864	8.1
Haines, AK	4 285	9 739	61.8	125	0.0	10.4	4.0	28	10.2
Juneau, AK	43 697	7 546	66.0	1 692	0.4	13.2	1.2	363	6.1

. . . = Not available.

Table C-1. Population, School, and Student Characteristics by County—*Continued*

County	High school graduates, 2000			College enrollment, 2000		College graduates, 2000 (percent)						
	Population 25 years and over	High school diploma or less (percent)	High school diploma or more (percent)	Number	Percent public	Bachelor's degree or more	+/- U.S. percent with bachelor's degree or more	Non-Hispanic White	Black or African American	American Indian and Alaska Native	Asian, Hawaiian, and Pacific Islander	Hispanic or Latino[1]
	30	31	32	33	34	35	36	37	38	39	40	41
UNITED STATES												
ALABAMA												
Autauga, AL	27 589	55.1	78.7	1 695	82.4	18.0	-6.4	20.0	7.6	12.3	16.7	15.1
Baldwin, AL	96 010	47.6	82.0	4 708	78.8	23.1	-1.3	24.8	7.5	14.2	29.2	17.9
Barbour, AL	18 896	67.8	64.7	743	92.2	10.9	-13.5	16.5	3.8	0.0	0.0	9.7
Bibb, AL	13 540	72.5	63.2	500	87.4	7.1	-17.3	8.5	1.2	11.5	0.0	16.2
Blount, AL	33 702	65.6	70.4	1 600	89.0	9.6	-14.8	9.8	2.5	2.6	62.7	4.4
Bullock, AL	7 570	74.8	60.5	282	82.6	7.7	-16.7	15.8	4.4	0.0	0.0	8.3
Butler, AL	13 767	66.7	67.8	673	94.4	10.4	-14.0	13.3	4.8	0.0	91.3	0.0
Calhoun, AL	74 015	58.3	73.9	7 129	94.0	15.2	-9.2	16.4	8.9	13.2	31.7	9.5
Chambers, AL	24 497	67.9	64.2	1 122	91.0	9.5	-14.9	12.2	4.3	0.0	40.0	15.9
Cherokee, AL	16 825	71.3	63.5	571	83.0	9.7	-14.7	9.8	7.2	14.0	46.9	5.0
Chilton, AL	25 902	69.6	66.2	935	88.7	9.9	-14.5	10.6	5.4	0.0	17.2	4.3
Choctaw, AL	10 569	69.8	65.0	424	95.3	9.6	-14.8	13.1	4.4	0.0	40.0	13.4
Clarke, AL	17 702	66.8	70.8	559	84.8	12.1	-12.3	16.4	5.2	22.2	34.5	0.0
Clay, AL	9 767	71.8	66.0	357	92.4	7.8	-16.6	8.8	2.7	0.0	0.0	0.7
Cleburne, AL	9 533	72.9	62.9	501	87.8	9.2	-15.2	9.5	4.2	6.7	. . .	13.3
Coffee, AL	28 885	53.1	73.2	1 991	91.4	19.3	-5.1	21.5	8.5	13.8	21.7	26.5
Colbert, AL	37 384	60.6	73.3	1 904	97.5	14.1	-10.3	15.2	7.6	8.4	37.0	16.5
Conecuh, AL	9 230	70.4	67.7	385	95.8	9.2	-15.2	10.4	7.6	0.0	0.0	15.0
Coosa, AL	8 255	72.6	65.7	247	88.3	8.0	-16.4	10.4	3.1	0.0	. . .	0.0
Covington, AL	25 705	64.5	68.4	1 166	93.6	12.2	-12.2	12.9	5.8	8.6	20.8	14.4
Crenshaw, AL	9 268	68.9	60.1	425	87.3	11.2	-13.2	13.0	5.4	40.0	. . .	3.8
Cullman, AL	51 787	61.6	70.4	3 327	94.3	11.9	-12.5	12.1	8.6	4.3	16.2	4.2
Dale, AL	31 390	51.4	77.8	2 353	89.9	14.0	-10.4	15.1	7.9	12.1	18.8	15.8
Dallas, AL	28 742	63.2	70.3	1 870	77.9	13.9	-10.5	20.4	9.0	7.9	40.7	14.9
De Kalb, AL	42 740	70.2	63.8	1 696	91.2	8.3	-16.1	8.4	2.5	11.3	27.1	1.9
Elmore, AL	43 177	56.2	77.6	2 245	83.1	16.6	-7.8	18.9	6.5	12.6	34.2	12.7
Escambia, AL	25 510	66.2	68.5	1 296	87.9	10.6	-13.8	12.7	6.1	2.6	8.1	9.8
Etowah, AL	69 829	58.2	74.1	4 130	91.9	13.4	-11.0	14.3	7.4	8.0	33.8	7.8
Fayette, AL	12 579	68.9	66.1	663	93.2	9.2	-15.2	9.2	8.7	0.0	46.9	0.0
Franklin, AL	20 860	68.4	62.1	945	90.2	9.7	-14.7	9.9	9.3	24.7	0.0	6.2
Geneva, AL	17 588	66.4	65.6	625	89.6	8.7	-15.7	9.4	1.4	9.0	76.7	1.4
Greene, AL	6 204	70.1	64.8	225	83.6	10.5	-13.9	15.8	8.6	. . .	100.0	30.0
Hale, AL	10 591	70.7	65.2	467	94.0	8.1	-16.3	11.1	5.2	47.4	100.0	9.2
Henry, AL	10 967	62.4	66.7	488	93.6	14.1	-10.3	17.6	5.8	66.7	. . .	3.8
Houston, AL	58 671	53.8	76.5	3 113	90.0	18.4	-6.0	21.1	8.3	9.6	34.8	13.1
Jackson, AL	36 435	67.8	67.0	1 435	94.1	10.4	-14.0	10.7	5.2	9.7	19.0	5.7
Jefferson, AL	434 158	47.0	80.9	38 365	76.4	24.6	0.2	30.0	14.3	23.0	63.9	18.8
Lamar, AL	10 758	72.5	65.1	443	95.7	7.8	-16.6	8.1	5.3	0.0	31.8	7.1
Lauderdale, AL	58 894	57.8	76.4	5 618	93.6	18.5	-5.9	19.3	9.5	17.3	50.8	16.0
Lawrence, AL	22 894	73.8	65.6	997	94.1	7.5	-16.9	7.4	5.2	10.4	30.2	18.2
Lee, AL	62 170	45.3	81.4	24 433	95.0	27.9	3.5	31.9	12.2	25.9	64.7	23.8
Limestone, AL	43 456	58.0	74.5	2 898	90.6	16.9	-7.5	18.2	8.8	14.7	41.0	3.3
Lowndes, AL	8 183	69.1	64.3	348	86.8	11.0	-13.4	21.4	6.1	0.0	. . .	20.0
Macon, AL	13 955	55.0	70.0	3 440	29.5	18.8	-5.6	15.2	18.7	10.7	90.1	4.0
Madison, AL	180 389	36.5	85.4	21 212	84.2	34.3	9.9	36.8	23.9	21.4	52.9	26.5
Marengo, AL	14 326	65.4	71.9	707	90.1	12.1	-12.3	18.4	4.9	0.0	0.0	17.2
Marion, AL	21 611	69.7	63.2	932	86.1	8.0	-16.4	8.2	3.5	0.0	0.0	6.4
Marshall, AL	54 961	61.1	69.4	2 441	92.7	13.9	-10.5	14.4	5.4	12.2	32.8	2.9
Mobile, AL	250 122	55.2	76.7	20 709	76.9	18.6	-5.8	21.9	10.7	7.8	33.9	21.5
Monroe, AL	15 378	66.5	67.9	768	88.4	11.8	-12.6	15.6	5.0	11.1	25.0	11.6
Montgomery, AL	141 342	44.1	80.3	16 879	82.4	28.5	4.1	36.5	18.2	11.3	32.7	25.2
Morgan, AL	73 331	54.0	76.3	3 925	91.4	18.4	-6.0	19.6	7.4	23.7	54.3	10.9
Perry, AL	6 978	68.0	62.4	551	72.2	10.0	-14.4	16.4	6.4	0.0	0.0	3.4
Pickens, AL	13 536	68.1	69.7	641	90.0	9.2	-14.6	12.3	5.7	0.0	35.3	0.0
Pike, AL	17 703	60.9	69.1	3 315	95.7	18.4	-6.0	24.7	6.6	8.3	35.0	4.6
Randolph, AL	14 762	70.1	61.9	745	93.8	10.0	-14.4	10.8	6.2	0.0	48.1	6.7
Russell, AL	32 107	66.5	66.5	1 766	92.9	9.7	-14.7	11.1	6.4	22.8	36.5	11.2
St. Clair, AL	43 101	63.3	71.3	1 905	81.3	11.1	-13.3	11.5	6.0	6.1	34.9	12.9
Shelby, AL	94 185	36.2	86.8	7 321	85.8	36.8	12.4	37.8	24.9	19.7	72.3	22.0
Sumter, AL	8 731	66.4	64.8	1 075	96.0	12.4	-12.0	27.4	6.1	0.0	0.0	12.8
Talladega, AL	53 060	64.8	69.7	2 625	84.4	11.2	-13.2	13.0	6.4	21.8	34.1	12.9
Tallapoosa, AL	28 373	62.9	70.1	1 221	87.8	14.1	-10.3	16.4	6.3	16.7	38.6	34.3
Tuscaloosa, AL	99 039	49.6	78.8	21 141	91.4	24.0	-0.4	27.9	12.1	15.7	65.6	22.7
Walker, AL	47 919	67.5	67.2	2 581	87.8	9.1	-15.3	9.0	8.4	7.8	37.3	5.0
Washington, AL	11 240	71.3	72.3	441	88.0	8.6	-15.8	9.8	6.6	4.5	0.0	0.0
Wilcox, AL	7 979	70.7	59.5	328	88.4	10.1	-14.3	18.0	6.1	0.0	0.0	0.0
Winston, AL	17 078	71.7	62.6	709	90.8	8.3	-16.1	7.9	0.0	34.7	82.6	13.3
ALASKA												
Aleutians East Borough, AK	2 007	74.2	74.7	28	82.1	4.9	-19.5	17.5	0.0	1.4	1.3	0.0
Aleutians West Census Area, AK	4 251	55.9	78.5	161	51.6	11.0	-13.4	22.9	0.8	3.2	3.4	6.8
Anchorage, AK	159 931	33.9	90.3	15 169	81.9	28.9	4.5	33.0	15.5	10.6	23.1	16.3
Bethel, AK	8 026	67.6	71.0	375	85.9	13.1	-11.3	46.5	7.4	4.5	24.7	30.9
Bristol Bay, AK	782	45.1	88.9	54	92.6	21.1	-3.3	28.9	0.0	8.9	22.2	40.0
Denali Borough, AK	1 316	38.7	91.7	88	89.8	22.7	-1.7	24.2	11.8	6.7	23.5	23.5
Dillingham, AK	2 655	57.3	76.6	176	87.5	16.4	-8.0	39.6	33.3	4.6	45.0	20.4
Fairbanks North Star, AK	47 974	33.7	91.8	6 952	91.7	27.0	2.6	30.0	12.5	9.8	24.6	15.5
Haines, AK	1 660	42.2	88.9	60	60.0	23.8	-0.6	26.3	0.0	8.5	20.0	31.3
Juneau, AK	19 899	28.8	93.2	1 890	93.0	36.0	11.6	41.5	23.0	7.9	32.1	19.9

[1]Hispanic or Latino persons may be of any race.
. . . = Not available.

Table C-1. Population, School, and Student Characteristics by County—*Continued*

County	State/County code	County type[1]	Population, 2000 Total	Population, 2000 Percent 5–17 years	Number of schools and students, 2000–2001 School districts	Number of schools and students, 2000–2001 Schools	Number of schools and students, 2000–2001 Students	Resident enrollment, 2000 Total	Resident enrollment, 2000 Percent public	Resident enrollment, 2000 K–12	Resident enrollment, 2000 Percent public
			1	2	3	4	5	6	7	8	9
Kenai Peninsula, AK	02122	5	49 691	23.3	1	41	9 925	14 004	90.4	11 739	92.8
Ketchikan Gateway, AK	02130	7	14 070	21.3	1	9	2 517	3 744	88.8	3 051	92.3
Kodiak Island, AK	02150	7	13 913	23.5	1	15	2 743	3 975	86.4	3 150	90.3
Lake and Peninsula Borough, AK	02164	...	1 823	29.8	1	15	528	645	92.7	555	94.8
Matanuska-Susitna, AK	02170	6	59 322	25.2	1	31	13 008	18 008	91.5	14 884	93.6
Nome, AK	02180	7	9 196	28.6	2	21	2 496	3 129	97.5	2 659	99.2
North Slope, AK	02185	7	7 385	28.6	1	10	2 187	2 623	97.6	2 148	99.0
Northwest Arctic Borough, AK	02188	7	7 208	30.8	1	13	2 188	2 505	98.0	2 202	99.2
Prince of Wales-Outer Ketchikan, AK	02201	7	6 146	23.6	5	20	1 441	1 694	95.6	1 473	96.6
Sitka, AK	02220	9	8 835	20.8	2	7	1 970	2 617	86.1	1 864	95.5
Skagway-Hoonah-Angoon, AK	02232	...	3 436	21.6	...	...	...	908	89.4	732	91.4
Southeast Fairbanks, AK	02240	5	6 174	25.7	1	8	490	1 970	85.3	1 574	85.9
Valdez-Cordova, AK	02261	7	10 195	23.0	4	18	2 218	2 929	91.9	2 337	95.9
Wade Hampton, AK	02270	9	7 028	36.0	3	13	2 354	2 968	99.1	2 583	99.5
Wrangell-Petersburg, AK	02280	7	6 684	23.0	3	8	1 341	1 783	93.7	1 542	96.2
Yakutat Borough, AK	02282	...	808	23.3	...	...	...	218	100.0	173	100.0
Yukon-Koyukuk, AK	02290	7	6 551	27.9	7	39	7 121	2 278	97.2	1 994	97.6
ARIZONA	04000										
Apache, AZ	04001	5	69 423	29.4	12	37	14 663	25 885	95.4	21 435	97.0
Cochise, AZ	04003	4	117 755	19.6	22	55	20 114	32 791	91.2	23 733	94.3
Coconino, AZ	04005	5	116 320	21.5	16	48	20 433	42 187	93.3	25 217	93.8
Gila, AZ	04007	4	51 335	19.0	10	28	8 585	12 718	92.8	10 261	94.1
Graham, AZ	04009	7	33 489	22.3	9	18	5 698	10 949	93.8	7 879	94.6
Greenlee, AZ	04011	7	8 547	23.4	4	8	1 919	2 476	95.0	2 070	97.1
La Paz, AZ	04012	7	19 715	16.2	7	12	2 859	3 969	95.3	3 303	96.0
Maricopa, AZ	04013	0	3 072 149	19.1	166	794	533 770	833 554	88.2	584 324	93.4
Mohave, AZ	04015	2	155 032	17.1	21	75	25 094	32 934	91.7	25 729	94.2
Navajo, AZ	04017	5	97 470	26.9	17	69	24 347	32 682	95.1	26 882	96.5
Pima, AZ	04019	2	843 746	18.0	45	281	131 404	236 404	89.2	153 693	91.7
Pinal, AZ	04021	1	179 727	18.4	19	60	24 379	42 725	92.5	33 416	95.3
Santa Cruz, AZ	04023	6	38 381	25.0	10	24	9 787	12 026	94.1	10 092	97.2
Yavapai, AZ	04025	4	167 517	16.0	35	79	24 124	37 187	86.8	26 770	93.2
Yuma, AZ	04027	3	160 026	21.0	12	45	30 520	43 353	95.3	34 014	96.9
ARKANSAS	05000										
Arkansas, AR	05001	7	20 749	18.3	4	13	3 683	5 072	88.9	3 938	93.0
Ashley, AR	05003	7	24 209	20.1	3	15	4 434	6 158	94.8	5 065	97.2
Baxter, AR	05005	7	38 386	14.5	3	10	5 012	7 019	92.6	5 533	96.7
Benton, AR	05007	3	153 406	19.0	7	44	25 110	36 954	86.6	29 280	92.0
Boone, AR	05009	7	33 948	17.7	6	18	5 938	7 417	91.1	6 016	93.0
Bradley, AR	05011	7	12 600	17.6	2	6	2 162	2 852	96.5	2 383	97.7
Calhoun, AR	05013	9	5 744	19.3	1	2	817	1 351	95.4	1 159	96.9
Carroll, AR	05015	7	25 357	17.5	3	8	3 562	5 062	91.2	4 297	92.2
Chicot, AR	05017	7	14 117	20.5	3	10	2 598	3 640	90.6	2 961	89.7
Clark, AR	05019	7	23 546	15.7	2	8	3 205	7 933	78.7	3 821	96.0
Clay, AR	05021	7	17 609	17.1	3	7	2 745	3 670	95.6	2 960	98.3
Cleburne, AR	05023	6	24 046	16.2	5	11	3 469	4 705	91.1	3 905	94.6
Cleveland, AR	05025	8	8 571	19.6	3	6	1 531	2 085	95.9	1 697	98.2
Columbia, AR	05027	7	25 603	19.0	6	14	4 490	7 482	95.4	4 889	97.0
Conway, AR	05029	6	20 336	19.0	3	10	3 371	4 962	91.2	3 877	93.4
Craighead, AR	05031	5	82 148	17.2	8	33	13 587	22 728	91.6	14 353	93.9
Crawford, AR	05033	3	53 247	20.8	5	23	10 334	13 483	92.9	10 961	96.2
Crittenden, AR	05035	1	50 866	22.7	5	25	10 727	14 577	92.1	11 592	95.2
Cross, AR	05037	6	19 526	21.1	3	10	4 034	5 275	94.9	4 316	97.7
Dallas, AR	05039	7	9 210	20.0	3	8	1 673	2 357	97.4	2 015	99.5
Desha, AR	05041	7	15 341	21.4	4	11	3 417	4 212	96.1	3 406	97.9
Drew, AR	05043	7	18 723	19.1	2	7	3 231	5 425	96.9	3 633	98.6
Faulkner, AR	05045	2	86 014	18.7	6	29	14 362	26 908	84.8	16 292	91.0
Franklin, AR	05047	5	17 771	19.4	5	11	3 601	4 051	94.6	3 379	96.5
Fulton, AR	05049	9	11 642	17.3	3	6	1 643	2 435	94.5	2 031	96.1
Garland, AR	05051	4	88 068	15.8	7	24	12 785	18 185	89.9	14 253	93.5
Grant, AR	05053	6	16 464	19.5	2	8	4 689	3 925	95.0	3 194	97.4
Greene, AR	05055	7	37 331	18.5	4	15	6 539	8 654	91.2	6 798	94.5
Hempstead, AR	05057	6	23 587	19.8	4	11	4 006	5 894	94.1	4 618	96.3
Hot Spring, AR	05059	6	30 353	18.8	5	16	5 528	7 183	93.2	5 578	96.6
Howard, AR	05061	7	14 300	20.1	4	10	3 063	3 353	93.0	2 847	95.5
Independence, AR	05063	7	34 233	18.1	7	21	5 573	8 165	87.9	6 268	95.4
Izard, AR	05065	9	13 249	15.8	4	8	1 962	2 658	93.1	2 093	94.8
Jackson, AR	05067	7	18 418	16.4	3	9	2 654	4 023	94.8	3 200	98.2
Jefferson, AR	05069	3	84 278	19.4	5	33	14 923	22 966	92.9	16 558	95.4
Johnson, AR	05071	7	22 781	18.5	4	11	4 012	5 363	93.9	4 256	97.9
Lafayette, AR	05073	8	8 559	19.4	3	6	1 549	2 064	97.1	1 706	98.2
Lawrence, AR	05075	7	17 774	17.6	6	13	3 244	4 345	89.3	3 181	96.8
Lee, AR	05077	6	12 580	19.6	1	4	1 874	3 184	89.4	2 646	88.1
Lincoln, AR	05079	8	14 492	16.5	3	7	2 085	2 933	93.8	2 397	94.9
Little River, AR	05081	6	13 628	18.3	2	7	2 095	3 128	92.9	2 481	94.9
Logan, AR	05083	6	22 486	19.4	4	10	3 553	5 033	92.9	4 293	95.1
Lonoke, AR	05085	2	52 828	21.6	4	21	10 697	14 008	93.0	11 362	96.9
Madison, AR	05087	8	14 243	20.4	3	7	2 663	3 198	95.4	2 875	96.3
Marion, AR	05089	9	16 140	17.1	3	7	2 307	3 301	92.2	2 770	93.4
Miller, AR	05091	3	40 443	19.1	4	17	6 596	9 869	89.4	7 692	92.2
Mississippi, AR	05093	4	51 979	21.5	6	26	9 850	13 939	92.7	11 331	93.9
Monroe, AR	05095	7	10 254	21.0	3	6	1 927	2 564	87.9	2 218	88.4
Montgomery, AR	05097	9	9 245	17.4	3	6	1 395	1 860	94.7	1 589	95.5
Nevada, AR	05099	7	9 955	18.8	3	7	1 928	2 425	96.9	1 927	99.0

[1]County type code is from the Economic Research Service of the USDA. See Notes and Definitions at the end of this section.
... = Not available.

Table C-1. School and Student Characteristics by County—*Continued*

County	Characteristics of students, 2000–2001			Staff and students, 2000–2001				Revenues, fiscal 1999			
	Percent with IEP[2]	Percent eligible for free lunch	Percent minority	Number of teachers	Student/ teacher ratio	Local school non-teaching staff	Central admin. staff	Total revenue ($1,000s)	Percentage of revenue from		
									Federal govt.	State govt.	Local govt.
	10	11	12	13	14	15	16	17	18	19	20
Kenai Peninsula, AK	12.2	28.4	15.6	593	16.7	442	66	$86 869	6.4	61.9	31.8
Ketchikan Gateway, AK	13.4	18.3	31.7	127	19.8	129	15	20 402	6.5	53.0	40.5
Kodiak Island, AK	13.7	30.5	48.4	167	16.4	149	18	25 549	13.6	60.5	25.8
Lake and Peninsula Borough, AK	12.3	57.8	92.4	50	10.6	63	12	12 747	27.1	60.0	12.9
Matanuska-Susitna, AK	15.3	28.1	13.4	716	18.2	628	47	107 225	6.1	66.2	27.7
Nome, AK	12.9	59.9	86.5	205	12.2	200	26	38 746	40.7	49.6	9.7
North Slope, AK	9.3	21.0	90.1	178	12.3	200	33	59 089	16.4	38.9	44.7
Northwest Arctic Borough, AK	10.6	67.6	97.6	165	13.3	194	48	31 028	25.4	58.4	16.1
Prince of Wales-Outer Ketchikan, AK	13.4	. . .	56.1	98	14.7	111	18	17 131	36.5	53.1	10.4
Sitka, AK	12.5	30.1	49.5	123	16.0	77	9	14 336	9.8	48.5	41.6
Skagway-Hoonah-Angoon, AK	. . .	. . .	. . .	. . .	. . .	. . .	. . .	6 046	19.0	49.9	31.1
Southeast Fairbanks, AK	18.2	54.5	51.0	30	16.3	35	7	8 117	12.2	82.3	5.5
Valdez-Cordova, AK	13.3	27.9	27.9	121	18.3	131	23	27 270	12.2	61.0	26.8
Wade Hampton, AK	10.4	63.4	99.4	174	13.5	233	31	32 213	43.9	47.7	8.4
Wrangell-Petersburg, AK	12.0	. . .	32.1	86	15.6	81	6	13 809	14.0	58.9	27.1
Yakutat Borough, AK	. . .	. . .	. . .	. . .	. . .	. . .	. . .	2 459	10.9	60.0	29.1
Yukon-Koyukuk, AK	6.3	. . .	28.1	229	31.1	260	56	47 452	20.0	75.9	4.1
ARIZONA											
Apache, AZ	10.6	. . .	84.4	926	15.8	1 240	58	145 469	41.0	38.0	21.1
Cochise, AZ	12.9	. . .	52.7	1 106	18.2	1 237	75	127 708	16.1	55.4	28.5
Coconino, AZ	12.6	. . .	53.7	1 172	17.4	1 201	54	133 100	21.0	36.0	43.0
Gila, AZ	15.1	. . .	43.3	500	17.2	531	26	60 565	18.6	43.4	38.0
Graham, AZ	12.4	. . .	42.1	315	18.1	286	24	38 139	14.0	68.7	17.3
Greenlee, AZ	11.5	. . .	49.8	112	17.1	112	11	12 728	4.2	20.2	75.6
La Paz, AZ	15.2	. . .	61.3	174	16.4	218	12	21 121	32.0	38.0	30.0
Maricopa, AZ	9.4	. . .	43.7	25 885	20.6	24 433	562	2 973 988	6.1	41.8	52.1
Mohave, AZ	11.9	. . .	22.5	1 095	22.9	1 157	48	118 180	7.7	42.2	50.1
Navajo, AZ	11.5	. . .	57.9	1 149	21.2	1 419	64	168 108	28.8	49.3	21.8
Pima, AZ	11.9	. . .	52.2	6 948	18.9	7 512	250	764 876	9.3	47.2	43.5
Pinal, AZ	15.2	. . .	54.9	1 355	18.0	1 673	67	173 125	11.4	56.0	32.6
Santa Cruz, AZ	7.1	. . .	92.7	438	22.3	478	14	55 646	12.0	53.3	34.7
Yavapai, AZ	12.5	. . .	18.6	1 195	20.2	1 202	58	119 117	6.2	40.0	53.8
Yuma, AZ	9.4	. . .	75.2	1 475	20.7	1 589	67	173 956	11.4	63.3	25.3
ARKANSAS											
Arkansas, AR	9.9	48.8	36.0	283	13.0	242	27	20 917	9.9	55.0	35.2
Ashley, AR	10.9	47.9	39.1	303	14.6	326	19	25 538	9.4	60.0	30.5
Baxter, AR	12.4	40.2	1.9	336	14.9	261	15	27 457	8.8	53.0	38.2
Benton, AR	11.9	34.0	16.6	1 578	15.9	1 573	70	132 577	5.8	48.7	45.5
Boone, AR	10.4	41.7	1.1	428	13.9	352	20	34 955	7.5	59.8	32.7
Bradley, AR	10.5	61.4	47.1	160	13.5	146	12	13 399	10.8	64.0	25.2
Calhoun, AR	15.7	48.3	30.0	63	13.0	43	5	5 032	8.3	52.6	39.1
Carroll, AR	13.6	43.9	13.6	240	14.8	241	13	19 227	6.4	51.0	42.6
Chicot, AR	11.9	81.4	81.6	224	11.6	221	17	18 811	18.6	59.9	21.4
Clark, AR	13.3	44.8	38.9	226	14.2	194	13	21 907	14.3	51.8	33.8
Clay, AR	16.3	45.1	0.6	201	13.7	169	13	15 033	8.2	63.8	28.1
Cleburne, AR	13.0	44.0	1.2	273	12.7	222	15	19 309	6.9	53.5	39.7
Cleveland, AR	9.9	42.3	20.5	114	13.4	121	7	8 700	11.9	64.6	23.5
Columbia, AR	10.2	52.7	50.1	359	12.5	281	28	25 655	8.6	57.9	33.5
Conway, AR	14.0	49.6	22.5	239	14.1	222	14	33 724	9.1	40.5	50.4
Craighead, AR	12.1	37.4	15.7	967	14.1	850	46	71 939	6.5	59.7	33.8
Crawford, AR	13.9	41.6	7.4	678	15.2	552	29	57 549	7.8	68.4	23.8
Crittenden, AR	10.9	61.0	65.9	721	14.9	652	37	58 436	10.8	65.8	23.4
Cross, AR	13.1	54.2	34.1	310	13.0	254	25	22 584	10.2	62.4	27.4
Dallas, AR	14.6	49.6	51.9	137	12.2	105	11	10 362	7.7	67.4	24.9
Desha, AR	12.8	63.6	60.2	273	12.5	247	21	21 270	10.3	62.3	27.4
Drew, AR	11.6	47.6	36.3	229	14.1	212	15	24 467	17.1	59.4	23.5
Faulkner, AR	13.7	30.3	14.1	981	14.6	710	43	80 079	5.1	62.2	32.7
Franklin, AR	11.1	38.6	2.5	266	13.5	180	13	22 701	15.2	56.6	28.2
Fulton, AR	12.9	51.6	0.5	130	12.6	98	9	9 356	8.4	68.3	23.3
Garland, AR	13.1	40.8	17.0	837	15.3	708	53	72 990	7.4	48.5	44.1
Grant, AR	12.2	33.9	3.1	290	16.2	244	14	23 564	5.1	68.5	26.4
Greene, AR	14.9	44.2	1.4	456	14.3	380	28	33 174	8.1	66.0	26.0
Hempstead, AR	9.9	59.4	51.8	298	13.4	259	18	26 538	9.8	62.4	27.7
Hot Spring, AR	13.5	41.1	14.7	383	14.4	307	26	30 435	6.8	65.0	28.2
Howard, AR	10.3	47.7	32.9	242	12.7	170	13	17 381	7.4	61.8	30.8
Independence, AR	16.2	43.9	6.3	460	12.1	394	33	35 062	7.5	54.6	38.0
Izard, AR	15.6	51.9	1.5	175	11.2	159	19	13 617	12.7	59.5	27.8
Jackson, AR	13.2	54.3	24.4	219	12.1	200	13	16 091	9.9	56.9	33.2
Jefferson, AR	10.7	55.5	66.2	1 007	14.8	986	52	88 142	11.0	61.2	27.8
Johnson, AR	11.0	54.3	9.8	299	13.4	208	14	22 829	11.2	63.3	25.5
Lafayette, AR	12.3	63.8	55.0	136	11.4	126	10	10 039	12.3	58.2	29.5
Lawrence, AR	15.7	54.9	1.3	269	12.1	232	19	21 559	10.7	64.0	25.3
Lee, AR	6.2	91.5	91.5	121	15.5	145	18	12 351	20.0	63.3	16.7
Lincoln, AR	13.8	54.0	39.9	145	14.4	138	20	11 860	10.4	69.9	19.7
Little River, AR	11.2	43.1	31.9	163	12.9	166	10	12 600	8.0	37.2	54.7
Logan, AR	12.5	45.8	2.7	294	12.1	197	19	20 580	10.3	64.1	25.6
Lonoke, AR	13.7	29.0	10.1	700	15.3	612	31	57 472	6.7	69.0	24.3
Madison, AR	12.5	40.3	3.4	188	14.2	158	10	14 597	7.1	69.1	23.8
Marion, AR	14.4	54.6	0.8	168	13.7	140	12	13 114	9.0	65.2	25.8
Miller, AR	13.4	49.6	34.4	470	14.0	437	37	41 250	9.4	62.5	28.0
Mississippi, AR	14.4	64.8	52.2	711	13.9	669	40	55 445	11.8	64.8	23.4
Monroe, AR	12.1	71.6	58.0	170	11.3	129	17	11 596	15.0	61.8	23.1
Montgomery, AR	13.3	52.0	4.3	116	12.0	94	8	8 957	25.8	50.4	23.8
Nevada, AR	11.6	51.6	39.0	146	13.2	135	11	10 988	8.9	65.1	26.0

[2]IEP = Individual Education Program. See Notes and Definitions at the end of this section.
. . . = Not available.

Table C-1. Population, School, and Student Characteristics by County—*Continued*

County	Current expenditures, fiscal 1999			Resident population 16 to 19 years, 2000				Outcomes, 1999–2000	
	Amount ($1,000s)	Amount per student	Percent for instruction	Total population 16 to 19 years	Percent in Armed Forces	Percent high school graduates	Percent not enrolled, not grads, not Armed Forces, not empl.	Number of graduates	Dropouts grades 9–12 (percent)
	21	22	23	24	25	26	27	28	29
Kenai Peninsula, AK	$85 404	$8 292	62.3	3 224	0.9	12.4	2.8	680	6.4
Ketchikan Gateway, AK	20 107	7 293	62.3	866	2.5	14.3	7.0	124	10.8
Kodiak Island, AK	26 306	9 382	64.2	727	2.1	19.5	2.2	133	6.1
Lake and Peninsula Borough, AK	10 120	17 509	52.3	149	0.0	16.1	8.1	18	3.9
Matanuska-Susitna, AK	101 460	7 840	60.7	3 925	0.2	11.4	5.0	708	4.4
Nome, AK	37 154	13 895	62.2	644	0.0	13.0	14.8	103	4.0
North Slope, AK	51 149	24 345	54.8	556	0.0	17.6	7.2	103	8.4
Northwest Arctic Borough, AK	29 853	13 375	51.4	539	0.0	16.0	20.4	77	9.3
Prince of Wales-Outer Ketchikan, AK	16 442	11 786	64.1	361	0.0	11.1	4.2	96	2.4
Sitka, AK	14 072	8 220	67.5	501	5.8	19.8	3.0	160	2.8
Skagway-Hoonah-Angoon, AK	5 591	14 410	61.3	188	0.0	10.6	8.5	...	...
Southeast Fairbanks, AK	6 438	12 453	57.2	405	2.0	16.5	6.4	32	10.1
Valdez-Cordova, AK	23 569	10 660	62.1	611	0.8	12.9	5.9	125	6.3
Wade Hampton, AK	29 646	11 389	57.9	573	0.0	12.7	10.8	71	15.9
Wrangell-Petersburg, AK	12 922	8 767	65.9	345	0.0	13.0	3.5	86	3.0
Yakutat Borough, AK	2 352	13 754	53.4	46	0.0	13.0	6.5	...	...
Yukon-Koyukuk, AK	44 355	8 385	60.3	468	0.0	9.8	10.0	223	5.4
ARIZONA									
Apache, AZ	96 322	6 165	50.6	5 232	0.0	9.7	11.9	...	...
Cochise, AZ	101 682	4 914	57.6	7 562	10.4	19.8	6.1	...	...
Coconino, AZ	101 598	5 226	57.6	8 192	0.0	7.9	6.6	...	...
Gila, AZ	45 205	4 786	53.5	2 558	0.0	10.4	9.6	...	...
Graham, AZ	26 842	4 372	59.6	2 653	0.0	10.8	7.9	...	...
Greenlee, AZ	10 105	4 915	55.7	538	0.0	10.0	2.2	...	...
La Paz, AZ	16 103	5 433	52.3	923	0.0	10.9	8.2	...	...
Maricopa, AZ	2 297 225	4 768	59.4	168 713	0.2	11.3	8.4	...	...
Mohave, AZ	90 099	4 126	57.6	7 038	0.0	13.9	11.8	...	...
Navajo, AZ	117 555	5 225	49.2	7 191	0.0	10.3	10.5	...	...
Pima, AZ	622 146	4 962	56.5	49 172	0.7	10.0	6.8	...	...
Pinal, AZ	129 060	4 881	55.3	9 460	0.0	10.9	14.5	...	...
Santa Cruz, AZ	43 253	4 735	56.1	2 215	0.0	8.2	8.4	...	...
Yavapai, AZ	96 502	4 441	59.1	7 946	0.1	10.5	6.0	...	...
Yuma, AZ	132 679	4 587	55.9	9 194	3.3	11.4	9.6	...	...
ARKANSAS									
Arkansas, AR	18 491	4 843	59.9	1 142	0.0	11.6	6.5	269	4.8
Ashley, AR	23 294	5 040	59.6	1 373	0.0	9.7	4.4	282	6.8
Baxter, AR	23 992	4 725	61.6	1 655	0.0	22.9	2.8	341	5.0
Benton, AR	111 764	4 754	61.6	8 071	0.0	13.8	4.4	1 345	3.8
Boone, AR	32 567	5 607	57.6	1 867	0.0	15.3	4.2	388	4.6
Bradley, AR	12 334	5 511	60.0	679	1.2	23.3	3.5	158	5.3
Calhoun, AR	4 386	5 148	62.1	273	0.0	13.9	0.0	55	4.2
Carroll, AR	16 774	4 696	62.0	1 457	0.0	21.4	6.2	227	5.8
Chicot, AR	16 395	5 651	60.4	916	0.0	12.1	6.6	201	8.0
Clark, AR	20 340	6 416	53.7	2 054	0.0	5.9	1.3	200	3.7
Clay, AR	13 088	4 478	62.6	777	0.0	18.5	1.3	198	3.7
Cleburne, AR	16 809	4 775	61.3	1 131	0.0	14.1	4.7	216	6.5
Cleveland, AR	7 350	4 788	62.9	453	0.0	19.9	3.5	99	3.4
Columbia, AR	22 257	4 716	61.1	1 800	0.0	7.9	5.2	305	4.9
Conway, AR	32 517	9 106	37.2	1 158	0.0	14.6	5.4	240	4.2
Craighead, AR	64 323	5 019	62.0	5 400	0.0	14.2	2.0	816	4.4
Crawford, AR	50 145	4 844	62.3	3 033	0.0	12.2	4.0	600	4.8
Crittenden, AR	51 175	4 742	62.5	3 230	0.0	9.2	7.5	520	8.0
Cross, AR	18 961	4 656	61.1	1 232	0.0	13.3	6.7	251	5.4
Dallas, AR	9 009	5 101	63.0	602	0.0	11.3	11.8	107	6.0
Desha, AR	18 876	5 189	59.3	963	0.1	9.9	4.0	203	6.7
Drew, AR	19 695	5 972	55.1	1 343	0.0	10.3	3.9	197	2.5
Faulkner, AR	65 581	4 678	61.6	6 320	0.2	9.6	1.2	864	5.7
Franklin, AR	18 499	5 091	60.2	1 195	0.0	16.5	6.1	236	4.5
Fulton, AR	8 234	4 810	61.7	552	0.0	10.5	3.8	95	2.4
Garland, AR	64 743	5 069	60.3	4 158	0.0	15.6	6.3	771	3.9
Grant, AR	20 773	4 570	63.4	885	0.0	16.9	2.0	253	3.5
Greene, AR	31 118	4 855	60.4	2 054	0.0	15.9	6.4	367	6.4
Hempstead, AR	23 031	5 586	61.3	1 363	0.0	13.4	10.4	229	7.1
Hot Spring, AR	28 922	5 162	58.8	1 662	0.0	16.3	5.1	330	7.5
Howard, AR	15 137	4 875	62.7	855	0.0	11.6	9.6	217	3.2
Independence, AR	30 570	5 180	61.3	2 132	0.7	15.1	3.0	394	5.5
Izard, AR	11 735	5 807	58.4	610	0.0	15.1	5.9	108	3.1
Jackson, AR	14 338	5 132	60.8	1 108	0.2	7.3	15.2	169	5.0
Jefferson, AR	80 165	5 189	60.5	5 609	0.0	12.9	6.0	896	7.1
Johnson, AR	18 531	4 556	64.6	1 393	0.4	12.3	8.0	222	6.1
Lafayette, AR	8 903	5 328	60.3	513	0.0	9.4	4.5	108	5.7
Lawrence, AR	18 488	5 514	60.6	1 107	0.0	13.2	4.2	214	5.6
Lee, AR	11 610	5 811	53.8	818	0.0	10.9	9.5	100	5.2
Lincoln, AR	10 689	4 852	61.0	804	0.0	18.0	6.6	136	7.3
Little River, AR	12 013	5 551	59.8	695	0.0	19.9	3.3	149	2.3
Logan, AR	17 385	4 716	63.2	1 234	0.1	17.8	5.2	221	5.9
Lonoke, AR	48 116	4 569	61.9	3 102	0.7	15.0	5.6	658	6.2
Madison, AR	11 867	4 509	61.4	813	0.0	15.0	4.4	154	5.1
Marion, AR	11 211	4 701	60.8	774	0.0	11.1	1.7	164	2.9
Miller, AR	36 097	5 209	62.7	2 225	0.0	14.7	8.6	422	9.4
Mississippi, AR	52 357	5 125	60.6	3 268	0.0	14.4	10.4	525	9.3
Monroe, AR	10 393	5 070	57.8	566	0.0	14.1	4.9	151	3.8
Montgomery, AR	6 791	4 769	61.6	459	0.0	10.5	6.8	99	4.8
Nevada, AR	9 589	4 831	60.3	480	0.0	12.3	2.1	158	3.1

. . . = Not available.

Table C-1. Population, School, and Student Characteristics by County—*Continued*

County	High school graduates, 2000			College enrollment, 2000		College graduates, 2000 (percent)						
	Population 25 years and over	High school diploma or less (percent)	High school diploma or more (percent)	Number	Percent public	Bachelor's degree or more	+/- U.S. percent with bachelor's degree or more	Non-Hispanic White	Black or African American	American Indian and Alaska Native	Asian, Hawaiian, and Pacific Islander	Hispanic or Latino[1]
	30	31	32	33	34	35	36	37	38	39	40	41
Kenai Peninsula, AK	31 388	43.3	88.5	1 623	86.9	20.3	-4.1	22.1	5.4	3.4	20.5	14.1
Ketchikan Gateway, AK	8 999	40.1	89.6	456	86.0	20.2	-4.2	22.9	0.0	4.3	23.5	28.1
Kodiak Island, AK	8 187	45.9	85.4	543	83.4	18.7	-5.7	24.7	16.2	5.4	9.8	10.6
Lake and Peninsula Borough, AK	981	67.1	72.2	39	66.7	12.4	-12.0	40.2	. . .	2.0	0.0	0.0
Matanuska-Susitna, AK	35 721	43.2	88.1	2 100	88.7	18.3	-6.1	19.3	19.8	5.9	17.4	9.0
Nome, AK	4 916	63.3	74.8	278	91.4	14.7	-9.7	42.4	25.0	3.3	24.5	6.5
North Slope, AK	3 883	57.6	77.4	250	88.0	17.0	-7.4	48.0	39.5	3.3	24.7	13.8
Northwest Arctic Borough, AK	3 498	68.4	72.0	121	89.3	12.7	-11.7	44.8	0.0	3.3	39.5	34.8
Prince of Wales-Outer Ketchikan, AK	3 797	57.0	84.1	109	90.8	14.2	-10.2	19.7	33.3	5.1	12.5	7.7
Sitka, AK	5 608	34.7	90.6	575	65.9	29.5	5.1	36.6	45.2	8.2	20.4	14.7
Skagway-Hoonah-Angoon, AK	2 273	46.1	84.4	104	75.0	21.6	-2.8	27.4	0.0	6.7	15.4	44.7
Southeast Fairbanks, AK	3 693	48.3	86.8	286	85.0	18.2	-6.2	20.6	11.9	4.4	0.0	20.6
Valdez-Cordova, AK	6 441	41.4	88.5	416	78.1	21.2	-3.2	23.8	20.8	5.7	24.2	17.4
Wade Hampton, AK	3 082	74.9	66.3	119	94.1	9.1	-15.3	68.1	42.9	2.8	55.6	16.7
Wrangell-Petersburg, AK	4 359	50.6	85.8	140	83.6	16.3	-8.1	19.2	. . .	2.0	16.5	13.2
Yakutat Borough, AK	522	49.0	84.3	27	100.0	17.6	-6.8	20.4	100.0	10.9	20.0	0.0
Yukon-Koyukuk, AK	3 707	65.0	74.3	164	91.5	14.2	-10.2	35.0	0.0	4.3	33.3	24.2
ARIZONA												
Apache, AZ	36 217	61.2	63.6	3 235	87.5	11.3	-13.1	25.4	8.3	6.7	51.1	7.9
Cochise, AZ	75 774	45.2	79.5	7 459	86.4	18.8	-5.6	23.7	18.9	6.9	18.1	5.8
Coconino, AZ	65 976	37.9	83.8	14 842	95.6	29.9	5.5	40.2	21.8	7.8	45.3	15.3
Gila, AZ	35 150	50.5	78.2	1 886	90.5	13.9	-10.5	16.6	9.3	1.9	41.6	6.3
Graham, AZ	19 302	54.5	75.6	2 540	94.2	11.8	-12.6	17.6	4.0	2.5	27.5	2.2
Greenlee, AZ	5 207	52.6	82.5	222	89.6	12.2	-12.2	16.0	6.9	0.0	0.0	7.3
La Paz, AZ	14 389	64.6	69.3	437	90.4	8.7	-15.7	9.8	16.9	6.5	16.9	3.8
Maricopa, AZ	1 934 957	40.6	82.5	197 913	81.2	25.9	1.5	30.2	19.9	11.2	45.7	8.1
Mohave, AZ	109 347	57.4	77.5	5 259	91.3	9.9	-14.5	10.3	6.2	6.0	22.8	6.0
Navajo, AZ	54 215	56.6	71.2	3 956	88.5	12.3	-12.1	19.9	6.4	4.2	25.9	4.8
Pima, AZ	546 200	39.9	83.4	69 727	90.0	26.7	2.3	32.5	16.8	9.4	42.2	10.9
Pinal, AZ	119 102	57.7	72.7	6 840	85.5	11.9	-12.5	15.6	7.4	2.0	22.6	3.9
Santa Cruz, AZ	22 445	62.2	60.7	1 314	88.0	15.2	-9.2	37.5	11.2	6.3	16.5	7.9
Yavapai, AZ	120 223	43.5	84.7	8 408	72.2	21.1	-3.3	22.3	39.5	9.7	42.4	7.7
Yuma, AZ	97 680	59.9	65.8	7 061	93.1	11.8	-12.6	16.6	12.6	6.2	23.4	4.7
ARKANSAS												
Arkansas, AR	13 888	67.4	72.4	743	90.8	12.2	-12.2	14.0	4.8	0.0	31.1	0.0
Ashley, AR	15 722	70.7	72.5	671	88.1	10.1	-14.3	11.8	4.6	12.3	44.4	3.2
Baxter, AR	28 861	60.0	77.5	911	94.7	12.8	-11.6	12.8	0.0	13.1	18.8	5.4
Benton, AR	99 436	52.4	80.4	5 637	71.6	20.3	-4.1	21.3	27.2	11.7	35.9	6.2
Boone, AR	23 070	58.2	76.8	988	89.4	12.7	-11.7	12.7	0.0	5.9	30.0	16.2
Bradley, AR	8 368	70.2	66.6	345	92.2	11.9	-12.5	14.9	6.0	. . .	0.0	5.1
Calhoun, AR	3 906	74.8	68.7	115	83.5	7.3	-17.1	8.4	3.1	0.0	0.0	7.1
Carroll, AR	17 207	62.3	71.8	398	91.2	13.8	-10.6	14.5	0.0	17.8	18.2	4.8
Chicot, AR	9 062	71.0	64.2	348	98.6	11.7	-12.7	15.9	7.2	0.0	27.5	7.5
Clark, AR	13 735	57.1	75.3	3 738	61.6	19.8	-4.6	23.1	8.7	35.6	56.8	7.3
Clay, AR	12 175	77.2	60.6	402	91.5	7.4	-17.0	7.3	0.0	3.8	100.0	0.0
Cleburne, AR	17 299	61.6	74.8	538	86.4	13.9	-10.5	14.0	20.0	14.3	55.6	4.7
Cleveland, AR	5 659	70.3	73.1	253	88.1	10.0	-14.4	11.1	2.7	0.0	10.0	0.0
Columbia, AR	16 039	61.7	74.1	2 082	95.3	16.8	-7.6	22.0	6.5	4.2	33.3	7.2
Conway, AR	13 480	68.2	73.2	712	89.9	11.5	-12.9	12.3	7.5	23.8	19.4	4.6
Craighead, AR	50 725	55.5	77.3	6 945	95.3	20.9	-3.5	21.5	14.4	8.6	22.0	11.6
Crawford, AR	33 765	64.5	71.5	1 655	88.1	9.7	-14.7	9.9	8.7	4.6	7.0	9.4
Crittenden, AR	30 251	64.0	69.2	1 928	86.6	12.8	-11.6	18.0	5.4	11.3	15.4	0.0
Cross, AR	12 412	69.8	68.3	645	92.6	9.9	-14.5	10.8	6.4	14.5	22.2	0.0
Dallas, AR	5 989	74.3	66.8	212	88.2	9.6	-14.8	14.8	1.6	0.0	. . .	0.0
Desha, AR	9 574	71.0	65.0	457	92.3	11.1	-13.3	14.1	6.9	0.0	45.9	0.0
Drew, AR	11 553	61.3	73.1	1 484	97.3	17.3	-7.1	20.6	8.2	0.0	13.0	9.1
Faulkner, AR	50 849	47.9	83.3	9 182	79.8	25.2	0.8	26.2	14.9	18.3	41.1	15.4
Franklin, AR	11 654	64.3	71.1	466	92.5	11.0	-13.4	11.2	0.0	13.8	9.1	0.0
Fulton, AR	8 243	66.9	72.2	276	88.8	10.5	-13.9	10.5	. . .	5.0	27.8	6.1
Garland, AR	62 694	54.5	78.3	2 731	87.6	18.0	-6.4	18.8	8.2	18.3	34.0	11.6
Grant, AR	10 824	65.1	77.2	539	89.2	11.0	-13.4	11.0	14.7	23.6	16.1	0.0
Greene, AR	24 510	68.5	72.1	1 233	80.5	10.9	-13.5	11.1	0.0	10.1	0.0	0.0
Hempstead, AR	14 869	69.2	69.2	932	92.4	11.0	-13.4	13.2	7.2	0.0	41.7	2.0
Hot Spring, AR	20 260	66.4	73.3	1 005	89.5	11.2	-13.2	11.7	7.2	15.4	22.0	4.1
Howard, AR	9 271	67.1	70.7	328	89.0	11.6	-12.8	13.1	6.8	6.3	5.7	8.2
Independence, AR	22 705	64.2	75.5	1 382	62.2	13.7	-10.7	13.8	11.1	23.8	11.4	3.1
Izard, AR	9 524	63.2	73.3	457	86.7	11.7	-12.7	11.8	0.0	7.5	62.5	30.4
Jackson, AR	12 204	72.3	66.0	545	89.2	10.3	-14.1	10.8	6.4	4.9	47.8	5.3
Jefferson, AR	53 132	60.0	74.8	4 998	93.1	15.7	-8.7	15.6	15.7	8.6	49.5	5.2
Johnson, AR	14 901	69.0	67.6	841	85.0	13.1	-11.3	13.5	10.0	7.6	0.0	8.3
Lafayette, AR	5 692	70.7	65.3	218	91.7	9.5	-14.9	13.0	2.9	0.0	6.7	0.0
Lawrence, AR	11 824	73.5	63.3	809	57.1	8.5	-15.9	8.6	0.0	2.4	11.5	0.0
Lee, AR	7 924	73.4	56.2	361	95.8	7.3	-17.1	8.1	6.8	23.2	0.0	0.0
Lincoln, AR	9 533	72.8	65.0	307	93.5	7.6	-16.8	9.5	4.0	0.0	0.0	1.5
Little River, AR	9 009	64.7	73.4	385	91.9	9.9	-14.5	11.7	3.4	8.4	0.0	5.0
Logan, AR	15 004	68.6	69.8	508	86.8	9.4	-15.0	9.1	4.0	24.5	68.9	12.3
Lonoke, AR	33 468	58.0	77.6	1 678	90.2	14.6	-9.8	15.2	6.5	2.2	3.7	13.3
Madison, AR	9 327	71.0	67.8	182	97.3	10.1	-14.3	10.3	0.0	9.4	7.1	2.6
Marion, AR	11 593	62.3	76.0	400	86.8	10.4	-14.0	10.3	. . .	10.9	6.8	8.2
Miller, AR	25 790	61.5	74.3	1 392	90.5	12.5	-11.9	14.2	6.0	0.0	50.4	9.6
Mississippi, AR	31 612	67.4	64.7	1 655	94.6	11.3	-13.1	13.5	5.5	1.8	44.8	7.0
Monroe, AR	6 602	74.4	63.8	208	94.2	8.4	-16.0	9.6	6.1	0.0	0.0	2.2
Montgomery, AR	6 464	69.4	69.8	185	88.1	8.8	-15.6	8.8	. . .	27.0	0.0	3.1
Nevada, AR	6 575	70.2	69.1	366	94.5	10.7	-13.7	13.3	5.1	0.0	. . .	1.2

[1]Hispanic or Latino persons may be of any race.
. . . = Not available.

Table C-1. Population, School, and Student Characteristics by County—*Continued*

County	State/County code	County type[1]	Population, 2000		Number of schools and students, 2000–2001			Resident enrollment, 2000			
			Total	Percent 5–17 years	School districts	Schools	Students	Total	Percent public	K–12	Percent public
			1	2	3	4	5	6	7	8	9
Newton, AR	05101	9	8 608	19.1	4	8	1 345	1 944	94.8	1 656	94.5
Ouachita, AR	05103	7	28 790	19.7	4	16	5 373	7 398	93.4	5 915	94.7
Perry, AR	05105	8	10 209	19.0	3	6	1 844	2 325	91.9	1 958	94.7
Phillips, AR	05107	7	26 445	23.7	5	14	5 775	8 079	90.0	6 506	91.0
Pike, AR	05109	9	11 303	18.6	4	9	2 299	2 606	93.5	2 111	95.2
Poinsett, AR	05111	6	25 614	19.3	5	13	4 783	5 948	96.9	4 997	97.5
Polk, AR	05113	7	20 229	18.9	5	12	3 606	4 834	93.4	3 852	94.6
Pope, AR	05115	5	54 469	19.0	5	22	9 571	15 194	93.8	10 420	95.9
Prairie, AR	05117	8	9 539	18.0	3	6	1 558	2 040	93.6	1 761	95.6
Pulaski, AR	05119	2	361 474	18.1	5	112	53 360	94 618	80.0	66 912	81.2
Randolph, AR	05121	7	18 195	18.6	4	10	2 893	4 304	92.8	3 368	95.0
St. Francis, AR	05123	6	29 329	20.3	3	13	5 018	8 028	94.3	6 323	94.4
Saline, AR	05125	2	83 529	19.0	5	21	12 201	20 335	88.0	15 742	93.1
Scott, AR	05127	6	10 996	19.2	1	3	1 665	2 425	96.4	2 123	97.6
Searcy, AR	05129	9	8 261	17.1	4	8	1 318	1 770	96.8	1 471	97.5
Sebastian, AR	05131	3	115 071	18.7	6	40	18 747	27 690	88.4	21 523	90.9
Sevier, AR	05133	6	15 757	20.4	3	9	3 038	3 907	96.5	3 254	98.0
Sharp, AR	05135	7	17 119	16.4	4	9	3 081	3 404	92.6	2 774	94.9
Stone, AR	05137	9	11 499	16.8	3	6	1 719	2 284	94.0	1 962	95.5
Union, AR	05139	5	45 629	19.5	9	26	8 399	11 194	91.0	9 106	92.7
Van Buren, AR	05141	8	16 192	16.4	5	11	2 461	3 205	93.9	2 688	95.9
Washington, AR	05143	3	157 715	17.7	9	51	26 579	46 255	91.3	27 413	93.9
White, AR	05145	4	67 165	18.1	9	30	11 545	18 439	75.5	12 232	91.9
Woodruff, AR	05147	7	8 741	19.0	3	6	1 535	2 089	96.6	1 674	97.9
Yell, AR	05149	7	21 139	19.3	6	14	4 013	4 761	94.7	4 062	96.7
CALIFORNIA	06000										
Alameda, CA	06001	0	1 443 741	17.7	21	334	218 992	417 264	83.1	264 846	87.2
Alpine, CA	06003	9	1 208	17.8	2	8	150	296	91.2	208	88.9
Amador, CA	06005	6	35 100	16.4	3	16	5 526	8 110	87.8	6 659	92.5
Butte, CA	06007	3	203 171	18.3	15	87	34 433	66 431	93.1	38 232	93.0
Calaveras, CA	06009	6	40 554	18.4	5	27	6 967	9 406	93.3	7 597	96.1
Colusa, CA	06011	6	18 804	23.5	5	20	4 275	5 596	94.4	4 635	96.1
Contra Costa, CA	06013	0	948 816	19.6	19	239	159 714	270 131	83.3	189 347	89.2
Del Norte, CA	06015	7	27 507	19.5	2	14	4 834	7 135	87.9	5 685	87.7
El Dorado, CA	06017	1	156 299	20.4	16	62	28 795	44 193	89.6	32 460	92.8
Fresno, CA	06019	2	799 407	23.6	35	291	181 110	263 942	93.0	197 351	96.1
Glenn, CA	06021	6	26 453	23.2	10	30	6 167	7 721	95.1	6 253	97.0
Humboldt, CA	06023	5	126 518	17.6	33	84	21 195	38 481	93.2	22 774	93.3
Imperial, CA	06025	4	142 361	23.8	17	61	33 216	47 441	94.6	36 443	96.2
Inyo, CA	06027	7	17 945	19.0	8	23	3 404	4 326	92.1	3 460	95.8
Kern, CA	06029	2	661 645	23.5	48	240	147 988	205 960	91.8	161 296	94.5
Kings, CA	06031	4	129 461	20.9	15	53	25 364	37 449	90.4	29 332	92.6
Lake, CA	06033	6	58 309	18.8	8	34	10 163	14 144	93.6	11 232	95.3
Lassen, CA	06035	6	33 828	16.9	11	30	5 335	8 900	91.9	6 518	94.0
Los Angeles, CA	06037	0	9 519 338	20.3	83	1 787	1 681 787	2 931 076	84.3	2 041 738	89.2
Madera, CA	06039	2	123 109	22.0	12	58	24 780	35 998	92.7	28 604	95.2
Marin, CA	06041	0	247 289	14.9	20	74	28 703	57 014	74.3	37 704	81.2
Mariposa, CA	06043	8	17 130	17.2	3	17	2 619	4 096	88.6	3 096	90.9
Mendocino, CA	06045	4	86 265	19.6	13	69	15 358	22 795	92.5	17 157	94.3
Merced, CA	06047	3	210 554	25.6	21	87	51 595	70 396	93.2	55 741	94.9
Modoc, CA	06049	7	9 449	20.1	4	21	2 255	2 336	97.4	2 005	97.6
Mono, CA	06051	7	12 853	17.3	3	18	2 140	2 917	89.6	2 210	92.3
Monterey, CA	06053	2	401 762	20.6	25	118	72 529	117 126	89.3	86 811	92.7
Napa, CA	06055	0	124 279	18.1	6	48	19 341	33 203	81.7	23 590	88.0
Nevada, CA	06057	4	92 033	18.4	11	50	14 272	23 203	90.9	17 457	94.3
Orange, CA	06059	0	2 846 289	19.4	28	567	494 178	847 671	85.2	569 481	90.1
Placer, CA	06061	1	248 399	20.1	20	97	55 531	69 856	87.1	50 421	91.7
Plumas, CA	06063	6	20 824	18.2	2	18	3 406	5 030	93.2	3 871	95.1
Riverside, CA	06065	0	1 545 387	22.5	25	366	319 910	465 645	89.0	356 146	93.0
Sacramento, CA	06067	0	1 223 499	20.3	18	345	222 224	366 459	87.8	253 944	90.7
San Benito, CA	06069	6	53 234	23.4	12	23	11 501	16 010	89.1	12 580	91.7
San Bernardino, CA	06071	0	1 709 434	23.9	35	457	380 830	555 363	89.0	420 751	93.3
San Diego, CA	06073	0	2 813 833	18.7	43	612	488 377	827 975	86.6	539 834	91.8
San Francisco, CA	06075	0	776 733	10.5	2	119	61 766	182 963	73.6	88 461	76.2
San Joaquin, CA	06077	2	563 598	23.0	17	182	122 349	176 188	87.5	133 856	92.3
San Luis Obispo, CA	06079	3	246 681	16.6	12	81	37 561	77 496	91.1	42 791	91.7
San Mateo, CA	06081	0	707 161	16.5	24	173	91 205	184 928	77.1	121 187	81.6
Santa Barbara, CA	06083	2	399 347	18.4	24	110	66 012	127 198	86.6	74 970	92.2
Santa Clara, CA	06085	0	1 682 585	17.7	34	378	254 004	476 333	80.1	305 563	87.5
Santa Cruz, CA	06087	0	255 602	17.7	13	74	40 462	76 840	86.9	46 143	88.6
Shasta, CA	06089	3	163 256	20.2	26	93	30 440	45 010	88.2	33 592	91.8
Sierra, CA	06091	8	3 555	19.2	2	12	1 621	875	95.4	699	98.6
Siskiyou, CA	06093	7	44 301	18.9	29	61	7 423	11 200	92.9	8 563	95.0
Solano, CA	06095	0	394 542	21.1	7	99	73 061	116 471	87.1	85 648	90.9
Sonoma, CA	06097	0	458 614	18.4	41	163	73 689	125 553	86.4	86 107	89.9
Stanislaus, CA	06099	2	446 997	23.2	28	143	97 297	136 838	90.8	106 277	93.2
Sutter, CA	06101	3	78 930	21.7	13	37	16 091	22 869	92.2	17 600	94.8
Tehama, CA	06103	6	56 039	21.1	19	41	10 786	15 427	94.2	12 146	95.7
Trinity, CA	06105	6	13 022	18.6	12	22	2 204	3 112	94.8	2 548	95.1
Tulare, CA	06107	2	368 021	24.8	48	160	85 664	118 065	93.4	94 339	95.7
Tuolumne, CA	06109	6	54 501	16.2	13	36	7 947	13 347	89.5	9 741	90.2
Ventura, CA	06111	0	753 197	21.0	22	197	140 156	224 449	85.5	162 520	90.3
Yolo, CA	06113	0	168 660	18.7	6	55	28 646	64 875	92.0	32 000	92.9
Yuba, CA	06115	3	60 219	22.8	6	36	13 547	18 858	93.6	14 106	95.1

[1]County type code is from the Economic Research Service of the USDA. See Notes and Definitions at the end of this section.

Table C-1. School and Student Characteristics by County—*Continued*

County	Characteristics of students, 2000–2001			Staff and students, 2000–2001				Revenues, fiscal 1999			
	Percent with IEP[2]	Percent eligible for free lunch	Percent minority	Number of teachers	Student/ teacher ratio	Local school non-teaching staff	Central admin. staff	Total revenue ($1,000s)	Percentage of revenue from		
									Federal govt.	State govt.	Local govt.
	10	11	12	13	14	15	16	17	18	19	20
Newton, AR	16.9	62.6	1.0	124	10.8	97	10	$9 180	16.1	67.0	16.8
Ouachita, AR	9.6	51.2	52.6	408	13.2	419	30	35 599	9.8	66.5	23.8
Perry, AR	16.0	42.0	3.7	138	13.4	118	10	10 358	10.8	68.3	20.9
Phillips, AR	11.1	76.6	81.6	380	15.2	415	32	36 312	16.9	66.4	16.7
Pike, AR	13.4	46.6	10.5	209	11.0	147	16	12 522	7.1	59.0	33.9
Poinsett, AR	15.4	53.1	13.2	378	12.7	288	22	30 148	12.2	61.7	26.1
Polk, AR	11.5	52.6	7.7	287	12.6	216	17	20 020	13.1	63.5	23.3
Pope, AR	10.9	41.4	7.8	765	12.5	657	35	58 239	7.3	48.4	44.3
Prairie, AR	9.1	47.7	21.4	140	11.1	107	15	8 858	7.9	56.6	35.5
Pulaski, AR	10.0	46.0	57.9	3 560	15.0	3 936	245	383 269	6.8	49.8	43.3
Randolph, AR	14.5	53.5	2.0	216	13.4	190	18	15 819	8.2	68.7	23.0
St. Francis, AR	14.4	73.7	68.9	332	15.1	432	24	35 033	13.1	64.4	22.5
Saline, AR	12.2	21.7	4.7	800	15.3	504	31	63 644	4.5	65.3	30.3
Scott, AR	12.1	47.4	9.0	123	13.5	92	5	9 995	22.7	58.3	19.0
Searcy, AR	14.0	66.5	1.1	123	10.7	88	6	8 266	9.7	69.4	20.9
Sebastian, AR	12.8	39.7	25.0	1 277	14.7	1 133	71	105 170	7.1	55.2	37.7
Sevier, AR	10.7	55.1	33.7	223	13.6	221	15	18 849	10.7	65.7	23.6
Sharp, AR	13.8	51.9	1.8	238	12.9	193	14	16 399	8.2	64.1	27.6
Stone, AR	13.7	49.4	1.3	147	11.7	116	9	10 473	10.1	65.9	24.0
Union, AR	11.7	45.4	45.6	635	13.2	501	37	48 154	9.0	58.8	32.2
Van Buren, AR	15.3	54.4	3.2	209	11.8	189	13	14 204	9.4	62.5	28.2
Washington, AR	12.8	34.3	17.3	1 717	15.5	1 535	65	151 834	5.3	53.1	41.6
White, AR	12.7	41.7	7.2	841	13.7	644	45	67 200	8.4	60.8	30.7
Woodruff, AR	14.3	68.1	40.6	125	12.3	126	15	9 367	13.1	62.6	24.3
Yell, AR	12.9	54.1	18.0	312	12.9	252	21	22 936	13.6	63.9	22.5
CALIFORNIA											
Alameda, CA	10.4	31.8	68.3	10 888	20.1	6 799	1 213	1 613 796	5.9	54.9	39.2
Alpine, CA	29.5	54.8	46.0	15	10.0	18	4	3 013	21.6	43.7	34.7
Amador, CA	13.2	25.3	21.2	276	20.0	252	20	30 980	3.5	40.4	56.1
Butte, CA	12.9	45.1	26.8	1 773	19.4	1 491	159	245 458	13.4	55.3	31.3
Calaveras, CA	12.0	29.6	11.9	339	20.6	368	41	47 927	4.5	44.5	51.0
Colusa, CA	11.2	67.3	62.0	254	16.8	216	21	34 152	10.7	58.6	30.7
Contra Costa, CA	12.2	29.3	47.0	7 734	20.7	5 267	662	1 085 391	7.8	50.1	42.1
Del Norte, CA	12.7	64.0	32.2	251	19.3	226	28	33 049	14.7	63.1	22.2
El Dorado, CA	11.4	21.2	16.9	1 415	20.3	1 085	179	214 586	10.2	52.8	37.0
Fresno, CA	11.2	62.4	71.0	8 785	20.6	7 359	1 079	1 265 706	10.5	65.7	23.7
Glenn, CA	...	58.3	46.8	339	18.2	264	40	48 479	10.7	63.1	26.2
Humboldt, CA	13.6	42.2	24.3	1 163	18.2	1 190	120	163 798	7.7	62.5	29.8
Imperial, CA	9.8	68.0	87.7	1 681	19.8	1 552	267	248 827	14.2	61.4	24.4
Inyo, CA	12.1	31.5	32.8	199	17.1	165	38	32 267	9.6	38.6	51.8
Kern, CA	10.0	58.9	59.4	7 228	20.5	6 558	966	1 043 286	9.5	59.8	30.7
Kings, CA	10.7	56.1	64.3	1 260	20.1	1 124	171	176 127	9.7	69.3	21.0
Lake, CA	12.7	52.2	25.4	524	19.4	482	49	73 958	12.6	55.5	31.9
Lassen, CA	...	34.0	17.8	294	18.1	257	33	40 961	8.8	62.1	29.2
Los Angeles, CA	10.6	61.3	81.3	78 291	21.5	63 319	7 897	11 409 040	10.5	64.7	24.8
Madera, CA	13.0	62.9	62.2	1 196	20.7	1 098	163	162 640	10.4	58.6	31.0
Marin, CA	14.0	14.9	25.9	1 564	18.4	1 178	217	245 173	3.9	22.9	73.2
Mariposa, CA	13.5	36.2	14.7	136	19.3	165	13	18 533	5.6	44.9	49.5
Mendocino, CA	15.1	52.4	32.0	882	17.4	826	84	135 992	8.1	53.7	38.2
Merced, CA	11.3	69.8	68.2	2 500	20.6	2 294	273	337 948	11.0	67.4	21.5
Modoc, CA	11.4	53.0	31.0	138	16.3	130	27	21 999	15.7	57.6	26.8
Mono, CA	15.3	41.7	32.6	133	16.1	114	36	19 937	6.2	37.5	56.3
Monterey, CA	9.1	55.3	73.4	3 533	20.5	2 662	377	497 161	9.9	53.3	36.8
Napa, CA	14.1	33.9	40.9	958	20.2	667	110	137 868	6.2	35.4	58.4
Nevada, CA	9.9	18.2	9.7	692	20.6	548	70	85 672	3.9	49.9	46.2
Orange, CA	9.6	37.8	58.9	22 160	22.3	16 093	2 056	3 063 174	6.2	50.0	43.8
Placer, CA	10.2	18.3	17.7	2 683	20.7	2 065	251	391 275	5.0	46.7	48.3
Plumas, CA	10.8	36.0	18.4	184	18.5	194	17	27 430	12.5	38.6	48.9
Riverside, CA	11.1	49.7	59.7	14 825	21.6	10 835	1 616	2 024 431	10.6	63.5	25.9
Sacramento, CA	11.0	43.9	52.0	10 534	21.1	8 455	1 288	1 490 616	7.9	66.0	26.1
San Benito, CA	10.3	35.0	58.9	546	21.1	364	57	78 323	10.9	52.6	36.5
San Bernardino, CA	10.8	51.7	64.3	17 376	21.9	13 050	1 913	2 387 847	8.3	68.7	23.1
San Diego, CA	11.1	40.3	58.0	23 338	20.9	18 458	2 806	3 250 824	7.7	52.9	39.4
San Francisco, CA	10.9	54.3	88.5	3 235	19.1	1 999	433	624 687	8.4	37.9	53.7
San Joaquin, CA	10.6	48.0	61.8	6 026	20.3	4 417	682	745 284	7.2	67.1	25.7
San Luis Obispo, CA	11.7	30.5	28.9	1 934	19.4	1 508	216	271 349	4.5	34.5	61.0
San Mateo, CA	10.8	24.5	60.8	4 690	19.4	3 278	563	698 923	4.5	27.4	68.1
Santa Barbara, CA	10.2	42.1	59.1	3 260	20.2	2 674	428	441 057	8.2	46.2	45.6
Santa Clara, CA	10.3	27.9	65.9	12 309	20.6	8 135	1 245	1 984 180	6.0	33.2	60.7
Santa Cruz, CA	12.1	36.9	51.5	2 011	20.1	1 602	283	283 449	7.9	50.6	41.5
Shasta, CA	11.5	42.9	17.1	1 510	20.2	1 429	184	245 346	8.6	53.1	38.3
Sierra, CA	7.2	...	33.3	83	19.5	52	12	18 583	5.0	82.4	12.6
Siskiyou, CA	13.6	55.2	20.8	456	16.3	427	56	70 680	13.9	57.4	28.6
Solano, CA	11.8	30.2	56.6	3 554	20.6	2 291	328	445 951	6.0	66.0	27.9
Sonoma, CA	12.8	25.4	30.9	3 737	19.7	2 664	349	555 955	4.4	45.8	49.8
Stanislaus, CA	12.3	48.1	50.7	4 516	21.5	3 204	489	646 497	10.6	57.7	31.7
Sutter, CA	13.6	55.6	46.0	822	19.6	614	85	111 130	13.5	59.3	27.2
Tehama, CA	10.7	51.5	26.3	571	18.9	595	68	79 566	8.4	62.5	29.1
Trinity, CA	...	54.1	13.6	145	15.2	186	14	24 745	15.3	52.0	32.7
Tulare, CA	9.2	65.7	68.2	4 233	20.2	3 190	438	680 491	12.8	61.7	25.4
Tuolumne, CA	12.7	37.1	12.1	433	18.4	366	49	65 920	14.3	48.9	36.8
Ventura, CA	10.1	34.8	52.4	6 402	21.9	4 682	615	932 396	6.8	53.9	39.3
Yolo, CA	10.9	37.3	47.7	1 458	19.6	1 068	174	184 084	6.5	56.2	37.3
Yuba, CA	14.4	64.5	44.7	658	20.6	527	75	95 353	14.2	64.4	21.4

[2]IEP = Individual Education Program. See Notes and Definitions at the end of this section.
. . . = Not available.

Table C-1. Population, School, and Student Characteristics by County—*Continued*

County	Current expenditures, fiscal 1999			Resident population 16 to 19 years, 2000				Outcomes, 1999–2000	
	Amount ($1,000s)	Amount per student	Percent for instruction	Total population 16 to 19 years	Percent in Armed Forces	Percent high school graduates	Percent not enrolled, not grads, not Armed Forces, not empl.	Number of graduates	Dropouts grades 9–12 (percent)
	21	22	23	24	25	26	27	28	29
Newton, AR	$7 648	$5 386	60.3	500	0.0	14.6	4.4	120	2.6
Ouachita, AR	30 503	5 377	58.4	1 647	0.0	11.8	6.1	338	5.4
Perry, AR	9 062	4 851	61.6	579	0.0	15.4	8.8	114	8.5
Phillips, AR	34 090	5 603	59.1	1 854	0.2	8.0	7.2	364	9.6
Pike, AR	11 135	5 025	61.2	609	0.0	8.5	3.0	134	3.5
Poinsett, AR	26 942	5 533	59.6	1 520	0.0	12.4	8.8	322	7.4
Polk, AR	17 621	4 770	62.5	1 142	0.4	14.1	4.0	231	5.3
Pope, AR	49 502	5 130	61.8	3 688	0.1	10.9	5.4	589	6.4
Prairie, AR	7 517	4 767	61.4	490	0.0	12.9	3.9	112	3.4
Pulaski, AR	338 394	6 368	58.4	19 002	1.3	13.3	5.9	2 888	6.0
Randolph, AR	14 775	4 951	62.8	1 000	0.0	19.5	9.6	193	5.0
St. Francis, AR	31 932	5 301	59.1	1 853	0.0	12.3	6.4	329	7.5
Saline, AR	54 352	4 510	65.6	4 127	0.0	14.4	4.6	705	5.8
Scott, AR	7 371	4 408	61.4	604	0.0	15.2	6.5	96	3.7
Searcy, AR	7 522	5 369	57.3	473	0.0	17.3	3.2	119	5.2
Sebastian, AR	94 981	5 136	62.0	6 418	0.3	12.8	6.6	1 204	5.1
Sevier, AR	16 218	5 342	58.4	968	0.0	14.7	6.1	172	6.4
Sharp, AR	15 048	4 903	61.0	870	0.0	16.7	9.3	196	5.5
Stone, AR	8 736	4 872	63.7	587	0.0	25.6	4.1	114	5.3
Union, AR	43 928	4 997	63.0	2 802	0.0	14.2	7.1	587	8.2
Van Buren, AR	11 557	4 772	58.7	730	0.0	20.1	5.3	141	7.1
Washington, AR	130 248	5 187	64.5	10 993	0.0	11.7	4.5	1 578	6.1
White, AR	56 394	4 930	60.9	4 613	0.0	10.0	5.4	719	5.6
Woodruff, AR	8 437	5 224	60.5	498	0.0	8.6	11.8	108	3.9
Yell, AR	18 531	4 715	60.2	1 328	0.0	16.9	6.8	234	7.6
CALIFORNIA									
Alameda, CA	1 253 958	5 851	63.1	71 920	0.1	8.7	5.1	11 231	. . .
Alpine, CA	2 229	17 976	57.6	86	0.0	34.9	7.0	0	. . .
Amador, CA	28 011	5 630	59.4	2 350	0.0	10.5	8.1	349	. . .
Butte, CA	216 646	6 139	57.7	13 482	0.1	8.2	2.7	2 097	. . .
Calaveras, CA	41 684	6 062	57.3	2 061	0.0	12.8	5.1	485	. . .
Colusa, CA	30 279	7 061	58.8	1 480	0.0	8.6	11.8	296	. . .
Contra Costa, CA	854 116	5 546	63.6	48 997	0.0	9.1	3.9	8 764	. . .
Del Norte, CA	29 837	5 657	63.6	1 693	0.0	13.2	7.2	306	. . .
El Dorado, CA	165 904	5 748	60.1	8 592	0.0	11.7	2.2	1 763	. . .
Fresno, CA	1 028 178	5 765	59.5	54 287	0.0	9.1	6.9	9 306	. . .
Glenn, CA	41 033	6 602	58.6	1 596	0.0	10.8	4.2	334	. . .
Humboldt, CA	136 478	6 179	60.8	7 987	0.3	11.8	4.0	1 369	. . .
Imperial, CA	201 804	6 134	61.1	9 576	0.2	9.1	6.7	1 863	. . .
Inyo, CA	27 516	8 032	55.4	934	0.0	14.6	2.9	205	. . .
Kern, CA	880 846	6 131	58.0	42 920	0.5	11.6	7.2	7 995	. . .
Kings, CA	147 017	5 876	60.5	7 867	4.1	14.5	8.6	1 162	. . .
Lake, CA	64 211	6 479	57.0	2 895	0.0	11.8	7.1	563	. . .
Lassen, CA	36 615	6 636	58.6	1 735	0.0	16.4	4.8	325	. . .
Los Angeles, CA	9 648 637	5 968	62.5	539 900	0.1	8.0	7.1	77 238	. . .
Madera, CA	138 335	5 929	57.1	8 045	0.0	11.1	9.1	1 271	. . .
Marin, CA	208 962	7 257	61.6	9 466	0.1	8.2	3.6	1 744	. . .
Mariposa, CA	17 225	6 203	55.1	863	0.0	18.4	4.1	172	. . .
Mendocino, CA	109 945	6 959	60.8	5 310	0.3	14.3	6.8	1 041	. . .
Merced, CA	295 568	5 943	60.3	14 424	0.0	10.2	7.2	2 886	. . .
Modoc, CA	18 202	8 676	57.9	517	0.0	14.5	3.9	150	. . .
Mono, CA	15 979	7 577	56.7	680	5.3	30.6	4.3	115	. . .
Monterey, CA	421 393	6 060	63.4	25 375	3.6	11.9	7.6	3 339	. . .
Napa, CA	113 085	5 858	60.1	6 854	0.0	9.5	3.5	1 218	. . .
Nevada, CA	77 411	5 829	63.7	4 998	0.0	8.2	4.1	1 106	. . .
Orange, CA	2 545 277	5 399	63.1	151 675	0.1	8.0	4.9	26 897	. . .
Placer, CA	283 831	5 426	61.9	13 370	0.0	10.0	2.7	3 479	. . .
Plumas, CA	25 605	7 245	57.6	1 169	0.0	11.6	1.5	226	. . .
Riverside, CA	1 599 999	5 420	62.9	93 272	0.1	12.4	6.0	15 628	. . .
Sacramento, CA	1 211 793	5 794	61.4	67 282	0.4	11.8	5.6	11 851	. . .
San Benito, CA	62 690	5 745	62.1	2 807	0.0	14.9	4.5	573	. . .
San Bernardino, CA	1 991 988	5 460	60.9	109 876	1.8	12.9	6.7	18 893	. . .
San Diego, CA	2 716 606	5 774	62.0	158 984	5.9	14.7	4.6	25 681	. . .
San Francisco, CA	425 463	6 851	66.7	26 234	0.2	8.5	4.2	3 763	. . .
San Joaquin, CA	622 524	5 540	61.4	37 229	0.0	10.7	7.0	5 503	. . .
San Luis Obispo, CA	211 928	5 789	61.4	18 175	0.1	8.8	2.3	2 213	. . .
San Mateo, CA	568 972	6 124	60.6	32 251	0.0	7.4	4.4	5 073	. . .
Santa Barbara, CA	386 785	5 997	63.2	26 449	0.3	7.3	4.2	3 620	. . .
Santa Clara, CA	1 548 224	6 111	62.6	85 189	0.0	7.9	4.5	13 795	. . .
Santa Cruz, CA	237 410	5 870	61.3	15 913	0.0	8.1	4.6	2 276	. . .
Shasta, CA	192 476	6 314	58.3	9 897	0.0	10.3	4.1	1 859	. . .
Sierra, CA	7 897	2 637	60.7	206	0.0	19.9	0.0	140	. . .
Siskiyou, CA	57 280	7 215	58.9	2 597	0.0	9.5	3.6	492	. . .
Solano, CA	374 098	5 224	66.2	22 795	1.8	12.8	4.2	4 034	. . .
Sonoma, CA	437 255	6 103	61.8	25 183	0.5	11.3	4.5	3 856	. . .
Stanislaus, CA	533 142	5 707	65.2	28 694	0.0	12.5	6.4	5 258	. . .
Sutter, CA	96 049	6 108	59.2	4 725	0.0	11.7	5.8	973	. . .
Tehama, CA	70 107	6 444	60.8	3 288	0.0	12.3	3.2	596	. . .
Trinity, CA	20 579	8 955	56.6	628	0.0	10.4	2.5	162	. . .
Tulare, CA	504 792	5 958	62.3	25 935	0.0	10.0	7.5	4 304	. . .
Tuolumne, CA	51 092	6 216	62.4	2 911	0.0	10.3	4.6	493	. . .
Ventura, CA	729 846	5 435	63.1	43 659	0.8	9.5	4.6	7 398	. . .
Yolo, CA	151 036	5 605	59.4	14 269	0.0	6.5	3.0	1 566	. . .
Yuba, CA	79 896	6 065	61.8	3 927	3.6	13.0	6.7	571	. . .

. . . = Not available.

Table C-1. Population, School, and Student Characteristics by County—*Continued*

County	High school graduates, 2000			College enrollment, 2000		College graduates, 2000 (percent)						
	Population 25 years and over	High school diploma or less (percent)	High school diploma or more (percent)	Number	Percent public	Bachelor's degree or more	+/- U.S. percent with bachelor's degree or more	Non-Hispanic White	Black or African American	American Indian and Alaska Native	Asian, Hawaiian, and Pacific Islander	Hispanic or Latino[1]
	30	31	32	33	34	35	36	37	38	39	40	41
Newton, AR	5 814	67.6	70.2	156	96.8	11.8	-12.6	11.7	0.0	32.7	...	6.9
Ouachita, AR	18 975	61.4	73.5	965	93.7	12.7	-11.7	15.6	7.2	23.4	41.5	12.0
Perry, AR	6 859	67.6	73.8	257	80.5	11.1	-13.3	10.7	44.3	4.4	62.5	4.8
Phillips, AR	15 420	64.3	62.2	923	87.6	12.4	-12.0	16.6	8.0	0.0	40.5	5.1
Pike, AR	7 653	70.3	68.8	357	94.4	10.1	-14.3	10.1	6.5	20.7	15.4	7.6
Poinsett, AR	16 674	77.5	62.0	678	93.4	6.3	-18.1	6.7	2.2	0.0	0.0	0.0
Polk, AR	13 505	63.6	72.6	711	88.2	10.9	-13.5	11.2	0.0	0.0	24.0	6.3
Pope, AR	34 297	56.1	77.4	3 951	94.0	19.0	-5.4	19.3	14.8	14.1	12.4	12.8
Prairie, AR	6 550	70.6	68.2	167	89.2	9.0	-15.4	9.7	3.6	0.0	0.0	3.8
Pulaski, AR	235 921	42.7	84.4	20 254	85.3	28.1	3.7	32.9	15.5	21.3	47.1	16.2
Randolph, AR	12 207	69.1	69.2	571	94.9	10.6	-13.8	10.6	0.0	0.0	0.0	12.0
St. Francis, AR	18 173	67.6	65.1	1 147	96.8	9.6	-14.8	13.0	6.4	16.7	22.0	0.3
Saline, AR	55 796	55.4	82.3	3 030	85.3	16.4	-8.0	16.4	11.9	13.9	24.0	9.6
Scott, AR	7 141	71.8	65.4	177	88.7	8.4	-16.0	8.6	...	0.0	28.6	0.0
Searcy, AR	5 792	72.6	68.0	208	92.3	8.4	-16.0	8.4	0.0	8.8	11.1	20.8
Sebastian, AR	74 601	54.6	76.6	4 352	90.1	16.6	-7.8	18.3	7.9	15.3	7.0	4.6
Sevier, AR	9 828	69.2	64.6	479	92.7	9.2	-15.2	10.9	4.8	2.8	0.0	1.8
Sharp, AR	12 294	65.4	72.9	391	81.6	10.3	-14.1	10.4	0.0	9.8	7.7	12.2
Stone, AR	8 119	70.4	68.0	263	84.0	9.8	-14.6	9.9	0.0	0.0	100.0	0.0
Union, AR	29 986	61.0	74.5	1 427	91.9	14.9	-9.5	18.5	5.7	2.2	43.7	8.6
Van Buren, AR	11 602	65.2	71.6	363	87.1	11.5	-12.9	11.5	38.5	23.2	0.0	12.1
Washington, AR	94 019	51.0	79.5	16 443	93.0	24.5	0.1	25.3	25.0	13.0	50.6	6.1
White, AR	42 366	62.8	72.9	5 349	39.5	15.5	-8.9	15.8	12.6	2.1	14.4	11.3
Woodruff, AR	5 716	76.1	60.6	229	90.4	8.7	-16.4	8.7	6.4	0.0	0.0	9.7
Yell, AR	13 659	71.6	64.1	439	88.2	10.9	-13.5	12.1	2.7	11.5	1.0	1.2
CALIFORNIA												
Alameda, CA	953 716	36.7	82.4	126 921	81.5	34.9	10.5	42.7	18.8	16.7	45.3	12.7
Alpine, CA	797	37.6	88.3	67	95.5	28.2	3.8	34.1	...	3.0	0.0	8.7
Amador, CA	25 549	46.3	84.0	1 063	71.9	16.6	-7.8	18.0	0.5	14.4	32.9	7.8
Butte, CA	126 736	42.1	82.3	25 780	96.2	21.8	-2.6	23.2	14.6	10.5	25.6	11.7
Calaveras, CA	29 201	42.9	85.7	1 426	82.3	17.1	-7.3	17.9	25.2	7.4	54.7	5.5
Colusa, CA	10 912	60.1	64.0	722	89.6	10.6	-13.8	16.5	0.0	6.0	10.0	2.3
Contra Costa, CA	625 641	32.9	86.9	61 975	78.2	35.0	10.6	40.1	18.3	17.7	48.0	12.5
Del Norte, CA	18 459	55.8	71.6	1 127	92.0	11.0	-13.4	13.2	1.3	6.0	12.5	4.2
El Dorado, CA	105 034	33.1	89.1	9 288	88.8	26.5	2.1	27.6	50.6	11.9	35.5	10.7
Fresno, CA	455 540	53.6	67.5	54 663	86.9	17.5	-6.9	26.2	11.8	7.5	24.5	5.6
Glenn, CA	16 099	58.3	68.5	1 058	91.8	10.7	-13.7	12.8	11.0	6.7	9.6	2.8
Humboldt, CA	81 501	40.8	84.9	13 891	96.3	23.0	-1.4	24.2	11.4	12.4	28.9	15.4
Imperial, CA	83 632	62.9	59.0	8 705	93.1	10.3	-14.1	19.7	4.5	5.4	30.7	6.4
Inyo, CA	12 566	49.0	82.3	546	83.3	17.1	-7.3	20.0	0.0	4.1	20.9	3.0
Kern, CA	383 667	56.9	68.5	34 561	86.5	13.5	-10.9	18.6	7.4	6.9	28.0	3.7
Kings, CA	77 095	60.1	68.8	6 475	84.0	10.4	-14.0	16.7	3.3	4.0	21.1	3.3
Lake, CA	40 717	52.5	77.3	2 295	89.2	12.1	-12.3	12.9	5.8	1.8	31.2	5.0
Lassen, CA	22 963	51.2	79.6	2 013	89.2	10.7	-13.7	13.9	0.3	3.0	13.3	2.2
Los Angeles, CA	5 882 948	48.9	69.9	730 314	76.1	24.9	0.5	37.7	17.8	11.6	42.4	6.8
Madera, CA	74 830	59.9	65.4	5 995	84.4	12.0	-12.4	17.2	7.2	9.3	27.6	3.7
Marin, CA	183 694	21.2	91.2	14 513	72.1	51.3	26.9	56.0	16.8	26.2	54.7	18.1
Mariposa, CA	12 196	41.2	85.1	819	85.8	20.2	-4.2	20.8	51.6	7.8	25.4	19.6
Mendocino, CA	56 886	45.2	80.8	4 500	90.5	20.2	-4.2	22.6	14.7	4.9	35.5	7.1
Merced, CA	116 725	60.1	63.8	11 077	91.0	11.0	-13.4	16.6	11.1	7.4	13.2	3.5
Modoc, CA	6 464	52.3	77.1	192	97.9	12.4	-12.0	13.4	0.0	0.0	7.1	11.4
Mono, CA	8 674	32.7	87.9	601	83.2	28.9	4.5	32.8	58.3	12.2	46.8	4.9
Monterey, CA	244 128	50.1	68.4	24 295	82.3	22.5	-1.9	36.4	11.3	8.7	26.5	4.6
Napa, CA	83 938	40.1	80.4	7 765	71.5	26.4	2.0	30.5	11.3	12.1	40.0	7.4
Nevada, CA	65 148	33.5	90.3	4 524	88.7	26.1	1.7	26.8	37.2	14.1	23.8	15.0
Orange, CA	1 813 456	38.0	79.5	230 749	82.4	30.8	6.4	37.6	27.6	13.3	40.9	8.5
Placer, CA	165 894	30.8	90.5	14 728	85.1	30.3	5.9	31.1	39.4	20.3	45.4	15.7
Plumas, CA	14 786	39.7	88.0	922	90.5	17.5	-6.9	18.2	5.2	2.2	32.3	3.9
Riverside, CA	936 024	49.7	75.0	88 703	81.6	16.6	-7.8	20.7	15.1	9.5	36.7	5.8
Sacramento, CA	772 488	39.6	83.3	93 272	86.4	24.8	0.4	28.2	15.4	13.6	29.7	12.0
San Benito, CA	31 401	48.3	74.9	2 570	88.3	17.1	-7.3	25.5	16.3	15.5	27.3	5.6
San Bernardino, CA	983 273	50.8	74.2	108 262	79.3	15.9	-8.5	19.2	14.8	9.0	42.0	6.4
San Diego, CA	1 773 327	37.3	82.6	242 117	81.8	29.5	5.1	36.1	16.3	13.8	36.0	10.7
San Francisco, CA	595 805	32.7	81.2	85 159	74.0	45.0	20.6	63.2	18.1	28.0	31.6	20.3
San Joaquin, CA	333 572	54.0	71.2	33 087	75.1	14.5	-9.9	18.2	9.7	6.4	20.7	5.3
San Luis Obispo, CA	159 196	36.2	85.6	31 338	94.4	26.7	2.3	29.8	7.6	11.6	34.1	8.9
San Mateo, CA	490 285	32.2	85.3	51 250	76.4	39.0	14.6	45.2	20.0	20.4	48.3	12.3
Santa Barbara, CA	246 729	39.8	79.2	46 317	81.7	29.4	5.0	38.9	16.9	12.3	37.1	7.0
Santa Clara, CA	1 113 058	32.5	83.4	141 601	72.5	40.5	16.1	47.1	29.7	16.3	50.9	11.0
Santa Cruz, CA	164 999	33.3	83.2	27 005	89.5	34.2	9.8	41.0	22.7	18.1	40.7	9.3
Shasta, CA	107 272	44.4	83.3	8 952	81.3	16.6	-7.8	17.2	12.7	5.4	17.3	10.8
Sierra, CA	2 540	43.5	85.2	124	96.0	17.2	-7.2	18.0	...	8.3	100.0	5.9
Siskiyou, CA	30 682	44.4	83.8	2 109	90.9	17.7	-6.7	19.2	5.0	7.2	10.5	6.7
Solano, CA	246 488	40.7	83.8	24 612	81.6	21.4	-3.0	23.9	14.7	8.2	31.1	9.8
Sonoma, CA	306 564	35.5	84.9	32 351	86.5	28.5	4.1	31.7	21.6	10.6	35.3	9.6
Stanislaus, CA	264 578	55.7	70.4	24 120	87.9	14.1	-10.3	17.2	14.7	7.4	21.0	5.1
Sutter, CA	49 071	50.6	73.0	4 072	87.7	15.3	-9.1	17.3	12.6	11.3	19.2	5.3
Tehama, CA	36 261	55.1	75.7	2 501	93.2	11.3	-13.1	12.5	10.0	6.9	38.5	2.4
Trinity, CA	9 433	48.6	81.0	441	92.5	15.5	-8.9	16.6	0.0	1.4	6.8	5.5
Tulare, CA	204 888	61.3	61.7	17 959	87.5	11.5	-12.9	17.5	6.7	4.6	18.4	3.6
Tuolumne, CA	38 977	45.4	84.3	2 825	91.3	16.1	-8.3	17.4	2.5	5.3	46.5	4.8
Ventura, CA	471 756	39.6	80.1	48 445	81.6	26.9	2.5	33.3	27.1	15.1	46.3	7.6
Yolo, CA	95 423	40.0	79.8	30 104	95.1	34.1	9.7	40.7	22.3	14.2	55.3	9.6
Yuba, CA	35 218	55.4	71.8	3 732	90.6	10.3	-14.1	11.6	14.6	4.5	10.2	3.7

[1]Hispanic or Latino persons may be of any race.

Table C-1. Population, School, and Student Characteristics by County—*Continued*

County	State/County code	County type[1]	Population, 2000		Number of schools and students, 2000–2001			Resident enrollment, 2000			
			Total	Percent 5–17 years	School districts	Schools	Students	Total	Percent public	K–12	Percent public
			1	2	3	4	5	6	7	8	9
COLORADO	08000										
Adams, CO	08001	0	363 857	20.1	7	109	60 663	95 644	89.1	73 319	93.6
Alamosa, CO	08003	7	14 966	20.3	2	8	2 760	5 251	91.8	3 079	91.9
Arapahoe, CO	08005	0	487 967	19.8	7	140	96 450	134 175	84.5	97 404	91.0
Archuleta, CO	08007	9	9 898	20.0	1	4	1 558	2 222	87.8	1 975	90.7
Baca, CO	08009	9	4 517	18.6	5	12	918	1 117	95.6	909	96.1
Bent, CO	08011	9	5 998	17.8	2	7	974	1 547	94.4	1 197	95.2
Boulder, CO	08013	0	291 288	16.9	3	93	47 246	90 124	85.8	48 758	89.7
Chaffee, CO	08015	7	16 242	15.3	2	8	2 270	3 408	83.3	2 620	87.4
Cheyenne, CO	08017	9	2 231	22.4	2	5	472	606	96.9	508	97.2
Clear Creek, CO	08019	8	9 322	16.8	1	6	1 327	2 042	86.5	1 570	92.4
Conejos, CO	08021	9	8 400	24.3	3	10	1 959	2 611	98.0	2 119	98.8
Costilla, CO	08023	9	3 663	19.4	2	5	631	908	94.2	733	96.5
Crowley, CO	08025	8	5 518	14.4	1	3	610	1 362	89.3	930	88.1
Custer, CO	08027	8	3 503	17.0	1	2	471	687	87.3	579	87.7
Delta, CO	08029	7	27 834	18.3	1	15	4 799	5 975	87.7	5 042	89.1
Denver, CO	08031	0	554 636	15.1	2	128	71 164	130 485	80.6	83 908	88.2
Dolores, CO	08033	9	1 844	16.9	1	3	332	365	93.2	312	93.9
Douglas, CO	08035	1	175 766	21.9	1	51	34 918	51 934	80.4	37 565	90.0
Eagle, CO	08037	7	41 659	16.4	1	13	4 649	9 194	85.7	6 782	91.7
Elbert, CO	08039	8	19 872	23.6	5	18	4 028	5 926	87.9	4 876	92.2
El Paso, CO	08041	2	516 929	20.0	16	184	94 074	146 429	83.8	103 247	90.9
Fremont, CO	08043	6	46 145	15.8	3	17	6 468	10 309	87.4	7 865	90.2
Garfield, CO	08045	7	43 791	19.7	3	23	9 472	10 894	89.2	8 442	93.1
Gilpin, CO	08047	8	4 757	15.5	1	4	444	1 027	83.2	732	90.6
Grand, CO	08049	9	12 442	16.0	2	10	1 892	2 475	90.3	2 038	94.7
Gunnison, CO	08051	7	13 956	13.3	1	6	1 684	4 697	92.0	1 918	94.0
Hinsdale, CO	08053	9	790	13.4	1	3	63	138	78.3	111	82.0
Huerfano, CO	08055	6	7 862	16.6	2	6	1 125	1 747	83.3	1 349	84.7
Jackson, CO	08057	9	1 577	19.9	1	2	304	367	94.3	303	93.1
Jefferson, CO	08059	0	527 056	19.0	1	157	87 703	141 847	84.0	100 325	89.4
Kiowa, CO	08061	9	1 622	19.9	2	5	362	425	98.8	341	100.0
Kit Carson, CO	08063	7	8 011	20.6	5	12	1 682	2 120	93.8	1 743	96.2
Lake, CO	08065	7	7 812	19.0	2	7	1 406	2 047	95.7	1 521	98.9
La Plata, CO	08067	7	43 941	17.6	3	20	7 101	13 191	89.7	7 778	91.5
Larimer, CO	08069	3	251 494	17.7	3	75	40 084	80 102	89.3	44 334	90.9
Las Animas, CO	08071	7	15 207	18.7	6	16	2 374	3 954	91.0	2 816	89.6
Lincoln, CO	08073	8	6 087	18.9	3	6	1 001	1 595	88.7	1 323	88.9
Logan, CO	08075	7	20 504	18.4	4	15	3 490	5 725	90.8	4 078	91.6
Mesa, CO	08077	5	116 255	18.8	3	45	20 468	29 470	89.3	21 719	91.9
Mineral, CO	08079	9	831	16.0	1	2	163	178	96.6	138	98.6
Moffat, CO	08081	7	13 184	21.7	1	9	2 575	3 639	93.0	2 835	94.3
Montezuma, CO	08083	7	23 830	20.6	4	21	4 659	5 872	94.3	4 789	96.2
Montrose, CO	08085	7	33 432	20.0	2	19	5 845	7 732	91.9	6 780	93.4
Morgan, CO	08087	6	27 171	21.9	4	17	5 505	7 075	94.1	5 760	96.1
Otero, CO	08089	6	20 311	20.4	6	21	3 978	5 382	94.7	4 069	95.7
Ouray, CO	08091	9	3 742	17.7	2	6	574	779	94.4	664	97.6
Park, CO	08093	8	14 523	17.8	2	8	2 224	3 289	87.0	2 589	91.3
Phillips, CO	08095	9	4 480	20.0	2	4	966	1 133	94.4	905	96.7
Pitkin, CO	08097	7	14 872	12.5	1	3	1 236	2 799	81.6	1 922	91.7
Prowers, CO	08099	7	14 483	22.2	5	14	3 087	4 102	97.3	3 164	98.1
Pueblo, CO	08101	3	141 472	19.1	2	58	24 793	37 564	91.6	27 023	94.1
Rio Blanco, CO	08103	9	5 986	20.8	2	6	1 330	1 726	97.3	1 269	98.0
Rio Grande, CO	08105	7	12 413	21.2	3	12	2 528	3 385	93.7	2 585	95.4
Routt, CO	08107	7	19 690	17.1	3	10	2 889	4 656	88.0	3 316	91.5
Saguache, CO	08109	9	5 917	21.6	3	10	1 087	1 558	92.6	1 277	93.9
San Juan, CO	08111	9	558	15.4	1	2	79	111	93.7	88	95.5
San Miguel, CO	08113	9	6 594	13.1	2	5	813	1 155	81.6	873	89.9
Sedgwick, CO	08115	9	2 747	17.1	2	4	481	601	96.0	488	96.9
Summit, CO	08117	9	23 548	12.0	1	8	2 748	4 229	88.2	2 878	92.6
Teller, CO	08119	6	20 555	20.2	2	7	4 040	5 228	87.5	4 209	93.1
Washington, CO	08121	9	4 926	20.3	5	10	991	1 252	97.0	1 034	96.8
Weld, CO	08123	3	180 936	20.4	12	70	30 409	55 843	91.4	37 126	93.4
Yuma, CO	08125	7	9 841	21.7	2	11	1 955	2 574	93.2	2 159	96.9
CONNECTICUT	09000										
Fairfield, CT	09001	2	882 567	18.4	29	227	139 717	233 796	75.9	167 739	86.3
Hartford, CT	09003	0	857 183	18.2	37	273	146 347	226 420	84.6	162 211	91.4
Litchfield, CT	09005	4	182 193	18.8	25	70	29 287	45 238	83.7	34 508	90.2
Middlesex, CT	09007	1	155 071	17.0	15	69	33 562	39 840	77.0	26 978	90.9
New Haven, CT	09009	2	824 008	18.0	31	246	129 637	225 396	76.5	154 863	89.0
New London, CT	09011	2	259 088	18.1	24	102	42 897	67 054	83.1	48 220	91.7
Tolland, CT	09013	1	136 364	17.2	15	45	22 655	43 189	90.5	24 004	94.5
Windham, CT	09015	4	109 091	19.0	18	41	18 146	29 936	88.9	21 445	90.6
DELAWARE	10000										
Kent, DE	10001	3	126 697	20.0	8	46	25 011	35 984	86.8	25 303	92.2
New Castle, DE	10003	2	500 265	18.3	10	103	67 857	139 816	73.6	92 041	77.1
Sussex, DE	10005	6	156 638	16.8	8	42	21 808	34 179	88.0	26 436	92.8
DISTRICT OF COLUMBIA	11000										
District of Columbia	11001	0	572 059	14.4	1	165	68 925	157 475	67.3	88 568	84.9

[1]County type code is from the Economic Research Service of the USDA. See Notes and Definitions at the end of this section.

Table C-1. School and Student Characteristics by County—*Continued*

County	Characteristics of students, 2000–2001			Staff and students, 2000–2001				Revenues, fiscal 1999			
	Percent with IEP[2]	Percent eligible for free lunch	Percent minority	Number of teachers	Student/teacher ratio	Local school non-teaching staff	Central admin. staff	Total revenue ($1,000s)	Percentage of revenue from		
									Federal govt.	State govt.	Local govt.
	10	11	12	13	14	15	16	17	18	19	20
COLORADO											
Adams, CO	9.9	30.3	41.4	3 172	19.1	2 842	350	$370 898	5.3	51.2	43.6
Alamosa, CO	6.8	53.8	53.0	177	15.6	185	28	20 515	10.0	54.4	35.5
Arapahoe, CO	11.2	19.6	33.2	5 262	18.3	4 826	515	655 668	3.6	41.1	55.3
Archuleta, CO	8.7	35.6	21.1	88	17.7	69	8	10 907	3.2	33.5	63.3
Baca, CO	11.5	42.1	12.6	90	10.2	58	18	7 657	2.0	58.4	39.6
Bent, CO	12.8	57.9	39.9	80	12.2	66	9	6 977	5.9	65.1	29.0
Boulder, CO	9.9	14.4	22.0	2 617	18.1	2 313	314	311 778	4.1	26.3	69.6
Chaffee, CO	9.5	26.3	10.8	148	15.3	120	12	15 910	4.8	42.0	53.3
Cheyenne, CO	8.3	25.0	10.4	50	9.4	32	3	4 441	0.9	38.1	61.0
Clear Creek, CO	11.6	19.4	7.2	87	15.3	91	10	10 017	5.4	22.7	71.9
Conejos, CO	6.2	59.0	57.1	132	14.8	90	11	13 175	8.5	73.2	18.3
Costilla, CO	8.6	79.1	84.0	49	12.9	30	13	6 188	9.3	42.7	48.0
Crowley, CO	9.2	60.0	34.3	44	13.9	32	4	4 044	7.2	68.5	24.3
Custer, CO	7.6	25.1	6.2	33	14.3	22	2	2 853	4.8	26.4	68.8
Delta, CO	12.6	39.1	16.7	280	17.1	238	43	29 551	5.6	53.6	40.8
Denver, CO	10.8	59.9	77.7	4 170	17.1	4 115	539	514 052	8.2	30.7	61.1
Dolores, CO	9.0	29.8	7.2	26	12.8	27	4	2 660	3.6	52.7	43.6
Douglas, CO	8.4	1.8	9.8	2 036	17.2	1 680	157	206 702	1.5	37.9	60.6
Eagle, CO	7.7	21.1	36.3	323	14.4	231	20	39 859	2.2	2.5	95.3
Elbert, CO	15.7	8.4	7.3	266	15.1	226	21	25 971	0.8	56.2	43.0
El Paso, CO	7.5	24.0	27.8	5 358	17.6	4 265	539	567 022	5.8	51.3	42.9
Fremont, CO	11.2	33.8	10.7	384	16.8	325	36	37 916	6.4	60.0	33.6
Garfield, CO	8.1	22.4	24.2	571	16.6	453	34	57 444	2.8	38.1	59.2
Gilpin, CO	14.0	9.0	6.1	30	14.8	20	3	4 287	2.9	29.2	67.9
Grand, CO	10.7	. . .	7.1	141	13.4	108	10	15 942	2.0	13.9	84.1
Gunnison, CO	7.9	. . .	9.1	123	13.7	91	5	12 154	2.5	13.3	84.2
Hinsdale, CO	6.3	. . .	0.0	7	9.0	5	2	793	3.8	21.2	75.0
Huerfano, CO	9.8	49.3	49.4	80	14.1	78	8	7 845	6.5	41.7	51.8
Jackson, CO	0.7	33.6	8.9	23	13.2	9	2	2 669	2.2	49.4	48.4
Jefferson, CO	8.9	13.9	17.5	4 521	19.4	4 309	402	582 215	2.8	43.3	53.9
Kiowa, CO	11.0	36.7	5.8	36	10.1	25	5	3 158	1.5	43.7	54.8
Kit Carson, CO	7.9	39.5	18.3	136	12.4	95	14	12 894	3.9	53.2	42.9
Lake, CO	9.8	46.4	51.3	100	14.1	162	14	14 908	11.6	45.0	43.4
La Plata, CO	8.8	24.3	22.0	450	15.8	373	51	50 715	5.7	26.9	67.5
Larimer, CO	10.5	17.5	15.3	2 192	18.3	1 991	231	240 315	4.4	41.2	54.5
Las Animas, CO	8.1	54.4	55.6	173	13.7	119	22	18 010	6.5	58.8	34.7
Lincoln, CO	14.9	30.2	9.7	83	12.1	66	24	10 827	17.6	45.5	36.9
Logan, CO	11.5	35.7	16.8	222	15.7	196	23	23 309	5.9	58.8	35.3
Mesa, CO	12.9	35.7	16.7	1 163	17.6	1 045	146	123 337	5.7	55.5	38.9
Mineral, CO	9.8	23.3	1.2	18	9.1	8	1	1 492	0.8	49.6	49.6
Moffat, CO	13.1	22.9	10.6	150	17.2	170	14	17 330	4.6	14.9	80.5
Montezuma, CO	11.2	42.7	31.4	315	14.8	309	35	32 018	9.0	48.7	42.2
Montrose, CO	11.5	38.6	22.0	353	16.6	309	30	33 479	8.4	58.7	32.9
Morgan, CO	11.1	48.9	42.4	361	15.2	370	40	36 979	7.9	46.3	45.8
Otero, CO	10.7	54.8	49.4	300	13.3	256	34	29 629	8.4	68.4	23.3
Ouray, CO	9.8	16.7	5.4	45	12.8	25	8	5 004	3.1	40.5	56.4
Park, CO	8.6	12.5	8.0	145	15.3	139	11	15 696	2.9	37.9	59.2
Phillips, CO	12.5	30.3	15.8	68	14.2	87	10	9 628	11.5	38.5	50.1
Pitkin, CO	4.8	1.1	10.9	101	12.2	47	8	14 722	0.5	4.8	94.7
Prowers, CO	11.8	49.7	41.0	215	14.4	171	28	22 144	9.0	56.5	34.5
Pueblo, CO	10.1	47.1	50.0	1 347	18.4	1 169	120	138 757	8.2	60.0	31.8
Rio Blanco, CO	13.3	20.1	7.6	93	14.3	89	9	12 085	3.4	36.4	60.2
Rio Grande, CO	7.9	49.7	50.3	178	14.2	124	14	16 998	6.7	59.7	33.6
Routt, CO	13.7	. . .	4.6	199	14.5	187	17	27 327	4.3	11.3	84.4
Saguache, CO	7.3	74.8	67.8	96	11.3	77	12	8 849	8.7	61.3	29.9
San Juan, CO	12.7	46.8	10.1	11	7.2	4	2	1 191	1.7	31.2	67.1
San Miguel, CO	7.3	12.1	5.8	70	11.6	43	6	10 251	3.2	22.7	74.0
Sedgwick, CO	19.1	44.3	26.2	43	11.2	30	5	4 044	2.2	55.8	42.0
Summit, CO	8.9	12.9	14.8	189	14.5	171	11	24 117	1.2	2.1	96.7
Teller, CO	9.4	12.9	8.0	219	18.4	173	19	23 473	1.8	47.1	51.1
Washington, CO	11.0	35.7	10.9	97	10.2	61	11	9 218	3.1	52.8	44.1
Weld, CO	9.9	38.6	39.0	1 908	15.9	1 440	140	185 203	5.7	46.9	47.4
Yuma, CO	14.8	41.1	18.9	146	13.4	118	10	15 037	3.3	36.4	60.4
CONNECTICUT											
Fairfield, CT	11.9	. . .	33.4	10 012	14.0	8 835	840	1 402 421	3.2	23.5	73.2
Hartford, CT	13.8	. . .	37.7	10 405	14.1	9 205	893	1 412 492	4.5	41.9	53.6
Litchfield, CT	13.6	. . .	6.3	1 956	15.0	2 419	233	280 583	2.7	34.9	62.4
Middlesex, CT	13.7	. . .	21.1	2 739	12.3	2 167	150	229 614	2.4	29.6	68.0
New Haven, CT	13.9	. . .	34.7	9 097	14.3	8 410	722	1 292 622	4.6	43.9	51.4
New London, CT	15.1	. . .	18.9	3 276	13.1	3 175	294	445 381	4.3	44.8	50.9
Tolland, CT	12.0	. . .	7.5	1 645	13.8	1 628	137	211 048	2.0	47.9	50.1
Windham, CT	15.1	. . .	14.8	1 340	13.5	1 776	169	191 879	4.7	61.5	33.8
DELAWARE											
Kent, DE	14.2	31.9	33.7	1 598	15.7	1 058	173	173 037	11.8	70.7	17.5
New Castle, DE	13.4	31.8	43.8	4 216	16.1	2 417	401	607 515	4.3	60.1	35.6
Sussex, DE	14.9	37.8	31.8	1 512	14.4	958	145	223 920	6.7	71.2	22.2
DISTRICT OF COLUMBIA											
District of Columbia	15.4	73.8	95.5	5 033	13.7	5 711	52	758 072	16.2	0.0	83.8

[2]IEP = Individual Education Program. See Notes and Definitions at the end of this section.
. . . = Not available.

Table C-1. Population, School, and Student Characteristics by County—*Continued*

County	Current expenditures, fiscal 1999			Resident population 16 to 19 years, 2000				Outcomes, 1999–2000	
	Amount ($1,000s)	Amount per student	Percent for instruction	Total population 16 to 19 years	Percent in Armed Forces	Percent high school graduates	Percent not enrolled, not grads, not Armed Forces, not empl.	Number of graduates	Dropouts grades 9–12 (percent)
	21	22	23	24	25	26	27	28	29
COLORADO									
Adams, CO	$315 821	$5 534	60.0	20 522	0.1	15.5	9.7	2 733	...
Alamosa, CO	18 917	6 699	55.9	1 396	0.0	10.7	6.9	174	...
Arapahoe, CO	557 241	6 002	61.7	26 415	0.3	12.8	4.3	5 243	...
Archuleta, CO	8 040	5 180	62.1	543	0.0	11.0	5.5	107	...
Baca, CO	7 012	7 722	59.1	277	0.0	7.6	1.4	63	...
Bent, CO	6 055	5 850	59.4	306	0.0	11.4	5.9	56	...
Boulder, CO	251 369	5 552	62.5	18 302	0.0	8.2	3.1	2 637	...
Chaffee, CO	13 600	6 185	61.2	798	0.0	14.3	4.8	150	...
Cheyenne, CO	3 715	8 024	57.0	155	0.0	3.9	6.5	39	...
Clear Creek, CO	8 102	5 634	59.1	447	0.0	9.8	3.8	86	...
Conejos, CO	11 088	5 505	63.3	619	0.0	9.2	4.7	142	...
Costilla, CO	5 396	8 054	51.2	245	0.8	19.2	9.8	43	...
Crowley, CO	3 507	5 693	59.4	231	0.0	12.1	5.6	44	...
Custer, CO	2 728	6 449	57.5	127	0.0	5.5	6.3	25	...
Delta, CO	27 068	5 802	53.6	1 402	0.0	13.0	5.5	293	...
Denver, CO	405 629	5 897	59.3	26 299	0.0	13.3	12.6	2 581	...
Dolores, CO	2 183	6 346	55.0	88	0.0	12.5	1.1	21	...
Douglas, CO	180 219	6 038	60.4	7 620	0.0	7.7	2.0	1 474	...
Eagle, CO	30 675	7 061	58.7	1 872	0.0	9.4	13.5	240	...
Elbert, CO	21 733	6 050	56.0	1 308	0.0	7.0	4.4	226	...
El Paso, CO	508 210	5 703	58.4	30 763	6.7	18.6	5.0	4 890	...
Fremont, CO	34 487	5 218	62.0	2 245	0.0	9.4	6.4	376	...
Garfield, CO	44 703	4 888	62.6	2 408	0.3	14.4	6.3	444	...
Gilpin, CO	2 832	7 375	59.1	186	0.0	9.7	0.0	31	...
Grand, CO	12 550	6 999	62.6	627	0.0	20.1	1.0	123	...
Gunnison, CO	9 693	5 797	58.4	1 116	0.0	7.9	0.4	99	...
Hinsdale, CO	586	8 879	49.0	30	0.0	6.7	0.0	3	...
Huerfano, CO	7 184	5 903	60.7	348	0.0	11.8	4.9	51	...
Jackson, CO	2 256	7 373	49.2	99	0.0	11.1	3.0	24	...
Jefferson, CO	573 453	6 468	50.4	28 334	0.0	10.9	3.6	5 709	...
Kiowa, CO	3 169	8 043	56.8	119	0.0	7.6	0.0	31	...
Kit Carson, CO	11 061	6 405	61.0	464	0.0	8.0	3.0	104	...
Lake, CO	11 277	8 473	56.7	468	0.0	12.4	9.0	100	...
La Plata, CO	44 651	6 400	55.5	3 309	0.0	9.9	3.3	462	...
Larimer, CO	219 530	5 675	55.9	17 029	0.1	9.2	2.9	2 461	...
Las Animas, CO	15 741	6 695	56.9	875	0.0	9.6	8.6	175	...
Lincoln, CO	8 406	7 983	46.8	367	0.0	7.1	4.9	66	...
Logan, CO	20 298	5 968	61.0	1 477	0.0	11.8	3.0	238	...
Mesa, CO	104 580	5 261	64.6	7 200	0.0	13.8	6.9	1 188	...
Mineral, CO	1 344	8 506	65.5	31	0.0	0.0	0.0	11	...
Moffat, CO	16 459	6 103	58.2	830	0.0	15.4	12.7	177	...
Montezuma, CO	26 508	5 638	62.2	1 337	0.0	14.7	5.9	257	...
Montrose, CO	33 658	5 722	54.8	1 904	0.0	15.1	8.2	351	...
Morgan, CO	31 189	5 652	59.4	1 682	0.0	10.0	8.4	291	...
Otero, CO	26 487	6 219	59.7	1 281	0.0	11.5	5.3	302	...
Ouray, CO	3 971	7 104	63.1	161	0.0	1.2	0.0	46	...
Park, CO	12 730	5 763	61.8	710	0.0	10.4	1.3	171	...
Phillips, CO	7 681	7 960	52.7	240	0.0	10.4	0.0	61	...
Pitkin, CO	9 892	7 674	68.6	516	0.0	8.5	3.1	97	...
Prowers, CO	18 071	6 109	62.6	997	0.7	8.0	8.5	158	...
Pueblo, CO	127 791	5 271	58.1	8 387	0.0	9.9	8.6	1 337	...
Rio Blanco, CO	10 075	6 730	57.8	531	0.0	10.5	5.3	112	...
Rio Grande, CO	14 886	5 752	59.3	687	0.0	10.8	6.3	188	...
Routt, CO	21 070	7 113	54.3	979	0.0	14.6	1.3	161	...
Saguache, CO	7 983	7 160	59.5	392	0.0	9.9	8.9	64	...
San Juan, CO	1 301	15 128	48.2	31	0.0	0.0	0.0	10	...
San Miguel, CO	6 862	8 399	57.0	263	0.0	16.3	4.2	54	...
Sedgwick, CO	3 722	7 519	58.7	133	0.0	14.3	0.0	35	...
Summit, CO	16 903	6 692	56.1	912	0.0	32.9	3.0	137	...
Teller, CO	18 966	4 881	61.2	1 130	0.0	14.1	4.9	262	...
Washington, CO	8 374	8 194	58.7	312	0.0	5.8	1.3	84	...
Weld, CO	156 014	5 532	61.0	12 913	0.0	9.0	6.2	1 452	...
Yuma, CO	11 564	5 536	64.3	601	0.0	7.8	1.8	154	...
CONNECTICUT									
Fairfield, CT	1 262 256	9 515	63.4	39 493	0.0	7.5	3.6	6 996	3.2
Hartford, CT	1 223 815	8 965	65.1	42 608	0.1	8.6	5.5	7 308	3.6
Litchfield, CT	241 265	8 591	64.8	8 090	0.0	12.1	2.4	1 642	2.3
Middlesex, CT	198 365	8 894	65.0	7 196	0.0	6.9	3.1	4 848	1.2
New Haven, CT	1 099 698	8 809	63.3	42 794	0.1	8.7	5.4	6 168	3.0
New London, CT	349 000	8 938	64.3	13 209	6.6	17.1	3.4	2 296	3.4
Tolland, CT	182 330	8 383	65.3	9 564	0.1	4.4	1.6	1 297	2.3
Windham, CT	145 210	8 432	64.9	6 323	0.3	8.7	4.6	882	5.7
DELAWARE									
Kent, DE	147 399	7 076	60.8	7 812	1.3	11.1	5.1	1 385	4.8
New Castle, DE	516 503	7 788	63.2	29 102	0.1	11.4	5.4	3 513	3.8
Sussex, DE	189 636	7 535	60.1	7 240	0.1	12.2	7.2	1 209	4.3
DISTRICT OF COLUMBIA									
District of Columbia	693 386	9 645	45.3	32 400	1.0	8.2	6.7	2 695	7.2

... = Not available.

Table C-1. Population, School, and Student Characteristics by County—*Continued*

County	High school graduates, 2000			College enrollment, 2000		College graduates, 2000 (percent)						
	Population 25 years and over	High school diploma or less (percent)	High school diploma or more (percent)	Number	Percent public	Bachelor's degree or more	+/- U.S. percent with bachelor's degree or more	Non-Hispanic White	Black or African American	American Indian and Alaska Native	Asian, Hawaiian, and Pacific Islander	Hispanic or Latino[1]
	30	31	32	33	34	35	36	37	38	39	40	41
COLORADO												
Adams, CO	223 094	51.9	78.8	15 697	77.1	17.4	-7.0	20.8	16.9	6.2	24.0	6.8
Alamosa, CO	8 567	44.5	82.6	1 945	94.8	27.0	2.6	33.8	42.6	13.8	40.5	16.4
Arapahoe, CO	316 560	29.9	90.7	27 529	73.6	37.0	12.6	40.7	24.5	19.5	40.1	15.2
Archuleta, CO	6 821	39.5	87.3	141	82.3	29.0	4.6	32.2	0.0	14.1	33.3	9.7
Baca, CO	3 152	55.8	78.5	112	87.5	14.0	-10.4	14.6	. . .	13.2	71.4	3.4
Bent, CO	4 037	57.9	77.2	232	88.8	11.5	-12.9	15.8	2.5	0.0	21.9	1.3
Boulder, CO	186 126	22.3	92.8	35 657	88.4	52.4	28.0	55.2	45.0	31.2	64.9	18.2
Chaffee, CO	11 837	41.4	88.5	507	82.4	24.3	-0.1	26.4	0.0	8.4	40.0	7.3
Cheyenne, CO	1 431	50.7	84.1	51	90.2	14.2	-10.2	14.6	. . .	0.0	. . .	8.3
Clear Creek, CO	6 702	28.1	93.4	300	71.0	38.8	14.4	39.7	0.0	20.4	32.6	14.5
Conejos, CO	4 979	61.8	72.1	320	95.3	14.4	-10.0	22.5	0.0	1.0	33.3	9.1
Costilla, CO	2 506	59.2	68.2	100	73.0	12.8	-11.6	23.0	0.0	16.7	16.3	7.3
Crowley, CO	3 897	57.0	77.5	370	95.9	11.9	-12.5	16.7	0.0	1.1	9.1	1.6
Custer, CO	2 548	37.8	90.3	63	79.4	26.7	2.3	27.4	0.0	0.0	. . .	22.6
Delta, CO	19 330	53.9	80.1	538	89.4	17.6	-6.8	19.0	0.0	15.4	23.6	3.9
Denver, CO	374 478	41.1	78.9	38 309	67.5	34.5	10.1	47.8	17.8	13.7	40.3	7.8
Dolores, CO	1 323	57.2	76.0	33	90.9	13.5	-10.9	13.8	. . .	0.0	57.1	15.0
Douglas, CO	112 436	16.2	97.0	8 719	69.8	51.9	27.5	52.4	57.0	36.9	59.0	37.6
Eagle, CO	27 178	29.9	86.6	1 625	80.1	42.6	18.2	51.0	14.3	23.5	47.8	6.7
Elbert, CO	12 814	34.9	92.5	655	67.5	26.6	2.2	26.7	25.9	31.3	66.7	17.4
El Paso, CO	320 420	31.6	91.3	33 737	70.2	31.8	7.4	34.9	19.0	13.3	33.7	14.1
Fremont, CO	33 214	56.2	80.5	1 820	82.7	13.5	-10.9	15.9	0.2	4.9	6.1	3.8
Garfield, CO	27 884	41.5	85.4	1 676	86.1	23.8	-0.6	26.2	0.0	9.5	34.3	6.5
Gilpin, CO	3 501	31.5	94.1	210	72.4	31.2	6.8	31.9	65.5	0.0	36.7	3.6
Grand, CO	8 571	31.7	92.3	301	76.7	34.5	10.1	35.1	0.0	9.8	72.7	17.6
Gunnison, CO	8 504	23.7	94.1	2 556	93.4	43.6	19.2	45.0	23.7	31.4	7.7	20.1
Hinsdale, CO	593	27.7	93.1	16	56.3	34.9	10.5	35.5	. . .	0.0	100.0	0.0
Huerfano, CO	5 647	54.5	77.8	255	78.0	16.1	-8.3	21.4	3.4	4.6	48.5	5.7
Jackson, CO	1 098	49.8	86.2	26	100.0	19.9	-4.5	20.2	0.0	0.0	100.0	13.2
Jefferson, CO	351 579	30.8	91.8	31 045	77.2	36.5	12.1	38.2	33.2	21.3	47.8	17.5
Kiowa, CO	1 085	49.2	86.3	49	89.8	16.1	-8.3	16.1	0.0	0.0	. . .	26.7
Kit Carson, CO	5 254	54.6	77.0	204	86.3	15.4	-9.0	16.9	12.1	0.0	0.0	4.8
Lake, CO	4 710	47.8	79.5	403	88.3	19.5	-4.9	26.8	. . .	0.0	77.8	2.2
La Plata, CO	27 973	31.7	91.4	4 732	93.1	36.4	12.0	39.7	21.1	14.3	32.4	14.3
Larimer, CO	156 426	29.0	92.3	31 384	93.1	39.5	15.1	40.8	39.4	16.9	61.9	17.4
Las Animas, CO	10 279	50.3	76.9	885	95.7	16.2	-8.2	21.2	0.0	4.1	33.3	7.9
Lincoln, CO	4 214	53.2	81.8	166	84.3	13.2	-11.2	14.5	10.3	13.9	0.0	4.1
Logan, CO	13 074	49.7	82.3	1 291	94.3	14.6	-9.8	15.8	20.3	0.0	5.9	2.6
Mesa, CO	76 358	45.3	85.0	5 836	88.6	22.0	-2.4	23.2	16.8	4.7	24.5	9.9
Mineral, CO	631	36.8	91.6	25	84.0	31.2	6.8	31.7	. . .	0.0	. . .	0.0
Moffat, CO	8 404	53.8	79.6	496	92.5	12.5	-11.9	13.1	48.0	12.2	33.3	3.1
Montezuma, CO	15 512	51.9	81.1	723	87.8	21.0	-3.4	23.7	0.0	5.4	12.5	8.4
Montrose, CO	22 089	52.7	80.7	498	86.3	18.7	-5.7	20.2	8.5	21.0	13.4	6.1
Morgan, CO	16 661	59.6	71.4	796	89.6	13.5	-10.9	16.8	21.1	12.1	18.8	2.4
Otero, CO	13 172	55.0	75.7	963	92.9	15.4	-9.0	20.7	68.8	0.8	41.2	4.3
Ouray, CO	2 741	28.2	93.4	56	66.1	36.8	12.4	37.6	0.0	10.0	0.0	19.7
Park, CO	10 371	33.4	93.3	432	67.8	30.3	5.9	30.6	34.5	27.3	51.9	18.9
Phillips, CO	2 999	50.6	81.6	116	90.5	19.9	-4.5	21.3	0.0	50.0	25.0	5.7
Pitkin, CO	11 322	14.6	96.3	659	66.6	57.1	32.7	60.1	82.7	23.5	38.3	13.9
Prowers, CO	8 545	56.9	72.0	599	96.7	11.9	-12.5	14.4	100.0	3.6	23.5	4.7
Pueblo, CO	92 080	49.7	81.3	8 081	90.3	18.3	-6.1	22.8	15.7	11.0	42.1	9.5
Rio Blanco, CO	3 857	43.6	88.4	385	95.1	19.5	-4.9	19.8	. . .	15.8	66.7	9.0
Rio Grande, CO	7 959	51.9	78.1	500	90.4	18.8	-5.6	26.6	. . .	4.5	16.7	5.4
Routt, CO	13 267	22.4	95.3	1 014	86.9	42.5	18.1	43.3	77.8	22.0	14.7	23.2
Saguache, CO	3 760	54.8	70.0	166	85.5	19.6	-4.8	29.2	0.0	8.7	50.0	4.5
San Juan, CO	428	22.4	92.1	14	78.6	43.7	19.3	45.8	. . .	0.0	50.0	20.0
San Miguel, CO	4 762	21.4	93.6	182	57.1	48.5	24.1	50.6	20.0	15.4	49.0	11.3
Sedgwick, CO	1 938	56.2	79.3	69	92.8	13.4	-11.0	14.8	0.0	0.0	0.0	2.4
Summit, CO	15 795	24.4	93.3	1 056	83.4	48.3	23.9	51.7	21.7	26.1	42.4	14.8
Teller, CO	14 240	29.5	94.0	635	72.0	31.7	7.3	32.3	31.4	9.5	31.0	15.8
Washington, CO	3 314	51.9	81.7	116	95.7	14.3	-10.1	14.3	0.0	27.8	75.0	7.6
Weld, CO	106 245	47.2	79.6	15 531	92.4	21.6	-2.8	25.7	23.4	13.0	48.4	6.5
Yuma, CO	6 340	54.3	79.5	225	76.9	15.5	-8.9	16.5	100.0	25.0	. . .	4.1
CONNECTICUT												
Fairfield, CT	596 371	39.2	84.4	44 981	54.1	39.9	15.5	45.8	13.9	23.3	59.2	11.7
Hartford, CT	579 839	46.3	82.4	48 436	72.0	29.6	5.2	33.2	13.3	15.3	50.7	10.0
Litchfield, CT	127 305	45.5	85.9	7 392	68.9	27.5	3.1	27.5	20.4	15.0	42.4	24.1
Middlesex, CT	108 106	39.8	88.7	9 945	48.4	33.8	9.4	34.4	18.5	22.8	53.0	29.7
New Haven, CT	551 642	47.8	83.0	55 307	48.5	27.6	3.2	29.9	13.6	14.9	65.7	10.0
New London, CT	173 910	46.0	86.0	14 440	61.9	26.2	1.8	27.5	12.5	10.9	42.8	11.9
Tolland, CT	87 202	39.8	89.2	16 790	90.9	32.8	8.4	32.5	20.9	18.9	70.9	21.6
Windham, CT	71 242	56.1	79.6	6 921	88.2	19.0	-5.4	19.5	9.8	10.7	35.5	10.3
DELAWARE												
Kent, DE	79 249	53.5	79.4	8 588	77.9	18.6	-5.8	19.4	15.6	9.4	33.9	11.8
New Castle, DE	324 810	44.2	85.5	37 364	72.9	29.5	5.1	32.1	16.0	26.3	67.3	14.3
Sussex, DE	110 599	59.1	76.5	5 455	79.6	16.6	-7.8	18.3	6.5	5.5	35.6	11.2
DISTRICT OF COLUMBIA												
District of Columbia	384 535	42.8	77.8	59 498	41.0	39.1	14.7	80.6	17.5	28.1	58.1	24.8

[1]Hispanic or Latino persons may be of any race.
. . . = Not available.

Table C-1. Population, School, and Student Characteristics by County—*Continued*

County	State/ County code	County type[1]	Population, 2000 Total	Population, 2000 Percent 5–17 years	Number of schools and students, 2000–2001 School districts	Number of schools and students, 2000–2001 Schools	Number of schools and students, 2000–2001 Students	Resident enrollment, 2000 Total	Resident enrollment, 2000 Percent public	Resident enrollment, 2000 K–12	Resident enrollment, 2000 Percent public
			1	2	3	4	5	6	7	8	9
FLORIDA	12000										
Alachua, FL	12001	3	217 955	15.0	2	59	30 730	90 184	91.8	32 792	89.3
Baker, FL	12003	6	22 259	20.5	1	6	4 566	5 495	91.4	4 509	94.7
Bay, FL	12005	3	148 217	18.0	1	41	25 743	36 970	90.0	27 420	92.6
Bradford, FL	12007	6	26 088	16.4	1	11	4 161	5 921	90.6	4 735	91.4
Brevard, FL	12009	2	476 230	16.8	1	106	70 596	112 005	82.0	80 722	88.6
Broward, FL	12011	0	1 623 018	17.2	1	241	251 129	410 814	79.3	290 350	87.1
Calhoun, FL	12013	8	13 017	17.3	1	6	2 232	2 907	97.7	2 364	98.0
Charlotte, FL	12015	3	141 627	12.0	1	24	17 169	22 784	87.6	17 899	92.5
Citrus, FL	12017	4	118 085	13.4	1	23	15 199	19 963	89.2	16 026	93.2
Clay, FL	12019	2	140 814	21.4	1	30	28 115	40 121	86.9	30 688	91.8
Collier, FL	12021	3	251 377	14.5	1	49	34 196	46 873	86.2	36 873	91.5
Columbia, FL	12023	6	56 513	18.9	1	15	9 590	13 898	90.6	11 213	92.4
De Soto, FL	12027	6	32 209	16.9	1	10	4 618	6 014	93.5	5 087	95.5
Dixie, FL	12029	9	13 827	16.5	1	4	2 305	2 814	93.0	2 350	96.8
Duval, FL	12031	2	778 879	19.1	1	178	125 744	211 236	81.3	151 264	85.6
Escambia, FL	12033	2	294 410	17.4	1	80	44 922	78 198	81.3	53 184	87.2
Flagler, FL	12035	2	49 832	13.8	1	8	6 760	9 366	87.0	6 882	93.1
Franklin, FL	12037	7	11 057	13.4	1	4	1 472	1 962	94.4	1 583	95.5
Gadsden, FL	12039	3	45 087	19.7	1	23	7 582	11 903	88.7	9 547	89.5
Gilchrist, FL	12041	8	14 437	18.7	1	4	2 687	3 574	94.0	2 968	95.5
Glades, FL	12043	8	10 576	16.3	1	5	1 106	2 213	92.7	1 757	94.2
Gulf, FL	12045	6	13 332	16.7	1	6	2 264	3 072	94.6	2 321	97.0
Hamilton, FL	12047	9	13 327	17.2	1	8	2 171	2 853	91.8	2 466	92.6
Hardee, FL	12049	6	26 938	19.9	1	7	4 964	6 525	94.4	5 483	97.2
Hendry, FL	12051	6	36 210	22.2	1	15	7 571	9 811	93.4	8 191	95.8
Hernando, FL	12053	0	130 802	14.4	1	21	17 215	23 878	85.4	18 867	89.3
Highlands, FL	12055	6	87 366	14.3	1	17	11 201	15 766	88.8	12 420	93.7
Hillsborough, FL	12057	0	998 948	18.5	1	206	164 270	267 599	82.0	187 070	87.8
Holmes, FL	12059	7	18 564	17.5	1	9	3 588	4 161	92.6	3 444	93.2
Indian River, FL	12061	4	112 947	14.6	1	26	14 974	22 308	82.8	17 024	87.9
Jackson, FL	12063	6	46 755	16.9	1	17	7 430	11 144	90.5	8 562	93.0
Jefferson, FL	12065	6	12 902	17.4	1	7	1 842	3 050	78.3	2 422	80.6
Lafayette, FL	12067	9	7 022	16.1	1	2	1 085	1 406	92.0	1 052	98.3
Lake, FL	12069	1	210 528	15.1	1	48	29 023	40 624	85.9	32 367	89.6
Lee, FL	12071	2	440 888	14.4	1	72	58 369	81 283	84.3	62 918	88.9
Leon, FL	12073	3	239 452	15.6	3	58	33 720	93 932	89.9	38 023	87.6
Levy, FL	12075	8	34 450	17.9	1	14	6 173	7 753	93.1	6 303	95.9
Liberty, FL	12077	8	7 021	16.3	1	7	1 221	1 492	92.6	1 217	92.9
Madison, FL	12079	7	18 733	19.5	1	10	3 471	4 656	89.5	3 840	89.0
Manatee, FL	12081	2	264 002	15.1	1	70	36 554	52 553	85.4	40 225	90.5
Marion, FL	12083	3	258 916	16.2	1	59	38 545	54 173	85.6	42 621	88.9
Martin, FL	12085	2	126 731	14.2	1	28	16 306	24 414	82.2	18 261	89.0
Miami-Dade, FL	12086	0	2 253 362	18.3	1	348	368 356	643 727	80.6	443 852	87.6
Monroe, FL	12087	4	79 589	12.7	1	18	9 371	14 277	85.8	10 266	93.4
Nassau, FL	12089	2	57 663	18.9	1	18	10 212	14 083	88.6	10 897	94.1
Okaloosa, FL	12091	3	170 498	18.4	1	48	30 335	44 445	89.2	31 577	93.0
Okeechobee, FL	12093	6	35 910	18.9	1	15	6 856	8 521	94.2	6 898	97.1
Orange, FL	12095	0	896 344	18.4	1	171	150 681	248 040	82.6	167 077	88.3
Osceola, FL	12097	1	172 493	20.0	1	42	34 566	44 944	86.6	35 247	92.5
Palm Beach, FL	12099	2	1 131 184	15.7	2	177	154 294	254 671	79.6	183 941	86.0
Pasco, FL	12101	0	344 765	14.9	1	60	49 607	67 546	86.5	51 677	92.4
Pinellas, FL	12103	0	921 482	14.3	1	159	113 017	190 563	79.3	133 945	85.0
Polk, FL	12105	2	483 924	18.0	1	137	79 463	114 180	84.6	88 103	91.0
Putnam, FL	12107	6	70 423	18.4	1	19	12 624	16 240	92.0	13 307	94.4
St. Johns, FL	12109	2	123 135	17.7	2	38	20 728	30 609	77.5	22 042	86.6
St. Lucie, FL	12111	2	192 695	17.0	1	40	29 489	43 393	86.7	33 356	90.1
Santa Rosa, FL	12113	2	117 743	20.0	1	36	22 633	31 346	88.5	23 695	91.0
Sarasota, FL	12115	2	325 957	12.3	1	44	35 504	55 269	81.6	40 983	87.2
Seminole, FL	12117	0	365 196	19.0	1	68	60 869	99 337	81.4	69 909	86.8
Sumter, FL	12119	6	53 345	12.1	1	12	6 132	8 862	88.8	7 121	92.5
Suwannee, FL	12121	7	34 844	18.0	1	8	5 810	7 960	86.7	6 459	89.4
Taylor, FL	12123	7	19 256	18.7	1	8	3 717	4 676	92.4	3 760	94.5
Union, FL	12125	8	13 442	16.4	1	5	2 228	2 866	93.2	2 297	96.0
Volusia, FL	12127	2	443 343	15.4	1	91	61 340	101 190	78.4	68 193	89.9
Wakulla, FL	12129	8	22 863	19.7	1	9	4 677	5 852	94.7	4 542	97.7
Walton, FL	12131	6	40 601	16.3	1	15	5 877	8 374	91.9	6 868	95.6
Washington, FL	12133	6	20 973	17.3	2	11	3 822	4 640	94.6	3 819	97.6
GEORGIA	13000										
Appling, GA	13001	7	17 419	19.8	1	6	3 281	4 329	93.0	3 615	94.3
Atkinson, GA	13003	9	7 609	20.9	1	3	1 550	1 770	96.0	1 561	96.9
Bacon, GA	13005	7	10 103	18.7	1	3	1 920	2 262	95.9	1 788	95.6
Baker, GA	13007	8	4 074	20.1	1	1	416	1 114	90.3	913	90.6
Baldwin, GA	13009	4	44 700	16.6	1	8	6 336	13 169	80.0	8 038	84.0
Banks, GA	13011	8	14 422	18.6	1	5	2 326	3 185	91.8	2 631	94.9
Barrow, GA	13013	1	46 144	20.2	1	13	8 666	11 251	88.4	9 130	93.2
Bartow, GA	13015	1	76 019	20.1	2	21	15 999	18 576	90.5	15 176	94.8
Ben Hill, GA	13017	7	17 484	20.2	1	4	3 472	4 520	91.9	3 554	96.7
Berrien, GA	13019	7	16 235	20.2	1	4	3 131	4 085	94.9	3 090	96.6

[1]County type code is from the Economic Research Service of the USDA. See Notes and Definitions at the end of this section.

Table C-1. School and Student Characteristics by County—*Continued*

County	Characteristics of students, 2000–2001			Staff and students, 2000–2001				Revenues, fiscal 1999			
	Percent with IEP[2]	Percent eligible for free lunch	Percent minority	Number of teachers	Student/ teacher ratio	Local school non-teaching staff	Central admin. staff	Total revenue ($1,000s)	Percentage of revenue from		
									Federal govt.	State govt.	Local govt.
	10	11	12	13	14	15	16	17	18	19	20
FLORIDA											
Alachua, FL	16.9	43.8	44.3	1 750	17.6	1 977	377	$207 566	9.8	54.3	35.9
Baker, FL	11.9	38.3	16.6	227	20.1	246	52	29 585	6.3	77.3	16.4
Bay, FL	17.9	44.3	19.3	1 505	17.1	1 505	228	180 271	8.2	52.5	39.3
Bradford, FL	21.8	54.4	25.8	255	16.3	259	29	27 875	7.4	68.9	23.8
Brevard, FL	15.7	30.9	20.8	3 870	18.2	3 455	338	448 084	5.8	56.1	38.1
Broward, FL	11.5	37.1	58.8	11 681	21.5	10 216	941	1 616 902	6.4	50.9	42.7
Calhoun, FL	18.3	48.4	15.9	149	15.0	106	26	13 037	8.5	74.6	16.9
Charlotte, FL	19.2	40.5	13.8	918	18.7	1 113	139	120 676	6.3	34.3	59.3
Citrus, FL	20.2	32.8	9.1	909	16.7	869	149	107 666	6.3	48.7	45.0
Clay, FL	19.2	22.6	15.4	1 650	17.0	1 471	224	176 117	4.1	70.0	25.9
Collier, FL	15.6	31.7	43.2	1 811	18.9	2 065	279	267 174	7.6	17.1	75.2
Columbia, FL	17.7	50.9	27.7	562	17.1	578	80	74 158	7.3	75.4	17.3
De Soto, FL	19.3	60.7	42.4	266	17.4	281	62	31 368	11.7	61.4	26.9
Dixie, FL	24.2	63.3	10.0	129	17.9	158	35	30 562	6.9	83.8	9.3
Duval, FL	16.3	46.6	49.8	6 321	19.9	3 940	1 157	850 191	7.4	56.8	35.7
Escambia, FL	16.3	56.6	41.9	2 565	17.5	2 646	367	319 194	9.4	60.3	30.3
Flagler, FL	17.7	39.4	20.3	390	17.3	485	112	53 096	5.3	35.7	59.0
Franklin, FL	15.8	64.7	16.7	94	15.7	81	18	10 523	10.2	37.4	52.5
Gadsden, FL	17.7	73.8	93.9	458	16.6	562	60	54 381	17.2	67.5	15.4
Gilchrist, FL	19.0	46.7	6.6	165	16.3	156	32	29 237	4.5	83.9	11.6
Glades, FL	16.3	69.2	53.1	70	15.8	54	12	8 455	12.0	45.6	42.4
Gulf, FL	13.9	50.7	19.9	140	16.2	133	18	16 823	11.0	56.6	32.4
Hamilton, FL	18.2	68.8	55.0	139	15.6	180	34	18 021	16.8	51.1	32.1
Hardee, FL	21.8	64.8	56.7	294	16.9	310	73	35 707	11.1	61.6	27.3
Hendry, FL	17.0	64.4	60.6	364	20.8	458	59	47 450	12.6	57.4	30.0
Hernando, FL	15.9	40.0	14.4	932	18.5	1 189	93	110 395	6.2	48.3	45.5
Highlands, FL	18.2	58.1	40.0	627	17.9	645	131	77 894	9.6	54.8	35.6
Hillsborough, FL	14.6	47.4	48.2	9 818	16.7	9 079	1 189	1 139 989	10.1	56.0	33.9
Holmes, FL	16.1	55.7	4.9	228	15.7	206	19	25 032	9.6	74.8	15.7
Indian River, FL	14.9	45.9	28.2	728	20.6	838	85	106 431	6.4	29.1	64.5
Jackson, FL	19.7	55.1	35.5	447	16.6	528	74	52 507	10.6	69.3	20.1
Jefferson, FL	24.3	69.2	68.7	120	15.4	147	27	13 794	13.3	65.2	21.5
Lafayette, FL	12.6	52.0	20.6	70	15.5	85	13	7 180	15.2	62.3	22.6
Lake, FL	17.2	39.4	25.2	1 509	19.2	1 602	208	176 113	7.0	51.3	41.8
Lee, FL	15.9	43.6	33.2	3 028	19.3	2 818	429	412 253	7.2	33.9	58.9
Leon, FL	19.4	30.3	44.8	1 987	17.0	2 163	301	241 922	6.4	55.7	37.9
Levy, FL	20.4	57.8	21.0	364	17.0	453	61	41 656	7.2	67.8	25.0
Liberty, FL	23.7	48.8	17.9	82	14.9	67	16	18 291	4.3	87.3	8.4
Madison, FL	23.5	63.5	59.4	196	17.7	206	38	25 119	13.9	69.4	16.6
Manatee, FL	19.2	37.8	33.2	2 034	18.0	2 432	248	278 352	5.9	46.4	47.7
Marion, FL	16.4	52.6	30.6	2 194	17.6	2 636	294	264 484	8.1	60.0	31.9
Martin, FL	16.8	31.2	24.9	896	18.2	848	137	123 072	6.1	19.6	74.3
Miami-Dade, FL	11.1	59.4	88.7	18 472	19.9	15 290	2 360	2 818 299	8.2	55.0	36.8
Monroe, FL	15.8	37.1	30.8	549	17.1	781	107	89 038	7.8	17.3	74.9
Nassau, FL	16.1	33.3	11.9	523	19.5	610	65	69 826	5.2	58.3	36.5
Okaloosa, FL	15.1	29.2	19.1	1 675	18.1	1 676	155	213 651	7.2	50.0	42.8
Okeechobee, FL	19.4	51.6	32.5	335	20.5	445	54	43 277	10.5	63.3	26.2
Orange, FL	15.8	47.8	55.9	8 609	17.5	7 854	1 724	969 240	6.1	43.7	50.3
Osceola, FL	14.5	46.6	49.8	1 633	21.2	2 009	258	206 446	4.7	54.6	40.8
Palm Beach, FL	13.7	39.7	50.3	8 161	18.9	7 566	1 189	1 233 974	7.6	39.2	53.3
Pasco, FL	19.4	45.0	12.3	2 882	17.2	3 253	447	338 798	7.1	61.2	31.6
Pinellas, FL	18.3	36.4	27.3	6 083	18.6	6 500	1 023	779 336	6.8	47.9	45.3
Polk, FL	15.3	50.5	36.5	4 860	16.4	5 153	425	511 310	8.1	61.0	30.8
Putnam, FL	16.2	61.1	36.0	711	17.8	972	81	83 814	9.5	59.9	30.7
St. Johns, FL	17.8	23.5	14.5	1 039	19.9	1 342	183	161 247	4.6	50.5	44.9
St. Lucie, FL	14.6	53.6	42.0	1 995	14.8	1 944	271	200 075	8.5	48.4	43.0
Santa Rosa, FL	16.2	31.7	9.2	1 263	17.9	908	95	143 223	7.3	63.5	29.3
Sarasota, FL	17.3	36.0	18.3	1 945	18.3	2 192	162	292 739	4.6	21.5	73.9
Seminole, FL	12.3	22.5	29.9	3 433	17.7	2 798	181	391 736	4.1	55.9	40.0
Sumter, FL	18.1	59.5	31.3	314	19.5	464	58	41 613	9.1	67.6	23.3
Suwannee, FL	13.6	47.8	23.6	296	19.6	296	47	39 400	7.5	71.6	20.9
Taylor, FL	17.0	50.4	25.7	211	17.6	252	35	26 318	14.3	56.9	28.7
Union, FL	16.7	42.2	20.1	128	17.4	149	19	14 141	7.6	76.6	15.8
Volusia, FL	16.7	38.8	26.1	3 788	16.2	4 010	349	408 348	6.8	50.2	43.0
Wakulla, FL	19.6	33.2	12.7	256	18.3	274	44	40 440	4.4	80.0	15.6
Walton, FL	16.8	52.2	12.1	342	17.2	424	40	43 784	7.6	25.4	67.0
Washington, FL	20.7	60.0	24.3	229	16.7	275	72	44 360	9.1	73.8	17.2
GEORGIA											
Appling, GA	14.1	58.6	32.2	216	15.2	234	15	23 234	9.9	51.1	39.0
Atkinson, GA	14.5	82.6	43.7	92	16.8	105	7	9 425	15.9	67.2	16.9
Bacon, GA	13.1	52.0	27.1	124	15.5	134	7	12 477	10.6	66.8	22.6
Baker, GA	20.0	91.3	77.2	37	11.2	47	2	4 470	18.3	38.4	43.3
Baldwin, GA	16.9	57.8	64.1	414	15.3	472	21	47 179	9.5	56.9	33.6
Banks, GA	12.5	52.0	8.0	140	16.6	127	10	16 705	6.2	58.7	35.1
Barrow, GA	15.0	31.6	19.9	554	15.6	477	25	54 683	5.5	54.0	40.5
Bartow, GA	13.3	35.4	15.8	985	16.2	955	43	103 734	5.6	49.8	44.6
Ben Hill, GA	12.9	61.0	48.7	221	15.7	217	13	22 261	10.7	66.9	22.4
Berrien, GA	12.4	53.5	20.1	180	17.4	212	17	19 742	13.7	61.0	25.3

[2]IEP = Individual Education Program. See Notes and Definitions at the end of this section.

Table C-1. Population, School, and Student Characteristics by County—*Continued*

County	Current expenditures, fiscal 1999			Resident population 16 to 19 years, 2000				Outcomes, 1999–2000	
	Amount ($1,000s)	Amount per student	Percent for instruction	Total population 16 to 19 years	Percent in Armed Forces	Percent high school graduates	Percent not enrolled, not grads, not Armed Forces, not empl.	Number of graduates	Dropouts grades 9–12 (percent)
	21	22	23	24	25	26	27	28	29
FLORIDA									
Alachua, FL	$165 944	$5 592	55.1	19 335	0.0	5.6	1.9	1 578	. . .
Baker, FL	24 635	5 207	52.5	1 315	0.0	11.6	14.1	198	. . .
Bay, FL	137 071	5 285	58.7	7 949	2.3	13.4	5.2	1 216	. . .
Bradford, FL	22 177	5 328	55.8	1 382	0.4	12.9	7.7	200	. . .
Brevard, FL	345 023	5 024	60.9	22 865	0.2	9.1	6.1	3 443	. . .
Broward, FL	1 306 137	5 650	55.3	73 499	0.0	9.3	5.4	10 297	. . .
Calhoun, FL	11 752	5 182	59.5	663	0.0	16.6	5.3	104	. . .
Charlotte, FL	92 474	5 585	55.4	4 880	0.0	13.7	4.9	907	. . .
Citrus, FL	84 187	5 756	54.7	4 639	0.0	12.1	7.1	707	. . .
Clay, FL	135 456	4 954	59.0	8 239	0.3	9.8	4.8	1 435	. . .
Collier, FL	197 507	6 415	59.9	10 207	0.1	11.1	8.9	1 411	. . .
Columbia, FL	51 184	5 435	57.7	3 592	0.1	12.0	10.2	411	. . .
De Soto, FL	25 702	5 539	57.5	2 042	0.0	9.2	14.7	155	. . .
Dixie, FL	12 876	5 392	54.2	736	0.0	20.5	7.7	106	. . .
Duval, FL	667 703	5 241	58.5	42 483	2.0	12.2	6.5	4 768	. . .
Escambia, FL	249 847	5 471	54.5	19 846	15.0	23.7	4.4	2 044	. . .
Flagler, FL	37 006	6 093	51.1	1 749	0.0	13.0	4.5	326	. . .
Franklin, FL	9 310	6 166	59.1	517	0.0	19.3	4.6	77	. . .
Gadsden, FL	47 333	5 662	54.0	2 664	0.1	8.5	8.9	381	. . .
Gilchrist, FL	14 594	5 367	57.4	917	0.0	14.6	11.0	124	. . .
Glades, FL	6 798	5 795	54.3	491	0.0	19.1	5.3	44	. . .
Gulf, FL	13 644	5 912	55.8	559	0.0	13.4	4.5	130	. . .
Hamilton, FL	14 029	6 235	47.7	797	0.0	13.3	13.8	106	. . .
Hardee, FL	28 751	5 563	56.7	1 801	0.0	12.8	11.0	245	. . .
Hendry, FL	41 769	5 596	53.9	2 700	0.0	8.8	11.8	348	. . .
Hernando, FL	86 043	5 240	54.7	5 403	0.0	14.0	6.2	796	. . .
Highlands, FL	65 468	5 903	54.0	3 531	0.0	13.2	7.4	477	. . .
Hillsborough, FL	915 473	5 851	56.9	52 941	0.2	10.7	7.5	7 437	. . .
Holmes, FL	20 910	5 598	59.9	1 011	0.0	10.2	6.8	202	. . .
Indian River, FL	81 119	5 550	55.4	4 932	0.6	11.2	6.8	747	. . .
Jackson, FL	43 597	5 569	55.6	2 608	0.0	10.8	6.2	460	. . .
Jefferson, FL	12 151	6 187	52.4	691	0.0	8.1	8.4	71	. . .
Lafayette, FL	5 919	5 547	51.0	375	0.0	6.7	15.5	49	. . .
Lake, FL	144 356	5 189	57.5	8 260	0.0	11.0	6.6	1 315	. . .
Lee, FL	329 508	6 015	55.5	17 053	0.4	14.5	7.2	2 572	. . .
Leon, FL	180 946	5 724	55.9	21 304	0.1	5.4	1.9	1 773	. . .
Levy, FL	33 378	5 354	56.1	1 968	0.5	10.2	9.8	309	. . .
Liberty, FL	6 758	5 530	55.3	372	0.0	2.7	8.6	55	. . .
Madison, FL	19 649	5 651	57.2	1 005	0.0	6.6	10.6	129	. . .
Manatee, FL	192 435	5 646	58.1	10 524	0.6	11.6	6.8	1 480	. . .
Marion, FL	201 168	5 306	58.2	11 281	0.1	10.9	7.5	1 713	. . .
Martin, FL	94 060	5 902	57.2	4 579	0.0	6.1	9.2	756	. . .
Miami-Dade, FL	2 165 093	6 141	59.0	123 037	0.1	7.7	6.8	14 696	. . .
Monroe, FL	60 743	6 419	53.3	2 776	1.7	17.0	4.3	446	. . .
Nassau, FL	52 327	5 080	58.0	2 900	0.0	11.2	5.5	480	. . .
Okaloosa, FL	158 796	5 221	59.5	9 554	5.7	17.8	3.0	1 772	. . .
Okeechobee, FL	37 415	5 514	55.5	2 304	0.0	7.6	12.8	288	. . .
Orange, FL	766 290	5 518	54.9	49 260	0.1	10.1	6.2	6 482	. . .
Osceola, FL	158 047	5 246	54.9	9 337	0.0	10.1	6.2	1 497	. . .
Palm Beach, FL	860 464	5 871	61.3	49 015	0.0	8.5	6.9	6 591	. . .
Pasco, FL	258 987	5 622	56.6	14 076	0.1	11.7	5.8	2 043	. . .
Pinellas, FL	620 521	5 611	59.0	36 204	0.2	11.2	5.9	4 969	. . .
Polk, FL	422 236	5 462	59.0	25 278	0.0	9.9	8.1	3 455	. . .
Putnam, FL	72 546	5 658	55.2	3 725	0.0	10.2	9.1	491	. . .
St. Johns, FL	97 583	5 320	57.6	5 896	0.0	10.4	2.0	1 011	. . .
St. Lucie, FL	162 547	5 629	55.3	8 988	0.0	9.7	9.3	1 122	. . .
Santa Rosa, FL	112 176	5 094	57.0	6 309	0.2	9.1	3.6	1 119	. . .
Sarasota, FL	222 497	6 552	59.8	10 743	0.0	11.3	4.1	1 647	. . .
Seminole, FL	297 078	5 108	60.4	18 797	0.0	8.9	4.1	3 001	. . .
Sumter, FL	32 411	5 492	53.8	2 078	0.0	9.8	13.4	286	. . .
Suwannee, FL	31 051	5 352	56.9	1 987	0.0	10.9	9.5	313	. . .
Taylor, FL	21 701	5 593	56.8	1 093	0.0	6.0	11.2	163	. . .
Union, FL	13 002	5 559	53.8	665	0.3	10.2	16.1	110	. . .
Volusia, FL	329 511	5 500	58.8	22 260	0.1	9.9	6.0	2 740	. . .
Wakulla, FL	24 434	5 266	53.6	1 281	0.5	11.5	8.3	215	. . .
Walton, FL	33 123	5 687	57.6	1 863	0.5	10.6	4.5	267	. . .
Washington, FL	23 642	6 976	55.7	935	0.0	15.2	8.3	192	. . .
GEORGIA									
Appling, GA	21 889	6 301	63.9	1 130	0.0	11.3	8.3	189	9.4
Atkinson, GA	8 378	5 323	61.8	502	0.0	18.1	16.9	61	8.2
Bacon, GA	11 255	5 636	62.4	523	0.0	17.4	6.1	87	14.0
Baker, GA	3 823	8 689	57.3	249	0.0	3.2	5.6	0	. . .
Baldwin, GA	37 695	5 903	63.4	3 752	0.0	6.6	6.7	241	6.8
Banks, GA	10 957	4 844	61.5	815	0.0	13.5	6.4	73	7.4
Barrow, GA	45 838	5 844	65.1	2 225	0.0	11.4	8.2	293	7.8
Bartow, GA	85 173	5 799	63.6	3 768	0.0	13.6	12.2	546	9.2
Ben Hill, GA	20 258	5 646	64.7	1 111	0.0	9.2	9.0	179	8.5
Berrien, GA	16 420	5 177	60.8	857	0.0	15.4	8.5	140	8.6

. . . = Not available.

Table C-1. Population, School, and Student Characteristics by County—*Continued*

County	High school graduates, 2000			College enrollment, 2000		College graduates, 2000 (percent)						
	Population 25 years and over	High school diploma or less (percent)	High school diploma or more (percent)	Number	Percent public	Bachelor's degree or more	+/- U.S. percent with bachelor's degree or more	Non-Hispanic White	Black or African American	American Indian and Alaska Native	Asian, Hawaiian, and Pacific Islander	Hispanic or Latino[1]
	30	31	32	33	34	35	36	37	38	39	40	41
FLORIDA												
Alachua, FL	123 524	32.2	88.1	53 371	96.2	38.7	14.3	42.2	14.3	35.3	78.6	47.0
Baker, FL	13 953	69.5	71.9	723	84.4	8.2	-16.2	8.9	5.6	0.0	0.0	5.1
Bay, FL	99 771	49.6	81.0	6 965	90.3	17.7	-6.7	18.5	9.5	9.8	22.5	19.0
Bradford, FL	17 883	66.0	74.2	795	89.9	8.4	-16.0	10.2	2.2	0.0	30.4	5.4
Brevard, FL	339 738	42.5	86.3	23 877	70.4	23.6	-0.8	24.3	12.1	10.3	37.0	22.9
Broward, FL	1 126 502	46.4	82.0	88 536	68.6	24.5	0.1	27.2	14.7	15.2	38.4	23.0
Calhoun, FL	8 884	69.4	69.1	397	98.0	7.7	-16.7	8.6	3.3	15.8	31.7	0.0
Charlotte, FL	113 071	53.5	82.1	3 279	79.6	17.6	-6.8	17.6	14.0	8.8	42.7	17.3
Citrus, FL	92 594	59.7	78.3	2 722	82.0	13.2	-11.2	13.1	9.1	15.0	42.1	11.0
Clay, FL	90 382	45.3	86.4	6 892	82.8	20.1	-4.3	20.2	17.6	11.4	31.0	17.9
Collier, FL	185 357	44.5	81.8	6 692	73.3	27.9	3.5	32.4	8.9	8.5	43.8	7.1
Columbia, FL	36 880	60.2	74.7	1 874	88.3	10.9	-13.5	11.2	6.0	33.6	50.8	16.1
De Soto, FL	21 222	71.8	63.5	556	81.8	8.4	-16.0	10.7	2.8	0.0	33.6	2.3
Dixie, FL	9 643	73.5	65.9	358	70.4	6.8	-17.6	7.1	1.9	0.0	20.0	4.8
Duval, FL	499 602	46.3	82.7	43 351	79.1	21.9	-2.5	24.6	13.1	17.9	34.0	21.8
Escambia, FL	189 710	46.3	82.1	20 805	70.5	21.0	-3.4	23.9	9.8	9.3	23.2	22.8
Flagler, FL	38 616	46.1	85.9	1 784	79.7	21.2	-3.2	21.4	18.9	26.3	37.2	17.1
Franklin, FL	8 202	68.1	68.3	246	92.7	12.4	-12.0	14.0	3.7	18.5	63.2	7.2
Gadsden, FL	28 932	65.2	70.7	1 599	90.8	12.9	-11.5	20.8	6.8	18.8	43.5	4.3
Gilchrist, FL	8 866	63.7	72.4	431	88.9	9.4	-15.0	9.6	4.3	0.0	0.0	7.1
Glades, FL	7 403	67.0	69.8	285	87.7	9.8	-14.6	11.2	3.2	14.3	48.6	3.1
Gulf, FL	9 527	64.6	72.6	592	92.9	10.1	-14.3	11.1	6.6	8.2	23.5	6.4
Hamilton, FL	8 758	72.2	62.9	232	92.7	7.3	-17.1	9.3	3.9	0.0	16.0	3.0
Hardee, FL	16 509	73.5	58.0	627	78.1	8.4	-16.0	11.3	6.2	8.7	43.3	1.4
Hendry, FL	20 551	74.9	54.2	873	86.8	8.2	-16.2	12.4	3.8	9.4	36.5	2.7
Hernando, FL	99 082	59.3	78.5	3 490	79.0	12.7	-11.7	12.9	10.0	2.9	28.2	8.9
Highlands, FL	65 087	60.1	74.5	2 080	80.5	13.6	-10.8	14.2	5.1	22.9	48.5	9.2
Hillsborough, FL	653 841	45.9	80.8	60 920	76.1	25.1	0.7	28.5	14.6	21.1	42.7	15.7
Holmes, FL	12 659	72.6	65.2	524	91.8	8.8	-15.6	9.1	2.2	12.0	21.6	3.3
Indian River, FL	84 531	47.5	81.6	3 733	71.7	23.1	-1.3	24.8	7.6	19.2	44.9	9.1
Jackson, FL	31 771	63.5	69.1	2 115	81.7	12.8	-11.6	14.9	7.1	6.7	44.7	11.6
Jefferson, FL	8 911	59.1	73.2	392	75.5	16.9	-7.5	23.3	6.7	0.0	30.8	6.9
Lafayette, FL	4 745	71.9	68.2	226	80.1	7.2	-17.2	9.2	0.4	0.0	0.0	1.4
Lake, FL	155 572	54.5	79.8	5 504	81.6	16.6	-7.8	17.3	7.3	1.7	33.5	14.5
Lee, FL	327 672	50.2	82.3	12 539	79.1	21.1	-3.3	22.6	8.9	11.4	40.7	8.9
Leon, FL	137 537	29.8	89.1	50 886	95.7	41.7	17.3	46.2	27.3	28.0	65.5	38.2
Levy, FL	24 030	64.3	73.9	930	85.4	10.6	-13.8	10.6	8.0	12.8	57.1	14.0
Liberty, FL	4 828	74.9	65.6	218	96.8	7.4	-17.0	8.9	1.8	0.0	17.6	0.0
Madison, FL	12 254	66.7	67.5	597	93.1	10.2	-14.2	13.5	4.7	0.0	0.0	6.9
Manatee, FL	192 789	50.4	81.4	8 183	78.7	20.8	-3.6	22.3	10.9	10.9	32.6	8.3
Marion, FL	187 187	57.7	78.2	8 078	81.5	13.7	-10.7	14.0	10.5	16.5	34.9	9.5
Martin, FL	96 467	43.0	85.3	4 372	73.5	26.3	1.9	27.7	7.4	4.3	42.9	14.1
Miami-Dade, FL	1 491 789	54.5	67.9	160 435	69.4	21.7	-2.7	38.0	11.5	15.8	44.7	18.1
Monroe, FL	61 161	44.0	84.9	3 028	74.1	25.5	1.1	28.2	8.8	13.0	47.3	13.9
Nassau, FL	38 972	53.4	81.0	2 188	80.1	18.9	-5.5	19.8	8.4	12.7	26.1	10.8
Okaloosa, FL	112 429	39.1	88.0	9 816	89.6	24.2	-0.2	26.1	11.9	15.4	14.8	19.6
Okeechobee, FL	23 388	68.8	65.1	1 136	84.4	8.9	-15.5	9.1	6.4	21.1	51.3	5.0
Orange, FL	574 101	44.0	81.8	64 155	77.9	26.1	1.7	30.7	14.7	14.5	40.6	17.0
Osceola, FL	110 607	54.8	79.1	7 092	70.5	15.7	-8.7	16.3	11.6	6.3	40.0	12.5
Palm Beach, FL	817 899	43.3	83.6	50 064	72.1	27.7	3.3	31.3	11.4	16.5	47.3	15.3
Pasco, FL	255 472	59.2	77.6	11 290	74.4	13.1	-11.3	12.7	13.0	5.9	45.2	14.2
Pinellas, FL	686 094	45.6	84.0	41 446	74.6	22.9	-1.5	23.8	10.5	18.1	33.6	20.0
Polk, FL	326 208	58.9	74.8	18 134	66.2	14.9	-9.5	16.0	8.9	13.0	40.0	8.6
Putnam, FL	47 761	67.0	70.4	1 984	84.9	9.4	-15.0	10.1	6.6	9.2	24.3	2.1
St. Johns, FL	86 199	37.3	87.2	6 425	59.5	33.1	8.7	34.2	12.6	50.0	58.7	25.9
St. Lucie, FL	136 448	55.0	77.7	7 060	83.1	15.1	-9.3	16.2	8.9	7.9	30.2	11.5
Santa Rosa, FL	78 166	43.8	85.4	5 600	91.2	22.9	-1.5	23.7	6.2	11.3	28.8	23.9
Sarasota, FL	256 802	43.0	87.1	10 210	75.7	27.4	3.0	28.2	10.5	24.4	35.0	19.5
Seminole, FL	243 216	35.7	88.7	22 095	79.8	31.0	6.6	32.8	18.5	26.6	47.6	23.3
Sumter, FL	41 509	61.6	77.3	1 221	70.7	12.2	-12.2	12.9	5.1	13.8	56.4	13.5
Suwannee, FL	23 492	65.6	73.2	953	81.4	10.5	-13.9	10.9	6.5	25.2	56.1	7.7
Taylor, FL	12 914	70.9	70.0	585	87.7	8.9	-15.5	10.9	3.1	0.0	57.6	5.0
Union, FL	9 363	66.4	72.5	429	78.3	7.5	-16.9	9.3	2.1	4.0	15.8	5.8
Volusia, FL	317 225	50.2	82.0	26 362	57.6	17.6	-6.8	18.1	14.7	16.9	35.8	11.7
Wakulla, FL	15 211	56.6	78.4	794	89.8	15.7	-8.7	17.4	4.5	0.0	10.0	16.1
Walton, FL	28 838	56.4	76.0	1 108	85.8	16.2	-8.2	17.4	2.6	12.6	25.8	12.6
Washington, FL	14 338	67.6	71.2	566	84.5	9.2	-15.2	9.5	6.1	8.6	0.0	8.0
GEORGIA												
Appling, GA	11 004	69.9	67.3	394	86.3	8.4	-16.0	9.6	3.8	0.0	32.7	0.0
Atkinson, GA	4 503	79.6	56.3	100	87.0	6.9	-17.5	9.0	3.4	0.0	20.0	0.5
Bacon, GA	6 525	76.3	67.7	317	98.1	6.6	-17.8	7.3	1.1	0.0	52.8	4.4
Baker, GA	2 543	74.4	66.0	103	97.1	10.7	-13.7	16.3	3.9	. . .	100.0	4.3
Baldwin, GA	28 445	62.8	72.6	4 231	73.8	16.2	-8.2	21.7	7.4	0.0	45.1	29.8
Banks, GA	9 401	72.9	65.4	328	81.7	8.6	-15.8	8.8	11.0	6.3	0.0	0.0
Barrow, GA	29 317	62.7	73.3	1 143	82.3	10.9	-13.5	11.6	5.8	21.5	16.6	2.0
Bartow, GA	48 709	62.4	71.8	2 093	80.0	14.1	-10.3	14.5	10.3	22.3	29.0	6.3
Ben Hill, GA	10 990	71.4	65.8	591	72.1	9.5	-14.9	12.8	2.6	19.4	0.0	0.0
Berrien, GA	10 451	68.6	66.0	604	94.2	9.4	-15.0	10.0	4.0	24.6	17.8	8.6

[1]Hispanic or Latino persons may be of any race.
. . . = Not available.

Table C-1. Population, School, and Student Characteristics by County—*Continued*

County	State/County code	County type[1]	Population, 2000 Total	Population, 2000 Percent 5–17 years	Number of schools and students, 2000–2001 School districts	Number of schools and students, 2000–2001 Schools	Number of schools and students, 2000–2001 Students	Resident enrollment, 2000 Total	Resident enrollment, 2000 Percent public	Resident enrollment, 2000 K–12	Resident enrollment, 2000 Percent public
			1	2	3	4	5	6	7	8	9
Bibb, GA	13021	2	153 887	19.1	1	42	24 739	42 862	78.9	30 324	86.2
Bleckley, GA	13023	6	11 666	20.2	1	4	2 387	3 502	93.5	2 406	97.5
Brantley, GA	13025	9	14 629	21.0	1	6	3 137	3 729	94.8	3 109	96.0
Brooks, GA	13027	7	16 450	20.4	1	4	2 707	4 275	93.1	3 509	94.7
Bryan, GA	13029	2	23 417	23.4	1	7	5 308	6 744	91.0	5 370	94.5
Bulloch, GA	13031	6	55 983	16.5	1	15	8 334	23 132	93.9	9 391	91.9
Burke, GA	13033	6	22 243	23.3	1	5	4 890	6 592	90.9	5 529	91.8
Butts, GA	13035	6	19 522	17.8	1	4	3 235	4 354	92.9	3 567	96.2
Calhoun, GA	13037	8	6 320	16.0	1	2	758	1 498	80.5	1 132	80.7
Camden, GA	13039	6	43 664	23.0	1	12	9 712	13 254	92.9	10 149	97.1
Candler, GA	13043	7	9 577	19.7	1	3	1 893	2 343	92.9	1 917	95.3
Carroll, GA	13045	1	87 268	18.9	2	22	15 939	24 665	92.9	16 383	94.4
Catoosa, GA	13047	2	53 282	19.0	1	12	9 588	13 012	90.1	10 040	93.7
Charlton, GA	13049	8	10 282	20.9	1	4	2 027	2 586	93.6	2 221	94.7
Chatham, GA	13051	2	232 048	18.3	1	49	35 344	64 990	77.4	44 375	82.8
Chattahoochee, GA	13053	2	14 882	20.0	1	2	493	4 158	90.9	3 027	95.5
Chattooga, GA	13055	7	25 470	16.4	2	10	4 130	5 264	91.5	4 234	95.5
Cherokee, GA	13057	1	141 903	20.0	1	31	26 043	36 937	84.1	27 510	92.5
Clarke, GA	13059	3	101 489	12.6	1	19	11 423	44 372	91.8	13 088	88.5
Clay, GA	13061	9	3 357	19.2	1	1	405	867	92.2	675	93.6
Clayton, GA	13063	0	236 517	21.6	1	48	46 930	68 358	88.8	51 453	94.3
Clinch, GA	13065	7	6 878	20.5	1	4	1 458	1 784	97.5	1 477	99.8
Cobb, GA	13067	0	607 751	18.8	2	102	103 149	165 032	82.3	114 905	90.4
Coffee, GA	13069	7	37 413	20.4	1	11	7 707	9 786	92.7	7 661	95.3
Colquitt, GA	13071	7	42 053	19.9	1	13	8 373	10 489	94.5	8 422	97.1
Columbia, GA	13073	2	89 288	22.7	1	24	18 756	26 407	86.9	20 242	91.0
Cook, GA	13075	7	15 771	20.5	1	3	3 256	4 164	95.4	3 266	98.1
Coweta, GA	13077	1	89 215	20.6	1	23	16 766	23 339	85.2	18 412	90.0
Crawford, GA	13079	8	12 495	20.9	1	3	2 149	3 288	90.5	2 663	91.7
Crisp, GA	13081	6	21 996	21.2	1	6	4 541	5 839	92.2	4 751	94.2
Dade, GA	13083	2	15 154	18.0	1	4	2 668	3 991	77.8	2 698	92.3
Dawson, GA	13085	8	15 999	18.0	1	4	2 773	3 395	92.2	2 804	95.6
Decatur, GA	13087	6	28 240	20.9	1	9	5 838	7 686	92.9	6 026	94.7
De Kalb, GA	13089	0	665 865	17.5	2	132	98 620	182 326	77.6	119 724	88.8
Dodge, GA	13091	7	19 171	19.7	1	4	3 558	4 906	96.1	3 963	98.4
Dooly, GA	13093	6	11 525	18.8	1	4	1 726	3 117	86.4	2 513	86.7
Dougherty, GA	13095	3	96 065	20.0	1	28	16 799	28 401	88.7	19 974	89.7
Douglas, GA	13097	0	92 174	20.3	1	25	17 489	25 409	84.8	19 159	91.4
Early, GA	13099	6	12 354	21.6	1	3	2 812	3 276	93.7	2 617	94.5
Echols, GA	13101	9	3 754	21.3	1	1	732	999	98.6	831	98.8
Effingham, GA	13103	2	37 535	22.3	1	11	8 458	10 636	93.0	8 498	96.6
Elbert, GA	13105	6	20 511	19.5	1	7	3 782	4 834	94.5	4 043	98.0
Emanuel, GA	13107	7	21 837	21.1	1	7	4 750	5 720	94.1	4 745	94.5
Evans, GA	13109	8	10 495	20.6	1	3	2 027	2 588	91.7	2 265	92.5
Fannin, GA	13111	9	19 798	15.6	1	5	3 112	3 861	93.6	3 128	96.0
Fayette, GA	13113	1	91 263	23.3	1	23	19 590	27 262	85.2	21 549	89.8
Floyd, GA	13115	4	90 565	18.0	2	30	15 624	23 133	81.5	16 375	93.0
Forsyth, GA	13117	1	98 407	18.4	1	21	17 131	23 873	82.1	17 633	91.0
Franklin, GA	13119	8	20 285	17.6	1	5	3 584	5 002	84.6	3 659	98.5
Fulton, GA	13121	0	816 006	17.5	2	169	126 813	219 663	76.6	145 409	86.9
Gilmer, GA	13123	8	23 456	17.2	1	5	3 723	4 750	89.8	3 934	94.1
Glascock, GA	13125	9	2 556	17.1	1	1	558	564	91.3	474	94.5
Glynn, GA	13127	5	67 568	18.8	1	15	12 048	16 443	88.8	12 887	91.2
Gordon, GA	13129	6	44 104	18.9	2	12	8 594	10 354	92.3	8 291	95.4
Grady, GA	13131	6	23 659	20.2	1	7	4 559	6 185	92.5	4 966	94.0
Greene, GA	13133	6	14 406	18.4	1	4	2 374	3 385	85.6	2 693	87.1
Gwinnett, GA	13135	0	588 448	20.2	2	89	112 228	161 510	85.8	119 551	92.9
Habersham, GA	13137	7	35 902	17.2	1	10	5 653	8 166	85.7	6 134	95.9
Hall, GA	13139	6	139 277	18.7	2	34	24 312	33 309	89.6	26 158	95.1
Hancock, GA	13141	9	10 076	18.3	1	3	1 742	2 704	91.5	2 155	92.3
Haralson, GA	13143	6	25 690	19.2	2	9	5 209	5 956	93.3	4 784	95.1
Harris, GA	13145	2	23 695	19.7	1	6	4 264	6 252	86.8	4 797	87.0
Hart, GA	13147	6	22 997	17.2	1	8	3 440	4 886	92.8	3 969	97.3
Heard, GA	13149	8	11 012	20.8	1	4	2 112	2 767	93.9	2 286	94.4
Henry, GA	13151	1	119 341	21.1	1	28	23 601	32 860	84.7	25 449	90.0
Houston, GA	13153	2	110 765	21.2	1	33	21 529	32 495	89.5	24 077	92.6
Irwin, GA	13155	7	9 931	22.0	1	3	1 897	2 682	95.9	2 266	95.8
Jackson, GA	13157	6	41 589	19.4	3	15	7 935	9 885	91.2	8 057	94.7
Jasper, GA	13159	8	11 426	20.3	1	4	2 083	2 876	86.9	2 373	87.8
Jeff Davis, GA	13161	7	12 684	19.5	1	4	2 650	2 880	92.6	2 328	96.4
Jefferson, GA	13163	8	17 266	21.2	1	6	3 680	4 628	88.6	3 911	89.5
Jenkins, GA	13165	7	8 575	21.4	1	3	1 794	2 381	94.3	1 969	96.8
Johnson, GA	13167	9	8 560	23.3	1	3	1 400	2 318	94.4	1 858	95.3
Jones, GA	13169	2	23 639	20.6	1	5	4 790	6 342	89.0	5 160	92.6
Lamar, GA	13171	6	15 912	18.4	1	3	2 647	4 354	90.7	2 824	92.5
Lanier, GA	13173	9	7 241	20.2	1	3	1 337	1 834	93.5	1 530	93.9
Laurens, GA	13175	6	44 874	19.9	2	14	9 090	11 544	93.4	9 240	94.7
Lee, GA	13177	3	24 757	23.4	1	6	5 392	7 626	90.8	6 043	92.7
Liberty, GA	13179	4	61 610	21.6	1	13	11 467	17 177	91.7	13 082	95.6
Lincoln, GA	13181	8	8 348	19.0	1	3	1 465	1 953	96.5	1 648	97.9

[1]County type code is from the Economic Research Service of the USDA. See Notes and Definitions at the end of this section.

Table C-1. School and Student Characteristics by County—*Continued*

County	Characteristics of students, 2000–2001			Staff and students, 2000–2001				Revenues, fiscal 1999			
	Percent with IEP[2]	Percent eligible for free lunch	Percent minority	Number of teachers	Student/ teacher ratio	Local school non-teaching staff	Central admin. staff	Total revenue ($1,000s)	Percentage of revenue from		
									Federal govt.	State govt.	Local govt.
	10	11	12	13	14	15	16	17	18	19	20
Bibb, GA	10.9	60.1	71.4	1 440	17.2	1 507	92	$157 644	11.0	54.9	34.1
Bleckley, GA	12.7	49.4	31.8	149	16.0	172	8	14 734	9.3	69.3	21.5
Brantley, GA	11.8	54.0	4.6	214	14.7	203	10	18 398	9.6	70.3	20.1
Brooks, GA	10.3	74.1	67.2	170	15.9	173	11	16 583	15.4	62.6	22.0
Bryan, GA	8.7	34.2	18.7	292	18.2	330	16	31 050	7.4	57.8	34.7
Bulloch, GA	14.8	53.5	40.3	545	15.3	642	21	67 169	9.1	61.8	29.1
Burke, GA	9.1	75.1	68.7	295	16.6	397	18	33 977	10.4	28.1	61.5
Butts, GA	12.1	46.1	38.6	196	16.5	205	15	24 285	6.2	61.3	32.4
Calhoun, GA	19.3	94.1	95.9	57	13.3	62	6	8 069	18.1	59.1	22.8
Camden, GA	10.7	34.9	28.7	534	18.2	562	26	60 822	12.5	59.2	28.3
Candler, GA	13.6	64.5	44.2	110	17.2	131	9	12 372	10.0	64.1	25.9
Carroll, GA	14.1	39.3	24.7	831	19.2	1 105	47	105 788	6.9	59.6	33.5
Catoosa, GA	11.5	31.6	3.4	556	17.2	563	27	55 713	5.3	60.2	34.5
Charlton, GA	12.2	57.6	34.4	110	18.4	111	9	13 260	9.2	62.6	28.2
Chatham, GA	11.6	52.0	68.6	2 025	17.5	1 823	106	249 856	7.3	47.5	45.2
Chattahoochee, GA	16.8	71.6	38.3	32	15.4	50	3	5 000	13.9	70.7	15.4
Chattooga, GA	17.0	43.3	11.3	277	14.9	269	12	30 146	7.4	55.5	37.0
Cherokee, GA	11.8	14.9	9.3	1 611	16.2	1 360	64	181 410	2.6	49.3	48.1
Clarke, GA	12.5	56.0	70.3	722	15.8	892	37	110 561	7.3	41.4	51.3
Clay, GA	16.0	91.9	95.1	23	17.6	30	2	3 944	19.7	51.5	28.8
Clayton, GA	9.3	55.1	76.9	2 581	18.2	3 077	197	323 381	5.8	48.3	45.9
Clinch, GA	17.0	66.0	40.2	90	16.2	107	9	10 067	13.3	62.2	24.4
Cobb, GA	12.3	21.2	36.7	6 835	15.1	5 340	378	744 098	4.1	47.4	48.6
Coffee, GA	11.1	63.7	41.6	460	16.8	486	32	51 008	8.7	61.2	30.0
Colquitt, GA	12.1	57.6	42.1	472	17.7	580	23	51 650	10.1	66.5	23.3
Columbia, GA	9.5	19.6	18.4	1 076	17.4	1 156	42	110 326	3.5	57.1	39.4
Cook, GA	11.5	57.8	42.7	189	17.2	244	12	20 758	9.2	60.6	30.2
Coweta, GA	14.1	27.7	26.9	1 017	16.5	1 085	61	111 482	4.5	49.3	46.1
Crawford, GA	13.6	54.8	30.5	134	16.0	820	12	13 160	7.6	66.1	26.2
Crisp, GA	10.6	69.2	61.2	274	16.6	331	16	31 876	11.6	61.5	26.8
Dade, GA	11.4	38.0	0.9	165	16.2	171	7	16 891	6.9	64.8	28.3
Dawson, GA	10.4	26.4	1.8	179	15.5	183	14	19 870	4.2	42.8	53.0
Decatur, GA	11.5	61.5	55.8	370	15.8	387	15	38 297	9.4	60.8	29.9
De Kalb, GA	8.6	55.4	86.5	5 867	16.8	5 982	447	749 486	4.7	41.3	54.0
Dodge, GA	12.3	60.1	38.0	204	17.4	259	11	24 631	15.9	67.6	16.5
Dooly, GA	8.5	85.1	84.0	94	18.4	144	12	13 246	12.4	58.9	28.7
Dougherty, GA	12.0	67.1	83.8	1 076	15.6	1 382	64	155 439	9.2	58.8	32.0
Douglas, GA	12.6	29.5	28.4	1 022	17.1	969	49	114 061	4.4	53.5	42.1
Early, GA	11.8	69.8	62.4	155	18.1	174	11	20 112	10.5	56.2	33.3
Echols, GA	10.7	55.6	26.0	45	16.3	55	6	4 500	9.7	66.3	24.0
Effingham, GA	12.2	29.5	17.1	487	17.4	579	24	48 638	5.5	59.7	34.8
Elbert, GA	11.3	54.1	42.4	242	15.6	294	12	27 015	8.0	65.0	27.0
Emanuel, GA	17.4	69.1	47.1	286	16.6	316	17	33 220	13.1	68.7	18.3
Evans, GA	17.0	70.6	49.9	113	17.9	110	12	12 385	11.4	66.1	22.5
Fannin, GA	14.0	40.8	1.0	183	17.0	236	8	18 385	10.3	62.1	27.7
Fayette, GA	11.1	6.9	19.3	1 352	14.5	1 078	55	133 593	2.0	47.3	50.7
Floyd, GA	17.1	43.1	25.7	973	16.1	847	50	100 327	6.9	57.6	35.5
Forsyth, GA	9.9	12.0	10.1	1 101	15.6	1 013	48	115 082	1.9	35.2	62.9
Franklin, GA	15.8	42.9	13.7	239	15.0	244	11	25 032	6.4	58.2	35.4
Fulton, GA	9.0	53.0	70.7	8 272	15.3	7 402	550	1 282 530	5.3	30.1	64.6
Gilmer, GA	8.8	43.6	7.8	217	17.2	233	10	23 920	17.3	54.9	27.9
Glascock, GA	14.0	45.5	10.4	39	14.3	49	1	3 613	14.0	54.6	31.4
Glynn, GA	12.6	41.5	42.0	713	16.9	788	52	85 078	7.2	46.9	45.9
Gordon, GA	14.7	36.3	12.5	534	16.1	501	35	57 068	5.7	54.2	40.1
Grady, GA	11.2	51.4	46.1	292	15.6	299	24	28 377	12.2	68.0	19.8
Greene, GA	12.7	79.8	77.5	155	15.3	170	18	18 652	11.2	48.1	40.7
Gwinnett, GA	10.4	21.4	35.8	7 279	15.4	5 574	195	788 088	2.6	44.3	53.1
Habersham, GA	13.2	32.2	14.3	350	16.2	349	14	41 065	4.7	50.0	45.3
Hall, GA	9.5	39.2	33.9	1 526	15.9	1 196	67	162 407	5.9	49.4	44.7
Hancock, GA	14.6	85.5	98.5	97	18.0	189	6	12 463	17.3	59.2	23.5
Haralson, GA	16.1	35.9	6.3	322	16.2	349	18	32 115	7.1	64.2	28.7
Harris, GA	9.4	36.6	25.3	267	16.0	303	16	27 828	5.6	52.9	41.5
Hart, GA	11.8	41.7	29.5	231	14.9	240	8	23 738	6.7	55.3	38.0
Heard, GA	12.1	44.2	13.6	131	16.1	134	9	11 985	8.5	58.6	32.8
Henry, GA	10.2	18.8	23.4	1 386	17.0	1 328	37	144 857	2.6	50.3	47.2
Houston, GA	12.1	36.4	36.0	1 417	15.2	1 203	86	144 763	6.0	56.8	37.1
Irwin, GA	15.6	67.5	40.3	128	14.8	140	10	13 736	11.6	62.7	25.7
Jackson, GA	18.8	39.4	12.9	508	15.6	501	27	53 891	6.9	52.9	40.2
Jasper, GA	15.8	58.0	41.6	133	15.7	164	10	14 599	12.8	53.3	33.9
Jeff Davis, GA	11.2	53.7	23.2	160	16.6	158	14	16 121	9.5	68.2	22.2
Jefferson, GA	12.0	81.9	76.9	204	18.0	244	15	23 327	12.7	63.9	23.3
Jenkins, GA	12.2	76.8	55.6	115	15.6	121	7	10 012	13.3	72.9	13.8
Johnson, GA	12.6	71.9	52.1	95	14.7	95	6	9 424	15.6	69.2	15.1
Jones, GA	11.1	30.6	25.2	261	18.4	265	10	24 879	7.2	67.1	25.7
Lamar, GA	9.1	53.4	43.3	149	17.8	163	11	16 901	8.0	56.9	35.2
Lanier, GA	13.6	64.6	35.3	92	14.5	92	11	8 560	10.3	69.9	19.8
Laurens, GA	9.8	59.9	47.6	620	14.7	569	27	63 283	8.6	59.5	31.9
Lee, GA	7.6	24.8	16.0	309	17.4	291	15	30 345	5.3	64.9	29.8
Liberty, GA	9.5	47.5	64.6	615	18.6	714	33	72 187	16.8	58.8	24.4
Lincoln, GA	18.0	55.2	42.9	95	15.4	108	7	10 289	12.8	63.9	23.3

[2]IEP = Individual Education Program. See Notes and Definitions at the end of this section.

Table C-1. Population, School, and Student Characteristics by County—*Continued*

County	Current expenditures, fiscal 1999			Resident population 16 to 19 years, 2000				Outcomes, 1999–2000	
	Amount ($1,000s)	Amount per student	Percent for instruction	Total population 16 to 19 years	Percent in Armed Forces	Percent high school graduates	Percent not enrolled, not grads, not Armed Forces, not empl.	Number of graduates	Dropouts grades 9–12 (percent)
	21	22	23	24	25	26	27	28	29
Bibb, GA	$150 840	$6 127	61.9	8 916	0.1	9.5	9.5	904	9.5
Bleckley, GA	13 067	5 504	63.5	984	0.0	12.2	4.5	120	3.4
Brantley, GA	15 965	5 094	62.8	812	0.0	12.8	4.7	134	11.6
Brooks, GA	15 536	5 643	59.3	1 120	2.0	12.4	10.4	92	14.7
Bryan, GA	27 443	5 353	62.4	1 355	0.0	9.8	8.3	226	5.9
Bulloch, GA	53 976	6 447	58.6	6 536	0.1	4.9	2.7	388	7.6
Burke, GA	29 132	5 960	58.5	1 541	0.8	8.0	10.6	205	9.4
Butts, GA	17 911	5 641	58.1	1 027	0.0	13.0	13.5	140	9.7
Calhoun, GA	7 809	9 701	44.8	333	0.0	10.8	6.0	45	4.8
Camden, GA	50 907	5 249	59.1	2 816	11.7	20.7	5.0	395	7.2
Candler, GA	10 710	5 541	63.1	491	0.0	5.7	8.8	85	10.4
Carroll, GA	93 484	6 145	62.0	5 999	0.0	8.7	8.0	669	6.6
Catoosa, GA	48 447	5 286	63.5	2 754	0.0	10.1	5.7	397	7.3
Charlton, GA	10 935	5 290	58.9	675	0.0	15.7	12.7	92	7.5
Chatham, GA	216 044	5 882	63.9	13 182	2.8	13.4	6.0	1 270	12.5
Chattahoochee, GA	3 423	6 725	62.5	1 303	67.8	71.1	3.1	0	. . .
Chattooga, GA	24 459	5 856	65.1	1 417	0.4	17.7	10.6	196	9.1
Cherokee, GA	139 035	5 712	63.4	7 243	0.1	9.8	5.6	1 164	4.8
Clarke, GA	87 302	7 780	56.7	10 245	1.1	5.6	4.7	454	8.9
Clay, GA	2 746	7 041	57.2	232	0.0	10.8	6.5	0	. . .
Clayton, GA	252 809	5 737	61.4	13 381	0.3	12.7	7.4	1 685	10.0
Clinch, GA	9 392	6 179	61.9	395	0.0	6.3	3.3	67	11.0
Cobb, GA	645 779	6 594	68.6	31 156	0.0	9.9	5.3	5 365	4.4
Coffee, GA	41 613	5 568	62.9	2 275	0.0	7.6	9.0	286	9.9
Colquitt, GA	47 709	5 727	62.7	2 754	2.9	10.8	10.7	359	10.7
Columbia, GA	92 767	4 983	65.8	5 336	0.0	8.8	3.3	1 085	6.0
Cook, GA	17 001	5 432	61.6	915	0.0	15.2	7.2	138	6.4
Coweta, GA	87 767	5 558	64.5	4 522	0.0	9.9	7.4	677	6.4
Crawford, GA	11 427	5 340	55.5	578	0.0	12.6	6.7	98	2.2
Crisp, GA	28 453	6 172	62.4	1 270	0.0	9.8	15.1	153	14.2
Dade, GA	14 726	5 688	64.0	1 042	0.0	8.1	8.5	140	5.3
Dawson, GA	14 420	5 836	58.8	752	0.0	19.4	10.0	98	7.0
Decatur, GA	31 887	5 456	61.8	1 605	0.0	8.8	9.3	260	7.0
De Kalb, GA	627 383	6 544	60.8	35 836	0.1	9.0	6.8	4 295	8.6
Dodge, GA	22 982	6 525	55.9	1 113	0.0	4.5	11.3	151	7.0
Dooly, GA	12 226	6 758	60.6	681	1.0	6.9	9.5	66	10.1
Dougherty, GA	111 920	6 466	57.4	6 697	10.6	12.7	7.0	652	11.8
Douglas, GA	102 085	6 087	60.6	4 929	0.0	11.8	4.3	796	5.3
Early, GA	16 259	5 679	63.2	679	0.0	17.4	9.4	120	3.4
Echols, GA	4 201	5 950	59.5	235	0.0	3.0	5.5	31	3.4
Effingham, GA	41 609	5 166	62.7	2 334	0.0	12.1	6.8	380	8.0
Elbert, GA	23 023	5 929	62.1	1 142	0.0	14.7	9.8	145	12.1
Emanuel, GA	27 906	5 591	63.3	1 569	0.0	9.4	10.5	261	8.6
Evans, GA	10 582	5 223	62.6	629	0.0	6.4	14.8	72	6.1
Fannin, GA	18 252	5 943	61.3	848	0.0	13.7	4.7	161	6.3
Fayette, GA	109 076	5 768	65.6	5 421	0.2	6.1	2.0	1 270	2.9
Floyd, GA	95 103	6 225	61.1	5 395	0.1	11.7	9.5	697	6.7
Forsyth, GA	86 115	6 022	59.5	3 849	0.0	7.3	4.3	588	6.3
Franklin, GA	20 097	5 721	66.6	1 120	0.0	11.3	5.1	176	14.1
Fulton, GA	928 516	7 358	59.8	44 610	0.2	7.9	8.0	4 973	6.0
Gilmer, GA	23 017	6 528	54.6	1 144	0.0	7.2	13.0	125	8.5
Glascock, GA	3 034	5 714	61.7	140	0.0	9.3	12.1	28	3.4
Glynn, GA	78 575	6 595	63.9	3 714	0.0	13.8	7.5	564	9.2
Gordon, GA	47 566	5 759	62.3	2 497	0.0	14.3	5.8	351	10.3
Grady, GA	26 971	5 723	62.2	1 473	0.0	12.5	9.0	176	8.1
Greene, GA	16 000	6 491	59.4	821	0.0	13.0	14.1	79	4.1
Gwinnett, GA	588 285	5 841	66.0	31 269	0.0	9.8	5.0	5 349	4.0
Habersham, GA	33 700	6 083	61.2	2 244	0.4	11.8	16.5	283	5.1
Hall, GA	129 361	5 785	64.9	8 005	0.0	8.5	12.8	896	6.3
Hancock, GA	10 853	6 135	55.6	587	0.0	11.6	8.9	64	4.6
Haralson, GA	29 072	5 671	62.2	1 523	0.0	10.2	7.6	184	8.3
Harris, GA	22 376	5 500	61.3	1 150	0.0	5.9	2.1	192	9.4
Hart, GA	20 843	6 038	65.8	1 096	0.3	12.9	7.8	159	10.1
Heard, GA	11 020	5 329	64.1	534	0.0	9.2	14.2	86	10.4
Henry, GA	104 182	5 132	66.4	6 124	0.0	11.9	4.6	929	4.8
Houston, GA	121 711	5 844	63.8	6 690	5.7	15.1	4.7	1 159	5.8
Irwin, GA	12 084	6 091	62.7	743	0.0	10.5	5.2	88	10.9
Jackson, GA	42 155	5 654	61.6	2 284	0.0	11.9	10.2	303	8.1
Jasper, GA	11 302	5 654	60.6	680	0.0	19.1	6.5	81	6.4
Jeff Davis, GA	14 942	5 598	63.4	739	0.0	17.3	6.0	127	6.9
Jefferson, GA	20 524	5 348	61.7	1 085	0.0	10.2	7.6	145	5.7
Jenkins, GA	9 474	5 226	63.6	516	0.0	8.9	10.1	80	7.5
Johnson, GA	8 910	6 279	61.4	731	0.0	5.6	25.2	59	10.5
Jones, GA	22 123	4 660	62.9	1 553	0.0	13.8	1.9	252	1.8
Lamar, GA	14 081	5 346	57.9	1 065	0.0	7.0	6.6	148	8.7
Lanier, GA	8 380	6 130	56.9	424	0.0	12.3	7.1	47	7.6
Laurens, GA	54 989	6 012	65.0	2 591	0.3	10.7	6.8	431	7.2
Lee, GA	26 812	5 102	63.8	1 666	0.0	6.7	2.1	298	0.2
Liberty, GA	56 390	4 942	64.2	4 433	26.0	35.6	5.8	389	4.6
Lincoln, GA	9 034	5 710	61.5	450	4.0	4.7	9.3	75	3.2

. . . = Not available.

Table C-1. Population, School, and Student Characteristics by County—*Continued*

County	High school graduates, 2000			College enrollment, 2000		College graduates, 2000 (percent)						
	Population 25 years and over	High school diploma or less (percent)	High school diploma or more (percent)	Number	Percent public	Bachelor's degree or more	+/- U.S. percent with bachelor's degree or more	Non-Hispanic White	Black or African American	American Indian and Alaska Native	Asian, Hawaiian, and Pacific Islander	Hispan-ic or Latino[1]
	30	31	32	33	34	35	36	37	38	39	40	41
Bibb, GA	97 463	54.5	77.2	8 815	59.1	21.3	-3.1	29.1	10.1	19.2	47.3	25.8
Bleckley, GA	7 268	64.0	71.7	867	90.1	12.5	-11.9	14.5	5.6	...	0.0	0.0
Brantley, GA	9 282	74.9	72.5	379	89.2	6.2	-18.2	6.4	2.8	100.0	11.1	0.0
Brooks, GA	10 455	69.6	67.5	518	90.3	11.3	-13.1	15.1	4.3	0.0	0.0	4.4
Bryan, GA	14 333	53.8	79.0	825	86.8	19.3	-5.1	20.2	7.4	0.0	49.3	39.3
Bulloch, GA	28 740	51.7	77.9	12 889	96.8	25.4	1.0	29.6	11.5	0.0	70.4	15.8
Burke, GA	13 338	72.1	64.9	613	87.9	9.5	-14.9	14.0	4.5	0.0	60.0	0.0
Butts, GA	13 055	70.1	69.8	511	79.8	8.6	-15.8	9.5	5.6	0.0	43.8	25.0
Calhoun, GA	4 277	68.2	65.5	228	71.1	11.7	-12.7	18.6	6.4	...	...	8.3
Camden, GA	24 073	49.9	83.3	2 121	81.8	16.0	-8.4	17.1	10.0	30.5	22.7	16.2
Candler, GA	6 166	72.3	56.9	240	90.8	10.2	-14.2	13.6	3.0	0.0	...	3.6
Carroll, GA	53 464	63.2	71.1	6 435	94.8	16.5	-7.9	17.7	8.6	23.5	49.3	15.8
Catoosa, GA	35 231	58.8	76.0	2 014	88.1	13.8	-10.6	13.8	14.1	12.6	23.3	6.8
Charlton, GA	6 404	77.0	65.1	250	88.4	6.4	-18.0	8.0	1.7	5.9	28.3	0.0
Chatham, GA	147 849	46.7	80.2	15 613	69.0	25.0	0.6	32.1	12.6	12.9	36.2	23.4
Chattahoochee, GA	6 417	34.3	88.8	837	80.0	25.0	0.6	32.5	11.2	25.0	21.3	29.4
Chattooga, GA	17 054	74.2	60.4	619	74.5	7.7	-16.7	8.0	3.9	40.9	33.3	6.6
Cherokee, GA	91 141	42.9	84.4	5 781	71.0	27.0	2.6	27.6	21.7	22.7	39.9	14.5
Clarke, GA	51 845	40.6	81.0	29 695	94.7	39.8	15.4	52.9	11.3	14.8	76.4	21.3
Clay, GA	2 215	71.2	64.3	114	85.1	10.1	-14.3	15.8	4.3	85.7	0.0	60.0
Clayton, GA	141 554	51.8	80.1	11 042	74.8	16.6	-7.8	13.9	20.2	21.3	15.9	6.1
Clinch, GA	4 380	73.6	58.9	162	90.1	10.4	-14.0	12.8	3.0	0.0	61.5	41.7
Cobb, GA	395 349	32.0	88.8	35 713	73.6	39.8	15.4	42.7	31.9	32.0	54.0	19.3
Coffee, GA	22 798	68.1	64.8	1 299	91.1	10.0	-14.4	11.9	4.1	22.7	55.8	5.3
Colquitt, GA	26 127	70.9	64.9	1 159	89.6	11.4	-13.0	14.5	3.6	7.0	36.8	1.4
Columbia, GA	56 562	37.9	87.9	3 983	86.6	32.0	7.6	32.2	24.4	19.4	53.0	31.2
Cook, GA	9 876	71.4	64.6	530	93.6	8.1	-16.3	10.1	3.0	0.0	4.2	3.2
Coweta, GA	56 821	51.2	81.6	2 735	79.6	20.6	-3.8	22.7	11.1	11.3	44.2	12.2
Crawford, GA	8 050	72.4	67.3	410	85.9	6.8	-17.6	7.5	5.0	0.0	...	0.0
Crisp, GA	13 709	68.6	65.9	606	85.3	12.8	-11.6	17.7	3.9	0.0	48.8	7.9
Dade, GA	9 728	63.3	67.0	1 047	35.8	10.9	-13.5	10.8	0.0	0.0	36.1	12.5
Dawson, GA	10 752	53.7	79.5	358	81.3	18.1	-6.3	18.3	83.3	0.0	0.0	4.5
Decatur, GA	17 633	63.9	69.7	1 019	94.5	12.1	-12.3	14.0	8.2	14.1	37.1	13.0
De Kalb, GA	429 981	35.3	85.1	47 609	57.6	36.3	11.9	55.7	22.8	24.5	46.6	14.8
Dodge, GA	12 501	70.3	66.3	555	83.1	11.6	-12.8	13.7	5.5	0.0	49.3	0.9
Dooly, GA	7 309	69.4	68.5	384	82.3	9.6	-14.8	13.6	5.1	0.0	51.3	1.2
Dougherty, GA	58 024	54.6	73.7	6 215	89.0	17.8	-6.6	23.1	13.4	16.4	15.4	15.4
Douglas, GA	58 687	53.5	81.1	4 171	66.0	19.2	-5.2	17.6	25.6	18.3	50.2	16.9
Early, GA	7 872	65.0	68.4	393	94.7	12.6	-11.8	16.4	7.1	...	100.0	10.1
Echols, GA	2 167	75.2	60.5	97	95.9	8.4	-16.0	10.3	0.0	...	50.0	2.0
Effingham, GA	23 129	61.6	78.9	1 184	88.5	13.6	-10.8	13.8	11.0	14.3	28.3	16.5
Elbert, GA	13 617	72.0	67.2	492	75.8	9.8	-14.6	12.3	3.1	100.0	42.9	13.7
Emanuel, GA	13 465	73.7	61.4	658	94.1	10.1	-14.3	11.8	5.3	30.4	58.8	4.0
Evans, GA	6 540	73.5	65.7	205	82.9	9.0	-15.4	11.7	2.7	0.0	57.4	0.0
Fannin, GA	14 291	68.0	70.9	474	88.2	10.4	-14.0	10.4	66.7	14.3	20.5	8.0
Fayette, GA	59 016	31.6	92.4	3 663	79.5	36.2	11.8	35.5	42.5	25.5	46.0	26.5
Floyd, GA	58 651	61.8	71.5	4 971	50.4	15.8	-8.6	17.8	4.5	17.2	28.6	5.7
Forsyth, GA	65 027	37.8	85.7	2 978	77.2	34.6	10.2	35.0	25.3	27.9	64.0	18.1
Franklin, GA	13 448	70.4	67.0	1 013	36.0	10.3	-14.1	11.2	0.8	0.0	37.5	0.0
Fulton, GA	527 738	35.4	84.0	55 078	59.3	41.4	17.0	60.6	18.3	28.1	60.3	20.1
Gilmer, GA	15 718	67.3	66.0	471	76.9	12.9	-11.5	13.2	0.0	0.0	16.9	7.6
Glascock, GA	1 764	74.2	66.1	71	74.6	6.5	-17.9	7.2	0.0	0.0	...	0.0
Glynn, GA	44 806	47.0	82.2	2 300	88.0	23.8	-0.6	28.5	8.2	25.6	21.0	20.6
Gordon, GA	28 490	68.2	65.9	1 266	86.7	10.6	-13.8	11.1	3.5	12.3	30.1	4.5
Grady, GA	14 988	70.3	69.4	764	91.6	10.6	-13.8	13.3	3.7	16.9	84.6	6.0
Greene, GA	9 508	63.2	70.1	330	74.2	17.6	-6.8	26.8	3.0	0.0	27.7	6.0
Gwinnett, GA	372 628	34.7	87.3	27 694	75.5	34.1	9.7	36.2	31.4	17.1	42.2	14.7
Habersham, GA	23 501	62.9	70.9	1 506	51.7	15.8	-8.6	16.8	11.7	23.7	9.0	3.7
Hall, GA	86 821	59.1	70.5	4 668	76.6	18.7	-5.7	22.3	11.1	3.8	14.8	3.3
Hancock, GA	6 618	72.2	62.2	330	88.5	9.8	-14.6	12.1	8.6	38.1	...	0.0
Haralson, GA	16 814	73.1	63.0	635	92.9	9.0	-15.4	9.3	3.9	0.0	0.0	25.0
Harris, GA	16 231	50.5	79.0	879	92.2	21.1	-3.3	24.5	6.1	0.0	37.8	50.0
Hart, GA	15 838	65.8	71.1	613	71.3	13.5	-10.9	15.6	2.8	31.8	30.9	28.1
Heard, GA	7 020	75.7	66.0	252	91.7	7.3	-17.1	7.8	3.2	0.0	12.8	2.9
Henry, GA	75 501	50.1	84.2	4 652	78.5	19.5	-4.9	18.0	24.5	22.2	42.9	26.3
Houston, GA	69 038	48.1	84.3	5 898	86.2	19.8	-4.6	21.2	13.9	9.6	31.1	17.6
Irwin, GA	6 196	70.8	67.7	268	98.1	9.9	-14.5	10.8	5.8	0.0	71.4	15.6
Jackson, GA	26 849	67.5	68.1	1 032	85.3	11.7	-12.7	12.4	5.3	14.6	18.3	4.8
Jasper, GA	7 531	67.4	69.7	236	90.3	11.5	-12.9	13.4	6.0	0.0	16.3	17.7
Jeff Davis, GA	8 036	72.1	63.3	289	73.0	9.4	-15.0	9.7	4.9	0.0	69.4	1.6
Jefferson, GA	10 799	75.4	58.5	366	81.7	9.1	-15.3	13.8	4.9	0.0	0.0	10.7
Jenkins, GA	5 335	70.8	62.0	267	87.6	10.8	-13.6	15.2	2.5	0.0	100.0	0.0
Johnson, GA	5 206	77.0	62.4	287	93.4	7.8	-16.6	9.3	3.5	...	100.0	12.7
Jones, GA	15 383	63.2	77.9	824	80.0	15.0	-9.4	15.1	14.1	0.0	35.1	37.6
Lamar, GA	10 227	65.7	71.3	1 151	91.6	11.3	-13.1	12.6	8.2	5.6	36.4	0.0
Lanier, GA	4 487	67.2	67.0	208	96.2	8.8	-15.6	10.4	4.2	14.0	0.0	0.0
Laurens, GA	28 875	66.8	70.3	1 517	91.0	14.4	-10.0	17.6	6.7	28.0	53.3	9.4
Lee, GA	15 036	54.6	81.3	1 136	88.5	17.0	-7.4	18.1	9.2	38.1	56.4	9.8
Liberty, GA	30 797	47.5	86.8	2 604	81.5	14.5	-9.9	18.2	10.4	10.2	19.5	12.1
Lincoln, GA	5 701	65.3	71.0	191	84.8	10.1	-14.3	13.2	3.6	0.0	0.0	8.0

[1]Hispanic or Latino persons may be of any race.
... = Not available.

Table C-1. Population, School, and Student Characteristics by County—*Continued*

County	State/County code	County type[1]	Population, 2000		Number of schools and students, 2000–2001			Resident enrollment, 2000			
			Total	Percent 5–17 years	School districts	Schools	Students	Total	Percent public	K–12	Percent public
			1	2	3	4	5	6	7	8	9
Long, GA	13183	9	10 304	22.1	1	2	1 979	2 788	93.2	2 211	95.3
Lowndes, GA	13185	5	92 115	19.0	2	19	16 206	30 067	91.0	18 445	92.5
Lumpkin, GA	13187	7	21 016	17.9	1	4	3 260	6 383	92.1	3 764	94.1
McDuffie, GA	13189	2	21 231	20.7	1	6	4 443	5 669	90.7	4 565	92.2
McIntosh, GA	13191	9	10 847	21.5	1	3	1 965	2 737	88.2	2 355	90.4
Macon, GA	13193	6	14 074	20.5	1	3	2 284	3 765	87.8	3 040	87.3
Madison, GA	13195	3	25 730	19.4	1	7	4 561	5 893	89.5	4 759	92.3
Marion, GA	13197	8	7 144	21.9	1	3	1 754	1 824	93.4	1 526	95.0
Meriwether, GA	13199	6	22 534	19.9	1	8	4 074	5 667	88.3	4 659	89.4
Miller, GA	13201	9	6 383	20.3	1	3	1 237	1 707	88.3	1 328	91.3
Mitchell, GA	13205	6	23 932	20.1	2	8	4 506	6 545	88.2	5 285	88.8
Monroe, GA	13207	6	21 757	19.9	1	4	3 759	5 835	84.2	4 410	84.9
Montgomery, GA	13209	9	8 270	18.2	1	3	1 323	2 506	76.9	1 594	96.3
Morgan, GA	13211	6	15 457	19.9	1	4	2 997	3 886	86.7	3 111	93.4
Murray, GA	13213	7	36 506	19.9	1	8	6 910	8 373	94.9	7 119	97.3
Muscogee, GA	13215	2	186 291	19.5	1	52	32 916	50 950	89.1	36 797	91.0
Newton, GA	13217	1	62 001	19.7	1	17	11 734	16 015	84.2	12 419	90.4
Oconee, GA	13219	3	26 225	23.3	1	7	5 427	7 782	83.3	6 034	88.5
Oglethorpe, GA	13221	8	12 635	18.9	1	4	2 149	3 078	87.4	2 396	91.8
Paulding, GA	13223	1	81 678	21.3	1	20	16 587	21 260	88.8	16 957	94.3
Peach, GA	13225	2	23 668	19.6	1	6	4 183	7 642	84.6	4 930	91.3
Pickens, GA	13227	1	22 983	17.2	1	5	3 760	4 808	92.4	3 842	95.8
Pierce, GA	13229	7	15 636	20.0	1	4	3 232	3 931	96.2	3 108	97.7
Pike, GA	13231	8	13 688	20.6	1	4	2 658	3 534	85.7	2 842	88.8
Polk, GA	13233	6	38 127	18.9	1	11	6 842	9 338	92.5	7 361	95.2
Pulaski, GA	13235	6	9 588	16.7	1	3	1 627	2 205	89.5	1 688	89.4
Putnam, GA	13237	6	18 812	17.1	1	3	2 521	4 207	81.1	3 332	82.1
Quitman, GA	13239	9	2 598	17.9	1	1	267	609	92.3	535	91.4
Rabun, GA	13241	9	15 050	16.1	1	5	2 134	2 961	85.6	2 450	89.6
Randolph, GA	13243	7	7 791	20.2	1	3	1 631	2 230	79.6	1 647	87.5
Richmond, GA	13245	2	199 775	19.7	1	56	35 424	56 607	88.4	41 134	91.8
Rockdale, GA	13247	1	70 111	21.1	1	16	13 519	19 019	88.6	14 818	93.0
Schley, GA	13249	9	3 766	20.8	1	2	961	1 062	88.4	851	90.8
Screven, GA	13251	6	15 374	21.3	1	3	3 160	4 374	94.3	3 439	96.0
Seminole, GA	13253	6	9 369	18.9	1	2	1 883	2 359	90.6	1 800	93.9
Spalding, GA	13255	1	58 417	19.8	1	16	10 340	14 632	87.9	11 806	90.9
Stephens, GA	13257	7	25 435	17.3	1	6	4 359	6 355	76.6	4 381	93.8
Stewart, GA	13259	8	5 252	18.5	1	3	803	1 265	87.2	991	85.4
Sumter, GA	13261	6	33 200	19.9	1	8	5 708	9 860	87.0	6 896	85.5
Talbot, GA	13263	8	6 498	18.2	1	1	846	1 505	85.0	1 236	85.9
Taliaferro, GA	13265	9	2 077	17.8	1	1	186	463	86.6	379	92.9
Tattnall, GA	13267	7	22 305	16.8	1	7	3 325	4 802	84.1	3 912	86.4
Taylor, GA	13269	8	8 815	19.8	1	3	1 782	2 199	95.5	1 805	96.2
Telfair, GA	13271	7	11 794	16.5	1	4	1 845	2 480	95.0	2 006	97.0
Terrell, GA	13273	6	10 970	20.6	1	3	1 835	2 960	87.0	2 402	85.6
Thomas, GA	13275	6	42 737	20.4	2	12	8 714	11 646	87.0	9 084	91.6
Tift, GA	13277	7	38 407	19.5	1	11	7 446	10 744	90.5	7 675	92.4
Toombs, GA	13279	7	26 067	20.8	2	8	5 187	6 704	93.0	5 445	94.9
Towns, GA	13281	9	9 319	11.9	1	1	1 066	1 865	74.0	1 156	95.8
Treutlen, GA	13283	7	6 854	18.6	1	2	1 211	1 671	92.1	1 385	95.7
Troup, GA	13285	4	58 779	20.6	1	19	11 623	15 898	86.2	12 477	92.0
Turner, GA	13287	7	9 504	21.7	1	4	2 000	2 621	96.5	2 117	97.5
Twiggs, GA	13289	2	10 590	20.3	1	5	1 727	2 644	81.7	2 237	81.6
Union, GA	13291	9	17 289	15.2	1	5	2 699	3 414	90.2	2 681	94.9
Upson, GA	13293	7	27 597	19.0	1	5	4 976	6 844	90.6	5 366	92.5
Walker, GA	13295	2	61 053	18.2	2	17	10 162	13 598	89.7	11 006	92.2
Walton, GA	13297	1	60 687	20.3	2	13	11 147	15 459	86.1	12 393	90.1
Ware, GA	13299	7	35 483	18.4	1	10	6 429	8 641	94.4	6 982	96.0
Warren, GA	13301	8	6 336	19.5	1	2	966	1 645	91.6	1 329	94.1
Washington, GA	13303	7	21 176	20.6	1	6	3 918	5 802	89.5	4 679	90.9
Wayne, GA	13305	7	26 565	19.3	1	9	5 190	6 292	93.4	5 194	95.0
Webster, GA	13307	8	2 390	18.2	1	1	379	549	85.8	469	86.8
Wheeler, GA	13309	9	6 179	16.4	1	2	1 120	1 358	94.6	1 071	97.6
White, GA	13311	9	19 944	16.9	1	5	3 490	4 506	83.9	3 284	95.4
Whitfield, GA	13313	4	83 525	19.2	2	25	17 003	19 439	92.5	16 101	95.1
Wilcox, GA	13315	9	8 577	16.5	1	3	1 383	1 855	91.8	1 519	91.6
Wilkes, GA	13317	6	10 687	18.1	1	4	1 924	2 461	93.3	1 976	95.4
Wilkinson, GA	13319	8	10 220	20.0	1	4	1 732	2 710	84.5	2 089	86.3
Worth, GA	13321	6	21 967	21.6	1	5	4 410	6 158	91.6	5 000	93.8
HAWAII	15000										
Hawaii, HI	15001	5	148 677	20.0	*	*	*	40 194	87.7	30 747	91.3
Honolulu, HI	15003	2	876 156	17.3	*1	*261	*184 360	234 038	76.7	155 556	81.8
Kalawao, HI	15005	5	147	2.0	*	*	*	0	...	0	...
Kauai, HI	15007	5	58 463	20.2	*	*	*	14 881	89.8	12 272	92.4
Maui, HI	15009	5	128 094	18.8	*	*	*	31 729	85.0	24 610	89.6

[1]County type code is from the Economic Research Service of the USDA. See Notes and Definitions at the end of this section.
* = Hawaii, Kalawao, Kauai, and Maui Counties are included with Honolulu County.
. . . = Not available.

Table C-1. School and Student Characteristics by County—*Continued*

County	Characteristics of students, 2000–2001			Staff and students, 2000–2001				Revenues, fiscal 1999			
	Percent with IEP[2]	Percent eligible for free lunch	Percent minority	Number of teachers	Student/ teacher ratio	Local school non-teaching staff	Central admin. staff	Total revenue ($1,000s)	Percentage of revenue from		
									Federal govt.	State govt.	Local govt.
	10	11	12	13	14	15	16	17	18	19	20
Long, GA	8.4	69.1	37.7	104	19.0	133	11	$11 831	11.4	67.6	21.0
Lowndes, GA	12.8	49.2	48.0	1 015	16.0	970	58	111 060	8.6	57.3	34.1
Lumpkin, GA	12.0	34.1	6.5	190	17.2	192	12	22 027	5.2	51.5	43.3
McDuffie, GA	12.2	56.9	50.5	275	16.2	297	16	31 502	8.0	64.7	27.3
McIntosh, GA	9.4	64.5	52.1	126	15.6	133	8	11 783	10.2	62.2	27.7
Macon, GA	8.6	81.0	87.2	141	16.2	229	9	17 134	12.4	55.6	32.0
Madison, GA	16.2	38.0	11.9	291	15.7	329	8	25 840	7.8	65.3	26.9
Marion, GA	8.8	64.3	47.3	105	16.7	142	8	11 316	10.0	63.8	26.1
Meriwether, GA	23.1	80.7	62.2	272	15.0	318	18	34 062	9.4	65.3	25.3
Miller, GA	14.6	56.3	40.7	88	14.1	94	6	8 691	11.6	65.1	23.4
Mitchell, GA	13.6	77.7	68.5	291	15.5	332	21	29 310	12.7	62.3	25.0
Monroe, GA	13.6	40.5	36.6	219	17.2	256	15	23 626	6.3	48.0	45.7
Montgomery, GA	10.5	63.0	41.2	88	15.0	86	9	7 672	11.7	70.8	17.5
Morgan, GA	14.9	39.9	36.4	192	15.6	187	13	20 686	7.0	51.4	41.7
Murray, GA	10.4	43.2	6.6	382	18.1	420	17	40 516	7.0	63.2	29.8
Muscogee, GA	11.0	56.3	64.6	1 932	17.0	2 329	132	255 322	8.2	52.2	39.6
Newton, GA	13.3	40.6	33.7	707	16.6	739	21	65 486	6.9	56.7	36.4
Oconee, GA	11.4	16.4	12.3	333	16.3	374	14	32 954	3.5	55.2	41.3
Oglethorpe, GA	16.3	40.7	26.1	138	15.6	145	8	13 524	8.5	62.9	28.6
Paulding, GA	12.4	20.0	10.6	1 007	16.5	853	32	85 062	3.8	57.8	38.4
Peach, GA	10.2	60.4	59.3	260	16.1	259	15	29 559	10.5	60.0	29.4
Pickens, GA	12.9	34.3	3.2	235	16.0	344	16	26 099	6.6	52.7	40.7
Pierce, GA	14.5	55.9	16.5	213	15.2	208	15	19 204	10.0	65.9	24.1
Pike, GA	9.1	29.7	19.0	141	18.9	181	9	13 762	6.6	65.4	28.0
Polk, GA	12.8	41.5	25.5	418	16.4	402	15	42 906	7.3	64.5	28.1
Pulaski, GA	14.6	58.7	43.9	109	14.9	110	13	11 931	9.9	62.9	27.2
Putnam, GA	14.6	60.8	55.3	164	15.4	206	8	17 296	12.4	46.3	41.3
Quitman, GA	15.7	94.0	83.5	21	12.7	32	2	2 922	15.1	53.2	31.8
Rabun, GA	12.4	41.4	6.5	133	16.0	139	9	17 824	5.4	39.9	54.7
Randolph, GA	9.8	93.3	87.5	104	15.7	155	9	13 383	21.2	55.9	22.9
Richmond, GA	8.7	63.8	72.1	2 117	16.7	2 200	85	255 236	8.4	49.9	41.7
Rockdale, GA	11.1	27.3	31.6	844	16.0	939	41	95 943	4.2	46.1	49.7
Schley, GA	9.9	56.7	28.8	51	18.8	55	6	4 081	9.9	60.5	29.6
Screven, GA	15.5	75.3	56.8	185	17.1	196	9	20 739	10.3	65.5	24.2
Seminole, GA	11.2	71.6	54.1	123	15.3	121	5	12 381	13.8	61.7	24.4
Spalding, GA	13.0	53.1	47.4	634	16.3	658	67	83 256	7.5	57.7	34.9
Stephens, GA	12.5	38.5	17.9	294	14.8	295	16	29 679	6.2	57.9	35.9
Stewart, GA	11.2	89.0	95.5	63	12.7	74	6	6 794	13.4	61.1	25.5
Sumter, GA	9.4	74.3	75.6	336	17.0	399	24	47 780	11.8	57.9	30.3
Talbot, GA	14.9	90.0	97.4	48	17.6	66	10	8 154	14.4	48.0	37.7
Taliaferro, GA	9.7	94.6	89.2	15	12.4	24	3	1 839	13.5	46.6	39.9
Tattnall, GA	10.0	61.9	44.9	216	15.4	225	11	22 404	14.3	63.4	22.3
Taylor, GA	8.2	70.4	54.9	99	18.0	126	9	11 073	11.6	67.0	21.3
Telfair, GA	11.3	72.5	50.9	122	15.1	133	9	12 717	11.5	68.3	20.2
Terrell, GA	14.1	76.6	96.3	113	16.2	143	7	12 962	15.5	63.9	20.6
Thomas, GA	15.2	57.4	51.5	485	18.0	577	39	54 342	10.6	68.7	20.6
Tift, GA	11.9	52.8	47.3	445	16.7	459	24	50 337	8.0	62.7	29.2
Toombs, GA	11.1	60.8	44.0	336	15.4	297	19	33 683	11.7	64.2	24.1
Towns, GA	12.9	45.3	0.0	61	17.5	81	3	6 643	11.5	45.8	42.7
Treutlen, GA	12.6	68.3	43.1	72	16.8	83	8	7 604	13.5	74.4	12.1
Troup, GA	12.7	49.4	43.0	787	14.8	714	44	79 632	7.1	54.9	38.0
Turner, GA	11.2	65.6	57.0	135	14.8	118	14	13 715	13.7	65.5	20.8
Twiggs, GA	9.0	77.6	61.2	103	16.8	127	10	14 039	11.5	54.9	33.6
Union, GA	14.4	41.5	0.8	160	16.9	184	13	17 940	7.1	58.2	34.8
Upson, GA	13.1	52.0	37.3	311	16.0	342	12	28 943	9.6	65.4	25.0
Walker, GA	12.2	44.0	5.9	595	17.1	653	26	68 733	6.8	64.9	28.3
Walton, GA	12.5	32.8	23.3	656	17.0	580	33	68 709	5.6	58.4	36.0
Ware, GA	14.3	57.2	40.1	424	15.2	444	23	49 586	9.0	61.2	29.8
Warren, GA	12.1	85.3	95.4	59	16.4	74	7	7 292	16.8	57.9	25.2
Washington, GA	8.9	68.0	69.7	222	17.6	239	12	27 973	9.4	57.1	33.6
Wayne, GA	11.6	50.1	29.3	305	17.0	390	17	32 481	7.8	58.7	33.5
Webster, GA	9.5	76.0	55.7	24	15.8	36	5	2 918	10.1	66.0	23.9
Wheeler, GA	13.4	74.2	40.4	78	14.4	86	4	7 008	13.6	71.7	14.7
White, GA	13.4	34.0	4.2	204	17.1	219	13	29 761	8.9	47.1	44.0
Whitfield, GA	10.2	43.2	33.1	1 088	15.6	1 066	43	126 893	5.5	47.4	47.1
Wilcox, GA	9.8	64.9	45.8	87	15.9	82	10	8 653	12.6	69.6	17.9
Wilkes, GA	11.6	63.4	56.5	115	16.7	152	8	12 828	10.7	61.4	27.9
Wilkinson, GA	13.7	71.7	61.0	121	14.3	135	8	15 130	9.4	49.8	40.8
Worth, GA	8.0	58.1	42.3	284	15.5	336	21	27 238	11.2	68.0	20.8
HAWAII											
Hawaii, HI	*	*	*	*	*	*	*	*	*	*	*
Honolulu, HI	*11.9	*43.8	*79.6	*10 839	*17.0	*6 593	*832	*1 328 572	*9.8	*87.8	*2.3
Kalawao, HI	*	*	*	*	*	*	*	*	*	*	*
Kauai, HI	*	*	*	*	*	*	*	*	*	*	*
Maui, HI	*	*	*	*	*	*	*	*	*	*	*

[2]IEP = Individual Education Program. See Notes and Definitions at the end of this section.
* = Hawaii, Kalawao, Kauai, and Maui Counties are included with Honolulu County.

Table C-1. Population, School, and Student Characteristics by County—*Continued*

County	Current expenditures, fiscal 1999			Resident population 16 to 19 years, 2000				Outcomes, 1999–2000	
	Amount ($1,000s)	Amount per student	Percent for instruction	Total population 16 to 19 years	Percent in Armed Forces	Percent high school graduates	Percent not enrolled, not grads, not Armed Forces, not empl.	Number of graduates	Dropouts grades 9–12 (percent)
	21	22	23	24	25	26	27	28	29
Long, GA	$8 661	$4 705	64.1	617	2.4	8.6	11.3	63	13.2
Lowndes, GA	94 063	5 843	62.9	6 030	2.5	9.9	6.0	714	9.4
Lumpkin, GA	17 786	5 549	64.6	1 663	1.1	10.8	4.8	111	4.4
McDuffie, GA	27 072	6 048	59.7	1 224	0.0	10.5	9.6	235	8.3
McIntosh, GA	10 763	5 615	59.0	641	0.0	11.4	8.9	71	10.7
Macon, GA	13 808	5 692	59.6	929	0.0	9.3	11.9	89	14.8
Madison, GA	23 662	5 248	65.9	1 342	0.0	15.9	7.0	209	10.0
Marion, GA	9 463	5 107	59.2	386	0.0	17.4	4.4	114	9.8
Meriwether, GA	26 427	6 347	60.7	1 359	0.0	17.3	9.8	144	8.6
Miller, GA	7 930	6 181	64.5	413	0.0	16.0	4.8	72	5.7
Mitchell, GA	26 499	5 705	61.8	1 467	0.0	11.4	11.7	232	9.1
Monroe, GA	21 342	5 696	63.5	1 241	0.0	15.0	5.6	142	8.0
Montgomery, GA	7 016	5 189	64.4	526	0.0	5.3	6.1	56	5.4
Morgan, GA	18 316	6 283	62.5	820	0.0	11.5	11.1	162	4.2
Murray, GA	33 798	5 284	65.8	1 995	0.3	13.3	12.5	205	16.0
Muscogee, GA	209 130	6 271	62.7	12 458	14.4	23.2	6.9	1 547	6.4
Newton, GA	60 180	5 669	63.0	3 508	0.0	10.2	8.2	320	6.5
Oconee, GA	27 012	5 338	64.3	1 493	0.0	10.6	2.5	293	2.7
Oglethorpe, GA	12 224	5 951	61.3	671	0.0	13.6	8.5	69	8.5
Paulding, GA	71 986	5 024	65.3	3 607	0.0	13.4	6.2	552	7.9
Peach, GA	25 993	5 841	58.3	1 796	0.0	6.5	9.6	210	6.3
Pickens, GA	22 273	6 272	61.1	1 029	0.0	10.2	10.0	162	8.3
Pierce, GA	16 808	5 230	64.7	760	0.0	18.7	11.2	152	9.6
Pike, GA	11 596	4 618	63.5	717	0.0	6.4	9.2	109	8.9
Polk, GA	37 801	5 482	66.7	2 229	0.0	9.2	15.2	274	12.3
Pulaski, GA	10 620	6 421	62.6	587	0.0	9.5	10.6	73	8.6
Putnam, GA	14 830	5 855	64.7	952	0.0	9.7	10.5	120	9.9
Quitman, GA	2 181	7 989	56.7	144	0.0	6.9	11.1	0	. . .
Rabun, GA	12 583	6 141	61.9	715	0.0	15.0	4.8	111	6.4
Randolph, GA	11 972	6 651	57.0	653	0.0	2.3	11.3	66	10.9
Richmond, GA	204 691	5 635	60.6	13 139	12.5	20.5	5.7	1 609	6.8
Rockdale, GA	79 398	5 984	61.0	4 315	0.0	12.4	5.8	740	4.2
Schley, GA	3 360	5 316	56.1	203	0.0	2.5	5.4	0	. . .
Screven, GA	18 577	5 693	59.5	899	0.0	9.8	2.3	140	6.6
Seminole, GA	11 266	5 868	61.8	525	6.1	14.7	8.2	89	6.1
Spalding, GA	66 056	6 254	61.6	3 477	0.0	8.9	15.4	438	12.7
Stephens, GA	26 339	6 027	64.1	1 448	0.0	11.3	6.8	195	8.9
Stewart, GA	5 984	6 511	54.4	335	0.0	10.4	14.9	31	17.3
Sumter, GA	34 549	5 888	58.5	2 313	0.0	8.6	8.6	209	13.9
Talbot, GA	6 606	7 228	58.5	310	0.0	17.1	4.5	18	9.8
Taliaferro, GA	1 399	8 968	52.0	109	0.0	14.7	18.3	0	. . .
Tattnall, GA	19 593	5 776	59.8	1 224	0.4	13.0	15.5	127	12.2
Taylor, GA	9 877	5 406	62.2	538	0.0	5.2	20.3	62	9.5
Telfair, GA	12 364	6 302	66.0	654	0.0	7.0	12.5	58	6.9
Terrell, GA	12 155	6 476	61.8	719	0.0	2.4	13.4	90	10.9
Thomas, GA	53 053	5 979	61.8	2 440	0.0	11.7	6.9	373	4.7
Tift, GA	42 464	5 670	62.8	2 630	0.0	7.6	9.4	297	8.9
Toombs, GA	31 438	6 091	59.3	1 484	0.0	9.7	10.8	243	9.3
Towns, GA	5 852	5 536	64.1	557	0.0	5.9	2.3	47	. . .
Treutlen, GA	7 108	5 562	62.5	489	0.0	9.0	19.8	62	7.4
Troup, GA	68 920	6 163	60.8	3 493	0.0	8.7	8.4	486	6.1
Turner, GA	12 624	6 284	65.7	605	0.0	15.5	4.5	85	13.0
Twiggs, GA	12 291	6 055	57.0	624	0.0	14.6	14.6	89	9.4
Union, GA	14 574	5 424	63.0	737	0.0	20.1	4.1	150	10.4
Upson, GA	27 629	5 573	63.9	1 272	0.0	14.9	6.0	209	10.8
Walker, GA	56 674	5 714	62.7	3 095	0.3	10.7	11.7	424	10.7
Walton, GA	60 819	5 835	66.1	3 385	0.0	12.8	7.8	436	5.5
Ware, GA	42 790	6 597	62.5	1 782	0.0	14.3	7.2	276	9.1
Warren, GA	6 458	6 234	61.4	401	0.0	10.7	16.2	51	7.3
Washington, GA	24 256	6 069	55.6	1 209	0.0	8.4	9.1	183	7.9
Wayne, GA	28 735	5 456	62.5	1 463	0.0	8.5	6.4	237	9.8
Webster, GA	2 737	6 877	55.0	110	0.0	12.7	4.5	0	. . .
Wheeler, GA	6 439	6 007	61.4	334	0.0	2.7	16.8	39	7.9
White, GA	25 120	8 145	57.6	1 070	0.0	9.9	5.6	121	3.0
Whitfield, GA	104 929	6 594	62.8	4 452	0.0	11.2	15.7	626	9.7
Wilcox, GA	7 847	5 856	65.0	449	0.0	10.0	6.7	82	7.9
Wilkes, GA	12 549	6 281	60.6	628	0.0	10.2	7.5	119	2.9
Wilkinson, GA	12 741	6 795	60.9	603	0.0	7.3	6.3	77	7.4
Worth, GA	25 204	5 388	60.7	1 355	0.0	7.3	2.4	191	11.1
HAWAII									
Hawaii, HI	*	*	*	8 798	0.0	13.6	5.0	*	*
Honolulu, HI	*114 389	*6 802	*62.8	45 427	5.9	17.8	3.2	*10 437	. . .
Kalawao, HI	*	*	*	0	. . .	. . .	. . .	*	*
Kauai, HI	*	*	*	3 275	0.0	16.1	2.5	*	*
Maui, HI	*	*	*	6 843	0.0	17.5	5.1	*	*

. . . = Not available.
* = Hawaii, Kalawao, Kauai, and Maui Counties are included with Honolulu County.

Table C-1. Population, School, and Student Characteristics by County—*Continued*

County	High school graduates, 2000			College enrollment, 2000		College graduates, 2000 (percent)						
	Population 25 years and over	High school diploma or less (percent)	High school diploma or more (percent)	Number	Percent public	Bachelor's degree or more	+/- U.S. percent with bachelor's degree or more	Non-Hispanic White	Black or African American	American Indian and Alaska Native	Asian, Hawaiian, and Pacific Islander	Hispanic or Latino[1]
	30	31	32	33	34	35	36	37	38	39	40	41
Long, GA	5 527	67.3	74.3	286	83.9	5.8	-18.6	6.5	4.1	16.7	12.9	3.6
Lowndes, GA	54 237	52.9	77.7	9 466	94.5	19.7	-4.7	24.2	10.3	12.4	16.9	17.3
Lumpkin, GA	12 665	58.4	72.0	2 321	93.4	17.6	-6.8	18.4	13.8	10.2	0.0	7.5
McDuffie, GA	13 442	68.5	66.7	614	87.8	11.7	-12.7	15.2	4.3	36.1	35.7	2.1
McIntosh, GA	6 978	66.7	71.2	231	82.7	11.1	-13.3	13.9	5.8	0.0	25.0	0.0
Macon, GA	8 844	72.0	63.2	542	90.6	10.0	-14.4	14.0	6.8	10.3	33.3	9.2
Madison, GA	16 881	70.0	70.8	669	83.0	10.9	-13.5	11.3	6.3	8.3	18.7	8.2
Marion, GA	4 437	70.7	65.4	166	89.8	8.9	-15.5	11.6	3.9	47.1	0.0	0.0
Meriwether, GA	14 434	69.9	65.8	473	79.9	10.8	-13.6	14.4	5.2	0.0	35.0	15.8
Miller, GA	4 281	66.9	69.0	195	88.2	11.3	-13.1	14.4	1.3	...	54.5	0.0
Mitchell, GA	14 972	70.1	65.3	825	89.2	9.1	-15.3	12.6	4.5	0.0	41.9	13.9
Monroe, GA	14 185	61.0	77.7	1 012	82.5	17.1	-7.3	20.9	6.4	39.4	71.2	0.0
Montgomery, GA	5 108	68.0	71.4	729	36.4	13.5	-10.9	16.2	5.4	...	48.8	0.0
Morgan, GA	10 125	63.1	74.0	397	67.5	18.7	-5.7	22.8	6.9	39.1	66.7	33.3
Murray, GA	22 803	74.3	61.1	779	85.0	7.2	-17.2	7.4	4.8	34.0	0.0	1.0
Muscogee, GA	114 045	49.3	78.9	10 058	90.7	20.3	-4.1	26.4	12.0	21.4	33.7	15.8
Newton, GA	39 144	60.0	74.7	2 259	61.8	14.5	-9.9	16.0	8.5	5.2	45.3	11.5
Oconee, GA	16 470	36.7	86.7	1 045	78.1	39.8	15.4	42.0	12.0	9.8	63.1	17.7
Oglethorpe, GA	8 436	65.4	72.1	441	83.7	15.6	-8.8	19.0	1.4	9.1	0.0	19.1
Paulding, GA	50 422	58.3	80.8	2 407	75.9	15.2	-9.2	14.3	24.4	13.9	27.9	26.2
Peach, GA	14 055	59.8	73.4	2 274	71.7	16.8	-7.6	18.0	15.7	32.0	38.5	3.9
Pickens, GA	15 868	62.9	70.2	504	82.5	15.6	-8.8	15.8	4.8	0.0	62.5	6.8
Pierce, GA	10 131	71.4	69.8	593	95.8	10.1	-14.3	10.5	4.0	0.0	...	22.2
Pike, GA	8 833	64.8	75.3	501	82.4	14.0	-10.4	15.5	6.2	25.0	0.0	4.8
Polk, GA	24 703	71.8	63.3	1 270	84.0	8.0	-16.4	8.3	8.4	0.0	0.0	1.5
Pulaski, GA	6 445	62.8	73.4	311	88.4	12.9	-11.5	16.0	5.4	0.0	86.4	8.6
Putnam, GA	12 931	65.1	75.5	549	79.8	14.4	-10.0	18.8	2.5	0.0	0.0	6.6
Quitman, GA	1 773	76.3	57.8	34	97.1	6.1	-18.3	9.0	2.1	0.0	...	0.0
Rabun, GA	10 675	59.6	75.4	270	63.7	17.6	-6.8	18.3	7.4	2.9	0.0	4.2
Randolph, GA	4 783	70.1	62.4	428	51.2	9.5	-14.9	15.7	4.2	...	...	21.9
Richmond, GA	122 592	51.7	78.0	11 630	81.8	18.7	-5.7	24.2	12.5	8.9	27.8	16.6
Rockdale, GA	44 794	47.0	82.4	2 578	81.8	23.4	-1.0	24.0	21.9	0.0	41.8	12.1
Schley, GA	2 364	70.1	70.0	102	93.1	13.7	-10.7	16.2	8.1	0.0	...	11.1
Screven, GA	9 685	71.7	66.9	580	91.4	10.2	-14.2	15.4	2.2	30.0	22.9	20.7
Seminole, GA	6 114	68.9	67.9	387	83.5	8.6	-15.8	9.9	6.1	0.0	50.0	0.0
Spalding, GA	37 110	67.0	67.8	1 678	85.3	12.5	-11.9	14.9	5.3	12.0	44.0	7.5
Stephens, GA	16 771	64.7	71.1	1 500	30.3	14.1	-10.3	15.0	6.3	29.6	12.9	0.0
Stewart, GA	3 495	73.9	63.2	152	91.4	9.3	-15.1	15.4	4.2	0.0	65.5	0.0
Sumter, GA	20 040	60.3	69.9	2 219	92.0	19.3	-5.1	28.1	8.4	39.5	55.6	5.6
Talbot, GA	4 403	75.5	64.8	178	80.3	7.9	-16.5	15.6	2.4	0.0	...	0.0
Taliaferro, GA	1 434	76.4	56.2	46	41.3	8.4	-16.0	13.0	5.1	...	...	0.0
Tattnall, GA	14 688	72.9	66.3	568	70.8	7.9	-16.5	11.0	2.7	0.0	20.0	0.0
Taylor, GA	5 594	75.4	63.6	256	92.2	8.5	-15.9	10.5	5.0	0.0	100.0	0.0
Telfair, GA	7 906	76.5	63.6	247	81.8	8.3	-16.1	11.0	4.0	...	...	0.0
Terrell, GA	6 741	68.3	64.5	336	97.6	10.7	-13.7	16.3	5.7	0.0	0.0	25.7
Thomas, GA	27 697	60.0	73.5	1 646	65.4	16.8	-7.6	22.0	7.1	11.7	33.3	8.4
Tift, GA	23 433	62.4	67.9	2 390	96.2	15.6	-8.8	19.8	5.6	13.1	37.6	5.2
Toombs, GA	16 212	67.6	67.3	731	88.1	12.7	-11.7	15.8	4.8	0.0	17.0	2.8
Towns, GA	6 935	58.3	75.1	582	34.2	17.4	-7.0	17.5	...	0.0	16.7	14.3
Treutlen, GA	4 292	77.8	61.8	216	72.2	8.5	-15.9	9.7	5.3	0.0	8.2	0.0
Troup, GA	36 815	60.7	73.0	2 079	62.2	18.0	-6.4	22.5	6.5	5.7	37.8	15.5
Turner, GA	5 707	71.0	67.7	299	95.0	10.5	-13.9	14.5	3.5	0.0	9.1	1.5
Twiggs, GA	6 702	77.6	63.2	243	82.3	5.4	-19.0	6.9	2.5	0.0	34.0	19.6
Union, GA	12 730	60.9	74.2	552	73.7	12.5	-11.9	12.7	0.0	26.2	0.0	0.0
Upson, GA	18 325	70.5	66.7	952	90.7	11.5	-12.9	14.7	2.1	7.0	15.0	0.0
Walker, GA	40 837	68.2	66.8	1 683	82.8	10.2	-14.2	10.3	4.1	0.0	46.1	12.0
Walton, GA	38 527	62.1	73.5	1 606	80.5	13.0	-11.4	14.1	5.2	8.5	36.0	11.2
Ware, GA	23 380	68.4	70.3	1 061	86.8	11.4	-13.0	13.0	6.6	31.0	13.6	4.6
Warren, GA	4 061	77.6	57.1	165	86.1	8.0	-16.4	13.7	2.9	0.0	71.4	20.0
Washington, GA	13 626	70.5	68.3	615	89.8	10.5	-13.9	16.7	4.3	0.0	0.0	0.0
Wayne, GA	17 531	66.9	70.1	711	86.5	11.6	-12.8	13.1	7.2	0.0	1.3	3.4
Webster, GA	1 588	72.7	61.3	47	97.9	9.1	-15.3	15.0	2.7	...	0.0	0.0
Wheeler, GA	4 144	74.0	67.9	146	69.9	7.1	-17.3	9.2	3.2	0.0	0.0	2.6
White, GA	13 473	59.2	76.0	970	48.4	15.4	-9.0	15.5	2.0	11.8	29.8	15.5
Whitfield, GA	52 570	66.0	63.0	2 007	89.4	12.8	-11.6	15.1	6.5	5.8	29.8	2.2
Wilcox, GA	5 761	75.5	68.2	200	93.0	7.0	-17.4	8.4	4.1	33.3	25.0	4.2
Wilkes, GA	7 265	70.9	65.0	289	92.4	12.0	-12.4	17.4	5.1	16.0	0.0	0.0
Wilkinson, GA	6 509	71.0	70.4	391	79.8	9.6	-14.8	12.5	4.9	0.0	0.0	4.7
Worth, GA	13 979	69.8	68.3	692	93.6	8.6	-15.8	8.7	8.6	0.0	0.0	0.0
HAWAII												
Hawaii, HI	97 708	46.8	84.6	7 220	84.9	22.1	-2.3	32.4	14.3	17.4	19.4	9.4
Honolulu, HI	579 998	43.0	84.8	65 507	71.8	27.9	3.5	40.4	20.9	22.8	26.3	15.1
Kalawao, HI	147	80.3	39.5	0	...	10.2	...	0.0	...	0.0	...	...
Kauai, HI	38 872	46.4	83.3	1 736	88.5	19.4	-5.0	30.9	23.0	19.3	14.9	7.7
Maui, HI	85 752	46.1	83.4	5 285	80.7	22.4	-2.0	33.1	31.8	24.0	17.8	11.2

[1]Hispanic or Latino persons may be of any race.
. . . = Not available.

186 THE ALMANAC OF AMERICAN EDUCATION (BERNAN PRESS)

Table C-1. Population, School, and Student Characteristics by County—*Continued*

County	State/County code	County type[1]	Population, 2000		Number of schools and students, 2000–2001			Resident enrollment, 2000			
			Total	Percent 5–17 years	School districts	Schools	Students	Total	Percent public	K–12	Percent public
			1	2	3	4	5	6	7	8	9
IDAHO	16000										
Ada, ID	16001	2	300 904	19.6	3	91	53 393	81 730	87.7	58 736	91.6
Adams, ID	16003	9	3 476	19.9	2	4	522	774	90.6	688	91.4
Bannock, ID	16005	5	75 565	20.0	2	35	13 908	25 491	92.5	15 052	94.0
Bear Lake, ID	16007	7	6 411	26.0	1	6	1 567	1 933	97.1	1 724	99.7
Benewah, ID	16009	8	9 171	20.4	2	7	1 687	2 139	89.4	1 868	89.9
Bingham, ID	16011	7	41 735	26.2	5	32	10 347	13 297	95.5	11 100	98.7
Blaine, ID	16013	7	18 991	18.2	1	8	3 012	4 341	82.8	3 440	86.5
Boise, ID	16015	8	6 670	20.3	3	8	1 061	1 611	89.3	1 327	89.4
Bonner, ID	16017	6	36 835	19.8	2	17	5 567	8 413	81.5	7 188	84.0
Bonneville, ID	16019	5	82 522	23.9	3	37	18 532	24 784	92.8	19 682	97.5
Boundary, ID	16021	9	9 871	22.2	1	7	1 601	2 237	81.7	1 996	83.7
Butte, ID	16023	9	2 899	22.5	1	5	584	758	95.9	651	96.5
Camas, ID	16025	9	991	20.4	1	2	179	250	94.8	210	98.1
Canyon, ID	16027	2	131 441	21.8	8	47	25 456	35 560	85.4	28 095	91.9
Caribou, ID	16029	7	7 304	24.2	3	10	1 796	2 190	96.5	1 795	98.4
Cassia, ID	16031	7	21 416	25.4	1	16	5 126	6 560	93.5	5 641	95.0
Clark, ID	16033	9	1 022	26.3	1	2	237	289	96.9	243	97.1
Clearwater, ID	16035	7	8 930	18.2	1	9	1 452	2 056	89.0	1 720	90.1
Custer, ID	16037	9	4 342	20.2	2	8	872	1 018	97.2	909	98.2
Elmore, ID	16039	6	29 130	19.6	3	15	5 143	7 773	91.3	5 757	96.2
Franklin, ID	16041	7	11 329	27.4	2	7	2 958	3 506	95.9	3 142	98.6
Fremont, ID	16043	7	11 819	24.7	1	8	2 346	3 534	93.0	3 039	98.4
Gem, ID	16045	6	15 181	20.9	1	8	2 983	3 788	91.1	3 180	94.8
Gooding, ID	16047	7	14 155	21.9	5	11	2 960	3 470	93.7	2 944	95.0
Idaho, ID	16049	7	15 511	19.7	2	11	2 158	3 608	86.8	3 080	87.9
Jefferson, ID	16051	7	19 155	27.4	3	15	5 357	6 224	93.4	5 235	98.5
Jerome, ID	16053	7	18 342	23.3	2	8	3 775	5 187	89.9	4 311	92.7
Kootenai, ID	16055	4	108 685	20.3	4	37	18 272	28 610	86.9	21 760	88.8
Latah, ID	16057	7	34 935	14.9	5	20	4 460	14 797	91.5	5 153	85.6
Lemhi, ID	16059	7	7 806	20.4	2	8	1 325	1 763	89.6	1 580	93.7
Lewis, ID	16061	9	3 747	20.6	3	7	1 071	885	92.8	753	93.1
Lincoln, ID	16063	9	4 044	22.8	3	4	871	1 127	97.6	946	99.2
Madison, ID	16065	7	27 467	19.0	2	15	5 308	15 041	42.0	5 209	98.1
Minidoka, ID	16067	7	20 174	23.6	1	10	4 476	5 884	92.9	4 896	96.2
Nez Perce, ID	16069	5	37 410	17.7	3	16	5 812	9 620	90.5	6 565	91.5
Oneida, ID	16071	9	4 125	24.6	1	4	966	1 245	97.0	1 053	98.7
Owyhee, ID	16073	8	10 644	24.1	4	13	2 467	2 883	92.3	2 532	94.2
Payette, ID	16075	7	20 578	23.1	3	11	4 351	5 547	94.0	4 757	94.7
Power, ID	16077	7	7 538	25.4	3	6	1 866	2 319	95.2	1 898	97.0
Shoshone, ID	16079	7	13 771	17.3	4	14	2 326	2 907	95.7	2 463	97.8
Teton, ID	16081	9	5 999	23.3	1	6	1 327	1 655	85.2	1 375	90.5
Twin Falls, ID	16083	5	64 284	20.6	8	31	11 895	17 741	90.5	13 204	92.0
Valley, ID	16085	9	7 651	19.3	2	9	1 414	1 634	94.6	1 474	96.8
Washington, ID	16087	7	9 977	20.7	3	8	1 981	2 400	94.4	2 052	97.9
ILLINOIS	17000										
Adams, IL	17001	5	68 277	18.7	5	29	10 429	17 661	76.2	13 042	81.7
Alexander, IL	17003	7	9 590	19.6	2	7	1 662	2 413	94.0	1 937	94.5
Bond, IL	17005	6	17 633	16.3	2	8	2 451	4 596	74.4	2 917	95.7
Boone, IL	17007	2	41 786	22.2	3	14	7 997	11 539	82.7	9 317	85.6
Brown, IL	17009	9	6 950	13.7	1	3	826	1 306	90.7	1 086	91.0
Bureau, IL	17011	7	35 503	18.8	15	30	6 070	8 576	89.4	6 738	91.9
Calhoun, IL	17013	8	5 084	17.6	2	5	693	1 192	82.8	919	83.4
Carroll, IL	17015	7	16 674	18.7	5	15	3 126	4 020	95.3	3 177	97.2
Cass, IL	17017	6	13 695	18.5	3	10	2 265	3 273	89.2	2 571	92.4
Champaign, IL	17019	3	179 669	15.3	17	62	23 995	73 433	92.7	27 413	89.4
Christian, IL	17021	6	35 372	18.0	6	21	5 504	8 254	88.2	6 481	90.3
Clark, IL	17023	6	17 008	18.9	3	10	3 095	4 100	96.3	3 248	98.4
Clay, IL	17025	7	14 560	18.0	3	11	2 700	3 331	98.9	2 665	99.1
Clinton, IL	17027	1	35 535	18.8	13	25	5 877	9 052	84.0	6 852	84.7
Coles, IL	17029	5	53 196	14.4	5	29	7 610	19 136	95.0	7 503	95.5
Cook, IL	17031	0	5 376 741	18.8	154	1 257	809 391	1 491 276	76.2	1 025 425	84.2
Crawford, IL	17033	7	20 452	17.3	4	10	3 544	5 498	94.9	4 035	96.3
Cumberland, IL	17035	9	11 253	20.1	2	7	2 036	2 845	92.5	2 274	93.7
De Kalb, IL	17037	1	88 969	16.9	9	38	15 451	35 173	93.4	14 995	93.1
De Witt, IL	17039	6	16 798	18.4	2	10	3 263	4 046	92.8	3 168	94.7
Douglas, IL	17041	6	19 922	20.1	4	11	3 085	4 859	87.3	3 988	86.9
Du Page, IL	17043	0	904 161	19.5	49	247	156 429	254 238	77.4	175 369	86.8
Edgar, IL	17045	6	19 704	18.1	5	18	3 640	4 346	92.8	3 580	94.9
Edwards, IL	17047	9	6 971	17.4	1	3	1 038	1 626	94.7	1 220	97.4
Effingham, IL	17049	7	34 264	21.4	5	21	6 440	9 514	84.7	7 337	85.2
Fayette, IL	17051	6	21 802	17.7	5	16	3 321	4 939	92.8	3 925	94.2
Ford, IL	17053	6	14 241	19.4	2	7	2 485	3 420	92.5	2 677	93.9
Franklin, IL	17055	7	39 018	17.3	12	23	6 486	9 032	94.8	6 783	96.7
Fulton, IL	17057	6	38 250	16.4	8	26	5 850	8 460	94.8	6 491	97.4
Gallatin, IL	17059	8	6 445	17.0	1	3	1 020	1 474	96.3	1 113	97.3

[1]County type code is from the Economic Research Service of the USDA. See Notes and Definitions at the end of this section.

Table C-1. School and Student Characteristics by County—*Continued*

County	Characteristics of students, 2000–2001			Staff and students, 2000–2001				Revenues, fiscal 1999			
	Percent with IEP[2]	Percent eligible for free lunch	Percent minority	Number of teachers	Student/teacher ratio	Local school non-teaching staff	Central admin. staff	Total revenue ($1,000s)	Percentage of revenue from		
									Federal govt.	State govt.	Local govt.
	10	11	12	13	14	15	16	17	18	19	20
IDAHO											
Ada, ID	10.5	22.1	8.5	2 845	18.8	2 050	185	$305 414	3.9	53.6	42.5
Adams, ID	12.5	43.1	2.7	42	12.4	21	5	4 300	8.4	71.0	20.5
Bannock, ID	13.8	36.5	12.0	746	18.6	506	54	81 179	7.3	66.7	26.0
Bear Lake, ID	12.5	37.4	4.4	90	17.4	67	4	8 698	6.3	77.7	15.9
Benewah, ID	13.9	43.7	20.0	114	14.8	91	9	11 876	10.5	58.3	31.3
Bingham, ID	11.2	45.1	22.0	566	18.3	415	33	58 499	10.8	71.2	18.0
Blaine, ID	13.6	19.5	13.9	207	14.6	145	14	22 837	2.3	29.2	68.6
Boise, ID	13.2	40.5	3.4	79	13.4	57	7	7 520	6.4	65.5	28.1
Bonner, ID	12.0	41.4	3.5	321	17.3	234	28	29 281	7.6	54.6	37.8
Bonneville, ID	11.3	25.6	10.9	962	19.3	710	58	98 229	5.5	68.1	26.3
Boundary, ID	10.7	45.7	7.3	97	16.5	79	9	9 797	14.9	59.1	26.0
Butte, ID	13.2	49.1	9.6	38	15.4	32	3	4 475	5.8	69.5	24.7
Camas, ID	15.1	34.6	2.2	16	11.2	11	1	1 518	4.9	67.0	28.1
Canyon, ID	12.6	45.9	29.7	1 342	19.0	877	90	124 349	7.6	67.0	25.4
Caribou, ID	11.8	29.0	3.8	112	16.0	87	10	13 022	5.5	64.1	30.4
Cassia, ID	12.2	45.5	22.8	283	18.1	228	12	29 985	7.9	63.6	28.5
Clark, ID	11.8	46.0	46.0	18	13.2	11	3	1 571	14.4	63.1	22.5
Clearwater, ID	16.7	45.7	5.5	95	15.3	79	6	9 978	8.9	63.2	28.0
Custer, ID	15.1	32.3	6.5	62	14.1	47	5	6 185	6.5	63.8	29.6
Elmore, ID	14.7	36.4	21.8	291	17.7	191	19	28 386	15.7	64.9	19.4
Franklin, ID	9.8	48.7	6.3	147	20.1	87	6	14 285	5.9	78.4	15.7
Fremont, ID	14.3	42.8	15.8	139	16.9	112	8	14 963	8.7	64.7	26.5
Gem, ID	10.6	41.2	11.6	159	18.8	120	6	14 950	6.9	73.4	19.8
Gooding, ID	15.5	47.4	22.7	196	15.1	122	13	17 579	8.1	69.9	21.9
Idaho, ID	14.2	44.0	4.7	138	15.6	94	8	16 106	10.8	63.3	25.8
Jefferson, ID	11.4	42.4	12.3	290	18.5	210	17	29 647	7.4	74.7	17.8
Jerome, ID	11.5	49.6	23.6	211	17.9	131	14	19 441	8.0	71.8	20.2
Kootenai, ID	10.7	36.0	4.2	948	19.3	686	56	95 669	5.6	56.1	38.3
Latah, ID	13.3	26.1	5.2	307	14.5	220	34	32 906	5.1	53.0	41.9
Lemhi, ID	14.4	39.7	5.1	87	15.2	66	8	8 028	8.1	68.4	23.4
Lewis, ID	16.3	45.5	13.5	76	14.1	54	10	8 292	8.9	65.5	25.7
Lincoln, ID	16.2	53.2	19.4	66	13.2	43	7	6 273	8.6	69.6	21.8
Madison, ID	11.3	41.1	6.5	288	18.4	213	17	28 340	9.1	74.1	16.8
Minidoka, ID	11.8	54.7	36.0	259	17.3	187	14	25 590	9.2	71.4	19.4
Nez Perce, ID	12.9	30.3	13.6	363	16.0	275	33	39 908	8.0	48.0	44.0
Oneida, ID	11.4	. . .	5.3	59	16.4	37	3	5 562	5.2	74.0	20.7
Owyhee, ID	11.0	55.2	32.7	160	15.4	130	16	16 548	11.1	67.0	21.9
Payette, ID	11.4	40.1	19.1	241	18.1	176	12	23 078	8.6	72.2	19.1
Power, ID	13.3	51.4	33.2	114	16.4	84	9	13 199	9.2	52.3	38.5
Shoshone, ID	13.9	41.3	3.1	156	14.9	128	18	19 038	10.6	55.7	33.7
Teton, ID	11.9	32.7	19.7	71	18.7	51	3	6 892	5.5	58.8	35.7
Twin Falls, ID	11.4	39.4	15.4	680	17.5	432	42	68 607	6.9	65.3	27.9
Valley, ID	10.9	26.4	3.5	94	15.0	59	6	10 926	9.1	40.9	50.1
Washington, ID	9.6	43.5	20.9	125	15.8	96	9	12 324	8.0	70.2	21.9
ILLINOIS											
Adams, IL	14.7	. . .	8.3	641	16.3	78	31	70 951	9.6	46.3	44.1
Alexander, IL	21.4	. . .	61.9	126	13.2	18	5	13 965	13.1	66.7	20.2
Bond, IL	16.4	. . .	6.6	147	16.7	19	3	15 009	4.4	59.8	35.9
Boone, IL	12.5	. . .	18.1	404	19.8	48	12	48 877	3.9	31.6	64.6
Brown, IL	15.5	. . .	0.7	62	13.3	5	1	4 962	3.7	55.1	41.2
Bureau, IL	16.2	. . .	9.2	466	13.0	56	18	52 318	4.8	48.7	46.5
Calhoun, IL	21.1	. . .	0.4	59	11.7	8	2	4 928	5.1	60.7	34.2
Carroll, IL	14.1	. . .	4.9	231	13.5	21	5	23 633	3.4	42.3	54.3
Cass, IL	17.6	. . .	13.8	169	13.4	18	5	15 638	7.8	58.6	33.6
Champaign, IL	17.3	. . .	29.0	1 687	14.2	257	77	173 303	6.7	36.3	56.9
Christian, IL	15.8	. . .	1.8	348	15.8	72	17	50 560	7.0	47.0	46.0
Clark, IL	18.0	. . .	1.5	199	15.6	27	4	18 421	4.3	65.3	30.4
Clay, IL	19.6	. . .	2.1	197	13.7	30	6	18 202	8.4	64.2	27.3
Clinton, IL	14.8	. . .	3.4	378	15.5	32	23	34 015	4.1	55.4	40.5
Coles, IL	21.6	. . .	5.1	507	15.0	113	36	62 020	10.1	40.5	49.4
Cook, IL	12.7	. . .	68.5	47 345	17.1	7 360	2 506	7 107 678	8.6	28.7	62.7
Crawford, IL	16.8	. . .	3.0	241	14.7	53	10	22 522	5.6	45.2	49.3
Cumberland, IL	20.4	. . .	0.1	135	15.1	13	2	12 187	5.6	65.1	29.3
De Kalb, IL	11.2	. . .	12.1	959	16.1	141	54	128 922	6.4	26.6	67.0
De Witt, IL	15.9	. . .	3.5	228	14.3	30	3	25 776	3.5	17.3	79.2
Douglas, IL	18.8	. . .	5.9	229	13.5	26	5	20 329	4.9	41.4	53.7
Du Page, IL	12.1	. . .	23.5	9 527	16.4	1 556	395	1 277 309	2.6	15.4	82.0
Edgar, IL	19.2	. . .	1.0	278	13.1	33	13	25 530	6.5	47.9	45.7
Edwards, IL	14.0	. . .	1.7	68	15.3	6	3	7 020	3.6	60.1	36.3
Effingham, IL	16.9	. . .	1.7	401	16.1	49	13	40 771	3.8	52.1	44.2
Fayette, IL	15.0	. . .	1.2	210	15.8	24	8	23 871	4.7	53.3	42.0
Ford, IL	15.4	. . .	2.1	149	16.7	18	6	21 904	6.5	37.0	56.5
Franklin, IL	20.6	. . .	0.4	431	15.0	40	28	50 533	10.9	66.9	22.2
Fulton, IL	18.0	. . .	1.9	456	12.8	46	10	51 238	5.7	51.5	42.8
Gallatin, IL	17.1	. . .	0.5	75	13.6	10	1	7 127	6.0	58.7	35.2

[2]IEP = Individual Education Program. See Notes and Definitions at the end of this section.
. . . = Not available.

Table C-1. Population, School, and Student Characteristics by County—*Continued*

County	Current expenditures, fiscal 1999			Resident population 16 to 19 years, 2000				Outcomes, 1999–2000	
	Amount ($1,000s)	Amount per student	Percent for instruction	Total population 16 to 19 years	Percent in Armed Forces	Percent high school graduates	Percent not enrolled, not grads, not Armed Forces, not empl.	Number of graduates	Dropouts grades 9–12 (percent)
	21	22	23	24	25	26	27	28	29
IDAHO									
Ada, ID	$264 065	$5 133	63.1	17 019	0.1	17.3	2.5	3 285	...
Adams, ID	3 860	6 196	64.7	207	0.0	13.0	3.9	35	...
Bannock, ID	71 650	4 940	62.4	5 556	0.2	15.8	3.2	990	...
Bear Lake, ID	7 778	4 674	56.1	510	0.0	15.3	1.0	133	...
Benewah, ID	10 353	5 676	55.9	524	0.0	10.7	7.1	132	...
Bingham, ID	51 957	4 847	61.4	3 155	0.4	12.3	4.3	785	...
Blaine, ID	20 233	7 134	66.5	889	0.0	8.3	4.0	173	...
Boise, ID	6 225	5 475	52.5	332	0.0	11.7	4.8	65	...
Bonner, ID	28 290	4 864	59.5	2 159	0.4	14.8	6.3	377	...
Bonneville, ID	86 250	4 631	62.8	5 848	0.0	13.8	3.3	1 363	...
Boundary, ID	8 825	5 313	63.1	595	0.0	19.0	8.6	106	...
Butte, ID	3 517	5 700	58.7	183	0.0	14.2	0.0	61	...
Camas, ID	1 377	6 885	65.1	59	0.0	5.1	8.5	19	...
Canyon, ID	108 880	4 652	62.4	8 576	0.0	13.7	8.4	1 309	...
Caribou, ID	11 195	5 703	65.1	542	0.0	6.8	2.6	172	...
Cassia, ID	24 462	4 667	60.2	1 547	0.0	13.8	5.6	342	...
Clark, ID	1 471	6 596	53.8	86	0.0	14.0	5.8	13	...
Clearwater, ID	9 530	5 997	59.9	453	0.0	15.7	2.4	111	...
Custer, ID	5 586	6 052	59.2	202	0.0	13.4	5.0	56	...
Elmore, ID	24 805	4 782	61.5	1 564	9.2	30.0	4.2	270	...
Franklin, ID	12 169	4 096	64.9	834	0.0	14.0	1.8	217	...
Fremont, ID	13 858	5 480	65.3	1 036	0.2	11.6	5.2	198	...
Gem, ID	13 849	4 630	67.9	950	0.0	19.6	6.4	168	...
Gooding, ID	15 447	5 135	63.7	1 005	0.0	12.3	7.1	223	...
Idaho, ID	13 570	5 673	61.6	1 023	0.0	10.7	7.1	201	...
Jefferson, ID	25 490	4 622	62.3	1 528	0.1	15.6	5.4	425	...
Jerome, ID	17 018	4 528	61.5	1 189	0.0	10.9	7.1	218	...
Kootenai, ID	79 641	4 543	63.7	6 362	0.1	16.1	3.6	1 047	...
Latah, ID	29 296	6 402	62.4	3 480	0.5	7.4	0.2	343	...
Lemhi, ID	7 305	4 942	61.2	473	0.0	16.9	3.2	107	...
Lewis, ID	7 344	6 505	56.2	208	0.0	8.7	1.9	86	...
Lincoln, ID	5 453	6 232	61.0	244	0.0	9.8	5.7	56	...
Madison, ID	25 702	4 653	61.9	6 308	0.0	4.0	0.4	490	...
Minidoka, ID	21 442	4 408	64.0	1 525	0.0	15.7	7.3	301	...
Nez Perce, ID	36 556	6 181	63.0	2 165	0.0	15.5	3.0	389	...
Oneida, ID	4 943	4 889	68.1	287	0.0	17.1	3.8	79	...
Owyhee, ID	13 981	5 442	62.7	698	0.0	12.3	9.3	155	...
Payette, ID	19 961	4 606	63.7	1 340	0.0	12.1	4.1	254	...
Power, ID	12 219	6 555	55.9	508	0.0	13.4	1.8	113	...
Shoshone, ID	16 552	6 674	59.2	678	0.0	12.8	4.9	153	...
Teton, ID	6 091	4 759	57.9	366	0.0	15.6	4.4	79	...
Twin Falls, ID	56 869	4 605	59.5	4 434	0.0	13.5	4.4	808	...
Valley, ID	9 727	6 555	59.0	447	1.1	13.0	1.1	110	...
Washington, ID	11 004	5 505	62.8	640	0.0	14.2	6.9	153	...
ILLINOIS									
Adams, IL	64 933	6 152	55.0	4 153	0.0	10.8	2.9	620	3.6
Alexander, IL	12 553	7 198	57.6	490	0.0	9.6	2.9	77	4.0
Bond, IL	11 889	4 981	59.0	1 053	0.0	7.6	5.0	143	4.2
Boone, IL	35 703	4 912	61.5	2 341	0.0	11.0	4.6	384	1.6
Brown, IL	4 306	5 403	56.8	329	0.6	8.8	16.7	64	2.1
Bureau, IL	39 049	6 159	60.0	2 049	0.0	9.3	4.3	424	4.4
Calhoun, IL	4 581	5 980	58.4	269	0.0	6.7	4.8	57	1.1
Carroll, IL	18 248	5 644	60.7	915	0.0	12.9	3.0	227	3.0
Cass, IL	12 979	5 570	63.6	772	0.0	9.1	8.2	150	3.3
Champaign, IL	147 343	6 177	63.0	17 484	0.1	5.6	1.4	1 554	4.6
Christian, IL	42 938	6 477	63.9	1 722	0.5	13.1	7.5	357	5.4
Clark, IL	15 097	4 764	60.7	928	0.0	5.6	4.0	206	4.2
Clay, IL	14 993	5 366	62.8	773	0.0	10.6	4.3	178	5.3
Clinton, IL	29 241	5 141	64.0	2 018	0.0	12.0	4.5	307	3.8
Coles, IL	50 367	6 970	58.2	4 817	0.0	7.2	2.0	450	5.9
Cook, IL	6 088 963	7 685	60.5	287 976	0.1	10.3	7.4	38 273	9.5
Crawford, IL	19 692	5 394	55.2	1 127	0.0	11.1	1.8	240	2.7
Cumberland, IL	9 828	4 727	60.4	682	0.0	11.6	3.2	125	1.7
De Kalb, IL	97 916	6 573	57.5	8 241	0.0	6.8	1.4	965	2.6
De Witt, IL	22 099	6 521	62.5	915	0.0	7.4	3.5	194	5.6
Douglas, IL	16 384	5 165	60.8	1 293	0.0	10.2	4.1	224	3.5
Du Page, IL	1 072 026	7 141	61.8	47 205	0.0	7.7	2.8	10 038	2.6
Edgar, IL	22 072	5 853	61.7	1 068	0.0	13.7	7.2	244	3.4
Edwards, IL	5 041	4 765	60.0	398	0.0	11.6	0.8	76	1.6
Effingham, IL	31 731	4 852	61.1	1 943	0.0	13.6	2.2	447	1.2
Fayette, IL	19 445	5 763	59.8	1 268	0.0	16.4	8.3	218	4.4
Ford, IL	19 798	7 983	57.3	666	0.3	7.8	5.7	162	2.9
Franklin, IL	43 572	6 632	61.5	1 948	0.2	10.0	6.1	421	4.4
Fulton, IL	44 200	5 957	60.2	1 980	0.1	11.6	7.1	436	5.4
Gallatin, IL	6 457	6 399	63.8	393	0.0	10.7	3.6	63	4.7

... = Not available.

Table C-1. Population, School, and Student Characteristics by County—*Continued*

County	High school graduates, 2000			College enrollment, 2000		College graduates, 2000 (percent)						
	Population 25 years and over	High school diploma or less (percent)	High school diploma or more (percent)	Number	Percent public	Bachelor's degree or more	+/- U.S. percent with bachelor's degree or more	Non-Hispanic White	Black or African American	American Indian and Alaska Native	Asian, Hawaiian, and Pacific Islander	Hispanic or Latino[1]
	30	31	32	33	34	35	36	37	38	39	40	41
IDAHO												
Ada, ID	188 662	32.3	90.8	17 989	88.2	31.2	6.8	31.7	27.3	16.0	41.0	16.2
Adams, ID	2 468	56.6	80.8	57	86.0	14.9	-9.5	14.6	0.0	18.9	...	6.7
Bannock, ID	43 285	38.4	87.5	9 013	97.0	24.9	0.5	25.5	23.1	8.8	41.8	14.3
Bear Lake, ID	3 837	56.7	85.5	101	91.1	11.7	-12.7	11.9	0.0	0.0	100.0	2.6
Benewah, ID	6 051	61.3	79.8	156	94.2	11.4	-13.0	11.9	0.0	6.1	0.0	3.5
Bingham, ID	23 155	50.5	80.6	1 423	85.2	14.4	-10.0	16.7	0.0	4.2	20.3	1.8
Blaine, ID	13 021	25.7	90.2	648	77.2	43.1	18.7	46.3	11.1	25.0	29.7	8.1
Boise, ID	4 547	46.2	86.3	165	89.7	19.9	-4.5	20.2	...	6.8	22.2	12.5
Bonner, ID	25 043	47.9	85.6	761	82.5	16.9	-7.5	17.1	0.0	13.1	29.8	9.1
Bonneville, ID	48 502	38.7	87.8	3 547	86.3	26.1	1.7	27.1	40.7	6.6	35.1	10.4
Boundary, ID	6 314	55.9	80.0	151	82.1	14.7	-9.7	15.0	...	15.8	20.0	4.8
Butte, ID	1 873	50.4	82.6	74	89.2	13.0	-11.4	13.8	0.0	0.0	...	4.0
Camas, ID	675	43.0	88.4	34	91.2	22.2	-2.2	22.7	0.0	0.0	...	0.0
Canyon, ID	76 619	54.3	76.0	5 511	62.9	14.9	-9.5	16.6	21.0	5.5	20.4	4.4
Caribou, ID	4 391	47.6	86.6	214	93.5	15.9	-8.5	16.2	0.0	18.2	0.0	7.8
Cassia, ID	12 206	52.9	76.9	596	95.8	13.9	-10.5	15.9	0.0	16.0	15.1	1.1
Clark, ID	580	60.5	64.0	6	100.0	12.6	-11.8	16.0	100.0	66.7	...	1.2
Clearwater, ID	6 352	57.2	80.1	244	88.9	13.4	-11.0	13.5	...	4.6	50.0	11.0
Custer, ID	3 012	53.0	84.5	69	89.9	17.4	-7.0	17.6	...	28.6	...	12.4
Elmore, ID	17 034	37.8	87.2	1 494	84.5	17.3	-7.1	18.6	13.2	2.4	26.7	8.5
Franklin, ID	6 069	51.8	88.2	187	90.9	13.6	-10.8	14.0	...	12.5	33.3	0.0
Fremont, ID	6 790	54.2	80.4	327	66.4	12.0	-12.4	13.1	...	0.0	0.0	0.8
Gem, ID	9 663	55.6	79.4	417	80.8	11.4	-13.0	11.6	...	5.7	32.2	3.5
Gooding, ID	8 761	62.1	72.6	363	93.1	12.0	-12.4	13.7	...	0.0	6.7	0.6
Idaho, ID	10 638	55.4	82.9	284	91.2	14.4	-10.0	14.7	...	6.7	27.3	13.4
Jefferson, ID	10 335	45.0	84.4	602	79.2	15.2	-9.2	16.3	0.0	6.8	50.0	1.2
Jerome, ID	10 946	51.7	75.1	570	92.1	14.0	-10.4	15.7	0.0	14.3	29.1	3.5
Kootenai, ID	69 872	43.0	87.3	5 072	89.5	19.1	-5.3	19.3	10.8	8.1	33.2	13.3
Latah, ID	19 493	31.6	91.0	9 171	96.9	41.0	16.6	40.1	48.3	37.1	78.8	32.0
Lemhi, ID	5 373	48.8	82.5	66	75.8	17.9	-6.5	17.9	...	0.0	100.0	11.6
Lewis, ID	2 596	50.5	84.2	92	87.0	14.8	-9.6	14.7	22.2	7.4	20.0	7.4
Lincoln, ID	2 458	55.5	77.4	120	90.0	13.0	-11.4	14.2	0.0	7.1	14.3	1.3
Madison, ID	9 320	33.8	88.5	9 416	11.2	24.4	0.0	25.3	...	12.5	33.7	4.1
Minidoka, ID	11 940	59.1	73.7	670	85.7	10.1	-14.3	12.2	0.0	0.0	20.0	1.8
Nez Perce, ID	24 759	46.3	85.5	2 459	94.8	18.9	-5.5	19.2	20.0	11.7	37.4	5.8
Oneida, ID	2 493	45.3	86.4	113	86.7	15.0	-9.4	15.1	...	0.0	100.0	0.0
Owyhee, ID	6 372	67.0	67.6	207	76.8	10.2	-14.2	12.1	28.6	4.5	22.8	1.6
Payette, ID	12 761	57.5	74.5	536	89.6	10.6	-13.8	11.6	0.0	14.8	20.5	0.2
Power, ID	4 344	58.1	74.7	275	93.1	14.3	-10.1	17.4	...	2.7	0.0	0.9
Shoshone, ID	9 670	62.4	77.9	285	91.6	10.2	-14.2	10.3	62.5	5.1	23.8	9.0
Teton, ID	3 614	35.3	87.3	170	66.5	28.1	3.7	30.4	0.0	0.0	100.0	2.8
Twin Falls, ID	39 544	49.1	81.3	3 482	94.6	16.0	-8.4	16.9	0.0	8.7	9.8	4.7
Valley, ID	5 525	40.2	88.9	91	86.8	26.3	1.9	26.8	...	0.0	23.8	16.1
Washington, ID	6 542	58.9	76.6	164	80.5	12.7	-11.7	13.7	0.0	28.6	44.4	0.0
ILLINOIS												
Adams, IL	45 101	53.8	83.7	3 338	57.8	17.6	-6.8	17.8	6.3	0.0	45.5	24.4
Alexander, IL	6 395	67.7	67.0	275	89.5	6.9	-17.5	8.6	3.6	0.0	8.3	0.0
Bond, IL	11 731	61.4	72.8	1 371	30.4	15.0	-9.4	16.4	2.1	4.2	23.1	9.6
Boone, IL	26 061	57.5	80.8	1 392	80.0	14.5	-9.9	15.4	15.4	1.6	42.0	4.6
Brown, IL	4 844	65.6	63.3	142	87.3	9.2	-15.2	11.7	0.0	0.0	10.0	5.5
Bureau, IL	24 085	54.9	84.1	1 147	86.1	15.7	-8.7	15.8	24.0	9.1	52.2	6.1
Calhoun, IL	3 528	64.7	79.9	179	86.6	9.4	-15.0	9.3	...	27.8	0.0	14.3
Carroll, IL	11 516	60.7	83.3	503	89.1	13.1	-11.3	13.1	7.1	0.0	57.1	1.7
Cass, IL	9 056	64.3	80.0	410	81.0	12.6	-11.8	13.1	0.0	13.3	77.3	2.1
Champaign, IL	100 559	33.3	91.0	42 713	97.6	38.0	13.6	37.7	16.6	11.1	79.4	41.4
Christian, IL	24 202	62.6	81.0	1 063	87.5	10.5	-13.9	10.7	2.0	9.8	23.0	7.0
Clark, IL	11 569	59.3	80.0	554	93.1	13.6	-10.8	13.6	0.0	0.0	0.0	35.0
Clay, IL	9 898	62.3	75.9	452	96.9	9.7	-14.7	9.7	...	0.0	23.9	0.0
Clinton, IL	23 463	57.6	77.4	1 666	82.2	13.0	-11.4	13.6	1.2	0.0	11.9	10.6
Coles, IL	30 326	49.7	82.9	10 787	97.9	20.8	-3.6	20.3	21.5	7.7	66.4	31.4
Cook, IL	3 454 738	46.5	77.7	359 786	58.3	28.0	3.6	36.7	15.0	15.3	54.5	8.8
Crawford, IL	13 995	57.6	79.3	1 063	98.1	10.3	-14.1	10.7	1.7	0.0	32.0	8.0
Cumberland, IL	7 352	62.8	80.2	436	92.4	10.1	-14.3	10.1	0.0	15.4	66.7	3.7
De Kalb, IL	48 912	42.4	87.5	18 467	96.3	26.8	2.4	26.8	30.4	23.3	58.6	14.6
De Witt, IL	11 354	60.1	83.5	542	90.0	13.4	-11.0	13.3	0.0	0.0	89.3	0.0
Douglas, IL	12 923	60.3	79.3	581	96.6	13.8	-10.6	13.9	0.0	0.0	48.8	3.8
Du Page, IL	589 120	30.6	90.0	57 695	59.4	41.7	17.3	41.8	33.5	14.3	66.4	14.8
Edgar, IL	13 395	60.5	81.4	477	81.3	13.3	-11.1	13.5	0.0	2.4	100.0	8.2
Edwards, IL	4 815	56.6	82.3	297	88.9	9.8	-14.6	9.5	0.0	36.4	45.5	...
Effingham, IL	21 635	54.7	83.4	1 366	91.5	15.1	-9.3	15.1	45.5	14.3	33.8	12.7
Fayette, IL	14 611	68.7	72.2	646	85.0	9.0	-15.4	9.7	0.0	0.0	0.0	0.0
Ford, IL	9 557	56.0	86.0	456	97.4	13.9	-10.5	13.8	15.8	100.0	55.6	4.7
Franklin, IL	26 965	57.7	76.7	1 697	93.0	11.3	-13.1	11.2	0.0	33.8	50.0	2.8
Fulton, IL	26 529	59.7	78.3	1 358	88.1	11.4	-13.0	11.8	2.0	0.0	13.9	1.7
Gallatin, IL	4 481	63.3	73.6	294	95.2	7.7	-16.7	7.7	37.5	0.0	40.0	4.3

[1]Hispanic or Latino persons may be of any race.
. . . = Not available.

Table C-1. Population, School, and Student Characteristics by County—*Continued*

County	State/County code	County type[1]	Population, 2000 Total	Population, 2000 Percent 5–17 years	Number of schools and students, 2000–2001 School districts	Number of schools and students, 2000–2001 Schools	Number of schools and students, 2000–2001 Students	Resident enrollment, 2000 Total	Resident enrollment, 2000 Percent public	Resident enrollment, 2000 K–12	Resident enrollment, 2000 Percent public
			1	2	3	4	5	6	7	8	9
Greene, IL	17061	6	14 761	19.2	3	8	2 484	3 569	90.2	2 830	93.3
Grundy, IL	17063	1	37 535	20.0	13	29	8 516	10 016	89.8	7 686	94.9
Hamilton, IL	17065	7	8 621	18.0	1	8	1 388	1 983	92.4	1 530	92.3
Hancock, IL	17067	7	20 121	19.0	8	23	4 033	4 985	93.3	3 940	94.7
Hardin, IL	17069	9	4 800	15.0	1	3	671	953	95.9	708	95.8
Henderson, IL	17071	9	8 213	17.4	2	5	1 184	1 882	92.3	1 461	94.8
Henry, IL	17073	2	51 020	19.3	9	28	9 449	12 859	91.2	9 918	94.3
Iroquois, IL	17075	6	31 334	19.3	11	32	5 496	7 606	91.0	6 120	93.6
Jackson, IL	17077	5	59 612	14.2	10	27	8 030	26 116	95.2	8 336	92.1
Jasper, IL	17079	7	10 117	20.2	1	10	1 690	2 708	91.7	2 078	92.2
Jefferson, IL	17081	7	40 045	18.4	19	27	6 767	9 817	93.1	7 349	94.5
Jersey, IL	17083	1	21 668	19.5	1	8	3 129	5 988	79.6	4 232	86.8
Jo Daviess, IL	17085	6	22 289	17.6	7	20	3 559	5 104	86.0	3 967	88.3
Johnson, IL	17087	9	12 878	13.7	6	8	1 769	2 829	95.3	2 159	96.2
Kane, IL	17089	0	404 119	21.5	12	146	102 187	114 833	82.1	85 895	88.0
Kankakee, IL	17091	3	103 833	20.1	14	47	18 768	28 166	81.7	20 874	87.8
Kendall, IL	17093	1	54 544	21.5	7	21	11 088	15 369	83.7	11 607	90.1
Knox, IL	17095	4	55 836	16.3	7	32	8 158	13 125	82.0	9 142	92.8
Lake, IL	17097	0	644 356	21.2	49	201	126 978	185 035	81.0	135 526	89.4
La Salle, IL	17099	4	111 509	18.8	30	51	17 327	27 018	86.3	21 364	87.8
Lawrence, IL	17101	7	15 452	17.2	2	10	2 415	3 396	95.0	2 703	95.9
Lee, IL	17103	7	36 062	18.7	6	18	5 404	9 047	85.7	6 980	87.7
Livingston, IL	17105	6	39 678	19.0	13	26	7 661	9 388	90.3	7 786	92.1
Logan, IL	17107	6	31 183	16.5	9	18	3 890	7 826	74.7	5 382	89.0
McDonough, IL	17109	5	32 913	13.3	6	20	4 048	13 645	95.9	4 459	95.6
McHenry, IL	17111	0	260 077	22.1	20	74	44 609	76 811	85.8	57 221	91.0
McLean, IL	17113	3	150 433	17.0	12	59	24 342	52 781	87.1	25 605	89.0
Macon, IL	17115	3	114 706	18.2	9	53	18 571	29 235	80.1	20 713	88.7
Macoupin, IL	17117	6	49 019	18.9	10	36	9 758	12 504	89.7	9 305	95.0
Madison, IL	17119	0	258 941	18.6	16	92	42 818	70 430	84.6	48 026	86.6
Marion, IL	17121	7	41 691	19.1	15	34	7 998	10 286	91.0	8 022	92.3
Marshall, IL	17123	6	13 180	18.0	2	7	1 606	3 090	93.1	2 381	95.3
Mason, IL	17125	6	16 038	18.7	3	9	3 528	3 734	95.6	2 923	99.2
Massac, IL	17127	7	15 161	16.8	2	13	2 587	3 373	97.4	2 595	98.4
Menard, IL	17129	3	12 486	20.8	3	11	2 810	3 307	91.7	2 558	94.3
Mercer, IL	17131	3	16 957	19.1	3	12	3 485	4 186	93.7	3 312	98.0
Monroe, IL	17133	1	27 619	19.9	4	12	4 615	7 520	79.5	5 685	82.2
Montgomery, IL	17135	6	30 652	18.0	4	19	5 372	7 203	93.0	5 680	93.7
Morgan, IL	17137	4	36 616	17.3	7	26	5 563	9 652	75.6	6 607	88.3
Moultrie, IL	17139	6	14 287	19.2	3	7	1 911	3 304	88.3	2 739	89.2
Ogle, IL	17141	2	51 032	21.1	11	33	10 536	13 620	93.3	10 898	95.8
Peoria, IL	17143	2	183 433	18.3	18	85	29 149	49 942	74.4	33 553	83.9
Perry, IL	17145	7	23 094	16.7	5	8	3 038	5 382	90.4	4 020	91.5
Piatt, IL	17147	6	16 365	19.0	5	15	3 406	4 303	93.6	3 156	98.1
Pike, IL	17149	7	17 384	18.3	5	15	3 148	4 152	92.4	3 443	95.8
Pope, IL	17151	9	4 413	16.7	1	2	641	959	94.4	731	97.5
Pulaski, IL	17153	9	7 348	21.0	3	7	1 510	2 064	96.9	1 572	96.3
Putnam, IL	17155	9	6 086	19.2	1	4	1 016	1 497	90.0	1 164	92.4
Randolph, IL	17157	6	33 893	16.7	7	17	4 690	7 438	83.6	5 795	84.4
Richland, IL	17159	7	16 149	18.4	3	9	2 767	4 095	91.3	2 941	91.6
Rock Island, IL	17161	2	149 374	17.4	10	58	22 951	37 839	82.5	26 365	88.9
St. Clair, IL	17163	0	256 082	20.8	29	99	46 108	73 803	84.9	54 017	87.8
Saline, IL	17165	7	26 733	18.2	5	15	4 447	6 262	97.4	4 663	97.5
Sangamon, IL	17167	3	188 951	18.5	16	115	41 836	48 266	82.1	34 965	82.8
Schuyler, IL	17169	7	7 189	17.3	1	4	1 161	1 580	94.6	1 282	98.4
Scott, IL	17171	9	5 537	18.8	2	5	1 019	1 315	88.3	1 031	92.6
Shelby, IL	17173	6	22 893	19.2	7	22	4 248	5 454	92.6	4 273	94.2
Stark, IL	17175	8	6 332	18.8	2	6	1 215	1 457	89.2	1 200	91.3
Stephenson, IL	17177	4	48 979	19.1	5	22	7 928	12 693	85.9	9 402	88.3
Tazewell, IL	17179	2	128 485	18.2	20	53	19 948	31 754	87.6	23 416	91.2
Union, IL	17181	7	18 293	17.9	7	16	3 404	4 290	94.8	3 292	95.2
Vermilion, IL	17183	4	83 919	18.3	14	45	14 272	19 917	90.8	15 297	92.0
Wabash, IL	17185	7	12 937	18.5	2	5	2 148	3 334	91.6	2 379	91.6
Warren, IL	17187	7	18 735	17.5	6	17	3 027	5 142	77.1	3 344	94.6
Washington, IL	17189	6	15 148	19.7	7	10	2 266	3 895	86.6	2 962	86.7
Wayne, IL	17191	7	17 151	17.7	8	15	2 872	3 981	96.9	3 053	98.0
White, IL	17193	6	15 371	16.4	3	12	2 725	3 321	96.0	2 567	97.7
Whiteside, IL	17195	4	60 653	18.6	11	32	10 406	14 998	88.7	11 644	91.4
Will, IL	17197	0	502 266	21.6	31	129	81 776	147 354	82.1	107 495	89.1
Williamson, IL	17199	5	61 296	17.0	6	24	9 473	14 961	90.8	10 550	91.6
Winnebago, IL	17201	2	278 418	19.3	12	93	44 643	72 350	78.6	54 037	81.9
Woodford, IL	17203	2	35 469	20.1	9	24	7 577	9 879	85.8	7 307	91.0
INDIANA	18000										
Adams, IN	18001	2	33 625	23.1	3	11	5 091	9 020	80.5	7 246	81.3
Allen, IN	18003	2	331 849	20.0	4	90	51 765	91 489	75.3	65 971	79.1
Bartholomew, IN	18005	4	71 435	19.2	2	18	11 617	17 865	84.4	13 359	88.7
Benton, IN	18007	8	9 421	21.2	1	6	2 122	2 424	85.6	1 963	89.5
Blackford, IN	18009	6	14 048	18.2	1	5	2 310	3 178	90.2	2 579	93.4
Boone, IN	18011	1	46 107	21.0	3	15	8 624	11 649	87.8	9 369	93.0
Brown, IN	18013	8	14 957	18.0	1	6	2 408	3 303	90.9	2 724	94.5
Carroll, IN	18015	6	20 165	19.5	2	6	2 916	4 612	89.4	3 813	92.3
Cass, IN	18017	6	40 930	18.9	3	12	6 949	9 488	90.3	7 749	93.5
Clark, IN	18019	2	96 472	17.5	3	32	14 278	21 962	85.5	16 552	88.2

[1]County type code is from the Economic Research Service of the USDA. See Notes and Definitions at the end of this section.

Table C-1. School and Student Characteristics by County—*Continued*

County	Characteristics of students, 2000–2001			Staff and students, 2000–2001				Revenues, fiscal 1999			
	Percent with IEP2	Percent eligible for free lunch	Percent minority	Number of teachers	Student/teacher ratio	Local school non-teaching staff	Central admin. staff	Total revenue ($1,000s)	Percentage of revenue from		
									Federal govt.	State govt.	Local govt.
	10	11	12	13	14	15	16	17	18	19	20
Greene, IL	17.8	...	0.6	178	14.0	20	4	$14 141	6.2	58.7	35.1
Grundy, IL	15.2	...	6.1	494	17.2	81	43	69 468	2.4	15.0	82.6
Hamilton, IL	18.4	...	1.3	87	16.0	10	5	9 635	6.8	68.3	25.0
Hancock, IL	16.0	...	1.1	315	12.8	50	16	25 337	5.2	55.8	39.0
Hardin, IL	18.9	...	4.0	49	13.7	5	1	5 228	9.1	74.4	16.5
Henderson, IL	13.8	...	2.7	100	11.8	10	2	8 820	6.1	52.4	41.5
Henry, IL	16.8	...	6.6	616	15.3	82	23	64 852	4.8	51.9	43.3
Iroquois, IL	17.3	...	8.7	397	13.8	62	15	33 706	3.9	51.3	44.9
Jackson, IL	18.6	...	25.8	549	14.6	88	34	67 025	9.4	50.2	40.5
Jasper, IL	18.0	...	1.4	122	13.9	17	4	16 290	15.4	36.4	48.2
Jefferson, IL	21.0	...	13.9	441	15.3	62	38	44 091	8.1	57.0	34.9
Jersey, IL	13.6	...	0.6	193	16.2	29	6	19 373	4.4	61.6	34.0
Jo Daviess, IL	20.1	...	2.2	274	13.0	29	11	30 462	2.3	28.6	69.1
Johnson, IL	19.9	...	1.0	118	15.0	11	6	11 290	4.7	61.3	34.0
Kane, IL	11.7	...	37.5	5 945	17.2	844	214	687 527	4.2	28.9	66.8
Kankakee, IL	16.8	...	34.1	1 115	16.8	148	71	136 855	8.6	45.1	46.3
Kendall, IL	12.3	...	14.9	609	18.2	110	25	77 314	2.2	26.1	71.7
Knox, IL	13.1	...	14.5	543	15.0	74	23	59 513	6.4	46.9	46.6
Lake, IL	14.7	...	30.3	7 753	16.4	1 328	426	1 052 803	3.5	20.2	76.2
La Salle, IL	16.8	...	9.7	1 180	14.7	170	62	150 501	5.5	30.9	63.6
Lawrence, IL	16.0	...	3.1	178	13.6	22	7	17 384	7.6	67.0	25.4
Lee, IL	15.0	...	7.0	371	14.6	50	18	39 999	4.5	42.0	53.5
Livingston, IL	15.4	...	5.2	542	14.1	64	22	59 127	4.7	40.2	55.1
Logan, IL	17.3	...	4.9	296	13.1	34	12	30 604	4.9	34.7	60.4
McDonough, IL	22.0	...	6.3	306	13.2	37	21	32 789	5.6	43.1	51.3
McHenry, IL	14.8	...	10.5	2 553	17.5	471	96	315 098	3.9	21.7	74.4
McLean, IL	14.2	...	15.7	1 645	14.8	239	57	156 916	4.8	28.9	66.2
Macon, IL	13.6	...	28.0	996	18.6	192	63	127 751	8.0	47.5	44.4
Macoupin, IL	17.9	...	1.9	602	16.2	84	15	61 767	5.4	61.2	33.4
Madison, IL	16.1	...	15.1	2 540	16.9	417	101	294 317	7.3	46.9	45.8
Marion, IL	17.9	...	7.8	545	14.7	75	28	58 819	11.6	57.5	30.9
Marshall, IL	17.1	...	2.2	126	12.7	28	8	12 348	3.9	41.1	55.0
Mason, IL	18.8	...	1.2	259	13.6	33	8	23 501	5.8	51.0	43.1
Massac, IL	18.7	...	9.2	153	16.9	19	2	15 262	5.9	52.4	41.8
Menard, IL	15.0	...	1.5	177	15.9	18	3	18 062	3.0	47.4	49.6
Mercer, IL	13.3	...	1.7	260	13.4	31	4	23 076	4.2	57.6	38.2
Monroe, IL	12.9	...	1.6	284	16.3	33	15	29 374	2.7	47.5	49.8
Montgomery, IL	15.9	...	1.8	317	16.9	38	8	36 441	5.2	52.7	42.0
Morgan, IL	18.9	...	8.4	410	13.6	63	25	40 067	7.9	37.6	54.5
Moultrie, IL	18.2	...	1.2	136	14.1	17	3	12 850	5.0	47.0	48.1
Ogle, IL	13.6	...	8.3	693	15.2	92	27	79 020	3.0	32.8	64.1
Peoria, IL	18.8	...	36.3	1 920	15.2	258	79	212 197	7.7	39.4	52.9
Perry, IL	17.6	...	6.2	207	14.7	18	7	20 668	6.2	57.7	36.0
Piatt, IL	12.1	...	1.2	233	14.6	24	7	21 858	1.7	25.6	72.8
Pike, IL	21.3	...	0.3	239	13.2	30	9	22 406	5.1	60.0	34.9
Pope, IL	14.4	...	1.4	48	13.4	6	1	4 197	6.7	72.4	21.0
Pulaski, IL	19.9	...	46.3	99	15.3	27	18	14 422	20.5	58.4	21.0
Putnam, IL	13.1	...	4.7	65	15.6	10	2	6 839	3.2	21.7	75.1
Randolph, IL	17.4	...	6.9	335	14.0	49	12	33 460	7.6	48.6	43.8
Richland, IL	16.9	...	1.9	204	13.6	22	9	18 809	7.1	57.0	36.0
Rock Island, IL	16.1	...	28.2	1 425	16.1	226	61	174 827	6.6	39.4	54.0
St. Clair, IL	16.3	...	46.2	2 734	16.9	381	108	337 140	10.8	54.6	34.7
Saline, IL	15.0	...	5.9	303	14.7	28	18	29 174	7.1	65.8	27.1
Sangamon, IL	14.4	...	37.7	2 251	18.6	371	125	227 741	6.0	36.3	57.7
Schuyler, IL	17.1	...	0.5	78	14.9	9	2	7 858	5.1	56.0	38.9
Scott, IL	19.6	...	0.2	76	13.4	9	2	7 001	5.2	58.2	36.6
Shelby, IL	17.8	...	1.4	329	12.9	41	11	20 486	4.7	57.2	38.1
Stark, IL	16.5	...	1.2	109	11.1	8	4	8 452	6.0	38.1	55.8
Stephenson, IL	14.9	...	18.2	519	15.3	77	16	54 389	5.7	43.7	50.6
Tazewell, IL	15.3	...	2.6	1 292	15.4	170	63	151 067	6.0	38.7	55.3
Union, IL	17.4	...	6.3	236	14.4	25	7	22 905	9.6	63.9	26.6
Vermilion, IL	19.9	...	20.0	982	14.5	145	34	105 501	9.5	50.5	40.0
Wabash, IL	15.2	...	0.9	143	15.0	12	4	14 847	7.8	56.2	35.9
Warren, IL	16.5	...	6.0	228	13.3	25	9	20 661	6.1	51.0	43.0
Washington, IL	14.8	...	0.7	155	14.6	14	7	15 498	3.6	49.3	47.0
Wayne, IL	16.9	...	0.8	215	13.4	19	9	19 462	5.8	61.3	32.9
White, IL	17.5	...	1.3	199	13.7	52	17	24 139	14.7	51.7	33.6
Whiteside, IL	14.7	...	13.5	693	15.0	89	28	86 947	5.6	40.1	54.3
Will, IL	14.0	...	28.0	4 306	19.0	701	214	553 760	4.0	30.0	66.0
Williamson, IL	20.2	...	6.4	479	19.8	87	18	69 389	7.1	51.9	41.0
Winnebago, IL	15.8	...	32.9	2 759	16.2	427	180	354 043	5.9	33.2	60.8
Woodford, IL	15.2	...	2.3	520	14.6	73	17	50 505	3.5	50.5	46.0
INDIANA											
Adams, IN	12.6	18.5	4.8	311	16.4	354	27	39 069	5.3	54.1	40.5
Allen, IN	15.0	30.3	27.0	2 834	18.3	2 980	101	409 410	4.1	47.6	48.4
Bartholomew, IN	14.9	25.5	5.9	668	17.4	758	32	97 100	5.4	45.2	49.4
Benton, IN	22.1	22.8	4.4	139	15.3	169	6	17 348	1.2	51.1	47.7
Blackford, IN	20.3	30.1	0.8	151	15.3	174	8	18 750	3.8	57.4	38.9
Boone, IN	13.3	13.0	1.9	471	18.3	471	24	64 822	1.9	49.8	48.3
Brown, IN	14.1	21.6	1.7	140	17.2	155	11	19 164	2.1	56.7	41.2
Carroll, IN	13.0	22.3	3.3	160	18.2	214	8	23 319	2.7	49.3	48.0
Cass, IN	14.0	30.6	11.6	374	18.6	586	36	61 981	5.7	49.4	45.0
Clark, IN	18.5	32.2	11.9	847	16.9	981	63	115 887	5.8	56.1	38.1

2IEP = Individual Education Program. See Notes and Definitions at the end of this section.
. . . = Not available.

Table C-1. Population, School, and Student Characteristics by County—*Continued*

County	Current expenditures, fiscal 1999			Resident population 16 to 19 years, 2000				Outcomes, 1999–2000	
	Amount ($1,000s)	Amount per student	Percent for instruction	Total population 16 to 19 years	Percent in Armed Forces	Percent high school graduates	Percent not enrolled, not grads, not Armed Forces, not empl.	Number of graduates	Dropouts grades 9–12 (percent)
	21	22	23	24	25	26	27	28	29
Greene, IL	$13 470	$5 282	61.9	854	0.0	14.8	7.3	151	4.6
Grundy, IL	55 172	6 819	57.0	2 354	0.0	13.3	3.2	680	3.5
Hamilton, IL	8 619	6 048	60.5	490	0.0	9.8	3.3	77	5.7
Hancock, IL	21 418	5 124	62.5	1 156	0.6	9.9	3.3	306	2.8
Hardin, IL	5 366	7 136	62.4	297	0.0	12.8	8.1	50	5.6
Henderson, IL	7 409	5 712	59.5	470	0.0	10.9	3.4	86	6.5
Henry, IL	52 868	5 436	61.8	2 885	0.0	12.8	2.0	672	3.8
Iroquois, IL	29 478	5 135	57.9	1 832	0.0	10.9	5.9	376	4.3
Jackson, IL	54 294	6 780	59.7	5 741	0.1	6.8	4.1	534	2.9
Jasper, IL	14 683	7 728	53.4	752	0.0	12.4	1.3	146	3.4
Jefferson, IL	38 953	5 697	61.5	2 131	0.0	12.3	7.0	404	4.2
Jersey, IL	17 530	5 298	59.7	1 480	0.0	10.9	4.0	223	5.1
Jo Daviess, IL	22 266	6 398	62.2	1 150	0.0	9.7	2.7	263	3.7
Johnson, IL	9 905	5 472	58.1	705	0.0	7.8	14.6	117	1.5
Kane, IL	567 905	6 036	63.0	23 853	0.1	10.3	7.7	4 788	4.3
Kankakee, IL	112 909	6 074	61.2	6 115	0.0	14.0	5.7	981	3.8
Kendall, IL	55 441	5 689	59.7	3 225	0.0	6.8	3.6	650	2.8
Knox, IL	50 227	5 963	62.0	3 154	0.0	9.2	7.4	530	4.6
Lake, IL	868 954	7 370	58.5	38 104	12.6	20.6	3.7	6 848	3.3
La Salle, IL	113 794	6 472	58.2	6 275	0.1	13.0	5.1	1 121	7.3
Lawrence, IL	14 508	5 710	61.8	721	0.0	12.9	4.7	149	7.3
Lee, IL	33 003	5 898	60.3	1 955	0.0	12.0	4.3	343	6.2
Livingston, IL	48 540	6 172	61.1	2 204	0.0	11.7	9.8	522	3.7
Logan, IL	24 899	6 197	61.9	2 055	0.6	9.2	4.1	278	5.2
McDonough, IL	26 640	6 261	60.5	3 482	0.0	3.0	1.9	343	5.4
McHenry, IL	246 622	5 942	61.4	13 662	0.1	8.8	2.5	2 566	3.1
McLean, IL	136 562	5 961	58.9	11 738	0.0	6.8	2.1	1 459	3.8
Macon, IL	107 390	5 723	56.8	6 574	0.0	11.9	7.5	1 070	6.4
Macoupin, IL	50 139	5 066	62.4	2 969	0.1	11.2	4.2	631	5.1
Madison, IL	257 459	5 902	58.0	14 923	0.0	10.1	4.7	2 744	5.7
Marion, IL	49 812	6 118	61.4	2 234	0.2	13.8	6.8	569	8.3
Marshall, IL	9 728	5 712	66.4	715	0.0	11.7	4.1	114	4.0
Mason, IL	21 014	5 919	62.9	914	0.0	9.2	7.8	237	4.6
Massac, IL	14 484	5 351	63.1	817	0.0	12.4	6.6	175	8.0
Menard, IL	13 899	4 906	60.8	717	0.0	8.5	1.4	193	3.3
Mercer, IL	18 283	4 997	59.9	1 074	0.0	14.9	2.0	273	4.1
Monroe, IL	22 453	5 108	61.3	1 704	0.0	13.0	1.3	335	2.1
Montgomery, IL	29 850	5 391	55.8	1 646	0.2	11.8	5.7	336	4.0
Morgan, IL	35 333	6 325	58.1	2 557	0.3	8.7	5.5	428	8.6
Moultrie, IL	9 740	5 164	59.1	816	0.0	11.9	4.4	127	3.3
Ogle, IL	65 768	6 325	63.5	2 985	0.0	11.3	2.8	701	2.7
Peoria, IL	176 274	6 340	58.9	10 361	0.1	9.4	5.0	1 701	7.2
Perry, IL	17 918	5 629	60.4	1 378	0.0	10.4	12.0	219	4.0
Piatt, IL	18 723	5 403	58.0	972	0.0	11.9	0.5	240	2.3
Pike, IL	17 853	5 639	62.2	922	0.0	10.5	6.7	198	4.2
Pope, IL	4 051	6 064	64.1	264	0.0	18.9	17.8	46	5.5
Pulaski, IL	12 733	8 152	58.4	472	0.0	8.7	16.3	116	13.6
Putnam, IL	5 556	5 410	57.8	334	0.0	8.1	1.8	66	3.6
Randolph, IL	28 481	5 863	59.9	1 757	0.0	14.3	9.0	342	3.5
Richland, IL	15 345	5 396	60.8	938	0.0	9.3	6.8	206	7.1
Rock Island, IL	143 056	6 157	64.4	9 001	0.1	10.2	5.0	1 414	7.0
St. Clair, IL	286 122	6 208	60.5	15 449	1.1	12.4	6.0	2 715	4.5
Saline, IL	25 411	5 661	63.7	1 971	0.0	7.6	24.6	254	7.0
Sangamon, IL	181 477	6 276	56.0	9 836	0.3	12.6	4.5	1 633	3.3
Schuyler, IL	6 718	5 409	63.9	353	1.4	4.2	2.8	77	1.1
Scott, IL	5 807	5 463	64.1	323	0.0	17.3	2.5	74	3.2
Shelby, IL	17 516	5 191	60.2	1 271	1.1	10.4	4.9	273	3.6
Stark, IL	7 431	5 945	63.8	352	0.0	6.0	6.8	78	3.6
Stephenson, IL	45 745	5 686	57.7	2 799	0.0	11.4	5.0	536	5.4
Tazewell, IL	122 350	6 011	58.7	6 903	0.0	12.6	2.4	1 403	3.6
Union, IL	19 653	5 522	62.0	1 033	0.0	12.6	4.2	196	5.3
Vermilion, IL	90 934	6 303	59.8	4 512	0.2	13.6	7.9	771	8.1
Wabash, IL	12 250	5 491	59.9	840	0.0	11.5	2.0	159	4.2
Warren, IL	16 868	5 193	61.1	1 374	0.0	7.2	4.7	217	12.6
Washington, IL	13 104	5 595	62.2	854	0.0	10.8	4.1	171	4.1
Wayne, IL	16 987	5 627	61.9	904	0.0	14.6	6.1	211	3.6
White, IL	22 017	7 647	60.3	811	0.0	14.1	9.4	182	5.2
Whiteside, IL	65 996	6 250	61.8	3 411	0.0	12.7	4.6	661	5.2
Will, IL	427 446	5 774	57.9	28 159	0.0	10.7	5.3	4 382	3.4
Williamson, IL	54 113	5 720	61.0	3 199	0.0	12.3	5.7	546	2.9
Winnebago, IL	297 833	6 785	60.2	14 919	0.2	10.5	6.6	2 213	7.3
Woodford, IL	42 109	5 436	61.6	2 259	0.0	9.1	1.1	576	1.9
INDIANA									
Adams, IN	31 340	5 992	58.5	2 229	0.0	7.9	7.9	406	...
Allen, IN	349 436	6 773	62.6	19 231	0.1	10.4	4.1	3 035	...
Bartholomew, IN	74 233	6 031	65.2	3 330	0.0	9.8	4.4	668	...
Benton, IN	14 707	6 869	60.1	557	0.0	16.5	4.8	154	...
Blackford, IN	15 254	6 254	62.7	702	0.0	11.3	4.1	147	...
Boone, IN	47 896	5 790	61.6	2 357	0.0	12.6	4.2	491	...
Brown, IN	16 078	6 357	59.1	772	0.0	14.2	4.3	162	...
Carroll, IN	16 519	5 655	58.9	1 051	0.0	14.5	5.9	197	...
Cass, IN	49 123	7 247	63.9	2 406	0.0	11.4	7.8	442	...
Clark, IN	94 889	6 639	64.6	5 178	0.1	13.4	6.1	822	...

. . . = Not available.

Table C-1. Population, School, and Student Characteristics by County—*Continued*

County	High school graduates, 2000			College enrollment, 2000		College graduates, 2000 (percent)						
	Population 25 years and over	High school diploma or less (percent)	High school diploma or more (percent)	Number	Percent public	Bachelor's degree or more	+/- U.S. percent with bachelor's degree or more	Non-Hispanic White	Black or African American	American Indian and Alaska Native	Asian, Hawaiian, and Pacific Islander	Hispanic or Latino[1]
	30	31	32	33	34	35	36	37	38	39	40	41
Greene, IL	9 688	64.9	78.9	436	78.9	10.1	-14.3	10.2	0.0	0.0	23.1	14.8
Grundy, IL	24 297	52.0	86.9	1 710	77.9	15.2	-9.2	15.3	0.0	0.0	55.8	12.5
Hamilton, IL	5 866	57.6	74.3	324	92.6	10.5	-13.9	10.4	0.0	0.0	100.0	0.0
Hancock, IL	13 724	55.8	85.7	731	93.0	15.6	-8.8	15.7	0.0	0.0	0.0	16.4
Hardin, IL	3 442	60.9	68.1	214	95.8	9.6	-14.8	9.7	0.0	. . .	61.1	0.0
Henderson, IL	5 680	63.9	82.4	278	84.2	10.0	-14.4	10.1	0.0	0.0	100.0	0.0
Henry, IL	34 183	52.7	84.5	2 008	86.1	15.7	-8.7	16.0	14.0	16.7	34.9	3.0
Iroquois, IL	21 111	60.3	80.3	1 007	86.2	11.8	-12.6	11.8	8.7	31.6	78.2	5.0
Jackson, IL	32 659	39.7	85.2	16 882	97.9	32.0	7.6	30.9	24.9	30.6	77.8	27.1
Jasper, IL	6 579	58.0	82.6	459	96.5	11.2	-13.2	11.1	. . .	0.0	0.0	0.0
Jefferson, IL	26 841	56.0	77.0	1 631	92.7	13.7	-10.7	14.2	7.0	10.9	44.1	5.1
Jersey, IL	13 982	56.8	82.5	1 427	61.3	12.6	-11.8	12.4	28.0	14.6	29.5	53.1
Jo Daviess, IL	15 625	58.0	83.6	725	72.3	15.2	-9.2	15.4	0.0	9.4	20.0	1.6
Johnson, IL	9 057	60.7	67.1	501	94.6	11.7	-12.7	13.9	0.0	0.0	53.8	4.1
Kane, IL	245 486	44.8	80.2	19 754	69.9	27.7	3.3	33.6	15.2	4.5	46.6	4.9
Kankakee, IL	65 844	56.0	79.8	5 437	62.2	15.0	-9.4	16.3	7.1	17.7	38.6	7.2
Kendall, IL	34 362	40.2	89.9	2 555	73.3	25.3	0.9	26.1	24.0	30.8	41.4	8.5
Knox, IL	38 049	54.9	81.8	3 207	53.4	14.6	-9.8	15.2	4.7	0.0	47.0	6.0
Lake, IL	398 265	34.8	86.6	32 659	64.8	38.6	14.2	43.1	17.3	14.1	64.6	8.4
La Salle, IL	74 431	57.2	81.4	3 807	88.8	13.3	-11.1	13.5	3.0	5.7	57.2	6.7
Lawrence, IL	10 752	60.6	81.3	537	94.6	9.7	-14.7	9.7	14.3	0.0	0.0	0.0
Lee, IL	24 540	56.5	80.2	1 434	87.2	13.2	-11.2	13.9	2.0	0.0	32.0	4.0
Livingston, IL	26 496	63.2	78.1	1 009	84.4	12.6	-11.8	13.5	0.4	28.3	13.0	0.8
Logan, IL	20 714	60.0	80.4	1 933	37.2	14.2	-10.2	15.2	1.7	0.0	46.6	4.5
McDonough, IL	17 944	46.5	86.9	8 722	96.3	26.9	2.5	25.6	33.1	0.0	85.1	44.9
McHenry, IL	163 780	39.1	89.2	12 583	81.6	27.7	-8.4	28.4	46.6	17.4	55.4	9.3
McLean, IL	87 220	37.5	90.7	24 570	88.4	36.2	11.8	35.8	30.7	7.3	73.1	23.9
Macon, IL	75 195	54.9	83.2	6 495	56.2	16.9	-7.5	18.3	5.2	14.5	53.6	11.0
Macoupin, IL	32 878	59.5	82.1	2 312	71.3	11.8	-12.6	11.8	5.2	12.5	35.9	18.0
Madison, IL	170 432	49.7	84.3	17 380	87.5	19.2	-5.2	19.6	11.1	16.4	48.9	18.3
Marion, IL	27 710	56.8	79.1	1 491	93.0	12.1	-12.3	12.1	7.6	16.7	55.2	20.3
Marshall, IL	9 135	55.2	85.0	468	84.8	14.5	-9.9	14.7	0.0	0.0	0.0	0.0
Mason, IL	10 890	62.2	79.9	476	89.5	11.2	-13.2	11.3	0.0	0.0	0.0	0.0
Massac, IL	10 471	58.3	76.5	597	92.6	10.7	-13.7	10.9	6.7	0.0	33.3	4.1
Menard, IL	8 298	50.0	88.3	445	81.3	20.5	-3.9	20.7	7.1	10.5	7.1	34.1
Mercer, IL	11 529	58.7	84.9	605	84.8	12.6	-11.8	12.6	0.0	0.0	35.5	30.6
Monroe, IL	18 277	45.4	87.2	1 344	79.5	20.4	-4.0	20.3	0.0	26.5	60.4	10.4
Montgomery, IL	20 874	63.9	77.1	899	90.8	11.2	-13.2	11.7	1.0	13.3	13.2	6.1
Morgan, IL	24 276	57.2	79.9	2 407	42.9	19.9	-4.5	20.8	4.0	11.9	63.5	6.7
Moultrie, IL	9 515	59.1	78.8	357	80.7	14.7	-9.7	14.6	0.0	0.0	53.8	33.8
Ogle, IL	33 317	53.3	83.1	1 842	88.0	17.0	-7.4	17.5	18.5	9.7	64.9	4.5
Peoria, IL	118 498	45.6	83.8	12 443	52.1	23.3	-1.1	24.4	10.1	6.0	68.7	19.3
Perry, IL	15 727	61.9	72.3	977	94.6	10.1	-14.3	10.9	1.1	0.0	28.6	5.5
Piatt, IL	11 118	48.5	88.7	728	94.0	21.0	-3.4	21.0	0.0	0.0	57.1	5.0
Pike, IL	11 864	64.2	79.6	473	73.8	9.9	-14.5	9.7	0.0	0.0	55.6	31.1
Pope, IL	2 989	57.3	75.8	186	80.6	10.5	-13.9	10.6	6.1	0.0	0.0	0.0
Pulaski, IL	4 704	60.9	70.7	326	98.2	7.1	-17.3	6.7	8.8	0.0	0.0	0.0
Putnam, IL	4 136	54.2	83.8	210	83.3	12.1	-12.3	12.2	0.0	25.0	0.0	4.1
Randolph, IL	23 141	65.9	71.3	1 095	85.5	8.6	-15.8	9.3	2.9	0.0	21.4	2.4
Richland, IL	10 827	49.4	83.4	898	94.3	15.2	-9.2	15.2	. . .	0.0	61.8	0.0
Rock Island, IL	98 865	51.5	82.6	8 734	68.0	17.1	-7.3	18.0	7.7	4.8	56.0	7.3
St. Clair, IL	162 715	48.2	80.9	14 400	80.6	19.3	-5.1	21.8	11.4	16.0	32.1	17.3
Saline, IL	18 111	54.1	76.1	1 248	97.0	12.1	-12.3	12.2	11.4	16.3	21.6	0.0
Sangamon, IL	126 620	43.0	88.1	9 460	87.1	28.6	4.2	29.3	15.8	24.4	63.6	29.9
Schuyler, IL	5 022	62.6	83.6	186	79.0	11.7	-12.7	11.7	66.7	0.0	0.0	0.0
Scott, IL	3 718	63.5	83.1	165	72.7	12.1	-12.3	12.1	100.0	0.0	0.0	0.0
Shelby, IL	15 448	61.0	82.9	772	90.7	11.5	-12.9	11.4	0.0	18.2	45.1	0.0
Stark, IL	4 312	55.7	83.4	151	73.5	13.4	-11.0	13.5	0.0	0.0	0.0	0.0
Stephenson, IL	32 851	54.2	84.1	2 375	86.4	15.6	-8.8	16.1	7.0	22.9	70.5	10.7
Tazewell, IL	86 666	49.4	85.0	5 906	84.1	18.1	-6.3	18.4	0.5	7.5	30.6	14.2
Union, IL	12 695	56.2	74.8	717	95.7	15.8	-8.6	16.0	2.2	19.6	55.2	4.5
Vermilion, IL	55 778	59.6	78.7	3 097	91.1	12.5	-11.9	12.8	5.9	12.1	58.9	7.6
Wabash, IL	8 627	48.7	82.2	730	96.7	12.5	-11.9	12.3	70.6	0.0	57.1	26.0
Warren, IL	12 131	57.3	82.3	1 492	37.2	15.8	-8.6	15.8	15.6	10.0	73.8	3.7
Washington, IL	10 168	55.8	79.1	689	89.1	13.4	-11.0	13.3	0.0	0.0	29.4	39.3
Wayne, IL	11 723	59.5	75.2	676	93.9	10.0	-14.4	9.8	0.0	0.0	38.0	7.8
White, IL	10 863	61.0	74.6	499	91.8	10.4	-14.0	10.3	18.2	13.3	0.0	20.0
Whiteside, IL	40 585	58.0	79.8	2 286	81.5	11.3	-13.1	11.8	15.1	19.8	30.4	3.9
Will, IL	310 918	42.2	86.9	26 437	69.2	25.5	1.1	26.7	19.1	9.5	58.2	9.5
Williamson, IL	41 973	52.6	79.8	3 462	94.5	17.2	-7.2	17.2	9.6	27.1	50.9	10.6
Winnebago, IL	181 803	51.4	81.4	12 464	74.5	19.4	-5.0	20.8	9.0	3.9	36.4	7.6
Woodford, IL	22 945	47.5	87.8	1 945	70.7	21.1	-3.3	21.1	0.0	0.0	42.7	14.2
INDIANA												
Adams, IN	20 158	65.1	80.0	1 145	85.8	10.7	-13.7	10.7	0.0	40.0	89.1	1.4
Allen, IN	208 769	46.3	85.7	18 136	73.8	22.7	-1.7	24.4	9.6	8.0	39.1	7.8
Bartholomew, IN	47 109	52.4	83.8	2 882	84.5	22.0	-2.4	21.4	16.3	11.4	72.4	12.8
Benton, IN	6 158	61.9	86.3	247	87.9	13.0	-11.4	13.4	0.0	50.0	11.1	0.0
Blackford, IN	9 550	68.2	81.3	369	83.5	10.3	-14.1	10.1	. . .	44.4	55.6	11.4
Boone, IN	30 048	49.6	88.3	1 276	80.5	27.6	3.2	27.7	0.0	0.0	51.1	4.4
Brown, IN	10 530	55.2	83.6	496	76.8	18.5	-5.9	18.5	19.6	29.0	100.0	0.0
Carroll, IN	13 299	64.5	83.2	485	83.3	12.9	-11.5	13.1	0.0	0.0	100.0	6.8
Cass, IN	26 747	63.7	81.8	1 161	87.5	12.0	-12.4	12.3	0.0	10.4	46.9	7.4
Clark, IN	64 389	56.6	79.9	3 884	85.5	14.3	-10.1	14.5	10.0	4.6	45.7	13.5

[1]Hispanic or Latino persons may be of any race.
. . . = Not available.

Table C-1. Population, School, and Student Characteristics by County—*Continued*

County	State/County code	County type[1]	Population, 2000		Number of schools and students, 2000–2001			Resident enrollment, 2000			
			Total	Percent 5–17 years	School districts	Schools	Students	Total	Percent public	K–12	Percent public
			1	2	3	4	5	6	7	8	9
Clay, IN	18021	3	26 556	19.5	1	10	4 672	6 549	90.5	5 323	93.3
Clinton, IN	18023	3	33 866	20.2	4	12	6 336	7 947	91.8	6 832	95.2
Crawford, IN	18025	8	10 743	19.2	1	6	1 851	2 346	90.8	2 049	92.4
Daviess, IN	18027	7	29 820	21.3	3	13	4 484	7 094	81.5	5 947	82.9
Dearborn, IN	18029	1	46 109	20.8	3	14	8 796	11 922	83.2	9 685	87.8
Decatur, IN	18031	6	24 555	18.8	2	10	4 229	5 684	88.3	4 608	92.9
De Kalb, IN	18033	2	40 285	20.4	3	12	7 023	10 316	89.6	8 065	93.5
Delaware, IN	18035	3	118 769	16.2	8	39	17 663	37 225	94.1	19 279	95.4
Dubois, IN	18037	7	39 674	20.2	4	17	7 400	10 124	88.8	8 012	92.2
Elkhart, IN	18039	3	182 791	20.8	7	53	32 751	44 933	85.4	36 607	90.5
Fayette, IN	18041	7	25 588	17.9	1	11	4 239	5 544	89.8	4 439	91.6
Floyd, IN	18043	2	70 823	19.3	1	17	11 115	18 474	82.8	13 808	84.5
Fountain, IN	18045	6	17 954	19.6	3	7	3 287	4 260	92.1	3 520	95.7
Franklin, IN	18047	6	22 151	21.2	1	5	3 014	5 644	78.2	4 611	82.1
Fulton, IN	18049	7	20 511	19.4	2	6	2 827	4 904	91.8	4 084	95.5
Gibson, IN	18051	6	32 500	18.4	3	13	5 052	7 933	81.5	6 100	88.5
Grant, IN	18053	4	73 403	17.7	4	29	11 358	19 117	73.4	12 773	93.1
Greene, IN	18055	6	33 157	18.5	5	12	5 828	7 678	92.3	5 980	95.3
Hamilton, IN	18057	0	182 740	21.7	6	47	34 498	51 209	79.2	38 339	86.9
Hancock, IN	18059	1	55 391	19.8	4	20	10 233	14 151	85.2	10 799	91.7
Harrison, IN	18061	2	34 325	19.5	3	15	6 045	8 341	85.3	6 637	87.6
Hendricks, IN	18063	1	104 093	20.7	6	32	19 194	27 181	86.2	21 421	92.0
Henry, IN	18065	6	48 508	17.9	5	22	8 457	10 911	91.6	8 779	94.8
Howard, IN	18067	3	84 964	18.6	5	30	14 111	20 385	87.3	15 619	91.6
Huntington, IN	18069	2	38 075	19.5	1	11	6 523	9 918	81.5	7 419	91.1
Jackson, IN	18071	7	41 335	18.5	4	16	6 376	9 233	84.7	7 554	87.5
Jasper, IN	18073	6	30 043	20.5	2	8	4 946	8 012	78.8	6 113	87.5
Jay, IN	18075	6	21 806	19.7	1	10	3 927	5 006	92.7	4 202	95.1
Jefferson, IN	18077	6	31 705	18.2	2	12	4 982	8 115	76.6	5 619	90.4
Jennings, IN	18079	7	27 554	20.2	1	9	5 121	6 562	86.2	5 392	89.1
Johnson, IN	18081	0	115 209	19.7	6	34	20 838	29 119	81.9	22 205	89.2
Knox, IN	18083	5	39 256	17.1	3	14	5 949	11 067	93.0	6 828	93.3
Kosciusko, IN	18085	6	74 057	20.3	4	28	14 073	18 081	85.2	14 606	90.2
Lagrange, IN	18087	8	34 909	24.0	3	14	6 378	7 998	77.9	7 099	78.0
Lake, IN	18089	0	484 564	19.6	16	146	82 294	130 977	84.7	96 754	88.8
La Porte, IN	18091	4	110 106	18.1	7	39	17 865	27 395	85.7	20 758	88.9
Lawrence, IN	18093	6	45 922	18.1	2	19	7 395	9 850	91.5	8 125	94.9
Madison, IN	18095	3	133 358	17.4	5	39	20 100	31 151	83.5	23 306	92.4
Marion, IN	18097	0	860 454	18.4	13	198	128 130	218 164	77.9	156 431	83.7
Marshall, IN	18099	6	45 128	20.8	5	15	7 861	11 369	85.5	9 285	89.7
Martin, IN	18101	7	10 369	18.9	2	5	1 858	2 269	89.5	1 942	90.8
Miami, IN	18103	6	36 082	19.5	4	18	7 573	8 768	90.3	6 949	92.2
Monroe, IN	18105	3	120 563	12.9	2	25	13 275	52 065	93.0	15 547	90.6
Montgomery, IN	18107	6	37 629	19.3	3	18	6 698	9 352	85.2	7 207	95.9
Morgan, IN	18109	1	66 689	20.0	4	24	11 288	15 760	89.3	13 108	93.8
Newton, IN	18111	8	14 566	20.2	2	7	2 822	3 438	91.9	2 961	93.5
Noble, IN	18113	6	46 275	21.0	3	16	7 955	11 357	87.3	9 512	91.1
Ohio, IN	18115	1	5 623	19.0	1	2	1 027	1 310	92.5	1 082	96.5
Orange, IN	18117	7	19 306	19.0	3	6	3 449	4 377	91.9	3 605	93.7
Owen, IN	18119	6	21 786	20.3	1	6	3 174	5 037	91.0	4 296	94.2
Parke, IN	18121	6	17 241	18.4	3	7	2 675	4 019	90.2	3 225	94.1
Perry, IN	18123	7	18 899	17.5	3	6	3 135	4 257	93.0	3 477	97.1
Pike, IN	18125	8	12 837	17.8	1	5	2 202	2 792	94.1	2 279	97.5
Porter, IN	18127	1	146 798	19.3	7	46	25 580	39 988	81.0	28 392	92.8
Posey, IN	18129	2	27 061	21.0	3	11	4 708	7 225	82.4	5 659	84.6
Pulaski, IN	18131	9	13 755	20.8	2	6	2 538	3 478	92.8	2 877	96.6
Putnam, IN	18133	6	36 019	17.4	4	16	6 823	9 600	73.8	6 440	97.1
Randolph, IN	18135	6	27 401	18.5	5	14	4 794	6 095	94.9	5 132	97.0
Ripley, IN	18137	6	26 523	20.7	4	10	5 411	6 526	85.1	5 318	89.1
Rush, IN	18139	6	18 261	19.9	1	6	2 668	4 229	86.4	3 477	91.0
St. Joseph, IN	18141	3	265 559	18.7	5	70	39 649	76 955	67.2	49 543	81.2
Scott, IN	18143	2	22 960	18.9	2	9	4 102	5 152	91.3	4 284	94.1
Shelby, IN	18145	1	43 445	19.9	4	14	7 859	10 554	90.3	8 496	94.7
Spencer, IN	18147	8	20 391	20.2	2	9	3 856	5 109	90.0	4 199	93.6
Starke, IN	18149	6	23 556	20.3	3	9	4 406	5 722	90.2	4 739	93.7
Steuben, IN	18151	6	33 214	19.0	3	10	5 002	8 611	82.3	6 285	96.2
Sullivan, IN	18153	6	21 751	17.0	2	11	3 559	5 101	92.9	4 013	96.3
Switzerland, IN	18155	8	9 065	20.0	1	4	1 639	2 017	94.0	1 752	95.3
Tippecanoe, IN	18157	3	148 955	15.1	3	33	18 992	60 819	92.2	22 061	90.8
Tipton, IN	18159	3	16 577	18.9	2	5	2 900	3 883	88.7	3 108	93.1
Union, IN	18161	8	7 349	20.3	1	4	1 609	1 818	93.8	1 492	96.2
Vanderburgh, IN	18163	2	171 922	16.9	1	38	22 875	44 775	77.5	29 035	81.2
Vermillion, IN	18165	3	16 788	17.5	2	7	2 795	3 892	93.3	3 044	95.7
Vigo, IN	18167	3	105 848	16.8	1	30	16 545	31 055	87.2	17 768	93.5
Wabash, IN	18169	7	34 960	18.6	3	16	6 011	8 948	81.3	6 638	95.4
Warren, IN	18171	8	8 419	20.0	1	4	1 369	2 032	92.2	1 663	96.3
Warrick, IN	18173	2	52 383	20.3	1	16	8 981	13 756	84.5	10 431	89.8
Washington, IN	18175	6	27 223	19.8	3	9	4 772	6 407	91.0	5 241	93.8
Wayne, IN	18177	5	71 097	18.0	5	29	11 519	17 570	87.4	12 838	94.8
Wells, IN	18179	2	27 600	20.7	3	9	5 167	7 028	88.6	5 604	93.7.
White, IN	18181	6	25 267	19.4	4	16	5 595	5 855	94.8	4 895	98.3
Whitley, IN	18183	2	30 707	19.9	2	11	5 056	7 674	89.1	6 205	91.9

[1]County type code is from the Economic Research Service of the USDA. See Notes and Definitions at the end of this section.

Table C-1. School and Student Characteristics by County—*Continued*

County	Characteristics of students, 2000–2001			Staff and students, 2000–2001				Revenues, fiscal 1999			
	Percent with IEP[2]	Percent eligible for free lunch	Percent minority	Number of teachers	Student/ teacher ratio	Local school non-teaching staff	Central admin. staff	Total revenue ($1,000s)	Percentage of revenue from		
									Federal govt.	State govt.	Local govt.
	10	11	12	13	14	15	16	17	18	19	20
Clay, IN	18.8	30.7	0.6	287	16.3	339	9	$35 062	4.2	56.9	39.0
Clinton, IN	12.6	29.8	7.9	376	16.9	374	23	46 611	5.8	55.7	38.5
Crawford, IN	17.9	45.0	0.2	103	18.0	116	3	14 610	5.1	61.6	33.4
Daviess, IN	19.8	30.8	2.9	241	18.6	260	16	36 230	6.8	50.5	42.7
Dearborn, IN	16.4	15.3	1.0	477	18.4	527	24	67 138	3.9	54.6	41.5
Decatur, IN	14.6	20.5	1.0	235	18.0	242	15	30 295	2.5	56.5	41.0
De Kalb, IN	15.4	17.7	1.8	387	18.1	481	35	59 419	6.7	45.1	48.3
Delaware, IN	19.0	34.5	11.9	1 132	15.6	1 054	56	151 222	6.5	53.8	39.7
Dubois, IN	12.3	12.2	2.9	393	18.8	488	28	62 423	4.1	43.5	52.4
Elkhart, IN	15.4	29.2	18.9	1 829	17.9	1 932	89	267 112	4.1	45.5	50.5
Fayette, IN	20.9	35.8	2.5	262	16.2	386	16	43 328	9.6	46.9	43.4
Floyd, IN	18.0	33.2	8.1	615	18.1	787	19	110 740	4.5	44.0	51.5
Fountain, IN	15.1	24.7	0.6	205	16.0	209	13	25 539	3.7	56.1	40.2
Franklin, IN	15.7	26.7	0.2	159	19.0	172	15	24 991	1.6	55.9	42.6
Fulton, IN	12.5	23.7	2.3	165	17.1	162	9	21 747	2.6	49.8	47.6
Gibson, IN	16.9	21.8	3.1	287	17.6	414	16	44 725	5.5	44.0	50.4
Grant, IN	13.9	36.6	15.5	727	15.6	892	50	91 166	7.1	57.8	35.1
Greene, IN	15.8	30.9	0.5	348	16.7	376	21	44 933	5.4	59.9	34.8
Hamilton, IN	13.7	6.8	5.8	1 968	17.5	2 220	77	278 426	1.4	37.6	61.0
Hancock, IN	18.6	10.3	1.2	529	19.3	668	30	82 526	2.8	47.8	49.4
Harrison, IN	16.2	23.0	0.4	339	17.8	359	16	45 391	4.0	58.4	37.7
Hendricks, IN	13.5	9.7	2.2	1 049	18.3	1 259	53	142 570	1.3	48.0	50.8
Henry, IN	20.9	24.3	1.9	542	15.6	637	66	70 495	5.3	56.9	37.8
Howard, IN	18.2	29.4	12.7	909	15.5	1 000	44	134 636	5.0	40.6	54.3
Huntington, IN	14.2	20.9	1.0	386	16.9	389	56	52 772	3.7	55.9	40.3
Jackson, IN	15.5	27.0	4.1	366	17.4	390	19	47 369	3.2	52.4	44.4
Jasper, IN	16.8	23.5	3.3	274	18.1	378	17	35 383	2.3	47.5	50.2
Jay, IN	16.2	32.5	1.7	241	16.3	255	13	29 039	4.5	58.2	37.3
Jefferson, IN	23.6	32.8	3.0	287	17.4	459	32	44 208	8.1	47.6	44.3
Jennings, IN	18.9	26.7	2.0	270	19.0	267	11	33 975	3.6	63.7	32.7
Johnson, IN	13.6	15.3	2.3	1 066	19.5	1 349	85	160 809	3.7	45.5	50.8
Knox, IN	16.1	35.2	1.7	376	15.8	362	18	48 522	5.7	55.0	39.3
Kosciusko, IN	12.2	23.7	6.5	792	17.8	813	52	111 910	3.2	47.2	49.6
Lagrange, IN	12.5	19.4	4.3	364	17.5	405	18	48 178	3.2	52.4	44.4
Lake, IN	13.3	38.0	46.5	4 390	18.7	6 096	249	732 826	5.9	53.6	40.5
La Porte, IN	15.7	28.5	16.4	1 109	16.1	1 271	51	151 478	4.5	49.6	45.9
Lawrence, IN	15.9	28.5	2.1	394	18.8	495	13	58 437	4.3	55.2	40.4
Madison, IN	17.6	32.5	12.6	1 230	16.3	1 193	74	156 759	6.1	58.8	35.1
Marion, IN	15.7	44.8	42.3	7 457	17.2	7 625	371	1 150 131	6.0	49.6	44.4
Marshall, IN	11.5	26.9	7.6	420	18.7	574	42	65 830	5.0	46.4	48.6
Martin, IN	17.5	31.2	0.4	101	18.4	101	8	13 863	5.6	62.2	32.2
Miami, IN	15.0	26.6	5.3	454	16.7	473	26	56 671	3.3	64.5	32.2
Monroe, IN	15.3	24.6	7.8	767	17.3	1 174	30	104 515	4.2	45.0	50.7
Montgomery, IN	16.3	24.1	2.6	408	16.4	506	31	57 016	5.3	42.4	52.3
Morgan, IN	14.8	19.1	0.5	672	16.8	746	25	80 358	2.8	59.9	37.3
Newton, IN	14.6	28.3	3.0	175	16.1	208	8	22 883	2.7	52.1	45.2
Noble, IN	13.4	...	10.6	439	18.1	515	29	55 887	2.8	56.6	40.6
Ohio, IN	16.0	15.2	0.7	54	19.0	62	4	7 697	1.9	54.6	43.5
Orange, IN	17.4	33.1	2.3	181	19.1	201	19	26 037	4.9	59.1	36.1
Owen, IN	18.0	32.4	0.5	191	16.6	197	7	25 792	2.8	57.8	39.4
Parke, IN	17.9	31.5	0.7	163	16.4	152	11	19 497	3.4	58.6	38.0
Perry, IN	13.5	24.2	0.3	177	17.7	187	11	23 562	4.2	63.6	32.2
Pike, IN	18.4	33.3	0.5	132	16.7	121	8	15 278	4.0	48.3	47.6
Porter, IN	13.9	15.4	6.5	1 335	19.2	1 651	89	225 388	2.7	43.4	53.9
Posey, IN	17.6	20.3	1.7	304	15.5	288	17	41 943	3.4	36.5	60.0
Pulaski, IN	14.6	27.1	1.7	144	17.6	172	11	20 182	8.5	49.0	42.6
Putnam, IN	21.4	23.6	1.6	370	18.4	521	27	60 208	4.7	51.0	44.3
Randolph, IN	17.9	27.7	1.1	319	15.0	347	28	36 275	4.1	61.2	34.7
Ripley, IN	16.0	20.7	0.7	312	17.3	357	19	44 505	3.0	51.3	45.8
Rush, IN	17.2	23.7	1.9	166	16.1	217	8	21 487	2.5	52.7	44.8
St. Joseph, IN	18.8	38.1	28.5	2 428	16.3	2 772	119	338 084	4.6	50.2	45.2
Scott, IN	13.0	37.3	0.9	216	19.0	232	25	31 225	5.9	59.4	34.7
Shelby, IN	16.4	17.5	2.4	414	19.0	504	25	58 964	3.5	50.8	45.7
Spencer, IN	11.8	18.3	2.2	216	17.9	230	6	30 024	2.4	44.9	52.8
Starke, IN	13.5	37.8	2.6	254	17.3	325	22	34 247	3.5	61.4	35.1
Steuben, IN	12.7	20.7	2.7	279	17.9	269	15	38 655	3.3	44.8	51.9
Sullivan, IN	21.0	35.6	0.6	229	15.5	181	8	28 978	3.1	49.8	47.1
Switzerland, IN	16.2	35.9	0.7	80	20.5	81	5	11 202	3.9	64.8	31.3
Tippecanoe, IN	15.7	23.4	13.0	1 108	17.1	1 084	43	162 102	3.2	40.7	56.1
Tipton, IN	15.1	14.2	2.7	170	17.1	173	10	21 929	2.2	53.2	44.6
Union, IN	14.1	27.8	0.4	90	17.9	120	7	11 653	2.1	56.8	41.1
Vanderburgh, IN	18.8	40.3	16.5	1 430	16.0	1 392	66	186 126	6.8	50.6	42.5
Vermillion, IN	15.6	31.1	0.9	189	14.8	208	10	24 071	4.5	44.9	50.6
Vigo, IN	17.8	37.7	8.8	986	16.8	1 069	38	125 033	6.6	54.8	38.6
Wabash, IN	18.0	20.9	1.7	355	16.9	471	22	52 657	4.4	51.8	43.8
Warren, IN	18.3	20.4	0.4	88	15.6	97	3	9 604	3.8	55.7	40.5
Warrick, IN	16.0	16.9	2.1	474	18.9	345	16	64 026	2.2	48.7	49.0
Washington, IN	16.4	30.1	0.2	256	18.6	365	20	37 137	6.7	58.4	34.9
Wayne, IN	19.4	35.5	7.8	697	16.5	793	42	91 463	6.1	58.5	35.4
Wells, IN	13.4	15.0	3.4	289	17.9	393	22	43 131	3.7	51.9	44.5
White, IN	15.9	31.1	5.9	342	16.4	343	23	44 561	2.5	43.4	54.1
Whitley, IN	11.6	12.3	1.2	281	18.0	307	18	37 437	1.6	55.2	43.2

[2]IEP = Individual Education Program. See Notes and Definitions at the end of this section.

Table C-1. Population, School, and Student Characteristics by County—*Continued*

County	Current expenditures, fiscal 1999			Resident population 16 to 19 years, 2000				Outcomes, 1999–2000	
	Amount ($1,000s)	Amount per student	Percent for instruction	Total population 16 to 19 years	Percent in Armed Forces	Percent high school graduates	Percent not enrolled, not grads, not Armed Forces, not empl.	Number of graduates	Dropouts grades 9–12 (percent)
	21	22	23	24	25	26	27	28	29
Clay, IN	$27 786	$5 901	64.9	1 574	0.3	10.3	7.4	276	...
Clinton, IN	37 807	5 835	61.3	2 077	0.0	11.0	5.7	393	...
Crawford, IN	12 030	6 328	62.7	582	0.0	17.0	4.0	110	...
Daviess, IN	28 423	6 291	65.1	1 704	0.0	9.5	9.7	248	...
Dearborn, IN	53 028	6 018	62.2	2 819	0.0	11.2	6.1	639	...
Decatur, IN	26 569	6 119	63.8	1 235	0.0	17.3	3.1	297	...
De Kalb, IN	48 662	6 526	60.6	2 225	0.0	12.5	2.5	442	...
Delaware, IN	121 680	7 177	60.1	8 631	0.1	6.1	2.4	1 153	...
Dubois, IN	48 866	6 552	64.8	2 132	0.0	13.2	2.0	517	...
Elkhart, IN	215 787	6 747	60.5	10 334	0.1	12.1	7.8	1 646	...
Fayette, IN	35 607	7 821	66.5	1 192	0.0	17.4	8.6	240	...
Floyd, IN	81 438	7 055	64.4	3 882	0.0	8.8	5.1	681	...
Fountain, IN	20 648	6 057	64.5	1 060	0.0	13.0	2.8	245	...
Franklin, IN	16 602	5 579	59.9	1 322	0.4	13.5	6.5	203	...
Fulton, IN	15 321	5 380	62.1	1 120	0.0	12.1	1.8	217	...
Gibson, IN	36 326	7 123	59.5	1 772	0.0	9.3	3.5	383	...
Grant, IN	79 035	6 721	60.7	4 635	0.1	10.8	4.1	660	...
Greene, IN	38 319	6 458	65.5	1 729	0.0	11.6	7.6	347	...
Hamilton, IN	200 841	6 467	60.3	8 025	0.1	6.3	1.7	1 894	...
Hancock, IN	62 017	6 223	60.0	2 726	0.0	9.2	1.0	698	...
Harrison, IN	36 580	5 936	61.6	2 153	0.0	17.7	2.8	430	...
Hendricks, IN	101 869	5 704	58.0	5 661	0.0	9.7	4.1	1 184	...
Henry, IN	58 902	6 826	63.4	2 528	0.0	10.5	7.6	527	...
Howard, IN	101 902	7 283	61.6	4 479	0.5	11.9	5.4	818	...
Huntington, IN	40 418	6 023	62.0	2 324	0.0	11.0	3.1	413	...
Jackson, IN	37 585	5 724	64.2	2 036	0.0	16.6	3.2	408	...
Jasper, IN	28 962	5 894	62.9	2 000	0.0	14.0	1.7	355	...
Jay, IN	26 619	6 687	62.1	1 169	0.0	15.0	2.5	243	...
Jefferson, IN	37 328	7 562	65.5	2 024	0.3	13.4	5.9	337	...
Jennings, IN	26 724	5 536	60.6	1 389	0.2	19.7	7.5	273	...
Johnson, IN	116 865	5 857	61.7	6 470	0.2	11.0	4.2	1 275	...
Knox, IN	39 509	6 408	63.1	3 422	0.0	6.3	4.4	413	...
Kosciusko, IN	90 010	6 347	61.7	4 018	0.0	11.4	5.2	837	...
Lagrange, IN	37 131	5 788	62.2	2 399	0.2	5.4	13.3	316	...
Lake, IN	606 575	7 209	58.1	28 733	0.1	11.5	5.1	4 927	...
La Porte, IN	119 843	6 641	61.3	5 774	0.0	11.5	6.6	1 053	...
Lawrence, IN	46 773	6 225	61.0	2 320	0.0	12.3	6.6	444	...
Madison, IN	132 221	6 493	65.5	7 413	0.0	13.0	4.8	1 163	...
Marion, IN	940 266	7 511	61.3	45 632	0.0	12.6	8.0	6 049	...
Marshall, IN	52 819	6 623	61.9	2 884	0.0	13.1	4.3	576	...
Martin, IN	11 165	5 818	62.2	598	0.0	9.2	2.3	130	...
Miami, IN	45 836	5 983	61.5	2 034	0.0	12.2	7.8	474	...
Monroe, IN	86 279	6 486	59.1	12 966	0.0	5.5	1.7	875	...
Montgomery, IN	42 297	6 372	58.8	2 146	0.0	11.5	5.0	394	...
Morgan, IN	65 733	5 748	62.1	3 889	0.0	10.7	5.6	687	...
Newton, IN	17 883	6 131	58.6	924	0.0	15.8	8.9	204	...
Noble, IN	45 503	5 765	61.3	2 693	0.0	10.7	8.6	494	...
Ohio, IN	5 450	5 364	64.9	294	0.0	16.3	3.1	69	...
Orange, IN	21 266	6 216	64.5	985	0.0	15.9	7.2	197	...
Owen, IN	18 530	5 903	66.6	1 327	0.0	16.4	6.5	185	...
Parke, IN	15 348	5 545	59.4	909	0.0	8.3	5.3	192	...
Perry, IN	20 391	6 060	65.8	1 074	0.0	13.9	11.1	214	...
Pike, IN	14 143	6 334	63.3	693	0.0	8.7	3.9	137	...
Porter, IN	169 942	6 580	59.7	9 342	0.0	9.8	2.6	1 873	...
Posey, IN	34 096	7 225	62.9	1 495	0.0	10.1	3.0	356	...
Pulaski, IN	15 991	6 179	55.9	821	0.6	10.2	2.4	181	...
Putnam, IN	45 995	6 854	57.4	2 567	0.0	6.7	7.3	382	...
Randolph, IN	31 719	6 405	62.9	1 419	0.0	13.3	4.2	353	...
Ripley, IN	34 908	6 420	58.6	1 414	0.0	15.8	3.7	345	...
Rush, IN	16 666	6 074	62.0	965	0.0	8.4	8.2	161	...
St. Joseph, IN	276 641	7 056	63.4	17 831	0.1	8.2	4.6	2 125	...
Scott, IN	24 017	5 864	63.0	1 222	0.0	12.5	9.1	239	...
Shelby, IN	46 066	5 933	63.2	2 308	0.0	16.2	5.6	481	...
Spencer, IN	23 346	5 942	65.0	1 102	0.0	12.3	1.8	261	...
Starke, IN	26 298	5 892	61.4	1 364	0.0	10.8	9.7	263	...
Steuben, IN	30 991	6 133	59.7	2 035	0.4	9.9	1.4	287	...
Sullivan, IN	23 222	6 376	65.7	1 130	0.0	12.7	3.1	258	...
Switzerland, IN	9 721	5 884	59.0	517	0.0	14.1	5.8	97	...
Tippecanoe, IN	125 074	6 669	61.3	14 890	0.0	5.0	2.0	1 149	...
Tipton, IN	17 792	6 035	60.6	887	0.0	10.5	1.9	222	...
Union, IN	8 685	5 525	59.7	361	0.0	17.2	4.2	84	...
Vanderburgh, IN	160 245	6 869	63.1	10 788	0.0	8.9	6.2	1 437	...
Vermillion, IN	18 376	6 248	62.0	967	0.0	11.3	4.4	205	...
Vigo, IN	102 934	6 103	59.3	7 380	0.0	7.5	3.7	939	...
Wabash, IN	42 347	6 839	62.5	2 283	0.0	8.7	2.5	400	...
Warren, IN	8 043	5 918	59.9	422	0.0	6.4	2.8	71	...
Warrick, IN	50 525	5 546	64.9	2 868	0.0	12.5	3.8	608	...
Washington, IN	30 755	6 422	64.3	1 488	0.0	14.9	4.9	297	...
Wayne, IN	75 313	6 366	62.1	4 143	0.0	11.7	7.9	661	...
Wells, IN	34 048	6 442	60.9	1 633	0.0	12.2	2.8	382	...
White, IN	32 667	5 817	59.3	1 331	0.0	11.8	3.8	386	...
Whitley, IN	30 954	6 171	58.6	1 684	0.2	16.9	2.1	332	...

. . . = Not available.

Table C-1. Population, School, and Student Characteristics by County—*Continued*

County	High school graduates, 2000			College enrollment, 2000		College graduates, 2000 (percent)						
	Population 25 years and over	High school diploma or less (percent)	High school diploma or more (percent)	Number	Percent public	Bachelor's degree or more	+/- U.S. percent with bachelor's degree or more	Non-Hispanic White	Black or African American	American Indian and Alaska Native	Asian, Hawaiian, and Pacific Islander	Hispanic or Latino[1]
	30	31	32	33	34	35	36	37	38	39	40	41
Clay, IN	17 304	63.3	82.3	872	88.1	12.8	-11.6	12.8	15.4	0.0	40.6	13.2
Clinton, IN	21 744	70.2	80.1	726	75.2	10.1	-14.3	10.2	0.0	0.0	37.9	5.0
Crawford, IN	7 088	74.5	70.6	224	79.9	8.4	-16.0	8.3	0.0	31.6	0.0	10.0
Daviess, IN	18 655	68.1	71.8	653	91.3	9.7	-14.7	9.6	0.0	14.1	65.8	0.7
Dearborn, IN	29 712	59.2	82.0	1 518	73.6	15.4	-9.0	15.3	13.4	56.0	16.9	25.3
Decatur, IN	15 948	68.4	79.1	647	83.2	11.5	-12.9	11.1	0.0	0.0	51.8	6.7
De Kalb, IN	25 500	61.2	84.7	1 537	80.1	12.4	-12.0	12.3	14.3	0.0	12.1	18.0
Delaware, IN	72 444	55.6	81.6	16 227	96.4	20.4	-4.0	20.7	11.1	3.3	68.8	26.1
Dubois, IN	25 733	64.3	80.2	1 112	85.3	14.5	-9.9	14.6	0.0	0.0	78.6	9.4
Elkhart, IN	112 908	61.3	75.7	5 271	70.4	15.5	-8.9	16.6	5.9	1.6	36.3	5.4
Fayette, IN	17 125	72.8	73.7	734	91.3	7.8	-16.6	7.9	0.0	18.2	0.0	9.8
Floyd, IN	46 609	50.7	82.4	3 412	88.1	20.4	-4.0	20.6	13.4	2.9	53.0	13.0
Fountain, IN	11 914	66.8	80.7	415	80.5	10.1	-14.3	10.2	0.0	9.1	0.0	0.0
Franklin, IN	14 218	68.1	76.1	684	67.7	12.5	-11.9	12.6	0.0	0.0	10.3	13.9
Fulton, IN	13 613	69.0	80.2	503	83.1	10.3	-14.1	10.5	0.0	30.2	38.9	3.8
Gibson, IN	21 694	60.1	80.9	1 215	64.6	12.4	-12.0	12.3	2.2	0.0	63.2	11.9
Grant, IN	47 408	62.7	79.2	5 296	27.9	14.1	-10.3	14.4	7.4	22.7	53.2	5.7
Greene, IN	22 396	64.3	79.2	1 162	89.7	10.5	-13.9	10.5	0.0	0.0	31.3	8.9
Hamilton, IN	116 457	25.6	94.2	7 048	77.2	48.9	24.5	48.6	48.8	13.7	69.5	43.9
Hancock, IN	37 073	49.7	87.8	2 262	70.7	22.2	-2.2	22.1	29.2	20.9	38.6	39.0
Harrison, IN	22 457	60.8	80.3	1 159	82.0	13.1	-11.3	13.1	0.0	2.1	42.5	7.7
Hendricks, IN	67 683	48.7	88.5	3 655	75.6	23.1	-1.3	23.1	13.5	11.2	55.0	19.8
Henry, IN	33 198	64.8	79.6	1 428	84.1	11.7	-12.7	11.7	8.1	0.0	40.4	4.0
Howard, IN	56 222	54.7	83.3	2 932	85.7	18.1	-6.3	18.0	13.3	41.8	57.5	14.2
Huntington, IN	24 386	61.7	85.0	1 885	51.9	14.2	-10.2	14.1	74.1	6.6	39.1	16.6
Jackson, IN	27 131	66.9	79.8	1 091	86.5	11.5	-12.9	11.3	7.8	16.3	35.2	11.1
Jasper, IN	18 751	64.0	82.4	1 392	46.3	13.0	-11.4	13.2	47.6	0.0	27.8	4.4
Jay, IN	14 280	71.0	78.5	526	88.0	9.9	-14.5	9.8	0.0	25.0	22.2	5.3
Jefferson, IN	20 605	59.1	81.0	2 077	44.1	16.4	-8.0	16.5	7.8	0.0	42.9	20.9
Jennings, IN	17 709	70.8	76.2	734	79.0	8.4	-16.0	8.0	17.1	16.9	73.3	9.3
Johnson, IN	73 966	50.5	85.7	4 952	66.3	23.1	-1.3	22.9	22.1	1.5	56.3	17.5
Knox, IN	24 865	55.6	81.7	3 756	95.1	14.4	-10.0	14.2	26.9	0.0	27.7	25.5
Kosciusko, IN	47 103	60.5	81.6	2 247	69.4	14.9	-9.5	15.1	15.0	13.1	18.4	8.1
Lagrange, IN	19 519	73.7	60.2	568	78.9	8.9	-15.5	8.9	0.0	0.0	35.9	3.2
Lake, IN	310 220	56.6	80.7	24 644	78.0	16.2	-8.2	18.7	10.8	3.2	58.6	8.5
La Porte, IN	73 723	60.4	80.6	4 525	83.9	14.0	-10.4	14.9	6.3	13.0	30.1	7.3
Lawrence, IN	31 175	69.0	77.4	979	85.8	10.7	-13.7	10.6	10.5	0.0	61.3	20.2
Madison, IN	89 458	59.9	80.1	5 680	59.2	14.4	-10.0	15.0	8.4	4.9	13.9	11.7
Marion, IN	553 459	48.0	81.6	45 864	69.8	25.4	1.0	28.7	13.6	12.2	55.8	14.2
Marshall, IN	28 555	61.3	79.8	1 346	75.2	14.9	-9.5	15.4	40.9	15.4	16.9	4.8
Martin, IN	7 066	68.1	74.2	199	80.4	8.8	-15.6	8.9	0.0	0.0	0.0	0.0
Miami, IN	23 741	64.3	81.9	1 208	89.2	10.4	-14.0	10.7	5.2	3.4	60.0	0.6
Monroe, IN	65 489	37.7	88.5	34 916	96.7	39.6	15.2	38.0	36.8	37.4	81.4	59.7
Montgomery, IN	24 501	61.2	85.7	1 508	45.8	14.7	-9.7	14.5	25.4	30.3	0.0	18.1
Morgan, IN	43 397	64.3	80.7	1 800	72.6	12.6	-11.8	12.4	72.0	1.6	30.5	30.9
Newton, IN	9 576	71.1	78.7	243	84.4	9.6	-14.8	9.7	0.0	0.0	28.6	3.5
Noble, IN	28 554	66.3	77.3	1 061	74.0	11.1	-13.3	11.4	17.0	0.0	7.5	4.6
Ohio, IN	3 780	66.3	78.4	169	71.0	11.6	-12.8	11.7	0.0	. . .	. . .	23.5
Orange, IN	12 818	71.4	73.8	471	91.1	10.2	-14.2	10.2	0.0	0.0	0.0	32.6
Owen, IN	14 384	68.6	74.9	495	85.5	9.2	-15.2	9.0	0.0	0.0	29.2	14.5
Parke, IN	11 891	65.1	80.5	488	87.9	11.6	-12.8	11.7	4.2	24.6	22.7	9.4
Perry, IN	12 734	70.7	74.8	608	72.5	9.6	-14.8	9.5	7.2	0.0	0.0	24.4
Pike, IN	8 753	69.9	75.6	333	82.3	8.4	-16.0	8.5	0.0	0.0	0.0	13.2
Porter, IN	94 462	49.8	88.3	8 959	53.7	22.6	-1.8	22.7	38.1	20.7	45.7	12.7
Posey, IN	17 671	57.4	84.4	1 022	90.5	14.8	-9.6	14.9	9.7	7.3	33.3	14.1
Pulaski, IN	9 038	65.3	79.8	403	71.0	10.3	-14.1	10.4	10.6	0.0	0.0	5.1
Putnam, IN	22 740	67.0	81.2	2 674	18.6	13.1	-11.3	13.4	2.3	0.0	42.7	8.9
Randolph, IN	18 310	67.9	79.6	660	89.8	9.9	-14.5	9.9	0.0	48.3	57.7	0.0
Ripley, IN	17 027	67.9	78.9	770	73.8	11.5	-12.9	11.3	. . .	36.5	51.4	14.3
Rush, IN	12 020	71.3	79.6	450	83.6	10.3	-14.1	10.1	0.0	0.0	100.0	26.1
St. Joseph, IN	166 060	50.1	82.4	22 170	40.3	23.6	-0.8	25.0	10.8	8.6	59.0	12.1
Scott, IN	14 760	71.1	71.4	582	86.8	8.8	-15.6	8.7	0.0	21.7	100.0	14.3
Shelby, IN	28 351	64.9	79.8	1 443	78.5	12.7	-11.7	12.6	13.3	72.1	28.2	0.0
Spencer, IN	13 491	61.6	81.2	573	79.6	13.0	-11.4	13.0	4.6	0.0	91.7	1.9
Starke, IN	15 290	71.5	72.0	616	77.6	8.4	-16.0	8.2	0.0	0.0	58.1	1.8
Steuben, IN	21 170	58.7	84.3	1 935	40.7	15.5	-8.9	15.5	10.7	0.0	63.2	19.4
Sullivan, IN	14 782	63.6	80.8	825	84.2	9.4	-15.0	10.0	0.0	0.0	0.0	7.6
Switzerland, IN	5 889	73.1	71.4	184	83.2	7.6	-16.8	7.3	. . .	0.0	90.5	0.0
Tippecanoe, IN	79 911	42.7	87.8	36 162	96.3	33.2	8.8	31.6	29.4	12.4	81.7	18.8
Tipton, IN	11 247	64.7	83.7	490	80.4	12.4	-12.0	12.4	. . .	0.0	5.1	1.3
Union, IN	4 784	65.7	79.9	227	88.1	11.1	-13.3	11.0	0.0	0.0	63.6	. . .
Vanderburgh, IN	112 178	52.6	83.1	12 739	76.6	19.3	-5.1	19.9	7.0	7.1	54.8	16.6
Vermillion, IN	11 410	64.0	81.2	618	88.8	11.2	-13.2	11.3	0.0	0.0	26.9	9.5
Vigo, IN	66 714	53.8	81.0	11 618	82.5	21.4	-3.0	21.4	15.2	8.0	66.0	15.0
Wabash, IN	22 744	64.3	81.7	1 794	37.7	13.7	-10.7	13.8	23.5	5.1	32.8	0.0
Warren, IN	5 648	61.7	85.0	239	86.2	14.0	-10.4	14.2	. . .	0.0	0.0	0.0
Warrick, IN	34 571	47.3	86.3	2 181	85.7	21.8	-2.6	21.6	30.0	22.7	54.9	10.7
Washington, IN	17 648	68.9	75.2	809	91.1	10.2	-14.2	10.1	0.0	0.0	25.0	21.0
Wayne, IN	47 322	61.4	78.1	3 686	67.5	13.7	-10.7	13.9	8.4	0.0	33.5	13.1
Wells, IN	17 767	59.2	87.3	904	73.5	14.3	-10.1	14.4	13.3	15.0	47.6	2.9
White, IN	16 829	65.6	82.1	511	89.0	10.5	-13.9	10.5	55.6	12.1	56.2	4.7
Whitley, IN	19 995	59.2	86.2	905	82.1	13.3	-11.1	13.2	21.4	26.3	5.3	13.5

[1]Hispanic or Latino persons may be of any race.
. . . = Not available.

Table C-1. Population, School, and Student Characteristics by County—*Continued*

County	State/ County code	County type[1]	Population, 2000		Number of schools and students, 2000–2001			Resident enrollment, 2000			
			Total	Percent 5–17 years	School districts	Schools	Students	Total	Percent public	K–12	Percent public
			1	2	3	4	5	6	7	8	9
IOWA	19000										
Adair, IA	19001	8	8 243	18.5	2	6	1 193	1 856	94.4	1 524	98.2
Adams, IA	19003	9	4 482	18.4	2	4	704	1 039	96.6	802	96.8
Allamakee, IA	19005	7	14 675	19.6	3	10	2 575	3 436	87.7	2 922	89.6
Appanoose, IA	19007	7	13 721	18.2	3	12	2 353	3 296	92.3	2 593	95.7
Audubon, IA	19009	7	6 830	20.1	2	5	1 145	1 616	97.0	1 384	99.0
Benton, IA	19011	6	25 308	20.9	3	15	4 273	6 744	91.0	5 344	96.2
Black Hawk, IA	19013	3	128 012	17.0	5	40	17 349	40 461	87.0	22 272	84.1
Boone, IA	19015	6	26 224	18.8	5	17	4 202	6 393	91.4	4 980	94.4
Bremer, IA	19017	6	23 325	18.6	6	24	4 981	6 970	75.3	4 434	95.2
Buchanan, IA	19019	6	21 093	21.7	3	15	3 113	5 468	88.0	4 565	90.0
Buena Vista, IA	19021	7	20 411	19.5	5	18	3 810	5 960	72.1	4 165	87.9
Butler, IA	19023	8	15 305	18.9	5	10	2 101	3 667	95.0	2 989	97.4
Calhoun, IA	19025	9	11 115	17.9	4	14	2 428	2 485	95.2	2 081	96.7
Carroll, IA	19027	7	21 421	20.9	4	12	3 373	5 715	69.9	4 556	69.7
Cass, IA	19029	6	14 684	18.3	4	11	2 919	3 431	93.1	2 815	98.6
Cedar, IA	19031	6	18 187	19.3	5	15	3 670	4 574	94.1	3 549	98.5
Cerro Gordo, IA	19033	5	46 447	17.8	5	21	6 935	11 271	86.8	8 435	88.7
Cherokee, IA	19035	7	13 035	19.1	3	12	2 156	2 998	94.9	2 556	98.2
Chickasaw, IA	19037	7	13 095	20.4	3	9	2 538	3 365	86.4	2 675	87.7
Clarke, IA	19039	6	9 133	19.9	2	5	1 878	2 192	94.2	1 843	99.1
Clay, IA	19041	7	17 372	18.6	3	11	2 822	4 161	91.5	3 230	93.2
Clayton, IA	19043	9	18 678	19.6	5	15	3 397	4 406	90.9	3 812	94.0
Clinton, IA	19045	4	50 149	19.2	6	23	8 623	12 977	86.9	9 837	93.2
Crawford, IA	19047	7	16 942	20.2	4	11	2 690	4 224	88.0	3 525	90.4
Dallas, IA	19049	2	40 750	19.9	7	24	8 629	10 346	86.7	8 120	93.4
Davis, IA	19051	7	8 541	20.1	1	3	1 304	2 038	83.8	1 670	84.7
Decatur, IA	19053	9	8 689	17.5	3	8	1 456	2 733	64.7	1 531	92.7
Delaware, IA	19055	6	18 404	22.6	3	12	3 535	5 181	83.6	4 200	86.2
Des Moines, IA	19057	5	42 351	18.1	4	23	6 965	10 167	85.5	7 642	89.6
Dickinson, IA	19059	7	16 424	16.6	4	10	2 800	3 611	94.2	2 760	98.6
Dubuque, IA	19061	3	89 143	18.9	2	27	12 484	24 497	60.9	17 029	71.7
Emmet, IA	19063	7	11 027	18.8	2	8	1 944	2 916	93.8	2 159	95.0
Fayette, IA	19065	6	22 008	19.0	5	16	4 273	5 850	86.1	4 351	95.2
Floyd, IA	19067	7	16 900	18.9	3	9	2 897	4 072	87.7	3 255	91.4
Franklin, IA	19069	7	10 704	18.6	3	11	1 861	2 506	94.7	2 067	97.2
Fremont, IA	19071	9	8 010	19.5	4	8	1 613	1 936	96.2	1 588	98.7
Greene, IA	19073	7	10 366	19.8	3	9	2 088	2 518	92.6	2 143	95.2
Grundy, IA	19075	8	12 369	19.8	4	12	2 501	3 156	93.9	2 530	96.5
Guthrie, IA	19077	8	11 353	18.0	4	10	2 354	2 510	94.6	2 110	98.2
Hamilton, IA	19079	7	16 438	19.0	4	11	2 914	4 022	90.3	3 100	93.2
Hancock, IA	19081	7	12 100	20.4	4	11	2 039	3 128	90.9	2 584	95.8
Hardin, IA	19083	7	18 812	19.0	5	14	3 252	4 772	95.0	3 602	98.1
Harrison, IA	19085	6	15 666	20.2	5	13	3 334	3 914	92.1	3 208	96.7
Henry, IA	19087	7	20 336	18.7	4	12	3 800	5 245	83.1	3 950	93.3
Howard, IA	19089	7	9 932	20.3	2	8	2 023	2 395	84.1	1 961	86.4
Humboldt, IA	19091	7	10 381	19.4	3	8	1 888	2 621	88.0	2 040	90.5
Ida, IA	19093	8	7 837	20.0	2	9	1 399	1 914	96.0	1 640	97.6
Iowa, IA	19095	8	15 671	20.2	5	10	2 907	3 952	89.1	3 199	90.9
Jackson, IA	19097	6	20 296	20.1	5	14	3 522	5 091	85.0	4 218	87.2
Jasper, IA	19099	6	37 213	18.4	5	20	6 381	8 568	90.2	6 798	94.7
Jefferson, IA	19101	7	16 181	19.0	1	7	2 038	4 260	71.0	3 191	79.9
Johnson, IA	19103	3	111 006	14.3	4	29	13 185	45 029	91.6	16 189	89.9
Jones, IA	19105	6	20 221	18.5	4	14	3 456	4 977	88.9	3 906	93.7
Keokuk, IA	19107	9	11 400	19.8	4	10	2 317	2 751	97.3	2 307	99.2
Kossuth, IA	19109	7	17 163	20.4	5	13	2 411	4 259	80.0	3 502	80.2
Lee, IA	19111	5	38 052	18.4	3	17	5 942	8 838	84.6	7 169	86.1
Linn, IA	19113	3	191 701	18.3	11	72	32 929	51 126	80.5	35 536	88.6
Louisa, IA	19115	8	12 183	20.5	4	10	2 960	3 131	96.0	2 529	98.6
Lucas, IA	19117	6	9 422	19.3	2	7	1 552	2 236	90.7	1 852	94.7
Lyon, IA	19119	6	11 763	21.3	4	10	1 950	3 024	85.7	2 574	88.3
Madison, IA	19121	6	14 019	20.1	3	11	2 961	3 444	92.3	2 823	98.0
Mahaska, IA	19123	7	22 335	19.1	3	12	3 370	5 587	82.0	4 223	88.4
Marion, IA	19125	6	32 052	19.1	5	18	5 991	8 619	74.7	6 153	90.1
Marshall, IA	19127	5	39 311	18.8	3	16	6 658	9 625	90.8	7 783	93.4
Mills, IA	19129	6	14 547	20.4	3	10	2 768	3 900	90.5	3 041	95.7
Mitchell, IA	19131	7	10 874	20.4	2	7	1 856	2 586	88.7	2 183	89.5
Monona, IA	19133	6	10 020	17.9	4	11	1 602	2 215	94.4	1 850	97.7
Monroe, IA	19135	7	8 016	19.0	1	4	1 268	1 956	93.9	1 540	96.2
Montgomery, IA	19137	6	11 771	18.9	3	11	2 075	2 706	93.2	2 186	97.8
Muscatine, IA	19139	4	41 722	20.0	3	17	7 557	10 777	92.2	8 391	95.8
O'Brien, IA	19141	7	15 102	18.9	3	11	2 744	3 545	83.1	2 939	84.5
Osceola, IA	19143	7	7 003	20.2	1	4	956	1 719	88.7	1 466	90.9
Page, IA	19145	7	16 976	17.7	4	15	2 939	3 956	91.7	3 201	94.1
Palo Alto, IA	19147	7	10 147	18.6	4	13	1 839	2 695	87.6	1 937	88.8
Plymouth, IA	19149	6	24 849	21.7	5	19	4 471	6 856	80.1	5 590	82.1
Pocahontas, IA	19151	9	8 662	20.5	2	9	1 321	2 189	89.6	1 826	91.7
Polk, IA	19153	2	374 601	18.2	9	119	62 079	96 530	80.2	68 002	90.5
Pottawattamie, IA	19155	2	87 704	19.4	8	44	17 536	21 969	89.5	16 929	92.7
Poweshiek, IA	19157	7	18 815	17.1	3	10	3 071	5 335	73.5	3 304	98.2
Ringgold, IA	19159	9	5 469	18.2	2	4	933	1 271	90.4	996	91.8

[1]County type code is from the Economic Research Service of the USDA. See Notes and Definitions at the end of this section.

Table C-1. School and Student Characteristics by County—*Continued*

County	Characteristics of students, 2000–2001			Staff and students, 2000–2001				Revenues, fiscal 1999			
	Percent with IEP[2]	Percent eligible for free lunch	Percent minority	Number of teachers	Student/ teacher ratio	Local school non-teaching staff	Central admin. staff	Total revenue ($1,000s)	Percentage of revenue from		
									Federal govt.	State govt.	Local govt.
	10	11	12	13	14	15	16	17	18	19	20
IOWA											
Adair, IA	16.6	31.7	1.7	66	18.1	77	7	$10 030	5.8	41.9	52.3
Adams, IA	16.9	30.8	0.3	43	16.4	49	5	5 419	5.6	50.0	44.4
Allamakee, IA	13.8	29.1	3.7	187	13.8	154	13	18 485	4.9	54.5	40.7
Appanoose, IA	16.8	38.9	3.6	198	11.9	139	9	17 610	7.1	54.1	38.7
Audubon, IA	10.1	28.6	2.0	89	12.9	90	10	7 967	4.1	48.3	47.5
Benton, IA	13.9	20.1	1.5	323	13.2	282	14	28 582	3.2	56.7	40.1
Black Hawk, IA	15.7	39.1	21.0	1 085	16.0	1 276	48	153 451	10.2	42.7	47.1
Boone, IA	14.2	21.5	2.0	323	13.0	253	20	31 105	2.9	50.1	47.1
Bremer, IA	11.6	16.0	1.3	342	14.6	227	22	34 602	3.1	53.0	43.9
Buchanan, IA	13.9	24.2	2.0	232	13.4	155	15	22 569	4.5	52.3	43.2
Buena Vista, IA	12.9	37.1	25.0	282	13.5	229	20	28 529	5.6	49.2	45.2
Butler, IA	11.3	22.6	0.9	164	12.8	98	19	16 195	2.4	46.7	50.9
Calhoun, IA	10.6	28.3	1.7	209	11.6	136	17	18 888	4.1	45.4	50.5
Carroll, IA	11.2	25.0	2.5	293	11.5	235	15	23 676	3.6	45.4	51.0
Cass, IA	14.2	31.1	2.0	215	13.6	181	14	21 616	4.7	49.3	46.1
Cedar, IA	10.8	16.5	2.0	271	13.5	211	18	25 597	2.8	47.1	50.1
Cerro Gordo, IA	17.1	30.2	8.2	515	13.5	548	63	61 494	7.1	42.8	50.1
Cherokee, IA	13.1	20.0	3.2	151	14.3	136	12	16 834	4.1	48.7	47.2
Chickasaw, IA	11.0	22.2	2.0	190	13.4	147	13	16 998	3.8	51.6	44.6
Clarke, IA	14.5	34.2	6.7	112	16.8	112	8	11 869	5.6	55.2	39.2
Clay, IA	12.5	22.5	3.4	204	13.8	183	9	19 508	3.0	51.5	45.5
Clayton, IA	14.3	27.9	1.7	269	12.6	379	43	38 367	12.4	34.9	52.6
Clinton, IA	15.5	28.6	6.6	611	14.1	558	33	63 657	3.5	52.5	44.0
Crawford, IA	12.4	37.3	11.5	192	14.0	156	13	19 520	5.2	51.0	43.8
Dallas, IA	11.6	17.0	8.4	610	14.1	467	37	57 492	2.5	48.4	49.1
Davis, IA	16.4	32.9	2.0	95	13.7	63	6	8 773	6.7	55.4	37.8
Decatur, IA	19.3	39.1	2.3	129	11.3	103	11	12 323	7.6	53.1	39.3
Delaware, IA	10.2	22.7	1.1	217	16.3	183	14	24 371	3.7	53.7	42.6
Des Moines, IA	16.7	36.7	11.7	492	14.2	515	36	58 833	6.9	47.1	46.0
Dickinson, IA	12.6	18.1	2.1	211	13.3	181	17	20 246	3.3	39.1	57.7
Dubuque, IA	17.6	24.6	4.6	844	14.8	775	30	84 992	4.4	52.0	43.6
Emmet, IA	15.5	33.0	7.9	149	13.0	209	19	15 092	4.0	53.2	42.7
Fayette, IA	13.7	33.1	2.6	299	14.3	240	24	30 421	5.3	54.8	39.9
Floyd, IA	14.9	31.8	3.1	221	13.1	187	12	21 805	4.8	52.0	43.1
Franklin, IA	13.2	27.4	8.8	135	13.8	123	12	13 905	3.3	48.6	48.0
Fremont, IA	13.2	32.5	1.5	124	13.0	90	12	11 987	4.6	45.9	49.5
Greene, IA	13.0	30.8	2.7	168	12.4	116	10	14 840	4.4	47.5	48.1
Grundy, IA	12.2	21.0	2.8	174	14.4	121	15	18 791	2.4	43.9	53.7
Guthrie, IA	11.6	27.6	1.5	169	13.9	154	14	16 496	3.6	46.6	49.8
Hamilton, IA	12.7	21.4	4.7	224	13.0	188	15	22 766	2.9	44.1	53.0
Hancock, IA	13.4	24.6	3.6	166	12.3	121	13	15 557	2.8	47.9	49.3
Hardin, IA	11.2	27.2	5.3	246	13.2	187	17	25 986	3.6	46.0	50.5
Harrison, IA	14.1	29.1	1.1	241	13.8	237	19	23 874	4.2	50.3	45.6
Henry, IA	12.7	24.7	6.1	277	13.7	166	17	26 782	2.6	49.1	48.3
Howard, IA	17.2	26.9	1.9	164	12.3	111	8	15 024	4.1	48.9	47.0
Humboldt, IA	10.2	20.6	1.7	139	13.6	108	7	14 353	3.1	45.8	51.0
Ida, IA	13.2	25.8	2.0	114	12.3	88	8	10 443	3.6	48.3	48.0
Iowa, IA	14.5	17.3	2.6	213	13.6	145	15	23 328	2.4	42.3	55.3
Jackson, IA	14.6	28.4	1.7	292	12.1	228	25	25 372	4.8	52.3	43.0
Jasper, IA	13.2	16.5	2.1	474	13.5	357	22	44 275	2.7	50.4	46.9
Jefferson, IA	12.0	22.5	5.6	156	13.1	136	6	14 076	3.4	49.8	46.9
Johnson, IA	12.5	17.0	16.0	788	16.7	685	39	93 717	2.5	43.3	54.2
Jones, IA	14.2	24.6	2.7	281	12.3	244	15	25 284	3.6	50.9	45.5
Keokuk, IA	16.7	24.4	1.6	208	11.1	137	14	17 427	3.4	48.3	48.3
Kossuth, IA	18.9	30.2	2.6	204	11.8	182	18	20 818	3.6	44.0	52.5
Lee, IA	15.7	37.0	8.5	438	13.6	343	17	42 881	5.0	54.6	40.4
Linn, IA	14.3	20.4	9.5	2 093	15.7	2 650	312	231 925	2.6	46.4	51.0
Louisa, IA	11.4	32.3	21.0	230	12.9	180	17	22 401	3.5	47.4	49.1
Lucas, IA	14.4	36.2	1.4	122	12.7	105	5	11 312	4.0	55.1	40.8
Lyon, IA	14.7	20.6	1.4	148	13.2	91	11	16 452	3.5	45.3	51.2
Madison, IA	12.4	19.4	1.2	193	15.3	148	16	20 058	2.9	53.8	43.3
Mahaska, IA	12.7	29.6	3.4	209	16.1	185	9	22 014	3.3	55.5	41.2
Marion, IA	11.8	17.9	3.5	402	14.9	368	22	39 932	2.8	52.5	44.8
Marshall, IA	14.8	36.0	19.5	432	15.4	587	37	56 544	6.9	47.2	45.9
Mills, IA	13.8	29.2	2.9	214	12.9	178	12	20 769	4.5	48.1	47.4
Mitchell, IA	12.0	22.5	1.3	127	14.6	109	6	12 645	2.9	50.0	47.0
Monona, IA	17.4	30.5	2.3	111	14.4	100	12	13 019	6.0	46.8	47.2
Monroe, IA	15.2	32.9	3.3	95	13.3	63	4	9 019	4.2	56.5	39.3
Montgomery, IA	15.6	32.3	0.6	149	13.9	119	13	14 373	4.8	55.1	40.1
Muscatine, IA	14.5	32.8	22.2	532	14.2	412	14	52 218	4.8	53.7	41.5
O'Brien, IA	15.5	25.5	4.0	193	14.2	292	23	20 476	3.6	49.0	47.4
Osceola, IA	15.2	22.2	4.2	67	14.3	55	4	7 191	3.0	48.5	48.5
Page, IA	12.0	27.5	6.6	244	12.0	182	17	20 919	5.2	48.0	46.8
Palo Alto, IA	16.4	28.6	2.5	164	11.2	136	15	19 848	10.1	35.2	54.7
Plymouth, IA	9.7	16.5	3.5	325	13.8	198	22	29 767	3.0	47.1	50.0
Pocahontas, IA	14.2	29.4	2.8	115	11.5	74	6	10 042	3.5	49.0	47.5
Polk, IA	13.2	28.4	17.8	4 079	15.2	3 277	148	497 875	5.5	43.2	51.2
Pottawattamie, IA	13.4	29.5	6.3	1 153	15.2	1 035	69	127 256	6.3	50.7	43.1
Poweshiek, IA	13.1	22.8	3.8	237	13.0	179	11	21 536	3.1	49.5	47.4
Ringgold, IA	18.0	38.8	1.4	77	12.1	39	7	8 612	5.6	49.8	44.6

[2]IEP = Individual Education Program. See Notes and Definitions at the end of this section.

Table C-1. Population, School, and Student Characteristics by County—*Continued*

County	Current expenditures, fiscal 1999			Resident population 16 to 19 years, 2000				Outcomes, 1999–2000	
	Amount ($1,000s)	Amount per student	Percent for instruction	Total population 16 to 19 years	Percent in Armed Forces	Percent high school graduates	Percent not enrolled, not grads, not Armed Forces, not empl.	Number of graduates	Dropouts grades 9–12 (percent)
	21	22	23	24	25	26	27	28	29
IOWA									
Adair, IA	$7 456	$6 052	59.6	427	0.0	6.3	3.3	86	3.5
Adams, IA	4 310	5 864	61.4	202	0.0	7.9	2.0	50	2.6
Allamakee, IA	15 228	5 521	63.6	797	0.0	8.4	1.0	226	1.3
Appanoose, IA	14 398	6 002	64.3	786	0.0	9.0	4.6	155	1.8
Audubon, IA	6 704	5 830	59.6	338	0.0	9.8	0.6	65	1.4
Benton, IA	23 582	5 429	61.7	1 402	0.0	12.6	1.2	276	1.4
Black Hawk, IA	132 556	7 932	50.6	8 922	0.2	7.8	2.3	1 183	2.8
Boone, IA	24 366	5 852	62.8	1 533	0.0	10.2	1.5	288	2.0
Bremer, IA	26 506	4 985	59.3	1 796	0.2	7.2	0.4	418	1.8
Buchanan, IA	18 226	5 515	64.3	1 202	0.0	6.7	7.8	283	1.1
Buena Vista, IA	22 957	5 886	61.0	1 487	0.3	5.0	4.2	312	2.5
Butler, IA	12 119	5 645	60.0	854	0.0	7.1	0.5	172	0.3
Calhoun, IA	15 199	5 986	58.4	604	0.0	7.1	1.2	173	1.4
Carroll, IA	19 165	5 560	59.7	1 344	0.0	8.5	1.1	239	0.8
Cass, IA	17 394	5 682	61.3	821	0.0	12.4	3.0	238	1.7
Cedar, IA	20 249	5 552	60.7	1 128	0.3	11.1	0.8	271	1.9
Cerro Gordo, IA	50 586	6 984	52.9	2 655	0.0	8.4	1.7	442	2.9
Cherokee, IA	13 957	5 922	62.1	796	0.0	9.2	0.9	181	1.7
Chickasaw, IA	14 058	5 249	62.6	726	0.0	7.9	2.5	203	1.5
Clarke, IA	10 399	5 546	60.2	464	0.0	14.2	5.8	117	1.6
Clay, IA	16 631	5 613	64.2	993	0.0	11.5	1.2	211	0.8
Clayton, IA	34 984	9 707	37.2	1 085	0.0	9.2	1.4	312	0.9
Clinton, IA	52 432	5 904	63.2	2 828	0.0	7.8	4.4	615	3.2
Crawford, IA	15 704	5 942	62.8	1 054	0.0	5.9	7.6	179	0.8
Dallas, IA	45 807	5 632	61.9	2 066	0.0	8.5	3.1	516	1.8
Davis, IA	7 168	5 776	60.6	511	0.0	4.5	5.9	95	3.5
Decatur, IA	9 236	6 283	58.6	735	0.0	9.9	3.4	99	5.8
Delaware, IA	19 567	5 308	61.2	1 122	0.0	7.3	2.2	292	3.0
Des Moines, IA	48 114	6 745	57.7	2 397	0.0	11.3	3.3	493	4.5
Dickinson, IA	16 179	5 614	63.4	772	0.3	5.1	1.8	226	1.2
Dubuque, IA	76 162	6 167	61.7	5 357	0.1	8.3	1.2	978	2.2
Emmet, IA	12 601	6 198	63.5	834	0.0	6.5	0.8	163	1.9
Fayette, IA	26 361	6 005	61.6	1 379	0.0	5.7	2.2	350	1.1
Floyd, IA	18 553	6 113	63.3	920	0.0	12.7	3.8	227	2.7
Franklin, IA	11 705	5 888	60.1	643	0.0	5.3	2.5	184	2.2
Fremont, IA	9 439	5 690	62.5	430	1.2	10.0	4.0	124	1.4
Greene, IA	12 044	5 684	60.5	585	0.0	3.8	5.0	170	2.2
Grundy, IA	14 558	5 734	58.1	661	0.0	8.3	1.1	155	1.7
Guthrie, IA	13 390	5 725	58.9	568	0.0	10.2	1.1	192	1.2
Hamilton, IA	17 594	5 801	60.0	859	0.0	7.2	0.8	217	0.4
Hancock, IA	12 771	6 076	59.7	746	0.0	8.2	0.4	197	2.2
Hardin, IA	21 187	6 060	62.9	1 236	0.0	9.0	1.9	333	2.0
Harrison, IA	18 958	5 555	59.5	902	0.0	9.9	2.4	283	1.6
Henry, IA	20 839	5 385	61.4	1 126	0.0	8.1	2.6	309	0.6
Howard, IA	11 998	5 659	59.3	546	0.0	9.5	5.3	189	3.5
Humboldt, IA	10 657	5 527	61.1	603	0.0	7.1	0.0	150	0.7
Ida, IA	8 654	5 832	61.6	456	0.0	10.1	0.4	114	0.2
Iowa, IA	16 299	5 605	62.7	840	0.0	10.6	0.8	216	0.2
Jackson, IA	21 904	6 081	63.8	1 134	0.0	8.6	1.7	279	2.2
Jasper, IA	35 890	5 543	61.4	1 872	0.0	10.7	1.2	395	4.5
Jefferson, IA	12 263	5 582	59.8	942	0.0	6.8	4.8	152	4.3
Johnson, IA	76 019	5 814	60.9	9 749	0.2	5.4	0.9	902	1.1
Jones, IA	19 781	5 732	59.5	1 058	0.0	8.4	3.0	253	1.7
Keokuk, IA	14 249	5 804	62.8	596	0.0	12.2	1.8	188	1.5
Kossuth, IA	17 227	6 543	63.7	1 072	0.9	8.1	1.7	201	0.7
Lee, IA	36 461	5 842	66.5	1 967	0.0	10.8	2.7	429	3.0
Linn, IA	187 249	5 791	59.7	11 277	0.0	10.4	2.2	1 965	2.5
Louisa, IA	17 466	6 056	63.7	704	0.0	6.3	8.7	175	5.9
Lucas, IA	8 665	5 523	63.8	591	0.0	9.5	7.4	112	2.1
Lyon, IA	12 294	5 843	62.0	763	0.0	10.6	1.0	189	1.0
Madison, IA	16 069	5 312	58.9	758	0.7	13.5	3.4	195	0.8
Mahaska, IA	18 000	5 362	62.3	1 416	0.0	10.2	4.7	221	4.3
Marion, IA	32 151	5 427	61.7	2 152	0.0	7.6	0.4	401	2.4
Marshall, IA	49 014	6 907	53.5	2 313	0.0	10.1	5.5	441	2.0
Mills, IA	16 953	6 178	61.8	778	0.0	8.6	1.8	189	2.4
Mitchell, IA	10 781	5 787	61.7	563	0.0	8.5	2.0	148	1.8
Monona, IA	10 084	5 918	61.0	534	0.0	8.6	4.9	130	3.0
Monroe, IA	7 754	5 689	61.2	477	0.0	13.0	1.0	99	0.5
Montgomery, IA	12 138	5 766	61.1	664	0.0	5.6	6.5	139	3.4
Muscatine, IA	43 612	5 776	68.5	2 300	0.0	9.7	6.5	502	3.2
O'Brien, IA	16 294	5 671	62.7	933	0.0	8.9	2.6	224	2.4
Osceola, IA	5 694	5 326	62.7	366	0.0	7.1	4.4	74	0.6
Page, IA	17 813	5 833	62.3	939	0.4	13.5	3.4	214	3.7
Palo Alto, IA	17 776	9 107	43.7	707	0.0	5.4	1.3	157	0.8
Plymouth, IA	24 570	5 382	60.5	1 610	0.0	9.2	0.9	344	1.3
Pocahontas, IA	8 307	5 862	62.3	473	0.0	7.4	0.8	102	1.3
Polk, IA	418 634	6 908	55.4	19 619	0.1	12.6	3.9	3 364	3.4
Pottawattamie, IA	106 940	6 201	54.1	5 187	0.0	11.7	5.0	842	3.9
Poweshiek, IA	17 794	5 729	62.6	1 369	0.0	8.0	0.7	216	1.6
Ringgold, IA	6 672	6 979	59.2	340	0.0	5.6	8.2	81	1.7

Table C-1. Population, School, and Student Characteristics by County—*Continued*

County	High school graduates, 2000			College enrollment, 2000		College graduates, 2000 (percent)						
	Population 25 years and over	High school diploma or less (percent)	High school diploma or more (percent)	Number	Percent public	Bachelor's degree or more	+/- U.S. percent with bachelor's degree or more	Non-Hispanic White	Black or African American	American Indian and Alaska Native	Asian, Hawaiian, and Pacific Islander	Hispanic or Latino[1]
	30	31	32	33	34	35	36	37	38	39	40	41
IOWA												
Adair, IA	5 695	60.6	87.8	206	78.2	11.2	-13.2	11.2	0.0	0.0	100.0	5.3
Adams, IA	3 131	56.9	84.5	132	97.7	12.0	-12.4	12.1	. . .	0.0	0.0	0.0
Allamakee, IA	9 946	62.8	81.4	334	79.9	14.4	-10.0	14.6	0.0	9.1	31.3	0.0
Appanoose, IA	9 401	59.7	81.4	527	81.2	12.2	-12.2	12.1	13.8	0.0	52.9	3.9
Audubon, IA	4 704	62.2	82.5	121	81.0	12.3	-12.1	12.3	0.0	0.0	100.0	0.0
Benton, IA	16 567	55.5	87.8	868	76.5	13.9	-10.5	14.0	0.0	0.0	0.0	0.0
Black Hawk, IA	78 401	48.7	86.5	15 933	95.1	23.0	-1.4	23.7	9.9	22.7	60.0	15.4
Boone, IA	17 529	49.2	89.0	994	87.2	18.8	-5.6	18.8	6.1	15.2	42.9	17.5
Bremer, IA	14 835	50.0	87.7	2 064	36.8	21.5	-2.9	21.4	0.0	0.0	34.5	38.5
Buchanan, IA	13 383	59.0	84.6	546	82.1	12.7	-11.7	12.5	17.6	0.0	30.6	22.9
Buena Vista, IA	12 736	54.8	81.3	1 449	24.3	18.7	-5.7	21.1	0.0	33.3	14.3	1.1
Butler, IA	10 563	59.3	82.2	420	80.5	12.4	-12.0	12.4	. . .	0.0	33.3	6.7
Calhoun, IA	7 877	52.7	85.4	284	88.0	15.4	-9.0	15.5	13.3	0.0	0.0	6.1
Carroll, IA	14 074	56.1	83.7	772	81.9	16.0	-8.4	16.0	33.3	. . .	5.7	5.8
Cass, IA	10 296	54.5	85.9	381	78.2	16.6	-7.8	16.6	0.0	0.0	54.3	12.3
Cedar, IA	12 291	54.2	87.7	686	84.3	16.3	-8.1	16.2	0.0	0.0	33.3	20.0
Cerro Gordo, IA	31 215	46.0	87.3	2 055	88.1	20.3	-4.1	20.7	0.0	0.0	17.8	7.8
Cherokee, IA	8 918	55.2	87.5	209	75.6	15.2	-9.2	15.3	0.0	. . .	7.7	0.0
Chickasaw, IA	8 797	61.8	83.4	446	84.3	12.2	-12.2	12.2	0.0	0.0	0.0	35.3
Clarke, IA	6 070	58.6	84.4	179	59.2	12.1	-12.3	12.3	. . .	0.0	16.7	8.7
Clay, IA	11 692	48.8	88.0	502	86.1	16.3	-8.1	16.3	29.4	0.0	7.3	14.6
Clayton, IA	12 743	63.0	82.6	382	69.1	12.8	-11.6	12.7	19.2	0.0	38.9	16.0
Clinton, IA	33 158	55.9	85.6	2 145	67.1	14.4	-10.0	14.4	7.1	4.5	44.6	11.8
Crawford, IA	11 068	64.3	78.5	422	79.6	12.4	-12.0	13.1	0.0	0.0	36.4	2.5
Dallas, IA	26 483	43.2	89.5	1 400	64.4	26.8	2.4	27.5	14.9	0.0	45.8	10.2
Davis, IA	5 578	62.5	78.9	263	81.0	11.4	-13.0	11.6	0.0	0.0	. . .	0.0
Decatur, IA	5 283	59.8	81.7	1 075	22.3	15.1	-9.3	15.0	0.0	0.0	45.5	20.4
Delaware, IA	11 784	62.1	85.1	557	74.0	13.0	-11.4	12.9	. . .	0.0	61.5	10.8
Des Moines, IA	28 425	53.5	85.8	1 820	82.1	16.0	-8.4	16.4	5.2	10.4	31.8	6.6
Dickinson, IA	11 730	46.1	89.2	599	78.6	21.3	-3.1	21.4	0.0	0.0	21.4	7.5
Dubuque, IA	57 236	55.0	85.2	5 714	34.3	21.3	-3.1	21.3	22.7	24.4	50.4	17.3
Emmet, IA	7 265	53.8	82.2	613	92.7	13.0	-11.4	13.3	0.0	0.0	100.0	2.1
Fayette, IA	14 632	59.0	84.8	1 055	50.7	13.8	-10.6	13.8	40.6	0.0	23.2	8.6
Floyd, IA	11 451	55.0	85.9	515	82.5	14.8	-9.6	14.8	0.0	0.0	75.0	0.0
Franklin, IA	7 362	54.6	84.0	303	82.5	14.5	-9.9	15.0	. . .	37.5	5.0	1.7
Fremont, IA	5 557	57.4	85.0	213	87.8	14.0	-10.4	14.1	100.0	36.4	0.0	2.5
Greene, IA	7 048	56.7	85.6	235	75.7	14.6	-9.8	14.9	0.0	0.0	0.0	0.0
Grundy, IA	8 465	51.7	86.5	441	82.1	17.2	-7.2	17.1	100.0	0.0	31.3	25.0
Guthrie, IA	7 976	59.5	85.4	239	73.2	14.9	-9.5	15.0	0.0	0.0	100.0	8.1
Hamilton, IA	11 094	53.1	87.3	539	80.7	17.5	-6.9	17.6	0.0	0.0	20.4	16.1
Hancock, IA	8 084	52.8	85.8	342	66.1	15.4	-9.0	15.6	. . .	33.3	77.8	4.0
Hardin, IA	12 615	51.3	85.7	877	93.2	17.1	-7.3	17.4	0.0	. . .	22.2	0.6
Harrison, IA	10 487	59.1	85.0	459	80.0	12.7	-11.7	12.5	61.5	33.3	40.0	7.7
Henry, IA	13 509	53.5	86.1	974	47.8	16.2	-8.2	16.5	3.0	5.9	19.3	8.8
Howard, IA	6 645	63.7	79.3	234	78.2	12.6	-11.8	12.6	100.0	. . .	66.7	0.0
Humboldt, IA	7 078	52.0	86.3	325	93.8	15.4	-9.0	15.3	0.0	0.0	50.0	14.7
Ida, IA	5 349	58.3	85.0	157	84.1	13.6	-10.8	13.6	. . .	0.0	50.0	25.0
Iowa, IA	10 565	55.1	87.0	490	85.1	15.8	-8.6	15.6	25.0	0.0	23.5	35.2
Jackson, IA	13 596	63.2	81.5	523	79.3	12.1	-12.3	11.9	0.0	28.6	66.7	28.6
Jasper, IA	25 291	58.0	86.8	1 015	74.4	15.9	-8.5	15.9	4.8	8.2	40.2	7.2
Jefferson, IA	10 893	43.3	88.1	875	42.2	31.2	6.8	31.0	31.0	31.4	50.0	52.4
Johnson, IA	62 859	26.1	93.7	26 885	96.3	47.6	23.2	47.0	34.9	41.1	76.5	34.5
Jones, IA	13 776	57.0	85.3	736	79.5	12.7	-11.7	13.0	3.1	16.1	17.2	3.7
Keokuk, IA	7 667	62.3	84.0	298	86.6	11.6	-12.8	11.5	0.0	0.0	64.7	11.8
Kossuth, IA	11 694	53.4	85.6	475	79.4	13.6	-10.8	13.6	0.0	0.0	7.7	2.5
Lee, IA	25 828	59.1	83.6	1 153	87.3	12.5	-11.9	12.6	4.7	0.0	42.1	10.2
Linn, IA	123 896	39.8	90.6	11 547	65.6	27.7	3.3	27.7	13.2	20.3	55.1	22.7
Louisa, IA	7 828	61.3	79.7	405	81.5	12.7	-11.7	13.5	27.3	0.0	32.5	2.8
Lucas, IA	6 336	65.4	79.1	225	70.2	11.1	-13.3	11.0	0.0	0.0	33.3	60.0
Lyon, IA	7 539	59.6	78.7	298	70.1	14.2	-10.2	14.1	20.0	0.0	100.0	52.6
Madison, IA	9 254	53.4	87.6	408	69.6	14.4	-10.0	14.4	0.0	0.0	35.3	12.5
Mahaska, IA	14 504	58.6	82.6	1 000	56.9	16.5	-7.9	16.5	0.0	0.0	29.9	4.8
Marion, IA	20 684	56.6	84.0	1 856	27.4	18.9	-5.5	18.9	19.1	12.9	18.4	9.8
Marshall, IA	26 179	54.9	82.3	1 316	83.9	17.0	-7.4	18.1	8.1	0.0	15.3	1.7
Mills, IA	9 662	53.5	83.2	541	72.5	16.3	-8.1	16.4	0.0	32.1	9.7	12.5
Mitchell, IA	7 320	60.0	84.4	268	85.8	12.8	-11.6	12.9	0.0	0.0	0.0	0.0
Monona, IA	7 072	61.2	81.7	197	72.1	13.4	-11.0	13.6	0.0	12.5	0.0	0.0
Monroe, IA	5 400	62.1	82.2	263	89.0	12.6	-11.8	12.7	0.0	0.0	. . .	0.0
Montgomery, IA	8 124	58.8	81.8	278	68.0	12.9	-11.5	13.0	. . .	. . .	27.3	0.0
Muscatine, IA	26 877	54.2	80.3	1 688	83.1	17.2	-7.2	18.0	10.8	4.7	27.6	7.9
O'Brien, IA	10 174	58.3	80.7	385	83.6	14.7	-9.7	14.8	25.0	0.0	25.0	1.6
Osceola, IA	4 647	56.5	81.1	172	77.9	13.4	-11.0	13.5	0.0	33.3	0.0	8.7
Page, IA	11 655	53.8	85.5	502	79.3	16.6	-7.8	17.0	0.0	6.8	20.0	5.2
Palo Alto, IA	6 692	51.3	83.7	591	88.7	13.9	-10.5	14.0	. . .	0.0	0.0	0.0
Plymouth, IA	15 994	51.7	87.4	816	74.6	19.3	-5.1	19.4	57.9	0.0	8.7	5.2
Pocahontas, IA	6 002	53.2	86.6	209	77.5	15.0	-9.4	15.1	0.0	0.0	0.0	0.0
Polk, IA	243 458	41.1	88.3	21 022	56.1	29.7	5.3	31.2	16.3	13.3	28.0	11.6
Pottawattamie, IA	57 013	55.3	84.0	3 618	82.1	15.0	-9.4	15.1	5.5	15.0	35.3	12.1
Poweshiek, IA	12 176	55.8	86.7	1 742	27.7	18.5	-5.9	18.3	46.2	20.0	34.4	17.1
Ringgold, IA	3 781	61.6	82.8	196	79.6	13.4	-11.0	13.3	. . .	0.0	88.9	66.7

[1]Hispanic or Latino persons may be of any race.
. . . = Not available.

Table C-1. Population, School, and Student Characteristics by County—*Continued*

County	State/County code	County type[1]	Population, 2000		Number of schools and students, 2000–2001			Resident enrollment, 2000			
			Total	Percent 5–17 years	School districts	Schools	Students	Total	Percent public	K–12	Percent public
			1	2	3	4	5	6	7	8	9
Sac, IA	19161	9	11 529	18.5	4	11	2 178	2 717	94.6	2 218	96.9
Scott, IA	19163	2	158 668	19.6	4	55	27 318	44 556	80.1	30 835	89.7
Shelby, IA	19165	6	13 173	20.5	3	11	2 474	3 210	88.6	2 779	91.1
Sioux, IA	19167	7	31 589	20.5	5	15	4 195	10 299	51.4	6 808	67.0
Story, IA	19169	4	79 981	13.9	7	29	10 847	35 450	95.3	11 147	95.6
Tama, IA	19171	6	18 103	19.6	4	14	3 484	4 440	93.6	3 602	95.5
Taylor, IA	19173	9	6 958	18.4	4	7	1 225	1 605	96.9	1 332	97.9
Union, IA	19175	7	12 309	17.4	2	10	2 116	3 013	91.5	2 186	94.6
Van Buren, IA	19177	9	7 809	19.2	3	8	1 371	1 753	87.3	1 477	89.4
Wapello, IA	19179	5	36 051	17.3	3	19	6 552	8 657	92.1	6 430	95.0
Warren, IA	19181	2	40 671	20.2	5	19	7 697	11 429	83.1	8 312	96.8
Washington, IA	19183	6	20 670	19.4	3	14	3 517	4 958	88.1	4 083	90.7
Wayne, IA	19185	9	6 730	18.8	3	7	1 199	1 566	94.1	1 276	96.8
Webster, IA	19187	5	40 235	18.2	3	18	5 600	10 158	86.0	7 580	86.2
Winnebago, IA	19189	7	11 723	18.5	3	9	2 801	3 008	86.1	2 287	97.2
Winneshiek, IA	19191	7	21 310	17.9	3	9	2 787	7 105	56.2	3 900	83.0
Woodbury, IA	19193	3	103 877	19.7	7	48	18 490	27 592	81.3	20 752	88.6
Worth, IA	19195	9	7 909	18.6	2	4	1 129	1 848	96.4	1 493	99.3
Wright, IA	19197	7	14 334	18.8	4	13	2 916	3 218	96.1	2 679	98.0
KANSAS	20000										
Allen, KS	20001	7	14 385	19.3	3	12	2 582	3 682	95.9	2 790	97.1
Anderson, KS	20003	6	8 110	20.0	2	9	1 430	1 952	90.0	1 660	89.8
Atchison, KS	20005	6	16 774	20.3	2	8	2 507	4 863	66.1	3 549	78.8
Barber, KS	20007	9	5 307	19.9	2	6	1 045	1 355	92.4	1 108	94.9
Barton, KS	20009	7	28 205	19.6	4	16	4 763	7 446	88.7	5 651	92.9
Bourbon, KS	20011	7	15 379	19.6	2	6	2 651	4 181	87.1	3 162	87.8
Brown, KS	20013	7	10 724	20.0	2	6	1 823	2 732	94.0	2 160	96.2
Butler, KS	20015	2	59 482	21.7	9	40	13 191	16 975	88.0	12 933	90.4
Chase, KS	20017	9	3 030	18.1	1	3	479	709	94.1	599	95.5
Chautauqua, KS	20019	9	4 359	18.9	2	4	714	1 055	93.2	874	94.1
Cherokee, KS	20021	6	22 605	19.6	4	19	3 891	5 494	94.2	4 460	95.6
Cheyenne, KS	20023	9	3 165	19.1	2	4	612	734	97.0	619	98.4
Clark, KS	20025	9	2 390	20.5	2	5	531	582	97.8	499	98.6
Clay, KS	20027	7	8 822	19.6	1	9	1 556	2 148	97.7	1 746	98.5
Cloud, KS	20029	7	10 268	17.4	2	8	1 519	2 741	94.9	1 847	96.5
Coffey, KS	20031	7	8 865	20.9	3	11	1 858	2 325	94.8	1 880	98.2
Comanche, KS	20033	9	1 967	16.5	1	3	326	393	97.7	337	98.5
Cowley, KS	20035	4	36 291	19.7	5	23	6 533	10 397	83.8	7 205	93.0
Crawford, KS	20037	4	38 242	16.5	5	17	5 885	11 944	92.3	6 338	90.0
Decatur, KS	20039	9	3 472	19.1	2	4	600	833	97.7	675	98.2
Dickinson, KS	20041	7	19 344	20.0	5	20	4 075	4 917	93.1	3 963	95.9
Doniphan, KS	20043	8	8 249	18.9	5	10	1 635	2 377	96.0	1 599	96.6
Douglas, KS	20045	3	99 962	14.8	3	34	12 966	42 645	90.7	15 063	92.0
Edwards, KS	20047	9	3 449	18.8	2	5	486	836	89.7	676	90.4
Elk, KS	20049	8	3 261	18.2	2	5	755	730	96.6	603	97.3
Ellis, KS	20051	7	27 507	16.7	3	13	4 066	9 329	90.6	4 663	87.5
Ellsworth, KS	20053	9	6 525	17.2	2	7	1 216	1 343	95.7	1 085	98.5
Finney, KS	20055	5	40 523	23.8	2	20	8 787	12 187	93.6	9 588	95.0
Ford, KS	20057	5	32 458	21.7	3	14	6 211	8 955	92.8	7 038	93.4
Franklin, KS	20059	6	24 784	20.7	4	16	4 758	6 652	86.1	5 217	93.3
Geary, KS	20061	5	27 947	20.2	1	17	6 360	8 115	91.0	5 664	93.2
Gove, KS	20063	9	3 068	20.2	3	7	705	753	95.5	640	98.0
Graham, KS	20065	9	2 946	18.0	2	5	476	685	95.9	560	98.2
Grant, KS	20067	9	7 909	24.1	1	4	1 745	2 281	93.2	1 954	95.1
Gray, KS	20069	7	5 904	23.8	4	8	1 214	1 565	82.5	1 343	83.2
Greeley, KS	20071	9	1 534	21.5	1	2	320	395	95.2	359	94.7
Greenwood, KS	20073	6	7 673	18.2	3	8	1 154	1 640	97.6	1 418	99.2
Hamilton, KS	20075	9	2 670	21.5	1	2	555	711	90.6	584	93.3
Harper, KS	20077	7	6 536	19.0	2	5	1 149	1 554	94.7	1 337	96.1
Harvey, KS	20079	2	32 869	19.4	5	18	5 830	8 739	79.9	6 503	88.9
Haskell, KS	20081	9	4 307	23.8	2	5	936	1 258	90.4	1 071	90.8
Hodgeman, KS	20083	9	2 085	24.1	2	4	488	615	95.4	519	98.1
Jackson, KS	20085	6	12 657	21.3	3	9	2 393	3 284	91.2	2 712	94.2
Jefferson, KS	20087	8	18 426	21.0	6	20	4 273	4 722	92.8	3 942	96.2
Jewell, KS	20089	9	3 791	17.4	3	9	595	773	95.9	656	98.5
Johnson, KS	20091	0	451 086	19.6	6	137	75 227	124 515	78.8	88 153	84.8
Kearny, KS	20093	9	4 531	25.5	2	6	1 147	1 379	92.8	1 147	95.8
Kingman, KS	20095	6	8 673	21.3	2	7	1 545	2 284	90.8	1 916	92.6
Kiowa, KS	20097	9	3 278	18.5	3	6	474	826	83.9	621	91.6
Labette, KS	20099	7	22 835	19.5	4	17	4 266	5 956	95.9	4 570	96.9
Lane, KS	20101	9	2 155	20.1	2	5	414	514	96.5	440	98.9
Leavenworth, KS	20103	1	68 691	19.7	6	29	12 219	18 935	84.1	13 771	89.6
Lincoln, KS	20105	9	3 578	18.3	2	4	591	803	94.8	657	96.8
Linn, KS	20107	8	9 570	18.7	3	11	2 037	2 094	89.1	1 788	91.3
Logan, KS	20109	9	3 046	19.0	2	6	575	723	89.5	576	93.2
Lyon, KS	20111	5	35 935	18.9	3	19	6 342	11 701	95.8	6 992	95.8
McPherson, KS	20113	7	29 554	19.5	5	20	5 045	8 098	85.6	5 809	89.4
Marion, KS	20115	6	13 361	19.3	5	13	2 527	3 472	81.0	2 604	92.7
Marshall, KS	20117	7	10 965	20.0	4	14	2 378	2 606	87.0	2 317	87.9
Meade, KS	20119	9	4 631	21.6	2	4	688	1 272	90.6	1 027	92.7

[1]County type code is from the Economic Research Service of the USDA. See Notes and Definitions at the end of this section.

Table C-1. School and Student Characteristics by County—*Continued*

County	Characteristics of students, 2000–2001			Staff and students, 2000–2001				Revenues, fiscal 1999			
	Percent with IEP[2]	Percent eligible for free lunch	Percent minority	Number of teachers	Student/ teacher ratio	Local school non-teaching staff	Central admin. staff	Total revenue ($1,000s)	Percentage of revenue from		
									Federal govt.	State govt.	Local govt.
	10	11	12	13	14	15	16	17	18	19	20
Sac, IA	10.3	30.0	2.5	169	12.9	111	15	$15 663	4.6	52.6	42.9
Scott, IA	11.5	27.8	19.4	1 862	14.7	1 710	90	216 467	6.2	46.7	47.1
Shelby, IA	12.2	29.8	1.2	177	14.0	146	10	17 675	3.6	51.0	45.4
Sioux, IA	13.2	25.5	7.0	308	13.6	202	19	36 217	6.6	39.0	54.5
Story, IA	12.2	15.2	9.0	685	15.8	562	39	80 619	2.2	44.6	53.2
Tama, IA	13.3	28.8	14.8	253	13.8	190	16	28 953	4.1	52.6	43.3
Taylor, IA	17.3	37.6	7.0	127	9.6	92	12	10 849	6.4	51.0	42.6
Union, IA	15.8	37.7	1.6	128	16.5	220	24	21 453	12.7	41.0	46.3
Van Buren, IA	12.3	29.8	0.9	118	11.6	116	12	10 690	4.3	55.1	40.7
Wapello, IA	15.6	33.5	7.3	424	15.5	484	33	53 413	9.8	45.2	45.0
Warren, IA	13.3	13.0	2.8	534	14.4	508	29	52 238	2.3	55.6	42.1
Washington, IA	15.1	22.8	6.2	267	13.2	194	13	25 380	5.4	50.4	44.3
Wayne, IA	14.6	42.0	1.0	97	12.4	79	9	8 873	6.0	52.4	41.6
Webster, IA	18.5	38.7	10.6	463	12.1	623	41	52 717	8.1	42.9	49.0
Winnebago, IA	14.7	23.9	3.6	224	12.5	170	15	20 266	3.1	49.7	47.2
Winneshiek, IA	18.8	18.3	1.8	172	16.2	166	15	20 643	3.4	49.1	47.5
Woodbury, IA	14.6	31.3	24.3	1 139	16.2	1 068	65	146 304	5.9	49.1	45.0
Worth, IA	13.0	27.0	3.0	90	12.5	76	6	8 776	2.7	46.3	51.0
Wright, IA	14.2	28.7	7.2	204	14.3	176	18	22 213	3.0	47.4	49.6
KANSAS											
Allen, KS	21.1	41.6	7.3	187	13.8	166	13	18 125	5.9	72.0	22.1
Anderson, KS	16.4	40.2	2.0	115	12.4	65	7	10 327	4.2	70.0	25.8
Atchison, KS	19.7	45.3	11.4	187	13.4	156	14	20 548	9.2	68.4	22.4
Barber, KS	11.6	36.3	4.5	83	12.6	57	8	8 053	3.6	70.1	26.3
Barton, KS	14.4	41.2	16.6	358	13.3	324	25	36 429	6.4	63.8	29.8
Bourbon, KS	13.4	42.2	6.5	190	14.0	148	17	16 192	7.2	74.2	18.5
Brown, KS	23.2	42.8	19.1	129	14.1	106	9	13 211	5.7	73.4	20.9
Butler, KS	12.7	18.5	6.0	886	14.9	989	56	86 121	3.8	69.8	26.4
Chase, KS	15.4	34.4	2.9	43	11.1	33	5	4 249	3.9	64.5	31.6
Chautauqua, KS	17.6	50.7	10.6	60	11.9	39	3	5 709	2.9	79.4	17.7
Cherokee, KS	12.7	45.5	7.1	296	13.1	218	22	26 284	4.1	76.7	19.2
Cheyenne, KS	15.4	38.1	5.1	59	10.4	40	2	5 275	4.1	69.2	26.7
Clark, KS	18.9	34.7	4.7	49	10.8	51	4	4 528	3.0	63.0	34.0
Clay, KS	17.1	34.1	3.1	127	12.3	122	7	11 884	7.3	68.6	24.1
Cloud, KS	22.0	41.3	1.3	136	11.2	135	19	13 224	7.7	70.7	21.6
Coffey, KS	17.2	25.8	3.4	183	10.2	120	12	24 006	3.2	27.3	69.5
Comanche, KS	21.2	36.2	0.3	33	9.9	35	5	3 428	3.8	52.4	43.8
Cowley, KS	18.3	38.4	14.4	486	13.4	467	34	48 371	5.7	67.8	26.5
Crawford, KS	14.4	39.2	6.3	400	14.7	455	23	47 317	8.5	68.6	22.8
Decatur, KS	18.6	37.8	0.7	63	9.5	41	4	5 237	3.2	73.3	23.4
Dickinson, KS	15.1	31.6	4.9	298	13.7	254	22	28 306	4.0	73.2	22.7
Doniphan, KS	17.9	34.1	5.7	147	11.1	99	13	12 727	4.7	78.7	16.6
Douglas, KS	20.2	27.7	18.7	911	14.2	925	74	93 513	4.8	54.2	41.0
Edwards, KS	11.2	47.1	21.8	43	11.3	41	7	4 898	5.5	66.1	28.4
Elk, KS	25.4	52.2	4.2	62	12.2	106	8	7 394	8.5	76.2	15.3
Ellis, KS	18.0	26.9	5.2	328	12.4	303	30	32 201	8.4	59.9	31.7
Ellsworth, KS	18.7	28.5	4.4	113	10.8	73	9	11 258	2.9	61.5	35.6
Finney, KS	14.2	49.0	58.3	569	15.4	534	32	58 010	7.1	58.2	34.7
Ford, KS	15.8	56.1	52.7	377	16.5	306	29	37 746	13.1	63.6	23.3
Franklin, KS	16.2	27.7	5.2	339	14.0	228	25	31 817	4.3	70.8	24.9
Geary, KS	16.1	55.0	47.6	423	15.0	448	33	40 616	25.4	60.4	14.2
Gove, KS	17.6	29.5	2.4	74	9.5	69	8	6 830	2.0	73.7	24.3
Graham, KS	20.7	38.2	5.7	47	10.1	44	5	4 576	4.3	71.0	24.6
Grant, KS	13.3	41.4	45.0	118	14.8	123	10	13 513	4.4	5.4	90.3
Gray, KS	12.6	27.8	17.1	106	11.5	107	11	10 858	3.6	66.3	30.1
Greeley, KS	14.7	28.1	13.4	29	11.0	19	3	2 814	5.3	57.2	37.5
Greenwood, KS	18.8	39.9	3.6	103	11.2	101	10	9 824	5.3	74.8	19.9
Hamilton, KS	14.1	44.7	31.2	45	12.3	35	7	4 255	6.1	46.2	47.7
Harper, KS	15.8	37.9	5.2	93	12.4	71	11	8 756	5.3	74.9	19.8
Harvey, KS	16.8	30.4	15.4	405	14.4	356	32	42 438	4.9	67.4	27.7
Haskell, KS	12.2	39.7	34.6	80	11.7	54	9	9 206	3.9	21.2	75.0
Hodgeman, KS	11.1	26.4	7.4	44	11.1	41	4	4 114	3.0	71.0	26.0
Jackson, KS	13.1	27.8	11.5	178	13.4	217	16	19 561	6.1	75.3	18.5
Jefferson, KS	15.4	22.1	3.1	309	13.8	271	29	30 595	2.8	77.8	19.4
Jewell, KS	13.7	43.9	2.4	60	9.9	44	7	5 928	2.2	75.8	22.0
Johnson, KS	15.6	8.2	11.2	5 264	14.3	4 277	268	563 733	2.3	46.0	51.7
Kearny, KS	10.4	41.8	39.1	91	12.6	83	7	10 924	4.1	16.2	79.7
Kingman, KS	15.9	37.3	3.6	115	13.4	85	7	10 848	3.7	62.8	33.5
Kiowa, KS	20.9	35.7	5.3	55	8.6	43	7	5 809	3.5	55.1	41.4
Labette, KS	14.6	42.2	13.2	281	15.2	213	16	26 707	6.1	76.4	17.5
Lane, KS	22.3	29.5	1.2	49	8.4	37	8	4 206	3.4	62.9	33.7
Leavenworth, KS	15.8	21.0	17.5	833	14.7	712	57	85 122	17.3	59.9	22.8
Lincoln, KS	15.6	32.3	1.4	53	11.2	55	6	5 230	2.4	73.7	23.9
Linn, KS	17.0	35.5	2.4	148	13.8	103	12	16 367	3.3	51.9	44.8
Logan, KS	19.8	38.8	3.5	61	9.4	69	7	5 627	4.3	66.0	29.7
Lyon, KS	14.1	43.0	31.3	444	14.3	438	38	50 522	9.5	67.1	23.5
McPherson, KS	17.4	18.3	4.7	389	13.0	333	38	40 702	4.6	61.6	33.8
Marion, KS	20.3	31.4	3.9	205	12.3	151	14	19 608	3.0	73.5	23.4
Marshall, KS	17.9	28.5	2.3	199	11.9	211	13	19 401	3.6	73.7	22.7
Meade, KS	15.0	27.5	9.9	59	11.7	52	8	5 671	2.7	49.5	47.8

[2]IEP = Individual Education Program. See Notes and Definitions at the end of this section.

Table C-1. Population, School, and Student Characteristics by County—*Continued*

County	Current expenditures, fiscal 1999			Resident population 16 to 19 years, 2000				Outcomes, 1999–2000	
	Amount ($1,000s)	Amount per student	Percent for instruction	Total population 16 to 19 years	Percent in Armed Forces	Percent high school graduates	Percent not enrolled, not grads, not Armed Forces, not empl.	Number of graduates	Dropouts grades 9–12 (percent)
	21	22	23	24	25	26	27	28	29
Sac, IA	$12 847	$5 632	61.7	618	0.0	6.3	0.6	198	0.9
Scott, IA	191 744	6 837	57.6	8 960	0.0	11.8	4.0	1 834	2.8
Shelby, IA	16 403	6 425	53.7	762	0.0	9.7	2.0	207	2.2
Sioux, IA	28 857	6 603	49.2	2 865	0.0	7.2	0.6	345	0.8
Story, IA	66 137	5 957	64.8	8 266	0.0	4.3	0.6	857	1.7
Tama, IA	23 704	5 412	58.7	941	0.0	9.6	4.3	239	4.5
Taylor, IA	8 414	6 284	58.9	402	0.0	10.0	3.2	91	1.7
Union, IA	18 324	8 140	44.8	809	0.0	9.6	3.3	173	5.1
Van Buren, IA	8 719	6 101	56.8	418	0.0	13.2	7.9	113	0.4
Wapello, IA	46 683	7 038	51.1	2 061	0.0	10.8	6.0	432	6.0
Warren, IA	43 012	5 593	59.4	2 609	0.0	11.2	2.3	522	1.5
Washington, IA	20 849	5 871	60.5	1 020	0.0	10.7	2.8	218	1.0
Wayne, IA	7 062	6 041	64.5	355	0.0	8.5	3.4	67	2.2
Webster, IA	44 813	7 651	50.5	2 648	0.0	11.6	4.8	404	4.4
Winnebago, IA	16 178	5 548	63.5	938	0.0	6.4	2.9	209	1.8
Winneshiek, IA	16 516	5 807	61.9	1 974	0.0	4.1	1.4	240	1.0
Woodbury, IA	122 925	6 637	61.0	6 334	0.1	11.1	4.6	1 194	4.1
Worth, IA	6 696	5 608	61.1	412	0.0	7.0	0.5	81	1.0
Wright, IA	18 043	5 935	61.0	778	0.0	16.3	4.9	212	3.2
KANSAS									
Allen, KS	14 929	5 493	55.9	1 114	0.0	11.1	3.5	192	...
Anderson, KS	8 552	5 763	52.4	496	0.0	2.4	1.8	100	...
Atchison, KS	16 247	6 414	57.2	1 171	0.0	9.3	0.1	170	...
Barber, KS	6 840	6 037	50.8	332	0.0	3.6	1.8	97	...
Barton, KS	29 777	5 932	57.2	1 968	0.6	5.9	4.4	368	...
Bourbon, KS	13 658	5 016	62.4	991	0.0	11.2	1.5	196	...
Brown, KS	10 927	5 754	54.4	648	0.0	10.2	6.2	112	...
Butler, KS	73 883	5 503	59.1	3 806	0.3	11.0	4.1	802	...
Chase, KS	3 504	6 871	53.8	186	0.0	5.9	5.9	44	...
Chautauqua, KS	4 730	6 248	55.5	262	0.0	4.6	2.3	60	...
Cherokee, KS	22 625	5 577	54.0	1 334	0.0	10.6	7.3	225	...
Cheyenne, KS	4 408	6 740	59.1	177	0.0	9.6	0.0	53	...
Clark, KS	4 150	7 657	48.3	157	0.0	8.3	1.9	53	...
Clay, KS	10 316	6 286	59.6	416	0.0	12.5	7.0	112	...
Cloud, KS	11 753	7 162	59.4	805	0.0	6.2	1.0	114	...
Coffey, KS	13 869	7 193	59.1	489	0.0	6.1	2.9	138	...
Comanche, KS	3 007	8 105	53.0	71	0.0	5.6	0.0	20	...
Cowley, KS	40 813	6 025	58.7	2 626	0.0	8.7	4.5	447	...
Crawford, KS	40 939	6 787	63.5	2 708	1.0	9.7	2.4	370	...
Decatur, KS	4 633	6 874	58.9	190	0.0	10.5	0.0	60	...
Dickinson, KS	23 905	5 506	54.0	1 057	0.6	7.4	4.4	299	...
Doniphan, KS	10 833	6 418	52.7	711	0.0	5.9	1.3	115	...
Douglas, KS	77 629	6 027	57.0	9 344	0.1	5.4	1.3	887	...
Edwards, KS	4 033	6 978	53.6	196	0.0	9.7	3.1	47	...
Elk, KS	6 608	8 396	57.9	137	0.0	12.4	2.9	49	...
Ellis, KS	27 973	6 524	60.3	2 324	0.0	10.5	1.9	284	...
Ellsworth, KS	8 795	6 505	51.9	349	0.6	10.9	0.9	132	...
Finney, KS	46 680	5 452	52.9	2 803	0.0	7.3	10.0	336	...
Ford, KS	28 234	4 703	57.1	2 167	0.0	9.6	8.8	346	...
Franklin, KS	26 562	5 458	58.3	1 428	0.0	8.3	2.5	312	...
Geary, KS	35 251	5 455	52.7	1 724	9.2	22.4	3.8	242	...
Gove, KS	5 922	7 802	60.4	179	0.0	6.1	2.2	52	...
Graham, KS	4 082	7 616	58.2	168	0.0	4.8	2.4	49	...
Grant, KS	9 886	5 367	57.4	510	0.0	11.8	6.7	96	...
Gray, KS	8 541	6 515	51.1	371	0.0	7.8	10.2	89	...
Greeley, KS	2 266	6 867	56.5	98	0.0	7.1	5.1	17	...
Greenwood, KS	8 533	6 843	60.0	455	0.0	11.0	11.4	98	...
Hamilton, KS	3 500	6 629	48.5	158	0.0	4.4	3.8	42	...
Harper, KS	7 601	5 851	55.4	378	0.0	9.0	1.9	79	...
Harvey, KS	35 646	5 908	52.9	2 099	0.0	8.9	2.0	361	...
Haskell, KS	6 630	6 765	51.1	288	0.0	11.1	3.1	64	...
Hodgeman, KS	3 352	6 940	59.6	143	0.0	9.1	1.4	37	...
Jackson, KS	16 681	6 795	64.0	743	0.0	12.5	2.4	186	...
Jefferson, KS	26 130	5 948	52.7	1 081	0.0	11.3	2.1	285	...
Jewell, KS	5 109	7 448	51.1	175	0.0	5.7	1.7	57	...
Johnson, KS	437 926	5 956	57.9	23 106	0.0	8.0	1.7	4 833	...
Kearny, KS	7 918	6 940	58.6	309	0.0	8.7	7.1	51	...
Kingman, KS	8 943	5 453	55.4	516	0.0	4.3	0.8	135	...
Kiowa, KS	4 540	7 504	48.5	217	0.0	8.3	0.9	53	...
Labette, KS	22 699	5 100	54.8	1 454	0.0	10.6	2.6	293	...
Lane, KS	3 438	7 458	54.7	112	0.0	1.8	2.7	44	...
Leavenworth, KS	66 192	5 505	57.0	3 602	1.1	12.5	3.1	755	...
Lincoln, KS	4 162	6 423	54.7	178	0.0	9.0	3.9	49	...
Linn, KS	13 389	6 668	53.0	531	0.0	18.3	3.8	134	...
Logan, KS	4 873	7 936	50.5	184	0.0	14.7	0.5	57	...
Lyon, KS	39 815	6 384	60.0	2 942	0.0	10.5	3.9	395	...
McPherson, KS	32 811	6 225	55.7	2 018	0.1	6.4	2.6	349	...
Marion, KS	15 687	5 895	54.6	823	0.0	6.0	2.9	175	...
Marshall, KS	16 740	6 537	59.6	685	0.0	7.7	1.9	236	...
Meade, KS	4 605	7 207	51.2	270	0.0	7.8	2.2	51	...

. . . = Not available.

Table C-1. Population, School, and Student Characteristics by County—*Continued*

County	High school graduates, 2000			College enrollment, 2000		College graduates, 2000 (percent)						
	Population 25 years and over	High school diploma or less (percent)	High school diploma or more (percent)	Number	Percent public	Bachelor's degree or more	+/- U.S. percent with bachelor's degree or more	Non-Hispanic White	Black or African American	American Indian and Alaska Native	Asian, Hawaiian, and Pacific Islander	Hispanic or Latino[1]
	30	31	32	33	34	35	36	37	38	39	40	41
Sac, IA	7 946	58.8	84.2	295	80.3	13.6	-10.8	13.6	0.0	0.0	16.7	13.3
Scott, IA	102 149	44.4	86.3	10 824	60.9	24.9	0.5	25.8	12.2	10.3	35.9	14.2
Shelby, IA	8 957	59.3	86.6	252	81.7	15.3	-9.1	15.1	0.0	0.0	72.0	8.6
Sioux, IA	18 172	53.3	80.4	2 920	14.0	19.8	-4.6	19.9	4.9	0.0	47.4	7.3
Story, IA	42 148	27.8	93.5	23 057	97.5	44.5	20.1	42.5	62.9	7.3	80.0	43.4
Tama, IA	12 011	56.6	84.2	561	89.7	12.9	-11.5	13.3	0.0	5.2	48.2	3.1
Taylor, IA	4 766	63.3	83.3	194	92.8	12.0	-12.4	12.2	...	18.2	0.0	2.9
Union, IA	8 342	55.9	87.3	597	88.4	14.7	-9.7	14.7	...	0.0	0.0	41.2
Van Buren, IA	5 322	63.5	82.7	171	77.2	11.8	-12.6	11.9	...	33.3	0.0	8.3
Wapello, IA	24 120	58.4	81.5	1 607	85.6	14.6	-9.8	14.6	24.6	33.3	23.0	10.6
Warren, IA	25 756	47.8	90.0	2 431	41.0	21.2	-3.2	21.3	20.3	0.0	26.4	20.2
Washington, IA	13 876	56.6	82.5	584	81.3	16.4	-8.0	16.5	10.9	13.3	100.0	9.7
Wayne, IA	4 722	62.0	83.9	191	80.6	12.1	-12.3	12.1	0.0	0.0	58.8	0.0
Webster, IA	25 981	52.6	84.2	1 918	91.5	16.9	-7.5	17.1	8.5	14.8	38.3	5.6
Winnebago, IA	7 772	50.8	87.3	567	40.9	16.5	-7.9	16.5	0.0	0.0	0.0	20.8
Winneshiek, IA	12 864	53.2	84.1	2 830	20.0	20.5	-3.9	20.7	15.4	0.0	2.4	0.0
Woodbury, IA	64 932	53.6	81.4	4 797	57.6	18.9	-5.5	20.6	10.9	2.1	11.8	3.0
Worth, IA	5 476	53.6	86.0	241	86.7	12.7	-11.7	13.0	0.0	0.0	0.0	0.0
Wright, IA	9 882	54.7	84.4	270	75.9	13.5	-10.9	13.9	0.0	0.0	0.0	3.9
KANSAS												
Allen, KS	9 292	52.7	83.1	647	97.1	15.2	-9.2	15.5	10.8	8.6	22.2	5.9
Anderson, KS	5 459	60.4	81.9	173	89.6	11.7	-12.7	11.7	0.0	0.0	0.0	11.8
Atchison, KS	10 375	56.9	84.7	1 058	26.5	18.0	-6.4	17.8	19.5	0.0	44.4	29.6
Barber, KS	3 646	47.0	85.8	112	88.4	21.0	-3.4	21.2	0.0	0.0	0.0	22.2
Barton, KS	18 265	49.1	82.3	1 206	78.4	16.6	-7.8	17.5	4.4	26.8	53.5	1.3
Bourbon, KS	9 965	47.5	84.2	684	93.1	17.8	-6.6	18.2	6.7	23.5	...	15.6
Brown, KS	7 080	54.5	84.6	349	87.7	19.0	-5.4	18.8	39.8	15.0	54.8	15.2
Butler, KS	37 560	45.0	87.3	3 044	87.7	20.4	-4.0	20.8	7.6	13.3	33.6	8.5
Chase, KS	2 081	52.6	87.1	86	94.2	19.6	-4.8	20.1	17.6	0.0	0.0	0.0
Chautauqua, KS	3 058	59.7	81.0	124	87.1	12.3	-12.1	12.1	...	18.2	37.5	13.6
Cherokee, KS	14 704	58.5	80.3	781	94.0	11.3	-13.1	11.2	5.4	17.9	19.4	5.4
Cheyenne, KS	2 257	50.2	85.5	71	91.5	16.0	-8.4	16.1	...	0.0	0.0	0.0
Clark, KS	1 640	40.1	87.4	56	94.6	22.1	-2.3	22.3	0.0	27.3	0.0	15.2
Clay, KS	6 026	52.5	87.0	244	97.1	16.5	-7.9	16.6	15.4	0.0	36.4	5.0
Cloud, KS	6 909	52.6	85.5	710	94.1	18.0	-6.4	17.8	0.0	29.4	46.2	50.0
Coffey, KS	5 932	53.7	86.9	280	84.6	20.1	-4.3	19.9	0.0	21.6	66.7	20.8
Comanche, KS	1 440	45.8	91.3	31	87.1	15.1	-9.3	15.0	...	...	100.0	18.2
Cowley, KS	22 982	45.6	85.4	2 584	61.3	18.3	-6.1	19.1	17.2	10.8	3.1	8.4
Crawford, KS	23 395	46.2	84.5	5 069	97.7	23.9	-0.5	24.2	9.5	16.5	53.5	11.3
Decatur, KS	2 479	53.6	86.4	106	93.4	15.4	-9.0	15.2	0.0	0.0	50.0	25.0
Dickinson, KS	13 156	52.9	86.4	663	85.7	15.2	-9.2	15.3	0.0	7.1	33.3	6.4
Doniphan, KS	5 176	56.6	80.2	643	97.0	14.8	-9.6	15.0	9.1	0.0	23.1	10.5
Douglas, KS	53 257	29.9	92.4	25 640	93.2	42.7	18.3	42.8	33.2	25.9	71.3	33.0
Edwards, KS	2 378	51.1	81.2	118	95.8	16.3	-8.1	17.3	37.5	33.3	54.5	0.0
Elk, KS	2 354	61.6	80.0	92	90.2	10.6	-13.8	10.8	...	0.0	...	0.0
Ellis, KS	16 278	42.7	87.2	4 298	96.9	29.2	4.8	29.2	60.0	0.0	56.9	12.1
Ellsworth, KS	4 660	50.7	84.8	177	83.1	16.4	-8.0	17.6	0.0	13.0	0.0	2.4
Finney, KS	22 196	57.5	67.4	1 747	90.7	14.3	-10.1	20.9	0.0	14.2	18.0	2.8
Ford, KS	18 632	53.2	69.9	1 285	94.5	16.4	-8.0	22.7	9.4	5.3	0.0	3.7
Franklin, KS	15 753	54.2	85.3	1 069	56.8	16.5	-7.9	16.8	12.7	8.6	46.5	6.3
Geary, KS	15 744	44.0	86.0	1 899	90.2	17.1	-7.3	19.4	10.3	21.3	14.6	12.8
Gove, KS	2 120	50.7	84.5	61	95.1	18.4	-6.0	18.7	0.0	0.0	...	0.0
Graham, KS	2 125	50.4	83.6	81	91.4	17.4	-7.0	17.0	20.6	22.2	66.7	37.5
Grant, KS	4 712	56.5	71.5	199	75.4	15.2	-9.2	19.6	...	18.2	...	3.7
Gray, KS	3 536	52.1	73.6	133	93.2	16.3	-8.1	17.2	0.0	0.0	...	5.8
Greeley, KS	983	45.6	83.7	19	100.0	17.4	-7.0	18.6	...	0.0	...	1.5
Greenwood, KS	5 343	57.7	80.9	168	88.1	14.5	-9.9	14.8	...	5.7	6.9	0.0
Hamilton, KS	1 727	53.7	76.7	63	92.1	17.4	-7.0	20.0	0.0	0.0	25.0	2.2
Harper, KS	4 462	55.3	83.8	144	89.6	14.0	-10.4	13.9	44.0	0.0	33.3	11.8
Harvey, KS	21 278	44.9	85.3	1 711	49.6	23.0	-1.4	24.3	19.8	2.1	12.7	5.3
Haskell, KS	2 505	50.6	74.8	128	94.5	17.5	-6.9	20.7	0.0	0.0	70.4	0.9
Hodgeman, KS	1 376	43.8	86.9	64	78.1	19.7	-4.7	20.3	0.0	0.0	...	0.0
Jackson, KS	8 228	58.2	87.7	305	70.5	15.4	-9.0	15.8	11.4	11.9	63.6	10.2
Jefferson, KS	12 127	53.7	88.9	491	77.8	17.9	-6.5	17.9	17.4	30.4	20.0	19.8
Jewell, KS	2 798	51.9	87.6	73	95.9	13.8	-10.6	13.4	0.0	0.0	100.0	18.8
Johnson, KS	295 829	22.6	94.9	24 951	76.2	47.7	23.3	48.5	41.1	26.6	59.4	25.3
Kearny, KS	2 592	51.9	75.8	134	82.8	15.0	-9.4	17.8	0.0	25.0	100.0	3.7
Kingman, KS	5 809	49.0	84.7	248	89.1	17.8	-6.6	17.5	100.0	40.0	85.7	20.0
Kiowa, KS	2 227	44.8	85.2	150	48.7	18.9	-5.5	19.2	...	0.0	33.3	0.0
Labette, KS	15 007	48.9	83.0	1 066	98.1	15.9	-8.5	16.1	5.1	11.4	80.0	19.3
Lane, KS	1 491	45.6	88.5	28	92.9	18.5	-5.9	18.7	0.0	...	50.0	16.7
Leavenworth, KS	44 792	47.4	86.5	3 720	73.8	23.1	-1.3	24.1	16.4	11.1	22.6	15.1
Lincoln, KS	2 548	50.6	85.0	101	85.1	17.4	-7.0	17.6	0.0	0.0	33.3	17.6
Linn, KS	6 538	58.6	80.9	183	84.2	12.7	-11.7	12.7	7.7	0.0	100.0	12.5
Logan, KS	2 058	52.0	86.7	86	83.7	17.5	-6.9	17.5	0.0	100.0	100.0	6.9
Lyon, KS	20 559	50.0	81.8	4 142	97.9	23.0	-1.4	25.9	9.9	11.7	14.2	5.3
McPherson, KS	19 078	46.2	85.9	1 897	80.3	22.2	-2.2	22.0	20.6	30.8	42.9	18.4
Marion, KS	9 000	54.2	84.4	680	39.7	17.9	-6.5	18.3	0.0	0.0	0.0	6.8
Marshall, KS	7 460	60.6	85.1	153	88.9	13.2	-11.2	13.4	0.0	0.0	3.3	0.0
Meade, KS	2 946	48.2	80.3	146	93.2	19.6	-4.8	20.8	0.0	20.0	11.1	5.3

[1]Hispanic or Latino persons may be of any race.
... = Not available.

Table C-1. Population, School, and Student Characteristics by County—*Continued*

County	State/County code	County type[1]	Population, 2000		Number of schools and students, 2000–2001			Resident enrollment, 2000			
			Total	Percent 5–17 years	School districts	Schools	Students	Total	Percent public	K–12	Percent public
			1	2	3	4	5	6	7	8	9
Miami, KS	20121	1	28 351	21.1	3	13	4 711	7 575	88.0	6 086	91.2
Mitchell, KS	20123	7	6 932	19.4	2	8	1 307	1 866	85.6	1 424	83.6
Montgomery, KS	20125	5	36 252	19.0	4	15	5 983	9 206	90.1	7 003	91.3
Morris, KS	20127	9	6 104	19.6	1	5	1 035	1 419	96.3	1 202	97.5
Morton, KS	20129	9	3 496	21.3	2	5	763	1 005	95.7	812	97.3
Nemaha, KS	20131	9	10 717	21.4	3	9	1 862	2 698	91.9	2 303	92.7
Neosho, KS	20133	7	16 997	19.7	2	13	3 089	4 518	91.4	3 440	93.1
Ness, KS	20135	9	3 454	17.8	4	8	617	769	91.2	625	92.2
Norton, KS	20137	7	5 953	17.3	3	8	1 001	1 349	90.3	1 120	92.2
Osage, KS	20139	6	16 712	20.6	5	14	3 266	4 279	94.9	3 378	97.4
Osborne, KS	20141	9	4 452	19.2	1	3	465	1 033	95.2	925	96.0
Ottawa, KS	20143	9	6 163	20.0	2	7	1 326	1 514	90.8	1 244	94.5
Pawnee, KS	20145	7	7 233	18.5	2	9	1 214	1 676	91.9	1 420	93.0
Phillips, KS	20147	7	6 001	19.0	3	7	1 078	1 384	98.0	1 170	99.7
Pottawatomie, KS	20149	6	18 209	22.0	4	16	3 713	5 159	87.3	4 131	87.7
Pratt, KS	20151	7	9 647	18.6	2	6	1 611	2 533	90.5	1 874	91.0
Rawlins, KS	20153	9	2 966	19.5	2	4	484	666	95.3	593	97.6
Reno, KS	20155	4	64 790	18.1	6	37	10 065	15 601	88.4	11 953	89.4
Republic, KS	20157	7	5 835	17.8	3	8	993	1 306	96.0	1 109	99.3
Rice, KS	20159	7	10 761	18.8	4	14	1 930	3 243	88.3	2 089	97.1
Riley, KS	20161	5	62 843	13.1	3	18	6 528	28 110	94.9	8 195	92.5
Rooks, KS	20163	9	5 685	19.6	3	7	1 023	1 330	91.7	1 122	92.8
Rush, KS	20165	9	3 551	17.3	2	6	644	790	95.1	644	96.7
Russell, KS	20167	7	7 370	17.4	2	8	1 237	1 627	93.5	1 340	97.5
Saline, KS	20169	5	53 597	19.3	3	19	8 743	14 039	84.4	10 731	89.8
Scott, KS	20171	7	5 120	21.1	1	4	1 050	1 229	93.1	1 033	95.1
Sedgwick, KS	20173	2	452 869	20.3	10	147	76 438	129 180	82.4	92 478	85.8
Seward, KS	20175	7	22 510	22.4	2	13	5 015	6 348	95.3	5 207	97.5
Shawnee, KS	20177	3	169 871	18.5	5	59	26 460	43 314	83.1	31 221	87.2
Sheridan, KS	20179	9	2 813	21.4	1	2	430	757	99.2	630	99.2
Sherman, KS	20181	7	6 760	18.5	1	5	1 174	1 793	95.3	1 203	98.1
Smith, KS	20183	9	4 536	17.4	2	4	774	979	96.3	817	100.0
Stafford, KS	20185	9	4 789	20.6	3	7	1 070	1 201	96.8	1 020	97.7
Stanton, KS	20187	9	2 406	23.0	1	5	567	644	92.2	538	95.9
Stevens, KS	20189	7	5 463	23.0	2	5	1 280	1 570	96.5	1 292	97.1
Sumner, KS	20191	6	25 946	21.9	7	21	4 615	7 299	91.7	5 745	94.6
Thomas, KS	20193	7	8 180	19.6	3	8	1 425	2 545	91.5	1 622	90.8
Trego, KS	20195	9	3 319	18.8	1	2	511	807	94.1	631	99.0
Wabaunsee, KS	20197	8	6 885	20.5	2	9	1 112	1 699	94.4	1 407	95.5
Wallace, KS	20199	9	1 749	23.5	2	4	410	470	90.9	415	89.6
Washington, KS	20201	9	6 483	18.0	4	12	1 338	1 403	88.0	1 161	88.5
Wichita, KS	20203	9	2 531	20.4	1	3	471	617	91.2	546	93.6
Wilson, KS	20205	7	10 332	19.6	3	10	2 080	2 434	96.9	2 047	98.8
Woodson, KS	20207	9	3 788	16.7	1	2	568	862	96.2	680	99.0
Wyandotte, KS	20209	0	157 882	20.4	4	59	27 999	42 334	86.9	32 339	89.1
KENTUCKY	21000										
Adair, KY	21001	7	17 244	17.4	1	6	2 556	4 198	77.2	2 934	92.0
Allen, KY	21003	7	17 800	19.3	1	4	2 951	3 983	91.1	3 357	92.9
Anderson, KY	21005	6	19 111	19.1	1	6	3 448	4 641	93.2	3 715	95.4
Ballard, KY	21007	9	8 286	17.0	1	3	1 386	1 785	96.0	1 417	96.8
Barren, KY	21009	7	38 033	17.8	3	16	6 687	8 256	90.5	6 748	92.9
Bath, KY	21011	8	11 085	17.5	1	6	1 891	2 341	94.9	1 962	95.5
Bell, KY	21013	7	30 060	18.3	3	16	5 378	6 872	91.7	5 616	94.2
Boone, KY	21015	0	85 991	20.7	2	23	14 192	23 160	77.5	17 525	81.0
Bourbon, KY	21017	2	19 360	18.6	2	9	3 365	4 539	91.9	3 554	93.1
Boyd, KY	21019	2	49 752	16.3	3	18	7 379	11 748	89.7	8 720	92.0
Boyle, KY	21021	7	27 697	17.1	2	11	4 479	7 043	79.4	4 994	95.0
Bracken, KY	21023	8	8 279	18.9	2	5	1 472	1 978	93.1	1 606	93.0
Breathitt, KY	21025	9	16 100	19.7	2	10	2 756	4 131	90.3	3 269	92.6
Breckinridge, KY	21027	9	18 648	18.6	2	9	2 977	4 228	88.6	3 621	89.1
Bullitt, KY	21029	2	61 236	19.9	1	19	10 621	14 974	85.7	12 247	88.8
Butler, KY	21031	9	13 010	19.0	1	7	2 256	2 925	96.3	2 482	97.2
Caldwell, KY	21033	6	13 060	16.9	1	4	1 991	2 797	93.2	2 182	96.2
Calloway, KY	21035	7	34 177	13.8	2	8	4 500	11 875	95.1	5 013	96.5
Campbell, KY	21037	0	88 616	18.7	7	29	12 057	23 663	76.0	16 747	74.8
Carlisle, KY	21039	9	5 351	17.4	1	3	853	1 185	89.8	956	91.2
Carroll, KY	21041	6	10 155	18.7	1	5	1 760	2 243	90.6	1 768	92.2
Carter, KY	21043	2	26 889	18.1	1	10	4 635	6 517	87.5	4 789	95.8
Casey, KY	21045	9	15 447	18.2	1	8	2 335	3 103	90.7	2 740	91.4
Christian, KY	21047	3	72 265	18.4	1	18	8 901	18 278	88.3	13 514	89.4
Clark, KY	21049	2	33 144	18.3	1	13	5 156	7 482	86.2	6 084	89.5
Clay, KY	21051	9	24 556	19.7	1	12	4 092	5 678	89.9	4 815	89.5
Clinton, KY	21053	9	9 634	16.4	1	3	1 477	2 011	95.3	1 570	96.6
Crittenden, KY	21055	7	9 384	17.8	1	4	1 389	2 030	89.5	1 663	90.7
Cumberland, KY	21057	9	7 147	18.0	1	3	1 146	1 566	95.8	1 375	98.5
Daviess, KY	21059	3	91 545	19.1	2	31	13 956	23 030	78.9	17 533	82.8

[1]County type code is from the Economic Research Service of the USDA. See Notes and Definitions at the end of this section.

Table C-1. School and Student Characteristics by County—*Continued*

County	Characteristics of students, 2000–2001			Staff and students, 2000–2001				Revenues, fiscal 1999			
	Percent with IEP[2]	Percent eligible for free lunch	Percent minority	Number of teachers	Student/ teacher ratio	Local school non-teaching staff	Central admin. staff	Total revenue ($1,000s)	Percentage of revenue from		
									Federal govt.	State govt.	Local govt.
	10	11	12	13	14	15	16	17	18	19	20
Miami, KS	14.8	23.1	4.9	296	15.9	409	20	$35 440	3.8	64.0	32.1
Mitchell, KS	18.6	34.4	2.7	121	10.8	119	8	13 025	5.3	66.0	28.6
Montgomery, KS	13.8	43.1	22.6	412	14.5	268	25	36 417	4.2	73.3	22.5
Morris, KS	20.2	40.0	4.7	81	12.8	78	4	6 869	5.1	75.5	19.5
Morton, KS	11.1	43.0	20.2	70	10.9	67	12	9 109	4.4	24.5	71.1
Nemaha, KS	13.6	23.6	1.8	158	11.8	112	13	14 375	4.5	72.9	22.6
Neosho, KS	18.2	43.2	6.8	229	13.5	182	13	20 359	5.6	73.5	20.9
Ness, KS	16.4	28.0	2.9	65	9.5	52	9	6 429	3.0	63.0	34.0
Norton, KS	21.1	33.4	3.8	103	9.7	69	7	8 207	3.3	77.1	19.6
Osage, KS	18.5	31.1	4.0	246	13.3	153	18	22 801	3.7	76.8	19.6
Osborne, KS	18.1	39.8	1.1	40	11.6	31	3	3 572	4.3	79.8	16.0
Ottawa, KS	16.5	30.8	2.1	102	13.0	73	6	9 731	2.9	77.8	19.3
Pawnee, KS	16.6	37.8	8.9	98	12.4	116	10	13 215	8.5	58.0	33.5
Phillips, KS	13.1	38.3	2.2	104	10.4	142	13	12 190	2.9	73.7	23.5
Pottawatomie, KS	17.4	24.1	5.0	291	12.8	266	25	31 989	4.4	51.2	44.4
Pratt, KS	17.4	35.9	7.0	118	13.7	87	9	11 305	3.9	71.3	24.7
Rawlins, KS	13.2	34.5	0.8	52	9.3	40	4	4 419	3.3	77.2	19.5
Reno, KS	16.6	37.1	11.8	741	13.6	640	56	74 018	5.1	63.4	31.5
Republic, KS	24.9	39.0	2.5	91	10.9	76	10	8 949	3.4	72.7	23.8
Rice, KS	18.3	43.4	12.5	175	11.0	170	21	17 580	7.5	67.4	25.1
Riley, KS	17.0	28.1	16.1	527	12.4	455	25	54 481	8.1	63.6	28.3
Rooks, KS	21.6	39.1	2.5	92	11.1	73	9	8 579	2.3	70.6	27.1
Rush, KS	14.2	40.7	2.3	51	12.6	43	5	5 613	3.9	70.3	25.8
Russell, KS	17.8	38.5	3.6	120	10.3	92	13	10 131	5.2	67.2	27.6
Saline, KS	18.0	38.0	17.1	594	14.7	701	43	64 885	8.0	65.7	26.3
Scott, KS	15.2	32.0	9.8	78	13.5	45	11	7 565	3.7	64.2	32.1
Sedgwick, KS	16.6	41.0	33.4	4 820	15.9	3 567	458	485 912	7.0	66.3	26.7
Seward, KS	10.4	52.6	58.5	344	14.6	357	22	33 500	8.9	67.2	23.9
Shawnee, KS	18.3	38.2	28.7	1 814	14.6	1 780	106	196 564	9.4	60.1	30.5
Sheridan, KS	10.9	24.4	0.9	40	10.8	35	4	3 939	3.1	67.8	29.1
Sherman, KS	14.4	34.5	13.9	90	13.0	106	5	8 350	4.6	68.0	27.4
Smith, KS	16.1	39.0	1.8	66	11.7	56	6	6 235	4.3	75.6	20.0
Stafford, KS	25.9	45.5	11.6	90	11.9	77	6	9 404	4.6	62.6	32.8
Stanton, KS	8.8	38.6	36.0	44	12.9	31	3	4 900	5.3	23.6	71.1
Stevens, KS	7.9	39.1	34.6	98	13.1	72	13	14 163	3.5	5.0	91.5
Sumner, KS	17.0	32.4	7.6	346	13.3	324	35	33 177	2.9	76.4	20.7
Thomas, KS	16.4	30.8	5.1	123	11.6	93	17	12 622	3.6	67.8	28.6
Trego, KS	16.0	28.0	1.6	40	12.8	31	6	4 762	3.7	71.1	25.2
Wabaunsee, KS	16.7	21.7	3.4	108	10.3	96	7	9 092	3.5	77.7	18.8
Wallace, KS	14.1	35.4	9.0	37	11.1	35	3	3 919	4.8	65.0	30.2
Washington, KS	15.3	36.1	0.7	133	10.1	81	16	11 372	3.8	70.0	26.2
Wichita, KS	17.3	33.5	22.5	40	11.8	35	4	4 006	5.5	66.6	27.9
Wilson, KS	12.5	42.1	3.4	164	12.7	115	11	15 104	5.0	75.1	19.9
Woodson, KS	16.1	40.8	2.5	43	13.2	42	4	4 503	4.6	78.8	16.5
Wyandotte, KS	14.5	61.9	61.6	1 716	16.3	1 960	117	207 071	6.1	68.7	25.2
KENTUCKY											
Adair, KY	14.4	59.2	3.6	152	16.8	187	21	17 683	9.4	70.2	20.5
Allen, KY	12.2	43.4	1.7	139	21.2	203	23	18 304	8.3	72.3	19.5
Anderson, KY	18.1	28.0	3.4	168	20.5	217	9	19 197	7.6	62.8	29.6
Ballard, KY	20.1	43.1	4.6	67	20.7	120	13	9 302	8.3	70.5	21.2
Barren, KY	14.8	43.5	7.0	402	16.6	490	42	41 629	7.2	65.4	27.4
Bath, KY	13.3	65.5	2.1	115	16.4	161	9	12 591	11.4	70.8	17.8
Bell, KY	14.4	79.5	2.9	330	16.3	415	35	37 683	14.0	70.5	15.4
Boone, KY	14.0	18.3	4.9	735	19.3	834	105	82 670	4.2	46.1	49.7
Bourbon, KY	15.7	43.9	9.9	190	17.7	289	15	23 868	12.4	64.9	22.7
Boyd, KY	16.3	46.5	3.3	442	16.7	583	52	52 363	11.6	61.7	26.8
Boyle, KY	17.3	34.7	13.5	260	17.2	329	35	28 422	8.9	61.2	29.9
Bracken, KY	15.8	43.4	1.2	76	19.4	104	4	9 129	9.8	72.5	17.8
Breathitt, KY	19.1	79.6	0.7	168	16.4	276	20	21 759	14.1	74.5	11.3
Breckinridge, KY	17.1	61.2	4.4	152	19.6	255	9	21 412	17.1	63.3	19.6
Bullitt, KY	12.6	34.0	1.2	496	21.4	576	61	58 945	6.3	69.6	24.1
Butler, KY	14.4	53.5	1.4	130	17.4	167	13	14 841	9.0	76.1	14.9
Caldwell, KY	13.3	42.1	7.9	140	14.2	146	11	13 320	9.4	70.7	19.9
Calloway, KY	15.5	38.7	5.9	264	17.0	424	23	34 426	16.9	55.0	28.2
Campbell, KY	16.0	37.1	2.3	692	17.4	722	62	81 685	6.6	58.8	34.6
Carlisle, KY	12.4	52.4	2.4	50	17.1	62	2	5 309	9.6	72.3	18.1
Carroll, KY	14.1	53.3	3.9	99	17.8	170	16	13 173	14.2	56.1	29.7
Carter, KY	16.6	61.6	0.3	264	17.6	385	21	30 525	11.6	75.3	13.0
Casey, KY	16.7	63.0	1.6	137	17.0	211	1	15 588	11.5	73.3	15.2
Christian, KY	18.5	66.3	38.3	473	18.8	650	57	57 799	12.4	68.9	18.7
Clark, KY	13.3	41.9	6.8	257	20.1	415	39	30 334	8.9	62.4	28.7
Clay, KY	24.6	79.8	1.1	292	14.0	423	30	30 173	13.5	76.1	10.4
Clinton, KY	18.7	77.6	0.4	104	14.2	138	21	11 738	21.7	64.1	14.2
Crittenden, KY	17.0	46.1	1.3	89	15.6	114	6	10 193	9.9	69.6	20.5
Cumberland, KY	16.0	64.7	4.2	74	15.5	91	5	8 082	11.4	72.0	16.6
Daviess, KY	14.8	40.4	7.9	839	16.6	1 201	77	95 502	8.7	61.4	30.0

[2]IEP = Individual Education Program. See Notes and Definitions at the end of this section.

Table C-1. Population, School, and Student Characteristics by County—*Continued*

County	Current expenditures, fiscal 1999			Resident population 16 to 19 years, 2000				Outcomes, 1999–2000	
	Amount ($1,000s)	Amount per student	Percent for instruction	Total population 16 to 19 years	Percent in Armed Forces	Percent high school graduates	Percent not enrolled, not grads, not Armed Forces, not empl.	Number of graduates	Dropouts grades 9–12 (percent)
	21	22	23	24	25	26	27	28	29
Miami, KS	$30 069	$6 262	59.0	1 588	0.2	8.8	2.3	319	...
Mitchell, KS	11 503	8 158	54.3	579	0.0	2.1	2.1	125	...
Montgomery, KS	30 358	4 790	57.8	2 291	0.0	7.4	3.9	384	...
Morris, KS	5 712	5 333	57.3	352	0.0	15.6	2.6	77	...
Morton, KS	6 266	7 784	59.1	233	0.0	5.6	2.6	57	...
Nemaha, KS	12 382	6 416	57.1	620	0.0	9.5	1.3	162	...
Neosho, KS	16 321	5 036	58.6	1 126	0.0	7.4	2.2	226	...
Ness, KS	5 373	7 878	54.8	164	0.0	4.3	0.0	64	...
Norton, KS	7 079	6 549	54.1	278	0.0	10.4	6.1	85	...
Osage, KS	19 061	5 688	54.9	944	1.0	13.2	2.0	237	...
Osborne, KS	3 097	5 979	54.2	240	0.0	5.0	0.8	44	...
Ottawa, KS	8 098	5 968	53.5	387	0.0	4.4	2.6	100	...
Pawnee, KS	10 848	8 502	60.2	594	0.0	11.1	15.0	92	...
Phillips, KS	10 956	9 619	60.9	316	0.0	7.0	2.2	78	...
Pottawatomie, KS	25 446	6 666	60.0	1 181	0.0	11.7	1.5	310	...
Pratt, KS	9 634	5 443	58.3	697	0.0	9.3	0.9	118	...
Rawlins, KS	4 006	7 297	59.3	181	0.0	7.2	1.7	40	...
Reno, KS	59 347	5 485	53.7	3 815	0.0	10.5	4.0	692	...
Republic, KS	7 694	7 039	57.0	275	0.0	4.4	0.0	81	...
Rice, KS	14 648	7 320	56.9	894	0.0	4.0	2.9	131	...
Riley, KS	41 984	5 984	55.5	6 991	9.5	15.9	1.9	550	...
Rooks, KS	7 513	6 775	53.6	314	0.0	13.4	3.2	102	...
Rush, KS	4 915	6 874	48.3	145	0.0	13.1	0.0	53	...
Russell, KS	8 978	6 621	54.8	431	0.0	6.5	0.2	96	...
Saline, KS	54 710	6 215	60.5	3 217	0.0	8.4	3.9	540	...
Scott, KS	6 228	5 332	61.2	297	0.0	6.1	5.7	71	...
Sedgwick, KS	419 549	5 541	58.6	25 400	0.6	11.2	5.4	3 912	...
Seward, KS	26 226	5 256	61.7	1 483	0.0	6.3	12.1	258	...
Shawnee, KS	162 433	6 023	53.8	9 610	0.0	13.8	5.9	1 560	...
Sheridan, KS	3 513	7 670	59.4	175	0.0	1.7	0.0	44	...
Sherman, KS	7 239	6 022	56.8	548	0.0	12.4	9.9	78	...
Smith, KS	5 359	6 674	60.4	253	0.0	2.8	3.2	62	...
Stafford, KS	7 468	6 758	52.7	272	0.0	6.6	7.4	72	...
Stanton, KS	3 865	6 618	57.3	138	0.0	8.0	8.0	44	...
Stevens, KS	8 010	6 625	52.2	420	0.0	6.2	2.4	74	...
Sumner, KS	28 298	5 767	57.5	1 637	0.0	11.6	2.1	325	...
Thomas, KS	9 604	6 360	55.6	632	0.0	4.1	0.8	113	...
Trego, KS	4 057	6 853	58.4	181	0.0	0.0	3.9	46	...
Wabaunsee, KS	8 213	6 555	53.9	374	0.0	8.3	3.7	94	...
Wallace, KS	3 160	7 069	54.3	133	0.0	12.8	1.5	44	...
Washington, KS	9 829	6 751	55.9	329	0.0	8.8	0.9	119	...
Wichita, KS	3 088	6 213	49.5	149	0.0	4.7	4.0	40	...
Wilson, KS	12 734	6 105	54.1	554	0.0	12.5	4.5	138	...
Woodson, KS	4 020	6 301	46.6	212	0.0	6.6	0.0	60	...
Wyandotte, KS	183 097	6 441	54.7	9 384	0.0	14.5	10.6	1 281	...
KENTUCKY									
Adair, KY	15 846	5 980	61.6	1 172	0.0	8.2	9.4	128	8.0
Allen, KY	14 510	4 759	64.2	1 015	0.0	15.5	9.4	202	5.9
Anderson, KY	16 434	4 690	63.5	900	0.0	11.7	4.2	184	3.0
Ballard, KY	7 856	5 251	61.4	380	0.0	9.2	3.7	92	3.0
Barren, KY	37 317	5 449	62.1	2 012	0.0	14.4	7.9	430	4.6
Bath, KY	10 722	5 555	62.1	621	0.8	8.2	11.4	121	7.6
Bell, KY	32 017	5 512	61.6	1 676	0.0	10.1	10.6	428	4.7
Boone, KY	73 212	5 321	62.3	4 691	0.0	13.2	6.0	751	2.0
Bourbon, KY	21 258	5 970	64.0	932	0.0	7.9	7.1	207	3.5
Boyd, KY	45 157	5 676	63.7	2 790	0.0	10.4	4.5	498	2.7
Boyle, KY	25 713	5 601	59.5	1 635	0.0	10.9	7.3	222	3.3
Bracken, KY	7 800	5 210	63.0	410	0.0	7.3	4.6	98	3.4
Breathitt, KY	18 738	6 000	59.3	1 033	0.0	13.7	8.9	143	10.6
Breckinridge, KY	17 646	5 582	60.9	1 038	0.0	10.0	4.1	230	4.6
Bullitt, KY	57 836	5 372	60.3	3 475	0.4	12.5	3.2	711	3.9
Butler, KY	13 401	5 752	59.2	824	0.0	12.6	3.2	112	4.2
Caldwell, KY	10 934	5 114	58.7	722	0.0	10.2	4.3	136	3.7
Calloway, KY	30 364	6 485	71.3	2 686	0.0	9.1	1.7	295	1.0
Campbell, KY	71 692	5 615	62.4	5 010	0.0	11.0	5.9	723	3.1
Carlisle, KY	4 635	5 267	63.6	275	0.0	12.0	6.2	59	1.5
Carroll, KY	12 229	6 817	57.1	532	0.0	15.0	11.8	120	7.2
Carter, KY	26 722	5 602	61.7	1 586	0.0	12.2	5.9	301	4.6
Casey, KY	14 055	5 734	63.3	807	0.0	13.8	12.4	155	5.4
Christian, KY	51 395	5 607	61.1	4 276	21.3	31.5	8.2	458	7.2
Clark, KY	28 292	5 373	63.7	1 844	0.0	11.9	10.5	277	8.0
Clay, KY	26 211	5 982	60.0	1 504	0.0	13.3	16.8	186	9.5
Clinton, KY	10 692	6 828	59.8	470	0.0	14.0	11.1	95	8.4
Crittenden, KY	8 399	5 472	63.6	534	0.9	12.7	20.0	121	3.7
Cumberland, KY	7 101	5 731	60.9	372	0.0	6.7	9.9	74	8.9
Daviess, KY	82 654	5 688	59.8	5 545	0.0	10.5	3.1	956	3.9

. . . = Not available.

Table C-1. Population, School, and Student Characteristics by County—*Continued*

County	High school graduates, 2000 — Population 25 years and over	High school diploma or less (percent)	High school diploma or more (percent)	College enrollment, 2000 — Number	Percent public	College graduates, 2000 (percent) — Bachelor's degree or more	+/- U.S. percent with bachelor's degree or more	Non-Hispanic White	Black or African American	American Indian and Alaska Native	Asian, Hawaiian, and Pacific Islander	Hispanic or Latino[1]
	30	31	32	33	34	35	36	37	38	39	40	41
Miami, KS	18 444	49.2	87.5	838	88.1	19.4	-5.0	19.7	7.1	17.9	36.2	4.7
Mitchell, KS	4 645	48.1	88.1	374	97.3	16.9	-7.5	16.8	...	0.0	77.8	0.0
Montgomery, KS	24 090	49.0	81.2	1 733	93.4	16.0	-8.4	17.1	5.1	8.9	20.2	6.0
Morris, KS	4 224	56.1	84.7	133	97.7	16.0	-8.4	16.2	0.0	0.0	0.0	13.7
Morton, KS	2 165	52.7	81.9	108	89.8	17.6	-6.8	18.1	0.0	14.7	70.2	1.0
Nemaha, KS	7 038	62.5	83.7	234	85.5	14.6	-9.8	14.7	10.5	0.0	62.5	0.0
Neosho, KS	11 113	51.7	83.5	751	97.5	15.0	-9.4	15.1	12.9	29.9	0.0	2.7
Ness, KS	2 498	52.1	84.4	92	92.4	17.9	-6.5	18.1	0.0	...	50.0	0.0
Norton, KS	4 178	52.8	84.8	138	71.7	15.4	-9.0	16.5	0.0	0.0	58.3	0.0
Osage, KS	11 117	56.8	85.5	581	87.4	14.3	-10.1	14.5	0.0	10.0	29.7	7.6
Osborne, KS	3 115	55.5	84.8	72	97.2	15.5	-8.9	15.4	...	60.0	30.0	0.0
Ottawa, KS	4 228	51.7	86.2	149	83.2	16.3	-8.1	16.5	0.0	0.0	37.5	13.3
Pawnee, KS	4 875	45.0	84.8	177	91.0	21.8	-2.6	22.2	15.3	7.0	100.0	4.9
Phillips, KS	4 182	52.5	84.4	124	96.8	16.1	-8.3	16.2	0.0	0.0	30.8	11.1
Pottawatomie, KS	11 441	48.2	89.2	822	88.7	22.7	-1.7	22.8	3.2	16.0	0.0	21.7
Pratt, KS	6 365	41.4	86.3	533	92.7	21.0	-3.4	21.5	29.3	0.0	0.0	5.1
Rawlins, KS	2 152	49.9	84.7	36	88.9	15.9	-8.5	16.1	0.0	0.0	0.0	0.0
Reno, KS	43 082	47.8	82.7	2 673	90.8	17.3	-7.1	18.1	8.6	7.4	23.6	6.0
Republic, KS	4 256	52.7	88.6	110	83.6	14.9	-9.5	14.9	0.0	18.2	0.0	0.0
Rice, KS	6 701	50.2	83.4	989	73.0	17.5	-6.9	18.1	8.3	18.2	33.3	4.9
Riley, KS	29 358	28.6	93.8	19 026	97.4	40.5	16.1	41.5	18.8	36.7	69.1	23.1
Rooks, KS	3 901	54.3	87.1	100	98.0	15.4	-9.0	15.8	0.0	28.6	0.0	0.0
Rush, KS	2 568	49.6	82.8	104	96.2	16.4	-8.0	16.4	...	0.0	50.0	0.0
Russell, KS	5 323	52.7	83.1	135	88.1	16.7	-7.7	17.0	...	0.0	0.0	0.0
Saline, KS	34 680	47.5	87.0	2 260	72.4	20.4	-4.0	21.2	17.0	15.0	12.6	8.5
Scott, KS	3 376	44.3	84.5	130	91.5	23.0	-1.4	23.5	100.0	100.0	0.0	0.0
Sedgwick, KS	282 585	44.2	85.1	27 503	81.1	25.4	1.0	28.0	13.1	13.9	23.8	10.0
Seward, KS	12 690	63.1	63.7	766	91.5	13.6	-10.8	19.8	9.3	7.4	22.6	2.5
Shawnee, KS	111 709	45.5	88.1	8 815	77.4	26.0	1.6	28.0	12.2	15.5	48.7	13.9
Sheridan, KS	1 905	48.8	87.8	63	98.4	15.9	-8.5	15.6	...	0.0	100.0	33.3
Sherman, KS	4 319	49.3	86.6	484	95.5	15.0	-9.4	16.2	0.0	0.0	...	0.0
Smith, KS	3 338	53.4	84.6	69	76.8	16.7	-7.7	16.6	0.0	0.0	45.0	0.0
Stafford, KS	3 254	46.2	82.9	108	89.8	18.4	-6.0	19.1	0.0	9.5	17.6	1.7
Stanton, KS	1 468	53.0	78.0	50	76.0	16.9	-7.5	19.6	0.0	12.5	100.0	4.6
Stevens, KS	3 287	51.5	80.5	184	92.4	17.5	-6.9	19.7	...	26.5	50.0	3.3
Sumner, KS	16 662	51.4	86.3	997	81.1	15.7	-8.7	16.1	12.6	4.9	22.7	3.6
Thomas, KS	4 978	37.5	92.7	745	94.4	25.0	0.6	25.0	0.0	...	56.0	7.1
Trego, KS	2 342	53.3	84.3	131	81.7	14.0	-10.4	14.1	...	0.0	0.0	0.0
Wabaunsee, KS	4 623	55.6	89.9	195	91.3	17.3	-7.1	17.4	0.0	0.0	55.6	28.2
Wallace, KS	1 133	52.7	84.0	31	100.0	17.2	-7.2	17.9	0.0	0.0	...	4.2
Washington, KS	4 572	56.9	81.2	139	90.6	15.2	-9.2	15.3	0.0	16.7	...	0.0
Wichita, KS	1 625	55.1	77.7	37	81.1	15.5	-8.9	17.2	...	33.3	0.0	5.1
Wilson, KS	6 944	56.1	81.1	264	92.4	10.9	-13.5	10.7	0.0	2.2	27.8	22.2
Woodson, KS	2 667	56.8	83.4	120	100.0	11.4	-13.0	11.1	0.0	0.0	55.0	20.0
Wyandotte, KS	96 608	60.3	74.0	6 959	84.1	12.0	-12.4	13.8	10.6	3.7	21.0	5.6
KENTUCKY		59.4	74.1							13.9	52.0	13.0
Adair, KY	11 270	71.1	60.1	1 122	37.9	10.9	-13.5	10.9	12.7	0.0	27.8	0.0
Allen, KY	11 643	74.7	64.5	430	80.9	9.1	-15.3	8.9	5.5	0.0	28.6	12.4
Anderson, KY	12 600	62.6	80.4	539	79.2	12.0	-12.4	12.3	3.8	0.0	0.0	12.3
Ballard, KY	5 766	64.1	76.3	222	95.9	10.6	-13.8	10.8	0.0	100.0	70.0	0.0
Barren, KY	25 751	70.9	69.5	983	89.6	11.1	-13.3	11.1	8.1	0.0	43.9	7.0
Bath, KY	7 451	75.5	59.0	232	86.2	10.1	-14.3	10.0	0.0	0.0	46.7	47.6
Bell, KY	20 042	76.5	56.6	912	80.8	9.0	-15.4	8.9	13.2	22.2	30.4	0.0
Boone, KY	54 166	47.7	85.1	3 592	80.8	22.8	-1.6	22.5	20.2	16.1	61.8	14.6
Bourbon, KY	13 015	63.3	75.4	558	86.2	13.5	-10.9	14.0	5.8	0.0	0.0	6.5
Boyd, KY	34 697	57.3	78.0	2 318	87.7	14.1	-10.3	14.3	9.8	29.8	38.5	2.3
Boyle, KY	18 491	57.7	76.6	1 614	34.4	19.3	-5.1	20.6	8.0	0.0	63.7	5.7
Bracken, KY	5 460	71.0	69.6	263	95.4	9.5	-14.9	9.4	17.1	0.0	...	...
Breathitt, KY	10 393	73.6	57.5	677	77.0	10.0	-14.4	9.8	...	0.0	90.5	0.0
Breckinridge, KY	12 501	75.3	68.9	364	88.5	7.4	-17.0	7.4	4.4	0.0	60.0	11.6
Bullitt, KY	39 307	65.1	76.0	1 964	78.2	9.2	-15.2	9.2	16.9	6.1	34.6	11.8
Butler, KY	8 489	79.7	60.7	324	90.1	6.4	-18.0	6.2	0.0	...	9.8	15.3
Caldwell, KY	9 265	68.1	73.1	456	88.8	10.0	-14.4	10.4	3.0	0.0	31.3	10.2
Calloway, KY	21 032	52.4	77.9	6 520	95.5	24.0	-0.4	23.6	23.7	12.5	60.4	23.1
Campbell, KY	57 184	53.9	80.8	5 232	87.5	20.5	-3.9	20.5	10.2	0.0	55.0	23.4
Carlisle, KY	3 690	66.1	73.4	180	81.7	10.6	-13.8	10.6	9.5	0.0	...	0.0
Carroll, KY	6 690	69.4	68.1	281	80.8	8.3	-16.1	7.9	0.0	34.1	55.6	0.0
Carter, KY	17 394	72.9	64.4	1 317	56.1	8.9	-15.5	8.9	0.0	0.0	18.0	13.6
Casey, KY	10 423	79.3	57.4	259	86.1	7.4	-17.0	7.4	0.0	0.0	0.0	0.0
Christian, KY	40 344	56.1	77.2	3 364	90.3	12.5	-11.9	14.3	5.6	6.9	33.7	11.3
Clark, KY	22 187	61.2	75.0	951	83.3	15.6	-8.8	16.0	7.5	0.0	29.7	5.0
Clay, KY	16 083	79.5	49.4	518	87.3	8.0	-16.4	8.2	5.5	12.5	46.7	7.9
Clinton, KY	6 594	78.1	53.5	293	86.0	8.0	-16.4	8.1	0.0	...	0.0	7.4
Crittenden, KY	6 460	73.2	67.0	266	85.7	7.3	-17.1	7.2	0.0	0.0	100.0	17.2
Cumberland, KY	4 972	80.4	56.0	140	68.6	7.1	-17.3	7.1	8.5	0.0	20.0	0.0
Daviess, KY	59 745	56.9	80.7	3 889	67.5	17.0	-7.4	17.2	7.6	17.6	63.5	17.6

[1] Hispanic or Latino persons may be of any race.
. . . = Not available.

Table C-1. Population, School, and Student Characteristics by County—*Continued*

County	State/ County code	County type[1]	Population, 2000 Total	Population, 2000 Percent 5–17 years	Number of schools and students, 2000–2001 School districts	Number of schools and students, 2000–2001 Schools	Number of schools and students, 2000–2001 Students	Resident enrollment, 2000 Total	Resident enrollment, 2000 Percent public	Resident enrollment, 2000 K–12	Resident enrollment, 2000 Percent public
			1	2	3	4	5	6	7	8	9
Edmonson, KY	21061	9	11 644	17.6	1	4	1 914	2 541	98.4	2 170	98.9
Elliott, KY	21063	8	6 748	18.9	1	4	1 192	1 524	97.8	1 251	98.5
Estill, KY	21065	6	15 307	18.1	1	6	2 604	3 394	95.9	2 847	97.6
Fayette, KY	21067	2	260 512	15.1	1	59	32 455	76 330	84.6	40 156	85.6
Fleming, KY	21069	7	13 792	18.7	1	6	2 407	3 295	91.8	2 635	94.7
Floyd, KY	21071	7	42 441	17.7	1	18	7 133	9 447	91.7	7 480	94.5
Franklin, KY	21073	4	47 687	16.5	2	13	6 727	11 593	84.0	8 273	84.9
Fulton, KY	21075	7	7 752	18.4	2	5	1 288	1 835	94.0	1 546	96.2
Gallatin, KY	21077	1	7 870	21.0	1	5	1 465	1 911	92.0	1 630	94.3
Garrard, KY	21079	6	14 792	18.2	1	5	2 375	3 317	92.6	2 688	93.9
Grant, KY	21081	1	22 384	20.7	2	8	4 338	5 436	91.7	4 684	94.3
Graves, KY	21083	7	37 028	17.9	2	16	5 744	8 421	88.9	6 694	90.3
Grayson, KY	21085	7	24 053	18.2	1	7	4 081	5 375	94.0	4 304	96.1
Green, KY	21087	9	11 518	17.3	1	5	1 680	2 523	91.8	2 001	96.1
Greenup, KY	21089	2	36 891	17.8	3	16	6 180	8 244	91.8	6 591	95.5
Hancock, KY	21091	8	8 392	19.6	1	5	1 523	1 977	91.0	1 641	95.4
Hardin, KY	21093	4	94 174	20.4	3	29	15 089	25 768	89.6	19 560	92.6
Harlan, KY	21095	7	33 202	18.9	2	16	5 973	7 775	94.0	6 320	95.3
Harrison, KY	21097	6	17 983	18.7	1	6	3 128	4 119	92.9	3 420	94.6
Hart, KY	21099	9	17 445	19.2	1	6	2 295	3 765	91.8	3 178	92.2
Henderson, KY	21101	2	44 829	18.2	1	13	6 961	10 565	88.2	8 367	90.0
Henry, KY	21103	8	15 060	18.6	2	7	2 458	3 368	88.9	2 770	92.2
Hickman, KY	21105	9	5 262	16.7	1	2	804	1 077	97.2	923	98.8
Hopkins, KY	21107	7	46 519	18.0	2	17	7 548	10 750	90.9	8 418	92.9
Jackson, KY	21109	8	13 495	19.4	1	6	2 334	2 999	93.8	2 680	95.1
Jefferson, KY	21111	2	693 604	17.5	2	162	94 842	175 028	75.3	123 874	78.0
Jessamine, KY	21113	2	39 041	19.0	1	10	6 509	11 132	71.7	7 372	87.9
Johnson, KY	21115	7	23 445	17.9	2	11	4 472	5 335	95.9	4 333	97.0
Kenton, KY	21117	0	151 464	19.0	5	42	20 759	38 232	71.7	28 640	73.4
Knott, KY	21119	9	17 649	18.5	1	11	2 965	4 684	88.9	3 352	94.6
Knox, KY	21121	7	31 795	19.1	2	13	5 498	7 599	90.0	6 176	96.8
Larue, KY	21123	7	13 373	18.7	1	5	2 313	3 123	91.3	2 527	92.7
Laurel, KY	21125	7	52 715	18.3	2	17	8 854	11 653	91.1	9 704	93.7
Lawrence, KY	21127	8	15 569	19.4	1	5	2 740	3 631	96.7	3 083	97.2
Lee, KY	21129	9	7 916	17.5	1	4	1 342	1 738	86.0	1 513	87.0
Leslie, KY	21131	9	12 401	18.5	1	8	2 223	2 862	93.5	2 347	95.2
Letcher, KY	21133	7	25 277	18.0	2	14	4 210	5 801	94.8	4 656	95.8
Lewis, KY	21135	8	14 092	19.0	1	6	2 435	3 393	95.0	2 737	96.6
Lincoln, KY	21137	7	23 361	18.9	1	10	4 065	5 338	94.4	4 377	96.6
Livingston, KY	21139	9	9 804	17.1	1	6	1 435	2 160	94.4	1 758	95.4
Logan, KY	21141	7	26 573	18.8	2	9	4 429	5 915	92.2	4 992	92.3
Lyon, KY	21143	9	8 080	12.0	1	2	1 043	1 466	84.0	1 240	83.0
McCracken, KY	21145	5	65 514	17.3	2	21	9 697	15 279	86.2	11 690	89.5
McCreary, KY	21147	9	17 080	20.9	1	10	3 340	4 288	93.9	3 653	93.9
McLean, KY	21149	8	9 938	17.6	1	5	1 592	2 167	92.2	1 740	96.3
Madison, KY	21151	2	70 872	15.5	2	20	10 050	22 171	87.8	11 078	91.8
Magoffin, KY	21153	9	13 332	19.7	1	8	2 497	3 284	96.8	2 717	97.6
Marion, KY	21155	7	18 212	18.6	1	7	2 997	4 229	86.3	3 538	89.9
Marshall, KY	21157	7	30 125	16.7	1	10	4 721	6 568	90.5	5 122	93.5
Martin, KY	21159	9	12 578	21.1	1	6	2 206	3 166	97.8	2 630	99.5
Mason, KY	21161	6	16 800	17.8	1	4	2 645	3 816	90.0	3 002	92.5
Meade, KY	21163	6	26 349	21.0	1	9	4 512	6 800	92.6	5 499	94.8
Menifee, KY	21165	9	6 556	19.1	1	6	1 134	1 478	96.5	1 264	96.3
Mercer, KY	21167	6	20 817	18.0	3	9	3 491	4 555	91.5	3 691	96.2
Metcalfe, KY	21169	9	10 037	18.3	1	5	1 580	2 146	91.6	1 807	91.8
Monroe, KY	21171	7	11 756	17.6	1	5	1 981	2 660	95.9	2 077	99.1
Montgomery, KY	21173	6	22 554	17.9	1	9	3 916	4 925	92.4	4 032	94.1
Morgan, KY	21175	9	13 948	17.0	1	8	2 235	3 092	90.6	2 506	90.9
Muhlenberg, KY	21177	7	31 839	16.7	1	13	5 013	6 747	92.9	5 522	94.3
Nelson, KY	21179	6	37 477	20.3	2	11	5 991	9 404	81.7	7 711	83.7
Nicholas, KY	21181	8	6 813	17.4	1	2	1 153	1 392	99.4	1 178	99.4
Ohio, KY	21183	6	22 916	18.6	1	10	3 959	5 308	95.1	4 398	95.7
Oldham, KY	21185	2	46 178	20.8	1	14	8 655	13 104	79.2	10 171	84.6
Owen, KY	21187	8	10 547	19.5	1	4	1 882	2 396	93.9	2 076	95.2
Owsley, KY	21189	9	4 858	19.1	1	2	911	1 167	92.4	936	92.2
Pendleton, KY	21191	1	14 390	21.6	1	4	2 901	3 590	93.8	3 053	95.5
Perry, KY	21193	7	29 390	18.5	2	17	5 701	6 979	95.6	5 444	96.5
Pike, KY	21195	7	68 736	17.6	2	32	11 581	15 519	92.3	12 398	96.9
Powell, KY	21197	6	13 237	19.8	1	6	2 606	3 021	95.8	2 704	97.3
Pulaski, KY	21199	7	56 217	17.5	3	18	9 461	12 531	92.7	10 027	93.8
Robertson, KY	21201	9	2 266	18.3	1	2	380	519	94.8	425	96.7
Rockcastle, KY	21203	6	16 582	18.5	1	7	2 920	3 509	97.3	2 971	98.4
Rowan, KY	21205	7	22 094	14.8	1	8	2 968	8 071	93.8	3 346	90.6
Russell, KY	21207	9	16 315	17.0	1	6	2 681	3 471	94.6	2 771	97.3
Scott, KY	21209	2	33 061	18.7	1	10	5 750	9 002	76.7	6 358	90.1
Shelby, KY	21211	6	33 337	18.3	1	9	5 049	7 538	83.8	6 228	86.8
Simpson, KY	21213	6	16 405	18.8	1	6	2 946	3 705	91.2	3 074	91.8
Spencer, KY	21215	8	11 766	19.7	1	3	2 047	2 845	86.4	2 321	90.1
Taylor, KY	21217	7	22 927	17.4	2	7	3 765	5 780	77.5	4 009	94.4
Todd, KY	21219	8	11 971	19.1	1	4	1 950	2 687	90.0	2 208	90.6

[1]County type code is from the Economic Research Service of the USDA. See Notes and Definitions at the end of this section.

Table C-1. School and Student Characteristics by County—*Continued*

County	Characteristics of students, 2000–2001			Staff and students, 2000–2001				Revenues, fiscal 1999			
	Percent with IEP[2]	Percent eligible for free lunch	Percent minority	Number of teachers	Student/ teacher ratio	Local school non-teaching staff	Central admin. staff	Total revenue ($1,000s)	Percentage of revenue from		
									Federal govt.	State govt.	Local govt.
	10	11	12	13	14	15	16	17	18	19	20
Edmonson, KY	16.5	45.8	0.9	105	18.2	137	13	$11 970	9.4	72.7	17.9
Elliott, KY	22.2	69.7	0.4	70	17.0	107	10	8 590	13.3	74.9	11.8
Estill, KY	16.7	53.8	1.5	13	200.3	161	26	17 120	11.2	76.4	12.4
Fayette, KY	11.3	36.6	29.2	1 970	16.5	2 184	147	234 482	5.5	42.9	51.5
Fleming, KY	12.3	53.7	2.4	142	17.0	175	6	15 836	14.1	70.1	15.8
Floyd, KY	14.6	70.4	0.2	407	17.5	348	37	49 159	11.7	70.5	17.8
Franklin, KY	14.8	33.0	11.8	321	21.0	436	18	41 234	6.5	61.5	32.0
Fulton, KY	22.1	80.0	38.8	79	16.3	109	16	10 205	13.2	67.8	19.0
Gallatin, KY	14.5	47.6	1.9	75	19.5	90	13	8 364	6.6	68.4	25.0
Garrard, KY	14.7	45.1	3.7	127	18.7	153	10	14 161	8.1	69.2	22.7
Grant, KY	13.1	41.6	1.4	36	120.5	274	10	25 382	9.1	68.7	22.2
Graves, KY	13.6	44.3	9.9	333	17.2	417	16	34 804	9.0	68.1	22.9
Grayson, KY	13.2	47.3	0.8	218	18.7	289	10	24 257	8.8	72.4	18.8
Green, KY	12.8	51.8	3.1	104	16.2	132	10	10 186	8.1	72.4	19.5
Greenup, KY	14.4	41.1	1.5	328	18.8	400	35	39 624	8.1	68.7	23.3
Hancock, KY	14.3	34.0	2.0	91	16.7	123	5	10 099	8.6	60.5	30.9
Hardin, KY	13.7	43.2	20.3	813	18.6	1 139	85	96 152	7.4	68.5	24.1
Harlan, KY	16.6	77.2	3.4	337	17.7	515	43	41 577	14.4	71.5	14.1
Harrison, KY	14.6	44.9	4.3	169	18.5	204	20	19 855	9.0	71.2	19.8
Hart, KY	16.1	59.1	5.2	115	20.0	162	8	15 141	11.2	72.1	16.7
Henderson, KY	16.3	41.5	10.6	341	20.4	558	60	45 761	8.1	64.5	27.5
Henry, KY	13.9	47.1	4.9	146	16.8	210	14	16 327	9.4	68.1	22.5
Hickman, KY	17.5	58.7	15.8	53	15.2	63	6	5 752	11.0	67.4	21.6
Hopkins, KY	16.9	49.5	10.3	403	18.7	640	43	49 461	7.7	69.4	22.9
Jackson, KY	17.6	81.4	1.3	149	15.7	235	12	16 389	13.6	77.0	9.4
Jefferson, KY	13.5	48.0	37.8	2 611	36.3	6 877	643	686 868	8.0	48.0	44.0
Jessamine, KY	15.1	41.1	4.2	351	18.5	522	43	38 962	6.4	61.6	32.1
Johnson, KY	13.3	64.6	0.3	267	16.7	341	18	33 145	10.7	66.9	22.5
Kenton, KY	14.5	35.9	7.8	1 072	19.4	1 271	72	133 815	6.5	56.4	37.1
Knott, KY	16.7	72.5	1.0	179	16.6	223	9	22 666	12.3	70.3	17.3
Knox, KY	14.9	76.2	1.0	304	18.1	414	16	36 658	13.8	73.2	13.1
Larue, KY	15.2	43.8	5.3	135	17.1	163	18	14 732	11.1	71.8	17.1
Laurel, KY	14.4	52.8	2.0	418	21.2	847	53	53 121	10.3	69.2	20.5
Lawrence, KY	14.7	63.4	0.2	171	16.0	195	11	17 444	12.7	73.6	13.6
Lee, KY	15.5	76.2	0.3	74	18.1	104	12	9 485	12.6	74.3	13.1
Leslie, KY	17.1	78.9	0.1	130	17.1	191	12	16 807	11.7	73.5	14.8
Letcher, KY	17.0	68.0	1.1	263	16.0	365	17	30 617	10.5	72.6	16.9
Lewis, KY	14.6	66.2	0.2	129	18.9	212	23	15 239	10.9	74.2	14.9
Lincoln, KY	18.9	58.8	3.5	229	17.8	352	32	26 352	14.8	71.0	14.2
Livingston, KY	13.7	44.8	1.0	83	17.3	127	8	9 045	7.6	64.0	28.5
Logan, KY	20.4	. . .	10.7	244	18.2	331	30	29 076	8.9	68.9	22.2
Lyon, KY	10.3	29.7	2.6	54	19.3	57	5	5 661	8.0	54.2	37.7
McCracken, KY	12.8	44.1	19.4	487	19.9	684	67	66 271	9.2	59.6	31.2
McCreary, KY	15.9	87.5	1.9	194	17.2	297	13	23 367	14.0	74.6	11.4
McLean, KY	13.8	42.9	0.8	95	16.8	134	15	9 857	8.1	70.1	21.7
Madison, KY	16.0	47.3	8.2	539	18.6	607	28	62 162	9.0	66.1	24.9
Magoffin, KY	15.3	78.0	0.0	149	16.8	217	14	18 734	12.0	74.0	14.0
Marion, KY	14.8	55.1	9.7	167	17.9	239	9	19 327	10.4	67.3	22.3
Marshall, KY	12.7	34.7	0.4	243	19.4	304	16	29 163	6.5	60.9	32.6
Martin, KY	23.6	68.3	0.3	135	16.3	182	10	18 919	13.5	69.2	17.3
Mason, KY	13.4	47.8	11.2	161	16.4	100	6	17 409	8.8	62.9	28.4
Meade, KY	13.7	40.3	4.7	229	19.7	297	19	26 476	6.8	73.6	19.6
Menifee, KY	19.0	64.1	2.1	83	13.7	102	6	7 004	11.3	76.1	12.6
Mercer, KY	18.1	35.2	6.7	189	18.5	250	23	20 963	7.6	66.4	26.0
Metcalfe, KY	17.3	66.1	4.8	92	17.2	142	11	10 566	12.5	70.2	17.4
Monroe, KY	15.7	65.1	5.3	127	15.6	210	5	13 763	12.5	70.7	16.8
Montgomery, KY	13.2	54.5	4.2	227	17.3	276	19	24 921	11.8	67.1	21.1
Morgan, KY	16.5	71.7	0.7	158	14.1	198	7	15 586	12.4	75.5	12.1
Muhlenberg, KY	15.2	47.7	4.6	330	15.2	403	19	36 509	7.6	62.9	29.5
Nelson, KY	15.4	39.5	10.2	306	19.6	496	21	38 587	6.2	65.8	28.0
Nicholas, KY	10.7	52.1	0.5	68	17.0	75	10	7 536	12.6	69.3	18.1
Ohio, KY	17.0	53.6	1.3	215	18.4	348	2	27 150	7.7	67.8	24.6
Oldham, KY	15.6	12.1	4.5	478	18.1	536	65	48 749	4.3	59.4	36.3
Owen, KY	11.4	46.0	1.9	100	18.8	134	8	11 431	7.8	72.6	19.6
Owsley, KY	15.4	95.0	0.5	54	16.9	124	12	7 438	22.0	68.4	9.6
Pendleton, KY	12.3	. . .	1.2	153	19.0	196	15	16 497	8.1	74.8	17.1
Perry, KY	16.2	66.4	3.4	374	15.2	554	29	41 181	11.4	71.5	17.1
Pike, KY	12.2	64.4	0.8	691	16.8	918	29	88 543	9.8	60.7	29.5
Powell, KY	16.4	59.7	1.2	143	18.2	195	16	16 564	10.8	75.8	13.3
Pulaski, KY	13.6	63.1	2.5	561	16.9	745	38	60 591	10.2	67.0	22.8
Robertson, KY	17.1	51.3	1.8	29	13.1	33	2	2 604	13.6	70.1	16.3
Rockcastle, KY	14.1	66.4	0.2	175	16.7	249	12	19 174	12.4	74.7	12.9
Rowan, KY	18.9	51.4	2.1	174	17.1	205	18	20 872	11.4	67.5	21.1
Russell, KY	14.6	58.0	0.9	163	16.4	218	4	17 796	9.7	72.1	18.3
Scott, KY	14.5	32.0	8.1	320	18.0	371	35	36 751	6.4	56.3	37.2
Shelby, KY	13.5	32.3	16.0	238	21.2	278	28	30 551	5.9	56.5	37.6
Simpson, KY	12.1	36.3	14.2	141	20.9	253	16	18 156	11.1	62.6	26.3
Spencer, KY	16.1	27.0	2.0	98	20.9	153	13	11 849	9.9	68.4	21.7
Taylor, KY	13.3	44.7	6.4	207	18.2	300	36	24 324	8.6	70.8	20.7
Todd, KY	18.9	53.2	14.1	106	18.4	176	1	13 157	9.3	72.4	18.3

[2]IEP = Individual Education Program. See Notes and Definitions at the end of this section.
. . . = Not available.

Table C-1. Population, School, and Student Characteristics by County—*Continued*

County	Current expenditures, fiscal 1999			Resident population 16 to 19 years, 2000				Outcomes, 1999–2000	
	Amount ($1,000s)	Amount per student	Percent for instruction	Total population 16 to 19 years	Percent in Armed Forces	Percent high school graduates	Percent not enrolled, not grads, not Armed Forces, not empl.	Number of graduates	Dropouts grades 9–12 (percent)
	21	22	23	24	25	26	27	28	29
Edmonson, KY	$9 930	$5 053	60.9	675	0.0	11.6	5.9	131	4.6
Elliott, KY	7 497	6 002	59.3	400	0.0	17.3	11.3	75	5.2
Estill, KY	15 281	5 465	66.1	873	0.0	7.3	14.4	140	7.8
Fayette, KY	220 456	6 655	56.7	15 177	0.2	8.0	4.9	1 633	5.7
Fleming, KY	14 052	5 785	65.5	806	0.0	10.8	10.5	165	6.1
Floyd, KY	40 384	5 294	61.5	2 405	0.0	11.2	13.7	420	5.2
Franklin, KY	35 898	5 179	61.8	2 671	0.0	10.1	6.4	407	5.2
Fulton, KY	9 150	6 220	62.3	443	0.0	17.6	7.0	102	4.6
Gallatin, KY	6 610	4 415	57.5	445	0.0	12.8	13.5	74	6.9
Garrard, KY	11 744	4 837	62.7	836	0.0	19.1	8.5	113	7.5
Grant, KY	20 486	4 818	61.1	1 275	0.0	17.5	5.3	201	7.4
Graves, KY	30 054	5 074	63.2	1 907	0.0	12.0	8.5	356	4.3
Grayson, KY	20 399	4 942	64.4	1 296	0.0	14.4	8.2	241	4.8
Green, KY	9 016	5 304	59.6	557	0.0	9.3	3.1	110	4.4
Greenup, KY	34 028	5 239	59.4	1 879	0.0	11.4	4.5	404	3.7
Hancock, KY	8 799	5 762	59.3	434	0.0	6.2	2.8	117	1.6
Hardin, KY	83 128	5 272	62.5	6 193	12.9	25.3	3.3	1 044	4.1
Harlan, KY	35 238	5 391	62.7	1 960	0.0	9.3	15.5	363	6.2
Harrison, KY	17 155	5 270	64.3	978	0.0	8.4	2.6	209	3.7
Hart, KY	13 552	5 721	60.4	847	0.0	16.9	9.8	164	4.5
Henderson, KY	39 401	5 302	61.1	2 613	0.0	14.8	6.9	475	8.6
Henry, KY	14 681	5 454	58.9	774	0.0	15.8	7.8	146	4.4
Hickman, KY	5 770	6 994	60.7	261	0.0	4.2	6.1	51	6.2
Hopkins, KY	42 669	5 297	62.2	2 442	0.0	14.4	8.1	445	3.9
Jackson, KY	14 358	5 880	59.5	768	0.0	15.2	16.0	126	6.1
Jefferson, KY	629 178	6 175	56.1	35 085	0.1	10.6	6.7	4 851	7.6
Jessamine, KY	33 655	5 209	63.7	2 362	0.0	9.7	3.9	313	5.7
Johnson, KY	26 095	5 578	63.3	1 332	0.0	8.2	9.9	270	2.2
Kenton, KY	116 373	5 436	62.2	7 870	0.0	12.7	5.4	1 199	1.8
Knott, KY	21 539	6 389	61.5	1 250	0.0	6.0	11.1	195	9.1
Knox, KY	32 632	5 780	62.2	1 734	0.0	10.0	16.5	313	6.0
Larue, KY	12 884	5 373	60.4	663	0.0	8.6	2.7	141	4.2
Laurel, KY	46 494	5 204	61.3	2 800	0.0	16.6	10.4	414	6.2
Lawrence, KY	14 837	5 186	65.3	978	0.0	8.0	10.7	169	8.4
Lee, KY	7 824	5 545	59.5	431	0.0	16.9	16.0	87	6.2
Leslie, KY	15 348	6 115	55.3	682	0.0	8.7	7.5	120	4.2
Letcher, KY	26 723	5 809	59.9	1 577	0.0	11.0	10.3	266	3.8
Lewis, KY	13 611	5 423	61.2	838	0.0	19.1	6.4	134	1.6
Lincoln, KY	24 143	5 787	67.7	1 166	0.0	14.9	6.4	195	10.0
Livingston, KY	7 952	5 170	55.1	527	0.0	13.7	2.8	88	5.6
Logan, KY	23 759	4 875	61.7	1 479	0.0	12.6	5.3	277	3.8
Lyon, KY	4 699	4 690	57.9	214	0.0	24.3	0.0	49	2.5
McCracken, KY	60 000	5 817	61.8	3 145	0.2	8.5	5.7	646	2.7
McCreary, KY	20 047	5 736	61.4	1 091	0.0	9.0	20.2	179	4.2
McLean, KY	8 600	5 095	57.9	501	0.0	12.4	7.8	111	6.0
Madison, KY	53 060	5 132	66.0	5 219	0.0	9.1	4.1	503	4.6
Magoffin, KY	15 749	5 803	59.0	852	0.0	14.1	13.6	171	8.8
Marion, KY	16 660	5 524	65.6	1 008	0.0	13.7	9.3	207	3.6
Marshall, KY	24 609	4 983	63.1	1 377	0.0	12.6	4.1	284	3.6
Martin, KY	16 099	5 865	59.9	828	0.0	14.9	15.2	146	7.0
Mason, KY	16 558	6 004	66.9	958	0.3	17.0	3.1	158	2.8
Meade, KY	21 620	4 664	65.3	1 551	0.6	17.4	7.6	319	5.4
Menifee, KY	6 461	5 815	64.8	496	0.0	11.3	20.0	64	8.1
Mercer, KY	18 329	5 188	61.5	949	0.0	14.9	7.4	208	2.4
Metcalfe, KY	9 037	5 351	56.2	540	0.0	13.3	13.1	83	4.3
Monroe, KY	12 467	5 917	58.0	701	0.0	10.4	8.0	132	1.5
Montgomery, KY	22 042	5 568	64.8	1 145	0.0	14.5	10.3	232	6.0
Morgan, KY	13 855	5 809	61.2	809	0.0	17.3	11.6	150	5.3
Muhlenberg, KY	30 999	5 825	64.2	1 809	0.0	12.5	13.7	332	3.0
Nelson, KY	32 678	5 112	60.0	2 121	0.0	11.3	5.6	403	4.3
Nicholas, KY	6 697	5 558	64.6	364	0.0	18.7	4.4	68	5.2
Ohio, KY	21 887	5 312	57.6	1 317	0.0	9.3	5.4	220	3.2
Oldham, KY	43 960	5 325	61.0	2 389	0.0	6.4	3.9	546	1.2
Owen, KY	9 232	4 786	59.9	622	0.0	15.0	6.3	119	3.7
Owsley, KY	6 374	7 122	63.5	292	0.0	12.0	18.8	53	4.3
Pendleton, KY	13 999	4 723	61.8	885	0.0	12.5	5.2	145	2.9
Perry, KY	38 255	6 212	59.7	1 843	0.0	10.1	12.6	322	11.1
Pike, KY	69 403	5 601	61.7	3 840	0.0	10.6	9.0	824	4.0
Powell, KY	14 948	5 620	61.1	871	0.0	11.7	6.4	145	6.9
Pulaski, KY	51 948	5 348	62.9	3 108	0.0	9.7	6.7	464	3.6
Robertson, KY	2 267	5 611	58.5	130	0.0	13.8	6.2	21	...
Rockcastle, KY	16 836	5 545	59.7	832	0.0	13.6	8.2	161	5.1
Rowan, KY	18 635	5 855	65.3	2 245	0.0	5.1	2.6	184	3.5
Russell, KY	14 492	5 108	60.7	867	0.0	11.0	11.3	151	7.6
Scott, KY	31 579	5 572	63.1	2 233	0.0	7.5	3.0	326	6.3
Shelby, KY	24 356	5 010	60.6	1 923	1.0	9.6	8.4	261	5.4
Simpson, KY	15 754	5 262	65.9	708	0.0	18.9	3.2	173	3.7
Spencer, KY	10 077	5 074	65.0	631	0.0	11.7	4.3	96	5.1
Taylor, KY	21 231	5 424	63.1	1 385	0.0	12.9	7.1	265	4.5
Todd, KY	10 469	4 865	57.6	623	0.0	17.2	3.2	112	4.4

. . . = Not available.

Table C-1. Population, School, and Student Characteristics by County—*Continued*

County	High school graduates, 2000			College enrollment, 2000		College graduates, 2000 (percent)						
	Population 25 years and over	High school diploma or less (percent)	High school diploma or more (percent)	Number	Percent public	Bachelor's degree or more	+/- U.S. percent with bachelor's degree or more	Non-Hispanic White	Black or African American	American Indian and Alaska Native	Asian, Hawaiian, and Pacific Islander	Hispanic or Latino[1]
	30	31	32	33	34	35	36	37	38	39	40	41
Edmonson, KY	7 865	78.4	61.7	282	94.3	4.9	-19.5	4.9	0.0	33.3	0.0	0.0
Elliott, KY	4 422	78.5	52.6	176	100.0	7.8	-16.6	7.8	. . .	. . .	. . .	. . .
Estill, KY	10 189	78.8	58.5	385	83.4	6.9	-17.5	6.7	0.0	0.0	35.7	41.2
Fayette, KY	167 235	36.6	85.8	31 508	89.4	35.6	11.2	38.7	14.5	17.7	67.3	14.6
Fleming, KY	9 154	71.5	66.5	412	86.7	8.8	-15.6	9.0	5.0	0.0	. . .	0.0
Floyd, KY	28 370	68.6	61.3	1 534	85.0	9.7	-14.7	9.6	2.5	0.0	76.9	6.1
Franklin, KY	32 388	52.6	78.8	2 644	87.1	23.8	-0.6	23.7	24.9	20.0	74.2	14.3
Fulton, KY	5 111	69.4	69.5	133	81.2	11.5	-12.9	13.9	1.1	. . .	. . .	0.0
Gallatin, KY	5 007	76.4	68.0	155	78.1	6.9	-17.5	6.7	12.5	0.0	0.0	11.5
Garrard, KY	9 951	66.3	69.4	476	90.1	10.5	-13.9	10.5	0.0	100.0	36.8	17.9
Grant, KY	13 861	71.8	72.4	503	82.5	9.4	-15.0	9.3	0.0	65.5	13.4	0.0
Graves, KY	24 932	65.5	73.4	1 251	84.1	12.6	-11.8	12.7	7.7	20.0	56.9	1.5
Grayson, KY	15 940	74.3	62.8	684	88.0	7.7	-16.7	7.7	7.1	13.3	0.0	8.3
Green, KY	7 983	74.8	61.4	377	69.5	9.1	-15.3	8.9	6.1	0.0	40.0	0.0
Greenup, KY	25 323	62.6	75.1	1 152	88.5	11.5	-12.9	11.2	14.2	0.0	65.7	26.4
Hancock, KY	5 427	68.5	77.2	253	72.3	8.1	-16.3	8.3	0.0	0.0	0.0	0.0
Hardin, KY	58 358	52.0	82.3	4 879	84.1	15.4	-9.0	15.7	11.5	13.1	30.9	10.8
Harlan, KY	22 041	75.6	58.7	1 004	90.1	8.9	-15.5	8.7	5.6	13.0	51.3	19.4
Harrison, KY	12 009	68.5	74.2	518	89.8	10.6	-13.8	10.6	5.7	7.9	0.0	9.4
Hart, KY	11 474	76.9	58.2	420	87.6	7.0	-17.4	7.3	0.9	34.0	100.0	2.4
Henderson, KY	29 960	59.5	78.3	1 374	92.1	13.8	-10.6	13.9	6.7	15.8	63.2	32.4
Henry, KY	10 032	71.1	73.4	331	68.3	9.8	-14.6	9.8	9.3	0.0	35.0	9.4
Hickman, KY	3 734	74.7	64.4	113	83.2	8.8	-15.6	9.3	0.9	0.0	85.7	18.2
Hopkins, KY	31 464	67.0	71.3	1 433	92.3	10.6	-13.8	10.7	8.2	9.4	45.2	8.1
Jackson, KY	8 611	80.5	52.9	189	77.2	6.8	-17.6	6.8	. . .	0.0	0.0	0.0
Jefferson, KY	464 284	47.2	81.8	37 969	75.5	24.8	0.4	27.2	11.9	19.1	50.6	18.4
Jessamine, KY	24 182	53.3	79.1	3 131	36.0	21.5	-2.9	21.4	14.6	14.3	62.8	24.4
Johnson, KY	15 735	71.4	63.8	778	92.4	9.3	-15.1	9.0	22.2	0.0	61.7	9.1
Kenton, KY	97 727	50.4	82.1	6 815	75.5	22.9	-1.5	23.4	9.4	18.9	43.0	13.5
Knott, KY	11 427	72.1	58.7	1 107	71.2	10.2	-14.2	10.2	0.0	70.6	7.7	0.0
Knox, KY	20 401	78.5	54.1	987	49.4	8.8	-15.6	8.8	5.7	15.0	44.4	11.4
Larue, KY	9 017	69.2	71.0	400	90.0	10.9	-13.5	10.7	6.1	32.1	0.0	49.1
Laurel, KY	34 431	71.0	63.9	1 465	83.5	10.6	-13.8	10.6	5.6	13.5	50.5	13.8
Lawrence, KY	10 256	74.8	58.2	401	95.0	6.6	-17.8	6.5	0.0	50.0	. . .	0.0
Lee, KY	5 381	79.9	50.9	163	71.2	6.3	-18.1	6.5	0.0	0.0	0.0	0.0
Leslie, KY	8 214	77.6	52.5	342	82.2	6.3	-18.1	6.2	0.0	0.0	100.0	15.4
Letcher, KY	16 930	74.4	58.5	858	91.5	7.7	-16.7	7.5	11.7	0.0	68.0	0.0
Lewis, KY	9 256	77.3	57.4	374	83.2	6.4	-18.0	6.4	0.0	6.5	. . .	0.0
Lincoln, KY	15 440	76.1	64.6	603	81.9	8.4	-16.0	8.3	3.6	0.0	91.7	23.6
Livingston, KY	6 851	66.4	74.3	306	89.9	8.4	-16.0	8.3	0.0	8.7	0.0	0.0
Logan, KY	17 471	71.0	68.5	521	95.8	9.6	-14.8	9.9	4.8	0.0	69.7	5.7
Lyon, KY	6 185	68.5	68.0	160	90.6	10.1	-14.3	10.5	0.0	0.0	76.7	6.5
McCracken, KY	45 038	53.1	80.3	2 443	84.2	18.1	-6.3	19.2	6.9	9.7	46.4	16.9
McCreary, KY	10 668	78.4	52.6	433	91.5	6.7	-17.7	6.4	0.0	0.0	52.2	49.1
McLean, KY	6 737	67.8	70.8	327	78.3	8.7	-15.7	8.9	0.0	0.0	0.0	0.0
Madison, KY	42 125	54.5	75.2	10 200	86.2	21.8	-2.6	22.0	10.5	16.2	67.4	13.0
Magoffin, KY	8 410	78.1	50.1	410	91.0	6.3	-18.1	6.3	0.0	0.0	20.0	0.0
Marion, KY	11 772	73.4	70.5	462	60.4	9.1	-15.3	9.2	3.7	0.0	47.2	19.7
Marshall, KY	21 278	61.1	76.9	1 056	85.7	13.7	-10.7	13.8	0.0	11.8	27.0	13.2
Martin, KY	7 835	75.6	54.0	435	89.2	9.0	-15.4	9.2	0.0	0.0	. . .	0.0
Mason, KY	11 372	62.5	73.3	598	82.8	14.4	-10.0	15.0	6.6	0.0	27.3	0.0
Meade, KY	16 131	62.0	77.9	976	84.7	11.3	-13.1	11.0	16.6	0.0	33.0	14.8
Menifee, KY	4 213	81.7	57.6	177	97.7	8.4	-16.0	8.6	0.0	0.0	. . .	0.0
Mercer, KY	14 158	65.8	75.8	529	78.6	13.5	-10.9	13.9	8.3	0.0	19.1	0.0
Metcalfe, KY	6 729	79.6	58.0	258	93.0	6.6	-17.8	6.7	13.0	0.0	. . .	0.0
Monroe, KY	7 896	76.8	57.8	438	82.2	8.4	-16.0	8.6	0.0	0.0	100.0	0.0
Montgomery, KY	15 033	68.8	70.5	574	94.9	13.4	-11.0	13.5	9.3	0.0	85.7	18.9
Morgan, KY	9 321	76.4	56.4	420	89.5	7.7	-16.7	7.9	2.5	0.0	15.4	2.0
Muhlenberg, KY	21 676	74.9	65.8	919	89.2	8.1	-16.3	8.3	5.2	0.0	0.0	0.0
Nelson, KY	23 785	64.1	79.0	1 030	76.8	13.4	-11.0	13.4	9.4	0.0	52.5	15.6
Nicholas, KY	4 636	74.7	62.9	158	98.7	7.5	-16.9	7.2	21.7	0.0	. . .	0.0
Ohio, KY	15 237	74.5	67.0	646	91.0	7.4	-17.0	7.4	15.0	0.0	100.0	0.0
Oldham, KY	30 366	40.0	86.5	1 972	73.9	30.6	6.2	31.7	9.8	50.8	43.7	16.1
Owen, KY	6 999	73.3	67.9	227	86.3	9.1	-15.3	9.0	18.4	0.0	28.6	3.5
Owsley, KY	3 242	78.7	49.2	154	89.6	7.7	-16.7	7.8	. . .	0.0	. . .	0.0
Pendleton, KY	9 081	74.1	72.8	345	83.5	9.7	-14.7	9.8	6.9	0.0	33.3	0.0
Perry, KY	19 596	73.0	58.3	1 179	91.2	8.9	-15.5	8.6	7.4	0.0	78.6	0.0
Pike, KY	46 153	72.6	61.8	2 322	66.5	9.9	-14.5	9.9	0.0	0.0	35.2	13.0
Powell, KY	8 485	80.4	56.1	196	71.9	6.5	-17.9	6.5	0.0	13.3	. . .	10.4
Pulaski, KY	38 430	69.2	65.6	1 781	93.9	10.5	-13.9	10.4	5.7	8.6	40.2	0.7
Robertson, KY	1 566	75.5	60.9	81	84.0	8.7	-15.7	8.8	0.0	. . .	0.0	0.0
Rockcastle, KY	11 109	79.3	57.7	366	87.4	8.3	-16.1	8.3	0.0	0.0	. . .	2.9
Rowan, KY	12 455	58.1	70.9	4 503	98.0	21.9	-2.5	21.7	47.3	0.0	92.4	0.0
Russell, KY	11 437	72.6	61.8	541	78.9	9.6	-14.8	9.6	5.3	33.3	12.1	0.0
Scott, KY	20 459	52.8	80.5	2 150	40.1	20.3	-4.1	20.6	11.8	0.0	66.1	19.5
Shelby, KY	22 096	55.4	79.1	820	74.3	18.7	-5.7	20.4	7.5	0.0	0.0	5.7
Simpson, KY	10 680	67.4	73.6	394	93.4	11.9	-12.5	12.9	3.6	0.0	22.2	0.0
Spencer, KY	7 672	65.0	75.4	307	70.7	11.1	-13.3	11.2	0.0	0.0	0.0	0.0
Taylor, KY	15 253	68.1	68.0	1 403	32.3	12.2	-12.2	12.4	11.7	0.0	0.0	0.0
Todd, KY	7 758	73.2	63.5	237	92.8	9.2	-15.2	10.2	0.6	0.0	0.0	5.6

[1]Hispanic or Latino persons may be of any race.
. . . = Not available.

Table C-1. Population, School, and Student Characteristics by County—*Continued*

County	State/County code	County type[1]	Population, 2000		Number of schools and students, 2000–2001			Resident enrollment, 2000			
			Total	Percent 5–17 years	School districts	Schools	Students	Total	Percent public	K–12	Percent public
			1	2	3	4	5	6	7	8	9
Trigg, KY	21221	8	12 597	17.1	1	3	2 009	2 654	96.2	2 101	97.7
Trimble, KY	21223	8	8 125	19.7	1	4	1 509	2 007	92.5	1 683	94.8
Union, KY	21225	6	15 637	19.1	1	7	2 422	3 952	87.3	3 197	89.6
Warren, KY	21227	5	92 522	16.7	2	31	14 174	28 046	92.7	15 725	93.4
Washington, KY	21229	7	10 916	19.4	1	5	1 808	2 699	80.5	2 182	84.8
Wayne, KY	21231	7	19 923	18.6	2	10	3 392	4 496	97.7	3 808	98.7
Webster, KY	21233	6	14 120	18.1	2	8	2 353	3 296	92.1	2 617	93.3
Whitley, KY	21235	7	35 865	19.4	3	21	7 240	9 292	85.0	6 860	97.9
Wolfe, KY	21237	9	7 065	19.3	1	5	1 326	1 649	93.8	1 333	93.6
Woodford, KY	21239	2	23 208	19.1	1	7	3 762	5 753	76.3	4 442	83.3
LOUISIANA	22000										
Acadia, LA	22001	2	58 861	22.0	1	27	9 984	16 063	79.1	12 993	77.6
Allen, LA	22003	6	25 440	18.2	1	12	4 402	6 125	89.2	5 056	89.5
Ascension, LA	22005	2	76 627	21.9	1	20	14 942	21 867	82.9	17 104	86.7
Assumption, LA	22007	6	23 388	21.5	1	11	4 601	6 255	88.8	5 203	89.2
Avoyelles, LA	22009	6	41 481	20.0	2	14	7 321	10 352	87.9	8 525	88.2
Beauregard, LA	22011	6	32 986	20.5	1	12	6 041	8 255	89.3	6 966	91.3
Bienville, LA	22013	6	15 752	20.8	1	8	2 585	4 152	89.4	3 377	89.5
Bossier, LA	22015	2	98 310	20.4	1	34	18 797	27 569	90.6	20 323	94.4
Caddo, LA	22017	2	252 161	19.9	2	74	45 193	68 792	88.8	50 825	91.9
Calcasieu, LA	22019	3	183 577	20.2	1	59	32 261	50 285	86.2	37 247	88.0
Caldwell, LA	22021	8	10 560	18.6	1	6	1 879	2 531	96.1	2 067	97.4
Cameron, LA	22023	8	9 991	21.7	1	7	1 952	2 578	92.8	2 165	95.2
Catahoula, LA	22025	7	10 920	19.3	1	10	1 910	2 633	93.4	2 161	94.4
Claiborne, LA	22027	6	16 851	19.6	1	10	2 754	4 244	86.5	3 463	85.4
Concordia, LA	22029	7	20 247	20.5	1	10	3 919	5 092	89.8	4 294	91.7
De Soto, LA	22031	6	25 494	21.4	1	13	5 057	6 702	92.5	5 510	94.5
East Baton Rouge, LA	22033	0	412 852	19.1	8	130	57 715	134 817	78.3	79 781	74.4
East Carroll, LA	22035	7	9 421	22.7	1	6	1 848	2 997	87.8	2 518	87.3
East Feliciana, LA	22037	6	21 360	19.2	1	8	2 628	5 150	75.3	4 186	74.7
Evangeline, LA	22039	7	35 434	21.6	1	14	6 407	9 554	89.9	7 763	89.4
Franklin, LA	22041	7	21 263	20.7	1	11	3 930	5 329	86.2	4 430	86.6
Grant, LA	22043	8	18 698	20.8	1	8	3 592	4 695	93.0	3 868	94.3
Iberia, LA	22045	4	73 266	22.0	1	33	14 547	20 021	87.4	16 481	87.8
Iberville, LA	22047	0	33 320	19.7	1	9	4 962	8 553	79.2	6 794	79.4
Jackson, LA	22049	6	15 397	18.8	1	7	2 568	3 746	92.0	2 916	92.3
Jefferson, LA	22051	0	455 466	18.7	1	83	50 891	121 830	62.7	86 794	63.9
Jefferson Davis, LA	22053	6	31 435	21.7	1	14	5 875	8 365	86.9	6 879	88.4
Lafayette, LA	22055	2	190 503	20.1	1	40	28 885	56 319	80.0	38 737	78.9
Lafourche, LA	22057	3	89 974	20.4	1	28	15 165	24 776	84.3	18 800	84.5
La Salle, LA	22059	7	14 282	20.0	1	9	2 656	3 312	95.3	2 811	96.1
Lincoln, LA	22061	4	42 509	16.1	1	19	6 696	17 955	90.9	7 049	85.6
Livingston, LA	22063	2	91 814	22.0	1	36	19 723	25 283	91.1	20 338	95.0
Madison, LA	22065	7	13 728	24.4	1	7	2 584	4 076	87.9	3 448	88.3
Morehouse, LA	22067	6	31 021	20.5	1	15	5 378	7 885	86.5	6 574	85.8
Natchitoches, LA	22069	6	39 080	18.9	2	16	7 424	13 663	91.2	7 674	89.3
Orleans, LA	22071	0	484 674	19.8	4	128	77 861	150 096	73.0	99 998	81.9
Ouachita, LA	22073	3	147 250	20.7	3	51	28 237	44 054	89.0	30 577	90.2
Plaquemines, LA	22075	1	26 757	21.8	1	9	4 978	7 807	81.5	6 134	85.5
Pointe Coupee, LA	22077	6	22 763	20.4	1	9	3 369	5 974	72.8	4 852	71.9
Rapides, LA	22079	3	126 337	20.2	2	55	23 514	33 345	86.4	26 221	89.8
Red River, LA	22081	8	9 622	22.6	1	7	1 917	2 747	89.7	2 257	89.5
Richland, LA	22083	6	20 981	19.9	1	12	3 760	5 489	86.4	4 427	87.2
Sabine, LA	22085	7	23 459	19.7	1	13	4 376	5 663	94.7	4 685	95.4
St. Bernard, LA	22087	0	67 229	18.9	1	14	8 536	17 654	70.1	12 950	71.5
St. Charles, LA	22089	0	48 072	23.0	1	20	9 894	14 720	82.5	11 466	85.9
St. Helena, LA	22091	8	10 525	21.5	1	3	1 463	2 993	81.6	2 370	82.0
St. James, LA	22093	1	21 216	22.5	1	13	4 056	6 103	81.0	4 953	80.3
St. John the Baptist, LA	22095	1	43 044	23.1	1	12	6 436	13 204	67.3	10 116	67.5
St. Landry, LA	22097	2	87 700	21.7	2	37	15 872	24 609	86.7	19 809	86.9
St. Martin, LA	22099	2	48 583	21.8	1	17	8 624	13 235	84.2	10 914	84.6
St. Mary, LA	22101	4	53 500	22.3	2	28	10 990	14 750	86.8	12 006	88.5
St. Tammany, LA	22103	0	191 268	21.4	1	51	32 392	54 129	76.5	41 459	80.5
Tangipahoa, LA	22105	4	100 588	20.5	2	38	18 614	30 230	86.5	20 980	86.6
Tensas, LA	22107	9	6 618	19.9	2	6	1 145	1 750	82.3	1 428	84.8
Terrebonne, LA	22109	3	104 503	21.8	1	41	19 774	28 789	83.7	23 114	85.7
Union, LA	22111	6	22 803	18.7	1	10	3 589	5 345	91.2	4 340	92.5
Vermilion, LA	22113	6	53 807	20.9	1	20	8 901	14 156	87.8	11 657	89.3
Vernon, LA	22115	5	52 531	19.7	1	19	10 215	14 157	93.8	10 708	95.6
Washington, LA	22117	6	43 926	19.6	2	22	7 826	10 968	90.6	9 038	92.1
Webster, LA	22119	6	41 831	19.1	1	22	7 727	10 694	92.9	8 397	94.2
West Baton Rouge, LA	22121	2	21 601	21.0	1	10	3 781	5 967	82.2	4 728	84.0
West Carroll, LA	22123	9	12 314	19.6	1	8	2 467	2 913	96.7	2 498	97.8
West Feliciana, LA	22125	8	15 111	15.7	1	5	2 384	3 830	80.6	3 181	81.9
Winn, LA	22127	7	16 894	18.5	1	8	2 943	4 107	95.7	3 319	97.3

[1]County type code is from the Economic Research Service of the USDA. See Notes and Definitions at the end of this section.

Table C-1. School and Student Characteristics by County—*Continued*

County	Characteristics of students, 2000–2001			Staff and students, 2000–2001				Revenues, fiscal 1999			
	Percent with IEP[2]	Percent eligible for free lunch	Percent minority	Number of teachers	Student/ teacher ratio	Local school non-teaching staff	Central admin. staff	Total revenue ($1,000s)	Percentage of revenue from		
									Federal govt.	State govt.	Local govt.
	10	11	12	13	14	15	16	17	18	19	20
Trigg, KY	16.8	48.9	15.0	105	19.1	155	14	$12 367	7.7	64.8	27.5
Trimble, KY	12.0	47.7	2.1	60	25.2	96	9	8 613	12.5	62.7	24.8
Union, KY	23.1	50.5	12.5	150	16.1	220	22	18 726	8.7	64.2	27.2
Warren, KY	11.8	42.5	17.0	782	18.1	983	51	86 462	7.7	58.6	33.7
Washington, KY	17.5	44.4	11.9	107	16.9	124	4	11 084	9.6	68.1	22.3
Wayne, KY	15.4	70.1	3.0	193	17.6	374	30	23 413	13.1	73.1	13.8
Webster, KY	13.3	48.7	6.3	104	22.6	203	17	15 577	9.1	69.2	21.8
Whitley, KY	14.1	69.5	0.7	404	17.9	629	52	48 916	12.2	69.2	18.6
Wolfe, KY	17.9	86.6	0.5	97	13.7	149	4	10 298	13.7	75.5	10.8
Woodford, KY	11.5	19.6	9.4	193	19.5	310	15	22 949	4.7	56.0	39.3
LOUISIANA											
Acadia, LA	16.0	66.4	29.3	652	15.3	724	24	61 112	16.4	56.0	27.6
Allen, LA	10.4	57.9	26.3	332	13.3	319	15	27 382	10.1	63.5	26.4
Ascension, LA	14.6	39.8	32.4	999	15.0	966	41	104 707	7.8	38.0	54.2
Assumption, LA	12.2	68.1	45.0	318	14.5	376	31	30 206	14.6	60.5	24.9
Avoyelles, LA	10.3	75.3	41.9	431	17.0	408	30	38 365	14.8	66.2	19.0
Beauregard, LA	11.9	43.1	18.5	412	14.7	432	22	36 907	8.1	55.5	36.4
Bienville, LA	13.0	71.2	61.0	191	13.5	195	14	19 596	11.6	47.5	40.9
Bossier, LA	11.4	37.7	33.6	1 101	17.1	1 175	60	103 918	7.7	53.4	38.9
Caddo, LA	14.0	52.9	64.0	2 947	15.3	3 552	177	298 555	9.8	50.2	39.9
Calcasieu, LA	14.2	44.0	34.8	2 107	15.3	2 099	96	194 241	8.7	44.5	46.8
Caldwell, LA	11.4	54.2	20.1	141	13.3	136	9	11 513	12.5	65.0	22.4
Cameron, LA	14.1	37.9	6.2	153	12.8	151	10	14 235	5.9	40.3	53.8
Catahoula, LA	9.7	59.9	37.8	145	13.2	161	14	13 010	15.5	62.9	21.7
Claiborne, LA	15.4	74.1	69.1	208	13.2	213	13	17 157	12.7	60.0	27.3
Concordia, LA	9.2	71.5	51.4	258	15.2	272	23	25 603	16.7	57.8	25.5
De Soto, LA	14.0	64.4	58.7	353	14.3	391	15	37 016	10.0	47.8	42.2
East Baton Rouge, LA	12.1	62.8	71.6	4 117	14.0	4 097	132	346 933	10.9	45.3	43.8
East Carroll, LA	10.3	90.9	92.5	126	14.7	137	16	11 714	19.2	63.8	17.0
East Feliciana, LA	11.9	85.1	81.2	172	15.3	203	16	17 696	13.4	61.6	25.0
Evangeline, LA	14.9	75.0	40.8	403	15.9	445	30	35 193	14.7	67.2	18.1
Franklin, LA	10.4	71.5	48.3	292	13.5	239	15	21 903	17.3	67.2	15.5
Grant, LA	13.1	58.7	16.7	245	14.7	247	13	19 875	12.4	72.9	14.7
Iberia, LA	16.1	60.0	45.9	999	14.6	917	48	93 171	10.2	57.1	32.8
Iberville, LA	13.9	77.3	76.4	335	14.8	347	15	36 287	12.3	40.9	46.8
Jackson, LA	10.9	55.5	37.4	174	14.8	198	13	16 245	10.2	62.2	27.6
Jefferson, LA	15.2	67.0	59.8	3 285	15.5	3 586	101	355 392	12.3	39.6	48.1
Jefferson Davis, LA	16.9	56.8	25.4	370	15.9	410	24	36 724	11.3	58.7	30.0
Lafayette, LA	11.3	46.4	39.6	1 855	15.6	1 510	71	173 826	10.8	45.3	43.9
Lafourche, LA	14.0	55.2	28.1	1 156	13.1	960	74	98 707	10.3	54.3	35.3
La Salle, LA	8.5	48.8	14.5	176	15.1	180	13	16 646	9.0	62.7	28.3
Lincoln, LA	11.1	54.5	50.3	470	14.2	365	19	37 178	9.2	53.7	37.1
Livingston, LA	9.3	40.5	6.4	1 196	16.5	1 034	41	102 476	6.8	67.5	25.8
Madison, LA	10.1	86.8	87.7	163	15.9	181	16	16 880	19.1	63.9	17.0
Morehouse, LA	15.0	72.6	64.6	354	15.2	342	20	32 677	15.0	57.2	27.8
Natchitoches, LA	11.7	66.7	55.7	509	14.6	514	16	44 008	16.7	53.7	29.6
Orleans, LA	9.4	74.6	96.0	4 506	17.3	3 914	204	485 828	15.0	48.5	36.5
Ouachita, LA	11.2	52.4	50.7	1 835	15.4	1 863	86	167 599	11.4	50.7	37.9
Plaquemines, LA	10.8	53.3	39.4	322	15.5	350	25	34 300	10.1	33.1	56.8
Pointe Coupee, LA	19.6	38.6	66.8	210	16.0	239	13	20 233	15.6	49.4	35.0
Rapides, LA	13.2	61.7	45.3	1 549	15.2	1 767	56	146 334	11.4	53.3	35.3
Red River, LA	13.9	80.6	62.1	159	12.1	155	12	14 036	13.6	57.9	28.5
Richland, LA	15.0	68.1	57.8	265	14.2	266	20	22 648	15.5	64.9	19.6
Sabine, LA	15.0	62.9	49.5	304	14.4	323	23	25 686	14.6	62.4	23.0
St. Bernard, LA	14.2	51.8	21.3	581	14.7	502	33	54 015	9.7	51.1	39.2
St. Charles, LA	10.5	42.2	37.6	765	12.9	689	41	87 030	5.9	28.2	65.8
St. Helena, LA	18.0	78.9	92.7	101	14.5	122	12	9 135	16.0	67.9	16.1
St. James, LA	11.1	70.7	68.4	265	15.3	319	21	30 504	11.2	36.8	51.9
St. John the Baptist, LA	20.2	77.7	77.9	457	14.1	397	28	46 214	12.3	46.5	41.2
St. Landry, LA	15.4	76.5	56.0	1 080	14.7	1 094	58	84 133	15.6	65.3	19.2
St. Martin, LA	15.3	69.5	49.0	576	15.0	509	23	51 504	11.9	61.6	26.5
St. Mary, LA	14.3	66.3	51.3	728	15.1	774	38	68 295	12.6	49.9	37.5
St. Tammany, LA	16.1	27.5	17.7	2 178	14.9	2 292	73	218 261	5.6	52.8	41.6
Tangipahoa, LA	14.6	66.2	46.4	1 078	17.3	1 146	45	107 083	13.5	59.5	27.0
Tensas, LA	20.1	83.4	81.0	86	13.3	141	14	8 556	27.5	58.4	14.0
Terrebonne, LA	15.8	57.9	37.7	1 351	14.6	1 231	60	117 417	11.2	53.8	35.1
Union, LA	10.5	58.6	44.1	226	15.9	245	13	17 730	12.9	68.8	18.3
Vermilion, LA	15.2	53.0	25.6	576	15.5	509	36	49 780	12.8	53.5	33.8
Vernon, LA	13.2	52.4	30.2	692	14.8	761	30	60 688	17.0	63.6	19.4
Washington, LA	16.1	74.9	43.3	563	13.9	582	34	47 680	14.2	65.4	20.4
Webster, LA	12.6	50.9	44.2	484	16.0	453	20	44 963	10.3	56.3	33.4
West Baton Rouge, LA	12.0	60.0	49.5	240	15.8	238	14	22 534	10.3	44.5	45.2
West Carroll, LA	10.9	63.6	22.2	186	13.3	133	12	13 104	11.9	72.3	15.9
West Feliciana, LA	13.6	44.3	45.1	189	12.6	196	20	20 232	10.1	37.1	52.8
Winn, LA	11.0	61.8	39.0	211	13.9	231	15	19 271	12.8	58.7	28.6

[2]IEP = Individual Education Program. See Notes and Definitions at the end of this section.

Table C-1. Population, School, and Student Characteristics by County—*Continued*

County	Current expenditures, fiscal 1999			Resident population 16 to 19 years, 2000				Outcomes, 1999–2000	
	Amount ($1,000s)	Amount per student	Percent for instruction	Total population 16 to 19 years	Percent in Armed Forces	Percent high school graduates	Percent not enrolled, not grads, not Armed Forces, not empl.	Number of graduates	Dropouts grades 9–12 (percent)
	21	22	23	24	25	26	27	28	29
Trigg, KY	$10 480	$5 293	62.0	492	0.0	11.2	5.7	98	4.5
Trimble, KY	7 218	5 208	63.7	407	0.0	17.9	4.7	92	3.8
Union, KY	16 118	6 211	63.8	1 607	0.0	13.8	16.9	178	2.5
Warren, KY	81 990	5 767	58.3	6 961	0.0	8.4	4.6	885	2.6
Washington, KY	9 467	5 090	61.7	684	0.0	14.0	8.0	124	1.7
Wayne, KY	21 220	5 867	61.9	1 151	0.0	13.7	12.4	204	6.5
Webster, KY	13 924	5 523	58.8	853	0.0	9.4	7.9	157	4.3
Whitley, KY	40 922	5 515	62.4	2 382	0.0	9.4	9.2	429	3.0
Wolfe, KY	8 869	6 507	66.1	413	0.0	10.4	19.6	93	4.1
Woodford, KY	20 294	5 306	65.2	1 151	0.0	14.5	5.2	225	4.8
LOUISIANA									
Acadia, LA	52 875	5 040	60.6	3 945	0.2	10.3	10.3	511	8.6
Allen, LA	23 365	5 235	57.0	1 453	0.0	13.8	11.2	220	3.3
Ascension, LA	82 680	5 623	62.1	4 719	0.2	10.8	4.9	710	8.1
Assumption, LA	27 169	5 778	59.5	1 438	0.0	5.6	12.7	197	9.4
Avoyelles, LA	36 116	4 830	59.1	2 560	0.0	10.2	18.3	405	10.0
Beauregard, LA	33 163	5 406	57.2	2 068	0.2	13.9	8.0	351	3.1
Bienville, LA	17 536	6 131	58.7	979	0.3	11.5	6.8	150	9.1
Bossier, LA	99 111	5 307	58.6	5 796	4.4	13.7	6.1	972	7.2
Caddo, LA	268 771	5 708	61.0	15 746	0.3	11.3	9.5	2 279	11.3
Calcasieu, LA	176 262	5 323	61.2	11 513	0.1	12.7	5.8	1 817	6.2
Caldwell, LA	10 634	5 280	59.6	512	0.0	11.3	18.8	83	7.7
Cameron, LA	13 336	6 430	56.0	612	0.0	12.6	7.4	134	2.5
Catahoula, LA	11 794	5 673	56.0	843	0.0	14.9	16.6	115	11.3
Claiborne, LA	15 251	5 154	59.8	1 032	0.0	11.2	12.8	157	5.6
Concordia, LA	22 499	5 476	58.4	1 161	0.6	9.8	14.3	168	8.7
De Soto, LA	32 748	6 286	56.7	1 533	0.0	14.6	10.8	286	8.7
East Baton Rouge, LA	327 092	5 786	59.4	30 936	0.0	8.2	6.0	2 916	13.6
East Carroll, LA	10 825	5 354	54.3	622	0.0	10.6	10.3	79	8.8
East Feliciana, LA	14 330	5 009	58.0	1 273	0.0	11.9	8.4	156	8.5
Evangeline, LA	32 872	4 823	59.5	2 313	0.0	8.7	13.7	283	12.6
Franklin, LA	21 886	5 232	58.2	1 346	0.0	15.1	13.4	194	13.7
Grant, LA	18 859	5 108	55.3	1 052	0.0	13.4	9.2	146	8.0
Iberia, LA	84 676	5 618	61.0	4 571	0.0	11.5	10.2	714	8.3
Iberville, LA	33 331	6 296	55.7	2 182	0.0	12.6	14.5	234	9.0
Jackson, LA	15 375	5 617	59.4	961	0.0	13.2	11.9	154	7.1
Jefferson, LA	315 888	5 892	61.7	25 239	0.1	9.7	6.5	2 530	12.1
Jefferson Davis, LA	32 507	5 308	57.4	2 076	0.0	16.3	9.7	329	7.2
Lafayette, LA	159 507	5 210	66.2	12 509	0.1	9.9	6.7	1 684	10.7
Lafourche, LA	86 848	5 517	62.8	6 126	0.0	12.7	5.4	888	7.1
La Salle, LA	14 608	4 812	60.0	1 078	0.0	9.1	18.8	152	6.8
Lincoln, LA	34 103	4 996	63.2	4 912	0.0	4.2	2.5	370	7.3
Livingston, LA	90 999	4 743	63.0	5 829	0.0	12.0	6.2	995	1.2
Madison, LA	15 058	4 659	56.4	1 402	0.0	6.8	20.3	115	13.6
Morehouse, LA	29 475	5 219	60.7	2 109	0.0	12.5	14.2	243	10.1
Natchitoches, LA	39 524	5 500	58.6	3 932	0.0	6.3	5.7	339	9.9
Orleans, LA	433 962	5 281	62.8	30 841	0.3	9.6	8.0	3 608	9.9
Ouachita, LA	141 288	5 017	65.0	10 101	0.1	10.9	8.8	1 219	10.3
Plaquemines, LA	31 404	6 109	57.0	1 648	0.0	12.0	4.3	261	3.0
Pointe Coupee, LA	17 646	4 857	54.5	1 517	0.5	12.3	8.0	184	11.0
Rapides, LA	129 882	5 427	59.4	8 535	0.2	11.7	9.8	1 190	7.6
Red River, LA	12 261	5 966	59.4	689	0.0	8.9	10.2	90	13.2
Richland, LA	21 119	5 407	61.4	1 283	0.0	12.2	13.4	209	10.0
Sabine, LA	22 967	5 049	57.8	1 334	0.0	8.5	8.0	262	6.4
St. Bernard, LA	48 309	5 400	61.6	3 813	0.2	11.6	5.8	554	8.6
St. Charles, LA	77 272	7 630	61.2	3 070	0.0	7.0	6.6	579	7.9
St. Helena, LA	8 575	5 586	58.0	740	0.0	13.4	9.3	64	11.3
St. James, LA	28 049	6 111	53.7	1 450	0.0	10.8	9.2	260	9.5
St. John the Baptist, LA	39 185	5 914	61.6	2 839	0.3	7.2	9.5	326	8.6
St. Landry, LA	76 184	4 767	63.2	5 787	0.0	9.0	9.8	898	6.3
St. Martin, LA	46 430	5 339	62.9	3 133	0.0	9.2	10.2	446	7.6
St. Mary, LA	63 813	5 635	59.2	3 311	0.0	10.9	9.5	547	8.1
St. Tammany, LA	187 344	5 755	63.1	10 690	0.1	8.3	5.1	1 841	8.4
Tangipahoa, LA	88 512	4 726	63.3	7 310	0.1	9.8	10.0	1 085	9.1
Tensas, LA	7 984	6 213	56.6	456	0.0	9.6	14.5	58	10.5
Terrebonne, LA	109 651	5 320	63.6	7 026	0.0	8.5	8.6	1 070	11.1
Union, LA	16 325	4 358	56.9	1 297	0.0	8.9	7.2	203	7.8
Vermilion, LA	49 769	5 285	61.6	3 486	0.3	8.8	10.4	520	6.1
Vernon, LA	57 484	5 492	60.4	3 387	18.1	30.5	4.2	465	8.3
Washington, LA	43 763	5 521	60.5	2 637	0.3	13.7	11.4	391	4.9
Webster, LA	39 265	4 939	60.3	2 383	0.0	9.9	9.7	413	10.0
West Baton Rouge, LA	19 279	4 898	55.5	1 482	0.0	14.2	6.3	218	10.9
West Carroll, LA	12 221	4 715	61.5	773	0.0	14.4	7.6	138	6.9
West Feliciana, LA	17 664	7 450	57.0	749	0.0	11.3	8.9	125	6.6
Winn, LA	18 100	5 826	58.4	966	0.0	6.3	10.1	130	5.2

Table C-1. Population, School, and Student Characteristics by County—*Continued*

County	High school graduates, 2000			College enrollment, 2000		College graduates, 2000 (percent)						
	Population 25 years and over	High school diploma or less (percent)	High school diploma or more (percent)	Number	Percent public	Bachelor's degree or more	+/- U.S. percent with bachelor's degree or more	Non-Hispanic White	Black or African American	American Indian and Alaska Native	Asian, Hawaiian, and Pacific Islander	Hispanic or Latino[1]
	30	31	32	33	34	35	36	37	38	39	40	41
Trigg, KY	8 897	64.6	72.1	399	90.0	12.0	-12.4	12.7	4.6	0.0	41.7	5.0
Trimble, KY	5 340	70.2	70.7	215	81.4	7.6	-16.8	7.7	18.2	0.0	...	0.0
Union, KY	9 524	66.0	76.9	530	77.5	10.9	-13.5	11.4	6.0	0.0	21.6	0.0
Warren, KY	56 069	51.0	80.3	10 926	95.6	24.7	0.3	25.8	10.6	17.1	50.1	9.5
Washington, KY	7 144	69.7	68.8	369	48.0	13.3	-11.1	14.1	2.7	39.1	18.2	0.0
Wayne, KY	13 153	78.0	57.8	423	87.5	7.2	-17.2	7.4	0.0	13.5	0.0	0.0
Webster, KY	9 424	72.6	70.9	543	92.4	7.1	-17.3	7.3	4.5	...	0.0	0.0
Whitley, KY	22 708	70.1	61.3	1 972	38.1	13.4	-11.0	13.3	0.0	28.0	53.2	13.0
Wolfe, KY	4 571	77.1	53.6	217	91.7	10.6	-13.8	10.2	0.0	...	84.6	61.5
Woodford, KY	15 546	46.9	82.6	960	59.8	25.9	1.5	27.1	11.8	100.0	90.0	3.7
LOUISIANA		57.6	74.8								9.2	35.2	19.5
Acadia, LA	35 573	73.4	64.7	1 884	89.0	9.4	-15.0	10.2	5.0	0.0	19.0	14.5
Allen, LA	16 817	74.8	63.2	646	87.2	9.3	-15.1	11.3	4.2	0.7	6.4	10.3
Ascension, LA	46 258	62.1	79.6	3 105	83.8	14.5	-9.9	15.9	7.8	6.6	26.1	15.0
Assumption, LA	14 411	77.5	59.4	666	89.2	7.4	-17.0	7.9	6.4	0.0	8.8	0.0
Avoyelles, LA	26 606	77.3	59.8	1 013	86.8	8.3	-16.1	9.4	4.4	4.8	28.7	17.2
Beauregard, LA	21 036	64.5	75.0	853	88.2	13.8	-10.6	14.2	8.6	20.2	14.3	28.4
Bienville, LA	10 172	69.4	71.9	514	91.6	11.5	-12.9	13.6	8.5	7.7	0.0	8.3
Bossier, LA	61 237	49.5	83.0	5 161	87.3	18.1	-6.3	20.5	8.5	12.7	23.8	13.1
Caddo, LA	159 011	53.5	78.7	13 004	84.7	20.6	-3.8	27.1	10.6	11.6	43.8	17.8
Calcasieu, LA	114 563	57.5	77.0	9 274	90.3	16.9	-7.5	19.0	8.3	6.3	37.0	19.5
Caldwell, LA	6 922	73.2	65.4	311	90.4	8.8	-15.6	9.8	4.2	0.0	22.2	6.3
Cameron, LA	6 257	74.7	68.1	230	95.2	7.9	-16.5	8.3	4.2	0.0	0.0	6.8
Catahoula, LA	6 904	75.3	61.4	325	92.3	9.4	-15.0	10.4	6.0	0.0	...	12.5
Claiborne, LA	11 169	69.5	65.7	455	93.0	12.4	-12.0	17.4	6.0	25.0	0.0	14.9
Concordia, LA	12 814	69.9	64.6	406	85.0	9.6	-14.8	10.9	6.6	3.8	41.9	7.4
De Soto, LA	16 118	70.3	70.3	782	85.5	10.2	-14.2	12.6	6.7	0.8	40.0	7.3
East Baton Rouge, LA	245 296	42.5	83.9	45 355	91.7	30.8	6.4	37.4	17.8	27.3	51.6	35.8
East Carroll, LA	5 542	73.3	57.9	218	93.6	12.3	-12.1	18.1	8.4	100.0	70.6	0.0
East Feliciana, LA	13 877	68.8	70.7	530	84.2	11.3	-13.1	16.4	4.8	0.0	18.6	8.5
Evangeline, LA	21 511	75.2	55.5	1 127	94.9	9.5	-14.9	11.4	3.6	0.0	22.1	2.0
Franklin, LA	13 423	75.1	61.4	464	89.9	9.8	-14.6	10.6	7.1	0.0	25.0	0.0
Grant, LA	11 921	68.5	73.1	436	90.8	9.8	-14.6	10.1	5.6	18.3	22.9	15.4
Iberia, LA	43 965	71.6	66.9	2 222	89.9	11.2	-13.2	13.1	6.4	20.5	7.9	12.0
Iberville, LA	21 101	73.2	65.7	1 124	88.6	9.6	-14.8	11.9	6.6	0.0	11.1	13.1
Jackson, LA	10 062	66.1	73.6	541	94.6	12.9	-11.5	12.9	13.1	0.0	29.4	0.0
Jefferson, LA	298 761	50.7	79.3	25 389	68.5	21.5	-2.9	23.6	12.2	10.9	35.4	18.6
Jefferson Davis, LA	19 352	71.8	69.4	903	90.7	9.9	-14.5	10.8	6.2	4.5	15.2	0.0
Lafayette, LA	116 183	49.2	79.8	13 951	91.8	25.5	1.1	29.1	11.1	17.5	46.2	20.5
Lafourche, LA	55 891	71.7	66.3	4 683	90.6	12.4	-12.0	13.1	5.1	3.7	42.4	13.9
La Salle, LA	9 219	70.0	68.5	371	91.4	11.2	-13.2	12.2	4.3	0.0	3.4	3.1
Lincoln, LA	22 059	44.3	80.4	10 157	96.7	31.8	7.4	35.1	22.9	27.1	84.5	22.0
Livingston, LA	56 528	66.0	77.2	3 235	89.4	11.4	-13.0	11.6	6.5	9.6	26.5	11.7
Madison, LA	7 670	70.3	63.4	325	87.7	11.0	-13.4	14.8	8.0	0.0	28.6	6.9
Morehouse, LA	19 446	72.2	66.6	810	97.5	9.7	-14.7	11.6	6.7	14.7	0.0	6.8
Natchitoches, LA	22 033	59.4	72.7	5 204	95.8	18.4	-6.0	23.8	8.6	12.3	50.7	26.7
Orleans, LA	300 568	48.8	74.7	39 625	53.9	25.8	1.4	47.6	13.4	17.1	31.5	27.1
Ouachita, LA	88 430	51.4	78.6	10 363	92.5	22.7	-1.7	26.6	13.1	9.1	48.0	12.2
Plaquemines, LA	16 448	65.5	68.7	1 234	70.9	10.8	-13.6	13.4	3.3	1.6	10.3	7.7
Pointe Coupee, LA	14 577	70.0	69.1	683	85.9	12.8	-11.6	14.7	9.0	0.0	3.0	12.3
Rapides, LA	79 811	59.1	74.6	4 620	75.2	16.5	-7.9	19.5	8.5	9.0	37.3	14.9
Red River, LA	5 792	74.4	67.4	285	93.7	8.7	-15.7	11.0	4.7	0.0	0.0	0.0
Richland, LA	13 060	70.3	61.9	647	87.0	12.8	-11.6	16.9	3.9	0.0	100.0	19.0
Sabine, LA	15 388	70.1	70.8	705	89.9	11.1	-13.3	12.6	4.7	7.2	39.1	6.0
St. Bernard, LA	44 127	64.8	73.1	3 378	78.1	8.9	-15.5	9.1	5.6	7.9	20.3	7.4
St. Charles, LA	29 551	56.1	80.0	2 134	81.6	17.5	-6.9	19.5	9.7	0.0	42.3	19.3
St. Helena, LA	6 489	72.0	67.5	453	77.5	11.2	-13.2	13.6	8.9	0.0	0.0	14.6
St. James, LA	12 840	71.2	73.9	712	84.7	10.1	-14.3	11.1	8.7	0.0	13.3	18.4
St. John the Baptist, LA	25 377	62.1	76.9	1 978	77.5	12.9	-11.5	14.5	10.0	9.6	44.5	13.5
St. Landry, LA	53 592	71.2	62.0	3 169	89.9	10.7	-13.7	12.7	7.4	4.7	24.6	9.7
St. Martin, LA	29 617	74.9	62.9	1 475	85.3	8.5	-15.9	10.6	3.4	9.6	5.5	14.4
St. Mary, LA	33 158	72.3	65.9	1 563	83.9	9.4	-15.0	10.8	6.1	3.9	9.5	11.5
St. Tammany, LA	122 959	42.6	83.9	8 143	79.8	28.3	3.9	29.7	15.0	20.7	38.0	28.9
Tangipahoa, LA	59 909	62.8	71.5	7 455	92.1	16.3	-8.1	19.2	7.2	11.1	30.4	17.9
Tensas, LA	4 208	68.3	63.2	179	92.2	14.8	-9.6	23.3	6.7	0.0	0.0	9.6
Terrebonne, LA	63 271	68.7	67.1	3 785	86.9	12.3	-12.1	13.6	7.0	2.0	32.0	15.7
Union, LA	14 819	68.4	71.7	670	91.5	11.8	-12.6	13.5	6.5	17.0	0.0	10.5
Vermilion, LA	33 616	72.4	65.6	1 667	88.9	10.7	-13.7	11.4	6.9	14.6	4.0	5.9
Vernon, LA	29 329	56.3	80.1	2 577	91.3	13.5	-10.9	14.3	8.9	9.1	22.7	15.2
Washington, LA	27 954	71.9	68.2	1 262	85.1	10.9	-13.5	12.7	6.6	10.6	0.0	10.2
Webster, LA	27 687	65.1	70.8	1 480	90.8	12.6	-11.8	14.3	8.4	8.1	27.7	4.7
West Baton Rouge, LA	13 347	67.2	73.4	838	86.0	11.1	-13.3	12.2	9.2	17.6	0.0	15.5
West Carroll, LA	7 994	75.3	59.5	305	95.4	9.5	-14.9	10.9	2.8	0.0	0.0	0.0
West Feliciana, LA	10 749	70.8	53.3	447	74.0	10.6	-13.8	19.1	2.7	0.0	11.8	8.8
Winn, LA	11 093	74.6	65.4	494	89.7	9.4	-15.0	11.8	4.1	0.0	11.8	0.0

[1]Hispanic or Latino persons may be of any race.
. . . = Not available.

Table C-1. Population, School, and Student Characteristics by County—*Continued*

County	State/County code	County type[1]	Population, 2000 Total	Population, 2000 Percent 5–17 years	Number of schools and students, 2000–2001 School districts	Number of schools and students, 2000–2001 Schools	Number of schools and students, 2000–2001 Students	Resident enrollment, 2000 Total	Resident enrollment, 2000 Percent public	Resident enrollment, 2000 K–12	Resident enrollment, 2000 Percent public
			1	2	3	4	5	6	7	8	9
MAINE	23000										
Androscoggin, ME	23001	3	103 793	18.0	12	42	16 564	25 970	80.3	18 993	89.2
Aroostook, ME	23003	5	73 938	17.6	30	51	12 309	17 892	95.5	13 414	96.9
Cumberland, ME	23005	3	265 612	17.5	17	95	40 333	68 515	82.4	47 766	91.4
Franklin, ME	23007	6	29 467	18.4	9	18	5 085	8 413	92.4	5 706	94.5
Hancock, ME	23009	6	51 791	17.4	32	38	7 878	12 336	86.0	9 173	92.8
Kennebec, ME	23011	4	117 114	18.4	21	57	18 331	30 287	83.7	22 240	93.4
Knox, ME	23013	7	39 618	17.1	11	28	6 972	8 546	85.7	6 908	90.1
Lincoln, ME	23015	9	33 616	17.9	18	16	3 728	7 510	82.4	6 137	86.9
Oxford, ME	23017	6	54 755	18.9	13	41	10 608	12 792	87.9	10 674	91.4
Penobscot, ME	23019	3	144 919	17.5	30	89	24 590	40 435	88.0	26 268	92.8
Piscataquis, ME	23021	6	17 235	18.6	9	19	2 970	3 892	89.8	3 221	93.5
Sagadahoc, ME	23023	6	35 214	19.7	8	20	6 932	8 939	88.0	7 054	94.2
Somerset, ME	23025	7	50 888	19.0	12	38	9 129	11 942	90.2	9 920	93.6
Waldo, ME	23027	6	36 280	18.6	7	26	5 204	8 692	88.5	6 873	95.6
Washington, ME	23029	7	33 941	17.8	37	36	4 933	8 044	92.2	6 122	94.0
York, ME	23031	4	186 742	18.9	15	72	32 492	46 836	84.1	35 798	91.4
MARYLAND	24000										
Allegany, MD	24001	3	74 930	15.5	1	24	10 416	18 070	91.9	11 666	92.6
Anne Arundel, MD	24003	0	489 656	18.5	1	117	74 491	131 201	79.4	93 322	83.5
Baltimore, MD	24005	0	754 292	17.6	1	161	106 898	201 904	76.6	135 001	80.3
Calvert, MD	24009	1	74 563	22.8	1	23	16 170	21 773	87.6	17 349	91.4
Caroline, MD	24011	6	29 772	20.6	1	9	5 557	7 456	90.4	6 178	91.3
Carroll, MD	24013	1	150 897	21.0	1	38	27 528	41 776	81.6	31 629	90.2
Cecil, MD	24015	2	85 951	20.7	1	30	15 905	22 438	85.5	17 589	89.5
Charles, MD	24017	1	120 546	21.6	1	32	23 468	35 134	82.5	26 224	85.9
Dorchester, MD	24019	7	30 674	17.9	1	11	4 869	7 043	88.6	5 525	90.6
Frederick, MD	24021	1	195 277	20.4	1	53	36 885	54 005	84.0	39 734	92.6
Garrett, MD	24023	8	29 846	19.0	1	16	4 946	6 978	91.6	5 660	93.9
Harford, MD	24025	0	218 590	20.7	1	53	39 520	61 532	82.3	45 281	87.5
Howard, MD	24027	0	247 842	20.7	1	65	44 946	73 343	80.2	51 631	87.8
Kent, MD	24029	6	19 197	16.1	1	8	2 795	4 940	68.5	3 114	90.1
Montgomery, MD	24031	0	873 341	18.5	1	191	134 180	240 098	74.9	164 578	81.9
Prince George's, MD	24033	0	801 515	19.5	1	190	133 723	249 844	80.3	162 830	84.6
Queen Anne's, MD	24035	1	40 563	19.0	1	12	7 217	9 899	87.0	7 714	89.9
St. Mary's, MD	24037	4	86 211	20.7	1	25	15 151	25 031	82.0	17 963	84.1
Somerset, MD	24039	7	24 747	13.7	1	10	3 063	7 036	89.1	3 949	92.8
Talbot, MD	24041	6	33 812	16.5	1	9	4 521	7 292	76.9	5 584	80.7
Washington, MD	24043	3	131 923	17.3	1	45	19 782	29 792	86.4	23 374	90.7
Wicomico, MD	24045	5	84 644	18.5	1	25	14 138	24 554	88.3	16 004	90.0
Worcester, MD	24047	7	46 543	15.7	1	13	6 892	9 832	89.5	7 510	92.3
Baltimore city, MD	24510	0	651 154	18.4	1	182	99 859	184 513	76.9	125 546	84.7
MASSACHUSETTS	25000										
Barnstable, MA	25001	3	222 230	15.7	20	60	32 505	47 762	85.2	35 283	93.5
Berkshire, MA	25003	3	134 953	17.2	18	55	20 689	34 081	81.2	23 446	90.9
Bristol, MA	25005	2	534 678	18.2	27	177	93 311	137 870	82.2	99 120	90.3
Dukes, MA	25007	9	14 987	17.2	7	8	2 593	3 307	89.4	2 622	97.0
Essex, MA	25009	0	723 419	18.5	38	222	118 199	194 443	78.6	138 179	87.6
Franklin, MA	25011	4	71 535	18.3	18	40	11 260	18 575	87.9	13 222	89.7
Hampden, MA	25013	2	456 228	19.5	22	152	78 380	127 601	81.9	90 633	89.9
Hampshire, MA	25015	2	152 251	15.0	20	55	21 057	55 111	77.6	23 193	89.2
Middlesex, MA	25017	0	1 465 396	16.2	66	383	210 488	391 638	67.9	239 751	88.1
Nantucket, MA	25019	7	9 520	13.7	1	3	1 201	1 800	76.3	1 412	87.6
Norfolk, MA	25021	0	650 308	17.0	35	188	97 989	169 601	69.6	112 513	85.9
Plymouth, MA	25023	1	472 822	19.8	31	136	80 207	128 952	83.2	95 640	91.8
Suffolk, MA	25025	0	689 807	14.6	15	164	79 633	209 914	57.7	110 369	82.7
Worcester, MA	25027	2	750 963	19.0	53	255	132 081	205 456	78.7	144 395	89.5
MICHIGAN	26000										
Alcona, MI	26001	9	11 719	14.7	1	3	1 048	2 113	94.6	1 764	95.7
Alger, MI	26003	7	9 862	16.0	4	6	1 570	2 015	94.5	1 715	96.5
Allegan, MI	26005	2	105 665	21.6	10	43	18 388	28 058	85.3	23 175	87.7
Alpena, MI	26007	7	31 314	18.2	1	14	5 516	7 992	89.4	5 933	91.4
Antrim, MI	26009	9	23 110	18.6	6	13	4 164	5 301	95.0	4 437	96.2
Arenac, MI	26011	8	17 269	18.0	3	6	2 946	4 010	94.8	3 230	97.3
Baraga, MI	26013	9	8 746	17.4	3	7	1 407	2 051	93.4	1 668	93.6
Barry, MI	26015	6	56 755	20.5	3	17	8 249	14 796	89.3	11 597	91.4
Bay, MI	26017	2	110 157	18.4	9	41	17 444	27 880	83.7	20 593	85.3
Benzie, MI	26019	9	15 998	17.5	2	7	2 551	3 445	90.0	2 795	92.2
Berrien, MI	26021	3	162 453	19.5	17	81	28 475	42 978	79.6	32 070	86.6
Branch, MI	26023	6	45 787	19.2	3	16	6 432	11 468	90.1	9 109	92.1
Calhoun, MI	26025	2	137 985	19.5	12	70	24 448	36 415	86.1	27 015	92.2
Cass, MI	26027	6	51 104	19.5	4	22	7 595	12 592	91.2	10 025	92.7
Charlevoix, MI	26029	7	26 090	19.4	5	14	4 429	6 278	91.1	5 162	94.1
Cheboygan, MI	26031	7	26 448	17.8	4	12	3 930	5 790	89.2	4 839	90.0
Chippewa, MI	26033	7	38 543	15.9	9	23	7 046	10 308	93.6	6 715	94.1
Clare, MI	26035	7	31 252	18.6	3	14	5 664	7 307	93.6	5 985	94.8
Clinton, MI	26037	2	64 753	21.2	6	31	10 004	18 094	87.5	13 925	89.6
Crawford, MI	26039	9	14 273	19.1	1	5	2 122	3 404	94.6	2 843	95.9

[1]County type code is from the Economic Research Service of the USDA. See Notes and Definitions at the end of this section.

Table C-1. School and Student Characteristics by County—*Continued*

County	Characteristics of students, 2000–2001			Staff and students, 2000–2001				Revenues, fiscal 1999			
	Percent with IEP[2]	Percent eligible for free lunch	Percent minority	Number of teachers	Student/ teacher ratio	Local school non-teaching staff	Central admin. staff	Total revenue ($1,000s)	Percentage of revenue from		
									Federal govt.	State govt.	Local govt.
	10	11	12	13	14	15	16	17	18	19	20
MAINE											
Androscoggin, ME	16.3	33.6	3.5	1 233	13.4	1 204	52	$125 483	5.0	52.2	42.9
Aroostook, ME	13.9	42.6	4.5	890	13.8	1 041	50	102 168	7.6	57.3	35.1
Cumberland, ME	13.8	20.5	6.0	2 889	14.0	3 033	130	326 757	3.7	33.9	62.4
Franklin, ME	14.5	37.8	2.0	368	13.8	383	16	42 254	6.0	41.7	52.4
Hancock, ME	18.6	25.2	2.2	665	11.8	617	36	72 346	5.7	26.6	67.7
Kennebec, ME	15.9	30.8	2.5	1 345	13.6	1 459	55	158 079	7.5	49.2	43.4
Knox, ME	15.1	. . .	1.6	540	12.9	554	35	41 763	3.8	26.3	69.9
Lincoln, ME	15.9	25.2	1.5	313	11.9	324	13	57 238	3.8	32.0	64.2
Oxford, ME	15.6	40.3	1.7	726	14.6	875	38	90 862	4.9	46.1	49.0
Penobscot, ME	14.5	33.4	3.0	1 751	14.0	1 849	83	185 170	5.2	47.7	47.1
Piscataquis, ME	12.3	50.3	1.7	183	16.2	263	9	25 854	9.2	54.0	36.7
Sagadahoc, ME	18.6	27.9	4.0	480	14.4	516	28	56 865	3.7	42.3	54.0
Somerset, ME	17.1	43.2	1.6	636	14.4	761	28	86 884	7.0	50.4	42.6
Waldo, ME	18.2	43.3	1.3	368	14.1	487	21	43 649	6.6	48.8	44.6
Washington, ME	16.0	51.9	5.8	431	11.4	439	21	49 625	8.5	44.2	47.3
York, ME	15.6	22.9	2.5	2 171	15.0	2 255	74	243 136	3.5	43.7	52.7
MARYLAND											
Allegany, MD	18.1	45.8	4.8	641	16.2	578	39	85 689	8.8	55.7	35.5
Anne Arundel, MD	13.5	15.6	24.9	4 232	17.6	3 222	172	548 398	4.2	34.1	61.7
Baltimore, MD	12.4	26.5	38.3	6 718	15.9	5 266	363	842 932	5.0	34.7	60.3
Calvert, MD	13.4	12.3	17.5	878	18.4	783	51	110 321	3.6	39.3	57.0
Caroline, MD	14.0	40.8	22.9	325	17.1	289	26	38 787	8.2	57.3	34.5
Carroll, MD	13.7	8.2	4.4	1 530	18.0	1 051	83	202 775	2.9	42.6	54.5
Cecil, MD	16.1	20.8	8.6	1 012	15.7	689	51	112 034	4.5	47.5	48.0
Charles, MD	11.4	21.2	40.1	1 289	18.2	918	95	163 535	3.8	44.9	51.3
Dorchester, MD	12.8	44.7	44.4	322	15.1	225	24	38 202	9.0	50.5	40.5
Frederick, MD	12.1	13.4	13.6	2 205	16.7	1 671	94	258 407	3.5	41.3	55.2
Garrett, MD	16.0	44.6	0.5	358	13.8	240	25	38 748	10.1	50.2	39.7
Harford, MD	14.4	15.4	18.7	2 431	16.3	1 741	112	266 980	3.9	45.0	51.1
Howard, MD	10.4	9.4	30.1	2 951	15.2	2 302	171	356 291	1.9	29.8	68.3
Kent, MD	12.3	37.9	30.0	179	15.6	144	19	23 157	9.0	37.6	53.4
Montgomery, MD	12.2	21.8	51.0	8 440	15.9	7 636	538	1 305 960	3.2	20.3	76.5
Prince George's, MD	10.9	41.6	88.6	7 628	17.5	6 703	482	1 026 408	5.2	45.3	49.5
Queen Anne's, MD	14.0	15.0	11.9	429	16.8	339	35	57 696	4.2	35.3	60.5
St. Mary's, MD	13.7	20.0	23.6	894	16.9	171	25	120 896	4.0	44.5	51.5
Somerset, MD	12.9	56.8	47.9	207	14.8	598	58	27 445	17.2	47.6	35.3
Talbot, MD	11.2	29.7	27.9	292	15.5	260	30	34 965	6.1	20.9	73.0
Washington, MD	15.0	27.7	10.4	1 277	15.5	857	74	141 671	6.1	48.4	45.5
Wicomico, MD	12.1	34.9	39.8	963	14.7	746	65	116 832	6.5	48.7	44.9
Worcester, MD	13.1	32.9	29.0	461	15.0	400	38	57 229	6.9	20.0	73.0
Baltimore city, MD	16.9	71.6	89.2	5 935	16.8	3 774	801	874 926	12.6	61.5	25.9
MASSACHUSETTS											
Barnstable, MA	14.6	14.4	8.1	. . .	. . .	1 713	143	265 206	4.3	24.2	71.5
Berkshire, MA	15.9	24.2	7.2	. . .	. . .	1 017	104	197 292	4.7	48.0	47.4
Bristol, MA	16.2	24.6	12.4	. . .	. . .	3 537	312	678 926	5.4	58.5	36.1
Dukes, MA	17.7	9.2	13.0	. . .	. . .	176	38	31 333	2.4	24.0	73.5
Essex, MA	16.1	27.4	26.0	. . .	. . .	5 410	921	964 587	5.4	45.9	48.7
Franklin, MA	18.7	27.2	6.1	. . .	. . .	793	80	112 678	4.6	51.9	43.5
Hampden, MA	19.1	40.5	38.6	. . .	. . .	5 010	656	676 434	7.3	64.2	28.6
Hampshire, MA	17.0	16.5	10.9	. . .	. . .	1 183	178	174 794	4.3	45.3	50.3
Middlesex, MA	16.0	16.9	20.2	. . .	. . .	9 453	1 621	1 903 679	4.1	30.0	65.8
Nantucket, MA	14.5	4.5	6.7	. . .	. . .	132	13	13 457	2.4	12.3	85.3
Norfolk, MA	16.8	9.1	13.9	. . .	. . .	4 270	620	791 214	3.5	26.4	70.1
Plymouth, MA	15.0	15.8	17.2	. . .	. . .	3 880	853	667 679	4.1	46.8	49.1
Suffolk, MA	18.4	69.0	78.7	. . .	. . .	5 437	450	867 550	6.6	39.8	53.6
Worcester, MA	15.1	22.3	18.0	. . .	. . .	6 282	701	1 043 428	4.9	53.0	42.1
MICHIGAN											
Alcona, MI	12.6	. . .	0.6	67	15.6	69	3	7 972	6.2	38.8	55.0
Alger, MI	13.5	. . .	15.2	98	16.0	93	9	11 998	5.1	65.0	29.9
Allegan, MI	12.7	20.1	7.1	1 026	17.9	1 175	65	151 100	5.0	62.1	32.9
Alpena, MI	12.1	35.2	2.3	303	18.2	399	20	45 794	6.6	60.6	32.8
Antrim, MI	10.5	33.4	3.3	243	17.1	254	21	32 537	3.9	47.5	48.6
Arenac, MI	11.9	44.4	2.5	165	17.9	157	7	22 358	6.3	66.3	27.4
Baraga, MI	13.0	. . .	29.1	93	15.1	74	10	11 351	10.1	67.3	22.6
Barry, MI	11.5	18.1	3.8	460	17.9	499	23	60 846	4.1	71.9	24.0
Bay, MI	12.5	30.6	8.9	887	19.7	1 081	55	145 543	7.0	62.7	30.3
Benzie, MI	9.0	44.7	6.4	139	18.4	146	4	16 786	4.4	52.5	43.1
Berrien, MI	14.5	41.0	29.8	1 755	16.2	2 023	136	264 737	14.1	60.3	25.7
Branch, MI	16.2	29.1	4.7	349	18.4	428	30	66 955	7.3	68.4	24.3
Calhoun, MI	13.8	36.5	22.9	1 472	16.6	1 540	119	226 859	8.3	64.6	27.1
Cass, MI	12.5	35.9	16.3	428	17.7	484	33	59 000	10.3	65.9	23.8
Charlevoix, MI	13.5	26.0	6.3	261	17.0	345	45	50 920	5.4	47.2	47.4
Cheboygan, MI	13.1	34.0	3.5	233	16.9	283	25	36 283	9.1	51.3	39.6
Chippewa, MI	12.2	41.4	40.3	448	15.7	410	63	50 446	12.7	62.5	24.9
Clare, MI	17.2	49.0	2.8	338	16.8	411	27	46 324	9.3	63.8	26.9
Clinton, MI	13.6	13.4	3.8	538	18.6	589	45	80 480	3.5	70.7	25.8
Crawford, MI	14.5	55.0	2.5	123	17.3	143	8	15 556	6.0	56.5	37.5

[2]IEP = Individual Education Program. See Notes and Definitions at the end of this section.
. . . = Not available.

Table C-1. Population, School, and Student Characteristics by County—*Continued*

County	Current expenditures, fiscal 1999			Resident population 16 to 19 years, 2000				Outcomes, 1999–2000	
	Amount ($1,000s)	Amount per student	Percent for instruction	Total population 16 to 19 years	Percent in Armed Forces	Percent high school graduates	Percent not enrolled, not grads, not Armed Forces, not empl.	Number of graduates	Dropouts grades 9–12 (percent)
	21	22	23	24	25	26	27	28	29
MAINE									
Androscoggin, ME	$109 941	$6 875	68.1	5 914	0.1	12.6	3.9	905	3.3
Aroostook, ME	91 108	7 138	64.4	4 324	0.0	9.4	4.5	848	2.6
Cumberland, ME	293 128	7 385	66.3	13 901	0.6	8.9	2.2	2 147	3.8
Franklin, ME	37 402	6 994	64.3	2 046	0.0	5.5	4.3	359	3.0
Hancock, ME	61 496	7 501	67.4	2 771	0.8	8.8	4.8	441	4.7
Kennebec, ME	140 205	7 278	65.5	6 528	0.0	8.6	3.2	1 113	2.5
Knox, ME	35 956	7 579	66.0	1 781	0.4	14.6	4.0	427	2.5
Lincoln, ME	49 952	8 010	70.3	1 605	0.2	12.3	5.1	149	2.7
Oxford, ME	75 705	7 093	63.4	2 969	0.1	12.4	3.9	560	3.1
Penobscot, ME	157 687	6 873	67.8	9 564	0.1	8.9	2.8	1 523	3.7
Piscataquis, ME	23 077	7 273	66.4	971	0.0	12.3	5.0	148	3.2
Sagadahoc, ME	49 502	7 121	66.6	1 848	0.6	10.3	3.2	446	4.5
Somerset, ME	80 331	6 967	67.4	2 737	0.1	9.7	4.4	553	3.1
Waldo, ME	37 588	7 173	64.7	1 860	0.3	10.1	3.2	281	2.3
Washington, ME	40 873	7 906	64.5	1 912	0.8	11.7	6.0	296	3.3
York, ME	218 461	6 758	67.7				3.2	1 803	
MARYLAND									
Allegany, MD	77 903	7 096	63.5	4 583	0.0	13.3	3.9	771	3.5
Anne Arundel, MD	490 785	6 625	61.3	24 457	5.6	15.8	4.1	4 324	4.7
Baltimore, MD	759 633	7 172	62.6	39 091	0.0	11.5	3.9	6 495	3.6
Calvert, MD	102 123	6 701	58.7	4 209	0.0	14.0	1.8	895	3.6
Caroline, MD	37 086	6 523	60.0	1 692	0.1	17.8	5.3	314	6.5
Carroll, MD	174 606	6 414	59.7	8 043	0.0	12.4	2.5	1 863	2.7
Cecil, MD	100 263	6 448	60.0	4 586	0.2	19.6	6.0	802	4.9
Charles, MD	146 608	6 585	57.5	6 551	0.3	15.2	3.7	1 531	4.4
Dorchester, MD	36 241	7 047	59.6	1 435	0.0	16.6	7.6	305	7.1
Frederick, MD	243 437	6 880	63.2	10 177	0.1	11.5	1.9	2 276	2.9
Garrett, MD	36 463	7 175	61.4	1 783	0.0	11.0	6.1	301	4.0
Harford, MD	237 590	6 106	63.1	10 922	0.5	13.0	2.2	2 342	4.2
Howard, MD	315 034	7 526	62.2	11 305	0.1	8.4	1.8	2 804	1.8
Kent, MD	21 884	7 570	58.7	1 140	0.0	11.8	2.5	157	3.7
Montgomery, MD	1 100 781	8 604	62.8	38 934	0.2	7.1	3.3	7 651	1.8
Prince George's, MD	909 134	6 979	51.1	46 313	0.4	10.0	4.1	7 364	2.8
Queen Anne's, MD	49 718	7 218	54.2	1 952	0.6	11.6	5.1	374	4.0
St. Mary's, MD	96 728	6 561	59.4	5 076	2.5	14.8	4.7	887	3.2
Somerset, MD	23 968	7 699	57.4	1 704	0.2	12.3	2.1	184	5.2
Talbot, MD	30 915	6 735	61.7	1 267	0.0	13.5	9.2	253	2.5
Washington, MD	126 795	6 290	63.8	6 116	0.1	16.4	8.0	1 126	6.1
Wicomico, MD	94 484	6 593	62.6	5 618	0.0	11.5	4.5	766	5.5
Worcester, MD	51 460	7 441	61.1	1 930	0.0	14.4	4.1	412	4.3
Baltimore city, MD	775 840	7 282	64.7	38 950	0.0	12.0	11.6	3 652	10.5
MASSACHUSETTS									
Barnstable, MA	248 901	7 721	65.1	8 984	0.5	10.1	2.9	1 851	3.9
Berkshire, MA	174 436	8 155	67.2	7 721	0.0	10.2	3.0	1 369	5.0
Bristol, MA	632 457	7 394	66.3	28 560	0.1	9.7	5.0	5 387	4.8
Dukes, MA	25 965	10 734	68.0	693	0.0	11.8	6.3	153	4.0
Essex, MA	898 595	7 772	68.2	35 775	0.1	7.8	3.4	5 852	3.4
Franklin, MA	100 531	8 443	65.8	3 862	0.1	7.8	5.7	608	4.7
Hampden, MA	630 562	8 298	68.1	26 293	0.1	8.2	6.8	4 100	5.4
Hampshire, MA	159 745	7 568	64.7	14 283	0.0	4.0	1.0	1 375	3.1
Middlesex, MA	1 785 131	8 680	67.5	70 607	0.0	7.8	2.5	12 001	2.9
Nantucket, MA	13 167	10 636	56.0	263	0.0	11.8	1.9	76	1.5
Norfolk, MA	750 034	7 869	66.7	28 590	0.0	6.7	1.9	5 625	2.2
Plymouth, MA	621 951	7 337	66.1	24 590	0.0	9.3	3.3	4 058	3.7
Suffolk, MA	807 379	10 452	64.5	41 057	0.1	7.4	4.9	3 675	9.7
Worcester, MA	951 541	7 495	68.0	39 549	0.1	10.2	4.2	6 747	3.6
MICHIGAN									
Alcona, MI	6 946	6 615	64.7	516	0.6	8.7	5.0	69	...
Alger, MI	10 104	6 280	61.9	488	0.0	13.9	4.1	128	...
Allegan, MI	117 761	6 474	58.0	6 337	0.0	12.4	4.8	1 122	...
Alpena, MI	38 139	6 869	54.8	1 803	0.0	7.0	3.8	429	...
Antrim, MI	26 723	6 472	61.8	1 093	0.0	9.0	3.8	276	...
Arenac, MI	17 588	5 845	65.7	927	0.0	13.1	6.8	205	...
Baraga, MI	9 297	6 231	65.6	449	0.0	11.1	4.7	107	...
Barry, MI	50 996	6 215	64.4	3 145	0.1	9.9	4.4	516	...
Bay, MI	124 840	7 140	58.8	5 860	0.3	7.9	4.3	1 210	...
Benzie, MI	15 011	6 048	62.6	767	0.0	14.1	2.9	117	...
Berrien, MI	216 418	7 374	54.8	9 364	0.0	7.8	6.8	1 582	...
Branch, MI	55 606	7 076	61.6	2 534	0.0	9.6	5.4	445	...
Calhoun, MI	172 988	7 317	58.0	7 887	0.0	9.3	7.7	1 347	...
Cass, MI	47 593	6 321	53.9	2 834	0.0	9.1	7.2	392	...
Charlevoix, MI	39 641	8 944	55.1	1 357	0.0	12.7	3.2	295	...
Cheboygan, MI	30 797	7 651	55.1	1 358	0.0	10.7	4.1	274	...
Chippewa, MI	42 537	7 057	57.2	2 214	0.0	11.2	4.0	368	...
Clare, MI	39 075	6 925	61.0	1 582	0.0	12.4	5.5	339	...
Clinton, MI	63 086	6 358	58.5	3 817	0.0	7.2	2.0	764	...
Crawford, MI	12 754	5 633	60.9	745	0.0	10.5	3.6	143	...

. . . = Not available.

Table C-1. Population, School, and Student Characteristics by County—*Continued*

County	High school graduates, 2000			College enrollment, 2000		College graduates, 2000 (percent)						
	Population 25 years and over	High school diploma or less (percent)	High school diploma or more (percent)	Number	Percent public	Bachelor's degree or more	+/- U.S. percent with bachelor's degree or more	Non-Hispanic White	Black or African American	American Indian and Alaska Native	Asian, Hawaiian, and Pacific Islander	Hispanic or Latino[1]
	30	31	32	33	34	35	36	37	38	39	40	41

MAINE

County	30	31	32	33	34	35	36	37	38	39	40	41
Androscoggin, ME	69 560	60.3	79.8	5 688	54.1	14.4	-10.0	14.3	14.9	19.8	29.7	14.5
Aroostook, ME	51 439	61.6	76.9	3 541	91.4	14.6	-9.8	14.6	33.9	2.5	41.1	12.1
Cumberland, ME	181 276	38.1	90.1	16 414	67.6	34.2	9.8	34.6	26.3	16.4	28.0	30.3
Franklin, ME	19 260	55.8	85.2	2 382	90.1	20.9	-3.5	20.8	0.0	27.3	25.6	46.3
Hancock, ME	36 416	46.7	87.8	2 559	69.1	27.1	2.7	27.1	41.7	10.9	42.6	10.6
Kennebec, ME	79 362	52.4	85.2	6 428	58.0	20.7	-3.7	20.7	20.4	6.2	28.8	16.4
Knox, ME	28 303	48.9	87.5	1 146	73.9	26.2	1.8	26.3	0.0	30.4	36.5	18.6
Lincoln, ME	24 094	47.2	87.9	976	70.4	26.6	2.2	26.6	0.0	17.0	57.8	19.6
Oxford, ME	37 929	60.7	82.4	1 405	77.3	15.7	-8.7	15.8	37.9	6.2	29.4	9.4
Penobscot, ME	95 505	52.7	85.7	12 276	82.8	20.3	-4.1	20.2	15.0	11.0	47.8	26.1
Piscataquis, ME	12 240	63.4	80.3	432	79.2	13.3	-11.1	13.5	16.7	3.3	0.0	8.3
Sagadahoc, ME	23 862	47.8	88.0	1 396	69.7	25.0	0.6	25.0	26.0	50.0	36.2	26.4
Somerset, ME	34 750	64.5	80.8	1 445	76.3	11.8	-12.6	11.9	16.7	8.6	2.6	9.6
Waldo, ME	24 818	54.2	84.6	1 306	59.1	22.3	-2.1	22.4	21.4	11.1	35.6	24.7
Washington, ME	23 488	62.0	79.9	1 543	87.8	14.7	-9.7	14.6	12.1	6.5	38.2	20.0
York, ME	127 591	48.5	86.5	8 279	64.8	22.9	-1.5	22.9	22.6	20.2	25.1	17.3

MARYLAND

County	30	31	32	33	34	35	36	37	38	39	40	41
Allegany, MD	51 205	62.5	79.9	5 521	94.3	14.1	-10.3	14.0	9.3	7.9	58.7	17.3
Anne Arundel, MD	326 999	41.5	86.4	29 356	78.2	30.6	6.2	32.1	19.4	22.8	40.7	28.2
Baltimore, MD	511 434	43.2	84.3	53 162	75.0	30.6	6.2	30.9	24.6	17.9	54.8	29.1
Calvert, MD	47 768	47.5	86.9	3 148	81.4	22.5	-1.9	24.4	8.4	9.9	56.1	28.2
Caroline, MD	19 550	67.0	75.0	836	90.3	12.1	-12.3	13.3	4.2	35.9	50.0	3.4
Carroll, MD	98 684	48.0	85.3	7 232	61.6	24.8	0.4	24.8	16.4	38.2	39.9	28.3
Cecil, MD	55 809	56.7	81.2	3 383	74.0	16.4	-8.0	16.3	11.1	29.9	50.1	22.9
Charles, MD	76 987	47.5	85.8	6 299	80.7	20.0	-4.4	21.2	15.9	7.6	31.5	26.4
Dorchester, MD	21 435	67.8	74.2	1 012	85.5	12.0	-12.4	14.0	5.6	0.0	37.0	11.9
Frederick, MD	127 256	43.0	87.1	10 587	66.2	30.0	5.6	30.8	11.5	20.9	54.4	27.1
Garrett, MD	20 004	64.4	79.2	1 015	84.3	13.8	-10.6	13.8	0.0	25.0	100.0	15.8
Harford, MD	143 056	41.5	86.7	11 837	75.8	27.3	2.9	27.8	20.3	38.7	36.6	23.3
Howard, MD	163 308	23.1	93.1	16 025	73.7	52.9	28.5	54.5	42.9	35.1	62.0	37.5
Kent, MD	13 103	57.1	78.8	1 568	25.9	21.7	-2.7	25.3	5.6	21.4	96.3	5.9
Montgomery, MD	594 034	24.2	90.3	57 291	68.7	54.6	30.2	62.1	39.6	32.2	59.7	22.1
Prince George's, MD	503 698	42.4	84.9	72 662	77.7	27.2	2.8	34.4	23.9	17.6	46.6	12.8
Queen Anne's, MD	28 018	46.0	84.2	1 540	83.5	25.4	1.0	27.2	6.7	23.5	25.9	27.2
St. Mary's, MD	54 552	49.6	85.3	5 548	82.0	22.6	-1.8	23.9	8.6	11.7	50.6	31.5
Somerset, MD	16 321	67.2	69.5	2 785	83.9	11.6	-12.8	13.7	7.3	0.0	52.7	6.5
Talbot, MD	24 809	46.3	84.4	1 167	75.5	27.8	3.4	31.4	6.6	22.2	34.5	22.3
Washington, MD	90 371	61.1	77.8	4 852	74.6	14.6	-9.8	15.2	4.1	8.5	32.3	15.3
Wicomico, MD	53 521	53.7	80.7	7 234	89.4	21.9	-2.5	24.9	9.9	22.9	32.5	25.7
Worcester, MD	34 092	52.5	81.7	1 681	86.6	21.6	-2.8	24.1	6.9	0.0	35.4	10.4
Baltimore city, MD	419 581	59.8	68.4	48 736	58.6	19.1	-5.3	32.9	10.0	16.7	51.8	24.6

MASSACHUSETTS

County	30	31	32	33	34	35	36	37	38	39	40	41
Barnstable, MA	165 115	35.4	91.8	8 492	70.8	33.6	9.2	34.4	20.0	15.5	42.4	21.3
Berkshire, MA	93 339	49.1	85.1	8 313	59.4	26.0	1.6	26.2	12.3	4.3	53.4	19.9
Bristol, MA	357 829	56.4	73.2	28 891	64.3	19.9	-4.5	20.1	16.9	16.6	39.6	9.5
Dukes, MA	10 693	32.8	90.4	409	64.1	38.4	14.0	39.4	32.0	14.7	42.6	40.6
Essex, MA	487 103	43.5	84.6	41 131	61.0	31.3	6.9	33.4	16.6	20.1	40.3	9.1
Franklin, MA	49 121	43.3	88.0	4 171	86.8	29.1	4.7	29.2	31.5	14.5	43.3	17.2
Hampden, MA	295 837	53.4	79.2	28 292	62.5	20.5	-3.9	22.7	14.4	10.2	31.5	6.2
Hampshire, MA	93 193	36.4	89.4	29 423	70.9	37.9	13.5	37.0	55.6	49.4	67.8	36.7
Middlesex, MA	1 006 497	34.9	88.5	121 081	35.7	43.6	19.2	43.9	30.3	34.1	61.2	24.1
Nantucket, MA	6 976	36.1	91.6	250	44.0	38.4	14.0	42.4	7.5	. . .	43.1	7.1
Norfolk, MA	452 517	33.0	91.3	42 232	38.0	42.9	18.5	42.8	37.3	19.4	52.0	37.3
Plymouth, MA	312 683	43.1	87.6	23 274	65.0	27.8	3.4	29.1	16.0	12.6	36.4	14.3
Suffolk, MA	446 504	47.6	78.1	91 260	27.6	32.5	8.1	42.7	15.7	12.9	35.7	13.2
Worcester, MA	495 868	46.7	83.5	46 184	52.9	26.9	2.5	27.6	19.3	17.3	42.7	11.5

MICHIGAN

County	30	31	32	33	34	35	36	37	38	39	40	41
Alcona, MI	8 958	62.1	79.7	211	86.3	10.9	-13.5	10.8	0.0	0.0	46.7	0.0
Alger, MI	7 169	60.8	81.5	190	92.1	14.7	-9.7	15.8	0.0	9.3	33.3	13.6
Allegan, MI	66 925	56.8	82.3	3 319	79.7	15.8	-8.6	16.3	7.8	8.5	31.6	6.2
Alpena, MI	21 399	52.6	83.1	1 635	87.1	13.2	-11.2	13.1	24.1	1.5	48.7	14.0
Antrim, MI	16 025	52.5	84.6	565	90.1	19.4	-5.0	19.5	20.8	4.3	50.0	23.7
Arenac, MI	11 868	65.4	76.8	567	84.8	9.1	-15.3	9.7	3.9	7.7	57.5	1.9
Baraga, MI	6 097	58.4	80.6	224	87.1	10.9	-13.5	12.1	0.0	6.7	30.8	0.0
Barry, MI	37 132	52.5	86.8	2 195	87.2	14.7	-9.7	14.7	13.6	12.0	47.6	19.7
Bay, MI	74 146	54.5	82.4	5 444	89.5	14.2	-10.2	14.3	7.0	8.8	42.0	6.3
Benzie, MI	11 283	51.0	85.4	435	89.0	20.0	-4.4	20.4	0.0	5.5	28.6	11.1
Berrien, MI	106 690	49.9	81.9	8 218	59.4	19.6	-4.8	20.5	10.9	11.1	61.0	18.2
Branch, MI	30 300	60.8	80.0	1 547	86.2	10.6	-13.8	11.0	2.8	1.5	49.2	4.0
Calhoun, MI	90 137	52.4	83.2	7 216	68.8	16.0	-8.4	16.6	9.7	7.7	41.7	11.2
Cass, MI	34 286	57.2	80.4	1 816	87.7	12.1	-12.3	12.6	7.2	6.2	24.2	5.2
Charlevoix, MI	17 528	49.1	86.0	761	83.4	19.8	-4.6	20.1	29.2	10.8	34.4	11.4
Cheboygan, MI	18 562	58.7	81.9	587	88.9	13.9	-10.5	14.3	0.0	4.4	31.5	0.0
Chippewa, MI	25 683	53.6	82.4	3 124	93.6	15.0	-9.4	16.7	4.2	10.4	25.4	10.5
Clare, MI	21 333	64.3	76.1	953	90.6	8.8	-15.6	8.8	0.0	5.9	36.4	8.8
Clinton, MI	41 864	43.7	89.2	3 148	89.6	21.2	-3.2	21.3	34.1	14.2	38.3	12.8
Crawford, MI	9 871	56.8	80.8	400	88.8	12.9	-11.5	13.2	0.0	3.2	29.2	27.7

[1]Hispanic or Latino persons may be of any race.
. . . = Not available.

Table C-1. Population, School, and Student Characteristics by County—*Continued*

County	State/County code	County type[1]	Population, 2000		Number of schools and students, 2000–2001			Resident enrollment, 2000			
			Total	Percent 5–17 years	School districts	Schools	Students	Total	Percent public	K–12	Percent public
			1	2	3	4	5	6	7	8	9
Delta, MI	26041	7	38 520	18.4	6	20	6 966	9 845	91.8	7 366	92.8
Dickinson, MI	26043	7	27 472	19.6	4	11	5 174	6 743	93.9	5 563	94.8
Eaton, MI	26045	2	103 655	19.8	9	36	16 679	28 631	87.0	21 041	91.3
Emmet, MI	26047	7	31 437	19.2	4	15	5 341	7 935	90.2	6 103	91.4
Genesee, MI	26049	2	436 141	20.2	22	159	80 645	120 255	88.8	90 051	91.8
Gladwin, MI	26051	6	26 023	17.7	2	9	3 880	5 597	90.4	4 696	91.4
Gogebic, MI	26053	7	17 370	15.9	5	9	2 254	3 902	88.9	2 933	89.9
Grand Traverse, MI	26055	7	77 654	19.3	3	27	12 668	19 918	84.3	15 076	85.4
Gratiot, MI	26057	6	42 285	17.9	6	21	7 676	11 080	82.3	7 956	93.5
Hillsdale, MI	26059	6	46 527	19.9	10	24	7 735	12 176	84.2	9 235	93.3
Houghton, MI	26061	7	36 016	16.4	9	18	5 688	12 652	94.3	6 172	96.1
Huron, MI	26063	7	36 079	18.7	17	28	6 059	8 425	87.9	6 984	90.1
Ingham, MI	26065	2	279 320	17.1	12	107	46 630	102 939	91.2	49 177	91.5
Ionia, MI	26067	6	61 518	20.0	10	35	12 112	15 973	88.1	13 143	90.3
Iosco, MI	26069	7	27 339	17.7	4	17	6 104	5 740	93.0	4 899	93.9
Iron, MI	26071	9	13 138	16.3	35	43	12 805	2 727	97.4	2 246	97.9
Isabella, MI	26073	4	63 351	15.1	19	34	13 480	28 337	93.7	9 886	88.7
Jackson, MI	26075	3	158 422	19.1	12	57	25 983	41 089	84.6	31 331	88.8
Kalamazoo, MI	26077	2	238 603	17.6	9	80	34 145	78 268	87.1	42 746	88.4
Kalkaska, MI	26079	9	16 571	19.1	3	11	2 815	3 785	94.0	3 169	95.4
Kent, MI	26081	2	574 335	20.5	24	243	96 856	165 304	78.8	120 383	84.0
Keweenaw, MI	26083	9	2 301	18.0	1	1	11	501	86.8	423	89.1
Lake, MI	26085	9	11 333	16.7	1	4	793	2 313	92.1	1 939	92.8
Lapeer, MI	26087	1	87 904	21.3	6	32	14 985	24 153	88.2	19 201	90.2
Leelanau, MI	26089	9	21 119	19.3	4	8	2 760	5 224	85.0	4 165	87.4
Lenawee, MI	26091	1	98 890	19.6	12	45	18 898	26 304	84.1	20 161	91.7
Livingston, MI	26093	1	156 951	21.5	5	41	27 303	44 359	87.8	34 074	92.0
Luce, MI	26095	9	7 024	16.4	1	4	1 244	1 638	89.6	1 391	88.4
Mackinac, MI	26097	7	11 943	17.5	6	11	1 763	2 544	96.2	2 148	96.9
Macomb, MI	26099	0	788 149	17.6	21	225	126 474	200 126	86.4	141 959	89.0
Manistee, MI	26101	7	24 527	17.3	5	16	3 597	5 638	87.8	4 633	89.6
Marquette, MI	26103	5	64 634	16.3	11	30	10 069	18 785	94.2	11 017	94.3
Mason, MI	26105	7	28 274	18.8	4	17	5 218	6 780	90.6	5 450	93.0
Mecosta, MI	26107	7	40 553	16.5	18	32	10 876	14 409	94.0	6 865	91.7
Menominee, MI	26109	7	25 326	18.1	4	13	3 782	5 896	92.6	4 709	94.2
Midland, MI	26111	2	82 874	20.4	6	33	14 478	23 890	84.9	17 269	92.8
Missaukee, MI	26113	9	14 478	20.7	2	7	2 415	3 629	87.0	3 056	89.4
Monroe, MI	26115	1	145 945	20.8	9	50	24 944	39 786	86.3	30 708	88.3
Montcalm, MI	26117	6	61 266	20.5	7	33	13 466	15 656	90.9	12 865	92.3
Montmorency, MI	26119	9	10 315	15.9	2	4	1 104	1 978	93.8	1 700	95.2
Muskegon, MI	26121	2	170 200	20.7	12	73	32 509	46 749	90.3	36 265	93.7
Newaygo, MI	26123	6	47 874	22.2	5	21	9 728	12 809	90.6	10 726	92.2
Oakland, MI	26125	0	1 194 156	18.5	37	356	193 368	326 864	82.5	225 089	87.2
Oceana, MI	26127	8	26 873	21.7	4	17	4 102	7 065	92.4	5 974	94.4
Ogemaw, MI	26129	7	21 645	18.3	1	4	2 704	5 004	91.3	4 137	92.2
Ontonagon, MI	26131	9	7 818	15.8	3	5	1 162	1 534	97.3	1 281	99.0
Osceola, MI	26133	9	23 197	21.0	4	17	5 534	5 867	90.9	4 933	92.7
Oscoda, MI	26135	9	9 418	18.1	2	4	1 348	2 015	89.6	1 704	91.3
Otsego, MI	26137	7	23 301	20.6	3	11	4 552	5 748	83.6	4 899	85.4
Ottawa, MI	26139	2	238 314	21.0	36	108	48 302	73 944	77.8	51 323	81.8
Presque Isle, MI	26141	7	14 411	16.1	5	9	2 007	3 000	87.3	2 388	88.4
Roscommon, MI	26143	7	25 469	15.7	2	12	3 999	5 232	90.7	4 212	92.9
Saginaw, MI	26145	2	210 039	19.8	22	99	37 863	58 489	88.1	43 311	88.6
St. Clair, MI	26147	0	164 235	20.1	9	58	28 100	42 822	89.1	33 310	92.4
St. Joseph, MI	26149	6	62 422	20.3	9	39	12 076	15 335	90.1	12 532	91.4
Sanilac, MI	26151	8	44 547	20.4	7	21	8 724	11 139	92.8	9 257	95.1
Schoolcraft, MI	26153	7	8 903	17.1	1	5	1 176	1 881	89.3	1 618	88.9
Shiawassee, MI	26155	1	71 687	20.1	8	33	14 545	19 093	89.1	14 847	92.6
Tuscola, MI	26157	6	58 266	20.7	8	32	12 315	15 594	87.9	12 490	89.9
Van Buren, MI	26159	2	76 263	21.3	12	43	17 543	20 117	91.1	16 500	93.5
Washtenaw, MI	26161	0	322 895	15.8	19	94	47 911	117 309	89.4	51 410	90.0
Wayne, MI	26163	0	2 061 162	20.6	62	610	348 669	587 853	85.7	438 464	89.3
Wexford, MI	26165	7	30 484	20.5	3	17	5 727	7 690	89.8	6 305	93.2
MINNESOTA	27000										
Aitkin, MN	27001	9	15 301	16.4	3	8	2 291	3 142	96.6	2 584	97.8
Anoka, MN	27003	0	298 084	21.3	8	97	64 458	83 625	87.7	64 379	92.6
Becker, MN	27005	6	30 000	20.4	5	12	4 881	7 526	95.1	6 313	96.2
Beltrami, MN	27007	7	39 650	21.6	5	27	8 085	13 148	92.9	8 628	92.6
Benton, MN	27009	3	34 226	19.8	2	9	5 221	9 595	88.1	7 027	87.3
Big Stone, MN	27011	9	5 820	20.1	2	7	1 228	1 443	95.4	1 200	96.1
Blue Earth, MN	27013	5	55 941	15.8	5	32	10 129	20 028	88.9	9 039	87.9
Brown, MN	27015	7	26 911	19.9	5	13	4 244	7 413	62.9	5 538	69.2
Carlton, MN	27017	6	31 671	19.5	7	18	6 404	8 607	91.4	6 397	94.5
Carver, MN	27019	1	70 205	22.7	6	26	12 284	21 079	74.9	16 043	82.4
Cass, MN	27021	9	27 150	19.9	6	17	4 872	6 556	95.3	5 583	96.4
Chippewa, MN	27023	7	13 088	19.5	3	11	2 645	3 082	94.7	2 643	95.6
Chisago, MN	27025	1	41 101	22.6	3	17	8 298	11 266	90.6	9 221	94.7
Clay, MN	27027	3	51 229	18.8	5	22	8 956	17 797	80.3	9 873	92.7
Clearwater, MN	27029	9	8 423	20.2	2	4	1 760	2 066	95.9	1 734	96.4
Cook, MN	27031	9	5 168	15.9	1	6	741	962	93.6	826	95.6
Cottonwood, MN	27033	7	12 167	19.2	3	8	1 882	2 897	90.2	2 391	91.9
Crow Wing, MN	27035	7	55 099	18.8	5	25	10 232	13 331	93.3	10 486	94.9
Dakota, MN	27037	0	355 904	21.4	10	131	72 767	101 596	84.1	76 682	90.3
Dodge, MN	27039	6	17 731	22.6	3	11	3 976	4 988	93.9	4 102	96.1

[1]County type code is from the Economic Research Service of the USDA. See Notes and Definitions at the end of this section.

Table C-1. School and Student Characteristics by County—*Continued*

County	Characteristics of students, 2000–2001			Staff and students, 2000–2001				Revenues, fiscal 1999			
	Percent with IEP[2]	Percent eligible for free lunch	Percent minority	Number of teachers	Student/ teacher ratio	Local school non-teaching staff	Central admin. staff	Total revenue ($1,000s)	Percentage of revenue from		
									Federal govt.	State govt.	Local govt.
	10	11	12	13	14	15	16	17	18	19	20
Delta, MI	13.7	30.6	8.4	390	17.9	436	41	$61 400	7.7	62.6	29.7
Dickinson, MI	13.3	24.6	2.7	289	17.9	277	31	45 963	9.5	61.4	29.1
Eaton, MI	15.4	17.5	4.7	935	17.8	1 149	63	138 596	6.1	66.4	27.4
Emmet, MI	9.6	25.9	6.5	291	18.4	265	15	40 630	3.0	41.5	55.6
Genesee, MI	12.8	34.1	33.0	4 221	19.1	4 798	272	724 971	7.9	68.4	23.7
Gladwin, MI	14.5	38.6	2.2	224	17.3	272	11	27 367	6.7	68.1	25.3
Gogebic, MI	15.9	43.9	8.1	149	15.1	161	27	19 976	10.7	63.1	26.2
Grand Traverse, MI	16.1	26.5	4.2	741	17.1	1 134	66	127 595	10.4	52.2	37.4
Gratiot, MI	17.4	34.1	7.4	447	17.2	679	43	71 615	10.1	70.9	19.0
Hillsdale, MI	13.3	33.1	1.8	441	17.5	465	33	61 774	5.4	73.7	20.9
Houghton, MI	9.3	40.4	2.9	358	15.9	307	40	49 852	7.1	67.6	25.3
Huron, MI	11.5	37.0	2.6	346	17.5	402	45	58 299	6.6	64.9	28.6
Ingham, MI	15.9	28.9	31.2	2 699	17.3	3 015	191	477 121	6.0	60.6	33.4
Ionia, MI	16.3	27.2	4.2	697	17.4	825	46	96 150	6.5	71.6	21.9
Iosco, MI	13.9	55.1	2.9	347	17.6	380	27	49 477	8.1	60.5	31.5
Iron, MI	7.8	. . .	56.4	675	19.0	560	86	80 296	4.2	86.9	8.9
Isabella, MI	10.2	. . .	38.3	711	19.0	657	69	54 528	5.2	67.7	27.1
Jackson, MI	14.6	35.2	14.6	1 391	18.7	1 747	83	224 934	5.5	65.0	29.5
Kalamazoo, MI	11.3	31.1	23.8	2 013	17.0	2 332	140	298 055	6.1	60.3	33.7
Kalkaska, MI	13.9	49.9	3.0	161	17.5	126	9	13 304	4.9	50.3	44.8
Kent, MI	15.6	31.1	27.6	5 333	18.2	5 802	284	890 589	6.2	57.9	35.9
Keweenaw, MI	14.3	. . .	0.0	1	11.0	1	. . .	77	0.0	1.3	98.7
Lake, MI	18.0	92.4	40.9	53	15.0	51	6	7 332	13.0	32.1	54.9
Lapeer, MI	11.5	20.2	5.2	745	20.1	901	49	110 564	4.0	72.4	23.6
Leelanau, MI	11.8	25.8	16.4	173	16.0	152	11	20 937	3.7	45.7	50.5
Lenawee, MI	15.7	20.7	12.4	1 002	18.9	1 233	78	159 841	5.2	68.0	26.8
Livingston, MI	13.5	6.8	3.0	1 381	19.8	1 367	61	212 063	3.0	63.0	34.0
Luce, MI	15.3	. . .	9.4	87	14.3	68	5	8 352	8.5	62.4	29.1
Mackinac, MI	9.7	. . .	46.6	119	14.8	110	15	15 679	6.5	45.0	48.5
Macomb, MI	13.5	16.8	8.6	6 538	19.3	7 734	424	1 136 656	4.4	63.5	32.0
Manistee, MI	14.9	43.6	9.1	229	15.7	254	27	32 155	10.0	53.5	36.5
Marquette, MI	16.2	28.2	8.6	624	16.1	582	59	91 021	11.4	60.6	28.0
Mason, MI	14.2	37.1	6.2	310	16.8	349	32	46 657	7.5	51.9	40.6
Mecosta, MI	13.0	54.7	38.8	588	18.5	676	40	68 298	7.4	64.9	27.8
Menominee, MI	13.7	34.9	1.9	235	16.1	237	20	31 898	5.8	71.1	23.0
Midland, MI	15.0	20.3	5.8	823	17.6	1 110	58	125 594	4.3	57.0	38.7
Missaukee, MI	9.9	. . .	1.9	139	17.4	130	7	16 341	5.5	69.0	25.5
Monroe, MI	16.9	18.3	6.3	1 260	19.8	1 515	105	214 184	3.9	57.4	38.7
Montcalm, MI	16.7	37.5	3.3	747	18.0	879	56	108 059	6.1	72.8	21.1
Montmorency, MI	11.9	43.2	0.5	76	14.5	123	8	9 175	6.5	46.7	46.8
Muskegon, MI	16.3	39.6	25.0	1 857	17.5	2 127	130	288 364	7.8	66.8	25.5
Newaygo, MI	16.8	39.1	8.4	549	17.7	708	36	85 299	8.3	64.6	27.1
Oakland, MI	11.9	15.4	21.8	10 817	17.9	12 739	617	2 022 249	4.0	52.9	43.1
Oceana, MI	16.3	45.3	25.7	264	15.5	230	18	33 183	9.7	62.9	27.5
Ogemaw, MI	12.2	42.1	2.1	160	16.9	164	9	18 427	6.6	66.9	26.6
Ontonagon, MI	12.9	33.9	3.7	85	13.7	59	9	14 080	11.4	54.5	34.2
Osceola, MI	14.0	43.8	2.7	320	17.3	311	19	39 536	6.3	71.9	21.8
Oscoda, MI	18.3	. . .	1.1	88	15.3	85	9	10 238	10.1	53.0	36.9
Otsego, MI	12.0	30.8	1.5	263	17.3	228	15	33 576	3.6	48.3	48.1
Ottawa, MI	12.1	20.8	18.1	2 649	18.2	2 694	147	380 063	3.6	59.4	37.0
Presque Isle, MI	9.6	45.2	1.7	128	15.7	104	10	14 159	5.7	63.8	30.5
Roscommon, MI	14.0	48.9	2.3	235	17.0	273	26	43 705	26.3	41.9	31.8
Saginaw, MI	17.0	43.1	41.6	2 172	17.4	2 526	145	308 862	8.2	69.3	22.4
St. Clair, MI	13.0	21.7	8.1	1 569	17.9	1 473	87	229 910	4.9	62.0	33.1
St. Joseph, MI	12.8	32.8	9.1	689	17.5	797	64	93 473	6.6	66.5	26.9
Sanilac, MI	12.1	31.3	4.0	466	18.7	501	48	64 408	5.7	72.4	21.9
Schoolcraft, MI	13.6	38.6	16.1	65	18.1	62	4	8 833	8.6	64.9	26.5
Shiawassee, MI	13.3	21.1	3.1	750	19.4	872	65	116 452	4.9	73.2	21.9
Tuscola, MI	15.6	32.7	5.7	656	18.8	847	43	111 028	18.2	66.0	15.7
Van Buren, MI	11.4	40.1	19.5	1 020	17.2	1 232	78	148 813	7.7	64.5	27.8
Washtenaw, MI	14.1	23.7	28.2	2 603	18.4	3 011	167	469 624	3.4	53.1	43.6
Wayne, MI	12.7	44.4	56.2	18 179	19.2	21 844	1 153	3 230 607	9.0	67.4	23.7
Wexford, MI	11.8	. . .	3.0	319	18.0	321	32	52 003	6.3	60.3	33.4
MINNESOTA											
Aitkin, MN	14.3	44.0	6.8	153	15.0	107	29	17 895	5.5	58.8	35.7
Anoka, MN	11.9	15.6	9.2	3 534	18.2	2 494	530	454 546	2.9	63.8	33.2
Becker, MN	16.0	36.3	12.4	331	14.7	271	57	36 426	5.6	67.3	27.1
Beltrami, MN	14.6	50.2	32.2	579	14.0	568	99	77 312	15.1	61.0	23.9
Benton, MN	13.6	20.8	2.5	316	16.5	232	58	36 484	2.9	69.9	27.2
Big Stone, MN	12.5	42.3	3.0	89	13.8	85	16	11 404	3.9	60.5	35.6
Blue Earth, MN	14.2	23.7	6.3	604	16.8	616	109	76 553	4.4	54.1	41.5
Brown, MN	10.0	21.0	6.4	271	15.7	174	49	35 580	10.1	57.3	32.5
Carlton, MN	12.1	27.4	8.9	397	16.1	299	75	51 319	5.8	68.5	25.7
Carver, MN	11.5	9.9	5.9	691	17.8	532	150	98 728	3.1	50.8	46.0
Cass, MN	17.2	49.3	28.0	349	14.0	338	64	40 466	9.6	50.8	39.6
Chippewa, MN	14.7	27.8	5.2	180	14.7	175	33	25 514	4.8	56.1	39.1
Chisago, MN	10.7	17.2	3.7	412	20.1	310	90	57 111	3.2	66.9	29.8
Clay, MN	16.5	28.4	10.9	584	15.3	550	95	64 905	4.8	71.6	23.6
Clearwater, MN	14.1	48.0	14.3	118	14.9	79	20	14 070	6.7	62.0	31.3
Cook, MN	13.9	19.2	15.5	46	16.1	37	10	6 321	5.4	24.1	70.5
Cottonwood, MN	17.6	32.9	10.6	144	13.1	144	27	16 305	4.3	55.4	40.2
Crow Wing, MN	13.4	30.0	2.9	626	16.3	529	105	71 188	5.2	55.5	39.3
Dakota, MN	13.4	11.1	11.0	4 212	17.3	2 952	686	544 489	2.4	53.7	43.8
Dodge, MN	10.5	15.8	4.6	250	15.9	159	42	26 721	2.1	70.5	27.4

[2]IEP = Individual Education Program. See Notes and Definitions at the end of this section.
. . . = Not available.

Table C-1. Population, School, and Student Characteristics by County—*Continued*

County	Current expenditures, fiscal 1999			Resident population 16 to 19 years, 2000				Outcomes, 1999–2000	
	Amount ($1,000s)	Amount per student	Percent for instruction	Total population 16 to 19 years	Percent in Armed Forces	Percent high school graduates	Percent not enrolled, not grads, not Armed Forces, not empl.	Number of graduates	Dropouts grades 9–12 (percent)
	21	22	23	24	25	26	27	28	29
Delta, MI	$51 652	$7 152	60.1	2 386	0.0	12.0	1.8	534	...
Dickinson, MI	37 267	7 049	58.4	1 513	0.0	11.0	3.7	403	...
Eaton, MI	110 720	6 597	58.8	6 355	0.0	11.8	4.0	1 165	...
Emmet, MI	33 383	6 406	65.3	1 778	0.0	9.4	2.6	346	...
Genesee, MI	584 149	7 025	57.5	24 358	0.0	10.6	6.8	4 387	...
Gladwin, MI	24 812	6 283	62.1	1 282	0.2	9.5	8.1	254	...
Gogebic, MI	17 644	6 752	61.6	1 080	0.0	10.5	6.4	200	...
Grand Traverse, MI	108 795	7 975	51.4	4 385	0.0	8.1	2.2	865	...
Gratiot, MI	58 598	7 132	58.4	2 718	0.0	9.4	4.7	555	...
Hillsdale, MI	52 343	6 727	62.5	3 098	0.0	8.5	6.9	397	...
Houghton, MI	41 125	6 860	58.2	3 162	0.3	5.7	2.9	423	...
Huron, MI	50 076	6 888	57.0	1 908	0.6	9.6	3.0	472	...
Ingham, MI	382 949	7 973	55.7	22 172	0.0	5.2	3.2	2 113	...
Ionia, MI	78 362	6 301	59.8	3 880	0.0	12.9	9.8	796	...
Iosco, MI	41 452	6 431	60.2	1 337	0.3	10.9	8.4	404	...
Iron, MI	72 684	5 901	52.7	629	0.2	7.8	2.1	307	...
Isabella, MI	44 072	6 245	60.7	7 903	0.0	3.5	1.7	469	...
Jackson, MI	197 353	7 639	53.7	8 107	0.0	8.6	7.0	1 489	...
Kalamazoo, MI	249 752	7 369	59.2	16 967	0.1	6.9	2.9	1 930	...
Kalkaska, MI	11 460	5 574	61.5	868	0.0	14.9	7.4	195	...
Kent, MI	699 098	7 298	59.0	34 941	0.0	9.8	5.2	5 236	...
Keweenaw, MI	67	11 167	56.7	171	0.0	4.1	5.3	0	...
Lake, MI	6 055	8 009	63.8	824	0.0	16.5	23.1	39	...
Lapeer, MI	94 489	6 275	60.2	5 230	0.0	10.4	3.4	962	...
Leelanau, MI	17 717	6 362	61.8	1 082	0.0	6.7	1.2	183	...
Lenawee, MI	132 107	7 101	57.1	5 962	0.0	10.0	2.9	1 192	...
Livingston, MI	163 975	6 380	58.2	8 764	0.0	8.1	4.5	1 598	...
Luce, MI	7 661	6 374	67.5	377	0.0	8.5	16.7	77	...
Mackinac, MI	12 903	6 960	60.0	592	0.5	9.6	7.6	110	...
Macomb, MI	917 977	7 411	58.4	37 980	0.1	9.5	3.5	7 743	...
Manistee, MI	27 119	7 639	56.9	1 350	0.0	9.2	5.9	296	...
Marquette, MI	76 634	7 138	58.9	4 651	0.0	8.8	2.0	798	...
Mason, MI	41 390	7 943	60.2	1 587	0.3	8.1	4.2	357	...
Mecosta, MI	55 990	7 098	56.7	3 794	0.2	5.3	2.7	446	...
Menominee, MI	27 038	6 569	60.0	1 422	0.1	12.1	3.0	297	...
Midland, MI	108 400	7 389	59.3	4 905	0.0	7.7	2.4	964	...
Missaukee, MI	13 020	5 409	61.7	866	0.0	9.4	3.6	166	...
Monroe, MI	176 402	7 161	55.2	8 547	0.0	10.3	4.0	1 607	...
Montcalm, MI	90 495	6 585	58.5	3 461	0.0	8.4	7.7	782	...
Montmorency, MI	7 482	6 204	61.1	491	0.0	11.4	3.9	80	...
Muskegon, MI	235 027	7 079	57.8	9 731	0.0	9.6	5.5	1 656	...
Newaygo, MI	69 126	6 915	60.9	2 708	0.0	13.0	5.6	536	...
Oakland, MI	1 580 215	8 267	57.1	57 371	0.0	7.1	2.6	11 515	...
Oceana, MI	27 522	6 649	63.4	1 736	1.2	9.6	7.0	263	...
Ogemaw, MI	16 011	5 495	63.8	1 151	0.0	7.5	5.2	202	...
Ontonagon, MI	11 926	9 288	53.2	347	0.3	5.2	4.3	90	...
Osceola, MI	33 248	5 728	62.8	1 443	0.0	12.8	4.3	380	...
Oscoda, MI	8 214	5 842	62.6	485	0.0	5.2	6.8	76	...
Otsego, MI	28 883	6 191	63.5	1 223	0.0	8.9	1.6	330	...
Ottawa, MI	297 601	6 689	58.6	16 429	0.0	8.9	1.9	2 389	...
Presque Isle, MI	12 386	5 774	64.1	806	0.0	8.8	4.7	182	...
Roscommon, MI	33 228	7 767	53.4	1 180	0.0	9.2	4.2	279	...
Saginaw, MI	266 120	7 063	56.6	11 932	0.1	7.7	6.4	2 125	...
St. Clair, MI	185 778	6 631	58.7	9 089	0.0	10.4	5.2	1 658	...
St. Joseph, MI	78 516	6 508	58.1	3 779	0.4	9.9	7.2	624	...
Sanilac, MI	54 349	6 134	60.8	2 566	0.2	9.4	3.4	584	...
Schoolcraft, MI	7 893	6 200	60.7	386	0.0	13.2	7.8	114	...
Shiawassee, MI	96 704	6 735	60.0	4 146	0.0	8.9	3.6	883	...
Tuscola, MI	86 671	7 029	58.4	3 616	0.0	6.4	5.8	836	...
Van Buren, MI	121 236	6 870	60.1	4 696	0.0	9.5	5.8	1 071	...
Washtenaw, MI	352 408	7 824	56.0	23 697	0.0	5.2	2.0	2 652	...
Wayne, MI	2 737 403	7 714	58.6	108 591	0.0	11.4	7.6	10 403	...
Wexford, MI	41 268	7 146	56.7	1 908	0.1	10.5	5.6	373	...
MINNESOTA									
Aitkin, MN	15 175	6 427	61.0	789	0.0	8.7	2.2	184	3.1
Anoka, MN	374 368	5 905	64.8	16 477	0.0	9.6	3.4	3 833	5.0
Becker, MN	31 343	6 355	64.4	1 887	0.0	9.2	4.9	372	1.9
Beltrami, MN	64 737	7 766	67.2	3 157	0.0	5.9	5.8	443	4.4
Benton, MN	29 031	5 632	63.1	2 105	0.8	15.5	1.3	367	1.1
Big Stone, MN	8 949	6 678	57.1	364	0.0	1.6	9.3	110	1.5
Blue Earth, MN	65 645	6 308	61.5	5 277	0.0	5.7	0.7	805	4.2
Brown, MN	27 199	6 050	63.7	1 820	0.0	7.3	0.4	334	1.0
Carlton, MN	42 616	6 496	64.7	1 856	0.0	8.6	2.5	476	3.5
Carver, MN	74 773	6 836	60.5	3 635	0.0	9.3	0.6	830	2.7
Cass, MN	33 971	6 850	62.4	1 495	0.0	9.7	3.9	288	6.6
Chippewa, MN	19 973	7 543	62.6	777	0.0	9.1	3.0	229	4.4
Chisago, MN	45 467	5 710	61.6	2 258	0.0	8.4	3.7	530	2.7
Clay, MN	57 118	6 145	67.6	4 649	0.0	5.2	2.0	580	1.6
Clearwater, MN	12 134	6 730	61.0	565	0.0	10.4	4.6	126	5.1
Cook, MN	5 142	6 874	63.1	210	0.0	14.8	0.0	52	4.1
Cottonwood, MN	14 445	7 226	65.2	686	0.0	8.6	2.8	186	2.1
Crow Wing, MN	61 597	6 075	66.3	3 131	0.0	11.3	3.6	679	6.1
Dakota, MN	442 962	6 282	64.6	19 283	0.2	8.8	1.8	4 372	3.1
Dodge, MN	21 790	5 509	64.1	1 207	0.0	7.7	2.9	293	2.1

... = Not available.

Table C-1. Population, School, and Student Characteristics by County—*Continued*

County	High school graduates, 2000			College enrollment, 2000		College graduates, 2000 (percent)						
	Population 25 years and over	High school diploma or less (percent)	High school diploma or more (percent)	Number	Percent public	Bachelor's degree or more	+/- U.S. percent with bachelor's degree or more	Non-Hispanic White	Black or African American	American Indian and Alaska Native	Asian, Hawaiian, and Pacific Islander	Hispanic or Latino[1]
	30	31	32	33	34	35	36	37	38	39	40	41
Delta, MI	26 362	49.7	86.1	1 968	91.4	17.1	-7.3	17.3	46.2	4.1	36.2	10.3
Dickinson, MI	18 831	55.6	88.8	775	89.7	16.7	-7.7	16.5	53.1	1.6	42.3	14.5
Eaton, MI	67 044	40.8	89.5	5 893	76.9	21.7	-2.7	21.2	29.1	18.9	48.2	14.8
Emmet, MI	21 258	42.4	89.0	1 372	92.0	26.2	1.8	26.9	0.0	8.2	41.7	11.0
Genesee, MI	277 660	50.2	83.1	22 250	80.8	16.2	-8.2	17.3	10.3	9.1	58.1	10.1
Gladwin, MI	18 308	63.3	78.3	660	89.1	9.2	-15.2	9.1	8.3	7.3	32.4	16.2
Gogebic, MI	12 311	53.0	85.5	725	92.1	15.8	-8.6	16.2	0.0	0.0	33.3	4.0
Grand Traverse, MI	51 801	38.6	89.3	3 729	89.2	26.1	1.7	26.5	12.9	15.2	31.1	6.2
Gratiot, MI	27 322	58.6	83.5	2 560	48.3	12.9	-11.5	13.5	4.2	3.5	49.1	6.5
Hillsdale, MI	29 595	59.8	83.1	2 261	49.5	12.0	-12.4	12.0	31.0	2.4	43.7	1.0
Houghton, MI	21 233	51.4	84.6	6 142	92.3	23.0	-1.4	22.4	21.1	16.2	71.3	9.3
Huron, MI	24 954	64.7	78.3	888	85.6	10.9	-13.5	10.8	12.5	5.3	56.6	3.2
Ingham, MI	162 909	35.3	88.1	49 242	93.2	33.0	8.6	34.0	22.8	16.8	63.3	15.4
Ionia, MI	37 835	57.0	83.4	1 877	82.0	10.8	-13.6	11.1	3.9	11.2	25.2	6.5
Iosco, MI	19 764	62.3	77.9	569	88.0	11.3	-13.1	11.3	0.0	18.2	38.5	6.1
Iron, MI	9 670	60.8	84.8	253	90.9	13.7	-10.7	13.9	0.0	13.5	23.8	9.3
Isabella, MI	31 677	47.8	86.1	17 635	97.3	23.9	-0.5	23.9	21.9	6.3	70.9	12.8
Jackson, MI	104 880	48.6	84.2	7 379	72.2	16.3	-8.1	17.2	5.2	7.6	56.1	9.2
Kalamazoo, MI	144 995	37.2	88.8	31 709	89.4	31.2	6.8	32.1	16.3	19.1	69.9	18.0
Kalkaska, MI	11 073	64.7	80.0	399	87.2	9.7	-14.7	9.8	8.0	7.1	33.3	0.0
Kent, MI	351 875	43.6	84.6	34 031	66.8	25.8	1.4	28.1	11.7	8.2	32.9	9.1
Keweenaw, MI	1 634	53.5	83.7	57	64.9	19.1	-5.3	18.9	. . .	. . .	0.0	50.0
Lake, MI	7 964	67.5	72.2	237	84.4	7.8	-16.6	8.1	7.5	0.0	0.0	5.8
Lapeer, MI	56 454	54.0	84.5	3 526	84.7	12.7	-11.7	12.9	2.8	9.4	42.1	6.5
Leelanau, MI	14 785	35.7	90.7	769	83.9	31.4	7.0	32.5	0.0	7.3	33.3	10.9
Lenawee, MI	64 311	55.1	83.4	4 573	59.3	16.3	-8.1	16.6	13.1	5.2	59.7	8.0
Livingston, MI	101 381	36.9	91.4	7 127	82.3	28.2	3.8	28.2	15.1	10.8	52.4	26.5
Luce, MI	4 927	61.9	75.5	147	99.3	11.8	-12.6	13.4	0.0	10.4	100.0	0.0
Mackinac, MI	8 588	58.8	82.5	246	93.9	14.9	-9.5	16.9	0.0	3.6	33.3	9.5
Macomb, MI	535 836	49.8	82.9	45 059	83.4	17.6	-6.8	17.1	15.2	11.5	44.2	17.9
Manistee, MI	17 298	58.0	81.4	651	80.6	14.2	-10.2	14.7	0.0	2.8	8.7	6.1
Marquette, MI	41 934	46.9	88.5	6 988	97.0	23.7	-0.7	24.2	6.3	8.3	21.0	14.7
Mason, MI	19 449	52.8	82.7	965	89.7	15.9	-8.5	16.4	5.0	5.3	30.6	3.2
Mecosta, MI	23 314	52.7	83.8	7 024	97.7	19.1	-5.3	19.0	14.3	11.2	82.4	15.5
Menominee, MI	17 342	62.9	83.5	831	87.2	11.0	-13.4	11.1	0.0	6.3	0.0	16.7
Midland, MI	53 497	41.0	89.0	5 050	69.7	29.3	4.9	28.4	54.5	6.0	75.1	41.7
Missaukee, MI	9 466	64.0	78.6	369	80.5	10.2	-14.2	10.2	0.0	0.0	30.8	5.4
Monroe, MI	94 281	54.2	83.1	6 669	85.5	14.3	-10.1	14.4	6.6	3.9	40.2	11.1
Montcalm, MI	39 560	58.8	81.2	1 937	85.1	10.8	-13.6	11.0	6.3	4.0	23.6	4.6
Montmorency, MI	7 604	66.9	74.8	186	87.1	8.2	-16.2	8.3	0.0	9.5	0.0	5.7
Muskegon, MI	108 661	52.4	83.1	7 581	79.0	13.9	-10.5	15.5	5.5	8.2	26.9	5.4
Newaygo, MI	30 329	61.7	78.7	1 354	81.6	11.4	-13.0	11.7	7.2	4.2	28.9	3.5
Oakland, MI	807 910	32.8	89.3	76 393	78.5	38.2	13.8	37.9	30.2	17.2	72.6	25.8
Oceana, MI	17 134	59.6	79.8	734	82.0	12.6	-11.8	13.5	6.5	11.1	27.3	1.5
Ogemaw, MI	15 191	64.9	75.0	611	89.4	9.6	-14.8	9.5	0.0	4.3	60.7	3.4
Ontonagon, MI	5 899	59.7	83.8	186	84.9	13.0	-11.4	12.9	. . .	3.2	33.3	38.2
Osceola, MI	15 033	63.3	80.5	652	79.4	11.3	-13.1	11.2	14.3	17.9	36.0	7.9
Oscoda, MI	6 716	66.8	73.7	221	87.3	8.0	-16.4	8.0	42.9	0.0	100.0	0.0
Otsego, MI	15 468	50.9	85.5	534	80.1	17.4	-7.0	17.5	0.0	9.6	31.6	14.0
Ottawa, MI	141 870	44.5	86.6	18 166	71.9	24.0	1.6	27.1	12.2	18.1	26.5	8.3
Presque Isle, MI	10 463	61.3	77.0	443	87.1	11.5	-12.9	11.6	33.3	0.0	0.0	6.5
Roscommon, MI	18 930	59.8	79.5	763	87.4	10.9	-13.5	10.9	20.0	9.9	25.4	7.1
Saginaw, MI	135 198	54.6	81.6	11 612	91.6	15.9	-8.5	17.5	8.5	10.5	57.4	7.7
St. Clair, MI	107 583	54.4	82.8	6 578	82.5	12.6	-11.8	12.7	8.3	8.6	39.1	5.3
St. Joseph, MI	39 807	59.7	78.6	1 819	87.4	12.7	-11.7	13.1	2.6	3.8	30.7	6.4
Sanilac, MI	29 197	64.2	79.7	1 231	82.0	10.0	-14.4	10.0	0.0	9.3	42.6	1.5
Schoolcraft, MI	6 272	64.5	79.4	144	91.0	11.3	-13.1	12.1	0.0	1.9	18.2	4.8
Shiawassee, MI	46 557	54.1	84.4	2 940	75.6	13.7	-10.7	13.8	22.6	5.2	51.4	8.2
Tuscola, MI	37 898	60.6	81.2	2 369	83.4	10.6	-13.8	10.7	8.9	0.6	43.0	3.3
Van Buren, MI	48 920	57.0	78.9	2 430	86.5	14.3	-10.1	15.6	4.3	5.8	26.2	4.1
Washtenaw, MI	197 414	25.6	91.5	60 032	93.3	48.1	23.7	49.1	25.0	27.2	82.3	44.1
Wayne, MI	1 305 288	53.7	77.0	110 846	77.8	17.2	-7.2	21.4	10.3	12.9	57.3	10.6
Wexford, MI	19 965	56.7	82.0	914	78.4	15.3	-9.1	15.2	25.0	18.2	52.8	14.2
MINNESOTA												
Aitkin, MN	11 263	59.2	80.4	349	89.7	11.3	-13.1	11.5	37.5	3.6	0.0	0.0
Anoka, MN	187 122	41.4	91.0	13 340	74.1	21.3	-3.1	21.3	20.4	8.8	31.3	13.3
Becker, MN	19 834	51.7	82.9	784	89.8	16.7	-7.7	17.5	29.2	4.6	17.5	19.2
Beltrami, MN	22 748	45.2	83.4	3 916	94.7	23.5	-0.9	26.4	45.6	4.5	31.4	11.5
Benton, MN	20 789	49.9	84.9	2 068	91.1	17.2	-7.2	17.2	27.1	23.7	14.0	11.0
Big Stone, MN	4 050	61.1	79.0	113	87.6	11.4	-13.0	11.3	0.0	18.2	. . .	0.0
Blue Earth, MN	31 684	40.4	87.7	10 105	92.1	26.6	2.2	26.6	26.0	15.1	44.1	20.1
Brown, MN	17 485	56.8	81.7	1 418	38.8	16.5	-7.9	16.7	0.0	3.7	43.5	4.6
Carlton, MN	21 238	53.1	84.3	1 582	82.1	14.9	-9.5	15.3	1.0	12.4	11.9	7.6
Carver, MN	43 218	35.3	91.4	2 867	57.2	34.3	9.9	34.8	37.0	14.1	40.1	9.7
Cass, MN	18 721	52.5	83.9	582	89.2	16.6	-7.8	17.4	100.0	6.4	14.0	11.3
Chippewa, MN	8 819	56.0	81.6	263	89.0	13.7	-10.7	13.8	50.0	3.2	14.3	11.0
Chisago, MN	25 859	48.4	88.7	1 228	78.1	15.3	-9.1	15.4	7.8	9.4	19.8	11.3
Clay, MN	29 580	41.5	86.7	7 152	64.3	24.7	0.3	25.5	29.3	4.4	23.3	6.6
Clearwater, MN	5 576	59.0	76.4	202	92.1	14.7	-9.7	15.4	. . .	6.5	38.5	0.0
Cook, MN	3 864	39.9	88.7	71	81.7	28.8	4.4	30.8	0.0	6.4	0.0	66.7
Cottonwood, MN	8 344	56.8	80.4	287	83.3	14.2	-10.2	14.1	0.0	100.0	32.9	7.7
Crow Wing, MN	37 092	47.2	86.3	1 951	89.2	18.4	-6.0	18.4	13.9	10.2	54.5	24.8
Dakota, MN	224 313	30.3	93.2	17 197	70.0	34.9	10.5	35.4	30.9	11.2	42.0	13.7
Dodge, MN	10 989	49.2	86.7	525	85.1	17.1	-7.3	17.2	0.0	20.0	38.1	7.1

[1]Hispanic or Latino persons may be of any race.
. . . = Not available.

Table C-1. Population, School, and Student Characteristics by County—*Continued*

County	State/ County code	County type[1]	Population, 2000		Number of schools and students, 2000–2001			Resident enrollment, 2000			
			Total	Percent 5–17 years	School districts	Schools	Students	Total	Percent public	K–12	Percent public
			1	2	3	4	5	6	7	8	9
Douglas, MN	27041	7	32 821	18.5	6	19	5 608	8 170	90.0	6 271	91.8
Faribault, MN	27043	7	16 181	19.2	2	8	2 519	3 880	92.3	3 224	93.2
Fillmore, MN	27045	8	21 122	20.4	5	14	3 278	5 095	91.7	4 306	92.0
Freeborn, MN	27047	7	32 584	18.2	3	13	4 929	7 375	93.1	6 153	94.2
Goodhue, MN	27049	6	44 127	20.4	6	21	7 773	11 305	91.1	9 219	93.9
Grant, MN	27051	9	6 289	19.0	3	7	1 397	1 476	96.1	1 215	97.5
Hennepin, MN	27053	0	1 116 200	17.4	30	345	159 788	297 966	82.1	197 828	88.2
Houston, MN	27055	3	19 718	21.4	5	12	3 653	5 283	85.9	4 268	86.7
Hubbard, MN	27057	9	18 376	19.1	3	9	2 809	4 254	94.0	3 538	95.6
Isanti, MN	27059	1	31 287	22.1	3	11	5 987	8 631	91.9	7 169	93.9
Itasca, MN	27061	6	43 992	19.1	4	28	7 587	10 950	92.7	8 676	93.8
Jackson, MN	27063	7	11 268	19.3	2	7	1 712	2 795	91.7	2 261	91.9
Kanabec, MN	27065	6	14 996	21.5	2	6	2 748	3 844	94.6	3 324	97.5
Kandiyohi, MN	27067	7	41 203	20.4	2	19	6 401	10 814	91.3	8 630	92.9
Kittson, MN	27069	9	5 285	18.7	3	7	1 040	1 288	91.5	1 093	90.9
Koochiching, MN	27071	7	14 355	18.4	3	10	2 360	3 451	90.1	2 770	91.4
Lac qui Parle, MN	27073	9	8 067	19.5	3	7	1 915	1 860	94.7	1 588	96.4
Lake, MN	27075	6	11 058	17.2	1	7	2 045	2 402	93.0	1 956	93.7
Lake of the Woods, MN	27077	9	4 522	20.6	1	2	786	1 073	97.1	940	97.9
Le Sueur, MN	27079	6	25 426	21.1	5	17	4 857	6 677	88.7	5 495	91.6
Lincoln, MN	27081	9	6 429	18.2	4	5	916	1 465	94.0	1 187	95.7
Lyon, MN	27083	7	25 425	19.6	8	17	4 773	7 659	86.7	5 024	85.1
McLeod, MN	27085	6	34 898	20.8	5	20	6 180	9 193	84.1	7 328	86.6
Mahnomen, MN	27087	9	5 190	22.1	2	7	1 344	1 414	94.3	1 161	94.4
Marshall, MN	27089	8	10 155	19.7	4	11	1 670	2 429	96.0	2 029	96.2
Martin, MN	27091	7	21 802	19.4	5	19	3 899	5 316	86.9	4 421	88.9
Meeker, MN	27093	6	22 644	20.5	4	16	6 179	5 764	95.1	4 762	96.7
Mille Lacs, MN	27095	6	22 330	20.8	4	15	6 340	5 643	89.3	4 771	91.0
Morrison, MN	27097	6	31 712	21.4	5	16	5 986	8 143	90.5	6 879	91.9
Mower, MN	27099	4	38 603	19.0	5	20	5 955	9 295	89.0	7 306	90.1
Murray, MN	27101	9	9 165	19.7	2	4	1 453	2 144	88.3	1 812	90.2
Nicollet, MN	27103	7	29 771	18.8	4	11	2 473	9 887	65.3	5 666	84.1
Nobles, MN	27105	7	20 832	19.6	5	13	3 641	5 134	90.8	4 207	93.0
Norman, MN	27107	8	7 442	19.6	3	8	1 374	1 769	96.7	1 479	97.9
Olmsted, MN	27109	3	124 277	19.8	8	47	21 463	34 049	82.9	25 301	87.4
Otter Tail, MN	27111	7	57 159	19.4	10	26	9 037	14 133	90.9	11 462	92.6
Pennington, MN	27113	7	13 584	18.4	2	6	2 357	3 589	93.4	2 556	93.5
Pine, MN	27115	6	26 530	20.0	4	14	4 500	6 412	91.4	5 447	93.8
Pipestone, MN	27117	7	9 895	20.0	3	10	2 043	2 509	87.8	2 079	88.3
Polk, MN	27119	3	31 369	20.0	7	21	5 827	8 889	91.8	6 352	91.6
Pope, MN	27121	6	11 236	19.9	2	5	1 708	2 750	94.0	2 357	95.2
Ramsey, MN	27123	0	511 035	18.7	28	194	88 768	148 722	74.7	98 122	85.2
Red Lake, MN	27125	9	4 299	20.0	3	6	804	1 072	91.4	871	91.7
Redwood, MN	27127	7	16 815	20.4	6	16	3 467	4 054	88.4	3 504	89.0
Renville, MN	27129	7	17 154	20.5	4	9	2 651	4 278	89.9	3 651	90.4
Rice, MN	27131	4	56 665	19.1	6	20	8 387	18 631	62.2	11 284	86.7
Rock, MN	27133	6	9 721	20.4	2	6	1 673	2 525	90.3	2 019	93.5
Roseau, MN	27135	9	16 338	22.5	4	15	3 664	4 373	96.5	3 729	97.2
St. Louis, MN	27137	3	200 528	17.1	17	96	30 313	54 961	89.1	35 402	92.2
Scott, MN	27139	1	89 498	22.0	6	41	14 064	25 390	82.6	19 902	87.7
Sherburne, MN	27141	1	64 417	22.5	3	20	14 063	19 430	88.3	14 644	92.0
Sibley, MN	27143	8	15 356	21.1	4	11	2 529	3 952	86.8	3 274	87.8
Stearns, MN	27145	3	133 166	19.3	14	51	24 586	43 624	80.0	26 236	85.1
Steele, MN	27147	7	33 680	21.0	3	14	6 512	8 991	86.4	7 229	90.4
Stevens, MN	27149	7	10 053	16.3	4	8	1 619	3 536	95.2	1 680	94.0
Swift, MN	27151	7	11 956	17.7	2	5	1 848	2 722	94.7	2 212	95.6
Todd, MN	27153	6	24 426	21.4	6	16	4 592	6 472	88.7	5 498	89.0
Traverse, MN	27155	9	4 134	19.9	2	4	693	1 000	97.6	825	98.2
Wabasha, MN	27157	6	21 610	21.4	5	11	5 350	5 671	91.3	4 651	91.9
Wadena, MN	27159	7	13 713	19.5	4	8	3 094	3 538	93.9	2 792	94.9
Waseca, MN	27161	7	19 526	19.1	3	12	3 935	4 864	88.2	3 883	90.6
Washington, MN	27163	0	201 130	21.8	9	72	36 627	58 157	83.6	44 185	89.6
Watonwan, MN	27165	7	11 876	20.4	3	7	2 139	3 074	89.5	2 536	91.3
Wilkin, MN	27167	6	7 138	21.5	3	7	1 352	1 839	87.4	1 530	88.6
Winona, MN	27169	4	49 985	17.2	6	24	6 682	17 104	79.6	8 791	82.1
Wright, MN	27171	1	89 986	22.8	10	44	19 064	25 341	89.4	20 802	92.2
Yellow Medicine, MN	27173	7	11 080	20.0	3	7	2 083	2 864	95.4	2 282	95.8
MISSISSIPPI	28000										
Adams, MS	28001	7	34 340	20.0	1	6	5 069	9 809	80.4	7 561	79.0
Alcorn, MS	28003	7	34 558	17.4	2	14	5 436	7 421	92.2	5 928	95.7
Amite, MS	28005	9	13 599	20.1	1	3	1 621	3 261	76.9	2 697	77.2
Attala, MS	28007	6	19 661	19.5	2	9	3 506	5 044	88.4	4 109	90.4
Benton, MS	28009	8	8 026	19.5	1	4	1 239	2 002	90.5	1 627	93.0
Bolivar, MS	28011	5	40 633	22.2	6	21	8 260	14 277	92.7	9 559	91.5
Calhoun, MS	28013	9	15 069	18.7	1	8	2 519	3 470	88.6	2 950	91.3
Carroll, MS	28015	9	10 769	18.9	1	3	1 209	2 647	75.0	2 175	74.8
Chickasaw, MS	28017	7	19 440	21.0	3	7	3 430	4 950	91.3	4 121	92.9
Choctaw, MS	28019	9	9 758	21.0	1	4	1 918	2 513	88.2	2 091	87.8

[1]County type code is from the Economic Research Service of the USDA. See Notes and Definitions at the end of this section.

Table C-1. School and Student Characteristics by County—*Continued*

County	Characteristics of students, 2000–2001			Staff and students, 2000–2001				Revenues, fiscal 1999			
	Percent with IEP2	Percent eligible for free lunch	Percent minority	Number of teachers	Student/ teacher ratio	Local school non-teaching staff	Central admin. staff	Total revenue ($1,000s)	Percentage of revenue from		
									Federal govt.	State govt.	Local govt.
	10	11	12	13	14	15	16	17	18	19	20
Douglas, MN	12.9	25.6	1.6	348	16.1	290	65	$40 523	5.2	58.4	36.4
Faribault, MN	13.2	31.6	7.5	165	15.3	162	35	19 451	4.4	59.5	36.1
Fillmore, MN	14.2	26.9	1.3	237	13.8	168	35	25 191	5.7	69.2	25.1
Freeborn, MN	15.1	28.6	12.2	286	17.2	225	59	38 344	4.2	63.4	32.4
Goodhue, MN	11.5	16.5	5.7	473	16.4	395	76	69 988	2.5	50.7	46.8
Grant, MN	11.5	31.3	2.9	101	13.8	58	18	11 256	4.6	58.7	36.6
Hennepin, MN	11.7	30.9	35.5	9 601	16.6	6 918	1 970	1 495 799	4.2	43.8	51.9
Houston, MN	11.4	16.8	2.1	240	15.2	175	36	23 540	2.7	74.1	23.1
Hubbard, MN	16.3	43.9	8.5	188	14.9	133	27	21 163	7.1	60.4	32.4
Isanti, MN	8.2	21.2	3.5	331	18.1	252	64	42 925	5.1	66.4	28.6
Itasca, MN	14.4	33.8	9.7	482	15.7	321	80	67 104	6.4	53.8	39.9
Jackson, MN	12.3	30.1	6.5	129	13.3	105	21	14 023	3.5	59.1	37.4
Kanabec, MN	9.5	33.2	3.6	171	16.1	124	22	18 219	5.5	76.3	18.1
Kandiyohi, MN	14.0	32.5	17.0	450	14.2	356	45	51 756	4.7	63.1	32.2
Kittson, MN	12.8	40.2	4.4	87	12.0	40	14	10 498	2.7	45.6	51.7
Koochiching, MN	13.1	29.0	5.4	161	14.7	113	33	20 682	4.8	67.3	27.9
Lac qui Parle, MN	14.2	32.5	5.0	133	14.4	129	23	16 103	5.7	63.0	31.3
Lake, MN	12.8	23.2	1.7	112	18.3	99	20	14 723	4.2	59.0	36.9
Lake of the Woods, MN	10.7	42.5	3.2	54	14.6	27	11	6 786	2.9	60.2	36.9
Le Sueur, MN	14.8	24.6	8.5	292	16.6	212	53	33 580	3.4	70.0	26.6
Lincoln, MN	11.8	35.5	1.1	72	12.7	49	12	8 358	3.9	64.6	31.4
Lyon, MN	12.2	27.4	12.9	329	14.5	287	60	44 039	11.9	47.6	40.5
McLeod, MN	10.2	17.8	6.7	380	16.3	291	61	43 942	3.1	65.2	31.7
Mahnomen, MN	18.2	64.7	59.7	122	11.0	98	17	13 330	16.0	70.1	13.9
Marshall, MN	13.1	38.8	7.9	130	12.8	107	26	15 751	5.6	50.7	43.7
Martin, MN	15.5	32.1	4.5	236	16.5	305	50	33 210	4.5	53.6	41.9
Meeker, MN	12.4	25.3	3.2	390	15.8	328	56	43 227	3.6	69.5	26.9
Mille Lacs, MN	11.6	29.3	6.0	373	17.0	269	57	46 913	4.4	67.0	28.6
Morrison, MN	14.7	36.5	1.9	382	15.7	240	58	50 126	5.8	70.1	24.1
Mower, MN	15.0	29.1	9.8	390	15.3	250	67	45 340	4.3	65.3	30.3
Murray, MN	11.8	29.2	3.0	96	15.1	92	16	10 573	4.1	62.7	33.1
Nicollet, MN	18.3	22.7	6.8	173	14.3	172	39	23 862	9.8	53.7	36.5
Nobles, MN	12.7	34.8	23.6	254	14.3	303	46	26 995	5.4	65.0	29.6
Norman, MN	12.4	37.9	10.8	112	12.3	69	18	21 115	39.3	43.8	16.9
Olmsted, MN	11.1	18.9	14.6	1 264	17.0	911	237	176 761	2.8	52.0	45.2
Otter Tail, MN	13.4	28.6	5.8	566	16.0	428	115	93 513	4.3	46.2	49.5
Pennington, MN	17.3	29.8	4.2	166	14.2	109	26	20 863	5.2	67.1	27.7
Pine, MN	10.1	35.6	6.7	300	15.0	200	52	33 173	4.3	68.1	27.6
Pipestone, MN	12.8	30.7	5.6	138	14.8	112	21	13 853	6.4	66.5	27.1
Polk, MN	12.8	36.0	13.3	384	15.2	292	73	65 943	20.9	60.1	19.0
Pope, MN	13.0	36.8	1.8	115	14.9	88	16	14 110	4.7	66.3	29.0
Ramsey, MN	12.9	41.7	43.2	5 252	16.9	5 528	871	770 419	5.3	56.6	38.1
Red Lake, MN	13.8	45.0	2.9	66	12.2	49	18	9 060	11.7	56.3	32.0
Redwood, MN	13.6	31.4	8.1	233	14.9	204	39	25 261	4.5	57.2	38.3
Renville, MN	13.2	29.2	14.4	185	14.3	159	28	18 896	4.9	55.0	40.1
Rice, MN	16.4	24.5	11.2	496	16.9	461	93	64 495	3.2	61.4	35.5
Rock, MN	12.9	25.7	4.9	120	13.9	88	15	13 645	4.2	60.5	35.3
Roseau, MN	14.5	27.6	6.9	235	15.6	194	32	28 643	4.1	69.4	26.5
St. Louis, MN	13.9	29.0	7.8	1 892	16.0	1 231	317	253 958	5.6	64.0	30.5
Scott, MN	11.5	. . .	6.8	817	17.2	608	134	100 498	2.8	56.3	40.9
Sherburne, MN	12.0	10.8	3.0	814	17.3	466	119	89 002	2.1	58.8	39.0
Sibley, MN	11.0	27.2	10.5	169	15.0	139	24	18 069	6.6	55.7	37.7
Stearns, MN	14.1	22.6	5.3	1 568	15.7	1 432	257	191 254	4.3	63.4	32.3
Steele, MN	12.6	18.1	10.9	361	18.0	263	61	45 562	3.2	62.8	34.1
Stevens, MN	15.3	20.4	4.0	110	14.7	85	21	12 904	6.1	55.9	38.0
Swift, MN	15.5	32.8	4.4	119	15.5	110	22	13 719	3.4	67.4	29.1
Todd, MN	13.0	46.1	3.6	305	15.1	257	74	55 425	6.8	51.0	42.3
Traverse, MN	15.2	42.9	12.0	50	13.9	50	10	5 663	4.1	60.2	35.7
Wabasha, MN	13.1	16.3	3.4	333	16.1	226	45	25 610	2.5	70.4	27.0
Wadena, MN	14.9	45.4	1.6	227	13.6	151	37	25 505	7.4	69.0	23.5
Waseca, MN	15.9	23.3	6.1	252	15.6	245	55	33 096	4.8	58.6	36.5
Washington, MN	12.1	8.6	6.4	2 087	17.6	1 563	374	261 444	2.2	55.1	42.7
Watonwan, MN	10.9	40.3	25.0	154	13.9	138	28	15 890	6.7	65.0	28.3
Wilkin, MN	14.4	29.7	6.5	103	13.1	71	14	11 884	9.3	51.9	38.9
Winona, MN	14.4	27.1	7.4	414	16.1	337	88	51 626	5.0	61.3	33.7
Wright, MN	12.3	14.5	2.4	1 131	16.9	800	197	140 192	3.2	56.8	40.0
Yellow Medicine, MN	16.3	35.9	8.7	137	15.2	154	28	17 441	4.4	59.3	36.2
MISSISSIPPI											
Adams, MS	9.6	87.6	83.8	285	17.8	402	45	29 648	17.7	44.8	37.5
Alcorn, MS	16.3	46.6	17.1	386	14.1	317	26	30 262	11.5	58.1	30.4
Amite, MS	11.7	91.0	84.9	97	16.7	112	15	9 360	21.8	53.0	25.2
Attala, MS	16.5	70.6	58.0	216	16.2	229	19	22 218	10.5	44.9	44.6
Benton, MS	17.1	89.2	60.5	77	16.1	88	10	6 366	19.2	62.4	18.4
Bolivar, MS	15.2	85.0	85.0	540	15.3	502	71	44 693	19.5	60.2	20.3
Calhoun, MS	17.9	70.5	47.1	165	15.3	163	16	13 342	13.5	63.8	22.7
Carroll, MS	12.8	88.2	75.4	76	15.9	77	10	7 059	14.1	54.0	31.9
Chickasaw, MS	12.0	75.4	61.9	212	16.2	193	21	17 592	13.4	63.7	22.9
Choctaw, MS	9.3	67.0	43.5	117	16.4	120	10	9 268	16.1	61.4	22.5

2IEP = Individual Education Program. See Notes and Definitions at the end of this section.
. . . = Not available.

Table C-1. Population, School, and Student Characteristics by County—*Continued*

County	Current expenditures, fiscal 1999			Resident population 16 to 19 years, 2000				Outcomes, 1999–2000	
	Amount ($1,000s)	Amount per student	Percent for instruction	Total population 16 to 19 years	Percent in Armed Forces	Percent high school graduates	Percent not enrolled, not grads, not Armed Forces, not empl.	Number of graduates	Dropouts grades 9–12 (percent)
	21	22	23	24	25	26	27	28	29
Douglas, MN	$32 311	$5 754	65.9	2 089	0.0	7.5	1.5	515	5.2
Faribault, MN	16 019	5 911	64.9	973	0.0	7.6	2.0	246	1.7
Fillmore, MN	21 511	6 197	63.7	1 294	0.0	6.6	4.7	291	1.8
Freeborn, MN	31 001	6 030	63.7	1 850	0.0	9.0	5.9	386	5.0
Goodhue, MN	55 625	5 966	63.8	2 867	0.0	10.6	2.8	595	2.1
Grant, MN	9 455	6 022	60.9	376	0.0	8.5	3.2	148	0.4
Hennepin, MN	1 221 302	7 854	63.3	56 930	0.0	8.6	3.7	8 605	6.9
Houston, MN	21 360	5 849	64.3	1 148	0.0	12.5	1.7	307	3.1
Hubbard, MN	18 524	6 284	64.6	1 044	0.0	10.5	5.7	219	2.9
Isanti, MN	35 779	6 198	69.2	2 105	0.0	9.4	3.9	476	4.6
Itasca, MN	56 939	7 010	64.5	2 789	0.0	8.1	3.4	651	5.6
Jackson, MN	11 826	6 074	64.4	679	0.0	4.6	1.3	178	. . .
Kanabec, MN	15 773	5 562	67.1	940	0.0	10.0	4.3	199	4.8
Kandiyohi, MN	43 586	6 658	64.6	2 842	0.0	10.2	2.7	461	2.4
Kittson, MN	7 966	7 248	60.3	252	0.0	7.5	0.0	93	0.3
Koochiching, MN	17 900	7 072	63.0	829	0.0	10.5	3.4	196	2.3
Lac qui Parle, MN	13 044	6 271	62.4	466	0.0	8.6	3.0	164	0.9
Lake, MN	13 747	6 427	62.7	573	0.0	18.8	1.7	135	4.9
Lake of the Woods, MN	5 179	5 973	58.5	195	0.0	8.2	0.5	67	3.4
Le Sueur, MN	27 780	5 511	64.1	1 640	0.0	8.4	2.3	406	2.3
Lincoln, MN	6 643	6 412	61.5	318	0.0	3.1	0.0	130	0.6
Lyon, MN	38 392	7 959	61.7	1 885	0.0	7.6	2.3	443	1.5
McLeod, MN	36 061	5 731	61.5	1 949	0.0	8.4	1.4	440	2.3
Mahnomen, MN	11 559	7 966	65.5	370	0.0	7.3	5.9	122	22.1
Marshall, MN	13 216	7 071	61.3	600	0.0	5.7	3.0	144	1.6
Martin, MN	26 984	6 811	62.8	1 363	0.0	10.8	0.2	324	2.4
Meeker, MN	36 360	5 687	63.0	1 431	0.0	10.6	3.7	473	1.9
Mille Lacs, MN	36 762	5 858	63.1	1 375	0.0	9.3	4.9	407	2.5
Morrison, MN	41 384	6 635	64.4	2 052	0.1	13.0	1.7	503	6.2
Mower, MN	38 825	6 351	65.5	2 263	0.0	9.1	6.5	435	5.5
Murray, MN	9 612	6 258	60.4	523	0.0	8.0	3.6	106	0.6
Nicollet, MN	17 631	7 515	65.8	2 757	0.0	5.1	1.6	194	1.4
Nobles, MN	23 654	6 509	66.0	1 283	0.0	5.0	3.1	293	4.8
Norman, MN	10 687	7 416	60.7	418	0.0	6.9	1.0	112	3.2
Olmsted, MN	150 119	7 118	54.7	6 769	0.0	7.5	1.9	1 486	3.3
Otter Tail, MN	82 529	8 803	46.1	3 746	0.0	8.2	2.3	777	4.8
Pennington, MN	16 961	6 691	59.2	949	0.0	7.2	1.8	179	0.2
Pine, MN	27 660	6 070	63.8	1 564	0.0	10.5	6.2	305	8.2
Pipestone, MN	13 647	6 203	64.9	599	0.0	8.0	0.8	162	3.3
Polk, MN	39 971	6 566	62.7	2 145	0.4	9.0	2.7	475	3.2
Pope, MN	11 442	6 152	64.0	707	0.0	3.4	1.8	142	0.6
Ramsey, MN	648 951	7 599	65.1	30 219	0.1	9.0	3.9	5 172	6.8
Red Lake, MN	7 972	9 049	63.1	311	0.0	10.6	1.9	74	0.9
Redwood, MN	21 240	6 032	63.4	1 004	0.0	6.7	2.4	283	1.4
Renville, MN	17 744	6 315	63.9	1 024	0.0	7.2	2.8	232	2.2
Rice, MN	51 589	6 334	62.8	4 870	0.0	6.6	1.6	616	4.7
Rock, MN	10 456	5 877	64.1	583	0.0	4.8	1.4	161	0.7
Roseau, MN	23 653	6 117	61.7	1 001	0.0	8.9	2.1	290	1.8
St. Louis, MN	213 309	6 863	63.6	13 530	0.1	8.4	2.4	2 420	4.3
Scott, MN	78 632	6 193	63.2	4 375	0.0	10.9	1.9	864	0.7
Sherburne, MN	74 399	5 770	63.7	3 971	0.1	13.2	2.9	810	3.6
Sibley, MN	16 672	6 973	67.2	888	0.0	9.5	0.5	243	3.5
Stearns, MN	158 976	6 524	64.8	11 213	0.0	6.5	1.3	2 031	2.1
Steele, MN	37 833	5 891	61.9	2 056	0.0	6.9	1.3	481	4.0
Stevens, MN	11 379	6 725	65.4	1 126	0.0	3.5	1.1	173	0.4
Swift, MN	10 584	5 513	63.3	617	0.0	4.2	0.6	162	2.5
Todd, MN	47 071	9 912	45.0	1 777	0.0	7.3	3.9	463	2.8
Traverse, MN	4 952	6 984	64.8	243	0.0	5.3	0.8	49	. . .
Wabasha, MN	22 571	5 430	65.0	1 296	0.0	9.4	1.8	424	0.8
Wadena, MN	20 336	6 187	66.6	757	0.0	6.6	1.8	272	1.4
Waseca, MN	26 796	6 553	63.3	1 133	0.0	7.4	3.3	329	4.0
Washington, MN	207 172	6 035	63.8	10 958	0.0	7.6	1.7	2 520	2.5
Watonwan, MN	14 022	6 391	64.6	706	0.0	6.5	1.6	171	1.7
Wilkin, MN	9 261	6 304	66.9	417	0.0	2.6	2.6	115	2.8
Winona, MN	41 965	6 345	67.9	4 572	0.0	6.7	1.0	484	5.2
Wright, MN	109 067	5 988	64.7	5 251	0.0	9.8	2.2	1 290	2.8
Yellow Medicine, MN	14 217	6 576	62.6	750	0.0	6.5	1.3	155	1.6
MISSISSIPPI									
Adams, MS	25 435	4 718	60.1	2 125	0.0	8.3	6.4	262	2.1
Alcorn, MS	27 327	4 891	65.7	1 759	0.0	13.5	6.9	301	5.4
Amite, MS	8 726	5 047	59.2	854	0.0	11.6	8.3	82	3.5
Attala, MS	16 193	4 527	58.2	1 173	0.0	6.5	8.1	180	1.8
Benton, MS	6 005	4 648	58.4	483	0.0	8.3	10.6	82	5.7
Bolivar, MS	45 399	5 121	56.7	3 414	0.1	7.2	6.6	434	2.6
Calhoun, MS	12 070	4 691	60.2	935	0.0	14.1	6.3	141	6.1
Carroll, MS	6 637	5 242	52.7	633	0.0	5.7	13.6	75	6.2
Chickasaw, MS	15 493	4 427	62.0	1 159	0.0	8.6	7.9	156	6.9
Choctaw, MS	8 697	4 513	59.0	670	0.0	7.3	6.6	84	8.1

. . . = Not available.

Table C-1. Population, School, and Student Characteristics by County—*Continued*

County	High school graduates, 2000			College enrollment, 2000		College graduates, 2000 (percent)						
	Population 25 years and over	High school diploma or less (percent)	High school diploma or more (percent)	Number	Percent public	Bachelor's degree or more	+/- U.S. percent with bachelor's degree or more	Non-Hispanic White	Black or African American	American Indian and Alaska Native	Asian, Hawaiian, and Pacific Islander	Hispanic or Latino[1]
	30	31	32	33	34	35	36	37	38	39	40	41
Douglas, MN	21 961	47.5	85.6	1 348	89.6	17.3	-7.1	17.4	0.0	28.1	17.5	23.6
Faribault, MN	11 128	57.2	83.6	369	85.4	13.8	-10.6	14.0	66.7	0.0	3.6	4.8
Fillmore, MN	14 116	55.2	81.7	493	86.4	15.1	-9.3	15.0	0.0	0.0	42.1	17.4
Freeborn, MN	22 363	56.5	81.2	789	88.7	12.8	-11.6	13.2	4.9	0.0	23.9	3.7
Goodhue, MN	29 127	49.8	86.7	1 302	79.8	19.1	-5.3	19.3	19.4	5.6	22.5	7.7
Grant, MN	4 370	51.8	83.5	165	84.8	15.7	-8.7	15.8	. . .	0.0	0.0	0.0
Hennepin, MN	740 444	30.5	90.6	78 624	74.9	39.1	14.7	42.0	17.8	10.1	38.6	18.0
Houston, MN	13 063	49.2	85.5	645	88.2	20.5	-3.9	20.2	55.6	0.0	49.2	33.8
Hubbard, MN	12 694	48.3	86.1	467	86.9	20.2	-4.2	20.5	0.0	9.3	27.6	0.0
Isanti, MN	19 915	51.8	86.6	959	87.0	14.5	-9.9	14.5	19.7	17.7	32.6	11.4
Itasca, MN	29 931	47.7	85.6	1 681	90.5	17.6	-6.8	18.0	27.0	8.0	4.5	5.1
Jackson, MN	7 768	53.9	84.1	350	95.7	14.2	-10.2	14.2	0.0	13.3	20.7	9.7
Kanabec, MN	9 797	61.6	80.6	269	80.7	10.5	-13.9	10.4	22.2	4.7	25.9	4.3
Kandiyohi, MN	26 419	47.7	83.5	1 628	88.9	18.3	-6.1	19.1	3.4	6.7	61.3	2.3
Kittson, MN	3 661	54.8	79.7	101	95.0	14.8	-9.6	14.7	42.9	0.0	0.0	6.7
Koochiching, MN	9 999	55.5	81.9	475	88.8	15.1	-9.3	15.4	0.0	4.4	40.0	0.0
Lac qui Parle, MN	5 644	56.9	80.8	128	79.7	13.0	-11.4	12.8	0.0	50.0	38.9	14.3
Lake, MN	7 847	51.1	86.4	322	87.0	19.5	-4.9	19.5	0.0	28.1	. . .	6.3
Lake of the Woods, MN	3 155	52.8	84.6	85	87.1	17.2	-7.2	17.3	0.0	0.0	0.0	60.0
Le Sueur, MN	16 499	53.7	84.6	729	77.1	16.9	-7.5	17.2	3.6	5.2	25.0	3.6
Lincoln, MN	4 516	58.7	79.8	169	85.8	14.1	-10.3	14.0	. . .	. . .	100.0	0.0
Lyon, MN	15 355	49.8	82.6	2 194	94.4	21.4	-3.0	21.7	20.0	26.8	44.1	3.2
McLeod, MN	22 495	52.6	84.7	1 188	83.8	15.4	-9.0	15.5	3.6	20.0	44.6	3.4
Mahnomen, MN	3 292	59.0	75.0	149	93.3	12.4	-12.0	14.8	0.0	6.8	17.1	0.0
Marshall, MN	6 914	57.9	79.1	248	95.6	12.0	-12.4	12.1	40.0	8.3	20.0	1.8
Martin, MN	14 935	54.2	83.7	492	85.2	16.1	-8.3	16.2	0.0	0.0	25.8	2.6
Meeker, MN	14 841	56.8	81.5	570	87.2	13.9	-10.5	14.0	0.0	4.4	0.0	5.8
Mille Lacs, MN	14 622	59.0	81.3	536	80.8	12.2	-12.2	12.3	20.0	3.8	53.1	7.4
Morrison, MN	20 347	59.0	79.7	850	80.4	14.7	-11.8	12.6	37.5	10.0	36.6	6.1
Mower, MN	25 749	53.0	82.3	1 309	88.2	14.7	-9.7	15.0	7.4	8.1	30.6	3.6
Murray, MN	6 320	58.7	79.1	211	87.2	11.9	-12.5	11.9	28.6	18.2	13.3	1.5
Nicollet, MN	17 496	37.6	90.1	3 662	36.3	29.3	4.9	29.9	7.8	50.0	22.8	7.0
Nobles, MN	13 654	58.5	75.8	593	89.2	13.5	-10.9	14.3	12.5	12.9	13.2	4.7
Norman, MN	5 105	54.8	80.0	147	89.8	13.1	-11.3	13.4	0.0	0.0	54.5	3.8
Olmsted, MN	80 277	32.9	91.1	6 285	77.2	34.7	10.3	34.7	16.8	21.2	54.1	14.5
Otter Tail, MN	38 739	51.7	81.4	1 858	91.8	17.2	-7.2	17.4	10.5	2.9	23.8	4.7
Pennington, MN	8 848	49.8	81.3	795	93.7	14.9	-9.5	14.8	33.3	0.0	35.8	9.5
Pine, MN	17 714	61.9	79.0	690	75.5	10.3	-14.1	10.7	2.2	5.8	20.4	3.7
Pipestone, MN	6 671	58.5	77.6	256	91.8	13.9	-10.5	14.2	0.0	3.0	0.0	11.5
Polk, MN	20 203	49.8	82.0	2 029	94.0	17.6	-6.8	18.0	15.4	7.8	27.8	6.6
Pope, MN	7 719	51.7	81.8	247	87.0	14.7	-9.7	14.7	50.0	0.0	0.0	0.0
Ramsey, MN	323 214	37.7	87.6	41 484	54.3	34.3	9.9	37.0	18.6	16.2	29.6	16.1
Red Lake, MN	2 879	59.4	78.8	122	91.8	10.7	-13.7	10.9	. . .	0.0	50.0	0.0
Redwood, MN	11 269	56.8	80.2	303	85.8	13.4	-11.0	13.8	0.0	1.7	6.7	11.9
Renville, MN	11 464	57.1	80.9	367	86.1	12.6	-11.8	13.0	0.0	0.0	20.0	2.6
Rice, MN	33 400	47.8	85.2	6 359	21.2	22.4	-2.0	23.2	11.8	3.4	27.7	8.0
Rock, MN	6 485	54.2	81.5	276	83.7	15.4	-9.0	15.2	27.5	58.3	38.9	6.1
Roseau, MN	10 366	55.3	82.5	303	91.7	14.9	-9.5	15.1	44.4	0.0	14.5	0.0
St. Louis, MN	132 801	44.6	87.2	16 743	85.8	21.9	-2.5	22.1	21.0	9.0	28.8	13.8
Scott, MN	55 564	37.4	91.0	3 500	70.4	29.4	5.0	30.1	15.7	7.5	30.6	7.6
Sherburne, MN	38 349	42.6	89.9	3 410	81.6	19.4	-5.0	19.5	12.5	10.2	33.1	16.7
Sibley, MN	9 970	60.9	79.2	370	78.9	11.6	-12.8	11.8	0.0	0.0	56.3	2.9
Stearns, MN	77 519	47.1	86.2	15 315	73.1	22.0	-2.4	21.9	13.9	8.7	31.1	18.7
Steele, MN	21 550	49.4	86.6	1 184	73.0	20.1	-4.3	20.4	3.4	0.0	28.8	9.7
Stevens, MN	5 790	49.7	84.4	1 713	97.6	20.6	-3.8	20.2	42.1	0.0	55.6	47.2
Swift, MN	8 336	54.8	80.4	347	87.0	14.0	-10.4	15.0	0.6	7.7	9.3	2.3
Todd, MN	15 758	62.0	79.3	663	91.3	10.0	-14.4	10.1	0.0	2.9	4.4	6.4
Traverse, MN	2 850	57.4	82.2	122	92.6	10.7	-13.7	10.8	. . .	0.0	20.0	20.0
Wabasha, MN	14 189	51.8	85.6	654	87.6	16.9	-7.5	16.9	40.0	52.6	19.7	15.0
Wadena, MN	9 047	57.4	79.5	569	95.1	13.4	-11.0	13.2	6.5	7.5	82.9	0.0
Waseca, MN	12 818	53.7	84.8	582	88.1	16.2	-8.2	16.8	0.3	2.0	93.3	8.9
Washington, MN	128 215	32.0	94.0	9 321	71.4	33.9	9.5	33.9	28.9	11.3	52.2	26.0
Watonwan, MN	7 745	63.1	75.9	261	80.1	13.7	-10.7	15.1	0.0	26.7	17.0	2.2
Wilkin, MN	4 673	48.0	84.5	175	86.9	14.0	-10.4	14.3	0.0	0.0	42.9	0.0
Winona, MN	29 165	46.2	84.0	7 565	59.4	23.2	-1.2	23.3	5.8	13.5	39.1	11.9
Wright, MN	55 234	48.7	88.1	2 738	77.5	17.9	-6.5	18.0	12.4	9.0	36.4	3.6
Yellow Medicine, MN	7 394	53.4	81.9	405	93.8	14.4	-10.0	14.4	0.0	14.7	71.4	0.0
MISSISSIPPI												
Adams, MS	22 211	58.3	73.4	1 538	92.6	17.5	-6.9	24.0	10.7	14.3	9.4	16.6
Alcorn, MS	23 159	66.8	68.1	1 016	88.3	11.7	-12.7	12.1	7.5	21.7	43.6	9.9
Amite, MS	8 981	68.4	67.2	392	80.1	9.4	-15.0	11.7	6.0	0.0	0.0	9.8
Attala, MS	12 674	66.4	63.4	576	84.2	11.6	-12.8	14.9	5.9	0.0	0.0	14.0
Benton, MS	5 073	73.3	58.8	210	66.2	7.8	-16.6	7.7	8.2	0.0	. . .	0.0
Bolivar, MS	22 956	59.1	65.3	3 752	96.2	18.8	-5.6	33.3	9.4	6.9	50.6	9.0
Calhoun, MS	10 021	70.2	64.4	338	91.4	10.2	-14.2	11.8	4.7	0.0	50.0	21.9
Carroll, MS	7 121	68.1	66.6	335	79.7	10.9	-13.5	12.6	6.7	. . .	44.4	5.7
Chickasaw, MS	12 159	71.0	59.4	487	88.9	9.5	-14.9	11.1	7.1	0.0	0.0	0.6
Choctaw, MS	6 171	67.6	65.1	276	86.6	11.2	-13.2	14.1	3.6	27.3	. . .	0.0

[1]Hispanic or Latino persons may be of any race.
. . . = Not available.

Table C-1. Population, School, and Student Characteristics by County—*Continued*

County	State/County code	County type[1]	Population, 2000		Number of schools and students, 2000–2001			Resident enrollment, 2000			
			Total	Percent 5–17 years	School districts	Schools	Students	Total	Percent public	K–12	Percent public
			1	2	3	4	5	6	7	8	9
Claiborne, MS	28021	8	11 831	19.5	1	3	2 011	4 792	95.1	2 350	92.1
Clarke, MS	28023	7	17 955	20.0	2	7	3 415	4 411	93.3	3 627	94.8
Clay, MS	28025	7	21 979	21.4	2	8	4 027	6 257	84.6	4 843	85.1
Coahoma, MS	28027	7	30 622	24.1	3	16	6 302	9 446	89.1	7 404	89.1
Copiah, MS	28029	6	28 757	20.3	2	6	4 911	8 378	82.8	6 183	83.9
Covington, MS	28031	7	19 407	21.3	1	6	3 558	5 285	92.8	4 337	93.2
De Soto, MS	28033	1	107 199	20.4	1	21	19 812	27 677	83.6	21 613	88.0
Forrest, MS	28035	5	72 604	17.6	4	20	11 606	24 754	88.3	12 986	91.2
Franklin, MS	28037	9	8 448	20.8	1	4	1 662	2 176	93.4	1 809	94.1
George, MS	28039	6	19 144	21.4	1	8	4 053	4 817	94.9	4 096	97.1
Greene, MS	28041	8	13 299	17.1	1	5	1 905	2 768	94.1	2 292	96.6
Grenada, MS	28043	7	23 263	20.3	1	4	4 625	6 164	88.2	4 888	90.3
Hancock, MS	28045	2	42 967	18.8	2	11	6 464	10 176	82.8	8 068	84.2
Harrison, MS	28047	2	189 601	18.9	6	49	30 701	48 256	85.4	35 754	89.0
Hinds, MS	28049	2	250 800	20.5	7	77	43 281	78 720	80.5	53 035	86.7
Holmes, MS	28051	6	21 609	24.4	2	9	4 543	7 369	90.9	5 799	91.3
Humphreys, MS	28053	7	11 206	24.9	1	3	2 267	3 643	86.5	3 076	86.3
Issaquena, MS	28055	9	2 274	21.9	. . .	. . .	9 999	658	90.9	560	90.7
Itawamba, MS	28057	7	22 770	18.1	1	7	3 790	5 744	96.5	4 215	98.5
Jackson, MS	28059	2	131 420	20.6	4	46	25 617	34 736	91.7	27 188	94.4
Jasper, MS	28061	9	18 149	21.0	2	6	3 089	4 891	90.7	3 964	90.8
Jefferson, MS	28063	9	9 740	21.5	1	3	1 714	2 748	93.8	2 133	92.9
Jefferson Davis, MS	28065	9	13 962	21.2	1	4	2 401	3 815	86.2	2 991	85.6
Jones, MS	28067	5	64 958	18.8	3	19	11 085	16 331	91.8	12 363	95.1
Kemper, MS	28069	9	10 453	18.8	1	3	1 411	2 955	86.3	2 011	82.7
Lafayette, MS	28071	7	38 744	14.2	3	10	5 180	16 076	94.0	5 569	95.0
Lamar, MS	28073	1	39 070	20.6	2	10	7 476	11 465	88.3	8 107	90.8
Lauderdale, MS	28075	5	78 161	19.5	3	22	13 692	20 890	90.1	15 416	92.7
Lawrence, MS	28077	9	13 258	20.5	1	5	2 459	3 493	92.5	2 808	93.4
Leake, MS	28079	6	20 940	19.6	1	7	3 236	5 007	80.3	4 251	80.0
Lee, MS	28081	5	75 755	20.2	3	23	14 881	19 509	91.7	15 438	94.8
Leflore, MS	28083	7	37 947	21.9	2	13	6 859	11 798	87.3	8 537	86.5
Lincoln, MS	28085	7	33 166	19.6	2	9	5 952	8 437	88.9	6 673	90.3
Lowndes, MS	28087	5	61 586	20.9	3	21	11 036	18 414	85.2	13 298	86.6
Madison, MS	28089	2	74 674	20.8	2	16	12 611	21 716	72.7	15 931	79.0
Marion, MS	28091	7	25 595	20.9	2	12	4 607	6 517	89.1	5 432	90.4
Marshall, MS	28093	6	34 993	19.5	2	10	5 192	8 919	78.3	7 008	83.0
Monroe, MS	28095	7	38 014	20.6	3	15	6 495	9 518	92.2	7 890	93.9
Montgomery, MS	28097	7	12 189	20.1	2	5	2 186	3 213	91.0	2 600	92.7
Neshoba, MS	28099	7	28 684	20.5	2	5	3 959	7 642	82.0	6 084	82.1
Newton, MS	28101	7	21 838	19.0	3	6	3 698	6 028	89.4	4 247	88.4
Noxubee, MS	28103	9	12 548	22.6	1	5	2 307	3 505	82.6	2 955	80.5
Oktibbeha, MS	28105	7	42 902	15.1	2	12	5 340	19 744	90.9	6 653	83.2
Panola, MS	28107	7	34 274	21.7	2	11	6 726	9 472	90.9	7 843	91.4
Pearl River, MS	28109	2	48 621	19.9	3	14	8 614	12 637	90.0	9 827	92.4
Perry, MS	28111	9	12 138	21.0	2	6	2 288	2 986	93.6	2 470	95.6
Pike, MS	28113	7	38 940	20.3	3	14	7 101	10 215	87.7	7 868	88.8
Pontotoc, MS	28115	7	26 726	20.4	2	6	5 217	6 412	93.6	5 267	96.6
Prentiss, MS	28117	7	25 556	18.2	3	12	4 776	6 548	97.1	4 658	97.5
Quitman, MS	28119	9	10 117	23.9	1	3	1 690	2 901	87.0	2 433	86.4
Rankin, MS	28121	2	115 327	18.9	4	29	18 774	28 701	85.8	21 903	92.0
Scott, MS	28123	6	28 423	21.2	2	10	5 617	7 148	91.2	6 012	93.2
Sharkey, MS	28125	9	6 580	24.4	1	3	1 561	2 026	88.5	1 716	88.2
Simpson, MS	28127	6	27 639	20.8	1	7	4 420	6 941	88.4	5 802	90.0
Smith, MS	28129	8	16 182	20.5	1	4	3 136	4 070	91.1	3 404	95.3
Stone, MS	28131	6	13 622	19.9	1	4	2 665	3 916	93.5	2 687	97.2
Sunflower, MS	28133	7	34 369	20.9	3	16	5 958	10 048	86.8	7 690	87.0
Tallahatchie, MS	28135	9	14 903	23.1	2	5	3 006	4 489	91.8	3 664	91.4
Tate, MS	28137	6	25 370	20.2	2	8	4 646	7 177	87.7	5 059	87.7
Tippah, MS	28139	7	20 826	18.6	2	9	4 073	4 775	91.2	3 900	95.6
Tishomingo, MS	28141	7	19 163	17.3	1	6	3 182	3 842	95.8	3 228	98.2
Tunica, MS	28143	8	9 227	23.1	1	4	2 005	2 471	90.1	2 166	89.6
Union, MS	28145	7	25 362	18.6	2	8	4 641	5 916	95.0	4 833	95.9
Walthall, MS	28147	9	15 156	21.3	1	5	2 720	4 094	95.1	3 329	96.7
Warren, MS	28149	4	49 644	21.0	1	13	9 180	13 651	85.1	10 568	88.9
Washington, MS	28151	5	62 977	23.1	4	26	12 482	19 083	86.3	15 260	86.2
Wayne, MS	28153	7	21 216	21.6	1	6	4 038	5 535	91.7	4 731	93.5
Webster, MS	28155	9	10 294	19.4	1	4	1 952	2 474	89.7	1 992	92.8
Wilkinson, MS	28157	9	10 312	20.0	1	3	1 660	2 669	78.7	2 241	77.4
Winston, MS	28159	7	20 160	20.0	1	6	3 308	5 032	83.9	4 234	84.8
Yalobusha, MS	28161	7	13 051	19.1	2	4	2 094	3 267	90.3	2 646	92.8
Yazoo, MS	28163	6	28 149	21.0	2	8	4 717	7 155	80.7	6 117	82.0
MISSOURI	29000										
Adair, MO	29001	7	24 977	13.9	3	8	2 956	10 082	90.1	3 520	90.4
Andrew, MO	29003	3	16 492	20.0	3	10	2 911	4 144	90.3	3 290	94.0
Atchison, MO	29005	9	6 430	19.6	3	7	1 203	1 417	94.6	1 144	97.8
Audrain, MO	29007	6	25 853	18.2	3	9	3 681	5 632	86.0	4 572	89.4
Barry, MO	29009	7	34 010	19.4	7	19	6 629	7 860	94.4	6 700	95.9
Barton, MO	29011	6	12 541	19.8	3	9	2 168	2 959	92.9	2 446	95.4
Bates, MO	29013	6	16 653	20.4	7	13	3 083	3 883	90.3	3 379	92.1
Benton, MO	29015	9	17 180	15.7	3	10	2 765	3 197	92.4	2 727	95.0
Bollinger, MO	29017	9	12 029	20.1	4	8	2 072	2 686	90.2	2 402	90.6
Boone, MO	29019	3	135 454	16.6	6	45	20 949	49 784	89.3	22 625	93.1

[1]County type code is from the Economic Research Service of the USDA. See Notes and Definitions at the end of this section.
. . . = Not available.

Table C-1. School and Student Characteristics by County—*Continued*

County	Characteristics of students, 2000–2001			Staff and students, 2000–2001				Revenues, fiscal 1999			
	Percent with IEP[2]	Percent eligible for free lunch	Percent minority	Number of teachers	Student/ teacher ratio	Local school non-teaching staff	Central admin. staff	Total revenue ($1,000s)	Percentage of revenue from		
									Federal govt.	State govt.	Local govt.
	10	11	12	13	14	15	16	17	18	19	20
Claiborne, MS	9.5	95.4	99.8	117	17.2	138	19	$12 438	15.8	45.6	38.6
Clarke, MS	12.6	61.6	45.2	210	16.3	210	28	17 398	12.0	54.1	33.9
Clay, MS	9.9	81.6	79.9	208	19.4	229	27	19 040	16.9	57.2	25.9
Coahoma, MS	13.9	85.0	91.1	386	16.3	404	44	32 714	19.2	57.2	23.6
Copiah, MS	10.1	82.7	76.1	282	17.4	281	33	23 164	17.5	53.2	29.4
Covington, MS	13.7	75.9	52.0	209	17.0	216	20	16 320	16.7	62.0	21.3
De Soto, MS	11.9	28.0	19.7	1 004	19.7	1 001	53	75 659	6.4	59.2	34.4
Forrest, MS	15.4	61.2	49.6	820	14.2	691	90	64 079	12.8	52.6	34.7
Franklin, MS	15.3	69.0	50.0	108	15.4	117	13	9 552	20.5	56.2	23.4
George, MS	13.1	57.2	12.4	237	17.1	254	21	16 870	12.0	65.7	22.3
Greene, MS	13.5	70.8	26.2	117	16.3	132	12	9 600	13.7	64.3	22.0
Grenada, MS	10.5	59.6	54.7	246	18.8	270	27	21 311	13.5	55.4	31.1
Hancock, MS	13.2	60.2	11.9	396	16.3	330	42	35 279	10.4	44.3	45.3
Harrison, MS	13.0	57.1	36.0	1 870	16.4	1 763	185	167 223	11.9	46.6	41.5
Hinds, MS	9.7	71.8	83.1	2 626	16.5	3 222	325	235 159	11.5	45.4	43.1
Holmes, MS	7.8	97.0	98.4	229	19.8	260	29	22 444	24.2	59.3	16.5
Humphreys, MS	8.7	95.9	97.7	111	20.4	141	25	11 775	26.8	55.8	17.4
Issaquena, MS	. . .	. . .	. . .	. . .	. . .	. . .	. . .	. . .	. . .	. . .	. . .
Itawamba, MS	15.0	53.5	8.9	233	16.3	220	14	18 564	10.3	66.0	23.7
Jackson, MS	12.4	47.9	30.8	1 471	17.4	1 596	171	130 745	9.0	49.4	41.6
Jasper, MS	14.0	84.5	76.3	196	15.8	195	32	17 458	15.2	51.6	33.2
Jefferson, MS	13.9	97.1	99.7	98	17.5	99	23	10 241	24.9	53.5	21.5
Jefferson Davis, MS	16.5	93.9	85.4	153	15.7	155	18	13 336	18.8	58.2	23.0
Jones, MS	13.3	65.9	41.1	703	15.8	692	73	56 125	12.5	57.5	30.1
Kemper, MS	5.8	88.4	96.1	88	16.0	97	13	8 178	19.7	50.4	29.9
Lafayette, MS	17.5	49.8	42.6	337	15.4	303	35	28 862	10.0	54.6	35.4
Lamar, MS	12.9	38.8	17.4	472	15.8	413	39	33 582	8.0	59.2	32.8
Lauderdale, MS	14.0	59.0	55.1	861	15.9	768	97	69 506	12.1	56.6	31.3
Lawrence, MS	10.7	60.1	42.4	149	16.5	140	18	12 034	13.6	55.5	30.9
Leake, MS	13.0	74.9	62.1	192	16.9	197	20	14 211	16.4	62.0	21.6
Lee, MS	15.2	50.2	36.6	899	16.6	832	78	79 746	8.8	52.4	38.9
Leflore, MS	14.1	89.9	91.5	414	16.6	423	53	35 840	20.6	54.9	24.5
Lincoln, MS	10.9	57.4	39.8	342	17.4	382	32	29 245	12.2	58.0	29.8
Lowndes, MS	10.4	61.7	59.5	683	16.2	686	63	57 498	12.9	50.6	36.5
Madison, MS	9.0	48.7	57.1	683	18.5	584	78	59 999	12.2	49.6	38.1
Marion, MS	16.3	76.7	46.3	294	15.7	280	32	23 686	15.3	61.0	23.7
Marshall, MS	14.0	86.8	77.7	286	18.2	293	33	23 223	18.2	63.4	18.4
Monroe, MS	13.2	60.9	41.4	396	16.4	360	38	33 047	12.5	57.8	29.7
Montgomery, MS	12.2	68.8	62.7	137	16.0	153	20	11 480	18.3	58.7	23.0
Neshoba, MS	12.7	57.1	37.9	258	15.3	241	29	18 699	15.5	58.5	26.0
Newton, MS	12.2	63.4	46.2	215	17.2	235	24	19 898	13.7	56.9	29.5
Noxubee, MS	13.5	94.3	100.0	128	18.0	175	17	11 821	22.1	55.6	22.3
Oktibbeha, MS	13.4	67.8	70.8	356	15.0	399	45	34 180	16.3	49.2	34.5
Panola, MS	12.4	75.6	69.4	367	18.3	414	39	32 690	17.9	57.0	25.1
Pearl River, MS	11.1	57.1	18.5	484	17.8	545	61	40 071	10.8	57.5	31.6
Perry, MS	13.3	69.1	34.0	151	15.2	141	16	12 074	16.7	58.7	24.7
Pike, MS	12.6	77.5	66.1	427	16.6	442	59	35 375	16.6	58.9	24.4
Pontotoc, MS	15.2	46.5	19.1	309	16.9	268	28	22 205	9.4	65.6	25.0
Prentiss, MS	18.0	54.3	18.9	327	14.6	262	35	25 166	10.4	63.9	25.7
Quitman, MS	15.1	97.0	97.4	92	18.4	112	18	8 108	22.8	54.6	22.6
Rankin, MS	10.0	34.6	22.7	1 110	16.9	978	87	84 477	7.5	55.1	37.3
Scott, MS	12.2	72.9	54.0	326	17.2	291	28	24 199	16.4	62.0	21.6
Sharkey, MS	11.1	96.0	97.2	93	16.8	101	16	8 587	23.6	54.5	21.9
Simpson, MS	10.8	76.6	51.9	252	17.5	246	25	20 957	14.2	58.6	27.2
Smith, MS	13.1	58.1	33.0	187	16.8	179	14	14 871	12.2	62.0	25.7
Stone, MS	10.5	57.9	25.9	167	16.0	173	20	12 491	13.1	58.5	28.5
Sunflower, MS	11.2	93.8	94.9	363	16.4	368	52	30 404	20.8	58.5	20.7
Tallahatchie, MS	13.0	91.1	81.1	179	16.8	213	28	15 806	19.8	59.9	20.3
Tate, MS	15.9	58.8	44.2	268	17.3	281	32	21 083	13.2	65.2	21.6
Tippah, MS	16.3	55.9	22.6	248	16.4	212	18	19 332	11.4	67.6	21.0
Tishomingo, MS	14.7	52.5	4.4	194	16.4	177	12	15 693	12.7	60.1	27.2
Tunica, MS	8.2	89.2	98.6	119	16.8	146	23	16 939	12.8	33.8	53.3
Union, MS	12.5	53.0	23.1	277	16.8	286	21	22 476	9.4	63.2	27.4
Walthall, MS	15.8	82.7	65.8	182	14.9	163	15	14 286	16.6	60.6	22.8
Warren, MS	11.4	61.3	59.8	533	17.2	699	69	50 088	11.5	47.6	40.9
Washington, MS	12.5	88.5	88.1	742	16.8	810	90	64 663	19.8	54.8	25.4
Wayne, MS	13.5	73.4	54.2	238	17.0	273	21	19 699	16.3	60.4	23.3
Webster, MS	14.5	57.7	31.6	118	16.5	131	10	9 240	11.6	64.8	23.6
Wilkinson, MS	11.6	91.6	99.8	98	16.9	107	15	8 458	21.9	57.3	20.8
Winston, MS	13.3	76.9	66.2	207	16.0	218	20	17 112	16.3	58.6	25.1
Yalobusha, MS	14.9	72.3	60.1	133	15.7	129	21	10 759	16.0	65.6	18.4
Yazoo, MS	12.3	90.6	83.8	275	17.2	306	45	24 331	19.5	57.7	22.9
MISSOURI											
Adair, MO	17.5	30.8	2.7	220	13.4	154	47	19 051	10.7	35.5	53.8
Andrew, MO	10.3	24.7	1.4	208	14.0	109	26	15 424	5.0	47.6	47.4
Atchison, MO	20.5	44.0	9.0	111	10.8	59	14	8 273	8.1	37.8	54.0
Audrain, MO	13.1	34.8	10.8	252	14.6	184	47	22 779	9.0	37.9	53.1
Barry, MO	14.0	44.9	8.0	452	14.7	370	66	37 459	9.0	47.1	43.9
Barton, MO	13.1	. . .	3.3	159	13.6	99	25	12 830	4.7	45.5	49.8
Bates, MO	11.6	35.8	2.5	229	13.5	141	34	16 707	7.5	44.6	47.9
Benton, MO	16.1	43.9	1.5	183	15.1	132	23	14 903	8.5	39.7	51.8
Bollinger, MO	11.9	42.7	1.2	150	13.8	110	22	10 836	7.3	54.9	37.8
Boone, MO	15.3	25.3	20.7	1 489	14.1	802	254	130 321	5.4	34.9	59.6

[2]IEP = Individual Education Program. See Notes and Definitions at the end of this section.
. . . = Not available.

Table C-1. Population, School, and Student Characteristics by County—*Continued*

County	Current expenditures, fiscal 1999			Resident population 16 to 19 years, 2000				Outcomes, 1999–2000	
	Amount ($1,000s)	Amount per student	Percent for instruction	Total population 16 to 19 years	Percent in Armed Forces	Percent high school graduates	Percent not enrolled, not grads, not Armed Forces, not empl.	Number of graduates	Dropouts grades 9–12 (percent)
	21	22	23	24	25	26	27	28	29
Claiborne, MS	$10 040	$4 975	64.4	1 275	0.0	7.1	6.4	108	1.6
Clarke, MS	14 929	4 245	59.2	1 063	0.5	9.0	7.8	163	5.5
Clay, MS	17 282	4 125	58.1	1 445	0.3	7.1	12.6	160	11.7
Coahoma, MS	31 553	4 746	58.2	2 163	0.0	8.2	14.2	256	4.1
Copiah, MS	22 721	4 585	55.0	2 235	7.7	10.6	2.1	258	8.4
Covington, MS	16 383	4 541	62.9	1 244	0.0	9.6	8.1	190	3.0
De Soto, MS	66 383	3 651	61.8	5 314	0.0	9.7	8.8	729	2.2
Forrest, MS	58 182	4 900	61.6	5 766	1.6	9.4	6.4	608	2.4
Franklin, MS	9 111	5 124	59.2	566	0.0	7.4	12.4	78	7.1
George, MS	14 556	3 669	64.9	1 128	0.0	12.2	6.1	171	0.5
Greene, MS	9 066	4 812	57.7	813	0.2	14.1	17.7	123	1.2
Grenada, MS	18 590	4 009	61.2	1 257	0.0	9.1	14.4	159	5.9
Hancock, MS	28 333	4 456	57.7	2 214	0.0	8.4	5.2	294	6.6
Harrison, MS	147 425	4 846	61.9	11 619	11.9	22.2	7.4	1 309	6.8
Hinds, MS	212 038	4 918	57.9	17 271	0.1	6.8	6.5	2 045	5.8
Holmes, MS	19 828	4 121	57.0	1 697	0.0	7.0	7.7	235	2.7
Humphreys, MS	11 022	4 453	56.0	904	0.0	2.9	8.5	96	5.4
Issaquena, MS	. . .	. . .	. . .	. . .	. . .	. . .	11.4	. . .	. . .
Itawamba, MS	15 857	4 170	66.1	1 538	0.0	7.0	5.9	183	8.4
Jackson, MS	116 941	4 595	59.9	7 461	1.4	12.4	6.4	1 245	4.6
Jasper, MS	15 103	4 659	56.8	1 226	0.0	10.9	6.5	172	3.4
Jefferson, MS	9 051	5 223	62.9	705	0.0	11.6	9.6	109	16.8
Jefferson Davis, MS	12 217	4 962	59.0	951	0.0	10.3	10.3	131	5.4
Jones, MS	52 958	4 711	62.2	4 375	0.0	6.8	6.4	652	6.7
Kemper, MS	7 550	5 098	60.7	832	0.0	8.7	4.1	56	10.4
Lafayette, MS	24 449	4 750	62.9	3 715	0.1	3.5	2.8	273	3.2
Lamar, MS	29 509	3 951	63.3	2 298	0.3	11.7	5.0	454	3.0
Lauderdale, MS	65 032	4 636	61.1	5 091	4.3	12.9	6.1	703	4.0
Lawrence, MS	11 504	4 613	60.8	898	0.0	8.7	7.5	139	4.7
Leake, MS	13 585	4 241	58.6	1 227	0.0	9.0	10.4	158	6.8
Lee, MS	69 033	4 665	63.5	4 086	0.0	10.2	7.2	689	4.6
Leflore, MS	33 698	4 772	58.8	2 781	0.0	6.9	12.8	243	9.2
Lincoln, MS	26 759	4 370	62.1	1 912	0.0	14.6	4.6	347	4.1
Lowndes, MS	51 251	4 633	58.3	3 766	1.1	8.4	5.9	682	4.5
Madison, MS	49 927	4 083	59.3	4 043	0.3	7.6	5.8	577	5.5
Marion, MS	21 685	4 521	60.6	1 605	0.0	10.6	9.3	240	3.3
Marshall, MS	22 424	4 285	58.7	2 362	0.0	9.1	13.9	241	1.5
Monroe, MS	28 494	4 306	63.1	2 347	0.0	9.6	6.1	361	4.7
Montgomery, MS	11 172	5 099	60.4	779	0.0	7.2	7.6	106	4.3
Neshoba, MS	17 134	4 207	64.1	1 808	0.0	13.4	8.8	191	4.3
Newton, MS	17 755	4 814	59.8	1 523	0.3	7.4	2.9	179	4.3
Noxubee, MS	11 071	4 588	55.7	881	0.2	9.1	7.9	116	10.1
Oktibbeha, MS	29 449	5 275	59.8	4 337	0.1	4.0	2.8	303	7.3
Panola, MS	27 890	4 153	61.4	2 449	0.0	8.3	10.1	289	3.2
Pearl River, MS	35 132	4 153	60.8	2 788	0.0	8.1	6.2	403	3.7
Perry, MS	11 491	4 898	62.0	878	0.8	9.8	8.9	138	6.9
Pike, MS	34 509	4 738	58.0	2 711	0.3	15.0	8.3	375	6.0
Pontotoc, MS	20 766	4 054	62.4	1 509	0.0	13.3	11.2	235	0.9
Prentiss, MS	22 219	4 525	62.8	1 819	0.3	6.1	5.9	239	3.5
Quitman, MS	7 424	4 311	52.3	655	0.0	11.5	13.9	75	4.8
Rankin, MS	73 605	3 923	63.1	6 799	0.0	11.3	9.6	1 008	2.3
Scott, MS	24 228	4 240	62.3	1 756	0.2	9.5	10.0	244	6.9
Sharkey, MS	8 069	4 956	56.8	500	0.0	2.8	16.8	77	8.2
Simpson, MS	18 711	4 234	59.9	1 566	0.6	7.1	11.2	218	6.0
Smith, MS	13 460	4 315	62.3	883	0.0	11.3	5.4	190	4.0
Stone, MS	12 366	4 638	59.4	1 060	0.0	7.4	4.2	127	0.7
Sunflower, MS	27 796	4 317	60.4	2 833	0.1	9.5	18.1	263	7.1
Tallahatchie, MS	14 654	4 739	62.0	975	0.0	5.5	13.5	139	5.1
Tate, MS	20 235	4 328	59.7	1 923	0.0	10.5	6.8	217	3.5
Tippah, MS	18 016	4 397	61.0	1 213	0.0	11.8	8.4	246	3.1
Tishomingo, MS	14 473	4 507	62.4	901	0.0	11.3	6.7	177	4.5
Tunica, MS	11 968	5 987	51.3	591	1.0	10.0	14.2	72	6.4
Union, MS	20 213	4 455	61.8	1 405	0.0	4.3	10.5	258	4.6
Walthall, MS	12 688	4 584	66.0	1 099	0.0	17.0	6.8	138	5.3
Warren, MS	46 459	4 941	57.6	3 021	0.0	9.6	9.5	406	7.0
Washington, MS	59 000	4 549	60.1	4 186	0.0	6.7	8.9	491	6.7
Wayne, MS	18 246	4 333	63.7	1 424	0.0	12.3	7.4	206	6.4
Webster, MS	8 845	4 346	65.2	677	0.0	8.1	10.3	115	4.8
Wilkinson, MS	8 411	4 733	55.8	683	0.0	17.0	10.8	98	5.4
Winston, MS	15 862	4 629	62.9	1 230	0.0	8.3	13.9	160	2.1
Yalobusha, MS	9 964	4 460	59.6	828	0.0	8.8	8.9	97	6.8
Yazoo, MS	23 155	4 747	57.3	1 783	0.0	8.9	11.8	202	9.6
MISSOURI									
Adair, MO	15 570	5 283	60.3	2 820	0.0	4.7	0.6	215	5.4
Andrew, MO	13 938	4 838	63.4	925	0.0	10.7	1.8	169	2.1
Atchison, MO	7 066	5 533	65.6	376	0.0	8.0	13.3	89	9.5
Audrain, MO	19 835	5 246	62.2	1 323	0.0	12.9	9.8	255	3.0
Barry, MO	33 142	4 994	65.4	1 877	0.0	12.3	7.7	385	4.1
Barton, MO	11 289	5 181	65.3	701	0.0	8.7	6.0	128	4.7
Bates, MO	14 537	4 857	62.7	967	0.0	15.0	5.4	173	4.1
Benton, MO	12 872	4 650	63.2	790	0.0	10.9	2.7	182	3.3
Bollinger, MO	9 830	4 679	58.1	699	0.0	14.6	8.0	139	3.7
Boone, MO	113 766	5 510	61.8	11 018	0.0	7.0	2.1	1 252	5.4

. . . = Not available.

Table C-1. Population, School, and Student Characteristics by County—*Continued*

County	High school graduates, 2000			College enrollment, 2000		College graduates, 2000 (percent)						
	Population 25 years and over	High school diploma or less (percent)	High school diploma or more (percent)	Number	Percent public	Bachelor's degree or more	+/- U.S. percent with bachelor's degree or more	Non-Hispanic White	Black or African American	American Indian and Alaska Native	Asian, Hawaiian, and Pacific Islander	Hispanic or Latino[1]
	30	31	32	33	34	35	36	37	38	39	40	41
Claiborne, MS	5 954	53.7	71.6	2 118	98.6	18.9	-5.5	28.6	15.9	0.0	...	16.7
Clarke, MS	11 541	68.0	68.8	488	91.6	9.6	-14.8	12.1	4.0	0.0	52.4	7.0
Clay, MS	13 441	63.1	68.6	1 013	86.3	14.6	-9.8	19.8	9.3	21.9	31.8	8.1
Coahoma, MS	17 403	59.3	62.2	1 099	95.7	16.2	-8.2	25.1	10.5	0.0	61.8	6.6
Copiah, MS	17 405	60.9	69.3	1 605	84.0	11.6	-12.8	15.0	7.6	31.3	24.0	0.0
Covington, MS	11 923	64.7	67.2	648	97.8	11.4	-13.0	13.7	6.4	0.0	0.0	12.5
De Soto, MS	68 302	52.5	81.6	4 155	79.2	14.3	-10.1	14.9	9.0	10.4	27.2	9.3
Forrest, MS	41 526	48.6	79.3	10 506	88.3	22.8	-1.6	28.2	10.2	0.0	39.0	12.5
Franklin, MS	5 377	66.3	67.5	235	95.3	10.5	-13.9	12.4	6.8	3.0	0.0	0.0
George, MS	11 838	68.9	69.8	452	87.4	9.1	-15.3	9.8	2.9	0.0	0.0	6.8
Greene, MS	8 352	70.6	67.4	311	87.8	8.0	-16.4	9.2	4.0	0.0	60.0	13.1
Grenada, MS	14 675	63.8	63.8	740	91.5	13.5	-10.9	17.0	7.1	24.1	23.2	8.8
Hancock, MS	28 840	51.4	77.9	1 463	86.5	17.3	-7.1	17.9	8.7	13.9	37.5	16.3
Harrison, MS	119 169	48.1	80.3	8 867	84.4	18.4	-6.0	20.3	10.8	12.9	16.7	15.8
Hinds, MS	150 287	41.5	80.4	19 813	70.5	27.2	2.8	37.7	18.5	13.9	58.0	24.5
Holmes, MS	12 071	67.0	59.7	1 087	89.6	11.2	-13.2	20.0	7.9	50.0	22.2	8.6
Humphreys, MS	6 379	67.9	53.7	337	91.7	11.6	-12.8	16.9	8.9	12.5	0.0	14.5
Issaquena, MS	1 380	72.4	58.8	63	90.5	7.1	-17.3	10.6	4.6	...	...	0.0
Itawamba, MS	14 833	65.6	65.9	1 268	91.6	8.8	-15.6	8.8	6.5	0.0	38.5	16.5
Jackson, MS	82 818	51.1	81.0	5 397	92.3	16.5	-7.9	18.1	9.1	12.0	21.4	11.8
Jasper, MS	11 263	67.8	66.7	576	90.3	9.8	-14.6	13.8	5.3	0.0	25.0	5.7
Jefferson, MS	5 785	68.5	59.7	419	95.5	10.6	-13.8	16.9	9.4	0.0	100.0	0.0
Jefferson Davis, MS	8 613	68.4	66.4	445	87.2	10.4	-14.0	13.6	7.6	0.0	0.0	0.0
Jones, MS	41 403	58.4	73.9	3 040	89.1	14.0	-10.4	16.1	6.9	7.4	44.9	7.4
Kemper, MS	6 498	67.8	60.5	729	97.1	10.3	-14.1	16.1	5.5	0.0	0.0	0.0
Lafayette, MS	20 628	44.2	78.5	9 856	96.1	31.1	6.7	36.8	11.9	8.6	70.7	30.5
Lamar, MS	23 855	44.0	83.0	2 681	91.1	26.8	2.4	28.1	15.7	15.0	49.5	33.1
Lauderdale, MS	49 511	53.2	74.9	3 921	91.6	16.2	-8.2	19.7	8.7	3.6	51.1	16.7
Lawrence, MS	8 394	61.2	72.9	458	93.9	12.0	-12.4	12.2	11.1	77.8	9.1	12.0
Leake, MS	13 160	67.7	64.1	436	88.3	11.6	-12.8	14.2	6.9	7.6	20.8	12.7
Lee, MS	48 382	53.5	74.7	2 574	92.4	18.1	-6.3	20.7	8.8	16.7	47.5	4.5
Leflore, MS	21 581	63.7	61.9	2 418	92.4	15.9	-8.5	23.2	10.9	28.6	52.0	13.2
Lincoln, MS	21 074	59.6	72.0	1 149	90.1	12.4	-12.0	13.5	9.3	0.0	57.8	0.0
Lowndes, MS	37 520	54.3	75.5	3 480	91.6	20.5	-3.9	27.2	9.2	31.0	32.2	12.1
Madison, MS	46 773	35.3	83.0	3 713	64.2	37.9	13.5	48.7	16.3	0.0	48.1	16.6
Marion, MS	16 025	66.9	66.5	726	93.1	11.5	-12.9	12.7	8.1	0.0	18.2	15.2
Marshall, MS	21 519	71.5	61.0	1 444	58.0	9.0	-15.4	8.1	10.0	0.0	30.8	2.5
Monroe, MS	24 288	66.9	65.5	889	90.7	10.9	-13.5	12.6	6.1	15.0	50.0	4.3
Montgomery, MS	7 830	69.9	62.1	363	95.3	11.0	-13.4	15.1	4.9	0.0	0.0	4.5
Neshoba, MS	17 780	64.0	67.7	891	92.9	11.4	-13.0	13.0	8.7	3.3	20.0	0.0
Newton, MS	13 663	60.5	72.9	1 443	97.8	12.1	-12.3	15.8	3.0	0.0	21.4	5.5
Noxubee, MS	7 456	72.2	58.4	387	91.2	10.9	-13.5	19.8	6.2	0.0	0.0	5.3
Oktibbeha, MS	21 250	41.8	80.0	12 335	96.7	34.8	10.4	45.9	12.6	65.9	80.7	39.5
Panola, MS	20 668	66.1	63.5	1 070	91.7	10.8	-13.6	15.7	3.7	0.0	35.7	1.1
Pearl River, MS	30 940	56.6	74.6	2 015	90.1	13.9	-10.5	14.6	7.7	6.3	26.8	18.8
Perry, MS	7 400	66.1	72.0	326	78.8	7.7	-16.7	8.0	6.5	12.0	3.4	0.0
Pike, MS	24 139	61.7	70.3	1 453	93.8	12.5	-11.9	17.1	5.8	20.8	34.8	5.9
Pontotoc, MS	17 082	67.1	66.7	787	88.9	11.4	-13.0	11.8	8.1	6.1	31.8	8.3
Prentiss, MS	16 114	66.4	64.9	1 586	96.8	9.9	-14.5	10.8	2.9	44.4	0.0	11.2
Quitman, MS	5 906	69.9	55.1	237	88.2	10.6	-13.8	15.8	7.2	28.6	58.3	0.0
Rankin, MS	74 885	45.6	81.8	4 647	74.2	23.8	-0.6	26.0	11.7	23.0	42.3	16.0
Scott, MS	17 496	70.0	62.0	669	81.9	8.6	-15.8	11.4	4.1	0.0	90.9	2.8
Sharkey, MS	3 704	68.2	60.6	156	93.6	12.6	-11.8	21.5	7.4	...	29.4	0.0
Simpson, MS	17 269	66.5	68.8	777	90.1	10.9	-13.5	12.7	5.9	0.0	68.3	7.6
Smith, MS	10 274	67.5	70.8	444	87.4	9.1	-15.3	11.0	1.8	0.0	0.0	0.0
Stone, MS	8 258	55.4	74.8	970	94.3	12.4	-12.0	13.5	4.3	0.0	0.0	26.5
Sunflower, MS	19 976	66.3	59.3	1 673	90.1	12.0	-12.4	18.8	8.3	18.2	21.1	9.9
Tallahatchie, MS	8 979	69.8	54.4	519	94.0	10.9	-13.5	16.3	5.8	100.0	31.8	0.0
Tate, MS	15 460	60.8	71.7	1 708	92.7	12.3	-12.1	14.6	6.2	0.0	33.3	0.0
Tippah, MS	13 557	70.3	65.5	607	65.1	9.0	-15.4	10.1	2.9	0.0	0.0	11.5
Tishomingo, MS	13 276	71.3	64.6	375	95.5	8.7	-15.7	8.9	3.5	6.1	18.2	6.5
Tunica, MS	5 263	69.6	60.5	132	95.5	9.1	-15.3	19.2	3.5	14.3	0.0	5.2
Union, MS	16 499	65.3	68.5	819	91.2	13.2	-11.2	13.8	8.5	0.0	67.2	5.4
Walthall, MS	9 366	67.1	67.0	493	96.1	10.4	-14.0	12.8	5.9	0.0	74.3	12.2
Warren, MS	30 955	49.5	77.0	1 814	85.4	20.8	-3.6	26.8	10.5	14.3	53.0	26.8
Washington, MS	36 852	62.2	66.5	2 144	90.8	16.4	-8.0	23.8	10.7	17.6	46.3	13.4
Wayne, MS	12 933	70.1	64.7	453	91.2	9.5	-14.9	10.9	5.9	0.0	100.0	0.0
Webster, MS	6 717	66.3	67.7	309	76.7	13.0	-11.4	13.8	8.1	0.0	0.0	32.5
Wilkinson, MS	6 515	75.0	58.1	251	89.2	10.0	-14.4	15.9	6.8	0.0	...	23.7
Winston, MS	12 896	65.1	68.2	534	88.8	13.8	-10.6	18.4	6.8	0.0	46.2	6.3
Yalobusha, MS	8 539	68.6	69.0	453	87.2	9.6	-14.8	12.4	3.5	23.3	0.0	21.4
Yazoo, MS	17 308	66.0	65.0	618	67.8	11.8	-12.6	16.8	7.4	0.0	31.7	5.3
MISSOURI												
Adair, MO	13 316	48.9	84.6	6 226	91.7	28.5	4.1	28.0	32.6	7.7	79.8	11.9
Andrew, MO	10 847	56.8	84.7	597	86.4	18.8	-5.6	18.7	18.4	13.3	61.8	14.6
Atchison, MO	4 500	59.2	80.0	163	83.4	16.6	-7.8	16.8	0.0	0.0	30.8	11.1
Audrain, MO	17 476	67.8	75.1	636	74.8	12.7	-11.7	13.4	2.7	11.3	30.0	5.0
Barry, MO	22 381	65.4	75.7	710	86.2	10.7	-13.7	10.9	13.8	0.0	52.3	4.5
Barton, MO	8 070	65.7	77.3	289	94.5	10.6	-13.8	10.6	12.5	22.7	3.1	10.2
Bates, MO	10 977	68.4	76.9	323	85.8	10.1	-14.3	10.1	0.0	8.3	31.8	0.0
Benton, MO	12 669	66.8	71.8	293	90.4	8.8	-15.6	8.7	0.0	9.5	0.0	6.1
Bollinger, MO	7 956	75.8	70.7	220	87.3	6.9	-17.5	7.0	0.0	4.7	0.0	9.1
Boone, MO	77 919	34.1	89.2	24 827	89.7	41.7	17.3	42.6	22.3	28.7	71.2	38.9

[1]Hispanic or Latino persons may be of any race.
. . . = Not available.

Table C-1. Population, School, and Student Characteristics by County—*Continued*

County	State/County code	County type[1]	Population, 2000 Total	Percent 5–17 years	Number of schools and students, 2000–2001 School districts	Schools	Students	Resident enrollment, 2000 Total	Percent public	K–12	Percent public
			1	2	3	4	5	6	7	8	9
Buchanan, MO	29021	3	85 998	18.1	4	36	13 909	21 945	87.5	15 543	89.5
Butler, MO	29023	7	40 867	17.8	3	16	6 597	9 296	91.3	7 334	94.0
Caldwell, MO	29025	8	8 969	20.8	8	14	1 857	2 186	94.9	1 840	97.0
Callaway, MO	29027	6	40 766	19.2	5	56	6 433	10 500	80.2	7 820	92.3
Camden, MO	29029	7	37 051	15.6	4	13	5 341	6 943	91.5	5 598	96.0
Cape Girardeau, MO	29031	5	68 693	17.5	5	23	9 674	19 596	85.5	12 003	82.9
Carroll, MO	29033	6	10 285	18.8	5	12	1 876	2 272	94.1	1 921	97.0
Carter, MO	29035	9	5 941	18.9	2	4	1 343	1 441	96.7	1 168	97.7
Cass, MO	29037	1	82 092	21.0	10	37	15 678	21 176	85.1	16 705	90.7
Cedar, MO	29039	7	13 733	19.0	2	6	2 399	3 058	88.2	2 529	95.5
Chariton, MO	29041	9	8 438	18.6	4	9	1 346	1 908	89.4	1 604	90.8
Christian, MO	29043	2	54 285	20.2	7	25	10 147	14 178	87.5	10 704	93.6
Clark, MO	29045	9	7 416	18.8	4	10	1 302	1 778	92.1	1 383	96.2
Clay, MO	29047	0	184 006	18.6	6	60	32 295	47 240	82.8	33 951	90.5
Clinton, MO	29049	1	18 979	20.2	3	11	3 335	4 790	92.5	3 836	95.5
Cole, MO	29051	4	71 397	17.7	5	59	11 853	18 439	73.1	12 875	71.8
Cooper, MO	29053	6	16 670	17.0	6	14	2 519	4 281	84.2	3 264	88.7
Crawford, MO	29055	6	22 804	19.8	3	9	3 469	5 230	90.3	4 525	92.4
Dade, MO	29057	8	7 923	18.5	4	8	1 293	1 758	90.3	1 528	92.3
Dallas, MO	29059	8	15 661	20.8	1	4	2 179	3 824	89.9	3 218	91.5
Daviess, MO	29061	9	8 016	20.0	5	10	1 382	1 830	90.6	1 560	90.9
De Kalb, MO	29063	8	11 597	15.5	4	8	1 444	2 508	90.0	2 096	92.4
Dent, MO	29065	7	14 927	18.5	5	8	2 571	3 282	91.6	2 739	96.1
Douglas, MO	29067	6	13 084	19.8	3	5	1 859	3 163	89.5	2 584	93.5
Dunklin, MO	29069	7	33 155	18.8	7	19	6 245	7 596	95.5	6 185	97.2
Franklin, MO	29071	1	93 807	20.4	10	40	17 063	23 737	83.6	19 146	85.5
Gasconade, MO	29073	6	15 342	18.9	2	9	3 120	3 449	90.0	2 906	91.8
Gentry, MO	29075	8	6 861	19.8	3	7	1 375	1 682	93.2	1 402	93.5
Greene, MO	29077	2	240 391	16.1	8	80	35 976	67 577	82.9	38 501	91.5
Grundy, MO	29079	7	10 432	17.1	5	8	1 820	2 421	94.4	1 766	98.9
Harrison, MO	29081	7	8 850	17.3	5	11	1 504	1 871	92.5	1 565	94.1
Henry, MO	29083	6	21 997	17.8	7	13	3 270	4 848	93.4	4 055	95.1
Hickory, MO	29085	9	8 940	15.6	4	11	1 892	1 551	95.5	1 371	97.0
Holt, MO	29087	8	5 351	19.0	3	6	911	1 239	96.0	1 062	96.9
Howard, MO	29089	6	10 212	18.4	3	7	1 584	3 018	66.7	1 894	89.5
Howell, MO	29091	7	37 238	19.3	8	15	7 364	9 017	92.9	7 057	95.3
Iron, MO	29093	9	10 697	19.1	4	8	2 400	2 522	96.4	2 038	97.8
Jackson, MO	29095	0	654 880	18.8	12	212	107 594	171 287	82.2	123 402	87.4
Jasper, MO	29097	3	104 686	18.5	7	46	18 480	26 027	88.0	19 008	92.8
Jefferson, MO	29099	1	198 099	20.7	11	55	35 345	52 378	85.3	40 986	90.0
Johnson, MO	29101	6	48 258	18.4	7	25	8 140	17 035	93.8	8 573	95.6
Knox, MO	29103	9	4 361	18.8	1	2	684	900	87.1	780	89.4
Laclede, MO	29105	6	32 513	19.8	4	11	5 971	7 953	92.0	6 408	95.8
Lafayette, MO	29107	1	32 960	20.1	6	16	5 933	8 064	88.5	6 574	91.2
Lawrence, MO	29109	6	35 204	20.1	6	18	5 971	8 171	89.1	6 744	91.3
Lewis, MO	29111	7	10 494	17.8	2	5	1 721	2 870	70.7	1 904	90.9
Lincoln, MO	29113	1	38 944	22.7	4	15	7 302	10 611	84.1	8 749	89.3
Linn, MO	29115	7	13 754	19.3	5	12	2 863	3 150	94.2	2 630	94.9
Livingston, MO	29117	7	14 558	18.3	3	9	2 431	3 413	91.2	2 700	94.4
McDonald, MO	29119	8	21 681	21.1	1	7	3 429	5 135	92.1	4 447	93.3
Macon, MO	29121	7	15 762	17.8	6	12	2 492	3 393	91.5	2 833	93.5
Madison, MO	29123	9	11 800	18.7	2	6	2 115	2 620	95.5	2 177	97.7
Maries, MO	29125	9	8 903	19.4	2	5	1 439	2 034	85.2	1 704	86.8
Marion, MO	29127	5	28 289	18.9	3	13	5 237	6 983	80.2	5 474	89.1
Mercer, MO	29129	9	3 757	17.4	2	4	663	809	93.9	671	93.9
Miller, MO	29131	7	23 564	19.5	5	14	5 114	5 473	91.5	4 555	95.7
Mississippi, MO	29133	7	13 427	19.2	2	8	2 524	3 143	96.1	2 592	97.8
Moniteau, MO	29135	6	14 827	19.2	6	11	2 419	3 474	84.1	2 923	86.9
Monroe, MO	29137	9	9 311	19.4	5	10	1 822	2 126	88.5	1 817	90.6
Montgomery, MO	29139	8	12 136	19.7	2	8	1 981	2 798	89.9	2 364	93.7
Morgan, MO	29141	9	19 309	17.8	2	7	2 326	3 916	86.1	3 290	87.5
New Madrid, MO	29143	7	19 760	19.8	4	12	3 535	4 677	96.6	3 895	96.6
Newton, MO	29145	3	52 636	19.2	5	18	8 346	12 541	87.7	9 905	89.5
Nodaway, MO	29147	9	21 912	14.7	7	15	3 053	8 420	92.5	3 338	91.4
Oregon, MO	29149	9	10 344	18.4	4	8	1 984	2 232	95.1	1 838	96.0
Osage, MO	29151	9	13 062	19.6	3	7	1 747	3 316	76.6	2 661	74.4
Ozark, MO	29153	9	9 542	16.7	5	9	1 805	1 902	92.7	1 584	92.7
Pemiscot, MO	29155	7	20 047	21.9	7	15	4 511	5 262	98.0	4 356	99.1
Perry, MO	29157	7	18 132	19.3	2	5	2 461	4 250	72.9	3 386	72.6
Pettis, MO	29159	7	39 403	19.3	6	17	6 221	9 733	86.6	7 583	89.3
Phelps, MO	29161	7	39 825	18.0	4	12	6 675	12 582	89.6	7 081	90.3
Pike, MO	29163	6	18 351	18.0	4	11	2 961	4 039	87.6	3 415	90.1
Platte, MO	29165	0	73 781	18.9	4	26	12 505	19 324	84.3	14 016	92.3
Polk, MO	29167	6	26 992	19.0	6	18	5 093	7 619	71.3	4 889	94.6
Pulaski, MO	29169	7	41 165	19.9	6	22	8 291	11 608	89.6	8 183	95.4
Putnam, MO	29171	9	5 223	17.5	1	3	839	1 139	94.6	924	96.4
Ralls, MO	29173	9	9 626	19.6	1	5	908	2 197	90.4	1 817	96.6
Randolph, MO	29175	6	24 663	17.5	5	13	3 807	5 935	87.4	4 618	91.6
Ray, MO	29177	1	23 354	20.9	5	13	3 878	5 815	91.5	4 916	96.1
Reynolds, MO	29179	9	6 689	18.2	4	9	1 263	1 519	95.5	1 250	96.2

[1]County type code is from the Economic Research Service of the USDA. See Notes and Definitions at the end of this section.

Table C-1. School and Student Characteristics by County—*Continued*

County	Characteristics of students, 2000–2001			Staff and students, 2000–2001				Revenues, fiscal 1999			
	Percent with IEP[2]	Percent eligible for free lunch	Percent minority	Number of teachers	Student/ teacher ratio	Local school non-teaching staff	Central admin. staff	Total revenue ($1,000s)	Percentage of revenue from		
									Federal govt.	State govt.	Local govt.
	10	11	12	13	14	15	16	17	18	19	20
Buchanan, MO	12.6	42.3	8.7	984	14.1	610	107	$82 131	9.0	41.1	49.9
Butler, MO	14.3	49.2	10.5	441	15.0	340	71	38 998	11.9	45.2	42.9
Caldwell, MO	17.9	40.6	1.0	180	10.3	102	22	13 247	6.5	51.2	42.2
Callaway, MO	13.3	32.9	11.7	514	12.5	265	62	33 437	5.1	38.1	56.8
Camden, MO	12.8	40.6	1.5	354	15.1	315	65	30 945	6.9	28.9	64.2
Cape Girardeau, MO	14.5	28.4	11.7	664	14.6	447	95	57 067	6.3	33.3	60.4
Carroll, MO	15.8	41.1	3.4	159	11.8	103	31	12 255	7.3	43.9	48.9
Carter, MO	16.7	65.2	0.2	109	12.3	79	20	8 793	11.1	59.5	29.4
Cass, MO	10.5	. . .	4.8	1 038	15.1	569	143	92 293	4.2	41.6	54.3
Cedar, MO	12.1	39.7	1.5	172	13.9	117	26	12 995	7.3	49.1	43.5
Chariton, MO	14.6	34.4	4.2	116	11.6	92	16	9 083	7.3	37.6	55.1
Christian, MO	12.8	25.9	2.1	708	14.3	382	88	51 588	5.3	49.5	45.2
Clark, MO	15.0	36.4	0.5	119	10.9	75	18	8 487	7.5	42.8	49.7
Clay, MO	13.1	17.7	9.4	2 046	15.8	2 054	306	193 223	3.5	27.9	68.6
Clinton, MO	15.5	25.6	5.0	260	12.8	177	41	21 530	4.4	49.5	46.1
Cole, MO	27.8	30.1	15.4	927	12.8	1 184	175	62 767	5.4	25.0	69.5
Cooper, MO	14.6	33.5	8.9	206	12.2	126	31	17 040	6.5	43.0	50.5
Crawford, MO	15.3	40.8	0.6	238	14.6	193	30	18 368	7.9	47.1	45.0
Dade, MO	11.8	46.0	0.9	120	10.8	68	15	8 645	6.9	48.6	44.5
Dallas, MO	12.9	45.0	1.7	137	15.9	144	19	12 386	7.5	52.2	40.4
Daviess, MO	14.3	. . .	1.7	137	10.1	91	22	10 776	6.7	49.0	44.3
De Kalb, MO	11.2	39.3	0.8	120	12.0	65	13	8 999	6.6	51.9	41.5
Dent, MO	15.4	40.1	1.6	191	13.5	140	26	16 526	8.1	46.2	45.7
Douglas, MO	14.6	54.8	0.9	133	14.0	80	15	10 710	9.6	54.9	35.4
Dunklin, MO	14.1	. . .	19.6	441	14.2	289	57	36 456	13.3	49.1	37.7
Franklin, MO	16.7	25.8	2.3	1 113	15.3	877	156	96 433	5.6	35.6	58.9
Gasconade, MO	14.2	27.2	0.5	214	14.6	178	31	18 877	4.3	36.1	59.6
Gentry, MO	16.9	38.6	0.8	119	11.6	89	14	9 327	6.8	47.4	45.8
Greene, MO	13.0	31.6	7.4	2 251	16.0	1 644	293	204 876	6.5	33.3	60.2
Grundy, MO	11.5	42.3	1.5	138	13.2	90	21	10 637	7.5	44.4	48.1
Harrison, MO	12.3	41.9	1.7	142	10.6	115	26	11 986	10.0	45.2	44.8
Henry, MO	18.5	40.1	3.0	262	12.5	180	37	20 967	7.7	38.2	54.2
Hickory, MO	13.4	53.4	2.9	147	12.9	122	20	12 009	9.2	49.1	41.6
Holt, MO	14.2	40.5	1.5	89	10.2	47	11	5 519	6.3	36.8	56.9
Howard, MO	17.6	. . .	9.4	136	11.6	79	21	9 546	6.9	45.2	47.9
Howell, MO	14.2	47.8	1.8	494	14.9	396	78	45 752	10.2	50.4	39.4
Iron, MO	15.0	51.5	3.3	173	13.9	121	29	15 027	8.9	38.4	52.6
Jackson, MO	12.0	39.6	44.3	6 942	15.5	5 995	1 035	880 072	6.6	42.4	50.9
Jasper, MO	13.6	40.1	8.1	1 252	14.8	1 034	200	101 619	7.4	40.6	52.0
Jefferson, MO	15.4	22.8	2.1	2 198	16.1	1 622	289	197 697	4.0	44.3	51.7
Johnson, MO	17.0	30.7	11.5	577	14.1	477	83	50 510	14.8	42.1	43.1
Knox, MO	14.2	45.3	1.9	66	10.4	57	10	5 824	7.1	47.3	45.6
Laclede, MO	12.2	38.8	2.3	355	16.8	322	61	30 849	7.7	46.3	45.9
Lafayette, MO	16.6	28.0	5.9	423	14.0	244	68	42 015	10.9	40.1	49.1
Lawrence, MO	15.3	43.8	4.2	434	13.8	290	61	33 385	7.4	48.6	44.0
Lewis, MO	13.4	37.6	6.3	127	13.6	73	19	10 517	6.9	45.9	47.3
Lincoln, MO	16.4	27.2	3.4	433	16.9	326	117	36 061	5.0	44.3	50.7
Linn, MO	15.5	32.2	1.5	238	12.0	137	39	20 063	5.3	55.8	38.9
Livingston, MO	17.5	35.4	2.1	176	13.8	156	26	16 779	6.7	44.5	48.8
McDonald, MO	12.7	54.6	14.7	211	16.3	176	23	16 482	10.4	50.8	38.8
Macon, MO	16.5	39.5	4.0	198	12.6	143	31	16 531	7.2	46.6	46.2
Madison, MO	11.6	44.1	0.4	144	14.7	97	22	11 509	8.9	52.2	39.0
Maries, MO	13.8	35.9	1.5	112	12.8	96	18	8 336	6.9	44.8	48.3
Marion, MO	15.6	37.1	7.4	363	14.4	253	64	30 836	7.8	43.7	48.5
Mercer, MO	13.0	38.9	1.1	67	9.9	39	10	5 071	5.6	36.7	57.7
Miller, MO	14.6	42.9	1.5	353	14.5	259	61	30 339	6.5	34.0	59.5
Mississippi, MO	14.2	60.9	34.1	183	13.8	167	23	15 044	12.7	48.4	38.9
Moniteau, MO	16.6	32.9	5.5	194	12.5	134	25	14 547	5.5	41.8	52.7
Monroe, MO	13.7	30.6	6.4	155	11.8	117	18	11 605	6.0	41.3	52.7
Montgomery, MO	15.1	36.4	3.4	140	14.2	107	26	11 615	7.5	43.3	49.2
Morgan, MO	15.0	. . .	1.8	163	14.3	134	24	11 724	9.6	29.5	60.8
New Madrid, MO	16.0	56.6	30.8	269	13.1	161	44	23 449	11.4	39.0	49.6
Newton, MO	13.9	42.5	7.1	533	15.7	398	81	43 043	8.5	49.3	42.3
Nodaway, MO	16.8	30.5	0.9	276	11.1	188	45	24 510	6.6	38.2	55.2
Oregon, MO	13.6	59.9	1.6	164	12.1	123	19	11 105	10.7	54.8	34.5
Osage, MO	17.0	29.0	0.4	140	12.5	96	19	11 222	7.0	38.9	54.1
Ozark, MO	16.2	54.0	0.6	146	12.4	132	24	11 303	10.9	49.0	40.1
Pemiscot, MO	. . .	61.6	41.7	321	14.1	191	65	30 539	12.5	53.4	34.1
Perry, MO	20.6	32.9	0.9	165	14.9	114	38	15 044	9.2	32.4	58.4
Pettis, MO	15.0	38.7	9.9	441	14.1	329	66	35 362	8.0	43.1	48.9
Phelps, MO	14.3	42.6	5.9	417	16.0	363	84	43 449	9.5	48.3	42.2
Pike, MO	14.0	34.4	8.1	225	13.2	177	39	18 525	10.0	36.6	53.4
Platte, MO	13.2	11.1	9.4	832	15.0	492	124	89 685	2.9	22.5	74.7
Polk, MO	14.9	44.3	1.5	380	13.4	283	55	28 755	8.0	54.2	37.7
Pulaski, MO	14.6	40.2	24.4	598	13.9	452	90	50 544	24.3	48.7	27.0
Putnam, MO	13.6	36.9	0.7	68	12.3	42	8	5 350	7.0	44.8	48.3
Ralls, MO	17.6	31.3	2.0	74	12.3	36	8	5 083	5.5	40.8	53.7
Randolph, MO	18.5	41.9	8.2	293	13.0	218	54	25 517	7.5	36.9	55.6
Ray, MO	13.9	23.9	3.5	288	13.5	136	42	22 490	5.0	47.9	47.0
Reynolds, MO	16.4	. . .	4.4	112	11.3	99	20	8 466	11.7	33.3	55.0

[2]IEP = Individual Education Program. See Notes and Definitions at the end of this section.
. . . = Not available.

Table C-1. Population, School, and Student Characteristics by County—*Continued*

County	Current expenditures, fiscal 1999			Resident population 16 to 19 years, 2000				Outcomes, 1999–2000	
	Amount ($1,000s)	Amount per student	Percent for instruction	Total population 16 to 19 years	Percent in Armed Forces	Percent high school graduates	Percent not enrolled, not grads, not Armed Forces, not empl.	Number of graduates	Dropouts grades 9–12 (percent)
	21	22	23	24	25	26	27	28	29
Buchanan, MO	$76 041	$5 292	64.0	5 210	0.0	11.5	7.3	830	3.1
Butler, MO	33 321	4 902	63.3	2 111	0.0	10.7	10.5	348	3.8
Caldwell, MO	11 103	5 828	59.4	488	0.4	15.6	3.1	109	3.4
Callaway, MO	29 229	5 490	59.6	2 679	0.0	14.6	7.4	327	5.0
Camden, MO	27 004	5 125	61.7	1 571	0.0	13.7	3.9	307	4.3
Cape Girardeau, MO	46 154	4 797	64.0	4 820	0.1	9.4	4.9	600	4.3
Carroll, MO	10 896	5 678	61.4	527	0.0	14.8	10.6	149	2.5
Carter, MO	8 085	5 682	64.4	317	3.2	7.6	5.0	92	3.3
Cass, MO	76 167	4 934	60.1	4 374	0.2	13.3	4.8	916	3.9
Cedar, MO	11 620	4 733	63.1	737	0.0	9.4	13.3	146	3.0
Chariton, MO	8 065	5 505	64.5	509	0.0	10.4	3.5	106	1.8
Christian, MO	43 649	4 626	64.2	3 004	0.0	12.3	4.7	565	3.5
Clark, MO	7 258	5 137	63.3	438	0.0	13.0	4.1	100	4.1
Clay, MO	165 359	5 270	64.7	9 711	0.2	10.0	4.1	2 042	5.6
Clinton, MO	18 778	5 462	68.0	1 150	0.0	11.0	4.2	220	4.2
Cole, MO	54 565	5 094	64.8	3 815	0.0	11.2	3.3	692	5.1
Cooper, MO	15 432	5 961	61.4	1 103	0.0	14.1	9.4	187	2.5
Crawford, MO	16 352	4 723	65.2	1 325	0.0	11.0	6.9	196	7.0
Dade, MO	7 828	5 520	60.7	467	0.0	13.5	4.7	121	3.8
Dallas, MO	10 930	4 968	63.2	859	0.0	7.2	6.5	160	4.4
Daviess, MO	9 308	6 769	62.4	419	0.0	11.5	8.8	89	1.7
De Kalb, MO	7 917	5 615	62.4	569	0.0	13.5	6.7	96	1.8
Dent, MO	12 728	4 928	64.8	776	0.0	12.9	9.0	139	4.6
Douglas, MO	9 464	4 896	60.3	736	0.0	19.6	5.3	95	3.6
Dunklin, MO	31 593	5 072	65.0	1 923	0.0	10.3	10.5	292	3.6
Franklin, MO	82 886	4 864	63.0	5 360	0.1	13.0	4.5	1 003	5.0
Gasconade, MO	15 425	4 781	64.2	833	0.0	12.5	5.9	238	4.7
Gentry, MO	8 070	5 707	63.5	404	0.0	8.4	3.2	120	0.9
Greene, MO	181 651	5 028	63.2	15 093	0.1	10.9	4.3	2 073	5.8
Grundy, MO	9 666	5 394	60.9	639	0.0	6.6	10.2	102	7.7
Harrison, MO	10 155	6 335	60.0	458	0.0	18.8	3.7	95	5.0
Henry, MO	18 418	5 508	66.4	1 033	0.0	15.5	9.0	229	3.9
Hickory, MO	10 072	5 243	59.9	379	0.0	12.1	6.6	118	2.2
Holt, MO	5 374	5 417	63.3	272	0.0	7.7	2.2	67	0.7
Howard, MO	9 003	5 430	62.1	813	0.0	6.2	1.2	110	4.5
Howell, MO	37 878	5 181	66.1	2 134	0.0	12.2	6.1	442	3.0
Iron, MO	13 423	5 459	62.1	638	0.0	13.5	5.2	156	2.3
Jackson, MO	685 812	6 353	59.7	34 885	0.0	12.5	7.1	5 352	6.5
Jasper, MO	88 072	4 848	64.2	6 416	0.2	12.4	7.3	943	7.0
Jefferson, MO	174 409	4 905	64.9	11 789	0.0	11.5	6.0	1 923	5.0
Johnson, MO	41 276	5 124	60.2	4 128	4.6	14.2	3.3	485	3.6
Knox, MO	4 884	6 681	56.3	202	0.0	23.3	0.0	44	1.5
Laclede, MO	26 882	4 526	66.0	1 948	0.0	13.7	7.0	302	6.6
Lafayette, MO	32 722	5 509	66.4	1 906	0.0	11.9	3.9	347	4.6
Lawrence, MO	29 455	5 012	62.9	1 799	0.0	13.6	9.9	343	3.5
Lewis, MO	8 671	5 062	63.3	702	0.0	7.4	3.7	139	2.2
Lincoln, MO	30 257	4 402	65.8	2 353	0.0	12.0	5.4	387	4.7
Linn, MO	17 092	5 761	65.1	776	0.0	8.9	4.3	206	3.2
Livingston, MO	14 719	5 866	70.5	856	0.0	8.5	5.1	174	2.0
McDonald, MO	13 195	3 704	64.4	1 275	0.0	13.6	6.3	155	5.7
Macon, MO	14 035	5 556	64.7	913	0.8	13.9	5.4	160	3.4
Madison, MO	11 064	5 092	62.0	635	0.0	16.4	4.7	114	4.9
Maries, MO	7 792	5 171	62.5	470	0.0	12.3	7.4	88	4.5
Marion, MO	26 488	5 022	65.0	1 823	0.4	11.2	6.1	355	4.5
Mercer, MO	4 657	6 930	59.0	209	0.0	14.8	1.4	59	4.4
Miller, MO	26 943	5 367	63.7	1 341	0.0	11.9	8.2	304	5.4
Mississippi, MO	13 909	5 153	64.7	824	0.0	9.5	13.8	120	3.1
Moniteau, MO	12 752	5 203	63.0	768	0.0	12.0	3.6	182	3.2
Monroe, MO	10 021	5 263	63.0	565	0.0	18.2	2.7	155	3.0
Montgomery, MO	10 748	5 094	63.3	730	0.0	14.1	8.5	134	4.4
Morgan, MO	10 647	4 734	64.7	898	0.0	9.4	5.3	137	4.5
New Madrid, MO	20 273	5 485	60.9	1 160	0.0	11.6	8.9	212	1.9
Newton, MO	36 544	4 358	62.7	3 040	0.1	12.9	8.3	450	3.9
Nodaway, MO	20 447	6 520	60.5	2 357	0.2	4.0	1.7	243	2.2
Oregon, MO	9 779	5 005	65.5	574	0.0	13.1	10.6	141	2.9
Osage, MO	10 002	5 859	59.0	770	0.0	9.1	2.6	151	1.5
Ozark, MO	9 365	5 090	61.4	505	0.4	18.2	6.7	137	2.8
Pemiscot, MO	25 915	5 644	64.9	1 248	0.0	11.7	12.8	225	3.7
Perry, MO	13 324	5 281	58.4	992	0.0	14.6	4.6	170	7.4
Pettis, MO	31 911	5 099	62.1	2 403	0.0	11.3	8.9	342	5.5
Phelps, MO	35 728	5 351	64.2	2 892	0.3	9.4	4.2	459	3.6
Pike, MO	15 688	5 112	65.5	1 082	0.0	9.3	14.1	189	4.6
Platte, MO	74 695	6 193	59.4	3 765	0.0	12.3	1.1	742	2.1
Polk, MO	26 061	5 220	60.6	1 976	0.1	10.3	2.0	305	3.3
Pulaski, MO	44 686	5 646	63.0	3 777	48.4	55.2	1.9	457	3.7
Putnam, MO	4 918	5 692	67.1	265	0.0	3.0	5.7	56	3.2
Ralls, MO	4 384	4 581	64.2	524	0.0	13.2	4.4	54	1.4
Randolph, MO	20 627	5 372	64.1	1 322	0.0	12.2	6.7	239	4.0
Ray, MO	19 743	5 120	63.8	1 424	0.0	16.3	3.9	224	2.3
Reynolds, MO	8 479	6 458	61.0	379	0.0	6.1	7.9	70	1.8

Table C-1. Population, School, and Student Characteristics by County—*Continued*

County	High school graduates, 2000			College enrollment, 2000		College graduates, 2000 (percent)						
	Population 25 years and over	High school diploma or less (percent)	High school diploma or more (percent)	Number	Percent public	Bachelor's degree or more	+/- U.S. percent with bachelor's degree or more	Non-Hispanic White	Black or African American	American Indian and Alaska Native	Asian, Hawaiian, and Pacific Islander	Hispanic or Latino[1]
	30	31	32	33	34	35	36	37	38	39	40	41
Buchanan, MO	55 583	56.5	81.5	4 905	91.7	16.9	-7.5	17.2	9.6	28.7	35.3	8.9
Butler, MO	27 596	63.8	70.5	1 257	86.2	11.6	-12.8	11.5	3.5	5.1	47.7	32.2
Caldwell, MO	5 890	64.7	81.5	199	91.5	11.7	-12.7	11.8	28.6	18.2	22.2	0.0
Callaway, MO	25 848	58.2	78.9	2 025	38.5	16.5	-7.9	17.1	7.6	1.4	42.0	12.6
Camden, MO	27 303	54.4	82.9	952	72.9	17.7	-6.7	17.8	42.2	8.6	46.7	3.2
Cape Girardeau, MO	43 440	52.2	81.1	6 507	96.1	24.2	-0.2	24.4	17.2	14.6	61.6	14.5
Carroll, MO	6 945	67.3	79.1	173	82.7	14.0	-10.4	14.3	5.6	12.8	0.0	5.6
Carter, MO	3 959	68.7	66.6	186	93.0	10.8	-13.6	10.4	. . .	0.0	0.0	16.7
Cass, MO	52 767	51.0	86.7	2 813	71.8	17.7	-6.7	17.7	22.9	14.6	26.7	17.3
Cedar, MO	9 473	69.8	74.0	376	55.9	10.0	-14.4	9.9	0.0	4.8	23.9	16.7
Chariton, MO	5 900	68.6	79.6	179	84.4	11.4	-13.0	11.6	4.9	0.0	0.0	25.0
Christian, MO	34 790	48.3	85.9	2 318	75.8	20.9	-3.5	21.1	57.4	9.8	22.6	8.1
Clark, MO	4 976	65.7	79.6	284	75.0	10.7	-13.7	10.6	. . .	100.0	100.0	0.0
Clay, MO	120 500	43.3	88.7	9 442	68.2	24.9	0.5	25.2	21.4	15.9	39.2	15.8
Clinton, MO	12 496	56.4	86.1	582	87.1	14.5	-9.9	14.7	9.1	11.0	8.1	14.0
Cole, MO	47 339	46.7	85.3	4 429	86.2	27.4	3.0	28.1	18.2	11.5	65.0	24.5
Cooper, MO	10 545	63.5	80.3	738	69.2	13.7	-10.7	14.5	2.3	0.0	11.1	35.9
Crawford, MO	15 057	69.8	69.4	480	79.2	8.4	-16.0	8.5	0.0	2.0	13.3	0.9
Dade, MO	5 451	66.9	78.5	134	82.8	9.9	-14.5	9.7	0.0	19.4	0.0	32.0
Dallas, MO	10 251	68.7	72.8	446	80.7	9.5	-14.9	9.6	0.0	10.2	21.4	0.0
Daviess, MO	5 213	63.2	79.1	179	86.0	12.0	-12.4	12.0	50.0	0.0	0.0	0.0
De Kalb, MO	8 252	64.2	77.0	280	86.1	10.7	-13.7	11.6	2.5	6.7	67.6	0.0
Dent, MO	10 098	69.5	66.3	402	66.2	10.1	-14.3	10.1	0.0	6.7	0.0	21.6
Douglas, MO	8 774	69.1	69.7	387	74.2	9.9	-14.5	10.0	. . .	4.9	50.0	1.8
Dunklin, MO	21 890	73.7	63.7	817	88.5	9.1	-15.3	9.6	2.1	5.7	49.3	1.0
Franklin, MO	60 467	57.9	77.7	3 167	79.7	12.8	-11.6	12.9	8.0	3.2	19.9	12.2
Gasconade, MO	10 530	66.2	74.0	322	94.4	10.4	-14.0	10.4	20.0	0.0	0.0	17.1
Gentry, MO	4 599	63.8	81.8	129	88.4	14.5	-9.9	14.6	0.0	0.0	66.7	0.0
Greene, MO	153 930	46.1	84.7	25 481	73.2	24.2	-0.2	24.5	14.0	11.3	41.6	17.3
Grundy, MO	7 149	60.4	79.0	450	86.7	12.5	-11.9	12.6	0.0	23.1	21.7	5.0
Harrison, MO	6 101	67.8	80.1	171	80.7	9.3	-15.1	9.2	0.0	0.0	63.6	7.7
Henry, MO	15 050	66.6	77.3	486	88.5	11.7	-12.7	11.6	8.2	11.1	25.6	12.1
Hickory, MO	6 712	68.8	73.4	107	82.2	7.7	-16.7	7.6	0.0	0.0	28.6	22.0
Holt, MO	3 736	67.6	81.9	128	95.3	11.7	-12.7	11.7	. . .	0.0	0.0	0.0
Howard, MO	6 420	61.7	81.3	974	22.1	17.9	-6.5	18.6	7.0	64.0	0.0	3.8
Howell, MO	24 600	65.5	73.4	1 369	87.4	10.9	-13.5	10.9	5.6	4.7	33.8	2.9
Iron, MO	7 204	69.9	65.2	293	91.1	8.4	-16.0	8.2	6.6	2.3	30.0	10.7
Jackson, MO	427 077	46.6	83.4	34 768	73.0	23.4	-1.0	26.9	13.2	15.3	34.9	11.0
Jasper, MO	66 206	55.9	79.5	5 495	79.5	16.5	-7.9	16.7	12.9	11.5	34.2	7.9
Jefferson, MO	125 956	57.0	79.4	7 775	76.4	12.1	-12.3	12.1	8.2	10.1	34.5	14.8
Johnson, MO	26 558	46.5	86.0	7 687	95.2	23.2	-1.2	23.3	18.5	24.2	39.4	13.1
Knox, MO	2 990	66.6	80.0	90	73.3	12.8	-11.6	13.0	. . .	0.0	0.0	0.0
Laclede, MO	21 120	68.2	72.9	1 016	72.9	11.3	-13.1	11.5	4.9	0.0	7.0	5.3
Lafayette, MO	21 863	62.3	79.9	947	84.5	13.8	-10.6	13.8	12.1	2.3	29.7	26.1
Lawrence, MO	22 882	64.1	77.4	852	87.3	12.1	-12.3	12.2	0.0	10.0	14.3	13.4
Lewis, MO	6 533	65.0	79.5	776	19.7	13.0	-11.4	13.1	3.7	55.6	. . .	0.0
Lincoln, MO	24 092	66.5	76.4	1 230	64.9	9.7	-14.7	9.5	10.7	7.1	22.2	24.9
Linn, MO	9 279	69.0	80.0	298	87.9	10.8	-13.6	10.8	0.0	30.0	0.0	13.5
Livingston, MO	9 954	65.1	80.6	452	87.4	13.1	-11.3	13.3	8.8	8.0	13.3	35.1
McDonald, MO	13 418	69.1	69.4	382	80.9	7.0	-17.4	7.4	18.2	10.0	3.8	1.9
Macon, MO	10 718	67.0	77.8	339	92.6	13.0	-11.4	13.2	4.3	25.6	0.0	0.0
Madison, MO	7 964	70.4	68.6	261	87.4	7.8	-16.6	7.3	0.0	15.8	69.6	0.0
Maries, MO	5 969	67.7	74.5	212	79.2	11.0	-13.4	10.9	0.0	0.0	. . .	45.5
Marion, MO	18 322	61.4	79.4	1 080	41.5	15.6	-8.8	16.1	7.4	0.0	25.0	5.8
Mercer, MO	2 647	64.0	82.5	83	90.4	12.2	-12.2	12.3	. . .	0.0	0.0	0.0
Miller, MO	15 369	66.3	73.9	659	75.3	11.4	-13.0	11.6	0.0	0.0	11.9	0.0
Mississippi, MO	8 702	76.6	61.1	311	85.2	9.6	-14.8	9.9	8.0	0.0	18.8	0.0
Moniteau, MO	9 751	66.3	77.6	406	78.6	13.0	-11.4	13.9	3.9	0.0	24.5	0.0
Monroe, MO	6 212	67.9	78.7	170	78.2	9.5	-14.9	9.7	3.5	8.6	0.0	20.0
Montgomery, MO	8 182	70.4	71.1	269	70.6	9.9	-14.5	9.8	0.0	0.0	41.7	0.0
Morgan, MO	13 466	66.1	74.5	385	79.2	10.7	-13.7	10.8	4.5	9.4	57.1	6.6
New Madrid, MO	12 868	76.0	63.6	499	95.4	9.6	-14.8	10.5	2.8	31.8	100.0	0.0
Newton, MO	34 211	54.6	79.8	1 910	82.5	16.1	-8.3	16.3	4.8	17.2	22.3	12.1
Nodaway, MO	12 169	54.1	87.1	4 747	95.8	23.6	-0.8	23.4	12.5	0.0	75.8	0.0
Oregon, MO	7 134	72.3	72.0	240	92.5	9.1	-15.3	9.0	0.0	2.2	43.8	28.6
Osage, MO	8 375	68.9	75.2	531	93.8	10.4	-14.0	10.3	. . .	6.9	85.7	0.0
Ozark, MO	6 795	70.0	73.0	196	87.8	8.3	-16.1	8.2	0.0	35.0	13.3	17.2
Pemiscot, MO	12 228	75.6	58.2	499	96.8	8.4	-16.0	9.8	2.8	0.0	57.1	0.0
Perry, MO	11 865	73.2	71.2	497	88.1	9.9	-14.5	10.0	0.0	0.0	13.0	0.0
Pettis, MO	25 355	55.5	78.3	1 572	89.6	15.0	-9.4	15.0	12.3	10.8	71.3	4.0
Phelps, MO	24 665	53.9	79.0	4 814	94.5	21.1	-3.3	19.9	15.2	7.3	74.9	22.0
Pike, MO	12 242	68.2	76.0	429	69.5	10.2	-14.2	10.6	5.4	41.4	41.9	2.2
Platte, MO	48 721	34.8	91.8	3 735	71.9	33.3	8.9	33.7	26.9	22.6	45.7	19.6
Polk, MO	16 645	62.2	77.5	2 320	21.8	14.6	-9.8	14.3	40.5	28.9	70.3	27.4
Pulaski, MO	23 062	48.5	85.1	2 825	74.9	18.8	-5.6	18.5	21.2	12.9	26.8	16.0
Putnam, MO	3 649	64.8	80.0	174	89.7	11.2	-13.2	11.2	0.0	0.0	100.0	0.0
Ralls, MO	6 506	67.8	78.7	221	63.8	12.3	-12.1	12.3	4.9	0.0	53.3	34.8
Randolph, MO	16 452	61.2	77.1	944	78.6	11.7	-12.7	12.3	3.5	10.8	47.7	16.2
Ray, MO	15 165	66.6	79.3	554	67.9	10.8	-13.6	11.0	0.0	0.0	23.8	3.7
Reynolds, MO	4 639	74.5	65.2	175	89.7	7.5	-16.9	7.7	0.0	0.0	55.6	0.0

[1]Hispanic or Latino persons may be of any race.
. . . = Not available.

Table C-1. Population, School, and Student Characteristics by County—*Continued*

County	State/County code	County type[1]	Population, 2000		Number of schools and students, 2000–2001			Resident enrollment, 2000			
			Total	Percent 5–17 years	School districts	Schools	Students	Total	Percent public	K–12	Percent public
			1	2	3	4	5	6	7	8	9
Ripley, MO	29181	9	13 509	18.8	4	7	2 325	2 972	92.4	2 501	93.1
St. Charles, MO	29183	0	283 883	21.3	5	61	49 519	82 278	76.8	60 232	83.1
St. Clair, MO	29185	9	9 652	17.5	4	7	1 506	1 941	94.8	1 738	97.1
Ste. Genevieve, MO	29186	6	17 842	20.6	1	4	2 185	4 398	76.2	3 636	77.3
St. Francois, MO	29187	6	55 641	17.9	5	24	10 448	13 139	91.6	10 223	93.3
St. Louis, MO	29189	0	1 016 315	18.9	24	258	153 823	281 608	68.5	193 194	75.2
Saline, MO	29195	7	23 756	18.2	8	16	3 903	6 338	78.7	4 267	95.8
Schuyler, MO	29197	9	4 170	18.6	1	3	776	919	95.0	783	97.3
Scotland, MO	29199	9	4 983	21.4	2	3	759	1 129	81.8	976	82.5
Scott, MO	29201	5	40 422	20.4	7	22	7 741	10 018	89.4	8 074	91.0
Shannon, MO	29203	9	8 324	20.3	2	4	895	2 042	95.5	1 680	97.5
Shelby, MO	29205	9	6 799	19.7	2	6	1 226	1 592	89.6	1 324	94.3
Stoddard, MO	29207	7	29 705	18.2	7	18	5 636	6 629	95.4	5 455	96.9
Stone, MO	29209	8	28 658	16.0	5	15	4 349	5 502	93.3	4 560	95.0
Sullivan, MO	29211	9	7 219	17.9	3	6	1 146	1 520	95.4	1 302	98.4
Taney, MO	29213	6	39 703	16.3	7	17	6 129	8 973	80.4	6 354	95.2
Texas, MO	29215	9	23 003	19.2	7	16	4 309	5 405	90.6	4 354	94.1
Vernon, MO	29217	7	20 454	19.9	4	12	3 369	5 081	85.5	4 047	91.6
Warren, MO	29219	1	24 525	20.3	2	7	3 905	5 978	81.2	4 928	84.6
Washington, MO	29221	6	23 344	20.0	4	11	4 058	5 577	92.7	4 737	93.7
Wayne, MO	29223	9	13 259	17.9	2	6	2 072	2 743	94.6	2 401	96.3
Webster, MO	29225	2	31 045	21.3	4	13	4 621	7 879	89.0	6 524	92.1
Worth, MO	29227	9	2 382	18.8	1	2	415	565	98.2	469	99.1
Wright, MO	29229	6	17 955	20.2	5	14	3 852	4 349	92.4	3 515	94.6
St. Louis city, MO	29510	0	348 189	19.0	1	116	44 361	98 331	72.6	67 241	80.7
MONTANA	30000										
Beaverhead, MT	30001	7	9 202	18.8	9	13	1 519	2 812	92.2	1 587	97.0
Big Horn, MT	30003	6	12 671	26.5	9	15	2 460	4 140	89.0	3 455	89.8
Blaine, MT	30005	9	7 009	24.5	11	18	1 470	2 097	92.9	1 724	93.3
Broadwater, MT	30007	9	4 385	19.9	1	3	762	1 046	90.5	869	93.0
Carbon, MT	30009	8	9 552	18.8	12	22	1 632	2 219	91.4	1 854	95.4
Carter, MT	30011	9	1 360	22.5	8	10	213	335	88.1	306	91.5
Cascade, MT	30013	3	80 357	19.4	14	43	13 793	20 212	86.0	15 730	92.4
Chouteau, MT	30015	8	5 970	22.4	13	17	908	1 675	94.7	1 369	96.4
Custer, MT	30017	7	11 696	19.2	12	18	2 051	2 903	91.5	2 237	93.2
Daniels, MT	30019	9	2 017	17.8	3	9	349	405	97.3	365	100.0
Dawson, MT	30021	7	9 059	18.0	7	10	1 491	2 206	93.6	1 678	93.9
Deer Lodge, MT	30023	7	9 417	17.9	2	6	1 516	2 218	94.6	1 811	97.0
Fallon, MT	30025	9	2 837	20.7	2	7	586	653	97.2	608	99.3
Fergus, MT	30027	7	11 893	19.4	14	24	2 162	2 689	95.0	2 340	97.9
Flathead, MT	30029	5	74 471	20.0	23	51	13 337	17 987	88.4	14 879	91.0
Gallatin, MT	30031	5	67 831	16.2	20	39	9 748	22 806	90.9	10 879	89.6
Garfield, MT	30033	9	1 279	17.7	10	11	208	277	93.5	250	94.0
Glacier, MT	30035	7	13 247	26.8	6	15	3 004	4 330	95.6	3 548	96.8
Golden Valley, MT	30037	8	1 042	22.5	2	6	205	242	90.5	227	90.7
Granite, MT	30039	9	2 830	19.4	4	7	466	622	90.8	556	91.4
Hill, MT	30041	7	16 673	21.1	12	21	3 254	5 291	92.0	3 528	93.1
Jefferson, MT	30043	9	10 049	22.6	8	12	1 837	2 611	91.6	2 312	94.4
Judith Basin, MT	30045	8	2 329	21.6	5	11	450	556	91.2	487	94.9
Lake, MT	30047	7	26 507	21.4	12	21	4 610	7 008	92.6	5 485	95.6
Lewis and Clark, MT	30049	5	55 716	19.4	10	28	9 898	14 412	84.3	10 836	95.1
Liberty, MT	30051	9	2 158	20.8	5	10	417	512	93.8	456	93.9
Lincoln, MT	30053	7	18 837	20.4	10	16	3 390	4 528	92.7	3 918	93.6
McCone, MT	30055	9	1 977	19.4	4	6	290	435	96.6	397	99.5
Madison, MT	30057	9	6 851	18.2	6	13	1 093	1 480	95.4	1 251	97.4
Meagher, MT	30059	8	1 932	20.0	4	5	309	428	94.2	384	96.6
Mineral, MT	30061	9	3 884	19.3	3	9	766	888	92.3	784	94.6
Missoula, MT	30063	5	95 802	17.2	14	42	13 903	30 019	91.5	16 769	92.2
Musselshell, MT	30065	8	4 497	18.4	4	6	758	1 008	92.9	847	94.1
Park, MT	30067	7	15 694	17.8	10	17	2 297	3 349	86.3	2 678	89.2
Petroleum, MT	30069	9	493	18.9	1	3	82	113	100.0	97	100.0
Phillips, MT	30071	9	4 601	22.4	7	16	968	1 174	94.4	1 043	97.4
Pondera, MT	30073	7	6 424	23.4	9	17	1 360	1 825	91.3	1 534	95.3
Powder River, MT	30075	9	1 858	20.7	4	5	377	437	93.1	388	97.7
Powell, MT	30077	7	7 180	16.6	8	9	1 064	1 483	86.7	1 245	92.1
Prairie, MT	30079	9	1 199	14.5	1	3	185	215	97.2	187	97.3
Ravalli, MT	30081	7	36 070	19.8	8	23	6 280	8 361	85.9	7 168	87.3
Richland, MT	30083	7	9 667	21.8	10	14	2 033	2 399	95.7	2 129	98.1
Roosevelt, MT	30085	7	10 620	26.5	12	22	2 809	3 651	95.2	2 891	97.3
Rosebud, MT	30087	7	9 383	25.8	11	17	2 169	2 924	89.7	2 426	91.1
Sanders, MT	30089	9	10 227	19.1	12	18	1 836	2 280	90.3	1 967	93.3
Sheridan, MT	30091	9	4 105	18.5	4	12	707	852	92.3	750	96.8
Silver Bow, MT	30093	5	34 606	17.9	5	14	5 269	9 439	86.7	6 390	87.0
Stillwater, MT	30095	8	8 195	19.8	13	18	1 583	1 888	93.5	1 657	96.0
Sweet Grass, MT	30097	9	3 609	20.1	5	6	638	808	91.5	713	96.2
Teton, MT	30099	8	6 445	21.1	11	17	1 337	1 586	90.0	1 398	92.9
Toole, MT	30101	7	5 267	20.2	4	10	979	1 297	90.0	1 135	94.5
Treasure, MT	30103	8	861	22.4	1	3	160	212	97.6	199	97.5
Valley, MT	30105	7	7 675	19.6	8	18	1 353	1 808	93.9	1 596	95.2
Wheatland, MT	30107	9	2 259	20.8	6	8	464	478	93.3	393	98.0
Wibaux, MT	30109	9	1 068	20.6	1	3	204	249	98.8	228	99.1
Yellowstone, MT	30111	3	129 352	18.9	19	61	21 866	33 876	88.4	24 867	92.4

[1]County type code is from the Economic Research Service of the USDA. See Notes and Definitions at the end of this section.

Table C-1. School and Student Characteristics by County—*Continued*

County	Characteristics of students, 2000–2001			Staff and students, 2000–2001				Revenues, fiscal 1999			
	Percent with IEP[2]	Percent eligible for free lunch	Percent minority	Number of teachers	Student/ teacher ratio	Local school non-teaching staff	Central admin. staff	Total revenue ($1,000s)	Percentage of revenue from		
									Federal govt.	State govt.	Local govt.
	10	11	12	13	14	15	16	17	18	19	20
Ripley, MO	13.2	59.7	1.1	168	13.8	123	21	$13 634	12.4	55.4	32.2
St. Charles, MO	15.8	10.9	6.5	3 058	16.2	1 926	603	310 264	2.9	31.2	65.9
St. Clair, MO	13.1	44.6	2.1	128	11.8	71	17	10 008	7.6	48.6	43.8
Ste. Genevieve, MO	15.3	37.5	1.5	141	15.5	91	20	12 065	6.6	23.0	70.4
St. Francois, MO	16.1	43.5	1.8	685	15.3	563	106	60 033	8.2	48.8	43.0
St. Louis, MO	. . .	29.9	40.8	10 281	15.0	7 713	2 157	1 296 058	3.7	25.9	70.3
Saline, MO	18.4	41.1	15.9	314	12.4	186	42	26 145	8.7	44.8	46.5
Schuyler, MO	15.5	49.2	1.4	64	12.1	42	2	4 648	7.7	46.3	46.1
Scotland, MO	15.2	. . .	0.3	63	12.0	67	7	5 160	8.5	43.3	48.2
Scott, MO	11.9	45.0	19.5	497	15.6	401	84	44 551	8.2	47.0	44.8
Shannon, MO	18.8	65.7	0.0	78	11.5	41	10	6 848	10.5	50.8	38.6
Shelby, MO	13.6	35.2	1.5	103	11.9	72	15	8 394	6.9	43.5	49.6
Stoddard, MO	14.8	46.9	2.8	403	14.0	276	48	31 646	7.9	45.8	46.2
Stone, MO	14.5	47.4	2.7	313	13.9	238	49	26 048	7.9	38.4	53.6
Sullivan, MO	11.9	51.3	12.1	98	11.7	58	13	6 775	7.1	44.3	48.5
Taney, MO	13.9	44.5	4.7	441	13.9	352	68	40 354	4.7	27.1	68.2
Texas, MO	13.0	46.8	1.7	332	13.0	242	46	26 285	9.0	55.4	35.6
Vernon, MO	14.7	40.5	2.6	246	13.7	160	42	21 057	9.2	46.3	44.5
Warren, MO	15.9	26.8	5.8	259	15.1	171	37	20 089	5.9	33.9	60.2
Washington, MO	14.6	51.5	1.7	273	14.9	202	47	23 439	10.7	52.9	36.4
Wayne, MO	18.2	62.5	0.9	154	13.5	124	24	12 795	10.8	52.2	37.0
Webster, MO	14.1	37.6	2.4	337	13.7	195	39	24 816	7.4	53.4	39.2
Worth, MO	12.3	43.9	0.7	39	10.6	29	4	2 759	7.2	47.6	45.2
Wright, MO	15.2	50.4	1.6	288	13.4	241	45	25 286	10.1	55.1	34.8
St. Louis city, MO	15.7	77.5	83.2	3 021	14.7	3 092	498	448 989	10.0	47.8	42.1
MONTANA											
Beaverhead, MT	9.9	20.1	6.0	100	15.2	14	3	10 862	4.5	44.8	50.7
Big Horn, MT	15.1	63.8	74.1	203	12.1	26	6	22 698	36.9	34.3	28.7
Blaine, MT	13.3	57.1	59.9	123	12.0	19	3	14 289	33.7	40.6	25.6
Broadwater, MT	12.5	32.3	3.4	51	14.9	6	1	3 932	5.5	51.4	43.0
Carbon, MT	10.9	25.5	3.8	129	12.7	18	4	11 349	5.6	47.4	47.0
Carter, MT	8.6	46.9	4.7	26	8.2	2	0	1 903	10.6	38.9	50.5
Cascade, MT	12.2	31.4	12.1	884	15.6	110	22	80 128	8.2	49.6	42.2
Chouteau, MT	12.9	35.0	1.3	85	10.7	10	4	8 320	3.7	39.7	56.6
Custer, MT	13.0	. . .	6.0	152	13.5	19	4	12 015	6.8	54.4	38.8
Daniels, MT	21.8	21.1	4.9	41	8.5	6	1	3 988	2.4	46.3	51.4
Dawson, MT	12.8	26.9	2.6	118	12.6	15	4	10 837	6.6	49.8	43.5
Deer Lodge, MT	12.6	34.7	11.3	91	16.7	13	4	8 917	6.9	55.2	37.9
Fallon, MT	8.4	19.3	1.2	57	10.3	7	1	5 360	2.6	57.1	40.3
Fergus, MT	12.1	30.7	4.5	165	13.1	18	5	16 456	6.0	48.3	45.7
Flathead, MT	10.3	27.9	4.4	832	16.0	113	18	76 498	5.9	46.6	47.5
Gallatin, MT	8.5	17.8	4.4	570	17.1	80	24	58 161	5.5	42.2	52.2
Garfield, MT	10.1	. . .	0.5	24	8.7	3	0	1 768	4.6	48.9	46.5
Glacier, MT	15.9	65.9	74.6	227	13.2	31	6	27 954	37.4	36.4	26.2
Golden Valley, MT	13.2	62.4	1.0	23	8.9	3	1	2 031	5.4	39.5	55.1
Granite, MT	15.7	33.2	1.1	41	11.4	5	2	3 735	5.8	41.5	52.6
Hill, MT	12.6	42.7	39.1	225	14.5	32	10	26 717	25.8	40.8	33.4
Jefferson, MT	10.5	20.6	5.2	129	14.2	18	4	11 442	2.3	50.0	47.7
Judith Basin, MT	11.6	36.4	1.6	47	9.6	4	1	3 810	4.1	38.5	57.5
Lake, MT	. . .	47.9	43.1	316	14.6	44	10	31 132	19.7	46.9	33.4
Lewis and Clark, MT	10.6	21.2	6.3	539	18.4	70	12	60 955	5.8	45.8	48.4
Liberty, MT	10.6	19.3	1.2	41	10.2	4	2	4 051	2.7	41.2	56.1
Lincoln, MT	12.4	41.9	3.9	220	15.4	26	8	19 988	7.8	55.2	37.0
McCone, MT	12.0	21.7	3.4	27	10.7	3	1	2 474	5.5	38.8	55.7
Madison, MT	8.6	30.4	4.7	88	12.4	11	3	10 094	3.8	33.9	62.4
Meagher, MT	12.0	45.2	5.8	27	11.4	4	1	2 254	6.1	34.5	59.4
Mineral, MT	13.4	50.1	6.0	66	11.6	8	3	6 616	9.9	45.1	45.1
Missoula, MT	14.1	28.8	6.8	878	15.8	117	18	88 783	7.8	43.1	49.2
Musselshell, MT	15.3	41.3	4.0	56	13.5	8	2	5 238	7.4	56.5	36.1
Park, MT	11.5	30.2	3.4	164	14.0	23	5	15 649	8.6	44.4	46.9
Petroleum, MT	8.5	53.7	1.2	11	7.5	1	1	1 031	6.8	46.7	46.6
Phillips, MT	11.6	41.9	17.3	93	10.4	10	3	9 732	7.8	43.6	48.6
Pondera, MT	11.7	41.6	25.7	104	13.1	14	3	12 570	20.8	43.6	35.6
Powder River, MT	11.3	27.1	4.2	32	11.8	4	1	2 976	5.3	50.7	44.0
Powell, MT	16.7	26.5	3.9	76	14.0	9	2	7 991	11.0	44.4	44.6
Prairie, MT	10.3	35.7	3.8	15	12.3	2	1	1 802	5.3	42.6	52.1
Ravalli, MT	11.6	30.4	3.6	399	15.7	50	11	39 841	6.7	49.9	43.3
Richland, MT	12.6	24.8	4.4	148	13.7	18	6	14 296	6.8	50.0	43.2
Roosevelt, MT	15.7	64.6	72.7	245	11.5	34	8	26 178	38.2	35.5	26.3
Rosebud, MT	17.5	49.5	47.7	178	12.2	28	13	25 890	34.4	25.1	40.5
Sanders, MT	11.1	49.8	10.6	132	13.9	19	5	13 123	9.9	43.3	46.8
Sheridan, MT	10.9	30.6	8.6	75	9.4	9	2	6 802	5.3	48.0	46.7
Silver Bow, MT	13.8	27.7	7.4	310	17.0	37	7	33 683	7.8	44.0	48.2
Stillwater, MT	11.8	17.6	5.3	112	14.1	17	5	11 674	6.1	41.8	52.1
Sweet Grass, MT	9.9	27.2	1.1	45	14.2	4	1	3 971	3.3	43.6	53.1
Teton, MT	11.2	25.1	5.7	108	12.4	14	4	9 301	4.4	48.8	46.9
Toole, MT	12.8	28.2	5.6	74	13.2	11	3	6 828	6.3	40.5	53.2
Treasure, MT	10.6	40.0	8.1	16	10.0	2	1	1 472	7.0	35.7	57.3
Valley, MT	14.0	33.2	16.7	124	10.9	15	6	12 018	11.2	39.3	49.5
Wheatland, MT	12.9	36.6	3.4	41	11.3	5	2	3 464	6.0	37.8	56.1
Wibaux, MT	14.7	48.0	2.5	20	10.2	3	1	1 556	9.3	50.8	39.9
Yellowstone, MT	14.3	25.3	11.9	1 337	16.4	186	38	132 734	6.1	45.1	48.8

[2]IEP = Individual Education Program. See Notes and Definitions at the end of this section.
. . . = Not available.

Table C-1. Population, School, and Student Characteristics by County—*Continued*

County	Current expenditures, fiscal 1999			Resident population 16 to 19 years, 2000				Outcomes, 1999–2000	
	Amount ($1,000s)	Amount per student	Percent for instruction	Total population 16 to 19 years	Percent in Armed Forces	Percent high school graduates	Percent not enrolled, not grads, not Armed Forces, not empl.	Number of graduates	Dropouts grades 9–12 (percent)
	21	22	23	24	25	26	27	28	29
Ripley, MO	$12 631	$5 354	65.4	718	0.0	18.1	11.0	128	3.0
St. Charles, MO	271 445	5 765	64.0	15 689	0.0	8.6	3.0	2 771	3.0
St. Clair, MO	8 918	5 347	62.6	426	0.0	11.0	7.0	96	2.1
Ste. Genevieve, MO	10 758	4 877	64.4	1 046	0.0	10.3	4.3	153	2.4
St. Francois, MO	51 385	4 904	60.9	3 248	0.0	10.3	12.4	638	4.4
St. Louis, MO	1 113 368	7 165	61.1	55 360	0.1	7.7	3.2	9 780	2.5
Saline, MO	22 851	5 708	68.0	1 637	0.0	10.8	5.1	276	4.5
Schuyler, MO	4 029	5 119	61.4	231	0.0	6.1	1.3	55	2.1
Scotland, MO	4 547	5 952	66.3	269	0.0	12.6	9.7	58	1.2
Scott, MO	37 204	4 717	65.3	2 275	0.0	10.4	9.5	447	2.6
Shannon, MO	5 088	5 604	65.0	483	0.0	20.1	14.5	60	0.7
Shelby, MO	7 425	5 783	63.7	406	0.0	16.5	6.9	88	3.5
Stoddard, MO	27 797	4 862	65.3	1 820	0.0	11.8	8.0	406	8.6
Stone, MO	22 743	5 200	61.5	1 443	0.0	15.5	7.6	271	4.5
Sullivan, MO	6 099	5 626	60.0	317	0.0	16.7	1.9	69	1.3
Taney, MO	30 392	5 235	62.0	2 329	0.0	13.1	4.6	316	6.0
Texas, MO	23 090	5 218	64.1	1 358	0.0	12.6	9.6	274	5.6
Vernon, MO	18 319	5 255	64.8	1 402	0.1	8.2	4.5	212	2.9
Warren, MO	16 811	4 432	61.5	1 369	0.0	12.3	6.4	218	3.2
Washington, MO	21 329	5 195	60.7	1 522	0.0	18.7	12.1	237	5.2
Wayne, MO	11 117	5 125	64.7	727	0.0	10.3	8.1	133	5.2
Webster, MO	20 814	4 534	62.4	1 745	0.0	11.6	8.9	258	6.5
Worth, MO	2 460	5 430	62.2	152	0.0	4.6	2.6	35	3.2
Wright, MO	22 583	5 595	67.9	1 128	0.0	15.4	9.1	272	4.5
St. Louis city, MO	361 185	7 855	54.2	19 036	0.0	10.4	10.3	1 407	9.4
MONTANA									
Beaverhead, MT	10 143	6 200	66.6	835	0.0	4.6	1.6	132	3.2
Big Horn, MT	21 055	8 435	58.9	908	0.0	8.9	12.4	134	5.2
Blaine, MT	12 280	7 792	57.4	506	0.0	9.9	8.5	99	4.7
Broadwater, MT	3 812	4 783	67.1	226	0.0	10.6	8.8	55	2.5
Carbon, MT	10 425	6 239	64.2	520	0.0	8.3	5.2	145	2.4
Carter, MT	1 673	7 639	63.0	86	0.0	0.0	0.0	22	. . .
Cascade, MT	72 768	5 060	66.6	4 335	7.0	21.6	3.9	970	4.0
Chouteau, MT	7 643	7 385	61.7	369	0.0	5.1	7.9	93	0.3
Custer, MT	11 042	5 276	63.0	756	0.0	11.9	0.7	151	2.6
Daniels, MT	3 402	8 569	60.1	114	0.0	2.6	0.0	40	. . .
Dawson, MT	10 785	6 633	57.9	605	0.0	9.6	0.2	131	2.0
Deer Lodge, MT	8 568	5 199	61.1	591	0.0	17.4	5.9	101	7.0
Fallon, MT	5 808	8 297	64.3	166	0.0	4.8	0.0	69	0.8
Fergus, MT	15 322	6 659	61.1	680	0.0	9.6	4.3	171	2.6
Flathead, MT	69 415	5 109	65.0	4 238	0.0	10.1	4.8	1 016	5.4
Gallatin, MT	49 858	5 244	61.6	5 008	0.0	8.2	1.5	652	4.2
Garfield, MT	1 791	7 280	58.6	81	0.0	13.6	3.7	19	. . .
Glacier, MT	23 803	7 469	57.8	913	0.0	11.1	9.2	132	7.1
Golden Valley, MT	1 715	7 588	65.0	50	0.0	4.0	6.0	13	. . .
Granite, MT	3 517	6 883	65.3	129	0.0	11.6	9.3	39	3.3
Hill, MT	23 232	6 680	58.7	1 207	0.0	8.8	5.0	251	5.8
Jefferson, MT	10 061	5 043	62.2	658	0.0	9.7	4.1	119	3.4
Judith Basin, MT	3 489	7 536	63.2	140	0.0	8.6	9.3	35	. . .
Lake, MT	27 909	5 848	63.1	1 805	0.0	9.4	14.0	271	8.0
Lewis and Clark, MT	55 217	5 471	65.7	3 520	0.4	11.3	1.2	605	5.0
Liberty, MT	3 760	7 899	59.4	149	0.0	2.7	14.8	43	0.7
Lincoln, MT	19 348	5 421	65.1	1 144	0.0	11.8	3.5	244	3.1
McCone, MT	2 330	7 420	63.8	114	0.0	5.3	7.9	27	1.0
Madison, MT	7 698	6 788	63.0	355	0.0	9.0	3.1	87	1.0
Meagher, MT	2 038	7 227	58.1	123	0.0	10.6	13.0	34	2.1
Mineral, MT	5 744	6 937	69.1	221	0.0	9.5	5.0	75	5.1
Missoula, MT	79 870	5 692	61.2	6 412	0.1	10.4	2.2	891	5.0
Musselshell, MT	5 035	6 286	65.2	274	0.0	6.6	4.4	59	5.1
Park, MT	14 527	5 966	61.5	742	0.0	20.1	4.0	169	4.7
Petroleum, MT	942	9 612	57.2	22	0.0	0.0	0.0	12	. . .
Phillips, MT	8 239	7 847	61.8	291	0.0	10.3	1.0	91	. . .
Pondera, MT	11 074	7 487	57.1	409	0.0	5.9	7.8	133	5.9
Powder River, MT	2 811	7 208	56.7	101	0.0	15.8	0.0	33	1.4
Powell, MT	7 297	6 504	62.8	336	1.5	5.1	12.5	76	3.3
Prairie, MT	1 581	7 154	63.0	47	0.0	0.0	4.3	15	1.4
Ravalli, MT	32 053	5 138	64.7	2 087	0.1	12.2	8.2	441	3.1
Richland, MT	13 549	6 284	63.0	587	0.0	11.2	2.7	174	2.3
Roosevelt, MT	22 611	7 757	58.7	766	0.4	7.3	12.4	148	10.2
Rosebud, MT	19 696	8 590	58.1	661	0.0	7.9	9.4	157	6.6
Sanders, MT	12 159	6 239	59.7	628	0.0	7.6	4.6	124	4.9
Sheridan, MT	6 453	8 348	59.4	212	0.0	6.1	0.0	68	0.4
Silver Bow, MT	30 469	5 399	60.7	1 981	0.0	9.7	4.0	382	3.3
Stillwater, MT	9 728	6 252	63.9	423	0.0	8.5	0.5	114	1.5
Sweet Grass, MT	3 571	6 063	68.0	175	0.0	8.0	1.1	40	0.6
Teton, MT	8 429	5 948	67.9	368	0.5	13.9	5.2	107	2.6
Toole, MT	6 500	6 366	61.0	348	0.0	7.5	8.3	81	4.8
Treasure, MT	1 443	7 885	60.0	53	0.0	11.3	1.9	15	1.5
Valley, MT	11 721	7 830	62.3	460	0.0	7.4	4.3	113	4.3
Wheatland, MT	3 145	8 023	62.2	124	0.0	9.7	4.8	33	3.2
Wibaux, MT	1 540	6 875	59.7	64	0.0	3.1	3.1	17	1.2
Yellowstone, MT	120 686	5 462	64.5	7 246	0.1	12.2	3.4	1 434	3.3

. . . = Not available.

Table C-1. Population, School, and Student Characteristics by County—*Continued*

County	High school graduates, 2000			College enrollment, 2000		College graduates, 2000 (percent)						
	Population 25 years and over	High school diploma or less (percent)	High school diploma or more (percent)	Number	Percent public	Bachelor's degree or more	+/- U.S. percent with bachelor's degree or more	Non-Hispanic White	Black or African American	American Indian and Alaska Native	Asian, Hawaiian, and Pacific Islander	Hispanic or Latino[1]
	30	31	32	33	34	35	36	37	38	39	40	41
Ripley, MO	9 092	71.0	62.1	272	91.5	7.8	-16.6	7.8	0.0	4.3	36.2	0.0
St. Charles, MO	178 498	40.5	89.1	15 745	65.4	26.3	1.9	26.3	22.7	16.4	51.9	26.7
St. Clair, MO	6 876	72.6	73.1	140	82.1	9.0	-15.4	8.9	0.0	3.3	70.8	11.4
Ste. Genevieve, MO	11 743	69.0	73.8	496	83.3	8.1	-16.3	8.0	25.5	0.0	100.0	11.4
St. Francois, MO	37 236	62.3	72.4	1 941	89.1	10.2	-14.2	10.2	4.3	23.6	24.8	19.6
St. Louis, MO	677 027	36.0	88.0	64 556	58.5	35.4	11.0	38.4	17.4	16.4	65.7	32.7
Saline, MO	15 185	64.2	74.0	1 643	36.3	15.8	-8.6	16.0	12.3	6.0	38.2	11.6
Schuyler, MO	2 870	65.2	81.4	76	94.7	11.6	-12.8	11.7	0.0	0.0	0.0	0.0
Scotland, MO	3 172	67.8	76.8	79	75.9	11.2	-13.2	11.3	...	0.0	0.0	6.7
Scott, MO	25 749	69.8	72.9	1 166	90.1	10.6	-13.8	11.3	2.6	14.3	28.6	2.9
Shannon, MO	5 552	75.6	67.6	220	77.7	7.6	-16.8	7.5	0.0	11.5	0.0	3.4
Shelby, MO	4 589	66.4	81.0	185	69.7	12.5	-11.9	12.6	0.0	0.0	0.0	27.8
Stoddard, MO	20 121	72.0	66.9	811	89.9	10.1	-14.3	10.0	0.6	8.3	48.2	18.4
Stone, MO	20 799	58.5	80.4	517	85.9	14.2	-10.2	14.1	0.0	14.6	0.0	37.0
Sullivan, MO	4 870	72.4	72.4	107	80.4	8.4	-16.0	8.8	0.0	0.0	0.0	3.2
Taney, MO	26 814	56.4	81.4	2 123	37.9	14.9	-9.5	15.1	19.3	8.1	11.0	16.8
Texas, MO	15 641	68.3	71.4	712	77.0	10.8	-13.6	10.8	22.2	4.3	23.1	9.6
Vernon, MO	13 169	63.3	76.6	704	59.9	14.2	-10.2	14.1	7.1	18.2	33.3	0.0
Warren, MO	16 137	60.8	79.5	664	70.9	11.1	-13.3	11.3	5.5	0.0	0.0	19.2
Washington, MO	14 796	72.9	62.5	634	92.7	7.5	-16.9	7.6	0.0	15.2	47.6	4.1
Wayne, MO	9 301	74.6	59.7	222	77.9	6.8	-17.6	6.7	0.0	3.1	53.8	28.6
Webster, MO	19 515	65.0	74.8	825	74.5	11.0	-13.4	11.2	1.5	9.3	43.1	2.1
Worth, MO	1 644	65.5	80.2	42	90.5	11.3	-13.1	11.3	...	18.2	...	0.0
Wright, MO	11 638	69.6	71.1	549	81.6	9.8	-14.6	10.0	14.8	15.5	0.0	3.0
St. Louis city, MO	221 951	56.2	71.3	24 410	51.8	19.1	-5.3	28.2	8.8	11.3	33.0	16.6
MONTANA												
Beaverhead, MT	5 825	39.8	89.3	1 117	89.3	26.4	2.0	27.0	0.0	3.4	...	5.2
Big Horn, MT	7 051	53.8	76.4	420	84.0	14.3	-10.1	20.3	...	9.3	36.7	0.0
Blaine, MT	4 144	49.3	78.7	213	89.2	17.4	-7.0	22.1	0.0	9.6	0.0	10.3
Broadwater, MT	3 061	54.5	85.2	112	85.7	15.0	-9.4	15.3	0.0	0.0	100.0	0.0
Carbon, MT	6 701	48.0	88.1	215	87.9	23.3	-1.1	23.4	66.7	21.4	14.3	15.6
Carter, MT	946	52.5	83.3	15	53.3	13.6	-10.8	13.9	0.0	0.0	0.0	...
Cascade, MT	52 333	46.2	87.1	3 154	69.8	21.5	-2.9	22.1	27.2	7.2	25.4	17.1
Chouteau, MT	3 837	43.3	87.1	174	87.9	20.5	-3.9	21.6	0.0	9.7	55.6	23.5
Custer, MT	7 819	44.9	84.9	514	93.8	18.8	-5.6	19.2	...	3.5	37.0	1.1
Daniels, MT	1 467	51.0	85.3	30	70.0	14.1	-10.3	14.3	...	0.0	33.3	0.0
Dawson, MT	6 161	47.8	82.7	445	94.4	15.1	-9.3	15.2	0.0	0.0	0.0	25.7
Deer Lodge, MT	6 584	58.4	84.5	330	82.1	14.7	-9.7	14.9	...	5.5	44.0	0.0
Fallon, MT	1 935	57.7	85.7	16	75.0	14.4	-10.0	14.3	50.0	0.0	100.0	20.0
Fergus, MT	8 290	50.4	86.3	187	85.0	19.1	-5.3	19.4	100.0	6.6	50.0	0.0
Flathead, MT	49 648	43.2	87.4	2 223	85.6	22.4	-2.0	22.5	64.0	15.5	31.9	20.8
Gallatin, MT	40 461	27.9	93.3	10 816	96.8	41.0	16.6	41.1	45.9	29.4	64.6	25.7
Garfield, MT	871	54.1	84.7	14	78.6	16.8	-7.6	16.8	...	...	...	0.0
Glacier, MT	7 383	48.7	78.6	469	88.1	16.5	-7.9	26.0	0.0	8.6	0.0	0.0
Golden Valley, MT	704	58.4	70.5	13	100.0	16.2	-8.2	16.4	...	0.0	...	0.0
Granite, MT	1 988	47.1	87.8	39	87.2	22.1	-2.3	22.5	...	0.0	0.0	13.3
Hill, MT	10 031	45.3	86.8	1 378	97.0	20.0	-4.4	20.9	0.0	12.3	32.1	22.4
Jefferson, MT	6 717	41.0	90.2	210	75.7	27.7	3.3	28.0	0.0	10.5	23.5	18.8
Judith Basin, MT	1 595	42.8	87.6	23	65.2	23.6	-0.8	23.9	...	0.0	0.0	0.0
Lake, MT	16 971	47.5	84.2	1 057	86.7	22.2	-2.2	24.6	8.3	11.1	35.5	24.9
Lewis and Clark, MT	36 690	37.9	91.4	2 691	52.5	31.6	7.2	32.1	34.8	11.4	52.3	25.8
Liberty, MT	1 470	50.0	75.0	34	94.1	17.6	-6.8	17.5	...	...	0.0	100.0
Lincoln, MT	13 008	57.8	80.2	428	89.5	13.7	-10.7	13.8	100.0	6.9	0.0	0.0
McCone, MT	1 374	52.1	86.1	24	79.2	16.4	-8.0	16.4	0.0	0.0	100.0	25.0
Madison, MT	4 945	42.8	89.8	138	92.0	25.5	1.1	25.8	...	12.5	0.0	22.9
Meagher, MT	1 334	53.8	83.4	10	40.0	18.7	-5.7	18.9	...	27.3	...	0.0
Mineral, MT	2 691	60.5	83.2	68	88.2	12.3	-12.1	12.5	...	6.7	20.0	21.4
Missoula, MT	59 298	35.5	91.0	11 985	94.4	32.8	8.4	33.1	50.7	19.3	39.9	29.4
Musselshell, MT	3 181	55.5	82.6	120	90.8	16.7	-7.7	16.8	...	0.0	50.0	3.0
Park, MT	11 013	44.7	87.6	376	84.8	23.1	-1.3	23.4	0.0	21.6	42.4	15.5
Petroleum, MT	333	52.9	82.9	12	100.0	17.4	-7.0	17.7	...	...	...	0.0
Phillips, MT	3 102	53.1	82.4	55	92.7	17.1	-7.3	17.6	...	11.9	22.6	0.0
Pondera, MT	4 108	53.4	81.6	159	81.1	19.8	-4.6	21.1	0.0	9.8	12.5	0.0
Powder River, MT	1 272	48.0	83.4	14	100.0	16.0	-8.4	16.0	...	16.7	0.0	0.0
Powell, MT	5 098	56.9	81.9	155	68.4	13.1	-11.3	13.3	68.2	1.1	44.0	0.0
Prairie, MT	913	53.6	78.8	25	100.0	14.8	-9.6	14.8	...	22.2	0.0	0.0
Ravalli, MT	24 565	44.1	87.4	798	87.3	22.5	-1.9	22.7	87.5	13.8	33.3	17.4
Richland, MT	6 398	51.9	83.5	162	82.1	17.2	-7.2	17.8	...	0.0	...	2.4
Roosevelt, MT	6 107	51.8	80.6	492	82.3	15.6	-8.8	20.9	...	8.9	29.8	38.2
Rosebud, MT	5 543	51.5	84.4	291	88.0	17.6	-6.8	20.2	...	10.2	23.1	8.9
Sanders, MT	7 242	56.0	81.2	229	78.6	15.5	-8.9	16.0	0.0	7.3	15.6	25.6
Sheridan, MT	2 931	50.3	81.2	70	67.1	18.4	-6.0	18.8	...	0.0	25.0	10.5
Silver Bow, MT	23 097	49.2	85.1	2 458	91.6	21.7	-2.7	22.2	18.2	8.4	45.6	9.8
Stillwater, MT	5 632	51.6	87.5	138	86.2	17.8	-6.6	17.8	50.0	28.6	42.9	18.3
Sweet Grass, MT	2 487	46.5	88.9	53	69.8	23.6	-0.8	24.1	...	0.0	0.0	0.0
Teton, MT	4 295	48.4	83.4	106	73.6	20.8	-3.6	21.3	...	9.6	42.9	17.2
Toole, MT	3 570	54.1	81.0	104	50.0	16.8	-7.6	17.7	0.0	3.4	0.0	0.0
Treasure, MT	577	54.8	86.3	9	100.0	18.2	-6.2	18.1	...	0.0	100.0	0.0
Valley, MT	5 345	55.8	83.9	129	87.6	15.7	-8.7	16.8	40.0	4.6	0.0	0.0
Wheatland, MT	1 508	61.8	69.0	40	77.5	13.5	-10.9	13.7	...	15.4	...	0.0
Wibaux, MT	738	58.0	76.8	17	100.0	16.0	-8.4	16.0	...	0.0	...	0.0
Yellowstone, MT	84 233	42.6	88.5	6 681	85.7	26.4	2.0	27.0	38.9	15.4	48.1	10.3

[1]Hispanic or Latino persons may be of any race.
. . . = Not available.

Table C-1. Population, School, and Student Characteristics by County—*Continued*

County	State/ County code	County type[1]	Population, 2000		Number of schools and students, 2000–2001			Resident enrollment, 2000			
			Total	Percent 5–17 years	School districts	Schools	Students	Total	Percent public	K–12	Percent public
			1	2	3	4	5	6	7	8	9
NEBRASKA	31000										
Adams, NE	31001	5	31 151	18.1	13	33	4 884	8 746	73.1	5 519	83.7
Antelope, NE	31003	9	7 452	21.5	6	15	1 296	1 892	88.2	1 636	88.8
Arthur, NE	31005	9	444	18.7	3	3	80	116	97.4	105	100.0
Banner, NE	31007	9	819	24.1	1	2	212	205	95.6	187	97.9
Blaine, NE	31009	9	583	20.8	1	2	145	136	99.3	125	100.0
Boone, NE	31011	9	6 259	23.2	8	13	1 224	1 676	88.2	1 459	90.1
Box Butte, NE	31013	7	12 158	21.6	6	14	2 551	3 384	92.1	2 779	96.9
Boyd, NE	31015	9	2 438	19.9	3	7	513	568	97.9	509	99.2
Brown, NE	31017	9	3 525	19.5	8	11	649	810	92.2	699	97.7
Buffalo, NE	31019	5	42 259	18.4	14	32	7 358	14 318	91.4	7 775	91.8
Burt, NE	31021	8	7 791	20.0	4	10	1 646	1 891	95.9	1 632	96.7
Butler, NE	31023	6	8 767	21.0	8	12	1 282	2 263	71.3	1 942	70.7
Cass, NE	31025	2	24 334	20.9	7	17	3 695	6 664	87.6	5 203	91.4
Cedar, NE	31027	9	9 615	23.4	5	11	1 623	2 646	73.7	2 293	73.9
Chase, NE	31029	9	4 068	19.6	5	8	908	969	94.2	822	97.1
Cherry, NE	31031	7	6 148	20.8	24	26	1 026	1 524	90.4	1 291	94.7
Cheyenne, NE	31033	7	9 830	19.9	6	15	1 926	2 414	95.7	2 060	98.6
Clay, NE	31035	9	7 039	21.5	4	14	2 183	1 891	92.2	1 568	93.4
Colfax, NE	31037	7	10 441	21.7	10	14	2 128	2 799	90.9	2 336	91.6
Cuming, NE	31039	7	10 203	20.7	5	11	1 613	2 552	66.3	2 182	65.7
Custer, NE	31041	7	11 793	20.6	14	23	2 204	2 835	92.8	2 520	95.1
Dakota, NE	31043	3	20 253	21.7	3	12	3 667	5 524	88.5	4 479	90.5
Dawes, NE	31045	7	9 060	16.2	12	16	1 547	3 367	96.2	1 535	95.5
Dawson, NE	31047	7	24 365	20.8	17	31	5 080	6 269	96.0	5 288	98.1
Deuel, NE	31049	9	2 098	19.0	2	5	487	466	92.5	421	94.3
Dixon, NE	31051	8	6 339	21.1	3	6	816	1 670	94.2	1 411	96.5
Dodge, NE	31053	4	36 160	18.5	6	32	6 215	9 093	80.1	6 752	89.5
Douglas, NE	31055	2	463 585	19.2	10	156	77 448	132 512	75.8	89 728	80.2
Dundy, NE	31057	9	2 292	18.0	1	3	338	530	94.7	421	99.3
Fillmore, NE	31059	9	6 634	20.5	8	16	1 289	1 609	92.3	1 361	94.4
Franklin, NE	31061	9	3 574	19.3	3	5	489	829	96.3	689	99.3
Frontier, NE	31063	9	3 099	20.5	3	8	786	947	96.6	664	98.3
Furnas, NE	31065	9	5 324	18.5	3	8	1 209	1 226	94.2	1 020	97.5
Gage, NE	31067	6	22 993	18.1	5	13	3 478	5 467	89.0	4 267	92.3
Garden, NE	31069	9	2 292	18.2	5	5	404	492	94.3	427	97.4
Garfield, NE	31071	9	1 902	18.7	6	6	359	437	95.0	385	98.4
Gosper, NE	31073	9	2 143	18.6	2	3	301	501	95.8	427	98.1
Grant, NE	31075	9	747	24.2	5	5	189	210	92.4	193	96.9
Greeley, NE	31077	9	2 714	21.3	4	8	608	725	82.6	593	80.1
Hall, NE	31079	5	53 534	19.5	9	28	9 019	12 912	89.4	10 391	92.0
Hamilton, NE	31081	7	9 403	22.4	3	7	1 679	2 594	91.8	2 143	94.4
Harlan, NE	31083	9	3 786	19.4	1	2	358	924	91.2	782	93.6
Hayes, NE	31085	9	1 068	22.2	1	2	169	289	97.2	259	97.7
Hitchcock, NE	31087	9	3 111	19.4	2	6	478	764	95.3	628	98.6
Holt, NE	31089	7	11 551	21.4	27	31	2 012	2 924	86.8	2 558	86.9
Hooker, NE	31091	9	783	19.9	1	2	192	181	94.5	160	100.0
Howard, NE	31093	9	6 567	22.3	5	8	1 539	1 723	95.0	1 495	96.1
Jefferson, NE	31095	7	8 333	18.0	3	7	1 718	1 844	87.6	1 528	89.1
Johnson, NE	31097	8	4 488	18.7	5	8	862	1 028	92.6	878	94.0
Kearney, NE	31099	7	6 882	20.6	3	7	1 405	1 779	94.7	1 467	96.4
Keith, NE	31101	7	8 875	19.5	6	11	1 496	2 090	92.9	1 814	95.5
Keya Paha, NE	31103	9	983	17.7	6	6	141	196	96.4	182	98.4
Kimball, NE	31105	6	4 089	19.3	1	3	710	913	95.1	778	98.2
Knox, NE	31107	9	9 374	19.8	6	12	1 696	2 258	91.1	1 957	93.0
Lancaster, NE	31109	3	250 291	16.8	12	78	35 953	76 553	83.1	42 543	84.1
Lincoln, NE	31111	5	34 632	19.6	11	28	5 802	8 777	89.8	6 868	92.2
Logan, NE	31113	9	774	22.1	1	2	207	201	98.0	171	98.8
Loup, NE	31115	9	712	20.4	1	2	125	168	89.3	150	89.3
McPherson, NE	31117	9	533	20.3	5	5	95	132	90.9	117	90.6
Madison, NE	31119	5	35 226	19.9	14	31	6 243	9 710	78.4	7 256	78.4
Merrick, NE	31121	7	8 204	21.2	4	8	1 403	2 058	86.5	1 682	88.5
Morrill, NE	31123	9	5 440	21.3	5	7	1 102	1 378	95.5	1 161	97.2
Nance, NE	31125	9	4 038	21.7	4	6	828	1 026	94.2	865	97.2
Nemaha, NE	31127	7	7 576	18.5	5	14	1 262	2 268	94.9	1 481	97.2
Nuckolls, NE	31129	9	5 057	18.5	1	3	512	1 187	92.2	981	93.1
Otoe, NE	31131	6	15 396	19.9	8	14	2 612	3 963	85.6	3 134	88.6
Pawnee, NE	31133	9	3 087	17.8	3	6	647	672	96.3	579	98.3
Perkins, NE	31135	9	3 200	21.2	3	5	523	779	88.1	694	89.6
Phelps, NE	31137	7	9 747	20.3	8	14	1 978	2 387	93.5	1 987	96.5
Pierce, NE	31139	9	7 857	23.0	4	8	1 541	2 264	86.4	1 865	88.3
Platte, NE	31141	7	31 662	21.8	7	26	4 599	8 809	70.8	6 970	70.4
Polk, NE	31143	9	5 639	19.4	4	10	1 249	1 408	95.2	1 140	97.3
Red Willow, NE	31145	7	11 448	18.6	5	14	2 021	2 925	93.5	2 257	95.6
Richardson, NE	31147	7	9 531	20.3	5	11	1 709	2 298	90.9	1 927	93.0
Rock, NE	31149	9	1 756	17.5	7	7	264	363	92.0	333	93.7
Saline, NE	31151	6	13 843	18.9	7	11	2 686	3 929	77.5	2 680	95.7
Sarpy, NE	31153	2	122 595	22.2	4	42	19 401	38 813	83.3	27 289	88.2
Saunders, NE	31155	6	19 830	21.5	16	26	2 989	5 208	79.9	4 334	80.9
Scotts Bluff, NE	31157	5	36 951	19.4	12	25	6 476	9 375	88.4	7 191	92.6
Seward, NE	31159	6	16 496	19.1	4	9	2 652	5 376	67.2	3 218	80.5

[1]County type code is from the Economic Research Service of the USDA. See Notes and Definitions at the end of this section.

Table C-1. School and Student Characteristics by County—*Continued*

County	Characteristics of students, 2000–2001			Staff and students, 2000–2001				Revenues, fiscal 1999			
	Percent with IEP2	Percent eligible for free lunch	Percent minority	Number of teachers	Student/teacher ratio	Local school non-teaching staff	Central admin. staff	Total revenue ($1,000s)	Percentage of revenue from		
									Federal govt.	State govt.	Local govt.
	10	11	12	13	14	15	16	17	18	19	20
NEBRASKA											
Adams, NE	18.7	28.7	10.0	363	13.5	264	55	$43 424	8.6	35.4	56.0
Antelope, NE	15.8	45.9	2.0	128	10.1	92	19	13 499	7.3	32.4	60.4
Arthur, NE	13.8	. . .	1.3	13	6.2	5	2	920	0.4	13.7	85.9
Banner, NE	11.3	35.8	8.5	20	10.6	21	3	1 764	6.3	19.0	74.6
Blaine, NE	11.0	34.5	2.1	18	8.1	13	3	1 625	5.1	18.8	76.1
Boone, NE	12.8	36.1	1.0	108	11.3	63	12	10 787	2.3	36.3	61.4
Box Butte, NE	13.8	29.7	17.4	196	13.0	184	26	18 870	7.8	46.9	45.3
Boyd, NE	17.7	45.2	1.9	56	9.2	41	6	4 707	6.0	49.7	44.3
Brown, NE	14.1	36.3	0.3	56	11.6	33	11	7 155	4.8	36.6	58.6
Buffalo, NE	16.1	30.5	9.6	504	14.6	419	63	56 313	5.4	35.6	59.0
Burt, NE	14.9	28.7	4.0	123	13.4	92	18	11 091	2.7	35.8	61.5
Butler, NE	16.7	27.3	3.2	102	12.6	80	12	9 521	2.6	19.0	78.4
Cass, NE	18.3	27.7	4.3	283	13.1	219	40	30 457	5.6	34.6	59.8
Cedar, NE	14.3	35.3	1.5	139	11.7	115	21	13 215	4.8	39.2	56.0
Chase, NE	14.0	35.0	5.5	83	10.9	61	14	8 567	2.5	30.4	67.0
Cherry, NE	9.9	46.2	6.9	107	9.6	66	10	9 038	5.6	29.4	65.0
Cheyenne, NE	14.4	37.0	8.9	158	12.2	133	22	16 276	5.1	35.8	59.1
Clay, NE	22.7	31.0	6.4	194	11.3	97	17	13 402	10.3	25.1	64.6
Colfax, NE	13.0	34.9	28.5	164	13.0	119	18	14 649	3.2	37.6	59.3
Cuming, NE	19.6	38.4	10.5	130	12.4	122	12	12 266	3.8	23.2	72.9
Custer, NE	12.2	37.4	2.3	185	11.9	142	22	18 206	3.5	36.2	60.3
Dakota, NE	16.7	33.1	40.0	248	14.8	223	17	21 556	7.2	51.1	41.7
Dawes, NE	21.0	. . .	16.8	115	13.5	83	19	11 184	5.1	49.7	45.2
Dawson, NE	13.4	51.1	35.6	350	14.5	225	43	32 620	6.4	39.9	53.7
Deuel, NE	10.5	37.4	4.9	46	10.6	26	6	4 369	2.9	27.5	69.6
Dixon, NE	11.6	24.9	1.8	68	12.0	45	7	12 522	6.8	35.8	57.3
Dodge, NE	18.9	28.7	7.5	424	14.7	309	62	46 973	5.4	38.6	56.0
Douglas, NE	14.2	34.0	30.7	5 090	15.2	4 211	592	562 799	7.2	37.3	55.5
Dundy, NE	14.5	30.2	7.4	31	10.9	38	4	3 215	3.4	20.9	75.8
Fillmore, NE	18.5	28.3	4.1	122	10.6	95	18	11 540	3.4	21.0	75.5
Franklin, NE	12.1	34.0	0.2	50	9.8	36	5	4 354	4.4	29.4	66.2
Frontier, NE	15.5	34.0	1.9	76	10.3	69	11	7 022	4.2	36.0	59.8
Furnas, NE	17.0	39.6	3.2	110	11.0	96	15	10 875	3.3	32.6	64.1
Gage, NE	16.6	24.3	3.6	253	13.7	155	38	29 919	7.9	37.2	54.9
Garden, NE	10.2	45.9	1.2	42	9.6	27	8	3 551	1.7	19.5	78.8
Garfield, NE	15.0	39.2	3.6	36	10.0	24	5	2 830	3.6	49.0	47.4
Gosper, NE	17.9	31.2	11.0	25	12.0	18	3	2 102	1.8	22.7	75.5
Grant, NE	8.7	. . .	6.9	22	8.6	16	3	2 427	1.2	21.6	77.2
Greeley, NE	17.9	58.7	3.3	65	9.4	48	9	5 269	7.5	36.2	56.3
Hall, NE	15.6	38.1	22.5	618	14.6	418	78	66 952	5.5	35.6	58.9
Hamilton, NE	15.0	25.7	2.9	123	13.7	94	15	12 903	3.5	25.2	71.3
Harlan, NE	12.3	27.4	1.7	29	12.3	25	4	3 181	11.0	41.3	47.7
Hayes, NE	16.6	55.6	6.5	19	8.9	18	3	1 728	3.1	19.6	77.3
Hitchcock, NE	17.7	40.6	3.8	51	9.4	45	10	7 533	10.1	28.3	61.6
Holt, NE	14.9	43.4	2.7	183	11.0	100	22	16 520	3.5	38.6	57.9
Hooker, NE	15.6	40.1	0.0	21	9.1	11	3	1 776	1.0	13.2	85.8
Howard, NE	17.3	34.3	1.9	118	13.0	89	13	10 980	3.2	42.6	54.1
Jefferson, NE	17.8	33.2	2.2	127	13.5	107	15	15 510	4.8	30.3	64.9
Johnson, NE	14.8	29.6	9.4	80	10.8	54	10	7 502	3.6	39.2	57.2
Kearney, NE	16.4	22.7	2.6	107	13.1	74	12	9 846	2.5	12.7	84.8
Keith, NE	15.0	27.9	7.1	115	13.0	93	21	15 531	12.5	32.6	54.9
Keya Paha, NE	9.9	48.2	0.7	21	6.7	7	2	1 281	6.3	14.4	79.2
Kimball, NE	17.0	36.2	8.7	49	14.5	46	8	4 900	3.9	35.7	60.5
Knox, NE	14.6	48.5	13.6	160	10.6	99	23	17 060	15.7	40.3	44.0
Lancaster, NE	16.3	23.8	12.5	2 612	13.8	2 038	459	284 894	5.3	30.5	64.2
Lincoln, NE	18.3	33.0	10.2	429	13.5	256	50	40 096	5.2	43.4	51.5
Logan, NE	15.5	45.9	3.4	19	10.9	14	2	1 782	3.8	35.0	61.2
Loup, NE	12.0	65.6	4.0	14	8.9	16	1	1 251	3.4	26.2	70.3
McPherson, NE	7.9	. . .	2.1	13	7.3	4	2	864	0.0	21.1	78.9
Madison, NE	15.1	31.4	19.5	454	13.8	350	63	45 524	4.4	40.3	55.2
Merrick, NE	13.5	26.5	3.3	105	13.4	70	14	11 935	3.4	27.4	69.2
Morrill, NE	10.6	49.7	17.6	84	13.1	75	10	8 686	6.1	44.4	49.5
Nance, NE	13.4	41.7	2.7	64	12.9	40	5	5 623	3.2	40.7	56.1
Nemaha, NE	12.7	27.7	4.4	97	13.0	71	15	12 082	6.5	38.5	55.0
Nuckolls, NE	18.8	21.1	2.1	49	10.4	60	7	6 836	6.7	44.2	49.1
Otoe, NE	16.9	20.8	4.7	192	13.6	158	24	19 616	3.4	32.2	64.4
Pawnee, NE	17.0	38.9	0.3	62	10.4	45	9	5 302	4.5	36.6	58.9
Perkins, NE	14.0	28.5	5.9	54	9.7	45	8	4 648	2.3	16.4	81.2
Phelps, NE	21.1	22.3	4.0	161	12.3	108	31	17 681	5.1	24.9	70.0
Pierce, NE	14.6	30.9	2.9	117	13.2	81	14	11 803	3.8	42.5	53.6
Platte, NE	18.1	27.9	13.8	321	14.3	253	54	36 949	6.9	31.9	61.3
Polk, NE	13.3	30.5	1.6	102	12.2	60	13	8 340	1.9	23.1	75.1
Red Willow, NE	22.5	36.7	4.2	167	12.1	128	26	15 738	4.7	44.7	50.6
Richardson, NE	16.8	39.1	6.3	142	12.0	94	18	12 734	3.8	45.6	50.5
Rock, NE	18.4	46.6	0.8	32	8.3	18	4	2 967	3.3	26.7	70.1
Saline, NE	14.5	26.2	11.3	176	15.3	139	21	18 810	5.2	37.6	57.2
Sarpy, NE	13.4	16.8	13.0	1 216	16.0	1 000	165	147 470	15.7	46.3	38.0
Saunders, NE	14.4	25.4	2.2	225	13.3	170	26	21 779	3.8	33.5	62.7
Scotts Bluff, NE	12.6	38.5	30.1	444	14.6	338	59	49 062	8.5	49.5	42.0
Seward, NE	15.9	19.9	2.9	193	13.7	180	32	24 150	8.0	28.2	63.8

2IEP = Individual Education Program. See Notes and Definitions at the end of this section.
. . . = Not available.

Table C-1. Population, School, and Student Characteristics by County—*Continued*

County	Current expenditures, fiscal 1999			Resident population 16 to 19 years, 2000				Outcomes, 1999–2000	
	Amount ($1,000s)	Amount per student	Percent for instruction	Total population 16 to 19 years	Percent in Armed Forces	Percent high school graduates	Percent not enrolled, not grads, not Armed Forces, not empl.	Number of graduates	Dropouts grades 9–12 (percent)
	21	22	23	24	25	26	27	28	29
NEBRASKA									
Adams, NE	$32 737	$6 525	71.1	2 035	0.6	5.7	1.7	336	3.5
Antelope, NE	10 746	8 737	63.9	496	0.0	9.3	0.2	114	0.4
Arthur, NE	898	9 978	64.7	26	0.0	0.0	0.0	12	...
Banner, NE	1 373	7 151	53.9	51	0.0	11.8	3.9	13	...
Blaine, NE	1 512	9 882	57.0	38	0.0	15.8	0.0	20	...
Boone, NE	8 131	6 174	69.5	362	0.0	7.2	0.8	89	1.6
Box Butte, NE	14 917	5 442	66.4	824	0.0	13.2	1.9	205	1.5
Boyd, NE	3 982	6 889	65.1	166	0.0	3.0	3.0	63	0.9
Brown, NE	5 142	7 887	62.6	179	0.0	7.8	0.6	54	1.7
Buffalo, NE	44 355	6 261	65.6	3 642	0.0	6.7	2.5	462	1.9
Burt, NE	9 351	5 630	66.2	443	0.0	4.7	2.3	113	3.0
Butler, NE	7 439	5 568	65.0	499	0.0	5.4	1.6	91	2.2
Cass, NE	22 183	5 819	65.8	1 461	0.0	9.7	3.7	272	2.8
Cedar, NE	10 518	6 094	66.1	615	0.0	7.3	0.7	136	0.4
Chase, NE	6 464	6 400	64.9	241	0.0	3.7	5.0	87	2.5
Cherry, NE	6 827	6 252	66.2	326	0.0	8.9	3.1	80	3.3
Cheyenne, NE	14 157	6 869	64.7	608	0.0	15.8	0.3	140	3.3
Clay, NE	10 642	6 992	64.8	468	0.0	6.2	1.9	135	1.8
Colfax, NE	11 582	5 357	67.6	720	0.0	9.7	9.3	176	4.4
Cuming, NE	9 780	5 746	66.3	598	0.0	8.0	3.7	144	1.9
Custer, NE	14 899	6 607	66.2	599	0.5	4.8	0.7	158	0.7
Dakota, NE	18 093	4 971	64.6	1 218	0.0	11.2	5.5	234	8.1
Dawes, NE	8 084	5 766	63.4	1 088	1.6	7.4	4.6	177	17.5
Dawson, NE	26 730	5 316	65.2	1 522	0.0	6.2	8.3	337	3.8
Deuel, NE	3 717	7 260	64.6	132	0.0	8.3	2.3	47	3.2
Dixon, NE	9 915	8 174	68.8	368	0.0	6.5	4.1	70	2.2
Dodge, NE	37 908	5 958	64.5	2 296	0.0	8.4	3.3	440	4.7
Douglas, NE	452 254	5 898	60.8	26 622	0.0	9.2	5.4	4 536	6.5
Dundy, NE	2 749	7 552	59.2	118	0.0	5.1	2.5	38	...
Fillmore, NE	9 500	7 175	65.8	399	0.0	10.0	2.8	101	1.0
Franklin, NE	3 431	6 624	67.1	170	0.0	6.5	1.8	40	...
Frontier, NE	6 250	7 225	56.7	290	0.0	4.5	0.7	68	1.0
Furnas, NE	9 115	7 149	64.2	317	0.0	5.7	1.3	107	2.0
Gage, NE	22 230	6 510	64.5	1 333	0.0	9.8	3.4	247	2.1
Garden, NE	3 475	8 517	66.0	118	0.0	12.7	3.4	21	1.6
Garfield, NE	2 482	6 159	63.7	100	0.0	4.0	0.0	43	1.5
Gosper, NE	1 720	5 870	65.4	112	0.0	1.8	2.7	16	...
Grant, NE	1 993	8 135	64.7	55	0.0	0.0	0.0	24	1.0
Greeley, NE	4 637	7 112	61.7	184	0.0	0.0	0.0	59	0.4
Hall, NE	51 577	5 481	69.1	3 014	0.0	13.7	6.4	551	4.2
Hamilton, NE	10 113	5 789	67.6	581	0.0	6.0	2.8	147	1.5
Harlan, NE	2 406	5 912	65.0	224	0.0	6.7	0.0	36	3.8
Hayes, NE	1 498	8 463	58.0	62	0.0	9.7	4.8	20	...
Hitchcock, NE	5 939	11 974	59.0	206	0.0	5.8	0.5	35	0.5
Holt, NE	13 257	6 073	65.6	722	0.0	5.0	0.7	189	1.3
Hooker, NE	1 655	8 444	63.7	52	0.0	5.8	0.0	25	...
Howard, NE	9 076	5 673	61.7	331	0.0	9.4	2.1	104	0.7
Jefferson, NE	12 243	6 278	65.2	464	0.0	12.1	5.6	147	3.1
Johnson, NE	6 143	6 542	62.4	240	0.0	7.5	2.1	87	3.5
Kearney, NE	8 217	5 560	62.8	413	0.0	2.9	3.4	119	1.9
Keith, NE	11 759	7 157	66.9	549	0.0	9.8	1.5	130	2.2
Keya Paha, NE	1 086	7 388	66.0	54	0.0	13.0	0.0	16	...
Kimball, NE	4 368	6 118	67.0	193	0.0	4.7	2.1	42	5.6
Knox, NE	13 495	6 648	64.1	490	0.0	5.1	1.2	153	1.5
Lancaster, NE	218 682	6 161	64.4	17 077	0.0	9.0	2.0	2 200	5.8
Lincoln, NE	33 799	5 569	66.6	2 168	0.0	11.5	3.6	435	4.3
Logan, NE	1 559	7 218	69.7	44	0.0	0.0	0.0	14	2.6
Loup, NE	999	7 929	57.5	28	0.0	17.9	7.1	5	...
McPherson, NE	781	6 791	73.4	30	0.0	0.0	0.0	11	...
Madison, NE	36 173	5 540	66.8	2 661	0.1	10.0	2.1	547	1.9
Merrick, NE	9 210	5 900	64.6	456	0.0	15.6	3.1	84	1.4
Morrill, NE	7 133	6 318	62.6	344	0.0	7.3	6.7	81	1.7
Nance, NE	4 692	5 736	65.9	228	0.0	8.8	2.2	52	1.2
Nemaha, NE	10 077	7 830	63.3	607	0.0	8.9	0.0	107	1.1
Nuckolls, NE	5 828	6 714	66.9	296	0.0	7.4	0.0	88	0.9
Otoe, NE	15 900	5 874	69.3	840	0.2	6.4	3.3	197	2.4
Pawnee, NE	4 622	6 612	62.8	160	0.0	6.9	2.5	51	0.9
Perkins, NE	4 662	7 835	65.7	211	0.0	7.6	1.4	50	1.0
Phelps, NE	14 979	7 580	71.3	544	0.0	8.3	1.7	146	3.0
Pierce, NE	8 828	5 573	65.5	548	0.0	5.3	3.8	157	0.9
Platte, NE	29 819	6 323	68.8	2 076	0.0	7.9	2.2	328	3.2
Polk, NE	7 042	5 978	64.7	333	0.0	5.4	4.8	86	0.6
Red Willow, NE	13 481	6 235	67.7	737	0.0	9.5	1.4	192	2.0
Richardson, NE	10 282	5 693	65.8	600	0.0	14.7	3.5	121	2.2
Rock, NE	2 318	7 335	67.9	109	0.0	3.7	1.8	40	...
Saline, NE	14 583	5 397	61.7	1 086	0.7	9.2	3.1	195	1.6
Sarpy, NE	107 573	5 533	66.0	7 065	3.6	13.9	1.6	1 418	1.7
Saunders, NE	17 480	5 802	68.7	1 094	0.0	7.9	4.7	222	2.0
Scotts Bluff, NE	37 120	5 414	67.0	2 264	0.3	10.7	6.8	479	3.4
Seward, NE	19 003	6 816	62.3	1 521	0.0	6.5	1.0	272	1.4

. . . = Not available.

Table C-1. Population, School, and Student Characteristics by County—*Continued*

County	High school graduates, 2000			College enrollment, 2000		College graduates, 2000 (percent)						
	Population 25 years and over	High school diploma or less (percent)	High school diploma or more (percent)	Number	Percent public	Bachelor's degree or more	+/- U.S. percent with bachelor's degree or more	Non-Hispanic White	Black or African American	American Indian and Alaska Native	Asian, Hawaiian, and Pacific Islander	Hispanic or Latino[1]
	30	31	32	33	34	35	36	37	38	39	40	41
NEBRASKA												
Adams, NE	19 814	46.8	86.3	2 565	54.2	19.9	-4.5	20.3	21.6	14.8	18.2	5.6
Antelope, NE	4 939	54.3	85.5	163	92.0	14.3	-10.1	14.3	0.0	11.1	...	40.0
Arthur, NE	306	42.5	89.5	11	72.7	15.7	-8.7	16.1	...	0.0	...	0.0
Banner, NE	551	38.8	94.2	13	92.3	19.6	-4.8	19.7	0.0	...	...	28.6
Blaine, NE	407	45.2	93.4	10	100.0	12.3	-12.1	11.9	...	...	...	...
Boone, NE	4 134	57.4	84.4	131	85.5	13.1	-11.3	13.1	...	0.0	50.0	0.0
Box Butte, NE	7 864	49.4	88.1	394	81.2	15.3	-9.1	16.4	0.0	6.7	0.0	4.1
Boyd, NE	1 698	59.9	83.0	33	93.9	12.8	-11.6	12.8	...	...	33.3	...
Brown, NE	2 478	54.0	83.3	44	88.6	17.2	-7.2	17.0	...	0.0	0.0	50.0
Buffalo, NE	24 177	37.5	89.2	5 852	94.9	30.2	5.8	30.8	52.9	9.0	61.3	11.0
Burt, NE	5 382	56.5	84.1	172	90.7	14.2	-10.2	14.4	0.0	0.0	0.0	4.0
Butler, NE	5 741	58.2	83.4	195	79.0	13.6	-10.8	13.6	0.0	0.0	71.4	0.0
Cass, NE	15 887	47.6	89.4	1 018	79.8	18.7	-5.7	18.8	33.3	11.8	20.0	6.7
Cedar, NE	6 208	56.7	83.5	215	81.4	13.0	-11.4	13.0	...	0.0	...	0.0
Chase, NE	2 791	53.2	86.4	57	93.0	16.6	-7.8	16.8	...	0.0	...	0.0
Cherry, NE	4 115	46.1	85.2	127	74.8	19.4	-5.0	19.7	...	11.5	0.0	22.2
Cheyenne, NE	6 543	48.5	86.7	256	82.4	16.8	-7.6	17.2	...	2.5	52.6	0.0
Clay, NE	4 685	50.7	86.7	193	85.5	16.2	-8.2	16.2	66.7	20.0	42.9	2.2
Colfax, NE	6 562	65.0	72.0	296	90.9	11.5	-12.9	13.2	...	0.0	0.0	3.8
Cuming, NE	6 755	61.8	78.7	200	90.0	12.3	-12.1	12.7	...	0.0	100.0	0.0
Custer, NE	8 026	51.3	87.5	168	85.7	16.1	-8.3	16.2	...	0.0	0.0	8.6
Dakota, NE	12 103	62.8	73.5	647	83.9	12.4	-12.0	14.1	32.7	8.0	8.6	4.8
Dawes, NE	5 018	39.2	86.9	1 769	97.9	28.4	4.0	29.0	0.0	21.1	0.0	6.6
Dawson, NE	15 175	61.9	73.6	530	87.0	14.4	-10.0	17.4	0.0	6.9	8.0	2.1
Deuel, NE	1 515	50.6	85.3	22	90.9	17.4	-7.0	17.1	...	0.0	81.8	0.0
Dixon, NE	4 147	57.4	82.1	179	86.6	14.1	-10.3	14.5	...	22.7	0.0	2.4
Dodge, NE	23 787	56.7	83.5	1 741	49.3	15.0	-9.4	15.4	32.6	0.0	22.5	4.7
Douglas, NE	293 076	38.9	87.3	33 759	70.9	30.6	6.2	33.6	12.0	7.6	57.0	11.1
Dundy, NE	1 630	48.5	82.4	59	86.4	16.7	-7.7	17.1	...	0.0	25.0	0.0
Fillmore, NE	4 561	54.5	88.2	133	86.5	15.7	-8.7	15.8	0.0	0.0	25.0	0.0
Franklin, NE	2 533	53.6	85.7	83	100.0	15.8	-8.6	15.9	...	0.0	0.0	0.0
Frontier, NE	1 941	46.4	88.3	240	99.2	17.9	-6.5	18.1	66.7	0.0	0.0	21.1
Furnas, NE	3 764	55.6	84.2	104	81.7	16.1	-8.3	16.3	...	0.0	0.0	9.5
Gage, NE	15 689	56.9	82.0	800	88.3	15.4	-9.0	15.4	11.1	0.0	81.6	10.6
Garden, NE	1 685	55.1	85.2	23	73.9	14.2	-10.2	14.5	...	0.0	0.0	0.0
Garfield, NE	1 374	55.5	81.1	31	93.5	13.4	-11.0	13.3	...	...	0.0	28.6
Gosper, NE	1 517	50.1	88.9	42	81.0	17.6	-6.8	17.6	...	...	100.0	10.0
Grant, NE	493	41.0	90.3	12	25.0	24.7	0.3	24.9	...	...	...	0.0
Greeley, NE	1 813	56.1	83.2	101	97.0	13.5	-10.9	13.5	0.0	...	...	0.0
Hall, NE	34 369	53.3	82.2	1 645	86.7	15.9	-8.5	17.4	4.7	10.3	24.7	2.9
Hamilton, NE	6 126	45.5	89.6	264	92.4	18.6	-5.8	18.6	0.0	...	...	29.0
Harlan, NE	2 675	52.1	85.8	62	95.2	15.3	-9.1	15.4	25.0	0.0	...	0.0
Hayes, NE	727	51.4	89.1	27	92.6	11.6	-12.8	11.8	...	...	...	0.0
Hitchcock, NE	2 180	52.0	85.6	101	94.1	13.8	-10.6	13.8	0.0	0.0	100.0	0.0
Holt, NE	7 748	56.6	84.5	216	92.1	14.5	-9.9	14.6	...	0.0	28.6	0.0
Hooker, NE	562	51.4	89.7	7	100.0	15.7	-8.7	15.4	...	0.0	...	40.0
Howard, NE	4 327	56.0	87.2	161	91.9	14.2	-10.2	14.4	0.0	0.0	0.0	0.0
Jefferson, NE	5 878	56.4	84.2	184	94.0	14.4	-10.0	14.0	0.0	64.7	0.0	22.2
Johnson, NE	3 143	63.0	80.4	95	85.3	14.7	-9.7	15.0	...	0.0	19.7	3.2
Kearney, NE	4 594	47.0	88.5	205	95.1	21.3	-3.1	21.4	100.0	0.0	0.0	19.0
Keith, NE	6 103	50.3	86.6	145	80.7	16.8	-7.6	17.0	...	19.0	14.7	6.2
Keya Paha, NE	681	53.9	82.2	12	83.3	15.7	-8.7	16.0	...	...	...	0.0
Kimball, NE	2 849	52.5	84.6	84	82.1	13.5	-10.9	13.6	0.0	12.0	60.0	5.7
Knox, NE	6 462	57.6	82.0	197	82.7	14.4	-10.0	14.8	0.0	5.1	26.7	0.0
Lancaster, NE	152 747	34.7	90.5	29 849	86.5	32.6	8.2	33.4	17.7	17.6	36.3	19.3
Lincoln, NE	22 736	47.0	86.3	1 332	90.4	16.2	-8.2	16.6	28.6	12.2	38.7	3.8
Logan, NE	524	47.1	90.8	13	100.0	10.5	-13.9	10.8	...	0.0	...	0.0
Loup, NE	487	50.9	91.8	8	75.0	13.3	-11.1	13.0	...	...	...	66.7
McPherson, NE	360	51.1	88.6	14	100.0	22.2	-2.2	22.5	...	0.0	...	...
Madison, NE	21 724	51.2	82.6	1 964	86.9	17.0	-7.4	18.1	5.0	6.0	29.8	2.8
Merrick, NE	5 432	56.3	85.3	197	79.2	14.9	-9.5	15.1	0.0	0.0	0.0	7.9
Morrill, NE	3 575	55.7	79.4	114	99.1	14.3	-10.1	15.2	0.0	22.2	0.0	3.7
Nance, NE	2 651	58.2	80.6	83	90.4	11.4	-13.0	11.4	...	0.0	33.3	0.0
Nemaha, NE	4 907	47.6	85.5	679	91.5	22.9	-1.5	23.0	0.0	0.0	43.6	8.0
Nuckolls, NE	3 567	55.5	84.5	119	94.1	13.1	-11.3	12.8	100.0	0.0	100.0	6.7
Otoe, NE	10 373	53.9	85.6	496	86.9	18.1	-6.3	18.2	30.8	13.3	26.5	11.3
Pawnee, NE	2 228	61.4	83.7	49	79.6	14.4	-10.0	14.4	...	12.5	0.0	40.0
Perkins, NE	2 159	47.7	87.1	53	90.6	17.6	-6.8	17.8	...	...	0.0	0.0
Phelps, NE	6 565	46.8	89.1	227	88.1	20.4	-4.0	20.8	...	9.1	100.0	0.0
Pierce, NE	5 019	57.6	84.6	282	87.9	13.3	-11.1	13.3	100.0	0.0	15.4	0.0
Platte, NE	19 988	51.5	84.7	1 155	85.4	17.2	-7.2	17.8	0.0	11.4	53.0	2.0
Polk, NE	3 886	53.4	86.6	152	88.8	13.5	-10.9	13.4	...	0.0	...	21.1
Red Willow, NE	7 490	47.0	87.9	454	93.4	15.2	-9.2	15.3	...	45.5	...	5.8
Richardson, NE	6 543	60.1	81.8	209	90.4	13.6	-10.8	13.6	0.0	13.3	26.4	0.0
Rock, NE	1 242	54.6	87.4	22	77.3	12.2	-12.2	12.2	...	0.0	40.0	0.0
Saline, NE	8 691	58.2	81.2	1 012	29.1	14.0	-10.4	15.1	0.0	0.0	12.0	0.0
Sarpy, NE	73 804	31.4	93.3	8 803	78.3	30.2	5.8	30.9	28.2	13.6	33.6	14.8
Saunders, NE	13 047	51.6	86.8	585	83.9	16.9	-7.5	16.9	0.0	0.0	44.4	15.9
Scotts Bluff, NE	24 314	50.0	79.6	1 541	84.8	17.3	-7.1	19.2	0.0	0.8	50.9	5.2
Seward, NE	10 009	44.4	87.5	1 915	47.7	22.6	-1.8	22.4	0.0	10.5	56.8	28.0

[1]Hispanic or Latino persons may be of any race.
. . . = Not available.

Table C-1. Population, School, and Student Characteristics by County—*Continued*

County	State/ County code	County type[1]	Population, 2000		Number of schools and students, 2000–2001			Resident enrollment, 2000			
			Total	Percent 5–17 years	School districts	Schools	Students	Total	Percent public	K–12	Percent public
			1	2	3	4	5	6	7	8	9
Sheridan, NE	31161	9	6 198	19.8	19	22	1 119	1 549	95.1	1 254	97.7
Sherman, NE	31163	9	3 318	19.3	3	5	551	770	97.3	676	98.7
Sioux, NE	31165	9	1 475	19.0	9	9	134	360	90.8	306	92.5
Stanton, NE	31167	9	6 455	23.1	3	4	474	1 832	83.2	1 498	89.3
Thayer, NE	31169	9	6 055	18.4	5	13	1 025	1 356	90.0	1 178	91.5
Thomas, NE	31171	9	729	17.7	2	3	121	166	98.2	141	100.0
Thurston, NE	31173	8	7 171	27.2	5	10	1 851	2 352	91.7	1 970	93.7
Valley, NE	31175	9	4 647	19.1	6	8	734	1 095	90.0	898	92.7
Washington, NE	31177	2	18 780	20.7	3	10	3 386	5 340	81.6	3 954	90.7
Wayne, NE	31179	7	9 851	16.3	5	10	1 685	4 077	95.6	1 673	93.7
Webster, NE	31181	9	4 061	18.4	2	4	655	953	91.3	795	93.8
Wheeler, NE	31183	9	886	21.3	1	3	152	236	94.9	205	94.1
York, NE	31185	7	14 598	19.7	4	12	2 103	4 000	76.6	2 860	89.7
NEVADA	32000										
Churchill, NV	32001	6	23 982	20.9	1	9	4 808	6 660	95.4	5 258	98.1
Clark, NV	32003	2	1 375 765	18.1	1	258	231 654	329 929	90.7	246 960	94.7
Douglas, NV	32005	7	41 259	18.9	1	15	7 033	10 499	90.3	7 885	94.7
Elko, NV	32007	5	45 291	24.0	1	27	10 102	13 237	93.6	10 760	96.7
Esmeralda, NV	32009	9	971	16.2	1	3	107	235	90.2	185	94.1
Eureka, NV	32011	9	1 651	21.9	1	3	305	440	96.1	379	96.6
Humboldt, NV	32013	7	16 106	23.4	1	14	3 805	4 563	95.7	3 824	99.1
Lander, NV	32015	7	5 794	24.7	1	7	1 449	1 755	96.4	1 456	99.0
Lincoln, NV	32017	8	4 165	23.8	1	9	1 018	1 192	98.0	1 007	98.3
Lyon, NV	32019	6	34 501	20.6	1	16	6 666	8 802	91.1	7 280	93.4
Mineral, NV	32021	7	5 071	19.1	1	6	872	1 176	93.5	973	92.8
Nye, NV	32023	2	32 485	17.8	1	16	5 290	6 644	91.6	5 747	94.0
Pershing, NV	32027	9	6 693	19.2	1	4	900	1 830	94.2	1 537	95.3
Storey, NV	32029	8	3 399	15.3	1	4	445	665	92.6	513	93.0
Washoe, NV	32031	2	339 486	17.9	1	89	56 268	89 970	90.4	62 229	93.8
White Pine, NV	32033	7	9 181	18.2	1	8	1 554	2 290	93.1	1 810	98.3
Carson City city, NV	32510	4	52 457	17.1	1	12	8 431	12 998	91.3	9 106	94.6
NEW HAMPSHIRE	33000										
Belknap, NH	33001	6	56 325	18.3	8	30	10 267	13 322	85.3	10 516	91.1
Carroll, NH	33003	6	43 666	17.8	9	26	7 384	9 809	87.8	8 026	92.9
Cheshire, NH	33005	4	73 825	18.1	12	37	10 765	21 073	81.0	13 485	90.1
Coos, NH	33007	7	33 111	17.8	11	30	5 649	7 435	92.0	6 106	94.3
Grafton, NH	33009	5	81 743	16.7	27	59	13 782	24 139	71.5	13 924	93.1
Hillsborough, NH	33011	2	380 841	19.6	24	120	66 091	103 468	76.1	75 632	87.4
Merrimack, NH	33013	4	136 225	19.0	16	58	21 383	36 957	78.0	26 380	89.7
Rockingham, NH	33015	2	277 359	19.9	37	97	49 211	73 404	79.2	55 638	87.7
Strafford, NH	33017	2	112 233	17.7	9	37	16 948	34 333	86.3	20 046	88.8
Sullivan, NH	33019	7	40 458	18.3	11	32	7 204	8 948	88.8	7 435	93.3
NEW JERSEY	34000										
Atlantic, NJ	34001	2	252 552	18.8	29	82	43 489	66 098	85.1	48 899	89.1
Bergen, NJ	34003	0	884 118	16.7	78	273	123 418	220 538	73.2	150 192	83.5
Burlington, NJ	34005	0	423 394	18.7	43	134	71 271	111 053	81.2	82 014	88.2
Camden, NJ	34007	0	508 932	20.0	40	162	87 236	141 671	81.8	104 979	86.8
Cape May, NJ	34009	2	102 326	17.2	18	33	15 419	23 063	83.3	18 054	88.5
Cumberland, NJ	34011	3	146 438	19.1	16	54	25 493	37 622	87.0	29 889	89.4
Essex, NJ	34013	0	793 633	18.8	33	235	121 842	221 424	77.2	155 379	84.8
Gloucester, NJ	34015	0	254 673	19.8	28	80	45 086	73 630	82.0	51 446	87.9
Hudson, NJ	34017	0	608 975	16.2	22	114	79 755	157 624	74.4	106 450	82.1
Hunterdon, NJ	34019	1	121 989	19.1	30	50	21 874	31 562	82.8	23 496	92.0
Mercer, NJ	34021	2	350 761	17.7	21	103	56 398	99 649	73.5	62 905	86.1
Middlesex, NJ	34023	0	750 162	17.1	26	179	108 968	200 431	81.3	130 731	87.9
Monmouth, NJ	34025	0	615 301	19.2	54	175	104 419	165 915	77.4	120 378	86.7
Morris, NJ	34027	0	470 212	17.8	41	153	73 278	122 655	74.7	84 319	87.1
Ocean, NJ	34029	0	510 916	17.0	29	101	74 891	118 859	77.6	88 689	85.9
Passaic, NJ	34031	0	489 049	18.7	24	130	75 058	129 731	77.9	94 172	84.1
Salem, NJ	34033	1	64 285	19.5	15	33	11 879	16 618	86.9	13 039	90.5
Somerset, NJ	34035	0	297 490	18.1	20	77	46 727	76 743	76.9	54 020	86.6
Sussex, NJ	34037	0	144 166	21.1	27	47	27 492	40 610	83.6	30 665	91.6
Union, NJ	34039	0	522 541	17.9	25	151	80 826	136 230	78.3	96 772	85.9
Warren, NJ	34041	1	102 437	19.2	24	41	18 164	26 106	83.3	19 619	91.5
NEW MEXICO	35000										
Bernalillo, NM	35001	2	556 678	18.4	1	131	85 276	156 057	85.3	102 911	87.6
Catron, NM	35003	9	3 543	16.9	2	6	460	714	89.8	583	92.1
Chaves, NM	35005	5	61 382	21.9	4	32	11 794	18 132	91.0	13 835	93.3
Cibola, NM	35006	6	25 595	22.7	1	11	3 623	7 644	86.3	5 833	86.7
Colfax, NM	35007	7	14 189	19.7	4	16	2 520	3 353	93.2	2 885	94.6
Curry, NM	35009	4	45 044	21.5	4	26	9 263	14 012	94.5	9 807	96.3
De Baca, NM	35011	9	2 240	19.0	1	3	382	532	99.6	439	99.5
Dona Ana, NM	35013	3	174 682	21.9	3	61	36 818	60 034	93.9	39 730	95.7
Eddy, NM	35015	5	51 658	21.5	3	27	10 636	14 292	91.9	11 526	94.5
Grant, NM	35017	7	31 002	19.4	2	15	5 464	8 657	92.3	6 107	94.1

[1]County type code is from the Economic Research Service of the USDA. See Notes and Definitions at the end of this section.

Table C-1. School and Student Characteristics by County—*Continued*

County	Characteristics of students, 2000–2001			Staff and students, 2000–2001				Revenues, fiscal 1999			
	Percent with IEP[2]	Percent eligible for free lunch	Percent minority	Number of teachers	Student/ teacher ratio	Local school non-teaching staff	Central admin. staff	Total revenue ($1,000s)	Percentage of revenue from		
									Federal govt.	State govt.	Local govt.
	10	11	12	13	14	15	16	17	18	19	20
Sheridan, NE	14.4	40.9	17.1	103	10.9	72	14	$9 467	5.1	44.0	50.9
Sherman, NE	14.5	45.9	2.7	52	10.6	32	7	6 075	5.7	39.1	55.1
Sioux, NE	15.5	. . .	5.2	24	5.6	5	1	1 690	1.2	11.4	87.5
Stanton, NE	13.5	32.4	5.7	33	14.4	24	5	3 718	2.6	44.8	52.6
Thayer, NE	16.4	29.3	2.3	100	10.3	64	17	9 284	3.4	26.7	69.9
Thomas, NE	18.2	55.7	0.0	15	8.1	13	4	1 172	1.7	25.6	72.7
Thurston, NE	23.1	64.7	60.2	185	10.0	118	25	15 627	36.8	44.1	19.1
Valley, NE	14.6	38.7	4.6	65	11.3	57	8	5 648	5.0	40.0	55.0
Washington, NE	14.6	11.4	1.8	215	15.7	197	23	23 177	3.0	38.1	59.0
Wayne, NE	12.7	24.1	8.7	131	12.9	89	19	12 022	4.4	42.8	52.8
Webster, NE	21.1	35.0	2.6	48	13.6	34	6	5 517	3.4	39.2	57.5
Wheeler, NE	8.6	56.3	0.0	17	8.9	12	3	1 446	1.9	12.0	86.2
York, NE	20.2	23.7	3.5	161	13.1	144	23	16 557	3.2	28.2	68.7
NEVADA											
Churchill, NV	13.8	29.2	23.4	278	17.3	211	21	34 392	7.7	55.0	37.3
Clark, NV	10.6	. . .	50.1	11 745	19.7	7 168	681	1 349 309	4.3	27.9	67.8
Douglas, NV	11.1	22.2	14.1	366	19.2	326	23	51 779	3.5	41.8	54.6
Elko, NV	10.7	24.9	29.6	599	16.9	409	16	76 990	4.6	48.0	47.5
Esmeralda, NV	7.5	. . .	29.9	8	13.4	14	3	1 614	5.4	52.7	41.9
Eureka, NV	22.3	23.6	15.4	29	10.5	34	6	5 926	2.8	4.6	92.6
Humboldt, NV	14.2	25.1	27.5	194	19.6	216	14	29 887	4.0	45.0	51.0
Lander, NV	12.2	19.7	24.1	85	17.0	59	6	14 697	5.1	50.2	44.6
Lincoln, NV	7.1	41.6	12.5	76	13.4	61	5	10 723	9.4	75.5	15.1
Lyon, NV	14.1	38.8	18.4	372	17.9	351	17	47 162	4.4	62.1	33.4
Mineral, NV	20.0	44.5	33.8	61	14.3	65	7	8 900	14.2	59.4	26.4
Nye, NV	16.8	37.5	17.8	334	15.8	254	23	39 956	4.8	56.5	38.7
Pershing, NV	21.0	35.3	31.2	53	17.0	59	5	10 009	5.6	58.0	36.4
Storey, NV	21.6	. . .	11.7	33	13.5	32	5	5 461	4.8	52.2	43.0
Washoe, NV	11.6	30.3	34.0	2 980	18.9	2 151	198	328 096	4.2	28.3	67.5
White Pine, NV	16.1	32.7	17.8	93	16.7	103	18	15 298	3.2	65.3	31.6
Carson City city, NV	14.2	29.4	25.8	468	18.0	317	21	58 849	4.4	40.0	55.6
NEW HAMPSHIRE											
Belknap, NH	14.3	19.6	1.8	738	13.9	687	40	77 311	3.4	7.0	89.6
Carroll, NH	12.6	20.5	1.6	545	13.5	529	38	64 809	4.0	4.4	91.6
Cheshire, NH	15.0	20.0	2.2	791	13.6	816	55	102 902	4.0	12.7	83.3
Coos, NH	13.8	25.8	1.6	434	13.0	395	38	42 469	6.4	15.1	78.5
Grafton, NH	14.0	18.4	3.1	1 100	12.5	967	105	128 646	3.0	8.5	88.5
Hillsborough, NH	14.1	14.1	8.2	4 265	15.5	3 385	354	412 797	4.6	6.6	88.8
Merrimack, NH	13.6	15.2	2.9	1 470	14.5	1 317	98	163 467	3.7	10.5	85.8
Rockingham, NH	15.6	9.3	3.1	3 339	14.7	2 994	176	349 031	2.8	6.1	91.0
Strafford, NH	15.0	19.3	3.4	1 131	15.0	1 007	82	114 118	4.9	14.1	81.0
Sullivan, NH	15.1	22.5	1.3	547	13.2	576	68	42 738	4.2	17.1	78.7
NEW JERSEY											
Atlantic, NJ	. . .	39.0	46.3	3 129	13.9	. . .	. . .	482 831	4.2	41.7	54.1
Bergen, NJ	. . .	12.7	32.8	8 818	14.0	. . .	. . .	1 468 599	2.5	16.0	81.5
Burlington, NJ	. . .	17.1	26.7	5 015	14.2	. . .	. . .	809 661	4.9	39.9	55.2
Camden, NJ	. . .	33.8	42.6	6 219	14.0	. . .	. . .	994 321	4.3	55.0	40.6
Cape May, NJ	. . .	29.6	15.6	1 278	12.1	. . .	. . .	194 536	4.0	33.3	62.7
Cumberland, NJ	. . .	49.4	53.2	2 048	12.4	. . .	. . .	303 237	4.9	74.8	20.3
Essex, NJ	. . .	52.5	69.8	8 750	13.9	. . .	. . .	1 498 547	4.8	51.8	43.3
Gloucester, NJ	. . .	19.8	16.9	3 078	14.6	. . .	. . .	490 787	3.2	50.6	46.2
Hudson, NJ	. . .	63.4	79.4	5 458	14.6	. . .	. . .	961 333	6.0	58.8	35.1
Hunterdon, NJ	. . .	3.6	5.5	1 436	15.2	. . .	. . .	260 557	1.3	21.4	77.3
Mercer, NJ	. . .	26.7	45.7	3 907	14.4	. . .	. . .	660 655	3.0	37.8	59.2
Middlesex, NJ	. . .	22.3	45.6	7 475	14.6	. . .	. . .	1 201 259	2.8	29.4	67.8
Monmouth, NJ	. . .	16.5	22.6	7 214	14.5	. . .	. . .	1 115 450	2.9	33.4	63.7
Morris, NJ	. . .	8.2	19.4	5 164	14.2	. . .	. . .	860 868	1.6	21.0	77.3
Ocean, NJ	. . .	17.0	12.0	4 923	15.2	. . .	. . .	745 200	3.0	38.5	58.5
Passaic, NJ	. . .	45.0	58.4	5 261	14.3	. . .	. . .	857 302	4.7	52.2	43.0
Salem, NJ	. . .	30.1	26.7	926	12.8	. . .	. . .	135 278	4.5	54.6	40.9
Somerset, NJ	. . .	11.3	30.1	3 375	13.8	. . .	. . .	519 572	1.5	20.3	78.2
Sussex, NJ	. . .	8.1	5.6	1 986	13.8	. . .	. . .	296 379	2.6	41.2	56.2
Union, NJ	. . .	37.4	55.6	5 690	14.2	. . .	. . .	907 670	3.6	38.2	58.2
Warren, NJ	. . .	13.5	7.7	1 337	13.6	. . .	. . .	213 471	2.3	40.7	57.1
NEW MEXICO											
Bernalillo, NM	20.1	44.9	60.0	5 479	15.6	4 672	943	528 303	8.3	74.9	16.8
Catron, NM	18.5	62.8	28.0	43	10.7	32	11	4 564	8.8	86.1	5.1
Chaves, NM	25.8	64.2	60.9	783	15.1	905	168	73 733	10.1	81.6	8.3
Cibola, NM	12.4	74.6	78.8	235	15.4	191	40	21 545	16.7	77.1	6.2
Colfax, NM	20.0	57.3	56.1	185	13.6	133	40	20 427	7.6	80.4	12.0
Curry, NM	20.8	60.0	50.4	635	14.6	501	117	53 653	11.1	78.7	10.2
De Baca, NM	26.4	63.9	41.6	34	11.2	31	15	3 555	7.7	82.8	9.6
Dona Ana, NM	20.9	66.2	79.3	2 333	15.8	2 252	498	222 975	11.5	78.6	10.0
Eddy, NM	23.6	48.8	51.7	635	16.7	555	82	69 148	8.5	74.2	17.3
Grant, NM	19.1	58.4	61.7	364	15.0	499	98	41 248	9.6	78.6	11.8

[2]IEP = Individual Education Program. See Notes and Definitions at the end of this section.
. . . = Not available.

Table C-1. Population, School, and Student Characteristics by County—*Continued*

County	Current expenditures, fiscal 1999			Resident population 16 to 19 years, 2000				Outcomes, 1999–2000	
	Amount ($1,000s)	Amount per student	Percent for instruction	Total population 16 to 19 years	Percent in Armed Forces	Percent high school graduates	Percent not enrolled, not grads, not Armed Forces, not empl.	Number of graduates	Dropouts grades 9–12 (percent)
	21	22	23	24	25	26	27	28	29
Sheridan, NE	$7 977	$6 449	66.4	378	0.0	5.6	2.1	104	1.2
Sherman, NE	4 164	7 082	67.6	194	0.0	7.7	0.0	45	2.5
Sioux, NE	1 448	8 994	70.0	86	0.0	3.5	2.3	11	2.1
Stanton, NE	2 865	5 552	65.2	418	0.0	4.5	3.3	40	0.6
Thayer, NE	8 281	7 145	66.7	327	0.0	4.0	0.6	104	0.7
Thomas, NE	1 117	8 398	62.7	45	0.0	0.0	0.0	11	. . .
Thurston, NE	11 542	7 029	59.8	465	0.0	9.9	15.7	103	6.3
Valley, NE	5 031	6 417	63.2	207	0.0	6.3	2.9	68	1.0
Washington, NE	18 553	5 305	62.9	1 189	0.0	6.9	0.4	289	3.0
Wayne, NE	9 892	5 468	65.8	1 133	0.0	5.5	1.1	145	1.0
Webster, NE	4 383	6 288	66.0	201	0.0	6.0	0.0	61	0.9
Wheeler, NE	1 467	9 715	62.9	57	0.0	7.0	3.5	14	. . .
York, NE	13 592	6 328	67.0	919	0.0	6.0	1.6	167	0.9
NEVADA									
Churchill, NV	30 008	6 208	62.2	1 249	1.8	15.1	3.0	278	2.4
Clark, NV	1 100 861	5 402	59.0	65 482	0.5	13.6	9.5	8 965	7.1
Douglas, NV	44 859	6 127	59.7	2 027	0.0	9.5	4.2	467	2.7
Elko, NV	65 497	6 272	61.4	3 053	0.0	8.1	6.8	564	4.1
Esmeralda, NV	1 456	12 772	44.9	68	0.0	8.8	0.0	0	. . .
Eureka, NV	5 172	14 447	56.1	93	0.0	5.4	8.6	23	. . .
Humboldt, NV	26 075	6 081	62.2	1 059	0.0	11.7	5.9	257	2.7
Lander, NV	10 687	6 275	62.1	327	0.0	5.2	0.0	83	3.4
Lincoln, NV	9 730	9 249	63.0	328	0.0	11.6	2.1	92	0.2
Lyon, NV	38 325	6 034	57.4	2 086	0.0	12.7	4.5	340	2.5
Mineral, NV	7 474	7 193	61.2	269	0.0	9.7	3.7	50	6.8
Nye, NV	34 962	6 640	61.3	1 235	0.0	11.2	5.9	313	4.3
Pershing, NV	7 396	7 509	62.9	355	0.0	8.5	6.8	55	1.6
Storey, NV	5 037	9 935	56.4	161	0.0	34.2	0.0	20	8.2
Washoe, NV	283 817	5 374	62.5	17 960	0.1	11.1	6.6	2 471	5.7
White Pine, NV	12 604	6 798	55.9	471	0.0	9.3	2.5	126	16.0
Carson City city, NV	50 437	6 035	61.8	2 290	0.0	10.5	7.0	447	3.9
NEW HAMPSHIRE									
Belknap, NH	66 564	6 572	63.5	2 705	0.0	9.9	4.1	586	. . .
Carroll, NH	53 691	7 292	63.8	2 073	0.0	11.4	2.3	439	. . .
Cheshire, NH	91 348	6 922	64.1	5 241	0.0	6.8	3.1	676	. . .
Coos, NH	36 205	6 283	62.5	1 721	0.0	8.7	5.1	376	. . .
Grafton, NH	113 465	7 629	65.4	6 267	0.0	6.7	2.9	929	. . .
Hillsborough, NH	361 383	5 770	66.8	19 010	0.1	9.0	3.3	3 713	. . .
Merrimack, NH	138 523	6 413	62.0	7 363	0.0	8.7	3.1	1 052	. . .
Rockingham, NH	309 371	7 011	67.9	13 218	0.1	9.2	2.8	2 713	. . .
Strafford, NH	98 529	6 031	66.5	8 166	0.0	9.9	2.6	921	. . .
Sullivan, NH	35 634	6 815	68.3	1 904	0.0	11.1	3.2	424	. . .
NEW JERSEY									
Atlantic, NJ	386 448	9 393	59.9	12 559	0.0	10.2	5.5	2 138	5.6
Bergen, NJ	1 308 915	11 203	62.2	37 929	0.0	6.7	1.7	7 652	1.3
Burlington, NJ	648 208	9 385	60.6	21 045	1.2	9.8	3.9	4 283	2.4
Camden, NJ	888 381	10 098	60.6	27 751	0.0	8.2	6.2	5 062	4.0
Cape May, NJ	157 294	10 348	60.5	4 563	3.3	11.6	4.0	874	3.6
Cumberland, NJ	265 275	10 531	61.1	7 976	0.0	11.4	6.0	1 507	5.6
Essex, NJ	1 378 022	11 608	58.9	41 257	0.1	10.3	6.9	6 140	4.1
Gloucester, NJ	402 850	9 179	59.1	14 528	0.0	9.4	2.8	2 617	3.3
Hudson, NJ	807 807	10 387	63.9	29 361	0.1	10.0	7.7	4 123	4.9
Hunterdon, NJ	217 138	10 543	58.1	5 282	0.0	5.9	2.2	1 452	0.9
Mercer, NJ	581 375	11 078	60.7	19 442	0.1	7.0	4.0	3 526	4.4
Middlesex, NJ	1 026 453	10 019	61.9	37 947	0.0	8.1	3.6	6 214	2.3
Monmouth, NJ	968 689	9 816	60.5	29 062	1.0	8.1	2.6	6 342	1.6
Morris, NJ	755 343	10 869	59.7	20 713	0.0	6.3	1.8	4 303	0.9
Ocean, NJ	643 641	8 976	61.3	21 495	0.2	10.7	2.8	4 133	3.0
Passaic, NJ	753 913	10 444	62.7	25 693	0.0	10.8	7.1	3 825	6.4
Salem, NJ	113 658	9 567	60.1	3 614	0.0	10.2	3.7	804	4.4
Somerset, NJ	435 583	10 312	59.9	11 724	0.0	7.4	2.0	2 411	1.2
Sussex, NJ	269 201	10 046	59.8	7 179	0.0	8.9	1.5	1 676	1.5
Union, NJ	803 634	10 552	61.0	24 207	0.0	9.8	3.9	4 437	3.5
Warren, NJ	169 411	9 788	59.9	4 860	0.0	11.6	2.3	1 067	3.2
NEW MEXICO									
Bernalillo, NM	445 559	5 190	60.0	31 866	0.5	12.3	7.0	4 668	8.8
Catron, NM	3 994	8 286	46.9	188	0.0	8.5	13.3	30	1.4
Chaves, NM	66 109	5 243	57.0	4 460	0.3	10.1	8.2	696	4.9
Cibola, NM	20 717	5 498	54.4	1 603	0.1	17.2	7.4	287	3.2
Colfax, NM	16 576	6 148	53.7	952	0.2	10.8	10.5	178	6.7
Curry, NM	48 854	5 036	58.0	2 839	7.6	19.2	5.5	597	5.1
De Baca, NM	3 233	7 249	56.9	131	0.0	7.6	3.8	35	0.7
Dona Ana, NM	196 227	5 370	54.6	12 338	0.1	8.2	6.6	1 952	7.1
Eddy, NM	60 049	5 320	56.7	3 339	0.0	11.7	7.7	699	2.4
Grant, NM	35 096	5 901	55.2	1 799	0.0	13.3	7.1	368	4.7

. . . = Not available.

Table C-1. Population, School, and Student Characteristics by County—*Continued*

County	Population 25 years and over	High school diploma or less (percent)	High school diploma or more (percent)	Number	Percent public	Bachelor's degree or more	+/- U.S. percent with bachelor's degree or more	Non-Hispanic White	Black or African American	American Indian and Alaska Native	Asian, Hawaiian, and Pacific Islander	Hispanic or Latino[1]
	30	31	32	33	34	35	36	37	38	39	40	41
Sheridan, NE	4 232	50.3	86.1	186	88.2	17.2	-7.2	17.9	0.0	5.2	10.0	21.6
Sherman, NE	2 355	58.8	82.0	67	85.1	10.8	-13.6	11.0	0.0	...	0.0	0.0
Sioux, NE	1 009	45.5	86.4	36	80.6	21.5	-2.9	22.0	...	50.0	0.0	0.0
Stanton, NE	4 065	51.8	86.2	193	80.3	13.7	-10.7	14.0	...	0.0	0.0	8.3
Thayer, NE	4 301	56.4	80.9	99	89.9	15.0	-9.4	15.0	...	0.0	...	16.0
Thomas, NE	528	48.5	83.7	19	100.0	17.2	-7.2	17.9	...	0.0	...	0.0
Thurston, NE	3 953	56.7	80.4	217	81.1	12.0	-12.4	14.9	14.3	6.7	33.3	0.0
Valley, NE	3 285	53.4	84.7	100	84.0	16.4	-8.0	16.5	...	0.0	0.0	0.0
Washington, NE	11 956	45.9	89.7	993	56.6	22.7	-1.7	22.7	45.2	34.2	24.2	10.0
Wayne, NE	5 115	44.1	87.0	2 296	98.6	28.0	3.6	28.2	100.0	0.0	35.7	3.3
Webster, NE	2 910	55.9	83.6	82	89.0	13.7	-10.7	13.7	0.0	0.0	24.0	0.0
Wheeler, NE	577	46.4	90.8	17	100.0	14.9	-9.5	15.1	...	...	...	0.0
York, NE	9 579	50.4	87.2	890	38.4	17.0	-7.4	17.3	0.0	12.5	100.0	3.5
NEVADA		42.7	87.4									
Churchill, NV	15 167	45.4	85.1	1 101	87.1	16.7	-7.7	17.6	21.4	7.1	21.8	7.4
Clark, NV	900 400	50.4	79.5	64 457	85.0	17.3	-7.1	20.0	11.9	10.1	26.2	6.4
Douglas, NV	29 279	35.0	91.6	1 924	88.8	23.2	-1.2	24.0	35.1	6.8	25.7	12.2
Elko, NV	26 798	51.3	79.1	1 917	85.2	14.8	-9.6	17.4	8.4	6.1	19.7	4.0
Esmeralda, NV	711	65.4	78.9	39	79.5	9.6	-14.8	9.9	...	0.0	0.0	0.0
Eureka, NV	1 104	55.0	76.7	39	89.7	13.6	-10.8	14.4	0.0	0.0	30.0	0.0
Humboldt, NV	9 846	53.0	78.3	432	88.7	14.2	-10.2	17.1	0.0	0.5	12.5	4.2
Lander, NV	3 581	57.6	79.2	210	83.3	10.8	-13.6	11.9	...	6.6	0.0	4.9
Lincoln, NV	2 654	54.7	83.0	116	94.0	15.1	-9.3	15.1	0.0	0.0	93.8	3.4
Lyon, NV	22 863	51.4	81.5	1 086	88.6	11.3	-13.1	12.0	24.6	5.0	17.8	3.3
Mineral, NV	3 527	59.1	77.1	142	95.1	10.1	-14.3	11.9	0.0	6.8	64.3	3.4
Nye, NV	23 234	62.0	79.2	601	83.5	10.1	-14.3	10.5	7.2	2.9	7.2	6.9
Pershing, NV	4 498	60.7	75.9	230	91.7	8.7	-15.7	11.1	0.8	4.2	4.3	3.1
Storey, NV	2 540	43.0	86.7	144	96.5	18.0	-6.4	16.8	...	30.5	36.7	32.5
Washoe, NV	221 837	41.2	83.9	22 839	89.9	23.7	-0.7	26.4	16.7	8.8	32.4	6.9
White Pine, NV	6 184	52.8	82.0	359	78.8	11.8	-12.6	13.5	2.1	6.0	9.5	4.8
Carson City city, NV	35 953	45.4	82.5	2 995	92.5	18.5	-5.9	20.1	3.6	13.4	40.3	4.8
NEW HAMPSHIRE		42.7	87.4	...	...	28.7	4.3	28.5	27.8	17.0	54.2	22.7
Belknap, NH	39 260	46.9	85.7	2 006	72.5	23.3	-1.1	23.4	37.0	10.4	24.9	26.9
Carroll, NH	31 534	44.0	88.2	1 231	71.3	26.5	2.1	26.5	31.0	17.8	25.6	31.9
Cheshire, NH	48 032	48.2	86.2	6 717	66.8	26.6	2.2	26.5	36.0	17.3	46.2	28.0
Coos, NH	23 490	64.7	76.9	932	82.3	11.9	-12.5	11.9	11.1	3.8	20.4	23.9
Grafton, NH	52 795	43.3	87.7	9 172	41.2	32.7	8.3	32.4	40.7	16.8	68.4	42.7
Hillsborough, NH	251 908	40.5	87.0	20 594	48.9	30.1	5.7	29.9	24.3	21.0	58.1	18.3
Merrimack, NH	91 278	41.5	88.2	8 216	50.1	29.1	4.7	29.0	26.4	1.5	59.1	28.7
Rockingham, NH	187 172	38.1	90.5	12 255	61.9	31.7	7.3	31.5	32.3	26.0	52.3	26.0
Strafford, NH	70 319	44.1	86.4	12 656	88.2	26.4	2.0	26.2	29.3	19.5	43.9	29.7
Sullivan, NH	28 199	55.5	83.0	1 053	71.4	19.7	-4.7	19.6	64.9	4.8	26.1	24.0
NEW JERSEY												
Atlantic, NJ	168 546	56.5	78.2	12 659	80.6	18.7	-5.7	21.0	10.8	21.1	30.7	7.2
Bergen, NJ	623 469	39.6	86.6	50 740	58.0	38.2	13.8	38.1	27.3	19.3	60.8	20.8
Burlington, NJ	285 553	44.0	87.2	20 140	71.3	28.4	4.0	29.7	19.8	22.5	48.0	18.8
Camden, NJ	331 765	51.9	80.3	25 699	72.9	24.0	-0.4	26.5	13.9	12.0	47.6	8.6
Cape May, NJ	72 878	54.5	81.9	3 466	72.4	22.0	-2.4	22.6	7.8	28.0	54.3	13.5
Cumberland, NJ	96 899	67.8	68.5	5 087	81.1	11.7	-12.7	14.4	6.0	7.5	46.4	5.6
Essex, NJ	513 570	51.6	75.6	47 684	62.1	27.5	3.1	41.5	14.6	12.7	62.9	10.7
Gloucester, NJ	164 801	52.6	84.3	17 149	76.0	22.0	-2.4	21.9	17.1	17.7	54.2	19.0
Hudson, NJ	408 799	56.3	70.5	41 431	58.0	25.3	0.9	31.8	16.5	19.2	56.4	12.1
Hunterdon, NJ	83 548	34.0	91.5	4 876	68.7	41.8	17.4	42.0	14.4	30.3	70.9	29.6
Mercer, NJ	231 139	43.8	81.8	28 687	54.5	34.0	9.6	39.5	12.8	17.3	71.1	11.6
Middlesex, NJ	501 552	44.7	84.4	54 877	77.1	33.0	8.6	29.7	26.1	22.5	70.4	11.4
Monmouth, NJ	413 058	39.5	87.9	30 358	61.6	34.6	10.2	36.0	14.8	18.1	63.5	16.6
Morris, NJ	323 881	33.4	90.6	25 292	56.0	44.1	19.7	44.8	26.8	27.9	69.9	18.5
Ocean, NJ	358 354	54.7	83.0	20 490	60.2	19.5	-4.9	19.5	15.3	11.3	47.1	12.2
Passaic, NJ	316 401	57.9	73.3	25 785	68.2	21.2	-3.2	27.9	8.7	4.7	48.1	7.8
Salem, NJ	42 789	59.8	79.4	2 436	79.6	15.2	-9.2	16.5	7.2	3.2	48.6	8.9
Somerset, NJ	204 343	31.9	89.6	14 627	65.9	46.5	22.1	47.4	31.5	29.9	76.0	18.5
Sussex, NJ	95 094	43.6	89.8	6 368	72.2	27.2	2.8	27.1	24.5	18.8	56.8	22.5
Union, NJ	351 903	50.4	79.3	28 216	65.1	28.5	4.1	35.0	16.6	16.9	61.0	12.7
Warren, NJ	69 457	50.5	84.9	4 235	64.1	24.4	0.0	24.4	24.7	12.5	51.9	18.5
NEW MEXICO												
Bernalillo, NM	358 680	40.3	84.4	44 365	87.1	30.5	6.1	42.2	22.9	15.0	38.8	13.8
Catron, NM	2 657	50.6	78.4	92	81.5	18.4	-6.0	20.7	100.0	9.4	100.0	8.3
Chaves, NM	37 811	53.9	72.6	3 290	86.4	16.2	-8.2	22.6	5.9	10.6	54.9	5.1
Cibola, NM	15 273	61.5	75.0	1 259	83.2	12.0	-12.4	23.4	11.8	7.4	29.7	6.0
Colfax, NM	9 518	53.4	80.8	324	81.2	18.5	-5.9	28.4	0.0	7.2	0.0	5.4
Curry, NM	26 403	49.5	78.4	3 355	94.7	15.3	-9.1	19.6	11.0	5.9	27.7	4.2
De Baca, NM	1 584	57.6	72.3	42	100.0	16.2	-8.2	23.2	...	0.0	0.0	2.2
Dona Ana, NM	99 893	52.4	70.0	17 779	93.3	22.3	-2.1	39.3	25.0	14.7	64.2	9.6
Eddy, NM	32 572	59.4	75.0	1 944	83.2	13.5	-10.9	17.3	13.7	8.4	51.4	4.8
Grant, NM	20 350	49.7	79.4	2 049	93.1	20.5	-3.9	28.5	40.0	10.0	28.2	9.8

[1]Hispanic or Latino persons may be of any race.
... = Not available.

Table C-1. Population, School, and Student Characteristics by County—*Continued*

County	State/County code	County type[1]	Population, 2000		Number of schools and students, 2000–2001			Resident enrollment, 2000			
			Total	Percent 5–17 years	School districts	Schools	Students	Total	Percent public	K–12	Percent public
			1	2	3	4	5	6	7	8	9
Guadalupe, NM	35019	9	4 680	19.0	2	7	922	1 279	92.0	1 017	93.9
Harding, NM	35021	9	810	17.2	2	4	167	174	89.7	151	91.4
Hidalgo, NM	35023	7	5 932	24.1	2	8	1 185	1 699	97.4	1 499	98.7
Lea, NM	35025	5	55 511	22.4	5	38	12 016	16 534	93.0	13 004	96.2
Lincoln, NM	35027	7	19 411	17.7	5	17	3 565	4 483	91.9	3 497	92.5
Los Alamos, NM	35028	3	18 343	20.2	1	7	3 636	5 057	87.5	3 656	94.1
Luna, NM	35029	6	25 016	22.3	1	11	5 325	6 401	97.3	5 600	98.7
McKinley, NM	35031	5	74 798	28.8	2	38	15 711	28 043	90.7	22 597	92.2
Mora, NM	35033	8	5 180	20.6	2	7	836	1 418	90.1	1 112	89.1
Otero, NM	35035	4	62 298	22.0	3	22	9 058	18 135	92.6	13 944	94.9
Quay, NM	35037	7	10 155	19.5	4	13	1 964	2 619	97.9	2 062	98.5
Rio Arriba, NM	35039	6	41 190	21.6	4	29	6 595	11 581	87.8	8 918	89.7
Roosevelt, NM	35041	7	18 018	20.6	4	15	3 437	6 636	94.3	3 739	95.8
Sandoval, NM	35043	2	89 908	22.2	4	28	15 075	26 442	87.1	20 360	89.8
San Juan, NM	35045	5	113 801	24.6	4	52	24 136	36 608	93.6	28 682	95.4
San Miguel, NM	35047	6	30 126	20.9	3	20	5 497	9 583	90.9	6 438	95.0
Santa Fe, NM	35049	3	129 292	17.9	2	36	15 356	33 486	79.4	23 538	85.6
Sierra, NM	35051	6	13 270	15.3	1	6	1 708	2 595	90.1	2 156	93.0
Socorro, NM	35053	7	18 078	21.4	2	10	2 509	5 817	94.3	3 840	97.1
Taos, NM	35055	7	29 979	18.7	4	23	5 264	7 505	87.0	5 752	87.8
Torrance, NM	35057	8	16 911	23.4	3	15	5 939	4 660	93.5	3 946	94.2
Union, NM	35059	9	4 174	21.3	2	7	846	1 084	91.6	977	92.5
Valencia, NM	35061	2	66 152	22.5	2	22	13 323	18 520	90.7	14 783	92.7
NEW YORK	36000										
Albany, NY	36001	2	294 565	16.9	14	65	41 808	83 713	77.0	50 548	87.1
Allegany, NY	36003	7	49 927	18.8	12	21	8 442	16 263	76.6	9 624	93.7
Bronx, NY	36005	0	1 332 650	21.6	*	*	*	419 114	78.5	310 307	85.0
Broome, NY	36007	2	200 536	17.4	13	57	33 468	56 153	89.7	35 644	91.1
Cattaraugus, NY	36009	4	83 955	20.0	14	36	17 700	22 211	82.6	16 729	93.4
Cayuga, NY	36011	2	81 963	19.2	8	26	12 438	20 377	88.5	15 927	93.1
Chautauqua, NY	36013	3	139 750	18.7	18	54	24 109	37 459	92.0	26 607	94.8
Chemung, NY	36015	3	91 070	18.4	4	24	13 810	22 739	79.9	17 140	88.2
Chenango, NY	36017	6	51 401	20.2	9	26	10 084	13 094	93.3	10 767	95.8
Clinton, NY	36019	5	79 894	17.8	9	33	13 749	22 184	90.3	14 676	90.5
Columbia, NY	36021	6	63 094	18.7	7	21	9 898	15 183	85.1	12 255	89.8
Cortland, NY	36023	4	48 599	17.8	5	17	7 753	15 221	92.8	8 751	93.4
Delaware, NY	36025	6	48 055	17.9	13	23	7 727	11 874	93.4	8 884	97.2
Dutchess, NY	36027	2	280 150	18.8	14	75	46 443	78 962	77.2	53 680	89.2
Erie, NY	36029	0	950 265	18.2	31	228	144 573	256 351	78.9	176 728	85.1
Essex, NY	36031	6	38 851	17.8	11	15	5 020	8 857	89.2	7 210	92.4
Franklin, NY	36033	7	51 134	17.8	8	22	9 214	12 024	87.7	9 270	96.0
Fulton, NY	36035	4	55 073	19.2	8	24	10 130	13 249	93.7	10 748	96.9
Genesee, NY	36037	1	60 370	20.0	8	21	10 747	16 129	87.5	12 183	90.8
Greene, NY	36039	6	48 195	17.6	6	18	7 731	10 810	88.9	8 504	93.9
Hamilton, NY	36041	8	5 379	15.4	7	7	698	1 059	92.0	868	94.2
Herkimer, NY	36043	2	64 427	18.8	12	26	12 110	16 600	92.9	12 567	97.5
Jefferson, NY	36045	5	111 738	19.1	12	38	19 311	28 331	89.9	21 771	92.0
Kings, NY	36047	0	2 465 326	19.5	*	*	*	731 672	73.8	512 325	79.7
Lewis, NY	36049	6	26 944	21.7	5	15	5 002	6 915	92.4	6 031	95.0
Livingston, NY	36051	1	64 328	18.0	9	22	10 673	19 552	88.4	11 944	92.1
Madison, NY	36053	2	69 441	19.0	11	30	12 845	20 630	79.0	13 451	95.8
Monroe, NY	36055	0	735 343	19.2	20	183	124 007	214 378	76.3	145 226	89.3
Montgomery, NY	36057	2	49 708	18.6	5	18	7 943	11 609	89.2	9 532	92.9
Nassau, NY	36059	0	1 334 544	18.2	57	315	207 709	357 675	73.7	246 184	86.3
New York, NY	36061	0	1 537 195	11.8	*1	*1 207	*1 066 945	358 066	60.2	195 948	78.0
Niagara, NY	36063	2	219 846	18.7	10	60	35 937	57 484	82.9	41 852	88.9
Oneida, NY	36065	2	235 469	18.2	16	75	38 332	60 218	84.4	44 252	92.7
Onondaga, NY	36067	2	458 336	19.2	19	126	78 522	132 420	76.0	89 450	91.3
Ontario, NY	36069	1	100 224	19.4	10	31	18 935	26 901	81.4	19 305	92.7
Orange, NY	36071	2	341 367	21.4	18	86	64 332	101 077	79.1	75 204	86.4
Orleans, NY	36073	1	44 171	19.9	6	15	8 785	10 701	92.0	8 851	95.3
Oswego, NY	36075	2	122 377	20.6	10	42	25 926	35 840	93.8	25 412	96.5
Otsego, NY	36077	6	61 676	17.9	12	23	9 748	19 248	90.9	11 317	95.1
Putnam, NY	36079	1	95 745	19.6	6	22	15 747	25 652	78.7	18 867	89.6
Queens, NY	36081	0	2 229 379	16.4	*	*	*	586 090	75.1	389 860	82.8
Rensselaer, NY	36083	2	152 538	18.2	13	47	23 576	42 526	73.1	27 840	88.2
Richmond, NY	36085	0	443 728	18.8	*	*	*	122 303	69.2	85 662	75.4
Rockland, NY	36087	0	286 753	20.4	10	67	41 313	84 629	62.3	60 015	69.8
St. Lawrence, NY	36089	5	111 931	18.0	18	41	18 502	32 990	80.4	20 580	94.6
Saratoga, NY	36091	2	200 635	18.6	12	53	34 803	51 400	82.0	37 384	93.5
Schenectady, NY	36093	2	146 555	18.2	6	41	22 329	37 662	81.0	26 871	92.1
Schoharie, NY	36095	2	31 582	18.4	6	13	5 570	8 606	89.5	5 836	95.9
Schuyler, NY	36097	8	19 224	19.5	2	6	2 454	4 643	90.4	3 770	93.8
Seneca, NY	36099	6	33 342	19.2	4	13	5 293	8 433	83.2	6 410	89.8
Steuben, NY	36101	4	98 726	19.9	15	42	19 652	24 686	90.3	19 977	93.6
Suffolk, NY	36103	0	1 419 369	19.0	73	338	253 754	387 491	82.8	273 741	92.7
Sullivan, NY	36105	6	73 966	19.1	9	26	11 566	18 389	86.8	14 622	91.8
Tioga, NY	36107	2	51 784	20.7	6	20	9 428	13 238	89.8	10 850	93.5
Tompkins, NY	36109	5	96 501	14.5	8	31	13 424	42 942	47.7	14 395	94.5
Ulster, NY	36111	4	177 749	18.0	11	54	28 998	46 266	87.5	32 223	92.1
Warren, NY	36113	3	63 303	18.6	9	21	11 290	15 874	88.8	11 896	96.7
Washington, NY	36115	3	61 042	19.0	12	24	11 410	14 653	92.8	12 040	96.9
Wayne, NY	36117	1	93 765	20.8	11	38	18 543	24 533	90.1	19 792	94.2
Westchester, NY	36119	0	923 459	18.0	49	252	143 970	244 926	71.3	170 768	84.4

[1]County type code is from the Economic Research Service of the USDA. See Notes and Definitions at the end of this section.
* = Bronx, Kings, Queens, and Richmond Counties are included with New York County.

Table C-1. School and Student Characteristics by County—*Continued*

County	Characteristics of students, 2000–2001			Staff and students, 2000–2001				Revenues, fiscal 1999			
	Percent with IEP2	Percent eligible for free lunch	Percent minority	Number of teachers	Student/ teacher ratio	Local school non-teaching staff	Central admin. staff	Total revenue ($1,000s)	Percentage of revenue from		
									Federal govt.	State govt.	Local govt.
	10	11	12	13	14	15	16	17	18	19	20
Guadalupe, NM	19.4	74.3	93.8	70	13.2	77	20	$9 148	11.2	75.5	13.2
Harding, NM	25.7	47.3	41.3	19	8.8	14	5	2 798	6.3	83.1	10.6
Hidalgo, NM	20.6	66.1	67.9	92	12.9	105	19	11 990	8.2	77.7	14.0
Lea, NM	20.5	58.7	56.7	746	16.1	588	115	70 799	9.9	76.3	13.7
Lincoln, NM	20.3	64.1	46.3	249	14.3	186	49	28 660	11.9	72.7	15.4
Los Alamos, NM	28.7	. . .	20.8	257	14.1	442	92	32 369	29.7	51.4	18.9
Luna, NM	9.3	75.9	78.9	317	16.8	273	37	29 453	12.4	78.7	8.9
McKinley, NM	15.9	77.5	92.7	1 067	14.7	1 087	223	106 375	47.1	44.2	8.7
Mora, NM	20.6	77.2	93.9	70	11.9	60	19	8 406	18.0	75.7	6.3
Otero, NM	16.9	46.4	43.2	584	15.5	578	98	52 340	13.0	75.5	11.5
Quay, NM	17.8	54.8	52.5	152	12.9	128	27	16 224	10.3	82.2	7.5
Rio Arriba, NM	12.7	73.4	95.2	423	15.6	483	110	52 225	15.5	69.4	15.1
Roosevelt, NM	18.2	54.9	44.5	239	14.4	187	32	21 981	8.7	79.2	12.1
Sandoval, NM	16.7	44.3	56.6	1 011	14.9	655	180	94 333	14.5	71.3	14.1
San Juan, NM	17.4	54.5	61.5	1 572	15.4	1 639	268	157 085	22.9	60.5	16.6
San Miguel, NM	16.3	66.4	91.5	372	14.8	352	98	41 644	13.9	75.7	10.3
Santa Fe, NM	18.2	49.2	74.1	1 084	14.2	889	180	92 517	7.7	72.5	19.8
Sierra, NM	20.0	66.8	43.7	110	15.5	97	20	11 493	10.7	79.8	9.5
Socorro, NM	17.5	60.0	73.4	173	14.5	159	33	18 571	15.3	74.6	10.0
Taos, NM	17.1	54.4	81.6	365	14.4	347	60	40 159	13.7	76.8	9.4
Torrance, NM	19.5	46.3	38.5	412	14.4	295	73	39 984	6.3	80.9	12.7
Union, NM	22.3	53.9	43.6	67	12.6	60	12	7 838	8.8	78.2	12.9
Valencia, NM	21.4	60.6	69.1	837	15.9	791	152	82 794	9.0	80.3	10.7
NEW YORK											
Albany, NY	15.8	26.4	24.1	2 903	14.4	3 685	487	426 551	4.8	31.4	63.8
Allegany, NY	13.1	38.9	1.7	658	12.8	676	99	94 961	5.1	71.3	23.5
Bronx, NY	*	*	*	*	*	*	*	*	*	*	*
Broome, NY	16.7	30.3	10.0	2 527	13.2	3 248	472	313 281	4.4	49.4	46.2
Cattaraugus, NY	18.9	38.5	8.8	1 223	14.5	1 620	231	170 635	6.2	67.3	26.5
Cayuga, NY	15.0	23.5	5.7	864	14.4	941	137	115 851	4.0	62.6	33.4
Chautauqua, NY	13.4	35.0	10.1	1 919	12.6	1 731	275	250 495	5.1	60.9	33.9
Chemung, NY	17.0	32.0	11.5	948	14.6	1 255	229	139 872	6.0	60.3	33.7
Chenango, NY	17.3	40.1	2.5	824	12.2	1 157	184	100 225	5.1	64.0	30.8
Clinton, NY	19.5	31.4	2.9	1 027	13.4	1 251	167	136 058	5.7	57.9	36.5
Columbia, NY	16.5	38.0	12.5	745	13.3	848	108	111 263	4.3	44.2	51.6
Cortland, NY	17.5	31.7	3.6	603	12.9	649	87	81 628	5.7	60.9	33.4
Delaware, NY	19.4	39.4	3.7	658	11.7	883	146	95 842	3.9	50.2	45.9
Dutchess, NY	15.4	19.3	21.2	2 996	15.5	3 375	500	449 465	2.5	38.8	58.7
Erie, NY	15.5	35.9	26.7	10 132	14.3	11 133	1 770	1 477 743	5.7	50.0	44.3
Essex, NY	14.7	38.7	1.7	443	11.3	437	61	55 817	4.3	39.4	56.3
Franklin, NY	20.0	40.3	11.2	684	13.5	946	132	99 197	5.6	62.4	32.0
Fulton, NY	17.1	37.8	3.3	720	14.1	882	131	97 082	5.1	62.1	32.8
Genesee, NY	13.9	25.2	5.1	859	12.5	816	111	108 258	3.4	57.3	39.2
Greene, NY	13.7	27.4	7.6	563	13.7	490	70	74 971	3.6	40.8	55.6
Hamilton, NY	13.0	26.6	1.6	91	7.7	90	18	13 239	1.8	14.6	83.6
Herkimer, NY	15.7	37.2	2.3	893	13.6	951	149	113 563	4.8	61.9	33.2
Jefferson, NY	17.4	41.4	11.5	1 334	14.5	1 585	216	196 094	12.3	60.7	27.0
Kings, NY	*	*	*	*	*	*	*	*	*	*	*
Lewis, NY	13.4	36.3	2.4	363	13.8	344	48	52 730	3.8	67.4	28.9
Livingston, NY	18.0	22.7	4.1	812	13.1	1 055	170	102 238	3.3	59.1	37.6
Madison, NY	18.3	24.4	3.2	877	14.6	1 215	182	124 623	3.5	59.4	37.1
Monroe, NY	16.3	31.1	31.8	9 090	13.6	11 410	1 717	1 299 902	4.9	43.6	51.5
Montgomery, NY	13.8	31.9	12.2	598	13.3	458	83	86 263	5.2	61.4	33.4
Nassau, NY	13.3	14.7	32.3	14 851	14.0	15 498	3 213	2 669 664	1.7	20.3	77.9
New York, NY	*14.0	*72.0	*84.7	*64 665	*16.5	*33 501	*1 455	*10 184 988	*10.4	*43.2	*46.3
Niagara, NY	13.7	28.3	14.6	2 509	14.3	2 355	385	382 839	4.1	55.4	40.4
Oneida, NY	15.1	33.8	12.5	2 642	14.5	2 733	382	375 649	4.1	58.8	37.1
Onondaga, NY	15.2	29.8	20.6	5 645	13.9	6 711	870	764 516	5.3	49.3	45.4
Ontario, NY	17.3	20.6	7.4	1 359	13.9	2 008	309	184 861	3.5	49.2	47.3
Orange, NY	13.8	26.9	27.1	4 273	15.1	4 789	816	632 060	4.3	45.1	50.6
Orleans, NY	19.4	28.3	9.4	602	14.6	840	153	75 308	4.1	65.0	30.9
Oswego, NY	15.8	33.9	2.6	1 749	14.8	2 195	307	250 856	4.7	53.7	41.6
Otsego, NY	14.3	34.9	3.9	775	12.6	805	102	100 678	4.2	56.9	39.0
Putnam, NY	13.1	6.1	9.2	1 107	14.2	1 168	147	183 852	1.2	25.2	73.5
Queens, NY	*	*	*	*	*	*	*	*	*	*	*
Rensselaer, NY	17.3	26.9	11.8	1 722	13.7	1 994	301	253 260	4.7	52.9	42.4
Richmond, NY	*	*	*	*	*	*	*	*	*	*	*
Rockland, NY	15.6	24.1	39.4	3 009	13.7	3 506	606	552 761	2.5	22.5	75.0
St. Lawrence, NY	17.6	40.2	3.1	1 334	13.9	1 643	233	196 066	4.9	66.0	29.1
Saratoga, NY	12.6	13.8	4.3	2 338	14.9	2 384	362	345 409	3.2	43.8	53.0
Schenectady, NY	14.6	28.1	19.9	1 460	15.3	1 557	210	222 853	4.7	44.7	50.6
Schoharie, NY	15.4	37.8	3.0	449	12.4	495	66	62 001	3.8	60.0	36.2
Schuyler, NY	12.5	24.6	2.1	177	13.9	181	21	25 469	5.5	64.5	30.0
Seneca, NY	15.1	34.9	3.1	397	13.3	471	42	54 060	3.9	62.9	33.2
Steuben, NY	14.7	36.1	3.6	1 427	13.8	1 656	238	200 476	4.2	64.8	31.0
Suffolk, NY	15.5	19.3	24.4	17 060	14.9	17 510	3 454	3 043 208	2.3	35.7	62.0
Sullivan, NY	18.3	40.1	24.0	923	12.5	687	91	139 013	4.0	42.2	53.8
Tioga, NY	11.9	31.9	1.8	670	14.1	687	91	88 360	4.6	64.3	31.1
Tompkins, NY	16.0	26.2	12.9	1 009	13.3	1 337	189	143 753	4.1	42.3	53.6
Ulster, NY	15.5	26.7	15.8	1 926	15.1	2 205	363	311 337	3.1	37.9	59.0
Warren, NY	14.2	24.1	2.9	860	13.1	837	131	114 678	3.9	40.9	55.1
Washington, NY	20.0	29.7	1.9	809	14.1	1 276	187	104 292	5.4	57.5	37.1
Wayne, NY	15.6	26.7	8.8	1 490	12.4	1 532	230	194 229	3.5	57.6	38.9
Westchester, NY	14.7	33.1	43.7	10 484	13.7	11 392	2 046	1 881 285	2.5	25.2	72.3

2IEP = Individual Education Program. See Notes and Definitions at the end of this section.
* = Bronx, Kings, Queens, and Richmond Counties are included with New York County.
. . . = Not available.

Table C-1. Population, School, and Student Characteristics by County—*Continued*

County	Current expenditures, fiscal 1999			Resident population 16 to 19 years, 2000				Outcomes, 1999–2000	
	Amount ($1,000s)	Amount per student	Percent for instruction	Total population 16 to 19 years	Percent in Armed Forces	Percent high school graduates	Percent not enrolled, not grads, not Armed Forces, not empl.	Number of graduates	Dropouts grades 9–12 (percent)
	21	22	23	24	25	26	27	28	29
Guadalupe, NM	$7 739	$7 693	49.1	279	0.0	20.1	5.0	83	1.9
Harding, NM	1 905	10 642	46.7	44	0.0	0.0	6.8	24	...
Hidalgo, NM	10 017	6 810	49.0	389	0.0	10.5	6.4	82	2.0
Lea, NM	65 457	5 073	57.0	4 063	0.1	9.1	7.1	759	1.6
Lincoln, NM	24 112	6 561	55.0	950	0.8	13.5	3.9	216	4.4
Los Alamos, NM	27 251	7 417	56.9	963	0.0	5.1	3.0	289	1.0
Luna, NM	25 753	4 624	59.1	1 570	0.0	10.3	13.1	237	5.4
McKinley, NM	91 157	5 665	53.3	5 677	0.0	9.0	9.0	942	3.4
Mora, NM	7 315	8 146	48.7	348	0.0	12.4	5.7	72	0.6
Otero, NM	47 500	4 832	55.6	3 602	2.3	14.4	8.9	581	1.6
Quay, NM	13 614	6 285	56.5	600	0.0	4.5	9.3	155	4.3
Rio Arriba, NM	41 575	6 011	49.6	2 409	0.0	8.2	11.7	238	9.5
Roosevelt, NM	19 745	5 559	54.5	1 397	0.0	9.6	6.2	212	8.3
Sandoval, NM	80 657	5 487	55.3	5 178	0.0	13.1	7.3	838	6.3
San Juan, NM	134 337	5 426	55.5	8 335	0.0	10.9	7.7	1 536	5.0
San Miguel, NM	34 135	5 935	51.9	2 274	0.0	5.0	3.8	298	2.1
Santa Fe, NM	80 920	5 154	56.1	6 863	0.0	11.6	8.3	708	9.5
Sierra, NM	10 189	5 437	53.3	602	0.0	5.6	8.8	83	3.8
Socorro, NM	16 027	5 828	52.7	1 361	0.5	11.1	8.1	146	2.3
Taos, NM	34 734	6 427	51.9	1 664	0.0	17.3	8.2	339	6.9
Torrance, NM	32 894	5 330	53.3	968	0.0	10.5	12.1	326	3.6
Union, NM	6 762	7 439	49.3	230	0.0	6.1	0.0	71	3.3
Valencia, NM	70 716	5 261	52.5	3 747	0.0	10.3	9.3	546	6.1
NEW YORK									
Albany, NY	364 447	8 834	64.9	17 925	0.0	6.4	3.0	2 430	...
Allegany, NY	78 321	8 938	65.4	4 482	0.0	5.5	2.3	542	...
Bronx, NY	*	*	*	80 832	0.0	7.7	11.1	*	*
Broome, NY	275 734	8 240	66.2	12 657	0.0	7.7	3.0	1 887	...
Cattaraugus, NY	142 748	8 261	67.7	5 430	0.0	10.3	6.4	1 074	...
Cayuga, NY	98 333	7 684	68.4	4 806	0.0	10.7	6.1	766	...
Chautauqua, NY	214 814	8 510	69.0	9 278	2.4	8.2	5.8	1 584	...
Chemung, NY	114 394	8 165	67.5	5 057	0.0	10.2	7.3	777	...
Chenango, NY	85 226	8 350	65.2	2 771	0.0	9.7	5.2	653	...
Clinton, NY	120 844	8 884	66.3	5 362	0.0	7.4	5.4	780	...
Columbia, NY	89 768	9 100	65.3	3 355	0.1	6.4	3.6	517	...
Cortland, NY	64 725	8 104	66.8	3 836	0.1	6.6	2.8	462	...
Delaware, NY	72 956	9 434	64.8	3 127	0.0	7.8	3.1	533	...
Dutchess, NY	399 364	8 940	65.6	16 633	0.1	7.0	5.3	2 370	...
Erie, NY	1 302 094	9 015	65.8	50 513	0.0	8.3	4.4	8 223	...
Essex, NY	49 629	9 906	66.2	1 895	0.0	9.8	4.2	354	...
Franklin, NY	84 357	9 254	67.4	2 877	0.0	8.9	5.0	627	...
Fulton, NY	81 516	8 142	69.2	2 993	0.2	7.4	6.3	584	...
Genesee, NY	96 321	8 556	68.6	3 500	1.0	11.7	3.2	701	...
Greene, NY	66 410	8 775	65.0	2 717	0.0	10.8	27.3	377	...
Hamilton, NY	11 059	15 511	63.2	272	0.0	9.9	5.5	59	...
Herkimer, NY	99 097	8 189	68.4	3 633	0.0	7.0	3.6	809	...
Jefferson, NY	159 977	8 361	66.1	6 514	12.1	21.0	4.7	1 117	...
Kings, NY	*	*	*	140 351	0.1	8.9	8.0	*	*
Lewis, NY	43 315	8 486	65.9	1 663	0.5	12.7	2.4	368	...
Livingston, NY	88 717	8 490	67.2	5 183	0.0	6.0	3.1	695	...
Madison, NY	103 801	8 136	66.3	5 586	0.0	4.9	2.6	836	...
Monroe, NY	1 109 545	8 985	64.6	41 721	0.0	7.5	3.8	6 464	...
Montgomery, NY	70 316	8 683	67.2	2 523	0.0	9.0	5.9	482	...
Nassau, NY	2 388 458	12 042	64.7	64 413	0.0	6.0	2.3	12 458	...
New York, NY	*9 458 777	*8 818	*71.7	61 349	0.0	6.1	7.0	*38 995	...
Niagara, NY	329 048	9 013	66.1	12 334	0.1	10.3	3.9	2 207	...
Oneida, NY	326 798	8 455	67.5	13 254	0.0	7.6	3.4	2 277	...
Onondaga, NY	668 195	8 391	66.3	26 156	0.0	7.7	4.5	4 203	...
Ontario, NY	156 439	8 547	67.4	5 640	0.3	7.8	3.5	1 059	...
Orange, NY	554 777	9 068	64.8	19 867	5.0	12.9	4.7	3 398	...
Orleans, NY	64 251	7 533	69.0	2 641	0.2	13.3	12.4	526	...
Oswego, NY	218 331	8 470	64.9	7 967	0.0	10.2	5.4	1 546	...
Otsego, NY	85 425	8 393	68.1	5 220	0.1	5.8	5.1	662	...
Putnam, NY	164 747	10 958	68.6	4 536	0.0	7.5	2.5	829	...
Queens, NY	*	*	*	108 616	0.0	9.0	6.2	*	*
Rensselaer, NY	210 750	8 942	63.6	9 232	0.1	6.9	5.3	1 158	...
Richmond, NY	*	*	*	22 953	0.1	7.9	4.2	*	*
Rockland, NY	495 343	12 398	65.6	15 172	0.1	5.2	3.9	2 539	...
St. Lawrence, NY	165 169	8 759	67.7	8 623	0.0	5.3	4.0	1 203	...
Saratoga, NY	297 471	8 542	68.1	10 398	1.2	7.9	3.0	2 129	...
Schenectady, NY	191 568	8 675	67.2	7 012	0.0	7.7	4.1	1 156	...
Schoharie, NY	51 378	8 892	68.3	2 544	0.1	6.8	3.7	356	...
Schuyler, NY	22 242	9 373	68.8	1 235	0.0	11.7	14.5	168	...
Seneca, NY	44 242	8 149	64.6	1 580	0.0	6.5	7.3	302	...
Steuben, NY	170 594	8 748	67.0	5 585	0.0	10.2	6.4	1 170	...
Suffolk, NY	2 745 819	11 532	66.6	68 844	0.0	8.9	3.3	13 779	...
Sullivan, NY	120 725	10 722	67.1	4 092	0.0	9.8	7.1	520	...
Tioga, NY	74 748	7 566	66.0	2 719	0.0	12.1	4.4	545	...
Tompkins, NY	121 538	9 095	65.2	10 977	0.2	3.9	1.3	782	...
Ulster, NY	275 013	9 614	67.3	9 585	0.3	9.0	5.1	1 542	...
Warren, NY	96 636	8 574	68.8	3 419	0.3	6.8	4.7	633	...
Washington, NY	90 729	8 351	68.6	3 197	0.0	7.5	11.5	598	...
Wayne, NY	163 833	8 625	65.4	4 896	0.0	10.8	5.0	1 106	...
Westchester, NY	1 653 041	12 202	64.7	41 585	0.0	6.7	4.9	7 211	...

. . . = Not available.
* = Bronx, Kings, Queens, and Richmond Counties are included with New York County.

Table C-1. Population, School, and Student Characteristics by County—*Continued*

County	High school graduates, 2000			College enrollment, 2000		College graduates, 2000 (percent)						
	Population 25 years and over	High school diploma or less (percent)	High school diploma or more (percent)	Number	Percent public	Bachelor's degree or more	+/- U.S. percent with bachelor's degree or more	Non-Hispanic White	Black or African American	American Indian and Alaska Native	Asian, Hawaiian, and Pacific Islander	Hispanic or Latino[1]
	30	31	32	33	34	35	36	37	38	39	40	41
Guadalupe, NM	3 099	69.2	68.3	218	83.9	10.3	-14.1	18.5	6.4	11.3	100.0	8.5
Harding, NM	609	59.6	72.2	20	75.0	18.1	-6.3	26.2	. . .	0.0	. . .	9.0
Hidalgo, NM	3 596	68.1	68.8	116	80.2	9.9	-14.5	17.4	0.0	3.6	0.0	2.9
Lea, NM	33 291	60.8	67.1	2 754	84.4	11.6	-12.8	15.7	5.3	4.4	37.5	4.1
Lincoln, NM	13 849	43.6	84.5	746	93.3	22.8	-1.6	26.5	12.5	16.5	29.1	8.8
Los Alamos, NM	12 822	15.7	96.3	997	88.3	60.5	36.1	63.4	0.0	61.7	76.1	31.7
Luna, NM	15 777	70.1	59.8	539	93.1	10.4	-14.0	15.6	8.1	21.3	26.1	3.7
McKinley, NM	38 988	62.7	65.2	3 502	87.1	12.0	-12.4	42.9	17.0	4.6	58.3	7.2
Mora, NM	3 348	61.9	69.8	212	96.7	15.5	-8.9	34.0	. . .	6.9	. . .	10.7
Otero, NM	38 061	48.1	81.0	3 323	90.3	15.4	-9.0	20.2	11.5	8.3	25.2	5.2
Quay, NM	6 970	62.9	73.8	413	94.2	13.7	-10.7	17.1	21.3	0.0	31.9	6.6
Rio Arriba, NM	25 930	58.3	73.0	2 050	81.4	15.4	-9.0	34.6	7.2	9.7	32.5	11.1
Roosevelt, NM	10 245	48.5	75.2	2 589	95.0	22.6	-1.8	28.0	7.6	25.8	77.4	9.2
Sandoval, NM	56 479	42.6	86.0	4 415	81.7	24.8	0.4	33.4	23.2	5.8	37.6	14.2
San Juan, NM	65 262	53.7	76.8	6 004	89.8	13.5	-10.9	19.8	27.5	5.4	25.2	6.5
San Miguel, NM	18 531	51.1	74.5	2 723	80.9	21.2	-3.2	37.5	10.4	25.7	68.1	15.4
Santa Fe, NM	87 870	35.2	84.5	8 294	67.7	36.9	12.5	56.2	30.2	16.8	56.6	14.0
Sierra, NM	9 906	55.3	76.1	352	77.0	13.1	-11.3	14.6	27.8	18.9	44.4	6.7
Socorro, NM	10 642	56.9	72.1	1 715	90.4	19.4	-5.0	31.6	13.5	11.2	73.3	7.6
Taos, NM	20 526	47.5	79.1	1 330	85.0	25.9	1.5	46.7	50.5	10.9	42.4	11.1
Torrance, NM	10 556	55.9	77.1	569	91.0	14.4	-10.0	19.1	1.1	18.1	31.7	4.9
Union, NM	2 786	64.0	79.9	50	82.0	13.0	-11.4	17.2	. . .	50.0	100.0	2.2
Valencia, NM	40 917	56.2	76.1	2 835	83.6	14.8	-9.6	20.6	15.7	9.4	27.3	8.9
NEW YORK												
Albany, NY	195 381	40.7	86.3	28 317	64.6	33.3	8.9	34.3	15.7	27.8	66.5	30.6
Allegany, NY	30 010	56.4	83.2	6 015	49.4	17.2	-7.2	16.8	8.8	21.5	67.7	20.2
Bronx, NY	794 792	63.5	62.3	86 014	57.5	14.6	-9.8	26.0	14.1	9.4	35.4	8.2
Broome, NY	132 541	48.9	83.8	17 211	92.1	22.7	-1.7	22.3	20.5	2.7	50.4	26.6
Cattaraugus, NY	54 154	60.0	81.2	4 328	44.1	14.9	-9.5	14.9	9.3	10.3	48.5	15.6
Cayuga, NY	54 649	56.9	79.1	3 240	74.6	15.5	-8.9	16.2	3.0	13.7	16.8	7.9
Chautauqua, NY	91 261	55.3	81.2	8 752	89.9	16.9	-7.5	17.5	5.7	6.6	47.0	5.2
Chemung, NY	60 796	54.0	82.1	4 239	55.3	18.6	-5.8	19.0	9.9	3.2	51.7	10.4
Chenango, NY	34 363	59.3	80.6	1 583	86.9	14.4	-10.0	14.4	4.9	11.7	51.9	19.6
Clinton, NY	51 598	57.1	76.4	6 653	95.8	17.8	-6.6	18.5	3.1	10.4	36.4	6.6
Columbia, NY	43 990	51.7	81.0	2 000	70.1	22.6	-1.8	23.3	6.4	13.2	34.7	13.1
Cortland, NY	29 527	53.0	82.8	5 898	94.6	18.8	-5.6	18.8	14.0	9.4	88.5	13.1
Delaware, NY	33 070	57.5	79.9	2 388	85.4	16.6	-7.8	16.5	23.2	13.9	65.9	10.7
Dutchess, NY	183 725	44.1	84.0	20 086	53.2	27.6	3.2	28.9	12.2	16.2	62.4	16.7
Erie, NY	637 676	47.0	82.9	63 289	68.4	24.5	0.1	26.0	11.5	13.1	64.0	15.3
Essex, NY	27 337	57.7	80.4	1 200	81.7	18.3	-6.1	19.0	2.3	17.2	28.0	4.0
Franklin, NY	34 482	64.1	69.7	2 202	58.9	13.0	-11.4	14.8	1.8	7.3	38.5	1.7
Fulton, NY	37 483	60.8	77.8	1 822	82.0	13.5	-10.9	13.6	6.9	0.0	46.0	8.7
Genesee, NY	40 125	53.7	84.4	2 893	82.3	16.3	-8.1	16.6	2.8	7.8	39.3	8.6
Greene, NY	32 570	57.9	78.6	1 577	78.7	16.4	-8.0	17.1	5.7	1.9	27.8	5.0
Hamilton, NY	4 022	53.9	83.4	131	80.9	18.4	-6.0	18.7	0.0	10.0	0.0	0.0
Herkimer, NY	43 455	56.0	79.4	3 133	80.5	15.7	-8.7	15.5	7.7	11.9	48.6	23.2
Jefferson, NY	68 965	53.4	82.9	4 962	89.3	16.0	-8.4	16.5	6.5	9.1	23.9	13.0
Kings, NY	1 552 870	57.9	68.8	174 210	60.1	21.8	-2.6	33.7	14.4	13.5	23.5	8.5
Lewis, NY	17 367	67.1	81.0	617	79.6	11.7	-12.7	11.7	10.6	11.7	35.3	11.1
Livingston, NY	40 081	51.5	82.3	6 866	87.2	19.2	-5.2	20.0	3.8	12.9	36.0	4.7
Madison, NY	43 762	49.8	83.3	6 099	46.9	21.6	-2.8	21.7	9.9	10.0	46.5	18.2
Monroe, NY	477 957	41.3	84.9	56 430	49.5	31.2	6.8	34.2	11.4	15.7	53.7	13.3
Montgomery, NY	33 900	61.1	78.1	1 456	79.7	13.6	-10.8	13.8	4.1	26.9	52.8	4.4
Nassau, NY	908 693	40.1	86.7	81 375	49.0	35.4	11.0	37.7	23.7	13.9	57.4	15.4
New York, NY	1 125 987	34.8	78.7	141 083	37.5	49.4	25.0	73.9	18.9	19.2	45.3	14.0
Niagara, NY	147 153	53.7	83.3	12 165	69.7	17.4	-7.0	17.8	8.0	14.7	46.7	19.2
Oneida, NY	158 846	53.5	79.0	12 772	61.8	18.3	-6.1	19.3	5.9	4.3	27.9	6.5
Onondaga, NY	296 914	43.4	85.7	35 188	40.9	28.5	4.1	29.5	10.5	19.7	55.8	23.3
Ontario, NY	66 539	44.2	87.4	5 865	52.2	24.7	0.3	25.0	10.5	13.1	51.7	13.3
Orange, NY	212 816	49.2	81.8	18 607	64.3	22.5	-1.9	24.1	13.4	11.2	50.3	11.6
Orleans, NY	29 043	63.2	76.4	1 208	84.4	13.0	-11.4	14.1	2.5	4.6	20.7	5.5
Oswego, NY	76 165	60.8	80.4	8 876	90.2	14.4	-10.0	14.2	28.3	18.9	46.5	14.0
Otsego, NY	38 808	51.7	83.0	7 215	86.6	22.0	-2.4	21.8	30.0	23.3	57.2	22.5
Putnam, NY	64 624	37.9	90.2	4 700	55.3	33.9	9.5	34.3	33.1	36.9	64.3	22.6
Queens, NY	1 509 502	53.4	74.4	164 114	61.2	24.3	-0.1	29.2	17.8	14.1	37.6	11.6
Rensselaer, NY	100 233	47.6	84.9	12 107	43.8	23.7	-0.7	23.5	17.1	24.6	71.3	21.2
Richmond, NY	293 795	51.1	82.6	28 243	57.9	23.2	-1.2	23.2	18.7	8.9	46.8	13.0
Rockland, NY	184 012	37.2	85.3	17 843	48.2	37.5	13.1	40.5	22.2	18.2	58.5	16.8
St. Lawrence, NY	70 201	58.5	79.2	11 180	55.1	16.4	-8.0	16.7	4.2	15.5	60.6	4.5
Saratoga, NY	135 015	40.8	88.2	10 297	53.9	30.9	6.5	30.6	20.9	16.4	63.0	38.8
Schenectady, NY	99 568	46.1	84.8	8 381	53.6	26.3	1.9	26.8	12.8	16.4	62.0	13.2
Schoharie, NY	20 695	56.4	81.7	2 354	76.6	17.3	-7.1	17.5	8.5	0.0	20.0	21.2
Schuyler, NY	12 842	57.5	82.4	610	76.4	15.5	-8.9	15.5	9.6	28.3	29.4	19.1
Seneca, NY	22 585	56.6	79.1	1 543	61.6	17.5	-6.9	17.8	7.5	23.4	31.6	6.7
Steuben, NY	65 765	54.5	82.8	3 253	81.1	17.9	-6.5	17.3	28.2	11.7	67.0	29.8
Suffolk, NY	942 401	45.1	86.2	82 092	65.5	27.5	3.1	29.1	16.5	23.0	56.7	12.0
Sullivan, NY	50 228	57.7	76.2	2 730	73.9	16.7	-7.7	18.1	6.6	4.1	38.1	8.7
Tioga, NY	34 223	52.6	84.8	1 571	78.7	19.7	-4.7	19.5	26.7	19.3	42.6	21.6
Tompkins, NY	53 075	30.9	91.4	27 205	22.6	47.5	23.1	45.0	37.7	45.4	87.9	61.2
Ulster, NY	120 670	48.3	81.7	11 682	83.4	25.0	0.6	26.3	11.5	16.7	51.6	12.1
Warren, NY	43 364	49.0	84.6	2 944	65.6	23.2	-1.2	23.2	26.3	8.8	45.2	17.4
Washington, NY	40 957	61.1	79.2	1 750	73.1	14.3	-10.1	14.8	2.0	22.3	14.5	3.5
Wayne, NY	61 731	53.9	82.3	3 271	76.6	17.0	-7.4	17.7	3.1	7.4	20.0	5.7
Westchester, NY	628 941	38.5	83.6	52 847	43.4	40.9	16.5	47.5	22.6	17.1	65.7	16.3

[1]Hispanic or Latino persons may be of any race.
. . . = Not available.

Table C-1. Population, School, and Student Characteristics by County—*Continued*

County	State/County code	County type[1]	Population, 2000		Number of schools and students, 2000–2001			Resident enrollment, 2000			
			Total	Percent 5–17 years	School districts	Schools	Students	Total	Percent public	K–12	Percent public
			1	2	3	4	5	6	7	8	9
Wyoming, NY	36121	6	43 424	18.8	5	12	5 845	10 379	90.0	8 372	94.0
Yates, NY	36123	6	24 621	20.0	2	6	3 053	6 376	74.7	4 836	85.5
NORTH CAROLINA	37000										
Alamance, NC	37001	3	130 800	17.4	3	34	21 058	32 488	79.8	23 114	92.3
Alexander, NC	37003	2	33 603	17.6	1	10	5 432	7 232	92.4	5 825	96.4
Alleghany, NC	37005	9	10 677	14.2	1	4	1 449	2 029	93.6	1 524	98.4
Anson, NC	37007	6	25 275	18.7	1	9	4 519	6 464	94.1	5 003	96.1
Ashe, NC	37009	9	24 384	14.5	1	6	3 250	4 610	94.8	3 566	95.8
Avery, NC	37011	9	17 167	14.6	3	11	2 522	3 841	81.1	2 609	92.2
Beaufort, NC	37013	6	44 958	17.4	2	15	7 543	10 641	91.0	8 251	93.0
Bertie, NC	37015	9	19 773	19.7	1	10	3 711	4 939	88.9	4 164	89.8
Bladen, NC	37017	6	32 278	18.0	1	14	5 829	7 732	92.5	5 739	94.0
Brunswick, NC	37019	3	73 143	15.7	2	16	10 394	14 593	88.9	11 662	91.4
Buncombe, NC	37021	3	206 330	16.2	4	49	29 086	47 002	85.1	33 328	90.9
Burke, NC	37023	2	89 148	17.8	1	25	14 588	20 594	91.6	16 382	96.3
Cabarrus, NC	37025	0	131 063	18.7	2	31	23 399	32 182	87.2	24 893	92.8
Caldwell, NC	37027	2	77 415	17.0	1	24	12 663	16 808	91.5	13 418	95.0
Camden, NC	37029	8	6 885	18.9	1	3	1 282	1 720	93.3	1 353	97.4
Carteret, NC	37031	6	59 383	15.8	3	17	8 531	12 345	86.8	9 458	90.1
Caswell, NC	37033	8	23 501	17.5	1	7	3 642	5 432	91.7	4 358	93.9
Catawba, NC	37035	2	141 685	17.7	4	41	23 879	32 637	88.3	25 244	95.3
Chatham, NC	37037	2	49 329	16.2	3	17	7 298	10 643	88.9	8 127	92.9
Cherokee, NC	37039	7	24 298	15.1	2	13	3 770	4 813	94.5	3 761	95.6
Chowan, NC	37041	7	14 526	18.1	1	4	2 510	3 709	81.9	2 579	95.9
Clay, NC	37043	9	8 775	14.3	1	3	1 262	1 774	95.7	1 279	98.8
Cleveland, NC	37045	4	96 287	18.5	3	27	17 395	23 444	87.2	17 800	95.4
Columbus, NC	37047	6	54 749	19.1	2	23	10 186	13 690	93.6	10 826	95.4
Craven, NC	37049	5	91 436	17.3	1	22	14 829	22 182	87.8	15 939	92.6
Cumberland, NC	37051	2	302 963	19.7	3	83	50 990	88 163	87.3	61 841	93.0
Currituck, NC	37053	1	18 190	19.3	1	7	3 213	4 264	88.2	3 441	92.9
Dare, NC	37055	7	29 967	16.2	1	9	4 683	6 006	88.7	4 960	94.2
Davidson, NC	37057	2	147 246	17.8	3	37	24 835	32 736	89.2	26 183	94.0
Davie, NC	37059	2	34 835	17.8	1	9	5 728	8 108	87.6	6 395	93.4
Duplin, NC	37061	6	49 063	18.7	1	15	8 606	11 574	93.7	9 674	95.6
Durham, NC	37063	2	223 314	16.0	11	57	32 080	63 107	71.0	36 078	87.3
Edgecombe, NC	37065	3	55 606	20.3	1	14	7 771	14 634	93.6	11 844	96.4
Forsyth, NC	37067	2	306 067	17.2	7	71	46 216	78 172	78.5	53 625	89.2
Franklin, NC	37069	2	47 260	18.3	1	12	7 773	11 252	84.8	8 663	91.6
Gaston, NC	37071	0	190 365	18.0	3	54	30 895	44 264	85.7	34 448	90.6
Gates, NC	37073	8	10 516	20.9	1	5	2 053	2 709	94.2	2 281	97.3
Graham, NC	37075	9	7 993	16.1	1	3	1 237	1 474	93.6	1 173	94.1
Granville, NC	37077	6	48 498	17.7	1	13	8 121	11 186	89.5	8 670	94.4
Greene, NC	37079	8	18 974	18.3	1	4	3 069	4 652	89.8	3 749	93.5
Guilford, NC	37081	2	421 048	17.1	4	98	64 311	114 435	84.0	74 078	89.8
Halifax, NC	37083	4	57 370	19.9	3	24	10 409	14 896	91.5	11 856	92.5
Harnett, NC	37085	6	91 025	19.3	2	26	16 440	25 203	84.0	17 716	95.5
Haywood, NC	37087	6	54 033	15.5	1	15	7 824	11 291	90.7	8 354	95.0
Henderson, NC	37089	6	89 173	15.2	2	22	11 776	17 967	87.2	13 934	90.7
Hertford, NC	37091	6	22 601	19.9	1	5	4 086	5 716	87.8	4 586	90.8
Hoke, NC	37093	6	33 646	20.6	1	11	6 286	9 385	91.2	7 050	94.9
Hyde, NC	37095	9	5 826	15.9	1	4	700	1 255	88.4	1 124	87.6
Iredell, NC	37097	4	122 660	18.7	6	41	21 735	28 540	89.4	22 667	93.4
Jackson, NC	37099	7	33 121	13.9	2	8	3 757	10 089	94.0	4 647	95.5
Johnston, NC	37101	2	121 965	18.2	1	29	21 334	28 470	91.0	22 380	96.0
Jones, NC	37103	8	10 381	19.6	1	6	1 534	2 635	86.7	2 091	87.6
Lee, NC	37105	6	49 040	18.7	2	13	8 935	11 864	89.0	9 442	91.4
Lenoir, NC	37107	4	59 648	18.7	2	20	10 385	14 821	90.2	11 328	93.2
Lincoln, NC	37109	1	63 780	18.5	2	19	11 058	14 743	90.1	11 777	94.1
McDowell, NC	37111	6	42 151	16.7	1	11	6 472	9 182	93.7	7 313	95.0
Macon, NC	37113	7	29 811	15.4	1	11	4 020	6 010	90.1	4 626	93.4
Madison, NC	37115	3	19 635	15.4	1	8	2 545	4 542	74.5	3 000	91.3
Martin, NC	37117	6	25 593	19.3	1	13	4 877	6 555	93.3	5 229	95.1
Mecklenburg, NC	37119	0	695 454	17.8	6	140	104 615	183 309	79.6	125 015	85.8
Mitchell, NC	37121	9	15 687	16.1	1	8	2 379	3 102	91.2	2 508	94.2
Montgomery, NC	37123	7	26 822	18.1	1	9	4 563	6 120	93.2	4 965	96.0
Moore, NC	37125	6	74 769	16.5	3	24	11 281	16 320	91.4	12 571	94.5
Nash, NC	37127	3	87 420	18.8	2	29	19 088	22 221	86.3	16 862	91.1
New Hanover, NC	37129	3	160 307	15.2	2	34	21 777	42 293	87.8	24 410	90.4
Northampton, NC	37131	9	22 086	18.6	1	10	3 767	5 438	90.1	4 343	90.7
Onslow, NC	37133	3	150 355	17.3	2	32	21 147	37 631	91.2	26 211	96.0
Orange, NC	37135	2	118 227	15.3	2	26	16 236	44 716	90.1	18 131	88.5
Pamlico, NC	37137	9	12 934	16.1	2	5	2 136	2 810	92.8	2 171	95.8
Pasquotank, NC	37139	7	34 897	18.6	1	12	6 042	10 325	89.6	6 789	95.0
Pender, NC	37141	8	41 082	17.3	1	12	6 567	9 203	91.6	7 385	95.1
Perquimans, NC	37143	9	11 368	17.8	1	4	1 850	2 592	90.9	2 100	93.1
Person, NC	37145	6	35 623	17.7	2	11	5 962	8 423	90.6	6 460	93.8
Pitt, NC	37147	3	133 798	17.1	2	32	20 200	45 735	91.7	23 462	91.2
Polk, NC	37149	8	18 324	14.9	1	6	2 506	3 529	85.3	2 662	87.3
Randolph, NC	37151	2	130 454	18.2	2	33	21 554	29 217	89.6	23 613	93.5
Richmond, NC	37153	7	46 564	19.0	1	18	8 342	11 419	93.4	9 150	96.2
Robeson, NC	37155	4	123 339	21.1	2	41	24 016	34 487	94.0	26 723	95.9
Rockingham, NC	37157	4	91 928	17.2	2	26	14 735	19 909	90.7	15 761	93.7
Rowan, NC	37159	1	130 340	18.1	2	30	20 612	31 855	84.4	24 024	92.1
Rutherford, NC	37161	6	62 899	17.6	2	20	10 336	14 178	90.5	11 037	93.7
Sampson, NC	37163	6	60 161	18.5	2	20	10 502	14 305	93.7	11 235	97.2

[1]County type code is from the Economic Research Service of the USDA. See Notes and Definitions at the end of this section.

Table C-1. School and Student Characteristics by County—*Continued*

County	Characteristics of students, 2000–2001 Percent with IEP[2]	Percent eligible for free lunch	Percent minority	Staff and students, 2000–2001 Number of teachers	Student/teacher ratio	Local school non-teaching staff	Central admin. staff	Revenues, fiscal 1999 Total revenue ($1,000s)	Percentage of revenue from Federal govt.	State govt.	Local govt.
	10	11	12	13	14	15	16	17	18	19	20
Wyoming, NY	13.5	22.4	1.5	418	14.0	379	59	$59 610	3.5	63.6	32.8
Yates, NY	13.7	32.6	2.1	244	12.5	259	35	30 131	5.0	48.8	46.3
NORTH CAROLINA											
Alamance, NC	14.3	...	36.2	1 370	15.4	1 050	25	126 804	5.8	63.4	30.8
Alexander, NC	12.9	...	12.8	323	16.8	319	8	35 719	6.9	77.0	16.2
Alleghany, NC	19.1	...	7.0	132	11.0	116	11	12 050	8.0	69.7	22.3
Anson, NC	17.3	...	65.9	329	13.7	267	10	30 260	10.9	68.6	20.5
Ashe, NC	14.2	...	3.2	222	14.6	219	12	25 553	6.6	71.4	22.0
Avery, NC	20.4	...	2.3	221	11.4	169	11	19 244	8.7	67.8	23.6
Beaufort, NC	16.0	...	46.1	573	13.2	424	17	58 769	10.7	70.6	18.8
Bertie, NC	12.8	...	83.4	274	13.5	201	15	25 361	16.5	70.2	13.3
Bladen, NC	12.2	...	55.1	417	14.0	371	18	38 619	11.2	69.5	19.3
Brunswick, NC	15.3	47.6	27.9	717	14.5	590	24	72 174	6.9	65.1	27.9
Buncombe, NC	13.9	33.2	16.5	2 191	13.3	1 774	61	201 736	6.0	62.3	31.7
Burke, NC	15.7	37.4	20.9	985	14.8	850	23	97 745	5.9	72.6	21.5
Cabarrus, NC	14.1	24.9	24.1	1 531	15.3	1 237	30	133 120	6.1	63.6	30.3
Caldwell, NC	12.0	35.3	11.2	889	14.2	750	21	76 413	5.8	72.1	22.1
Camden, NC	9.4	26.7	20.7	90	14.2	88	7	9 750	5.2	81.0	13.7
Carteret, NC	18.1	34.2	14.0	651	13.1	591	15	58 456	6.7	58.5	34.9
Caswell, NC	15.3	41.1	45.5	251	14.5	246	12	23 488	7.6	71.8	20.6
Catawba, NC	13.7	29.6	26.0	1 612	14.8	1 322	35	147 851	4.9	65.0	30.0
Chatham, NC	13.8	31.9	36.9	508	14.4	482	13	48 480	5.1	59.2	35.7
Cherokee, NC	16.4	50.1	6.2	271	13.9	236	6	29 972	8.3	71.6	20.1
Chowan, NC	11.2	54.0	51.8	181	13.9	172	11	18 974	6.7	70.9	22.3
Clay, NC	13.0	43.0	2.0	95	13.3	68	4	11 002	5.2	80.9	14.0
Cleveland, NC	14.4	38.5	32.3	1 140	15.3	1 109	38	114 396	7.5	66.9	25.6
Columbus, NC	12.4	59.8	49.6	683	14.9	622	28	66 374	10.9	76.1	13.0
Craven, NC	12.7	43.1	40.2	987	15.0	815	20	93 984	9.4	68.9	21.8
Cumberland, NC	11.8	52.1	57.1	2 844	17.9	2 946	54	322 274	8.0	69.3	22.6
Currituck, NC	17.0	25.9	12.7	279	11.5	240	16	24 268	5.3	57.7	37.1
Dare, NC	12.5	20.7	7.6	340	13.8	261	12	33 105	3.5	56.2	40.3
Davidson, NC	12.7	30.6	18.6	1 678	14.8	1 319	34	144 327	6.0	70.5	23.5
Davie, NC	13.0	22.1	14.2	378	15.2	319	9	33 088	4.3	65.8	29.9
Duplin, NC	11.3	59.6	51.9	541	15.9	491	14	52 810	8.6	73.8	17.7
Durham, NC	15.5	38.5	67.3	2 569	12.5	2 060	122	228 876	5.4	55.7	38.9
Edgecombe, NC	13.6	68.7	62.0	524	14.8	495	33	48 261	12.2	69.0	18.8
Forsyth, NC	13.8	35.8	46.9	3 495	13.2	2 152	76	311 970	5.1	61.2	33.7
Franklin, NC	13.5	45.6	45.9	461	16.9	436	27	43 580	8.0	70.8	21.2
Gaston, NC	12.3	33.4	24.9	2 043	15.1	1 815	60	182 099	6.2	67.8	26.0
Gates, NC	16.1	51.8	44.6	164	12.5	156	12	15 604	6.7	72.8	20.5
Graham, NC	14.5	49.0	13.2	102	12.1	115	7	10 197	9.9	76.6	13.5
Granville, NC	13.3	41.0	43.9	463	17.5	497	20	46 644	7.8	72.2	20.1
Greene, NC	17.6	60.4	63.5	217	14.1	205	9	23 011	12.0	74.0	14.1
Guilford, NC	15.3	39.4	50.0	4 754	13.5	3 874	47	436 664	5.6	59.7	34.7
Halifax, NC	14.9	70.1	73.5	775	13.4	768	41	81 773	10.5	73.4	16.1
Harnett, NC	12.7	48.4	39.3	978	16.8	936	17	103 879	6.9	77.8	15.3
Haywood, NC	15.3	32.4	4.4	556	14.1	452	15	52 665	6.0	65.7	28.3
Henderson, NC	13.5	35.0	15.1	820	14.4	657	18	78 850	5.1	71.7	23.2
Hertford, NC	13.2	69.6	82.4	264	15.5	334	14	28 096	12.2	72.0	15.8
Hoke, NC	14.9	58.5	68.9	420	15.0	390	16	41 768	9.1	80.4	10.5
Hyde, NC	17.3	73.9	49.9	75	9.3	77	8	12 636	7.9	79.5	12.5
Iredell, NC	12.8	29.9	25.1	1 346	16.1	1 281	32	136 220	4.7	62.2	33.1
Jackson, NC	16.2	39.8	13.3	268	14.0	257	6	24 004	8.2	67.2	24.6
Johnston, NC	14.9	34.2	30.8	1 490	14.3	1 333	27	142 908	4.8	68.3	26.9
Jones, NC	16.6	75.0	59.1	126	12.2	125	6	14 784	10.3	80.2	9.5
Lee, NC	11.9	39.2	44.5	554	16.1	513	20	54 804	8.9	62.7	28.4
Lenoir, NC	14.8	49.8	56.0	749	13.9	639	22	66 731	9.3	70.8	20.0
Lincoln, NC	14.0	30.5	16.9	650	17.0	592	19	65 105	5.2	74.4	20.5
McDowell, NC	14.2	33.9	10.4	408	15.9	317	17	36 347	7.0	73.0	20.0
Macon, NC	17.3	44.7	3.5	293	13.7	276	9	24 954	6.8	71.2	22.0
Madison, NC	16.2	45.1	1.4	189	13.5	235	12	17 751	8.6	72.4	19.0
Martin, NC	13.3	58.2	59.6	374	13.0	298	10	33 169	10.5	69.1	20.4
Mecklenburg, NC	11.7	35.3	53.5	6 406	16.3	6 535	214	739 099	5.2	55.1	39.7
Mitchell, NC	15.0	57.7	4.0	180	13.2	192	9	16 491	6.8	79.1	14.1
Montgomery, NC	12.8	51.3	46.5	290	15.7	339	20	28 885	9.8	67.7	22.5
Moore, NC	13.5	39.4	31.7	790	14.3	646	23	78 326	6.1	65.0	28.9
Nash, NC	15.0	49.0	60.1	1 337	14.3	1 090	33	111 088	8.0	68.0	24.0
New Hanover, NC	12.6	34.1	32.7	1 474	14.8	1 314	74	155 005	5.4	57.5	37.1
Northampton, NC	15.3	79.7	81.9	271	13.9	243	15	25 506	12.7	70.3	17.0
Onslow, NC	13.6	40.7	35.5	1 394	15.2	1 336	17	127 825	7.9	70.2	21.9
Orange, NC	16.1	20.8	31.0	1 178	13.8	1 116	46	131 584	3.7	52.0	44.4
Pamlico, NC	19.5	50.6	32.5	168	12.7	157	10	16 069	7.9	75.2	16.9
Pasquotank, NC	14.2	63.1	51.6	462	13.1	306	13	44 524	8.9	69.2	21.9
Pender, NC	15.7	49.7	35.4	471	13.9	356	13	38 483	8.1	68.6	23.3
Perquimans, NC	13.9	57.8	39.4	136	13.6	179	10	19 950	7.4	66.6	26.0
Person, NC	15.3	40.2	40.1	479	12.4	343	14	35 649	8.5	66.1	25.4
Pitt, NC	14.1	48.0	55.5	1 355	14.9	1 052	25	127 560	7.6	69.5	22.8
Polk, NC	14.5	34.1	16.0	189	13.3	138	10	16 965	4.8	63.5	31.7
Randolph, NC	13.2	28.4	17.6	1 447	14.9	1 254	37	129 374	5.0	72.3	22.6
Richmond, NC	12.2	59.9	46.8	594	14.0	508	17	56 161	9.2	76.0	14.8
Robeson, NC	15.9	74.1	78.1	1 548	15.5	1 452	29	140 076	12.5	73.5	14.1
Rockingham, NC	15.7	36.3	30.3	1 031	14.3	802	19	102 059	6.7	75.0	18.4
Rowan, NC	14.2	35.5	29.0	1 342	15.4	1 202	22	127 526	6.3	68.4	25.4

[2]IEP = Individual Education Program. See Notes and Definitions at the end of this section.
... = Not available.

Table C-1. Population, School, and Student Characteristics by County—*Continued*

County	Current expenditures, fiscal 1999			Resident population 16 to 19 years, 2000				Outcomes, 1999–2000	
	Amount ($1,000s)	Amount per student	Percent for instruction	Total population 16 to 19 years	Percent in Armed Forces	Percent high school graduates	Percent not enrolled, not grads, not Armed Forces, not empl.	Number of graduates	Dropouts grades 9–12 (percent)
	21	22	23	24	25	26	27	28	29
Yates, NY	$25 138	$7 771	67.3	1 798	0.0	12.8	5.3	211	...
NORTH CAROLINA									
Alamance, NC	101 922	5 153	61.7	7 316	0.0	10.1	7.3	972	...
Alexander, NC	27 586	5 214	64.9	1 582	0.0	11.2	4.9	282	...
Alleghany, NC	10 428	6 952	61.5	526	0.0	17.7	9.7	84	...
Anson, NC	26 284	5 791	62.0	1 194	0.0	14.2	6.2	207	...
Ashe, NC	19 926	6 033	62.5	1 108	0.0	16.8	4.9	198	...
Avery, NC	16 942	6 634	60.4	825	0.0	12.2	4.8	137	...
Beaufort, NC	43 918	5 753	63.9	2 219	0.0	14.8	6.4	403	...
Bertie, NC	23 677	6 132	55.5	1 092	0.0	4.6	9.3	219	...
Bladen, NC	34 615	5 861	61.3	1 877	0.0	11.7	12.7	307	...
Brunswick, NC	60 303	6 013	61.5	3 253	5.6	18.1	5.6	436	...
Buncombe, NC	173 801	5 964	62.9	9 782	0.1	13.1	6.7	1 588	...
Burke, NC	74 237	5 212	65.2	4 896	0.0	12.6	17.4	592	...
Cabarrus, NC	113 504	5 211	65.2	6 202	0.1	9.2	6.0	1 209	...
Caldwell, NC	64 934	5 310	64.3	3 415	0.0	13.1	8.0	607	...
Camden, NC	7 664	5 978	57.6	404	0.0	4.0	5.2	69	...
Carteret, NC	55 280	6 531	61.3	2 592	0.7	8.9	6.4	476	...
Caswell, NC	21 219	5 962	63.9	1 071	0.0	13.4	6.8	184	...
Catawba, NC	123 410	5 469	65.7	6 953	0.0	13.2	7.1	1 160	...
Chatham, NC	40 143	5 931	58.5	2 021	0.0	12.3	5.8	335	...
Cherokee, NC	21 820	6 093	64.8	1 110	0.0	6.2	6.9	211	...
Chowan, NC	15 653	6 027	59.7	940	0.0	12.2	1.3	143	...
Clay, NC	8 209	6 305	64.5	340	0.0	12.1	7.6	73	...
Cleveland, NC	97 429	5 645	64.0	4 941	0.0	11.2	8.0	806	...
Columbus, NC	58 249	5 668	62.3	3 173	0.2	10.6	7.8	543	...
Craven, NC	81 602	5 505	61.4	4 794	11.5	22.9	6.3	770	...
Cumberland, NC	264 848	5 163	62.7	18 240	13.2	21.5	4.6	2 576	...
Currituck, NC	20 301	6 503	60.4	831	1.0	15.8	5.4	145	...
Dare, NC	27 894	6 145	63.7	1 337	1.0	19.4	2.5	255	...
Davidson, NC	127 845	5 278	64.5	6 866	0.0	10.4	7.7	1 196	...
Davie, NC	29 439	5 492	63.2	1 620	0.0	9.3	6.2	280	...
Duplin, NC	43 652	5 131	63.5	2 630	0.1	10.0	9.8	382	...
Durham, NC	192 320	6 622	61.0	12 343	0.1	6.5	7.0	1 547	...
Edgecombe, NC	45 864	5 737	62.1	3 223	0.0	10.8	9.3	368	...
Forsyth, NC	261 210	6 096	65.8	15 448	0.0	9.7	6.1	2 117	...
Franklin, NC	38 221	5 192	63.0	2 375	0.0	10.9	6.8	348	...
Gaston, NC	160 219	5 278	65.9	9 162	0.0	11.1	9.2	1 392	...
Gates, NC	13 317	6 427	57.8	526	0.0	5.7	8.2	103	...
Graham, NC	8 798	7 112	61.3	368	0.0	13.9	12.2	71	...
Granville, NC	42 452	5 433	62.7	2 273	0.0	9.6	20.1	307	...
Greene, NC	18 368	6 193	61.4	982	0.0	5.6	5.3	147	...
Guilford, NC	369 973	6 050	60.2	24 144	0.0	8.4	3.3	3 020	...
Halifax, NC	65 273	6 063	62.2	2 911	0.0	15.5	7.9	521	...
Harnett, NC	79 749	5 111	65.7	4 959	1.1	12.7	8.8	636	...
Haywood, NC	45 191	5 858	63.3	2 318	0.0	14.7	4.2	397	...
Henderson, NC	63 283	5 511	65.8	3 764	0.0	12.1	7.1	639	...
Hertford, NC	23 535	5 509	59.1	1 408	0.0	7.7	7.0	213	...
Hoke, NC	31 542	5 078	63.7	1 896	0.5	19.6	10.4	221	...
Hyde, NC	7 460	9 419	58.6	265	0.0	7.5	17.4	44	...
Iredell, NC	105 233	5 301	62.3	5 937	0.0	13.7	7.9	968	...
Jackson, NC	21 349	5 924	62.2	2 707	0.1	6.1	2.5	216	...
Johnston, NC	102 522	5 308	64.0	5 837	0.0	12.0	7.7	846	...
Jones, NC	11 170	6 741	55.2	593	0.0	7.9	5.9	84	...
Lee, NC	47 620	5 435	64.5	2 655	0.0	8.7	9.6	412	...
Lenoir, NC	58 111	5 597	65.0	3 200	0.5	8.1	12.2	436	...
Lincoln, NC	51 421	5 037	65.2	2 958	0.0	9.4	5.5	549	...
McDowell, NC	34 071	5 330	64.7	1 966	0.0	13.7	7.3	365	...
Macon, NC	23 851	5 993	63.2	1 421	0.7	17.9	8.2	233	...
Madison, NC	15 915	6 140	60.7	1 162	0.3	11.5	5.0	128	...
Martin, NC	30 490	6 069	63.1	1 359	0.0	9.6	4.2	268	...
Mecklenburg, NC	611 574	6 193	59.3	34 198	0.0	8.6	5.7	4 702	...
Mitchell, NC	13 830	5 760	61.0	740	0.0	21.4	5.7	126	...
Montgomery, NC	25 721	5 882	63.9	1 425	0.1	8.8	11.8	222	...
Moore, NC	61 639	5 678	62.0	3 374	0.0	13.6	6.0	609	...
Nash, NC	99 189	5 492	64.5	4 745	0.0	11.9	6.8	861	...
New Hanover, NC	129 371	6 019	60.3	8 624	0.6	8.5	3.6	1 195	...
Northampton, NC	22 850	5 743	60.6	1 148	0.0	12.8	9.1	172	...
Onslow, NC	107 208	5 025	62.1	11 465	36.1	48.3	3.4	1 152	...
Orange, NC	103 569	7 067	63.9	10 630	0.0	4.0	1.8	841	...
Pamlico, NC	12 512	6 752	62.8	615	0.0	15.0	11.4	143	...
Pasquotank, NC	35 237	5 627	63.0	2 189	0.0	6.4	2.0	303	...
Pender, NC	34 600	5 446	59.4	2 057	0.0	10.7	8.5	319	...
Perquimans, NC	12 532	6 530	55.7	622	0.0	8.4	13.0	99	...
Person, NC	32 291	5 568	64.7	1 605	0.0	12.1	4.6	271	...
Pitt, NC	108 661	5 428	65.5	10 156	0.1	6.0	4.2	986	...
Polk, NC	14 940	6 301	63.7	637	0.0	10.4	6.6	108	...
Randolph, NC	105 404	5 110	62.9	6 383	0.0	10.3	8.9	917	...
Richmond, NC	45 913	5 503	64.7	2 850	2.7	15.5	13.4	364	...
Robeson, NC	123 350	5 125	64.7	7 841	0.0	10.3	11.6	980	...
Rockingham, NC	81 018	5 500	63.1	4 393	0.3	13.7	8.4	770	...
Rowan, NC	107 011	5 387	64.3	6 535	0.0	12.3	6.2	1 018	...

. . . = Not available.

Table C-1. Population, School, and Student Characteristics by County—*Continued*

County	Population 25 years and over	High school diploma or less (percent)	High school diploma or more (percent)	Number	Percent public	Bachelor's degree or more	+/- U.S. percent with bachelor's degree or more	Non-Hispanic White	Black or African American	American Indian and Alaska Native	Asian, Hawaiian, and Pacific Islander	Hispanic or Latino[1]
	30	31	32	33	34	35	36	37	38	39	40	41
Wyoming, NY	29 522	63.4	75.6	1 414	81.1	11.5	-12.9	12.6	0.3	24.4	43.8	1.9
Yates, NY	15 714	56.2	80.0	1 279	37.3	18.2	-6.2	18.4	3.4	36.7	60.0	1.3
NORTH CAROLINA												
Alamance, NC	86 635	54.6	76.5	7 545	49.3	19.2	-5.2	22.1	9.3	24.7	37.6	5.0
Alexander, NC	22 729	66.9	68.7	979	80.4	9.3	-15.1	9.6	2.9	0.0	14.1	2.2
Alleghany, NC	7 829	63.8	68.0	392	85.5	11.7	-12.7	12.0	0.0	27.3	26.7	2.3
Anson, NC	16 824	68.2	70.2	1 107	89.3	9.2	-15.2	12.7	4.9	0.0	52.6	22.6
Ashe, NC	17 722	64.7	68.6	795	92.6	12.1	-12.3	12.3	2.3	7.7	11.8	7.4
Avery, NC	12 058	61.2	70.6	1 024	51.5	14.5	-9.9	14.7	5.1	7.7	44.9	17.2
Beaufort, NC	30 868	58.7	75.0	1 728	91.1	16.0	-8.4	20.2	5.1	0.0	0.0	10.2
Bertie, NC	13 135	72.9	63.8	481	84.4	8.8	-15.6	11.4	6.7	44.1	45.8	15.2
Bladen, NC	21 409	63.2	70.6	1 484	94.1	11.3	-13.1	14.1	6.8	6.0	66.7	11.2
Brunswick, NC	52 605	55.0	78.3	2 062	89.9	16.1	-8.3	17.3	9.2	5.8	29.2	6.6
Buncombe, NC	143 649	46.4	81.9	10 777	78.6	25.3	0.9	26.5	9.9	14.3	41.3	13.7
Burke, NC	59 922	62.8	67.6	3 109	83.7	12.8	-11.6	13.6	6.6	12.0	7.9	3.0
Cabarrus, NC	86 732	51.9	78.2	5 028	78.8	19.1	-5.3	20.4	12.7	15.7	34.0	3.6
Caldwell, NC	53 539	65.9	66.2	2 403	87.8	10.4	-14.0	10.7	6.3	7.6	22.5	1.6
Camden, NC	4 770	51.9	82.1	264	85.6	16.2	-8.2	16.1	15.4	0.0	0.0	51.0
Carteret, NC	43 457	47.6	82.1	2 223	85.4	19.8	-4.6	20.7	6.4	14.8	5.5	26.9
Caswell, NC	16 212	67.5	69.2	786	89.1	8.3	-16.1	10.4	4.2	4.2	42.4	10.1
Catawba, NC	94 747	56.5	74.8	5 405	69.1	17.0	-7.4	18.6	7.8	3.9	13.5	4.3
Chatham, NC	34 920	48.8	77.9	1 797	86.0	27.6	3.2	33.2	10.8	30.8	62.0	3.7
Cherokee, NC	17 709	61.5	73.3	835	89.5	11.0	-13.4	11.1	12.6	7.0	0.0	12.1
Chowan, NC	9 583	60.5	73.1	899	50.3	16.4	-8.0	19.7	10.0	0.0	0.0	20.7
Clay, NC	6 578	57.3	76.5	426	89.4	15.4	-9.0	15.5	0.0	15.8	0.0	0.0
Cleveland, NC	63 396	61.9	72.2	4 276	59.9	13.3	-11.1	14.9	6.3	6.2	30.4	10.4
Columbus, NC	35 921	65.1	68.6	2 284	90.4	10.1	-14.3	12.0	6.1	5.8	36.6	3.5
Craven, NC	57 027	47.9	82.1	4 413	85.9	19.3	-5.1	23.4	7.0	16.7	23.2	10.6
Cumberland, NC	176 714	43.4	85.0	20 830	76.4	19.1	-5.3	22.5	14.6	10.9	19.6	13.6
Currituck, NC	12 361	56.9	77.6	555	79.1	13.3	-11.1	13.4	8.9	8.5	32.3	14.5
Dare, NC	21 713	39.0	88.6	682	83.6	27.7	3.3	28.2	6.6	19.4	28.6	18.0
Davidson, NC	100 128	61.2	72.0	4 371	82.5	12.8	-11.6	13.3	7.9	7.4	18.5	4.8
Davie, NC	23 840	56.6	78.1	1 180	77.4	17.6	-6.8	18.6	9.2	0.0	100.0	2.5
Duplin, NC	31 700	65.8	65.8	1 402	84.7	10.5	-13.9	12.9	7.4	0.0	12.9	5.1
Durham, NC	143 804	36.2	83.0	23 187	50.6	40.1	15.7	49.5	26.6	35.3	77.8	14.5
Edgecombe, NC	35 748	71.3	65.6	1 822	83.0	8.5	-15.9	12.0	5.8	0.0	8.6	4.3
Forsyth, NC	204 081	45.0	82.0	18 750	58.0	28.7	4.3	32.8	18.0	20.0	52.8	8.9
Franklin, NC	31 467	60.9	73.6	1 802	62.3	13.2	-11.2	16.1	6.4	5.7	48.1	6.0
Gaston, NC	127 748	58.2	71.4	7 020	75.9	14.2	-10.2	14.8	9.8	7.4	22.5	10.4
Gates, NC	7 095	63.9	71.4	324	86.4	10.5	-13.9	10.3	9.7	32.4	46.8	0.0
Graham, NC	5 622	67.6	68.4	220	88.2	11.2	-13.2	11.8	. . .	0.0	0.0	0.0
Granville, NC	32 641	61.1	73.0	1 852	84.2	13.0	-11.4	16.8	6.3	4.1	26.7	7.9
Greene, NC	12 380	69.3	65.4	628	85.0	8.2	-16.2	11.4	3.9	0.0	0.0	4.8
Guilford, NC	275 494	42.2	83.0	32 524	79.6	30.3	5.9	35.1	19.7	12.3	30.8	13.3
Halifax, NC	37 719	67.7	65.4	1 959	90.3	11.1	-13.3	15.6	7.0	2.8	32.7	10.1
Harnett, NC	57 138	57.6	75.0	6 071	56.8	12.8	-11.6	14.9	6.4	8.0	20.9	6.2
Haywood, NC	39 552	54.4	77.7	2 173	85.2	16.0	-8.4	16.0	7.0	27.3	64.7	5.9
Henderson, NC	65 039	46.0	83.2	2 843	88.0	24.1	-0.3	25.4	8.2	3.0	26.3	5.6
Hertford, NC	14 976	65.3	65.6	781	77.0	11.1	-13.3	14.2	8.8	12.1	17.0	7.3
Hoke, NC	19 934	58.9	73.5	1 723	81.3	10.9	-13.5	16.3	4.6	7.1	23.0	9.8
Hyde, NC	4 190	67.9	68.4	72	91.7	10.6	-13.8	12.7	6.4	0.0	. . .	0.0
Iredell, NC	82 036	53.7	78.4	4 050	83.5	17.4	-7.0	19.4	5.4	11.8	26.8	7.9
Jackson, NC	20 881	46.9	78.8	5 086	94.9	25.5	1.1	27.2	36.7	8.9	19.5	14.9
Johnston, NC	80 268	55.9	75.9	4 186	82.6	15.9	-8.5	17.5	9.5	20.7	25.8	6.9
Jones, NC	6 998	64.2	72.2	379	85.8	9.5	-14.9	10.8	7.1	0.0	37.5	1.6
Lee, NC	32 043	53.6	76.3	1 780	86.2	17.2	-7.2	21.2	6.7	13.0	40.8	5.6
Lenoir, NC	39 833	59.4	71.9	2 379	89.1	13.3	-11.1	17.1	7.4	8.1	39.7	0.9
Lincoln, NC	43 259	60.1	71.7	2 024	83.2	13.0	-11.4	13.6	4.8	12.8	15.2	11.1
McDowell, NC	29 157	65.9	70.2	1 318	85.5	9.0	-15.4	9.0	5.4	10.1	30.5	1.2
Macon, NC	21 908	54.9	77.3	1 062	88.2	16.2	-8.2	16.2	12.4	0.0	34.7	5.3
Madison, NC	13 409	62.5	69.3	1 267	35.8	16.1	-8.3	16.1	5.0	66.7	10.5	18.9
Martin, NC	17 014	63.9	70.7	930	89.0	11.6	-12.8	15.9	6.0	0.0	35.7	3.3
Mecklenburg, NC	455 163	33.7	86.2	42 462	74.5	37.1	12.7	45.2	20.3	20.7	39.7	14.3
Mitchell, NC	11 315	64.3	68.6	452	79.2	12.2	-12.2	12.0	0.0	0.0	56.7	13.0
Montgomery, NC	17 713	67.9	64.2	844	86.1	10.0	-14.4	12.3	4.6	8.1	14.4	1.7
Moore, NC	53 347	43.3	82.6	2 803	92.3	26.8	2.4	30.7	6.7	11.0	38.5	8.3
Nash, NC	57 522	58.3	75.6	3 925	78.3	17.2	-7.2	21.6	8.3	19.9	45.6	7.7
New Hanover, NC	107 671	38.2	86.3	14 962	91.5	31.0	6.6	34.4	13.2	21.5	49.9	17.0
Northampton, NC	15 199	69.0	62.5	733	89.9	10.8	-13.6	15.2	7.3	24.2	20.0	6.4
Onslow, NC	75 286	48.5	84.3	8 820	84.0	14.8	-9.6	16.1	10.0	14.3	11.6	12.7
Orange, NC	69 530	28.3	87.6	24 674	95.4	51.5	27.1	57.2	19.5	15.7	80.6	27.6
Pamlico, NC	9 332	56.1	75.2	457	89.3	14.7	-9.7	18.1	4.8	0.0	3.8	1.7
Pasquotank, NC	22 223	53.5	76.8	2 936	83.3	16.4	-8.0	16.1	16.2	32.5	29.3	20.8
Pender, NC	28 566	56.7	76.8	1 339	82.4	13.6	-10.8	15.8	6.8	0.0	27.5	6.3
Perquimans, NC	7 970	61.1	71.9	343	91.8	12.3	-12.1	13.3	9.6	0.0	. . .	19.1
Person, NC	24 473	63.2	74.9	1 268	88.9	10.3	-14.1	11.4	7.3	0.0	30.1	18.5
Pitt, NC	79 040	45.3	79.9	20 154	95.8	26.4	2.0	34.0	11.0	30.6	53.7	13.6
Polk, NC	13 653	47.6	80.6	582	83.5	25.7	1.3	26.7	6.4	49.1	74.1	14.0
Randolph, NC	87 450	65.7	70.0	3 898	84.9	11.1	-13.3	11.5	6.9	6.7	25.4	5.6
Richmond, NC	29 870	66.5	69.2	1 641	89.2	10.1	-14.3	11.6	6.6	7.6	14.0	6.1
Robeson, NC	74 458	65.8	64.9	5 683	91.7	11.4	-13.0	16.4	8.3	8.5	27.7	5.0
Rockingham, NC	63 470	64.4	68.9	2 722	85.3	10.8	-13.6	12.0	6.5	8.2	17.7	2.6
Rowan, NC	86 345	59.3	74.2	5 618	64.4	14.2	-10.2	14.8	12.2	10.6	15.9	4.4

[1]Hispanic or Latino persons may be of any race.
. . . = Not available.

Table C-1. Population, School, and Student Characteristics by County—*Continued*

County	State/ County code	County type[1]	Population, 2000		Number of schools and students, 2000–2001			Resident enrollment, 2000			
			Total	Percent 5–17 years	School districts	Schools	Students	Total	Percent public	K–12	Percent public
			1	2	3	4	5	6	7	8	9
Scotland, NC	37165	7	35 998	20.8	3	16	7 293	10 267	90.1	7 652	96.5
Stanly, NC	37167	6	58 100	18.8	2	21	10 230	14 133	87.9	11 004	95.0
Stokes, NC	37169	2	44 711	17.9	1	18	7 420	9 914	88.7	8 106	92.5
Surry, NC	37171	6	71 219	17.2	4	24	11 540	15 791	93.7	12 328	97.0
Swain, NC	37173	9	12 968	18.1	1	5	1 749	3 071	92.9	2 409	96.7
Transylvania, NC	37175	6	29 334	15.5	2	10	4 069	6 292	81.9	4 469	93.1
Tyrrell, NC	37177	9	4 149	17.7	1	2	745	994	93.9	803	94.3
Union, NC	37179	1	123 677	20.0	2	34	23 156	32 693	82.2	24 979	90.5
Vance, NC	37181	6	42 954	20.0	2	16	8 638	10 894	92.4	8 523	94.7
Wake, NC	37183	2	627 846	17.9	14	133	101 310	178 475	82.0	112 881	89.4
Warren, NC	37185	8	19 972	18.2	2	7	3 248	4 667	87.6	3 818	87.8
Washington, NC	37187	7	13 723	19.4	1	5	2 293	3 423	91.8	2 797	92.6
Watauga, NC	37189	7	42 695	12.4	1	9	4 891	16 832	91.9	5 355	92.7
Wayne, NC	37191	3	113 329	19.2	3	33	19 493	29 896	86.7	22 655	91.8
Wilkes, NC	37193	7	65 632	16.4	2	22	10 557	13 770	93.2	10 722	97.6
Wilson, NC	37195	4	73 814	18.7	2	24	12 641	18 243	86.3	13 997	93.2
Yadkin, NC	37197	2	36 348	17.3	1	10	5 851	7 982	90.0	6 360	93.6
Yancey, NC	37199	8	17 774	15.7	1	9	2 520	3 307	91.1	2 764	95.0
NORTH DAKOTA	38000										
Adams, ND	38001	9	2 593	18.7	1	2	406	577	96.7	526	99.6
Barnes, ND	38003	7	11 775	17.0	5	10	1 794	3 096	94.8	2 060	95.1
Benson, ND	38005	9	6 964	27.2	6	10	1 020	2 216	98.1	1 927	98.0
Billings, ND	38007	9	888	21.4	1	2	79	210	96.7	183	97.8
Bottineau, ND	38009	7	7 149	18.3	5	9	1 182	1 786	98.4	1 324	99.8
Bowman, ND	38011	9	3 242	19.5	3	6	740	752	97.7	665	98.6
Burke, ND	38013	9	2 242	17.2	3	6	357	438	94.3	408	94.6
Burleigh, ND	38015	3	69 416	18.5	11	35	10 826	18 617	79.3	12 849	86.6
Cass, ND	38017	3	123 138	16.8	8	42	19 036	37 145	91.8	20 881	93.2
Cavalier, ND	38019	9	4 831	20.3	5	9	832	1 094	91.2	1 031	91.3
Dickey, ND	38021	9	5 757	18.1	2	5	948	1 531	78.7	1 047	94.7
Divide, ND	38023	9	2 283	17.2	1	2	333	436	99.5	407	99.5
Dunn, ND	38025	9	3 600	21.7	4	6	558	972	95.8	862	96.2
Eddy, ND	38027	9	2 757	18.6	2	4	523	597	97.5	522	98.7
Emmons, ND	38029	8	4 331	19.5	5	8	784	923	96.1	840	98.3
Foster, ND	38031	9	3 759	20.9	1	2	713	982	95.0	816	98.2
Golden Valley, ND	38033	9	1 924	22.9	2	3	447	505	94.7	445	96.2
Grand Forks, ND	38035	3	66 109	17.4	7	31	10 546	23 794	95.1	11 757	94.6
Grant, ND	38037	8	2 841	19.1	2	5	389	629	96.8	552	98.9
Griggs, ND	38039	9	2 754	17.8	2	5	565	609	98.0	545	99.8
Hettinger, ND	38041	9	2 715	18.9	3	6	567	596	98.0	540	99.6
Kidder, ND	38043	8	2 753	18.2	5	7	497	539	97.4	507	99.0
La Moure, ND	38045	9	4 701	19.8	5	11	1 013	1 074	94.3	977	96.5
Logan, ND	38047	9	2 308	17.1	2	4	442	483	93.4	421	96.0
McHenry, ND	38049	9	5 987	19.0	6	12	1 136	1 351	99.0	1 183	99.8
McIntosh, ND	38051	9	3 390	15.2	3	6	533	654	94.3	569	96.8
McKenzie, ND	38053	9	5 737	24.4	7	12	1 097	1 675	94.0	1 454	95.0
McLean, ND	38055	8	9 311	19.1	7	14	1 840	2 082	98.1	1 858	99.3
Mercer, ND	38057	7	8 644	24.5	4	9	1 999	2 442	95.1	2 188	97.0
Morton, ND	38059	3	25 303	20.5	9	21	5 050	6 330	89.1	5 190	91.3
Mountrail, ND	38061	9	6 631	21.6	4	8	1 530	1 796	95.2	1 464	96.7
Nelson, ND	38063	8	3 715	18.4	2	5	694	823	93.2	730	95.2
Oliver, ND	38065	8	2 065	22.9	1	2	282	549	90.9	500	92.8
Pembina, ND	38067	9	8 585	19.9	7	15	1 754	1 954	97.5	1 734	99.0
Pierce, ND	38069	7	4 675	18.6	2	4	740	1 028	93.6	894	93.4
Ramsey, ND	38071	7	12 066	19.4	4	11	2 285	3 016	91.1	2 346	92.7
Ransom, ND	38073	5	5 890	19.1	5	9	1 120	1 311	95.7	1 181	97.1
Renville, ND	38075	9	2 610	19.0	3	6	731	596	95.3	521	99.0
Richland, ND	38077	6	17 998	18.7	7	15	2 954	5 726	93.6	3 497	93.8
Rolette, ND	38079	9	13 674	27.6	5	11	3 159	4 863	97.1	3 857	97.4
Sargent, ND	38081	3	4 366	20.8	3	7	876	988	96.4	874	97.8
Sheridan, ND	38083	9	1 710	18.2	2	4	197	339	98.5	322	100.0
Sioux, ND	38085	9	4 044	29.8	3	6	467	1 566	91.3	1 258	93.4
Slope, ND	38087	9	767	20.6	3	3	35	180	96.1	157	100.0
Stark, ND	38089	7	22 636	19.8	5	14	3 844	6 347	81.6	4 586	78.6
Steele, ND	38091	8	2 258	22.0	2	4	336	585	97.8	500	99.6
Stutsman, ND	38093	7	21 908	17.5	6	17	3 269	5 399	76.4	3 983	93.2
Towner, ND	38095	9	2 876	19.9	3	6	503	679	97.3	595	99.5
Traill, ND	38097	8	8 477	18.8	4	9	1 729	2 369	98.6	1 606	98.7
Walsh, ND	38099	6	12 389	19.2	8	15	2 172	2 811	95.5	2 438	97.1
Ward, ND	38101	5	58 795	18.8	11	35	9 778	16 316	91.5	11 203	91.8
Wells, ND	38103	9	5 102	18.1	5	8	925	1 158	95.3	998	97.4
Williams, ND	38105	7	19 761	20.4	7	21	3 569	5 133	91.4	4 161	91.7

[1]County type code is from the Economic Research Service of the USDA. See Notes and Definitions at the end of this section.

Table C-1. School and Student Characteristics by County—*Continued*

County	Characteristics of students, 2000–2001			Staff and students, 2000–2001				Revenues, fiscal 1999			
	Percent with IEP[2]	Percent eligible for free lunch	Percent minority	Number of teachers	Student/ teacher ratio	Local school non-teaching staff	Central admin. staff	Total revenue ($1,000s)	Percentage of revenue from		
									Federal govt.	State govt.	Local govt.
	10	11	12	13	14	15	16	17	18	19	20
Rutherford, NC	13.9	42.1	20.0	698	14.8	716	22	$73 557	7.5	67.6	24.8
Sampson, NC	12.9	57.3	50.6	715	14.7	627	24	67 606	9.5	71.7	18.8
Scotland, NC	15.3	54.6	60.2	556	13.1	467	15	48 930	9.8	68.3	21.9
Stanly, NC	16.8	36.8	23.4	633	16.2	577	3	65 242	5.3	78.3	16.3
Stokes, NC	15.9	24.6	7.8	497	14.9	404	7	47 954	5.4	68.2	26.4
Surry, NC	15.0	35.1	16.0	850	13.6	691	24	79 609	6.0	63.8	30.2
Swain, NC	18.7	56.3	22.8	147	11.9	114	12	13 489	13.2	73.3	13.6
Transylvania, NC	12.4	33.7	9.0	294	13.8	205	7	28 734	5.8	63.8	30.4
Tyrrell, NC	17.0	65.1	50.7	64	11.6	65	4	8 664	8.3	78.8	12.9
Union, NC	12.5	27.8	24.8	1 455	15.9	1 231	40	132 106	4.7	67.5	27.8
Vance, NC	13.0	63.9	68.4	438	19.7	647	22	58 338	8.7	71.7	19.6
Wake, NC	14.0	24.2	36.9	6 550	15.5	5 215	94	639 738	3.8	59.2	37.1
Warren, NC	15.2	67.9	80.4	214	15.2	219	13	23 479	9.9	72.3	17.9
Washington, NC	18.4	78.6	72.7	198	11.6	236	14	18 200	12.2	71.3	16.5
Watauga, NC	16.0	25.6	4.2	379	12.9	306	17	33 939	5.8	63.7	30.5
Wayne, NC	14.7	48.0	50.9	1 370	14.2	1 160	29	123 668	8.5	75.6	15.9
Wilkes, NC	14.7	35.6	10.1	684	15.4	633	13	62 354	6.5	67.4	26.1
Wilson, NC	12.7	53.9	61.0	854	14.8	736	31	77 050	9.1	65.6	25.3
Yadkin, NC	17.6	28.5	13.9	391	15.0	383	13	36 616	5.6	70.6	23.8
Yancey, NC	14.7	38.1	5.0	193	13.1	190	10	19 801	6.5	77.4	16.1
NORTH DAKOTA											
Adams, ND	9.9	34.0	1.5	29	14.0	21	4	3 217	3.2	39.5	57.3
Barnes, ND	13.9	31.8	2.5	123	14.6	105	15	13 373	9.8	42.3	48.0
Benson, ND	18.6	63.1	50.9	91	11.2	75	13	8 617	30.2	37.4	32.4
Billings, ND	12.7	35.4	0.0	11	7.2	10	2	1 690	26.6	1.0	72.4
Bottineau, ND	15.1	34.8	4.1	98	12.1	76	14	8 702	7.9	37.9	54.2
Bowman, ND	9.5	29.5	1.9	63	11.7	41	5	4 836	4.9	41.3	53.8
Burke, ND	12.9	38.1	2.2	45	7.9	25	5	3 173	4.7	38.1	57.2
Burleigh, ND	11.5	18.8	7.1	683	15.9	534	46	64 202	8.7	40.1	51.2
Cass, ND	11.3	18.5	6.4	1 182	16.1	953	79	134 982	4.4	31.4	64.2
Cavalier, ND	10.1	32.6	0.6	74	11.2	48	6	5 994	5.1	35.0	60.0
Dickey, ND	10.1	35.5	4.0	64	14.8	43	8	6 125	5.3	40.8	54.0
Divide, ND	6.0	29.7	1.8	28	11.9	22	3	2 511	7.0	37.8	55.2
Dunn, ND	9.3	42.8	16.7	56	10.0	49	10	3 787	5.1	40.2	54.7
Eddy, ND	10.9	37.9	14.3	41	12.8	33	6	3 946	9.5	41.0	49.4
Emmons, ND	11.7	48.1	0.9	64	12.3	54	7	7 296	5.7	30.6	63.7
Foster, ND	9.0	21.3	2.5	48	14.9	28	3	3 725	5.2	47.4	47.4
Golden Valley, ND	9.8	53.9	7.2	38	11.8	32	4	3 240	8.8	39.6	51.5
Grand Forks, ND	12.8	26.3	11.0	754	14.0	587	66	80 366	17.9	33.6	48.5
Grant, ND	12.3	73.8	5.9	43	9.0	28	6	3 469	10.4	41.3	48.3
Griggs, ND	8.5	40.2	0.7	48	11.8	32	6	4 546	4.7	38.2	57.0
Hettinger, ND	10.4	44.4	1.6	54	10.5	45	5	4 841	6.0	42.1	51.8
Kidder, ND	11.1	47.1	0.2	51	9.7	32	9	3 977	6.6	37.2	56.1
La Moure, ND	11.3	42.6	1.9	81	12.5	61	13	7 488	7.3	38.0	54.8
Logan, ND	13.6	41.2	1.8	40	11.1	19	6	3 747	12.4	41.1	46.5
McHenry, ND	13.5	34.5	1.8	104	10.9	68	11	7 261	7.3	45.0	47.7
McIntosh, ND	11.3	42.6	0.8	51	10.5	29	6	3 674	6.4	39.4	54.2
McKenzie, ND	14.1	42.4	26.0	105	10.4	94	13	10 438	32.4	29.4	38.1
McLean, ND	10.7	33.5	13.0	158	11.6	111	20	12 645	7.2	45.7	47.2
Mercer, ND	11.8	13.4	5.3	127	15.7	110	13	13 584	4.1	42.4	53.4
Morton, ND	12.7	30.2	7.6	325	15.5	275	26	26 584	8.0	46.0	46.0
Mountrail, ND	17.1	57.1	50.9	121	12.6	101	13	10 109	27.1	40.3	32.6
Nelson, ND	11.0	37.6	0.9	52	13.3	45	4	5 284	5.4	32.9	61.7
Oliver, ND	13.8	17.7	5.0	23	12.3	21	3	2 040	4.8	42.6	52.5
Pembina, ND	12.4	23.4	8.2	146	12.0	85	14	13 885	5.3	38.8	56.0
Pierce, ND	9.7	34.7	2.8	62	11.9	36	2	4 801	4.8	43.4	51.8
Ramsey, ND	14.0	39.5	19.3	165	13.8	190	30	15 860	9.1	40.9	50.0
Ransom, ND	14.3	18.8	4.1	82	13.7	44	7	6 777	3.9	39.8	56.3
Renville, ND	16.8	39.8	4.0	62	11.8	42	6	4 690	7.2	44.2	48.6
Richland, ND	12.2	23.7	4.6	217	13.6	191	21	20 729	7.2	39.2	53.6
Rolette, ND	9.4	63.6	78.5	302	10.5	264	29	24 084	45.0	39.2	15.8
Sargent, ND	12.9	20.0	1.5	61	14.4	36	6	4 949	3.5	41.3	55.2
Sheridan, ND	15.7	51.8	1.5	22	9.0	17	2	1 748	4.7	40.7	54.6
Sioux, ND	27.8	93.4	93.1	69	6.8	63	10	5 877	51.9	35.3	12.8
Slope, ND	...	...	0.0	5	7.0	2	1	480	18.8	30.0	51.3
Stark, ND	10.4	34.1	3.3	247	15.6	214	16	21 840	10.7	46.8	42.5
Steele, ND	11.3	37.2	0.3	31	10.8	17	2	2 749	4.4	34.2	61.4
Stutsman, ND	15.8	27.1	4.1	227	14.4	179	23	20 113	7.6	44.7	47.7
Towner, ND	10.3	43.5	3.0	47	10.7	27	4	3 640	6.2	39.5	54.3
Traill, ND	8.5	23.8	6.3	112	15.4	84	12	12 063	6.3	37.3	56.4
Walsh, ND	14.4	31.4	10.0	159	13.7	138	17	17 640	10.0	37.9	52.1
Ward, ND	14.4	30.8	8.9	694	14.1	557	39	75 896	21.2	32.7	46.1
Wells, ND	11.5	31.4	1.4	78	11.9	65	13	7 081	8.3	39.3	52.3
Williams, ND	13.0	28.0	10.8	274	13.0	193	22	25 723	12.4	40.2	47.3

[2]IEP = Individual Education Program. See Notes and Definitions at the end of this section.

Table C-1. Population, School, and Student Characteristics by County—*Continued*

County	Current expenditures, fiscal 1999			Resident population 16 to 19 years, 2000				Outcomes, 1999–2000	
	Amount ($1,000s)	Amount per student	Percent for instruction	Total population 16 to 19 years	Percent in Armed Forces	Percent high school graduates	Percent not enrolled, not grads, not Armed Forces, not empl.	Number of graduates	Dropouts grades 9–12 (percent)
	21	22	23	24	25	26	27	28	29
Rutherford, NC	$57 943	$5 627	64.7	3 047	0.3	11.9	10.1	494	...
Sampson, NC	56 137	5 525	63.1	3 314	0.1	10.6	9.8	528	...
Scotland, NC	43 490	6 075	62.8	2 083	0.0	10.6	5.8	337	...
Stanly, NC	52 645	5 206	66.6	3 090	0.2	10.9	6.6	590	...
Stokes, NC	40 468	5 669	61.5	2 042	0.0	13.4	6.2	371	...
Surry, NC	66 399	5 865	63.9	3 178	0.0	11.4	6.6	587	...
Swain, NC	11 154	6 612	63.9	813	0.0	24.8	7.3	98	...
Transylvania, NC	22 407	5 732	63.3	1 557	0.0	11.1	6.5	249	...
Tyrrell, NC	6 466	8 083	59.5	198	0.0	7.6	3.5	56	...
Union, NC	106 319	5 106	64.4	6 438	0.0	12.3	4.6	1 037	...
Vance, NC	45 195	5 516	63.2	2 354	0.1	14.1	18.8	273	...
Wake, NC	515 960	5 593	62.7	32 322	0.0	7.9	3.9	4 805	...
Warren, NC	19 512	6 024	57.8	1 056	0.0	11.0	10.4	140	...
Washington, NC	16 331	6 207	63.6	796	0.0	9.3	8.3	157	...
Watauga, NC	27 847	5 792	63.5	4 685	0.0	3.6	0.8	310	...
Wayne, NC	101 444	5 271	66.4	6 104	1.8	10.8	6.9	994	...
Wilkes, NC	56 698	5 678	63.9	3 082	0.0	10.3	6.0	505	...
Wilson, NC	68 364	5 675	66.7	4 250	0.0	8.7	11.3	553	...
Yadkin, NC	31 289	5 487	60.7	1 581	0.0	8.9	5.8	313	...
Yancey, NC	15 561	6 160	61.1	852	0.0	21.4	8.7	144	...
NORTH DAKOTA									
Adams, ND	2 722	5 499	55.0	142	0.0	6.3	1.4	40	0.6
Barnes, ND	11 637	5 913	63.2	860	0.1	6.9	2.9	160	0.3
Benson, ND	7 157	6 746	58.9	490	0.0	5.3	10.2	83	4.0
Billings, ND	1 557	14 551	49.6	59	0.0	6.8	0.0	0	...
Bottineau, ND	7 632	6 005	58.5	538	0.0	3.7	0.4	92	1.3
Bowman, ND	4 597	5 871	62.9	165	0.0	2.4	0.0	69	0.3
Burke, ND	2 852	7 148	62.4	120	0.0	2.5	1.7	38	0.7
Burleigh, ND	54 859	4 949	65.3	4 638	0.0	7.7	1.6	812	2.8
Cass, ND	101 686	5 277	63.9	7 786	0.1	8.6	2.1	1 295	3.6
Cavalier, ND	5 567	6 341	56.9	246	0.0	1.6	0.0	72	1.9
Dickey, ND	4 913	5 081	56.3	355	0.0	8.5	0.8	62	0.3
Divide, ND	2 361	6 038	55.7	122	0.0	2.5	4.1	34	0.8
Dunn, ND	3 310	5 932	59.3	203	0.0	8.4	2.5	50	...
Eddy, ND	3 457	5 940	58.6	140	0.0	7.1	2.1	55	...
Emmons, ND	4 670	5 661	56.8	215	0.0	2.8	0.0	63	1.6
Foster, ND	3 187	4 155	60.9	208	0.0	5.8	0.0	55	0.4
Golden Valley, ND	3 033	6 565	51.7	155	0.0	7.1	2.6	25	1.1
Grand Forks, ND	56 786	5 162	65.0	5 458	2.0	8.7	1.7	774	1.7
Grant, ND	3 052	7 032	51.7	175	0.0	5.7	2.3	41	0.6
Griggs, ND	3 906	6 200	52.3	171	0.0	2.3	0.6	68	1.2
Hettinger, ND	4 050	6 459	57.9	145	0.0	7.6	1.4	58	...
Kidder, ND	3 451	6 487	53.8	178	0.0	10.7	7.9	35	1.1
La Moure, ND	6 463	6 132	55.2	319	0.0	3.1	2.8	95	...
Logan, ND	2 829	5 931	54.6	98	0.0	5.1	2.0	39	0.6
McHenry, ND	6 595	5 455	59.8	355	0.0	6.8	0.8	99	...
McIntosh, ND	3 206	5 644	56.5	166	0.0	3.0	0.0	65	1.9
McKenzie, ND	9 486	8 199	54.6	400	0.0	5.0	2.3	83	4.3
McLean, ND	11 490	5 334	55.7	570	0.2	7.0	1.4	186	2.3
Mercer, ND	11 600	5 418	57.6	597	0.0	6.9	0.8	193	0.8
Morton, ND	23 525	4 761	61.6	1 511	0.2	9.7	5.6	407	3.0
Mountrail, ND	8 761	5 452	59.1	400	0.3	4.8	5.3	105	6.3
Nelson, ND	4 273	5 705	54.7	205	0.0	1.0	0.0	57	...
Oliver, ND	1 829	5 476	59.5	135	0.0	1.5	1.5	37	...
Pembina, ND	11 402	6 078	62.5	555	0.0	8.5	3.6	137	1.0
Pierce, ND	4 037	4 953	58.6	249	0.0	8.0	0.0	96	0.3
Ramsey, ND	13 220	5 688	57.3	844	0.0	11.7	6.0	182	2.8
Ransom, ND	5 559	4 668	55.2	329	0.0	4.6	2.7	98	1.0
Renville, ND	4 235	5 465	55.1	165	1.2	11.5	0.0	68	1.0
Richland, ND	17 592	5 620	63.7	1 655	0.0	5.5	0.3	245	1.8
Rolette, ND	20 987	6 274	58.2	1 027	0.0	6.3	11.9	208	10.5
Sargent, ND	4 173	4 819	58.7	194	0.0	7.2	0.0	66	0.4
Sheridan, ND	1 642	7 363	62.9	75	0.0	4.0	5.3	17	1.4
Sioux, ND	5 390	9 608	56.6	348	0.0	6.6	12.9	24	11.2
Slope, ND	281	6 854	64.1	52	0.0	7.7	0.0	0	...
Stark, ND	19 134	4 706	63.0	1 687	0.2	10.8	3.2	321	1.8
Steele, ND	2 376	6 492	55.9	139	0.0	2.9	2.2	14	3.0
Stutsman, ND	17 613	5 108	61.8	1 471	0.2	9.2	3.3	280	4.1
Towner, ND	3 205	5 555	58.5	165	0.0	2.4	2.4	43	0.5
Traill, ND	10 201	5 617	57.7	544	0.0	4.2	1.3	137	2.7
Walsh, ND	14 363	5 985	64.0	789	0.0	11.9	2.4	177	2.0
Ward, ND	51 612	5 032	61.3	3 782	7.7	17.8	2.7	741	3.2
Wells, ND	6 077	5 871	56.4	278	0.0	4.0	4.0	79	2.1
Williams, ND	22 226	5 625	62.1	1 400	0.1	6.6	2.0	326	3.1

. . . = Not available.

Table C-1. Population, School, and Student Characteristics by County—*Continued*

County	Population 25 years and over	High school diploma or less (percent)	High school diploma or more (percent)	College enrollment, 2000 Number	College enrollment, 2000 Percent public	Bachelor's degree or more	+/- U.S. percent with bachelor's degree or more	Non-Hispanic White	Black or African American	American Indian and Alaska Native	Asian, Hawaiian, and Pacific Islander	Hispanic or Latino[1]
	30	31	32	33	34	35	36	37	38	39	40	41
Rutherford, NC	42 889	62.9	70.4	2 368	86.7	12.5	-11.9	13.3	5.0	4.8	29.5	11.8
Sampson, NC	38 796	66.1	69.1	2 078	86.3	11.1	-13.3	13.5	6.9	9.8	10.4	6.6
Scotland, NC	22 563	58.1	71.4	1 881	72.7	15.9	-8.5	20.7	10.3	2.8	48.9	42.0
Stanly, NC	38 702	62.5	73.4	2 196	65.7	12.7	-11.7	13.4	6.5	4.9	30.0	9.2
Stokes, NC	30 598	66.9	73.2	1 163	77.2	9.3	-15.1	9.6	4.8	0.0	32.5	6.2
Surry, NC	49 018	62.5	67.0	2 652	84.5	12.0	-12.4	12.8	6.7	4.6	15.1	1.3
Swain, NC	8 739	59.6	70.5	438	81.3	13.9	-10.5	14.8	24.4	9.8	59.1	9.3
Transylvania, NC	20 973	47.5	82.5	1 462	57.2	23.7	-0.7	24.0	14.3	19.7	50.0	16.1
Tyrrell, NC	2 828	67.5	66.3	156	96.8	10.6	-13.8	13.9	5.0	0.0	0.0	15.7
Union, NC	78 878	50.6	80.2	4 781	66.7	21.3	-3.1	23.6	9.1	23.8	41.8	6.6
Vance, NC	27 360	66.2	68.1	1 332	87.4	10.7	-13.7	14.0	6.6	11.1	68.5	5.4
Wake, NC	403 481	28.4	89.3	51 713	78.9	43.9	19.5	49.2	24.3	29.8	65.6	17.8
Warren, NC	13 599	64.5	67.5	618	88.7	11.6	-12.8	16.8	7.2	2.0	17.0	20.5
Washington, NC	9 091	67.5	69.9	377	88.1	11.6	-12.8	15.9	5.9	...	63.3	3.9
Watauga, NC	23 939	42.2	81.6	10 952	93.2	33.2	8.8	33.5	27.0	28.3	56.1	33.6
Wayne, NC	72 894	55.3	77.2	5 211	78.5	15.0	-9.4	17.9	9.5	2.5	31.9	6.1
Wilkes, NC	45 498	65.5	66.0	2 024	87.8	11.3	-13.1	11.7	4.7	0.0	20.1	4.1
Wilson, NC	48 061	62.3	69.4	3 210	66.0	15.1	-9.3	21.4	5.5	31.0	38.9	3.1
Yadkin, NC	24 916	64.8	72.0	1 149	77.0	10.3	-14.1	10.5	4.4	0.0	82.9	6.5
Yancey, NC	12 709	65.7	71.1	444	70.3	13.1	-11.3	13.2	0.0	19.2	8.3	6.6
NORTH DAKOTA												
Adams, ND	1 885	52.3	83.1	35	80.0	16.6	-7.8	16.5	11.1	8.7	...	60.0
Barnes, ND	7 792	47.5	85.0	912	96.3	22.1	-2.3	22.1	13.3	14.9	38.9	56.3
Benson, ND	3 902	56.4	73.8	169	97.0	10.9	-13.5	14.1	...	4.4	0.0	8.0
Billings, ND	644	54.2	77.8	23	87.0	18.8	-5.6	18.9	...	...	...	...
Bottineau, ND	4 973	48.4	81.3	406	97.5	14.9	-9.5	14.8	...	20.0	100.0	0.0
Bowman, ND	2 290	49.9	82.2	61	93.4	17.9	-6.5	17.8	0.0	50.0	...	100.0
Burke, ND	1 687	56.1	78.8	21	100.0	12.0	-12.4	11.8	100.0	0.0	0.0	...
Burleigh, ND	44 636	35.8	87.9	4 801	63.5	28.7	4.3	29.2	6.7	6.8	38.1	26.6
Cass, ND	74 668	32.0	90.9	14 297	94.2	31.3	6.9	31.5	22.6	8.5	59.8	16.6
Cavalier, ND	3 462	51.6	78.8	28	78.6	13.1	-11.3	13.1	...	25.0	0.0	0.0
Dickey, ND	3 815	52.3	79.6	418	37.3	16.6	-7.8	16.4	0.0	26.3	100.0	15.6
Divide, ND	1 741	54.5	80.4	24	100.0	13.3	-11.1	13.2	...	0.0	50.0	0.0
Dunn, ND	2 393	54.7	77.5	71	94.4	16.3	-8.1	16.5	0.0	13.1	66.7	0.0
Eddy, ND	1 933	52.5	75.5	48	91.7	15.9	-8.5	15.8	...	17.4	100.0	0.0
Emmons, ND	3 125	64.1	65.9	60	90.0	12.3	-12.1	12.2	0.0	50.0	0.0	10.0
Foster, ND	2 569	51.9	78.0	77	64.9	19.8	-4.6	19.9	...	...	60.0	0.0
Golden Valley, ND	1 278	46.6	87.4	49	83.7	19.8	-4.6	19.9	...	...	...	0.0
Grand Forks, ND	37 366	35.2	89.2	11 022	97.4	27.8	3.4	28.3	16.6	17.0	40.2	16.9
Grant, ND	2 044	59.7	73.4	41	70.7	11.2	-13.2	10.9	...	18.2	100.0	0.0
Griggs, ND	1 993	53.9	78.7	40	82.5	15.7	-8.7	15.6	...	50.0	0.0	...
Hettinger, ND	1 978	57.8	74.8	37	81.1	14.4	-10.0	14.3	...	22.2	0.0	0.0
Kidder, ND	1 982	63.0	72.0	26	65.4	11.0	-13.4	11.1	...	0.0	...	0.0
La Moure, ND	3 297	58.5	75.3	65	73.8	13.9	-10.5	13.8	...	22.2	...	18.2
Logan, ND	1 693	63.7	66.0	42	88.1	12.9	-11.5	12.7	...	...	25.0	54.5
McHenry, ND	4 192	57.9	76.9	108	96.3	13.2	-11.2	13.1	33.3	25.0	60.0	20.0
McIntosh, ND	2 580	66.6	59.3	63	74.6	9.9	-14.5	9.6	...	0.0	60.0	16.7
McKenzie, ND	3 644	53.5	79.1	116	92.2	15.7	-8.7	16.4	33.3	10.5	31.6	12.5
McLean, ND	6 620	51.8	79.0	159	87.4	15.1	-9.3	15.2	...	12.4	60.0	11.8
Mercer, ND	5 780	52.0	79.0	151	81.5	14.4	-10.0	14.1	...	15.7	84.6	42.9
Morton, ND	16 520	51.7	80.2	716	76.5	17.0	-7.4	17.0	75.0	11.1	0.0	11.3
Mountrail, ND	4 309	51.7	77.9	235	85.5	15.6	-8.8	16.0	...	10.6	78.1	0.0
Nelson, ND	2 753	49.5	81.4	61	83.6	17.5	-6.9	17.2	100.0	12.5	88.9	...
Oliver, ND	1 402	55.4	79.9	39	64.1	12.0	-12.4	12.2	...	0.0	...	50.0
Pembina, ND	5 908	52.1	79.8	101	86.1	16.4	-8.0	16.7	50.0	5.6	80.0	9.4
Pierce, ND	3 300	53.3	76.7	101	98.0	14.7	-9.7	14.8	...	21.1	0.0	...
Ramsey, ND	8 123	45.1	80.1	518	97.1	18.8	-5.6	19.4	...	7.6	66.7	28.9
Ransom, ND	4 065	54.4	81.3	75	92.0	15.8	-8.6	15.7	0.0	0.0	80.0	23.5
Renville, ND	1 872	48.8	84.1	50	88.0	16.1	-8.3	15.6	...	18.2	57.1	0.0
Richland, ND	10 991	44.2	83.2	2 039	95.3	15.2	-9.2	15.3	...	5.1	23.3	3.5
Rolette, ND	7 406	52.9	73.7	719	95.5	14.7	-9.7	21.8	0.0	10.3	73.4	0.0
Sargent, ND	2 989	54.0	81.1	56	87.5	12.7	-11.7	12.6	100.0	28.6	...	0.0
Sheridan, ND	1 280	63.4	67.8	11	72.7	9.7	-14.7	9.8	...	0.0	...	0.0
Sioux, ND	1 919	53.5	78.5	196	74.5	11.2	-13.2	17.5	...	8.5	12.5	9.1
Slope, ND	538	53.9	82.5	8	100.0	16.0	-8.4	16.0	...	...	...	...
Stark, ND	14 252	47.9	79.9	1 509	95.4	22.3	-2.1	22.2	84.6	31.0	74.1	2.4
Steele, ND	1 529	42.2	86.1	59	88.1	19.8	-4.6	19.8	0.0	16.7	...	66.7
Stutsman, ND	14 618	52.9	81.1	1 215	23.7	19.7	-4.7	19.6	0.0	13.0	64.7	31.6
Towner, ND	2 057	51.9	81.9	49	91.8	16.1	-8.3	16.6	0.0	0.0	...	0.0
Traill, ND	5 542	42.2	83.7	670	98.5	21.8	-2.6	22.2	0.0	5.3	0.0	0.0
Walsh, ND	8 530	55.5	76.6	194	88.7	13.3	-11.1	13.8	0.0	0.0	0.0	0.7
Ward, ND	35 957	41.6	87.4	4 170	96.2	22.1	-2.3	22.4	21.1	8.5	20.0	25.6
Wells, ND	3 715	58.3	72.6	95	89.5	13.7	-10.7	13.8	0.0	0.0	...	0.0
Williams, ND	13 048	49.2	82.5	747	94.9	16.5	-7.9	17.1	...	8.5	23.8	2.4

[1]Hispanic or Latino persons may be of any race.
. . . = Not available.

Table C-1. Population, School, and Student Characteristics by County—*Continued*

County	State/County code	County type[1]	Population, 2000		Number of schools and students, 2000–2001			Resident enrollment, 2000			
			Total	Percent 5–17 years	School districts	Schools	Students	Total	Percent public	K–12	Percent public
			1	2	3	4	5	6	7	8	9
OHIO	39000										
Adams, OH	39001	6	27 330	19.9	1	9	5 151	6 202	93.6	5 423	94.0
Allen, OH	39003	3	108 473	19.2	9	43	19 216	28 722	80.7	21 705	85.9
Ashland, OH	39005	4	52 523	19.1	4	20	7 977	14 026	77.1	10 029	90.3
Ashtabula, OH	39007	1	102 728	19.6	7	44	18 664	24 547	90.2	20 225	93.1
Athens, OH	39009	4	62 223	13.6	5	22	9 858	28 058	96.2	8 535	95.6
Auglaize, OH	39011	3	46 611	20.8	6	20	9 050	12 239	90.0	9 877	93.5
Belmont, OH	39013	3	70 226	16.7	7	30	10 119	15 628	85.4	12 369	87.1
Brown, OH	39015	1	42 285	20.5	5	16	9 151	10 406	92.9	8 815	94.7
Butler, OH	39017	0	332 807	19.0	9	84	58 704	95 720	85.6	63 221	87.7
Carroll, OH	39019	2	28 836	19.1	2	10	4 030	6 740	91.2	5 595	94.0
Champaign, OH	39021	6	38 890	19.6	5	16	7 696	9 309	87.3	7 597	93.6
Clark, OH	39023	2	144 742	18.6	7	51	25 343	36 734	84.1	27 318	91.4
Clermont, OH	39025	0	177 977	20.3	9	45	28 783	46 454	82.1	36 411	85.9
Clinton, OH	39027	6	40 543	19.3	4	18	8 311	10 521	84.1	7 852	94.8
Columbiana, OH	39029	2	112 075	18.4	11	42	18 802	26 376	90.9	21 122	94.6
Coshocton, OH	39031	6	36 655	19.8	3	18	6 502	8 641	88.2	7 235	90.9
Crawford, OH	39033	3	46 966	18.4	6	26	8 033	10 769	87.0	8 889	90.6
Cuyahoga, OH	39035	0	1 393 978	18.4	41	353	203 588	365 498	75.7	263 086	81.1
Darke, OH	39037	6	53 309	19.6	7	24	9 261	13 068	89.9	10 595	92.2
Defiance, OH	39039	4	39 500	19.6	5	20	7 002	10 009	85.6	7 970	91.8
Delaware, OH	39041	1	109 989	20.3	4	26	15 293	30 948	74.6	22 024	86.2
Erie, OH	39043	4	79 551	18.7	7	33	15 112	19 104	85.8	15 363	89.6
Fairfield, OH	39045	1	122 759	19.8	8	42	21 964	31 818	85.4	24 594	90.4
Fayette, OH	39047	6	28 433	18.6	2	17	5 175	6 481	94.5	5 355	96.8
Franklin, OH	39049	0	1 068 978	17.9	20	319	179 979	307 823	83.0	191 642	88.0
Fulton, OH	39051	2	42 084	21.1	7	25	9 314	11 406	89.0	8 815	94.1
Gallia, OH	39053	6	31 069	18.7	2	14	5 984	7 742	84.0	5 887	91.8
Geauga, OH	39055	1	90 895	21.6	7	29	12 789	24 286	73.7	19 058	77.2
Greene, OH	39057	2	147 886	18.0	7	39	24 713	46 402	78.3	26 857	85.9
Guernsey, OH	39059	7	40 792	19.4	3	17	6 307	9 866	90.1	8 153	93.5
Hamilton, OH	39061	0	845 303	19.1	27	221	128 092	233 939	73.5	163 773	75.8
Hancock, OH	39063	4	71 295	19.0	8	32	11 862	19 271	78.5	13 404	92.4
Hardin, OH	39065	6	31 945	17.9	6	21	6 103	9 275	68.1	5 458	96.3
Harrison, OH	39067	6	15 856	17.2	2	9	2 569	3 343	91.6	2 750	94.0
Henry, OH	39069	6	29 210	20.9	4	14	6 122	7 621	85.8	6 173	88.5
Highland, OH	39071	6	40 875	19.9	5	19	8 102	9 963	92.9	8 190	96.3
Hocking, OH	39073	6	28 241	18.8	1	10	4 089	6 737	91.0	5 370	92.8
Holmes, OH	39075	7	38 943	25.3	2	17	4 618	8 965	65.2	8 145	64.2
Huron, OH	39077	4	59 487	20.8	7	30	11 569	15 240	82.8	12 304	85.4
Jackson, OH	39079	7	32 641	19.4	3	17	5 828	7 870	90.4	6 429	94.0
Jefferson, OH	39081	3	73 894	16.2	5	32	11 487	17 543	79.2	12 315	86.7
Knox, OH	39083	6	54 500	18.6	5	19	9 080	14 679	74.1	10 108	90.6
Lake, OH	39085	0	227 511	18.1	9	62	35 382	56 308	81.0	41 818	84.4
Lawrence, OH	39087	2	62 319	18.3	7	28	11 551	15 147	94.2	11 614	95.8
Licking, OH	39089	0	145 491	19.1	10	58	25 146	37 916	82.2	28 214	90.2
Logan, OH	39091	6	46 005	19.8	4	16	8 220	10 951	91.3	9 184	95.1
Lorain, OH	39093	0	284 664	19.3	14	89	47 226	75 017	79.6	55 489	85.9
Lucas, OH	39095	2	455 054	19.4	18	128	71 306	129 500	79.7	88 948	80.3
Madison, OH	39097	1	40 213	18.4	4	21	7 841	9 790	83.0	7 663	88.2
Mahoning, OH	39099	2	257 555	17.8	17	86	39 781	64 677	84.7	47 024	86.9
Marion, OH	39101	4	66 217	18.4	5	31	12 670	16 180	89.6	12 999	93.1
Medina, OH	39103	1	151 095	20.5	7	47	29 099	40 364	83.3	31 234	88.1
Meigs, OH	39105	6	23 072	18.2	3	16	3 794	5 161	94.0	4 275	96.6
Mercer, OH	39107	7	40 924	22.3	6	23	9 706	11 195	92.8	9 147	95.9
Miami, OH	39109	2	98 868	19.5	9	41	19 809	24 416	87.0	19 342	90.3
Monroe, OH	39111	6	15 180	18.3	1	10	2 842	3 438	88.5	2 778	88.3
Montgomery, OH	39113	2	559 062	18.1	23	157	84 224	150 213	78.3	101 609	85.8
Morgan, OH	39115	8	14 897	19.2	1	8	2 413	3 555	93.2	2 863	96.2
Morrow, OH	39117	6	31 628	20.8	4	16	5 681	7 830	89.9	6 556	93.0
Muskingum, OH	39119	4	84 585	19.3	6	41	17 076	21 558	83.9	16 340	91.6
Noble, OH	39121	8	14 058	17.6	2	4	2 403	3 540	89.7	2 613	93.3
Ottawa, OH	39123	6	40 985	18.0	6	21	6 637	9 895	90.6	7 672	94.0
Paulding, OH	39125	6	20 293	20.2	3	9	3 928	5 172	90.3	4 243	94.3
Perry, OH	39127	6	34 078	20.8	4	16	6 580	8 928	91.4	7 113	92.6
Pickaway, OH	39129	1	52 727	18.3	4	22	9 623	12 644	89.8	9 880	95.8
Pike, OH	39131	7	27 695	20.3	4	13	6 129	6 897	92.9	5 690	95.1
Portage, OH	39133	1	152 061	17.6	11	55	25 045	46 475	89.5	26 926	91.8
Preble, OH	39135	2	42 337	19.7	6	18	7 752	10 416	91.7	8 465	94.8
Putnam, OH	39137	6	34 726	22.4	9	23	7 249	9 685	87.8	7 856	90.3
Richland, OH	39139	3	128 852	18.4	9	52	23 003	31 084	86.6	24 217	90.0
Ross, OH	39141	4	73 345	17.8	7	32	15 725	17 385	92.1	13 531	95.3
Sandusky, OH	39143	4	61 792	19.7	5	27	13 784	16 006	86.0	12 286	88.6
Scioto, OH	39145	4	79 195	18.1	10	35	14 081	18 990	92.8	14 844	94.7
Seneca, OH	39147	5	58 683	19.7	7	30	9 346	16 006	77.3	11 688	88.2
Shelby, OH	39149	6	47 910	21.0	8	23	8 990	12 315	88.6	10 196	90.9
Stark, OH	39151	2	378 098	18.5	17	123	65 097	94 779	82.2	71 024	89.2
Summit, OH	39153	2	542 899	18.4	23	167	86 303	142 049	84.2	101 486	86.5
Trumbull, OH	39155	2	225 116	18.2	20	85	37 018	53 297	86.5	41 257	89.2
Tuscarawas, OH	39157	4	90 914	18.8	8	40	16 581	21 272	89.4	17 119	91.6
Union, OH	39159	6	40 909	20.0	3	14	6 479	10 216	87.1	8 259	91.7

[1]County type code is from the Economic Research Service of the USDA. See Notes and Definitions at the end of this section.

Table C-1. School and Student Characteristics by County—*Continued*

County	Characteristics of students, 2000–2001			Staff and students, 2000–2001				Revenues, fiscal 1999			
	Percent with IEP2	Percent eligible for free lunch	Percent minority	Number of teachers	Student/ teacher ratio	Local school non-teaching staff	Central admin. staff	Total revenue ($1,000s)	Percentage of revenue from		
									Federal govt.	State govt.	Local govt.
	10	11	12	13	14	15	16	17	18	19	20
OHIO											
Adams, OH	13.4	41.5	1.0	366	14.1	246	25	$35 710	8.6	36.8	54.6
Allen, OH	12.0	36.4	18.5	1 121	17.1	846	168	130 360	6.0	46.6	47.4
Ashland, OH	11.6	18.7	2.0	477	16.7	308	34	54 488	4.1	43.0	53.0
Ashtabula, OH	12.7	32.9	7.2	1 060	17.6	968	150	128 262	6.6	55.4	37.9
Athens, OH	14.5	35.8	3.6	656	15.0	498	105	69 457	9.0	54.7	36.3
Auglaize, OH	13.5	15.8	1.2	468	19.3	400	79	62 383	3.1	47.7	49.2
Belmont, OH	14.2	35.2	3.6	600	16.9	477	101	72 728	6.9	58.9	34.2
Brown, OH	9.5	27.9	1.0	491	18.6	431	68	62 497	4.7	68.4	26.9
Butler, OH	12.5	18.7	9.9	3 266	18.0	2 685	391	379 674	5.1	42.3	52.6
Carroll, OH	11.6	. . .	1.6	192	21.0	145	35	21 544	5.3	58.3	36.4
Champaign, OH	14.1	18.8	3.4	440	17.5	363	101	61 857	3.9	56.6	39.5
Clark, OH	11.4	26.4	13.2	1 604	15.8	1 332	194	180 348	6.5	52.0	41.5
Clermont, OH	11.1	18.2	1.8	1 553	18.5	1 175	245	198 702	3.3	41.9	54.8
Clinton, OH	9.8	19.5	2.7	438	19.0	366	137	57 425	5.2	52.4	42.3
Columbiana, OH	11.8	31.1	2.3	1 113	16.9	786	164	136 657	6.0	56.5	37.5
Coshocton, OH	14.9	28.8	1.8	349	18.6	317	40	41 160	5.3	43.0	51.7
Crawford, OH	13.7	29.1	1.9	512	15.7	475	87	54 281	4.4	47.1	48.5
Cuyahoga, OH	14.3	42.1	47.5	13 564	15.0	11 097	2 171	1 947 365	5.9	34.9	59.2
Darke, OH	10.7	20.5	1.6	567	16.3	404	83	59 940	4.7	50.3	45.0
Defiance, OH	13.1	. . .	10.7	389	18.0	288	34	44 094	3.0	46.7	50.3
Delaware, OH	13.3	8.8	4.2	919	16.6	694	127	111 578	1.8	28.7	69.5
Erie, OH	14.6	23.9	14.0	921	16.4	799	215	131 281	4.9	35.6	59.5
Fairfield, OH	9.7	17.5	4.5	1 241	17.7	787	172	151 612	2.9	46.1	51.0
Fayette, OH	11.4	23.3	2.9	281	18.4	223	35	31 007	6.2	50.0	43.8
Franklin, OH	11.7	31.7	33.4	10 707	16.8	7 780	1 470	1 439 913	4.7	32.1	63.2
Fulton, OH	11.4	15.7	7.0	505	18.4	500	159	76 686	4.6	40.9	54.4
Gallia, OH	16.5	30.5	3.8	356	16.8	255	37	40 634	10.8	44.5	44.7
Geauga, OH	10.9	8.7	2.7	736	17.4	612	144	99 073	2.3	31.4	66.3
Greene, OH	12.0	15.2	9.5	1 405	17.6	1 232	220	175 630	4.3	39.0	56.7
Guernsey, OH	11.8	33.8	3.2	359	17.6	296	83	43 120	6.9	56.3	36.8
Hamilton, OH	12.5	35.3	39.9	7 555	17.0	6 593	1 344	1 106 412	5.9	33.3	60.8
Hancock, OH	13.7	. . .	5.4	749	15.8	596	102	86 001	3.1	36.5	60.4
Hardin, OH	11.5	22.7	1.3	377	16.2	322	70	42 711	6.6	52.3	41.1
Harrison, OH	22.8	34.9	4.2	173	14.8	150	15	17 756	7.8	52.1	40.1
Henry, OH	14.6	. . .	8.0	390	15.7	277	55	49 708	3.1	45.0	51.9
Highland, OH	10.2	. . .	2.1	436	18.6	356	46	63 961	4.0	72.0	24.0
Hocking, OH	13.8	28.2	0.9	204	20.0	182	27	25 650	7.2	58.2	34.6
Holmes, OH	11.2	25.8	0.8	307	15.0	237	17	29 699	6.7	41.3	52.0
Huron, OH	14.1	23.1	6.1	658	17.6	452	72	77 146	4.4	49.2	46.4
Jackson, OH	13.0	37.8	1.0	311	18.7	241	38	36 819	7.8	64.1	28.1
Jefferson, OH	14.2	39.6	9.8	721	15.9	610	102	85 833	8.1	43.7	48.2
Knox, OH	16.2	20.6	1.3	519	17.5	405	91	59 643	5.9	47.4	46.7
Lake, OH	11.6	15.9	5.5	1 996	17.7	1 754	326	301 957	2.8	27.0	70.2
Lawrence, OH	14.3	38.4	3.0	724	16.0	539	95	86 312	10.2	67.7	22.1
Licking, OH	10.8	18.1	3.3	1 464	17.2	1 113	227	172 101	4.5	42.3	53.3
Logan, OH	13.7	19.2	3.5	434	18.9	407	103	62 588	5.7	43.4	50.8
Lorain, OH	12.1	29.2	20.7	2 937	16.1	1 982	397	345 410	5.7	44.0	50.3
Lucas, OH	14.7	36.9	33.9	4 409	16.2	3 341	588	547 966	7.0	42.9	50.1
Madison, OH	10.9	17.0	4.5	419	18.7	315	49	53 106	3.4	47.5	49.1
Mahoning, OH	12.9	37.8	27.0	2 236	17.8	1 992	364	312 507	7.1	51.2	41.7
Marion, OH	13.1	26.9	5.7	743	17.1	521	83	86 927	6.8	48.1	45.1
Medina, OH	12.0	10.7	2.4	1 696	17.2	1 162	217	202 409	2.6	36.7	60.7
Meigs, OH	14.8	48.8	1.3	275	13.8	175	25	27 168	8.1	65.0	26.9
Mercer, OH	12.7	. . .	1.2	530	18.3	409	138	74 935	3.9	53.9	42.3
Miami, OH	11.5	16.4	4.2	981	20.2	861	161	131 634	3.9	39.2	56.9
Monroe, OH	13.8	53.4	0.4	186	15.3	112	19	20 870	7.4	46.2	46.5
Montgomery, OH	12.6	36.5	30.9	5 062	16.6	4 198	845	687 652	6.5	41.3	52.2
Morgan, OH	11.7	36.4	3.7	167	14.4	114	15	15 359	9.6	60.4	30.0
Morrow, OH	11.4	24.1	0.7	322	17.6	258	23	33 776	4.8	60.6	34.6
Muskingum, OH	13.6	31.3	5.6	992	17.2	814	173	119 331	7.2	57.2	35.6
Noble, OH	14.2	25.1	0.1	139	17.3	114	23	14 901	6.4	56.8	36.8
Ottawa, OH	13.0	16.5	4.9	399	16.6	356	42	53 493	3.0	24.9	72.1
Paulding, OH	13.8	20.4	3.3	247	15.9	160	17	31 585	4.2	60.1	35.7
Perry, OH	14.3	. . .	0.5	375	17.5	319	69	44 642	6.8	69.7	23.5
Pickaway, OH	12.8	20.2	1.4	518	18.6	389	70	59 184	5.5	46.7	47.8
Pike, OH	12.6	40.0	1.4	308	19.9	298	43	48 626	7.4	71.2	21.4
Portage, OH	11.8	19.6	4.6	1 564	16.0	1 217	229	189 766	3.8	45.5	50.7
Preble, OH	9.3	. . .	0.7	455	17.0	382	70	56 681	3.8	46.7	49.6
Putnam, OH	11.2	. . .	5.5	441	16.4	328	77	53 734	4.2	55.9	39.9
Richland, OH	12.6	31.8	11.9	1 520	15.1	1 103	252	177 753	5.8	46.7	47.5
Ross, OH	11.8	25.5	4.3	687	22.9	594	136	107 177	5.8	60.8	33.4
Sandusky, OH	13.0	. . .	12.4	674	20.5	581	110	84 882	5.0	46.7	48.3
Scioto, OH	10.6	41.7	2.2	860	16.4	637	136	116 015	9.1	67.8	23.1
Seneca, OH	14.4	30.1	6.7	536	17.4	581	134	70 886	6.1	52.0	41.8
Shelby, OH	11.5	18.6	3.3	495	18.2	424	79	60 115	3.5	41.6	54.8
Stark, OH	12.6	29.2	12.0	3 860	16.9	2 944	608	477 335	6.0	45.5	48.5
Summit, OH	12.3	27.9	23.2	5 618	15.4	4 398	1 410	667 481	6.4	38.7	54.9
Trumbull, OH	12.0	29.5	12.3	2 246	16.5	1 713	352	281 071	5.2	48.8	45.9
Tuscarawas, OH	14.1	21.2	1.3	903	18.4	676	197	116 240	5.4	53.6	41.0
Union, OH	11.8	10.9	1.3	358	18.1	263	28	61 794	1.8	21.9	76.3

2IEP = Individual Education Program. See Notes and Definitions at the end of this section.
. . . = Not available.

Table C-1. Population, School, and Student Characteristics by County—*Continued*

County	Current expenditures, fiscal 1999			Resident population 16 to 19 years, 2000				Outcomes, 1999–2000	
	Amount ($1,000s)	Amount per student	Percent for instruction	Total population 16 to 19 years	Percent in Armed Forces	Percent high school graduates	Percent not enrolled, not grads, not Armed Forces, not empl.	Number of graduates	Dropouts grades 9–12 (percent)
	21	22	23	24	25	26	27	28	29
OHIO									
Adams, OH	$29 462	$5 450	59.4	1 538	0.0	16.2	6.2	306	5.7
Allen, OH	112 394	6 019	58.2	6 965	0.1	9.2	4.9	1 080	6.0
Ashland, OH	48 487	6 170	63.3	3 732	0.0	10.5	5.6	533	2.6
Ashtabula, OH	111 283	6 027	59.8	5 742	0.2	16.9	5.9	1 175	3.3
Athens, OH	63 244	6 954	58.9	7 591	0.0	4.0	1.1	605	4.5
Auglaize, OH	50 303	5 405	59.7	2 790	0.0	9.7	0.2	666	1.4
Belmont, OH	60 579	6 063	61.7	3 577	0.0	10.2	3.2	724	2.4
Brown, OH	46 779	5 528	55.9	2 323	0.2	12.6	4.4	505	6.3
Butler, OH	321 343	5 949	57.6	21 825	0.1	10.6	3.1	3 119	4.2
Carroll, OH	19 099	4 682	60.6	1 449	0.0	13.8	2.1	282	2.0
Champaign, OH	44 732	5 823	58.5	2 230	0.0	14.4	3.5	470	3.7
Clark, OH	154 978	6 191	58.2	8 403	0.2	9.6	6.8	1 425	5.4
Clermont, OH	167 426	5 807	60.1	9 787	0.0	11.1	5.1	1 653	5.4
Clinton, OH	46 909	5 577	58.3	2 584	0.0	12.9	1.2	543	2.7
Columbiana, OH	110 670	6 063	59.3	6 022	0.0	12.4	3.5	1 254	2.3
Coshocton, OH	36 884	5 713	59.7	2 168	0.0	10.7	5.2	435	2.2
Crawford, OH	48 580	5 894	59.9	2 618	0.0	14.2	3.3	575	5.5
Cuyahoga, OH	1 611 592	8 023	58.1	70 120	0.1	9.6	5.9	14 272	9.9
Darke, OH	52 237	5 563	60.4	2 868	0.0	10.5	2.8	608	1.8
Defiance, OH	38 997	5 319	63.7	2 452	0.0	10.6	3.4	520	4.4
Delaware, OH	87 108	6 266	60.9	5 872	0.0	9.6	2.3	901	1.9
Erie, OH	111 250	7 759	56.6	3 995	0.0	10.0	3.1	988	2.4
Fairfield, OH	122 921	5 668	59.9	6 316	0.2	10.5	3.6	1 458	2.7
Fayette, OH	27 194	5 127	57.9	1 575	0.0	16.1	4.5	301	4.7
Franklin, OH	1 154 197	6 907	58.8	59 036	0.0	10.1	4.6	8 663	8.8
Fulton, OH	65 567	6 952	56.8	2 467	0.0	11.2	1.9	634	2.7
Gallia, OH	35 368	6 478	58.5	2 026	0.4	10.6	6.5	326	2.9
Geauga, OH	83 403	6 468	56.2	5 057	0.0	7.5	7.8	976	1.6
Greene, OH	151 086	6 358	58.4	11 371	0.9	6.1	2.9	1 555	5.1
Guernsey, OH	37 527	5 834	58.5	2 326	0.0	11.3	4.5	409	4.7
Hamilton, OH	915 035	7 156	60.8	48 268	0.0	9.0	6.0	6 091	6.1
Hancock, OH	73 087	6 161	60.4	4 131	0.3	9.6	2.5	765	4.0
Hardin, OH	36 331	5 804	58.5	2 406	0.0	8.1	4.5	399	3.5
Harrison, OH	15 141	5 263	60.7	808	0.0	12.0	3.7	197	3.1
Henry, OH	38 009	7 037	58.8	1 818	0.0	8.9	9.5	381	2.3
Highland, OH	41 099	4 977	57.0	2 293	0.0	13.4	6.3	506	4.3
Hocking, OH	21 490	5 039	55.0	1 598	0.0	13.7	1.9	257	5.5
Holmes, OH	23 365	5 026	62.2	2 701	0.0	7.7	19.7	235	1.7
Huron, OH	64 501	5 483	60.0	3 327	0.0	12.5	6.2	759	2.4
Jackson, OH	31 285	5 219	61.7	1 734	0.0	16.4	3.4	328	3.5
Jefferson, OH	75 064	6 386	58.2	4 010	0.0	12.0	2.9	771	2.7
Knox, OH	51 546	6 114	59.3	3 711	0.0	7.8	2.7	634	1.9
Lake, OH	254 917	7 288	58.3	11 692	0.0	11.0	2.6	2 398	3.3
Lawrence, OH	68 520	5 956	57.2	3 417	0.1	10.1	7.2	676	3.9
Licking, OH	142 344	5 910	58.4	8 478	0.0	11.5	4.1	1 453	3.5
Logan, OH	49 513	6 226	58.3	2 484	0.0	11.3	3.1	519	2.9
Lorain, OH	294 084	6 478	60.8	15 543	0.0	11.5	4.5	2 443	0.2
Lucas, OH	491 075	7 050	57.5	25 237	0.0	10.1	5.9	3 635	6.4
Madison, OH	45 130	6 360	55.9	2 427	0.0	14.3	6.3	462	3.2
Mahoning, OH	255 102	6 511	57.5	13 145	0.0	10.7	4.5	2 514	5.9
Marion, OH	76 809	6 381	58.9	3 280	0.0	11.3	6.0	663	2.8
Medina, OH	171 702	6 212	60.6	7 814	0.0	9.6	2.0	1 849	1.1
Meigs, OH	22 422	5 638	58.8	1 308	0.0	13.9	7.6	279	3.2
Mercer, OH	56 529	5 627	61.1	2 664	0.0	12.0	2.1	732	2.1
Miami, OH	112 186	6 366	61.2	5 406	0.0	12.9	3.4	1 137	2.3
Monroe, OH	17 679	5 971	63.2	841	0.0	13.4	6.9	208	2.0
Montgomery, OH	616 842	7 279	55.6	30 764	0.2	11.2	6.0	4 367	7.1
Morgan, OH	14 947	5 936	59.9	873	0.0	12.0	4.7	148	3.8
Morrow, OH	28 741	5 131	58.7	1 811	0.0	15.0	2.9	375	1.8
Muskingum, OH	98 921	5 962	58.3	4 856	0.1	12.8	4.4	1 003	4.2
Noble, OH	12 309	4 910	61.6	762	0.0	16.0	3.3	165	1.1
Ottawa, OH	45 911	6 923	60.7	2 130	0.7	12.4	1.4	520	2.2
Paulding, OH	26 830	6 558	54.0	1 258	0.0	11.8	2.0	273	2.5
Perry, OH	36 998	5 587	58.3	2 012	0.0	13.0	5.7	420	3.5
Pickaway, OH	52 173	5 373	59.5	2 688	0.0	14.2	8.1	549	4.6
Pike, OH	35 225	6 003	54.5	1 664	0.0	14.2	7.4	351	5.1
Portage, OH	154 603	6 337	59.5	10 892	0.1	8.2	1.8	1 632	3.6
Preble, OH	46 276	5 869	59.0	2 336	0.0	12.8	2.5	520	4.4
Putnam, OH	42 786	5 673	60.3	2 204	0.0	8.7	1.9	584	2.3
Richland, OH	150 026	6 787	57.2	6 751	0.3	11.3	4.0	1 300	3.6
Ross, OH	78 668	6 328	59.4	3 851	0.1	12.0	4.7	766	3.6
Sandusky, OH	75 699	6 622	61.3	3 570	0.1	10.9	4.3	795	1.5
Scioto, OH	90 747	6 371	56.8	4 630	0.0	13.6	6.2	876	3.8
Seneca, OH	60 486	6 162	56.9	3 819	0.0	11.4	2.4	637	5.1
Shelby, OH	50 235	5 547	59.0	2 734	0.3	9.3	2.4	594	4.0
Stark, OH	393 487	6 053	60.4	20 471	0.0	10.3	4.0	4 169	4.2
Summit, OH	568 523	6 681	59.0	28 072	0.1	11.6	3.3	5 245	5.2
Trumbull, OH	237 742	6 413	57.5	11 881	0.0	12.0	5.6	2 327	4.7
Tuscarawas, OH	89 571	5 731	60.8	4 984	0.0	13.9	2.9	1 113	2.2
Union, OH	35 173	5 729	60.9	2 015	0.0	14.0	4.6	415	3.2

Table C-1. Population, School, and Student Characteristics by County—*Continued*

County	High school graduates, 2000			College enrollment, 2000		College graduates, 2000 (percent)						
	Population 25 years and over	High school diploma or less (percent)	High school diploma or more (percent)	Number	Percent public	Bachelor's degree or more	+/- U.S. percent with bachelor's degree or more	Non-Hispanic White	Black or African American	American Indian and Alaska Native	Asian, Hawaiian, and Pacific Islander	Hispanic or Latino[1]
	30	31	32	33	34	35	36	37	38	39	40	41
OHIO												
Adams, OH	17 775	75.8	68.6	550	91.3	7.2	-17.2	7.2	. . .	15.2	22.2	0.0
Allen, OH	69 669	60.1	82.5	5 414	65.1	13.4	-11.0	14.1	7.4	14.3	46.4	9.1
Ashland, OH	33 339	63.7	83.3	3 166	38.1	15.9	-8.5	15.7	12.3	0.0	56.3	11.8
Ashtabula, OH	67 994	65.9	79.9	2 903	82.2	11.1	-13.3	11.3	6.6	2.4	25.6	4.1
Athens, OH	31 563	51.2	82.9	18 795	97.2	25.7	1.3	24.3	31.5	19.1	76.6	49.4
Auglaize, OH	30 093	61.9	85.7	1 549	82.1	13.4	-11.0	13.4	8.7	0.0	53.6	11.9
Belmont, OH	49 616	65.5	80.9	2 477	85.2	11.1	-13.3	11.2	1.9	10.2	69.1	27.1
Brown, OH	27 209	70.5	74.8	1 164	79.0	8.8	-15.6	8.8	11.0	0.0	22.4	23.8
Butler, OH	207 213	50.3	83.3	26 012	89.4	23.5	-0.9	23.3	18.2	17.8	56.4	22.2
Carroll, OH	19 460	72.9	80.1	679	79.2	9.1	-15.3	9.1	11.8	24.4	27.8	13.7
Champaign, OH	25 644	65.8	82.3	1 085	55.4	10.6	-13.8	10.4	12.2	17.3	26.0	6.9
Clark, OH	95 298	58.4	81.2	7 419	64.6	14.9	-9.5	15.2	10.5	10.0	50.8	12.5
Clermont, OH	113 513	53.3	82.0	6 609	79.0	20.8	-3.6	20.4	28.7	16.9	55.4	22.9
Clinton, OH	25 720	59.0	83.1	2 142	47.5	14.1	-10.3	14.1	12.0	10.9	68.2	7.9
Columbiana, OH	76 022	67.1	80.6	3 521	81.5	10.8	-13.6	11.0	3.8	13.6	40.7	2.9
Coshocton, OH	24 172	72.4	78.7	758	77.4	9.8	-14.6	9.8	3.3	0.0	21.2	0.0
Crawford, OH	31 379	69.2	80.2	1 143	72.9	9.7	-14.7	9.5	9.0	10.1	57.1	6.9
Cuyahoga, OH	936 148	48.4	81.6	75 981	63.7	25.1	0.7	29.5	10.9	14.3	60.1	13.8
Darke, OH	35 206	67.6	82.8	1 540	88.4	10.1	-14.3	10.0	7.9	0.0	40.2	13.0
Defiance, OH	25 426	61.1	84.7	1 478	61.8	14.3	-10.1	14.9	10.2	0.0	8.3	6.9
Delaware, OH	70 617	32.1	92.9	6 126	50.6	41.0	16.6	40.7	36.5	33.3	71.1	38.5
Erie, OH	54 232	57.0	84.0	2 641	75.8	16.6	-7.8	17.6	6.5	0.0	40.1	8.0
Fairfield, OH	79 948	50.8	87.6	4 719	78.6	20.8	-3.6	20.5	29.8	7.3	44.6	21.2
Fayette, OH	18 954	68.9	78.7	718	89.0	10.7	-13.7	10.8	10.1	0.0	22.6	0.0
Franklin, OH	676 318	41.4	85.7	95 799	79.6	31.8	7.4	34.5	15.2	15.7	59.8	21.1
Fulton, OH	26 887	58.8	85.3	1 611	80.6	13.2	-11.2	13.6	4.0	0.0	25.7	4.4
Gallia, OH	20 207	67.9	73.7	1 494	55.5	11.6	-12.8	11.5	8.0	0.0	67.8	5.1
Geauga, OH	59 216	41.8	86.3	3 361	68.2	31.7	7.3	31.8	16.0	17.4	59.1	35.6
Greene, OH	92 414	41.1	87.8	16 907	70.3	31.1	6.7	30.2	35.9	27.2	56.0	40.4
Guernsey, OH	26 839	67.8	78.4	1 105	76.0	10.0	-14.4	9.9	6.6	0.0	50.0	22.0
Hamilton, OH	546 048	45.0	82.7	53 200	74.7	29.2	4.8	32.9	12.4	14.9	66.7	36.2
Hancock, OH	45 871	52.2	88.4	4 538	44.4	21.7	-2.7	21.5	17.5	19.5	62.7	10.7
Hardin, OH	19 220	69.9	80.6	3 395	22.2	11.4	-13.0	11.3	10.1	16.0	8.4	19.3
Harrison, OH	11 097	70.1	79.6	392	83.4	9.0	-15.4	9.1	0.0	0.0	. . .	30.0
Henry, OH	18 833	66.4	83.5	852	80.0	11.1	-13.3	11.3	0.0	14.1	52.8	0.9
Highland, OH	26 372	68.5	76.3	1 221	79.6	9.7	-14.7	9.6	0.0	18.0	68.5	8.1
Hocking, OH	18 720	68.2	78.0	979	85.6	9.8	-14.6	9.9	3.7	0.0	55.0	29.3
Holmes, OH	21 016	80.6	51.5	372	80.9	8.3	-16.1	8.3	0.0	0.0	21.6	1.9
Huron, OH	37 576	67.7	81.0	1 801	76.6	10.9	-13.5	11.1	7.6	7.7	24.1	6.9
Jackson, OH	21 306	69.6	73.5	917	75.5	11.0	-13.4	11.0	9.0	0.0	23.4	27.5
Jefferson, OH	51 819	64.8	81.7	4 123	56.6	11.8	-12.6	11.8	9.8	26.3	41.7	24.4
Knox, OH	34 485	60.3	81.8	3 824	30.9	16.7	-7.7	16.6	25.2	7.3	52.4	3.6
Lake, OH	156 177	48.0	86.4	10 082	76.5	21.5	-2.9	21.5	13.3	13.3	54.7	14.2
Lawrence, OH	41 685	67.8	75.6	2 743	91.4	10.3	-14.1	10.0	10.3	26.8	66.0	28.8
Licking, OH	95 009	56.0	84.7	7 135	59.0	18.4	-6.0	18.3	21.4	8.7	38.1	21.0
Logan, OH	29 962	68.2	83.6	1 230	73.5	11.5	-12.9	11.5	12.4	12.7	24.9	2.3
Lorain, OH	185 491	54.0	82.8	13 711	64.3	16.6	-7.8	17.8	7.7	10.6	48.9	6.2
Lucas, OH	291 022	49.4	82.9	31 806	85.7	21.3	-3.1	23.2	10.2	13.0	60.8	10.1
Madison, OH	26 655	62.7	79.0	1 584	64.3	13.0	-11.4	13.3	4.8	36.6	45.3	16.0
Mahoning, OH	174 803	57.7	82.4	12 736	86.6	17.5	-6.9	19.3	6.8	7.2	45.2	11.8
Marion, OH	44 466	64.7	80.3	2 291	80.2	11.1	-13.3	11.3	6.4	9.7	34.8	6.0
Medina, OH	99 005	47.6	88.8	5 804	77.7	24.8	0.4	24.7	13.5	13.8	55.1	27.4
Meigs, OH	15 602	73.4	73.2	688	82.0	7.4	-17.0	7.4	14.9	0.0	26.7	0.0
Mercer, OH	25 614	65.8	84.0	1 275	86.0	12.7	-11.7	12.5	0.0	0.0	62.0	21.6
Miami, OH	65 765	57.1	82.7	3 450	79.5	16.3	-8.1	16.2	6.3	0.0	43.3	14.9
Monroe, OH	10 544	71.3	78.8	493	90.5	8.4	-16.0	8.4	0.0	0.0	45.0	0.0
Montgomery, OH	367 099	46.9	83.5	38 583	63.4	22.8	-1.6	24.0	14.9	17.2	53.6	29.1
Morgan, OH	9 934	69.9	80.6	504	80.4	9.1	-15.3	9.4	0.9	0.0	73.9	0.0
Morrow, OH	20 591	68.7	78.6	871	79.0	9.5	-14.9	9.4	10.3	6.7	0.0	2.2
Muskingum, OH	54 616	63.7	80.6	3 766	57.0	12.6	-11.8	12.6	13.3	14.3	29.8	28.8
Noble, OH	9 210	69.3	78.6	798	78.4	8.1	-16.3	8.2	3.8	14.6	68.2	1.3
Ottawa, OH	28 829	56.3	84.2	1 503	84.8	16.0	-8.4	16.5	0.0	9.9	17.9	4.7
Paulding, OH	13 108	70.9	81.6	601	68.7	7.8	-16.6	7.9	7.5	7.4	40.0	3.7
Perry, OH	21 626	72.2	78.9	1 068	88.3	6.9	-17.5	6.8	1.6	0.0	44.6	12.5
Pickaway, OH	35 258	65.5	77.2	1 905	67.3	11.4	-13.0	12.2	2.2	0.0	27.1	14.8
Pike, OH	17 710	71.4	70.1	774	80.9	9.7	-14.7	9.5	4.3	5.2	79.7	9.3
Portage, OH	94 073	54.0	85.9	17 050	90.0	21.0	-3.4	20.7	16.2	6.8	76.1	20.1
Preble, OH	28 079	67.8	81.7	1 356	83.2	10.1	-14.3	10.0	3.7	3.8	44.6	16.3
Putnam, OH	21 524	61.6	86.1	1 215	75.9	12.9	-11.5	13.3	35.0	11.9	8.3	2.8
Richland, OH	86 184	62.8	80.2	4 997	79.1	12.6	-11.8	13.2	6.5	7.3	32.5	4.6
Ross, OH	49 443	66.1	76.1	2 809	83.9	11.3	-13.1	11.6	6.7	2.2	39.8	9.3
Sandusky, OH	40 565	61.6	82.1	2 609	84.2	11.9	-12.5	12.5	6.4	5.0	16.3	2.4
Scioto, OH	52 236	65.8	74.1	3 208	89.6	10.1	-14.3	10.2	4.5	6.5	50.3	2.0
Seneca, OH	37 271	63.2	83.1	3 270	43.7	12.5	-11.9	12.6	7.3	5.1	27.3	6.3
Shelby, OH	30 280	63.8	81.5	1 321	83.4	12.8	-11.6	12.4	16.2	15.6	49.0	17.1
Stark, OH	252 971	57.8	83.4	16 696	63.2	17.9	-6.5	18.6	7.0	11.6	48.0	19.4
Summit, OH	362 645	47.9	85.7	29 977	87.7	25.1	0.7	26.5	10.6	10.9	61.1	26.7
Trumbull, OH	153 044	61.8	82.5	8 496	85.1	14.5	-9.9	14.9	6.9	8.1	48.3	12.3
Tuscarawas, OH	60 653	67.9	80.3	2 663	86.7	12.2	-12.2	12.1	5.2	14.1	41.3	15.1
Union, OH	26 534	57.9	86.0	1 275	78.4	15.9	-8.5	16.2	2.5	0.0	53.0	18.6

[1]Hispanic or Latino persons may be of any race.
. . . = Not available.

Table C-1. Population, School, and Student Characteristics by County—*Continued*

County	State/ County code	County type[1]	Population, 2000		Number of schools and students, 2000–2001			Resident enrollment, 2000			
			Total	Percent 5–17 years	School districts	Schools	Students	Total	Percent public	K–12	Percent public
			1	2	3	4	5	6	7	8	9
Van Wert, OH	39161	6	29 659	19.7	3	14	4 809	7 501	86.7	5 933	91.3
Vinton, OH	39163	9	12 806	19.7	1	7	2 527	3 146	95.5	2 646	97.6
Warren, OH	39165	1	158 383	19.9	8	45	27 987	41 655	81.4	32 241	86.7
Washington, OH	39167	3	63 251	17.7	6	29	10 904	15 573	83.7	11 269	91.3
Wayne, OH	39169	4	111 564	20.4	10	51	19 315	29 064	80.3	22 085	86.8
Williams, OH	39171	7	39 188	19.8	7	20	7 213	9 356	91.3	7 807	93.8
Wood, OH	39173	2	121 065	17.9	10	50	20 033	42 352	90.4	22 026	90.0
Wyandot, OH	39175	7	22 908	19.4	3	11	3 949	5 557	85.0	4 476	88.0
OKLAHOMA	40000										
Adair, OK	40001	6	21 038	22.7	12	18	4 792	5 702	94.1	4 761	95.0
Alfalfa, OK	40003	8	6 105	14.9	3	9	879	1 228	95.7	982	97.4
Atoka, OK	40005	7	13 879	17.7	7	12	2 291	3 231	96.0	2 646	96.5
Beaver, OK	40007	9	5 857	21.1	5	9	1 249	1 434	97.6	1 254	98.6
Beckham, OK	40009	7	19 799	17.9	5	15	3 667	4 648	95.5	3 766	98.5
Blaine, OK	40011	6	11 976	18.3	4	11	2 192	2 801	96.6	2 336	97.6
Bryan, OK	40013	6	36 534	18.3	8	25	6 761	9 959	94.3	6 831	97.2
Caddo, OK	40015	6	30 150	21.9	11	32	6 594	8 304	95.5	6 832	96.7
Canadian, OK	40017	2	87 697	21.3	10	39	17 637	24 386	89.8	18 887	94.2
Carter, OK	40019	5	45 621	19.3	9	31	8 935	11 129	93.9	9 131	95.3
Cherokee, OK	40021	6	42 521	19.3	12	20	7 481	13 564	94.0	8 375	95.3
Choctaw, OK	40023	7	15 342	19.6	7	14	2 811	3 715	96.9	2 962	98.0
Cimarron, OK	40025	9	3 148	21.0	4	7	629	780	95.4	685	97.1
Cleveland, OK	40027	2	208 016	18.2	6	62	35 917	67 969	90.8	37 689	92.8
Coal, OK	40029	9	6 031	20.0	4	8	1 250	1 519	95.8	1 241	95.8
Comanche, OK	40031	3	114 996	19.8	10	60	22 284	32 582	93.0	23 102	95.8
Cotton, OK	40033	6	6 614	18.8	3	7	1 240	1 557	97.4	1 301	99.4
Craig, OK	40035	6	14 950	17.9	5	14	3 098	3 336	96.4	2 777	97.3
Creek, OK	40037	2	67 367	20.6	15	39	13 458	17 579	91.9	14 067	94.9
Custer, OK	40039	7	26 142	18.2	5	18	4 973	8 868	96.5	5 064	96.7
Delaware, OK	40041	6	37 077	18.3	9	18	6 592	7 983	94.4	6 721	96.2
Dewey, OK	40043	9	4 743	18.5	3	7	812	1 121	96.8	956	98.3
Ellis, OK	40045	9	4 075	16.8	4	8	722	848	96.0	729	96.2
Garfield, OK	40047	3	57 813	18.3	8	31	9 702	14 040	89.8	10 951	92.1
Garvin, OK	40049	6	27 210	18.4	8	23	5 444	6 197	96.6	5 211	97.4
Grady, OK	40051	6	45 516	19.8	12	35	8 351	12 198	93.7	9 242	95.8
Grant, OK	40053	8	5 144	20.1	4	8	1 048	1 322	95.6	1 115	96.7
Greer, OK	40055	7	6 061	15.3	2	5	922	1 265	94.9	971	96.0
Harmon, OK	40057	7	3 283	19.8	1	3	633	793	97.7	728	98.4
Harper, OK	40059	9	3 562	18.6	2	6	687	829	97.6	713	99.7
Haskell, OK	40061	6	11 792	19.2	5	10	2 360	2 759	98.8	2 301	99.3
Hughes, OK	40063	7	14 154	17.4	6	14	2 491	3 242	94.2	2 591	94.4
Jackson, OK	40065	5	28 439	21.0	6	20	5 943	8 036	96.0	5 965	98.4
Jefferson, OK	40067	9	6 818	17.8	4	9	1 276	1 494	97.9	1 255	98.6
Johnston, OK	40069	7	10 513	19.2	7	13	1 939	2 768	96.2	2 038	96.8
Kay, OK	40071	5	48 080	19.6	8	27	9 223	12 077	91.8	9 483	93.3
Kingfisher, OK	40073	6	13 926	21.0	6	15	3 194	3 504	91.3	3 003	92.6
Kiowa, OK	40075	6	10 227	18.5	4	10	1 865	2 390	98.1	1 934	98.5
Latimer, OK	40077	7	10 692	19.0	4	9	1 832	2 953	97.2	2 020	97.3
Le Flore, OK	40079	6	48 109	19.3	17	38	9 550	11 821	96.1	9 487	97.0
Lincoln, OK	40081	6	32 080	20.9	9	23	5 904	8 108	92.5	6 765	94.5
Logan, OK	40083	2	33 924	19.3	4	13	4 308	10 009	89.7	6 700	90.5
Love, OK	40085	9	8 831	19.6	4	8	1 655	2 124	95.0	1 740	96.6
McClain, OK	40087	2	27 740	20.2	7	20	5 485	7 367	91.8	5 761	94.0
McCurtain, OK	40089	7	34 402	20.9	15	32	7 667	8 723	97.5	7 167	98.4
McIntosh, OK	40091	7	19 456	17.2	8	15	3 300	4 197	94.3	3 409	95.1
Major, OK	40093	6	7 545	18.9	6	10	1 663	1 762	90.4	1 470	91.6
Marshall, OK	40095	6	13 184	17.3	2	6	2 422	2 820	96.8	2 290	98.0
Mayes, OK	40097	6	38 369	19.8	8	22	7 317	9 429	94.8	7 797	97.3
Murray, OK	40099	7	12 623	17.6	2	7	2 279	2 765	97.5	2 273	98.4
Muskogee, OK	40101	4	69 451	18.9	11	38	13 546	17 289	95.1	13 298	97.3
Noble, OK	40103	7	11 411	19.1	4	10	2 302	2 796	96.2	2 256	99.1
Nowata, OK	40105	6	10 569	19.6	3	8	2 006	2 578	96.4	2 114	98.2
Okfuskee, OK	40107	6	11 814	18.5	7	15	2 274	2 678	95.0	2 224	96.9
Oklahoma, OK	40109	2	660 448	18.3	15	208	108 142	177 872	84.6	122 501	90.4
Okmulgee, OK	40111	6	39 685	20.1	10	24	7 348	10 580	95.4	8 238	97.1
Osage, OK	40113	2	44 437	20.2	13	25	4 578	11 443	92.2	9 312	94.4
Ottawa, OK	40115	6	33 194	19.1	8	25	6 265	8 325	95.7	6 198	97.7
Pawnee, OK	40117	6	16 612	20.3	3	8	2 744	4 117	96.2	3 437	97.4
Payne, OK	40119	4	68 190	14.1	7	27	9 992	28 426	96.6	9 937	96.5
Pittsburg, OK	40121	7	43 953	17.9	14	32	8 166	10 214	95.1	8 296	97.2
Pontotoc, OK	40123	6	35 143	18.4	9	25	6 797	10 199	95.8	6 720	96.0
Pottawatomie, OK	40125	2	65 521	19.0	14	37	12 396	17 776	85.1	12 422	95.3
Pushmataha, OK	40127	7	11 667	19.7	7	14	2 417	2 777	98.0	2 361	99.1
Roger Mills, OK	40129	9	3 436	18.3	5	12	839	758	96.8	641	96.6
Rogers, OK	40131	2	70 641	21.7	6	31	13 595	19 354	90.4	15 430	93.5
Seminole, OK	40133	6	24 894	19.6	11	25	4 909	6 499	95.5	5 073	97.7
Sequoyah, OK	40135	3	38 972	20.4	12	25	8 466	9 537	96.5	7 874	97.6
Stephens, OK	40137	6	43 182	18.3	8	27	8 226	10 155	94.5	8 339	96.5
Texas, OK	40139	7	20 107	20.3	9	23	3 869	5 517	93.5	4 143	98.1

[1]County type code is from the Economic Research Service of the USDA. See Notes and Definitions at the end of this section.

Table C-1. School and Student Characteristics by County—*Continued*

County	Characteristics of students, 2000–2001			Staff and students, 2000–2001				Revenues, fiscal 1999			
	Percent with IEP2	Percent eligible for free lunch	Percent minority	Number of teachers	Student/teacher ratio	Local school non-teaching staff	Central admin. staff	Total revenue ($1,000s)	Percentage of revenue from		
									Federal govt.	State govt.	Local govt.
	10	11	12	13	14	15	16	17	18	19	20
Van Wert, OH	13.1	...	3.7	307	15.7	242	58	$33 841	3.6	46.9	49.5
Vinton, OH	16.2	51.1	0.2	152	16.6	121	15	18 357	7.4	64.9	27.7
Warren, OH	9.6	9.0	3.3	1 574	17.8	1 202	250	175 552	2.4	38.0	59.5
Washington, OH	11.8	22.6	1.4	639	17.1	493	92	73 628	5.9	43.9	50.2
Wayne, OH	11.6	21.0	3.7	1 169	16.5	932	219	146 346	5.7	42.3	52.0
Williams, OH	10.9	...	3.5	392	18.4	311	51	46 234	2.7	46.2	51.1
Wood, OH	11.9	12.9	5.5	1 149	17.4	975	188	152 928	3.9	35.4	60.7
Wyandot, OH	12.7	13.5	2.2	233	16.9	188	31	23 988	4.0	48.1	47.9
OKLAHOMA											
Adair, OK	15.9	71.5	64.8	357	13.4	345	35	32 669	21.5	66.5	12.1
Alfalfa, OK	15.5	44.6	6.5	75	11.7	42	7	6 588	5.8	50.8	43.5
Atoka, OK	15.4	70.4	34.0	167	13.7	139	14	14 298	12.3	67.8	19.9
Beaver, OK	9.6	39.5	20.9	97	12.9	69	14	9 242	4.5	45.2	50.2
Beckham, OK	12.2	51.5	19.9	271	13.5	150	17	22 091	8.1	59.1	32.8
Blaine, OK	12.9	63.0	32.8	172	12.7	109	11	14 261	9.8	62.2	28.0
Bryan, OK	14.2	63.1	33.6	450	15.0	369	35	39 366	12.1	66.3	21.6
Caddo, OK	14.6	69.4	45.4	502	13.1	365	36	46 380	14.5	60.5	25.0
Canadian, OK	9.5	24.9	16.3	1 082	16.3	713	56	98 907	4.8	56.4	38.7
Carter, OK	17.1	55.5	31.3	599	14.9	486	45	57 981	9.2	56.4	34.3
Cherokee, OK	15.7	73.7	60.9	503	14.9	399	35	44 038	17.3	65.1	17.6
Choctaw, OK	14.6	68.2	46.6	211	13.3	140	16	17 739	15.7	69.4	14.8
Cimarron, OK	11.4	56.0	25.8	65	9.7	35	8	5 100	6.9	56.9	36.2
Cleveland, OK	13.1	27.5	24.4	2 232	16.1	1 464	146	195 662	4.9	58.9	36.2
Coal, OK	23.4	69.0	37.0	95	13.2	78	11	8 134	13.0	61.5	25.5
Comanche, OK	13.0	53.8	43.8	1 362	16.4	1 170	83	133 269	11.2	63.7	25.1
Cotton, OK	15.9	50.2	22.1	92	13.5	56	9	6 726	9.7	68.1	22.2
Craig, OK	12.7	56.1	51.8	220	14.1	139	16	17 548	8.7	60.8	30.5
Creek, OK	12.2	48.4	27.1	833	16.2	592	53	79 247	6.7	63.2	30.1
Custer, OK	12.6	57.1	28.8	356	14.0	255	19	30 695	9.1	59.1	31.9
Delaware, OK	14.6	62.1	51.0	461	14.3	352	24	36 917	11.7	60.7	27.6
Dewey, OK	16.3	53.0	11.7	75	10.8	51	7	8 637	4.9	59.1	36.0
Ellis, OK	14.0	51.9	6.2	71	10.2	37	8	5 650	5.1	57.0	37.9
Garfield, OK	13.0	42.5	19.9	657	14.8	469	41	63 501	7.2	56.5	36.3
Garvin, OK	17.2	51.2	29.2	372	14.6	253	21	30 416	8.3	65.7	26.0
Grady, OK	12.7	39.6	15.4	567	14.7	370	38	44 765	6.8	63.6	29.6
Grant, OK	17.1	43.1	3.1	91	11.5	48	11	7 928	3.2	46.3	50.5
Greer, OK	15.5	58.7	19.6	78	11.8	44	6	6 366	9.9	66.3	23.8
Harmon, OK	14.5	64.9	48.2	56	11.3	38	3	4 380	9.4	69.2	21.4
Harper, OK	17.8	44.7	9.9	61	11.3	47	3	5 590	2.5	53.5	44.0
Haskell, OK	14.0	72.2	30.9	154	15.3	98	15	13 009	11.6	69.1	19.3
Hughes, OK	13.4	68.4	44.8	181	13.8	131	14	18 630	15.6	59.0	25.4
Jackson, OK	9.6	45.2	34.6	401	14.8	222	28	34 714	12.7	64.8	22.4
Jefferson, OK	19.8	66.0	24.1	103	12.4	72	9	8 615	7.0	70.1	22.8
Johnston, OK	13.5	69.6	39.5	151	12.8	93	11	12 656	13.0	64.8	22.2
Kay, OK	13.5	48.8	28.1	575	16.0	484	40	54 506	7.9	54.5	37.6
Kingfisher, OK	12.6	49.6	18.2	223	14.3	149	15	20 520	8.2	51.1	40.7
Kiowa, OK	13.4	56.0	27.6	149	12.5	105	12	12 656	11.5	62.7	25.8
Latimer, OK	16.3	65.5	38.9	128	14.3	88	12	29 644	10.2	45.5	44.4
Le Flore, OK	14.1	64.5	35.0	691	13.8	419	45	55 152	13.3	66.4	20.2
Lincoln, OK	12.0	45.1	17.0	387	15.3	224	22	30 098	7.0	67.1	26.0
Logan, OK	14.5	49.7	21.7	309	13.9	226	23	25 053	8.2	63.7	28.1
Love, OK	16.3	63.1	29.5	112	14.8	79	11	9 479	6.8	66.9	26.4
McClain, OK	12.4	35.6	26.9	364	15.1	225	19	32 680	6.9	63.2	29.9
McCurtain, OK	12.9	70.9	40.7	552	13.9	437	39	45 408	13.8	65.5	20.7
McIntosh, OK	16.3	74.6	43.4	232	14.2	175	15	19 865	15.0	64.7	20.3
Major, OK	18.6	42.8	8.7	123	13.5	79	11	8 453	16.0	51.5	32.5
Marshall, OK	10.4	63.3	48.2	159	15.2	117	9	12 865	9.8	62.7	27.5
Mayes, OK	12.1	50.9	44.6	495	14.8	312	30	38 929	11.5	64.5	24.0
Murray, OK	12.5	54.0	30.1	143	15.9	92	8	12 367	9.6	68.3	22.1
Muskogee, OK	13.9	55.2	52.5	873	15.5	629	65	97 114	10.6	55.4	34.0
Noble, OK	13.9	41.0	21.5	179	12.9	103	14	16 029	10.0	41.9	48.2
Nowata, OK	12.1	56.8	41.0	133	15.1	108	14	11 502	8.5	66.6	24.9
Okfuskee, OK	13.8	71.7	43.9	172	13.2	131	15	14 185	14.4	64.6	21.0
Oklahoma, OK	14.1	49.2	43.4	7 355	14.7	5 603	365	646 095	8.0	52.2	39.8
Okmulgee, OK	14.3	60.0	43.7	501	14.7	350	34	42 964	10.1	67.7	22.2
Osage, OK	15.6	58.8	45.0	329	13.9	253	32	29 372	14.4	62.7	22.9
Ottawa, OK	13.3	63.8	44.4	394	15.9	313	26	45 002	11.9	56.5	31.6
Pawnee, OK	12.7	55.4	21.9	180	15.2	106	7	14 353	9.2	66.1	24.7
Payne, OK	15.9	37.4	19.4	652	15.3	529	64	69 328	8.7	53.6	37.7
Pittsburg, OK	17.6	58.3	40.4	561	14.6	447	45	48 415	12.7	64.9	22.4
Pontotoc, OK	16.3	60.0	39.2	488	13.9	362	34	43 210	10.4	65.7	23.9
Pottawatomie, OK	13.1	51.4	29.3	815	15.2	548	45	75 289	11.3	62.5	26.2
Pushmataha, OK	13.8	71.1	40.2	197	12.3	141	15	15 507	11.1	73.3	15.6
Roger Mills, OK	10.6	52.2	16.3	100	8.4	66	10	4 267	11.3	42.2	46.5
Rogers, OK	13.0	31.3	35.6	818	16.6	607	64	69 471	5.8	55.5	38.7
Seminole, OK	14.2	68.2	43.6	361	13.6	245	33	30 700	13.7	62.7	23.6
Sequoyah, OK	16.1	64.9	45.7	554	15.3	425	27	46 366	14.6	68.9	16.5
Stephens, OK	11.6	44.7	17.4	539	15.3	404	40	47 579	8.7	63.7	27.6
Texas, OK	8.8	48.9	40.7	299	12.9	200	22	23 639	7.8	52.4	39.8

2IEP = Individual Education Program. See Notes and Definitions at the end of this section.

Table C-1. Population, School, and Student Characteristics by County—*Continued*

County	Current expenditures, fiscal 1999			Resident population 16 to 19 years, 2000				Outcomes, 1999–2000	
	Amount ($1,000s)	Amount per student	Percent for instruction	Total population 16 to 19 years	Percent in Armed Forces	Percent high school graduates	Percent not enrolled, not grads, not Armed Forces, not empl.	Number of graduates	Dropouts grades 9–12 (percent)
	21	22	23	24	25	26	27	28	29
Van Wert, OH	$28 364	$6 477	64.0	1 888	0.0	12.6	4.3	320	1.6
Vinton, OH	12 358	4 883	57.4	662	0.0	8.6	4.7	140	6.0
Warren, OH	145 425	5 790	57.3	7 779	0.1	11.5	2.9	1 508	2.6
Washington, OH	63 098	5 833	59.2	3 646	0.0	11.4	3.3	757	1.8
Wayne, OH	124 551	6 496	58.8	7 222	0.0	10.0	4.8	1 226	3.2
Williams, OH	39 912	5 541	62.7	2 325	0.0	15.4	6.2	496	2.8
Wood, OH	134 519	7 172	58.8	10 651	0.1	6.3	1.7	1 336	1.8
Wyandot, OH	20 730	5 171	60.5	1 258	0.0	12.7	2.8	336	2.1
OKLAHOMA									
Adair, OK	31 186	6 209	57.3	1 263	0.0	13.9	6.5	287	4.5
Alfalfa, OK	6 148	6 286	61.0	276	0.0	7.6	1.1	79	0.7
Atoka, OK	13 386	5 840	56.5	751	0.0	9.9	3.3	155	3.3
Beaver, OK	9 046	6 932	57.6	365	0.8	11.8	4.7	82	1.9
Beckham, OK	20 403	5 311	64.4	1 033	0.0	5.1	5.4	233	4.8
Blaine, OK	13 671	6 150	62.2	684	0.0	7.5	7.3	139	4.2
Bryan, OK	36 079	5 204	61.0	2 337	0.0	10.0	6.2	371	4.1
Caddo, OK	39 162	5 878	59.4	2 150	0.0	11.7	8.5	451	4.4
Canadian, OK	82 377	4 651	58.8	5 547	0.1	8.0	2.6	1 300	2.6
Carter, OK	49 682	5 459	57.7	2 472	0.2	10.2	5.6	529	4.4
Cherokee, OK	40 118	5 609	63.6	3 278	0.1	9.0	6.3	364	5.5
Choctaw, OK	17 260	5 782	60.5	847	0.0	9.7	11.6	204	3.5
Cimarron, OK	4 868	7 839	58.1	165	0.0	3.0	4.2	38	0.6
Cleveland, OK	169 592	4 695	60.0	14 804	0.3	7.6	2.8	2 268	6.4
Coal, OK	7 904	6 283	62.7	341	0.0	12.0	8.2	68	2.0
Comanche, OK	121 676	5 275	56.5	8 397	21.3	32.6	5.7	1 186	4.3
Cotton, OK	6 596	5 260	60.4	397	0.8	12.3	4.0	79	3.5
Craig, OK	16 419	5 221	58.0	862	0.0	8.7	5.3	217	6.1
Creek, OK	66 109	4 918	58.5	4 151	0.0	11.3	3.7	825	4.3
Custer, OK	29 211	5 500	61.8	2 358	0.0	6.2	3.4	315	4.9
Delaware, OK	33 164	5 018	60.6	1 901	0.0	13.5	7.8	355	5.7
Dewey, OK	8 268	7 336	60.5	329	0.0	7.3	1.5	90	0.6
Ellis, OK	5 650	7 272	59.7	236	0.0	4.2	5.5	86	1.2
Garfield, OK	56 347	5 371	59.1	3 212	0.0	8.3	6.4	659	4.0
Garvin, OK	28 721	5 144	62.4	1 646	0.0	10.9	5.0	397	5.6
Grady, OK	41 677	4 854	61.2	3 000	0.0	10.4	4.4	589	4.4
Grant, OK	7 032	6 404	60.8	301	0.0	8.3	0.7	95	1.1
Greer, OK	5 985	5 926	60.1	344	0.0	14.5	2.9	70	5.1
Harmon, OK	4 218	6 078	70.8	219	0.0	8.7	7.8	53	7.8
Harper, OK	5 298	7 102	57.9	212	0.0	7.1	2.4	67	1.5
Haskell, OK	12 557	5 230	61.3	710	0.0	18.5	3.7	150	4.8
Hughes, OK	15 941	6 169	57.0	643	0.0	10.6	6.8	182	11.7
Jackson, OK	31 342	5 100	63.5	1 801	6.6	16.0	6.9	389	1.2
Jefferson, OK	8 078	5 697	61.7	334	0.0	9.9	4.5	95	2.3
Johnston, OK	11 722	5 674	65.0	743	0.0	9.0	6.7	152	3.2
Kay, OK	45 867	4 838	59.8	2 970	0.0	9.6	6.7	618	6.2
Kingfisher, OK	17 877	5 489	60.2	877	0.0	8.9	2.9	242	2.6
Kiowa, OK	12 049	5 889	60.3	623	0.0	13.6	7.2	137	4.4
Latimer, OK	16 397	8 496	60.2	810	0.0	3.7	7.8	111	1.6
Le Flore, OK	52 895	5 374	62.6	3 001	0.0	13.9	6.4	614	6.1
Lincoln, OK	27 458	4 633	61.8	1 954	0.0	11.7	4.1	405	2.7
Logan, OK	23 039	5 133	58.8	2 637	0.0	8.6	4.1	288	4.0
Love, OK	8 308	5 066	63.2	521	0.0	5.2	6.1	113	5.1
McClain, OK	27 675	5 102	62.8	1 782	0.0	13.0	3.3	371	3.8
McCurtain, OK	43 732	5 747	56.6	2 022	0.0	12.6	8.5	439	3.9
McIntosh, OK	18 334	5 501	59.1	1 016	0.0	11.6	10.1	187	5.4
Major, OK	8 176	5 899	65.0	421	0.0	2.4	5.2	135	2.7
Marshall, OK	11 941	5 049	63.5	729	0.0	10.3	8.2	143	2.9
Mayes, OK	36 394	4 987	61.3	2 327	0.0	10.4	6.1	469	6.5
Murray, OK	11 585	5 079	60.7	765	0.0	14.2	0.4	172	2.2
Muskogee, OK	77 280	5 469	58.4	4 261	0.0	10.9	6.7	841	5.0
Noble, OK	14 156	6 206	61.8	622	0.0	9.0	2.1	138	2.4
Nowata, OK	10 584	5 411	60.2	576	0.0	10.2	3.8	141	5.5
Okfuskee, OK	13 518	5 745	61.7	703	0.0	13.1	10.8	158	5.6
Oklahoma, OK	574 473	5 313	57.6	38 506	0.7	11.9	6.7	5 545	7.6
Okmulgee, OK	38 503	5 095	60.4	2 682	0.1	9.3	8.7	476	4.1
Osage, OK	27 556	5 932	59.0	2 643	0.1	11.3	3.7	272	5.7
Ottawa, OK	36 427	5 731	58.2	2 180	0.0	8.5	6.8	336	7.5
Pawnee, OK	12 881	4 635	59.7	986	0.0	13.4	4.9	167	5.1
Payne, OK	56 187	5 560	55.2	6 044	0.5	6.9	1.9	744	4.0
Pittsburg, OK	45 593	5 426	58.8	2 398	0.0	11.0	5.6	531	5.4
Pontotoc, OK	37 943	5 427	62.2	2 380	0.0	9.6	4.3	428	4.7
Pottawatomie, OK	64 611	5 238	59.9	4 293	0.0	13.3	6.7	713	5.7
Pushmataha, OK	14 779	5 979	61.0	665	0.0	12.5	6.9	160	5.5
Roger Mills, OK	3 605	9 035	54.4	218	0.0	5.5	0.9	74	0.3
Rogers, OK	60 133	4 535	58.4	4 198	0.0	12.5	4.4	869	4.0
Seminole, OK	28 928	5 616	58.7	1 728	0.0	6.9	9.0	311	10.2
Sequoyah, OK	43 501	5 210	57.6	2 354	0.0	15.2	8.4	428	4.2
Stephens, OK	42 443	5 040	60.2	2 537	0.0	8.2	3.1	580	5.3
Texas, OK	21 636	5 680	60.3	1 478	0.0	7.2	7.8	230	8.5

Table C-1. Population, School, and Student Characteristics by County—*Continued*

County	High school graduates, 2000			College enrollment, 2000		College graduates, 2000 (percent)						
	Population 25 years and over	High school diploma or less (percent)	High school diploma or more (percent)	Number	Percent public	Bachelor's degree or more	+/- U.S. percent with bachelor's degree or more	Non-Hispanic White	Black or African American	American Indian and Alaska Native	Asian, Hawaiian, and Pacific Islander	Hispanic or Latino[1]
	30	31	32	33	34	35	36	37	38	39	40	41
Van Wert, OH	19 453	65.0	86.6	875	65.1	12.0	-12.4	12.0	20.0	0.0	15.2	4.3
Vinton, OH	8 223	76.9	70.7	296	75.3	6.0	-18.4	6.0	0.0	11.4	. . .	9.1
Warren, OH	103 306	45.0	86.2	5 886	76.4	28.4	4.0	28.3	13.9	12.3	66.1	29.3
Washington, OH	42 770	58.5	84.5	3 317	65.3	15.0	-9.4	15.0	14.7	0.0	57.7	10.2
Wayne, OH	69 953	62.0	80.0	5 283	58.6	17.2	-7.2	17.0	17.9	7.8	53.5	23.9
Williams, OH	25 690	65.6	83.1	983	82.8	10.7	-13.7	10.8	0.0	14.9	0.0	8.2
Wood, OH	71 551	46.2	88.6	18 158	95.0	26.2	1.8	26.1	34.6	28.3	59.3	11.0
Wyandot, OH	15 097	66.5	82.5	772	76.0	9.8	-14.6	9.8	0.0	0.0	25.9	7.5
OKLAHOMA												
Adair, OK	12 764	71.4	66.7	511	83.4	9.8	-14.6	11.3	0.0	7.1	27.3	3.9
Alfalfa, OK	4 543	59.4	81.4	170	88.2	14.9	-9.5	16.5	4.5	2.0	. . .	2.6
Atoka, OK	9 377	70.5	69.4	383	95.0	10.1	-14.3	10.7	1.6	10.3	0.0	0.0
Beaver, OK	3 898	55.1	81.2	119	98.3	17.6	-6.8	18.6	0.0	22.0	71.4	6.4
Beckham, OK	12 968	58.8	75.9	566	80.2	15.5	-8.9	16.8	0.0	15.7	76.7	5.4
Blaine, OK	8 118	65.7	75.5	266	96.2	14.0	-10.4	16.7	10.9	3.2	11.4	3.3
Bryan, OK	23 175	56.9	74.9	2 495	88.6	17.9	-6.5	17.6	13.9	16.9	53.5	11.7
Caddo, OK	19 020	64.6	75.9	1 024	90.5	14.2	-10.2	15.2	5.9	13.2	7.7	5.0
Canadian, OK	56 207	44.7	87.3	3 883	85.4	20.9	-3.5	21.4	13.5	16.2	32.1	9.8
Carter, OK	30 195	59.8	77.0	1 212	89.5	15.1	-9.3	15.8	9.7	8.6	53.1	18.8
Cherokee, OK	25 237	53.5	76.7	4 448	94.5	22.1	-2.3	23.8	26.2	18.1	22.7	9.9
Choctaw, OK	10 210	67.7	69.0	495	93.5	9.9	-14.5	9.6	5.2	13.2	22.7	28.2
Cimarron, OK	2 077	55.0	76.6	66	84.8	17.7	-6.7	19.7	0.0	16.7	0.0	1.3
Cleveland, OK	126 569	38.6	88.1	26 884	92.9	28.0	3.6	28.1	27.1	21.8	48.6	17.9
Coal, OK	3 964	68.4	68.6	172	93.6	12.4	-12.0	12.2	0.0	14.8	35.7	10.6
Comanche, OK	67 220	46.3	85.2	7 129	89.4	19.1	-5.3	21.8	11.6	13.0	21.5	11.2
Cotton, OK	4 436	62.2	77.0	155	92.9	14.0	-10.4	14.8	1.4	11.8	33.3	7.5
Craig, OK	10 197	63.8	76.9	386	94.6	10.5	-13.9	10.5	8.8	9.5	0.0	21.6
Creek, OK	43 523	62.4	77.6	2 269	83.4	11.7	-12.7	12.1	9.8	8.0	20.5	7.6
Custer, OK	15 156	50.2	81.2	3 431	97.8	22.8	-1.6	25.2	3.1	12.0	29.0	4.6
Delaware, OK	25 549	61.7	75.4	796	84.9	13.3	-11.1	14.0	15.4	11.2	24.0	5.8
Dewey, OK	3 310	61.0	79.8	107	90.7	16.6	-7.8	17.3	0.0	3.7	100.0	1.6
Ellis, OK	2 918	57.1	81.2	63	90.5	19.2	-5.2	19.5	. . .	16.7	. . .	8.9
Garfield, OK	38 067	53.4	82.2	2 079	87.8	19.6	-4.8	20.2	5.6	10.5	25.9	12.6
Garvin, OK	18 263	67.4	73.0	572	90.2	12.0	-12.4	12.2	14.7	9.3	26.0	5.6
Grady, OK	29 172	58.8	79.5	2 073	92.6	14.4	-10.0	14.7	7.0	17.4	29.9	4.3
Grant, OK	3 500	53.3	85.7	113	89.4	16.2	-8.2	16.0	0.0	22.9	22.2	34.5
Greer, OK	4 302	59.6	76.7	261	92.3	12.6	-11.8	14.6	4.1	2.7	58.8	0.0
Harmon, OK	2 192	69.0	63.2	43	86.0	12.1	-12.3	15.6	0.0	0.0	50.0	1.7
Harper, OK	2 507	54.2	82.1	74	81.1	19.2	-5.2	19.3	. . .	22.7	0.0	14.5
Haskell, OK	7 762	65.7	66.9	281	98.2	10.3	-14.1	10.6	10.5	8.1	0.0	2.5
Hughes, OK	9 762	68.3	70.8	434	92.6	9.7	-14.7	10.8	2.2	5.4	0.0	6.5
Jackson, OK	17 270	47.8	79.1	1 543	93.6	18.5	-5.9	20.5	10.6	21.3	35.1	5.6
Jefferson, OK	4 710	68.1	69.3	149	96.0	10.6	-13.8	10.8	0.0	13.3	5.9	8.5
Johnston, OK	6 759	61.4	69.1	536	97.4	13.3	-11.1	13.8	0.0	11.1	36.8	15.3
Kay, OK	31 106	52.3	80.9	1 774	92.8	18.3	-6.1	19.4	4.2	8.7	35.3	8.9
Kingfisher, OK	8 984	57.6	81.2	316	88.6	16.1	-8.3	17.5	4.8	11.3	0.0	1.8
Kiowa, OK	6 963	58.9	77.4	314	95.5	14.8	-9.6	16.1	2.0	5.3	. . .	11.1
Latimer, OK	6 716	61.1	73.8	754	96.4	12.0	-12.4	11.6	25.0	14.4	25.0	26.7
Le Flore, OK	30 966	64.7	70.4	1 658	95.4	11.3	-13.1	11.7	10.4	10.4	29.1	4.1
Lincoln, OK	20 746	64.5	77.5	883	83.5	11.1	-13.3	11.4	11.4	8.6	11.4	2.4
Logan, OK	21 195	53.1	81.5	2 817	93.2	19.1	-5.3	18.9	23.1	15.2	43.4	17.1
Love, OK	5 931	67.8	73.6	248	91.5	10.8	-13.6	11.1	1.8	19.7	0.0	3.2
McClain, OK	18 069	57.4	79.3	1 154	88.8	15.7	-8.7	16.1	8.8	18.8	28.6	4.6
McCurtain, OK	21 875	66.9	69.2	908	92.4	10.8	-13.6	11.7	7.3	9.0	8.0	1.9
McIntosh, OK	13 787	62.6	71.6	557	91.7	13.1	-11.3	12.5	9.1	16.1	20.0	15.1
Major, OK	5 191	61.8	78.6	136	90.4	14.4	-10.0	14.9	14.3	6.4	. . .	0.0
Marshall, OK	9 078	63.3	71.0	332	91.0	11.4	-13.0	12.1	0.7	10.8	0.0	4.1
Mayes, OK	24 849	62.0	76.1	1 062	83.1	12.1	-12.3	12.8	3.0	9.2	50.9	6.5
Murray, OK	8 566	61.5	74.3	325	90.2	14.9	-9.5	15.1	30.4	12.0	18.2	6.7
Muskogee, OK	44 890	56.8	75.1	2 819	87.0	15.4	-9.0	16.5	12.3	12.0	40.4	11.9
Noble, OK	7 635	58.6	81.5	371	89.2	15.8	-8.6	16.3	3.9	10.9	36.5	0.0
Nowata, OK	7 092	66.5	76.2	270	93.0	9.5	-14.9	9.9	11.6	10.6	. . .	12.7
Okfuskee, OK	7 904	70.2	69.4	288	84.7	9.2	-15.2	9.8	7.9	7.9	0.0	10.4
Oklahoma, OK	420 823	43.5	82.5	43 237	74.4	25.4	1.0	28.8	14.8	14.6	34.4	8.5
Okmulgee, OK	25 225	60.5	74.7	1 790	90.2	11.4	-13.0	11.8	9.3	11.1	9.7	13.5
Osage, OK	29 417	56.2	80.2	1 282	83.6	14.6	-9.8	14.1	22.3	11.5	35.9	9.6
Ottawa, OK	21 510	58.9	75.7	1 586	93.1	12.2	-12.2	12.5	13.3	11.9	19.7	2.7
Pawnee, OK	10 997	61.4	78.8	460	88.9	12.1	-12.3	12.5	8.6	10.4	18.2	2.7
Payne, OK	37 237	40.0	86.7	17 412	98.1	34.2	9.8	33.8	22.5	23.8	80.6	36.6
Pittsburg, OK	30 162	60.3	76.2	1 301	89.7	12.9	-11.5	13.3	7.7	12.4	35.7	7.0
Pontotoc, OK	22 031	53.5	78.2	2 957	96.0	21.8	-2.6	22.6	11.9	18.0	77.8	10.3
Pottawatomie, OK	41 142	56.4	79.3	4 315	59.4	15.5	-8.9	16.3	9.2	10.3	24.0	7.6
Pushmataha, OK	7 861	66.3	69.0	277	89.5	12.4	-12.0	12.1	4.4	11.5	64.7	14.5
Roger Mills, OK	2 396	59.3	79.3	59	100.0	15.8	-8.6	16.6	. . .	3.7	0.0	10.3
Rogers, OK	45 152	49.4	83.4	2 378	85.4	16.9	-7.5	17.4	12.8	13.1	30.9	23.2
Seminole, OK	15 988	61.6	73.2	1 022	84.5	12.1	-12.3	12.9	10.9	6.9	50.0	4.4
Sequoyah, OK	24 980	64.7	70.2	1 007	90.4	10.9	-13.5	10.3	12.9	13.6	42.9	6.3
Stephens, OK	29 111	60.3	77.0	1 230	88.6	16.6	-7.8	16.9	8.9	13.2	65.6	10.1
Texas, OK	11 776	56.7	71.9	1 065	83.5	17.7	-6.7	21.9	0.0	17.8	43.9	3.6

[1]Hispanic or Latino persons may be of any race.
. . . = Not available.

Table C-1. Population, School, and Student Characteristics by County—*Continued*

County	State/County code	County type[1]	Population, 2000		Number of schools and students, 2000–2001			Resident enrollment, 2000			
			Total	Percent 5–17 years	School districts	Schools	Students	Total	Percent public	K–12	Percent public
			1	2	3	4	5	6	7	8	9
Tillman, OK	40141	6	9 287	20.5	4	10	1 901	2 304	96.8	2 032	97.4
Tulsa, OK	40143	2	563 299	18.9	15	180	105 639	152 977	79.7	107 559	87.9
Wagoner, OK	40145	2	57 491	21.1	4	15	6 007	15 269	89.5	12 342	93.9
Washington, OK	40147	4	48 996	19.1	4	19	8 803	12 166	88.3	9 627	93.8
Washita, OK	40149	7	11 508	20.1	5	11	2 162	3 007	94.8	2 476	94.8
Woods, OK	40151	7	9 089	14.7	3	9	1 435	2 625	97.9	1 454	98.8
Woodward, OK	40153	7	18 486	19.2	4	13	3 562	4 392	95.6	3 724	97.8
OREGON	41000										
Baker, OR	41001	7	16 741	18.9	4	15	2 773	3 629	93.2	3 141	95.9
Benton, OR	41003	4	78 153	16.2	4	29	9 713	30 859	92.7	12 857	90.7
Clackamas, OR	41005	0	338 391	19.7	11	104	54 391	87 642	83.9	66 117	89.2
Clatsop, OR	41007	6	35 630	18.0	5	16	5 516	8 478	89.4	6 425	93.0
Columbia, OR	41009	1	43 560	20.9	5	24	8 593	10 694	91.2	8 920	94.8
Coos, OR	41011	5	62 779	17.1	6	28	9 392	14 249	93.6	10 859	96.6
Crook, OR	41013	7	19 182	20.1	1	7	3 170	4 562	91.1	3 743	95.6
Curry, OR	41015	7	21 137	15.1	3	10	3 065	3 801	93.4	3 197	96.5
Deschutes, OR	41017	5	115 367	18.6	4	36	19 807	27 802	87.9	21 359	91.3
Douglas, OR	41019	4	100 399	18.4	14	50	16 560	22 732	89.9	18 784	91.6
Gilliam, OR	41021	9	1 915	18.7	2	4	350	438	95.9	381	99.2
Grant, OR	41023	9	7 935	20.1	5	9	1 351	1 888	88.1	1 612	90.1
Harney, OR	41025	7	7 609	20.3	10	13	1 423	1 713	94.5	1 535	95.0
Hood River, OR	41027	6	20 411	20.6	1	9	3 759	5 124	88.1	4 269	90.3
Jackson, OR	41029	3	181 269	18.4	9	57	28 544	44 630	89.4	32 724	91.0
Jefferson, OR	41031	7	19 009	22.1	4	11	3 704	4 882	94.4	4 137	97.8
Josephine, OR	41033	4	75 726	17.7	2	26	11 332	16 787	86.6	13 426	88.8
Klamath, OR	41035	5	63 775	19.4	2	30	10 996	16 355	90.6	12 484	92.7
Lake, OR	41037	7	7 422	19.9	5	8	1 379	1 669	95.0	1 497	96.3
Lane, OR	41039	2	322 959	17.1	17	126	46 967	90 503	90.6	54 942	92.1
Lincoln, OR	41041	7	44 479	16.6	1	22	5 956	9 074	91.5	7 409	94.6
Linn, OR	41043	4	103 069	19.2	7	53	17 487	25 885	86.3	19 774	88.6
Malheur, OR	41045	7	31 615	20.1	9	23	5 602	8 244	90.9	6 489	92.6
Marion, OR	41047	2	284 834	19.7	11	115	49 046	73 702	85.2	55 606	91.0
Morrow, OR	41049	9	10 995	22.2	1	7	2 246	2 868	96.4	2 526	97.9
Multnomah, OR	41051	0	660 486	15.9	9	178	91 361	162 670	80.7	104 972	88.3
Polk, OR	41053	2	62 380	19.1	4	19	6 469	17 391	87.6	11 511	89.4
Sherman, OR	41055	9	1 934	21.4	1	3	364	465	94.0	411	94.6
Tillamook, OR	41057	6	24 262	17.4	3	12	3 764	5 039	91.0	4 214	92.4
Umatilla, OR	41059	4	70 548	20.3	10	34	12 832	18 290	92.0	14 484	94.9
Union, OR	41061	7	24 530	18.7	6	16	4 131	7 032	93.6	4 662	94.1
Wallowa, OR	41063	9	7 226	19.4	4	9	1 196	1 677	89.2	1 450	91.9
Wasco, OR	41065	7	23 791	18.8	5	13	3 671	5 507	87.8	4 426	89.5
Washington, OR	41067	0	445 342	19.0	8	110	73 146	116 491	82.5	83 868	88.7
Wheeler, OR	41069	9	1 547	18.0	3	4	255	358	86.0	296	84.5
Yamhill, OR	41071	1	84 992	19.9	7	33	15 308	23 412	77.3	16 901	90.8
PENNSYLVANIA	42000										
Adams, PA	42001	6	91 292	19.0	6	25	14 646	23 246	77.6	17 333	88.3
Allegheny, PA	42003	0	1 281 666	16.4	49	327	172 336	322 016	75.7	212 715	85.1
Armstrong, PA	42005	6	72 392	17.5	5	28	11 672	15 812	91.9	12 826	95.5
Beaver, PA	42007	0	181 412	17.2	16	60	28 238	41 572	84.1	31 636	91.7
Bedford, PA	42009	6	49 984	17.5	5	20	8 269	10 487	91.5	8 761	94.2
Berks, PA	42011	2	373 638	18.4	18	103	64 401	94 301	82.7	69 719	88.9
Blair, PA	42013	3	129 144	17.1	7	35	19 812	29 585	85.9	22 369	90.2
Bradford, PA	42015	6	62 761	19.5	7	33	11 467	14 740	88.0	12 501	91.4
Bucks, PA	42017	0	597 635	19.3	16	131	90 494	157 810	72.4	115 596	80.6
Butler, PA	42019	1	174 083	18.2	7	47	27 843	45 627	87.6	32 159	92.1
Cambria, PA	42021	3	152 598	16.0	14	40	19 958	34 592	81.5	24 953	86.4
Cameron, PA	42023	7	5 974	19.7	1	2	1 119	1 384	91.0	1 192	93.3
Carbon, PA	42025	2	58 802	17.0	7	21	8 614	12 781	86.3	10 303	90.0
Centre, PA	42027	3	135 758	13.4	7	31	14 440	56 564	92.9	18 306	92.4
Chester, PA	42029	0	433 501	19.4	17	95	64 932	119 787	73.0	84 718	80.4
Clarion, PA	42031	7	41 765	16.2	7	17	7 482	12 036	92.3	6 868	92.2
Clearfield, PA	42033	6	83 382	17.2	8	35	15 579	18 092	89.3	14 719	92.3
Clinton, PA	42035	6	37 914	16.1	2	14	5 111	9 857	90.2	6 141	91.3
Columbia, PA	42037	2	64 151	15.9	7	24	11 300	17 963	92.2	10 468	93.7
Crawford, PA	42039	4	90 366	18.8	3	23	11 874	22 134	80.6	16 917	90.0
Cumberland, PA	42041	2	213 674	16.5	10	71	51 903	54 249	77.8	35 816	87.0
Dauphin, PA	42043	2	251 798	18.1	13	71	38 237	60 052	82.9	46 556	87.7
Delaware, PA	42045	0	550 864	18.6	18	106	71 771	154 448	62.9	103 230	74.2
Elk, PA	42047	7	35 112	18.3	3	10	4 600	7 993	76.4	6 516	79.8
Erie, PA	42049	2	280 843	18.8	14	77	42 492	77 763	74.2	53 964	80.9
Fayette, PA	42051	1	148 644	17.0	6	46	20 909	32 185	88.4	25 608	91.8
Forest, PA	42053	9	4 946	19.1	1	4	753	1 101	76.0	993	74.8
Franklin, PA	42055	4	129 313	17.8	7	42	18 330	28 494	84.3	22 600	88.2
Fulton, PA	42057	8	14 261	18.3	3	6	2 440	2 996	94.1	2 580	96.1
Greene, PA	42059	6	40 672	16.9	5	15	6 413	9 468	86.9	7 221	95.6

[1]County type code is from the Economic Research Service of the USDA. See Notes and Definitions at the end of this section.

Table C-1. School and Student Characteristics by County—*Continued*

County	Characteristics of students, 2000–2001			Staff and students, 2000–2001				Revenues, fiscal 1999			
	Percent with IEP[2]	Percent eligible for free lunch	Percent minority	Number of teachers	Student/teacher ratio	Local school non-teaching staff	Central admin. staff	Total revenue ($1,000s)	Percentage of revenue from		
									Federal govt.	State govt.	Local govt.
	10	11	12	13	14	15	16	17	18	19	20
Tillman, OK	18.1	64.1	46.6	153	12.4	104	11	$12 298	9.9	69.1	20.9
Tulsa, OK	13.8	39.5	35.4	6 493	16.3	5 743	547	656 925	6.3	47.1	46.6
Wagoner, OK	14.9	52.3	37.9	401	15.0	257	21	30 359	8.5	67.4	24.1
Washington, OK	11.3	34.1	22.4	550	16.0	445	39	54 241	6.6	56.7	36.7
Washita, OK	10.3	54.4	12.0	159	13.6	92	20	17 890	8.0	54.9	37.1
Woods, OK	12.8	39.1	6.2	115	12.5	82	11	13 936	7.1	46.9	46.0
Woodward, OK	12.7	37.2	9.9	248	14.4	172	19	23 475	6.0	61.1	32.9
OREGON											
Baker, OR	14.0	36.7	6.0	176	15.8	165	18	21 803	4.5	68.1	27.4
Benton, OR	12.2	21.7	12.5	473	20.5	452	50	89 866	5.7	52.3	42.0
Clackamas, OR	12.0	20.7	10.3	2 660	20.4	2 433	229	396 545	3.5	55.0	41.5
Clatsop, OR	13.1	24.7	7.1	437	19.7	381	38	60 050	4.4	54.7	40.9
Columbia, OR	14.8	45.3	16.3	490	19.2	488	43	83 174	8.7	58.3	32.9
Coos, OR	13.2	42.3	10.3	162	19.6	174	9	20 682	6.2	59.0	34.8
Crook, OR	15.4	43.8	9.9	174	17.6	159	15	21 716	9.5	58.0	32.5
Curry, OR	13.1	29.5	5.9	942	21.0	846	161	141 186	6.6	49.7	43.8
Deschutes, OR	13.1	45.0	8.1	911	18.2	834	90	129 304	10.7	63.0	26.2
Gilliam, OR	11.3	34.6	6.0	33	10.6	30	4	9 047	2.1	63.0	34.9
Grant, OR	13.8	35.8	4.3	110	12.3	91	11	15 100	7.5	63.8	28.7
Harney, OR	15.1	48.4	14.6	100	14.2	90	15	14 317	6.5	69.4	24.1
Hood River, OR	12.3	43.7	38.4	212	17.7	222	21	30 128	8.1	61.1	30.8
Jackson, OR	11.4	35.8	14.7	1 409	20.3	1 175	131	204 779	5.9	62.5	31.6
Jefferson, OR	13.9	62.6	53.2	224	16.5	248	24	29 247	17.5	59.7	22.8
Josephine, OR	10.9	50.3	9.9	573	19.8	558	41	81 646	7.4	63.2	29.3
Klamath, OR	15.0	47.9	21.0	584	18.8	629	66	80 571	11.3	65.9	22.8
Lake, OR	13.2	42.2	8.8	93	14.8	89	12	12 733	8.3	63.9	27.8
Lane, OR	13.8	33.4	12.7	2 311	20.3	2 381	220	377 057	7.5	54.3	38.2
Lincoln, OR	14.5	53.8	15.8	290	20.5	273	20	50 038	8.3	40.3	51.4
Linn, OR	13.9	37.4	9.0	869	20.1	858	105	119 131	7.0	65.2	27.8
Malheur, OR	12.6	61.4	42.7	350	16.0	347	41	46 925	9.6	71.0	19.4
Marion, OR	12.3	46.3	26.7	2 626	18.7	2 313	299	362 902	9.9	64.8	25.3
Morrow, OR	11.8	49.2	36.2	148	15.2	151	8	17 422	3.8	57.7	38.6
Multnomah, OR	12.2	38.5	30.6	4 692	19.5	4 047	514	741 022	7.7	50.5	41.8
Polk, OR	13.2	37.7	19.4	337	19.2	280	30	42 797	6.7	63.3	30.0
Sherman, OR	17.3	29.7	10.4	33	11.0	29	3	4 164	2.5	67.9	29.6
Tillamook, OR	15.9	43.3	13.1	221	17.0	235	25	28 480	7.8	46.7	45.5
Umatilla, OR	12.9	43.7	29.6	739	17.4	638	68	98 705	9.2	64.8	26.1
Union, OR	14.9	32.6	7.4	258	16.0	188	29	41 768	11.5	58.8	29.7
Wallowa, OR	19.2	47.2	5.7	90	13.3	54	7	15 204	6.5	49.0	44.5
Wasco, OR	13.9	42.3	21.0	217	16.9	226	38	32 074	9.5	63.2	27.3
Washington, OR	11.7	21.9	24.8	3 521	20.8	3 218	284	507 347	3.8	51.0	45.2
Wheeler, OR	9.0	55.3	6.7	20	12.8	21	5	3 778	3.6	66.9	29.5
Yamhill, OR	13.0	33.6	16.7	770	19.9	655	77	113 422	5.4	58.5	36.1
PENNSYLVANIA											
Adams, PA	12.2	22.3	8.7	841	17.4	1 247	156	158 900	8.7	35.1	56.2
Allegheny, PA	12.6	29.9	24.0	10 935	15.8	9 313	890	1 833 122	5.4	30.3	64.3
Armstrong, PA	13.7	31.6	2.0	740	15.8	501	61	107 833	4.2	46.5	49.3
Beaver, PA	11.0	31.1	10.5	1 736	16.3	1 343	144	242 831	6.3	46.7	47.0
Bedford, PA	13.6	35.7	1.4	508	16.3	422	48	65 328	6.1	54.1	39.8
Berks, PA	10.9	22.2	21.0	3 788	17.0	3 439	431	542 703	4.7	32.4	62.9
Blair, PA	12.9	33.7	3.0	1 177	16.8	1 128	137	163 176	8.6	51.8	39.6
Bradford, PA	12.7	34.0	2.3	751	15.3	595	53	92 680	5.8	55.6	38.5
Bucks, PA	13.4	12.5	9.8	5 200	17.4	4 884	485	910 529	2.4	23.0	74.5
Butler, PA	11.9	18.3	2.0	1 646	16.9	1 047	98	204 862	2.6	43.6	53.7
Cambria, PA	12.9	44.5	5.2	1 318	15.1	1 122	126	206 441	9.1	50.9	40.0
Cameron, PA	12.8	34.3	1.7	66	17.0	58	6	8 000	2.1	55.0	42.9
Carbon, PA	11.5	30.1	5.8	534	16.1	435	53	78 574	3.2	35.9	60.9
Centre, PA	11.1	18.2	6.9	930	15.5	1 096	111	133 736	5.4	32.1	62.5
Chester, PA	11.5	12.2	15.8	4 066	16.0	3 422	417	630 393	3.2	22.7	74.1
Clarion, PA	13.4	34.7	1.7	502	14.9	467	31	77 186	9.9	54.1	36.0
Clearfield, PA	13.1	37.0	1.0	957	16.3	767	70	120 130	5.5	54.7	39.8
Clinton, PA	17.1	22.2	1.4	377	13.6	290	24	46 137	6.3	47.5	46.2
Columbia, PA	14.0	28.1	2.8	750	15.1	610	45	87 625	2.8	46.1	51.1
Crawford, PA	14.4	30.4	4.2	763	15.6	575	42	94 977	6.4	52.2	41.4
Cumberland, PA	. . .	. . .	10.0	2 347	22.1	2 128	297	320 228	3.8	31.0	65.3
Dauphin, PA	13.4	27.0	34.6	2 533	15.1	1 944	205	340 294	4.1	32.9	63.0
Delaware, PA	14.1	22.7	28.3	4 643	15.5	4 563	455	699 314	3.6	26.3	70.1
Elk, PA	12.5	27.2	1.9	297	15.5	173	23	38 086	3.8	46.1	50.1
Erie, PA	14.3	38.5	15.1	2 518	16.9	2 094	235	360 044	8.4	45.5	46.1
Fayette, PA	15.0	48.9	7.1	1 260	16.6	929	82	167 481	7.1	61.1	31.8
Forest, PA	17.0	43.6	0.5	53	14.2	58	3	8 666	5.4	35.2	59.4
Franklin, PA	14.0	22.2	9.5	1 050	17.5	838	153	136 322	3.6	40.7	55.7
Fulton, PA	9.1	32.1	2.0	166	14.7	127	10	22 310	5.7	53.5	40.8
Greene, PA	18.8	43.8	1.9	457	14.0	268	32	59 687	7.2	46.4	46.4

[2]IEP = Individual Education Program. See Notes and Definitions at the end of this section.
. . . = Not available.

Table C-1. Population, School, and Student Characteristics by County—*Continued*

County	Current expenditures, fiscal 1999			Resident population 16 to 19 years, 2000				Outcomes, 1999–2000	
	Amount ($1,000s)	Amount per student	Percent for instruction	Total population 16 to 19 years	Percent in Armed Forces	Percent high school graduates	Percent not enrolled, not grads, not Armed Forces, not empl.	Number of graduates	Dropouts grades 9–12 (percent)
	21	22	23	24	25	26	27	28	29
Tillman, OK	$11 595	$5 880	59.7	542	0.9	8.1	2.0	123	4.6
Tulsa, OK	528 731	5 075	55.1	31 914	0.0	10.4	6.3	5 875	6.0
Wagoner, OK	27 634	4 660	60.7	3 573	0.0	9.7	5.1	365	6.8
Washington, OK	46 278	5 118	58.3	2 723	0.1	11.6	4.9	579	3.3
Washita, OK	14 150	6 212	57.8	729	0.0	6.4	1.5	147	2.7
Woods, OK	10 617	7 237	57.2	623	0.0	3.4	1.8	128	1.3
Woodward, OK	20 391	5 541	62.1	1 153	0.0	12.1	7.6	207	5.9
OREGON									
Baker, OR	21 195	7 329	60.5	875	0.0	12.1	7.7	182	3.1
Benton, OR	76 647	7 498	48.9	6 792	0.1	5.5	0.7	751	3.2
Clackamas, OR	344 877	6 392	60.6	18 703	0.0	11.9	4.4	3 204	3.1
Clatsop, OR	34 445	6 721	63.0	2 291	1.0	12.7	8.7	322	3.4
Columbia, OR	56 829	6 214	60.4	2 267	1.0	15.1	4.1	494	4.4
Coos, OR	76 649	7 635	54.9	3 549	0.7	13.2	5.8	704	3.8
Crook, OR	18 932	6 045	60.8	1 073	0.0	14.7	10.1	163	3.4
Curry, OR	20 507	6 226	64.2	884	0.0	10.9	4.6	192	4.8
Deschutes, OR	117 492	6 194	60.6	5 855	0.0	14.4	2.8	1 247	6.0
Douglas, OR	120 350	6 986	54.9	5 456	0.2	12.0	5.6	1 001	4.8
Gilliam, OR	5 833	15 151	53.9	94	0.0	5.3	2.1	33	. . .
Grant, OR	12 460	8 357	58.9	466	0.0	9.7	3.0	102	1.5
Harney, OR	13 174	8 883	52.6	453	0.0	14.3	8.6	116	6.0
Hood River, OR	25 829	6 819	62.2	1 147	0.0	12.3	6.8	246	6.2
Jackson, OR	187 767	6 517	62.2	10 013	0.1	12.6	5.8	1 492	6.7
Jefferson, OR	26 938	7 618	57.4	921	0.0	11.2	9.6	159	4.2
Josephine, OR	71 916	6 103	64.2	3 650	0.0	14.5	7.6	638	4.9
Klamath, OR	75 093	6 774	63.7	3 556	0.0	13.4	4.3	565	4.9
Lake, OR	11 485	7 904	59.0	365	0.0	11.5	2.5	97	0.8
Lane, OR	350 873	7 147	56.0	19 632	0.0	12.9	3.6	2 877	5.0
Lincoln, OR	45 491	6 461	58.5	2 274	1.0	18.1	7.7	411	8.0
Linn, OR	110 893	6 208	59.0	6 161	0.0	12.1	6.9	1 015	6.3
Malheur, OR	42 162	7 194	60.0	1 807	0.0	11.8	5.9	278	2.8
Marion, OR	331 526	6 562	61.1	17 704	0.0	13.9	8.5	2 725	6.6
Morrow, OR	14 862	6 674	64.4	710	0.0	9.3	7.2	163	3.6
Multnomah, OR	707 750	7 606	57.5	33 149	0.0	12.7	5.7	4 786	9.2
Polk, OR	39 549	6 200	64.3	4 256	0.0	10.7	3.4	418	5.8
Sherman, OR	3 623	9 149	54.3	103	0.0	13.6	5.8	35	. . .
Tillamook, OR	27 005	7 056	59.7	1 322	0.7	14.7	4.8	271	3.7
Umatilla, OR	87 846	6 775	60.1	4 001	0.0	8.8	6.8	655	6.4
Union, OR	36 997	8 476	61.6	1 748	0.5	7.9	2.7	314	4.0
Wallowa, OR	11 276	8 575	65.9	341	0.0	10.3	2.1	89	. . .
Wasco, OR	29 494	7 782	57.5	1 182	0.0	8.6	5.6	233	4.9
Washington, OR	436 637	6 298	59.8	23 102	0.0	12.1	5.3	3 678	5.4
Wheeler, OR	3 269	12 243	54.9	99	0.0	12.1	0.0	21	0.9
Yamhill, OR	98 531	6 433	60.4	5 545	0.0	10.2	5.0	906	7.1
PENNSYLVANIA									
Adams, PA	135 902	9 339	59.7	5 427	0.1	11.0	3.2	921	3.7
Allegheny, PA	1 545 289	8 907	63.6	64 811	0.0	8.6	3.1	11 471	2.5
Armstrong, PA	89 930	7 800	62.8	3 837	0.0	11.6	4.1	897	1.9
Beaver, PA	206 012	7 158	62.6	9 127	0.0	10.2	3.6	2 053	2.5
Bedford, PA	53 814	6 312	62.2	2 431	0.0	14.7	4.2	555	3.5
Berks, PA	450 670	7 130	62.7	20 694	0.0	10.0	4.9	3 742	4.5
Blair, PA	130 898	6 299	62.1	7 576	0.1	13.1	3.4	1 388	3.6
Bradford, PA	82 463	6 889	63.1	3 428	0.0	12.0	5.1	787	4.6
Bucks, PA	780 619	8 785	66.0	29 976	0.1	9.1	2.2	5 825	2.0
Butler, PA	172 055	6 203	65.3	9 699	0.0	8.2	2.1	1 865	3.0
Cambria, PA	168 801	8 265	59.8	8 601	0.1	10.1	3.8	1 674	2.2
Cameron, PA	6 537	5 429	64.7	313	0.0	8.9	3.2	93	2.9
Carbon, PA	60 270	7 250	63.5	2 820	0.0	12.1	5.2	579	2.6
Centre, PA	117 967	8 181	60.4	11 929	0.1	4.8	1.6	1 007	1.9
Chester, PA	534 144	8 527	61.3	23 454	0.0	6.7	2.9	3 917	2.3
Clarion, PA	64 386	8 283	58.9	3 245	0.0	5.7	2.6	574	2.2
Clearfield, PA	98 885	6 247	63.7	4 163	0.2	11.4	7.4	1 012	3.2
Clinton, PA	41 400	7 851	66.8	2 646	0.4	7.6	5.3	375	3.7
Columbia, PA	74 096	6 786	63.3	4 862	0.2	5.7	2.8	839	2.5
Crawford, PA	80 370	6 577	61.9	5 741	0.1	9.7	4.8	837	3.1
Cumberland, PA	270 110	7 450	62.2	13 107	0.1	7.2	2.7	2 451	2.7
Dauphin, PA	271 573	7 198	64.5	12 418	0.0	10.4	4.6	2 151	4.4
Delaware, PA	598 994	8 546	65.1	32 263	0.0	6.7	3.2	4 384	2.7
Elk, PA	31 059	6 617	61.3	1 785	0.0	14.8	2.2	329	2.2
Erie, PA	304 519	7 137	62.0	18 122	0.0	8.2	3.5	2 754	3.9
Fayette, PA	137 295	6 371	61.6	7 221	0.1	13.3	5.1	1 387	4.1
Forest, PA	6 400	8 112	57.5	322	0.0	11.5	1.9	62	2.4
Franklin, PA	111 485	6 207	64.4	6 695	0.0	12.7	4.4	1 109	3.5
Fulton, PA	16 964	6 756	62.9	681	0.0	19.1	4.0	141	2.8
Greene, PA	50 997	7 687	61.1	2 254	0.2	12.7	3.3	446	2.4

. . . = Not available.

Table C-1. Population, School, and Student Characteristics by County—*Continued*

County	High school graduates, 2000			College enrollment, 2000		College graduates, 2000 (percent)						
	Population 25 years and over	High school diploma or less (percent)	High school diploma or more (percent)	Number	Percent public	Bachelor's degree or more	+/- U.S. percent with bachelor's degree or more	Non-Hispanic White	Black or African American	American Indian and Alaska Native	Asian, Hawaiian, and Pacific Islander	Hispanic or Latino[1]
	30	31	32	33	34	35	36	37	38	39	40	41
Tillman, OK	6 141	67.0	67.4	160	90.0	12.5	-11.9	15.4	5.0	2.8	27.6	1.3
Tulsa, OK	359 386	41.5	85.1	34 049	62.5	26.9	2.5	29.7	14.3	17.8	38.6	11.8
Wagoner, OK	36 895	54.5	81.3	1 948	75.7	15.4	-9.0	16.0	16.0	11.9	13.6	6.6
Washington, OK	32 905	46.9	85.2	1 783	65.8	25.8	1.4	28.0	12.1	10.2	19.4	16.8
Washita, OK	7 613	59.3	79.7	378	95.0	15.1	-9.3	15.5	0.0	10.3	0.0	8.3
Woods, OK	5 993	49.2	82.7	995	98.9	23.7	-0.7	24.9	8.0	27.6	84.6	13.9
Woodward, OK	11 992	58.2	79.9	397	95.7	15.2	-9.2	15.8	7.6	11.6	26.3	5.0
OREGON												
Baker, OR	11 712	51.0	80.3	284	76.1	16.4	-8.0	16.8	0.0	0.0	2.7	7.7
Benton, OR	45 758	22.2	93.1	16 823	97.4	47.4	23.0	47.6	49.0	30.7	67.2	28.0
Clackamas, OR	223 211	35.2	88.9	15 812	80.0	28.4	4.0	28.5	27.4	20.5	44.2	14.5
Clatsop, OR	24 069	43.5	85.6	1 633	84.1	19.1	-5.3	19.6	16.3	9.1	22.7	7.0
Columbia, OR	28 725	49.6	85.6	1 210	83.6	14.0	-10.4	14.1	20.0	9.3	32.1	11.1
Coos, OR	44 667	49.2	81.6	2 558	92.0	15.0	-9.4	15.3	23.5	8.5	26.9	10.9
Crook, OR	12 692	58.4	80.5	485	79.2	12.6	-11.8	13.1	...	12.1	14.7	1.6
Curry, OR	16 168	50.4	81.7	463	82.9	16.4	-8.0	17.1	28.0	6.4	2.4	7.4
Deschutes, OR	77 981	38.8	88.4	4 761	89.2	25.0	0.6	25.6	0.0	13.2	31.3	8.2
Douglas, OR	68 783	53.7	81.0	3 038	89.8	13.3	-11.1	13.3	8.9	9.9	22.6	13.8
Gilliam, OR	1 368	45.8	89.3	37	67.6	13.4	-11.0	13.5	0.0	20.0	0.0	0.0
Grant, OR	5 428	52.8	84.5	145	86.9	15.7	-8.7	16.9	...	9.1	85.7	4.5
Harney, OR	5 130	57.1	81.2	72	97.2	11.9	-12.5	11.9	...	15.1	19.3	9.7
Hood River, OR	12 972	48.5	78.2	562	86.8	23.1	-1.3	26.7	20.7	1.0	34.6	5.2
Jackson, OR	121 155	45.1	85.0	9 304	92.4	22.3	-2.1	23.0	16.1	14.2	26.0	10.4
Jefferson, OR	11 972	55.2	76.5	388	80.7	13.7	-10.7	17.1	30.0	4.4	14.4	1.6
Josephine, OR	53 427	49.3	81.8	2 498	89.2	14.1	-10.3	14.5	32.1	6.5	18.9	4.6
Klamath, OR	41 833	52.6	81.5	2 970	91.5	15.9	-8.5	16.8	15.5	10.2	24.5	5.3
Lake, OR	5 199	53.7	79.6	101	81.2	15.5	-8.9	16.0	...	10.0	16.7	7.8
Lane, OR	210 601	38.3	87.5	30 647	94.3	25.5	1.1	25.7	29.2	15.6	47.0	15.8
Lincoln, OR	32 000	44.1	84.9	1 053	91.3	20.8	-3.6	21.3	3.5	11.2	40.3	6.0
Linn, OR	67 605	51.1	81.9	4 574	86.9	13.4	-11.0	13.8	9.0	3.4	16.2	5.4
Malheur, OR	19 587	59.5	71.0	1 349	86.7	11.1	-13.3	13.2	3.0	3.9	22.2	1.7
Marion, OR	177 683	47.0	79.3	14 424	72.2	19.8	-4.6	22.1	10.9	10.2	24.8	5.0
Morrow, OR	6 627	57.9	74.1	209	92.8	11.0	-13.4	12.9	14.3	2.2	34.1	1.9
Multnomah, OR	446 322	37.4	85.6	47 924	71.1	30.7	6.3	33.3	15.2	13.5	27.2	12.7
Polk, OR	39 357	40.4	85.5	5 087	89.1	25.3	0.9	26.9	6.3	10.3	25.2	8.5
Sherman, OR	1 316	48.6	84.3	16	87.5	19.0	-5.4	18.9	100.0	31.6	0.0	20.0
Tillamook, OR	17 145	52.9	84.1	547	94.0	17.6	-6.8	18.1	0.0	2.8	14.5	6.6
Umatilla, OR	44 515	51.9	77.8	2 743	88.8	16.0	-8.4	17.6	15.4	9.9	17.2	5.9
Union, OR	15 562	45.3	85.6	2 077	96.2	21.8	-2.6	22.1	14.3	21.1	15.6	14.1
Wallowa, OR	5 099	49.2	87.5	161	83.2	20.3	-4.1	20.6	...	0.0	0.0	13.0
Wasco, OR	16 023	51.9	82.1	777	83.1	15.7	-8.7	16.5	15.9	5.6	34.8	6.3
Washington, OR	285 518	31.2	88.9	24 771	75.9	34.5	10.1	35.7	32.0	21.0	50.2	11.3
Wheeler, OR	1 143	57.8	79.4	31	90.3	14.3	-10.1	13.9	0.0	0.0	...	26.9
Yamhill, OR	52 645	48.1	82.8	5 277	40.0	20.6	-3.8	22.1	9.8	15.8	22.6	6.6
PENNSYLVANIA												
Adams, PA	60 173	64.1	79.7	4 694	43.3	16.7	-7.7	16.7	15.4	21.3	55.5	6.7
Allegheny, PA	891 171	47.5	86.3	87 059	60.5	28.3	3.9	29.3	13.4	19.1	72.5	37.9
Armstrong, PA	50 638	71.1	80.0	2 012	83.0	10.4	-14.0	10.5	3.9	4.8	15.4	24.2
Beaver, PA	126 933	58.8	83.6	6 954	60.6	15.8	-8.6	16.2	7.1	3.1	48.1	18.1
Bedford, PA	34 582	72.4	78.3	1 066	82.3	10.2	-14.2	10.2	10.3	19.2	8.5	12.9
Berks, PA	248 864	61.3	78.0	18 185	71.2	18.5	-5.9	19.6	8.4	9.0	38.6	4.7
Blair, PA	88 366	66.2	83.8	5 251	79.0	13.9	-10.5	13.8	9.9	3.6	55.1	14.1
Bradford, PA	42 428	65.4	81.7	1 436	75.8	14.8	-9.6	14.7	6.7	15.4	67.8	24.1
Bucks, PA	402 575	43.6	88.6	28 682	59.4	31.2	6.8	31.1	22.4	26.2	57.0	16.2
Butler, PA	116 072	52.2	86.8	10 254	85.6	23.5	-0.9	23.2	23.6	3.7	65.4	28.7
Cambria, PA	106 780	67.3	80.0	7 614	71.3	13.7	-10.7	13.9	5.1	5.4	41.4	8.7
Cameron, PA	4 150	70.2	79.8	95	78.9	12.1	-12.3	12.1	0.0	...	100.0	0.0
Carbon, PA	41 690	68.9	79.0	1 770	76.2	11.0	-13.4	10.9	31.5	62.9	19.0	8.6
Centre, PA	74 785	45.6	88.2	36 356	96.1	36.3	11.9	34.5	20.0	24.8	84.4	48.8
Chester, PA	285 816	36.7	89.3	25 130	64.9	42.5	18.1	44.2	17.5	21.0	70.0	16.6
Clarion, PA	26 334	68.7	81.8	4 650	96.1	15.3	-9.1	15.0	60.5	0.0	44.2	18.5
Clearfield, PA	58 138	71.9	79.1	2 156	81.9	11.1	-13.3	11.1	2.3	7.7	66.2	7.7
Clinton, PA	24 701	67.6	80.4	3 407	90.6	13.4	-11.0	13.4	2.4	5.9	27.0	7.0
Columbia, PA	41 658	65.8	80.6	6 640	95.2	15.8	-8.6	15.5	41.1	0.0	49.8	11.7
Crawford, PA	59 684	66.6	81.6	4 041	44.6	14.7	-9.7	14.7	8.3	9.3	37.7	8.0
Cumberland, PA	144 215	49.7	86.1	15 608	63.3	27.9	3.5	28.0	13.3	26.5	46.4	15.9
Dauphin, PA	171 783	54.0	83.4	9 782	76.3	23.5	-0.9	25.6	12.8	18.8	39.3	9.0
Delaware, PA	365 174	46.5	86.5	39 670	41.9	30.0	5.6	31.4	15.4	12.9	50.9	30.0
Elk, PA	24 337	66.8	82.7	882	78.9	12.3	-12.1	12.2	0.0	0.0	40.5	30.0
Erie, PA	180 106	57.1	84.6	18 832	62.3	20.9	-3.5	21.5	8.7	10.8	51.0	11.0
Fayette, PA	103 227	71.8	76.0	4 864	79.1	11.5	-12.9	11.5	10.1	0.0	27.0	7.1
Forest, PA	3 540	73.8	79.4	61	77.0	8.9	-15.5	9.0	0.0	6.3	50.0	0.0
Franklin, PA	87 959	66.0	78.9	4 467	74.0	14.8	-9.6	14.7	8.5	5.3	52.8	12.7
Fulton, PA	9 687	75.1	73.2	285	76.8	9.3	-15.1	9.3	0.0	33.3	30.0	0.0
Greene, PA	27 758	71.8	75.7	1 857	58.4	12.2	-12.2	12.7	2.2	0.0	46.9	2.7

[1]Hispanic or Latino persons may be of any race.

... = Not available.

Table C-1. Population, School, and Student Characteristics by County—*Continued*

County	State/County code	County type[1]	Population, 2000 Total	Population, 2000 Percent 5–17 years	Number of schools and students, 2000–2001 School districts	Number of schools and students, 2000–2001 Schools	Number of schools and students, 2000–2001 Students	Resident enrollment, 2000 Total	Resident enrollment, 2000 Percent public	Resident enrollment, 2000 K–12	Resident enrollment, 2000 Percent public
			1	2	3	4	5	6	7	8	9
Huntingdon, PA	42061	6	45 586	16.3	5	18	6 492	10 515	83.4	8 043	95.4
Indiana, PA	42063	6	89 605	16.1	7	23	12 418	27 443	92.8	14 434	93.1
Jefferson, PA	42065	7	45 932	18.0	4	18	6 715	10 163	89.7	8 348	92.0
Juniata, PA	42067	8	22 821	18.5	1	12	3 371	4 798	86.6	4 117	88.8
Lackawanna, PA	42069	2	213 295	16.5	12	50	27 452	52 278	68.5	36 314	81.2
Lancaster, PA	42071	2	470 658	19.7	18	125	68 373	115 931	76.3	89 947	81.2
Lawrence, PA	42073	4	94 643	17.5	10	31	15 638	21 804	86.3	16 641	94.6
Lebanon, PA	42075	2	120 327	17.6	6	34	17 880	26 552	80.4	21 104	87.6
Lehigh, PA	42077	2	312 090	17.9	11	70	45 708	77 729	76.8	57 231	86.4
Luzerne, PA	42079	2	319 250	16.1	12	67	40 359	73 449	74.2	53 178	81.7
Lycoming, PA	42081	3	120 044	17.8	8	40	19 094	29 073	84.5	21 522	92.6
McKean, PA	42083	7	45 936	18.0	5	14	7 712	10 674	88.1	8 417	92.3
Mercer, PA	42085	3	120 293	17.7	13	40	19 135	29 378	78.8	21 881	90.5
Mifflin, PA	42087	6	46 486	18.3	1	14	6 214	9 564	82.1	8 244	85.4
Monroe, PA	42089	6	138 687	20.8	4	37	28 145	39 478	87.1	28 869	91.9
Montgomery, PA	42091	0	750 097	17.8	23	149	99 654	194 722	66.6	134 756	77.7
Montour, PA	42093	6	18 236	18.7	3	8	2 911	4 244	83.3	3 479	88.3
Northampton, PA	42095	2	267 066	17.8	9	59	41 535	70 501	71.5	48 206	86.0
Northumberland, PA	42097	4	94 556	16.8	7	28	14 046	19 600	84.6	16 362	88.1
Perry, PA	42099	2	43 602	19.4	5	14	7 544	9 718	90.0	8 317	92.2
Philadelphia, PA	42101	0	1 517 550	18.8	35	295	213 224	440 307	66.9	298 504	77.0
Pike, PA	42103	1	46 302	20.8	1	7	4 911	11 944	88.2	9 714	95.9
Potter, PA	42105	7	18 080	19.8	5	9	3 239	4 194	92.1	3 590	94.8
Schuylkill, PA	42107	4	150 336	16.0	12	38	20 136	30 760	84.3	24 600	88.8
Snyder, PA	42109	7	37 546	18.4	2	12	5 599	9 512	70.1	6 727	87.4
Somerset, PA	42111	3	80 023	17.0	11	35	12 297	16 927	90.7	14 074	92.9
Sullivan, PA	42113	8	6 556	16.5	1	3	903	1 347	91.1	1 140	93.7
Susquehanna, PA	42115	8	42 238	19.8	6	14	8 401	10 047	89.8	8 458	93.5
Tioga, PA	42117	6	41 373	18.3	3	16	6 804	10 811	91.6	7 667	93.0
Union, PA	42119	6	41 624	15.3	2	10	4 475	10 801	62.4	6 646	88.6
Venango, PA	42121	4	57 565	18.6	5	31	10 459	13 090	88.1	11 097	90.1
Warren, PA	42123	6	43 863	18.5	1	20	6 550	10 028	88.9	8 301	91.6
Washington, PA	42125	0	202 897	16.6	15	58	30 764	46 477	84.7	34 487	92.4
Wayne, PA	42127	6	47 722	18.4	3	16	9 640	10 913	88.3	8 953	93.4
Westmoreland, PA	42129	0	369 993	16.8	19	101	56 571	84 043	83.5	63 187	90.1
Wyoming, PA	42131	2	28 080	19.7	2	8	4 806	7 072	84.9	5 615	94.4
York, PA	42133	2	381 751	18.5	19	100	57 701	90 912	82.1	71 383	90.5
RHODE ISLAND	44000										
Bristol, RI	44001	2	50 648	17.5	2	15	7 033	14 156	64.5	9 004	81.6
Kent, RI	44003	2	167 090	17.3	5	51	26 272	40 874	80.0	29 276	86.4
Newport, RI	44005	4	85 433	16.7	6	29	11 914	22 211	74.0	14 785	85.4
Providence, RI	44007	2	621 602	17.7	18	190	93 834	176 038	73.4	115 371	87.4
Washington, RI	44009	2	123 546	17.5	6	35	18 294	37 326	86.2	21 953	90.2
SOUTH CAROLINA	45000										
Abbeville, SC	45001	6	26 167	18.6	1	9	3 871	6 687	81.8	5 041	89.8
Aiken, SC	45003	2	142 552	19.5	1	36	25 147	37 855	86.9	28 650	89.6
Allendale, SC	45005	7	11 211	19.7	1	5	1 960	3 132	94.3	2 505	94.5
Anderson, SC	45007	2	165 740	17.9	5	45	27 685	39 271	86.3	29 839	92.7
Bamberg, SC	45009	7	16 658	19.2	2	8	2 899	4 940	84.5	3 485	91.9
Barnwell, SC	45011	6	23 478	21.0	3	9	5 244	6 391	93.1	5 287	95.3
Beaufort, SC	45013	5	120 937	16.6	1	23	16 721	27 897	82.8	20 802	85.2
Berkeley, SC	45015	2	142 651	20.8	1	34	26 635	39 541	87.1	30 440	91.1
Calhoun, SC	45017	8	15 185	18.7	1	6	2 216	3 652	83.9	2 971	84.3
Charleston, SC	45019	2	309 969	17.3	1	73	44 767	87 355	80.1	55 508	84.3
Cherokee, SC	45021	2	52 537	18.7	1	17	9 308	12 165	89.9	9 811	96.4
Chester, SC	45023	6	34 068	20.2	1	9	6 824	8 226	93.0	6 922	95.3
Chesterfield, SC	45025	6	42 768	19.9	1	15	8 160	10 526	90.0	8 840	92.8
Clarendon, SC	45027	6	32 502	19.7	3	12	6 136	8 452	89.9	7 083	91.9
Colleton, SC	45029	6	38 264	20.6	1	14	6 920	9 704	87.9	7 878	89.2
Darlington, SC	45031	4	67 394	19.4	1	21	11 581	17 661	86.3	14 074	90.7
Dillon, SC	45033	6	30 722	21.7	3	12	6 462	8 481	91.8	6 996	93.1
Dorchester, SC	45035	2	96 413	22.2	2	19	19 242	28 267	84.3	21 791	88.1
Edgefield, SC	45037	2	24 595	18.1	1	7	4 060	6 110	89.7	4 936	91.6
Fairfield, SC	45039	6	23 454	19.4	1	7	3 769	5 873	89.0	4 946	90.1
Florence, SC	45041	3	125 761	19.4	5	33	22 217	33 873	86.7	25 584	89.0
Georgetown, SC	45043	6	55 797	18.9	1	16	10 452	13 450	92.5	10 912	95.7
Greenville, SC	45045	2	379 616	17.8	1	89	59 875	96 798	76.2	69 888	86.0
Greenwood, SC	45047	5	66 271	18.6	3	20	12 299	17 843	88.9	12 478	90.5
Hampton, SC	45049	7	21 386	20.9	2	10	4 784	5 899	88.9	4 917	91.7
Horry, SC	45051	3	196 629	15.6	1	38	29 894	42 752	89.2	31 435	93.0
Jasper, SC	45053	8	20 678	19.5	1	4	2 973	5 407	78.9	4 429	81.3
Kershaw, SC	45055	6	52 647	19.6	1	17	9 817	12 532	90.5	10 443	94.7
Lancaster, SC	45057	6	61 351	18.9	1	19	11 342	14 891	92.2	12 038	94.9
Laurens, SC	45059	6	69 567	18.7	2	16	10 080	17 251	84.8	13 504	91.2
Lee, SC	45061	6	20 119	19.4	1	7	3 067	5 138	84.0	4 312	84.6
Lexington, SC	45063	2	216 014	19.2	5	58	47 825	55 402	89.8	41 574	94.3
McCormick, SC	45065	8	9 958	15.3	1	4	1 180	2 139	88.3	1 737	88.5
Marion, SC	45067	6	35 466	20.7	4	13	6 773	9 764	93.1	7 824	94.4
Marlboro, SC	45069	7	28 818	19.5	1	8	5 571	7 049	91.6	5 872	93.1
Newberry, SC	45071	6	36 108	17.7	1	13	5 817	8 802	83.0	6 688	93.7
Oconee, SC	45073	6	66 215	16.8	1	20	11 176	14 546	90.0	11 032	93.2
Orangeburg, SC	45075	4	91 582	19.4	3	29	16 499	27 308	85.3	18 826	88.1
Pickens, SC	45077	2	110 757	16.2	1	24	15 938	34 574	90.7	17 757	91.6
Richland, SC	45079	2	320 677	17.9	4	86	46 655	97 237	85.6	59 220	90.2

[1]County type code is from the Economic Research Service of the USDA. See Notes and Definitions at the end of this section.

Table C-1. School and Student Characteristics by County—*Continued*

County	Characteristics of students, 2000–2001			Staff and students, 2000–2001				Revenues, fiscal 1999			
	Percent with IEP[2]	Percent eligible for free lunch	Percent minority	Number of teachers	Student/ teacher ratio	Local school non-teaching staff	Central admin. staff	Total revenue ($1,000s)	Percentage of revenue from		
									Federal govt.	State govt.	Local govt.
	10	11	12	13	14	15	16	17	18	19	20
Huntingdon, PA	14.5	32.6	3.6	433	15.0	286	35	$50 447	6.0	55.7	38.2
Indiana, PA	12.5	38.0	2.4	843	14.7	723	91	128 889	6.5	50.0	43.5
Jefferson, PA	14.3	35.6	1.3	447	15.0	335	35	57 448	5.2	54.5	40.3
Juniata, PA	9.6	25.9	3.2	196	17.2	127	11	16 842	4.4	63.6	32.0
Lackawanna, PA	13.7	29.4	6.4	1 621	16.9	1 347	102	251 445	5.6	38.6	55.7
Lancaster, PA	13.8	21.8	17.3	4 115	16.6	3 241	401	603 152	6.1	30.5	63.4
Lawrence, PA	11.9	30.4	8.9	920	17.0	719	65	118 341	3.6	55.8	40.6
Lebanon, PA	11.7	20.3	12.5	1 072	16.7	904	80	139 291	2.8	38.2	59.0
Lehigh, PA	9.7	30.9	27.4	2 488	18.4	2 732	249	396 353	4.1	29.6	66.3
Luzerne, PA	11.2	30.6	4.9	2 267	17.8	1 823	166	355 933	5.5	40.0	54.5
Lycoming, PA	14.8	31.9	8.5	1 197	16.0	1 042	104	159 987	5.9	45.7	48.4
McKean, PA	12.1	32.2	2.7	468	16.5	492	58	80 194	8.4	49.5	42.2
Mercer, PA	13.0	32.5	11.3	1 195	16.0	1 268	128	183 867	10.6	47.6	41.8
Mifflin, PA	14.3	29.6	3.1	425	14.6	296	39	59 835	13.8	49.5	36.7
Monroe, PA	12.0	21.8	21.3	1 741	16.2	1 627	149	214 269	2.4	24.6	73.0
Montgomery, PA	12.1	12.7	19.5	6 485	15.4	5 774	646	1 069 044	2.6	19.2	78.2
Montour, PA	9.5	25.3	7.9	183	15.9	162	11	22 606	5.4	38.7	55.9
Northampton, PA	11.8	20.9	17.3	2 549	16.3	2 344	228	369 523	4.8	28.0	67.1
Northumberland, PA	10.4	32.2	3.3	856	16.4	609	83	103 624	4.8	52.9	42.3
Perry, PA	14.9	20.2	2.6	485	15.6	344	46	58 075	3.4	49.7	46.9
Philadelphia, PA	11.1	69.1	83.1	11 773	18.1	14 258	285	1 919 450	11.0	45.7	43.3
Pike, PA	6.9	16.0	6.4	301	16.3	199	11	37 534	2.1	25.4	72.5
Potter, PA	10.8	33.3	2.1	211	15.4	139	14	26 142	2.3	54.4	43.2
Schuylkill, PA	13.2	28.8	2.2	1 125	17.9	952	105	188 289	6.4	46.0	47.6
Snyder, PA	12.5	26.4	2.8	362	15.5	280	21	41 609	4.6	41.7	53.7
Somerset, PA	12.3	38.4	1.1	776	15.8	611	74	102 383	6.2	54.6	39.2
Sullivan, PA	11.2	35.3	1.6	65	13.9	54	5	8 641	6.1	35.2	58.7
Susquehanna, PA	14.8	32.0	2.2	543	15.5	372	42	65 708	4.5	54.2	41.3
Tioga, PA	9.8	37.0	2.6	483	14.1	356	32	52 036	6.2	54.0	39.8
Union, PA	8.8	18.9	4.4	272	16.5	680	89	71 815	22.8	31.6	45.6
Venango, PA	16.4	36.2	2.8	641	16.3	589	49	88 385	4.8	56.7	38.5
Warren, PA	17.0	27.7	1.3	404	16.2	365	39	48 810	5.2	52.5	42.3
Washington, PA	12.0	27.1	6.5	1 929	15.9	1 647	153	291 867	5.9	41.7	52.4
Wayne, PA	13.0	37.0	3.7	621	15.5	403	49	81 498	3.9	30.5	65.6
Westmoreland, PA	11.6	26.0	5.0	3 219	17.6	2 216	260	472 731	4.6	42.1	53.3
Wyoming, PA	11.3	29.1	1.6	306	15.7	186	19	38 727	3.8	49.7	46.4
York, PA	14.0	19.5	13.6	3 462	16.7	2 459	251	429 536	2.8	35.5	61.6
RHODE ISLAND											
Bristol, RI	19.0	18.2	3.2	513	13.7	276	29	62 927	2.9	35.2	61.8
Kent, RI	19.3	16.8	5.3	1 828	14.4	1 068	124	219 545	3.4	34.2	62.3
Newport, RI	20.3	21.5	13.9	880	13.5	456	62	110 246	5.9	29.7	64.4
Providence, RI	19.6	44.7	38.3	6 216	15.1	3 896	422	778 246	7.3	49.0	43.7
Washington, RI	18.1	13.1	6.3	1 209	15.1	742	46	187 602	2.7	30.7	66.7
SOUTH CAROLINA											
Abbeville, SC	18.7	55.5	44.3	269	14.4	42	5	23 424	9.0	59.1	32.0
Aiken, SC	13.3	45.9	38.6	1 496	16.8	207	33	140 114	7.5	58.0	34.5
Allendale, SC	20.5	88.4	95.8	162	12.1	35	3	15 594	14.5	52.0	33.5
Anderson, SC	15.6	36.9	24.2	1 739	15.9	290	31	172 239	6.4	54.1	39.5
Bamberg, SC	20.7	77.2	75.5	212	13.7	34	5	21 255	14.4	59.1	26.5
Barnwell, SC	18.8	57.1	53.1	336	15.6	52	13	32 840	10.9	61.1	28.0
Beaufort, SC	12.7	46.9	52.1	1 139	14.7	133	8	125 322	6.2	31.8	62.0
Berkeley, SC	14.9	47.8	40.5	1 727	15.4	260	42	156 981	8.1	60.6	31.3
Calhoun, SC	19.4	78.2	77.6	162	13.7	30	4	16 137	11.1	44.3	44.7
Charleston, SC	13.9	52.1	61.9	2 925	15.3	365	32	273 852	9.5	50.1	40.4
Cherokee, SC	10.7	47.5	31.7	576	16.2	99	10	60 455	6.2	48.5	45.3
Chester, SC	16.1	52.5	51.5	438	15.6	57	4	44 406	7.7	56.8	35.5
Chesterfield, SC	15.3	56.9	44.9	537	15.2	78	11	48 738	8.9	60.3	30.8
Clarendon, SC	16.5	73.4	70.3	397	15.5	65	11	38 736	12.2	61.9	25.9
Colleton, SC	14.3	67.5	58.9	462	15.0	72	8	42 892	10.9	59.3	29.8
Darlington, SC	17.5	63.8	58.3	830	14.0	123	10	75 879	9.9	53.0	37.1
Dillon, SC	13.4	75.0	63.8	376	17.2	60	10	34 661	14.3	65.5	20.3
Dorchester, SC	11.4	32.8	36.4	1 251	15.4	210	21	116 460	5.3	58.4	36.3
Edgefield, SC	16.8	54.7	52.6	269	15.1	44	4	26 558	8.4	57.6	34.0
Fairfield, SC	22.8	74.2	86.9	276	13.7	45	6	35 609	8.8	32.9	58.3
Florence, SC	17.3	57.4	57.0	1 488	14.9	239	45	135 392	11.0	58.5	30.5
Georgetown, SC	16.2	56.5	57.7	785	13.3	127	17	80 141	8.3	43.7	48.0
Greenville, SC	15.9	31.9	33.1	3 681	16.3	650	35	368 869	5.8	51.1	43.1
Greenwood, SC	16.6	45.2	44.6	799	15.4	131	18	71 875	8.4	53.2	38.5
Hampton, SC	14.4	68.4	70.5	304	15.7	49	11	29 841	12.2	59.1	28.8
Horry, SC	15.5	51.7	30.6	1 967	15.2	390	48	195 951	7.2	42.5	50.3
Jasper, SC	11.7	81.6	86.7	199	14.9	23	7	17 955	12.3	61.5	26.2
Kershaw, SC	12.4	44.5	35.9	609	16.1	109	10	60 476	7.4	57.3	35.3
Lancaster, SC	13.0	44.8	37.1	691	16.4	120	11	68 844	8.1	60.1	31.8
Laurens, SC	17.6	50.3	40.7	636	15.8	100	17	56 766	9.2	60.3	30.5
Lee, SC	15.1	81.9	93.6	221	13.9	42	11	21 354	15.8	58.4	25.8
Lexington, SC	13.7	28.9	22.3	3 279	14.6	483	43	303 699	4.6	55.1	40.3
McCormick, SC	47.6	68.3	83.4	95	12.4	15	3	9 265	17.9	49.9	32.3
Marion, SC	22.9	76.2	75.8	460	14.7	70	15	42 536	14.5	64.3	21.2
Marlboro, SC	3.6	77.8	65.9	345	16.1	55	9	31 882	12.1	63.0	24.9
Newberry, SC	18.3	58.2	53.3	414	14.1	81	9	45 855	7.2	50.6	42.2
Oconee, SC	19.0	38.9	17.4	729	15.3	120	9	76 259	5.9	40.0	54.2
Orangeburg, SC	16.2	75.8	79.9	1 077	15.3	187	25	120 418	10.9	53.3	35.8
Pickens, SC	13.0	29.1	11.2	1 055	15.1	138	12	90 937	5.5	58.9	35.6
Richland, SC	13.9	46.7	71.2	3 333	14.0	613	57	330 755	7.2	47.7	45.1

[2]IEP = Individual Education Program. See Notes and Definitions at the end of this section.

Table C-1. Population, School, and Student Characteristics by County—*Continued*

County	Current expenditures, fiscal 1999			Resident population 16 to 19 years, 2000				Outcomes, 1999–2000	
	Amount ($1,000s)	Amount per student	Percent for instruction	Total population 16 to 19 years	Percent in Armed Forces	Percent high school graduates	Percent not enrolled, not grads, not Armed Forces, not empl.	Number of graduates	Dropouts grades 9–12 (percent)
	21	22	23	24	25	26	27	28	29
Huntingdon, PA	$41 905	$6 397	63.8	2 532	0.0	9.9	4.7	427	3.9
Indiana, PA	104 795	7 931	62.1	7 091	0.0	6.4	3.2	1 034	2.8
Jefferson, PA	47 959	7 246	62.5	2 512	0.0	10.7	4.1	549	3.5
Juniata, PA	15 737	4 567	61.7	1 166	0.0	17.2	5.7	242	2.3
Lackawanna, PA	219 316	7 917	63.6	11 494	0.0	8.0	2.9	1 849	2.9
Lancaster, PA	487 601	7 160	62.2	26 608	0.1	10.2	5.3	4 137	4.3
Lawrence, PA	96 091	6 234	67.0	4 946	0.3	9.8	5.6	1 077	2.8
Lebanon, PA	114 843	6 368	63.9	6 325	0.0	11.1	4.6	1 175	3.3
Lehigh, PA	332 424	7 461	62.1	15 872	0.1	10.3	5.1	2 818	3.0
Luzerne, PA	302 806	7 504	64.9	16 639	0.0	8.5	3.9	2 838	3.3
Lycoming, PA	139 547	7 055	64.6	7 224	0.2	10.3	3.8	1 227	4.1
McKean, PA	67 352	8 667	64.5	2 437	0.0	9.2	3.2	474	3.5
Mercer, PA	159 913	8 284	65.6	7 085	0.0	7.1	3.7	1 344	3.0
Mifflin, PA	52 014	8 239	57.3	2 298	0.1	14.8	8.6	369	5.7
Monroe, PA	167 698	6 397	61.3	8 287	0.2	9.4	2.8	1 680	3.3
Montgomery, PA	913 512	9 434	62.7	35 196	0.1	8.0	1.7	6 268	2.1
Montour, PA	18 389	6 461	66.2	1 002	0.0	11.8	3.9	175	2.6
Northampton, PA	306 354	7 442	61.7	15 697	0.0	7.1	3.0	2 574	3.9
Northumberland, PA	86 272	5 988	65.7	4 801	0.0	11.4	4.5	948	5.1
Perry, PA	45 575	6 012	62.1	2 341	0.1	12.9	6.8	501	4.0
Philadelphia, PA	1 527 422	7 362	60.7	88 916	0.0	10.1	7.4	10 019	11.2
Pike, PA	29 637	6 415	68.1	2 212	0.0	9.2	2.3	270	2.8
Potter, PA	20 183	6 052	59.7	947	0.0	17.7	3.7	240	2.2
Schuylkill, PA	149 258	7 241	59.1	6 825	0.1	11.1	5.2	1 447	4.0
Snyder, PA	34 680	6 097	65.4	2 487	0.0	9.2	3.7	354	2.8
Somerset, PA	81 558	6 374	64.0	4 227	0.0	11.8	3.5	889	1.4
Sullivan, PA	7 681	8 322	60.7	535	0.0	11.0	11.8	60	1.0
Susquehanna, PA	57 054	6 538	62.2	2 370	0.0	10.8	4.6	578	3.4
Tioga, PA	45 726	6 436	63.9	2 805	0.0	9.6	1.8	520	1.9
Union, PA	65 064	14 510	45.5	3 014	0.0	6.7	3.8	295	1.9
Venango, PA	71 260	6 556	62.3	3 341	0.0	9.2	3.6	718	4.6
Warren, PA	42 981	6 163	63.3	2 277	0.1	11.0	4.7	511	3.9
Washington, PA	240 863	7 838	63.7	10 346	0.0	9.2	3.1	2 189	2.4
Wayne, PA	69 868	7 409	63.5	2 409	0.0	12.5	4.3	585	2.7
Westmoreland, PA	391 727	6 820	63.6	17 603	0.1	9.3	2.4	4 150	2.3
Wyoming, PA	35 011	7 125	61.9	1 662	0.0	9.3	1.6	331	2.8
York, PA	342 015	6 129	63.8	19 672	0.1	12.0	4.0	3 472	4.8
RHODE ISLAND									
Bristol, RI	57 459	8 197	67.3	3 024	0.0	6.8	2.2	416	4.3
Kent, RI	202 634	8 604	66.6	7 752	0.0	11.1	3.3	1 604	3.0
Newport, RI	98 919	8 384	65.3	4 400	3.6	11.1	3.9	657	2.3
Providence, RI	696 260	7 653	64.7	38 449	0.0	8.9	5.9	4 696	6.0
Washington, RI	164 056	8 053	63.3	7 784	0.0	4.6	0.8	1 104	3.5
SOUTH CAROLINA									
Abbeville, SC	21 546	5 580	62.3	1 566	0.0	8.0	4.9	193	. . .
Aiken, SC	121 506	4 969	61.9	8 068	0.1	10.1	5.9	1 254	. . .
Allendale, SC	14 457	6 861	54.8	699	0.0	8.0	14.6	88	. . .
Anderson, SC	145 801	5 523	59.9	8 498	0.0	13.2	8.0	1 334	. . .
Bamberg, SC	19 452	6 598	55.3	1 424	1.3	12.8	3.4	127	. . .
Barnwell, SC	29 093	5 873	59.7	1 439	0.0	11.0	5.0	257	. . .
Beaufort, SC	102 253	6 584	56.7	7 076	30.5	39.5	3.0	727	. . .
Berkeley, SC	139 223	5 277	58.1	10 369	18.0	31.1	4.1	1 316	. . .
Calhoun, SC	14 331	6 847	55.9	791	0.0	9.9	5.9	100	. . .
Charleston, SC	243 233	5 536	61.7	18 939	1.1	9.1	4.9	1 632	. . .
Cherokee, SC	47 839	5 572	59.6	2 788	0.0	15.7	10.5	346	. . .
Chester, SC	37 357	5 563	61.2	1 880	0.0	15.3	13.1	226	. . .
Chesterfield, SC	43 967	5 469	59.5	2 324	0.1	11.8	9.5	368	. . .
Clarendon, SC	33 075	5 428	59.0	2 077	0.0	10.2	9.1	283	. . .
Colleton, SC	39 987	5 740	57.1	2 146	0.0	10.1	11.4	320	. . .
Darlington, SC	64 238	5 880	60.8	3 497	0.0	9.7	7.1	484	. . .
Dillon, SC	32 340	5 161	57.0	1 941	0.3	11.3	9.6	301	. . .
Dorchester, SC	98 362	5 183	61.2	5 397	0.0	11.3	5.0	985	. . .
Edgefield, SC	23 515	5 677	56.4	1 542	0.0	10.6	14.7	165	. . .
Fairfield, SC	30 019	8 160	53.8	1 271	0.0	14.1	4.1	139	. . .
Florence, SC	121 632	5 415	58.7	7 754	0.1	10.5	6.1	1 039	. . .
Georgetown, SC	68 015	6 527	55.8	2 997	0.0	11.2	6.5	536	. . .
Greenville, SC	309 696	5 350	59.5	20 669	0.0	9.5	5.4	3 000	. . .
Greenwood, SC	63 921	5 638	60.3	3 786	0.3	9.6	10.7	534	. . .
Hampton, SC	26 665	6 229	56.5	1 292	0.2	11.7	5.7	202	. . .
Horry, SC	170 196	6 342	58.5	10 024	0.0	12.3	7.6	1 395	. . .
Jasper, SC	16 045	5 598	52.9	1 233	0.0	11.4	10.0	116	. . .
Kershaw, SC	52 906	5 566	56.9	2 747	0.0	15.4	6.6	513	. . .
Lancaster, SC	56 869	5 206	59.2	3 320	0.0	13.1	10.1	550	. . .
Laurens, SC	51 071	5 449	59.8	4 189	0.0	10.9	8.1	445	. . .
Lee, SC	18 463	5 762	53.8	1 109	0.0	14.4	7.6	121	. . .
Lexington, SC	262 623	5 903	59.7	10 975	0.2	12.6	3.8	2 458	. . .
McCormick, SC	8 157	6 659	49.9	521	0.0	9.0	13.8	51	. . .
Marion, SC	38 007	5 609	59.9	2 204	0.2	10.8	5.9	375	. . .
Marlboro, SC	29 568	5 444	59.0	1 682	0.0	12.5	11.4	244	. . .
Newberry, SC	35 133	5 997	57.8	2 200	0.0	8.5	9.5	294	. . .
Oconee, SC	64 747	6 455	58.7	3 211	0.4	13.9	6.7	537	. . .
Orangeburg, SC	100 496	6 189	57.6	6 474	0.0	9.2	5.8	821	. . .
Pickens, SC	80 741	5 117	62.2	8 600	0.0	6.3	4.4	714	. . .
Richland, SC	284 438	6 575	57.9	23 297	11.5	17.6	5.6	2 129	. . .

. . . = Not available.

Table C-1. Population, School, and Student Characteristics by County—*Continued*

County	High school graduates, 2000			College enrollment, 2000		College graduates, 2000 (percent)						
	Population 25 years and over	High school diploma or less (percent)	High school diploma or more (percent)	Number	Percent public	Bachelor's degree or more	+/- U.S. percent with bachelor's degree or more	Non-Hispanic White	Black or African American	American Indian and Alaska Native	Asian, Hawaiian, and Pacific Islander	Hispan-ic or Latino[1]
	30	31	32	33	34	35	36	37	38	39	40	41
Huntingdon, PA	31 152	72.7	74.6	2 034	40.4	11.9	-12.5	12.5	1.2	38.9	19.4	2.7
Indiana, PA	55 995	65.4	81.0	11 981	94.6	17.0	-7.4	16.6	27.3	8.5	60.5	21.4
Jefferson, PA	31 583	70.4	81.0	1 283	84.6	11.7	-12.7	11.5	9.5	0.0	58.5	24.4
Juniata, PA	15 225	77.2	74.5	433	78.1	8.8	-15.6	8.7	33.3	0.0	12.5	11.9
Lackawanna, PA	148 116	58.5	82.0	12 508	37.8	19.6	-4.8	19.6	8.6	8.4	46.6	11.0
Lancaster, PA	302 503	61.5	77.4	18 811	64.3	20.5	-3.9	21.2	11.8	9.6	24.6	7.4
Lawrence, PA	64 767	64.1	81.6	3 916	59.5	15.1	-9.3	15.3	3.8	2.5	54.0	29.9
Lebanon, PA	82 008	68.0	78.6	4 081	50.7	15.4	-9.0	15.7	12.7	31.4	35.1	3.8
Lehigh, PA	212 665	53.8	81.1	15 378	52.4	23.3	-1.1	24.3	10.4	5.4	52.8	7.0
Luzerne, PA	226 374	60.4	81.1	15 918	56.1	16.4	-8.0	16.4	5.8	10.3	50.3	10.4
Lycoming, PA	80 500	61.3	80.6	6 190	64.9	15.1	-9.3	15.2	6.9	12.1	38.6	13.8
McKean, PA	31 529	65.7	82.2	1 656	80.4	14.0	-10.4	14.5	1.3	10.0	29.8	3.5
Mercer, PA	81 499	62.2	82.9	5 921	41.5	17.3	-7.1	17.7	6.2	12.5	44.9	21.1
Mifflin, PA	31 722	74.8	77.2	722	68.3	10.9	-13.5	10.8	35.6	0.0	35.2	7.8
Monroe, PA	89 793	54.8	83.8	8 213	81.1	20.5	-3.9	20.6	21.5	27.2	47.1	13.9
Montgomery, PA	515 871	38.8	88.5	43 540	46.3	38.7	14.3	39.4	22.4	21.6	57.4	28.6
Montour, PA	12 573	59.8	82.3	498	65.3	22.1	-2.3	21.3	23.3	78.9	86.0	30.3
Northampton, PA	180 018	55.8	80.7	17 800	39.2	21.2	-3.2	21.5	15.7	16.3	55.7	10.1
Northumberland, PA	67 112	72.3	77.8	2 148	71.9	11.1	-13.3	11.0	9.3	8.2	35.2	17.6
Perry, PA	29 250	69.7	79.9	982	84.0	11.3	-13.1	11.2	6.3	14.3	53.6	21.1
Philadelphia, PA	966 197	62.1	71.2	115 671	43.2	17.9	-6.5	24.1	10.3	9.9	32.6	9.2
Pike, PA	31 525	54.5	86.8	1 412	59.3	19.0	-5.4	18.8	29.0	6.9	31.4	18.0
Potter, PA	12 144	66.7	80.6	301	78.1	12.3	-12.1	12.2	0.0	0.0	41.1	12.8
Schuylkill, PA	108 010	71.1	77.2	4 303	70.4	10.7	-13.7	10.9	1.8	1.5	41.1	3.7
Snyder, PA	24 217	73.2	73.2	2 379	22.4	12.5	-11.9	12.6	4.6	0.0	0.0	6.2
Somerset, PA	55 956	72.9	77.5	1 978	84.9	10.8	-13.6	11.0	1.6	0.0	6.7	5.2
Sullivan, PA	4 659	67.6	78.0	165	74.5	12.8	-11.7	12.9	0.0	0.0	0.0	0.0
Susquehanna, PA	28 581	64.7	82.5	1 028	70.0	13.2	-11.2	13.2	8.1	11.1	36.6	25.8
Tioga, PA	27 176	64.2	80.5	2 767	92.7	14.2	-10.2	14.1	23.9	9.8	51.0	23.3
Union, PA	27 521	65.9	73.1	3 717	14.8	18.0	-6.4	20.5	1.8	8.0	18.0	2.9
Venango, PA	39 366	68.4	81.0	1 398	81.5	13.1	-11.3	13.2	7.2	0.0	14.7	4.9
Warren, PA	30 535	63.7	84.8	1 060	79.1	14.2	-10.2	14.2	17.2	20.4	41.0	13.8
Washington, PA	142 118	60.0	82.6	8 902	69.5	18.8	-5.6	19.0	10.2	6.1	45.2	13.2
Wayne, PA	33 326	62.8	80.7	1 318	63.0	14.6	-9.8	14.7	6.8	10.5	24.0	9.1
Westmoreland, PA	263 593	55.6	85.6	14 834	69.7	20.2	-4.2	20.2	12.3	13.2	59.9	20.1
Wyoming, PA	18 741	61.6	83.7	1 011	43.5	15.4	-9.0	15.3	16.0	27.6	26.0	45.1
York, PA	259 040	60.9	80.7	13 146	54.2	18.4	-6.0	18.7	9.8	7.3	36.3	10.8
RHODE ISLAND												
Bristol, RI	34 218	42.7	80.7	4 188	35.7	34.3	9.9	34.1	32.4	32.3	75.8	37.3
Kent, RI	116 628	47.2	83.9	8 945	70.9	24.8	0.4	24.5	34.0	7.0	46.8	23.8
Newport, RI	59 084	36.4	87.7	6 086	52.6	38.3	13.9	39.3	17.8	22.3	48.3	26.1
Providence, RI	403 779	55.6	72.5	51 819	46.1	21.3	-3.1	23.4	15.6	12.4	31.2	7.0
Washington, RI	80 864	37.4	88.6	12 971	87.3	35.5	11.1	35.7	20.6	17.5	49.3	31.2
SOUTH CAROLINA												
Abbeville, SC	17 068	65.8	70.1	1 241	57.9	12.8	-11.6	15.9	4.2	0.0	46.5	37.3
Aiken, SC	92 922	54.0	77.7	6 691	88.3	19.9	-4.5	23.4	9.0	12.1	40.7	10.0
Allendale, SC	7 094	71.3	60.0	439	97.7	9.3	-15.1	19.2	4.7	0.0	0.0	0.0
Anderson, SC	111 037	59.3	73.4	6 724	73.5	15.9	-8.5	17.3	7.4	8.1	42.8	17.9
Bamberg, SC	10 213	63.6	64.7	1 135	59.2	15.4	-9.0	19.7	11.6	100.0	0.0	37.5
Barnwell, SC	14 770	67.2	67.5	669	90.6	11.6	-12.8	14.8	6.4	6.7	65.2	13.2
Beaufort, SC	78 502	36.3	87.8	4 807	83.9	33.2	8.8	40.7	10.8	10.7	31.9	13.1
Berkeley, SC	86 015	54.1	80.2	6 897	80.1	14.4	-10.0	15.4	10.0	12.8	28.4	14.8
Calhoun, SC	10 266	62.5	72.8	462	84.0	14.2	-10.2	20.4	6.5	22.6	9.4	0.0
Charleston, SC	199 361	41.4	81.5	25 683	78.4	30.7	6.3	40.4	10.7	19.6	41.2	18.9
Cherokee, SC	34 283	69.9	66.7	1 664	63.9	11.8	-12.6	13.1	6.0	0.0	28.6	14.5
Chester, SC	22 043	69.0	67.1	800	87.8	9.6	-14.8	11.9	5.0	0.0	22.7	21.2
Chesterfield, SC	27 769	69.4	65.2	1 026	81.2	9.7	-14.7	11.7	4.2	12.8	52.7	20.0
Clarendon, SC	20 698	69.2	65.3	883	81.3	11.4	-13.0	17.7	5.0	36.5	0.0	5.9
Colleton, SC	24 716	67.3	69.6	1 129	88.8	11.5	-12.9	14.7	6.6	0.0	33.3	7.7
Darlington, SC	43 512	63.2	69.3	2 538	71.8	13.5	-10.9	17.4	6.7	10.2	30.1	18.4
Dillon, SC	18 867	72.9	60.7	835	93.4	9.2	-15.2	12.1	5.1	2.7	8.9	5.7
Dorchester, SC	61 334	47.5	82.2	4 471	79.8	21.4	-3.0	24.4	11.7	14.3	46.9	9.6
Edgefield, SC	16 227	64.0	71.4	829	87.8	12.5	-11.9	17.7	5.0	17.2	34.2	0.0
Fairfield, SC	15 244	68.7	67.0	646	85.3	11.7	-12.7	20.5	4.5	0.0	100.0	2.1
Florence, SC	80 904	57.8	73.1	6 166	88.9	18.7	-5.7	23.6	9.0	17.3	58.6	13.2
Georgetown, SC	37 340	55.0	75.2	1 500	83.2	20.0	-4.4	26.0	7.7	47.6	53.8	10.5
Greenville, SC	250 258	46.8	79.5	20 732	54.4	26.2	1.8	29.6	11.1	7.4	43.5	14.6
Greenwood, SC	42 412	56.6	73.1	4 024	93.2	18.9	-5.5	24.0	7.1	9.0	37.6	5.0
Hampton, SC	13 668	70.8	66.9	633	67.8	10.1	-14.3	14.5	6.3	18.4	22.5	2.9
Horry, SC	136 551	51.0	81.1	8 531	87.3	18.7	-5.7	20.4	8.0	12.4	28.4	10.8
Jasper, SC	13 112	70.8	65.2	578	67.6	8.7	-15.7	11.5	5.9	6.0	32.2	6.3
Kershaw, SC	34 863	60.1	75.4	1 348	82.6	16.3	-8.1	18.5	9.9	7.0	8.3	11.8
Lancaster, SC	40 520	65.8	69.8	1 936	85.8	10.2	-14.2	11.6	5.5	10.5	26.5	14.4
Laurens, SC	45 470	67.3	67.7	2 822	55.7	11.7	-12.7	13.7	5.2	14.2	39.6	7.2
Lee, SC	12 918	73.7	61.4	495	78.3	9.2	-15.2	14.3	5.7	0.0	0.0	5.8
Lexington, SC	142 083	46.5	83.0	10 063	87.6	24.6	0.2	26.0	13.2	8.6	46.9	17.8
McCormick, SC	7 192	64.4	66.1	255	88.6	16.0	-8.4	26.9	4.3	...	100.0	6.9
Marion, SC	22 224	70.5	68.0	1 234	87.9	10.2	-14.2	14.2	6.5	0.0	73.7	0.3
Marlboro, SC	18 482	74.1	60.9	698	89.4	8.3	-16.1	10.4	5.8	5.6	58.0	19.8
Newberry, SC	23 881	64.4	69.1	1 525	45.4	14.8	-9.6	19.8	4.2	27.5	52.6	5.2
Oconee, SC	45 896	59.3	73.9	2 461	86.1	18.2	-6.2	18.9	7.3	14.4	67.4	12.5
Orangeburg, SC	57 037	60.1	71.5	6 858	81.3	16.3	-8.1	18.1	15.0	7.8	25.6	4.1
Pickens, SC	66 787	57.1	73.7	15 364	93.5	19.1	-5.3	19.2	9.5	5.6	68.6	12.8
Richland, SC	198 703	37.7	85.2	31 645	83.4	32.5	8.1	43.5	18.0	21.9	50.1	23.0

[1]Hispanic or Latino persons may be of any race.

Table C-1. Population, School, and Student Characteristics by County—*Continued*

County	State/County code	County type[1]	Population, 2000		Number of schools and students, 2000–2001			Resident enrollment, 2000			
			Total	Percent 5–17 years	School districts	Schools	Students	Total	Percent public	K–12	Percent public
			1	2	3	4	5	6	7	8	9
Saluda, SC	45081	6	19 181	18.4	1	4	2 200	4 394	94.2	3 701	94.9
Spartanburg, SC	45083	2	253 791	18.2	8	66	42 877	61 998	86.2	46 790	93.2
Sumter, SC	45085	3	104 646	20.6	2	28	19 063	30 345	85.0	22 355	88.1
Union, SC	45087	6	29 881	17.5	1	9	5 212	6 799	94.1	5 463	97.2
Williamsburg, SC	45089	6	37 217	21.7	1	13	6 395	10 681	92.4	8 584	92.9
York, SC	45091	2	164 614	19.5	4	42	30 136	44 094	89.0	32 418	92.4
SOUTH DAKOTA	**46000**										
Aurora, SD	46003	9	3 058	21.9	4	11	610	759	94.5	664	97.6
Beadle, SD	46005	7	17 023	19.0	5	23	2 965	4 139	81.1	3 358	90.6
Bennett, SD	46007	9	3 574	27.4	1	5	606	1 257	94.9	983	97.3
Bon Homme, SD	46009	9	7 260	18.1	4	16	1 397	1 529	92.9	1 341	95.4
Brookings, SD	46011	7	28 220	15.1	4	16	4 197	11 458	96.8	4 361	96.8
Brown, SD	46013	5	35 460	17.2	6	24	5 020	9 554	85.5	6 207	86.5
Brule, SD	46015	9	5 364	24.8	2	8	1 214	1 475	93.8	1 315	97.0
Buffalo, SD	46017	9	2 032	30.7	. . .	. . .	. . .	779	89.7	662	89.1
Butte, SD	46019	6	9 094	22.2	2	7	1 849	2 361	89.2	2 000	92.8
Campbell, SD	46021	9	1 782	21.2	2	6	310	410	96.6	380	98.7
Charles Mix, SD	46023	9	9 350	23.4	4	16	1 794	2 522	87.5	2 178	88.7
Clark, SD	46025	9	4 143	21.6	2	9	774	974	97.1	880	98.0
Clay, SD	46027	7	13 537	13.4	2	7	1 588	6 399	96.7	1 853	96.6
Codington, SD	46029	7	25 897	19.7	5	20	4 695	6 730	87.3	5 198	91.0
Corson, SD	46031	9	4 181	27.9	3	9	811	1 410	96.7	1 181	97.6
Custer, SD	46033	8	7 275	19.4	3	9	1 208	1 731	89.1	1 476	92.5
Davison, SD	46035	7	18 741	18.8	3	13	3 128	5 217	77.9	3 642	88.4
Day, SD	46037	9	6 267	20.0	4	11	1 119	1 449	96.0	1 284	97.9
Deuel, SD	46039	9	4 498	19.9	1	3	628	1 079	95.7	922	97.8
Dewey, SD	46041	9	5 972	29.7	3	9	752	2 154	97.1	1 745	98.2
Douglas, SD	46043	9	3 458	21.9	2	6	450	842	76.6	761	79.0
Edmunds, SD	46045	9	4 367	21.0	3	13	767	1 050	88.8	919	89.1
Fall River, SD	46047	7	7 453	18.0	3	10	1 217	1 418	90.2	1 209	93.2
Faulk, SD	46049	9	2 640	21.1	2	10	489	606	85.6	539	86.6
Grant, SD	46051	7	7 847	20.7	3	8	1 435	1 871	90.4	1 591	94.2
Gregory, SD	46053	9	4 792	19.4	3	10	931	1 051	97.8	957	97.8
Haakon, SD	46055	9	2 196	20.4	2	12	478	517	97.5	461	98.7
Hamlin, SD	46057	9	5 540	22.9	3	10	1 291	1 477	92.3	1 267	93.3
Hand, SD	46059	9	3 741	19.4	2	6	589	825	96.2	723	99.7
Hanson, SD	46061	9	3 139	22.0	2	8	536	763	95.7	685	96.8
Harding, SD	46063	9	1 353	28.3	1	8	307	395	91.9	365	92.6
Hughes, SD	46065	7	16 481	21.2	2	10	2 882	4 081	91.2	3 589	94.3
Hutchinson, SD	46067	9	8 075	18.9	4	21	1 721	1 797	89.3	1 538	92.3
Hyde, SD	46069	9	1 671	18.0	1	3	275	357	94.1	305	97.7
Jackson, SD	46071	9	2 930	28.2	1	4	391	964	97.9	803	99.8
Jerauld, SD	46073	9	2 295	17.7	2	7	433	473	96.6	402	98.5
Jones, SD	46075	9	1 193	21.4	1	3	216	303	98.0	281	99.3
Kingsbury, SD	46077	9	5 815	19.1	3	9	901	1 360	94.5	1 177	96.1
Lake, SD	46079	6	11 276	18.2	4	17	2 063	3 471	94.1	2 085	94.8
Lawrence, SD	46081	6	21 802	18.3	3	11	3 301	6 595	93.3	4 091	95.1
Lincoln, SD	46083	3	24 131	21.6	3	14	3 364	6 784	86.8	5 286	92.7
Lyman, SD	46085	9	3 895	23.5	1	4	435	1 128	96.5	934	98.0
McCook, SD	46087	8	5 832	21.7	4	13	1 045	1 493	89.4	1 281	90.6
McPherson, SD	46089	9	2 904	16.7	2	9	500	546	94.1	497	96.2
Marshall, SD	46091	9	4 576	21.1	3	11	900	1 110	94.6	925	97.3
Meade, SD	46093	6	24 253	20.7	2	20	3 048	6 506	89.0	5 047	91.9
Mellette, SD	46095	9	2 083	26.3	2	7	524	647	98.0	533	98.1
Miner, SD	46097	9	2 884	20.4	2	4	541	678	96.9	611	98.4
Minnehaha, SD	46099	3	148 281	18.9	9	64	25 522	38 766	79.6	27 965	88.9
Moody, SD	46101	8	6 595	22.9	2	8	1 148	1 788	94.7	1 535	96.1
Pennington, SD	46103	3	88 565	19.5	5	44	17 054	24 276	88.3	17 352	92.2
Perkins, SD	46105	9	3 363	18.3	3	11	616	732	95.9	652	97.1
Potter, SD	46107	9	2 693	18.5	2	6	521	583	91.9	535	93.6
Roberts, SD	46109	9	10 016	23.3	4	14	1 872	2 692	97.8	2 294	98.4
Sanborn, SD	46111	9	2 675	19.9	2	7	503	653	95.4	570	98.9
Shannon, SD	46113	7	12 466	34.4	1	4	976	4 956	94.2	4 036	94.7
Spink, SD	46115	7	7 454	19.9	6	21	1 475	1 700	92.6	1 483	95.4
Stanley, SD	46117	9	2 772	21.5	1	7	588	698	93.3	603	97.2
Sully, SD	46119	9	1 556	19.9	2	7	348	358	96.6	330	97.6
Todd, SD	46121	9	9 050	31.9	1	12	2 050	3 548	98.6	2 824	99.8
Tripp, SD	46123	7	6 430	21.4	2	10	1 231	1 609	95.3	1 421	96.7
Turner, SD	46125	8	8 849	20.1	5	15	1 538	2 149	91.9	1 860	94.7
Union, SD	46127	8	12 584	20.1	5	14	2 625	3 301	87.3	2 602	90.1
Walworth, SD	46129	7	5 974	17.8	2	7	925	1 323	92.4	1 134	94.2
Yankton, SD	46135	7	21 652	19.4	3	12	3 666	5 720	82.3	4 219	92.2
Ziebach, SD	46137	9	2 519	29.9	1	3	250	883	92.6	735	92.7
TENNESSEE	**47000**										
Anderson, TN	47001	2	71 330	17.6	3	26	12 365	16 224	92.3	12 729	95.5
Bedford, TN	47003	6	37 586	18.4	1	12	6 210	8 678	90.2	7 088	93.7
Benton, TN	47005	7	16 537	16.8	1	6	2 527	3 320	91.5	2 861	94.5
Bledsoe, TN	47007	8	12 367	17.2	1	5	1 746	2 571	91.8	2 178	92.3
Blount, TN	47009	2	105 823	17.0	3	26	16 226	23 856	87.5	18 075	94.8
Bradley, TN	47011	4	87 965	17.1	2	24	13 402	22 171	79.1	15 197	93.2
Campbell, TN	47013	6	39 854	17.0	1	16	6 219	7 939	95.1	6 799	96.7
Cannon, TN	47015	8	12 826	18.7	1	7	2 077	2 831	90.2	2 358	91.3
Carroll, TN	47017	6	29 475	17.3	5	13	5 026	6 547	89.7	5 136	97.1
Carter, TN	47019	2	56 742	15.8	2	21	8 287	12 454	91.3	9 100	97.9

[1]County type code is from the Economic Research Service of the USDA. See Notes and Definitions at the end of this section.
. . . = Not available.

Table C-1. School and Student Characteristics by County—*Continued*

County	Characteristics of students, 2000–2001			Staff and students, 2000–2001				Revenues, fiscal 1999			
	Percent with IEP[2]	Percent eligible for free lunch	Percent minority	Number of teachers	Student/teacher ratio	Local school non-teaching staff	Central admin. staff	Total revenue ($1,000s)	Percentage of revenue from		
									Federal govt.	State govt.	Local govt.
	10	11	12	13	14	15	16	17	18	19	20
Saluda, SC	22.8	57.5	48.6	163	13.5	33	6	$15 150	10.7	54.1	35.3
Spartanburg, SC	15.1	40.3	33.0	2 909	14.7	499	47	292 352	6.2	49.5	44.3
Sumter, SC	15.3	62.3	63.9	1 256	15.2	210	36	118 745	12.9	58.7	28.4
Union, SC	16.6	56.6	40.5	378	13.8	56	4	32 218	9.6	59.6	30.7
Williamsburg, SC	21.3	86.6	91.9	383	16.7	69	11	42 851	15.5	60.9	23.6
York, SC	12.0	28.0	29.1	1 948	15.5	305	33	202 814	4.5	43.0	52.5
SOUTH DAKOTA											
Aurora, SD	12.3	51.8	7.9	59	10.3	42	9	3 831	6.7	39.3	54.0
Beadle, SD	13.4	33.0	4.2	216	13.7	211	22	18 310	6.0	39.6	54.4
Bennett, SD	13.9	67.8	58.1	56	10.8	56	6	6 031	46.5	30.2	23.2
Bon Homme, SD	12.8	33.3	4.1	109	12.8	91	21	9 169	6.9	43.3	49.7
Brookings, SD	12.0	15.9	5.4	280	15.0	198	29	25 608	3.8	34.6	61.6
Brown, SD	13.2	. . .	13.5	343	14.6	316	46	30 766	5.7	30.4	64.0
Brule, SD	12.0	36.5	18.6	100	12.1	68	10	8 334	12.3	34.1	53.6
Buffalo, SD	. . .	. . .	. . .	. . .	. . .	. . .	. . .	. . .	. . .	. . .	. . .
Butte, SD	12.4	39.1	7.0	133	13.9	112	12	12 527	6.8	41.4	51.8
Campbell, SD	7.4	35.8	1.0	27	11.5	22	5	2 264	12.7	43.5	43.8
Charles Mix, SD	12.9	52.3	34.6	153	11.7	125	26	13 617	26.4	38.4	35.2
Clark, SD	14.0	41.5	3.1	63	12.3	45	6	5 431	9.2	33.7	57.2
Clay, SD	11.4	31.0	13.3	118	13.5	66	14	10 343	5.7	31.5	62.8
Codington, SD	13.3	22.5	4.5	300	15.7	224	34	27 148	4.5	37.2	58.2
Corson, SD	26.1	80.3	73.7	75	10.8	78	18	6 210	25.5	53.1	21.5
Custer, SD	16.7	35.0	10.9	96	12.6	69	12	6 948	15.2	26.7	58.1
Davison, SD	14.1	26.3	4.7	202	15.5	163	14	18 729	5.9	40.2	53.9
Day, SD	13.0	45.6	10.4	96	11.7	74	17	7 916	9.0	42.1	48.9
Deuel, SD	11.3	24.8	1.4	41	15.3	42	5	3 461	6.2	38.9	54.9
Dewey, SD	30.6	66.4	60.9	81	9.3	63	16	7 389	41.9	37.9	20.2
Douglas, SD	11.3	30.9	2.9	44	10.2	34	6	3 033	6.9	49.6	43.6
Edmunds, SD	11.5	41.8	2.0	67	11.4	42	6	4 874	7.8	30.6	61.6
Fall River, SD	14.0	39.3	18.9	95	12.8	89	12	8 294	11.1	37.1	51.8
Faulk, SD	9.2	42.7	0.0	44	11.1	30	5	3 424	6.8	38.3	54.8
Grant, SD	13.9	22.6	2.8	106	13.5	73	11	9 461	4.7	25.1	70.2
Gregory, SD	11.1	58.0	11.5	80	11.6	71	15	6 276	10.4	46.6	43.0
Haakon, SD	8.4	31.4	4.4	45	10.6	23	6	3 310	6.0	38.7	55.3
Hamlin, SD	11.5	39.0	2.1	91	14.2	124	17	8 687	6.0	36.1	57.9
Hand, SD	12.6	41.6	0.2	51	11.5	40	7	4 253	8.5	28.2	63.3
Hanson, SD	14.0	38.2	0.6	53	10.1	30	5	3 436	8.8	47.8	43.4
Harding, SD	6.5	. . .	0.3	30	10.2	10	4	2 237	7.3	30.4	62.3
Hughes, SD	12.2	28.8	13.6	181	15.9	161	16	16 965	6.1	38.1	55.8
Hutchinson, SD	13.3	33.1	2.8	138	12.5	79	14	11 136	7.2	42.6	50.2
Hyde, SD	13.1	33.8	9.1	24	11.5	20	3	1 971	7.0	32.7	60.4
Jackson, SD	15.1	51.9	36.1	39	10.0	27	3	2 681	18.9	40.4	40.7
Jerauld, SD	12.2	35.6	1.6	43	10.1	40	10	3 112	9.3	39.1	51.6
Jones, SD	13.0	. . .	1.4	23	9.4	19	4	1 668	4.2	34.2	61.6
Kingsbury, SD	11.2	27.1	1.8	79	11.4	62	9	8 197	4.8	41.4	53.8
Lake, SD	9.0	24.4	2.7	151	13.7	101	16	13 348	4.8	39.2	56.0
Lawrence, SD	12.3	23.1	6.8	242	13.6	317	79	22 319	6.1	23.2	70.7
Lincoln, SD	14.1	14.9	2.2	225	15.0	163	28	19 359	3.7	42.9	53.4
Lyman, SD	13.3	48.0	26.9	36	12.1	38	3	2 947	13.7	22.0	64.3
McCook, SD	15.7	32.7	1.5	87	12.0	62	13	7 225	5.7	37.9	56.4
McPherson, SD	10.8	43.0	1.4	45	11.1	34	7	3 576	10.7	24.0	65.3
Marshall, SD	9.3	36.6	3.3	71	12.7	50	6	5 776	7.1	34.4	58.6
Meade, SD	10.7	29.0	6.4	228	13.4	145	33	17 486	7.5	44.1	48.4
Mellette, SD	14.1	80.4	68.5	49	10.7	49	6	3 596	27.2	44.4	28.4
Miner, SD	13.9	30.1	1.7	41	13.2	45	6	3 535	7.7	38.5	53.8
Minnehaha, SD	12.5	21.7	10.3	1 604	15.9	1 167	107	148 007	5.8	27.7	66.5
Moody, SD	11.1	25.3	22.8	92	12.5	62	9	7 245	7.3	46.1	46.6
Pennington, SD	11.8	27.2	18.4	1 124	15.2	842	158	103 281	11.1	39.8	49.1
Perkins, SD	11.9	46.1	4.5	58	10.6	45	10	4 516	9.7	35.1	55.3
Potter, SD	9.8	31.7	2.1	48	10.9	26	5	3 575	7.4	27.5	65.1
Roberts, SD	15.5	53.3	38.0	155	12.1	134	20	13 099	18.7	42.5	38.9
Sanborn, SD	12.7	40.0	4.2	49	10.3	35	6	3 551	10.3	49.5	40.2
Shannon, SD	26.9	78.1	99.3	105	9.3	172	23	10 742	43.9	48.9	7.1
Spink, SD	10.6	34.6	2.7	131	11.3	97	17	9 948	7.0	39.0	54.0
Stanley, SD	13.6	27.5	17.3	38	15.5	25	6	3 438	11.9	32.2	55.9
Sully, SD	14.9	23.9	6.9	39	8.9	21	7	3 124	3.4	16.7	79.9
Todd, SD	16.9	82.5	94.8	165	12.4	248	31	21 639	54.1	37.5	8.3
Tripp, SD	11.2	46.5	18.8	95	13.0	66	13	7 841	9.6	42.2	48.2
Turner, SD	14.8	20.7	1.8	119	12.9	91	23	9 890	5.2	45.5	49.3
Union, SD	14.0	19.9	4.6	186	14.1	150	26	18 143	3.9	25.4	70.6
Walworth, SD	14.6	39.6	20.8	73	12.7	61	14	6 195	9.4	42.8	47.8
Yankton, SD	13.7	21.7	4.3	218	16.8	195	23	22 331	5.4	37.7	56.9
Ziebach, SD	24.8	69.2	75.2	29	8.6	29	4	3 072	45.4	40.2	14.4
TENNESSEE											
Anderson, TN	18.1	. . .	. . .	. . .	. . .	796	15	85 141	9.0	45.3	45.6
Bedford, TN	14.7	. . .	. . .	. . .	. . .	458	6	29 575	8.7	56.2	35.2
Benton, TN	16.7	. . .	. . .	. . .	. . .	166	3	14 175	9.9	54.7	35.4
Bledsoe, TN	21.8	. . .	. . .	. . .	. . .	159	4	9 845	11.7	67.6	20.8
Blount, TN	15.1	. . .	. . .	. . .	. . .	903	13	89 969	6.5	47.3	46.2
Bradley, TN	12.6	. . .	. . .	. . .	. . .	620	11	69 472	9.8	48.7	41.5
Campbell, TN	13.3	. . .	. . .	. . .	. . .	386	4	33 628	12.5	61.4	26.2
Cannon, TN	11.2	. . .	. . .	. . .	. . .	120	3	10 380	8.9	66.6	24.5
Carroll, TN	14.8	. . .	. . .	. . .	. . .	321	7	29 781	10.1	56.3	33.7
Carter, TN	16.7	. . .	. . .	. . .	. . .	456	12	47 098	10.9	56.9	32.2

[2]IEP = Individual Education Program. See Notes and Definitions at the end of this section.
. . . = Not available.

Table C-1. Population, School, and Student Characteristics by County—*Continued*

County	Current expenditures, fiscal 1999			Resident population 16 to 19 years, 2000				Outcomes, 1999–2000	
	Amount ($1,000s)	Amount per student	Percent for instruction	Total population 16 to 19 years	Percent in Armed Forces	Percent high school graduates	Percent not enrolled, not grads, not Armed Forces, not empl.	Number of graduates	Dropouts grades 9–12 (percent)
	21	22	23	24	25	26	27	28	29
Saluda, SC	$12 568	$5 816	57.1	1 109	0.0	9.0	9.7	106	...
Spartanburg, SC	249 976	6 135	61.3	13 520	0.1	11.4	7.6	1 974	...
Sumter, SC	100 142	5 284	57.6	6 376	2.5	13.2	6.6	888	...
Union, SC	29 709	6 105	62.0	1 531	0.0	11.7	9.6	221	...
Williamsburg, SC	38 794	5 861	56.1	2 407	0.5	9.5	6.6	266	...
York, SC	161 076	5 719	60.2	9 025	0.0	10.5	5.8	1 443	...
SOUTH DAKOTA									
Aurora, SD	3 331	5 753	60.9	230	0.0	4.8	11.7	54	6.2
Beadle, SD	15 389	5 274	59.9	987	0.0	14.1	2.8	238	2.5
Bennett, SD	3 734	6 318	68.4	245	0.0	6.5	15.1	32	6.5
Bon Homme, SD	7 649	5 253	59.0	432	0.0	12.5	5.1	116	2.7
Brookings, SD	21 078	4 908	64.9	2 817	0.1	6.1	0.2	350	1.1
Brown, SD	26 734	5 055	61.0	2 384	0.0	9.2	1.4	415	2.8
Brule, SD	6 837	5 470	63.7	372	0.0	5.1	7.5	91	2.6
Buffalo, SD	...	...	...	...	...	...	14.5	...	...
Butte, SD	9 523	5 036	61.2	583	0.0	16.8	1.5	116	3.3
Campbell, SD	1 852	5 879	63.4	96	0.0	5.2	0.0	24	2.5
Charles Mix, SD	9 793	5 279	64.6	580	0.0	5.9	13.8	99	3.5
Clark, SD	4 240	4 753	61.6	268	0.0	9.0	4.9	61	0.4
Clay, SD	8 368	5 131	60.6	1 472	0.0	2.4	0.7	142	1.7
Codington, SD	21 319	4 485	65.7	1 741	0.0	12.2	2.3	410	3.4
Corson, SD	5 229	6 844	60.4	290	0.0	6.9	13.1	42	9.1
Custer, SD	6 170	5 499	63.7	609	0.0	9.4	1.8	78	2.6
Davison, SD	16 924	5 258	61.7	1 338	0.0	6.7	3.3	244	2.0
Day, SD	6 674	5 511	57.9	351	0.0	10.3	2.8	89	2.5
Deuel, SD	2 943	4 809	55.6	248	0.0	9.3	2.0	48	1.5
Dewey, SD	5 545	7 028	64.8	467	0.0	13.3	13.7	42	7.8
Douglas, SD	2 498	5 046	57.8	208	0.0	7.2	2.4	49	0.6
Edmunds, SD	4 154	5 238	60.2	239	0.0	3.8	7.1	68	0.8
Fall River, SD	7 262	5 621	60.2	347	0.0	7.8	2.6	82	6.1
Faulk, SD	2 746	5 211	62.3	167	0.0	4.2	10.8	42	2.0
Grant, SD	8 205	5 300	58.3	442	0.0	9.5	6.1	122	1.9
Gregory, SD	5 381	5 281	59.8	257	0.0	8.9	1.2	87	1.4
Haakon, SD	2 675	4 945	64.4	156	0.0	8.3	0.0	55	0.5
Hamlin, SD	6 143	4 668	60.0	380	0.0	8.4	5.3	116	0.9
Hand, SD	3 610	5 667	60.7	222	0.0	2.7	0.9	55	0.5
Hanson, SD	2 917	5 218	60.4	188	0.0	8.5	6.9	51	0.6
Harding, SD	1 874	5 802	64.4	128	0.0	0.0	16.4	28	...
Hughes, SD	14 676	4 796	65.0	992	0.0	13.0	3.9	212	2.6
Hutchinson, SD	9 250	5 153	62.2	453	0.0	2.9	10.2	129	0.7
Hyde, SD	1 752	5 492	58.0	86	0.0	5.8	0.0	27	...
Jackson, SD	2 167	4 993	64.5	211	0.0	15.6	2.4	24	2.4
Jerauld, SD	2 891	6 023	64.9	122	0.0	2.5	2.5	44	3.4
Jones, SD	1 283	4 649	63.1	83	0.0	0.0	0.0	27	3.3
Kingsbury, SD	6 811	5 449	58.1	351	0.0	6.6	2.3	90	2.1
Lake, SD	11 144	4 966	61.0	1 055	0.4	6.9	2.7	194	2.1
Lawrence, SD	18 823	5 443	64.2	1 900	0.0	11.9	4.6	256	3.7
Lincoln, SD	15 384	4 609	60.2	1 421	0.5	7.4	0.6	225	1.9
Lyman, SD	2 579	5 998	57.8	213	0.0	4.7	4.7	31	4.5
McCook, SD	5 825	5 276	59.7	326	0.0	9.2	4.9	100	1.4
McPherson, SD	2 863	5 433	62.5	118	0.0	6.8	12.7	35	2.9
Marshall, SD	4 638	5 165	62.9	271	0.0	7.4	14.0	53	2.2
Meade, SD	15 709	4 847	64.7	1 376	8.0	21.7	4.8	238	2.1
Mellette, SD	3 234	6 316	61.9	136	0.0	14.7	5.9	22	5.2
Miner, SD	2 723	4 880	60.0	175	0.0	5.1	1.1	40	2.6
Minnehaha, SD	123 241	5 043	61.0	8 653	0.0	12.3	3.7	1 620	3.9
Moody, SD	6 058	4 893	60.5	466	0.0	5.4	5.6	83	4.2
Pennington, SD	90 353	5 140	65.3	5 548	0.3	13.7	4.5	1 028	5.2
Perkins, SD	4 159	5 950	57.6	186	0.0	10.2	3.8	57	1.9
Potter, SD	3 172	5 842	66.9	137	0.0	2.2	0.0	58	1.5
Roberts, SD	10 396	5 392	61.6	627	0.0	6.9	10.7	126	3.7
Sanborn, SD	3 021	5 463	57.3	174	0.0	7.5	6.9	60	0.5
Shannon, SD	10 517	9 500	54.2	1 015	0.0	12.2	27.6	0	...
Spink, SD	8 747	5 463	62.2	462	0.6	5.6	8.9	139	1.9
Stanley, SD	2 868	4 694	56.3	178	0.0	6.2	2.2	42	2.8
Sully, SD	2 530	6 504	63.3	92	0.0	13.0	0.0	27	0.8
Todd, SD	16 589	7 759	58.3	754	0.0	10.1	12.9	60	23.1
Tripp, SD	6 065	4 691	63.8	391	0.0	8.4	9.7	105	1.7
Turner, SD	7 914	5 057	62.1	490	0.4	9.6	1.0	122	1.8
Union, SD	13 656	5 208	60.9	721	0.0	11.0	1.4	216	2.9
Walworth, SD	5 371	5 220	60.0	320	0.0	10.0	9.7	70	12.0
Yankton, SD	16 445	4 416	61.6	1 157	0.0	7.8	3.0	257	5.7
Ziebach, SD	2 036	7 712	60.0	201	0.0	9.5	23.4	15	3.1
TENNESSEE									
Anderson, TN	77 284	6 111	64.3	3 567	0.0	15.7	2.1	715	2.9
Bedford, TN	25 722	4 288	64.1	2 189	0.0	9.5	8.3	280	5.1
Benton, TN	12 255	4 800	66.6	759	0.0	14.2	5.1	146	0.9
Bledsoe, TN	8 209	4 694	61.7	615	0.0	13.5	10.1	56	3.3
Blount, TN	85 949	5 346	67.6	5 248	0.1	12.1	3.3	798	3.1
Bradley, TN	66 013	4 939	66.8	5 067	0.0	14.6	3.7	634	3.7
Campbell, TN	30 031	4 708	66.4	1 994	0.3	15.9	11.7	251	6.9
Cannon, TN	8 877	4 326	64.6	641	0.0	14.0	5.5	103	5.1
Carroll, TN	24 295	4 682	65.0	1 578	0.0	15.2	4.6	323	1.7
Carter, TN	42 845	5 423	65.0	2 857	0.0	14.9	4.3	416	1.8

... = Not available.

Table C-1. Population, School, and Student Characteristics by County—*Continued*

County	Population 25 years and over	High school diploma or less (percent)	High school diploma or more (percent)	College enrollment, 2000 Number	Percent public	Bachelor's degree or more	+/- U.S. percent with bachelor's degree or more	Non-Hispanic White	Black or African American	American Indian and Alaska Native	Asian, Hawaiian, and Pacific Islander	Hispanic or Latino[1]
	30	31	32	33	34	35	36	37	38	39	40	41
Saluda, SC	12 654	69.3	69.3	509	96.7	11.9	-12.5	15.6	3.9	0.0	25.7	1.3
Spartanburg, SC	167 802	56.8	73.1	11 226	67.4	18.2	-6.2	20.6	8.0	10.0	26.1	14.2
Sumter, SC	64 144	55.4	74.3	5 724	77.8	15.8	-8.6	19.9	10.5	13.8	22.4	14.1
Union, SC	20 222	69.5	66.9	967	86.9	9.8	-14.6	11.3	5.8	0.0	26.8	0.0
Williamsburg, SC	23 189	69.6	65.5	1 289	92.4	11.5	-12.9	15.1	9.2	12.8	46.2	2.4
York, SC	105 757	51.2	77.2	8 717	90.1	20.9	-3.5	23.7	8.8	5.6	28.6	16.0
SOUTH DAKOTA												
Aurora, SD	2 020	56.5	79.5	75	68.0	12.7	-11.7	12.9	...	0.0	0.0	8.0
Beadle, SD	11 368	51.9	83.0	517	36.9	18.3	-6.1	18.0	13.8	46.9	9.3	0.0
Bennett, SD	1 972	56.4	71.3	170	81.2	12.7	-11.7	16.4	23.1	5.9	...	14.3
Bon Homme, SD	5 026	57.1	79.0	96	80.2	15.3	-9.1	15.7	0.0	4.0	...	14.3
Brookings, SD	14 819	38.0	90.2	6 622	98.8	32.2	7.8	31.8	78.1	5.2	68.7	20.6
Brown, SD	22 959	45.8	85.8	2 787	88.6	23.6	-0.8	23.8	37.9	14.0	63.0	16.4
Brule, SD	3 371	50.5	81.1	78	92.3	20.6	-3.8	20.7	...	21.5	0.0	30.8
Buffalo, SD	948	69.7	63.9	49	91.8	5.4	-19.0	13.8	0.0	2.9	0.0	0.0
Butte, SD	5 859	57.2	79.8	258	87.6	12.2	-12.2	12.3	...	2.9	0.0	13.3
Campbell, SD	1 251	54.1	79.2	16	87.5	14.8	-9.6	14.9	...	0.0	...	...
Charles Mix, SD	5 676	59.9	74.7	160	73.1	14.1	-10.3	16.2	0.0	6.1	25.0	8.2
Clark, SD	2 781	63.3	76.6	53	81.1	11.4	-13.0	11.3	...	0.0	33.3	0.0
Clay, SD	6 719	33.6	89.5	4 397	97.5	38.7	14.3	38.0	59.5	23.8	77.5	53.6
Codington, SD	16 377	52.8	85.3	1 100	87.0	18.8	-5.6	19.1	0.0	1.5	7.5	15.7
Corson, SD	2 238	61.9	76.0	116	84.5	11.3	-13.1	15.4	0.0	7.1	50.0	0.0
Custer, SD	5 099	44.4	88.9	185	73.0	24.4	0.0	24.7	...	19.4	0.0	36.0
Davison, SD	11 719	50.0	83.9	1 283	54.3	20.2	-4.2	20.2	56.4	6.0	37.0	0.0
Day, SD	4 354	58.3	80.0	102	79.4	15.4	-9.0	15.7	...	6.9	30.8	0.0
Deuel, SD	3 094	60.3	81.9	89	78.7	13.3	-11.1	13.3	0.0	0.0	...	22.2
Dewey, SD	3 107	54.8	77.4	262	90.8	12.2	-12.2	20.4	100.0	7.5	14.8	28.6
Douglas, SD	2 332	59.8	68.8	41	78.0	14.5	-9.9	14.5	...	14.3	...	0.0
Edmunds, SD	2 975	59.7	73.6	59	78.0	15.5	-8.9	15.6	...	...	0.0	0.0
Fall River, SD	5 313	51.9	82.5	125	64.0	19.2	-5.2	19.9	0.0	6.2	25.0	24.1
Faulk, SD	1 803	60.4	73.7	27	74.1	13.1	-11.3	13.3	...	0.0	0.0	0.0
Grant, SD	5 303	63.1	79.5	119	71.4	14.8	-9.6	14.8	...	0.0	0.0	80.0
Gregory, SD	3 367	61.3	77.7	43	95.3	12.0	-12.4	12.4	0.0	0.7	0.0	0.0
Haakon, SD	1 477	54.4	86.3	32	97.5	15.4	-9.0	15.1	...	14.8	0.0	100.0
Hamlin, SD	3 507	62.9	79.9	123	95.1	12.8	-11.6	12.7	0.0	26.3	50.0	18.8
Hand, SD	2 627	58.1	80.1	33	63.6	15.6	-8.8	15.6	0.0	0.0	0.0	0.0
Hanson, SD	1 962	61.1	75.1	61	85.2	14.0	-10.4	13.8	...	...	60.0	50.0
Harding, SD	850	46.6	87.8	28	82.1	17.8	-6.6	17.5	...	50.0	...	0.0
Hughes, SD	10 853	38.1	89.5	183	84.7	32.0	7.6	33.3	13.0	8.4	72.7	12.2
Hutchinson, SD	5 629	57.6	71.7	139	82.7	14.1	-10.3	14.1	100.0	18.8	...	25.0
Hyde, SD	1 147	56.2	80.5	20	95.0	16.0	-8.4	16.0	...	12.1	...	...
Jackson, SD	1 662	51.6	82.7	137	86.9	16.2	-8.2	21.7	...	5.9	0.0	100.0
Jerauld, SD	1 661	61.0	79.6	49	81.6	12.3	-12.1	12.2	...	50.0	...	0.0
Jones, SD	811	53.3	86.2	12	83.3	17.8	-6.6	18.2	...	12.5	...	...
Kingsbury, SD	4 015	59.6	82.3	97	89.7	16.2	-8.2	16.2	...	12.5	25.0	0.0
Lake, SD	6 917	50.9	85.7	1 213	97.4	21.1	-3.3	20.6	0.0	19.0	86.5	22.0
Lawrence, SD	13 746	44.2	87.5	2 245	95.7	24.0	-0.4	24.1	0.0	18.4	44.8	15.1
Lincoln, SD	15 093	41.4	89.4	994	75.8	25.5	1.1	25.5	27.3	17.1	36.5	25.6
Lyman, SD	2 344	59.7	81.1	101	94.1	15.9	-8.5	17.9	0.0	8.7	37.5	0.0
McCook, SD	3 827	55.8	82.9	140	86.4	16.3	-8.1	16.3	...	0.0	100.0	8.7
McPherson, SD	2 128	68.7	58.8	23	78.3	10.7	-13.7	10.7	...	...	...	0.0
Marshall, SD	3 111	57.8	75.6	99	93.9	16.2	-8.2	16.7	...	8.3	...	0.0
Meade, SD	14 816	46.1	87.7	1 061	82.2	16.8	-7.6	17.0	19.7	5.8	23.5	20.6
Mellette, SD	1 199	56.3	78.1	66	95.5	16.6	-7.8	25.3	...	4.6	66.7	0.0
Miner, SD	1 982	60.8	79.6	40	95.0	13.5	-10.9	13.4	0.0	40.0	0.0	0.0
Minnehaha, SD	93 400	42.3	88.5	7 981	58.9	26.0	1.6	26.8	20.0	7.7	28.7	7.6
Moody, SD	4 193	51.8	84.7	191	91.1	17.4	-7.0	17.9	23.1	9.5	37.1	33.3
Pennington, SD	55 535	41.5	87.8	5 409	84.0	25.0	0.6	26.5	10.5	9.7	29.9	8.8
Perkins, SD	2 367	56.9	80.3	27	59.3	14.6	-9.8	14.9	0.0	0.0	33.3	0.0
Potter, SD	1 969	56.6	80.8	26	76.9	16.2	-8.2	16.1	...	22.2	50.0	...
Roberts, SD	6 301	61.4	75.8	210	93.8	13.4	-11.0	14.4	0.0	8.4	77.8	0.0
Sanborn, SD	1 788	56.2	82.7	67	70.1	14.8	-9.6	15.1	...	0.0	0.0	5.6
Shannon, SD	5 524	56.4	70.0	537	89.4	12.1	-12.3	41.3	0.0	9.3	64.0	9.5
Spink, SD	5 024	57.5	81.4	90	78.9	14.4	-10.0	14.4	0.0	17.7	0.0	0.0
Stanley, SD	1 823	47.3	87.7	42	52.4	22.1	-2.3	22.3	0.0	11.3	100.0	0.0
Sully, SD	1 065	53.2	84.9	13	84.6	16.4	-8.0	16.6	...	0.0	...	0.0
Todd, SD	4 173	57.2	74.1	504	93.3	12.1	-12.3	22.2	...	8.4	73.3	0.0
Tripp, SD	4 218	58.7	80.2	65	92.3	13.5	-10.9	14.0	...	2.6	0.0	9.1
Turner, SD	6 019	54.1	83.2	203	77.3	17.0	-7.4	17.0	0.0	0.0	0.0	0.0
Union, SD	8 262	45.6	87.2	477	85.5	26.3	1.9	25.5	19.0	24.3	74.6	30.8
Walworth, SD	4 083	58.7	78.1	113	77.0	15.8	-8.6	15.8	...	9.6	0.0	0.0
Yankton, SD	14 178	47.9	86.1	1 130	54.0	23.0	-1.4	23.9	9.4	2.5	0.0	10.5
Ziebach, SD	1 223	64.3	71.4	84	95.2	12.0	-12.4	17.1	...	8.4	22.2	...
TENNESSEE												
Anderson, TN	49 499	54.0	78.9	2 453	87.0	20.8	-3.6	20.7	14.6	19.4	67.8	20.8
Bedford, TN	24 232	69.3	69.7	966	88.6	11.1	-13.3	12.3	4.3	0.0	16.4	4.5
Benton, TN	11 798	76.6	65.8	246	77.2	6.3	-18.1	6.1	12.7	0.0	14.6	30.2
Bledsoe, TN	8 455	75.1	66.0	228	87.7	7.1	-17.3	7.5	0.0	0.0	0.0	3.3
Blount, TN	72 938	56.0	78.4	4 291	67.1	17.9	-6.5	18.1	9.6	7.0	47.7	19.4
Bradley, TN	57 163	56.0	73.3	5 736	48.4	15.9	-8.5	15.8	10.3	11.2	39.0	28.4
Campbell, TN	27 359	76.8	58.7	809	81.5	7.0	-17.4	6.9	7.5	0.0	40.4	19.5
Cannon, TN	8 486	76.0	67.2	323	88.9	8.4	-16.0	8.4	12.5	0.0	0.0	0.0
Carroll, TN	20 238	70.5	67.9	1 042	60.6	11.1	-13.3	11.6	7.2	22.2	17.4	11.7
Carter, TN	39 450	64.4	69.1	2 710	71.3	12.8	-11.6	12.8	11.7	16.7	14.7	10.6

[1]Hispanic or Latino persons may be of any race.
... = Not available.

Table C-1. Population, School, and Student Characteristics by County—*Continued*

County	State/ County code	County type[1]	Population, 2000		Number of schools and students, 2000–2001			Resident enrollment, 2000			
			Total	Percent 5–17 years	School districts	Schools	Students	Total	Percent public	K–12	Percent public
			1	2	3	4	5	6	7	8	9
Cheatham, TN	47021	2	35 912	20.5	1	14	6 861	8 906	87.4	7 369	92.0
Chester, TN	47023	6	15 540	17.5	1	6	2 459	4 531	67.8	2 770	93.3
Claiborne, TN	47025	6	29 862	17.9	1	11	4 659	6 863	88.1	5 431	94.5
Clay, TN	47027	9	7 976	16.4	1	4	1 197	1 712	99.1	1 388	100.0
Cocke, TN	47029	7	33 565	16.9	2	12	5 311	6 849	95.1	5 823	97.3
Coffee, TN	47031	5	48 014	18.5	3	18	8 967	11 485	91.2	8 906	95.4
Crockett, TN	47033	8	14 532	18.7	3	7	2 677	3 233	91.1	2 787	94.1
Cumberland, TN	47035	7	46 802	15.9	1	10	6 562	9 432	92.3	7 599	93.9
Davidson, TN	47037	2	569 891	15.6	1	125	67 669	141 200	70.8	90 547	82.3
Decatur, TN	47039	9	11 731	16.1	1	5	1 753	2 284	94.2	1 897	96.5
De Kalb, TN	47041	6	17 423	17.2	1	4	2 111	3 693	92.3	3 071	95.3
Dickson, TN	47043	2	43 156	19.7	1	13	7 966	10 311	89.9	8 621	93.0
Dyer, TN	47045	7	37 279	19.1	2	12	6 788	8 964	91.3	7 032	94.7
Fayette, TN	47047	1	28 806	19.0	1	8	3 555	6 736	73.9	5 551	73.8
Fentress, TN	47049	9	16 625	18.0	1	7	2 364	3 601	95.6	3 084	96.4
Franklin, TN	47051	7	39 270	17.1	1	12	5 796	9 706	78.1	6 782	93.9
Gibson, TN	47053	4	48 152	17.7	5	20	8 431	10 813	92.8	8 732	95.7
Giles, TN	47055	6	29 447	18.4	1	8	4 617	6 974	88.0	5 637	94.2
Grainger, TN	47057	8	20 659	16.8	1	6	3 263	4 193	95.4	3 564	97.3
Greene, TN	47059	6	62 909	16.5	2	21	9 538	13 201	88.6	10 392	94.9
Grundy, TN	47061	6	14 332	18.3	1	7	2 292	3 040	94.1	2 654	95.8
Hamblen, TN	47063	5	58 128	16.7	1	20	9 082	11 928	92.6	9 572	96.0
Hamilton, TN	47065	2	307 896	17.2	1	76	40 709	77 307	78.1	53 191	81.5
Hancock, TN	47067	9	6 786	17.8	1	4	1 146	1 401	94.1	1 218	93.7
Hardeman, TN	47069	6	28 105	18.0	1	9	4 569	6 246	89.2	5 433	92.1
Hardin, TN	47071	6	25 578	17.2	1	10	3 810	5 325	89.2	4 457	92.0
Hawkins, TN	47073	2	53 563	17.1	2	17	7 656	11 234	92.0	9 175	94.6
Haywood, TN	47075	6	19 797	20.0	1	7	3 631	4 975	93.8	4 095	95.7
Henderson, TN	47077	6	25 522	17.9	2	9	4 287	5 456	91.1	4 547	93.8
Henry, TN	47079	7	31 115	16.5	2	9	4 651	6 506	93.8	5 384	96.8
Hickman, TN	47081	6	22 295	18.1	1	7	3 726	4 976	85.2	4 174	89.9
Houston, TN	47083	8	8 088	17.7	1	3	1 417	1 742	93.9	1 490	95.8
Humphreys, TN	47085	6	17 929	17.9	1	5	2 994	3 901	90.0	3 242	93.9
Jackson, TN	47087	9	10 984	16.5	1	4	1 627	2 188	94.6	1 807	96.1
Jefferson, TN	47089	6	44 294	16.7	1	11	6 816	10 701	80.7	7 627	95.1
Johnson, TN	47091	8	17 499	14.8	1	8	2 296	3 316	93.5	2 768	95.3
Knox, TN	47093	2	382 032	16.2	1	84	51 934	102 622	85.6	62 407	86.8
Lake, TN	47095	9	7 954	12.7	1	3	894	1 424	93.8	1 167	95.9
Lauderdale, TN	47097	6	27 101	18.0	1	7	4 588	6 156	91.3	5 096	93.6
Lawrence, TN	47099	6	39 926	19.5	1	12	6 903	9 223	90.9	7 663	93.7
Lewis, TN	47101	7	11 367	19.3	1	3	1 925	2 649	86.5	2 176	90.2
Lincoln, TN	47103	6	31 340	17.8	2	11	5 177	7 089	92.7	5 671	95.9
Loudon, TN	47105	2	39 086	16.1	2	12	6 707	7 829	92.3	6 232	95.2
McMinn, TN	47107	7	49 015	17.6	3	15	7 905	10 614	89.7	8 587	95.6
McNairy, TN	47109	7	24 653	17.5	1	8	4 127	5 328	89.6	4 393	92.3
Macon, TN	47111	6	20 386	19.0	1	7	3 539	4 610	96.6	3 926	97.9
Madison, TN	47113	3	91 837	18.9	1	23	13 840	24 814	72.1	17 759	82.5
Marion, TN	47115	2	27 776	17.8	2	11	4 385	6 125	92.9	5 111	94.8
Marshall, TN	47117	6	26 767	19.0	1	7	4 765	6 342	94.3	5 294	96.4
Maury, TN	47119	4	69 498	19.4	1	17	11 286	16 743	83.1	13 184	86.8
Meigs, TN	47121	8	11 086	18.2	1	4	1 770	2 335	88.4	2 017	90.1
Monroe, TN	47123	6	38 961	18.4	2	14	6 434	8 665	89.7	7 117	95.3
Montgomery, TN	47125	3	134 768	19.9	1	30	23 966	38 242	90.2	27 284	94.1
Moore, TN	47127	9	5 740	17.6	1	2	955	1 312	92.8	1 015	95.5
Morgan, TN	47129	8	19 757	17.4	1	6	3 243	4 260	94.8	3 480	95.5
Obion, TN	47131	7	32 450	17.0	2	11	5 470	7 182	95.0	5 636	98.5
Overton, TN	47133	7	20 118	16.9	1	8	3 081	4 459	95.6	3 473	97.1
Perry, TN	47135	9	7 631	18.3	1	4	1 170	1 594	93.7	1 392	93.9
Pickett, TN	47137	9	4 945	15.6	1	2	730	1 021	96.0	825	97.0
Polk, TN	47139	9	16 050	16.2	1	6	2 316	3 089	91.4	2 577	92.9
Putnam, TN	47141	5	62 315	16.2	1	16	9 505	17 803	92.9	9 895	94.5
Rhea, TN	47143	6	28 400	17.6	2	6	4 446	6 583	91.1	5 023	94.6
Roane, TN	47145	4	51 910	16.5	2	19	7 306	10 736	91.7	8 612	93.6
Robertson, TN	47147	2	54 433	20.0	1	16	9 755	12 851	87.3	10 877	90.0
Rutherford, TN	47149	2	182 023	18.9	2	41	31 510	53 906	90.4	34 723	92.4
Scott, TN	47151	6	21 127	19.1	2	9	3 860	4 995	97.3	4 182	98.7
Sequatchie, TN	47153	6	11 370	17.7	1	3	1 831	2 422	88.6	1 943	92.6
Sevier, TN	47155	2	71 170	17.0	1	23	12 288	15 086	90.7	12 154	94.0
Shelby, TN	47157	0	897 472	20.6	2	203	161 186	259 171	83.5	189 061	87.7
Smith, TN	47159	8	17 712	19.0	1	8	3 151	3 995	94.2	3 366	97.4
Stewart, TN	47161	8	12 370	18.1	1	3	2 064	2 710	94.5	2 300	96.5
Sullivan, TN	47163	2	153 048	16.2	3	49	23 063	32 281	88.3	25 279	93.6
Sumner, TN	47165	2	130 449	19.6	1	36	21 789	32 250	85.4	25 901	89.2
Tipton, TN	47167	1	51 271	22.3	2	13	10 905	14 163	89.9	11 411	94.2
Trousdale, TN	47169	6	7 259	18.2	1	3	1 292	1 609	90.9	1 398	93.2
Unicoi, TN	47171	2	17 667	15.0	1	6	2 472	3 316	95.9	2 692	97.6
Union, TN	47173	2	17 808	19.0	1	7	3 006	3 890	95.8	3 345	97.3
Van Buren, TN	47175	9	5 508	17.0	1	2	781	1 203	96.1	1 016	96.5
Warren, TN	47177	7	38 276	17.7	1	11	6 277	7 910	93.9	6 653	95.8
Washington, TN	47179	2	107 198	15.4	2	23	14 903	26 774	91.7	16 544	93.5
Wayne, TN	47181	8	16 842	16.3	1	7	2 623	3 539	95.1	2 826	98.0
Weakley, TN	47183	7	34 895	15.9	1	11	4 885	10 280	95.3	5 595	97.0
White, TN	47185	7	23 102	17.5	1	9	3 830	4 904	94.4	4 215	95.7
Williamson, TN	47187	2	126 638	22.3	2	38	23 505	35 558	77.1	28 159	83.5
Wilson, TN	47189	2	88 809	19.4	1	21	14 357	21 923	80.8	17 549	85.5

[1]County type code is from the Economic Research Service of the USDA. See Notes and Definitions at the end of this section.

Table C-1. School and Student Characteristics by County—*Continued*

County	Characteristics of students, 2000–2001			Staff and students, 2000–2001				Revenues, fiscal 1999			
	Percent with IEP2	Percent eligible for free lunch	Percent minority	Number of teachers	Student/ teacher ratio	Local school non-teaching staff	Central admin. staff	Total revenue ($1,000s)	Percentage of revenue from		
									Federal govt.	State govt.	Local govt.
	10	11	12	13	14	15	16	17	18	19	20
Cheatham, TN	11.5	...	...	...	...	494	3	$32 209	5.9	62.6	31.5
Chester, TN	11.5	...	...	...	...	142	3	11 910	9.0	66.5	24.5
Claiborne, TN	18.8	...	...	...	...	260	12	28 287	13.3	59.8	26.9
Clay, TN	17.1	...	...	...	...	96	3	7 008	12.7	64.6	22.7
Cocke, TN	16.0	...	...	...	...	323	6	28 608	12.6	57.5	29.9
Coffee, TN	18.6	...	...	...	...	521	16	50 770	7.5	45.2	47.3
Crockett, TN	13.4	...	...	...	...	156	5	13 680	10.8	64.9	24.3
Cumberland, TN	14.8	...	...	...	...	358	4	33 455	9.8	56.1	34.2
Davidson, TN	15.1	...	...	...	...	3 277	62	446 326	8.6	30.8	60.5
Decatur, TN	19.3	...	...	...	...	109	5	10 661	10.1	59.6	30.3
De Kalb, TN	21.3	...	...	...	...	182	1	12 581	11.5	63.1	25.5
Dickson, TN	19.7	...	...	...	...	553	3	41 478	7.4	53.1	39.5
Dyer, TN	18.1	...	...	...	...	440	4	39 540	8.6	46.8	44.6
Fayette, TN	14.5	...	...	...	...	307	5	21 733	16.9	57.0	26.1
Fentress, TN	14.5	...	...	...	...	149	3	12 842	13.3	62.3	24.4
Franklin, TN	21.5	...	...	...	...	367	3	31 453	8.2	57.3	34.5
Gibson, TN	14.4	...	...	...	...	449	9	44 713	9.5	55.9	34.6
Giles, TN	15.2	...	...	...	...	270	8	24 737	7.9	55.2	36.9
Grainger, TN	16.6	...	...	...	...	144	9	16 657	10.6	66.9	22.5
Greene, TN	21.7	...	...	...	...	618	10	52 909	9.2	51.4	39.4
Grundy, TN	23.8	...	...	...	...	169	4	13 426	11.7	66.3	21.9
Hamblen, TN	14.8	...	...	...	...	486	15	49 390	8.9	45.6	45.4
Hamilton, TN	17.5	...	...	...	...	2 694	81	238 929	9.5	37.6	52.9
Hancock, TN	17.6	...	...	...	...	98	7	7 237	17.1	67.1	15.8
Hardeman, TN	18.2	...	...	...	...	330	4	24 707	12.0	61.0	27.0
Hardin, TN	15.7	...	...	...	...	263	5	21 219	9.7	57.5	32.8
Hawkins, TN	20.2	...	...	...	...	609	11	40 554	9.5	57.2	33.3
Haywood, TN	14.0	...	...	...	...	296	5	20 905	15.2	55.9	28.9
Henderson, TN	16.0	...	...	...	...	231	7	21 091	8.3	64.0	27.7
Henry, TN	15.2	...	...	...	...	325	10	29 784	8.6	50.0	41.3
Hickman, TN	17.8	...	...	...	...	213	2	18 126	8.5	65.8	25.6
Houston, TN	14.2	...	...	...	...	94	3	7 279	8.7	68.3	23.0
Humphreys, TN	13.0	...	...	...	...	195	3	15 787	9.3	57.3	33.4
Jackson, TN	17.6	...	...	...	...	113	4	9 040	11.3	65.4	23.3
Jefferson, TN	17.5	...	...	...	...	440	9	31 696	9.5	61.0	29.5
Johnson, TN	18.5	...	...	...	...	211	1	14 279	13.8	59.1	27.1
Knox, TN	17.9	...	...	...	...	2 724	96	293 738	5.9	36.9	57.1
Lake, TN	20.1	...	...	...	...	56	1	5 447	13.2	61.2	25.5
Lauderdale, TN	12.8	...	...	...	...	282	3	24 485	12.1	63.7	24.2
Lawrence, TN	17.3	...	...	...	...	464	2	32 977	8.6	58.9	32.6
Lewis, TN	14.8	...	...	...	...	111	1	9 132	11.6	66.5	21.9
Lincoln, TN	12.8	...	...	...	...	368	9	26 701	7.3	58.9	33.8
Loudon, TN	11.7	...	...	...	...	351	7	36 515	7.7	52.8	39.5
McMinn, TN	18.4	...	...	...	...	387	7	40 789	8.7	53.9	37.4
McNairy, TN	12.9	...	...	...	...	258	9	21 226	8.9	61.6	29.4
Macon, TN	12.9	...	...	...	...	226	4	17 647	8.6	66.9	24.5
Madison, TN	22.3	...	...	...	...	876	20	91 811	7.9	36.3	55.7
Marion, TN	15.6	...	...	...	...	235	8	23 419	9.3	59.3	31.4
Marshall, TN	17.3	...	...	...	...	310	6	25 168	6.9	51.3	41.8
Maury, TN	17.6	...	...	...	...	733	11	62 297	7.8	55.7	36.5
Meigs, TN	17.6	...	...	...	...	114	2	9 015	10.9	64.3	24.8
Monroe, TN	12.6	...	...	...	...	344	7	31 596	10.0	58.8	31.2
Montgomery, TN	13.4	...	...	...	...	1 382	10	116 048	6.9	53.2	39.9
Moore, TN	13.5	...	...	...	...	76	1	5 612	5.1	58.0	36.9
Morgan, TN	16.8	...	...	...	...	188	2	16 950	10.5	68.7	20.8
Obion, TN	15.9	...	...	...	...	354	6	29 993	8.6	49.2	42.1
Overton, TN	19.6	...	...	...	...	215	1	16 948	11.2	62.8	26.0
Perry, TN	18.2	...	...	...	...	96	3	6 606	11.1	65.4	23.4
Pickett, TN	13.0	...	...	...	...	53	4	6 590	12.1	48.3	39.6
Polk, TN	7.0	...	...	...	...	158	3	13 083	11.6	58.3	30.1
Putnam, TN	14.8	...	...	...	...	568	17	46 771	8.2	50.1	41.7
Rhea, TN	12.5	...	...	...	...	261	9	22 605	9.9	62.0	28.0
Roane, TN	19.0	...	...	...	...	453	7	43 059	8.6	52.9	38.5
Robertson, TN	17.5	...	...	...	...	685	13	48 162	7.0	58.8	34.2
Rutherford, TN	14.9	...	...	...	...	1 590	53	156 227	4.7	49.7	45.5
Scott, TN	12.2	...	...	...	...	281	7	22 764	12.6	57.6	29.8
Sequatchie, TN	19.7	...	...	...	...	125	4	10 596	11.0	56.6	32.3
Sevier, TN	14.1	...	...	...	...	789	12	68 389	6.5	39.0	54.5
Shelby, TN	13.9	...	...	...	...	7 422	191	953 233	8.6	41.1	50.3
Smith, TN	15.9	...	...	...	...	168	4	14 547	7.5	62.8	29.7
Stewart, TN	16.4	...	...	...	...	188	2	10 772	9.2	72.2	18.6
Sullivan, TN	20.4	...	...	...	...	1 516	24	158 080	6.1	35.4	58.4
Sumner, TN	19.3	...	...	...	...	1 283	16	112 501	5.9	53.2	40.8
Tipton, TN	21.2	...	...	...	...	725	9	51 797	9.7	65.3	25.0
Trousdale, TN	16.9	...	...	...	...	75	3	6 372	8.3	67.3	24.4
Unicoi, TN	21.0	...	...	...	...	141	1	13 320	11.0	61.4	27.6
Union, TN	23.8	...	...	...	...	152	2	16 286	9.6	69.2	21.3
Van Buren, TN	10.5	...	...	...	...	64	2	4 758	10.2	63.8	26.0
Warren, TN	17.7	...	...	...	...	404	6	32 282	9.0	55.1	35.9
Washington, TN	14.5	...	...	...	...	902	9	97 922	6.2	36.7	57.1
Wayne, TN	18.5	...	...	...	...	181	7	14 330	10.9	65.6	23.5
Weakley, TN	13.3	...	...	...	...	288	3	24 428	7.8	59.4	32.8
White, TN	15.1	...	...	...	...	255	4	18 311	9.3	66.2	24.5
Williamson, TN	14.9	...	...	...	...	1 093	33	131 586	3.2	42.5	54.3
Wilson, TN	16.4	...	...	...	...	606	12	72 621	5.0	52.6	42.4

2IEP = Individual Education Program. See Notes and Definitions at the end of this section.
... = Not available.

Table C-1. Population, School, and Student Characteristics by County—*Continued*

County	Current expenditures, fiscal 1999			Resident population 16 to 19 years, 2000				Outcomes, 1999–2000	
	Amount ($1,000s)	Amount per student	Percent for instruction	Total population 16 to 19 years	Percent in Armed Forces	Percent high school graduates	Percent not enrolled, not grads, not Armed Forces, not empl.	Number of graduates	Dropouts grades 9–12 (percent)
	21	22	23	24	25	26	27	28	29
Clay, TN	$6 211	$5 017	65.4	419	2.1	27.9	2.9	92	0.3
Cocke, TN	25 141	4 626	65.6	1 631	0.0	12.4	7.4	246	2.9
Coffee, TN	46 302	5 310	65.2	2 636	0.3	10.5	4.7	516	2.4
Crockett, TN	12 224	4 651	62.4	794	0.0	10.7	7.6	125	3.5
Cumberland, TN	28 849	4 301	65.4	2 124	0.0	18.3	3.2	339	2.4
Davidson, TN	442 847	6 608	65.4	32 378	0.0	10.0	6.6	2 493	6.2
Decatur, TN	8 255	4 467	69.9	572	0.0	16.4	2.8	123	2.4
De Kalb, TN	10 776	4 085	68.0	940	0.0	17.6	5.3	132	4.8
Dickson, TN	36 425	4 628	64.0	2 410	0.0	13.4	4.1	374	7.4
Dyer, TN	36 664	5 331	64.7	1 898	0.0	14.3	7.1	337	2.7
Fayette, TN	19 485	5 113	61.1	1 663	0.0	15.6	4.9	120	10.8
Fentress, TN	11 215	4 764	66.5	818	0.0	10.6	6.5	48	6.3
Franklin, TN	28 212	4 798	71.2	2 411	0.0	10.0	4.8	286	6.3
Gibson, TN	38 758	4 524	64.5	2 453	0.0	16.3	4.6	431	3.3
Giles, TN	22 143	4 678	64.2	1 705	0.0	18.2	2.9	269	3.0
Grainger, TN	14 212	4 434	68.7	985	0.0	13.2	5.2	191	3.2
Greene, TN	47 507	5 011	65.3	2 947	0.5	19.2	3.8	486	2.0
Grundy, TN	11 934	5 019	66.3	802	0.0	12.5	10.8	128	8.9
Hamblen, TN	47 094	5 280	70.0	3 083	0.2	20.1	4.4	451	1.8
Hamilton, TN	232 820	5 505	65.2	16 060	0.0	10.6	5.2	1 788	5.8
Hancock, TN	6 125	5 321	63.8	428	0.0	13.3	4.4	74	2.1
Hardeman, TN	20 656	4 363	67.6	1 500	0.0	9.0	9.4	213	7.3
Hardin, TN	18 925	4 762	64.8	1 275	0.0	14.7	5.8	209	3.5
Hawkins, TN	36 613	4 795	66.7	2 464	0.0	15.7	5.7	304	5.8
Haywood, TN	19 227	5 243	63.9	1 174	0.0	14.1	7.3	371	5.3
Henderson, TN	19 531	4 517	69.4	1 211	0.0	18.8	7.2	224	2.4
Henry, TN	23 126	4 797	63.9	1 608	0.0	15.5	7.0	235	4.0
Hickman, TN	15 793	4 435	65.4	1 114	0.0	20.6	5.2	157	3.1
Houston, TN	6 053	4 444	60.4	366	1.1	21.3	0.5	75	1.1
Humphreys, TN	14 333	4 681	64.5	956	0.0	15.6	2.6	181	2.6
Jackson, TN	7 508	4 663	65.4	604	0.0	12.3	4.6	80	3.3
Jefferson, TN	29 216	4 569	64.4	2 513	0.0	10.3	5.1	317	4.1
Johnson, TN	12 190	5 243	62.8	747	0.0	7.1	9.9	87	3.6
Knox, TN	279 799	5 415	63.2	22 203	0.0	9.8	3.7	2 597	2.7
Lake, TN	4 760	5 324	67.1	429	0.0	6.5	20.3	37	4.2
Lauderdale, TN	22 366	4 752	63.8	1 509	0.0	15.4	8.0	214	4.3
Lawrence, TN	31 222	4 503	65.3	2 081	0.0	10.3	6.6	371	4.4
Lewis, TN	7 839	4 064	64.4	708	0.0	13.3	8.8	104	3.5
Lincoln, TN	23 382	4 401	68.2	1 543	0.0	14.4	5.3	269	2.8
Loudon, TN	31 496	4 254	65.7	1 748	0.0	14.7	3.4	337	5.4
McMinn, TN	37 439	4 756	66.4	2 446	0.0	14.6	6.5	362	4.6
McNairy, TN	18 179	4 389	67.3	1 289	0.0	16.4	3.1	195	2.1
Macon, TN	15 532	4 425	65.3	1 135	0.1	13.4	4.3	154	4.8
Madison, TN	80 206	5 862	67.3	5 751	0.0	10.9	4.3	692	5.4
Marion, TN	21 424	4 678	66.6	1 481	0.0	11.3	7.6	224	2.3
Marshall, TN	23 761	5 034	63.9	1 554	0.0	13.4	6.4	258	3.1
Maury, TN	57 122	4 889	65.4	4 198	0.0	16.7	4.7	473	3.2
Meigs, TN	7 939	4 616	66.7	520	0.0	12.7	7.7	70	2.6
Monroe, TN	28 147	4 506	64.4	2 095	0.0	15.6	7.0	282	3.8
Montgomery, TN	107 370	4 601	62.9	7 580	7.2	19.2	3.0	1 048	3.5
Moore, TN	4 847	4 997	60.7	254	0.0	6.3	5.1	54	4.1
Morgan, TN	15 377	4 695	65.4	1 042	0.0	17.6	3.4	229	3.0
Obion, TN	27 912	5 001	66.8	1 554	0.0	14.7	4.2	273	4.6
Overton, TN	14 068	4 469	65.6	1 142	0.0	14.3	3.1	179	2.3
Perry, TN	6 267	5 356	64.5	350	0.0	13.1	2.6	52	3.0
Pickett, TN	4 572	5 961	56.1	261	0.0	17.2	4.6	57	0.9
Polk, TN	11 217	4 837	67.8	660	0.0	16.1	8.0	88	1.9
Putnam, TN	44 429	4 679	65.3	4 098	0.0	12.6	4.1	497	1.6
Rhea, TN	20 630	4 408	66.1	1 649	0.0	15.3	2.9	191	7.2
Roane, TN	38 585	5 255	65.4	2 421	0.0	15.1	4.7	388	3.5
Robertson, TN	44 402	4 558	70.5	3 183	0.0	20.7	3.7	383	4.5
Rutherford, TN	143 290	4 725	68.7	11 646	0.0	11.3	3.0	1 402	4.1
Scott, TN	20 685	5 186	65.6	1 185	0.0	13.2	6.6	184	4.8
Sequatchie, TN	8 249	4 575	65.3	490	0.0	22.2	1.2	88	5.1
Sevier, TN	58 919	4 947	61.8	3 433	0.0	14.3	4.2	557	2.4
Shelby, TN	859 295	5 375	63.9	51 491	0.1	9.5	7.1	6 342	6.3
Smith, TN	12 002	3 817	67.0	1 003	0.0	14.6	5.3	177	3.6
Stewart, TN	9 342	4 613	60.5	672	0.0	25.9	1.5	120	4.2
Sullivan, TN	144 679	6 246	60.9	7 230	0.1	12.0	5.3	1 144	2.9
Sumner, TN	109 659	4 947	66.4	7 587	0.0	13.4	4.0	1 361	2.8
Tipton, TN	47 148	4 433	67.9	3 060	0.0	15.0	5.8	505	3.3
Trousdale, TN	5 372	4 375	68.6	436	0.0	16.1	5.7	72	3.5
Unicoi, TN	12 510	5 038	64.0	824	1.6	19.2	5.3	122	4.9
Union, TN	14 348	4 661	62.8	1 041	0.0	25.8	4.3	109	1.7
Van Buren, TN	3 823	4 803	59.5	287	0.0	17.8	5.9	40	3.4
Warren, TN	28 756	4 554	65.6	1 748	0.0	18.1	3.1	317	2.1
Washington, TN	76 976	5 158	68.2	5 817	0.1	10.0	3.3	757	3.5
Wayne, TN	12 536	4 667	67.4	758	0.0	12.9	7.5	114	3.7
Weakley, TN	22 634	4 416	66.7	2 710	0.0	10.8	2.8	257	1.8
White, TN	15 474	4 002	67.6	1 244	0.0	16.9	5.3	195	3.6
Williamson, TN	120 801	5 495	64.8	6 880	0.0	7.4	1.5	1 221	1.2
Wilson, TN	67 503	4 676	61.3	4 623	0.0	14.1	2.8	582	5.3

Table C-1. Population, School, and Student Characteristics by County—*Continued*

County	High school graduates, 2000			College enrollment, 2000		College graduates, 2000 (percent)						
	Population 25 years and over	High school diploma or less (percent)	High school diploma or more (percent)	Number	Percent public	Bachelor's degree or more	+/- U.S. percent with bachelor's degree or more	Non-Hispanic White	Black or African American	American Indian and Alaska Native	Asian, Hawaiian, and Pacific Islander	Hispanic or Latino[1]
	30	31	32	33	34	35	36	37	38	39	40	41
Cheatham, TN	23 341	61.7	75.4	989	73.7	15.1	-9.3	15.1	10.0	22.5	32.7	20.4
Chester, TN	9 531	65.3	67.8	1 525	22.3	11.2	-13.2	11.6	7.1	. . .	85.7	0.0
Claiborne, TN	20 200	74.2	60.3	1 005	55.5	8.9	-15.5	9.0	3.8	0.0	68.8	0.0
Clay, TN	5 623	80.2	58.4	245	94.7	6.8	-17.6	6.4	0.0	0.0	72.7	0.0
Cocke, TN	23 070	76.9	61.2	713	84.9	6.2	-18.2	6.2	1.8	0.0	35.5	0.0
Coffee, TN	32 079	59.2	73.7	1 738	82.3	17.5	-6.9	17.3	13.3	19.8	46.7	15.6
Crockett, TN	9 690	72.1	65.1	302	70.9	9.1	-15.3	10.3	2.8	0.0	60.0	3.4
Cumberland, TN	33 595	63.1	72.5	1 259	88.6	13.7	-10.7	13.6	37.7	13.6	25.5	13.4
Davidson, TN	377 734	43.1	81.5	41 321	50.5	30.5	6.1	34.1	20.2	15.9	50.0	14.4
Decatur, TN	8 247	76.3	63.6	280	85.7	7.3	-17.1	7.4	2.7	0.0	50.0	0.0
De Kalb, TN	11 870	72.9	64.6	389	90.5	11.3	-13.1	11.0	21.1	88.9	45.5	6.7
Dickson, TN	28 108	67.1	72.6	1 006	78.7	11.3	-13.1	11.6	4.0	13.5	31.0	15.1
Dyer, TN	24 356	67.3	66.3	1 232	85.1	12.0	-12.4	12.6	5.7	0.0	37.0	10.2
Fayette, TN	18 991	64.3	70.6	775	86.8	12.8	-11.6	15.4	7.5	8.6	33.3	5.1
Fentress, TN	11 275	79.9	57.3	341	92.4	8.3	-16.1	8.3	0.0	. . .	0.0	19.6
Franklin, TN	25 963	61.7	73.8	2 292	36.3	15.3	-9.1	15.8	6.6	3.4	31.8	15.4
Gibson, TN	32 751	68.4	70.9	1 395	85.2	10.1	-14.3	10.8	6.8	0.0	13.0	10.7
Giles, TN	19 829	70.1	72.5	1 011	65.3	10.6	-13.8	11.2	4.1	39.6	51.3	3.4
Grainger, TN	14 210	77.1	60.1	523	83.6	7.8	-16.6	7.8	0.0	47.4	0.0	1.3
Greene, TN	43 752	67.8	69.6	2 118	68.1	12.8	-11.6	12.8	8.7	0.0	40.4	6.9
Grundy, TN	9 441	80.3	55.2	244	81.1	7.1	-17.3	7.1	0.0	10.5	50.0	6.6
Hamblen, TN	39 340	63.7	69.3	1 719	86.0	13.3	-11.1	13.5	8.6	5.8	35.7	9.8
Hamilton, TN	207 180	46.5	80.7	18 563	77.6	23.9	-0.5	26.6	10.6	22.1	48.9	19.4
Hancock, TN	4 617	76.0	55.9	116	94.8	10.2	-14.2	10.1	0.0	0.0	46.2	16.7
Hardeman, TN	18 595	71.3	66.7	607	66.7	7.8	-16.6	9.4	5.1	2.7	16.2	0.0
Hardin, TN	17 644	72.1	66.9	588	80.6	9.8	-14.6	10.0	4.4	0.0	17.0	7.6
Hawkins, TN	37 146	69.3	70.4	1 552	82.5	10.0	-14.4	9.7	13.4	0.0	60.6	19.4
Haywood, TN	12 421	71.8	65.6	451	80.9	11.1	-13.3	15.9	5.7	25.0	52.2	0.0
Henderson, TN	17 140	70.5	69.3	577	78.0	9.3	-15.1	9.3	8.8	15.9	0.0	16.4
Henry, TN	21 791	69.6	70.5	716	90.6	12.1	-12.3	12.5	7.4	0.0	61.1	11.5
Hickman, TN	14 899	73.1	64.3	457	72.0	6.7	-17.7	6.9	2.4	0.0	0.0	5.9
Houston, TN	5 539	71.0	70.1	138	91.3	10.3	-14.1	10.0	2.4	0.0	87.5	19.6
Humphreys, TN	12 270	71.2	72.0	424	80.0	9.3	-15.1	9.1	2.7	4.8	47.8	8.3
Jackson, TN	7 671	77.2	61.6	212	88.2	8.4	-16.0	7.8	0.0	21.9	71.4	0.0
Jefferson, TN	29 455	64.6	71.0	2 593	41.0	12.8	-11.6	12.8	14.5	0.0	50.8	6.3
Johnson, TN	12 755	76.1	58.4	392	92.9	6.9	-17.5	6.9	2.1	0.0	40.7	6.4
Knox, TN	252 530	44.6	82.5	33 984	90.2	29.0	4.6	29.7	16.4	19.4	63.3	30.0
Lake, TN	5 492	79.3	56.0	205	90.7	5.4	-19.0	7.3	0.9	0.0	. . .	0.0
Lauderdale, TN	17 507	75.9	62.3	702	88.3	7.7	-16.7	9.3	4.1	24.4	6.0	18.1
Lawrence, TN	26 145	72.8	65.5	1 058	84.2	8.7	-15.7	8.8	9.7	0.0	13.8	4.8
Lewis, TN	7 466	70.7	69.5	346	83.2	8.5	-15.9	8.3	7.7	46.2	50.0	0.0
Lincoln, TN	21 361	67.1	69.6	943	86.4	11.9	-12.5	12.5	4.3	0.0	0.0	13.2
Loudon, TN	27 899	57.6	75.6	1 118	87.8	17.0	-7.4	17.3	4.1	42.4	31.8	8.4
McMinn, TN	33 110	66.9	69.3	1 433	63.2	10.8	-13.6	10.7	10.4	5.1	69.7	6.5
McNairy, TN	16 787	71.7	68.5	592	80.6	8.8	-15.6	8.8	6.2	0.0	67.9	0.0
Macon, TN	13 331	78.8	60.2	378	96.8	5.6	-18.8	5.6	0.0	0.0	51.9	1.3
Madison, TN	58 038	52.1	78.8	5 342	43.3	21.5	-2.9	25.6	11.4	16.8	50.8	15.1
Marion, TN	18 815	69.8	64.6	763	89.8	9.5	-14.9	9.8	3.7	0.0	16.7	8.3
Marshall, TN	17 615	67.6	73.6	784	87.6	10.6	-13.8	11.2	4.7	0.0	50.0	6.3
Maury, TN	45 288	58.4	77.9	2 338	83.0	13.6	-10.8	14.9	6.0	4.3	65.5	7.1
Meigs, TN	7 405	73.2	63.5	223	79.4	7.0	-17.4	7.1	0.0	0.0	100.0	0.0
Monroe, TN	25 955	70.5	66.7	1 196	64.9	10.1	-14.3	10.1	7.3	8.2	24.5	9.4
Montgomery, TN	79 823	46.1	84.3	8 526	88.2	19.3	-5.1	21.6	10.6	6.5	18.1	16.0
Moore, TN	3 939	63.4	76.6	245	82.9	11.8	-12.6	12.1	6.6	0.0	0.0	. . .
Morgan, TN	13 371	77.1	63.8	556	91.4	6.0	-18.4	6.2	0.0	61.1	0.0	0.0
Obion, TN	22 119	70.3	71.0	980	90.8	10.3	-14.1	10.8	3.7	0.0	60.0	11.5
Overton, TN	13 751	78.9	59.0	661	94.1	8.3	-16.1	8.2	0.0	14.0	57.1	10.1
Perry, TN	5 209	74.6	63.8	146	93.2	7.1	-17.3	7.2	3.8	0.0	. . .	0.0
Pickett, TN	3 466	76.5	62.9	162	95.1	9.1	-15.3	8.7	0.0	37.5	. . .	68.8
Polk, TN	11 113	75.4	62.2	304	82.2	7.5	-16.9	7.5	100.0	0.0	0.0	10.0
Putnam, TN	39 403	59.5	72.6	6 958	95.5	20.2	-4.2	20.1	25.1	6.5	60.1	9.7
Rhea, TN	18 894	68.9	65.3	1 202	85.3	9.1	-15.3	9.3	1.4	8.0	21.9	4.9
Roane, TN	36 455	61.3	74.8	1 573	91.7	14.8	-9.6	14.7	6.9	22.6	53.9	10.2
Robertson, TN	35 252	64.2	74.8	1 227	81.0	11.9	-12.5	12.7	4.4	4.9	17.6	3.3
Rutherford, TN	109 913	50.0	81.8	16 117	92.4	22.9	-1.5	23.5	18.8	17.5	31.1	11.8
Scott, TN	13 480	77.4	60.7	608	91.8	7.5	-16.9	7.5	0.0	14.3	0.0	0.0
Sequatchie, TN	7 610	71.8	66.7	316	87.0	10.2	-14.2	9.6	0.0	. . .	63.8	20.8
Sevier, TN	48 843	61.8	74.6	2 101	84.0	13.5	-10.9	13.4	16.5	24.2	35.5	8.4
Shelby, TN	558 056	45.4	80.8	50 931	77.9	25.3	0.9	35.1	12.8	16.2	48.6	15.2
Smith, TN	11 798	73.0	67.5	391	77.2	9.3	-15.1	9.1	6.9	23.2	58.5	1.2
Stewart, TN	8 486	67.7	74.3	329	90.9	10.2	-14.2	9.9	8.0	0.0	31.4	82.6
Sullivan, TN	108 605	57.2	75.8	4 970	76.9	18.1	-6.3	18.2	13.2	2.4	41.7	12.2
Sumner, TN	85 651	52.4	79.7	4 410	79.6	18.6	-5.8	18.8	11.8	17.3	38.2	13.2
Tipton, TN	31 856	62.1	74.0	1 769	79.4	10.8	-13.6	11.5	6.7	14.0	37.1	6.9
Trousdale, TN	4 852	73.8	61.4	154	76.6	8.9	-15.5	9.5	5.3	36.4	0.0	0.0
Unicoi, TN	12 744	68.3	67.7	495	92.1	10.6	-13.8	10.6	. . .	0.0	100.0	4.1
Union, TN	11 632	79.2	56.3	379	88.7	5.8	-18.6	5.8	0.0	0.0	0.0	0.0
Van Buren, TN	3 738	80.4	62.0	149	98.0	7.8	-16.6	7.9	0.0	0.0	. . .	0.0
Warren, TN	25 691	72.0	67.2	864	95.1	9.1	-15.3	9.4	1.8	0.0	60.4	5.5
Washington, TN	72 947	51.8	77.2	8 627	93.0	22.9	-1.5	22.7	17.2	46.6	71.1	21.3
Wayne, TN	11 733	76.7	61.3	553	88.1	8.0	-16.4	7.5	14.1	0.0	23.1	4.9
Weakley, TN	21 908	65.6	70.3	4 274	94.6	15.3	-9.1	15.0	12.3	0.0	58.8	19.1
White, TN	15 806	74.3	64.8	477	91.2	7.9	-16.5	8.0	2.8	0.0	33.3	0.0
Williamson, TN	81 620	29.8	90.1	4 118	69.3	44.4	20.0	46.2	20.9	26.7	56.5	17.6
Wilson, TN	58 683	53.0	80.9	2 961	71.5	19.6	-4.8	20.1	10.9	38.3	41.1	20.5

[1]Hispanic or Latino persons may be of any race.
. . . = Not available.

Table C-1. Population, School, and Student Characteristics by County—*Continued*

County	State/ County code	County type[1]	Population, 2000		Number of schools and students, 2000–2001			Resident enrollment, 2000			
			Total	Percent 5–17 years	School districts	Schools	Students	Total	Percent public	K–12	Percent public
			1	2	3	4	5	6	7	8	9
TEXAS	48000										
Anderson, TX	48001	6	55 109	15.2	7	24	8 491	11 231	92.4	9 247	93.9
Andrews, TX	48003	6	13 004	24.2	1	7	3 166	3 864	95.8	3 345	98.1
Angelina, TX	48005	5	80 130	20.0	7	40	16 131	21 101	92.6	16 317	94.6
Aransas, TX	48007	6	22 497	18.3	1	6	3 360	5 072	90.5	4 278	93.1
Archer, TX	48009	3	8 854	21.9	4	8	2 012	2 406	93.5	1 914	98.2
Armstrong, TX	48011	8	2 148	20.4	1	2	394	546	95.6	441	98.2
Atascosa, TX	48013	6	38 628	23.5	5	23	8 342	11 272	94.5	9 568	95.8
Austin, TX	48015	6	23 590	20.4	3	12	5 398	5 952	91.2	4 954	94.0
Bailey, TX	48017	7	6 594	22.2	2	7	1 515	1 775	96.3	1 520	98.9
Bandera, TX	48019	8	17 645	19.1	2	7	2 925	4 107	90.7	3 514	94.3
Bastrop, TX	48021	2	57 733	20.4	4	22	11 434	14 375	91.1	12 022	94.0
Baylor, TX	48023	7	4 093	18.5	1	2	726	878	96.8	725	97.5
Bee, TX	48025	6	32 359	17.3	4	14	5 152	7 807	92.1	6 038	92.8
Bell, TX	48027	2	237 974	20.0	12	93	50 018	65 774	88.3	47 400	94.6
Bexar, TX	48029	0	1 392 931	20.6	33	420	262 236	407 384	85.9	293 733	91.0
Blanco, TX	48031	8	8 418	18.2	2	6	1 555	1 847	91.6	1 529	93.5
Borden, TX	48033	9	729	20.9	1	1	149	201	94.5	169	97.6
Bosque, TX	48035	6	17 204	18.7	8	14	3 198	3 846	95.6	3 183	98.2
Bowie, TX	48037	3	89 306	18.4	14	44	16 330	22 200	93.7	17 634	96.3
Brazoria, TX	48039	1	241 767	20.8	8	77	47 681	68 391	88.6	51 867	92.2
Brazos, TX	48041	3	152 415	15.3	4	35	21 056	73 264	94.2	23 599	93.2
Brewster, TX	48043	7	8 866	16.7	4	8	1 471	2 971	95.1	1 557	97.3
Briscoe, TX	48045	9	1 790	20.7	1	1	256	436	94.5	391	95.9
Brooks, TX	48047	7	7 976	23.3	2	5	1 858	2 428	97.9	1 946	99.2
Brown, TX	48049	7	37 674	19.6	7	32	7 229	9 963	85.6	7 533	96.7
Burleson, TX	48051	6	16 470	20.2	3	12	3 213	3 971	91.2	3 357	94.7
Burnet, TX	48053	6	34 147	18.0	2	11	6 417	7 243	91.2	6 182	94.2
Caldwell, TX	48055	2	32 194	21.0	3	18	6 245	8 294	91.5	6 758	96.2
Calhoun, TX	48057	6	20 647	20.7	1	9	4 124	5 469	90.7	4 555	94.2
Callahan, TX	48059	6	12 905	20.7	4	12	2 886	3 130	95.8	2 652	99.0
Cameron, TX	48061	2	335 227	24.3	12	128	83 738	109 790	93.9	85 966	95.3
Camp, TX	48063	6	11 549	19.5	1	4	2 236	3 000	90.2	2 441	93.3
Carson, TX	48065	8	6 516	21.7	3	8	1 277	1 779	95.0	1 445	97.9
Cass, TX	48067	6	30 438	18.9	8	21	6 001	7 138	93.6	5 920	96.3
Castro, TX	48069	7	8 285	24.6	3	6	1 926	2 425	94.6	2 104	99.0
Chambers, TX	48071	1	26 031	22.0	3	17	5 240	7 139	93.6	5 800	96.6
Cherokee, TX	48073	6	46 659	19.3	5	18	7 878	11 603	88.8	9 174	94.7
Childress, TX	48075	7	7 688	16.4	1	3	1 217	1 691	91.4	1 356	98.7
Clay, TX	48077	6	11 006	19.0	5	8	2 032	2 661	95.2	2 156	97.9
Cochran, TX	48079	7	3 730	25.0	2	7	971	1 081	98.4	945	98.7
Coke, TX	48081	8	3 864	20.1	2	8	823	937	97.2	803	98.4
Coleman, TX	48083	6	9 235	17.9	4	16	1 631	2 018	94.3	1 748	98.2
Collin, TX	48085	0	491 675	20.1	14	143	91 203	136 630	82.7	96 997	90.6
Collingsworth, TX	48087	9	3 206	20.5	2	4	711	797	95.6	671	98.7
Colorado, TX	48089	7	20 390	19.6	3	12	3 769	5 113	86.6	4 002	92.2
Comal, TX	48091	1	78 021	19.3	3	29	16 685	19 006	87.4	15 339	90.6
Comanche, TX	48093	7	14 026	19.0	4	9	2 494	3 192	96.0	2 762	98.6
Concho, TX	48095	8	3 966	12.4	2	6	488	740	92.2	544	95.2
Cooke, TX	48097	6	36 363	20.6	8	20	6 145	9 620	88.5	7 465	90.8
Coryell, TX	48099	2	74 978	18.4	5	22	10 503	19 217	90.1	13 801	96.0
Cottle, TX	48101	9	1 904	18.9	1	2	324	399	98.5	365	99.5
Crane, TX	48103	6	3 996	24.2	1	3	1 017	1 256	97.3	1 055	96.8
Crockett, TX	48105	7	4 099	22.2	1	4	835	1 129	98.8	1 026	100.0
Crosby, TX	48107	8	7 072	22.9	3	11	1 593	1 992	96.4	1 671	98.4
Culberson, TX	48109	7	2 975	24.6	1	3	698	888	96.4	741	97.2
Dallam, TX	48111	7	6 222	23.2	2	6	1 703	1 650	93.0	1 394	93.8
Dallas, TX	48113	0	2 218 899	19.7	40	606	410 063	591 553	84.7	441 372	90.6
Dawson, TX	48115	7	14 985	19.3	4	9	3 009	3 867	94.6	3 057	97.6
Deaf Smith, TX	48117	6	18 561	24.3	2	10	4 174	5 645	92.4	4 821	94.0
Delta, TX	48119	8	5 327	20.0	2	5	1 199	1 344	93.8	1 091	94.8
Denton, TX	48121	0	432 976	19.6	11	121	70 495	130 034	87.2	82 738	92.5
De Witt, TX	48123	6	20 013	18.3	6	17	4 548	4 753	92.9	3 894	94.2
Dickens, TX	48125	9	2 762	14.3	2	2	423	545	96.0	443	97.1
Dimmit, TX	48127	7	10 248	24.9	1	7	2 460	3 249	95.8	2 679	97.3
Donley, TX	48129	9	3 828	17.6	2	4	667	1 031	96.9	716	98.0
Duval, TX	48131	7	13 120	22.1	4	12	3 166	3 856	96.7	2 972	97.9
Eastland, TX	48133	7	18 297	17.4	5	12	3 191	4 568	94.5	3 255	97.1
Ector, TX	48135	3	121 123	22.4	1	41	26 831	36 067	94.1	27 951	96.3
Edwards, TX	48137	9	2 162	22.7	2	5	758	598	97.8	510	98.4
Ellis, TX	48139	1	111 360	22.6	11	43	24 825	32 112	88.6	25 302	92.2
El Paso, TX	48141	2	679 622	23.3	13	210	156 466	226 320	91.9	167 423	94.2
Erath, TX	48143	6	33 001	18.1	8	15	5 425	11 111	93.0	5 998	95.4
Falls, TX	48145	6	18 576	21.7	4	11	3 174	5 024	91.7	4 202	94.4
Fannin, TX	48147	6	31 242	17.4	8	21	5 303	7 106	91.7	5 730	93.9
Fayette, TX	48149	7	21 804	17.8	5	13	3 663	4 935	86.7	4 067	89.1
Fisher, TX	48151	9	4 344	18.2	2	5	726	971	97.6	832	99.5
Floyd, TX	48153	7	7 771	23.2	2	8	1 828	2 161	95.5	1 888	99.0
Foard, TX	48155	9	1 622	20.1	1	2	337	402	98.3	336	98.8
Fort Bend, TX	48157	0	354 452	24.3	5	92	74 585	114 365	85.7	87 855	91.4
Franklin, TX	48159	9	9 458	18.6	1	4	1 454	2 230	95.4	1 781	97.2

[1]County type code is from the Economic Research Service of the USDA. See Notes and Definitions at the end of this section.

Table C-1. School and Student Characteristics by County—*Continued*

County	Characteristics of students, 2000–2001			Staff and students, 2000–2001				Revenues, fiscal 1999			
	Percent with IEP[2]	Percent eligible for free lunch	Percent minority	Number of teachers	Student/ teacher ratio	Local school non-teaching staff	Central admin. staff	Total revenue ($1,000s)	Percentage of revenue from		
									Federal govt.	State govt.	Local govt.
	10	11	12	13	14	15	16	17	18	19	20
Anderson, TX	14.5	47.2	33.9	663	12.8	590	44	$53 742	7.6	52.5	39.9
Andrews, TX	21.5	32.6	54.6	242	13.1	245	6	27 205	5.4	9.1	85.5
Angelina, TX	13.9	51.7	40.6	1 174	13.7	1 135	36	99 155	9.0	53.1	37.9
Aransas, TX	13.9	48.1	37.7	267	12.6	275	3	23 920	7.8	31.0	61.2
Archer, TX	8.7	25.0	6.5	156	12.9	117	15	13 211	5.1	58.9	36.0
Armstrong, TX	15.2	31.0	6.1	39	10.1	26	2	2 796	2.5	60.2	37.3
Atascosa, TX	15.5	61.4	67.8	629	13.3	657	30	56 754	9.5	64.7	25.8
Austin, TX	14.2	35.1	38.7	392	13.8	330	14	32 713	5.2	45.8	49.0
Bailey, TX	14.6	64.4	67.2	137	11.1	113	5	11 837	9.2	57.6	33.2
Bandera, TX	17.1	37.8	18.7	241	12.1	214	9	18 016	4.2	47.1	48.8
Bastrop, TX	14.0	43.3	42.5	856	13.4	786	38	71 946	6.8	54.3	39.0
Baylor, TX	15.6	50.4	21.5	63	11.5	42	1	5 861	5.5	63.0	31.5
Bee, TX	12.6	62.2	70.9	377	13.7	441	10	35 561	10.6	64.9	24.4
Bell, TX	13.7	46.5	52.9	3 454	14.5	3 583	140	325 951	15.9	54.2	29.9
Bexar, TX	14.8	46.6	73.7	17 382	15.1	18 229	366	1 747 464	10.5	48.6	40.9
Blanco, TX	17.0	33.2	25.2	140	11.1	103	6	11 701	3.2	51.4	45.3
Borden, TX	6.7	35.6	23.5	21	7.1	26	1	4 702	3.1	4.2	92.7
Bosque, TX	15.6	44.5	23.3	280	11.4	221	33	23 994	7.0	58.8	34.3
Bowie, TX	14.6	45.0	34.6	1 196	13.7	969	43	107 955	8.5	49.7	41.8
Brazoria, TX	12.5	34.5	40.7	3 056	15.6	2 661	44	294 930	5.0	34.3	60.7
Brazos, TX	13.1	45.9	50.1	1 460	14.4	1 111	26	144 276	7.8	35.7	56.5
Brewster, TX	8.8	63.4	63.1	141	10.4	91	14	10 796	9.6	54.0	36.3
Briscoe, TX	14.8	52.7	37.9	28	9.1	20	2	2 118	6.9	62.0	31.1
Brooks, TX	12.8	73.2	95.5	138	13.5	142	4	12 401	11.8	40.3	47.9
Brown, TX	14.0	46.6	29.1	546	13.2	512	15	46 853	7.8	57.7	34.4
Burleson, TX	12.5	47.1	40.8	258	12.5	237	27	23 925	7.4	44.8	47.7
Burnet, TX	13.0	40.2	25.7	453	14.2	439	8	40 898	5.9	35.4	58.7
Caldwell, TX	15.6	52.4	57.6	424	14.7	433	7	39 898	9.3	61.3	29.4
Calhoun, TX	11.7	48.3	59.2	276	14.9	289	9	43 408	5.1	7.1	87.8
Callahan, TX	17.5	41.9	9.3	250	11.5	205	5	20 123	5.5	67.5	27.0
Cameron, TX	11.5	42.2	94.1	5 577	15.0	7 379	100	558 384	12.9	67.8	19.3
Camp, TX	15.9	57.0	45.5	170	13.2	144	3	13 636	11.7	51.9	36.4
Carson, TX	15.3	25.8	9.7	120	10.6	94	6	10 591	2.5	15.2	82.3
Cass, TX	18.7	48.9	26.5	513	11.7	419	16	41 688	8.3	46.4	45.3
Castro, TX	9.9	66.5	69.2	181	10.6	158	6	14 713	12.2	52.2	35.5
Chambers, TX	11.9	29.8	24.6	366	14.3	322	9	51 172	2.7	19.0	78.4
Cherokee, TX	13.6	58.0	43.8	599	13.2	509	22	51 160	10.4	59.6	30.0
Childress, TX	16.9	44.9	38.9	94	12.9	120	2	9 567	9.4	60.7	29.9
Clay, TX	14.6	31.0	6.5	177	11.5	136	8	13 995	4.3	62.1	33.5
Cochran, TX	9.7	67.5	58.6	107	9.1	90	4	11 597	7.4	34.2	58.4
Coke, TX	16.2	54.3	37.5	79	10.4	59	2	6 784	5.4	50.1	44.5
Coleman, TX	16.2	52.5	25.6	157	10.4	141	6	13 789	7.6	68.0	24.4
Collin, TX	11.3	12.1	26.3	6 374	14.3	4 419	172	593 562	2.4	19.6	77.9
Collingsworth, TX	16.9	58.5	42.8	73	9.7	58	3	5 989	7.0	71.0	22.0
Colorado, TX	16.6	48.4	48.2	293	12.9	229	13	25 907	8.4	43.7	47.9
Comal, TX	14.2	28.2	30.9	1 141	14.6	1 242	18	101 517	4.8	30.6	64.6
Comanche, TX	15.2	54.6	34.2	196	12.7	152	12	15 955	9.1	61.7	29.2
Concho, TX	16.0	54.0	41.6	50	9.8	45	2	4 635	5.5	51.0	43.5
Cooke, TX	12.9	37.3	20.1	463	13.3	357	21	38 577	6.3	52.2	41.5
Coryell, TX	13.1	34.5	35.0	767	13.7	825	18	73 726	20.9	56.2	22.9
Cottle, TX	17.3	67.0	49.7	35	9.3	29	1	3 798	7.1	61.3	31.6
Crane, TX	21.3	28.7	56.9	91	11.2	67	5	13 002	3.2	5.1	91.6
Crockett, TX	8.0	51.3	64.8	80	10.4	74	3	12 158	4.3	5.7	90.0
Crosby, TX	19.8	72.0	69.5	148	10.8	138	29	13 580	11.8	63.3	24.9
Culberson, TX	11.2	77.1	81.5	63	11.1	50	2	5 835	9.3	26.8	63.9
Dallam, TX	14.2	50.5	33.6	143	11.9	135	5	11 692	10.0	41.9	48.1
Dallas, TX	10.2	50.6	70.2	26 681	15.4	21 059	473	2 530 156	6.9	26.3	66.8
Dawson, TX	11.4	59.6	67.7	229	13.1	239	11	22 389	9.8	40.1	50.2
Deaf Smith, TX	13.3	70.0	76.5	307	13.6	298	8	27 139	13.5	54.8	31.7
Delta, TX	18.3	48.9	25.9	95	12.6	98	2	8 382	8.9	68.7	22.4
Denton, TX	12.9	16.9	24.4	5 050	14.0	3 682	150	418 316	3.9	29.2	66.9
De Witt, TX	13.0	47.5	46.5	369	12.3	394	13	32 677	8.8	59.4	31.8
Dickens, TX	18.7	. . .	34.3	47	9.0	43	3	4 604	6.3	61.4	32.3
Dimmit, TX	10.2	59.1	91.4	185	13.3	233	6	18 845	15.1	65.5	19.4
Donley, TX	16.9	48.3	21.1	71	9.4	50	2	5 474	5.1	64.6	30.3
Duval, TX	10.1	76.5	93.1	254	12.5	268	6	23 989	11.1	56.8	32.1
Eastland, TX	17.8	52.1	19.7	265	12.0	230	39	21 923	9.7	63.0	27.2
Ector, TX	11.0	57.0	61.3	1 762	15.2	1 520	79	156 599	8.9	52.0	39.1
Edwards, TX	15.7	70.7	54.7	77	9.8	87	4	6 746	8.1	38.8	53.1
Ellis, TX	14.8	33.1	35.1	1 683	14.8	1 626	46	143 195	5.0	51.8	43.2
El Paso, TX	10.0	62.9	89.7	10 022	15.6	9 671	158	981 001	13.0	59.3	27.7
Erath, TX	13.4	39.2	28.0	398	13.6	337	19	31 927	7.9	47.8	44.3
Falls, TX	16.4	60.3	59.8	253	12.5	239	26	22 339	11.8	61.1	27.2
Fannin, TX	15.3	37.9	13.1	417	12.7	366	16	34 783	8.4	60.9	30.7
Fayette, TX	11.7	37.8	33.2	285	12.9	251	8	27 313	4.6	28.0	67.4
Fisher, TX	18.9	53.6	39.4	74	9.8	60	2	6 385	5.8	67.1	27.1
Floyd, TX	11.7	59.3	67.0	158	11.6	142	7	13 624	11.1	62.0	26.9
Foard, TX	19.6	70.0	35.0	34	9.9	33	1	2 815	5.9	64.0	30.1
Fort Bend, TX	10.6	26.4	62.1	4 582	16.3	4 223	86	427 300	4.0	41.5	54.5
Franklin, TX	14.3	32.6	20.1	114	12.8	87	2	9 023	6.1	28.1	65.8

[2]IEP = Individual Education Program. See Notes and Definitions at the end of this section.

Table C-1. Population, School, and Student Characteristics by County—*Continued*

County	Current expenditures, fiscal 1999			Resident population 16 to 19 years, 2000				Outcomes, 1999–2000	
	Amount ($1,000s)	Amount per student	Percent for instruction	Total population 16 to 19 years	Percent in Armed Forces	Percent high school graduates	Percent not enrolled, not grads, not Armed Forces, not empl.	Number of graduates	Dropouts grades 9–12 (percent)
	21	22	23	24	25	26	27	28	29
TEXAS									
Anderson, TX	$47 545	$5 391	63.1	2 368	0.0	18.1	7.3	484	4.2
Andrews, TX	24 021	6 926	61.9	1 054	0.0	8.8	8.9	226	1.8
Angelina, TX	84 956	5 317	61.8	4 890	0.0	11.5	5.4	975	4.1
Aransas, TX	21 863	6 304	59.9	1 352	0.4	16.3	4.7	251	2.7
Archer, TX	12 266	6 004	65.8	542	0.0	12.5	1.8	134	1.8
Armstrong, TX	2 612	6 749	68.0	120	0.0	9.2	5.0	30	1.5
Atascosa, TX	49 559	6 040	60.9	2 596	0.0	13.4	5.3	406	4.2
Austin, TX	28 391	5 431	63.8	1 567	0.0	9.3	2.9	349	2.9
Bailey, TX	10 715	7 182	61.8	412	0.5	6.6	2.2	106	3.8
Bandera, TX	16 211	5 800	62.8	907	0.0	6.5	2.0	174	4.3
Bastrop, TX	60 573	5 795	61.1	3 217	0.0	16.1	6.6	550	4.9
Baylor, TX	4 829	6 430	68.2	182	0.0	8.8	8.8	38	1.4
Bee, TX	31 949	5 862	61.5	2 204	0.0	6.9	12.6	344	5.5
Bell, TX	264 737	5 428	60.3	14 633	8.5	21.9	5.4	2 583	4.3
Bexar, TX	1 517 384	5 986	60.4	87 106	4.4	14.3	6.8	13 546	6.6
Blanco, TX	10 023	6 483	66.5	427	0.0	8.9	7.3	94	1.6
Borden, TX	2 793	13 493	52.6	48	0.0	0.0	8.3	23	5.9
Bosque, TX	19 472	6 164	62.7	938	0.0	10.8	4.4	223	3.8
Bowie, TX	86 783	5 254	64.5	4 819	0.0	13.7	4.8	1 020	4.1
Brazoria, TX	253 075	5 339	60.1	13 901	0.1	10.6	6.3	2 595	3.8
Brazos, TX	120 323	5 769	61.8	17 536	0.1	5.0	1.8	1 151	5.4
Brewster, TX	10 958	6 971	63.8	601	0.0	9.2	2.5	96	2.8
Briscoe, TX	1 968	7 182	63.4	110	0.0	5.5	6.4	16	. . .
Brooks, TX	11 853	6 212	60.3	597	0.0	9.2	16.2	101	9.2
Brown, TX	41 536	5 759	64.2	2 771	0.0	12.6	7.1	477	5.1
Burleson, TX	19 931	6 155	61.6	980	0.0	12.0	5.1	196	5.3
Burnet, TX	34 537	5 536	62.0	1 721	0.0	16.8	4.6	359	4.1
Caldwell, TX	32 294	5 330	61.0	1 963	0.0	16.1	7.5	353	5.4
Calhoun, TX	24 426	5 649	60.8	1 206	0.0	12.7	6.6	219	7.5
Callahan, TX	17 785	5 940	66.3	731	0.0	11.9	3.4	186	2.2
Cameron, TX	485 394	5 909	60.9	23 139	0.1	8.2	8.1	4 300	5.1
Camp, TX	12 283	5 897	68.5	723	0.0	16.5	3.7	111	2.6
Carson, TX	9 805	6 934	63.1	394	0.0	13.5	1.0	103	. . .
Cass, TX	36 476	5 889	64.8	1 700	0.0	14.1	6.1	442	1.5
Castro, TX	13 846	6 562	63.7	561	0.0	8.9	6.2	121	3.7
Chambers, TX	32 546	6 426	61.9	1 623	0.0	9.1	5.5	296	2.5
Cherokee, TX	43 464	5 500	61.3	2 826	0.0	14.6	6.0	478	3.7
Childress, TX	7 559	6 136	68.6	424	0.0	9.4	18.2	78	3.6
Clay, TX	12 572	6 187	65.0	607	0.0	9.1	7.4	138	2.4
Cochran, TX	9 749	8 529	60.6	310	0.0	9.7	3.5	69	3.6
Coke, TX	6 069	8 383	66.2	411	0.0	5.4	21.7	56	21.6
Coleman, TX	12 318	7 055	61.6	473	0.0	14.0	2.3	103	3.7
Collin, TX	454 618	5 638	63.3	23 575	0.0	10.8	3.5	4 470	1.4
Collingsworth, TX	5 008	6 607	67.2	203	0.0	10.3	3.9	53	3.1
Colorado, TX	21 887	5 725	63.3	1 417	0.0	10.3	4.0	250	2.5
Comal, TX	87 086	5 422	62.1	4 523	0.0	15.8	5.1	1 004	4.6
Comanche, TX	13 723	5 392	66.6	814	0.0	5.7	4.5	154	3.9
Concho, TX	4 012	7 443	62.3	210	0.0	7.1	18.1	46	2.7
Cooke, TX	34 968	5 753	65.6	2 350	0.1	10.3	5.8	336	4.1
Coryell, TX	58 923	5 649	63.0	4 827	31.6	41.0	4.3	587	4.6
Cottle, TX	3 230	8 303	67.5	92	0.0	6.5	5.4	18	3.6
Crane, TX	9 194	8 351	61.5	341	0.0	10.3	6.5	75	3.2
Crockett, TX	7 594	7 773	57.5	203	0.0	0.0	0.0	91	1.7
Crosby, TX	12 687	7 831	62.3	456	0.0	11.2	6.8	101	4.9
Culberson, TX	5 357	6 738	62.4	257	0.0	9.3	5.1	52	6.1
Dallam, TX	10 860	6 192	62.1	397	0.0	14.6	7.8	110	2.5
Dallas, TX	2 106 562	5 426	59.4	126 851	0.0	10.6	9.6	18 194	4.7
Dawson, TX	18 770	5 831	63.4	880	0.0	11.8	9.5	194	3.9
Deaf Smith, TX	29 107	6 554	65.5	1 254	0.0	16.8	6.4	259	3.7
Delta, TX	7 009	5 851	60.3	317	0.0	12.0	7.9	76	4.6
Denton, TX	351 809	5 524	62.4	24 095	0.1	10.6	3.0	3 439	2.6
De Witt, TX	29 683	6 364	65.8	1 062	0.0	9.8	9.2	314	3.3
Dickens, TX	4 229	9 154	63.3	120	0.0	8.3	10.8	28	3.3
Dimmit, TX	16 889	6 451	60.9	637	0.0	7.5	6.8	145	7.0
Donley, TX	5 072	7 383	67.8	300	0.0	6.3	0.7	43	2.2
Duval, TX	19 953	6 113	57.8	867	0.0	11.3	4.0	194	3.7
Eastland, TX	20 190	6 129	66.9	1 262	0.0	5.5	5.9	220	2.4
Ector, TX	141 994	5 002	58.6	8 435	0.1	10.4	5.9	1 479	8.0
Edwards, TX	6 286	7 666	64.0	120	0.0	1.7	0.0	58	2.5
Ellis, TX	122 003	5 233	62.9	7 342	0.0	11.7	4.2	1 408	3.1
El Paso, TX	862 966	5 626	60.0	45 857	1.3	9.9	6.6	8 457	5.6
Erath, TX	29 326	5 235	65.8	2 435	0.0	7.2	3.8	297	1.8
Falls, TX	19 292	6 012	62.5	1 445	0.1	11.7	12.5	189	4.2
Fannin, TX	31 145	5 930	64.0	1 694	0.0	17.0	9.4	311	2.8
Fayette, TX	20 797	5 574	63.6	1 245	0.0	7.9	5.4	241	2.9
Fisher, TX	5 516	7 567	63.6	269	0.0	13.0	1.9	62	2.2
Floyd, TX	13 202	6 725	63.4	509	0.0	3.7	6.3	111	3.0
Foard, TX	2 547	7 340	61.6	90	0.0	4.4	15.3	11	2.0
Fort Bend, TX	374 439	5 283	60.0	22 536	0.0	8.0	4.6	4 431	3.3
Franklin, TX	7 992	5 176	67.5	545	0.0	10.6	5.0	102	5.2

. . . = Not available.

Table C-1. Population, School, and Student Characteristics by County—*Continued*

County	Population 25 years and over	High school diploma or less (percent)	High school diploma or more (percent)	College enrollment, 2000 Number	College enrollment, 2000 Percent public	Bachelor's degree or more	+/- U.S. percent with bachelor's degree or more	Non-Hispanic White	Black or African American	American Indian and Alaska Native	Asian, Hawaiian, and Pacific Islander	Hispanic or Latino[1]
	30	31	32	33	34	35	36	37	38	39	40	41
TEXAS												
Anderson, TX	38 506	63.8	64.4	1 438	88.0	11.1	-13.3	14.9	4.3	17.9	27.3	2.3
Andrews, TX	7 815	64.6	68.0	334	83.8	12.4	-12.0	16.9	6.3	16.3	0.0	3.8
Angelina, TX	50 290	58.1	71.2	3 308	92.4	14.7	-9.7	17.5	5.9	7.3	26.0	5.0
Aransas, TX	15 728	54.5	74.6	498	86.1	16.7	-7.7	19.7	1.8	1.1	7.1	4.9
Archer, TX	5 729	54.9	81.1	316	90.2	15.9	-8.5	15.9	0.0	32.1	85.7	7.9
Armstrong, TX	1 458	45.4	82.4	81	95.1	20.5	-3.9	20.9	...	50.0	...	0.0
Atascosa, TX	22 751	66.8	65.2	1 183	89.9	10.5	-13.9	17.3	0.0	19.2	28.1	4.3
Austin, TX	15 280	57.8	74.5	647	91.5	17.3	-7.1	21.0	3.5	20.0	72.0	3.0
Bailey, TX	3 960	70.0	61.5	139	92.1	9.3	-15.1	14.5	0.0	0.0	...	1.3
Bandera, TX	12 287	47.1	84.8	423	71.4	19.4	-5.0	20.8	0.0	14.7	8.3	9.0
Bastrop, TX	37 249	54.8	76.9	1 514	83.0	17.0	-7.4	21.0	6.6	4.4	14.6	6.5
Baylor, TX	2 939	62.6	70.1	99	89.9	12.1	-12.3	13.4	0.0	15.8	0.0	2.8
Bee, TX	20 568	61.1	73.7	1 373	91.5	12.2	-12.2	20.4	3.7	0.0	25.9	7.5
Bell, TX	137 430	42.8	84.7	13 867	75.4	19.8	-4.6	24.5	11.1	17.0	22.3	9.5
Bexar, TX	849 004	47.4	76.9	88 075	77.0	22.7	-1.7	36.6	17.8	13.3	38.0	10.8
Blanco, TX	5 895	49.9	80.6	196	75.5	22.2	-2.2	24.8	23.2	26.2	0.0	3.0
Borden, TX	490	49.0	83.9	29	75.9	21.4	-3.0	23.2	...	0.0	100.0	0.0
Bosque, TX	11 910	56.2	75.9	456	89.5	15.4	-9.0	16.7	5.1	9.0	64.3	2.5
Bowie, TX	58 767	54.6	77.3	3 226	91.1	16.1	-8.3	19.1	7.5	18.2	48.1	3.7
Brazoria, TX	152 244	47.7	79.5	11 894	87.4	19.6	-4.8	22.3	17.2	11.8	51.2	7.6
Brazos, TX	70 708	38.8	81.3	47 039	97.8	37.0	12.6	43.7	10.4	24.4	80.6	14.9
Brewster, TX	5 519	42.5	78.6	1 330	95.6	27.7	3.3	36.9	44.0	0.0	38.1	12.7
Briscoe, TX	1 181	55.6	74.8	26	84.6	17.5	-6.9	20.9	6.7	...	...	1.1
Brooks, TX	4 717	73.5	49.9	280	96.8	6.8	-17.6	9.7	0.0	21.8	...	6.3
Brown, TX	24 016	60.4	74.6	1 805	41.5	15.0	-9.4	16.7	10.1	11.9	35.3	2.6
Burleson, TX	10 787	66.4	71.1	413	85.0	13.2	-11.2	16.4	4.5	19.5	85.7	2.7
Burnet, TX	23 436	54.7	77.8	599	86.5	17.4	-7.0	19.2	2.4	10.8	12.9	3.5
Caldwell, TX	20 337	63.5	71.3	948	82.3	13.3	-11.1	19.9	3.9	7.3	35.2	4.7
Calhoun, TX	13 012	64.1	69.0	541	80.6	12.1	-12.3	15.0	3.0	0.0	65.0	3.1
Callahan, TX	8 658	58.8	79.3	308	78.9	12.3	-12.1	12.8	7.4	4.2	62.5	1.1
Cameron, TX	187 064	64.9	55.2	16 722	91.1	13.4	-11.0	28.9	28.0	10.4	56.6	8.9
Camp, TX	7 474	63.1	69.5	333	93.4	12.2	-12.2	15.2	5.4	0.0	50.9	1.1
Carson, TX	4 305	48.4	82.6	264	85.6	15.5	-8.9	16.1	0.0	0.0	50.0	5.9
Cass, TX	20 546	63.2	75.0	817	85.3	12.0	-12.4	13.6	4.8	8.5	4.3	6.0
Castro, TX	4 871	64.3	65.4	140	90.0	14.7	-9.7	24.7	7.7	0.0	0.0	2.4
Chambers, TX	16 348	55.5	76.9	942	91.8	12.1	-12.3	13.0	8.3	18.0	21.4	6.1
Cherokee, TX	30 008	63.6	68.4	1 712	64.1	11.4	-13.0	13.4	5.7	16.7	43.5	3.3
Childress, TX	5 173	66.0	65.0	237	61.6	8.6	-15.8	10.9	6.0	0.0	50.0	0.0
Clay, TX	7 549	59.2	80.4	372	91.1	13.9	-10.5	14.1	0.0	0.0	0.0	8.0
Cochran, TX	2 236	65.6	62.7	85	94.1	10.2	-14.2	15.1	9.5	0.0	...	2.5
Coke, TX	2 620	59.8	74.2	80	87.5	14.7	-9.7	15.7	0.0	40.0	100.0	5.4
Coleman, TX	6 373	67.2	71.0	180	71.1	11.7	-12.7	12.7	2.3	19.6	0.0	4.1
Collin, TX	315 665	23.2	91.8	25 951	82.3	47.3	22.9	48.2	42.9	28.7	72.0	22.4
Collingsworth, TX	2 159	54.2	71.3	81	95.1	15.3	-9.1	18.0	9.7	0.0	100.0	1.9
Colorado, TX	13 383	64.3	69.1	821	72.5	14.4	-10.0	18.6	5.0	38.9	0.0	3.1
Comal, TX	52 549	44.6	83.9	2 441	86.6	26.2	1.8	30.0	26.3	20.7	46.6	9.0
Comanche, TX	9 411	64.4	70.2	291	80.1	13.0	-11.4	14.8	0.0	0.0	9.1	2.6
Concho, TX	2 921	67.9	59.3	144	86.1	14.1	-10.3	19.8	15.2	50.0	0.0	5.9
Cooke, TX	23 148	52.3	79.2	1 538	91.1	15.7	-8.7	16.6	10.8	11.6	57.5	3.5
Coryell, TX	41 764	51.0	81.1	4 134	77.0	12.4	-12.0	14.8	7.4	7.6	17.8	6.6
Cottle, TX	1 342	64.5	66.1	17	82.4	15.3	-9.1	19.0	0.0	...	...	2.1
Crane, TX	2 394	64.2	68.7	127	100.0	12.8	-11.6	17.6	0.0	0.0	89.5	2.1
Crockett, TX	2 659	66.8	62.1	42	85.7	10.4	-14.0	19.4	0.0	31.8	0.0	1.9
Crosby, TX	4 299	68.8	61.8	184	81.0	10.5	-13.9	17.8	2.9	0.0	0.0	1.4
Culberson, TX	1 781	71.5	56.1	111	90.1	13.9	-10.5	31.0	66.7	0.0	80.0	4.5
Dallam, TX	3 703	67.1	65.0	138	94.2	9.6	-14.8	12.7	0.0	17.3	...	0.1
Dallas, TX	1 365 848	46.7	75.0	108 942	72.2	27.0	2.6	38.0	17.0	16.2	45.2	7.0
Dawson, TX	9 949	69.6	65.2	579	85.3	10.5	-13.9	20.2	1.3	54.5	15.4	1.4
Deaf Smith, TX	10 539	65.6	60.9	553	85.2	11.8	-12.6	20.7	2.4	0.0	21.8	2.2
Delta, TX	3 618	60.6	75.5	186	86.0	13.9	-10.5	15.1	3.1	14.8	0.0	0.0
Denton, TX	265 220	30.5	89.4	37 656	88.8	36.6	12.2	38.7	33.8	24.1	47.1	17.9
De Witt, TX	13 969	65.0	67.9	578	92.6	11.8	-12.6	17.1	2.3	0.0	53.8	2.4
Dickens, TX	1 940	67.9	70.6	63	88.9	8.4	-16.0	10.8	0.0	44.4	25.0	0.8
Dimmit, TX	5 982	72.0	54.3	419	89.7	10.1	-14.3	19.1	27.2	42.1	45.5	7.5
Donley, TX	2 586	48.3	78.2	282	93.6	15.8	-8.6	16.6	0.0	6.4	0.0	7.2
Duval, TX	8 042	70.0	59.7	583	91.3	8.9	-15.5	13.7	0.0	0.0	0.0	8.3
Eastland, TX	12 171	60.9	72.6	1 000	90.8	12.7	-11.7	13.6	18.4	4.5	100.0	2.4
Ector, TX	71 756	58.8	68.0	5 731	93.0	12.0	-12.4	16.2	7.7	8.3	56.4	4.5
Edwards, TX	1 418	62.3	67.1	44	93.2	17.3	-7.1	26.1	0.0	0.0	0.0	3.5
Ellis, TX	67 470	53.0	77.8	4 799	81.8	17.1	-7.3	19.8	11.6	16.0	62.9	4.2
El Paso, TX	391 540	56.8	65.8	46 798	87.3	16.6	-7.8	35.1	21.1	13.6	40.8	10.6
Erath, TX	19 350	49.5	77.1	4 587	94.7	25.0	0.6	27.4	50.9	0.0	50.6	4.2
Falls, TX	12 013	67.9	66.2	539	82.6	9.6	-14.8	12.8	5.3	0.0	37.5	1.8
Fannin, TX	21 120	63.2	72.5	945	85.1	12.6	-11.8	13.9	3.0	10.0	31.7	3.2
Fayette, TX	15 183	64.5	71.3	585	86.8	14.6	-9.8	16.7	1.5	37.9	77.3	2.8
Fisher, TX	3 036	65.1	73.3	77	88.3	12.4	-12.0	15.1	0.0	0.0	100.0	0.8
Floyd, TX	4 773	67.5	63.5	122	72.1	12.3	-12.1	18.9	0.0	0.0	0.0	1.5
Foard, TX	1 116	65.1	70.0	40	92.5	10.5	-13.9	12.1	8.3	0.0	0.0	2.6
Fort Bend, TX	214 461	35.1	84.3	18 037	81.3	36.9	12.5	44.1	30.0	18.0	56.1	11.9
Franklin, TX	6 421	58.2	77.4	308	93.8	16.2	-8.2	17.5	5.0	4.5	16.7	2.1

[1]Hispanic or Latino persons may be of any race.
. . . = Not available.

Table C-1. Population, School, and Student Characteristics by County—*Continued*

County	State/ County code	County type[1]	Population, 2000		Number of schools and students, 2000–2001			Resident enrollment, 2000			
			Total	Percent 5–17 years	School districts	Schools	Students	Total	Percent public	K–12	Percent public
			1	2	3	4	5	6	7	8	9
Freestone, TX	48161	7	17 867	18.1	4	12	3 184	4 486	92.0	3 443	93.7
Frio, TX	48163	7	16 252	21.0	2	10	3 151	4 659	96.2	3 752	97.7
Gaines, TX	48165	7	14 467	26.7	3	10	2 984	4 369	88.8	3 831	89.2
Galveston, TX	48167	0	250 158	19.7	11	101	66 294	69 639	89.0	50 267	92.4
Garza, TX	48169	6	4 872	21.6	2	5	1 192	1 384	94.4	1 104	96.9
Gillespie, TX	48171	7	20 814	16.5	3	10	3 198	4 229	84.5	3 474	88.7
Glasscock, TX	48173	8	1 406	25.5	1	2	345	458	98.3	389	100.0
Goliad, TX	48175	8	6 928	20.1	1	3	1 401	1 652	92.4	1 429	93.9
Gonzales, TX	48177	6	18 628	21.0	3	12	3 897	4 671	95.0	3 989	96.7
Gray, TX	48179	7	22 744	18.2	4	10	3 976	5 609	91.4	4 460	94.3
Grayson, TX	48181	3	110 595	18.8	13	55	19 823	27 885	88.0	20 779	95.4
Gregg, TX	48183	3	111 379	19.7	8	51	23 298	29 686	88.2	22 659	94.4
Grimes, TX	48185	6	23 552	18.6	4	13	4 297	5 846	94.2	4 727	97.6
Guadalupe, TX	48187	1	89 023	21.2	4	33	16 346	25 322	85.7	19 460	92.8
Hale, TX	48189	4	36 602	21.9	5	22	8 045	10 891	88.6	8 463	96.1
Hall, TX	48191	9	3 782	19.9	2	5	840	880	94.9	767	97.8
Hamilton, TX	48193	6	8 229	18.2	2	6	1 582	1 863	95.4	1 544	98.8
Hansford, TX	48195	7	5 369	22.5	3	7	1 298	1 408	95.6	1 193	98.7
Hardeman, TX	48197	7	4 724	18.8	2	5	873	1 135	97.7	928	100.0
Hardin, TX	48199	2	48 073	20.8	5	25	10 679	12 456	93.2	10 212	96.6
Harris, TX	48201	0	3 400 578	20.7	59	838	661 815	973 905	87.8	722 117	92.6
Harrison, TX	48203	3	62 110	20.4	6	31	12 655	17 187	83.7	12 987	94.2
Hartley, TX	48205	7	5 537	15.1	2	2	320	1 190	79.4	942	84.3
Haskell, TX	48207	7	6 093	18.8	4	5	1 091	1 375	97.8	1 172	98.6
Hays, TX	48209	2	97 589	18.2	5	35	19 525	35 718	92.5	17 740	92.6
Hemphill, TX	48211	9	3 351	22.3	1	5	774	908	97.2	784	100.0
Henderson, TX	48213	1	73 277	17.9	8	29	10 081	16 770	92.0	13 310	94.5
Hidalgo, TX	48215	2	569 463	25.1	21	217	144 376	188 181	96.2	148 929	97.5
Hill, TX	48217	6	32 321	19.0	12	25	6 075	7 820	93.1	6 183	96.5
Hockley, TX	48219	6	22 716	21.9	6	21	4 921	6 942	96.0	5 043	97.3
Hood, TX	48221	1	41 100	17.8	3	15	7 121	9 233	90.7	7 446	94.4
Hopkins, TX	48223	6	31 960	19.6	7	17	6 123	7 986	92.9	6 452	95.6
Houston, TX	48225	7	23 185	18.0	5	15	3 768	5 478	87.6	4 723	88.0
Howard, TX	48227	5	33 627	18.3	3	15	5 617	8 543	93.7	6 459	96.6
Hudspeth, TX	48229	8	3 344	25.5	3	3	871	1 000	96.0	857	97.9
Hunt, TX	48231	1	76 596	19.8	10	43	14 104	21 088	91.0	15 431	93.6
Hutchinson, TX	48233	6	23 857	20.6	4	15	4 790	6 379	93.5	4 939	95.8
Irion, TX	48235	8	1 771	21.0	1	3	359	474	94.5	392	96.7
Jack, TX	48237	6	8 763	17.7	3	7	1 640	2 103	89.2	1 705	93.6
Jackson, TX	48239	6	14 391	20.3	3	12	3 300	3 738	96.3	3 043	98.5
Jasper, TX	48241	6	35 604	19.7	5	15	7 187	8 698	93.3	7 329	95.2
Jeff Davis, TX	48243	9	2 207	20.3	2	4	407	555	89.9	486	89.1
Jefferson, TX	48245	2	252 051	19.2	9	80	44 348	67 831	89.7	51 343	92.3
Jim Hogg, TX	48247	6	5 281	23.7	1	3	1 180	1 506	96.7	1 255	99.1
Jim Wells, TX	48249	4	39 326	23.2	5	22	8 810	11 609	95.9	9 350	97.3
Johnson, TX	48251	1	126 811	21.4	9	56	25 833	34 577	86.7	27 610	92.2
Jones, TX	48253	6	20 785	17.6	5	15	3 168	5 352	91.2	4 722	92.9
Karnes, TX	48255	6	15 446	16.4	4	13	2 559	3 494	95.5	2 936	97.0
Kaufman, TX	48257	1	71 313	22.0	7	34	17 216	19 166	88.7	15 607	92.8
Kendall, TX	48259	6	23 743	20.9	2	11	6 048	6 471	88.4	5 062	93.5
Kenedy, TX	48261	9	414	20.3	1	1	68	104	97.1	94	100.0
Kent, TX	48263	9	859	17.1	1	1	144	179	98.9	165	98.8
Kerr, TX	48265	7	43 653	17.3	5	18	6 888	9 399	85.1	7 821	93.2
Kimble, TX	48267	7	4 468	17.6	1	3	752	1 035	95.7	908	99.3
King, TX	48269	9	356	27.0	1	1	86	84	97.6	82	97.6
Kinney, TX	48271	9	3 379	19.5	1	4	663	807	98.0	699	98.1
Kleberg, TX	48273	4	31 549	19.7	4	20	6 089	11 650	92.4	6 437	93.0
Knox, TX	48275	9	4 253	21.3	4	7	893	1 129	96.5	985	97.9
Lamar, TX	48277	6	48 499	19.1	5	23	9 000	12 054	91.2	9 355	93.8
Lamb, TX	48279	6	14 709	22.2	6	18	3 400	3 793	96.1	3 310	98.4
Lampasas, TX	48281	6	17 762	20.8	3	8	3 547	4 706	93.2	3 831	96.6
La Salle, TX	48283	6	5 866	22.0	1	6	1 294	1 545	97.7	1 318	99.5
Lavaca, TX	48285	6	19 210	18.3	6	12	2 161	4 471	83.9	3 668	86.0
Lee, TX	48287	6	15 657	21.9	3	10	2 977	3 941	88.3	3 331	89.7
Leon, TX	48289	8	15 335	18.7	5	12	2 980	3 454	94.7	2 957	97.4
Liberty, TX	48291	1	70 154	20.5	7	38	14 409	17 632	93.0	15 097	95.6
Limestone, TX	48293	6	22 051	18.9	3	12	4 163	5 437	95.5	4 356	97.1
Lipscomb, TX	48295	9	3 057	21.3	4	5	721	737	98.4	664	98.9
Live Oak, TX	48297	6	12 309	17.3	2	7	1 948	2 803	91.8	2 360	94.7
Llano, TX	48299	7	17 044	12.1	1	4	1 682	2 364	92.4	2 070	95.0
Loving, TX	48301	9	67	16.4	. . .	. . .	27	85.2	16	100.0	
Lubbock, TX	48303	3	242 628	18.5	12	95	42 230	80 919	90.8	46 144	94.0
Lynn, TX	48305	6	6 550	23.9	4	8	1 534	1 884	95.3	1 625	97.0
McCulloch, TX	48307	7	8 205	19.9	3	6	1 650	1 813	97.1	1 587	98.6
McLennan, TX	48309	3	213 517	19.5	21	116	39 227	68 392	76.0	41 749	92.7
McMullen, TX	48311	9	851	19.4	1	1	168	191	94.8	172	97.1
Madison, TX	48313	6	12 940	15.7	2	6	2 352	2 887	93.2	2 184	98.3
Marion, TX	48315	8	10 941	16.8	1	3	1 516	2 167	90.8	1 872	92.1
Martin, TX	48317	6	4 746	25.3	2	4	1 055	1 383	96.2	1 176	98.6
Mason, TX	48319	9	3 738	17.3	1	3	605	756	95.4	666	96.1

[1]County type code is from the Economic Research Service of the USDA. See Notes and Definitions at the end of this section.
. . . = Not available.

Table C-1. School and Student Characteristics by County—*Continued*

County	Characteristics of students, 2000–2001			Staff and students, 2000–2001				Revenues, fiscal 1999			
	Percent with IEP[2]	Percent eligible for free lunch	Percent minority	Number of teachers	Student/ teacher ratio	Local school non-teaching staff	Central admin. staff	Total revenue ($1,000s)	Percentage of revenue from		
									Federal govt.	State govt.	Local govt.
	10	11	12	13	14	15	16	17	18	19	20
Freestone, TX	13.9	36.9	30.9	237	13.4	201	22	$21 745	7.5	21.8	70.7
Frio, TX	11.7	67.1	87.3	250	12.6	263	5	23 279	12.6	66.0	21.3
Gaines, TX	14.4	55.3	50.9	254	11.7	271	7	38 076	5.2	12.2	82.6
Galveston, TX	9.9	29.4	39.8	4 334	15.3	3 870	115	415 018	6.7	24.6	68.7
Garza, TX	19.1	56.9	50.3	98	12.2	78	2	9 001	5.6	34.5	60.0
Gillespie, TX	13.9	38.7	30.3	241	13.3	222	10	21 944	6.7	27.8	65.5
Glasscock, TX	11.6	39.1	37.4	29	11.9	27	1	5 531	2.7	6.4	91.0
Goliad, TX	14.8	41.1	47.2	106	13.2	112	15	10 254	11.1	28.4	60.4
Gonzales, TX	13.4	64.0	63.4	297	13.1	311	15	25 764	9.8	58.3	31.8
Gray, TX	12.9	42.8	24.9	306	13.0	254	10	26 728	6.9	35.2	57.8
Grayson, TX	15.6	33.9	18.4	1 430	13.9	1 184	34	133 758	6.4	48.1	45.5
Gregg, TX	13.4	42.8	38.8	1 653	14.1	1 510	71	149 492	10.5	32.7	56.7
Grimes, TX	11.6	50.7	46.0	327	13.1	279	13	27 023	7.3	42.4	50.2
Guadalupe, TX	12.9	39.8	48.7	1 123	14.6	1 086	27	98 541	7.0	51.2	41.8
Hale, TX	14.6	56.3	69.7	602	13.4	484	25	51 417	10.4	59.0	30.5
Hall, TX	16.3	64.0	55.6	86	9.8	79	3	7 233	9.0	61.0	30.0
Hamilton, TX	15.0	46.1	13.8	141	11.2	116	16	12 047	8.0	58.8	33.2
Hansford, TX	11.9	47.1	45.1	132	9.8	85	5	11 497	4.3	21.9	73.8
Hardeman, TX	16.8	52.1	33.6	79	11.1	75	10	7 633	11.5	43.0	45.5
Hardin, TX	15.6	31.3	13.4	771	13.9	809	26	70 608	7.4	58.1	34.4
Harris, TX	10.0	50.6	69.5	39 264	16.9	41 615	583	4 067 668	6.9	36.0	57.1
Harrison, TX	12.7	45.6	36.4	920	13.8	929	33	79 157	8.8	35.0	56.1
Hartley, TX	13.8	38.1	16.6	37	8.6	22	2	3 130	3.8	31.7	64.4
Haskell, TX	18.8	65.8	35.8	108	10.1	105	5	10 213	8.3	62.5	29.2
Hays, TX	14.0	35.5	48.1	1 304	15.0	1 195	40	119 209	5.4	43.0	51.5
Hemphill, TX	15.6	34.4	33.2	73	10.6	55	. . .	8 459	2.4	10.4	87.2
Henderson, TX	14.4	44.0	22.8	733	13.8	675	39	63 070	6.9	49.2	44.0
Hidalgo, TX	8.6	57.4	96.5	9 395	15.4	12 379	187	951 740	13.9	65.2	20.9
Hill, TX	16.7	50.5	31.1	491	12.4	492	46	41 078	6.6	60.7	32.7
Hockley, TX	13.3	52.5	54.0	419	11.7	360	31	40 229	8.2	30.7	61.1
Hood, TX	13.5	27.7	11.6	489	14.6	500	12	43 270	4.3	36.2	59.5
Hopkins, TX	15.3	41.2	23.7	465	13.2	394	20	37 157	9.0	52.0	39.0
Houston, TX	15.5	54.3	45.2	326	11.6	307	14	28 159	10.2	50.7	39.1
Howard, TX	11.4	44.9	47.4	420	13.4	383	9	36 031	8.3	44.4	47.3
Hudspeth, TX	7.6	81.6	84.4	75	11.6	66	3	7 054	15.2	49.0	35.8
Hunt, TX	15.4	41.6	25.5	1 057	13.3	906	53	86 884	7.9	58.5	33.6
Hutchinson, TX	13.7	37.1	26.2	378	12.7	336	18	35 554	7.3	42.0	50.8
Irion, TX	12.0	41.6	32.6	33	10.9	32	1	3 967	2.4	7.9	89.7
Jack, TX	13.4	36.5	11.0	151	10.9	106	2	11 892	4.2	54.2	41.5
Jackson, TX	12.5	38.8	37.9	269	12.3	209	18	28 038	4.7	35.5	59.7
Jasper, TX	15.3	45.0	29.0	544	13.2	557	33	54 677	6.7	49.0	44.4
Jeff Davis, TX	30.0	. . .	45.7	52	7.8	37	3	4 566	3.0	61.7	35.3
Jefferson, TX	11.2	52.0	61.4	3 147	14.1	2 949	77	303 938	11.2	25.7	63.1
Jim Hogg, TX	15.6	42.2	96.4	96	12.3	106	1	9 115	10.4	47.0	42.6
Jim Wells, TX	11.7	66.2	84.1	624	14.1	664	19	56 628	10.1	65.9	24.0
Johnson, TX	13.7	35.1	18.6	1 774	14.6	1 644	48	149 632	5.7	56.8	37.5
Jones, TX	19.3	56.8	32.2	296	10.7	248	21	25 068	10.5	69.2	20.3
Karnes, TX	15.0	58.0	62.7	229	11.2	215	8	19 785	10.1	63.9	26.0
Kaufman, TX	15.1	36.0	26.5	1 180	14.6	1 060	32	102 669	7.5	56.6	35.9
Kendall, TX	12.8	22.1	23.2	430	14.1	395	6	34 233	4.5	29.5	66.0
Kenedy, TX	11.8	1.5	77.9	7	9.7	8	1	2 637	0.0	2.4	97.6
Kent, TX	17.4	32.6	12.5	22	6.5	18	2	6 209	1.0	2.8	96.2
Kerr, TX	13.3	45.0	35.4	521	13.2	506	28	44 015	8.9	40.3	50.8
Kimble, TX	16.5	41.6	30.2	73	10.3	63	2	5 261	4.0	60.4	35.6
King, TX	15.1	40.7	14.0	16	5.4	2	1	2 628	0.6	3.9	95.5
Kinney, TX	14.2	64.1	67.9	59	11.2	44	1	5 202	7.7	65.2	27.1
Kleberg, TX	14.4	64.0	80.8	443	13.7	473	24	42 334	10.1	55.1	34.8
Knox, TX	15.5	59.1	51.2	96	9.3	74	12	8 889	10.9	68.7	20.4
Lamar, TX	13.7	43.6	26.0	684	13.2	656	15	57 109	9.7	51.3	38.9
Lamb, TX	14.3	59.2	63.4	275	12.4	252	19	28 085	8.5	46.5	45.0
Lampasas, TX	14.6	43.7	25.3	250	14.2	266	9	21 255	7.9	60.7	31.4
La Salle, TX	11.8	76.2	88.3	98	13.2	95	5	10 848	9.0	60.2	30.8
Lavaca, TX	13.0	37.3	20.8	173	12.5	147	6	15 016	4.4	43.4	52.2
Lee, TX	11.8	43.5	43.7	237	12.6	219	16	18 713	7.6	47.0	45.4
Leon, TX	14.6	37.7	23.3	242	12.3	209	18	23 166	4.9	39.5	55.6
Liberty, TX	11.8	43.2	26.4	962	15.0	933	45	80 367	6.0	54.5	39.5
Limestone, TX	17.4	55.5	43.6	317	13.1	313	11	36 895	8.2	34.5	57.3
Lipscomb, TX	12.5	53.0	34.0	84	8.6	54	5	7 460	3.6	24.1	72.3
Live Oak, TX	13.8	41.7	47.9	154	12.6	150	4	14 900	6.1	27.5	66.4
Llano, TX	16.5	36.0	13.2	141	11.9	136	4	16 403	4.5	7.2	88.3
Loving, TX	. . .	. . .	. . .	. . .	. . .	. . .	. . .	. . .	. . .	. . .	. . .
Lubbock, TX	14.5	50.4	53.2	3 022	14.0	2 134	101	277 380	10.2	47.4	42.4
Lynn, TX	13.2	59.0	56.1	143	10.7	125	4	13 377	7.9	65.8	26.3
McCulloch, TX	16.6	59.5	37.6	153	10.8	159	9	13 456	9.5	62.2	28.3
McLennan, TX	16.4	48.9	46.9	2 693	14.6	2 510	196	260 431	9.5	54.9	35.6
McMullen, TX	12.5	55.4	53.6	19	8.8	21	1	4 572	0.9	5.6	93.5
Madison, TX	12.2	55.1	34.9	169	13.9	154	7	14 911	9.2	57.0	33.8
Marion, TX	17.9	51.5	45.6	119	12.7	123	6	10 422	11.1	39.6	49.3
Martin, TX	11.4	42.1	55.2	92	11.5	73	13	8 477	6.2	45.7	48.1
Mason, TX	19.7	51.2	36.9	57	10.6	56	1	5 480	6.3	51.2	42.5

[2]IEP = Individual Education Program. See Notes and Definitions at the end of this section.
. . . = Not available.

Table C-1. Population, School, and Student Characteristics by County—*Continued*

County	Current expenditures, fiscal 1999			Resident population 16 to 19 years, 2000				Outcomes, 1999–2000	
	Amount ($1,000s)	Amount per student	Percent for instruction	Total population 16 to 19 years	Percent in Armed Forces	Percent high school graduates	Percent not enrolled, not grads, not Armed Forces, not empl.	Number of graduates	Dropouts grades 9–12 (percent)
	21	22	23	24	25	26	27	28	29
Freestone, TX	$19 505	$6 204	62.2	984	0.7	10.9	6.0	189	2.4
Frio, TX	21 656	6 492	60.7	978	0.0	11.7	7.5	197	7.2
Gaines, TX	24 231	7 385	61.4	1 139	0.0	7.1	15.0	183	2.3
Galveston, TX	352 235	5 416	61.7	14 462	0.1	9.2	5.6	3 680	5.2
Garza, TX	7 761	6 611	65.3	294	0.0	18.4	3.7	56	4.7
Gillespie, TX	18 477	5 701	61.6	936	0.0	13.0	4.3	236	1.8
Glasscock, TX	3 439	8 619	62.6	124	0.0	1.6	6.5	25	. . .
Goliad, TX	9 518	6 765	56.6	417	0.0	8.9	5.3	96	2.3
Gonzales, TX	21 887	5 691	64.0	1 060	0.0	11.1	10.8	221	5.4
Gray, TX	23 272	5 511	63.9	1 261	0.0	19.2	4.0	271	2.7
Grayson, TX	112 812	5 665	63.9	6 426	0.0	11.5	7.2	1 217	4.5
Gregg, TX	130 975	5 544	57.2	7 360	0.0	10.5	9.5	1 345	4.5
Grimes, TX	24 656	5 673	59.8	1 213	0.0	13.7	6.7	246	4.9
Guadalupe, TX	82 611	5 331	61.9	5 454	0.7	13.0	4.0	1 027	4.1
Hale, TX	49 839	5 864	59.4	2 597	0.0	11.4	6.8	460	7.7
Hall, TX	6 172	7 236	68.6	204	0.0	5.4	6.4	70	5.4
Hamilton, TX	10 829	6 867	64.5	385	0.0	5.7	4.7	114	1.2
Hansford, TX	9 876	7 442	65.2	357	0.0	3.9	5.6	86	2.1
Hardeman, TX	7 322	7 916	63.9	306	0.0	14.1	5.6	70	1.0
Hardin, TX	62 589	5 700	62.5	3 021	0.0	11.0	3.3	709	3.2
Harris, TX	3 525 792	5 590	59.5	199 589	0.0	9.4	8.4	30 685	6.3
Harrison, TX	68 644	5 107	62.9	4 405	0.1	10.6	5.0	767	4.2
Hartley, TX	2 760	8 415	61.2	179	0.0	6.1	2.2	24	2.2
Haskell, TX	9 611	7 950	64.7	349	0.0	11.7	2.0	107	2.5
Hays, TX	99 774	5 582	59.7	8 049	0.1	8.9	5.3	1 134	4.1
Hemphill, TX	6 725	8 161	65.6	263	0.0	6.8	3.0	50	2.3
Henderson, TX	54 105	5 403	62.7	3 964	0.0	12.9	4.8	603	4.7
Hidalgo, TX	805 301	5 937	59.4	40 746	0.0	7.2	11.1	7 084	6.8
Hill, TX	36 237	6 130	63.0	2 009	0.0	7.5	8.9	332	3.9
Hockley, TX	35 323	6 588	64.0	1 843	0.0	10.6	4.5	357	4.4
Hood, TX	34 973	5 054	61.0	2 183	0.0	11.5	4.2	429	4.5
Hopkins, TX	33 655	5 637	65.1	1 918	0.2	13.7	3.8	367	3.1
Houston, TX	24 062	5 935	64.1	1 282	0.0	13.4	10.1	233	3.3
Howard, TX	34 104	5 683	62.5	2 044	0.0	15.0	10.7	346	3.0
Hudspeth, TX	5 746	7 050	58.4	233	0.0	9.9	6.9	42	3.0
Hunt, TX	77 647	5 601	61.8	4 659	0.0	12.3	4.9	756	3.7
Hutchinson, TX	29 924	5 804	67.1	1 654	0.0	11.3	5.0	362	3.4
Irion, TX	3 295	9 578	57.5	96	0.0	5.2	0.0	26	. . .
Jack, TX	10 972	6 029	65.5	513	0.0	15.2	7.6	113	4.9
Jackson, TX	20 760	6 217	62.3	912	0.0	12.8	3.1	221	2.2
Jasper, TX	44 248	5 908	61.5	2 086	0.4	9.7	5.7	478	2.6
Jeff Davis, TX	3 374	8 111	67.1	116	0.0	4.3	1.7	34	4.5
Jefferson, TX	268 880	5 963	59.5	15 411	0.1	10.8	7.1	2 516	5.9
Jim Hogg, TX	8 426	6 768	61.6	344	0.0	10.8	1.2	69	3.5
Jim Wells, TX	51 520	5 792	61.7	2 643	0.0	8.5	9.1	525	6.3
Johnson, TX	125 020	5 218	64.5	8 065	0.2	12.1	6.7	1 393	4.0
Jones, TX	22 831	7 023	66.0	1 529	0.0	8.2	23.9	197	3.0
Karnes, TX	17 348	6 366	62.8	817	0.0	12.0	8.0	197	2.7
Kaufman, TX	85 870	5 196	60.8	4 403	0.0	10.2	8.5	923	4.3
Kendall, TX	28 352	4 900	64.4	1 296	0.0	7.9	3.2	381	1.2
Kenedy, TX	899	15 500	50.9	27	0.0	7.4	11.1	0	. . .
Kent, TX	2 286	12 357	52.8	42	0.0	0.0	0.0	17	3.2
Kerr, TX	39 715	5 658	63.3	2 204	0.0	10.7	3.5	404	5.2
Kimble, TX	5 008	6 624	66.9	249	0.0	10.0	9.2	46	3.4
King, TX	1 420	15 778	58.9	9	0.0	0.0	0.0	4	. . .
Kinney, TX	4 349	6 711	67.3	180	0.0	6.7	2.8	53	1.5
Kleberg, TX	39 847	6 179	60.7	2 384	0.2	6.4	4.5	413	3.8
Knox, TX	7 679	7 804	64.8	249	0.0	8.0	0.8	70	1.1
Lamar, TX	50 906	5 618	64.5	2 750	0.0	9.5	5.6	521	3.1
Lamb, TX	22 998	6 637	64.1	992	0.0	9.2	7.0	219	4.4
Lampasas, TX	19 168	5 410	62.8	1 187	0.8	7.1	3.4	231	4.5
La Salle, TX	8 882	6 216	59.0	367	0.0	10.1	16.9	68	3.7
Lavaca, TX	12 713	5 633	65.3	1 116	0.0	9.8	6.2	171	2.5
Lee, TX	17 101	5 833	63.4	1 236	0.0	10.4	19.0	223	1.0
Leon, TX	18 215	6 154	62.1	896	0.0	8.6	3.7	211	3.5
Liberty, TX	70 575	5 170	61.5	4 116	0.0	12.9	7.9	706	4.0
Limestone, TX	27 259	6 744	62.1	1 204	0.0	12.1	5.2	234	4.5
Lipscomb, TX	6 105	8 538	65.2	193	0.0	8.3	2.6	48	2.2
Live Oak, TX	13 732	6 705	64.6	741	0.0	13.5	5.7	138	2.2
Llano, TX	11 726	7 431	59.9	527	0.0	16.5	5.1	88	2.8
Loving, TX	. . .	. . .	. . .	. . .	. . .	. . .	0.0	. . .	. . .
Lubbock, TX	247 853	5 876	60.7	17 939	0.1	10.6	3.8	2 624	3.8
Lynn, TX	11 477	6 819	63.3	449	0.0	11.1	5.6	107	1.4
McCulloch, TX	11 925	6 941	61.4	374	0.0	12.8	8.3	101	2.7
McLennan, TX	225 103	5 775	59.3	16 641	0.1	8.6	5.5	2 120	5.6
McMullen, TX	1 871	9 899	44.2	46	0.0	17.4	0.0	11	. . .
Madison, TX	13 321	5 592	59.2	496	0.0	11.5	5.4	116	5.7
Marion, TX	9 164	6 017	64.2	554	0.0	14.1	6.0	86	4.3
Martin, TX	7 984	7 604	61.3	334	0.0	6.3	9.9	67	1.9
Mason, TX	5 005	8 398	63.4	182	0.0	7.7	8.8	51	1.3

. . . = Not available.

Table C-1. Population, School, and Student Characteristics by County—*Continued*

County	High school graduates, 2000			College enrollment, 2000		College graduates, 2000 (percent)						
	Population 25 years and over	High school diploma or less (percent)	High school diploma or more (percent)	Number	Percent public	Bachelor's degree or more	+/- U.S. percent with bachelor's degree or more	Non-Hispanic White	Black or African American	American Indian and Alaska Native	Asian, Hawaiian, and Pacific Islander	Hispanic or Latino[1]
	30	31	32	33	34	35	36	37	38	39	40	41
Freestone, TX	12 085	60.9	76.8	826	94.4	10.9	-13.5	11.6	10.3	22.9	32.0	2.8
Frio, TX	9 807	70.7	57.7	584	87.2	8.4	-16.0	20.8	14.0	14.3	30.0	3.1
Gaines, TX	8 006	70.2	56.2	268	81.0	10.5	-13.9	15.2	0.0	0.0	100.0	2.0
Galveston, TX	161 503	45.5	80.9	14 654	89.1	22.7	-1.7	27.0	10.7	22.4	47.9	10.1
Garza, TX	3 131	68.3	70.1	164	95.7	10.0	-14.4	14.8	4.3	...	...	1.2
Gillespie, TX	15 255	49.4	80.1	397	73.8	22.9	-1.5	25.3	0.0	22.2	13.0	4.4
Glasscock, TX	836	54.3	69.9	40	92.5	18.7	-5.7	24.7	100.0	0.0	...	1.4
Goliad, TX	4 603	57.2	72.4	159	87.4	12.3	-12.1	16.5	10.9	20.0	0.0	3.2
Gonzales, TX	11 797	71.8	62.0	312	85.9	10.7	-13.7	17.1	2.0	6.7	35.3	1.4
Gray, TX	15 420	58.3	75.3	920	86.7	11.9	-12.5	12.9	8.0	9.7	66.0	3.8
Grayson, TX	72 382	49.8	80.2	5 331	70.6	17.2	-7.2	17.9	10.5	12.7	46.6	8.0
Gregg, TX	70 006	48.6	79.1	5 017	72.8	19.5	-4.9	22.8	10.3	17.7	33.9	6.5
Grimes, TX	16 080	65.5	67.3	787	86.9	10.3	-14.1	13.7	3.4	9.8	25.6	2.7
Guadalupe, TX	55 679	52.0	78.1	4 172	65.9	19.1	-5.3	24.2	21.1	28.2	16.9	6.3
Hale, TX	21 498	62.8	65.9	1 730	55.3	14.4	-10.0	21.7	4.2	6.3	78.1	4.3
Hall, TX	2 527	71.1	61.7	54	87.0	10.3	-14.1	13.6	0.0	0.0	0.0	1.3
Hamilton, TX	5 792	59.2	73.8	196	88.3	16.8	-7.6	17.6	...	0.0	...	2.8
Hansford, TX	3 420	59.9	69.9	94	97.9	18.6	-5.8	24.3	...	6.8	...	0.5
Hardeman, TX	3 135	62.6	70.7	99	94.9	12.8	-11.6	14.3	2.4	26.7	70.6	1.4
Hardin, TX	30 747	60.8	79.5	1 418	92.8	13.0	-11.4	13.5	5.7	4.5	29.8	10.1
Harris, TX	2 067 399	47.0	74.6	186 214	81.5	26.9	2.5	38.5	17.4	18.1	45.6	8.2
Harrison, TX	39 130	55.8	78.3	3 252	50.4	15.4	-9.0	16.6	11.7	3.0	31.4	10.0
Hartley, TX	4 136	56.6	77.3	174	72.4	17.6	-6.8	21.3	8.3	0.0	0.0	5.5
Haskell, TX	4 314	65.4	71.1	90	84.4	14.4	-10.0	17.4	9.8	0.0	0.0	0.3
Hays, TX	53 635	38.2	84.7	16 274	95.7	31.3	6.9	39.6	11.0	23.3	48.5	10.8
Hemphill, TX	2 190	49.3	79.9	59	84.7	17.9	-6.5	20.0	0.0	0.0	...	2.7
Henderson, TX	49 886	58.9	73.5	2 412	88.6	12.1	-12.3	12.7	7.6	27.3	26.5	3.4
Hidalgo, TX	304 670	69.8	50.5	27 046	91.8	12.9	-11.5	27.8	16.7	7.4	65.1	9.6
Hill, TX	21 209	61.5	71.8	1 100	84.9	12.5	-11.9	14.4	3.0	17.8	51.3	1.6
Hockley, TX	13 466	58.0	68.2	1 511	93.4	13.6	-10.8	19.0	3.1	7.4	83.8	2.4
Hood, TX	28 621	46.1	83.5	1 234	87.3	20.5	-3.9	21.1	70.0	23.9	44.6	7.5
Hopkins, TX	21 003	62.1	73.6	1 000	90.7	15.1	-9.3	16.6	5.3	2.7	80.3	4.0
Houston, TX	16 244	64.7	70.0	487	91.6	12.2	-12.2	15.0	7.8	6.1	7.1	1.1
Howard, TX	22 544	60.7	70.6	1 702	86.6	11.1	-13.3	15.7	12.6	0.0	39.6	2.8
Hudspeth, TX	1 910	74.5	46.1	69	68.1	9.7	-14.7	26.5	0.0	25.0	0.0	2.5
Hunt, TX	48 548	57.4	76.9	4 348	90.4	16.8	-7.6	18.1	7.7	12.3	56.6	7.1
Hutchinson, TX	15 282	54.5	79.6	1 034	93.8	14.3	-10.1	15.4	4.8	16.9	58.6	7.1
Irion, TX	1 217	52.2	78.8	54	90.7	21.5	-2.9	26.9	0.0	0.0	...	3.8
Jack, TX	5 830	60.8	75.8	315	73.0	12.8	-11.6	13.5	8.6	0.0	58.6	3.5
Jackson, TX	9 278	61.6	72.7	397	97.7	12.8	-11.6	16.9	3.3	0.0	69.2	2.0
Jasper, TX	23 420	66.6	73.0	751	85.4	10.5	-13.9	12.0	3.4	11.6	31.5	5.3
Jeff Davis, TX	1 560	44.3	74.7	54	94.4	35.1	10.7	46.0	...	...	...	12.0
Jefferson, TX	161 261	54.7	78.5	11 596	91.4	16.3	-8.1	21.2	8.2	7.5	32.5	7.9
Jim Hogg, TX	3 203	70.3	58.0	168	86.3	9.5	-14.9	11.8	0.0	0.0	0.0	9.3
Jim Wells, TX	23 525	67.5	64.8	1 531	92.6	10.9	-13.5	17.3	10.6	13.6	64.9	8.2
Johnson, TX	79 417	55.7	77.6	4 806	67.4	13.8	-10.6	14.7	8.9	13.0	27.7	4.6
Jones, TX	13 780	70.3	64.3	438	74.0	8.2	-16.2	11.3	1.3	0.0	5.1	1.1
Karnes, TX	10 352	73.2	59.1	336	87.5	9.4	-15.0	17.2	1.6	6.6	50.0	2.7
Kaufman, TX	44 859	59.3	74.5	2 336	78.6	12.3	-12.1	13.4	8.1	8.5	38.5	4.3
Kendall, TX	15 827	37.6	85.4	820	81.2	31.4	7.0	34.5	0.0	24.3	69.7	11.8
Kenedy, TX	261	64.0	57.9	6	50.0	20.3	-4.1	45.7	0.0	...	...	14.9
Kent, TX	643	58.9	78.1	12	100.0	15.1	-9.3	16.1	0.0	0.0	...	7.5
Kerr, TX	31 006	48.0	81.2	1 142	39.1	23.3	-1.1	26.9	2.6	11.0	19.7	4.9
Kimble, TX	3 146	62.1	72.1	42	61.9	17.3	-7.1	20.3	0.0	0.0	50.0	2.3
King, TX	228	47.8	78.1	2	100.0	24.6	0.2	26.0	...	...	...	0.0
Kinney, TX	2 335	60.4	66.9	57	94.7	17.7	-6.7	28.4	0.0	0.0	63.6	3.7
Kleberg, TX	17 896	54.8	68.2	4 469	94.0	20.4	-4.0	32.8	8.8	21.9	48.5	13.5
Knox, TX	2 819	66.9	66.8	78	84.6	11.8	-12.6	14.6	1.2	33.3	53.3	2.7
Lamar, TX	31 612	56.9	76.3	1 847	92.5	14.5	-9.9	15.9	5.7	13.1	34.2	7.9
Lamb, TX	9 202	64.7	63.7	284	84.5	11.1	-13.3	16.7	2.0	0.0	0.0	2.9
Lampasas, TX	11 491	51.7	78.8	605	78.8	16.2	-8.2	18.0	9.2	0.0	13.1	6.5
La Salle, TX	3 602	75.6	50.1	157	81.5	6.4	-18.0	20.7	0.0	0.0	10.0	2.2
Lavaca, TX	13 214	68.1	68.6	546	86.1	11.4	-13.0	12.6	7.1	4.8	30.8	3.4
Lee, TX	9 804	65.0	71.7	323	85.1	13.1	-11.3	15.5	6.9	0.0	0.0	4.2
Leon, TX	10 652	64.1	73.8	338	87.9	12.1	-12.3	13.6	6.7	0.0	0.0	0.7
Liberty, TX	44 206	66.6	69.6	1 634	85.9	8.1	-16.3	9.3	4.5	11.4	11.3	2.0
Limestone, TX	14 564	62.6	67.4	785	89.8	11.1	-13.3	14.3	3.2	10.7	0.0	1.1
Lipscomb, TX	2 047	54.8	74.5	37	91.9	18.9	-5.5	21.3	37.5	0.0	...	5.6
Live Oak, TX	8 399	61.2	67.1	284	81.0	12.0	-12.4	17.3	1.8	9.4	20.0	3.0
Llano, TX	13 571	49.1	83.5	182	75.3	21.0	-3.4	21.9	0.0	0.0	0.0	2.8
Loving, TX	51	51.0	86.3	11	63.6	5.9	-18.5	6.3	...	...	...	0.0
Lubbock, TX	141 363	46.9	78.4	30 844	90.4	24.4	0.0	31.1	10.0	14.6	64.2	7.2
Lynn, TX	4 037	66.1	61.9	168	82.1	13.4	-11.0	21.7	2.7	38.5	33.3	0.4
McCulloch, TX	5 550	64.5	70.5	84	83.3	14.0	-10.4	16.4	15.9	0.0	...	5.0
McLennan, TX	125 961	51.3	76.6	22 657	46.9	19.1	-5.3	23.2	9.1	9.0	47.7	6.8
McMullen, TX	613	60.5	74.7	19	73.7	16.2	-8.2	20.8	0.0	100.0	...	3.9
Madison, TX	8 907	71.1	72.8	542	87.6	11.5	-12.9	16.2	1.5	27.3	82.8	3.8
Marion, TX	7 792	65.7	67.5	238	81.9	8.5	-15.9	9.4	5.4	9.9	...	0.0
Martin, TX	2 785	65.6	65.8	103	83.5	11.8	-12.6	16.4	0.0	0.0	45.5	3.1
Mason, TX	2 701	49.7	78.1	44	79.5	18.7	-5.7	21.4	0.0	35.1	...	2.9

[1]Hispanic or Latino persons may be of any race.
. . . = Not available.

Table C-1. Population, School, and Student Characteristics by County—*Continued*

County	State/County code	County type[1]	Population, 2000		Number of schools and students, 2000–2001			Resident enrollment, 2000			
			Total	Percent 5–17 years	School districts	Schools	Students	Total	Percent public	K–12	Percent public
			1	2	3	4	5	6	7	8	9
Matagorda, TX	48321	4	37 957	22.6	5	22	8 073	10 524	92.2	8 924	94.3
Maverick, TX	48323	5	47 297	27.0	1	23	12 515	15 541	96.5	13 100	98.3
Medina, TX	48325	6	39 304	21.8	5	22	8 382	10 809	92.4	8 698	96.2
Menard, TX	48327	8	2 360	19.6	1	3	469	544	98.5	482	99.0
Midland, TX	48329	3	116 009	22.7	5	42	23 048	34 805	86.7	26 914	88.4
Milam, TX	48331	6	24 238	20.6	6	15	4 846	6 297	93.9	5 256	96.1
Mills, TX	48333	9	5 151	20.2	4	7	1 025	1 128	97.3	1 050	98.7
Mitchell, TX	48335	7	9 698	15.1	3	6	1 444	2 012	95.2	1 662	95.5
Montague, TX	48337	6	19 117	18.0	7	15	3 237	4 192	95.2	3 510	97.9
Montgomery, TX	48339	1	293 768	21.8	7	80	59 643	81 114	87.7	63 588	91.9
Moore, TX	48341	6	20 121	24.3	2	12	4 731	5 772	96.8	4 854	98.5
Morris, TX	48343	6	13 048	19.3	2	8	2 623	3 217	95.6	2 607	98.1
Motley, TX	48345	9	1 426	18.1	1	1	210	294	85.0	241	88.0
Nacogdoches, TX	48347	5	59 203	17.5	9	26	10 031	21 373	93.8	10 692	94.1
Navarro, TX	48349	4	45 124	20.1	7	21	8 811	12 175	93.4	9 301	95.5
Newton, TX	48351	8	15 072	19.7	3	9	2 568	3 518	93.3	3 083	93.6
Nolan, TX	48353	6	15 802	20.4	4	14	3 211	4 262	95.6	3 396	99.1
Nueces, TX	48355	2	313 645	20.7	18	122	61 426	91 444	91.4	67 291	93.8
Ochiltree, TX	48357	7	9 006	22.5	1	5	1 990	2 357	94.4	2 020	97.7
Oldham, TX	48359	8	2 185	28.5	4	7	872	715	96.8	641	96.4
Orange, TX	48361	2	84 966	20.6	5	29	16 866	22 128	91.4	17 626	94.4
Palo Pinto, TX	48363	6	27 026	19.3	6	13	5 030	6 254	95.2	5 296	97.4
Panola, TX	48365	6	22 756	19.0	4	9	3 852	5 765	93.9	4 667	95.6
Parker, TX	48367	1	88 495	21.2	8	36	16 313	23 189	90.0	18 732	93.6
Parmer, TX	48369	7	10 016	24.3	4	11	2 469	3 082	96.2	2 689	97.2
Pecos, TX	48371	7	16 809	21.1	3	12	3 086	4 947	94.9	3 906	95.9
Polk, TX	48373	6	41 133	17.0	6	16	6 739	9 215	93.4	7 149	95.3
Potter, TX	48375	3	113 546	19.7	4	59	31 774	31 113	92.1	22 798	93.9
Presidio, TX	48377	7	7 304	24.9	2	6	1 954	2 151	98.6	1 869	99.6
Rains, TX	48379	8	9 139	18.2	1	4	1 572	2 022	95.0	1 696	96.2
Randall, TX	48381	3	104 312	19.2	1	13	7 424	30 922	89.2	19 793	91.2
Reagan, TX	48383	6	3 326	26.0	1	3	886	1 036	99.1	910	100.0
Real, TX	48385	9	3 047	18.6	1	1	302	742	96.5	596	98.3
Red River, TX	48387	6	14 314	18.0	4	12	2 765	3 114	94.7	2 610	96.4
Reeves, TX	48389	7	13 137	22.9	2	9	3 002	3 606	98.5	3 116	99.5
Refugio, TX	48391	6	7 828	20.2	3	8	1 601	1 906	96.0	1 640	98.1
Roberts, TX	48393	9	887	20.1	1	1	166	217	92.6	184	96.7
Robertson, TX	48395	6	16 000	21.0	5	14	3 288	4 049	94.2	3 339	96.6
Rockwall, TX	48397	0	43 080	22.6	2	17	10 333	12 565	86.6	9 821	92.9
Runnels, TX	48399	6	11 495	20.6	4	16	2 473	2 833	95.6	2 481	97.3
Rusk, TX	48401	6	47 372	18.8	8	23	7 508	11 399	91.2	9 081	95.0
Sabine, TX	48403	9	10 469	15.9	2	5	1 618	2 043	93.5	1 747	95.9
San Augustine, TX	48405	9	8 946	18.0	2	6	1 446	1 961	95.8	1 657	97.7
San Jacinto, TX	48407	8	22 246	19.1	2	8	3 645	5 092	92.8	4 384	94.0
San Patricio, TX	48409	2	67 138	23.0	7	38	15 589	19 646	94.4	15 739	97.1
San Saba, TX	48411	7	6 186	22.6	3	7	1 142	1 514	96.7	1 329	98.0
Schleicher, TX	48413	8	2 935	21.8	1	5	662	798	99.5	669	100.0
Scurry, TX	48415	7	16 361	18.9	3	11	3 040	4 259	95.6	3 247	99.2
Shackelford, TX	48417	8	3 302	21.3	2	3	713	882	95.6	732	97.1
Shelby, TX	48419	7	25 224	19.6	6	15	4 806	6 145	94.0	5 129	96.5
Sherman, TX	48421	9	3 186	24.5	2	4	1 031	927	93.9	774	94.7
Smith, TX	48423	3	174 706	19.5	10	67	30 812	46 077	88.1	34 152	90.0
Somervell, TX	48425	8	6 809	22.0	2	6	1 671	1 907	92.4	1 502	96.9
Starr, TX	48427	6	53 597	27.0	3	23	14 775	18 163	97.8	14 828	98.7
Stephens, TX	48429	7	9 674	18.8	1	6	1 787	2 381	93.1	1 944	96.7
Sterling, TX	48431	8	1 393	23.6	1	5	307	395	94.4	336	93.5
Stonewall, TX	48433	9	1 693	17.7	1	3	266	363	92.6	312	94.2
Sutton, TX	48435	7	4 077	21.6	1	4	933	1 085	96.5	937	98.0
Swisher, TX	48437	6	8 378	20.5	3	8	1 804	2 196	93.9	1 823	96.4
Tarrant, TX	48439	0	1 446 219	20.1	23	413	270 155	399 208	84.2	291 485	91.1
Taylor, TX	48441	3	126 555	19.4	6	57	23 501	37 937	75.0	25 143	94.5
Terrell, TX	48443	9	1 081	21.0	1	3	200	277	91.0	249	93.6
Terry, TX	48445	6	12 761	21.0	3	7	2 635	3 351	97.4	2 833	98.9
Throckmorton, TX	48447	9	1 850	19.7	2	3	372	443	99.1	386	100.0
Titus, TX	48449	7	28 118	21.7	4	14	5 976	7 916	94.7	6 333	98.0
Tom Green, TX	48451	3	104 010	19.2	6	66	19 142	29 720	94.2	20 707	95.8
Travis, TX	48453	2	812 280	16.5	17	182	115 687	235 906	88.5	133 691	92.5
Trinity, TX	48455	7	13 779	17.0	4	12	2 397	2 836	96.0	2 369	97.7
Tyler, TX	48457	6	20 871	17.4	5	15	3 718	4 466	93.2	3 784	95.7
Upshur, TX	48459	3	35 291	20.4	7	20	6 643	8 817	92.0	7 267	95.4
Upton, TX	48461	8	3 404	23.8	2	5	819	959	99.3	868	99.4
Uvalde, TX	48463	7	25 926	23.0	5	16	6 336	7 779	93.5	6 142	94.6
Val Verde, TX	48465	3	44 856	23.1	3	17	10 141	12 850	92.4	10 622	95.6
Van Zandt, TX	48467	6	48 140	19.2	8	31	9 267	11 226	91.4	9 289	93.2
Victoria, TX	48469	3	84 088	21.5	3	30	15 522	24 141	87.9	18 552	89.7
Walker, TX	48471	4	61 758	13.1	3	14	7 642	20 291	90.2	10 092	88.0
Waller, TX	48473	1	32 663	18.8	3	15	7 155	11 274	94.0	6 445	95.3
Ward, TX	48475	6	10 909	24.0	2	8	2 224	3 113	94.8	2 640	96.4
Washington, TX	48477	6	30 373	18.7	2	10	5 164	8 413	86.7	5 844	88.7
Webb, TX	48479	3	193 117	25.6	7	71	50 803	67 101	93.2	51 488	95.4

[1]County type code is from the Economic Research Service of the USDA. See Notes and Definitions at the end of this section.

Table C-1. School and Student Characteristics by County—*Continued*

County	Characteristics of students, 2000–2001			Staff and students, 2000–2001				Revenues, fiscal 1999			
	Percent with IEP[2]	Percent eligible for free lunch	Percent minority	Number of teachers	Student/ teacher ratio	Local school non-teaching staff	Central admin. staff	Total revenue ($1,000s)	Percentage of revenue from		
									Federal govt.	State govt.	Local govt.
	10	11	12	13	14	15	16	17	18	19	20
Matagorda, TX	13.2	59.5	57.9	570	14.2	633	17	$81 326	10.1	23.9	66.0
Maverick, TX	7.1	81.3	98.5	753	16.6	932	6	69 557	16.3	69.0	14.7
Medina, TX	13.1	45.2	57.4	591	14.2	620	18	51 691	8.1	63.6	28.3
Menard, TX	16.2	60.8	55.4	45	10.4	36	12	4 862	13.9	58.7	27.3
Midland, TX	9.0	35.8	51.3	1 492	15.4	1 417	22	149 373	10.5	40.5	49.0
Milam, TX	13.7	50.7	43.5	360	13.5	328	12	30 390	7.2	52.0	40.9
Mills, TX	26.3	51.0	27.0	114	9.0	80	5	9 081	6.9	70.9	22.2
Mitchell, TX	13.9	53.5	50.0	132	10.9	117	4	12 414	7.1	39.0	53.9
Montague, TX	15.5	40.5	10.4	274	11.8	238	23	23 448	6.7	60.9	32.3
Montgomery, TX	11.9	30.3	21.4	3 880	15.4	3 789	62	345 798	4.6	41.7	53.6
Moore, TX	11.2	47.4	60.7	341	13.9	290	12	27 226	8.7	17.8	73.5
Morris, TX	15.9	52.2	41.1	220	11.9	193	7	18 761	8.0	29.7	62.3
Motley, TX	15.2	72.9	33.8	25	8.4	22	1	2 042	12.9	50.8	36.3
Nacogdoches, TX	13.7	52.0	40.3	762	13.2	625	50	66 353	8.1	58.0	33.8
Navarro, TX	14.1	50.8	42.6	646	13.6	588	20	56 517	7.9	58.3	33.9
Newton, TX	18.7	56.1	30.7	217	11.8	206	4	21 899	7.7	55.4	36.9
Nolan, TX	15.4	50.6	43.3	281	11.4	258	18	24 500	8.9	46.6	44.6
Nueces, TX	14.5	53.1	71.9	4 056	15.1	4 010	127	416 575	10.3	46.0	43.6
Ochiltree, TX	9.4	50.2	43.7	155	12.8	127	6	12 202	7.0	35.6	57.5
Oldham, TX	18.9	. . .	20.3	116	7.5	81	8	9 372	6.8	44.9	48.2
Orange, TX	16.5	38.7	17.5	1 185	14.2	1 163	25	113 356	8.1	40.8	51.1
Palo Pinto, TX	18.4	47.7	23.1	389	12.9	312	30	36 651	6.8	50.0	43.2
Panola, TX	16.5	41.5	29.4	302	12.8	340	9	33 355	4.9	8.4	86.7
Parker, TX	13.0	26.2	10.3	1 144	14.3	923	52	95 548	4.8	54.4	40.8
Parmer, TX	13.2	66.7	64.4	213	11.6	202	8	17 348	10.1	59.8	30.1
Pecos, TX	16.0	56.4	71.4	266	11.6	277	9	43 488	5.3	7.5	87.2
Polk, TX	17.7	50.4	29.7	470	14.3	521	19	49 415	6.5	42.8	50.7
Potter, TX	11.9	49.5	44.8	2 173	14.6	1 929	30	210 359	13.3	40.9	45.8
Presidio, TX	9.7	59.3	95.9	158	12.4	146	5	13 235	14.5	64.8	20.7
Rains, TX	14.8	41.2	11.0	116	13.6	108	3	9 328	4.2	56.3	39.5
Randall, TX	12.1	19.9	14.4	463	16.0	521	8	35 581	5.2	44.4	50.5
Reagan, TX	21.3	41.4	60.8	78	11.4	74	3	7 937	6.4	15.0	78.5
Real, TX	21.5	60.3	27.2	29	10.4	23	3	1 994	5.3	34.6	60.2
Red River, TX	15.1	56.1	34.0	227	12.2	223	16	19 863	12.7	61.5	25.7
Reeves, TX	11.5	68.4	89.1	208	14.4	246	9	21 456	11.5	55.8	32.8
Refugio, TX	16.0	47.1	62.1	144	11.1	119	5	13 117	6.6	33.3	60.1
Roberts, TX	9.0	27.7	5.4	22	7.5	20	1	3 372	0.9	4.9	94.2
Robertson, TX	12.3	61.7	54.0	272	12.1	248	18	27 234	8.5	42.4	49.1
Rockwall, TX	11.0	17.4	18.6	663	15.6	565	16	51 515	3.1	34.0	62.9
Runnels, TX	13.3	57.8	43.5	220	11.2	174	8	19 427	8.2	68.9	22.9
Rusk, TX	14.2	49.2	36.9	599	12.5	594	25	53 961	8.6	44.1	47.3
Sabine, TX	14.2	49.6	17.3	132	12.3	126	9	12 052	17.4	49.2	33.4
San Augustine, TX	15.4	71.1	48.1	131	11.0	139	5	11 381	12.7	60.8	26.5
San Jacinto, TX	12.8	54.1	27.9	260	14.0	261	9	21 725	9.6	49.6	40.8
San Patricio, TX	12.3	53.9	61.3	1 089	14.3	1 115	43	100 399	10.3	53.6	36.2
San Saba, TX	18.5	56.6	31.5	105	10.9	95	6	9 302	7.7	64.4	27.9
Schleicher, TX	12.5	57.2	63.0	63	10.5	57	4	5 661	5.1	45.2	49.7
Scurry, TX	18.5	45.8	46.3	248	12.3	189	6	21 960	8.4	48.5	43.2
Shackelford, TX	17.5	41.7	13.6	62	11.5	46	2	5 405	5.8	56.4	37.8
Shelby, TX	14.3	54.4	40.5	389	12.4	348	15	34 020	11.7	63.6	24.6
Sherman, TX	6.0	55.5	38.3	71	14.5	47	3	5 866	6.7	20.6	72.7
Smith, TX	11.1	43.3	45.3	2 161	14.3	1 907	50	181 264	8.3	40.9	50.8
Somervell, TX	13.4	36.6	21.1	166	10.1	166	4	63 709	0.7	2.0	97.3
Starr, TX	11.8	67.0	99.7	975	15.2	1 569	20	93 840	17.4	65.6	17.0
Stephens, TX	14.5	50.0	27.4	123	14.5	112	3	11 696	7.5	45.4	47.1
Sterling, TX	19.9	43.9	39.7	34	9.0	24	1	3 701	2.6	7.5	89.9
Stonewall, TX	18.0	39.5	22.6	30	8.9	23	1	3 358	3.9	27.8	68.3
Sutton, TX	15.8	42.2	60.6	88	10.6	66	3	7 571	5.0	13.1	81.9
Swisher, TX	14.7	60.6	53.9	171	10.5	147	9	13 735	8.7	64.4	26.9
Tarrant, TX	10.6	35.4	47.9	17 109	15.8	15 444	313	1 575 568	6.0	34.8	59.2
Taylor, TX	17.6	45.3	35.3	1 813	13.0	1 558	56	166 796	16.5	50.8	32.7
Terrell, TX	12.0	42.5	67.5	23	8.7	25	2	4 556	2.9	4.1	93.0
Terry, TX	13.9	59.4	63.8	203	13.0	194	9	19 946	12.2	44.2	43.6
Throckmorton, TX	14.0	50.8	10.5	39	9.5	31	2	3 529	11.4	40.9	47.7
Titus, TX	14.3	57.5	54.9	453	13.2	470	14	46 532	20.5	40.0	39.5
Tom Green, TX	14.0	48.0	48.5	1 330	14.4	1 302	88	136 486	10.6	48.9	40.5
Travis, TX	12.4	41.3	59.1	7 771	14.9	6 383	200	811 549	6.3	15.5	78.2
Trinity, TX	15.1	57.5	27.1	193	12.4	182	11	16 569	10.7	55.5	33.7
Tyler, TX	15.3	46.5	19.4	311	12.0	292	15	26 055	7.2	57.7	35.1
Upshur, TX	14.1	38.0	18.0	512	13.0	469	23	43 769	5.8	56.2	38.0
Upton, TX	16.5	51.2	52.9	89	9.2	72	11	12 434	4.5	6.4	89.2
Uvalde, TX	12.1	72.7	79.6	474	13.4	550	9	44 398	11.9	61.7	26.3
Val Verde, TX	11.1	69.2	88.4	630	16.1	691	15	61 517	16.2	64.6	19.2
Van Zandt, TX	12.7	38.1	13.7	641	14.5	594	47	54 865	6.9	59.0	34.1
Victoria, TX	12.3	50.6	60.8	1 123	13.8	1 270	27	111 306	12.9	39.4	47.7
Walker, TX	13.2	45.5	47.3	532	14.4	600	13	57 169	16.6	52.1	31.3
Waller, TX	12.1	49.6	56.0	502	14.3	517	16	44 822	6.7	52.0	41.3
Ward, TX	13.0	47.9	54.1	175	12.7	192	4	16 529	7.8	26.0	66.2
Washington, TX	12.2	40.4	43.4	371	13.9	313	9	33 612	8.3	30.6	61.1
Webb, TX	12.5	73.7	97.9	3 087	16.5	3 926	59	287 314	11.6	61.7	26.7

[2]IEP = Individual Education Program. See Notes and Definitions at the end of this section.
. . . = Not available.

Table C-1. Population, School, and Student Characteristics by County—*Continued*

County	Current expenditures, fiscal 1999			Resident population 16 to 19 years, 2000				Outcomes, 1999–2000	
	Amount ($1,000s)	Amount per student	Percent for instruction	Total population 16 to 19 years	Percent in Armed Forces	Percent high school graduates	Percent not enrolled, not grads, not Armed Forces, not empl.	Number of graduates	Dropouts grades 9–12 (percent)
	21	22	23	24	25	26	27	28	29
Matagorda, TX	$51 267	$6 219	58.9	2 573	0.0	12.5	8.0	497	4.2
Maverick, TX	64 738	5 303	60.9	3 350	0.0	7.0	13.9	591	4.5
Medina, TX	44 106	5 408	63.5	2 431	0.0	10.8	4.9	497	3.5
Menard, TX	4 409	8 836	57.7	150	0.0	9.3	4.0	33	1.3
Midland, TX	134 476	5 472	58.4	7 590	0.0	9.4	5.4	1 444	6.4
Milam, TX	27 572	5 866	65.8	1 463	0.0	13.3	2.6	293	4.4
Mills, TX	7 625	7 557	65.6	284	0.0	8.1	7.4	66	2.3
Mitchell, TX	11 014	7 157	64.3	723	0.0	15.6	19.4	108	4.5
Montague, TX	21 695	6 554	62.8	1 067	0.0	15.1	9.0	199	4.1
Montgomery, TX	287 245	5 262	60.5	17 271	0.1	10.0	6.3	3 059	3.1
Moore, TX	24 643	5 250	64.6	1 300	0.0	18.0	6.4	251	2.9
Morris, TX	17 143	6 373	64.0	741	0.0	14.2	6.2	163	3.6
Motley, TX	2 257	9 687	63.3	80	0.0	13.8	2.5	19	2.4
Nacogdoches, TX	57 518	5 695	59.9	5 187	0.0	6.0	3.2	633	3.5
Navarro, TX	47 335	5 560	62.5	3 172	0.0	6.7	8.0	501	4.3
Newton, TX	17 042	6 231	62.4	1 053	0.0	16.2	11.5	173	1.7
Nolan, TX	22 513	6 387	64.1	999	0.0	14.3	3.9	229	5.0
Nueces, TX	364 221	5 804	60.1	20 381	0.6	10.6	7.3	3 620	7.0
Ochiltree, TX	11 445	5 550	66.5	477	0.0	6.7	6.1	111	2.9
Oldham, TX	8 676	10 996	66.7	195	0.0	5.6	3.6	74	2.4
Orange, TX	98 196	5 684	60.6	5 240	0.0	12.0	4.4	1 130	3.0
Palo Pinto, TX	29 841	6 076	63.6	1 644	0.0	10.0	11.4	266	3.6
Panola, TX	25 565	6 393	62.0	1 545	0.0	8.9	2.7	283	5.0
Parker, TX	80 363	5 243	63.2	5 353	0.0	10.8	6.1	829	5.4
Parmer, TX	16 044	6 243	66.5	677	0.0	9.3	5.5	155	3.3
Pecos, TX	27 017	7 820	59.8	1 395	0.0	18.6	10.7	255	6.6
Polk, TX	37 939	5 787	61.5	1 972	0.1	9.8	9.0	376	3.1
Potter, TX	179 496	5 619	61.0	7 166	0.0	14.0	15.2	1 687	5.3
Presidio, TX	11 068	5 922	63.6	512	0.0	8.4	12.1	102	5.0
Rains, TX	7 760	5 374	64.3	548	0.0	16.4	4.4	94	2.3
Randall, TX	31 179	4 264	64.9	6 773	0.1	11.7	2.3	450	3.9
Reagan, TX	7 638	7 669	62.9	251	0.0	5.6	0.0	83	0.3
Real, TX	2 002	7 612	67.4	172	0.0	11.0	4.1	28	2.2
Red River, TX	17 666	6 160	63.5	860	0.0	12.3	8.8	176	5.5
Reeves, TX	18 380	5 624	61.8	825	0.0	9.9	7.0	178	6.2
Refugio, TX	11 608	6 812	64.2	492	0.0	12.0	4.5	135	4.4
Roberts, TX	1 727	9 489	55.9	54	0.0	0.0	3.7	17	. . .
Robertson, TX	20 991	6 371	61.3	925	0.0	16.5	12.3	184	7.2
Rockwall, TX	44 919	4 947	61.0	2 275	0.0	9.5	3.9	497	2.6
Runnels, TX	17 271	6 661	65.7	681	0.0	8.4	5.0	147	4.3
Rusk, TX	48 285	6 279	61.6	2 579	0.0	11.4	6.9	471	4.4
Sabine, TX	10 407	6 492	63.2	471	0.0	5.5	4.7	96	3.8
San Augustine, TX	10 570	6 968	60.6	421	1.2	10.7	1.7	114	2.2
San Jacinto, TX	19 703	5 499	60.7	1 249	0.0	11.4	7.7	168	5.2
San Patricio, TX	88 541	5 623	62.1	4 600	3.3	15.5	7.7	848	4.3
San Saba, TX	7 901	6 823	65.3	640	0.0	12.7	28.1	67	1.8
Schleicher, TX	5 027	6 915	64.7	180	0.0	9.4	3.3	50	1.3
Scurry, TX	21 772	6 309	65.0	1 306	0.0	10.4	15.0	250	3.2
Shackelford, TX	4 571	6 654	64.2	182	0.0	9.9	1.1	37	2.3
Shelby, TX	28 314	5 825	63.4	1 477	0.0	11.0	9.6	253	4.8
Sherman, TX	5 188	6 534	65.8	193	0.0	8.3	5.7	59	3.3
Smith, TX	154 935	5 144	62.2	11 093	0.0	11.7	5.8	1 677	4.4
Somervell, TX	14 160	9 106	57.5	385	0.0	8.8	2.3	92	2.5
Starr, TX	81 932	5 678	56.8	4 069	0.0	7.0	13.0	684	8.5
Stephens, TX	9 780	5 194	64.8	599	0.0	6.3	12.5	118	4.5
Sterling, TX	2 786	7 983	63.1	84	0.0	11.9	0.0	27	. . .
Stonewall, TX	2 909	8 408	66.4	115	0.0	13.9	0.0	31	1.7
Sutton, TX	7 103	7 146	61.4	241	0.0	6.6	3.3	71	2.9
Swisher, TX	12 976	6 713	64.2	499	0.0	13.4	8.6	130	2.1
Tarrant, TX	1 355 608	5 299	60.6	81 998	0.1	11.4	6.9	13 169	5.4
Taylor, TX	141 289	5 785	62.0	9 283	3.0	14.0	4.9	1 375	5.7
Terrell, TX	2 442	10 617	52.9	70	0.0	8.6	2.9	11	1.4
Terry, TX	18 198	6 332	62.6	874	0.0	15.1	5.1	166	4.8
Throckmorton, TX	3 119	8 059	66.7	122	0.0	6.6	1.6	26	1.9
Titus, TX	38 564	6 741	51.7	1 766	0.0	10.8	7.2	271	4.9
Tom Green, TX	114 642	5 830	59.1	7 663	6.7	17.7	4.1	1 168	5.1
Travis, TX	627 287	5 612	59.3	48 677	0.1	9.7	6.5	5 409	6.3
Trinity, TX	15 487	6 560	62.5	721	0.0	15.3	9.0	134	5.5
Tyler, TX	23 134	6 031	61.0	1 026	0.7	12.8	6.2	265	3.4
Upshur, TX	38 389	5 676	66.5	2 166	0.0	10.5	6.9	458	3.2
Upton, TX	9 043	9 265	60.9	274	0.0	5.8	2.6	83	3.2
Uvalde, TX	38 424	6 107	60.4	1 758	0.0	8.0	7.1	334	8.5
Val Verde, TX	54 557	5 364	60.6	2 750	1.1	10.0	10.2	545	5.7
Van Zandt, TX	46 562	5 073	63.4	2 568	0.0	11.3	4.2	542	3.6
Victoria, TX	97 973	6 050	58.5	5 069	0.0	11.8	4.5	976	6.9
Walker, TX	47 779	6 333	50.2	5 932	0.2	14.3	13.4	448	3.8
Waller, TX	39 109	5 867	58.0	3 146	0.0	8.0	3.5	342	4.8
Ward, TX	16 718	6 396	62.1	873	0.0	13.5	9.3	159	6.5
Washington, TX	29 013	5 586	61.1	2 541	0.0	7.9	3.6	313	4.7
Webb, TX	263 458	5 577	60.4	13 908	0.0	8.0	10.3	2 342	4.5

. . . = Not available.

Table C-1. Population, School, and Student Characteristics by County—*Continued*

| County | High school graduates, 2000 | | | College enrollment, 2000 | | College graduates, 2000 (percent) | | | | | | |
	Population 25 years and over	High school diploma or less (percent)	High school diploma or more (percent)	Number	Percent public	Bachelor's degree or more	+/- U.S. percent with bachelor's degree or more	Non-Hispanic White	Black or African American	American Indian and Alaska Native	Asian, Hawaiian, and Pacific Islander	Hispanic or Latino[1]
	30	31	32	33	34	35	36	37	38	39	40	41
Matagorda, TX	23 509	60.9	70.3	932	88.6	12.5	-11.9	17.6	8.1	15.4	14.3	2.1
Maverick, TX	25 468	76.7	42.1	1 552	87.8	9.1	-15.3	33.0	17.1	2.9	25.2	8.0
Medina, TX	24 629	61.2	72.2	1 529	84.3	13.3	-11.1	19.5	0.4	23.1	29.6	5.3
Menard, TX	1 660	61.6	69.4	33	90.9	17.2	-7.2	23.0	42.9	0.0	100.0	1.1
Midland, TX	71 008	43.8	79.2	5 824	91.8	24.8	0.4	32.1	10.4	21.9	50.0	6.0
Milam, TX	15 641	66.1	70.9	647	93.0	11.6	-12.8	14.1	3.4	16.5	0.0	2.4
Mills, TX	3 582	59.2	76.7	57	71.9	20.2	-4.2	21.6	50.0	80.0	. . .	2.5
Mitchell, TX	6 634	69.3	71.7	248	97.2	10.4	-14.0	16.6	0.4	5.0	0.0	2.7
Montague, TX	13 208	62.4	73.0	446	92.4	11.3	-13.1	11.4	0.0	4.4	43.5	5.5
Montgomery, TX	183 743	45.8	81.6	11 460	87.7	25.3	0.9	27.1	15.4	14.5	50.0	11.3
Moore, TX	11 460	66.4	62.1	612	95.8	11.0	-13.4	16.7	0.0	0.0	34.8	1.2
Morris, TX	8 776	60.7	73.7	419	88.3	11.2	-13.2	13.6	4.1	11.5	21.7	4.5
Motley, TX	987	60.2	73.5	28	78.6	14.7	-9.7	16.1	0.0	100.0	. . .	3.9
Nacogdoches, TX	33 175	53.6	73.7	9 575	96.7	22.8	-1.6	27.3	8.6	10.5	61.1	5.3
Navarro, TX	28 324	61.0	71.7	2 132	90.0	12.2	-12.2	15.0	4.2	31.3	26.0	3.6
Newton, TX	9 738	76.7	68.7	214	95.3	5.5	-18.9	5.5	4.8	0.0	68.0	5.1
Nolan, TX	10 203	62.2	69.9	559	91.2	13.2	-11.2	17.2	4.8	0.0	10.6	1.7
Nueces, TX	191 848	50.7	74.4	18 244	91.9	18.8	-5.6	29.3	13.8	11.5	43.2	9.4
Ochiltree, TX	5 441	58.2	69.2	178	82.6	16.1	-8.3	19.9	. . .	26.2	0.0	3.7
Oldham, TX	1 250	46.6	80.5	57	100.0	19.4	-5.0	19.4	80.0	0.0	. . .	17.1
Orange, TX	54 229	59.7	79.0	2 925	90.2	11.0	-13.4	11.3	7.3	3.4	19.4	6.4
Palo Pinto, TX	17 764	60.5	71.2	610	88.0	12.1	-12.3	13.4	4.2	2.9	9.0	1.9
Panola, TX	14 848	58.9	75.9	831	90.9	13.4	-11.0	15.7	4.6	0.0	0.0	0.5
Parker, TX	57 072	49.9	80.5	3 105	84.5	18.6	-5.8	19.7	4.9	16.4	18.1	4.9
Parmer, TX	5 868	64.7	60.7	280	92.5	13.4	-11.0	22.0	0.0	15.6	27.3	1.4
Pecos, TX	9 870	66.9	62.5	787	91.7	12.9	-11.5	22.9	9.3	25.0	8.6	6.2
Polk, TX	28 453	66.5	70.0	1 496	91.8	10.4	-14.0	12.1	2.2	2.3	44.8	5.3
Potter, TX	69 427	58.2	71.1	5 877	92.0	13.5	-10.9	17.8	5.6	10.0	16.5	3.6
Presidio, TX	4 303	75.2	44.7	164	87.8	11.7	-12.7	34.5	28.6	60.0	44.0	6.0
Rains, TX	6 298	64.5	73.0	216	90.3	11.5	-12.9	11.7	7.6	12.1	47.6	2.7
Randall, TX	65 628	33.8	89.5	9 190	94.8	28.9	4.5	30.3	14.5	26.5	46.7	12.8
Reagan, TX	1 955	66.9	63.0	40	100.0	9.2	-15.2	15.1	0.0	31.6	0.0	0.5
Real, TX	2 150	55.3	73.0	95	90.5	17.3	-7.1	19.7	0.0	0.0	0.0	6.3
Red River, TX	9 801	68.0	65.7	306	92.2	9.0	-15.4	10.2	4.2	1.5	88.9	0.9
Reeves, TX	7 692	78.2	46.6	297	93.3	8.0	-16.4	22.0	5.6	5.4	68.6	2.2
Refugio, TX	5 178	64.4	68.1	166	95.2	11.6	-12.8	19.1	0.6	0.0	16.7	3.4
Roberts, TX	623	38.5	90.0	25	92.0	25.4	1.0	25.4	. . .	. . .	0.0	0.0
Robertson, TX	10 218	67.8	68.1	368	81.5	12.7	-11.7	16.5	6.4	0.0	0.0	1.7
Rockwall, TX	27 113	36.2	86.7	1 854	77.0	32.7	8.3	34.8	27.4	37.1	41.4	10.0
Runnels, TX	7 723	66.3	68.9	227	86.3	13.1	-11.3	15.9	0.0	25.4	12.5	3.1
Rusk, TX	31 843	58.9	74.1	1 715	81.5	12.8	-11.6	15.8	3.8	28.4	24.3	1.5
Sabine, TX	7 676	65.2	72.5	188	79.8	10.6	-13.8	10.9	7.6	18.8	50.0	4.5
San Augustine, TX	6 221	68.7	69.9	178	96.6	11.8	-12.6	14.0	5.3	27.8	0.0	6.8
San Jacinto, TX	15 040	66.0	72.6	386	84.7	9.6	-14.8	10.4	4.9	50.0	0.0	1.9
San Patricio, TX	39 551	58.4	71.4	2 740	87.4	13.0	-11.4	19.2	13.1	13.0	22.2	5.7
San Saba, TX	3 997	61.2	70.0	136	83.8	15.8	-8.6	18.2	0.0	15.4	33.3	3.4
Schleicher, TX	1 913	60.2	60.4	75	100.0	17.6	-6.8	26.3	0.0	0.0	80.0	2.3
Scurry, TX	10 632	59.6	72.3	704	94.2	11.8	-12.6	15.3	5.6	0.0	43.3	1.6
Shackelford, TX	2 221	53.4	79.2	82	86.6	20.8	-3.6	21.8	0.0	0.0	66.7	5.1
Shelby, TX	16 266	66.6	68.9	653	90.0	12.2	-12.2	14.8	4.2	8.3	24.5	3.7
Sherman, TX	1 968	53.8	73.1	95	96.8	20.4	-4.0	25.6	25.0	0.0	0.0	2.8
Smith, TX	111 020	44.6	80.2	9 012	91.3	22.5	-1.9	26.9	11.2	17.9	47.6	3.4
Somervell, TX	4 372	54.4	78.0	263	82.5	17.2	-7.2	18.9	0.0	28.0	14.3	0.9
Starr, TX	27 716	82.2	34.7	2 009	91.7	6.9	-17.5	26.0	34.6	0.0	79.8	6.2
Stephens, TX	6 471	57.0	72.3	346	84.1	13.4	-11.0	14.2	17.7	0.0	46.9	0.0
Sterling, TX	916	57.5	70.4	42	100.0	17.1	-7.3	23.0	. . .	0.0	. . .	2.0
Stonewall, TX	1 211	66.9	71.0	23	60.9	12.6	-11.8	14.1	5.7	0.0	. . .	2.8
Sutton, TX	2 632	65.4	64.4	63	92.1	13.0	-11.4	21.4	. . .	0.0	82.4	3.0
Swisher, TX	5 200	61.3	69.7	193	80.3	16.2	-8.2	23.6	0.0	13.6	0.0	1.5
Tarrant, TX	898 850	42.2	81.3	78 661	72.2	26.6	2.2	31.7	17.1	18.5	35.9	9.6
Taylor, TX	75 496	47.2	81.2	10 826	32.0	22.5	-1.9	25.9	15.3	13.4	27.2	6.5
Terrell, TX	736	56.5	70.9	17	47.1	19.0	-5.4	31.9	. . .	0.0	. . .	4.7
Terry, TX	8 008	69.3	62.5	304	83.9	9.5	-14.9	15.0	2.1	0.0	100.0	0.6
Throckmorton, TX	1 272	56.1	77.4	38	89.5	18.2	-6.2	19.4	. . .	0.0	. . .	1.4
Titus, TX	16 899	63.9	65.5	929	89.9	13.2	-11.2	16.9	8.8	17.9	40.0	2.1
Tom Green, TX	63 430	52.3	76.2	7 281	95.7	19.5	-4.9	24.7	12.4	17.0	27.3	6.1
Travis, TX	501 361	32.7	84.7	87 661	89.8	40.6	16.2	51.0	20.5	24.9	63.3	15.8
Trinity, TX	9 623	66.4	73.1	256	91.0	9.4	-15.0	9.9	5.7	0.0	50.0	10.4
Tyler, TX	14 433	69.6	71.9	491	82.3	9.7	-14.7	10.9	2.6	3.6	66.7	4.0
Upshur, TX	22 977	60.0	76.3	1 046	82.1	11.1	-13.3	11.6	7.5	8.5	24.6	6.6
Upton, TX	2 165	67.1	67.1	57	96.5	11.8	-12.6	17.6	0.0	17.4	. . .	2.7
Uvalde, TX	15 280	62.8	59.6	1 099	93.4	13.8	-10.6	25.6	0.0	6.0	30.1	5.4
Val Verde, TX	26 281	66.1	58.7	1 443	82.6	14.1	-10.3	27.0	25.2	15.2	42.5	9.0
Van Zandt, TX	32 427	62.4	72.0	1 205	91.4	11.6	-12.8	12.3	3.3	10.3	19.0	2.8
Victoria, TX	51 985	52.8	76.2	3 966	92.7	16.2	-8.2	22.3	9.4	6.8	50.3	6.0
Walker, TX	36 678	58.6	73.1	9 404	95.1	18.3	-6.1	25.3	6.4	7.4	45.5	4.3
Waller, TX	18 395	57.6	73.9	4 267	95.3	16.8	-7.6	18.2	21.4	13.7	19.7	4.9
Ward, TX	6 765	64.4	70.1	253	92.5	12.4	-12.0	17.9	0.0	3.9	100.0	4.5
Washington, TX	19 451	56.5	72.1	1 938	95.4	19.0	-5.4	23.0	5.9	0.0	21.4	2.8
Webb, TX	101 182	65.0	53.0	11 089	89.6	13.9	-10.5	36.7	23.4	6.1	43.9	12.3

[1]Hispanic or Latino persons may be of any race.
. . . = Not available.

Table C-1. Population, School, and Student Characteristics by County—*Continued*

County	State/County code	County type[1]	Population, 2000		Number of schools and students, 2000–2001			Resident enrollment, 2000			
			Total	Percent 5–17 years	School districts	Schools	Students	Total	Percent public	K–12	Percent public
			1	2	3	4	5	6	7	8	9
Wharton, TX	48481	6	41 188	21.7	5	18	8 571	11 527	92.0	9 347	94.3
Wheeler, TX	48483	9	5 284	18.9	5	7	945	1 214	94.4	1 098	95.0
Wichita, TX	48485	3	131 664	18.2	6	46	22 478	35 683	90.5	24 628	94.5
Wilbarger, TX	48487	6	14 676	21.3	3	8	2 732	3 816	94.2	2 881	95.9
Willacy, TX	48489	6	20 082	23.4	4	13	4 752	6 058	97.9	5 013	98.9
Williamson, TX	48491	2	249 967	21.4	11	95	62 549	70 940	85.8	53 372	93.3
Wilson, TX	48493	1	32 408	22.3	4	22	6 949	8 879	92.5	7 296	95.6
Winkler, TX	48495	6	7 173	22.8	2	6	1 727	1 938	99.5	1 698	99.6
Wise, TX	48497	6	48 793	21.5	7	28	8 356	12 621	92.9	10 784	95.1
Wood, TX	48499	6	36 752	16.6	6	20	5 897	7 855	89.5	6 157	95.1
Yoakum, TX	48501	7	7 322	24.6	2	7	1 928	2 286	99.0	1 972	100.0
Young, TX	48503	7	17 943	19.0	3	11	3 413	4 167	93.9	3 556	96.5
Zapata, TX	48505	6	12 182	23.9	1	6	2 904	3 703	97.1	3 093	97.9
Zavala, TX	48507	7	11 600	25.2	2	7	2 451	3 883	96.7	3 147	97.2
UTAH	49000										
Beaver, UT	49001	9	6 005	24.2	1	5	1 426	1 757	95.5	1 488	99.3
Box Elder, UT	49003	6	42 745	26.8	1	26	10 917	13 949	95.7	11 538	97.9
Cache, UT	49005	4	91 391	21.4	2	31	18 958	37 654	95.8	19 663	98.0
Carbon, UT	49007	7	20 422	21.5	1	14	4 285	6 264	94.8	4 291	95.9
Daggett, UT	49009	9	921	16.6	1	3	164	192	100.0	165	100.0
Davis, UT	49011	0	238 994	25.4	1	83	59 578	80 293	92.2	60 679	96.6
Duchesne, UT	49013	7	14 371	27.7	1	15	4 140	4 687	96.0	4 002	98.2
Emery, UT	49015	9	10 860	27.2	1	10	2 714	3 518	96.9	3 042	99.0
Garfield, UT	49017	9	4 735	24.1	1	9	1 115	1 301	96.8	1 119	99.6
Grand, UT	49019	7	8 485	19.9	1	4	1 560	2 054	93.1	1 649	94.6
Iron, UT	49021	7	33 779	21.9	1	14	7 176	13 246	96.2	7 356	98.1
Juab, UT	49023	6	8 238	27.4	2	9	2 121	2 607	93.2	2 251	95.5
Kane, UT	49025	7	6 046	22.8	1	7	1 335	1 688	93.8	1 371	95.3
Millard, UT	49027	7	12 405	29.2	1	9	3 363	4 187	96.5	3 704	97.5
Morgan, UT	49029	8	7 129	28.9	1	3	2 032	2 628	93.8	2 103	98.6
Piute, UT	49031	9	1 435	22.5	1	4	407	392	97.4	313	96.8
Rich, UT	49033	9	1 961	27.4	1	4	473	640	95.3	544	97.8
Salt Lake, UT	49035	0	898 387	21.6	4	234	176 334	275 773	88.7	193 851	93.9
San Juan, UT	49037	7	14 413	29.6	1	13	3 165	5 470	98.0	4 410	98.8
Sanpete, UT	49039	6	22 763	24.9	2	14	5 305	8 638	95.2	5 588	97.5
Sevier, UT	49041	7	18 842	25.7	1	15	4 520	5 971	94.5	4 876	97.1
Summit, UT	49043	6	29 736	22.7	3	12	6 227	8 606	87.1	6 661	94.3
Tooele, UT	49045	6	40 735	24.0	1	18	9 177	12 109	92.5	9 805	96.6
Uintah, UT	49047	7	25 224	26.3	1	13	6 014	7 936	95.2	6 634	97.7
Utah, UT	49049	2	368 536	23.1	3	114	81 513	148 809	70.4	83 763	96.7
Wasatch, UT	49051	6	15 215	25.0	1	7	3 678	4 874	91.5	3 926	96.2
Washington, UT	49053	4	90 354	22.1	1	31	18 374	26 270	91.4	19 539	94.9
Wayne, UT	49055	9	2 509	23.6	1	4	550	719	97.8	599	99.0
Weber, UT	49057	0	196 533	22.0	4	68	41 293	59 292	93.1	43 794	96.2
VERMONT	50000										
Addison, VT	50001	6	35 974	19.2	21	22	5 563	10 568	68.8	6 890	92.0
Bennington, VT	50003	6	36 994	18.5	15	20	6 861	9 380	77.4	6 897	89.2
Caledonia, VT	50005	7	29 702	19.8	20	21	4 057	7 986	80.0	5 971	82.3
Chittenden, VT	50007	3	146 571	17.8	24	52	23 376	45 835	79.4	25 849	89.3
Essex, VT	50009	9	6 459	20.2	9	9	1 300	1 543	92.5	1 322	93.1
Franklin, VT	50011	3	45 417	21.0	18	20	8 942	11 338	93.8	9 512	97.3
Grand Isle, VT	50013	3	6 901	19.3	6	6	796	1 629	89.6	1 327	95.4
Lamoille, VT	50015	8	23 233	18.8	12	15	3 980	6 279	89.5	4 237	93.1
Orange, VT	50017	9	28 226	20.0	22	21	5 323	7 349	85.9	5 634	89.9
Orleans, VT	50019	7	26 277	19.5	22	22	4 581	6 344	86.0	5 214	92.2
Rutland, VT	50021	7	63 400	18.1	31	37	10 840	16 135	86.4	11 748	94.2
Washington, VT	50023	6	58 039	18.1	22	27	9 847	15 111	79.1	10 728	93.5
Windham, VT	50025	7	44 216	18.3	27	34	6 718	10 936	77.0	8 180	88.8
Windsor, VT	50027	7	57 418	18.4	33	45	9 643	13 723	84.8	10 809	93.9
VIRGINIA	51000										
Accomack, VA	51001	7	38 305	18.2	1	12	5 340	8 559	89.2	7 110	92.0
Albemarle, VA	51003	3	79 236	18.6	1	24	12 237	21 699	82.4	14 705	86.2
Alleghany, VA	51005	6	12 926	17.3	◊2	◊11	◊3 583	2 731	93.8	2 198	96.0
Amelia, VA	51007	8	11 400	19.1	1	3	1 788	2 734	84.5	2 238	87.3
Amherst, VA	51009	3	31 894	17.8	1	10	4 630	7 838	74.9	5 609	88.0
Appomattox, VA	51011	8	13 705	18.5	1	4	2 397	3 174	87.4	2 628	92.2
Arlington, VA	51013	0	189 453	11.0	1	30	18 870	40 996	66.7	21 548	88.2
Augusta, VA	51015	4	65 615	18.1	1	20	10 746	14 577	85.5	12 054	90.8
Bath, VA	51017	9	5 048	16.6	1	3	821	1 034	93.3	836	95.0
Bedford, VA	51019	3	60 371	18.2	*1	*21	*10 697	13 656	82.2	10 747	89.3
Bland, VA	51021	9	6 871	14.9	1	4	903	1 436	87.7	1 104	91.5
Botetourt, VA	51023	3	30 496	17.7	1	11	4 583	6 949	84.9	5 518	91.1
Brunswick, VA	51025	8	18 419	15.5	1	6	2 426	4 414	81.8	3 224	89.7
Buchanan, VA	51027	9	26 978	16.6	1	14	4 063	5 598	95.4	4 398	97.1
Buckingham, VA	51029	8	15 623	17.4	1	6	2 260	3 417	92.7	2 914	93.5
Campbell, VA	51031	3	51 078	18.1	1	14	8 654	12 058	84.6	9 357	89.8
Caroline, VA	51033	8	22 121	18.5	1	6	3 888	4 940	92.3	4 191	95.0
Carroll, VA	51035	7	29 245	15.5	1	10	3 990	5 729	94.4	4 542	95.7
Charles City County, VA	51036	2	6 926	16.5	1	3	941	1 543	84.5	1 216	87.9
Charlotte, VA	51037	8	12 472	18.8	1	6	2 217	2 876	92.0	2 414	94.6

[1]County type code is from the Economic Research Service of the USDA. See Notes and Definitions at the end of this section.
◊ = Clifton Forge City and Covington City are included with Alleghany County.
* = Bedford City is included in Bedford County.

Table C-1. School and Student Characteristics by County—*Continued*

County	Characteristics of students, 2000–2001			Staff and students, 2000–2001				Revenues, fiscal 1999			
	Percent with IEP[2]	Percent eligible for free lunch	Percent minority	Number of teachers	Student/ teacher ratio	Local school non-teaching staff	Central admin. staff	Total revenue ($1,000s)	Percentage of revenue from		
									Federal govt.	State govt.	Local govt.
	10	11	12	13	14	15	16	17	18	19	20
Wharton, TX	12.6	49.8	59.7	623	13.8	626	17	$53 298	7.7	51.0	41.3
Wheeler, TX	9.4	49.0	25.4	118	8.0	87	22	11 744	5.6	24.6	69.9
Wichita, TX	12.1	42.3	30.9	1 642	13.7	1 426	24	142 565	11.5	44.3	44.1
Wilbarger, TX	15.4	52.8	42.5	216	12.6	145	14	17 709	7.4	35.7	56.9
Willacy, TX	11.0	...	95.6	358	13.3	452	27	37 194	15.6	61.3	23.2
Williamson, TX	11.7	18.2	30.2	4 505	13.9	3 793	103	373 017	3.4	29.5	67.1
Wilson, TX	13.4	40.7	43.0	496	14.0	456	17	40 842	6.8	63.8	29.5
Winkler, TX	17.6	43.2	55.3	155	11.1	154	10	16 176	7.1	25.9	66.9
Wise, TX	12.4	32.0	18.5	614	13.6	491	31	50 845	4.9	52.9	42.1
Wood, TX	13.5	40.2	16.8	441	13.4	368	39	37 940	6.7	46.3	47.1
Yoakum, TX	10.5	57.3	60.3	168	11.5	125	5	24 894	5.3	7.2	87.5
Young, TX	14.3	39.5	18.5	254	13.4	190	14	20 646	8.6	58.5	32.9
Zapata, TX	9.7	69.8	96.6	216	13.4	306	3	22 861	10.6	7.6	81.8
Zavala, TX	10.0	89.9	98.1	182	13.5	266	8	20 250	19.6	65.2	15.2
UTAH											
Beaver, UT	11.1	34.3	8.2	70	20.4	59	5	8 057	5.3	60.7	34.1
Box Elder, UT	14.2	30.0	8.8	509	21.4	475	38	53 260	6.2	67.1	26.7
Cache, UT	11.5	28.6	10.0	889	21.3	707	35	92 117	5.4	66.6	28.0
Carbon, UT	15.9	42.2	12.5	227	18.9	233	21	28 790	12.9	57.2	29.9
Daggett, UT	11.0	36.3	3.7	15	10.9	17	3	2 446	5.9	57.6	36.4
Davis, UT	9.2	19.7	8.1	2 619	22.7	2 282	199	287 547	6.1	64.0	29.9
Duchesne, UT	15.5	46.5	11.5	220	18.8	254	13	24 325	7.7	69.7	22.6
Emery, UT	14.5	40.5	6.3	151	18.0	162	7	20 285	5.6	44.3	50.1
Garfield, UT	14.7	46.5	8.3	64	17.4	61	5	8 438	8.0	62.6	29.4
Grand, UT	14.2	42.9	13.6	86	18.1	95	11	9 501	5.7	50.0	44.4
Iron, UT	12.6	39.1	9.1	328	21.9	337	26	46 718	6.7	51.6	41.7
Juab, UT	15.1	38.4	3.1	104	20.4	110	7	13 009	6.1	64.1	29.7
Kane, UT	15.8	43.0	6.1	75	17.8	74	4	9 172	7.4	61.7	30.9
Millard, UT	7.0	46.5	10.5	178	18.9	237	9	24 768	6.8	41.4	51.8
Morgan, UT	7.4	14.8	2.6	100	20.3	75	6	10 341	4.2	61.3	34.5
Piute, UT	19.9	58.6	5.9	28	14.5	31	3	3 530	8.3	78.4	13.3
Rich, UT	15.2	49.9	1.3	30	15.8	24	3	4 302	5.2	60.7	34.1
Salt Lake, UT	10.9	28.3	19.3	7 847	22.5	6 171	529	883 417	7.6	58.5	33.9
San Juan, UT	12.1	65.5	59.4	210	15.1	235	31	30 382	29.8	51.1	19.1
Sanpete, UT	16.3	43.0	9.7	257	20.6	309	18	31 281	11.1	68.2	20.8
Sevier, UT	12.3	42.3	5.3	215	21.0	202	12	25 238	8.7	66.4	24.9
Summit, UT	11.3	16.2	8.5	345	18.0	260	30	46 454	2.7	24.9	72.4
Tooele, UT	10.9	34.6	14.0	411	22.3	335	21	38 582	7.3	66.3	26.3
Uintah, UT	15.5	43.2	14.9	310	19.4	269	23	34 364	10.2	61.5	28.4
Utah, UT	10.5	24.3	9.8	3 509	23.2	1 997	223	377 482	6.3	66.9	26.8
Wasatch, UT	13.3	16.5	6.0	194	19.0	203	13	19 042	5.7	57.0	37.3
Washington, UT	11.2	34.7	9.4	827	22.2	608	25	89 086	5.2	60.0	34.8
Wayne, UT	10.0	54.4	1.1	36	15.3	32	4	4 079	7.3	75.2	17.5
Weber, UT	13.6	34.3	19.1	1 994	20.7	1 322	210	199 587	6.9	66.4	26.7
VERMONT											
Addison, VT	...	20.9	1.8	480	11.6	510	40	84 047	3.2	52.9	43.9
Bennington, VT	...	24.3	3.6	644	10.7	606	80	72 070	5.6	56.8	37.6
Caledonia, VT	20.5	40.8	2.4	373	10.9	449	27	44 959	5.5	75.5	19.0
Chittenden, VT	...	15.8	5.7	1 750	13.4	1 664	158	233 916	3.6	60.6	35.8
Essex, VT	...	26.6	1.2	114	11.4	96	12	10 324	5.5	75.9	18.6
Franklin, VT	...	26.5	5.9	741	12.1	700	67	82 314	5.7	71.3	23.0
Grand Isle, VT	24.6	32.9	1.0	72	11.1	64	6	10 001	6.1	74.2	19.7
Lamoille, VT	...	26.0	2.9	336	11.8	322	22	40 628	4.3	62.4	33.3
Orange, VT	...	30.2	1.9	483	11.0	480	40	59 785	4.1	58.0	37.9
Orleans, VT	...	44.5	3.1	414	11.1	441	34	55 590	8.0	55.9	36.1
Rutland, VT	...	27.2	2.2	931	11.6	896	85	120 919	4.5	57.1	38.4
Washington, VT	...	21.6	2.9	804	12.2	822	78	118 798	3.9	57.0	39.2
Windham, VT	...	25.9	4.0	637	10.5	632	56	100 701	5.5	47.8	46.7
Windsor, VT	...	22.3	2.6	850	11.3	887	79	113 548	4.6	58.3	37.1
VIRGINIA											
Accomack, VA	11.0	58.7	55.8	379	14.1	351	32	39 354	8.0	53.7	38.3
Albemarle, VA	16.4	17.9	19.1	961	12.7	847	101	100 051	2.8	21.2	76.0
Alleghany, VA	◊17.6	◊31.1	◊10.6	◊264	◊14.6	◊260	◊37	◊30 979	◊5.2	◊42.9	◊52.0
Amelia, VA	15.4	34.4	37.9	125	14.3	119	19	12 429	5.1	46.3	48.6
Amherst, VA	11.9	29.7	28.4	330	14.0	240	34	28 046	4.2	51.8	44.1
Appomattox, VA	14.5	31.3	31.2	186	12.9	141	18	15 206	5.3	52.7	42.0
Arlington, VA	16.5	40.7	58.7	1 442	13.1	1 077	429	221 653	3.3	9.8	86.9
Augusta, VA	14.2	21.5	4.1	778	13.8	614	96	79 910	3.5	37.8	58.7
Bath, VA	16.4	26.7	2.8	75	10.9	60	11	7 473	5.9	15.3	78.8
Bedford, VA	*12.6	*25.0	*11.9	*713	*15.0	*514	*35	*51 655	*4.6	*43.8	*51.6
Bland, VA	19.0	...	1.1	72	12.5	50	11	6 576	5.4	59.3	35.3
Botetourt, VA	18.9	11.3	4.5	325	14.1	259	22	31 400	3.3	40.8	55.9
Brunswick, VA	12.7	68.1	78.4	184	13.2	195	40	18 764	9.4	53.8	36.8
Buchanan, VA	18.5	68.3	0.2	354	11.5	245	59	32 044	9.3	51.9	38.9
Buckingham, VA	17.1	...	49.4	165	13.7	158	32	15 485	7.8	55.7	36.5
Campbell, VA	11.2	28.2	19.7	585	14.8	450	61	57 498	4.2	42.5	53.3
Caroline, VA	11.4	38.8	44.7	251	15.5	240	20	24 881	6.3	47.0	46.7
Carroll, VA	21.2	41.0	3.0	329	12.1	264	41	26 384	7.3	49.9	42.8
Charles City County, VA	14.8	42.8	78.3	...	...	80	20	9 334	5.2	38.4	56.5
Charlotte, VA	13.9	47.6	39.8	152	14.6	142	26	15 183	7.8	58.2	34.0

[2]IEP = Individual Education Program. See Notes and Definitions at the end of this section.
. . . = Not available.
◊ = Clifton Forge City and Covington City are included with Alleghany County.
* = Bedford City is included in Bedford County.

Table C-1. Population, School, and Student Characteristics by County—*Continued*

County	Current expenditures, fiscal 1999			Resident population 16 to 19 years, 2000				Outcomes, 1999–2000	
	Amount ($1,000s)	Amount per student	Percent for instruction	Total population 16 to 19 years	Percent in Armed Forces	Percent high school graduates	Percent not enrolled, not grads, not Armed Forces, not empl.	Number of graduates	Dropouts grades 9–12 (percent)
	21	22	23	24	25	26	27	28	29
Wharton, TX	$48 862	$5 628	64.0	2 943	0.0	11.1	6.8	567	1.9
Wheeler, TX	9 683	9 204	64.5	333	0.0	9.6	2.7	82	2.8
Wichita, TX	129 200	5 691	62.2	10 345	24.1	35.5	5.8	1 384	2.8
Wilbarger, TX	15 551	5 445	66.0	1 235	0.0	14.3	14.8	175	5.1
Willacy, TX	32 664	6 554	60.0	1 527	0.0	11.3	13.2	287	8.0
Williamson, TX	296 223	5 344	63.2	13 778	0.0	11.0	2.4	3 312	2.8
Wilson, TX	35 948	5 385	64.0	1 950	0.0	7.5	7.4	395	2.8
Winkler, TX	14 271	7 535	58.8	506	0.0	9.9	5.3	124	2.8
Wise, TX	45 120	5 732	63.7	2 800	0.0	15.1	5.2	522	1.9
Wood, TX	34 129	5 653	63.6	2 096	0.0	14.7	6.9	378	2.9
Yoakum, TX	16 694	7 693	62.5	588	0.0	5.8	3.7	144	1.2
Young, TX	20 052	5 582	65.2	1 041	0.0	7.5	5.3	230	1.6
Zapata, TX	18 271	6 246	60.4	938	0.0	13.1	13.6	164	7.3
Zavala, TX	17 388	6 870	58.1	901	0.0	6.7	11.1	142	8.8
UTAH									
Beaver, UT	6 687	4 593	62.8	384	0.5	14.1	1.6	112	1.1
Box Elder, UT	46 124	4 117	66.2	3 425	0.0	15.0	4.9	777	2.6
Cache, UT	76 219	3 996	67.0	8 606	0.0	12.9	2.4	1 383	3.7
Carbon, UT	23 048	4 968	65.1	1 724	0.0	8.5	3.0	315	1.4
Daggett, UT	1 985	10 847	52.8	59	0.0	10.2	3.4	12	...
Davis, UT	242 005	4 082	62.9	18 896	0.7	15.9	2.9	4 567	0.4
Duchesne, UT	20 842	4 820	60.1	1 158	0.0	15.4	7.8	295	3.3
Emery, UT	15 270	4 924	70.6	943	0.0	9.1	3.0	263	1.2
Garfield, UT	6 916	6 219	66.6	344	0.0	17.4	0.9	93	...
Grand, UT	7 901	4 859	58.7	539	0.0	13.5	6.9	111	2.8
Iron, UT	32 005	4 606	64.9	3 214	0.0	8.3	1.9	404	1.1
Juab, UT	10 312	4 774	60.8	643	0.0	9.5	1.9	167	1.0
Kane, UT	7 657	5 303	66.3	425	0.0	9.2	3.5	109	0.4
Millard, UT	19 382	5 375	64.3	1 107	0.0	8.8	3.6	279	3.5
Morgan, UT	9 045	4 419	62.1	726	0.0	9.6	1.5	185	0.8
Piute, UT	2 893	6 921	63.5	105	0.0	12.4	1.9	33	...
Rich, UT	3 620	7 154	59.9	152	0.0	10.5	2.6	43	0.5
Salt Lake, UT	736 493	4 113	66.6	62 241	0.0	13.9	4.6	11 878	7.3
San Juan, UT	25 234	7 357	56.0	1 122	0.0	10.8	4.1	204	3.3
Sanpete, UT	24 559	4 489	68.2	2 615	0.3	6.8	2.3	368	3.0
Sevier, UT	20 890	4 374	65.2	1 548	0.0	8.6	5.6	332	7.4
Summit, UT	31 548	5 179	61.9	1 752	0.0	10.4	5.7	384	3.7
Tooele, UT	33 588	4 112	63.8	3 169	0.1	15.1	9.1	483	1.9
Uintah, UT	28 224	4 361	65.3	2 151	0.4	15.9	4.9	466	5.4
Utah, UT	308 810	3 921	67.5	34 454	0.0	14.1	2.5	4 950	2.1
Wasatch, UT	13 926	3 889	68.3	1 040	0.0	10.7	2.4	297	2.9
Washington, UT	71 605	3 868	66.7	6 967	0.0	14.5	3.3	1 316	2.6
Wayne, UT	3 639	6 569	57.4	164	0.0	12.8	0.0	37	...
Weber, UT	175 532	4 302	63.6	14 074	0.1	14.7	5.4	2 647	3.6
VERMONT									
Addison, VT	51 140	8 621	60.2	2 868	0.0	8.7	5.0	380	3.8
Bennington, VT	47 454	8 390	66.5	2 015	0.0	11.7	1.6	689	4.8
Caledonia, VT	36 746	9 082	72.4	1 941	0.0	12.1	4.8	105	5.6
Chittenden, VT	176 539	7 549	64.9	9 953	0.0	5.9	1.5	1 387	4.4
Essex, VT	7 891	8 169	58.3	342	0.0	18.1	6.4	103	5.0
Franklin, VT	55 153	6 756	63.9	2 438	0.1	18.9	3.2	626	5.4
Grand Isle, VT	6 749	8 426	60.1	321	0.0	5.9	2.2	0	...
Lamoille, VT	29 206	7 405	64.4	1 316	0.0	9.8	2.4	220	5.0
Orange, VT	40 094	7 754	63.2	1 679	0.0	11.4	1.9	295	5.7
Orleans, VT	36 345	7 751	58.9	1 408	0.0	14.3	4.3	317	5.0
Rutland, VT	81 985	7 597	65.1	3 623	0.2	11.5	2.7	791	3.6
Washington, VT	77 733	7 669	64.1	3 245	0.3	11.0	1.1	666	3.1
Windham, VT	66 645	9 396	63.9	2 438	0.0	9.1	3.2	434	7.3
Windsor, VT	78 985	8 251	62.9	2 845	0.0	12.1	2.1	630	4.9
VIRGINIA									
Accomack, VA	31 659	5 826	61.5	1 972	0.0	13.8	8.2	306	13.0
Albemarle, VA	80 222	6 696	60.7	3 371	0.0	9.1	3.9	713	2.1
Alleghany, VA	◊	◊	◊	599	0.0	13.2	1.5	◊	◊
Amelia, VA	10 352	5 738	61.1	533	0.0	10.7	2.1	110	4.4
Amherst, VA	23 834	5 112	63.2	2 053	0.0	14.7	6.3	299	5.1
Appomattox, VA	12 549	5 266	65.4	667	0.0	6.9	1.6	142	4.0
Arlington, VA	187 024	10 321	56.0	5 912	3.9	12.1	3.7	988	2.7
Augusta, VA	61 803	5 669	66.1	3 215	0.0	15.2	2.9	742	2.1
Bath, VA	7 474	8 379	54.2	181	0.0	4.4	0.0	55	4.2
Bedford, VA	*	*	*	2 735	0.0	16.6	3.7	*	*
Bland, VA	5 694	5 919	59.5	325	0.0	7.4	4.9	67	2.9
Botetourt, VA	26 929	5 828	65.3	1 502	0.0	13.3	1.3	310	3.1
Brunswick, VA	16 956	6 567	52.3	990	0.7	12.0	9.0	141	5.8
Buchanan, VA	29 849	6 652	59.8	1 585	0.0	13.3	12.6	352	4.8
Buckingham, VA	13 559	6 034	61.7	672	0.0	19.2	10.3	89	6.4
Campbell, VA	44 758	5 267	60.8	2 394	0.0	14.3	1.5	468	3.3
Caroline, VA	21 279	5 594	62.8	1 117	0.0	19.3	6.4	195	4.3
Carroll, VA	22 183	5 546	63.8	1 200	0.0	13.8	5.0	243	3.9
Charles City County, VA	7 918	7 725	56.5	353	0.0	14.7	1.1	65	3.4
Charlotte, VA	13 331	5 899	62.5	671	0.0	15.6	8.5	139	3.0

. . . = Not available.
◊ = Clifton Forge City and Covington City are included with Alleghany County.
* = Bedford city is included in Bedford County.

Table C-1. Population, School, and Student Characteristics by County—*Continued*

County	High school graduates, 2000			College enrollment, 2000		College graduates, 2000 (percent)						
	Population 25 years and over	High school diploma or less (percent)	High school diploma or more (percent)	Number	Percent public	Bachelor's degree or more	+/- U.S. percent with bachelor's degree or more	Non-Hispanic White	Black or African American	American Indian and Alaska Native	Asian, Hawaiian, and Pacific Islander	Hispanic or Latino[1]
	30	31	32	33	34	35	36	37	38	39	40	41
Wharton, TX	25 567	59.5	69.8	1 417	94.6	14.3	-10.1	20.2	9.2	8.3	47.1	2.6
Wheeler, TX	3 601	58.6	72.0	82	84.1	13.0	-11.4	13.8	0.0	0.0	62.5	7.0
Wichita, TX	80 740	49.9	79.9	8 736	87.6	20.0	-4.4	22.5	10.5	16.1	21.0	8.6
Wilbarger, TX	9 313	57.3	72.2	665	97.1	17.1	-7.3	20.2	4.8	77.1	41.9	2.8
Willacy, TX	11 332	75.6	48.7	620	91.1	7.5	-16.9	23.3	0.7	0.0	0.0	4.7
Williamson, TX	155 565	33.4	88.8	11 436	75.6	33.6	9.2	36.3	29.0	24.1	55.3	16.7
Wilson, TX	20 590	60.3	73.8	1 099	80.9	12.8	-11.6	15.8	7.8	16.2	28.7	6.5
Winkler, TX	4 380	67.0	60.3	135	97.0	10.5	-13.9	16.0	0.0	25.0	0.0	1.6
Wise, TX	31 130	58.7	76.1	1 230	81.7	13.0	-11.4	13.8	5.8	7.7	34.5	4.1
Wood, TX	25 895	56.5	76.3	1 175	68.4	14.5	-9.9	15.4	8.2	6.7	29.0	3.8
Yoakum, TX	4 322	67.1	59.4	182	87.9	10.2	-14.2	14.9	19.4	0.0	100.0	2.3
Young, TX	12 265	60.0	72.1	443	84.0	14.4	-10.0	15.1	20.1	9.8	75.9	4.2
Zapata, TX	6 945	74.6	53.1	359	88.3	8.7	-15.7	12.2	...	...	0.0	7.6
Zavala, TX	6 371	76.9	43.4	460	98.3	7.6	-16.8	26.3	0.0	0.0	100.0	5.4
UTAH												
Beaver, UT	3 442	55.2	83.2	127	85.0	12.1	-12.3	12.5	0.0	0.0	35.7	1.1
Box Elder, UT	22 766	43.6	87.8	1 685	91.6	19.5	-4.9	20.4	0.0	20.6	22.5	4.0
Cache, UT	42 544	32.2	90.4	16 337	97.7	31.9	7.5	32.9	38.1	6.5	51.7	7.7
Carbon, UT	12 090	50.3	81.1	1 565	93.3	12.3	-12.1	13.4	0.0	3.7	26.1	2.9
Daggett, UT	632	51.6	83.7	11	100.0	11.9	-12.5	13.0	...	...	0.0	0.0
Davis, UT	125 532	31.1	92.2	14 267	88.1	28.8	4.4	29.9	19.2	11.3	24.9	10.9
Duchesne, UT	7 752	56.7	81.0	445	88.3	12.7	-11.7	13.2	...	7.1	30.8	8.4
Emery, UT	5 980	51.1	84.2	283	93.6	11.6	-12.8	12.1	0.0	11.5	0.0	2.3
Garfield, UT	2 829	46.7	85.8	82	86.6	20.3	-4.1	20.8	0.0	0.0	0.0	18.5
Grand, UT	5 486	44.3	82.5	248	91.9	22.9	-1.5	23.7	0.0	0.0	25.0	15.7
Iron, UT	16 318	35.5	88.6	5 249	96.5	23.8	-0.6	24.5	0.0	11.1	39.0	7.2
Juab, UT	4 290	52.4	82.9	186	83.9	12.2	-12.2	12.3	...	0.0	...	0.0
Kane, UT	3 842	39.8	86.4	243	94.2	21.1	-3.3	21.4	0.0	0.0	0.0	12.5
Millard, UT	6 769	43.9	86.7	216	90.3	16.8	-7.6	17.4	...	22.5	17.9	2.6
Morgan, UT	3 805	37.0	92.6	377	93.1	23.3	-1.1	23.6	...	0.0	33.3	4.8
Piute, UT	893	51.1	85.7	35	100.0	14.4	-10.0	14.8	...	0.0	0.0	0.0
Rich, UT	1 144	42.5	91.5	51	100.0	22.0	-2.4	22.4	...	0.0	...	0.0
Salt Lake, UT	509 453	37.2	86.8	63 514	84.2	27.4	3.0	29.5	22.5	11.4	30.0	10.0
San Juan, UT	7 290	54.0	69.6	725	96.7	13.9	-10.5	26.2	0.0	3.5	20.0	5.7
Sanpete, UT	11 522	44.3	84.6	2 563	93.0	17.3	-7.1	17.9	22.6	5.6	14.0	7.3
Sevier, UT	10 480	48.5	85.8	661	94.1	15.2	-9.2	15.7	0.0	0.0	11.1	7.8
Summit, UT	18 366	24.6	92.5	1 350	74.5	45.5	21.1	48.1	22.2	58.5	60.5	9.9
Tooele, UT	21 752	47.4	85.6	1 318	88.2	15.9	-8.5	17.1	8.7	11.0	20.8	5.1
Uintah, UT	13 736	56.2	79.8	773	91.5	13.2	-11.2	13.9	0.0	4.0	41.3	9.1
Utah, UT	166 240	28.3	90.9	57 002	35.6	31.5	7.1	32.5	25.7	20.6	41.6	16.2
Wasatch, UT	8 448	35.7	89.3	620	81.8	26.3	1.9	27.0	...	11.1	47.4	8.1
Washington, UT	51 842	39.1	87.6	5 019	91.4	21.0	-3.4	21.7	17.0	9.1	19.0	5.2
Wayne, UT	1 493	37.8	88.5	76	92.1	20.9	-3.5	20.9	100.0	10.0	0.0	0.0
Weber, UT	111 156	42.6	85.0	11 715	91.6	19.9	-4.5	21.7	10.1	13.7	27.9	5.9
VERMONT												
Addison, VT	22 468	47.4	86.4	3 126	20.9	29.8	5.4	29.9	45.5	14.5	57.7	32.6
Bennington, VT	25 311	48.2	84.9	1 816	41.6	27.1	2.7	27.2	34.4	0.0	45.6	25.1
Caledonia, VT	19 596	55.0	82.6	1 584	73.0	22.5	-1.9	22.6	15.4	6.3	42.5	28.7
Chittenden, VT	92 651	32.9	90.6	17 217	69.8	41.2	16.8	41.1	38.3	33.2	46.3	47.1
Essex, VT	4 384	71.0	75.0	121	85.1	10.8	-13.6	10.4	0.0	5.4	18.2	62.5
Franklin, VT	29 485	58.5	82.6	1 223	75.5	16.6	-7.8	16.8	30.0	8.1	36.1	4.9
Grand Isle, VT	4 796	49.6	84.2	192	68.2	25.0	0.6	25.2	50.0	0.0	30.0	20.0
Lamoille, VT	15 281	43.6	87.0	1 637	84.5	31.2	6.8	31.5	31.3	26.6	37.5	42.3
Orange, VT	18 821	53.4	84.1	1 232	77.1	23.9	-0.5	23.8	29.6	10.7	55.0	32.3
Orleans, VT	17 814	62.5	78.2	811	75.2	16.1	-8.3	16.1	38.1	8.7	31.8	17.1
Rutland, VT	43 289	51.5	84.3	3 396	65.6	23.2	-1.2	23.2	12.7	14.4	45.7	37.5
Washington, VT	39 167	43.1	88.4	3 593	40.1	32.2	7.8	32.3	29.7	33.6	39.1	38.0
Windham, VT	30 542	45.4	87.3	2 145	40.4	30.5	6.1	30.3	47.5	14.3	51.1	44.6
Windsor, VT	40 618	44.2	88.1	2 225	51.2	30.2	5.8	30.1	33.3	33.8	53.4	24.5
VIRGINIA												
Accomack, VA	25 894	66.2	67.9	881	87.6	13.5	-10.9	17.8	4.7	0.0	44.2	2.3
Albemarle, VA	53 847	30.4	87.4	5 379	87.8	47.7	23.3	49.8	20.7	27.7	77.5	32.0
Alleghany, VA	9 168	61.7	77.5	382	93.7	13.6	-10.8	13.3	10.0	...	74.5	0.0
Amelia, VA	7 789	67.9	68.3	219	91.8	9.8	-14.6	10.9	7.1	0.0	0.0	100.0
Amherst, VA	21 293	62.8	70.6	1 757	40.4	13.1	-11.3	15.0	4.7	9.8	43.1	9.7
Appomattox, VA	9 421	67.6	70.7	350	73.1	10.5	-13.9	12.4	2.6	0.0	50.0	59.0
Arlington, VA	138 844	23.9	87.8	16 371	43.9	60.2	35.8	73.8	29.9	31.7	59.8	20.6
Augusta, VA	45 609	62.1	78.2	1 580	73.5	15.4	-9.0	15.7	8.2	0.0	32.1	17.3
Bath, VA	3 705	65.1	74.0	135	83.7	11.1	-13.3	11.5	0.0	...	0.0	33.9
Bedford, VA	42 413	52.6	80.1	1 752	69.1	20.9	-3.5	21.8	3.6	27.8	42.7	17.8
Bland, VA	4 989	67.2	70.9	258	84.9	9.2	-15.2	9.3	0.0	...	...	57.1
Botetourt, VA	21 621	52.5	81.4	937	73.0	19.6	-4.8	19.9	12.3	4.0	36.4	25.7
Brunswick, VA	12 777	67.8	63.2	908	54.0	10.8	-13.6	10.9	10.9	22.2	0.0	7.6
Buchanan, VA	18 851	74.7	52.9	905	86.1	8.0	-16.4	7.9	11.7	...	29.8	3.0
Buckingham, VA	10 893	75.3	62.8	336	82.4	8.5	-15.9	10.1	6.1	...	100.0	13.7
Campbell, VA	35 018	59.9	73.4	1 918	70.2	14.6	-9.8	15.9	4.6	7.3	59.4	24.1
Caroline, VA	15 082	66.3	71.3	459	77.6	12.1	-12.3	15.3	5.8	6.0	21.1	14.4
Carroll, VA	21 006	69.6	64.3	935	93.9	9.5	-14.9	9.5	0.0	0.0	20.0	15.9
Charles City County, VA	4 845	68.9	65.7	240	82.9	10.5	-13.9	19.1	5.3	1.2	0.0	0.0
Charlotte, VA	8 570	71.6	63.2	284	81.7	10.3	-14.1	12.2	5.9	...	0.0	17.9

[1]Hispanic or Latino persons may be of any race.
. . . = Not available.

Table C-1. Population, School, and Student Characteristics by County—*Continued*

County	State/County code	County type[1]	Population, 2000 Total	Percent 5–17 years	Number of schools and students, 2000–2001 School districts	Schools	Students	Resident enrollment, 2000 Total	Percent public	K–12	Percent public
			1	2	3	4	5	6	7	8	9
Chesterfield, VA	51041	2	259 903	21.5	1	58	51 212	76 024	86.8	56 777	92.4
Clarke, VA	51043	1	12 652	18.2	1	5	1 947	2 927	82.6	2 349	88.3
Craig, VA	51045	8	5 091	17.9	1	2	711	1 057	87.1	883	91.7
Culpeper, VA	51047	1	34 262	19.3	1	7	5 627	8 160	86.7	6 702	89.7
Cumberland, VA	51049	8	9 017	18.5	1	3	1 309	2 035	78.7	1 712	81.0
Dickenson, VA	51051	9	16 395	16.7	1	8	2 712	3 605	97.9	2 829	99.1
Dinwiddie, VA	51053	2	24 533	18.4	1	7	4 318	5 586	89.1	4 508	93.2
Essex, VA	51057	8	9 989	17.7	1	3	1 637	2 300	88.2	1 912	89.7
Fairfax, VA	51059	0	969 749	18.4	+1	+194	+156 412	265 920	78.8	181 731	86.8
Fauquier, VA	51061	1	55 139	20.4	1	16	9 613	14 403	80.3	11 091	84.5
Floyd, VA	51063	8	13 874	16.6	1	5	1 957	2 800	90.3	2 169	93.5
Fluvanna, VA	51065	3	20 047	17.1	1	5	3 048	4 657	85.8	3 538	89.7
Franklin, VA	51067	6	47 286	16.8	1	15	7 140	10 503	84.8	7 814	94.2
Frederick, VA	51069	4	59 209	19.9	1	15	10 634	14 489	88.7	11 715	94.3
Giles, VA	51071	9	16 657	16.4	1	5	2 538	3 462	94.1	2 747	95.9
Gloucester, VA	51073	1	34 780	20.4	1	10	6 451	9 365	89.1	7 144	93.6
Goochland, VA	51075	2	16 863	16.1	1	5	1 984	3 725	69.6	2 779	73.3
Grayson, VA	51077	9	17 917	14.7	1	11	2 263	3 280	91.2	2 667	94.4
Greene, VA	51079	3	15 244	19.8	1	5	2 607	3 751	84.9	3 014	87.2
Greensville, VA	51081	6	11 560	14.4	°1	°5	°2 766	2 619	86.4	2 063	84.3
Halifax, VA	51083	6	37 355	17.5	1	19	6 030	8 208	92.8	6 553	94.7
Hanover, VA	51085	2	86 320	20.6	1	19	16 611	23 954	84.3	17 536	94.8
Henrico, VA	51087	2	262 300	17.8	1	62	41 655	65 953	83.8	46 900	90.5
Henry, VA	51089	4	57 930	16.8	1	21	8 807	12 980	90.0	9 981	94.4
Highland, VA	51091	9	2 536	16.2	1	2	334	483	93.0	412	98.1
Isle of Wight, VA	51093	1	29 728	19.4	1	8	4 973	7 272	81.0	5 731	84.0
James City County, VA	51095	0	48 102	17.7	§1	§12	§8 191	11 808	85.0	8 630	89.3
King and Queen, VA	51097	8	6 630	17.4	1	3	945	1 339	88.6	1 132	90.6
King George, VA	51099	1	16 803	20.2	1	4	2 939	4 551	86.1	3 444	93.2
King William, VA	51101	6	13 146	19.2	2	6	2 598	3 138	89.6	2 537	93.8
Lancaster, VA	51103	9	11 567	14.8	1	3	1 513	2 169	86.5	1 805	89.3
Lee, VA	51105	9	23 589	16.9	1	13	3 815	5 068	93.1	3 985	96.4
Loudoun, VA	51107	1	169 599	20.1	1	46	31 804	46 444	79.9	33 317	88.9
Louisa, VA	51109	8	25 627	18.5	1	5	4 219	5 754	89.9	4 854	91.8
Lunenburg, VA	51111	9	13 146	16.4	1	4	1 836	2 602	90.7	2 160	92.3
Madison, VA	51113	8	12 520	18.3	1	5	1 849	2 711	79.7	2 212	83.6
Mathews, VA	51115	1	9 207	15.3	1	3	1 297	1 744	89.5	1 390	95.0
Mecklenburg, VA	51117	7	32 380	16.2	1	12	4 997	6 732	93.2	5 325	95.2
Middlesex, VA	51119	8	9 932	15.4	1	4	1 357	1 929	91.0	1 552	92.7
Montgomery, VA	51121	4	83 629	12.4	1	20	9 114	37 615	94.8	10 341	92.1
Nelson, VA	51125	8	14 445	16.4	1	4	2 058	2 892	89.2	2 353	93.0
New Kent, VA	51127	2	13 462	19.3	1	4	2 342	3 026	92.6	2 549	95.4
Northampton, VA	51131	9	13 093	17.7	1	4	2 198	3 230	87.2	2 566	88.1
Northumberland, VA	51133	9	12 259	14.3	1	3	1 488	2 114	87.0	1 753	92.1
Nottoway, VA	51135	6	15 725	17.3	1	6	2 499	3 322	91.5	2 965	93.1
Orange, VA	51137	6	25 881	17.0	1	7	3 955	5 494	86.3	4 492	90.7
Page, VA	51139	6	23 177	17.4	1	7	3 537	4 692	92.7	4 080	95.9
Patrick, VA	51141	9	19 407	16.0	1	7	2 640	3 770	93.4	2 997	97.4
Pittsylvania, VA	51143	3	61 745	17.4	1	18	9 241	13 858	87.5	11 025	92.3
Powhatan, VA	51145	2	22 377	18.1	1	4	3 573	5 353	85.6	4 188	90.5
Prince Edward, VA	51147	7	19 720	15.3	1	3	2 623	7 257	80.7	3 130	86.5
Prince George, VA	51149	2	33 047	19.1	1	10	5 855	8 720	88.5	6 578	92.3
Prince William, VA	51153	0	280 813	21.9	1	66	54 646	83 548	83.5	61 279	90.4
Pulaski, VA	51155	7	35 127	15.1	1	11	5 015	6 831	96.0	5 145	99.6
Rappahannock, VA	51157	8	6 983	17.2	1	2	1 020	1 453	80.2	1 166	84.0
Richmond, VA	51159	9	8 809	14.3	1	3	1 256	1 743	89.0	1 374	92.6
Roanoke, VA	51161	3	85 778	17.4	1	27	13 869	20 624	81.6	15 132	91.7
Rockbridge, VA	51163	6	20 808	16.8	1	8	3 053	4 498	84.6	3 550	95.5
Rockingham, VA	51165	5	67 725	18.4	1	20	10 703	16 106	81.9	12 333	89.3
Russell, VA	51167	6	30 308	15.8	1	12	4 263	6 333	93.7	4 934	95.9
Scott, VA	51169	2	23 403	15.5	1	13	3 671	4 540	97.0	3 654	99.1
Shenandoah, VA	51171	6	35 075	16.7	1	9	5 447	7 076	86.5	5 774	89.4
Smyth, VA	51173	6	33 081	16.3	1	13	5 189	6 761	95.2	5 448	97.7
Southampton, VA	51175	6	17 482	17.6	1	7	2 862	3 963	85.2	3 189	85.7
Spotsylvania, VA	51177	0	90 395	22.4	1	25	18 876	25 581	85.7	20 291	90.9
Stafford, VA	51179	1	92 446	23.8	1	23	21 124	29 156	87.5	22 283	93.0
Surry, VA	51181	8	6 829	19.6	1	3	1 232	1 750	83.4	1 443	84.8
Sussex, VA	51183	8	12 504	15.0	1	5	1 433	2 713	83.6	2 200	82.6
Tazewell, VA	51185	7	44 598	16.2	1	16	7 116	9 714	90.6	7 262	96.0
Warren, VA	51187	1	31 584	18.9	1	8	4 935	7 320	79.6	5 905	85.7
Washington, VA	51191	2	51 103	15.7	1	15	7 360	10 974	85.2	7 994	93.8
Westmoreland, VA	51193	6	16 718	17.8	2	5	2 630	3 622	91.1	3 019	92.7
Wise, VA	51195	7	40 123	17.2	1	15	6 938	9 569	94.3	7 019	96.8
Wythe, VA	51197	7	27 599	16.4	1	10	4 318	5 862	92.7	4 471	98.4
York, VA	51199	0	56 297	22.8	1	19	11 756	17 228	85.1	12 874	91.1
Alexandria City, VA	51510	0	128 283	10.6	1	18	11 167	26 509	72.1	14 135	83.5
Bedford City, VA	51515	3	6 299	16.0	*	*	*	1 345	89.0	1 022	94.8
Bristol City, VA	51520	2	17 367	15.0	1	6	2 408	3 677	80.3	2 616	93.2
Buena Vista City, VA	51530	6	6 349	16.3	1	4	1 118	1 501	82.2	1 018	98.1
Charlottesville City, VA	51540	3	45 049	10.8	1	10	4 458	20 969	93.6	4 959	91.9

[1]County type code is from the Economic Research Service of the USDA. See Notes and Definitions at the end of this section.
+ = Fairfax City is included with Fairfax County.
° = Emporia City is included with Greensville County.
§ = Williamsburg City is included with James City County.
* = Bedford City is included in Bedford County.

Table C-1. School and Student Characteristics by County—*Continued*

County	Characteristics of students, 2000–2001			Staff and students, 2000–2001				Revenues, fiscal 1999			
	Percent with IEP[2]	Percent eligible for free lunch	Percent minority	Number of teachers	Student/ teacher ratio	Local school non-teaching staff	Central admin. staff	Total revenue ($1,000s)	Percentage of revenue from		
									Federal govt.	State govt.	Local govt.
	10	11	12	13	14	15	16	17	18	19	20
Chesterfield, VA	15.3	. . .	28.2	3 466	14.8	2 413	218	$319 137	3.3	37.4	59.3
Clarke, VA	10.4	12.0	8.7	140	13.9	143	20	13 134	3.4	32.1	64.5
Craig, VA	14.3	22.6	1.0	57	12.5	34	9	4 838	6.7	51.8	41.5
Culpeper, VA	12.7	. . .	24.7	430	13.1	345	45	38 416	3.9	38.8	57.3
Cumberland, VA	17.3	. . .	57.7	98	13.4	94	23	9 049	7.5	48.1	44.4
Dickenson, VA	15.0	57.0	0.6	200	13.6	165	18	20 555	10.2	52.9	37.0
Dinwiddie, VA	12.3	35.1	41.8	298	14.5	281	33	29 379	5.9	49.8	44.4
Essex, VA	18.3	48.9	55.2	131	12.5	92	13	11 107	6.3	42.4	51.3
Fairfax, VA	+13.9	+17.7	+39.2	+11 006	+14.2	+8 450	+1 487	+1 367 606	+3.0	+13.8	+83.2
Fauquier, VA	14.9	15.0	12.3	707	13.6	591	45	72 351	2.5	24.2	73.3
Floyd, VA	18.5	28.9	4.2	136	14.4	129	14	12 044	5.7	52.0	42.3
Fluvanna, VA	14.7	18.0	23.8	207	14.7	160	15	18 073	3.5	46.3	50.1
Franklin, VA	17.2	40.0	14.9	494	14.5	439	46	44 042	5.6	43.1	51.3
Frederick, VA	13.8	14.8	7.0	797	13.3	603	57	73 868	3.0	35.0	62.0
Giles, VA	13.1	27.8	2.3	175	14.5	159	17	17 241	5.2	47.6	47.2
Gloucester, VA	11.5	. . .	14.5	477	13.5	397	43	42 587	4.0	45.4	50.6
Goochland, VA	18.6	19.3	34.0	157	12.6	139	22	14 893	4.3	15.8	79.9
Grayson, VA	13.3	54.3	4.2	153	14.8	153	20	15 405	6.3	58.0	35.7
Greene, VA	19.2	21.6	11.8	227	11.5	200	40	19 077	4.8	45.8	49.4
Greensville, VA	°4.6	°58.0	°73.4	°200	°13.8	°130	°23	°17 414	°8.4	°59.0	°32.6
Halifax, VA	19.7	49.4	49.9	496	12.2	451	36	41 045	7.7	56.0	36.3
Hanover, VA	13.1	. . .	11.6	1 133	14.7	684	83	102 075	2.4	32.7	64.9
Henrico, VA	13.9	. . .	39.4	2 559	16.3	1 786	201	260 239	3.3	31.8	64.9
Henry, VA	18.2	35.3	32.9	707	12.5	612	58	56 829	6.8	50.7	42.5
Highland, VA	15.3	31.1	38.9	35	9.5	22	6	2 992	5.7	45.2	49.0
Isle of Wight, VA	11.9	32.2	36.9	310	16.0	258	35	34 288	4.9	40.0	55.1
James City County, VA	§10.9	. . .	§27.7	§626	§13.1	§474	§71	§79 155	§2.4	§17.3	§80.3
King and Queen, VA	20.1	61.9	53.3	79	12.0	77	16	8 523	6.8	39.8	53.4
King George, VA	17.8	21.0	26.8	214	13.7	165	23	19 078	4.3	44.7	50.9
King William, VA	17.7	24.7	29.4	206	12.6	127	31	19 244	4.7	43.2	52.1
Lancaster, VA	10.4	48.3	52.5	. . .	. . .	92	10	10 847	6.5	26.8	66.7
Lee, VA	18.0	60.0	0.9	302	12.6	224	43	28 143	11.1	60.4	28.5
Loudoun, VA	12.1	8.3	22.1	1 996	15.9	1 605	147	206 210	1.7	18.1	80.2
Louisa, VA	12.4	32.6	29.0	304	13.9	307	42	28 578	4.1	23.8	72.1
Lunenburg, VA	17.6	61.5	50.9	140	13.1	126	20	12 942	8.7	58.8	32.6
Madison, VA	18.5	19.1	18.3	145	12.8	120	16	11 118	5.5	48.1	46.4
Mathews, VA	15.8	22.5	16.3	94	13.8	95	15	9 279	4.6	36.6	58.8
Mecklenburg, VA	14.7	49.8	49.5	370	13.5	304	45	29 457	7.8	54.4	37.8
Middlesex, VA	18.4	28.3	27.0	107	12.7	98	17	9 673	7.5	32.0	60.5
Montgomery, VA	13.6	27.5	8.8	717	12.7	623	83	64 268	5.3	40.6	54.1
Nelson, VA	16.9	33.3	21.2	161	12.8	146	27	21 132	4.7	25.3	70.0
New Kent, VA	18.9	13.0	19.3	186	12.6	175	13	13 911	3.7	42.8	53.5
Northampton, VA	12.4	65.2	61.1	178	12.3	190	42	16 863	8.6	49.7	41.8
Northumberland, VA	11.9	47.8	48.5	104	14.3	134	16	11 786	7.0	22.7	70.3
Nottoway, VA	19.4	52.3	48.7	186	13.4	154	28	16 481	10.0	59.0	30.9
Orange, VA	15.2	26.4	20.4	312	12.7	242	38	26 804	3.6	38.7	57.8
Page, VA	12.2	34.1	3.6	267	13.2	203	27	21 535	5.7	52.7	41.5
Patrick, VA	16.6	38.7	11.6	200	13.2	186	16	16 867	5.6	52.0	42.4
Pittsylvania, VA	12.5	32.4	33.1	636	14.5	520	43	53 100	6.4	54.5	39.1
Powhatan, VA	15.4	12.4	13.4	263	13.6	240	30	22 675	5.2	38.6	56.1
Prince Edward, VA	18.1	53.9	60.6	201	13.0	152	31	17 332	9.8	49.2	41.0
Prince George, VA	10.3	. . .	42.8	389	15.1	316	33	36 467	14.1	49.3	36.5
Prince William, VA	12.8	21.4	39.8	3 343	16.3	2 392	375	371 496	2.7	36.4	60.9
Pulaski, VA	17.8	32.5	8.6	355	14.1	305	23	30 922	7.2	49.8	43.0
Rappahannock, VA	17.6	17.2	8.5	75	13.6	66	15	7 321	4.2	25.0	70.8
Richmond, VA	9.0	34.2	36.0	84	15.0	74	20	8 768	5.5	45.0	49.6
Roanoke, VA	17.2	11.8	7.7	1 035	13.4	766	56	98 529	2.6	34.8	62.6
Rockbridge, VA	16.5	25.5	5.7	268	11.4	184	27	21 292	5.2	40.1	54.7
Rockingham, VA	13.6	23.9	6.3	801	13.4	602	49	75 407	3.6	38.0	58.4
Russell, VA	15.5	42.8	0.9	295	14.5	223	25	27 631	8.9	54.7	36.4
Scott, VA	16.9	51.5	1.0	257	14.3	215	18	23 236	7.7	61.0	31.2
Shenandoah, VA	14.7	22.7	6.2	414	13.2	319	36	33 262	4.6	44.3	51.0
Smyth, VA	16.0	40.2	2.7	403	12.9	226	31	31 256	8.0	57.7	34.2
Southampton, VA	15.3	40.3	53.6	212	13.5	211	32	20 044	6.6	47.1	46.3
Spotsylvania, VA	15.3	17.0	21.0	1 281	14.7	1 082	93	122 465	3.3	36.7	60.0
Stafford, VA	10.3	14.0	21.6	1 374	15.4	979	138	128 187	3.0	39.1	57.9
Surry, VA	15.8	49.3	71.1	104	11.8	107	19	12 856	4.6	12.6	82.8
Sussex, VA	15.2	. . .	78.9	114	12.6	113	23	12 548	7.9	43.7	48.4
Tazewell, VA	17.1	49.8	4.2	509	14.0	326	38	45 714	8.2	54.0	37.9
Warren, VA	13.6	19.7	9.6	357	13.8	277	38	29 547	2.8	40.6	56.6
Washington, VA	12.1	35.2	2.6	15	490.7	339	50	47 324	6.9	45.0	48.1
Westmoreland, VA	10.5	. . .	51.5	139	18.9	157	22	17 608	7.3	47.6	45.1
Wise, VA	14.4	43.2	2.4	480	14.5	376	61	47 454	8.3	54.7	37.0
Wythe, VA	12.6	31.8	4.4	249	17.3	259	26	26 011	7.9	52.5	39.6
York, VA	10.1	15.3	24.0	729	16.1	734	81	82 787	18.1	33.8	48.0
Alexandria City, VA	17.0	49.9	77.8	1 027	10.9	763	121	130 609	3.6	9.5	86.9
Bedford City, VA	*	*	*	*	*	*	*	*	*	*	*
Bristol City, VA	18.4	41.9	10.6	143	16.8	101	22	17 854	4.9	45.9	49.2
Buena Vista City, VA	17.1	29.9	6.9	85	13.2	52	7	8 621	4.6	49.5	46.0
Charlottesville City, VA	17.3	44.8	53.0	368	12.1	309	62	42 063	6.0	26.4	67.6

[2]IEP = Individual Education Program. See Notes and Definitions at the end of this section.
. . . = Not available.
+ = Fairfax City is included with Fairfax County.
° = Emporia City is included with Greensville County.
§ = Williamsburg City is included with James City County.
* = Bedford City is included in Bedford County.

Table C-1. Population, School, and Student Characteristics by County—*Continued*

County	Current expenditures, fiscal 1999			Resident population 16 to 19 years, 2000				Outcomes, 1999–2000	
	Amount ($1,000s)	Amount per student	Percent for instruction	Total population 16 to 19 years	Percent in Armed Forces	Percent high school graduates	Percent not enrolled, not grads, not Armed Forces, not empl.	Number of graduates	Dropouts grades 9–12 (percent)
	21	22	23	24	25	26	27	28	29
Chesterfield, VA	$276 423	$5 461	63.1	15 826	0.2	8.9	3.1	3 191	4.1
Clarke, VA	11 514	6 089	61.4	535	0.0	8.6	3.7	136	1.8
Craig, VA	4 494	6 190	64.2	206	0.0	21.4	11.2	29	0.5
Culpeper, VA	32 865	5 952	64.6	2 106	0.0	10.6	13.2	312	3.8
Cumberland, VA	8 174	6 371	53.0	453	0.0	20.5	4.6	55	7.3
Dickenson, VA	18 054	6 077	57.8	969	0.0	16.1	4.3	233	5.2
Dinwiddie, VA	22 697	5 319	60.7	1 075	0.0	12.7	4.4	194	4.9
Essex, VA	10 261	6 159	60.8	421	0.0	9.0	1.0	84	3.8
Fairfax, VA	+	+	+	45 985	0.2	7.0	3.3	+	+
Fauquier, VA	59 305	6 371	63.2	2 883	0.5	16.6	1.7	589	4.2
Floyd, VA	10 547	5 508	62.1	651	0.0	17.5	2.3	132	1.2
Fluvanna, VA	16 321	5 638	66.4	868	0.0	9.3	0.6	166	5.2
Franklin, VA	38 251	5 494	59.7	2 227	0.0	14.1	3.1	421	3.6
Frederick, VA	62 422	6 016	60.4	3 070	0.1	14.4	3.7	632	4.3
Giles, VA	14 714	5 732	66.1	745	0.0	18.7	2.7	158	3.4
Gloucester, VA	35 805	5 379	60.8	1 902	0.0	11.5	2.6	384	6.0
Goochland, VA	12 977	6 551	59.5	691	0.0	10.9	1.3	91	4.8
Grayson, VA	13 826	5 972	60.5	769	0.0	20.5	5.6	156	2.8
Greene, VA	15 550	6 122	64.4	805	0.0	15.8	4.8	143	7.5
Greensville, VA	°	°	°	459	0.0	13.1	3.5	°	°
Halifax, VA	37 731	6 065	62.2	1 799	0.0	18.6	5.1	378	2.9
Hanover, VA	80 644	5 094	66.3	4 777	0.0	7.4	2.7	978	0.5
Henrico, VA	227 635	5 692	61.2	11 991	0.1	10.4	3.1	2 284	3.7
Henry, VA	51 375	5 566	62.5	2 787	0.5	15.5	6.6	501	2.5
Highland, VA	2 626	7 503	62.2	113	0.0	20.4	0.0	19	...
Isle of Wight, VA	28 516	5 687	62.9	1 477	0.0	8.3	4.8	271	3.6
James City County, VA	§	§	§	2 111	0.0	12.2	3.8	§	§
King and Queen, VA	7 165	7 763	54.4	337	0.0	20.8	5.0	43	2.4
King George, VA	17 900	6 021	60.7	940	6.5	24.5	1.1	185	0.9
King William, VA	15 994	6 257	63.4	567	0.0	10.8	1.2	167	1.3
Lancaster, VA	9 243	5 720	62.2	437	0.0	10.5	3.4	82	4.6
Lee, VA	25 257	6 351	65.3	1 185	0.0	12.9	8.8	228	...
Loudoun, VA	181 835	6 972	63.2	6 931	0.1	8.3	3.1	1 438	2.0
Louisa, VA	23 634	5 739	58.7	1 131	0.0	14.4	5.0	216	4.8
Lunenburg, VA	11 607	6 052	58.6	610	0.0	11.8	8.9	103	7.4
Madison, VA	11 664	6 261	59.0	649	0.0	28.8	4.3	131	3.6
Mathews, VA	7 471	5 668	63.1	284	1.1	14.8	0.0	101	3.5
Mecklenburg, VA	26 962	5 347	63.7	1 577	0.0	13.8	3.7	276	5.1
Middlesex, VA	7 941	5 759	58.5	401	0.0	11.0	6.7	64	3.0
Montgomery, VA	54 981	5 959	61.2	9 640	0.1	3.9	0.7	597	4.3
Nelson, VA	12 830	6 148	56.4	714	1.0	15.1	4.8	153	2.9
New Kent, VA	12 336	5 361	61.5	662	0.0	15.3	5.3	147	3.2
Northampton, VA	15 004	6 270	63.0	780	0.0	8.2	4.7	149	6.6
Northumberland, VA	9 777	6 340	62.5	421	0.0	10.9	0.7	99	4.1
Nottoway, VA	14 580	5 886	61.4	737	0.0	7.6	6.5	150	8.4
Orange, VA	23 644	6 185	64.7	1 159	0.0	15.0	5.9	248	2.6
Page, VA	18 858	5 215	66.5	1 196	0.0	16.5	4.3	237	2.9
Patrick, VA	14 903	5 443	62.8	838	0.0	23.2	4.2	166	4.7
Pittsylvania, VA	48 553	5 215	61.7	3 202	0.0	10.6	2.7	595	3.8
Powhatan, VA	19 684	5 886	61.7	1 094	0.0	14.4	4.8	182	4.3
Prince Edward, VA	14 330	5 335	63.5	2 403	0.0	3.7	4.2	122	4.6
Prince George, VA	30 484	5 377	60.4	2 557	33.9	42.3	4.0	307	3.4
Prince William, VA	318 293	6 227	59.9	15 375	1.5	11.9	3.6	3 020	3.5
Pulaski, VA	28 966	5 750	61.5	1 341	0.0	24.7	7.8	314	4.8
Rappahannock, VA	6 446	6 127	58.5	258	0.0	8.1	4.3	83	0.6
Richmond, VA	7 478	5 739	62.3	359	0.0	9.2	17.5	78	2.4
Roanoke, VA	86 668	6 237	63.9	4 242	0.0	8.4	1.6	969	2.4
Rockbridge, VA	18 834	5 887	63.1	1 027	0.0	17.4	4.9	222	3.5
Rockingham, VA	59 863	5 653	61.9	3 724	0.0	14.6	4.9	667	3.4
Russell, VA	23 915	5 423	62.5	1 583	0.4	12.6	3.8	320	3.0
Scott, VA	21 630	5 782	63.5	1 015	0.0	16.1	3.6	243	2.8
Shenandoah, VA	31 254	5 789	62.4	1 614	0.0	18.4	3.7	341	4.8
Smyth, VA	28 441	5 333	66.0	1 645	0.4	14.3	3.7	295	1.1
Southampton, VA	17 701	6 138	60.7	910	0.0	10.2	7.3	125	3.3
Spotsylvania, VA	99 207	5 744	62.8	4 902	0.0	13.0	2.9	1 137	2.2
Stafford, VA	106 338	5 594	63.7	5 363	0.5	12.8	0.9	1 239	2.0
Surry, VA	11 326	9 268	59.6	375	0.0	6.4	0.5	79	6.4
Sussex, VA	11 168	7 455	58.3	451	0.0	16.2	3.8	74	6.3
Tazewell, VA	41 459	5 360	62.8	2 341	0.0	11.9	5.6	500	5.7
Warren, VA	25 557	5 386	57.6	1 522	0.0	12.4	3.4	248	3.8
Washington, VA	42 181	5 664	62.1	2 728	0.2	13.5	3.4	519	3.1
Westmoreland, VA	14 783	5 117	61.4	768	0.0	13.9	1.6	143	2.6
Wise, VA	41 308	5 623	65.4	2 621	0.0	11.5	5.5	547	2.8
Wythe, VA	23 989	5 478	65.2	1 421	0.0	21.5	2.1	255	3.1
York, VA	61 503	5 370	59.9	3 212	3.1	8.5	3.4	745	1.7
Alexandria City, VA	107 778	9 977	59.7	3 819	0.2	11.8	5.3	537	6.8
Bedford City, VA	*	*	*	244	0.0	7.4	11.9	*	*
Bristol City, VA	15 571	6 542	64.3	792	0.0	13.0	4.2	112	4.2
Buena Vista City, VA	6 759	6 133	64.3	377	0.0	4.5	0.0	71	2.2
Charlottesville City, VA	38 789	8 824	62.2	5 798	0.2	3.8	1.5	220	4.0

+ = Fairfax City is included with Fairfax County.
° = Emporia City is included with Greensville County.
§ = Williamsburg City is included with James City County.
* = Bedford city is included in Bedford County.

Table C-1. Population, School, and Student Characteristics by County—_Continued_

County	High school graduates, 2000			College enrollment, 2000		College graduates, 2000 (percent)						
	Population 25 years and over	High school diploma or less (percent)	High school diploma or more (percent)	Number	Percent public	Bachelor's degree or more	+/- U.S. percent with bachelor's degree or more	Non-Hispanic White	Black or African American	American Indian and Alaska Native	Asian, Hawaiian, and Pacific Islander	Hispanic or Latino[1]
	30	31	32	33	34	35	36	37	38	39	40	41
Chesterfield, VA	167 037	36.7	88.1	13 958	83.8	32.6	8.2	33.9	26.4	21.0	45.0	20.8
Clarke, VA	9 015	50.8	82.1	385	69.4	23.9	-0.5	24.9	10.5	32.4	37.2	14.9
Craig, VA	3 561	64.2	76.6	110	69.1	10.8	-13.6	10.9	0.0	0.0	18.2	. . .
Culpeper, VA	22 628	62.0	73.7	919	88.6	15.7	-8.7	17.4	5.0	22.9	46.0	18.5
Cumberland, VA	6 183	69.8	63.8	193	67.9	11.8	-12.6	14.0	7.8	0.0	100.0	12.4
Dickenson, VA	11 308	76.0	58.9	668	92.8	6.7	-17.7	6.7	0.0	0.0	15.4	0.0
Dinwiddie, VA	17 199	68.0	70.0	686	90.5	11.0	-13.4	12.5	7.8	9.3	54.0	5.8
Essex, VA	7 052	61.3	73.5	311	87.5	17.4	-7.0	21.4	9.7	75.0	55.9	37.5
Fairfax, VA	653 237	23.1	90.7	62 896	73.1	54.8	30.4	62.0	37.5	38.2	51.6	23.3
Fauquier, VA	36 792	43.4	84.5	2 217	80.6	27.1	2.7	29.1	6.3	26.4	35.0	25.7
Floyd, VA	9 836	68.2	70.1	405	80.0	12.5	-11.9	12.6	9.0	. . .	52.4	0.0
Fluvanna, VA	14 125	52.5	80.0	827	84.8	24.5	0.1	28.1	9.0	0.0	37.8	24.1
Franklin, VA	33 037	60.4	72.2	2 126	54.4	14.8	-9.6	15.3	8.1	25.6	23.5	14.5
Frederick, VA	39 271	57.1	78.6	1 918	79.8	18.6	-5.8	18.6	13.9	28.3	38.4	10.7
Giles, VA	11 856	64.9	75.9	504	91.9	12.4	-12.0	12.3	12.0	100.0	61.1	10.8
Gloucester, VA	23 273	49.9	81.7	1 627	86.8	17.6	-6.8	18.4	11.1	34.9	32.1	8.2
Goochland, VA	12 248	50.6	78.8	587	72.7	29.4	5.0	36.0	8.4	0.0	71.3	35.0
Grayson, VA	13 086	73.6	64.1	439	81.5	8.0	-16.4	8.1	6.9	0.0	11.1	10.6
Greene, VA	10 120	56.3	78.4	492	89.8	19.8	-4.6	21.1	2.5	0.0	32.0	0.0
Greensville, VA	8 610	77.1	62.1	445	93.3	11.0	-13.4	7.9	12.9	0.0	100.0	13.0
Halifax, VA	26 073	69.9	63.9	1 112	85.4	9.5	-14.9	11.6	5.2	5.3	31.8	20.1
Hanover, VA	56 892	42.2	86.6	4 301	63.7	28.7	4.3	29.8	17.5	14.1	41.3	26.4
Henrico, VA	177 191	37.1	86.6	13 581	80.0	34.9	10.5	39.2	20.1	9.1	50.3	21.4
Henry, VA	40 518	67.8	64.9	2 200	84.4	9.4	-15.0	10.4	6.0	10.9	23.1	4.5
Highland, VA	1 929	65.4	72.8	43	48.8	13.2	-11.2	13.3	0.0	0.0	. . .	0.0
Isle of Wight, VA	20 121	54.3	76.2	969	89.2	17.5	-6.9	21.1	6.7	5.9	28.6	37.6
James City County, VA	34 042	31.6	89.3	2 277	87.7	41.5	17.1	46.5	10.8	8.7	60.2	32.8
King and Queen, VA	4 663	69.0	68.2	136	80.9	10.3	-14.1	13.4	4.6	25.6	. . .	12.1
King George, VA	10 803	52.0	80.4	735	79.7	23.6	-0.8	26.3	9.5	11.5	50.0	48.2
King William, VA	8 960	59.1	79.1	348	85.9	14.8	-9.6	16.2	9.5	7.1	32.4	8.8
Lancaster, VA	8 841	53.5	74.4	197	88.3	24.5	0.1	31.7	1.6	100.0	68.9	47.8
Lee, VA	16 314	71.2	60.6	833	78.4	9.5	-14.9	9.3	0.0	25.0	67.2	0.0
Loudoun, VA	109 567	25.1	92.5	8 012	73.7	47.2	22.8	49.6	32.0	23.9	53.0	24.7
Louisa, VA	17 697	63.1	71.7	677	82.1	14.0	-10.4	16.0	6.4	8.1	32.2	0.0
Lunenburg, VA	9 305	68.2	63.4	281	84.0	9.2	-15.2	12.7	3.4	0.0	14.3	7.8
Madison, VA	8 644	61.2	75.0	374	74.6	19.4	-5.0	20.7	5.1	0.0	47.4	32.8
Mathews, VA	6 926	53.0	80.8	261	87.7	19.2	-5.2	20.8	5.0	61.5	. . .	19.1
Mecklenburg, VA	22 981	66.3	67.8	1 027	91.4	12.1	-12.3	15.3	5.6	13.3	68.3	18.1
Middlesex, VA	7 436	56.2	73.7	310	89.0	18.9	-5.5	22.1	5.5	0.0	0.0	0.0
Montgomery, VA	43 106	41.0	82.8	26 224	97.7	35.9	11.5	34.2	29.6	7.4	85.6	37.8
Nelson, VA	10 403	57.6	69.0	393	80.7	20.8	-3.6	22.9	7.9	. . .	27.3	24.4
New Kent, VA	9 285	54.1	80.6	319	91.8	16.3	-8.1	18.6	6.9	6.6	40.0	6.5
Northampton, VA	9 133	61.8	67.4	486	87.7	15.7	-8.7	23.3	5.6	0.0	85.7	3.5
Northumberland, VA	9 476	55.0	75.9	211	75.4	21.7	-2.7	25.8	6.4	63.9	55.6	0.0
Nottoway, VA	10 841	67.4	64.4	226	89.4	11.1	-13.3	15.0	5.7	0.0	19.6	0.0
Orange, VA	18 202	58.8	75.2	720	80.8	18.5	-5.9	20.1	6.7	0.0	21.4	28.3
Page, VA	16 085	74.9	64.8	373	81.2	9.8	-14.6	9.8	9.3	0.0	18.4	9.9
Patrick, VA	13 815	72.2	62.2	543	86.2	8.6	-15.8	8.3	3.3	47.4	94.9	19.5
Pittsylvania, VA	43 120	67.9	67.3	1 891	80.7	9.3	-15.1	10.6	4.4	22.6	0.0	20.9
Powhatan, VA	15 411	53.3	78.9	807	82.4	19.1	-5.3	21.2	8.9	38.9	0.0	45.1
Prince Edward, VA	11 089	58.5	69.9	3 885	76.9	19.2	-5.2	27.2	6.0	0.0	60.6	46.2
Prince George, VA	20 272	50.1	81.6	1 738	83.0	19.4	-5.0	21.5	14.6	8.8	30.1	15.5
Prince William, VA	171 058	36.1	88.8	16 310	75.6	31.5	7.1	34.5	24.9	30.8	40.5	15.2
Pulaski, VA	25 362	59.6	74.2	1 296	89.4	12.5	-11.9	12.9	7.2	7.1	0.0	0.0
Rappahannock, VA	5 059	54.1	76.0	216	79.2	22.9	-1.5	23.6	7.0	0.0	46.7	8.3
Richmond, VA	6 552	71.3	60.0	298	80.9	9.9	-14.5	13.5	3.0	0.0	8.3	8.5
Roanoke, VA	60 771	42.1	85.8	3 952	62.7	28.2	3.8	28.1	22.7	9.8	50.8	34.7
Rockbridge, VA	14 556	61.4	71.0	779	45.2	18.7	-5.7	19.2	8.9	0.0	17.9	4.6
Rockingham, VA	45 123	63.0	72.4	2 824	58.1	17.6	-6.8	18.0	7.2	6.9	16.4	7.9
Russell, VA	21 362	69.9	62.5	1 011	88.1	9.4	-15.0	9.7	1.8	0.0	0.0	4.1
Scott, VA	16 846	71.9	64.4	634	91.0	8.3	-16.1	8.3	5.1	62.1	41.2	2.7
Shenandoah, VA	24 926	63.1	75.3	824	81.9	14.7	-9.7	14.9	10.5	0.0	14.9	12.2
Smyth, VA	23 255	66.9	67.5	1 040	85.8	10.6	-13.8	10.5	13.1	0.0	34.4	12.9
Southampton, VA	12 070	63.3	63.2	565	91.3	11.7	-12.7	15.6	6.3	16.7	. . .	0.0
Spotsylvania, VA	56 633	47.8	83.8	3 690	80.9	22.8	-1.6	23.7	15.4	19.1	26.8	23.1
Stafford, VA	56 029	39.3	88.6	4 879	83.1	29.6	5.2	29.9	25.9	29.7	33.5	31.5
Surry, VA	4 569	62.6	70.4	211	72.5	12.8	-11.6	16.0	9.8	16.7	0.0	15.6
Sussex, VA	8 899	75.6	57.6	442	89.6	10.0	-14.4	16.6	6.1	0.0	0.0	0.0
Tazewell, VA	31 291	65.0	67.5	1 954	76.0	11.0	-13.4	10.5	15.2	0.0	71.4	37.9
Warren, VA	21 127	62.2	75.5	1 085	63.8	15.0	-9.4	15.2	8.6	0.0	49.2	5.1
Washington, VA	35 958	58.9	72.3	2 539	61.8	16.1	-8.3	16.1	14.7	0.0	27.0	40.6
Westmoreland, VA	11 808	64.1	69.3	428	85.3	13.3	-11.1	17.3	3.3	33.3	42.9	9.1
Wise, VA	26 731	67.4	62.5	2 059	91.2	10.8	-13.6	10.6	12.1	0.0	65.6	3.5
Wythe, VA	19 528	62.2	70.2	1 024	82.7	12.1	-12.3	12.0	9.2	0.0	65.8	9.8
York, VA	36 168	29.5	91.7	3 066	81.1	37.4	13.0	39.2	23.5	45.4	44.7	41.3
Alexandria City, VA	95 730	25.8	86.8	10 296	63.8	54.3	29.9	70.0	28.3	55.6	55.4	21.3
Bedford City, VA	4 494	61.5	70.9	232	68.5	15.2	-9.2	17.6	5.4	0.0	45.0	52.6
Bristol City, VA	12 366	56.9	72.4	792	44.7	17.0	-7.4	17.3	5.9	21.7	34.1	34.1
Buena Vista City, VA	4 250	65.0	69.0	419	42.5	10.5	-13.9	10.4	7.8	0.0	100.0	. . .
Charlottesville City, VA	22 868	40.6	80.8	15 501	95.7	40.8	16.4	49.1	8.6	41.9	75.2	47.8

[1]Hispanic or Latino persons may be of any race.
. . . = Not available.

Table C-1. Population, School, and Student Characteristics by County—*Continued*

County	State/County code	County type[1]	Population, 2000		Number of schools and students, 2000–2001			Resident enrollment, 2000			
			Total	Percent 5–17 years	School districts	Schools	Students	Total	Percent public	K–12	Percent public
	1	2			3	4	5	6	7	8	9
Chesapeake City, VA	51550	0	199 184	21.6	1	43	37 645	58 385	84.7	43 542	90.6
Clifton Forge City, VA	51560	6	4 289	15.8	◊	◊	◊	886	92.1	708	97.6
Colonial Heights City, VA	51570	2	16 897	17.3	1	5	2 773	3 884	90.2	2 991	95.4
Covington City, VA	51580	6	6 303	15.2	◊	◊	◊	1 202	94.5	937	99.4
Danville City, VA	51590	3	48 411	17.3	1	15	7 659	11 141	88.7	8 649	91.8
Emporia City, VA	51595	6	5 665	19.0	°	°	°	1 282	92.7	1 113	94.2
Fairfax City, VA	51600	0	21 498	14.5	+	+	+	5 133	80.7	3 157	86.0
Falls Church City, VA	51610	0	10 377	17.9	1	4	1 721	2 683	72.8	1 828	84.2
Franklin City, VA	51620	6	8 346	20.1	1	3	1 423	2 175	88.8	1 709	89.4
Fredericksburg City, VA	51630	0	19 279	11.9	1	3	2 143	6 061	90.1	2 329	90.3
Galax City, VA	51640	7	6 837	16.6	1	3	1 320	1 446	97.0	1 171	98.5
Hampton City, VA	51650	0	146 437	17.9	1	34	23 290	42 305	77.6	27 044	90.1
Harrisonburg City, VA	51660	5	40 468	10.7	1	6	3 743	19 504	90.7	4 247	91.5
Hopewell City, VA	51670	2	22 354	19.2	1	5	3 967	5 474	91.3	4 204	92.7
Lexington City, VA	51678	6	6 867	8.0	1	2	475	3 467	53.6	533	97.6
Lynchburg City, VA	51680	3	65 269	16.3	1	17	9 212	19 578	61.8	10 830	89.3
Manassas City, VA	51683	0	35 135	21.0	1	7	6 411	9 941	82.1	7 433	87.1
Manassas Park City, VA	51685	0	10 290	21.1	1	5	2 013	2 862	84.9	2 118	91.7
Martinsville City, VA	51690	4	15 416	16.9	1	6	2 711	3 540	93.6	2 630	96.7
Newport News City, VA	51700	0	180 150	19.6	1	39	33 008	50 215	87.2	35 994	91.6
Norfolk City, VA	51710	0	234 403	17.0	1	54	37 349	63 867	85.5	40 850	90.2
Norton City, VA	51720	7	3 904	16.6	1	2	709	906	94.7	699	95.1
Petersburg City, VA	51730	2	33 740	18.7	1	10	5 984	8 191	90.9	6 381	93.8
Poquoson City, VA	51735	0	11 566	21.7	1	4	2 474	3 260	87.9	2 524	93.3
Portsmouth City, VA	51740	0	100 565	18.6	1	27	16 473	26 135	86.3	19 171	89.1
Radford City, VA	51750	4	15 859	9.4	1	4	1 582	8 502	95.8	1 435	94.7
Richmond City, VA	51760	2	197 790	15.6	2	64	28 200	54 048	80.8	31 524	87.5
Roanoke City, VA	51770	3	94 911	16.1	1	30	13 800	20 600	88.7	15 292	93.3
Salem City, VA	51775	3	24 747	16.0	1	6	3 955	6 792	73.2	4 103	98.3
Staunton City, VA	51790	4	23 853	14.6	1	6	2 786	5 314	70.3	3 528	84.6
Suffolk City, VA	51800	0	63 677	20.6	1	19	11 983	17 697	84.3	13 372	87.3
Virginia Beach City, VA	51810	0	425 257	20.3	1	82	76 586	121 415	84.5	86 963	91.2
Waynesboro City, VA	51820	4	19 520	17.3	1	6	3 030	4 309	90.6	3 412	95.4
Williamsburg City, VA	51830	0	11 998	6.9	§	§	§	6 365	90.1	832	90.7
Winchester City, VA	51840	4	23 585	15.6	1	7	3 399	5 762	76.0	3 690	95.7
WASHINGTON	53000										
Adams, WA	53001	6	16 428	24.7	5	11	3 789	4 945	93.9	4 249	94.6
Asotin, WA	53003	7	20 551	18.7	2	10	3 511	5 037	93.3	3 900	94.5
Benton, WA	53005	3	142 475	22.2	6	51	28 810	40 139	89.9	31 831	93.5
Chelan, WA	53007	5	66 616	20.8	7	34	13 024	18 093	88.7	14 315	92.2
Clallam, WA	53009	5	64 525	16.8	5	29	10 021	14 410	89.1	11 058	91.0
Clark, WA	53011	1	345 238	20.9	9	108	65 862	92 185	88.1	70 778	92.0
Columbia, WA	53013	9	4 064	18.6	2	4	654	918	90.5	759	92.6
Cowlitz, WA	53015	4	92 948	20.1	6	39	17 711	23 679	90.4	18 394	94.3
Douglas, WA	53017	7	32 603	21.9	6	18	6 767	8 929	93.8	7 284	96.7
Ferry, WA	53019	9	7 260	21.4	5	6	1 192	1 875	92.1	1 554	92.2
Franklin, WA	53021	3	49 347	24.6	4	22	10 892	14 657	93.8	12 379	95.8
Garfield, WA	53023	9	2 397	21.4	1	2	463	586	97.1	496	98.4
Grant, WA	53025	5	74 698	23.3	9	44	15 911	21 570	94.8	17 754	96.9
Grays Harbor, WA	53027	4	67 194	19.4	13	40	12 861	16 737	94.2	13 316	96.0
Island, WA	53029	1	71 558	18.8	3	23	9 861	17 742	88.0	13 317	92.4
Jefferson, WA	53031	6	25 953	15.7	5	13	3 603	5 042	87.4	3 934	93.3
King, WA	53033	0	1 737 034	16.4	19	476	251 712	444 560	81.9	287 823	87.7
Kitsap, WA	53035	3	231 969	20.1	5	79	41 612	62 794	87.1	46 929	91.8
Kittitas, WA	53037	6	33 362	15.5	6	13	4 779	12 277	95.5	5 204	94.7
Klickitat, WA	53039	7	19 161	20.7	10	17	3 819	4 850	90.6	4 081	93.7
Lewis, WA	53041	6	68 600	20.1	14	39	12 858	17 267	90.7	13 805	92.8
Lincoln, WA	53043	8	10 184	19.5	8	15	2 108	2 355	89.3	1 980	91.6
Mason, WA	53045	6	49 405	18.1	7	20	8 454	11 233	92.4	9 123	94.8
Okanogan, WA	53047	7	39 564	21.4	9	27	8 284	10 277	93.5	8 692	95.5
Pacific, WA	53049	7	20 984	16.9	6	19	3 356	4 621	93.5	3 735	95.1
Pend Oreille, WA	53051	8	11 732	20.9	3	9	2 042	2 986	89.1	2 413	90.9
Pierce, WA	53053	2	700 820	20.1	15	238	127 160	191 320	85.7	142 171	91.3
San Juan, WA	53055	8	14 077	15.4	4	13	1 843	2 789	83.8	2 184	89.5
Skagit, WA	53057	4	102 979	19.8	7	48	18 894	26 225	91.1	20 524	94.4
Skamania, WA	53059	8	9 872	20.2	4	8	1 294	2 385	91.2	1 955	94.0
Snohomish, WA	53061	0	606 024	20.2	14	194	105 741	163 166	87.5	122 466	92.0
Spokane, WA	53063	2	417 939	19.1	14	160	72 588	117 842	84.5	80 540	90.5
Stevens, WA	53065	6	40 066	22.6	12	28	6 469	10 414	90.2	8 901	92.4
Thurston, WA	53067	3	207 355	19.1	8	74	37 764	56 997	87.4	40 428	92.4
Wahkiakum, WA	53069	9	3 824	18.1	1	2	509	912	87.4	690	94.9
Walla Walla, WA	53071	4	55 180	18.3	7	26	8 965	16 905	71.1	10 530	87.9
Whatcom, WA	53073	3	166 814	18.0	7	65	25 749	51 210	88.7	29 602	88.7
Whitman, WA	53075	5	40 740	13.2	13	24	4 838	20 964	95.7	5 320	91.6
Yakima, WA	53077	3	222 581	23.1	15	93	47 813	63 808	91.2	53 034	94.3

[1]County type code is from the Economic Research Service of the USDA. See Notes and Definitions at the end of this section.
◊ = Clifton Forge City and Covington City are included with Alleghany County.
° = Emporia City is included with Greensville County.
+ = Fairfax City is included with Fairfax County.
§ = Williamsburg City is included with James City County.

Table C-1. School and Student Characteristics by County—*Continued*

	Characteristics of students, 2000–2001			Staff and students, 2000–2001				Revenues, fiscal 1999			
County	Percent with IEP2	Percent eligible for free lunch	Percent minority	Number of teachers	Student/ teacher ratio	Local school non-teaching staff	Central admin. staff	Total revenue ($1,000s)	Percentage of revenue from		
									Federal govt.	State govt.	Local govt.
	10	11	12	13	14	15	16	17	18	19	20
Chesapeake City, VA	16.1	23.2	38.5	2 429	15.5	2 268	313	$237 222	5.3	40.6	54.1
Clifton Forge City, VA	◊	◊	◊	◊	◊	◊	◊	◊	◊	◊	◊
Colonial Heights City, VA	13.4	. . .	12.5	210	13.2	133	20	20 591	2.6	28.8	68.6
Covington City, VA	◊	◊	◊	◊	◊	◊	◊	◊	◊	◊	◊
Danville City, VA	12.0	53.6	68.6	544	14.1	382	88	53 399	7.9	44.0	48.0
Emporia City, VA	°	°	°	°	°	°	°	°	°	°	°
Fairfax City, VA	+	+	+	+	+	+	+	+	+	+	+
Falls Church City, VA	17.8	. . .	21.3	141	12.2	119	19	18 449	1.4	9.4	89.2
Franklin City, VA	19.0	59.3	75.7	120	11.9	79	27	14 759	6.3	51.5	42.2
Fredericksburg City, VA	15.9	42.0	50.6	168	12.8	158	48	18 751	5.0	22.4	72.6
Galax City, VA	10.6	. . .	24.8	95	13.9	52	18	7 892	6.9	47.8	45.3
Hampton City, VA	12.0	36.8	62.8	1 475	15.8	1 295	186	158 541	7.2	43.4	49.5
Harrisonburg City, VA	16.9	41.3	30.1	328	11.4	180	48	30 220	5.1	25.5	69.4
Hopewell City, VA	17.6	49.2	55.2	241	16.5	208	56	29 722	7.3	45.4	47.2
Lexington City, VA	18.3	17.3	12.4	39	12.2	17	13	4 415	3.9	45.5	50.6
Lynchburg City, VA	15.2	41.9	51.9	690	13.4	587	58	69 643	7.0	37.7	55.3
Manassas City, VA	12.8	19.2	38.9	438	14.6	279	55	60 853	1.9	26.0	72.2
Manassas Park City, VA	14.1	28.4	39.0	153	13.2	90	87	17 547	2.1	35.6	62.2
Martinsville City, VA	18.9	46.6	59.6	258	10.5	147	19	19 290	6.4	42.2	51.3
Newport News City, VA	12.1	. . .	62.2	1 436	23.0	1 926	230	220 682	8.4	44.3	47.3
Norfolk City, VA	12.8	59.0	71.6	2 717	13.7	1 964	506	276 068	7.5	44.3	48.2
Norton City, VA	15.1	45.3	12.3	60	11.8	38	10	4 864	9.4	53.4	37.2
Petersburg City, VA	12.3	71.0	98.0	465	12.9	339	85	44 344	8.7	55.0	36.3
Poquoson City, VA	11.1	4.4	3.7	164	15.1	96	21	13 647	3.2	43.9	53.0
Portsmouth City, VA	14.6	59.0	70.7	1 145	14.4	973	176	120 242	10.5	56.2	33.2
Radford City, VA	14.9	17.3	13.5	122	13.0	53	20	10 474	4.2	44.6	51.2
Richmond City, VA	16.1	66.0	92.1	1 782	15.8	1 449	241	241 591	8.3	33.1	58.6
Roanoke City, VA	17.2	54.5	47.7	999	13.8	867	98	109 481	7.6	35.5	56.9
Salem City, VA	12.9	15.0	9.0	283	14.0	177	25	31 456	2.5	29.3	68.2
Staunton City, VA	16.5	39.7	24.8	230	12.1	154	27	20 735	5.2	46.0	48.8
Suffolk City, VA	12.3	42.2	59.9	802	14.9	668	51	82 164	6.1	42.7	51.2
Virginia Beach City, VA	12.8	25.4	36.7	5 420	14.1	3 927	437	516 939	5.9	39.9	54.1
Waynesboro City, VA	11.7	36.8	20.9	219	13.8	156	28	23 442	4.4	33.2	62.4
Williamsburg City, VA	§	§	§	§	§	§	§	§	§	§	§
Winchester City, VA	18.9	33.2	26.8	297	11.4	209	29	31 652	3.8	22.8	73.4
WASHINGTON											
Adams, WA	10.2	. . .	60.4	210	18.0	179	15	27 661	7.6	72.0	20.4
Asotin, WA	12.6	. . .	5.9	180	19.5	145	13	23 766	8.2	74.8	17.0
Benton, WA	11.5	. . .	20.7	1 414	20.4	1 215	84	193 580	5.4	70.3	24.2
Chelan, WA	10.3	. . .	33.5	660	19.7	592	75	95 666	11.3	63.8	24.8
Clallam, WA	11.5	. . .	17.7	551	18.2	402	38	74 725	9.9	70.0	20.1
Clark, WA	11.0	. . .	13.7	3 156	20.9	2 774	237	472 356	5.8	67.5	26.7
Columbia, WA	11.0	. . .	15.1	39	16.8	29	4	5 345	6.9	68.7	24.4
Cowlitz, WA	12.4	. . .	11.3	842	21.0	783	55	117 614	6.0	69.0	25.0
Douglas, WA	11.2	. . .	32.2	340	19.9	277	25	43 340	5.3	74.3	20.5
Ferry, WA	11.3	. . .	27.7	74	16.1	63	11	10 246	20.7	67.3	12.0
Franklin, WA	10.8	. . .	67.2	588	18.5	536	67	77 502	9.3	72.1	18.6
Garfield, WA	12.3	. . .	6.5	28	16.5	18	3	4 554	3.2	77.6	19.2
Grant, WA	11.1	. . .	43.1	831	19.1	710	60	123 845	7.9	74.8	17.3
Grays Harbor, WA	13.2	. . .	18.1	668	19.3	573	54	91 995	8.8	69.1	22.1
Island, WA	10.8	. . .	20.6	461	21.4	370	30	64 577	8.4	72.2	19.4
Jefferson, WA	13.2	. . .	9.9	174	20.7	159	16	28 777	9.2	60.9	29.9
King, WA	10.9	. . .	32.9	12 271	20.5	10 764	781	1 965 170	4.9	57.6	37.5
Kitsap, WA	12.1	. . .	19.7	2 033	20.5	1 868	152	302 609	9.9	64.5	25.6
Kittitas, WA	12.4	. . .	11.4	221	21.6	180	24	35 588	6.9	70.7	22.4
Klickitat, WA	14.3	. . .	18.2	214	17.8	176	21	29 840	6.7	76.3	16.9
Lewis, WA	12.5	. . .	11.9	666	19.3	529	56	89 490	7.5	71.0	21.5
Lincoln, WA	9.2	. . .	6.7	138	15.3	122	19	20 871	4.9	71.8	23.3
Mason, WA	12.1	. . .	17.0	432	19.6	366	33	55 755	7.9	69.3	22.7
Okanogan, WA	12.2	. . .	38.5	455	18.2	416	49	55 469	12.5	70.4	17.1
Pacific, WA	12.2	. . .	19.9	206	16.3	170	19	28 738	7.4	71.7	20.9
Pend Oreille, WA	13.8	. . .	7.3	73	28.0	91	14	15 318	11.1	74.1	14.9
Pierce, WA	11.6	. . .	27.8	6 218	20.5	5 113	389	873 965	6.9	64.4	28.7
San Juan, WA	12.1	. . .	7.2	104	17.7	79	12	16 858	2.3	58.0	39.7
Skagit, WA	12.9	. . .	22.9	941	20.1	913	98	140 616	7.6	61.8	30.7
Skamania, WA	14.8	. . .	12.7	75	17.3	70	8	11 064	33.8	47.6	18.5
Snohomish, WA	11.2	. . .	17.5	4 880	21.7	4 067	337	710 999	3.9	65.4	30.7
Spokane, WA	11.7	. . .	10.0	3 627	20.0	3 238	235	524 951	8.3	64.8	26.9
Stevens, WA	11.9	. . .	13.9	348	18.6	290	38	44 730	10.9	75.2	13.9
Thurston, WA	12.0	. . .	19.5	1 924	19.6	1 870	123	290 139	6.5	65.0	28.5
Wahkiakum, WA	14.7	. . .	7.7	27	18.9	23	3	5 114	1.7	51.6	46.6
Walla Walla, WA	11.7	. . .	29.8	475	18.9	397	38	68 307	9.8	65.2	25.0
Whatcom, WA	12.0	. . .	17.9	1 266	20.3	1 089	84	177 890	5.3	65.6	29.1
Whitman, WA	10.4	. . .	10.4	298	16.2	243	31	41 389	3.6	71.4	25.0
Yakima, WA	11.8	. . .	57.2	2 397	19.9	2 103	187	327 724	12.5	72.6	14.9

2IEP = Individual Education Program. See Notes and Definitions at the end of this section.
◊ = Clifton Forge City and Covington City are included with Alleghany County.
. . . = Not available.
° = Emporia City is included with Greensville County.
+ = Fairfax City is included with Fairfax County.
§ = Williamsburg City is included with James City County.

Table C-1. Population, School, and Student Characteristics by County—*Continued*

County	Current expenditures, fiscal 1999			Resident population 16 to 19 years, 2000				Outcomes, 1999–2000	
	Amount ($1,000s)	Amount per student	Percent for instruction	Total population 16 to 19 years	Percent in Armed Forces	Percent high school graduates	Percent not enrolled, not grads, not Armed Forces, not empl.	Number of graduates	Dropouts grades 9–12 (percent)
	21	22	23	24	25	26	27	28	29
Chesapeake City, VA	$216 350	$5 891	63.5	11 484	1.8	12.3	4.0	2 396	3.9
Clifton Forge City, VA	◊	◊	◊	221	0.0	14.0	1.8	◊	◊
Colonial Heights City, VA	18 695	6 811	68.5	841	0.0	14.0	2.1	155	5.6
Covington City, VA	◊	◊	◊	264	0.0	25.8	3.4	◊	◊
Danville City, VA	44 855	5 702	65.2	2 475	0.0	11.6	9.5	419	5.5
Emporia City, VA	°	°	°	°	°	°	13.6	°	°
Fairfax City, VA	+	+	+	983	0	7.8	4.9	+	+
Falls Church City, VA	15 474	10 042	60.5	426	0.0	4.2	0.0	141	0.2
Franklin City, VA	10 396	6 141	61.9	477	0.0	8.4	6.7	91	4.4
Fredericksburg City, VA	16 661	7 643	63.1	1 904	0.8	14.4	2.8	117	3.9
Galax City, VA	6 808	5 319	63.6	302	0.0	14.9	2.0	74	2.5
Hampton City, VA	140 336	5 961	62.8	9 310	1.3	13.3	3.0	1 345	3.9
Harrisonburg City, VA	25 220	7 055	63.0	6 261	0.0	2.8	2.5	221	4.2
Hopewell City, VA	25 199	6 292	62.7	1 112	0.0	17.0	6.7	191	4.0
Lexington City, VA	3 823	8 384	68.8	1 238	0.0	1.5	0.6	0	…
Lynchburg City, VA	59 921	6 383	62.1	4 792	0.3	6.9	4.2	544	2.3
Manassas City, VA	40 046	6 466	61.4	1 923	0.0	8.6	5.6	342	1.9
Manassas Park City, VA	11 361	6 354	61.6	499	0.0	11.4	5.2	82	2.2
Martinsville City, VA	18 141	6 662	62.4	703	0.0	7.7	4.6	166	1.8
Newport News City, VA	187 828	5 635	61.5	10 506	7.7	19.2	4.0	1 583	5.9
Norfolk City, VA	240 815	6 362	59.5	16 165	19.0	27.0	5.6	1 413	4.9
Norton City, VA	4 459	5 821	69.0	218	0.0	18.8	3.2	48	1.4
Petersburg City, VA	35 241	5 558	59.3	1 704	0.3	13.3	11.2	242	7.3
Poquoson City, VA	12 584	5 166	66.5	651	0.0	5.5	3.8	181	1.5
Portsmouth City, VA	102 928	5 879	60.6	5 791	9.8	19.7	7.4	852	7.7
Radford City, VA	9 003	5 756	64.7	2 507	0.0	2.4	0.0	78	2.1
Richmond City, VA	207 659	7 518	57.2	11 559	0.1	9.9	6.2	1 045	4.3
Roanoke City, VA	91 101	6 743	63.2	4 030	0.0	18.1	12.8	544	6.8
Salem City, VA	28 010	7 095	68.6	1 715	0.0	5.4	0.5	245	3.1
Staunton City, VA	18 280	6 286	65.0	1 364	0.0	9.7	2.3	164	6.7
Suffolk City, VA	61 774	5 495	64.7	3 204	0.0	8.7	6.6	538	3.5
Virginia Beach City, VA	421 291	5 440	65.2	23 384	5.4	15.8	3.7	4 330	4.9
Waynesboro City, VA	18 152	6 089	63.4	845	0.0	12.3	6.2	155	2.1
Williamsburg City, VA	§	§	§	2 080	0	1.6	0.0	§	§
Winchester City, VA	26 815	8 060	64.3	1 688	0.0	10.5	9.5	179	3.6
WASHINGTON									
Adams, WA	24 142	6 392	62.4	1 110	0.0	6.8	9.8	222	…
Asotin, WA	22 545	6 175	64.3	1 155	0.0	10.8	3.7	246	…
Benton, WA	168 599	5 933	60.7	8 530	0.0	8.6	6.1	1 744	…
Chelan, WA	83 783	6 385	57.1	4 091	0.0	11.4	8.9	823	…
Clallam, WA	63 575	5 980	62.2	3 460	0.0	12.5	7.1	660	…
Clark, WA	387 880	6 128	57.4	18 895	0.1	11.3	5.9	3 442	…
Columbia, WA	4 840	6 722	61.9	251	1.6	15.5	6.4	73	…
Cowlitz, WA	106 313	5 929	59.5	5 382	0.3	12.0	6.5	953	…
Douglas, WA	38 196	5 865	64.5	1 883	0.0	7.5	5.1	387	…
Ferry, WA	9 439	7 479	58.7	587	0.0	16.2	11.8	69	…
Franklin, WA	66 231	6 346	58.0	3 692	0.0	8.5	12.5	469	…
Garfield, WA	3 392	7 156	60.7	153	0.0	8.5	1.3	40	…
Grant, WA	97 667	5 896	61.6	5 232	0.0	10.6	7.9	825	…
Grays Harbor, WA	81 832	6 140	61.9	3 943	0.2	8.7	6.0	798	…
Island, WA	54 410	5 400	63.6	3 514	7.8	16.8	3.2	494	…
Jefferson, WA	22 868	6 116	58.0	1 118	0.0	13.8	5.3	279	…
King, WA	1 572 567	6 259	59.0	85 185	0.1	10.3	3.2	14 226	…
Kitsap, WA	253 866	5 983	59.0	13 475	4.6	14.7	4.4	2 369	…
Kittitas, WA	29 627	6 035	62.1	2 752	0.0	7.9	2.9	304	…
Klickitat, WA	25 111	6 524	60.9	1 038	0.0	13.8	3.9	226	…
Lewis, WA	79 416	6 066	61.6	4 210	0.1	11.0	7.7	762	…
Lincoln, WA	19 015	8 157	58.2	549	0.0	8.7	1.8	184	…
Mason, WA	50 977	5 978	59.8	2 739	0.0	14.2	9.3	455	…
Okanogan, WA	48 088	6 124	61.9	2 277	0.0	9.2	6.0	454	…
Pacific, WA	25 243	7 024	60.3	1 017	0.7	8.8	4.2	216	…
Pend Oreille, WA	14 427	6 636	59.4	715	0.0	11.3	9.2	147	…
Pierce, WA	741 517	5 924	59.1	40 956	3.4	13.8	5.2	6 249	…
San Juan, WA	12 999	6 725	59.5	567	0.0	13.1	4.8	126	…
Skagit, WA	119 874	6 492	60.0	6 523	0.2	12.1	7.3	961	…
Skamania, WA	9 478	6 995	60.2	614	0.0	12.1	5.7	98	…
Snohomish, WA	589 408	5 751	61.2	33 396	1.2	11.8	3.9	5 110	…
Spokane, WA	461 106	6 290	59.3	26 628	0.7	12.1	3.1	4 558	…
Stevens, WA	41 759	6 292	60.8	2 621	0.0	12.1	5.3	440	…
Thurston, WA	244 185	6 421	59.3	12 447	0.0	11.4	2.8	2 339	…
Wahkiakum, WA	3 187	5 784	57.6	202	0.0	6.4	3.5	42	…
Walla Walla, WA	60 190	6 556	61.2	4 044	0.0	3.7	3.3	500	…
Whatcom, WA	147 008	5 712	61.0	11 267	0.1	9.6	2.7	1 522	…
Whitman, WA	37 198	7 391	60.2	4 413	0.0	2.9	0.8	336	…
Yakima, WA	281 938	5 901	60.9	14 451	0.0	11.8	8.7	2 270	…

◊ = Clifton Forge City and Covington City are included with Alleghany County.
° = Emporia City is included with Greensville County.
+ = Fairfax City is included with Fairfax County.
... = Not available.
§ = Williamsburg City is included with James City County.

Table C-1. Population, School, and Student Characteristics by County—*Continued*

County	High school graduates, 2000			College enrollment, 2000		College graduates, 2000 (percent)						
	Population 25 years and over	High school diploma or less (percent)	High school diploma or more (percent)	Number	Percent public	Bachelor's degree or more	+/- U.S. percent with bachelor's degree or more	Non-Hispanic White	Black or African American	American Indian and Alaska Native	Asian, Hawaiian, and Pacific Islander	Hispan-ic or Latino[1]
	30	31	32	33	34	35	36	37	38	39	40	41
Chesapeake City, VA	125 498	42.6	85.1	10 785	79.2	24.7	0.3	25.5	20.3	12.3	49.8	32.2
Clifton Forge City, VA	3 110	61.4	75.0	120	75.0	9.6	-14.8	9.4	9.1	. . .	100.0	0.0
Colonial Heights City, VA	11 675	50.8	83.7	690	84.3	19.0	-5.4	18.5	28.5	0.0	22.4	19.2
Covington City, VA	4 485	68.4	71.4	164	93.3	6.4	-18.0	7.0	3.8	. . .	0.0	0.0
Danville City, VA	33 196	62.2	68.5	1 709	78.8	13.9	-10.5	18.0	6.7	14.6	45.4	27.8
Emporia City, VA	3 775	70.3	58.5	106	78.3	14.2	-10.2	22.1	7.2	. . .	28.6	0.0
Fairfax City, VA	15 222	30.9	88.6	1 693	80.9	45.7	21.3	48.3	34.5	52.1	52.8	24.4
Falls Church City, VA	7 464	16.7	95.9	636	62.3	63.7	39.3	68.0	37.6	40.0	55.5	31.9
Franklin City, VA	5 642	56.6	71.0	356	93.3	16.4	-8.0	25.1	7.3	0.0	. . .	15.6
Fredericksburg City, VA	11 211	47.3	80.2	3 503	92.3	30.5	6.1	37.5	9.9	32.5	8.3	13.7
Galax City, VA	4 782	68.2	60.4	195	95.4	11.1	-13.3	12.4	0.0	0.0	0.0	3.4
Hampton City, VA	92 477	42.5	85.5	12 830	55.5	21.8	-2.6	24.1	18.7	18.3	24.4	17.4
Harrisonburg City, VA	17 448	46.7	76.8	14 822	91.8	31.2	6.8	34.6	18.5	0.0	29.4	7.2
Hopewell City, VA	14 323	64.1	71.8	859	84.6	10.2	-14.2	11.1	7.5	14.0	21.4	6.6
Lexington City, VA	3 285	40.2	77.1	2 876	45.9	42.6	18.2	47.4	15.9	0.0	0.0	78.9
Lynchburg City, VA	40 806	49.7	78.0	7 622	24.9	25.2	0.8	31.3	8.3	10.1	58.0	26.2
Manassas City, VA	21 188	42.7	81.3	1 916	75.0	28.1	3.7	33.7	17.2	0.0	31.2	9.9
Manassas Park City, VA	6 224	51.0	76.4	477	77.6	20.3	-4.1	18.6	26.7	65.4	68.0	6.2
Martinsville City, VA	10 843	60.8	68.5	661	87.9	16.6	-7.8	23.4	5.6	100.0	50.0	10.1
Newport News City, VA	110 083	45.6	84.5	10 611	81.9	19.9	-4.5	25.0	11.7	18.4	25.2	13.7
Norfolk City, VA	135 258	51.2	78.4	19 085	80.3	19.6	-4.8	26.3	9.7	9.3	34.3	16.5
Norton City, VA	2 665	60.3	66.5	180	100.0	14.0	-10.4	15.0	4.2	0.0	0.0	0.0
Petersburg City, VA	22 289	61.7	68.6	1 388	79.6	14.8	-9.6	21.1	12.4	23.9	34.9	17.0
Poquoson City, VA	7 759	38.5	88.5	527	86.9	31.6	7.2	30.7	40.0	0.0	76.6	39.7
Portsmouth City, VA	63 685	54.2	75.2	5 211	83.1	13.8	-10.6	17.0	10.0	18.2	23.1	18.6
Radford City, VA	6 766	36.3	83.4	6 952	96.9	34.1	9.7	35.6	11.0	0.0	90.2	29.4
Richmond City, VA	128 555	48.4	75.2	19 116	72.6	29.5	5.1	51.4	11.2	22.4	49.0	20.3
Roanoke City, VA	65 593	54.4	76.0	3 590	79.4	18.7	-5.7	22.2	7.8	20.9	37.4	19.4
Salem City, VA	16 657	50.2	82.0	2 195	29.7	19.8	-4.6	20.5	6.5	0.0	29.7	15.9
Staunton City, VA	16 703	55.5	75.6	1 387	42.4	20.4	-4.0	22.3	6.2	0.0	0.0	33.3
Suffolk City, VA	41 662	52.8	76.8	3 129	84.5	17.3	-7.1	21.5	10.8	17.0	40.6	17.0
Virginia Beach City, VA	266 627	35.5	90.4	26 275	76.9	28.1	3.7	30.6	18.1	12.7	33.3	19.1
Waynesboro City, VA	13 303	56.0	77.9	488	87.7	20.6	-3.8	22.4	7.2	18.4	42.9	12.5
Williamsburg City, VA	5 360	31.2	89.6	5 403	90.5	45.0	20.6	54.1	10.3	. . .	38.9	23.8
Winchester City, VA	15 316	51.3	75.4	1 688	39.6	23.7	-0.7	26.6	7.4	0.0	34.2	7.4
WASHINGTON		37.8	87.1	. . .	. . .	27.7	3.3	28.9	19.4	12.4	35.5	11.1
Adams, WA	9 242	62.9	63.3	466	93.6	12.2	-12.2	17.3	0.0	8.6	27.9	3.0
Asotin, WA	13 619	46.9	85.8	853	95.2	18.0	-6.4	17.9	62.5	29.2	57.1	11.6
Benton, WA	88 217	38.9	85.1	5 789	89.3	26.3	1.9	27.6	23.7	10.3	50.1	6.9
Chelan, WA	42 425	46.7	79.1	2 623	87.7	21.9	-2.5	24.9	24.6	6.8	19.0	3.7
Clallam, WA	45 711	42.3	85.5	2 425	89.6	20.8	-3.6	21.5	7.7	11.3	24.1	5.3
Clark, WA	217 293	39.2	87.8	15 495	85.7	22.1	-2.3	22.4	22.5	11.1	29.9	10.1
Columbia, WA	2 827	47.8	82.7	96	93.8	17.5	-6.9	18.3	0.0	28.6	35.7	3.8
Cowlitz, WA	60 355	49.6	83.2	3 602	89.8	13.3	-11.1	13.6	17.7	4.7	12.2	8.8
Douglas, WA	20 435	51.0	78.4	1 088	88.9	16.2	-8.2	18.3	19.3	11.4	16.2	3.5
Ferry, WA	4 748	51.7	82.7	230	91.3	13.5	-10.9	15.4	0.0	4.7	7.7	26.8
Franklin, WA	26 779	60.3	63.5	1 654	90.5	13.6	-10.8	19.4	12.2	5.3	23.1	2.9
Garfield, WA	1 655	45.1	84.4	54	90.7	17.0	-7.4	17.1	. . .	0.0	50.0	25.0
Grant, WA	43 309	55.6	72.2	2 622	92.1	13.7	-10.7	16.9	9.5	14.1	28.2	2.5
Grays Harbor, WA	44 588	53.2	81.1	2 347	93.1	12.7	-11.7	12.9	0.0	9.4	24.0	7.0
Island, WA	47 112	32.2	92.1	3 165	86.6	27.0	2.6	28.0	24.2	15.2	21.1	13.2
Jefferson, WA	19 551	35.6	91.6	678	78.5	28.4	4.0	29.5	12.3	9.9	24.9	4.9
King, WA	1 188 740	28.9	90.3	125 584	79.4	40.0	15.6	42.5	21.1	18.2	40.9	20.4
Kitsap, WA	148 704	34.7	90.8	11 528	83.9	25.3	0.9	26.4	17.7	15.9	24.0	14.1
Kittitas, WA	19 303	43.8	87.2	6 679	97.5	26.2	1.8	26.6	23.5	21.8	39.0	12.7
Klickitat, WA	12 806	52.6	81.7	441	78.0	16.4	-8.0	17.4	0.0	2.9	20.0	4.1
Lewis, WA	44 857	52.4	80.5	2 619	86.6	12.9	-11.5	13.2	30.1	8.8	24.7	4.2
Lincoln, WA	7 117	44.7	86.5	227	85.9	18.8	-5.6	19.0	11.1	15.9	31.3	16.4
Mason, WA	33 936	48.7	83.7	1 522	85.7	15.6	-8.8	16.0	4.2	8.2	28.4	8.7
Okanogan, WA	25 826	54.1	76.6	1 047	85.7	15.9	-8.5	17.9	0.0	11.2	25.0	3.9
Pacific, WA	15 298	52.6	78.9	606	91.4	15.2	-9.2	15.7	0.0	13.3	8.1	10.4
Pend Oreille, WA	7 995	52.4	81.0	365	81.6	12.3	-12.1	12.7	27.3	0.0	1.2	6.6
Pierce, WA	442 665	42.9	86.9	37 999	73.0	20.6	-3.8	21.8	15.0	13.0	19.5	11.8
San Juan, WA	10 691	24.3	94.4	348	87.1	40.2	15.8	41.3	. . .	0.0	8.2	7.4
Skagit, WA	66 959	42.4	84.0	4 095	86.6	20.8	-3.6	22.2	20.7	3.7	33.2	3.7
Skamania, WA	6 557	47.6	85.9	283	83.0	16.8	-7.6	17.4	20.0	3.1	51.6	3.6
Snohomish, WA	388 997	36.7	89.2	29 961	83.3	24.4	0.0	24.3	21.1	10.9	36.6	14.6
Spokane, WA	266 829	37.7	89.1	30 682	76.6	25.0	0.6	25.5	14.8	13.3	27.0	17.3
Stevens, WA	25 984	50.1	85.4	955	84.7	15.3	-9.1	15.7	17.8	6.9	19.2	12.3
Thurston, WA	135 686	34.3	89.5	13 181	81.4	29.8	5.4	30.8	28.7	16.4	24.9	18.9
Wahkiakum, WA	2 715	48.0	84.2	127	87.4	14.8	-9.6	14.7	. . .	23.6	100.0	0.0
Walla Walla, WA	34 372	43.0	81.1	5 541	41.6	23.3	-1.1	25.9	19.1	7.7	30.2	4.8
Whatcom, WA	102 787	40.1	87.5	19 135	93.9	27.2	2.8	28.3	26.7	7.1	31.0	12.5
Whitman, WA	20 070	26.4	92.8	15 058	98.2	44.0	19.6	41.5	58.3	10.8	73.0	66.7
Yakima, WA	130 747	58.7	68.7	7 244	82.2	15.3	-9.1	19.8	16.6	11.7	27.2	3.9

[1]Hispanic or Latino persons may be of any race.
. . . = Not available.

Table C-1. Population, School, and Student Characteristics by County—*Continued*

County	State/County code	County type[1]	Population, 2000		Number of schools and students, 2000–2001			Resident enrollment, 2000			
			Total	Percent 5–17 years	School districts	Schools	Students	Total	Percent public	K–12	Percent public
			1	2	3	4	5	6	7	8	9
WEST VIRGINIA	54000										
Barbour, WV	54001	7	15 557	17.7	1	9	2 653	3 687	85.1	2 726	98.7
Berkeley, WV	54003	3	75 905	19.1	1	25	13 076	17 453	90.2	14 127	94.3
Boone, WV	54005	6	25 535	16.9	1	18	4 477	5 551	95.9	4 458	97.5
Braxton, WV	54007	9	14 702	17.5	1	8	2 662	3 065	96.6	2 532	98.0
Brooke, WV	54009	3	25 447	15.4	1	12	3 744	5 883	81.6	3 926	95.1
Cabell, WV	54011	2	96 784	14.6	1	31	12 571	25 315	91.4	14 222	91.6
Calhoun, WV	54013	9	7 582	17.3	1	4	1 318	1 642	92.4	1 335	95.3
Clay, WV	54015	8	10 330	19.5	1	7	2 118	2 430	96.7	2 016	98.5
Doddridge, WV	54017	9	7 403	19.1	1	6	1 253	1 737	94.5	1 497	95.9
Fayette, WV	54019	6	47 579	16.1	1	28	7 277	10 243	92.1	7 779	95.6
Gilmer, WV	54021	9	7 160	15.4	1	5	1 129	2 212	98.5	1 154	99.3
Grant, WV	54023	8	11 299	16.4	1	5	1 980	2 273	94.3	1 877	96.8
Greenbrier, WV	54025	7	34 453	16.1	1	14	5 650	7 168	91.7	5 733	94.2
Hampshire, WV	54027	8	20 203	19.0	2	11	3 627	4 501	93.7	3 862	95.5
Hancock, WV	54029	3	32 667	15.5	1	12	4 496	6 671	86.4	5 263	89.4
Hardy, WV	54031	9	12 669	17.4	1	5	2 236	2 840	95.8	2 286	97.6
Harrison, WV	54033	5	68 652	17.4	1	29	11 495	15 737	89.9	12 116	94.8
Jackson, WV	54035	6	28 000	18.1	1	12	5 055	6 340	95.0	5 170	97.3
Jefferson, WV	54037	1	42 190	17.6	1	13	6 871	10 289	88.8	7 404	91.5
Kanawha, WV	54039	2	200 073	15.6	2	91	29 658	42 554	88.1	31 608	92.7
Lewis, WV	54041	7	16 919	16.8	1	7	2 764	3 644	90.8	2 923	93.8
Lincoln, WV	54043	8	22 108	17.6	1	11	3 900	4 652	97.3	3 861	98.1
Logan, WV	54045	7	37 710	16.4	1	21	6 334	7 911	94.9	6 299	96.6
McDowell, WV	54047	7	27 329	18.0	1	19	4 827	5 746	96.7	4 949	97.1
Marion, WV	54049	5	56 598	15.5	1	21	8 572	13 612	93.3	9 024	95.7
Marshall, WV	54051	3	35 519	17.5	1	16	5 567	7 980	90.8	6 370	93.9
Mason, WV	54053	6	25 957	16.9	1	13	4 326	5 443	96.2	4 444	98.3
Mercer, WV	54055	7	62 980	15.3	1	25	9 516	13 744	94.1	9 810	96.9
Mineral, WV	54057	3	27 078	17.8	1	14	4 610	6 308	94.5	4 814	96.4
Mingo, WV	54059	7	28 253	18.4	1	18	5 195	6 305	96.1	5 274	97.1
Monongalia, WV	54061	5	81 866	13.3	1	26	10 251	30 286	93.7	10 864	91.6
Monroe, WV	54063	9	14 583	15.2	1	4	2 101	2 971	96.0	2 379	98.2
Morgan, WV	54065	8	14 943	16.3	1	8	2 412	2 831	92.8	2 480	94.8
Nicholas, WV	54067	7	26 562	17.9	1	15	4 550	5 967	95.1	4 887	96.7
Ohio, WV	54069	3	47 427	16.1	1	14	5 892	12 425	74.9	7 815	79.2
Pendleton, WV	54071	9	8 196	16.5	1	4	1 281	1 718	92.4	1 384	94.0
Pleasants, WV	54073	8	7 514	17.9	1	4	1 432	1 690	94.4	1 379	96.7
Pocahontas, WV	54075	9	9 131	15.9	1	5	1 408	1 801	91.3	1 457	94.5
Preston, WV	54077	7	29 334	18.1	1	12	4 858	6 362	95.7	5 368	97.5
Putnam, WV	54079	2	51 589	18.4	1	21	8 755	12 580	88.3	9 541	92.6
Raleigh, WV	54081	5	79 220	16.0	1	33	11 998	17 797	86.6	13 215	95.2
Randolph, WV	54083	7	28 262	17.1	1	16	4 757	6 028	86.9	4 723	97.1
Ritchie, WV	54085	8	10 343	17.5	1	7	1 752	2 222	95.5	1 804	97.3
Roane, WV	54087	8	15 446	17.7	1	6	2 783	3 248	96.9	2 820	98.4
Summers, WV	54089	7	12 999	15.9	1	5	1 635	2 513	91.4	2 026	94.9
Taylor, WV	54091	7	16 089	17.5	1	6	2 492	3 632	92.7	2 944	96.2
Tucker, WV	54093	9	7 321	16.4	1	3	1 236	1 449	93.3	1 212	96.5
Tyler, WV	54095	9	9 592	18.0	1	4	1 551	2 073	95.7	1 721	98.8
Upshur, WV	54097	7	23 404	17.2	1	11	3 937	6 164	73.7	4 079	97.0
Wayne, WV	54099	2	42 903	17.6	1	21	7 465	9 488	95.2	7 637	97.2
Webster, WV	54101	9	9 719	17.8	1	5	1 754	2 084	97.2	1 752	97.6
Wetzel, WV	54103	6	17 693	18.1	1	9	3 513	3 967	97.2	3 238	99.0
Wirt, WV	54105	8	5 873	19.8	1	3	1 164	1 473	97.6	1 249	98.5
Wood, WV	54107	3	87 986	17.2	1	28	14 004	19 616	89.8	14 998	94.5
Wyoming, WV	54109	9	25 708	16.7	1	14	4 350	5 232	96.7	4 385	98.4
WISCONSIN	55000										
Adams, WI	55001	9	18 643	16.0	1	8	2 055	3 616	93.8	3 073	94.4
Ashland, WI	55003	7	16 866	19.1	4	12	3 091	4 768	78.3	3 243	91.6
Barron, WI	55005	7	44 963	19.7	7	29	8 418	10 864	91.6	8 961	93.6
Bayfield, WI	55007	8	15 013	19.4	4	12	2 134	3 665	89.9	2 996	92.6
Brown, WI	55009	3	226 778	19.2	9	71	38 463	61 176	79.7	43 878	82.9
Buffalo, WI	55011	8	13 804	19.3	4	11	2 561	3 261	90.5	2 687	92.0
Burnett, WI	55013	8	15 674	17.2	3	9	2 253	3 169	91.7	2 733	93.5
Calumet, WI	55015	2	40 631	21.6	5	14	4 307	11 173	82.3	8 975	85.1
Chippewa, WI	55017	3	55 195	20.2	7	25	8 981	14 029	83.5	11 414	84.3
Clark, WI	55019	6	33 557	22.3	8	24	5 819	8 564	81.3	7 381	81.4
Columbia, WI	55021	6	52 468	19.1	9	38	9 509	12 494	88.9	10 054	91.6
Crawford, WI	55023	7	17 243	20.2	4	11	2 670	4 180	86.4	3 496	86.8
Dane, WI	55025	2	426 526	16.5	19	164	65 853	132 595	88.9	71 417	91.2
Dodge, WI	55027	4	85 897	18.8	9	29	8 500	21 011	79.5	16 963	82.2
Door, WI	55029	7	27 961	17.5	5	17	4 253	5 892	88.8	4 918	90.8
Douglas, WI	55031	3	43 287	17.7	3	16	6 958	11 211	89.5	7 878	89.5
Dunn, WI	55033	6	39 858	17.6	4	18	6 080	14 115	92.7	7 115	91.2
Eau Claire, WI	55035	3	93 142	17.5	4	31	14 236	30 324	88.7	16 477	86.3
Florence, WI	55037	9	5 088	18.4	1	4	870	1 077	96.4	935	97.3
Fond du Lac, WI	55039	4	97 296	19.2	7	41	15 733	25 296	78.1	19 140	84.1

[1]County type code is from the Economic Research Service of the USDA. See Notes and Definitions at the end of this section.

Table C-1. School and Student Characteristics by County—*Continued*

County	Characteristics of students, 2000–2001			Staff and students, 2000–2001				Revenues, fiscal 1999			
	Percent with IEP[2]	Percent eligible for free lunch	Percent minority	Number of teachers	Student/ teacher ratio	Local school non-teaching staff	Central admin. staff	Total revenue ($1,000s)	Percentage of revenue from		
									Federal govt.	State govt.	Local govt.
	10	11	12	13	14	15	16	17	18	19	20
Forest, WI	16.6	44.7	22.3	132	15.4	122	16	$18 562	9.3	51.3	39.5
Grant, WI	16.1	24.9	1.9	633	13.4	478	97	74 963	3.9	66.5	29.6
Green, WI	16.0	15.6	2.6	446	13.4	354	42	48 456	3.1	58.7	38.1
Green Lake, WI	15.8	19.2	6.2	260	13.9	178	24	31 839	2.7	50.7	46.6
Iowa, WI	14.3	15.9	0.8	312	12.7	206	22	34 709	2.7	57.4	39.9
Iron, WI	13.9	36.0	2.2	76	13.2	53	6	10 052	3.6	48.1	48.3
Jackson, WI	14.1	28.8	12.4	236	14.2	208	19	26 936	5.2	64.4	30.4
Jefferson, WI	15.9	16.5	7.7	819	14.8	659	82	104 016	2.8	50.4	46.8
Juneau, WI	13.9	35.6	3.5	329	13.0	240	21	38 162	4.4	61.2	34.4
Kenosha, WI	13.6	23.0	20.8	1 744	15.5	1 140	155	206 356	4.7	56.8	38.5
Kewaunee, WI	15.6	11.0	2.3	245	15.2	159	13	29 278	2.9	59.5	37.7
La Crosse, WI	13.3	27.0	13.0	1 108	14.2	942	104	137 882	4.0	55.1	40.9
Lafayette, WI	15.4	16.2	0.5	286	12.3	172	22	31 713	2.6	63.4	34.0
Langlade, WI	16.3	38.5	3.5	268	13.9	210	28	33 491	5.8	54.7	39.5
Lincoln, WI	12.2	25.9	2.4	339	15.2	237	42	42 317	4.6	58.0	37.4
Manitowoc, WI	13.1	...	8.6	786	15.7	605	64	92 276	3.2	60.2	36.5
Marathon, WI	12.8	24.3	15.8	1 317	15.0	961	128	161 243	3.7	60.7	35.6
Marinette, WI	14.1	26.1	2.1	506	14.3	331	46	62 929	4.2	60.7	35.1
Marquette, WI	16.8	30.7	4.9	155	14.5	134	11	18 539	3.4	50.5	46.1
Menominee, WI	30.3	80.8	100.0	103	9.6	91	15	14 907	38.4	47.7	13.8
Milwaukee, WI	14.6	51.1	59.9	9 195	16.4	4 594	727	1 378 028	7.8	55.7	36.5
Monroe, WI	12.8	28.6	4.6	498	14.4	383	40	54 725	5.4	65.5	29.1
Oconto, WI	17.0	21.1	2.6	369	14.4	267	55	41 151	4.0	63.9	32.1
Oneida, WI	11.9	27.2	5.7	379	15.3	279	29	58 583	3.7	31.5	64.9
Outagamie, WI	13.4	13.7	10.6	1 960	15.5	1 249	148	227 162	2.8	57.0	40.2
Ozaukee, WI	11.3	4.1	5.9	825	15.4	544	82	110 109	1.3	31.2	67.6
Pepin, WI	16.5	25.5	1.3	112	13.6	92	10	14 893	3.6	63.0	33.5
Pierce, WI	13.3	13.2	3.5	510	14.6	433	37	60 549	2.9	61.6	35.5
Polk, WI	13.7	24.0	3.7	558	15.0	448	45	69 674	3.6	61.9	34.5
Portage, WI	13.0	20.5	9.8	694	14.5	563	52	82 290	3.6	60.0	36.4
Price, WI	11.8	26.8	2.9	199	13.5	160	16	21 085	4.0	62.7	33.3
Racine, WI	15.3	28.0	29.6	1 793	16.5	1 342	162	239 186	4.1	60.2	35.8
Richland, WI	19.5	25.9	2.3	157	12.7	122	15	19 279	3.4	63.3	33.3
Rock, WI	16.1	22.1	14.9	1 857	14.8	1 412	203	220 482	3.7	60.5	35.7
Rusk, WI	15.3	44.9	2.8	202	13.6	157	27	30 208	5.2	60.0	34.8
St. Croix, WI	14.4	10.9	3.0	718	15.2	555	56	86 939	2.6	59.1	38.4
Sauk, WI	15.9	20.7	5.5	839	14.2	746	75	81 157	3.8	54.7	41.6
Sawyer, WI	15.8	38.6	20.9	181	13.3	130	9	21 708	9.1	34.7	56.3
Shawano, WI	15.2	27.5	14.1	429	14.7	346	37	49 497	5.3	62.6	32.1
Sheboygan, WI	13.7	17.8	15.7	1 295	15.2	941	113	159 556	3.0	54.9	42.0
Taylor, WI	11.7	25.1	2.2	238	15.0	175	21	30 673	4.4	66.2	29.4
Trempealeau, WI	14.1	23.7	2.0	425	13.7	379	44	52 056	3.3	62.4	34.3
Vernon, WI	14.7	27.7	1.4	345	13.1	299	37	40 657	5.2	63.0	31.7
Vilas, WI	13.9	36.3	17.5	253	12.5	188	22	29 010	15.9	12.4	71.8
Walworth, WI	11.3	19.1	13.0	991	15.2	668	76	125 883	2.4	34.4	63.3
Washburn, WI	15.9	33.2	4.5	206	14.5	136	25	26 328	4.8	44.9	50.3
Washington, WI	12.3	8.5	3.8	1 215	16.0	841	96	153 212	2.4	45.0	52.6
Waukesha, WI	12.2	6.6	7.9	3 868	15.3	2 530	256	518 477	1.7	30.6	67.7
Waupaca, WI	11.9	20.1	4.0	717	14.5	615	62	82 820	3.2	60.6	36.3
Waushara, WI	11.8	36.4	12.8	223	14.8	151	14	25 493	4.5	46.5	49.0
Winnebago, WI	13.8	16.9	9.6	1 519	15.7	1 105	133	179 123	3.0	54.7	42.3
Wood, WI	13.4	19.3	6.9	917	15.1	646	75	110 298	3.4	60.7	35.9
WYOMING											
Albany, WY	16.1	45.8	15.1	313	12.2	257	32	30 943	5.5	66.2	28.3
Big Horn, WY	13.6	69.1	10.0	206	11.5	196	25	22 671	7.1	66.2	26.8
Campbell, WY	10.5	40.0	4.6	537	13.9	624	58	60 390	6.1	13.5	80.4
Carbon, WY	13.3	51.3	19.4	234	11.7	183	26	27 336	4.4	34.2	61.5
Converse, WY	10.6	57.6	7.7	197	12.4	182	17	20 950	5.9	40.7	53.4
Crook, WY	16.0	47.7	3.0	100	11.6	90	11	11 648	5.3	55.0	39.7
Fremont, WY	14.7	61.8	31.7	562	12.1	620	73	72 297	22.0	57.0	21.0
Goshen, WY	14.3	69.4	16.0	179	11.7	163	14	17 416	7.5	72.0	20.5
Hot Springs, WY	12.6	51.0	4.5	63	12.4	62	9	8 031	3.8	42.3	53.9
Johnson, WY	13.5	41.7	5.3	103	13.0	97	12	10 438	5.0	60.1	34.9
Laramie, WY	11.3	49.2	19.6	969	14.8	821	122	109 468	8.9	71.0	20.1
Lincoln, WY	9.5	43.5	2.1	232	14.0	206	20	34 411	3.9	56.6	39.5
Natrona, WY	13.6	52.9	9.0	796	15.1	757	83	91 844	6.2	70.6	23.2
Niobrara, WY	14.9	49.5	3.5	40	10.6	40	9	4 187	6.4	60.3	33.3
Park, WY	9.9	45.2	6.3	295	14.5	271	26	33 882	4.3	53.4	42.3
Platte, WY	14.1	...	7.2	148	10.9	119	14	14 005	8.3	55.6	36.1
Sheridan, WY	12.9	49.4	7.1	370	11.8	282	41	35 014	6.0	73.8	20.2
Sublette, WY	11.1	38.4	4.4	98	12.4	204	17	14 453	2.9	9.7	87.4
Sweetwater, WY	14.9	37.0	11.8	525	14.5	534	70	68 386	4.7	31.1	64.2
Teton, WY	9.9	17.9	6.7	166	13.9	138	16	19 424	2.6	12.3	85.1
Uinta, WY	15.5	46.6	6.3	344	13.8	330	50	47 982	5.0	40.7	54.4
Washakie, WY	16.9	54.0	16.2	124	12.9	139	10	14 595	6.3	61.8	31.9
Weston, WY	14.7	38.1	5.2	105	11.3	90	12	11 104	6.8	63.1	30.1

[2]IEP = Individual Education Program. See Notes and Definitions at the end of this section.
. . . = Not available.

Table C-1. Population, School, and Student Characteristics by County—*Continued*

County	Current expenditures, fiscal 1999			Resident population 16 to 19 years, 2000				Outcomes, 1999–2000	
	Amount ($1,000s)	Amount per student	Percent for instruction	Total population 16 to 19 years	Percent in Armed Forces	Percent high school graduates	Percent not enrolled, not grads, not Armed Forces, not empl.	Number of graduates	Dropouts grades 9–12 (percent)
	21	22	23	24	25	26	27	28	29
WEST VIRGINIA									
Barbour, WV	$16 792	$5 938	62.5	931	0.0	11.4	9.8	172	4.1
Berkeley, WV	80 117	6 352	59.8	4 037	0.0	19.3	8.1	735	6.2
Boone, WV	35 422	7 561	59.3	1 266	0.0	13.1	2.6	298	4.7
Braxton, WV	17 116	6 179	62.4	683	0.0	12.7	13.5	165	2.8
Brooke, WV	26 777	6 829	62.4	1 370	0.2	9.6	5.5	279	5.6
Cabell, WV	91 088	6 880	59.9	6 110	0.2	9.5	4.9	888	6.5
Calhoun, WV	10 131	6 864	59.9	445	0.0	12.1	11.2	103	5.1
Clay, WV	13 734	6 361	60.2	631	0.0	14.4	10.3	141	4.6
Doddridge, WV	9 038	6 821	55.0	519	0.0	15.4	3.3	107	3.8
Fayette, WV	52 313	6 726	64.9	2 559	0.1	15.4	7.2	577	5.0
Gilmer, WV	8 284	6 973	56.7	667	0.0	5.5	7.0	86	4.6
Grant, WV	12 144	6 161	61.5	427	0.0	15.9	4.0	132	3.8
Greenbrier, WV	36 163	6 191	66.2	1 691	0.0	13.2	5.2	409	4.2
Hampshire, WV	20 494	5 909	61.1	1 039	0.0	11.1	6.4	188	5.9
Hancock, WV	30 980	6 617	63.1	1 548	0.0	11.0	7.4	348	4.8
Hardy, WV	13 127	6 131	61.0	574	0.0	13.9	4.4	128	1.2
Harrison, WV	78 970	6 602	61.7	3 828	0.0	11.5	6.1	806	3.4
Jackson, WV	33 822	6 643	59.8	1 353	0.0	8.2	5.6	337	4.6
Jefferson, WV	43 019	6 170	64.0	2 565	0.4	12.9	4.0	454	6.7
Kanawha, WV	210 502	6 837	60.8	9 522	0.1	12.3	8.5	1 981	4.5
Lewis, WV	17 590	6 170	60.7	843	1.8	10.6	2.0	211	1.7
Lincoln, WV	29 176	7 101	61.8	1 319	0.0	13.4	11.2	280	3.6
Logan, WV	46 282	6 834	62.3	2 087	0.0	12.2	9.8	435	5.4
McDowell, WV	38 538	7 137	65.5	1 595	0.0	15.0	19.7	324	4.5
Marion, WV	60 094	6 730	61.3	3 165	0.0	11.4	3.8	672	1.5
Marshall, WV	41 266	7 126	62.9	1 707	0.0	10.3	4.7	418	4.0
Mason, WV	30 682	6 978	64.8	1 373	0.0	13.6	6.3	314	3.2
Mercer, WV	64 933	6 593	63.4	3 199	0.1	11.5	6.5	591	3.9
Mineral, WV	31 041	6 476	59.9	1 576	0.0	11.7	3.4	285	3.6
Mingo, WV	40 080	7 089	66.0	1 663	0.0	13.1	13.2	341	2.7
Monongalia, WV	67 919	6 545	59.7	7 414	0.1	6.6	2.7	699	3.4
Monroe, WV	12 703	6 200	61.9	633	0.0	14.1	7.6	147	4.3
Morgan, WV	13 841	6 041	57.3	568	0.0	10.7	5.5	107	6.0
Nicholas, WV	32 696	6 865	61.9	1 397	0.0	13.3	7.9	300	3.1
Ohio, WV	42 758	6 921	58.8	2 803	0.0	6.0	4.5	414	5.4
Pendleton, WV	8 839	6 538	62.7	338	2.1	18.3	2.7	80	2.0
Pleasants, WV	12 267	8 572	59.3	373	0.0	9.7	4.3	105	4.1
Pocahontas, WV	10 096	6 822	63.9	368	0.0	13.0	2.7	82	4.7
Preston, WV	30 623	6 013	64.3	1 729	0.0	15.4	4.4	329	5.7
Putnam, WV	54 180	6 170	63.0	2 514	0.1	10.5	1.7	575	2.5
Raleigh, WV	86 376	6 897	58.6	4 028	0.5	16.1	5.3	798	4.1
Randolph, WV	30 452	6 215	66.2	1 367	0.0	13.7	8.6	279	2.9
Ritchie, WV	12 638	6 842	59.8	601	0.0	15.3	5.7	123	4.7
Roane, WV	18 001	6 216	59.1	906	1.2	13.2	7.4	180	4.4
Summers, WV	11 378	6 539	60.2	715	0.0	9.7	16.2	145	3.9
Taylor, WV	17 330	6 392	59.5	794	0.0	8.9	6.8	169	2.3
Tucker, WV	8 113	6 353	59.3	393	0.0	14.0	7.6	88	0.7
Tyler, WV	11 788	7 349	60.3	478	0.0	10.0	4.0	111	3.9
Upshur, WV	25 101	6 130	63.7	1 641	0.2	7.1	4.5	245	5.4
Wayne, WV	51 028	6 486	63.2	2 342	0.0	14.1	9.3	505	5.2
Webster, WV	12 581	6 860	59.3	556	0.0	9.9	5.4	149	3.0
Wetzel, WV	24 023	6 487	61.2	945	0.0	8.6	5.4	242	4.1
Wirt, WV	7 531	6 345	61.4	373	0.0	6.7	4.6	65	1.3
Wood, WV	93 845	6 499	62.7	4 561	0.1	12.1	6.6	914	2.7
Wyoming, WV	35 548	7 584	65.3	1 316	0.0	11.7	9.3	381	4.3
WISCONSIN									
Adams, WI	15 546	7 651	63.7	805	0.0	16.8	2.6	145	. . .
Ashland, WI	26 230	7 917	59.8	1 212	0.0	12.0	3.9	256	. . .
Barron, WI	58 856	6 804	62.1	2 697	0.0	10.8	3.3	666	1.0
Bayfield, WI	17 360	7 788	60.6	824	0.0	8.6	0.8	155	2.9
Brown, WI	264 455	7 115	63.4	13 524	0.1	10.3	4.4	2 422	2.3
Buffalo, WI	18 072	6 956	61.8	755	0.0	12.7	0.3	177	2.2
Burnett, WI	16 439	7 216	63.2	812	0.0	13.3	3.9	162	0.9
Calumet, WI	27 846	6 391	61.5	2 233	0.0	11.2	1.4	396	0.6
Chippewa, WI	64 005	6 958	63.3	3 310	0.1	13.5	2.4	630	1.2
Clark, WI	42 764	7 084	60.4	2 251	0.1	10.8	6.8	491	1.2
Columbia, WI	77 119	6 748	62.6	2 849	0.0	13.2	2.9	677	1.3
Crawford, WI	19 864	7 027	64.8	1 216	0.0	18.8	5.8	239	1.0
Dane, WI	497 834	7 939	63.0	27 257	0.0	8.2	2.4	4 128	2.5
Dodge, WI	63 300	7 229	65.1	4 863	0.0	12.2	3.4	677	0.4
Door, WI	34 149	7 927	64.2	1 455	0.0	8.0	2.1	331	0.9
Douglas, WI	50 254	7 064	63.4	2 480	0.3	9.4	3.3	471	4.0
Dunn, WI	43 222	7 012	61.9	3 635	0.1	8.8	1.5	444	1.2
Eau Claire, WI	103 966	7 226	61.8	7 422	0.0	7.0	2.1	1 034	0.8
Florence, WI	6 341	6 892	63.2	250	0.0	11.6	4.0	62	0.3
Fond du Lac, WI	106 288	6 651	63.1	6 311	0.2	13.2	2.8	1 156	1.8

. . . = Not available.

Table C-1. Population, School, and Student Characteristics by County—*Continued*

County	High school graduates, 2000			College enrollment, 2000		College graduates, 2000 (percent)						
	Population 25 years and over	High school diploma or less (percent)	High school diploma or more (percent)	Number	Percent public	Bachelor's degree or more	+/- U.S. percent with bachelor's degree or more	Non-Hispanic White	Black or African American	American Indian and Alaska Native	Asian, Hawaiian, and Pacific Islander	Hispanic or Latino[1]
	30	31	32	33	34	35	36	37	38	39	40	41
WEST VIRGINIA												
Barbour, WV	10 510	73.4	72.7	827	39.5	11.8	-12.6	11.7	39.3	7.5	20.0	0.0
Berkeley, WV	50 092	62.8	77.6	2 424	81.8	15.1	-9.3	15.2	11.3	4.2	42.3	10.6
Boone, WV	17 282	77.0	64.0	808	87.0	7.2	-17.2	7.0	14.6	20.0	100.0	11.0
Braxton, WV	10 273	75.0	67.3	320	83.8	9.2	-15.2	9.2	0.0	33.3	100.0	0.0
Brooke, WV	17 855	63.9	79.7	1 611	52.2	13.4	-11.0	13.5	13.4	100.0	0.0	21.9
Cabell, WV	64 444	54.0	80.0	9 752	95.4	20.9	-3.5	21.1	10.6	20.3	48.9	16.4
Calhoun, WV	5 283	77.4	62.4	204	77.0	9.3	-15.1	8.9	. . .	0.0	100.0	41.7
Clay, WV	6 766	80.8	63.7	258	86.0	7.3	-17.1	7.4	0.0	0.0	0.0	0.0
Doddridge, WV	4 897	71.9	69.4	155	82.6	10.2	-14.2	10.3	. . .	0.0	50.0	0.0
Fayette, WV	32 721	71.2	68.6	2 079	82.6	10.7	-13.7	10.8	4.9	8.7	69.2	20.9
Gilmer, WV	4 515	66.9	70.0	953	98.1	17.1	-7.3	17.1	0.0	50.0	9.5	0.0
Grant, WV	7 859	72.3	70.8	323	82.0	11.4	-13.0	11.4	0.0	0.0	. . .	23.5
Greenbrier, WV	24 373	67.8	73.4	1 108	85.4	13.6	-10.8	13.9	4.6	10.1	62.5	7.5
Hampshire, WV	13 690	72.9	71.3	474	87.8	11.3	-13.1	11.3	5.8	50.0	42.5	0.0
Hancock, WV	23 502	64.7	82.9	927	85.9	11.5	-12.9	11.6	9.8	0.0	12.2	27.5
Hardy, WV	8 759	74.3	70.3	345	91.6	9.4	-15.0	9.7	3.3	28.6	. . .	0.0
Harrison, WV	46 870	62.0	78.4	2 738	75.2	16.3	-8.1	16.2	9.5	11.9	52.8	18.4
Jackson, WV	19 074	62.3	77.4	867	89.3	12.4	-12.0	12.1	100.0	20.6	72.7	14.7
Jefferson, WV	27 920	55.6	79.0	2 359	90.8	21.6	-2.8	22.3	9.5	20.5	35.0	9.5
Kanawha, WV	140 588	56.2	80.0	8 345	81.5	20.6	-3.8	20.4	15.5	24.0	70.3	21.9
Lewis, WV	11 872	70.4	73.7	459	87.8	11.2	-13.2	10.9	100.0	0.0	74.2	71.8
Lincoln, WV	14 864	79.5	62.7	541	90.4	5.9	-18.5	5.9	. . .	0.0	16.7	2.9
Logan, WV	25 824	71.7	63.1	1 181	85.7	8.8	-15.6	8.2	16.2	0.0	81.3	32.6
McDowell, WV	18 802	83.1	50.0	473	92.6	5.6	-18.8	5.1	9.5	0.0	44.0	2.8
Marion, WV	38 957	60.1	79.5	3 891	91.7	16.0	-8.4	16.1	9.6	0.0	55.6	25.5
Marshall, WV	24 707	66.8	79.7	1 228	85.6	10.7	-13.7	10.5	11.1	26.5	70.2	11.7
Mason, WV	17 947	73.8	72.4	752	87.6	8.8	-15.6	8.5	7.5	57.9	80.8	0.0
Mercer, WV	43 673	64.5	72.1	3 223	88.5	13.8	-10.6	13.5	13.4	28.1	72.6	8.5
Mineral, WV	18 443	66.1	80.3	1 189	93.3	11.7	-12.7	11.8	5.9	. . .	34.3	4.8
Mingo, WV	18 793	76.1	59.6	765	94.1	7.3	-17.1	6.9	12.1	0.0	71.8	4.8
Monongalia, WV	47 943	46.9	83.6	18 429	97.0	32.4	8.0	31.4	23.5	12.6	80.8	36.1
Monroe, WV	10 474	73.1	73.7	482	89.4	8.2	-16.2	8.8	1.1	30.0	25.0	0.0
Morgan, WV	10 591	70.2	75.8	238	81.9	11.2	-13.2	11.2	2.7	23.7	0.0	5.8
Nicholas, WV	18 149	73.6	70.0	797	88.3	9.8	-14.6	9.4	. . .	23.1	75.0	59.5
Ohio, WV	32 263	53.1	83.0	3 900	71.3	23.1	-1.3	23.2	10.2	0.0	69.0	29.7
Pendleton, WV	5 813	70.6	72.0	177	72.9	10.8	-13.6	10.9	0.7	0.0	100.0	0.0
Pleasants, WV	5 121	69.6	79.4	215	80.0	9.7	-14.7	9.5	12.5	23.8	40.0	46.2
Pocahontas, WV	6 556	71.7	70.9	234	76.9	11.8	-12.6	11.7	6.5	9.1	87.5	40.0
Preston, WV	20 050	73.1	74.0	691	88.4	10.8	-13.6	10.6	19.2	. . .	68.4	35.4
Putnam, WV	34 854	55.0	83.8	2 105	88.4	19.7	-4.7	19.2	56.3	0.0	48.9	38.0
Raleigh, WV	55 201	64.3	72.0	3 688	59.7	12.7	-11.7	12.6	5.9	0.0	64.5	12.8
Randolph, WV	19 498	69.4	73.5	998	44.9	13.6	-10.8	13.5	16.6	0.0	32.6	43.4
Ritchie, WV	7 177	70.3	73.4	294	94.2	7.1	-17.3	7.1	31.3	31.8	0.0	4.0
Roane, WV	10 442	74.9	66.8	278	81.7	9.0	-15.4	9.0	0.0	0.0	60.0	25.8
Summers, WV	9 302	74.9	65.4	415	74.0	10.1	-14.3	10.2	3.8	0.0	0.0	0.0
Taylor, WV	11 146	69.4	74.7	444	85.6	11.3	-13.1	11.2	15.2	6.5	31.3	11.3
Tucker, WV	5 301	73.0	75.5	192	72.9	10.6	-13.8	10.3	. . .	0.0	0.0	0.0
Tyler, WV	6 749	69.4	75.4	245	82.9	8.5	-15.9	8.4	100.0	0.0	71.4	0.0
Upshur, WV	15 222	69.8	74.6	1 781	22.5	13.8	-10.6	13.7	0.0	0.0	40.0	33.0
Wayne, WV	29 223	67.9	70.5	1 433	91.4	11.9	-12.5	11.7	37.5	3.6	43.8	35.6
Webster, WV	6 701	78.2	58.2	152	88.8	8.7	-15.7	8.7	. . .	0.0	100.0	. . .
Wetzel, WV	12 287	69.9	77.6	464	86.2	10.4	-14.0	10.3	0.0	19.2	100.0	0.0
Wirt, WV	3 944	72.6	72.4	140	97.1	9.9	-14.5	9.9	. . .	0.0	0.0	0.0
Wood, WV	60 697	56.9	81.4	3 348	80.0	15.2	-9.2	15.0	18.6	17.9	51.5	25.4
Wyoming, WV	17 722	77.5	64.3	610	85.2	7.1	-17.3	7.1	18.9	0.0	0.0	0.0
WISCONSIN												
Adams, WI	13 730	65.2	76.7	371	88.7	10.0	-14.4	9.9	7.1	3.9	49.1	5.9
Ashland, WI	10 668	56.4	84.1	1 192	45.8	16.5	-7.9	17.1	0.0	9.2	12.9	23.1
Barron, WI	29 942	57.1	82.4	1 371	88.8	14.9	-9.5	14.9	0.0	1.2	50.0	11.9
Bayfield, WI	10 526	47.2	86.9	453	81.5	21.6	-2.8	22.5	0.0	9.5	30.4	0.0
Brown, WI	144 172	48.6	86.3	13 385	77.3	22.5	-1.9	23.3	7.7	11.1	21.3	7.3
Buffalo, WI	9 384	59.7	84.1	374	85.3	14.0	-10.4	13.9	40.0	9.1	18.2	21.9
Burnett, WI	11 273	59.9	82.8	248	82.3	14.0	-10.4	14.4	0.0	3.3	12.5	0.0
Calumet, WI	26 068	53.2	87.3	1 476	79.3	20.8	-3.6	20.5	60.0	12.9	43.2	32.0
Chippewa, WI	36 330	56.7	84.3	1 800	89.2	14.7	-9.7	14.6	10.0	9.8	29.1	29.1
Clark, WI	20 991	67.3	75.4	711	86.9	10.3	-14.1	10.2	5.4	10.3	51.1	11.8
Columbia, WI	35 529	53.5	86.2	1 668	83.8	16.7	-7.7	16.8	7.6	1.6	42.5	12.5
Crawford, WI	11 301	61.2	81.3	432	85.2	13.2	-11.2	13.2	0.0	4.8	22.9	0.0
Dane, WI	269 998	30.1	92.2	53 744	91.4	40.6	16.2	41.1	19.2	23.1	65.0	27.2
Dodge, WI	57 453	61.2	82.3	2 735	75.2	13.2	-11.2	13.5	2.7	10.7	39.1	8.7
Door, WI	20 062	50.8	87.8	636	83.0	21.4	-3.0	21.5	11.8	8.4	38.9	13.0
Douglas, WI	28 653	50.3	85.9	2 719	93.4	18.3	-6.1	18.7	20.9	2.2	38.0	12.0
Dunn, WI	22 644	50.2	86.6	6 457	96.5	21.1	-3.3	21.2	13.6	29.3	16.0	18.1
Eau Claire, WI	55 290	42.2	88.9	12 337	96.6	27.0	2.6	27.1	29.9	8.6	26.5	25.7
Florence, WI	3 641	60.6	83.7	83	89.2	12.4	-12.0	12.6	0.0	0.0	0.0	0.0
Fond du Lac, WI	63 548	55.9	84.2	4 722	60.5	16.9	-7.5	17.0	8.0	10.5	38.8	8.3

[1]Hispanic or Latino persons may be of any race.
. . . = Not available.

Table C-1. Population, School, and Student Characteristics by County—*Continued*

County	State/County code	County type[1]	Population, 2000		Number of schools and students, 2000–2001			Resident enrollment, 2000			
			Total	Percent 5–17 years	School districts	Schools	Students	Total	Percent public	K–12	Percent public
			1	2	3	4	5	6	7	8	9
Forest, WI	55041	9	10 024	19.6	3	8	2 035	2 407	94.7	2 045	95.5
Grant, WI	55043	6	49 597	18.5	10	31	8 478	15 315	90.4	9 319	89.3
Green, WI	55045	6	33 647	20.1	6	19	5 982	8 301	92.6	6 905	95.6
Green Lake, WI	55047	6	19 105	18.5	4	10	3 618	4 182	84.8	3 554	85.6
Iowa, WI	55049	6	22 780	20.6	5	13	3 952	5 763	90.9	4 809	92.8
Iron, WI	55051	9	6 861	15.4	2	4	1 003	1 365	96.9	1 104	99.0
Jackson, WI	55053	6	19 100	18.5	3	11	3 354	4 439	93.7	3 728	95.0
Jefferson, WI	55055	4	74 021	18.9	7	32	12 091	18 482	79.5	13 994	82.4
Juneau, WI	55057	7	24 316	19.5	5	16	4 261	5 654	87.0	4 840	88.0
Kenosha, WI	55059	1	149 577	20.1	13	53	26 990	42 684	82.6	30 494	89.1
Kewaunee, WI	55061	6	20 187	19.9	3	8	3 713	4 977	83.3	4 139	84.2
La Crosse, WI	55063	3	107 120	17.6	5	39	15 751	33 296	85.1	19 081	85.1
Lafayette, WI	55065	9	16 137	21.3	7	17	3 513	4 218	93.6	3 525	95.3
Langlade, WI	55067	6	20 740	19.0	3	19	3 728	4 619	87.2	3 948	88.2
Lincoln, WI	55069	6	29 641	19.7	2	13	5 157	7 154	88.3	5 830	89.6
Manitowoc, WI	55071	4	82 887	19.6	6	28	12 361	20 954	77.8	16 665	80.5
Marathon, WI	55073	3	125 834	20.4	8	43	19 731	32 716	85.7	25 711	87.4
Marinette, WI	55075	7	43 384	18.4	8	24	7 254	10 876	83.4	8 300	91.0
Marquette, WI	55077	9	15 832	16.2	2	7	2 251	3 437	87.1	2 782	88.4
Menominee, WI	55078	6	4 562	29.4	1	3	991	1 645	95.3	1 335	96.0
Milwaukee, WI	55079	0	940 164	19.2	23	310	150 778	268 828	76.5	190 432	82.1
Monroe, WI	55081	6	40 899	21.4	4	22	7 158	10 296	84.8	8 652	85.5
Oconto, WI	55083	6	35 634	20.0	5	18	5 298	8 738	90.8	7 363	93.0
Oneida, WI	55085	7	36 776	17.6	4	16	5 794	8 435	88.7	6 676	91.3
Outagamie, WI	55087	2	160 971	20.8	8	56	30 452	44 269	78.8	33 537	81.3
Ozaukee, WI	55089	0	82 317	20.5	5	25	12 724	23 199	71.1	16 931	80.0
Pepin, WI	55091	8	7 213	20.6	2	5	1 522	1 844	84.8	1 498	84.1
Pierce, WI	55093	8	36 804	18.7	6	23	7 451	12 261	89.4	7 033	92.1
Polk, WI	55095	6	41 319	20.3	8	25	8 345	10 202	94.0	8 586	96.3
Portage, WI	55097	4	67 182	18.2	4	29	10 057	21 761	91.3	12 280	90.0
Price, WI	55099	7	15 822	19.0	3	12	2 696	3 685	90.3	3 111	92.9
Racine, WI	55101	3	188 831	20.0	12	57	29 648	51 249	78.4	38 957	80.6
Richland, WI	55103	7	17 924	19.6	2	12	1 993	4 510	85.9	3 620	86.1
Rock, WI	55105	3	152 307	19.8	8	61	27 420	39 380	86.7	30 300	92.0
Rusk, WI	55107	7	15 347	19.4	4	13	2 755	3 751	86.5	3 078	93.4
St. Croix, WI	55109	1	63 155	20.9	6	25	10 894	17 324	86.8	13 251	91.0
Sauk, WI	55111	6	55 225	19.6	6	38	11 914	13 531	87.0	10 922	89.3
Sawyer, WI	55113	9	16 196	18.6	2	9	2 400	3 740	88.0	3 075	91.3
Shawano, WI	55115	6	40 664	19.5	5	20	6 295	9 992	87.4	8 151	89.3
Sheboygan, WI	55117	3	112 646	19.1	9	45	19 715	28 868	78.5	22 043	83.2
Taylor, WI	55119	6	19 680	21.3	3	9	3 569	5 003	90.1	4 353	91.4
Trempealeau, WI	55121	8	27 010	19.2	7	23	5 805	6 266	91.6	5 212	93.3
Vernon, WI	55123	6	28 056	20.9	6	21	4 509	6 831	83.9	5 816	83.8
Vilas, WI	55125	9	21 033	16.4	5	11	3 171	4 346	92.0	3 520	94.1
Walworth, WI	55127	4	93 759	18.3	16	39	15 079	28 372	88.3	17 448	88.1
Washburn, WI	55129	9	16 036	18.7	4	9	2 990	3 591	92.1	3 056	93.8
Washington, WI	55131	1	117 493	19.9	9	34	19 380	30 427	77.3	23 736	81.2
Waukesha, WI	55133	0	360 767	19.9	19	105	59 274	97 499	75.3	72 586	80.9
Waupaca, WI	55135	6	51 731	19.6	7	29	10 416	12 254	86.4	10 414	87.9
Waushara, WI	55137	8	23 154	18.5	3	10	3 292	4 997	91.2	4 340	93.0
Winnebago, WI	55139	2	156 763	17.8	5	55	23 884	43 417	86.3	28 544	86.8
Wood, WI	55141	4	75 555	19.5	6	32	13 840	19 208	84.3	15 093	86.1
WYOMING	56000										
Albany, WY	56001	5	32 014	13.3	1	20	3 816	14 837	90.9	4 311	93.3
Big Horn, WY	56003	9	11 461	21.9	4	19	2 369	3 028	95.7	2 557	97.3
Campbell, WY	56005	7	33 698	23.7	3	22	7 491	9 726	94.7	7 977	97.6
Carbon, WY	56007	7	15 639	18.4	2	20	2 736	3 674	95.9	2 969	97.8
Converse, WY	56009	6	12 052	22.1	2	16	2 438	3 154	95.0	2 604	98.2
Crook, WY	56011	9	5 887	21.7	1	11	1 162	1 512	98.3	1 345	98.7
Fremont, WY	56013	7	35 804	20.9	8	27	6 787	9 531	94.6	7 484	96.7
Goshen, WY	56015	7	12 538	18.4	2	13	2 100	3 108	90.6	2 279	95.2
Hot Springs, WY	56017	7	4 882	17.2	1	4	783	1 043	95.0	900	96.2
Johnson, WY	56019	7	7 075	19.0	1	9	1 334	1 652	95.8	1 456	97.3
Laramie, WY	56021	3	81 607	19.2	3	40	14 293	21 266	89.9	15 626	93.3
Lincoln, WY	56023	7	14 573	24.1	2	12	3 259	4 113	95.1	3 620	97.2
Natrona, WY	56025	3	66 533	19.5	1	38	12 042	18 067	94.1	12 864	96.9
Niobrara, WY	56027	9	2 407	17.8	1	4	423	522	95.4	428	97.9
Park, WY	56029	7	25 786	18.9	3	14	4 292	6 815	92.6	5 000	93.3
Platte, WY	56031	7	8 807	20.2	2	13	1 618	2 147	93.0	1 841	93.9
Sheridan, WY	56033	7	26 560	18.8	4	24	4 356	6 752	88.1	5 051	88.9
Sublette, WY	56035	9	5 920	19.9	2	8	1 211	1 392	91.6	1 178	94.3
Sweetwater, WY	56037	5	37 613	22.0	2	33	7 592	11 129	95.1	8 471	98.2
Teton, WY	56039	7	18 251	14.7	2	9	2 313	3 101	86.3	2 438	90.6
Uinta, WY	56041	7	19 742	25.2	3	15	4 738	5 873	94.7	5 003	97.9
Washakie, WY	56043	7	8 289	21.4	2	8	1 602	2 112	95.3	1 850	97.6
Weston, WY	56045	7	6 644	18.8	2	8	1 185	1 585	97.6	1 310	98.5

[1]County type code is from the Economic Research Service of the USDA. See Notes and Definitions at the end of this section.

Table C-1. School and Student Characteristics by County—*Continued*

County	Characteristics of students, 2000–2001			Staff and students, 2000–2001				Revenues, fiscal 1999			
	Percent with IEP[2]	Percent eligible for free lunch	Percent minority	Number of teachers	Student/ teacher ratio	Local school non-teaching staff	Central admin. staff	Total revenue ($1,000s)	Percentage of revenue from		
									Federal govt.	State govt.	Local govt.
	10	11	12	13	14	15	16	17	18	19	20
WEST VIRGINIA											
Barbour, WV	18.4	64.9	1.6	193	13.7	122	24	$17 881	11.2	77.7	11.2
Berkeley, WV	15.8	37.7	9.5	880	14.9	687	101	90 975	10.3	57.7	32.0
Boone, WV	20.0	57.0	1.5	361	12.4	263	41	36 002	8.5	53.3	38.2
Braxton, WV	22.5	59.1	0.6	200	13.3	127	26	18 543	13.1	69.7	17.2
Brooke, WV	17.6	29.3	1.9	284	13.2	183	36	28 941	5.9	58.8	35.2
Cabell, WV	18.1	52.3	8.2	928	13.5	600	126	110 320	7.4	53.9	38.7
Calhoun, WV	17.8	70.4	0.4	94	14.0	70	15	12 833	9.4	77.3	13.3
Clay, WV	19.0	75.2	0.4	161	13.2	119	13	15 801	15.2	67.6	17.2
Doddridge, WV	21.2	55.3	0.5	90	13.9	76	12	9 547	7.8	63.9	28.3
Fayette, WV	16.0	64.1	7.4	529	13.8	380	72	54 913	10.3	65.1	24.6
Gilmer, WV	16.8	66.3	1.2	80	14.1	64	13	11 383	13.1	67.2	19.6
Grant, WV	19.2	54.7	1.5	135	14.7	115	15	13 544	7.5	55.6	36.9
Greenbrier, WV	19.3	54.0	4.7	385	14.7	323	42	39 866	9.2	66.5	24.3
Hampshire, WV	22.5	53.5	2.4	291	12.5	363	25	25 095	7.3	71.9	20.8
Hancock, WV	15.8	33.5	4.6	311	14.5	228	34	34 189	5.3	53.4	41.3
Hardy, WV	21.1	60.9	2.6	152	14.7	105	17	13 989	11.0	66.5	22.5
Harrison, WV	18.1	50.9	3.1	773	14.9	581	93	87 285	6.1	58.6	35.4
Jackson, WV	17.0	43.0	1.1	328	15.4	268	35	36 755	7.5	62.0	30.5
Jefferson, WV	16.9	32.8	12.0	505	13.6	316	67	46 943	5.3	57.6	37.1
Kanawha, WV	15.9	42.8	12.3	1 875	15.8	1 537	291	235 857	7.7	55.0	37.3
Lewis, WV	20.4	59.2	1.0	197	14.0	150	21	22 412	8.5	69.2	22.3
Lincoln, WV	21.3	69.4	0.1	296	13.2	191	37	30 392	13.9	70.9	15.3
Logan, WV	17.3	57.6	4.3	449	14.1	336	57	49 760	12.1	64.2	23.7
McDowell, WV	21.9	83.6	14.2	351	13.8	339	42	45 385	13.0	71.0	16.0
Marion, WV	14.6	43.7	5.7	609	14.1	455	96	64 304	10.1	61.9	28.0
Marshall, WV	19.4	43.8	1.1	395	14.1	291	38	42 438	5.8	56.7	37.5
Mason, WV	20.6	50.3	1.2	297	14.6	229	30	30 255	6.0	62.3	31.6
Mercer, WV	17.8	56.3	9.4	677	14.1	492	69	69 915	9.7	66.8	23.5
Mineral, WV	16.3	48.2	4.0	327	14.1	237	38	33 891	10.3	67.4	22.3
Mingo, WV	19.1	67.7	3.0	372	14.0	317	48	44 374	10.2	60.2	29.6
Monongalia, WV	14.8	40.8	7.7	661	15.5	564	83	79 473	9.0	48.9	42.2
Monroe, WV	19.1	52.3	2.2	138	15.2	113	24	17 782	10.1	78.6	11.3
Morgan, WV	16.2	45.1	1.8	159	15.2	107	23	15 315	6.1	58.9	35.0
Nicholas, WV	17.8	62.3	0.7	319	14.3	235	50	34 852	12.2	65.2	22.6
Ohio, WV	14.9	40.6	8.2	398	14.8	286	78	47 007	7.0	56.8	36.2
Pendleton, WV	18.5	46.1	4.2	88	14.6	71	12	11 415	8.0	75.5	16.5
Pleasants, WV	20.6	46.1	0.8	101	14.2	89	12	12 477	5.3	43.1	51.6
Pocahontas, WV	18.8	58.0	0.5	103	13.7	80	14	10 134	14.2	67.0	18.8
Preston, WV	19.3	60.3	0.9	333	14.6	243	39	32 633	8.8	74.4	16.8
Putnam, WV	19.0	33.0	1.8	579	15.1	408	72	58 105	5.4	59.6	35.0
Raleigh, WV	15.9	55.2	11.3	795	15.1	681	112	94 015	9.0	61.8	29.3
Randolph, WV	15.8	56.2	1.2	328	14.5	218	45	31 787	11.0	74.7	14.3
Ritchie, WV	18.6	60.1	1.2	121	14.5	107	14	13 719	11.7	65.7	22.6
Roane, WV	21.3	63.9	1.3	202	13.8	144	22	20 057	11.1	74.5	14.4
Summers, WV	20.7	69.0	4.5	106	15.4	100	13	12 117	11.2	75.4	13.5
Taylor, WV	18.8	57.7	1.4	164	15.2	141	23	19 361	9.0	69.9	21.1
Tucker, WV	15.9	57.7	1.1	85	14.5	61	10	8 830	10.9	64.0	25.1
Tyler, WV	18.4	48.8	0.5	114	13.6	76	14	14 066	6.3	60.7	33.0
Upshur, WV	18.0	56.7	1.4	263	15.0	203	35	26 007	9.4	75.5	15.2
Wayne, WV	19.0	58.1	0.8	543	13.7	429	61	57 738	7.2	67.6	25.2
Webster, WV	18.9	76.1	0.2	130	13.5	94	17	15 798	13.2	74.1	12.6
Wetzel, WV	19.3	45.6	0.8	254	13.8	157	27	27 071	6.8	68.3	24.9
Wirt, WV	17.4	47.3	0.5	82	14.2	52	11	8 359	8.5	74.2	17.3
Wood, WV	14.6	37.3	2.3	940	14.9	635	133	107 239	6.4	59.7	33.9
Wyoming, WV	20.5	63.6	1.7	323	13.5	223	37	41 270	8.4	66.9	24.7
WISCONSIN											
Adams, WI	19.3	53.3	6.3	152	13.5	125	11	18 053	6.4	54.0	39.6
Ashland, WI	15.4	41.9	14.3	238	13.0	204	51	29 363	6.3	69.6	24.1
Barron, WI	13.6	26.5	4.6	583	14.4	634	83	70 129	3.7	63.8	32.6
Bayfield, WI	14.7	44.1	22.1	151	14.1	121	23	21 409	12.4	41.7	45.9
Brown, WI	15.7	22.3	15.6	2 514	15.3	1 832	276	300 265	3.9	53.0	43.1
Buffalo, WI	13.1	26.3	2.3	173	14.8	157	25	21 603	3.3	61.5	35.2
Burnett, WI	14.7	44.1	14.0	158	14.3	110	24	19 653	5.1	51.4	43.5
Calumet, WI	14.8	10.4	1.6	312	13.8	235	24	34 382	2.0	59.6	38.5
Chippewa, WI	14.6	27.1	2.3	621	14.5	467	81	76 960	3.6	61.7	34.7
Clark, WI	14.3	31.4	2.8	436	13.3	301	45	52 316	4.3	64.6	31.2
Columbia, WI	14.1	14.6	3.9	680	14.0	565	82	91 632	3.1	49.1	47.9
Crawford, WI	16.2	28.7	1.8	212	12.6	139	22	23 629	5.0	64.6	30.4
Dane, WI	15.7	17.5	19.8	4 863	13.5	3 923	474	564 012	2.9	37.9	59.1
Dodge, WI	16.5	14.7	4.8	564	15.1	448	45	75 301	2.8	56.0	41.2
Door, WI	14.2	16.2	3.8	327	13.0	219	28	37 771	4.3	32.9	62.8
Douglas, WI	12.9	38.1	7.9	450	15.5	378	36	56 908	5.8	66.6	27.6
Dunn, WI	14.4	28.9	9.3	392	15.5	253	29	50 211	3.8	65.4	30.8
Eau Claire, WI	13.4	26.0	10.6	985	14.5	673	81	119 672	4.5	56.6	39.0
Florence, WI	10.9	39.1	2.2	52	16.7	45	8	7 506	7.2	54.1	38.7
Fond du Lac, WI	14.9	16.9	5.8	1 012	15.5	693	76	125 536	2.9	57.0	40.1

[2]IEP = Individual Education Program. See Notes and Definitions at the end of this section.

Table C-1. Population, School, and Student Characteristics by County—*Continued*

County	Current expenditures, fiscal 1999			Resident population 16 to 19 years, 2000				Outcomes, 1999–2000	
	Amount ($1,000s)	Amount per student	Percent for instruction	Total population 16 to 19 years	Percent in Armed Forces	Percent high school graduates	Percent not enrolled, not grads, not Armed Forces, not empl.	Number of graduates	Dropouts grades 9–12 (percent)
	21	22	23	24	25	26	27	28	29
Forest, WI	$14 423	$6 759	61.8	591	0.0	9.3	8.5	134	1.1
Grant, WI	66 113	7 431	63.3	4 046	0.2	6.9	2.0	673	0.8
Green, WI	42 740	7 123	65.8	1 822	0.0	10.8	3.0	411	1.4
Green Lake, WI	24 895	6 413	62.2	1 146	0.3	13.4	2.6	308	0.6
Iowa, WI	29 973	7 535	61.8	1 298	0.0	11.6	1.8	258	0.8
Iron, WI	7 995	7 607	59.9	365	0.5	7.4	1.6	103	0.6
Jackson, WI	22 592	6 694	61.6	1 038	0.0	12.6	6.8	211	1.4
Jefferson, WI	92 408	7 592	61.0	3 996	0.1	13.8	2.8	909	1.5
Juneau, WI	31 972	7 173	62.0	1 292	0.0	13.1	3.0	311	2.2
Kenosha, WI	183 036	6 985	61.5	8 661	0.2	11.5	3.9	1 477	3.7
Kewaunee, WI	24 538	6 677	64.2	1 142	0.0	11.5	0.6	310	0.9
La Crosse, WI	118 958	7 611	62.5	7 770	0.0	10.3	1.0	1 114	0.8
Lafayette, WI	26 879	7 224	64.1	1 063	0.4	6.3	0.8	305	1.2
Langlade, WI	29 390	7 620	59.4	1 131	0.0	14.3	2.7	273	1.2
Lincoln, WI	36 801	7 000	62.6	1 781	0.0	9.9	7.2	399	0.4
Manitowoc, WI	79 438	6 335	63.2	4 655	0.0	10.4	3.0	932	2.1
Marathon, WI	145 143	7 314	62.7	7 652	0.0	12.7	1.7	1 548	1.0
Marinette, WI	55 459	7 319	62.9	2 788	0.0	9.3	2.4	588	1.3
Marquette, WI	15 015	6 455	62.5	764	0.0	12.6	1.8	164	0.9
Menominee, WI	11 712	10 755	57.5	347	0.0	16.4	11.0	39	8.3
Milwaukee, WI	1 259 854	8 323	61.2	53 378	0.0	9.9	6.7	7 011	6.9
Monroe, WI	46 122	6 532	62.7	2 333	0.1	12.9	4.5	506	0.7
Oconto, WI	34 244	6 475	61.8	1 929	0.0	8.9	2.6	349	2.5
Oneida, WI	48 854	7 532	60.4	1 779	0.0	13.6	3.0	471	2.5
Outagamie, WI	199 061	6 748	63.5	9 485	0.1	12.2	2.3	2 016	1.0
Ozaukee, WI	99 910	7 840	63.5	4 502	0.0	8.2	1.6	1 046	1.0
Pepin, WI	13 273	7 967	59.2	457	0.0	9.4	1.3	142	1.8
Pierce, WI	54 575	7 302	65.5	3 203	0.3	8.3	1.4	608	0.6
Polk, WI	56 236	6 831	62.7	2 405	0.3	12.3	2.6	609	0.5
Portage, WI	73 413	6 963	65.5	5 331	0.0	8.9	1.3	835	2.4
Price, WI	19 085	6 804	61.5	858	0.0	11.1	1.6	246	0.4
Racine, WI	218 140	7 245	63.6	10 703	0.1	11.5	4.5	1 844	5.5
Richland, WI	16 463	7 784	62.0	1 151	0.0	9.5	2.4	178	2.4
Rock, WI	197 936	7 231	64.9	8 757	0.0	11.6	4.6	1 641	3.2
Rusk, WI	23 485	8 343	62.7	901	0.0	8.5	3.0	198	. . .
St. Croix, WI	72 678	6 890	62.2	3 525	0.0	10.2	1.8	738	1.0
Sauk, WI	70 355	6 964	62.0	3 029	0.0	15.1	3.8	786	2.1
Sawyer, WI	18 323	7 409	59.3	862	0.0	17.1	4.1	146	2.3
Shawano, WI	43 250	6 765	63.5	2 320	0.1	12.0	2.9	438	1.7
Sheboygan, WI	141 576	7 196	64.6	6 439	0.0	11.5	2.9	1 461	2.3
Taylor, WI	24 571	6 547	62.4	1 175	0.0	12.1	3.3	298	. . .
Trempealeau, WI	42 266	7 292	60.1	1 467	0.0	12.0	2.6	430	0.8
Vernon, WI	34 721	7 373	60.6	1 610	0.0	10.6	7.7	405	1.0
Vilas, WI	24 408	9 420	58.6	902	0.0	8.8	3.1	143	0.7
Walworth, WI	103 347	7 222	62.5	6 786	0.0	8.4	1.7	899	1.3
Washburn, WI	22 397	7 281	62.7	881	0.0	10.3	3.4	250	0.6
Washington, WI	137 136	7 077	62.5	6 175	0.0	14.5	1.5	1 590	1.4
Waukesha, WI	458 913	7 844	62.8	19 496	0.0	10.3	1.1	4 461	0.3
Waupaca, WI	69 718	6 557	63.6	2 753	0.0	13.4	3.6	775	1.8
Waushara, WI	20 649	6 253	62.7	1 232	0.0	12.5	2.6	207	1.1
Winnebago, WI	161 688	6 762	65.0	9 974	0.1	9.8	1.7	1 535	1.8
Wood, WI	99 712	7 053	64.5	4 431	0.0	11.7	3.3	1 097	2.0
WYOMING									
Albany, WY	28 143	7 276	58.9	3 357	0.0	6.1	1.4	281	6.6
Big Horn, WY	18 964	7 487	58.8	757	0.3	9.5	4.5	208	4.4
Campbell, WY	53 448	6 932	56.6	2 180	0.0	11.1	4.9	561	3.1
Carbon, WY	23 419	8 103	60.4	933	0.0	11.9	4.1	240	4.1
Converse, WY	18 632	7 095	60.7	731	0.7	11.4	4.8	187	2.9
Crook, WY	9 560	7 533	56.8	403	0.0	7.7	1.7	99	2.7
Fremont, WY	57 794	8 031	60.1	2 261	0.5	8.7	8.7	469	8.6
Goshen, WY	16 519	7 683	59.3	722	0.0	12.6	3.9	147	4.1
Hot Springs, WY	6 128	7 036	56.5	274	0.0	11.3	1.5	73	6.6
Johnson, WY	8 962	6 708	60.6	442	0.0	10.9	0.0	103	1.8
Laramie, WY	91 243	6 250	61.2	4 423	3.7	15.1	3.9	873	2.9
Lincoln, WY	24 308	7 087	58.9	1 019	0.5	12.2	3.2	251	3.6
Natrona, WY	79 819	6 505	63.9	4 204	0.0	12.7	4.5	783	10.6
Niobrara, WY	3 672	7 650	57.7	140	0.0	28.6	1.4	41	3.6
Park, WY	27 953	6 039	58.5	1 737	0.0	8.2	2.1	325	5.5
Platte, WY	12 114	6 962	62.6	477	0.2	3.8	4.0	126	5.9
Sheridan, WY	30 044	6 790	64.0	1 590	0.0	6.7	3.2	326	4.8
Sublette, WY	10 142	7 850	53.4	289	0.0	5.5	2.4	85	1.5
Sweetwater, WY	59 204	7 015	58.8	2 861	0.0	9.8	2.8	579	6.8
Teton, WY	14 694	6 364	60.6	800	0.0	29.5	6.6	146	6.6
Uinta, WY	35 513	6 788	57.0	1 567	0.0	13.1	2.8	338	7.4
Washakie, WY	11 921	6 514	61.8	519	0.0	17.3	3.7	94	7.7
Weston, WY	8 905	6 876	57.8	444	0.0	17.1	5.6	127	2.3

. . . = Not available.

Table C-1. Population, School, and Student Characteristics by County—*Continued*

County	High school graduates, 2000			College enrollment, 2000		College graduates, 2000 (percent)						
	Population 25 years and over	High school diploma or less (percent)	High school diploma or more (percent)	Number	Percent public	Bachelor's degree or more	+/- U.S. percent with bachelor's degree or more	Non-Hispanic White	Black or African American	American Indian and Alaska Native	Asian, Hawaiian, and Pacific Islander	Hispanic or Latino[1]
	30	31	32	33	34	35	36	37	38	39	40	41
Forest, WI	6 694	64.2	78.5	222	88.3	10.0	-14.4	10.1	0.0	6.0	66.7	5.0
Grant, WI	30 625	56.5	83.5	5 323	94.5	17.2	-7.2	17.1	5.2	6.6	63.3	21.0
Green, WI	22 523	56.2	84.1	933	84.0	16.7	-7.7	16.7	18.9	16.9	57.1	6.9
Green Lake, WI	13 229	60.0	81.9	402	82.8	14.5	-9.9	14.6	12.5	0.0	100.0	4.2
Iowa, WI	15 100	53.3	88.5	642	88.0	18.5	-5.9	18.4	0.0	16.2	15.4	3.0
Iron, WI	5 124	54.4	83.7	189	83.6	13.2	-11.2	13.1	0.0	0.0	16.7	0.0
Jackson, WI	12 779	62.8	79.0	493	84.8	11.3	-13.1	11.8	3.9	7.3	8.9	6.4
Jefferson, WI	49 057	53.8	84.7	3 174	75.2	17.4	-7.0	17.7	10.7	8.1	38.2	5.8
Juneau, WI	16 457	64.5	78.5	554	85.2	10.0	-14.4	10.0	5.6	4.3	30.6	7.6
Kenosha, WI	95 038	49.8	83.5	9 631	70.3	19.2	-5.2	19.7	11.3	16.2	51.1	9.5
Kewaunee, WI	13 336	63.5	84.0	602	80.2	11.4	-13.0	11.4	. . .	0.0	24.1	3.7
La Crosse, WI	65 263	42.2	89.7	12 713	88.0	25.4	1.0	25.6	15.3	11.4	27.6	16.8
Lafayette, WI	10 528	61.1	85.5	479	88.5	13.3	-11.1	13.3	0.0	20.0	33.3	3.3
Langlade, WI	14 372	64.4	80.9	446	83.2	11.7	-12.7	11.7	15.4	4.6	20.9	8.3
Lincoln, WI	20 120	59.8	81.6	855	91.5	13.6	-10.8	13.6	0.0	0.0	12.9	7.0
Manitowoc, WI	55 452	58.5	84.6	3 031	75.1	15.5	-8.9	15.6	12.0	2.5	21.5	6.7
Marathon, WI	81 925	54.2	83.8	4 793	91.0	18.3	-6.1	18.5	39.1	5.7	11.2	10.5
Marinette, WI	29 575	62.2	82.5	1 945	59.2	12.9	-11.5	12.9	0.0	3.8	32.8	4.5
Marquette, WI	11 428	62.6	78.8	509	85.3	10.1	-14.3	10.4	6.3	9.4	23.8	5.3
Menominee, WI	2 399	63.8	78.2	170	87.1	12.9	-11.5	27.8	60.0	8.8	7.9	0.0
Milwaukee, WI	594 387	49.2	80.2	65 887	63.6	23.6	-0.8	28.3	9.9	11.2	39.9	9.6
Monroe, WI	26 323	60.1	81.1	1 027	84.7	13.2	-11.2	13.2	15.6	10.5	39.6	3.5
Oconto, WI	24 186	64.5	80.6	870	85.6	10.6	-13.8	10.6	0.0	10.4	4.3	12.8
Oneida, WI	26 449	51.4	85.1	1 306	86.6	20.0	-4.4	20.2	5.5	0.0	51.1	11.4
Outagamie, WI	102 218	49.6	88.1	7 729	77.3	22.5	-1.9	22.7	21.5	14.3	28.2	12.3
Ozaukee, WI	54 912	32.3	91.9	4 454	54.2	38.6	14.2	38.5	46.1	23.0	72.0	24.9
Pepin, WI	4 733	60.2	82.6	247	91.1	13.3	-11.1	13.5	. . .	0.0	0.0	0.0
Pierce, WI	21 542	45.3	89.6	4 736	90.4	24.6	0.2	24.5	18.2	44.9	34.6	46.6
Polk, WI	27 725	55.2	85.9	1 120	83.6	15.6	-8.8	15.5	36.4	15.2	27.9	27.5
Portage, WI	40 143	50.8	86.5	8 526	97.2	23.4	-1.0	23.6	0.0	5.3	15.2	6.8
Price, WI	11 122	61.1	82.4	388	77.6	13.0	-11.4	13.0	0.0	6.1	9.1	5.7
Racine, WI	122 356	49.6	82.9	8 818	80.3	20.3	-4.1	22.1	7.1	11.2	43.6	8.3
Richland, WI	11 896	58.7	82.1	626	91.2	14.1	-10.3	14.0	0.0	8.3	61.5	6.2
Rock, WI	98 770	55.3	83.9	6 280	72.7	16.7	-7.7	17.3	6.0	16.7	39.0	5.2
Rusk, WI	10 296	64.3	79.1	477	42.1	11.2	-13.2	11.2	15.4	0.0	8.0	10.3
St. Croix, WI	40 357	41.7	91.6	2 913	80.0	26.3	1.9	26.3	25.9	25.4	49.0	20.6
Sauk, WI	36 701	54.3	83.5	1 768	87.1	17.6	-6.8	17.6	12.6	14.0	45.8	8.2
Sawyer, WI	11 343	55.2	84.7	465	72.3	16.5	-7.9	17.6	7.0	7.8	19.6	31.7
Shawano, WI	27 503	64.3	81.5	1 189	82.6	12.6	-11.8	12.7	0.0	11.5	34.3	7.1
Sheboygan, WI	74 561	55.5	84.4	4 720	64.2	17.9	-6.5	18.3	6.8	3.0	15.2	9.2
Taylor, WI	12 872	66.1	78.3	378	79.6	11.0	-13.4	10.9	0.0	15.2	58.8	3.6
Trempealeau, WI	18 317	59.9	80.9	694	87.8	13.3	-11.1	13.2	12.5	13.3	25.0	18.5
Vernon, WI	18 473	59.6	78.9	679	83.8	14.0	-10.4	14.0	7.1	0.0	19.0	8.1
Vilas, WI	15 667	54.3	85.4	547	84.8	17.6	-6.8	18.1	0.0	6.7	34.6	10.4
Walworth, WI	58 153	49.3	84.2	9 549	92.6	21.8	-2.6	22.5	24.0	3.1	42.1	4.3
Washburn, WI	11 248	55.9	83.7	355	90.1	15.2	-9.2	15.5	0.0	9.5	11.8	0.0
Washington, WI	77 709	46.4	88.8	4 500	76.2	21.9	-2.5	22.0	22.1	21.6	30.8	14.5
Waukesha, WI	241 299	35.7	92.0	17 704	67.2	34.1	9.7	34.0	34.5	9.9	67.9	18.5
Waupaca, WI	34 726	61.0	82.7	1 145	85.8	14.8	-9.6	14.9	27.8	12.1	21.0	10.2
Waushara, WI	16 310	64.3	78.8	437	82.4	11.7	-12.7	11.8	0.0	3.7	45.2	5.5
Winnebago, WI	101 095	51.2	86.3	12 191	92.0	22.8	-1.6	22.9	7.8	10.7	38.3	16.3
Wood, WI	50 259	56.3	84.8	2 792	88.0	16.9	-7.5	16.6	31.5	10.8	39.9	19.3
WYOMING												
Albany, WY	17 016	28.4	93.5	10 055	91.5	44.1	19.7	46.2	37.8	30.2	64.2	13.5
Big Horn, WY	7 343	50.9	83.2	302	91.7	15.9	-8.5	16.6	100.0	0.0	18.8	2.8
Campbell, WY	20 107	47.0	88.3	1 160	88.8	15.7	-8.7	15.9	0.0	3.2	44.7	3.2
Carbon, WY	10 508	51.5	83.5	389	89.2	17.2	-7.2	19.0	13.2	7.5	51.5	4.3
Converse, WY	7 818	49.0	86.4	350	86.3	14.7	-9.7	15.4	27.3	5.3	0.0	1.7
Crook, WY	3 888	52.3	85.8	86	97.7	17.5	-6.9	17.4	. . .	10.0	0.0	31.3
Fremont, WY	23 053	48.4	84.8	1 462	90.2	19.7	-4.7	22.7	37.5	6.4	9.1	10.4
Goshen, WY	8 406	48.7	84.7	660	80.0	18.6	-5.8	19.9	60.7	16.9	. . .	1.3
Hot Springs, WY	3 515	51.9	84.2	94	91.5	17.9	-6.5	18.4	100.0	6.1	0.0	0.0
Johnson, WY	4 981	40.8	90.1	134	97.8	22.2	-2.2	22.2	. . .	0.0	. . .	11.6
Laramie, WY	53 041	37.4	89.1	4 235	90.1	23.4	-1.0	25.3	14.2	12.9	24.9	8.0
Lincoln, WY	9 049	46.9	87.9	328	78.0	17.2	-7.2	17.4	0.0	18.0	27.3	4.4
Natrona, WY	42 656	42.3	88.3	3 904	94.1	20.0	-4.4	20.7	23.7	3.7	33.6	7.0
Niobrara, WY	1 731	51.6	87.3	67	89.6	15.3	-9.1	15.5	. . .	22.2	0.0	22.2
Park, WY	17 145	42.8	87.6	1 469	98.0	23.7	-0.7	23.9	0.0	19.6	26.0	18.0
Platte, WY	6 034	53.6	84.9	173	88.4	15.2	-9.2	15.8	. . .	0.0	0.0	2.5
Sheridan, WY	17 980	40.4	88.4	1 371	94.2	22.4	-2.0	22.8	0.0	4.4	14.6	17.6
Sublette, WY	4 044	46.4	89.0	105	78.1	21.6	-2.8	21.8	0.0	7.7	0.0	15.6
Sweetwater, WY	23 053	47.3	87.4	2 004	93.8	17.0	-7.4	18.0	18.5	3.4	29.4	5.9
Teton, WY	12 838	24.2	94.7	465	77.4	45.8	21.4	47.2	100.0	48.2	48.9	17.4
Uinta, WY	11 443	50.8	84.8	580	84.0	15.0	-9.4	15.5	0.0	10.6	56.3	5.7
Washakie, WY	5 460	48.2	85.6	105	89.5	18.7	-5.7	20.1	. . .	0.0	0.0	5.6
Weston, WY	4 554	55.0	85.2	199	92.5	14.5	-9.9	14.6	0.0	21.4	36.8	1.7

[1]Hispanic or Latino persons may be of any race.
. . . = Not available.

NOTES AND DEFINITIONS: COUNTY EDUCATION STATISTICS

Section C presents 41 data items for each county, county equivalent, or independent city. The counties are presented in alphabetical order within states, which are also in alphabetical order. Independent cities, which are found in Maryland, Missouri, Nevada, and Virginia are placed in alphabetical order at the end of the list of counties for those states. The District of Columbia is included as both a county and a state.

Common Core of Data. Items 3–5, 10–23, 28, 29, 33, and 34 in this section are from the Common Core of Data from the National Center for Education Statistics (NCES), U.S. Department of Education. NCES uses the Common Core of Data (CCD) system to acquire and maintain statistical data from each of the 50 states, the District of Columbia, and the outlying areas. Information about staff and students is collected annually at the school, local education agency (LEA) or school district, and state levels. Information about revenues and expenditures is also collected at the state level. In addition, information about revenues and expenditures at the school district level is assembled from the annual surveys of government finances conducted by the Bureau of the Census.

Data are collected for a particular school year (July 1 through June 30) via survey instruments sent to the state education agencies during the subsequent school year. States have one year in which to modify the data originally submitted. This volume uses the data from the school year 2000–2001, except for the revenue and expenditure data for counties, which is for school year 1998–1999 (fiscal year 1999).

Since the CCD is a universe survey, the CCD information is not subject to sampling error. However, nonsampling errors could come from two sources—nonreturn and inaccurate reporting. Almost all of the states submit the six CCD survey instruments each year, but submissions are sometimes incomplete or too late for publication.

Understandably, when 51 education agencies compile and submit data for approximately 90,000 public schools and 15,000 local school dis-

tricts, misreporting can occur. Typically, this results from varying interpretation of NCES definitions and differing record keeping systems. NCES attempts to minimize these errors by working closely with the Council of Chief State School Officers (CCSSO) and its Committee on Evaluation and Information Systems (CEIS).

The state education agencies report data to NCES from data collected and edited in their regular reporting cycles. NCES encourages the agencies to incorporate into their own survey systems the NCES items they do not already collect so that those items will also be available for the subsequent CCD survey. Over time, this has meant fewer missing data cells in each state's response, reducing the need to impute data.

NCES subjects data from the education agencies to a comprehensive edit. Where data are determined to be inconsistent, missing, or out of range, NCES contacts the education agencies for verification. NCES-prepared state summary forms are returned to the state education agencies for verification. States are also given an opportunity to revise their state-level aggregates from the previous survey cycle. The county-level data in this volume have not been adjusted.

The CCD data are collected at three levels—the school, the school district, and the state. In Section D, selected school and school district data items have been aggregated to the county level because the county is a widely used statistical area. School districts, and even some schools, can serve populations in different counties. In this volume, schools and school districts are assigned to the county where the school district office is located, as coded by NCES in their files. Consequently, the numbers do not necessarily represent the population of a given county. The structure of school districts ranges from states like West Virginia and Nevada, where most counties have a single school district, to Cook County, IL, which includes 154 separate school districts. Some counties have no school districts. Hawaii has a single statewide school district whose offices are located in Honolulu County. New York City has a single school system for all five boroughs (counties). A few other counties report no school districts, usually counties with very small populations or independent cities in

Virginia whose school systems are run by the neighboring or surrounding county.

For additional information about the Common Core of Data, see <www.nces.ed.gov/ccd/>.

2000 Census of Population and Housing. Items 1, 2, 6–9, 24–27, 30–32, and 35–41 are from the 2000 Census. The population totals and age data are from the complete count, while the education data are from the long-form questionnaire that was answered by a sample of the population. The sample data are estimates of the actual figures that would have been obtained from a complete count. Estimates derived from a sample are expected to be different from the 100-percent figures because they are subject to sampling and nonsampling errors. Sampling error in data arises from the selection of people and housing units included in the sample. Nonsampling error affects both sample and 100-percent data and is introduced as a result of errors that may occur during the data collection and processing phases of the census.

For additional information about the 2000 Census, see:
<http://www.census.gov/main/www/cen2000.html>.

Geographic identification. Data are presented for 3,141 counties and county equivalents. A five-digit state and county code is given for each entity. The first two digits indicate the state; the remaining three identify the county. Within each state, the counties are numbered in alphabetical order, beginning with 001, with even numbers usually omitted. Independent cities follow the counties and begin with the number 510.

These codes have been established by the U.S. government as Federal Information Processing Standards and are often referred to as "FIPS codes." They are used by U.S. government agencies and many other organizations for data presentation. They are provided in this volume for use in matching the data given here with other data sources in which counties may be identified by FIPS codes.

Independent cities. Independent cities are not included in any county; data are presented separately in this volume where available.

Maryland

  Baltimore (separate from Baltimore County)

Missouri

  St. Louis (separate from St. Louis County)

Nevada

  Carson City

Virginia

  Alexandria
  Bedford
  Bristol
  Buena Vista
  Charlottesville
  Chesapeake
  Clifton Forge
  Colonial Heights
  Covington
  Danville
  Emporia
  Fairfax
  Falls Church
  Franklin
  Fredericksburg
  Galax
  Hampton
  Harrisonburg
  Hopewell
  Lexington
  Lynchburg
  Manassas
  Manassas Park
  Martinsville
  Newport News
  Norfolk
  Norton
  Petersburg
  Poquoson
  Portsmouth
  Radford
  Richmond
  Roanoke
  Salem
  Staunton
  Suffolk
  Virginia Beach
  Waynesboro
  Williamsburg
  Winchester

County type. Table C provides, in the third column, a "county type" code which identifies each county by its metropolitan/nonmetropolitan status and its size. These codes were developed by the Economic Research Service of the U.S. Department of Agriculture and are commonly referred to as "Beale" codes after their originator, Calvin Beale. The ERS county typology scheme goes beyond the Beale codes to a detailed typology of economic and land use classifications. In this volume, the basic Beale codes are used and are as follows:

Metropolitan counties
(0)   Central county of a metropolitan area of 1 million population or more.
(1)   Fringe county of a metropolitan area of 1 million population or more.
(2)   County in a metropolitan area of 250,000 to 1,000,000 population.
(3)   County in a metropolitan area of less than 250,000 population.

Nonmetropolitan counties
(4)   Urban population of 20,000 or more, adjacent to a metropolitan area.
(5)   Urban population of 20,000 or more, not adjacent to a metropolitan area.
(6)   Urban population of 2,500–19,999, adjacent to a metropolitan area.
(7)   Urban population of 2,500–19,999, not adjacent to a metropolitan area.
(8)   Completely rural (no places with a population of 2,500 or more), adjacent to a metropolitan area.
(9)   Completely rural (no places with a population of 2,500 or more), not adjacent to a metropolitan area.

Data sources and explanations. Table C has been developed by Bernan from the individual school and school district data from the CCD. Some data items in Table B, such as revenues and expenditures, include statewide numbers that are inappropriate at the local level, so the two tables are not necessarily consistent.

TABLE C (COUNTIES)

POPULATION (ITEMS 1–2)
Source: U.S. Bureau of the Census.

The population data for 2000 are from the 2000 Census and represent the resident population as of April 1, 2000.

Age is defined as age at last birthday (that is, number of completed years from birth to April 1, 2000).

SCHOOL DISTRICTS (ITEM 3)
Source: U.S. Department of Education, National Center for Education Statistics, Common Core of Data, 2000–2001.

A School District or Local Education Agency (LEA) is an education agency at the local level that exists primarily to operate public schools or to contract for public school services.

The county totals in this volume include 15,507 regular and special school districts. Special districts typically offer research, administrative, or other support services to client agencies. Excluded are all regular and special districts that reported no students in membership.

NUMBER OF SCHOOLS AND STUDENTS (ITEMS 4–5)
Source: U.S. Department of Education, National Center for Education Statistics, Common Core of Data, 2000–2001.

The county data were aggregated from 90,640 individual schools in the CCD school universe.

RESIDENT ENROLLMENT AND TYPE OF SCHOOL (ITEMS 6–9 AND 33–34)
Source: U.S. Bureau of the Census, 2000 Census of Population and Housing.

Data on school enrollment were derived from answers to long-form questionnaire Items 8a and 8b, which were asked of a sample of the population. People were classified as enrolled in school if they reported attending a "regular" public or private school or college at any time between February 1, 2000, and the time of enumeration. The question included instructions to "include only nursery school or preschool, kindergarten, elementary school, and schooling which leads to a high school diploma or a college degree" as regular school or college. Respondents who did not answer the enrollment question were assigned the enrollment status and type of school of a person with the same age, sex, and race/Hispanic or Latino origin whose residence was in the same or a nearby area. All persons 3 years old and over are included.

Public and private schools. Public and private schools include people who attended school in the reference period and indicated they were enrolled by marking one of the questionnaire categories for either "public school, public college" or "private school, private college." Schools supported and controlled primarily by a federal, state, or local government are defined as public (including tribal schools). Those supported and controlled primarily by religious organizations or other private groups are private.

STUDENTS WITH INDIVIDUAL EDUCATION PROGRAMS (ITEM 10)

Source: U.S. Department of Education, National Center for Education Statistics, Common Core of Data, 2000–2001.

An Individualized Education Program (IEP) is a written instructional plan for students with disabilities designated as special education students under the Individuals with Disabilities Education Act (IDEA). This includes a statement of present levels of educational performance of a child; a statement of annual goals, including short-term instructional objectives; a statement of specific educational services to be provided and the extent to which the child will be able to participate in regular educational programs; a projected date for initiation and anticipated duration of services; appropriate objectives, criteria and evaluation procedures; and schedules for determining, on at least an annual basis, whether instructional objectives are being achieved.

IEP counts for the counties are from the agency universe. Some agencies did not report this information. If 20 percent or more of a county's student membership were represented by agencies with missing data, the county was considered "missing." Students with IEPs were counted as a percentage of students in agencies who reported this information, not as a percentage of all students in the county.

STUDENTS WHO ARE ELIGIBLE FOR FREE OR REDUCED-PRICE LUNCH (ITEM 11)

Source: U.S. Department of Education, National Center for Education Statistics, Common Core of Data, 2000–2001.

The Free or Reduced-Price Lunch Program is a program under the National School Lunch Act that provides cash subsidies for free lunches to students based on family size and income criteria. Because participation in the Free Lunch Program depends on income, eligibility is often used to estimate student needs.

The number of students who apply for and are eligible to receive free or reduced-price lunches is included in the CCD school universe, from which the county totals in this volume were derived. If 20 percent or more of a county's student membership were in schools with missing data, the county was considered "missing." Eligible students were counted as a percentage of students in schools who reported this information, not as a percentage of all students in the county.

MINORITY STUDENTS (ITEM 12)

Source: U.S. Department of Education, National Center for Education Statistics, Common Core of Data, 2000–2001.

The percentage of a county's students who were minority was tallied from the CCD school universe. Individual schools reported the number of students who were American Indian/Alaskan Native, Asian/Pacific Islander, Hispanic, Black non-Hispanic, and White non-Hispanic. "Minority" includes all categories except White non-Hispanic.

TEACHERS (ITEMS 13–14)

Source: U.S. Department of Education, National Center for Education Statistics, Common Core of Data, 2000–2001.

The number of teachers in each county is aggregated from the full-time-equivalent numbers in the CCD school universe. The student/teacher ratio is calculated from this school-based number and the number of students reported by individual schools in the county.

STAFF (ITEMS 15–16)
Source: U.S. Department of Education, National Center for Education Statistics, Common Core of Data, 2000–2001.

The county data are aggregated from the CCD agency universe. Staff in local schools who are not classroom teachers include teacher aides; guidance counselors; librarians and library/media support staff; principals and their assistants and support staff; and all noninstructional staff such as health services workers, bus drivers, social workers, and all others employed in the schools. Central administration staff and support include the Local Education Agency superintendents, deputies, assistant superintendents, all persons with district-wide responsibilities, and their support staffs, as well as all staff supervising instructional programs at the district or sub-district level, such as curriculum coordinators.

REVENUES (ITEMS 17–20)
Source: U.S. Department of Education, National Center for Education Statistics, Common Core of Data, Fiscal Year 1999.

The county data are aggregated from the 15,554 agencies in the Public School District Financial Survey data file for fiscal year 1999 (school year 1998–1999). Some of these school districts have no students in membership but they have revenues and expenditures, usually because of financial arrangements with neighboring counties or regional agencies. These revenue and expenditure data are obtained by the U.S. Bureau of the Census through its annual surveys of government finances and are supplied by the Bureau of the Census to the National Center for Education Statistics.

Revenues from federal sources include direct grants-in-aid from the federal government; federal grants-in-aid through the state or an intermediate agency; and other revenue that, in lieu of taxes, had the tax base been subject to taxation.

Revenues from state government sources, include those that can be used without restriction; those for categorical purposes; and revenues in lieu of taxation. Included are revenues from payments made by a state for the benefit of the LEA or contributions of equipment or supplies. Such revenues include the payment of a pension fund by the state on behalf of an LEA employee for services rendered to the LEA; contributions of fixed assets (property, plant, and equipment) such as school buses and textbooks.

Revenues from local sources include revenues from a local education agency, including local property and non-property tax revenues, local government, tuition, transportation, food services, student activities, textbook sales, donations, and property rentals. Revenues from local sources include taxes levied or assessed by an LEA; revenues from a local government to the LEA; tuition received; transportation fees; earnings on investments from LEA holdings; net revenues from food services (gross receipts less gross expenditures); net revenues from student activities (gross receipts less gross expenditures); and other revenues (textbook sales, donations, property rentals).

A fourth category, Intermediate Revenues, is not included in this volume but can be derived by subtracting the federal, state, and local revenues from the total revenue. Intermediate revenues come from sources that are not local or state education agencies, but operate at an intermediate level between local and state education agencies and possess independent fund-raising capability.

EXPENDITURES (ITEMS 21–23)
Source: U.S. Department of Education, National Center for Education Statistics, Common Core of Data, Fiscal Year 1999.

The county data are aggregated from the 15,554 agencies in the Public School District Financial Survey data file for fiscal year 1999 (school year 1998–1999). Some of these school districts have no students in membership but they have revenues and expenditures, usually because of financial arrangements with neighboring counties or regional agencies. These revenue and expenditure data are obtained by the U.S. Bureau of the Census through its annual surveys of government finances and are supplied by the Bureau of the Census to the National Center for Education Statistics.

Current expenditures are defined as expenditures for the categories of instruction, support services, and non-instructional services for salaries, employee benefits, purchased services and supplies; and payments by the state made for or on behalf of school systems. This does not include expenditures for debt service and capital outlay, and property (i.e., equipment); or direct costs (for Head Start, adult education, community colleges) and community services expenditures.

Current expenditures per student for counties is calculated by dividing current expenditures by the number of students in fall membership. Student membership is the count of students enrolled on or about October 1 and is comparable across all counties. However, comparisons should be made with caution because counties vary greatly in type of school districts as well as contractual arrangements with regional administrative school agencies or neighboring counties. For example, a county with a small population may have a school district that operates an elementary school and pays an intergovernmental fee to a neighboring county's school district for educational services to children in middle and high school. This hypothetical county would have artificially high per student expenditures because only the elementary school children would be included in the membership count.

Current expenditures for instruction are expenditures for activities dealing directly with the interaction between students and teachers (salaries, including sabbatical leave, employee benefits, and purchased instructional services).

POPULATION 16 TO 19 YEARS BY SCHOOL ENROLLMENT AND EMPLOYMENT STATUS (ITEMS 24–27)
Source: U.S. Bureau of the Census, 2000 Census of Population and Housing.

Tabulation of data on school enrollment, educational attainment, and employment status for the population 16 to 19 years old allows for calculating the proportion of people 16 to 19 years old who are not enrolled in school and not high school graduates ("dropouts") and an unemployment rate for the "dropout" population.

GRADUATES (ITEM 28)
Source: U.S. Department of Education, National Center for Education Statistics, Common Core of Data, 2000–2001.

The county data are from the CCD agency universe. The number of graduates includes individuals who received a regular diploma, individuals who received a diploma from other than the regular school program, and individuals who received a certificate of attendance or other certificate of completion in lieu of a diploma during the previous school year and subsequent summer school. Recipients of high school equivalency certificates are not included.

DROPOUTS (ITEM 29)
Source: U.S. Department of Education, National Center for Education Statistics, Common Core of Data, 1999–2000.

The county data are from the CCD agency universe dropout file. A dropout is a student who was enrolled in school at some time during the previous school year; was not enrolled at the beginning of the current school year; has not graduated from high school or completed a state or district-approved educational program; and does not meet any of the following exclusionary conditions; has transferred to another public school district, private school, or state- or district-approved educational program; is temporarily absent due to suspension or school-approved illness; or has died.

Dropout data for a particular year are reported the following year. For example, 1999–2000 dropout data are reported in the 2000–2001 Local Education Agency Universe file. Thus, the dropout rates are based on the prior year's enrollment from the 1999–2000 school universe.

EDUCATIONAL ATTAINMENT (ITEMS 30–32 AND 35–41)
Source: U.S. Bureau of the Census, 2000 Census of Population and Housing.

Data on educational attainment were derived from answers to long-form questionnaire Item 9, which was asked of a sample of the population. Data on attainment are tabulated for the population 25 years and over. People are classified according to the highest degree or level of school completed. The order in which degrees were listed on the questionnaire suggested that doctorate degrees were "higher" than professional school degrees, which were "higher" than master's degrees. The question included instructions for people currently enrolled in school to report the level of the previous grade attended or the highest degree received. Respondents who did not report educational attainment or enrollment level were assigned the attainment of a person of the same age, race, Hispanic or Latino origin, occupation and sex, where possible, who resided in the same or a nearby area. Respondents who filled more than one box were edited to the highest level or degree reported. The question included a response category that allowed respondents to report completing the 12th grade without receiving a high school diploma. It allowed people who received either a high school diploma or the equivalent, for example, passed the Test of General Educational Development (G.E.D.) and did not attend college, to be reported as "high school graduate(s)."

High school graduate or higher. This category includes people whose highest degree was a high school diploma or its equivalent, people who attended college but did not receive a degree, and people who received a college, university, or professional degree. People who reported completing the 12th grade but not receiving a diploma are not high school graduates.

Bachelor's degree or higher. This category includes people whose highest degree was a bachelor's, master's, professional, or doctorate degree. Master's degrees include the traditional M.A. and M.S. degrees and field-specific degrees, such as M.S.W., M.Ed., M.B.A., M.L.S., and M.Eng. Some examples of professional degrees include medicine, dentistry, chiropractic, optometry, osteopathic medicine, pharmacy, podiatry, veterinary medicine, law, and theology. Vocational and technical training, such as barber school training; business, trade, technical, and vocational schools; or other training for a specific trade, are specifically excluded.

The Internet has become a research tool for virtually every type of subject matter and for all levels of users. In terms of education, there are countless government and non-government resources online. Educators have embraced the potential of the Internet for reaching students and for sharing professional information with each other.

Resources described in this guide include sites made available by the federal government as well as others that are the work of academia, non-profits, or commercial services. This guide includes General resources followed by special sections for Higher Education, K-12, and Web Sites for Children.

GENERAL

ACT
http://www.act.org/
Description: ACT, founded in 1959 as the American College Testing Program but now known simply by its acronym, is a non-profit organization "that provides more than a hundred assessment, research, information, and program management services in the broad areas of education and workforce development." (from the Web site)

On the K–12 level, ACT develops and administers the widely known ACT Assessment college entrance exam as well as EXPLORE, PLAN, and WorkKeys tests. ACT also develops assessments and resources pertaining to postsecondary measures and institutional effectiveness. Information about ACT's various assessment and related services is posted on ACT's Educational and Career Planning page.

ACT's Workforce Productivity Solutions page contains information on training and testing for the business environment. Such resources are designed to provide employees with the tools they need to help their employers remain competitive.

Other useful information on ACT's Web site includes a Financial Aid Calculator and a College Search database.

AskERIC
http://ericir.syr.edu/
Description: AskERIC combines a question-answering service with a powerful Web interface to the ERIC database. Sections of the AskERIC system are About AskERIC, the ERIC database, Ask an ERIC Expert, Question Archive, Lesson Plans, and Mailing Lists. The home page also presents a subject guide to over 3000 selected resources, including Internet sites, discussion lists, ERIC publications, and organizations. AskERIC's implementation of the ERIC database is one of the best free versions available. Updated monthly, the AskERIC version includes coverage back to 1966. It offers both simple and advanced search options. The simple search allows keywords or phrases, and may be limited to journal articles or *ERIC Digest* and my year. The advanced search interface allows for fielded searching, using Boolean logic, of the following fields: Keyword, Author, Title, ERIC Number, Journal Citation, Descriptor, Identifier, Abstract, Geographic Source, Institution Name, Publication Type, Publication Date, ISBN, ISSN, Clearinghouse Number Government, Availability, Note, and Language. Users can access the ERIC Thesaurus for proper subject headings. The Ask an ERIC Expert service allows visitors to submit questions on educational topics to experts and receive responses by email. The responses consist of ERIC database citations or digests, Internet resources, and/or referrals to other sources of information. Users may also browse the Question Archive for previous answers to relevant information. The Lesson Plans section contains a collection of more than 2,000 lesson plans submitted by teachers. Lesson plans are arranged by subject or may be searched by keyword and grade level. Teachers may use this section to submit lesson plans, according to the posted instructions and criteria. The Mailing Lists section of the site has searchable archives for a number of education-related electronic discussion lists.

The variety of education resources available through AskERIC make this site an important resource for educators. Its straightforward interface to the ERIC database provides easy-access to this valuable warehouse of data.

Americans Communicating Electronically (ACE)
http://www.reeusda.gov/ecs/ace.htm
Description: ACE is an outreach initiative dedicated to improving technological literacy in underserved communities. The effort is co-sponsored by USDA's Cooperative State Research, Education, and Extension Service (CSREES) and the Small Business Administration (SBA) and members come from the public and private sectors. The ACE home page offers a list of links to sites that describe community and government efforts to connect schools to the Internet, recycle computers, and provide computers for schools and nonprofit organizations. Other topics include distance learning, the "digital divide," and technology assistance for small businesses. The site also features a calendar of events dealing with government and computing, youth education in technology, access for rural areas, and related topics.

Census 2000 Gateway
http://www.census.gov/main/www/cen2000.html
Description: As its name implies, the Census 2000 Gateway site is a starting point for finding products, data sets, news, documentation, and other information relating to the most recent Decennial Census. A Census in Schools section

includes teaching resources and lesson plans. The resources provided in this section are designed to provide educators with fun and interactive ways to teach students about the census—and what it tells us about our society.

Also available on the Census 2000 Gateway site is a link to The American FactFinder. The American FactFinder has tables and maps of Census 2000 data for all geographies to the block level. Another section is State and County Quick Facts, which has summaries of the most requested data for states and counties.

The Census Gateway also has data files that include rankings and comparisons; briefs and special reports; selected historical Census data; data release schedules; Census operations information; the Census Store; PDF copies of Census forms; and contact information for Bureau subject experts and state and local resource centers.

The College Board
`http://www.collegeboard.com/`

Description: The College Board, administrator of the SAT, is a non-profit organization that provides students with resources to facilitate the college admissions process. Such resources include information about testing; financial aid; scholarships; and application essays, as well as information on what questions to ask when planning for college. The College Board Web site also contains a useful Compare College database that allows students to compare and evaluate colleges based on criteria such as tuition costs and average GPAs of incoming freshmen.

In terms of testing, students may register for the SAT and other test via the College Board's Web site. The College Board also administers the PSAT/NMSQT, AP, and CLEP. Students may also register for these tests via the College Board Web site.

The College Board Web site also contains various downloadable PDF reports for students and educators. Such reports include the "2002 PSAT/NMSQT State Summary Reports for College-Bound Juniors and Sophomores" and Trends in College Pricing 2002." These and other reports are posted on the Professionals page.

DANTES—Defense Activity for Non-Traditional Education Support
`http://www.dantes.doded.mil/`

Description: DANTES provides support for the off-duty, voluntary education programs of the Defense Department. Their Web sites has information on certification programs, counselor support, distance learning, and tuition assistance. It also has a section about the Troops-to-Teachers program that assists military personnel interested in beginning a second career in public education as a teacher.

Department of Education
`http://www.ed.gov/`

Description: As the obvious starting point for government information on and about education, the U.S. Department of Education (ED) site delivers substantial information resources through a variety of access points. Major sections of the site are News, Grants and Contracts, Financial Aid, Education Resources, Research and Statistics, Policy, and About ED. The site also has special pages designed for specific groups, such as students, teachers, and parents and families. An ED Priorities section offers quick access to education-related initiatives of the Bush administration, such as "No Child Left Behind" and "Ready to Read, Ready to Learn." The site also has an A-Z Index and a personalization feature called My.ED.gov.

Department of Labor Educational Resources
`http://www.dol.gov/asp/fibre/main.htm`

Description: This DOL site features pages designed for the educational community, covering topics such as the History of the DOL, Child Labor and Youth Employment Laws, "Jobs for Kids Who Like. . .", Mine Safety, Safety and Health, Reference Materials, and "So You Are Thinking About Dropping Out of School...". Some of these links lead to the educational pages of component agencies. Most provide information geared towards children but do not necessarily provide curriculum or teacher resources. Reference Materials contain links to Women's Bureau resources. The section addressing dropping out of school presents data on employment rate and earnings by educational attainment.

Directorate for Education and Human Resources—NSF
`http://www.ehr.nsf.gov/`

Description: The Directorate for Education and Human Resources (EHR) provides leadership in the effort to improve science, mathematics, engineering, and technology education in the United States. Its Web site includes links to descriptions of the EHR divisions and the types of projects they sponsor: the Division of Graduate Education (DGE), the Division of Undergraduate Education (DUE), the Experimental Program to Stimulate Competitive Research (EPSCoR), and the Division of Elementary, Secondary and Informal Education (ESIE). The Publications category includes selected full-text documents. The Programs category has announcements of funding opportunities.

This site will be of assistance to science and engineering students and educators at all levels who are interested in pursuing grants or scholarships.

Economic Education from The Federal Reserve
`http://www.federalreserveeducation.org/`
Description: The resources of this site are listed under the rather long title of "When it Comes 2 Economic Education, the Federal Reserve is Where It's @." The site organizes links to the many educational resources made available by the Federal Reserve Banks. Resource categories include Web Curriculum, Newsletters and Periodicals, Interactive Web sites, and Non-Fed Web sites and Resources. Featured resources include a multimedia Fed 101 site and a free video, called "The Fed Today," which can be ordered online.

This Federal Reserve site does an excellent job of pulling together educational resources from a variety of sites and putting them under a helpful interface. There are many resources aimed at teachers, but the site is also helpful to anyone wanting to learn more about the Fed.

EDUGATE
`http://web.lmi.org/edugate/`
Description: This Web site provides general information about science, engineering, and mathematics educational programs sponsored in whole or in part by the DoD and provides informational resources for teachers. It features sections such as DoD Employee Programs, Student Aid, Faculty and Teacher Programs, Public Education Programs, and Equipment Donation Programs.

This is an excellent resource for finding educational materials and links to DoD educational resources at all educational levels.

Emergency Planning
`http://www.ed.gov/emergencyplan/`
Description: The Emergency Planning site was launched in March 2003 as a "one-stop shop that provides school leaders with information they need to plan for any emergency, including natural disasters, violent incidents and terrorist acts." (from the Web site) The site includes crisis planning resources and model emergency plans.

ERIC—Educational Resources Information Center
`http://www.eric.ed.gov/`
Description: While AskERIC is the preferred site for accessing the ERIC database, this Web site is the place to go for information about the ERIC system of 16 subject-specific clearinghouses, associated adjunct clearinghouses, and support components. The site has links to each of the clearinghouses as well as to the ERIC Document Reproduction Service (EDRS). This central ERIC site also has publications about ERIC and a Frequently Asked Questions section.

The ERIC system was established to provide ready access to education-related literature for practitioners in all aspects of education. When used along with the core ERIC database

at AskERIC, this site provides straightforward access to information on all ERIC services.

ERIC Clearinghouse on Assessment and Evaluation
`http://ericae.net/`
Description: In addition to the ERIC database and information on the ERIC system, the Assessment and Evaluation Clearinghouse site offers such sections as Library, Test Locator, Resources, and Calls for Papers. The Library provides access to full-text books and other publications; the online journal, *Practical Assessment, Research, and Evaluation*; ERIC/AE Digests; and other online journals. Substantial resources can be found under Test Locator, which connects to searchable bibliographic databases of tests from Buros, Pro-Ed, and the Educational Testing Service (ETS). The Assessment and Evaluation on the Internet section under Resources presents a pathfinder to numerous documents on such topics as alternative assessment, goals and standards, personnel evaluation, professional standards, qualitative research, test preparation, test reviews, and more.

There is a substantial body of test and assessment information on this site. Anyone interested in educational assessment, testing, and measuring learning should explore this site.

ERIC Clearinghouse on Counseling and Student Services
`http://ericcass.uncg.edu/`
Description: The ERIC Clearinghouse on Counseling and Student Services (CASS) is designed for school guidance counselors and therapists. The site includes information on the clearinghouse, online publications and a collection of *ERIC/CASS Digests*, links to selected Web resources, and Submit a Document section.

ERIC Clearinghouse on Educational Management
`http://eric.uoregon.edu/`
Description: The Clearinghouse on Educational Management acquires, indexes, abstracts, and enters into the ERIC database documents, papers, and articles on the governance, leadership, administration, and organizational structure of public and private schools. Sections of this site include Trends and Issues, Hot Topics, Publications, Directory of Organizations, Search/Find, Links, and About ERIC and ERIC/CEM. Each section is full of well-organized resources on school administration.

ERIC Clearinghouse on Information and Technology
`http://ericit.org/`
Description: The ERIC Clearinghouse on Information and Technology specializes in educational technology and library and information science. The site features *ERIC/IT Digests*

and various other documents and databases from the clearing-house. Featured sections include About, ERIC Database, Publications, Discussion Groups, Lesson Plans, Projects, Research, Educational Technology, and Library and Information Science.

ERIC Clearinghouse on Languages and Linguistics
http://www.cal.org/ericcll/
Description: This ERIC Clearinghouse focuses on providing services and materials for language educators. Among the many resources available on this site are such features as *ERIC/CLL Digests*, About ERIC/CLL, Resource Guides, Publications, ERIC/CLL Databases, and more. The home page presents the bulk of the information available, including links to the report, *What Teachers Need to Know about Language*, Publications, and ERIC/CLL Databases as well as information about ERIC/CLL. Under ERIC/CLL Databases are a variety of resources such as the *Directory of Resources for Foreign Language Programs*. The site also offers an opportunity to ask experts language-related questions.

ERIC Clearinghouse on Teaching and Teacher Education
http://www.ericsp.org/
Description: The ERIC Clearinghouse on Teaching and Teacher Education collects, abstracts, and indexes education materials in the subject areas of teaching, teacher education, health and physical education, recreation, and dance. It also produces special publications on current research, programs, and practices. Under Becoming a Teacher, the site connects to a number of full-text InfoCards on topics relevant to becoming a teacher, including information on colleges and universities for teacher education. The Resources for Teachers section links to pages on lesson plans and teaching with technology. The Digests and Publications heading features links to *ERIC/TTE Digests* from the clearinghouse and a publications list.

ERIC Clearinghouse on Urban Education
http://eric-web.tc.columbia.edu/
Description: The ERIC Clearinghouse on Urban Education focuses on information related to the development and education of urban children and adolescents of diverse ethnic groups. Their site provides several directories to resources from ERIC and from the Internet. The site also has a link to the ERIC Adjunct Clearinghouse for Homeless Education.

ERIC Document Reproduction Service
http://edrs.com/
Description: The ERIC Document Reproduction Service produces and sells microfiche and electronic collections of documents abstracted by ERIC as well as individual copies. The

site includes sections such as Download Center, E*Subscribe (an online subscription service to access ERIC documents), Products, and Search and Order. Users may search for documents by accession number only or by a variety of bibliographic fields. Documents are delivered as laser-printed copies of microfiche documents, PDF documents available immediately online, or microfiche. Products may be sent by mail or fax (limited to 50 pages).

ERIC Processing and Reference Facility
http://ericfac.piccard.csc.com/
Description: The facility provides technical support functions and services to the ERIC system. It produces and maintains the ERIC database and its thesaurus. Its Web site includes sections on Submitting Documents to ERIC, a Reproduction Release Form, Products, and Resources. A Ready Reference section provides documentation on the ERIC database, such as an index to ERIC accession number ranges by year and a guide to ERIC document price codes. Access to the ERIC Thesaurus is provided through the Resources section, where users can also search or browse through an index of source journals and link to online versions of *ERIC Digests*.

This site is primarily of interest to those submitting or managing ERIC documents.

Federal Highway Administration Education Pages
http://www.fhwa.dot.gov/education/
Description: The central education page from the Federal Highway Administration provides educational information and resources on the FHWA and its Garrett A. Morgan Technology and Transportation Futures Program. Featured sections include Kindergarten through Fifth Grade, Sixth Grade through Eighth Grade, Ninth Grade through Twelfth Grade, Life-Long Learning, Instructional Aids for Teachers, and Colleges, Universities, and Trade Schools.

Federal School Code Search Page
http://www.fafsa.ed.gov/fotw0203/fslookup.htm
Description: This site provides searchable access to the federal Title IV School Codes required on many financial aid forms. Access is by a form that offers searches by school name and state. Search results include the Title IV School Code and offer access to a school address. The database can also search for schools by their Title IV School Code.

This can be a handy source for these codes, especially when a print source is not readily available.

Federal Resources for Educational Excellence (FREE)
http://www.ed.gov/free/
Description: Federal Resources for Educational Excellence (FREE) is a central finding aid to hundreds of Internet-based

education resources supported by 50 agencies across the U.S. federal government. Users access the database by searching or browsing by subject. The Searches and Subjects page is the main access point, although the same subjects and search interface are also present on the home page. Note that the Search function actually searches the contents of the linked sites and not just titles or descriptions. Recently added materials are listed under the New Resources section. The More for Students page highlights resources particularly appropriate for K-12 students.

This is one of the most comprehensive finding aids for education-related U.S. government Web sites. Its primary focus is on K-12 resources.

The Gateway to Educational Materials
http://thegateway.org/

Description: The Gateway to Educational Materials (GEM) project is a consortium effort to provide educators with quick and easy access to the substantial but uncataloged collections of educational materials found on various federal, state, university, nonprofit, and commercial Internet sites. GEM can be browsed by keyword or subject. Its search feature allows users to specify grade levels while searching in title, subject, keywords, and description fields.

Learn and Serve America
http://www.learnandserve.org/

Description: Learn and Serve America is a program of the Corporation for National and Community Service that makes grants to governments and organizations for service-learning projects. The projects are designed to help students learn while the students help meet community needs. The Web site has information about the program and contact lists for state education agencies, Indian Tribes, and others administering service-learning grants. The site has resources about service-learning and a link to the National Service Learning Clearinghouse.

NASA Langley Research Center Office of Education
http://edu.larc.nasa.gov/

Description: The Langley Research Center Office of Education was created to promote programs between the center and the larger education community. The Office of Education provides education programs for students from kindergarten through the postdoctoral level, for K–12 teachers, and for university faculty. It offers distance learning programs for K–12 students. Some of the resources for educators include the NASA Educator Resource Center Network and the Virginia Science Resource Network. The site also links to the NASA Education Program and to NASA/CORE, Central Operation of Resources for Educators.

National Center for Education Statistics
http://nces.ed.gov/

Description: NCES collects and analyzes data relating to education in the United States and other nations. Their Web site is a primary source for education statistics for all educational levels and for data on educational assessment, libraries, and other nations' educational outcomes. The site packages NCES data in different formats for different needs. For example, there are sections for ED Stats at a Glance, Quick Tables and Figures, and NCES Fast Facts. Most data on the site are drawn from major NCES statistical publications, such as *Education Statistics Quarterly, The Condition of Education,* and *The Digest of Education Statistics.* NCES Fast Facts highlights frequently requested information, such as data on the effects of reading to children and on average tuition costs at colleges and universities. The site also includes a searchable directory of private and public schools and of colleges and public libraries.

For anyone searching for statistics related to any form of education, this site should be the first place to visit. Although statistical reports are only available from the past few years (in some cases from 1996), some of the reports include time-series data. In addition, the major reports are in PDF format, which permits easy browsing and keyword searching.

Office of Educational Technology, Department of Education
http://www.ed.gov/Technology/index.html

Description: The U.S. Department of Education's Office of Educational Technology (OET) develops national educational technology policy and works with the educational community and other offices within the Department of Education to promote national goals for educational technology. OET's Web site features information on educational technology grants, federal resources, and state and regional organizations. Topical sections cover distance learning, the digital divide, and the evaluation and assessment of educational technology.

HIGHER EDUCATION

Air Force Institute of Technology
http://www.afit.edu/

Description: A component of Air University, the Air Force Institute of Technology (AFIT) is the Air Force's graduate school of engineering and management and its institution for technical professional continuing education. General information about the school can be found in the Public Affairs section.

Air University
http://www.au.af.mil/au/index.html

Description: Air University, located at Maxwell Air Force

Base, conducts professional military education, graduate education, and professional continuing education for officers, enlisted personnel and civilians. This site links to each of the component schools that make up Air University, and provides information on the University's history and mission. The Other AU Links section links to the University's course catalogs and publications, Air University Press, and Air University Library.

Army Logistics Management College
http://www.almc.army.mil/
Description: The Army Logistics Management College site features information on the college and its schools. It offers an online course catalog, course schedule, curriculum areas, and an online version of *Army Logistician*.

Carlisle Barracks and the U.S. Army War College
http://carlisle-www.army.mil/
Description: Carlisle Barracks is the home of the Army War College, Military History Institute, Army Physical Fitness Research Institute, the Center for Strategic Leadership, and the Strategic Studies Institute. This site features information on the Barracks and the resident institutions. In addition to the resources and descriptions under each institution, the site features an online *Carlisle Barracks News and Banner Online*, the Carlisle Barracks online newspaper.

Command and General Staff College
http://www-cgsc.army.mil/
Description: The U.S. Army Command and General Staff College is focused on leadership development within the Army. This site offers information on the college, its training programs, and its organizations. The journal *Military Review* is available online in its English, Spanish, and Portuguese language editions.

Defense Language Institute Foreign Language Center
http://dli-www.army.mil/
Description: The Defense Language Institute Foreign Language Center (DLIFLC) is the primary foreign language training institution within the Defense Department. Most information about the center is available by clicking on the DLIFLC link at this site. The course catalog and DLI periodicals are available online, as is information about the school's language programs.

The site is primarily of interest to those eligible for and interested in DLI language training.

ERIC Clearinghouse for Community Colleges
http://www.gseis.ucla.edu/ERIC/eric.html
Description: ERIC Clearinghouse for Community Colleges site features a Frequently Asked Questions section about community colleges and tools for finding community colleges online. The Publications section has summaries and bibliographies of research on community college education. This clearinghouse also offers an online reference service under the heading Ask. Other sections include the ERIC database, Submit a Document, and What's New at the Clearinghouse.

ERIC Clearinghouse on Adult, Career, and Vocational Education
http://www.ericacve.org/
Description: The ERIC Clearinghouse on Adult, Career, and Vocational Education contains a substantial number of publications online. Under the Publications heading are such sections as ERIC Digests from ACVE, *Trends and Issues Alerts, Myths and Realities, Practitioner File* (P-File), *Practice Application Briefs*, and Major Clearinghouse Publications. Most of these publications are available in HTML and PDF formats. Other sections include Journals on the Web, New and Noteworthy, In-Process Abstracts, and Links to Full-Text Resources.

ERIC Clearinghouse on Higher Education
http://www.eriche.org/
Description: This ERIC Clearinghouse presents itself as both a resource for ERIC publications as well as a gateway to higher education information on the Web. Clearinghouse information is available under the headings What's New, About ERIC, and ERIC Database, which contains a quick guide on conducting advanced searches. The Publications page presents links to *ERIC/HE Digests, ERIC Trends, CRIB Sheets*, the *ASHE-ERIC Report Series*, and *ERIC Review: Early Intervention Programs for College*. The home page also presents links to pages of resources arranged by audience, comprising Administrators, Faculty, Parents, Librarians, and Students.

ERIC/Professional Development Schools
http://www.aacte.org/Eric/pro_dev_schools.htm
Description: The Adjunct ERIC Clearinghouse on Clinical Schools (ADJ/CL) provides sources of information on professional development schools, clinical schools, partner schools, and similar institutions proposed for teacher education. ADJ/CL acquires, abstracts, and indexes literature on professional development schools for the ERIC database; produces bibliographies, periodic papers, digests, and other material on

PDS issues, collects data on PDSs. Its site includes *ERIC/PDS Digests*, announcements, a Professional Development Schools Database, and general information on PDSs.

FAA Aerospace Medicine
http://www.cami.jccbi.gov/

Description: The Office of Aerospace Medicine has three main sections: OAM Program Information; Aeromedical Reference Material, which offers access to the *Federal Air Surgeon's Medical Bulletin*; and Aeromedical Certification Standards and Regulations, the documents of which are offered in HTML, Word, or PDF formats. The Civil Aeromedical Institute (CAMI) handles medical certification, research, and education in aviation safety. The CAMI Web site offers resources related to CAMI research areas, including Aeromedical Certification, Aeromedical Education, Human Resources Research, Aeromedical Research, and Occupational Health. Within these sections are links to Library, Publications, Aviation Links, and CAMI Video Page. The Publications page provides access to technical report citations, the *Federal Air Surgeon's Medical Bulletin*, some brochures, and the *Aviation Medical Examiners Directory*.

This is an excellent resource for researchers in aviation medicine and aviation safety.

Free Application for Federal Student Aid (FAFSA)
http://www.fafsa.ed.gov/

Description: For college students, FAFSA on the Web makes it possible to apply online for student financial aid. The FAFSA renewal application may also be completed online. The site provides guidance on applying for aid and the application process.

Fulbright Scholar Program
http://exchanges.state.gov/education/fulbright/

Description: The U.S.-sponsored Fulbright Program is a scholarly exchange program providing grants for graduate students, scholars, professionals, teachers, and administrators from the U.S. and other countries. This site for U.S. and non-U.S. applicants describes the program and links to the Fulbright Commissions around the world. Much of the program is administered for the State Department by the Institute of International Education (IIE) and its Council for the International Exchange of Scholars (CIES). The alternate URL for this entry leads to the IIE and CIES pages. These pages provide detailed information for U.S. and non-U.S. applicants. For U.S. applicants, the relevant applications are online. The site also links to related Fulbright information, including the Hubert H. Humphrey Fellowships and the Fulbright Teacher Exchange Program.

Information for Financial Aid Professionals
http://ifap.ed.gov

Description: Information for Financial Aid Professionals (IFAP) is an electronic library for financial aid professionals containing publications, regulations, and guidance regarding the administration of the Title IV Federal Student Aid (FSA) Programs. This site features technical documentation, online tools, worksheets, and schedules related to the Federal Student Aid programs. Further information is available through a link to the related Schools Portal.

LingNet—The Linguists' Network
http://www.lingnet.org/

Description: LingNet is dedicated to supporting the members of the foreign language community in learning and sustaining their abilities in new languages. The site includes access to discussion forums, software libraries, news, mailing lists, and reading material for LingNet members. In addition, the site offers a compendium of links to language resources on the Internet. It also provides information on how to sign up to be a member.

Marine Corps University
http://www.mcu.usmc.mil/

Description: The Marine Corps University site provides information about the university and its programs. Featured categories include History, Organization, Schools, and Student Information.

Minority University Space Interdisciplinary Network
http://muspin.gsfc.nasa.gov/

Description: Minority University Space Interdisciplinary Network (MU-SPIN) is designed for Historically Black Colleges and Universities (HBCUs), and Other Minority Universities (OMUs). The focus of the program is on the transfer of advanced computer networking technologies to HBCUs and OMUs and their use for supporting multidisciplinary research. The Web site includes sections such as About MU-SPIN, Network Resources and Training Sites (NRTS), Programs, News, Resources, and Annual Users' Conference. MU-SPIN offers services such as hands-on training to faculty and students in accessing resources available over the Internet, hands-on training to technical staff in local area and campus network installation, management and user support, technical sessions at annual conferences, and technical video lectures on network-related issues.

For minority colleges and universities, this is an important resource for high technology and computer networking information and training.

NASA Academy

http://www.nasa-academy.nasa.gov

Description: This is the central page for NASA Academy summer programs for college students in science, math, engineering, or computer science. The two NASA Academy programs are the NASA Academy at Goddard Space Flight Center Academy and the Ames Astrobiology Academy at Ames Research Center. The site has application forms and detailed program information.

The information on these pages will be of interest to college students interested in careers or further study with NASA and to those that advise such students.

National Defense University

http://www.ndu.edu/

Description: The National Defense University site provides an online course catalog and links to the University's component colleges: Africa Center for Strategic Studies, Joint Forces Staff College, Industrial College of the Armed Forces, Institute for National Strategic Studies, Information Resources Management College, Center for Hemispheric Defense Studies, Near East-South Asia Center for Strategic Studies, and the National War College. The site also includes an online phone book and more links to the library and various programs and centers, including the International Fellows Program, the National Security Education Program, and the Center for Counterproliferation Research.

Naval Postgraduate School

http://www.nps.navy.mil/

Description: The Naval Postgraduate School (NPS) emphasizes education and research programs that are relevant to the Navy, defense and national and international security interests. The NPS site offers information on the school, its research, and its courses. Information is presented by topic and audience, with sections on Academics, Research, and Executive Education; Students, Faculty, Administration, and Alumni and Friends; and Library, and About NPS.

Naval War College

http://www.nwc.navy.mil/

Description: The Web site for the Naval War College presents information about the institute and its programs. In addition to the latest news, speeches and presentations, upcoming events, and a set of related links, the home page links to the following sections: Welcome Aboard, About NWC, Academics, Library, Research, War Gaming, NWC Press, Museum, Reserve Affairs, Alumni Affairs, and more. Publications are accessible under the NWC Press section.

NSF Division of Graduate Education

http://www.ehr.nsf.gov/ehr/dge/

Description: The programs of the National Science Foundation's Division of Graduate Education promote the early career development of scientists and engineers by offering support at critical junctures of their careers. This Web site describes a number of the Division's programs and fellowships that offer assistance to graduate students in the sciences. The Publications sections include some program guidelines and other electronic publications. There is also a page to search Directorate for Education and Human Resources (EHR) awards.

NSF Division of Undergraduate Education

http://www.ehr.nsf.gov/EHR/DUE/default.asp

Description: The DUE focuses on improving undergraduate education in the sciences, mathematics, and engineering. This Web site describes the agency and its programs, including staff listings, award announcements, and press releases. The primary categories are Programs and Deadlines, Publications, Awards, About DUE, Outreach Activities, and Links. On the top page, under the category DUE Programs, are two sections entitled Workforce Development and Curriculum, Laboratory, and Instructional Development that link to various programs funded by DUE.

Office of Postsecondary Education, Department Of Education

http://www.ed.gov/offices/OPE/

Description: The OPE home page describes the 40 plus programs administered by the office. These cover such postsecondary education topics as policy, financing, international education, and minority education. OPE Web resources are accessible under such headings as Information for Students, Planning for College, and Policy and Student Aid Professionals. Current grant competitions and their deadlines are highlighted. The site also has contact information for postsecondary education accrediting agencies.

This is a very useful site, with a substantial body of information sources of interest to both students and financial aid offices.

Office of University Programs at NASA Goddard Space Flight Center

http://university.gsfc.nasa.gov/

Description: The OUP site describes the mission of the office and links to pages with descriptions of its programs for institutions and individuals. It also has links to University-Related Programs, Post-Doc Programs, and Other Programs: the Goddard Senior Fellows, NASA Academy, the Graduate

Student Researchers Program, the National Space Grant College and Fellowship Program, the NRC Resident Researchers Associateship Program, and the Director's Discretionary Fund among others.

Office of Vocational and Adult Education, Department Of Education
http://www.ed.gov/offices/OVAE/
Description: This site provides information about the Office of Vocational and Adult Education programs, grants, events, legislation, and resources concerning the fields of adult education and vocational education. Key sections are High Schools, Career and Technical Education, Community Colleges, and Adult Literacy and Education.

Students.gov
http://www.students.gov/
Description: Students.gov is the federal student gateway to U.S. government information. This "FirstGov for students" site is a government-wide initiative to deliver electronic services from federal agencies to postsecondary students. Featured sections include Plan Your Education, Pay for Your Education, Career Development, Community Service, Military Service, Government 101, Travel and Fun, and Additional Resources. A search interface allows users to search the site's database of links, all of FirstGov, the Education Department site, and other databases. The home page also presents featured services and links to other cross-agency federal portals.

Like the other cross-agency portals that FirstGov has spawned, this site provides an excellent single access point to the myriad of government sources providing information of use to high school and college students.

Uniformed Services University of the Health Sciences
http://www.usuhs.mil/
Description: The Uniformed Services University of the Health Sciences is the nation's federal health sciences university, committed to excellence in military medicine and public health during peace and war. This Web site provides basic information about the university under the following headings University Welcome, School of Medicine, Graduate School of Nursing, Graduate Education, Academics, Administration, Admissions, Affiliations, Alumni Affairs, Recruitment and Diversity Affairs, and Research. The home page also links to information on Disaster/Terrorism Care Resources and Biological, Chemical, and Nuclear Warfare and Terrorism.

United States Air Force Academy
http://www.usafa.af.mil/
Description: The United States Air Force Academy site provides information for cadets, staff, and faculty. It includes an Academy Virtual Tour and sections on Academics, Admissions, Athletics, Cadet Life, Current Events, Information Resources, Photos, and Newcomers Information. A link to the Academy's library system is listed under the Academics section. The system includes the Academic Library, the Base Library, and the Medical Library.

United States Military Academy at West Point
http://www.usma.edu/
Description: The West Point site has information for prospective and current students as well as for alumni, visitors, and the West Point community. There are sections on Admissions, Cadet Life, and the Academic, Physical, and Military Programs. A brief section on USMA History includes a timeline and list of notable graduates.

United States Naval Academy
http://www.usna.edu
Description: This site contains information on the Naval Academy, mainly for students, prospective students, and midshipmen. The top level listing includes such sections as About USNA, Academics, Administration, Admissions, Alumni/Foundation Information, Athletics, Library, Midshipmen Interests, Public Affairs/Events, and What's New.

USDA Graduate School
http://grad.usda.gov/
Description: The Graduate School, USDA is a continuing education institution offering career-related courses to federal workers and the public. The main sections include Course Catalog, Visitor Center, About Us, Course Information and Registration, and Programs and Services. It also has a section with information for faculty and students, and information about the Fulbright Teacher Exchange.

Woodrow Wilson International Center for Scholars
http://wwics.si.edu/
Description: The Wilson Center supports scholarship linked to public policy by offering fellowships and special opportunities for research and writing with a focus on history, political science, and international relations. As a public-private partnership, the Center receives roughly half of its operating funds from a U.S. government appropriation. The Web site has information on current Wilson Center projects and publications, and audio files of its weekly radio program, Dialogue. The site also carries essays and other items from the Center's journal, *The Wilson Quarterly*. There is information on applying for a fellowship or internship with the Center, and a Media Guide has a directory of the Center's subject experts.

K–12

Ames Educator Resource Center

Description: The page is almost exclusively descriptive of the Center, which is located at the National Aeronautic and Space Administration Ames Research Center at Moffett Field, California. It serves educators in the western states (Alaska, Arizona, Northern California, Hawaii, Idaho, Montana, Nevada, Oregon, Utah, Washington, Wyoming). This page provides contact information, hours, and a listing of the kinds of educational materials available, only a few of which are available online. The Online Resources section links to a variety of sites about space, science, and education including Cool Picks, Aeronautics, Space, Biology, Computing, and Classroom Resources. This page also links to a list of other NASA Educator Resource Centers around the country.

This site is most useful for those that want to visit or contact the center. It would be even more useful if the lesson plans, curriculum materials, or publications were available online.

ArtsEdge: The National Arts and Education Information Network

`http://artsedge.kennedy-center.org/`

Description: ArtsEdge from the Kennedy Center is a major arts resource for educators and students. Featured sections include NewsBreak, Teaching Materials, Professional Resources, User Guide, and Community Center. NewsBreak presents a daily update of events in the arts and includes sections on Job Opportunities, Grants and Funding, Competitions and Calls, Fellowships and Internships, and Professional Development News. Teaching Material offers sections on Curricula, Lessons, and Activities; Curriculum WebLinks; Get Published; Idea Exchange; and Using ArtsEdge Lessons. The Curriculum WebLinks section provides annotated lists of Web sites on such topics as ESL, Foreign Language, Mathematics, Physical Education, Science, Social Science, Design Arts, Language Arts, Performing Arts, and Visual Arts. The Sites We Host link on the home page leads to related sites such as: Duke Ellington Centennial, the African Odyssey Interactive, the National Forum, and more.

Well-designed, this site should be a primary stopping point for anyone involved in arts education.

Computers for Learning

`http://www.computers.fed.gov/School/user.asp`

Description: The Computers for Learning Web site is designed for public, private, parochial, or home schools serving the K–12 student population, and other nonprofit educational organizations. The service allows these groups of students and nonprofit organizations to request donations of surplus federal computer equipment. The site includes a listing of available equipment, registration, success stories, background, and a section that describes who is eligible.

Cosmic and Heliospheric Learning Center

`http://helios.gsfc.nasa.gov/`

Description: The Cosmic and Heliospheric Learning Center is designed to increase people's interest in cosmic and heliospheric science. (The site explains that "the heliosphere is the HUGE area in space affected by the Sun.") The information on the Learning Center Web site is aimed at the general public or at about a high school level of science understanding. It features sections for Astrophysics Basics, Cosmic Rays, The Sun, and Space Weather. On the top page there are a series of images taken by various spacecraft: TRACE, ASCA, and IMAGE, which lead to information about the images.

ECENET-L [email list]

`http://ericeece.org/listserv/ecenet-l.html`

Description: ECENET-L is an email discussion list for people interested in early childhood education. The list invites participation from representatives of professional associations and government agencies, faculty and researchers, students and teachers, parents, and librarians. The Web address includes access to archives of postings.

ECPOLICY-L [email list]

`http://ericeece.org/listserv/ecpol-l.html`

Description: ECPOLICY-L provides a forum for discussion of policy issues related to young children. Suggested topics include providing information about the development, care, and education of young children for state, federal, and local policymakers; raising the awareness of policymakers, educators, the media, and parents about the issues important to the future of young children; and encouraging responsiveness of the early childhood community to public issues affecting children. The Web address includes an archive of postings.

ECPROFDEV-L [email list]

`http://ericeece.org/listserv/ecprof-l.html`

Description: ECPROFDEV-L is intended to foster communication among those who teach pre-service and in-service early childhood educators, train Head Start or other early childhood program staff, and consult or facilitate learning with early childhood professionals in any setting. A link to the list's archives is provided on the Web site.

Eisenhower National Clearinghouse

`http://www.enc.org/`

Description: The mission of the Eisenhower National Clearinghouse (ENC) is to identify effective curriculum resources, create high-quality professional development materials, and disseminate useful information and products to improve K-12 mathematics and science teaching and learning. While not a government office, ENC is funded through a contract with the Education Department. The site has curriculum resources, useful Web links, and professional development information for teachers. Some of the special topics covered include incorporating math and science into other subjects and bringing real world math and science work into the classroom.

This site provides access to many documents with high-quality content in the broad fields of mathematics and science education.

ERIC Clearinghouse for Science, Mathematics, and Environmental Education
`http://www.ericse.org/`
Description: The Web server for the ERIC Clearinghouse for Science, Mathematics, and Environmental Education features Science Education Resources, Mathematics Education Resources, Environmental Education Resources, Online Publications, Web Companions, Contributing to the Database, Resources for Parents and Children, and a Conference Calendar. Each of the topical sections includes links to relevant *Digests*, bulletins, lesson plans, and information guides.

ERIC Clearinghouse for Social Studies/Social Science Education
`http://www.indiana.edu/~ssdc/eric-chess.html`
Description: ERIC/ChESS specializes in and monitors the literature and developments in the teaching and learning of social studies, social science education, music education, and art education. The ERIC/ChESS site features such sections as About ERIC and ERIC/ChESS, Publications and Services, *ERIC/ChESS Digests*, *Keeping Up* (a news bulletin), Resource Organizations Directory, Internet Resources, Indiana Social Studies Resources, What's New, and Standards and Curriculum. Standards and Curriculum contains links to national and state social studies, art, and music standards and curriculum information on the Internet.

ERIC Clearinghouse on Disabilities and Gifted Education
`http://ericec.org/`
Description: This ERIC Clearinghouse site provides information on the education of individuals of all ages who have disabilities as well as those who are gifted. It features information about the clearinghouse and the ERIC system, and sections on Searching the Databases, Submitting Documents to ERIC, the ERIC/OSEP Special Project, Research Connections, Digests, Fact Sheets and Minibibliographies, Frequently Asked Questions, Email Lists, Links to the Laws, and Gifted Education/Dual Exceptionalities.

ERIC Clearinghouse on Elementary and Early Childhood Education
`http://ericeece.org/`
Description: The ERIC Clearinghouse on Elementary and Early Childhood Education offers descriptive information on the clearinghouse, links to external education resources, connections to other components in the ERIC system, and lists of its available publications. A Popular Topics section has information on bullying, diversity, parenting, readiness for school, and other subjects. This site also lists electronic discussion groups sponsored by ERIC/EECE.

This is a useful collection of materials on elementary education, early childhood education, and parenting.

ERIC Clearinghouse on Reading, English, and Communications
`http://www.indiana.edu/~eric_rec/`
Description: This site is dedicated to providing educational materials, services, and course work to everyone interested in the language arts. On the home page, the site lists the latest reading research and reading news and links to resources for literacy education and children's literature. Featured sections include Family Information Center, Lesson Plans, Great Web Resources, Publications, and a Question and Answer Service. The Family Information Center category features parent involvement Web resources, free phonics information, books that help, helpful tips for parents, and information on parent workshops and a senior partners pen pal program.

ERIC Clearinghouse on Rural Education and Small Schools
`http://www.ael.org/eric/`
Description: The Clearinghouse on Rural Education and Small Schools covers a variety of topics, including American Indian and Alaska Native Education, Mexican American Education, Migrant Education, Outdoor Education, Rural Education, and Small Schools, each of which list relevant ERIC Digests. Other sections include Publications, Conferences, and About Us. Under Publications is a link to a newsletter, *ERIC/CRESS Bulletin!* and information on books.

GLOBE Program
`http://www.globe.gov/`
Description: Global Learning and Observations to Benefit the Environment (GLOBE) is a worldwide network of students, teachers, and scientists working together to study and understand the global environment. This site both offers information on the program and is used by participants in the program. This program involves students in taking environmental measurements. Over 10,000 schools in more than 95 countries have already submitted over hundreds of thousands of data

reports based on observations by GLOBE student scientists. The data is accessible to anyone, and there is information on how new schools can register to be included in the program. The site is available in a variety of languages including Spanish, French, German, and Arabic.

With participating schools from all over the world, this kind of collaborative project demonstrates how the Internet can be used in a K-12 environment. In addition, the Web site is well-designed and makes navigation easy even for those not familiar with GLOBE.

K12ASSESS-L [email list]
http://ericae.net/k12assess/
Description: The goal of K12ASSESS-L is to provide educators with a fast, convenient, and topical electronic discussion forum focusing on issues related to educational assessment in grades K-12. The Web site provides subscription information, a form for subscribing, and archives back to 1998.

Learning Page of the Library of Congress
http://lcweb2.loc.gov/ammem/ndlpedu/
Description: Designed for the educational community, this site helps students and teachers find relevant materials within the National Digital Library collection on the Library of Congress Web pages, particularly the American Memory project. This site features sections such as Lesson Plans, Features and Activities, and Professional Development.

Learning Web at the U.S. Geological Survey
http://www.usgs.gov/education/
Description: The Learning Web is dedicated to K-12 education, exploration, and life-long learning on topics of concern to USGS scientists. There are sections for Students (Homework Help and Project Ideas), Teachers (Lesson Plans, Paper Models), and Explorers (Research Tools, Special Topics). Topics include water, rocks, ecosystems, and maps and images. The site also has a variety of online games and printable projects for kids.

This is useful for teachers interested in finding educational resources in science and for students looking for basic earth science information.

Live from the Hubble Space Telescope
http://quest.arc.nasa.gov/hst/
Description: In the spring of 1996, students in grades K-12 had a chance to use the Hubble Space Telescope (HST). The Space Telescope Science Institute (which operates Hubble) contributed three HST orbits to the Passport to Knowledge educational project for this purpose. The planets Neptune and Pluto were selected as targets for original observations by students who served as Hubble Space Telescope co-investigators,

working alongside astronomers. The Web site features Live Video, Project News, Featured Events, Background, Teachers' Lounge, and a Kids' Corner. This site provides news, featured events, a video broadcast schedule, and background information on the project.

This is another excellent example of how the Internet can aid in collaborative projects with students and teachers in K-12. Users should be aware that while much of the material is still useful, the site only covers the 1996 project and is no longer updated.

MIDDLE-L [email list]
http://ericeece.org/listserv/middle-l.html
Description: MIDDLE-L is a forum for information related to middle school education. It is intended for middle school educators, teacher educators, and others interested in education at the middle level. The Web address includes access to archives of postings.

MUSIC-ED [email list]
http://artsedge.kennedy-center.org/user_guide/comment/listservs.html#musiced
Description: The MUSIC-ED email list discussion is focused specifically on music education. The discussions range from teaching tips among educators, to reviews of music education software, and to ideas for integrating music education with other subjects in the K-12 curriculum. The Web page provides a form interface for subscribing to this and other ArtsEdge email lists.

NASA Classroom of the Future Program
http://www.cotf.edu/
Description: The NASA Classroom of the Future program at Wheeling Jesuit College aims to bridge the gap between American schools and the expertise of NASA scientists. This site features descriptive information about the program and includes a virtual tour of the Center for Educational Technologies at Wheeling. Some of the projects available from the Products section are Astronomy Village, BioBLAST, the International Space Station Challenge. This site provides information on the projects and their current stage of development. Under Products is the NASA TV service, which streams NASA TV to viewers on the Internet. Other sections include Mission, Philosophy, Research, and a link to the main Center for Educational Technologies (CET) Web site.

NASA Glenn Learning Technologies Project
http://www.lerc.nasa.gov/Other_Groups/K-12/
Description: This Learning Technologies site from the Glenn Research Center features educational material on airplanes and aeronautics. Primary sections include Teachers' Corner,

Aeronautic Educational Resources, and Math/Sciences Resources. The site also has sections for Announcements, Publications, Resources, and Awards.

NASA Quest
http://quest.arc.nasa.gov/
Description: The NASA Quest Web site is the agency's vehicle for interacting with educators, students, and space enthusiasts. As a way to interest students in science and the space program, this site provides resources about the national space program and the people involved. Resources on this site are divided into four topical areas, covering space, aerospace, astrobiology, and women of NASA. In addition, the site provides detailed information about the scientists that work for NASA, information on live Web chats and webcasts, resources for teachers, and more information about NASA. The Educators and Parents section provides a discussion list, lesson plans, and lists of standards.

NASA Spacelink—An Aeronautics and Space Resource for Education
http://spacelink.nasa.gov/
Description: Spacelink is a NASA resource developed specifically for educators. It provides current and historical educational information on space, NASA, and aeronautics for the educational community. The main sections include Educator Focus, The Library, Hot Topics, Cool Picks, and Spacelink Express. Within The Library, there are links to NASA educational services and products, instructional materials, NASA projects and news, and frequently asked questions. Within these links there are teacher guides, pictures, computer software, science, mathematics, engineering and technology education lesson plans, information on NASA educational programs and services, current status reports on NASA projects and events, news releases, and television broadcasts schedules for NASA Television.

By creating this site specifically for the education community and building a large collection of relevant files, this is an essential stop for anyone in the education community interested in space and aeronautical sciences.

NASA's Learning Technologies Project
http://learn.arc.nasa.gov/
Description: The goal of NASA's Learning Technologies Project (LTP) is to promote the growth of a national information infrastructure using the vast amount of information the National Aeronautics and Space Administration (NASA) has acquired since its creation. Access to this knowledge will allow the public and industry to contribute to rapid and significant advances in science, engineering, and technology. The Web site includes Feature Stories, Education Resources, Movies, and Calendar of Events. Education Resources features a grants

page; a topic listing of LTP projects, with information about the programs with links to related NASA educational Web sites; and LTP product guides, where one can search various programs by grade level, by research and general interest, or by national standards for geography, science, mathematics, and technology.

National Child Care Information Center
http://nccic.org/
Description: NCCIC is an Adjunct ERIC Clearinghouse for Child Care. The site provides information on the center and has links to child care topics; directories of state contacts and regulatory agencies, national organizations, and state resource sheets; information on grant and funding opportunities; publications and other resources; and a searchable database. There are also links to various projects and centers, including the Tribal Child Care Technical Assistance Center and the Child Care Partnership Project. Access to the full text of NCCIC's *Child Care Bulletin* is available as well.

National Parent Information Network
http://npin.org/
Description: National Parent Information Network (NPIN) is designed and maintained by the ERIC Clearinghouse on Urban Education and the ERIC Clearinghouse on Elementary and Early Childhood Education. NPIN's mission is to provide access to research-based information about the process of parenting, and about family involvement in education. Major categories on this site include About NPIN, Virtual Library, Questions, Parent News, and Special Initiatives. The Virtual Library page features full-text publications including *ERIC Digests*, book summaries, and other brochures, pamphlets, and newsletters. Full-text materials have been reviewed for reliability and usefulness.

While many of the resources available through NPIN are available directly from the ERIC Clearinghouses or other sources, pulling them together in a clear organization, makes the materials more readily accessible for anyone interested in parenting topics.

No Child Left Behind
http://www.nochildleftbehind.gov/
Description: This Education Department site is dedicated to information about Public Law 107-110, the No Child Left Behind Act of 2001. The law concerns educational standards and testing, teacher training and recruitment, English language instruction, school safety, and other matters. Major sections of the site are What to Know, For Parents, and News Center. Along with fact sheets and key dates, the site includes a glossary of education policy terms related to the No Child Left Behind Act.

The No Child Left Behind Act site is different from many

government sites in that it concerns a single piece of legislation. The focus is on the George W. Bush administration's goals in promoting the provisions of the law and the policy behind it.

NSF Division of Elementary, Secondary, and Informal Education
http://www.ehr.nsf.gov/EHR/ESIE/
Description: Part of the National Science Foundation, the Division of Elementary, Secondary, and Informal Education (ESIE) focuses on improving preK-12 science, technology, engineering, and mathematics (STEM) education in the United States. Its Web site includes descriptions of the programs and funding opportunities offered by this agency. The site is divided into pages on Program Announcements, Publications, and Deadlines. Under Program Announcements, information is available for Teacher Enhancement programs, Instructional Materials Development programs, Informal Science Education programs, and Presidential Awards for Excellence in Science and Mathematics Teaching. The Publications page presents solicitations, documents, and other publications.

Office of Special Education Programs (OSEP), Department Of Education
http://www.ed.gov/offices/OSERS/OSEP/
Description: The Office of Special Education Programs (OSEP) has primary responsibility for administering programs and projects relating to the education of all children, youth, and adults with disabilities, from birth through age 21. Sections describe OSEP's Programs and Projects, Grants and Funding, Legislation and Policy, Publications and Products, and Research and Statistics.

PARENTING-L [email list]
http://ericeece.org/listserv/parent-l.html
Description: PARENTING-L is an Internet discussion group on topics related to parenting children (including child development, education, and child care) from birth through adolescence. Discussion ranges from family leave and parental rights issues, to parents as partners in their children's education, to the changes in children as they leave high school and begin college or get their first job. The Web address includes access to archives of postings.

PROJECTS-L [email list]
http://ericeece.org/listserv/projec-l.html
Description: This discussion group focuses on the project approach, which is an in-depth study of a topic undertaken by a class, a group, or an individual child. The group discusses how the approach is used in early childhood, elementary, and

middle school classrooms. The Web address includes access to archives of postings.

School District Demographics
http://nces.ed.gov/surveys/sdds/index.asp
Description: This site presents demographic and geographic data from the 2000 Census, 1990 Census, and from surveys and estimates made between the censuses. A School District Maps section allows for viewing state or individual district maps using the Map Viewer application. The 2000 Census section allows for selecting and downloading data tables in a comma delimited file format.

The data from this special census tabulation can be helpful for studying school districts as well as for general demographics of children and families with children.

United Nations Cyber School Bus
http://www.un.org/cyberschoolbus/index.html
Description: This UN site, designed for the education community, promotes education about international issues and the United Nations. The site features a wide range of resources in English with Spanish, French, Russian, Chinese, and Arabic versions. It features quizzes and games, current events information, and curriculum materials on such topics as human rights, peace education, and the United Nations itself.

WEB SITES FOR CHILDREN

America's Story from America's Library
http://www.americaslibrary.gov/
Description: This Library of Congress site is designed for kids and their families. It uses digitized images from the Library's collection, accompanied by text and graphics, to create educational pages about American history and culture. Sections include: Explore the States, Jump Back in Time, and Meet Amazing Americans.

Ben's Guide to U.S. Government for Kids
http://bensguide.gpo.gov/
Description: With Benjamin Franklin as a guide, this GPO site for children covers topics such as the U.S. Constitution, how laws are made, the branches of the federal government, and citizenship. It features sections for specific age groups, plus a special section for parents and educators. It also offers instruction on the use of the primary source materials on GPO Access. The primary links are About Ben, K–2, 3–5, 6–8, 9–12, Parents and Teachers, and About this Site.

CIA Home Page for Kids
http://www.cia.gov/cia/ciakids/
Description: The CIA offers a variety of information targeted

toward children. The page includes links to Who We Are and What We Do, CIA Canine Corps, CIA Seal, Aerial Photography Pigeons, Geography Trivial Quiz, Break the Code Word Puzzle, and History. It also links to the CIA's *World Factbook* with its wealth of country information.

Department of the Interior Kids Page
http://www.doi.gov/kids/
Description: This central DOI page for the children links to more than a dozen pages from DOI agencies. These include Wildlife Species, Butterfly Site, Coloring Book, Kids Eye View, Shorebirds, Learning Web, The Great American Landmarks Adventure, Ozark Junior Ranger, Blue Ridge, Coal Mining, Alaska, BLM Resource Explorers, and Hoover Dam.

DOJ Kids and Youth
http://www.usdoj.gov/kidspage/
Description: The Department of Justice page for youth provides information about the department and its agencies, primarily the FBI. Information is arranged by the following main categories: Kids (K–5th), Youth (6th–12th), Teachers and Parents, and Subjects. Links from the home page lead to special subject sections, such as Inside the Courtroom, Get It Straight (the Facts about Drugs), Civil Rights, Cyberethics for Kids, and Getting Involved in Crime Prevention.

Dr. E's Energy Lab: Energy Efficiency and Renewable Energy Network
http://www.eren.doe.gov/kids/
Description: This page for children from the Energy Efficiency and Renewable Energy Network (EREN) features links to the following headings: Energy Efficiency Tips, Wind Energy, Solar Energy, Geothermal Energy, Alternative Fuels, General Renewable Energy, and Ask an Energy Expert.

EIA Kids' Page: What is Energy?
http://www.eia.doe.gov/kids/
Description: The Information Administration of the Energy Department provides this educational page about energy. Sections of this general information site include What Is Energy, Kid's Corner, Online Resources, Fun Facts, Classroom Connection, and Energy Quiz.

Students and teachers seeking education resources about energy may prefer this site to the main DOE site for children.

Energy.gov Kidzone
http://www.energy.gov/kidz/kidzone.html
Description: The main Energy Department site for kids presents a mix of links, most of it appropriate for the higher grade levels. Major sections include a history of the Energy

Department with historical firsts in energy and links to energy glossaries at a variety of DOE sites. Teachers and parents may be interested in some of the site's Quick Links; Contests and Events links to Web sites for energy and science educational contests and Science Projects cover science fair information.

Parents and teachers will want to use this site to find useful material. However, due to the uneven nature of the materials it links to, this site may not be the best for kids to use themselves without guidance.

FBI Youth
http://www.fbi.gov/kids/6th12th/6th12th.htm
Description: The FBI Youth site is intended for young adults, grades 6 through 12. Sections like FBI Investigates and A Day In The Life are intended to demonstrate the type of work FBI employees do. Special Agent Challenge is a quiz the user can complete by finding the answers on the FBI Web site. The History section presents an FBI history timeline with links to more information on special topics such as Al Capone and the FBI Academy.

FDA Kids' Homepage
http://www.fda.gov/oc/opacom/kids/
Description: The FDA Web site for children and teens presents health and safety information with sections including: Food Safety Quiz, Mac and Molly Investigator, All About Vaccines, and The Teen Scene. There is also a Parents' Corner. Two additional links are Cosmetics Quiz for Teens and Powerful Girls Have Powerful Bones. The Teen Scene features *FDA Consumer* magazine articles with important health information for teenagers, ranging from nutrition and sun safety to eating disorders and attention deficit disorder.

FEMA for Kids
http://www.fema.gov/kids/
Description: This FEMA site provides information and resources to help children prepare for and prevent disasters. Get Ready, Get Set has information and activities about preparing for a disaster and the Disaster Area describes 10 kinds of disasters, including hurricanes and tornadoes. The Disaster Connections section has children's artwork, poems, and letters with their thoughts on disasters such as tornadoes and the September 11, 2001 attacks.

FEMA has done an excellent job pulling together a Web site of resources explaining disasters to children without scaring them.

FirstGov for Kids
http://www.kids.gov/
Description: This FirstGov for Kids site is a portal to Web pages designed for children. Annotated Web links are

arranged by topic, such as Careers, Geography, History, Homework, Money, Safety, and Space. Each topic lists U.S. government Web pages and most also have clearly-marked sections for selected sites from organizations, educational institutions, and commercial entities.

FirstGov for Kids is an easy way for kids, as well as teachers and parents, to find kid-friendly information on the Web. It is particularly helpful as an index to government Web pages for children. A few commercial sites require logging in or are more appropriate for the teacher's use, but many have appropriate content low in advertising.

Garrett A. Morgan Technology and Transportation Futures Program
http://education.dot.gov/

Description: This program aims to connect youth with the transportation community and improve education of those in the transportation workforce. The Web site features the following sections: Teen Zine, Home and School, Reading Room, DOT Kids, About Garrett A. Morgan, the Garrett A. Morgan Technology and Transportation Futures Program, Transportation Education and Careers, Essay Contest, and College, University, and Life-Long Learning. The Garrett A. Morgan Technology and Transportation Futures Program page has links to information for pre-kindergarten to secondary school students, information about transportation education at universities and community colleges and careers and training, and links to a virtual library and a life-long learning center.

HHS Pages for Kids
http://www.hhs.gov/kids/

Description: This page offers links to information for parents and teachers, but the primary content is links to other HHS and related agencies' Web sites for children. Featured topics include child health, smoke-free kids, and food safety.

HUD Kids Next Door
http://www.hud.gov/kids/kids.html

Description: HUD's page for children is subtitled "where kids can learn more about being good citizens." The page features Meet Cool People, See Neat Things, and Visit Awesome Places. Within each of these sections are activities and pages such as Help the Homeless, Kids Volunteer, Safe Places to Play, Build a Community, and Scavenger Hunt.

Kids' Corner, Endangered Species
http://endangered.fws.gov/kids/

Description: This children's site provides information on endangered species, featuring a Crossword Puzzle, Creature Features, Where Can I Find It?, Risky Critters Game, How

Can Kids Help?, and Hey Teachers. Links are also available to FWS endangered species resources.

NASAKIDS
http://kids.msfc.nasa.gov/

Description: This site features a colorful, graphical interface to NASA News by Kids, Space and Beyond, Rockets and Airplanes, Projects and Games, Astronauts Living in Space, Creation Station, Our Earth, NASA toons, and Teachers' Corner.

NCEH Kids' Page
http://www.cdc.gov/nceh/kids/99kidsday/default.htm

Description: Designed for the young reader, the site is based on *Take Your Children to Work Day*, a booklet that NCEH created for its employees' children to describe the important work their parents do to promote health and quality of life. It offers sections on Asthma, Birth Defects, Cruise Ship, Inspection, Disabilities, Emergency Response, Global Health, Laboratory Programs, Lead Poisoning, Refugee Health, and Activities. The booklet is available in Spanish and as a PDF version that may be downloaded and printed.

NIEHS' Kids Pages
http://www.niehs.nih.gov/kids/home.htm

Description: This Kids Page offering from the National Institute of Environmental Health Sciences has both a Spanish language version and a text version. It includes Games and Activities, Color Our World Bright and Beautiful, Science Word Scrambles, and Science Spelling Bee. There is also a section on Environmental Health and Sciences Hot Topics, Careers, and Projects which includes a section on Asthma and Allergies and one on Children's Health.

Patent and Trademark Office Kids' Page
http://www.uspto.gov/go/kids/

Description: The PTO site offers children's contests, games, and puzzles having to do with creativity, invention, and the operations of the PTO. The site has sections designed for students in K–6 and 6–12, and for parents, teachers, and coaches.

Peace Corps Kids' World
http://www.peacecorps.gov/kids/

Description: The Peace Corps offers this kids' page, with sections for What is the Peace Corps?, Make a Difference, Explore the World, Tell Me a Story, and Food, Friends, and Fun. An online quiz game called "Pack Your Bags" is also available. This site mainly provides information about the Peace Corps program. Some resources on foreign countries are listed under the sections: Explore the World and Food, Friends, and Fun.

Physical Oceanography from Space
`http://podaac.jpl.nasa.gov/kids/`
Description: This page for students covers What is Physical Oceanography?, How do Satellites Measure the Ocean?, How do Scientists use Satellite Measurements?, Oceanography History, and Oceanography News.

Safety City
`http://www.nhtsa.dot.gov/kids/`
Description: Vince and Larry, the NHTSA's crash test dummies, are the guides on this children's Web site, which provides information on vehicle safety. The site features sections such as Safety School, Bike Tour, Research Laboratory, and School Bus.

Space Place
`http://spaceplace.jpl.nasa.gov/spacepl.htm`
Description: This Web site, designed for students in grades K–6, features facts, activities, and contests related to space science. It offers such sections as Make Spacey Things, Do Spacey Things, Space Science in Action, Dr. Marc's Amazing Facts, and Friends Share. The section for teachers, Goodies for Teachers, presents classroom activity articles from the journal *The Technology Teacher*.

Tobacco Information and Prevention Source (TIPS) for Youth
`http://www.cdc.gov/tobacco/tips4youth.htm`
Description: TIPS4Youth links to an extensive list of resources providing information to young people about smoking and advertises public health events concerning tobacco use. Sections include: How to Quit, Educational Materials, Celebrities Against Smoking, Tobacco Quiz, and materials designed to make teens more savvy about cigarette and tobacco advertising. The site also features *SGR 4 Kids*, the Surgeon General's Report for Kids about Smoking.

USDA for Kids
`http://www.usda.gov/news/usdakids/index.html`
Description: This gateway site offers links to a wide variety of children's pages from USDA agencies. Linked sites include Smokey Bear, Backyard Conservation, Food Guide Pyramid, Agriculture for Kids, History of Agriculture, Team Nutrition, Woodsy Owl, George Washington Carver Coloring Book, and more.

WhiteHouseKids.Gov
`http://www.whitehouse.gov/kids/whlife/index.html`
Description: The White House for Kids Web site presents information about the White House and the nation through the pets of the Bush family: the dogs Spotty and Barney; India, the cat; and Ophelia, the longhorn. Spotty gives a tour of the White House; Barney presents the ABCs with brief messages from the president; India asks an historical question; and Ophelia presents a dream team of heroes who made a significant contribution to the country. In addition, there are brief biographies of the president, the first lady, the vice president, and Mrs. Cheney. The site also includes coloring pages, games, and a video tour of the White House.

Youthlink
`http://www.ssa.gov/kids`
Description: The Social Security kids' page offers Social Security Kids' Stuff and Hot Questions for Cool Teens. Other sections provide resources for Parents and Teachers. There is also a link for information about low-cost or free health care insurance for children.

Index